THE Enduring Vision

A History of the American People

Concise Seventh Edition

PAUL S. BOYER
University of Wisconsin, Madison

CLIFFORD E. CLARK, JR.
Carleton College

KAREN HALTTUNEN
University of Southern California

SANDRA MCNAIR HAWLEY
San Jacinto College

JOSEPH F. KETT
University of Virginia

ANDREW RIESER
State University of New York, Dutchess Community College

NEAL SALISBURY
Smith College

HARVARD SITKOFF
University of New Hampshire

NANCY WOLOCH
Barnard College

Australia • Brazil • Japan • Korea • Mexico • Singapore • Spain • United Kingdom • United States

***The Enduring Vision: A History of the American People*, Concise Seventh Edition**

Paul S. Boyer, Clifford E. Clark, Jr., Karen Halttunen, Sandra McNair Hawley, Joseph F. Kett, Andrew Rieser, Neal Salisbury, Harvard Sitkoff, Nancy Woloch

Senior Publisher: Suzanne Jeans

Senior Sponsoring Editor: Ann West

Senior Development Editor: Tonya Lobato

Assistant Editor: Megan Chrisman

Editorial Assistant: Patrick Roach

Senior Media Editor: Lisa Ciccolo

Marketing Coordinator: Lorreen Towle

Marketing Communications Manager: Glenn McGibbon

Senior Content Project Manager: Jane Lee

Senior Art Director: Cate Rickard Barr

Manufacturing Planner: Sandra Milewski

Rights Acquisition Specialist, Image: Jennifer Meyer Dare

Rights Acquisition Specialist, Text: Jennifer Meyer Dare

Production Service: S4Carlisle Publishing Services

Cover Designer: Yvo Riezebos, RHDG

Cover Image: Carl Rakeman, *Railroad Crossings, Bridged,* 1934. Oil on canvas. Courtesy of the Federal Highway Administration.

Compositor: S4Carlisle Publishing Services

Library of Congress Control Number: 2011935137

Student Edition:

ISBN-13: 978-1-111-83825-6

ISBN-10: 1-111-83825-9

Wadsworth
20 Channel Center Street
Boston, MA 02210
U.S.A.

Cengage Learning is a leading provider of customized learning solutions with office locations around the globe, including Singapore, the United Kingdom, Australia, Mexico, Brazil, and Japan. Locate your local office at **international.cengage.com/region**

Cengage Learning products are represented in Canada by Nelson Education, Ltd.

For your course and learning solutions, visit **www.cengage.com.**

Purchase any of our products at your local college store or at our preferred online store **www.cengagebrain.com.**

Instructors: Please visit **login.cengage.com** and log in to access instructor-specific resources.

Printed in Canada
1 2 3 4 5 6 7 15 14 13 12 11

Contents

31 Global Dangers, Global Challenges, 2001 to the Present 775

Maps

Charts, Graphs, and Tables

Preface

Much has changed in America and the world since we began planning *The Enduring Vision* for college survey students more than twenty-five years ago. Some of these developments have been welcome and positive; others deeply unsettling. This new Concise Seventh Edition fully documents all of these changes for today's new generation of students, as well as the continuities that offer reassurance for the future.

Vision and Goals

The Concise Seventh Edition builds on the underlying strategy that has guided us from the beginning. We want our history to be not only comprehensive and illuminating, but also lively, readable, and true to the lived experience of earlier generations of Americans. Within a clear political and chronological framework, we integrate the best recent scholarship in all areas of American history. Our interest in social and cultural history, which shapes our own teaching and scholarship, has suffused *The Enduring Vision* from the outset, and it remains central. We integrate the historical experience of women and men of all regions, ethnic groups, and social classes who make up the American mosaic.

As we pursue these purposes in this Concise Seventh Edition, we welcome Karen Halttunen to the team of authors. A distinguished historian of nineteenth-century American social and cultural history who teaches at the University of Southern California, Professor Halttunen brings impressive strengths to our mission.

New Interpretations, Expanded Coverage

This edition of *The Enduring Vision* brings the work fully up to date, incorporating major developments and scholarship since the previous edition went to press. We have included the best of the new political history, stressing the social, cultural, and economic issues at stake in political decisions and debates. Religious history remains an important focus, from the spiritual values of pre-Columbian communities to the political activism of contemporary conservative Christian groups. We again offer extensive coverage of medicine and disease, from the epidemics brought by European explorers to today's AIDS crisis, bioethics debates, and controversies over health-care financing.

As with previous editions, we have added a number of new chapter-opening vignettes, including new vignettes on Edmund Ruffin, a fanatical defender of the South and slavery, and Martin Luther King, Jr. These vignettes introduce a central theme of the chapter and remind us that, in the last analysis, history involves the choices and actions of individual men and women.

Streamlined Organization

In our continuing quest to make the text clear and reader-friendly, we have rearranged some sections and reorganized some chapters. The post–World War II chapters, in particular, have been heavily reorganized to consolidate topical coverage and tighten the narrative. We have edited rigorously but without sacrificing any substantive material. As a result, we have reduced the total number of chapters from thirty-two to thirty-one and shortened the text by about 10 percent.

Understanding history requires a firm grasp of geography, and *The Enduring Vision* has always emphasized the significance of the land in the interplay of historical events. Our extensive coverage of environmental history, the land, and the West is fully integrated into the narrative and treated analytically—not simply "tacked on" to a traditional account. An upgraded map program offers maps that are rich in information, easy to read, and visually appealing.

Visual Resources and Features

Based on the positive feedback we have received from readers, we have maintained the layout of the previous edition. Our one-column format allows for seamless integration of images and a smoother narrative flow. Each chapter begins with Focus Questions that correspond to the major sections of the chapter to give students a preview of the key topics to be covered. These questions are briefly answered at the end of the chapter in the "Chapter Summary." All maps in the text have been redesigned to be more visually dynamic and engaging; each map also features a corresponding online interactive map. Throughout the chapters, students get assistance from key terms that are boldfaced in the text and defined in the margins; "Checking In" boxes at the end of each section summarize the key points in that section.

Supplementary Resources

A wide array of supplements accompanies this text to help students master the material and guide instructors in teaching from *The Enduring Vision,* Concise Seventh Edition. For details on viewing or ordering these materials, please consult your Cengage Learning sales representative.

Instructor Resources

PowerLecture CD-ROM with ExamView® and JoinIn®. This dual platform, all-in-one multimedia resource includes the Instructor's Resource Manual, authored by Ken Blume of Albany College of Pharmacy and Health Sciences; the Test Bank, authored by Volker Janssen of California State University, Fullerton; Microsoft® PowerPoint® slides of lecture outlines as well as images and maps from the text that can be used as offered, or customized by importing personal lecture slides or other material; and JoinIn® PowerPoint® slides with clicker content. Also included is ExamView, an easy-to-use assessment and tutorial system that allows instructors to create, deliver, and customize tests in minutes. Instructors can build tests with as many as 250 questions using up to twelve question types; using ExamView's complete word-processing capabilities, they can enter an unlimited number of new questions or edit existing ones.

eInstructor's Resource Manual. This manual has many features, including chapter themes, lecture suggestions, directions for using print and nonprint resources, and additional instructional suggestions. This manual is available on the instructor's companion website.

WebTutor™ on Blackboard® and WebCT®. With WebTutor's text-specific, preformatted content and total flexibility, instructors can easily create and manage their own custom course website. WebTutor's course management tool gives instructors the ability to provide virtual office hours, post syllabi, set up threaded discussions, track student progress with the quizzing material, and much more. For students, WebTutor offers real-time access to a full array of study tools, including animations and videos that bring the book's topics to life, plus chapter outlines, summaries, glossary flashcards, practice quizzes, and weblinks.

CourseMate. Cengage Learning's History CourseMate brings course concepts to life with interactive learning, study, and exam preparation tools that support the printed textbook. Watch student comprehension soar as your class works with the printed textbook and the textbook-specific website. History CourseMate goes beyond the book to deliver what you need! History CourseMate includes an integrated eBook; interactive teaching and learning tools, including quizzes, flashcards, videos, and more; and EngagementTracker, a first-of-its-kind tool that monitors student engagement in the course. Learn more at **www.cengagebrain.com.**

CourseReader for U.S. History. CourseReader offers a way for instructors to build customized online readers for their courses. By selecting documents from a rich database of primary and secondary sources, including many from the Gale collections, instructors can create their own reader to match the specific needs of their course. An Editor's Choice developed for *The Enduring Vision* provides a useful starting point. Go to **Cengage.com/coursereader** for more information.

Student Resources

CourseMate. For students, CourseMate provides an additional source of interactive learning, study, and exam preparation outside the classroom. Students will find outlines and objectives, focus questions, flashcards, quizzes, primary source links, and video clips. In addition, CourseMate includes an integrated *The Enduring Vision* eBook. Students taking quizzes will be linked directly to relevant sections in the eBook for additional information. The eBook is fully searchable and students can even take notes and save them for later review. The eBook links out to rich media assets such as video and MP3 chapter summaries, primary source documents with critical thinking questions, and interactive (zoomable) maps. Students can use the eBook as their primary text or as a companion multimedia support. It is available at **www.cengagebrain.com.**

Book Companion Site. This website for students features a wide assortment of resources to help students master the subject matter. The website includes a glossary, chapter outlines, flashcards, crossword puzzles, tutorial quizzes, focus questions, and weblinks. Throughout the text, icons direct students to relevant exercises and self-testing material located on the student companion website.

Cengagebrain.com. Save your students time and money. Direct them to **www.cengagebrain.com** for additional choices in formats and savings and a better chance to succeed in your class. *Cengagebrain.com,* Cengage Learning's online store, is a single destination for more than 10,000 new textbooks, eTextbooks, eChapters, study tools, and audio supplements. Students have the freedom to purchase a-la-carte exactly what they need when they need it. Students can save 50 percent on the electronic textbook, and can pay as little as $1.99 for an individual eChapter.

Wadsworth American History Resource Center. Wadsworth's American History Resource Center gives your students access to a "virtual reader" with hundreds of primary sources, including speeches, letters, legal documents and transcripts, poems, maps, simulations, timelines, and additional images that bring history to life, along with interactive assignable exercises. A map feature including Google Earth™ coordinates and exercises will aid in student comprehension of geography and use of maps. Students can compare the traditional textbook map with an aerial view of the location today. It's an ideal resource for study, review, and research. In addition to this map feature, the resource center also provides blank maps for student review and testing.

Rand McNally Atlas of American History, 2e. This comprehensive atlas features more than eighty maps, with new content covering global perspectives, including events in the Middle East from 1945 to 2005, as well as population trends in the United States and around the world. Additional maps document voyages of discovery; the settling of the colonies; major U.S. military engagements, including the American Revolution and World Wars I and II; and sources of immigrations, ethnic populations, and patterns of economic change.

Reader Program. Cengage Learning publishes a number of readers, some containing exclusively primary sources, others a combination of primary and secondary sources, and some designed to guide students through the process of historical inquiry. Visit **Cengage.com/history** for a complete list of readers.

Custom Options

Nobody knows your students like you, so why not give them a text that is tailor-fit to their needs? Cengage Learning offers custom solutions for your course—whether it's making a small modification to *The Enduring Vision* to match your syllabus or combining multiple sources to create something truly unique. You can pick and choose chapters, include your own material, and add additional map exercises along with the Rand McNally Atlas to create a text that fits the way you teach. Ensure that your students get the most out of their textbook dollar by giving them exactly what they need. Contact your Cengage Learning representative to explore custom solutions for your course.

Acknowledgments

Any book, and this one in particular, is the result of the hard work of many people. In preparing this Concise Seventh Edition, we benefited from the critical readings of many colleagues. Our sincere thanks go in particular to the following instructors and teachers: Vanessa de los Reyes, Gateway Community and Technical College; Eva Mo, Modesto Junior College; Donald Trotter, Johnson Bible College; Jason McCollom, University of Arkansas; Charles Hubbard, Lincoln Memorial University; Verdis Robinson, Monroe Community College; Nicolas Rosenthal, Loyola Marymount University; and James Gillispie, Sampson Community College. As always, the editorial staff at Cengage has been outstanding. Particularly deserving of thanks are Ann West and Tonya Lobato, and also Roxanne Klaas of S4Carlisle Publishing Services. On behalf of everyone associated with *The Enduring Vision* over the years, Andrew Rieser expresses his condolences to the family of co-author Sandra McNair Hawley and dedicates this volume to her memory.

Chapter 1

Native Peoples of America

to 1500

Courtesy, National Museum of the American Indian, Smithsonian Institution #D115235

Kwakwaka'wakw Sun Transformation Mask, Northwest Coast

Chapter Preview

The First Americans, c. 13,000–2500 B.C.E.
How did environmental change shape the transition from Paleo-Indian to Archaic ways of life?

Cultural Diversity, c. 2500 B.C.E.–1500 C.E.
What were the principal differences among the Native American cultures that emerged after 2500 B.C.E.?

North American Peoples on the Eve of European Contact
What common values did Native Americans share despite their vast diversity?

American history began thousands of years before the arrival of Europeans. The earliest Native Americans lived in small hunter-gatherer bands, but as they spread across North and South America they adapted to a wide variety of regional environments. Consequently, their cultures diverged and diversified. Indian bands and communities ranged from a few dozen to thousands of members, with a large range of social structures. Hunters and gatherers, as well as farmers and fishers, depended on a wide variety of food sources. Nonetheless, many Indian cultures demonstrated common characteristics amid great diversity.

THE FIRST AMERICANS, C. 13,000–2500 B.C.E.

How did environmental change shape the transition from Paleo-Indian to Archaic ways of life?

Precisely how and when the Western Hemisphere was settled remains uncertain. Although many Indians believe that their ancestors originated in the Americas, most scientific theories point to the arrival of peoples from northeastern Asia during the last Ice Age (c. 33,000–10,700 B.C.E.), when land linked Siberia and Alaska. As the Ice Age waned, Native Americans adapted to environments that ranged from tropical to frigid and developed diverse cultures that nonetheless had many elements in common.

Peopling New Worlds

Monte Verde, Chile Site of human habitation by 12,000 B.C.E.

Bering land bridge Link between Northeast Asia and far Northwest North America during late Ice Age

Scientists now believe that the earliest migrants from Asia traveled by boat along the coastline around 13,000 B.C.E. Recent archaeological finds at **Monte Verde, Chile,** reveal evidence of human habitation by 12,000 B.C.E. Later migrants reached the Americas by crossing the **Bering land bridge** and fanned out in the interior as melting glaciers opened the way for eastward and southward migration.

Most Native Americans descend from these early migrations, but a later surge of migration brought Athapaskan (ath-a-PAS-kan)-speaking peoples to the Americas about 7000 B.C.E. Their descendants include the Apaches and Navajos. The arrival of non-Indian Inuits, Aleuts, and Eskimos after 3000 B.C.E. completed the peopling of the Americas.

Paleo-Indians Earliest peoples of the Americas, 13,000–8000 B.C.E.

Most **Paleo** (PAY-lee-oh)**-Indians** lived in small bands of fifteen to fifty people. The band lived together for the summer but split into smaller groups of one or two families for fall and winter. Although they moved constantly, they remained within informal boundaries except when they traveled to favored quarries to obtain jasper or flint for making tools. Here they encountered other bands, with whom they traded and joined in religious ceremonies. Most Paleo-Indians practiced **reciprocity,** the mutual bestowing of gifts and favors rather than competition for resources.

reciprocity Mutual bestowing of gifts and favors rather than competition for resources

By 9000 B.C.E. many big-game species, including mammoths and mastodons, had vanished. Paleo-Indian hunters contributed to this extinction, as did a warming climate and environmental changes. Human beings were major beneficiaries of these changes.

Archaic Societies

Climatic warming continued until about 4000 B.C.E. with dramatic effects for North America. Sea levels rose, flooding the shallow continental shelf, and glacial runoff filled the Great Lakes, the Mississippi River basin, and other waters. As the glaciers receded northward, so did the cold, icy arctic or subarctic environments that had covered much of what is now the United States. Treeless plains and evergreen forests yielded to deciduous forests in the East, grassland prairies on the Plains, and desert in much of the West. An immense range of plants and animals covered the landscape.

Archaic peoples Native Americans from 8000–2500 B.C.E.

The **Archaic** (ar-KAY-ick) **peoples,** as archaeologists term native North Americans from 8000 B.C.E. to sometime after 2500 B.C.E., lived off wide varieties of smaller

Chronology

c. 13,000 B.C.E.	People present in America
c. 10,500–9000 B.C.E.	Paleo-Indians spread throughout Western Hemisphere
c. 9000 B.C.E.	Extinction of big-game mammals
c. 8000 B.C.E.	Archaic era begins
c. 7000 B.C.E.	Athapaskan-speaking peoples arrive in North America
c. 5000 B.C.E.	First domesticated plants grown
c. 3000 B.C.E.	First maize grown in Mesoamerica
c. 3000–2000 B.C.E.	Eskimo and Aleut peoples arrive in North America
c. 2500 B.C.E.	Archaic societies yield before diverse cultures; first maize grown in North America
c. 1200 B.C.E.	Poverty Point flourishes in Louisiana
c. 400–100 B.C.E.	Adena culture flourishes in Ohio Valley
c. 250 B.C.E.	Hohokam culture begins in Southwest
c. 100 B.C.E.	Anasazi culture begins in Southwest
c. 100 B.C.E.– 600 C.E.	Hopewell culture thrives in Midwest
c. 1 C.E.	Rise of chiefdoms on Northwest Coast and in California
c. 100–700	Teotihuacán flourishes in Mesoamerica
c. 600–1400	Mayan kingdoms flourish
c. 700	Mississippian culture begins; Anasazi expansion begins
c. 900	Urban center arises at Cahokia
c.1000	Norse attempt, and fail, to colonize Vinland
c. 1200	Anasazi and Hohokam peoples disperse in Southwest
c. 1200–1400	Cahokia declines; inhabitants disperse
1428	Rise of Aztec empire
1438	Rise of Inca empire
1492	Christopher Columbus reaches Western Hemisphere

mammals, fish, and wild plants rather than big game. Greater efficiency in hunting and gathering permitted larger populations to inhabit smaller areas. In rich areas, such as the East and Midwest, large populations lived in villages for virtually the entire year. For example, a year-round village that flourished near present-day Kampsville, Illinois, from 3900 to 2800 B.C.E. supported 100 to 150 people. Its residents procured fish and mussels from local lakes to supplement the deer, birds, nuts, and seeds available in the surrounding area.

Over time, Archaic Americans sharpened distinctions between women's and men's roles. Generally men fished and hunted while women foraged for wild plant products. However, both genders apparently served as religious healers. As they foraged for wild plants, gatherers—usually women in North America—gradually learned how to manipulate their environments to favor plants that produced food and medicine. They then developed tools for digging and grinding, as well as effective methods of drying and storing seeds. Agricultural societies began domesticating wild animals such as sheep, goats, and cattle as early as 8000 B.C.E., but the Americas lacked large animals suitable for domestication; by the time Native Americans began farming, the only animals they found suitable for taming were llamas, turkeys, guinea pigs, and dogs, which seem to have been omnipresent in human societies as early as 30,000 B.C.E. This not only limited food sources but also forced American Indians to rely primarily on human power for carrying goods and dragging loads.

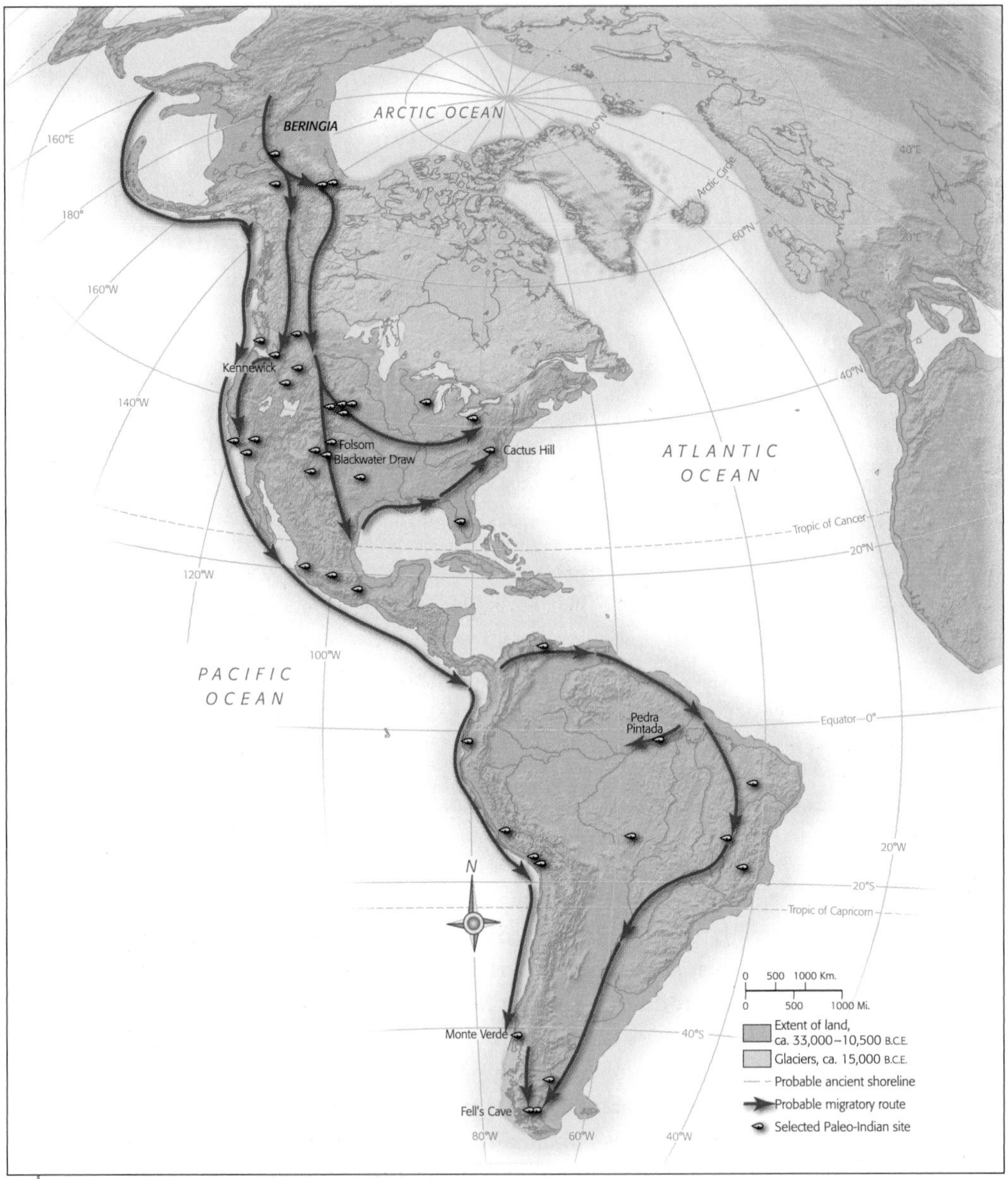

Map 1.1 The Peopling of the Americas

Scientists postulate two probable routes by which the earliest peoples reached America. By 9500 B.C.E., they had settled throughout the Western Hemisphere.

 Interactive Map

The most sophisticated of these early farmers lived in highland valleys in **Mesoamerica,** particularly Tehuacán (teh-wha-CAHN). By 3000 B.C.E. they were cultivating squash, gourds, beans, chili peppers, and fruits. At the same time Tehuacán farmers began the long process of domesticating a lowlands plant called teosinte, which ultimately became maize (maze), or corn. Maize agriculture spread rapidly; by 2500 B.C.E. maize was cultivated as far north as modern New Mexico and as far south as the Amazon basin.

At the same time, Indians in the Andes were already cultivating potatoes, while their counterparts along the Pacific coast harvested squash, beans, and peppers. Initially these domesticated plants constituted only a small part of the Native American diet, essentially a supplement to meat, fish, and wild plants. Centuries would pass before stable societies based primarily on agriculture emerged.

Checking In

- Historians believe that most Native Americans descended from Northeast Asian peoples who arrived in the Americas from around 33,000 to 9000 B.C.E.
- Paleo-Indians, the earliest peoples of the Americas, lived in small groups and were mainly hunters.
- Climatic warming created favorable environments for expansion, including the emergence of agriculture by 5000 B.C.E.

Mesoamerica Roughly, land extending from modern Mexico to Colombia; Central America plus Mexico

Cultural Diversity, c. 2500 B.C.E.–1500 C.E.

What were the principal differences among the Native American cultures that emerged after 2500 B.C.E.?

After 2500 B.C.E. many Native Americans moved far beyond the ways of their Archaic ancestors. The most far-reaching changes occurred among peoples whose environments permitted them to produce food surpluses by cultivating crops or by other means. Intensive farming radically changed the environment, and larger populations linked by trade and religion evolved into formal confederacies, and even hierarchical states joined by political and religious systems.

Mesoamerica and South America

Mesoamerican farmers rapidly developed sophisticated agricultural systems, improving both the quality and the quantity of their crops. In turn, the higher yields and improved nutrition led to the emergence of maize-based farming societies throughout Mesoamerica during the next eight centuries. According to geneticist Nina Fedoroff, the development of maize "arguably was the first, and perhaps man's greatest, feat of genetic engineering."

By 2000 B.C.E. some Mesoamerican farming societies were trading surplus crops to their nonfarming neighbors. Trade led to the development of wealthy and powerful urban centers that dominated surrounding communities. These chiefdoms generally dominated relatively small areas, but some developed into centralized states complete with taxes, public works, and armies. The capital of the largest early state, Teotihuacán (tehoh-tee-whah-KAHN), about fifty miles northeast of modern Mexico City, housed a population of one hundred thousand people. At its center was a complex of pyramids over which towered the

Richard Alexander Cooke III

Sun Pyramid, Teotihuacán

Built over several centuries, this pyramid remained the largest structure in the Americas until after the Spanish arrived.

Sun Pyramid, the largest structure in the Americas prior to the arrival of the Spanish. From 100 to 700 C.E., Teotihuacán dominated the Valley of Mexico, with trade networks extending throughout modern Mexico; its influence on the religion, government, and culture of its neighbors was enormous.

As Teotihuacán declined, the Maya (MY-uh) rose. Living in kingdom-states that flourished from southern Mexico to Honduras, the Maya developed a highly accurate calendar; a numerical system; and a system of phonetic, hieroglyphic writing. Mayan codices (singular, codex)—formed from bark paper glued into long folded strips—recorded religious ceremonies, historical traditions, and astronomical observations.

In the fifteenth century two powerful empires emerged: the Aztecs of Mexico and the Inca of Peru. In 1428 the Aztecs began asserting control over Lake Texcoco in the Valley of Mexico and its surrounding communities. After 1450 Aztec expansion became increasingly bloody, as Aztec priests maintained that their gods demanded to be served human blood and hearts; warriors sought captives for human sacrifice.

Tenochtitlán (teh-knowtch-teet-LAN), the Aztec capital, at its peak had some two hundred thousand inhabitants. At the center of the city was a massive temple complex. The Aztecs borrowed freely from other Mesoamerican societies, taking writing from Teotihuacán and the calendar from the Maya. To support the capital's population, the Aztecs developed intensive agriculture based on artificially created islands anchored in Lake Texcoco; Aztec engineers developed an elaborate irrigation system to provide fresh water for both people and crops.

The Aztecs collected taxes from conquered peoples living within a hundred miles of the capital; from those farther away, they exacted tribute. Aztec trading networks extended far from Tenochtitlán, reaching as far north as the American Southwest. However, by the early sixteenth century rebellions had flared up within the Aztec empire.

Far to the south, the Inca empire was expanding as well. After 1438, Inca conquests created an empire that stretched along the Andes and its adjacent areas. The Inca were highly successful farmers, producing enormous quantities of potatoes, maize, beans, and meats. They constructed terraced irrigation systems on their uneven terrain, perfected freeze-drying and other preservation techniques, and built a vast network of roads and bridges.

However, the arrival of the Spanish would destroy both empires.

The Southwest

The Southwest (the modern American Southwest and most of northern Mexico) is an arid region of diverse landscapes; however, various peoples managed to establish stable supplies of water there and become farmers. Although maize had reached the Southwest as early as 2500 c.e., large agricultural societies did not emerge until the introduction of drought-resistant strains of the plant around 400 b.c.e. The two most influential of these were the **Hohokam** (ho-HO-kum) and the **Anasazi** (an-uh-SAW-zee).

Hohokam Early agricultural society of Southwest

Anasazi Pueblo culture that dominated Southwest from 100 b.c.e.–1200 c.e.

Hohokam culture emerged in the third century b.c.e. when ancestors of Pima and Tohono O'odham Indians began farming in the Gila (HEE-la) River and Salt River valleys of southern Arizona. The Hohokam people built elaborate canal systems for irrigation that enabled them to harvest two crops each year. The construction and maintenance of the canals demanded large, coordinated workforces. The Hohokams therefore built permanent villages of several hundred residents, and many such communities were joined in confederations linked by canals. The central village in each confederation coordinated labor, trade, and religious and political life for all.

The Hohokam way of life drew on Mesoamerican materials and ideas. From about the sixth century c.e., the larger Hohokam villages had ball courts and platform mounds like those in Mesoamerica, and ball games became major public events. Mesoamerican art influenced Hohokam artists, who used clay, stone, turquoise, and shell. Archaeologists have found Mesoamerican items, such as rubber balls, macaw feathers, and copper bells, at Hohokam sites.

Anasazi culture originated during the first century b.c.e. in the Four Corners area where Arizona, New Mexico, Colorado, and Utah meet. Although they adopted village life and agriculture late, the Anasazis expanded rapidly in the eighth century c.e. and came to dominate a wide area. Modern Pueblo Indians are descendants of the Anasazi.

The Anasazis had a distinctive architecture. They constructed their early dwellings, round pit houses, in the shape of **kivas** (KEE-vahs), the partly underground, circular structures where Anasazi men conducted religious ceremonies. Anasazi-style apartments and kivas are characteristic of the architecture of the modern-day Pueblo Indians of the Southwest.

kivas A large chamber, often wholly or partially underground, in an Anasazi and later a Pueblo Indian village; used for religious ceremonies and other purposes

From the tenth through the mid-twelfth century, an unusually wet period, the Anasazis expanded over much of today's New Mexico and Arizona. Village populations grew to a thousand or more. In **Chaco** (CHAH-ko) **Canyon** in northwestern New Mexico, a cluster of twelve villages forged a powerful confederation numbering fifteen thousand people. Perfectly straight roads radiated from the canyon to satellite pueblos up to sixty-five miles away. The builders carved out stairs or footholds in the sides of steep cliffs. The canyon was a major trade center, importing and exporting a wide range of materials from and to Mesoamerica, the Great Plains, the Mississippi Valley, and California.

Chaco Canyon Center of powerful Anasazi confederation, 900–1200 c.e.

Devastating droughts in the late twelfth and thirteenth centuries destroyed classic Anasazi culture. Suddenly, the amount of farmland was drastically reduced for a population that had grown rapidly during the preceding centuries. The Indians abandoned the great Anasazi centers and scattered. Other large agricultural communities, such as those of the Hohokam, also dispersed when droughts came, clearing the way for the arrival of the nonfarming Navajos and Apaches at the end of the thirteenth century.

The Eastern Woodlands

Long before they developed agriculture, Indians of the Eastern Woodlands, the vast forests from the Mississippi Valley to the Atlantic coast, experimented with village life and political centralization. By 1200 B.C.E. about five thousand people had concentrated in a single village at Poverty Point on the Mississippi River in Louisiana. Two large mounds flanked the village, and six concentric embankments—the largest over half a mile in diameter—surrounded it. During the spring and autumn equinoxes, a person standing on the larger mound could watch the sun rise directly over the village center. Solar observations formed the basis for these Indians' religious beliefs as well as for their calendar.

Poverty Point lay at the center of a large political and economic unit. It imported quartz, copper, obsidian, crystal, and other sacred materials from long distances and distributed them to nearby communities. These communities almost certainly supplied the labor for the earthworks. The Olmec peoples of Mesoamerica clearly influenced the design and organization of Poverty Point. The settlement flourished for only three centuries and then declined, for reasons that are unclear. A different **mound-building culture,** the Adena, emerged in the Ohio Valley in the fifth century B.C.E. Adena villages rarely exceeded four hundred inhabitants, but the Adena people spread over a wide area and built hundreds of mounds, most of them containing graves that reflected an individual's social standing.

mound-building culture
Eastern Woodlands societies, which flourished from 1200 B.C.E.–1400 C.E.; included Poverty Point, Adena, Hopewell, and Mississippian

During the first century B.C.E., Adena culture evolved into a more developed and widespread culture known as Hopewell. Hopewell ceremonial centers, which were larger and more elaborate than those of the Adena, mushroomed along the Ohio River and Illinois River valleys. Some centers contained two or three dozen mounds within enclosures of several square miles. The graves of the elite contained elaborate burial goods: freshwater pearls, copper ornaments, mica, quartz, and other sacred substances. Hopewell artisans used raw materials from throughout America east of the Rockies. Through trade networks the Hopewell influence spread to communities as distant as places in modern-day Wisconsin, Florida, and New York.

The people who created the sophisticated Hopewell culture were primarily hunter-gatherers, not farmers. Although they did grow some crops, agriculture became a dietary mainstay for Woodlands people only between the seventh and twelfth centuries C.E.

The first full-time farmers in the East were the Mississippians, who lived on the flood plains of the Mississippi River and its major tributaries. Their culture, beginning sometime around 700 C.E., blended elements of the Hopewell culture and ideas from Mesoamerica with their own traditions. Mississippian towns, containing hundreds or even thousands of people, were built around open plazas like those of central Mexico. Religious temples and elite residences stood atop large mounds next to the plazas. Religious ceremonies focused on worship of the sun as the source of agricultural fertility. Chiefs claimed to be related to the sun, and when they died, wives and servants were killed to accompany them to the afterlife. Artisans produced sophisticated work in clay, stone, shell, copper, and wood, largely for religious and funeral rituals.

By the tenth century most Mississippian centers were part of larger confederacies based on trade and shared religious beliefs. Powerful "supercenters" and their chiefs dominated these confederacies. The most powerful confederacy revolved around the magnificent city of **Cahokia** (ka-HO-kee-uh), near modern St. Louis; its influence extended from the Appalachians to the edge of the Plains and from the Great Lakes to the Gulf of Mexico.

Cahokia Major mound-building "supercenter," which existed from 900–1200 C.E.

After 1200 C.E. Cahokia and other valley centers experienced shortages of food and other resources. Densely concentrated societies had taxed a fragile environment with a fluctuating climate. Competition for suddenly scarce resources led to debilitating warfare, and survivors fled to the surrounding prairies. By the fifteenth century, their descendants lived in villages linked by reciprocity instead of coercion.

The Spanish later encountered them as the forerunners of the Cherokee, Creek, and other Southeastern Indian peoples.

The Mississippians profoundly affected native culture in the Eastern Woodlands. They spread not only new strains of corn and beans but also the techniques and tools to cultivate them. However, northern New England and the upper Great Lakes had growing seasons too short for corn to become a reliable crop.

Cahokia Mounds Historic Site, painting by William R. Iseminger

Cahokia Mounds

This contemporary painting conveys Cahokia's grand scale. Not until the late eighteenth century did another North American city (Philadelphia) surpass the population of Cahokia, c. 1150.

Woodlands tribes employed slash-and-burn techniques, which were environmentally sound as well as economically productive. Indian men systematically burned hardwood forests to form open expanses of land. The grass and berry bushes that flourished there attracted deer and other game, and some areas of the ash-enriched soil were planted in corn, beans, and pumpkins. After several years of abundant harvests, yields declined, and the Indians repeated the process on another area; ground cover eventually restored the fertility of the abandoned areas, permitting the Indians to return.

Nonfarming Societies

Along the Pacific coast, from Alaska to southern California, improvements in the production and storage of food enabled Indians to develop more settled ways of life than their Archaic forebears. From the Alaskan panhandle to northern California, natives spent brief periods each year catching salmon and other fish. The Northwest Coast Indians dried and stored enough fish to last the year, and their seasonal movements gradually gave way to settled life in permanent villages of cedar-plank houses. On the Columbia Plateau, Indians built villages of pit houses and ate salmon through the summer. They left these communities in spring and fall for hunting and gathering.

By 1 C.E. many Northwest Coast villages numbered several hundred people. Trade and warfare strengthened the power of chiefs and other leaders, whose families had greater wealth and prestige than commoners. Leading families proclaimed their status in elaborate totem poles depicting supernatural beings linked to their ancestors and in potlatches, ceremonies in which the Indians gave away or destroyed much of their material wealth. The artistic and architectural achievements of Northwest Coast Indians awed Europeans.

At about the same time, Indians farther south, along the coast and in the interior valleys of what is now California, began to cluster in villages of one hundred or more people. Acorns dominated their diet, supplementing game, fish, and plants. After the fall harvest, Indians ground the acorns into meal, leached them of bitter tannic acid, and then roasted, boiled, or baked the nuts before eating or storing them.

The end of the Archaic period produced little change in the forbidding aridity of the Great Basin, encompassing present-day Nevada, western Utah, southern Idaho, and eastern Oregon. However, the area continued to support small hunting-and-gathering bands.

To the east of the Great Basin lay the grasslands of the Great Plains, which were too dry to support large human settlements but ideal for herds of game animals such as antelope, deer, and elk. Primary among the Great Plains animals were the buffalo, which served nomadic hunters as an ambulatory supermarket. In addition to meat, buffalo provided hides for clothing and tipis, as well as bones and horn for tools and arrowheads; Indians used most other buffalo parts as well. Following the great herds on foot, nomadic tribes killed individual animals with spears and arrows, but also stampeded hundreds at a time over cliffs. Despite such wasteful practices, humans were so few in number that they had no significant impact on the buffalo population before the arrival of the Europeans. There are no reliable estimates of the number of buffalo that roamed on the Great Plains, but they may well have numbered in the tens of millions.

In western Alaska, the Aleuts arrived around 3000 B.C.E., bringing with them sophisticated tools and weapons from their Siberian homeland. Most importantly, the Aleuts introduced the bow and arrow to the Americas. Over several thousand years, they spread eastward across Canada as far as Greenland.

The first verified contacts between Europe and America came when the **Norse** colonized Greenland in the 980s. The Norse traded with the Aleuts for furs and walrus ivory. In 1001 Leif Ericson led a group of Norse who planted a small settlement in **Vinland,** now known as Newfoundland. However, the Norse quickly settled into a pattern of hostility with local Indians. By 1015 the Norse had abandoned their Vinland settlement, although the Greenland settlements endured almost until the end of the fifteenth century; Europeans would later reap, at the expense of the native peoples, the fruits of a "new world."

Norse Also known as Vikings, a warrior culture from Scandinavia

Vinland Site of first known attempt at European settlement in the Americas

Checking In

- Powerful states, such as the Maya, Aztec, and Inca empires, developed in Mesoamerica and Peru.
- Pueblo society, featuring sophisticated agriculture and irrigation, developed in the Southwest.
- The Eastern Woodlands saw an increase of mound builders in Mississippian centers such as Cahokia.
- Along the Pacific coast, nonfarming societies flourished.

North American Peoples on the Eve of European Contact

What common values did Native Americans share despite their vast diversity?

In 1492 the Western Hemisphere numbered about 75 million people, clustered thickly in Mexico and Central America, the Caribbean islands, and Peru. Between 7 and 10 million Native Americans lived north of Mexico. Sparse nomad populations inhabited the Great Basin, the high plains, and the northern forests. Denser concentrations, however, thrived along the Pacific coast, in the Southwest and Southeast, in the Mississippi Valley, and along the Atlantic coast. Speaking many diverse languages and dialects, these people constituted several hundred Indian nations and tribes.

Despite the vast diversity of Native American cultures, they shared many characteristics. Kinship, reciprocity, and communal control of resources lay at the base of Indian societies, while trade ensured that the bow and arrow, ceramic pottery, and certain religious practices existed in almost all Indian societies.

Kinship and Gender

Kinship and gender cemented societies north of Mesoamerica together. Ties to cousins, aunts, and uncles created complex patterns of social obligation.

Kinship bonds were more important in Indian society than the bonds within **nuclear families,** that is, among married couples and their children. Indians did not necessarily expect spouses to be bound together forever, but kinship lasted for

nuclear families Married couples and their children

Map 1.2 Locations of Selected Native American Peoples, 1500 C.E.

Today's Indian nations were well established in homelands across the continent when Europeans first arrived. Many would combine with others or move in later centuries, either voluntarily or because they were forced.

Interactive Map

life. Customs regulating marriage varied, but strict rules prevailed. In most cultures young people married in their teens, generally after a period of sexual experimentation. Strong ties of residence and deference bound each couple to one or both sets of parents, producing what social scientists call **extended families.**

extended families Families that consist of several generations living together

In some Native American societies such as the Iroquois, the extended families of women took precedence over those of men. A new husband moved in with his wife's extended family. The mother's oldest brother was the primary male authority figure in a child's life. In many ways, a husband and father was simply the guest of his wife's family. Other Indian societies recognized men's extended families as primary, while still others did not distinguish sharply between the status of male and female family lines.

In addition, kinship was the basis for armed conflict. Indian societies typically considered homicide a matter to be resolved by the extended families of the victim and the perpetrator. If the perpetrator's family offered a gift that the victim's family considered appropriate, the question was settled. If not, the victim's kin might avenge the killing by armed retaliation. Chiefs or other leaders intervened to resolve disputes within the same village or tribe, but disputes between members of different groups could escalate into war. Densely populated societies that competed for scarce resources, as on the California coast, and centralized societies that attempted to dominate trade networks through coercion, such as the Hopewell culture, experienced frequent and intense warfare. However, warfare remained a low-level affair in most of North America. An exasperated New England officer, writing of his efforts to win Indian allies in the early seventeenth century, described a battle between two Indian groups as "more for pastime than to conquer and subdue enemies." He concluded that "they might fight seven years and not kill seven men."

Among almost all agricultural Indians except those in the Southwest (where men and women shared the work), women did most of the cultivating. With women producing most of the food supply, some communities gave women more power than European societies did. Among the Iroquois of what today is upstate New York, for example, women collectively owned the fields, distributed food, and played a major role in selecting chiefs. In New England, women often served as *sachems,* or chiefs.

Courtney Milne/Photographer's Choice/Getty Images

Big Horn Medicine Wheel, Wyoming

The medicine wheel was constructed between three and eight centuries ago as a center for religious ceremonies, including those relating to the summer solstice.

Manitou Powerful spiritual force that Algonquian-speaking Indians believed pervaded all of nature; other Native American languages had comparable terms

Spiritual and Social Values

Native American religions revolved around the conviction that nature was alive, pulsating with spiritual power—***Manitou*** (MAN-ih-too) in the Algonquian language. A mysterious, awe-inspiring force that affected human life for both good and evil, such power united all nature in an unbroken web. Belief in supernatural power led most Indians to seek constantly to conciliate all the spiritual forces in nature: living things, rocks, water, the sun and moon, even ghosts and witches.

Native Americans had several ways of gaining access to spiritual power. One was dreaming; most Native Americans took seriously the visions that came to them in sleep. They also sought access to the supernatural by using physical ordeals to alter their consciousness. Young men gained recognition as adults through a vision quest—a solitary venture that entailed fasting and waiting for the appearance of a spirit that would endow them with special powers. Girls went through comparable rituals at the onset of menstruation, to initiate them into the spiritual world from which female reproductive power flowed. Entire communities often engaged in collective power-seeking rituals, such as the Sun Dance (see Chapter 17).

Native Americans reinforced cooperation with a strong sense of order. Custom, the demands of social conformity, and the rigors of nature strictly regulated life and people's everyday affairs. Revenge was a ritualized way of restoring order. Failure to restore order could bring ominous consequences—blind hatred, unending violence, and, most feared of all, witchcraft. Indians would share this dread with both the Europeans and the Africans they would encounter after 1492.

The principle of reciprocity remained strong. Although it involved mutual give-and-take, the purpose of reciprocity was not equality, but the maintenance of equilibrium and interdependence among individuals of unequal power and prestige.

Most leaders' authority depended on the obligations they bestowed, rather than on coercion. The distribution of gifts obligated members of the community to support them and to accept their authority. In the same way, powerful communities distributed gifts to weaker neighbors who reciprocated with tribute in the form of material goods and submission.

CHECKING IN

- Kinship ties bound virtually all Native Americans.
- In most Native American societies, gender roles were clear: women farmed and men hunted.
- Native Americans lived in a world permeated by spiritual power that they could tap into through various rituals.
- Indian societies generally demanded cooperation and order from their members.
- Reciprocity dominated political and social relationships among individuals and between leaders and their followers.

Chapter Summary

How did environmental change shape the transition from Paleo-Indian to Archaic ways of life? (page 2)

Ancestors of most Native Americans reached North America from around 33,000 to 10,500 B.C.E., during an Ice Age when Asia and North America were directly connected. Warming weather facilitated the spread of these Paleo-Indians and granted them access to a wide range of food sources that could support large populations. Climate change also contributed to the extinction of many of the large animals that might have threatened early Americans.

KEY TERMS

Monte Verde, Chile *(p. 2)*
Bering land bridge *(p. 2)*
Paleo-Indians *(p. 2)*
reciprocity *(p. 2)*

What were the principal differences among the Native American cultures that emerged after 2500 B.C.E.? (page 5)

From 2500 B.C.E. to 1500 C.E. diverse Native American societies based on agriculture proliferated and adapted to widely varying environments. Among the most prominent were the centralized Mesoamerican societies, such as the Maya and the Aztec; the Inca of the Peruvian Andes; the Pueblo societies of what is now the southwestern United States; and the Eastern Woodlands mound builders of Hopewell, Adena, and Cahokia. Nonfarming societies like those of the Pacific Northwest also prospered. The vast grasslands of the Great Plains were home to nomadic hunters dependent on the great buffalo herds.

What common values did Native Americans share despite their vast diversity? (page 11)

Despite their diversity, the majority of these societies shared several common characteristics. In most, kinship played a critical social and political role, with extended families assuming greater importance than nuclear families. Gender also played a major role in organizing most societies, with women doing the farming and men primarily hunting. Indians believed that nature was spiritual as well as physical and sought to live in accord with the supernatural. Most people sought orderly societies and relied on reciprocity to maintain stability.

Native Americans never saw themselves as a single people. It was Europeans who emphasized differences between themselves and the Indians, a name bestowed by Christopher Columbus, who thought he had landed in the Indies. This new America, in which people were categorized according to continental ancestry, was radically different from the one that flourished for thousands of years before 1492.

KEY TERMS continued

Archaic peoples *(p. 2)*
Mesoamerica *(p. 5)*
Hohokam *(p. 7)*
Anasazi *(p. 7)*
kivas *(p. 7)*
Chaco Canyon *(p. 7)*
mound-building culture *(p. 8)*
Cahokia *(p. 9)*
Norse *(p. 11)*
Vinland *(p. 11)*
nuclear families *(p. 11)*
extended families *(p. 13)*
Manitou *(p. 14)*

Go to the CourseMate website at **www.cengagebrain.com** for additional study tools and review materials—including audio and video clips—for this chapter.

Chapter 2

The Rise of the Atlantic World

1400–1625

Courtesy of the John Carter Brown Library at Brown University

Bartholomew Gosnold Trading with Wampanoag Indians at Martha's Vineyard (1602), by Theodore Debry, 1634

Chapter Preview

African and European Backgrounds
What major changes were reshaping the African and European worlds in the fifteenth and sixteenth centuries?

Europe and the Atlantic World, 1440–1600
What was the Atlantic world, and how did it emerge?

Footholds in North America, 1512–1625
How did European exploration, conquest, and colonization of North America begin?

At ten o'clock on a moonlit night the tense crew spotted a glimmering light. At two o'clock the next morning came the shout "Land! Land!" It was October 12, 1492. At daybreak Christopher Columbus went ashore, the royal standard of Spain fluttering, knelt to give thanks, and rose to claim for Spain the island that he named San Salvador.

Columbus's meeting with the Tainos marked the first step in the formation of an Atlantic world. After 1492, peoples from Europe, Africa, and North and South America became intertwined in elaborate webs of trade, colonization, religion, and war. These interchanges constantly challenged customary ways of thinking and acting. They also led to far-reaching environmental changes, as not only people but also plants, animals, and germs crossed the Atlantic in both directions, a process known as the "Columbian exchange." European nations sought to increase their wealth and power by conquering and exploiting the inhabitants of the Americas, whom they deemed uncivilized.

In much of what is now Latin America, the arrival of the Europeans led to conquest. In the future United States and Canada, however, European mastery came more slowly; more than one hundred years would pass before self-sustaining colonies were established there.

African and European Backgrounds

What major changes were reshaping the African and European worlds in the fifteenth and sixteenth centuries?

When the Atlantic world emerged in the fifteenth and sixteenth centuries, enormous changes were engulfing the Atlantic basin. In the Americas, some societies rose, others fell, and still others adapted to the new circumstances (see Chapter 1). In both West Africa and western Europe, a market society emerged, and wealthy merchants financed dynastic rulers trying to extend their domains.

Western Europe's transformation was thoroughgoing. Its population nearly doubled, wealth and power changed hands, and new modes of thought and spirituality challenged established systems. Social, political, and religious upheaval accompanied a brilliant explosion of creativity and innovation.

West Africa: Tradition and Change

Before the beginning of Atlantic travel, the only link between sub-Saharan Africa and the Mediterranean was a broad belt of grassland, or **savannah,** which separated the desert from the forests to the south. Here caravan trade stimulated the rise of kingdoms and empires whose size and wealth rivaled those of any in Europe.

savannah Rich grasslands where West African civilizations prospered

The richest grassland kingdoms rose in West Africa, with its ample stores of gold. Chief among these in the fifteenth century was Mali, whose Muslim rulers enjoyed access to a network of wealthy Muslim rulers and merchants. Mali's wealth rested on the careful cultivation of trade, dominated by gold and slaves, and its fame extended throughout Africa, Europe, and the Middle East.

Gold had recently become the standard for all European currencies, and demand for the precious metal soared. Thousands of newcomers flooded into the region later known as the Gold Coast, and new states emerged to claim their share of the gold trade.

To the south of the savannah empires lay a region of small states and chiefdoms. During the first millennium C.E., Islamic states arose in Senegambia (seh-nuh-GAM-bee-ah), at Africa's westernmost bulge, and in Guinea's (GINN-ee) coastal forests. The best-known state was Benin (BEH-nin), where artisans fashioned magnificent ironwork for centuries.

Near the Congo River still farther south, four major kingdoms had arisen by the fifteenth century. The most powerful of these kingdoms was Kongo.

West African leaders wielded sharply different amounts and kinds of political power. Grassland emperors claimed semigodlike status, whereas rulers of smaller kingdoms depended on their ability to persuade, to conform to custom, and

Jenny Pate/Robert Harding World Imagery/Corbis

Sankore Mosque, Timbuktu, Mali

Sankore was one of three great mosques built during the fourteenth century when Timbuktu became the center of Islamic worship and learning in West Africa.

sometimes to redistribute wealth justly among their people.

In West Africa, kinship groups knit societies together. Parents, aunts, uncles, distant cousins, and those who shared clan ties formed networks of mutual obligation. In centuries to come, the tradition of strong extended families would help enslaved Africans to endure the breakup of nuclear families by sale. The region's high mortality rate from famine and tropical disease epidemics was a driving force behind marriage. Children were an essential part of the labor force, contributing to a family's wealth by increasing its food production and the amount of land it cultivated. Men of means frequently married more than one wife in order to produce more children; women generally married soon after puberty.

Both men and women farmed. Vast amounts of land and a relatively sparse population enabled African farmers to shift their fields periodically and thus maintain high soil quality and productivity. In areas of coastal rain forest, food crops such as yams, sugar cane, bananas, and eggplant flourished; so, too, did cotton. On the grasslands, cattle raising and fishing complemented the cultivation of millet, sorghum, and rice.

By the fifteenth century the market economy took in many small farmers, who traded surplus crops for other food and cloth. Artisans wove cotton or raffia palm leaves, made clothing and jewelry, and crafted tools and religious objects.

Religion permeated African life. People believed that another world lay beyond the one they perceived through their five senses, a world to which the souls of most people passed at death. Deities spoke to mortals through a variety of means, including priests, dreams, "speaking shrines," and magical charms. West African religions emphasized the importance of continuous revelations; consequently, there was no fixed dogma or hierarchy like those that characterized both Islam and Christianity. African religion also emphasized ancestor worship, venerating ancestors as spiritual guardians. Religious motifs saturated African art. West Africans used their ivory, cast-iron, and wood sculptures in ceremonies reenacting creation myths and honoring spirits. A strong moralistic streak ran through African folktales. Oral reciters transmitted these stories in dramatic public presentations with ritual masks, dance, and music of complex rhythmic structure. West African art and music powerfully influenced twentieth-century art and jazz.

Chronology

c. 1400–1600	European Renaissance
c. 1400–1600	Coastal West African kingdoms rise and expand
1440	Portuguese slave trade in West Africa begins
1488	Bartolomeu Días reaches the Cape of Good Hope
1492	Christian "reconquest" of Spain; Columbus lands at San Salvador
1498	Vasco da Gama rounds the Cape of Good Hope and reaches India
1517	Protestant Reformation begins in Germany
1519–1521	Hernán Cortés leads conquest of the Aztec empire
1519–1522	Magellan's expedition circumnavigates the globe
1532–1536	Spanish conquest of Inca empire
1534	Church of England breaks from the Roman Catholic church
1539–1543	De Soto attempts conquests in southeastern America
1541–1542	Cartier attempts to colonize eastern Canada
1558	Elizabeth I becomes queen of England
1565	St. Augustine founded by Spanish
1585–1590	English colony of Roanoke established, then disappears
1588	England defeats the Spanish Armada
1598	Oñate founds New Mexico
1603	James I becomes king of England
1607	English found colonies at Jamestown and Sagadahoc
1608	Champlain founds New France
1609	Henry Hudson explores the Hudson River
1610–1614	First Anglo-Powhatan War
1614	New Netherlands colony founded
1619	Large exports of tobacco from Virginia begin; House of Burgesses, first elected assembly in English North America, established in Virginia; first Africans arrive in Virginia
1620	Plymouth colony founded
1622–1632	Second Anglo-Powhatan War
1624	James I revokes Virginia Company's charter

Among Africans, Islam appealed primarily to merchants trading with Muslim North Africa and to grassland rulers eager to consolidate their power. By 1400, Islam had just begun to affect the daily lives of grassland cultivators and artisans.

European Culture and Society

When Columbus reached the Americas in 1492, Europe was approaching the height of a cultural revival known as the **Renaissance,** a rebirth of classical Greek and Roman culture. Intellectuals and poets believed that their age marked a return to the ideals

Renaissance "Rebirth" of classical Greek and Roman culture that swept Europe from the fifteenth to the seventeenth century

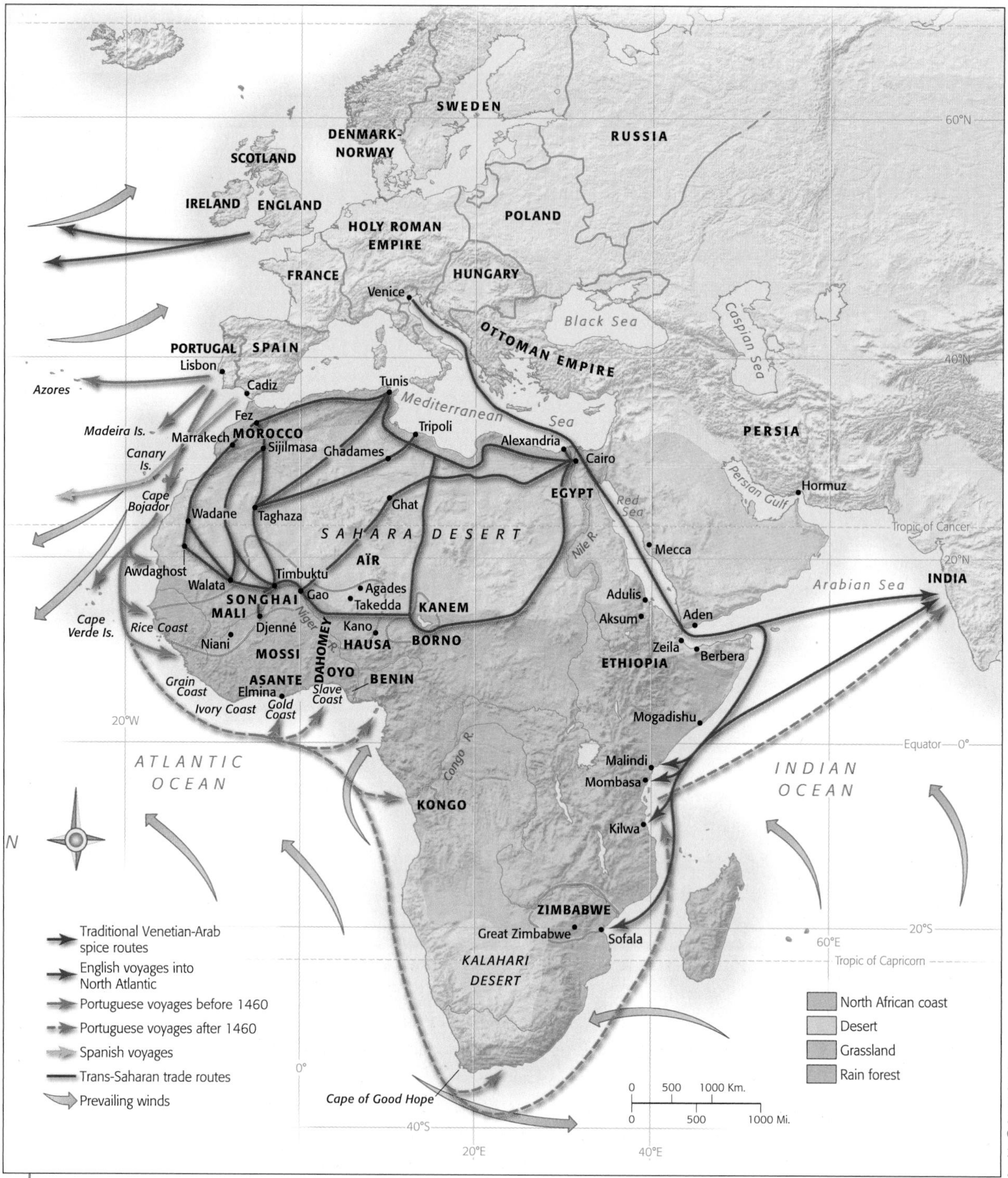

Map 2.1 Europe, Africa, and Southwestern Asia in 1500

During the fifteenth century, Portuguese voyages established maritime trade links between Africa and Europe, circumventing older trans-Saharan routes. Several voyages near the end of the century extended Europe's reach to India and the Americas.

Interactive Map

of the ancient Greeks and Romans. The writings of Muslim, Eastern Orthodox, and Jewish scholars provided a treasure trove of ancient texts in philosophy, science, medicine, geography, and other subjects. Scholars strove to reconcile Christian faith and ancient philosophy, to explore the mysteries of nature, to map the world, and to explain the motions of the heavens. Renaissance painters and sculptors created works based on close observations of nature and attention to perspective.

At the same time, European society quivered with tension. The era's artistic and intellectual creativity stemmed partly from intense social and spiritual stress, as Europeans groped for stability by glorifying order, hierarchy, and beauty. A concern for power and rank, or "degree," dominated European life in the fifteenth and sixteenth centuries. Gender, wealth, inherited position, and political power affected every European's status, and few people lived beyond the reach of some political authority's claim to tax and rule. But this order was shaky. Conflicts between states, between religions, and between rich and poor threatened the balance, making Europeans cling all the more eagerly to order and hierarchy.

Change lay at the heart of these conflicts. By the end of the fifteenth century, strong national monarchs in France and England had unified their realms and reduced the power of both the nobility and the Catholic church. On the Iberian Peninsula, the marriage of King Ferdinand of Aragon and Queen Isabella had created the Spanish monarchy and a unified Spain.

Between 70 and 80 percent of Europeans were peasants. Taxes, rents, and other dues to landlords and church officials were heavy. Poor harvests or war drove even well-to-do peasants to starvation.

By 1600 dramatic growth was driving up the population to 100 million. Food supplies, however, did not rise as rapidly. Peasant families survived on pitifully low yields of wheat, barley, and oats. Plowing, sowing, and harvesting together, they also grazed livestock on jointly owned "commons." But with new land at a premium, landlords, especially the English gentry, began to "enclose" the commons, thus making them private property. Peasants with no *written* title to their lands were particularly vulnerable.

Environmental factors worsened peasants' circumstances. A "little Ice Age" began in the fifteenth century and lasted more than four centuries, drastically reducing the food supply. Hunger and malnutrition were widespread, and full-scale famine struck in some areas. Population growth led to increased demand for wood and thus to deforestation of large areas; the subsequent disappearance of wild foods and game accelerated the exodus of rural Europeans to towns and cities.

Although numerous, European towns usually contained only a few thousand inhabitants. London, a great metropolis of 200,000 people by 1600, was an exception. Large or small, towns were dirty and disease ridden, and townspeople lived closely packed with their neighbors. People of the times saw towns as centers of opportunity, and immigration from the countryside swelled urban populations.

The consequences of rapid population growth were particularly acute in England, where the population doubled from 2.5 million in 1500 to 5 million by 1620. Some members of the gentry grew rich selling wool; however, because of technological stagnation, per capita output and household income among textile workers fell. In effect, more workers competed for fewer jobs as European markets for English cloth diminished and as food prices rose. Land **enclosure** aggravated

enclosure English practice of fencing off what had been common grazing land; left many peasants impoverished unemployment; large numbers of unemployed workers and displaced farmers wandered the countryside, seeming to threaten law and order. A handful of English writers began to speculate that overseas colonies could serve in effect as a safety valve.

As in the New World and Africa, traditional society in Europe rested on long-term, reciprocal relationships. Reciprocity required the upper classes to act with self-restraint and dignity, and the lower classes to show deference to their "betters." It demanded strict economic regulation, too, to ensure that sellers charged a "just" price—one that covered costs and allowed the seller to profit but barred him from taking advantage of buyers' and borrowers' misfortunes or of shortages to make "excessive" profits.

Yet the ideals of traditional economic behavior had been withering for centuries. By the sixteenth century, nothing could stop the practices of charging interest on borrowed money and of increasing prices in response to demand. New forms of business organization, such as the **joint-stock company,** the ancestor of the modern corporation, steadily spread. Demand for capital investment grew, and so too did the supply of accumulated wealth. Gradually, a new economic outlook arose that justified the unimpeded acquisition of wealth and unregulated economic competition. Its adherents insisted that individuals owed one another only the money necessary to settle each market transaction. This "market economy" capitalism stood counter to traditional demands for the strict regulation of economic activity to ensure social reciprocity and to maintain "just prices."

joint-stock company Forerunner of modern corporation; way to raise large sums of money by selling shares in an enterprise

Sixteenth- and seventeenth-century Europeans were ambivalent about economic enterprise and social change. A restless desire for opportunity kept life simmering with competitive tension. However, even those who prospered still sought the security and prestige of traditional social distinctions, and the poor longed for the age-old values that they hoped would restrain irresponsible greed.

Fundamental change in European society could also be seen in the rising importance of the nuclear family. Each member of the family—father, mother, children—had specific roles. The father exercised supreme authority; the wife bore and reared children, and assisted her husband in the unending labor of providing for the family's subsistence. Children were laborers from an early age. The family was thus the principal economic unit in European society and the household, the primary social organization. Those who lived outside a household were viewed with extreme suspicion and became easy targets for accusations of theft or even witchcraft.

Europeans frequently characterized the nuclear family as a "little commonwealth." A father's authority over his family supposedly mirrored God's rule of Creation and the king's over his subjects. According to a German writer, "wives should obey their husbands and not seek to dominate them. . . . Husbands . . . should treat their wives with consideration and occasionally close an eye to their faults." Repeated male complaints about "wives who think themselves every way as good as their husbands" suggest that male domination had its limits.

Religious Upheavals

Although predominantly Christian by 1400, Europe was also home to significant numbers of Muslims and Jews.

Although Jewish and Muslim European minorities shared Christians' worship of a single supreme being, based on the God of the Old

Testament, hatred and violence often marred their shared history. For more than three centuries, European Christians had conducted Crusades against Muslims in the Middle East; each side saw the conflict as "holy war" or "jihad" and labeled the other "infidel." Ultimately, ambitious rulers transformed religious conflicts into wars of conquest. At the same time as the Catholic empires of Spain and Portugal drove Muslims from their territory, the Islamic Ottoman empire conquered much of the Balkans and menaced Central Europe. In 1492, the Spanish completed the "reconquest" of the Iberian Peninsula from Muslims and forced Jews to convert or leave.

The medieval Christian church taught that Christ had founded the church to save sinners from hell. Every time a priest said Mass, Christ's sacrifice was repeated, and divine grace flowed to sinners through sacraments that priests alone could administer—especially baptism, confession, and communion. In most of Europe the "church" was a network of clergymen set apart from laypeople by ordination into the priesthood and by the fact that they did not marry. The pope, the "vicar (representative) of Christ," topped this hierarchy.

The papacy wielded awesome spiritual power. Fifteenth- and sixteenth-century popes claimed the authority to dispense extra blessings, or "indulgences," to repentant sinners in return for "good works," such as donating money to the church. Indulgences also promised time off from future punishment in purgatory. Given people's anxieties over sin, indulgences were enormously popular.

However, the sale of indulgences provoked charges of materialism and corruption. In 1517 Martin Luther, a German friar, attacked the practice. When the papacy tried to silence him, Luther broadened his criticism to include the Mass, priests, and the pope. His revolt sparked the **Protestant Reformation,** which changed Christianity forever.

Protestant Reformation Split of reformers from Roman Catholic church; triggered by Martin Luther

To Luther, the selling of indulgences was evil not only because it bilked people but also because the church did harm by falsely assuring people that they could "earn" salvation by doing good works. Luther believed instead that God alone chose whom to save and that believers should trust only God's love, not the word of priests and the pope. Luther's own spiritual struggle and experience of being "reborn" constituted a classic conversion experience—the heart of Protestant religion as it would be preached and practiced for centuries in England and North America.

Later reformers also abandoned Catholicism. For example, the French theologian **John Calvin** insisted on the doctrine of predestination, in which an omnipotent God "predestined" most sinful humans to hell, saving only a few to exemplify his grace.

John Calvin Early Protestant theologian who believed in "predestination"

Despite their differences, Protestants shared much common ground. Reading the Bible became an essential element of faith; translations into living languages made the Bible accessible, and the newly invented printing press allowed for wide circulation. Protestantism thus fostered education. Protestants also rejected the idea that priests had special powers; each individual had to assume responsibility for his or her own spiritual and moral condition. Finally, many Protestants felt displaced by the rapidly changing European world and yearned for greater simplicity. Thus, Protestantism condemned the replacement of traditional reciprocity by marketplace values.

Challenged by the rise of Protestantism, the Catholic church displayed remarkable resilience. Indeed, the papacy vigorously attacked church corruption and combated Protestant viewpoints. This Catholic revival, known as the Counter-Reformation, created the modern Roman Catholic church.

The Reformation also split Europe geographically. Many northern and western European areas, including England, most of the German states, the Netherlands, and parts of France, became predominantly Protestant; most southern European states—Portugal, Spain, and Italy—and most of France remained Roman Catholic.

The Reformation in England, 1533–1625

England's Reformation began when King Henry VIII, anxious for a male heir, tried to annul his marriage to Catherine of Aragon. When the pope refused to do so, Henry persuaded Parliament to annul the marriage and then to proclaim him "supreme head" of the Church of England (the Anglican church).

Religious strife troubled England for over a century after Henry's break with Rome. Under his son Edward VI (ruled 1547–1553), however, the English church veered sharply toward Protestantism. Then Henry's daughter Mary assumed the throne in 1553 and tried to restore Catholicism, in part by burning several hundred Protestants at the stake.

The reign of Mary's successor, Elizabeth I, who became queen in 1558, marked a crucial watershed. Most English people were now Protestant; *how* Protestant was the question. A militant Calvinist minority, the **Puritans,** demanded wholesale "purification" of the Church of England from "popish abuses." As Calvinists, they affirmed salvation by predestination, denied Christ's presence in the Eucharist, and believed that a learned sermon was the heart of true worship. They wished to free each congregation from outside interference and encouraged lay members to participate in parish affairs.

Puritans English followers of Calvin, dissenters from established Church of England

Puritanism appealed mainly to the growing middle sectors of English society—the gentry, university-educated clergymen and intellectuals, merchants, shopkeepers, artisans, and well-to-do farmers. Self-discipline had become central to both the worldly and the spiritual dimensions of these people's lives, and from their ranks would come the settlers of New England (see Chapter 3). Puritanism attracted few of the titled nobility, who enjoyed their wealth and privilege, and few of the desperately poor who struggled for mere survival.

Queen Elizabeth distrusted Puritan militancy until the pope declared her a heretic in 1570 and urged Catholics to overthrow her. By courting influential Puritans and embracing militant anti-Catholicism, Elizabeth maintained most Puritans' loyalty. After her death, however, religious tensions came to a boil.

Under Elizabeth, most Puritans expected to transform the Church of England into independent congregations of "saints." However, Stuart monarchs James I (ruled 1603–1625) and Charles I (ruled 1625–1649) bitterly opposed Puritan efforts to eliminate the office of bishop. Nonetheless, they quietly tolerated Calvinists who did not dissent loudly.

CHECKING IN

- In the fifteenth century the West African savannah fragmented politically, and Islam gained a foothold.
- From the fourteenth to seventeenth centuries, Europe was undergoing major changes. The Renaissance, the rise of nation-states, population growth, the emergence of a market economy, and the Reformation set the stage for territorial expansion and conflict.
- In the throes of religious transformation, Reformation England saw the rise of Puritanism.

Europe and the Atlantic World, 1440–1600

What was the Atlantic world, and how did it emerge?

The forces transforming Europe reverberated beyond that continent. In the fifteenth and sixteenth centuries, monarchs and merchants organized imperial ventures to Africa, Asia, and the Americas. Europeans proclaimed that their mission was to introduce Christianity and "civilizations" to the "savages" and "pagans" in alien lands—and to increase their own fortunes and power. Both the transatlantic slave trade and the colonization of the Americas grew out of this new imperialism, and the cascading exchanges that resulted created a new Atlantic world.

Portugal and the Atlantic, 1440–1600

Merchants realized that they could increase their profits by trading directly with Asia and Africa. Leading the shift from a Mediterranean to an Atlantic world was Portugal.

Improved maritime technology permitted this European expansion. In the early fifteenth century, shipbuilders added the triangular Arab sail to their heavy cargo ships, creating a highly maneuverable ship, the caravel, to sail the stormy Atlantic. Further, the growing use of the compass and astrolabe permitted mariners to calculate their bearings on the open sea. Hand in hand with the technological advances of this "maritime revolution," Renaissance scholars corrected ancient geographical data and drew increasingly accurate maps.

Led by **Prince Henry "the Navigator,"** Portugal was first to capitalize on these developments. Henry encouraged Portuguese seamen to pilot their caravels farther down the African coast searching for weak spots in Muslim defenses and for trade opportunities. By the time of Henry's death, the Portuguese had built a profitable slaving station at Arguin; shortly afterward, they had penetrated south of the equator. In 1488 Bartolomeu Días reached Africa's southern tip, the Cape of Good Hope, opening the possibility of direct trade with India, and in 1498 Vasco da Gama led a Portuguese fleet around the cape and on to India. For more than a century the Portuguese remained an imperial presence in the Indian Ocean and the East Indies (modern Indonesia). Far more significantly, they brought Europeans face to face with black Africans and an already flourishing slave trade.

Prince Henry "the Navigator" Member of Portuguese royal family who encouraged exploration of Africa and searched for routes to Asia

The "New Slavery" and Racism

Slavery was well established in fifteenth-century West Africa, as elsewhere. The grassland emperors as well as individual families depended on slave labor. However, most slaves or their children were absorbed into African families over time. In contrast, first Arabs, and then Europeans, turned African slavery into an intercontinental business.

In 1482, the Portuguese built an outpost, Elmina, on West Africa's Gold Coast, but they continued to rely primarily on African-controlled commercial networks. The local African kingdoms were too strong for the Portuguese to attack, and black rulers traded—or chose not to trade—according to their own self-interest.

African View of Portuguese, ca. 1650–1700

A carver in the kingdom of Benin, on Africa's west coast, created this salt holder depicting Portuguese officials and their ship.

"new slavery" Harsh form of slavery based on racism; arose as a result of Portuguese slave trade with Africa

The coming of the Portuguese slavers changed West African societies. Small kingdoms in Guinea and Senegambia expanded to "service" the trade, and some of their rulers became rich. Farther south, in modern Angola, the kings of Kongo used the slave trade to consolidate their power and adopted Christianity.

Europeans had used slaves since ancient Greece and Rome, but ominous changes took place once the Portuguese began making voyages to Africa. The **"new slavery"** was a high-volume business that expanded at a steady rate as Europeans colonized the Western Hemisphere and established plantation societies there. The "new slavery" had two devastating consequences. First, it became a demographic catastrophe for West Africa and its peoples. Before the Atlantic slave trade ended in the nineteenth century, nearly 12 million Africans would be shipped across the sea. Slavery on this scale had been unknown since the Roman Empire. Second, African slaves were subjected to new extremes of dehumanization. In medieval Europe, slaves had primarily performed domestic service, but by 1450 the Portuguese and Spanish had created large slave-labor plantations on their Atlantic and Mediterranean islands. Using African slaves who toiled until death, these plantations produced sugar for European markets. Enslaved Africans became property rather than persons of low status, consigned to endless, exhausting, mindless labor. By 1600 the "new slavery" had become a brutal link in an expanding commerce that ultimately would encompass all major Western nations.

Finally, race became the ideological basis of the "new slavery." Africans' blackness and alien religion dehumanized them in European eyes. As racial prejudice hardened, Europeans found it easy to justify black slavery. European Christianity, moreover, made few attempts to soften slavery's rigors. Because the victims of the "new slavery" were physically distinctive and culturally alien, slavery became a lifelong, hereditary, and despised status.

To America and Beyond, 1492–1541

The fascinating, contradictory figure of Christopher Columbus (1451–1506) embodied Europeans' varied motives for expansion. The son of an Italian weaver, Columbus became obsessed by the idea that Europeans could reach Asia by sailing westward across the Atlantic. Combining an overestimation of Asia's eastward thrust with an underestimation of Earth's circumference, he concluded that the world was much smaller than it actually is and that the open-sea distance from Europe to Asia was roughly three thousand miles, not the actual twelve thousand miles. Religious fervor led Columbus to dream of carrying Christianity around the globe, but he also hungered for wealth and glory.

Europeans had ventured far into the Atlantic before Columbus: besides the early Norse, fifteenth-century English fishing boats may have reached North America's coast. What distinguished Columbus was his persistence in hawking his "enterprise of the Indies" around Europe's royal courts. In 1492 the rulers of newly united Spain, Isabella of Castile and Ferdinand of Aragon, accepted Columbus's offer, hoping to break a threatened Portuguese monopoly on Asian trade. Picking up the westerly trade winds, Columbus's three small ships made landfall within a month off the North American coast at a small island that he named San Salvador.

Treaty of Tordesillas Agreement in which Portugal and Spain divided between them all future discoveries in the non-Christian world

Word of Columbus's discovery fired Europeans' imagination. It also induced the Spanish and Portuguese to sign the **Treaty of Tordesillas** (tore-day-SEE-yuss)

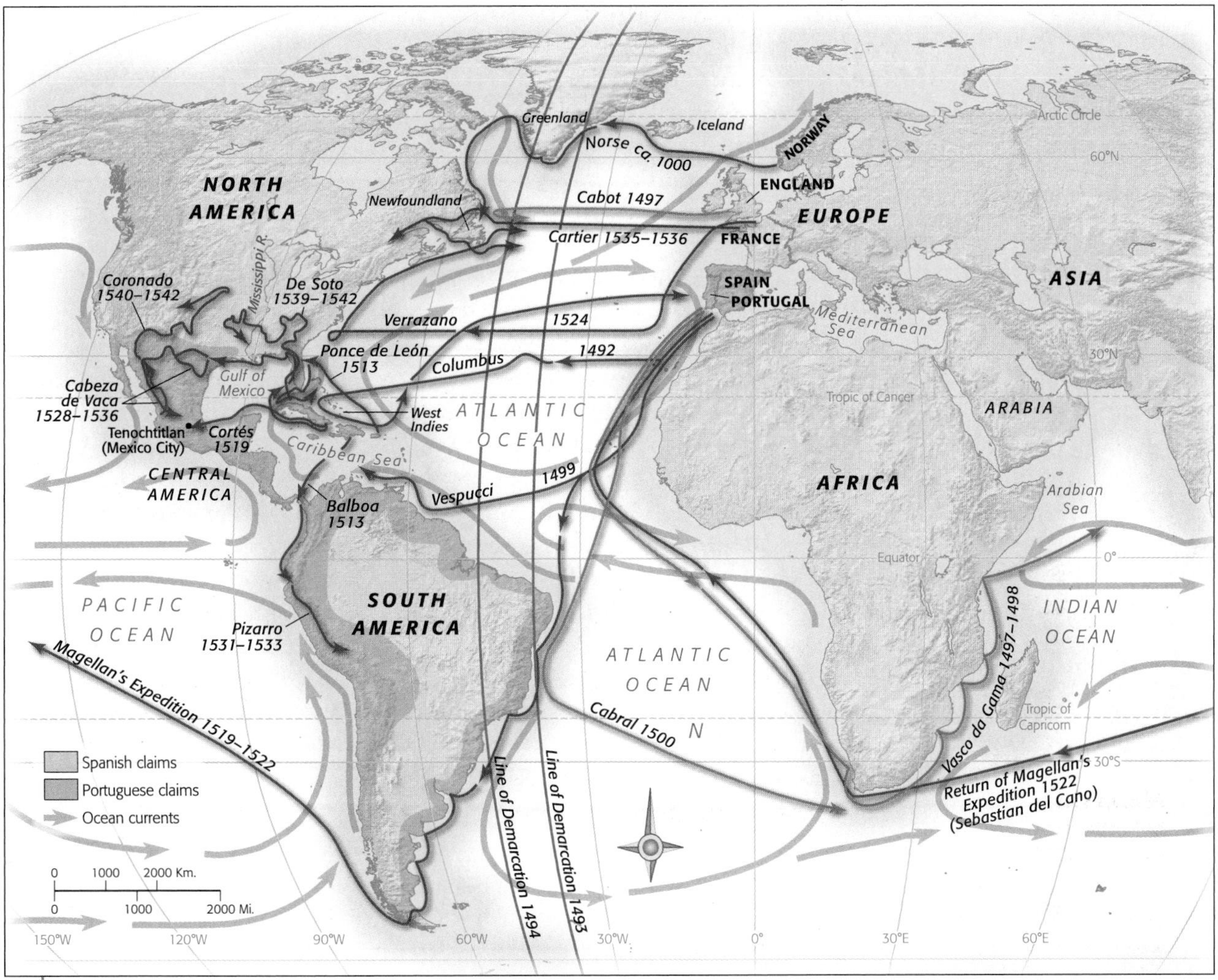

Map 2.2 Major Transatlantic Explorations, 1000–1542

Following Columbus's 1492 voyage, Spain's rivals began laying claim to parts of the New World based on the voyages of Cabot for England, Cabral for Portugal, and Verrazano for France.

in 1494, dividing all future discoveries between themselves. Columbus made three further voyages, in the course of which he established Spanish colonies but never fulfilled his promise of reaching Asia. In 1506 he died a bitter man, convinced that he had been cheated of his rightful rewards. Meanwhile, England's Henry VII (ruled 1485–1509) ignored the Treaty of Tordesillas and sent an Italian navigator known as **John Cabot** westward across the northern Atlantic in 1497. Cabot claimed Nova Scotia, Newfoundland, and the rich Grand Banks fisheries for England, but he vanished at sea on a second voyage. Eighty years would pass before England capitalized on Cabot's voyage.

John Cabot Italian explorer who established English claims to the New World

The more Europeans explored, the more apparent it became that a vast landmass blocked the western route to Asia. In 1500 the Portuguese claimed Brazil, and

Spanish Conquistadors vs. Aztec Defenders

After the Spanish conquest, a Mexica (Aztec) artist recalled this moment before the disastrous smallpox epidemic destroyed the Indians' ability to resist.

other voyages outlined a continuous coastline from the Caribbean to Brazil. In 1507 a publisher brought out a collection of voyagers' tales, including one from the Italian Amerigo Vespucci (ves-POO-chee). A shrewd marketer, the publisher devised a catchy name for the new continent: America.

Getting past America to Asia remained the early explorers' goal. In 1513 the Spaniard Vasco Núñez de Balboa crossed the narrow Isthmus of Panama and chanced upon the Pacific Ocean. In 1519 the Portuguese mariner Ferdinand Magellan, sailing under the Castilian flag, began a voyage around the world through the stormy straits at South America's southern tip, now named the Straits of Magellan. He crossed the Pacific to the Philippines, only to die fighting with natives. One of his five ships and fifteen emaciated sailors returned to Spain in 1522, the first people to have sailed around the world.

Spain's Conquistadors, 1492–1526

Columbus was America's first slave trader and the first Spanish *conquistador* (cone-KEES-ta-dohr), or conqueror. On Hispaniola he enslaved native people and created *encomiendas* (en-cohmee-EN-dahs), grants for both land and the labor of the Indians who lived on it. He also ignited the New World's first gold rush. Indians were forced to hunt for gold and to supply the Spanish with food. The gold rush quickly spilled from Hispaniola to Puerto Rico, Jamaica, and Cuba.

As disease, overwork, and malnutrition killed thousands of Indians, Portuguese slave traders supplied shiploads of Africans to replace them. Although shocked Spanish friars sent to convert the Native Americans reported the Indians' exploitation, and King Ferdinand attempted to forbid the practice, no one worried about African slaves' fate. Missionaries joined most other colonizers in condemning Africans as less than fully human and thus beyond hope of redemption. Blacks could therefore be exploited mercilessly.

Spanish settlers were soon fanning out across the Caribbean in pursuit of slaves and gold. In 1519 the young nobleman **Hernán Cortés** (core-TEZ) (1485–1547) led a small band of Spaniards to the Mexican coast. Destroying his boats and enlisting Indian allies, he marched inland to conquer Mexico.

Hernán Cortés Spanish conqueror of Aztec empire

Upon reaching the Aztec capital of Tenochtitlán (see Chapter 1), the Spanish were stunned by its size and wealth. The Spanish raided the imperial palace and treasury, melting down all the gold they could find. But the Aztecs regrouped and recaptured the city. Then an epidemic of smallpox, which the Aztecs and other Indians were ill equipped to resist, plus reinforcements from Cuba, enabled Cortés to defeat the Aztecs. By 1521 the Spanish had begun to build Mexico City on the ruins of Tenochtitlán. Within twenty years, Central America lay at the Spaniards' feet. Thus was New Spain born.

Over the remainder of the sixteenth century, conquistadors and officials established a great Spanish empire stretching from Mexico to Chile. The Inca empire represented the most important conquest, thanks to smallpox and Inca unfamiliarity with European weapons. The human cost of the Spanish empire was enormous. When Cortés landed in 1519, central Mexico had been home to between 13 and 25 million people. By 1600 the population had shrunk to 700,000. Peru and other regions witnessed similar devastation in the greatest demographic disaster in world history.

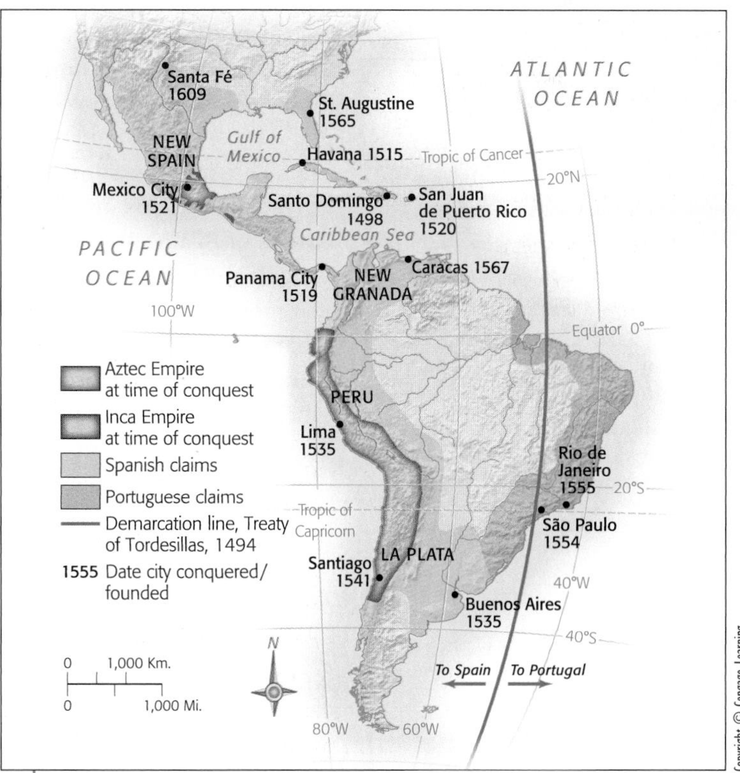

Map 2.3 The Spanish and Portuguese Empires, 1610

By 1610, Spain dominated Latin America, including Portugal's possessions. Having devoted its energies to exploiting Mexico and the Caribbean, Spain had not yet expanded into what is now the United States, beyond outposts in Florida and New Mexico.

Interactive Map

The Columbian Exchange

The Spanish conquest came at enormous human cost. Disease, not war or slavery, was the greatest killer. Native Americans lacked resistance to European and African infections, especially the deadly, highly communicable smallpox. From the first years of contact with Europeans, terrible epidemics decimated Indian communities. In the West Indies the native population vanished within a half-century, and disease opened the mainland for conquest as well.

"Columbian exchange" Exchange of people, plants, animals, and disease within the Atlantic world as a result of European voyages

The **"Columbian exchange"**—the biological encounter of the Old and New Worlds—went beyond deadly germs. Europeans brought horses, cattle, sheep, swine, chickens, wheat, coffee, sugar cane, and numerous fruits and vegetables with them, as well as an astonishing variety of weeds. African slaves carried rice and yams across the Atlantic. The list of American gifts to Europe and Africa was equally impressive: it included corn, white and sweet potatoes, many varieties of beans, tomatoes, squash, pumpkins, peanuts, vanilla, chocolate, avocados, pineapples, chilis, tobacco, and turkeys. European weeds and domesticated animals often overwhelmed indigenous plant life and drove away native animals, especially in North America. Settlers' crops, intensively cultivated on land never allowed to lie fallow, frequently exhausted American soil. Nonetheless, the worldwide exchange of food products enriched human diets and made possible enormous population growth. Today, nearly 60 percent of all food crops worldwide trace their roots to the Native American garden.

Another dimension of the emergence of the Atlantic world was the mixing of peoples. Within Spain's empire, a great human intermingling occurred. From 1500 to 1600 about 300,000 Spaniards immigrated to the New World, 90 percent of them male. A racially mixed population developed, particularly in towns. Spaniards fathered numerous children with African or Indian mothers; most of the former were slaves. Such racial mixing would occur, although far less commonly, in French and English colonies as well.

The Americas supplied seemingly endless wealth for Spain. West Indian sugar plantations and Mexican sheep and cattle ranches enriched many. Much of Spain's wealth, however, was dug from the silver mines of Mexico and Peru. After 1540, enormous amounts of silver flowed across the Atlantic, far more than the small Spanish economy could absorb, setting off inflation that eventually engulfed Europe. But, bent on dominating Europe, Spanish kings needed even more silver to pay for their ships and armies. Several times they went bankrupt, and in the 1560s their efforts to squeeze more taxes from their subjects provoked revolt in Spain's Dutch provinces. In the end, gaining access to American wealth cost the Spanish dearly.

CHECKING IN

- In the fifteenth century, Portugal undertook African exploration, beginning the creation of the Atlantic world.
- By 1600, a "new slavery" based on race arose.
- Early explorers, such as Columbus, Balboa, and Magellan, reached the Americas.
- The Spanish conquered Mexico.
- The "Columbian exchange" transported food, animals, drugs, and germs between Europe, the Americas, and Africa.

FOOTHOLDS IN NORTH AMERICA, 1512–1625

How did European exploration, conquest, and colonization of North America begin?

Spain's New World wealth attracted other Europeans. Throughout the sixteenth century, they sailed the North American coast, exploring, fishing, trading for furs, and smuggling. But, except for a Spanish fort at St. Augustine, Florida, all sixteenth-century attempts at colonizing North America failed. Unrealistic dreams of easy wealth and pliant Indians brought French, English, and Spanish attempts to grief. Only the ravaging of the Indians by disease, declining Spanish power, and rising French, Dutch, and English power finally made colonization possible.

In 1607–1608 the English and French established permanent colonies. By 1614 the Dutch had followed. Within a generation, North America's modern history took shape as each colony developed an economic orientation and its own approach to Native Americans.

Spain's Northern Frontier

The Spanish built their New World empire by subduing the Aztecs, Inca, and other Indian states. The dream of finding even more wealth drew would-be conquistadors to lands north of Mexico.

Earliest came Juan Ponce de León (wahn PON-say deh lee-OWN), the conqueror of Puerto Rico, who trudged through Florida in search of gold and slaves twice, in 1512–1513 and in 1521, and then died in an Indian skirmish. The most astonishing early expedition began when three hundred explorers left Florida in 1527 to explore the Gulf of Mexico. Indian attacks whittled their numbers until only a handful survived. Stranded in Texas, the survivors, led by Cabeza de Vaca (cuh-BAY-zuh deh VAH-cah), moved from Indian tribe to tribe, at first as slaves, then later as traders and medicine men. They finally made their way south to Mexico in 1536.

As de Soto roamed the Southeast, the Southwest drew others with dreams of conquest, lured by rumors that the fabled Seven Golden Cities of Cíbola (SEE-bow-lah) lay north of Mexico. In 1538 an expedition sighted the Zuñi (ZOO-nyee) pueblos and assumed them to be the golden cities.

For decades after these failures, Spain's principal interest in the lands north of Mexico lay in establishing a few strategic bases in Florida to keep out intruders. In 1565 Spain planted the first successful European settlement on mainland North America, the fortress of St. Augustine. Spanish missionaries moved north from the fortress to establish religious missions as far north as the Chesapeake (CHESS-uh-peak) Bay, but Indian resistance and epidemic disease ended their efforts shortly before 1600.

Meanwhile, in the 1580s, the Spanish returned to the southwestern pueblo country, preaching Christianity and scouting for wealth. In 1598 Juan de Oñate (oh-NYAH-tee) led five hundred Spaniards into the upper Rio Grande Valley, where he proclaimed the royal colony of New Mexico. When Acoma Indians refused his demands for provisions in December 1598, Oñate ordered massive retaliation. In January, Spanish troops captured the pueblo, killing more than eight hundred inhabitants. Oñate then forced surviving men to have one foot cut off and sent them, along with women and children, to become servants.

The new colony barely survived. In 1606 the Spanish replaced Oñate because of his excessive brutality. Determined to succeed, by 1630 Franciscan missionaries had established more than fifty pueblo missions stretching along the Rio Grande and had converted about 20,000 Indians.

Colonizing Canada

France made its first attempt at colonizing North America in 1541, when ten ships sailed into the St. Lawrence Valley. Having alienated many of the Indians along the St. Lawrence in two previous expeditions, Jacques Cartier built a fortified settlement on Indian land and thus ended all possibility of peaceful Indian-French relations. Steady Indian attacks and harsh winters drove the French off within two years.

George H. H. Huey

Navajo View of Spanish Colonizers

This pictograph (a painting or drawing on rock) was sketched in the early colonial period in Cañón del Muerto, Arizona.

In 1562 French Huguenots (HYEW-guh-nots) (Calvinists) made the next French attempt at colonization, establishing a base in modern South Carolina. Two years later they founded a settlement in Florida, which the Spanish quickly destroyed. These failures, as well as a civil war between French Catholics and Huguenots, ended France's first attempts at colonization.

Meanwhile, French and other European fishermen worked the teeming Grand Banks off the coast of Newfoundland. Going ashore to dry their catch, French sailors bartered with Indians for beaver pelts; by the late sixteenth century, as European demands for beaver hats soared, a French-dominated fur trade blossomed.

Most traders, unlike explorers or colonizers, recognized the need for reciprocity in dealing with Native Americans; consequently, trade flourished. Glass beads were a mainstay of this trade, for Indians believed that the beads possessed spiritual power comparable to that of quartz, mica, and other sacred substances. To deter potential competitors, the French dispatched Samuel de Champlain to establish the colony of New France at Quebec in 1608. Familiar with Indian politics and diplomacy,

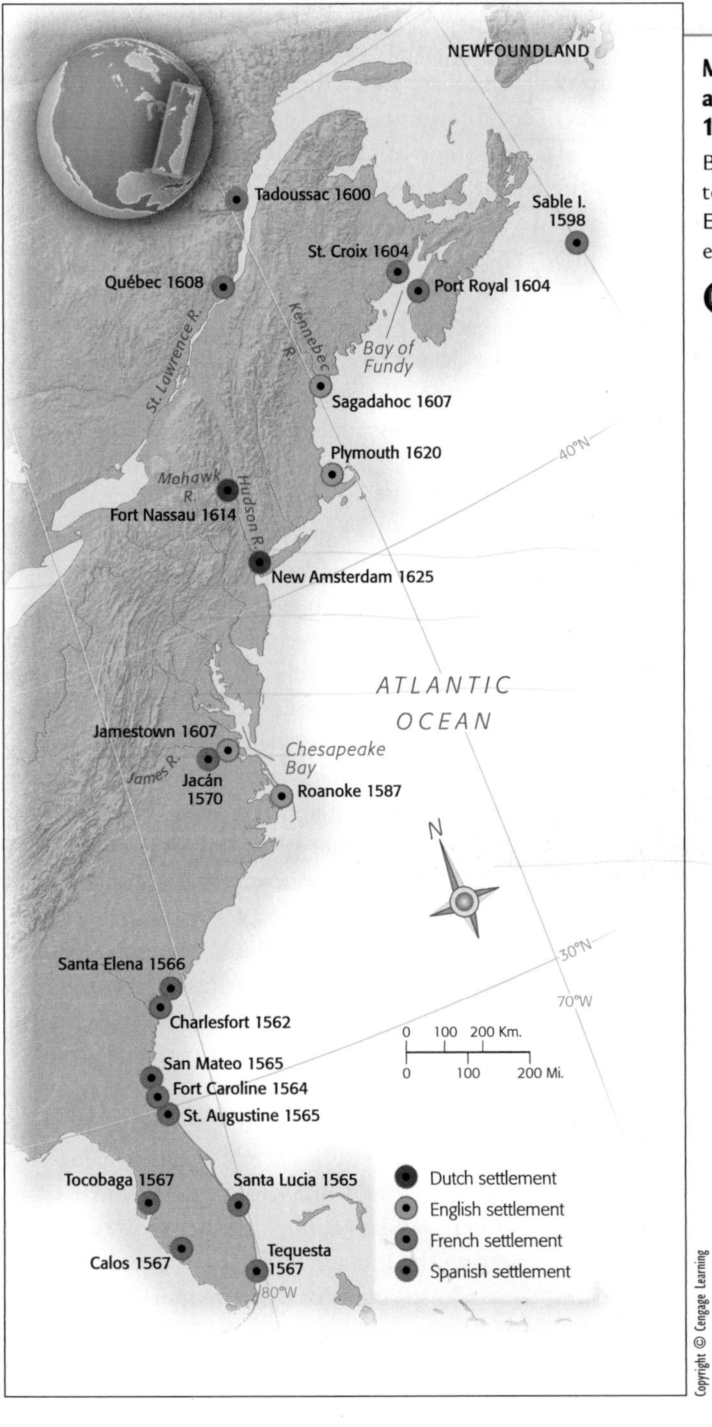

Map 2.4 European Imperial Claims and Settlements in Eastern North America, 1565–1625

By 1625, four European nations contended for territory on North America's Atlantic coast. Except for St. Augustine, Florida, all settlements established before 1607 were abandoned by 1625.

Interactive Map

Champlain built alliances with the Montagnais (MON-tan-yay) and Algonquins (al-GON-kwins) of the St. Lawrence and with the Hurons of the lower Great Lakes by promising to help them defeat their enemies, the Mohawks.

In July 1609 Champlain and Indian allies encountered a substantial Mohawk force near the southern tip of Lake Champlain (which the explorer had named for himself). In the ensuing Battle of Lake Champlain, more than fifty Mohawks died and a dozen were captured. The battle marked the beginning of a deadly era of trade, diplomacy, and warfare. Through their alliance with the Hurons, the French gained access to the thick beaver pelts of the interior in exchange for European goods and protection against the Mohawks and other Iroquois. These economic and diplomatic arrangements defined the course of New France's history for the rest of the seventeenth century.

England and the Atlantic World, 1558–1603

When Elizabeth I became queen in 1558, England, a second-rank power, stood on the sidelines as Spain and France grappled for European supremacy. Religious division and domestic instability preoccupied the English. They hoped to cure the country's economic woes by founding colonies overseas, but Spain blocked the way.

Meanwhile, England's position in Ireland had deteriorated. By 1565 English troops were fighting to impose Elizabeth's rule throughout the island, where a Protestant English government was battling Irish Catholic rebels aided by Spain. In a war that ground on through the 1580s, English troops drove the Irish clans from their strongholds and established "plantations," or settlements, of Scottish and English Protestants. The English resorted to a "scorched earth policy" of starvation and mass slaughter to break the Irish spirit. Elizabeth's generals justified these atrocities by calling the Irish "savages." The Irish experience gave England strategies that it later used against North American Indians, whose customs, religion, and methods of fighting seemed to absolve the English from guilt in waging exceptionally cruel warfare.

England had two objectives in the Western Hemisphere in the 1570s. The first was to find a northwest passage to Asia, preferably one lined with gold. The second, as Sir Francis Drake said, was to "singe the king of Spain's beard" by raiding Spanish fleets and cities. The search for a northwest passage proved fruitless, but the English did stage spectacularly successful and profitable privateering raids against the Spanish. The most breathtaking enterprise of the era was Drake's voyage around the world in 1577–1580 in quest of sites for colonies.

Roanoke Site of the first English attempt at New World colonization; it was a failure

In 1587 Sir Walter Raleigh, dreaming of founding an American colony where English, Indians, and even blacks freed from Spanish slavery could live together amicably, sponsored a colony on **Roanoke** Island, off the modern North Carolina coast. An earlier attempt (1585–1586) had failed, in part because the colonists refused to grow their own food, expecting the Indians to feed them, and wore out their welcome. One hundred and ten colonists, many of them members of families, reached Roanoke in late summer 1587. Almost immediately the colony's leader, John White, returned to England for more supplies, leaving the settlers behind.

Spain's attempt to crush England with the Great Armada in 1588 prevented White from returning to Roanoke until 1590. When he did, he found only rusty armor, moldy books, and the word CROATOAN (CROW-uh-tan) carved into a post. To this day, no one knows exactly what happened to the "Lost Colony," although they were probably living among the nearby Croatoan Indians. The miserable failure at Roanoke would postpone the establishment of English colonies for seventeen more years.

However, England's victory over the Spanish Armada in 1588 preserved English independence and confirmed its status as a major Atlantic power.

Failure and Success in Virginia, 1603–1625

Two events opened the way for English colonization: peace with Spain and the emergence of the joint-stock company. In the peace between England and Spain, concluded in 1604 by Elizabeth's successor, James I (ruled 1603–1625), the Spanish not only agreed to peace but also renounced their claims to Virginia, leaving England a free hand. At the same time, the development of joint-stock companies, which could amass money through sales of stock, created a way for potential colonizers to raise large sums of money with limited risk for the individual investor.

On April 10, 1606, James I granted charters to two separate joint-stock companies, one based in London and the other in Plymouth. The **Virginia Company of Plymouth** received a grant extending from modern Maine to the Potomac River; the **Virginia Company of London** received a grant from Cape Fear north to the Hudson River. The grants overlapped, with the land in question to go to the first successful colonizer. Both companies dispatched colonists in 1607.

Virginia Company of Plymouth Received charter to establish colonies from Chesapeake Bay northward

Virginia Company of London Received charter to establish colonies from Chesapeake Bay southward; founded Jamestown

The Virginia Company of Plymouth sent 120 men to Sagadahoc at the mouth of the Kennebec River in Maine. The following year, the colony disintegrated, the victim of Indian hostility (generally provoked) and the hard Maine winter. The company subsequently became dormant. The Virginia Company of London dispatched 105 settlers to a site on the James River near Chesapeake Bay that they named **Jamestown.** But the first colonists, who included many members of the gentry, hunted for gold and failed to plant crops. When relief ships arrived in January 1608, they found only thirty-eight survivors.

Jamestown First successful English colony, established in 1607

Near anarchy reigned at Jamestown until September 1608, when desperate councilors, representatives of the Virginia Company of London, turned to a brash soldier of fortune, Captain **John Smith.** Only twenty-eight, Smith found that his experiences fighting the Spanish and the Turks had prepared him well to assume control in Virginia. By instituting harsh discipline, organizing the settlers, and requiring them to build houses and plant food, he ensured Jamestown's survival. During the winter of 1608–1609, Smith lost just twelve men out of two hundred.

John Smith Soldier of fortune who "saved" Jamestown by establishing order and maintaining good relations with Indians

Smith also became the colony's best diplomat. After local Indians captured him late in 1607, Smith displayed such impressive courage that Powhatan (pow-uh-TAN), the leader of the nearby Powhatan Confederacy, arranged an elaborate ceremony in which Pocahontas, his daughter, "saved" Smith's life during a mock execution. This gesture was meant to remind the English that Powhatan's people were the stronger force and that reciprocity rather than force should govern their dealings with one another. Powhatan expected that the English would become his allies against local tribal enemies. Smith maintained satisfactory relations with the Powhatan Confederacy partly through his personality and partly through calculated demonstrations of English military strength.

When serious injuries forced Smith to return to England in 1609, discipline again crumbled. Expecting the Indians to furnish corn, the settlers did not store enough food for winter. One colonist reported that Jamestown residents ate dogs, cats, rats, and snakes in order to survive. He gruesomely added that "many besides fed on the corpses of dead men." Of the 500 residents at Jamestown in September 1609, only 100 lived to May 1610. An influx of new recruits and the imposition of military rule, however, enabled Virginia to win the First Anglo-Powhatan War (1610–1614) and, by 1611, to expand west to modern Richmond. The English population remained small—only 380 by 1616—and produced nothing of value for the stockholders.

John Rolfe Brought tobacco to Jamestown, thus ensuring its economic survival

Tobacco saved Virginia. **John Rolfe,** an Englishman who married Pocahontas, perfected a salable variety of tobacco for planting there, and by 1619 Virginia was exporting large, profitable amounts of the crop. Thereafter, the Virginia Company poured supplies and settlers into the colony.

To attract labor and capital, the company awarded fifty-acre land grants ("headrights") to anyone paying his or her own passage or that of a laborer. By financing the passage of indentured servants, planters could accumulate large tracts of land. Thousands of single young men and a few hundred women became indentured servants, choosing the uncertainty of Virginia over poverty in England. In return for their passage, they worked a fixed term, usually four to seven years.

House of Burgesses First elected representative legislature in New World, in Virginia; first met in 1619

In 1619 the Virginia Company ended military rule and provided for an elected assembly, the **House of Burgesses.** Although the company could veto the assembly's actions, 1619 marked the beginning of representative government in North America. However, Virginia still faced three serious problems. First, local officials systematically defrauded shareholders, in the process sinking the company deeply into debt. Second, the colony's death rate soared. Malnutrition, salt poisoning, typhus, and dysentery (from drinking polluted river water) killed thousands of immigrants. Third, Indian relations worsened. After Powhatan's death in 1618, the new leader, Opechancanough (oh-peh-can-CUH-noo), worried about the relentless expansion of the English colony. In 1622 the Indians killed 347 of the 1,200 settlers in a surprise attack. With their livestock destroyed, spring planting impossible, and disease spreading through crowded stockades, hundreds more colonists died in the ensuing months.

The Virginia Company sent more men, and Governor Francis Wyatt took the offensive. Using tactics developed during the Irish war, Wyatt destroyed the Indians' food supplies, conducted winter campaigns to drive them from their homes when they would suffer most, and fought (according to John Smith) as if he had "just cause to destroy them by all means possible." By 1625 the English had won the Second Powhatan War, and the Indians had lost their best chance of forcing out the intruders.

But the struggle bankrupted the Virginia Company. After a report critical of its management, James I revoked its charter and made Virginia a royal colony in 1624. Only five hundred Old World settlers lived there, including a handful of Africans who had been brought in since 1619. With its combination of fabulous profits, unfree labor, and massive mortality, Virginia was truly a land of contradictions.

New England Begins, 1614–1625

After Virginia, the next permanent English settlements appeared in New England. Along the coast, a terrible epidemic in 1616–1618 had devastated the Indian population by about 90 percent. Later visitors found the ground littered with the "bones and skulls" of the unburied dead, along with acres of overgrown cornfields.

In 1620 the Virginia Company of London granted a patent for a settlement to a group of English merchants, who dispatched eighteen families (102 people) in a small, leaky ship, the *Mayflower.* The colonists promised to send back lumber, furs, and fish for seven years, after which they would own the tract.

The expedition's leaders, and half its members, belonged to a small religious community from the northern English town of Scrooby. Separatist Puritans, they had earlier fled to the Netherlands to practice their religion freely. Fearing that their children were adopting Dutch ways, they decided to immigrate to America.

In November 1620 the *Mayflower* landed at **Plymouth,** outside the bounds of Virginia. Because they had no legal right to be there, the leaders insisted that adult males in the group sign the **Mayflower Compact** before they landed. By this document they constituted themselves a "civil body politic"—a civil government—under James I's sovereignty and established Plymouth Plantation.

Plymouth Colony established by Pilgrims in Massachusetts

Mayflower Compact Agreement signed by Pilgrims to govern themselves

Weakened by their journey and unprepared for winter, half the Pilgrims, as they were later called, died within four months. Two Indians helped the others to survive: Squanto, a local Patuxet, and Samoset (SAM-oh-sett), an Abenaki (aah-beh-NAH-key) from Maine who had traded with the English. To stop the Pilgrims from stealing their food, the Indians taught the newcomers how to grow corn. Squanto and Samoset also arranged an alliance between the Pilgrims and the local Wampanoag (wahm-puh-NO-ag) Indians, who were headed by Chief Massasoit (MASS-uh-soyt).

Plymouth's relations with the Indians soon worsened. Learning of the Virginia massacre of 1622, the Pilgrims militarized their colony and threatened their Indian "allies" with their monopoly of firepower. Within a decade, Plymouth had attracted several hundred colonists and had become economically self-sufficient. After they abandoned communal farming for individually owned plots, prosperous farmers produced corn surpluses that they traded for furs. Prosperity allowed Plymouth's elite to buy out the colony's London backers.

Plymouth colony had three lasting influences. It constituted an outpost of Puritans dissenting from the Church of England, proved that a self-governing society could exist in New England, and foreshadowed the aggressive methods that would give Europeans mastery over the Indians. The Pilgrims became the vanguard of a massive migration of Puritans to New England in the 1630s (see Chapter 3).

A "New Netherland" on the Hudson, 1609–1625

The Dutch-speaking provinces of the Netherlands were among the most fervently Calvinist regions of Europe. Ruled by the Spanish during the sixteenth century and alienated by high taxes and religious intolerance, the Dutch rebelled in 1566. More than forty years later, in 1609, Spain and the Dutch Republic signed a truce. By then the Netherlands was a wealthy commercial power whose empire stretched from Brazil to South Africa to Taiwan. It would play a key role in colonizing North America.

New Amsterdam Dutch colony that would become New York

In 1609 Henry Hudson sailed up the broad, deep river that today bears his name, and in the next year Dutch ships sailed up the Hudson to trade with Indians. In 1614 they began their New Netherland colony by establishing Fort Nassau at the site of modern Albany, New York, and in 1625 planted another fort on an island at the mouth of the Hudson. Within two years, Peter Minuit, director-general of the colony, bought the island from local Indians, named it Manhattan, and began a settlement christened **New Amsterdam.**

Furs, particularly beaver pelts, became the New Netherlanders' chief economic staple. The Mohawks, as well as the other nations of the Iroquois Confederacy, became the Dutch colonists' chief suppliers of furs and soon found themselves embroiled in competition with the French-supported Hurons.

CHECKING IN

- Pushing northward from their New World empire, Spanish explorers roamed the American Southwest, and conquistadors conquered the Pueblo Indians.
- Early French colonies based on agriculture barely survived, but the French fur trade with Indians of the interior prospered.
- The first English colony, Roanoke, failed, but Jamestown and Plymouth survived despite hardship.
- The Dutch established New Amsterdam at the mouth of the Hudson River and relied on the fur trade.

Chapter Summary

What major changes were reshaping the African and European worlds in the fifteenth and sixteenth centuries? (page 17)

The fifteenth and sixteenth centuries were times of tumultuous change in both West Africa and Europe. In the West African savannah, powerful kingdoms such as Mali gave way to more fragmented political structures. In Europe, the Renaissance, the Reformation, a population boom, and the emergence of the market economy created new tensions as well as new opportunities. In England, the Reformation led to the rise of Puritanism, which found itself in a tense relationship with the monarchy.

What was the Atlantic world, and how did it emerge? (page 25)

The Atlantic world began to open as Portuguese explorers traveled along the African coast; one sad result of this was the brutal "new slavery," based primarily on race. Spanish explorers such as Columbus, Balboa, and Magellan opened the way for the creation of an empire that would encompass both the Aztecs and the Inca in the Americas. Plants, animals, drugs, and diseases crossed the Atlantic in both directions in the "Columbian exchange."

How did European exploration, conquest, and colonization of North America begin? (page 30)

The Spanish explored large parts of North America, conquered the Pueblo Indians of the Southwest, and incorporated them into their empire. Although France attempted to plant agricultural colonies, its primary success lay in establishing the fur trade with the Indians of the interior. After failure at Roanoke, Englishmen successfully planted colonies at Jamestown in Virginia and at Plymouth in Massachusetts. The Dutch established New Amsterdam.

KEY TERMS

savannah *(p. 17)*
Renaissance *(p. 19)*
enclosure *(p. 21)*
joint-stock company *(p. 22)*
Protestant Reformation *(p. 23)*
John Calvin *(p. 23)*
Puritans *(p. 24)*
Prince Henry "the Navigator" *(p. 25)*
"new slavery" *(p. 26)*
Treaty of Tordesillas *(p. 26)*
John Cabot *(p. 27)*
Hernán Cortés *(p. 29)*
"Columbian exchange" *(p. 30)*
Roanoke *(p. 34)*
Virginia Company of Plymouth *(p. 35)*
Virginia Company of London *(p. 35)*
Jamestown *(p. 35)*
John Smith *(p. 35)*
John Rolfe *(p. 36)*
House of Burgesses *(p. 36)*
Plymouth *(p. 37)*
Mayflower Compact *(p. 37)*
New Amsterdam *(p. 37)*

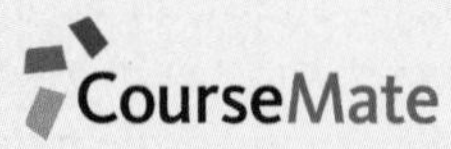

Go to the CourseMate website at **www.cengagebrain.com** for additional study tools and review materials—including audio and video clips—for this chapter.

Chapter 3

The Emergence of Colonial Societies 1625–1700

Lord Baltimore, by Gerard Soest (1670)

Courtesy of Enoch Pratt Free Library, Central Library/State Library Resource Center, Baltimore, MD

Chapter Preview

Chesapeake Society
How did tobacco shape the Chesapeake colonies?

Puritanism in New England
What was the "New England Way," and what challenges did it endure?

The Spread of Slavery: The Caribbean and Carolina
Why and how did plantation agriculture shape slavery in the Caribbean and Carolina?

The Middle Colonies
How did diversity distinguish the Middle Colonies?

Rivals for North America: France and Spain
How did the French and Spanish empires develop in the seventeenth century?

The seventeenth century witnessed a flood of English migration across the Atlantic. In 1600 no English person lived along the North American seacoast. By 1700, however, about 250,000 people of European birth or ancestry were dwelling in what would become the United States. In addition, nearly 30,000 enslaved Africans resided in North America in 1700, most of them in Chesapeake colonies and Carolina. Whereas English immigrants to America hoped to realize economic opportunity or religious freedom, Africans and their descendants were owned by others.

A devastating demographic upheaval, the depopulation and uprooting of Native Americans, made these two other migrations possible. Epidemic disease did much of the work of destroying the Indians, but warfare played an important role as well. About

1 million Indians had died as a result of contact with Europeans by 1700. European colonists built their farms, plantations, and cities not in wilderness but on lands long inhabited by Native Americans.

Indian depopulation and European and African immigration transformed North America in the seventeenth century. Europeans expanded their territorial domains and established colonial societies from the St. Lawrence River to the Rio Grande, increasing the continent's cultural diversity.

English immigrants, and English capital, ensured that England would dominate the East Coast as well as the Caribbean; by 1700 the English would force out the Dutch and leave France and Spain with lands less attractive to colonists. Four distinct regions emerged within England's mainland colonies: New England, the Chesapeake, Carolina, and the Middle Colonies, each shaped by its environment, the motives of white immigrants, and the concentrations of enslaved Africans.

CHESAPEAKE SOCIETY

How did tobacco shape the Chesapeake colonies?

Thanks to the tobacco boom of the 1620s, the English colonies on the Chesapeake Bay—Virginia and Maryland—were the first in North America to prosper. They shared similar economies, populations, and patterns of growth that gave them a distinct regional identity. Chesapeake society was highly unequal and unstable. Life for most colonists was short and living conditions poor. Not until English colonists seized large amounts of Native American land to grow tobacco and shifted from white indentured servants to black slaves did they finally achieve stability and at least minimal prosperity.

State and Church in Virginia

James I planned to rule Virginia through appointed officials, but Virginians petitioned repeatedly for the restoration of their elected assembly, the first in the New World.

View of Jamestown, 1625
As Virginia's tobacco production boomed, the capital expanded beyond the fort that had originally confined it.

Colonial National Historical Park

James I's successor, Charles I, grudgingly relented but only to induce the assembly to tax tobacco exports so as to transfer the cost of government from the crown to Virginia's taxpayers. After 1630, seeking more taxes, Virginia's royal governors called regular assemblies. During the 1650s the assembly split into two chambers, the elected House of Burgesses and the appointed Governor's Council.

Local government officials were appointed, rather than elected, during Virginia's first quarter-century. In 1634 Virginia adopted England's county-court system. Appointed by the royal governor, justices of the peace acted as judges, set local tax rates, paid county officials, and oversaw the construction and maintenance of roads, bridges, and public buildings. Thus, unelected county courts became the basic unit of local government south of New England.

Virginia had the Church of England as its established church. Anglican vestries governed each parish; elected vestrymen handled church finances, determined poor relief, and investigated complaints against the minister. Taxpayers were legally obliged to pay fixed rates to the Anglican church. Because of the large distances between settlements and churches, as well as a chronic shortage of clergymen, few Virginians regularly attended services. In 1662 Virginia had just ten ministers to serve its forty-five parishes.

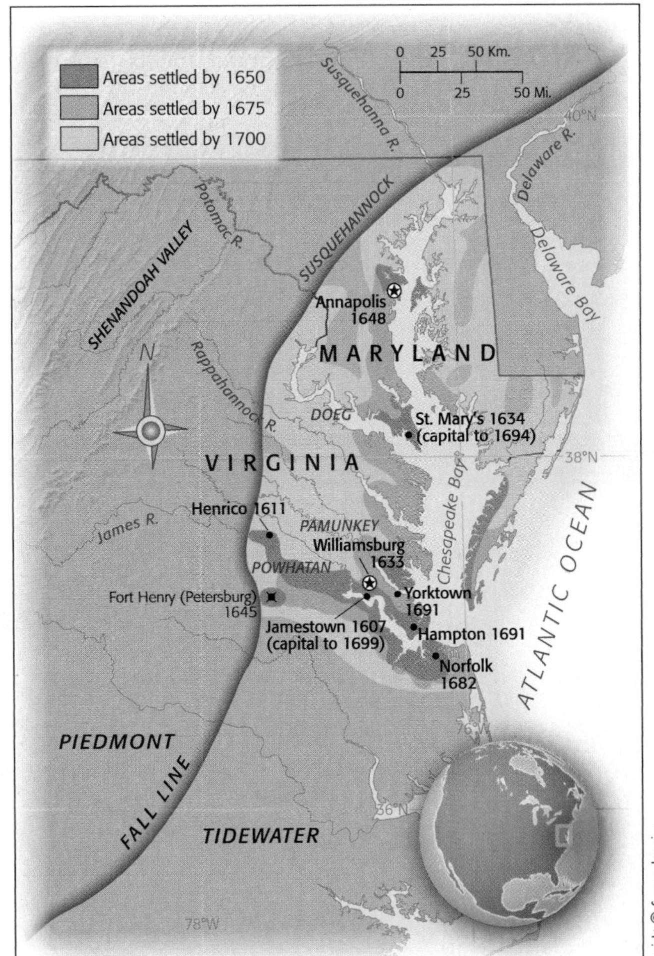

Map 3.1 Chesapeake Expansion, 1607–1700

The Chesapeake colonies expanded slowly before midcentury. By 1700, Anglo-Indian wars, a rising English population, and an influx of enslaved Africans permitted settlers to spread throughout the tidewater.

Interactive Map

State and Church in Maryland

Beginning in the 1630s, grants by the crown to reward English politicians replaced joint-stock companies as the primary mechanism of colonization. The first such grant, or proprietorship, went in 1632 to Lord Baltimore (Cecilius Calvert); he named the large tract east of Chesapeake Bay "Maryland" in honor of England's Queen Henrietta Maria. Lord Baltimore enjoyed broad power, lessened only by the stipulations that an elected assembly had to approve all laws and that the crown would control both war and trade.

Baltimore intended to make Maryland a refuge for England's Catholics, who could neither worship in public nor hold political office and who had to pay tithes to the Anglican church. To make Maryland a haven, Baltimore tried to install the old English manor system. In theory, a manor lord would employ a Catholic priest as chaplain and allow others to hear Mass and to receive the sacraments on the manor. In practice, this arrangement never worked, for relatively few Catholics settled in Maryland, which was overwhelmingly Protestant from the beginning. Cheap land lured settlers who did not need to become tenants on the manors, and Baltimore's scheme fell apart. By 1675 all sixty of Maryland's nonproprietary manors had become plantations.

Religious tension gradually developed in Maryland society. Until 1642, Catholics and Protestants shared the chapel at St. Mary's, the capital, but they began to argue over its use. As antagonisms intensified, Baltimore drafted, and the assembly passed, the Act for Religious Toleration (1649).

Unfortunately, the Toleration Act did not secure religious peace. In 1654 the Protestant majority barred Catholics from voting; ousted Governor William Stone, a pro-tolerance Protestant; and repealed the Toleration Act. Stone raised an army, both Protestant and Catholic, in an attempt to regain the government but was defeated. The victors imprisoned Stone and hanged three Catholic leaders. Although Lord Baltimore was restored to control in 1658, Protestant resistance to Catholic political influence continued to cause problems in Maryland.

Chronology

1628	Massachusetts Bay colony founded
1630–1642	"Great migration" to North America
1633	First English settlements in Connecticut
1634	Lord Baltimore founds Maryland
1636	Roger Williams founds Providence, Rhode Island; Harvard College established
1637	Antinomian crisis in Massachusetts Bay; Pequot War in Connecticut
1638	New Sweden established
1642–1648	English Civil War
1644–1646	Third Anglo-Powhatan War in Virginia
1649	Maryland's Act for Religious Toleration; King Charles I beheaded
1655	New Netherland annexes New Sweden
1660	Restoration in England; Charles II becomes king
1661	Maryland defines slavery as a lifelong, inheritable racial status
1662	Half-Way Covenant adopted
1664	English conquer New Netherland; establish New York and New Jersey
1670	Charles Town, Carolina, established; Virginia defines slavery as a lifelong, inheritable racial status
1675–1676	King Philip's War in New England
1675–1676	Bacon's Rebellion in Virginia
1680	Pueblo Revolt begins in New Mexico
1681	William Penn founds Pennsylvania
1682	La Salle claims Louisiana for France
1691	Spain establishes Texas
1692–1693	Salem witchcraft trials
1692–1700	Spain "reconquers" New Mexico
1698	First French settlements in Louisiana

Death, Gender, and Kinship

So few women immigrated to the Chesapeake Bay that, before 1650, only one-third of male servants could find brides and then only after completing their indenture. Female scarcity gave women an advantage in negotiating favorable marriages. Some female indentured servants married prosperous planters who paid off their remaining time of service.

Death ravaged Chesapeake society and left domestic life exceptionally fragile. In 1650 malaria joined the killer diseases typhoid, dysentery, and salt poisoning, as the marshy lowlands of the tidewater Chesapeake became fertile breeding grounds for the mosquitoes that spread malaria. Life expectancy in the 1600s was twenty years lower in the Chesapeake than in New England. Servants died at appalling rates; 40 percent were dead within a decade of arrival and 70 percent before reaching age fifty.

Chesapeake widows often enjoyed substantial property rights. The region's men wrote wills giving their wives perpetual and complete control of their estate, so that their own children could inherit it. Although a widow in such circumstances had a degree of economic independence, she faced enormous pressure to remarry, particularly a man who could produce income by farming her fields.

The lopsided sex ratio and high death rates contributed to slow population growth in the Chesapeake. Although perhaps 100,000 English immigrated to the Chesapeake between 1630 and 1700, the white population was just 70,000 in 1700. In contrast, the benign disease environment and more balanced gender ratio of New England allowed that region's 28,000 white immigrants to burgeon to 91,000 during the same time period. Change came gradually as children acquired childhood immunities, life-spans lengthened, and the sex ratio evened out. By 1720 most Chesapeake residents were native born.

Tobacco Shapes a Region, 1630–1670

Chesapeake settlers were scattered across the landscape. A typical community included only twenty-four families in a twenty-five-square-mile area, a mere six people per square mile. (In contrast, New England often had five hundred people squeezed onto one square mile.) Most Chesapeake inhabitants lived in a world of few friendships and considerable isolation.

Isolated Chesapeake settlers shared a life governed by one overriding factor: the price of tobacco. After an initial boom, tobacco prices plunged 97 percent in 1629 before stabilizing at 10 percent of their original high. Tobacco was still profitable as long as it was grown on fertile soil near navigable water. As a result, 80 percent of Chesapeake homes were located along a riverbank. Wealthy planters built wharves that served as depots for tobacco exports and distribution centers for imported goods. Consequently, a merchant class was slow to materialize, and towns grew painfully slowly; by 1678 St. Mary's, Maryland's capital, had just thirty scattered houses.

Chesapeake society became increasingly unequal. A few planters used the headright system to build up large landholdings and to profit from their servants' labor. Wretchedly exploited—and poorly fed, clothed, and housed—servants faced a bleak future even when their indenture ended. Although some were able to claim fifty acres of land in Maryland, the majority who went to Virginia had no such prospects.

Indeed, in Virginia after 1650 most riverfront land was held by large planters and speculators, and upward mobility became virtually impossible.

In 1660 Chesapeake tobacco prices plunged 50 percent, setting off a depression that lasted fifty years. Despite losses, large planters earned some income from rents, interest on loans, and shopkeeping, and many landowners scrambled to sell corn and cattle in the West Indies. A typical family in this depression era lived in a small wooden shack, slept on rags, and ate mush or stew cooked in their single pot. Ex-servants in particular became a frustrated and embittered underclass that seemed destined to remain landless and poor. Having fled poverty in England for the promise of a better life, they found utter destitution in the Chesapeake.

Bacon's Rebellion, 1675–1676

Virginia had been free of serious conflict with the Indians since the end of the Third Anglo-Powhatan War in 1646. By 1653 tribes encircled by English settlements had begun agreeing to remain within boundaries set by the government—in effect, on reservations. White settlement continued to expand northward to the Potomac River, and by 1675 whites outnumbered Indians by a ten-to-one ratio.

Tensions flared between Native Americans struggling to retain land and independence and settlers bent on expansion, especially white freedmen who often squatted illegally on tribal lands. The conflict also divided white society; Governor Berkeley, Lord Baltimore, and a few of their cronies held fur-trade monopolies that profited from friendly relations with some Indians. The monopolies alienated freedmen and wealthy planters. Colonists' resentment against Native Americans fused with resentment against the governor and the proprietor.

In June 1675 a dispute between some Doeg (Dohg) Indians and a Virginia farmer escalated. A force of Virginia and Maryland militia pursuing the Doegs murdered fourteen friendly Susquehannocks (suss-kweh-HAN-nocks) and later executed five of their chiefs. The violence was now unstoppable. Although Governor William Berkeley proposed defending the frontier with a costly system of forts, small farmers preferred the cheaper solution: a war of extermination against the Indians. Some three hundred settlers elected Nathaniel Bacon, a distant relative of Berkeley and a member of the Royal Council, to lead them against nearby Indians in April 1676. The expedition found only peaceful Indians but slaughtered them anyhow.

Returning to Jamestown in June 1676, Bacon asked for authority to wage war "against all Indians in general." The legislature voted for a program designed to appeal to both hard-pressed taxpayers and landless ex-servants. All Indians who had left their village without permission (even if fleeing Bacon) were declared enemies, and their lands were forfeited. Bacon's troops could seize any "enemy" property and enslave Indian prisoners.

However, Governor Berkeley soon had second thoughts about the slaughter and recalled Bacon and his thirteen hundred men. Forbidden to attack Indians, Bacon's forces turned against the government and burned Jamestown. The rebels offered freedom to any servants or slaves owned by Berkeley's allies who would join them, and then looted enemy plantations. What had begun as Indian warfare was now a social rebellion. Before the uprising could proceed further, however, Bacon died of dysentery in late 1676, and his followers dispersed.

Bacon's Rebellion revealed a society under deep internal stress. Begun as an effort to displace escalating tensions among whites onto the Indians, it became an excuse to plunder other whites. This rebellion was an outburst of pent-up frustrations by marginal taxpayers and ex-servants driven to desperation by the tobacco depression.

Bacon's Rebellion Uprising that showed deep stresses within the Virginia colony

From Servitude to Slavery

Race was fundamental in reshaping Chesapeake society. Whites drew racial boundaries between themselves and the region's growing African population and tried to avert class conflict by substituting black slaves for white servants.

Racial slavery developed in three stages. From 1619 to 1640, Anglo-Virginians carefully distinguished between whites and blacks in official documents but did not assume that every African sold was a slave for life. Some Africans gained their freedom, and a few even owned their own farms.

By 1640 blacks and some Indians were being treated as slaves, and their children inherited their status. Thus, their situation had become inferior to that of indentured white servants. In the final phase, after 1660, laws defined slavery as a lifelong, inheritable status based on color. By 1705 strict legal codes defined the place of slaves in society and set standards of racial etiquette.

Slavery was a system for blacks and Indians only. Whites never enslaved their white enemies; rather, they reserved the complete denial of human rights for nonwhites. To stabilize Chesapeake society and to defuse the resentment of poor whites, planter elites created a caste system based on race. This system simultaneously defined nonwhites as unfit for freedom and created a common, exclusive identity among whites.

Slavery grew slowly in the Chesapeake, with fewer than a thousand slaves in Virginia and Maryland as late as 1660. By 1680, however, the slave population had grown to twelve thousand; by 1700 slaves would make up nearly one-fourth of the Chesapeake population and much of the labor force.

The rise of a direct slave trade with Africa increased the growing gap between whites and blacks. Before 1690, most blacks in the Chesapeake, having spent long periods in West African ports or other American colonies, were familiar with English ways and spoke some English. They could carve out space for themselves as free landowners. After 1690, as slaves poured into the Chesapeake directly from the West African interior, language and culture became barriers rather than bridges, reinforcing increased racism among whites.

Racism was enforced by the changing composition of the white population, increasingly American-born and evenly distributed between male and female. Whites shared a sense of common racial identity vis-à-vis an increasingly fragmented and seemingly alien black population.

By 1700 the Chesapeake had been transformed; profits had fallen, but life expectancy had risen. As nonwhites' condition deteriorated, Virginia and Maryland expanded their territories, and their white colonists flourished.

CHECKING IN

- A cash-crop economy set the Chesapeake colonies apart from New England.
- Maryland was intended as a refuge for Catholics but became mainly Protestant.
- Tobacco shaped the economy and living conditions in Chesapeake colonies.
- Bacon's Rebellion began as an anti-Indian campaign but became a social and economic movement as well.
- Slavery developed in gradual stages in the Chesapeake colonies, eventually becoming a lifelong, inheritable status based on color.

Preparing a Slave Voyage
Africans weep as relatives or friends are taken to a slave vessel.

PURITANISM IN NEW ENGLAND

What was the "New England Way," and what challenges did it endure?

New England soon joined the Chesapeake as a prosperous colonial region. The Plymouth colony established in 1620 was dwarfed after 1630 as Puritans flooded into New England in the "Great Migration." By the time England's civil war halted the migration in 1642, about 21,000 newcomers had arrived. They established the colonies of Massachusetts Bay, Connecticut, New Haven (absorbed by Connecticut in 1662), and Rhode Island. New England's leaders endeavored to build colonies based on social and religious ideals. Even though the ideas ultimately weakened and then vanished, Puritanism shaped New England's distinctive regional identity.

In almost every way—the place of religion, economies, class structure, local communities, and living standards—New England contrasted sharply with the Chesapeake colonies. Both, however, shared English nationality and a determination to expand at Native Americans' expense.

A City upon a Hill, 1628–1632

Upon ascending the throne in 1625, Charles I scrapped James's policy of tolerance toward the Puritans and began a systematic campaign to eliminate Puritan influence within the Church of England. In response to continual harassment, in 1628 several Puritan merchants obtained a charter to settle north of the Separatist colony at Plymouth. Organized as the Massachusetts Bay Company, they moved the seat of their colony's government to New England, paving the way for Massachusetts to be self-governing.

In 1630 the company dispatched a "great fleet," eleven ships and seven hundred passengers, to New England. As the ships crossed the Atlantic, Governor John Winthrop delivered a lay sermon, "A Model of Christian Charity," in which he explained how and why the new colony would differ from England itself.

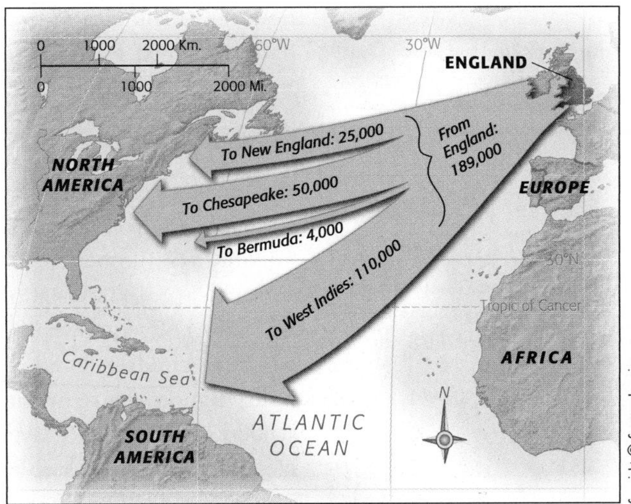

Map 3.2 English Migration, 1610–1660

During the first phase of English transatlantic migration, more than half of the colonists settled in the West Indies.

Interactive Map

Winthrop boldly announced that "we shall be as **a city upon a hill,** the eyes of all people are upon us." The settlers would build a godly community whose compelling example would shame England. The English government would then truly reform the church, and a revival of piety would create a nation of saints. Denouncing economic jealousy, Winthrop explained that God intended "in all times some must be rich and some poor." The rich would practice charity and mercy, and the poor show their faith in God's will by practicing patience and fortitude. In a godly state, the government would prevent the greedy among the rich from exploiting the poor and the lazy among the poor from burdening their fellow citizens.

a city upon a hill John Winthrop's vision of the Puritan settlement in New England as a model for the world

By 1631, thirteen hundred more settlers had arrived, and the colony was moving toward both economic and political stability. Most of the new colonists were landowning farm families of modest means, who had neither indentured servants nor slaves. More than fifteen thousand colonists had settled in New England by 1642.

Massachusetts established a broad-based political system, permitting every adult male church member to vote; the widespread suffrage contrasted sharply with England itself, where property requirements restricted the vote to less than 30 percent of adult males. Within a few years of their arrival, the colonists had established a bicameral legislature, the General Court, with an appointed Governor's Council as the upper house and two delegates from each town as the lower house.

New England Ways

Self-governing Puritan congregations ignored the authority of Anglican bishops. Male "saints," as Puritans termed those who had been saved, ran each congregation. By majority vote they chose ministers, elected a board of elders to handle finances, and decided who were saints. Thus, control of New England churches was broadly based.

The clergy quickly asserted its power in New England's religious life. In England, Puritans had focused on their common opposition to Anglican practices. In America,

the "New England Way" Puritan orthodoxy that was supposed to govern the Massachusetts Bay colony

however, theological differences began to undermine the harmony that Winthrop had envisioned. Puritan ministers struggled to define orthodox practices—**the "New England Way"**—that strengthened their authority at the expense of the laypersons (nonclergy) within their congregations.

Education was a key means of establishing orthodoxy. Like most Protestants, Puritans insisted on familiarity with the Bible and, thus, literacy. They felt education should begin in childhood and be promoted by each colony.

Old Deluder Act Law requiring Puritan towns to establish and maintain schools; foundation of public education in New England

In 1647 the Massachusetts Bay colony passed the **Old Deluder Act** because "one chief project of that old deluder, Satan [is] to keep men from knowledge of the Scriptures." Every town of fifty or more households was to appoint one teacher from whom all children could receive instruction, and every town of one hundred households or more was to maintain a grammar school with a teacher capable of preparing students for university-level learning. This law, echoed by other Puritan colonies, was New England's first step toward public education, although attendance remained optional and boys were more likely to be taught reading and writing than girls.

An educated clergy was essential, so in 1636 Massachusetts founded Harvard College to produce learned ministers. In its first thirty-five years, the college turned out 201 graduates, 111 of them ministers. These alumni made New England the only American colony with a college-educated elite during the seventeenth century.

Although agreeing that the church must be free of state control, Winthrop and other Massachusetts Bay leaders insisted that a holy commonwealth required cooperation between church and state. Therefore, the colony required all adults to attend services and pay tithes to support their local church. Massachusetts thus had a state-sponsored or "established" religion. Some Puritans, however, dissented from their leaders' vision of social order and religious conformity. **Roger Williams,** who arrived in America in 1631, argued that civil government had to remain absolutely uninvolved with religious matters. Williams opposed compulsory church service and interference with private religious beliefs because he feared that the state would eventually corrupt the church and its saints.

Roger Williams Dissenter seen as a threat to the New England Way; ultimately banished; founded Rhode Island

Believing that the purpose of the colony was to protect true religion and to prevent heresy, political authorities declared Williams's opinions subversive and banished him in 1635. Williams went south to the edge of Narragansett Bay to a place that he later named Providence, which he purchased from the Indians. A steady stream of dissenters drifted to the group of settlements near Providence, forming Rhode Island in 1647. The only New England colony to practice religious toleration, Rhode Island grew to eight hundred settlers by 1650.

Anne Hutchinson Dissenter feared not only for her theology but also because she challenged gender roles; banished from Massachusetts

Anne Hutchinson presented the second major challenge to the New England Way. "A woman of haughty and fierce carriage, of a nimble wit and active spirit," Hutchinson maintained that her fellow Puritans were too certain that they could tell whether or not a person was a saint on the basis of his or her behavior. She reminded them that their creed stressed predestination, not good works, and argued that New England's ministers had gone astray.

Hutchinson's ideas directly attacked the clergy's authority to interpret and teach Scripture; critics charged that her beliefs would delude individuals into imagining that they were accountable only to themselves. Her followers were labeled "antinomians," meaning those opposed to the rule of law. Anne Hutchinson bore the additional liability of being a woman challenging traditional male roles in church and state. Her gender made her seem an especially dangerous foe. "You have stepped out of your places; you [would] rather have been a husband than a wife, a preacher than a hearer," one of her foes railed against her.

Massachusetts Bay split into pro- and anti-Hutchinson forces. Her opponents prevailed, bringing Hutchinson to trial for sedition in 1637 before the Massachusetts Bay legislature (the General Court) and then for heresy before a panel of ministers. Hutchinson's knowledge of Scripture was so superior to that of her inquisitors that she might well have been acquitted had she not claimed to communicate directly with the Holy Spirit. Because Puritans believed that God had ceased to make matters of faith known by personal revelation since New Testament times, Hutchinson was condemned by her own words. Banished from the colony along with other antinomians, Hutchinson settled in Rhode Island and then moved to New Netherland, where she was killed in that colony's war with Indians in 1643. Her banishment effectively ended the last challenge capable of splitting congregationalism and ensured the survival of the New England Way for two more generations.

New restrictions on women's independence and on equality within Puritan congregations followed antinomianism's defeat. Increasingly, women were prohibited from assuming the kind of public religious role claimed by Hutchinson and were even required to relate their conversion experiences in private to their minister rather than publicly before their congregation.

Towns, Families, and Farm Life

To ensure that colonists would settle in communities with congregations, all New England colonies provided for the establishment of towns by awarding a grant of land to several dozen landowning church members. These men laid out the settlement, organized its church, distributed land among themselves, and established a town meeting. At the center of each town was the meetinghouse, which served as both church and town hall.

Local administration lay in the hands of the town meeting, which resulted in a highly decentralized authority over political and economic decisions. Each town determined its own qualifications for voting and for holding office; most allowed all male taxpayers, including nonsaints, to participate.

Most towns attempted to maintain communities of tightly clustered settlers by distributing only as much land as was necessary for each family to support itself. The remaining land would be distributed to future generations as needed. Forcing residents to live close together was an attempt to foster social reciprocity. New England's generally compact system of settlement made people interact with each other and established an atmosphere of mutual watchfulness that promoted godly order.

Despite the restriction of their public roles after the antinomian crisis, women remained a social force in their communities. Remaining at home while husbands and older sons tended the families, fields, and business, women exchanged goods—a pound of butter for a section of spun wool, for example—advice, and news. Women confided in one another, creating a community of women that helped enforce morals and protect the poor and vulnerable.

Puritans defined matrimony as a contract, not a sacrament; they were thus married by justices of the peace rather than ministers. As a civil institution, marriage could be dissolved by the courts in cases of desertion, bigamy, adultery, or physical cruelty. However, New England courts saw divorce as a remedy only for extremely wronged spouses, such as the Plymouth woman who found that her husband also had wives in Boston, Barbados (bar-BAY-dose), and England.

New England wives enjoyed significant legal protections against spousal violence and nonsupport and had more freedom to escape a failed marriage than their English counterparts. However, they suffered the legal disabilities borne by all women under English law. A wife had no property rights independent of her husband except by premarital agreement. Only if there were no other heirs, or if a will so specified, would a widow receive control of household property, although law entitled her to lifetime use of one-third of the estate.

New England's families enjoyed greater stability and lived longer lives than their English counterparts. The region's cold climate limited the impact of disease, especially in winter when limited travel between towns slowed the spread of infection. Easy access to land contributed to a healthy diet, which strengthened resistance to disease and lowered death rates associated with childbirth. Life expectancy for Puritan men reached sixty-five, and women lived nearly that long. These life-spans were ten years or more longer than those in England. More than 80 percent of all infants survived long enough to marry. Because so many of the twenty thousand immigrants who arrived in New England between 1630 and 1642 came as members of families, an even sex ratio and a rapid natural increase of population followed.

Families were economically interdependent. Male heads of families managed the household's crops and livestock, conducted its business transactions, and represented it at town meetings. Wives bore and nurtured children, and performed or oversaw work in the house, garden, and barn. Sons depended on parents to provide them with acreage for a farm, and parents encouraged sons to stay at home and work in return for a bequest of land later on. Young males often tended their father's fields until their late twenties before receiving their own land. The average family, raising four sons to adulthood, could count on thirty to forty years of work if their sons delayed marriage until age twenty-six.

There were other benefits as well. Prolonged dependence for sons ensured that the family line and property would continue in the hands of capable, experienced men. Although daughters performed vital labor, they would marry into another family. Young women with many childbearing years ahead of them were the most valuable potential wives, and first-generation women tended to marry by the age of twenty-one.

Economic and Religious Tensions

Saddled with a short growing season, rocky soil salted with gravel, and an inefficient system of land distribution that forced farmers to cultivate widely scattered strips, the colonists nevertheless managed to feed their families and to keep ahead of their debts. Few grew wealthy from farming. For wealth, New Englanders turned lumbering, shipbuilding, fishing, and rum distilling into major industries that employed perhaps one-fifth of all adults full time. As its economy diversified, New England prospered.

While most Puritans shared Winthrop's view of community, self-discipline, and mutual obligation, a large minority had come to America for prosperity and social mobility. The most visibly ambitious colonists were merchants, whose activities fueled New England's economy but whose way of life challenged its ideals.

Merchants fit uneasily into a religious society that equated financial shrewdness with greed. New England ministers attempted to curtail the acquisitive impulses transforming England itself. Merchants clashed with political leaders, who were trying to regulate prices so that consumers would not suffer from the chronic shortage of manufactured goods that afflicted New England. In 1635 the General Court forbade the sale of any item above 5 percent of its cost. Led by Robert Keayne, merchants protested that they needed to sell some goods at higher rates to offset losses incurred by shipwreck and inflation. In 1639 authorities fined Keayne for selling nails at 25 percent above cost and forced him to apologize in front of his congregation.

Keayne symbolized the fear that a headlong rush for prosperity would lead New Englanders to forget that they were their brothers' keepers. Controversies like these were part of a struggle for the New England soul. At stake was the Puritans' ability to insulate their city upon a hill from a market economy that threatened to strangle the spirit of community within a harsh world of frantic competition.

Other changes further undermined Winthrop's vision. After 1660 farmers voted themselves larger amounts of land and consolidated their scattered parcels of land. Farmers began to leave town centers to live on their outlying tracts. Friction grew between townspeople and "outlivers," whose distance from the town center limited their influence over town affairs. John Winthrop's vision of a society sustained by reciprocity was slowly giving way to the individualistic society that the original immigrants had fled in England.

As New England slowly prospered, old England fell into chaos and civil war. Alienated by years of religious harassment, Puritans gained control of the revolt, beheaded Charles I in 1649, and governed without a king for more than a decade. In 1660 a provisional English government recalled the Stuarts and restored Charles II to the throne.

The Stuart Restoration left American Puritans without a mission. Having conquered a wilderness and built their city upon a hill, they found that the eyes of the world were no longer fixed on them.

An internal crisis also gripped New England. First-generation Puritans had believed that they held a covenant, a holy contract, with God to establish a scripturally ordained church and to charge their descendants with its preservation. However, understandably reluctant to submit to a public review of their spirituality, relatively few second-generation Puritans were willing to join the elect by making the required conversion relation before the congregation. This generation also rejected the ritual of public conversion relation as an unnecessary source of division and bitterness that undermined Christian fellowship.

Because Puritan churches baptized only babies born to saints, first-generation Puritans faced the prospect that their own grandchildren would remain unbaptized unless the standards for church membership were lowered. They solved their dilemma in 1662 through a compromise known as the **Half-Way Covenant,** which permitted the children of all baptized members, including nonsaints, to be baptized. Church membership would pass down from generation to generation, but nonsaints would be "half-way" members, unable to take communion or to vote in church affairs. When forced to choose between a church system founded on a pure membership of

Half-Way Covenant Law to admit nonsaints to church membership; major blow to New England Way the elect and one that embraced the entire community, New Englanders opted for worldly power over spiritual purity.

The Half-Way Covenant signaled the dilution of the New England Way. Most adults chose to remain in "half-way" status for life, and the saints became a shrinking minority in the third and fourth generations. By the 1700s there were more female than male saints in most congregations. But because women could not vote in church affairs, religious authority stayed in male hands.

Expansion and Native Americans

In contrast to the settlement of Virginia, the Puritan colonization of New England initially met little resistance from Native Americans, whose numbers had been drastically reduced by disease. Settlers brought new diseases such as diphtheria, measles, tuberculosis, and new outbreaks of smallpox to rage through the Indian population. Between 1616 and 1618 an epidemic killed 90 percent of New England's coastal Indians, and a second epidemic in 1633–1634 inflicted comparable casualties on Indians throughout the Northeast. By 1675, New England's Native American population had shrunk from 125,000 in 1600 to about 10,000. During the 1640s, Massachusetts Bay passed laws prohibiting Indians from practicing their own religion and encouraging missionaries to convert them to Christianity. The Massachusetts Indians surrendered much of their independence and moved into "praying towns," such as Natick, a reservation established by the colony.

The expansion of English settlement farther inland, however, aroused Indian resistance. As settlers moved into the Connecticut River Valley, beginning in 1633, friction developed with the Pequots, who controlled the trade in furs and wampum with New Netherland. After tensions escalated into violence, the English waged a ruthless campaign against the Pequots, using tactics similar to those devised to break Irish resistance (see Chapter 2). In a predawn attack, troops led by Captain John Mason surrounded and set fire to a Pequot village at Mystic, Connecticut, and then cut down all who tried to escape. Several hundred Pequots, mostly women and children, were killed. By late 1637, Pequot resistance was crushed, and English settlement of the new colonies of Connecticut and New Haven could proceed unimpeded.

Indians felt the English presence in many ways. The fur trade, initially beneficial to Native Americans of the interior, became a burden. Once Indians began hunting for trade instead of for their subsistence needs alone, they quickly depleted the supply of beavers and other fur-bearing animals. Because English traders advanced trade goods on credit before the hunting season began, many Indians fell into debt. Traders increasingly took Indian land as collateral and sold it to settlers.

English townspeople, eager to expand their agricultural output and provide for their sons, voted themselves much larger amounts of land after 1660. For example, Dedham, Massachusetts, had distributed only three thousand acres from 1636 to 1656; by 1668 it had allocated another fifteen thousand acres. Many farmers built homes on their outlying tracts, crowding closer to the Indians' settlements and hunting, fishing, and gathering areas.

Expansion put pressure on the natives and the land alike. By clearing trees for fields and for use as fuel and building material, the colonists were altering the entire ecosystem by the mid-1600s. Deer no longer grazed freely, and the wild plants on which the Indians depended for food and medicine could not grow. Clear-cutting trees not only dried the soil but also brought frequent flooding. Encroaching white settlers allowed their livestock to run wild, according to English custom. Pigs damaged Indian cornfields and shellfish-gathering sites. Cattle and horses devoured native grasses, which the settlers replaced with English varieties.

Powerless to reverse the alarming decline of population, land, and food supplies, many Indians became demoralized. Some turned to alcohol, which became increasingly available during the 1660s despite colonial attempts to suppress its sale to Native Americans. Interpreting the crisis as one of belief, other Indians converted to Christianity. By 1675 Puritan missionaries had established about thirty "praying towns." Although missionaries struggled to convert the Indians to "civilization"—English culture and ways of life—most Indians integrated the new faith with their native cultural identities, reinforcing the hostility of settlers who believed that all Indians were irrevocably "savage" and heathen.

Anglo-Indian conflict became acute in the 1670s because of pressure on the Indians to sell their land and to accept missionaries and the legal authority of English courts. Tension was especially high in the Plymouth colony, where Puritans had engulfed the Wampanoag tribe and forced a series of humiliating concessions from their leader, Metacom (MEH-tuh-comb), or "King Philip," the son of the Pilgrims' onetime ally, Massasoit.

In 1675 Plymouth hanged three Wampanoags for killing a Christian Indian. Then several other Wampanoags were shot while burglarizing a farmhouse, touching off the conflict known as **King Philip's War**. In response to the escalation of violence, Metacom organized two-thirds of the Native Americans, including a few praying Indians, into a military alliance. The war raged across New England. Metacom's forces, as well armed as the Puritans, devastated the countryside, wiping out twelve of New England's ninety towns and killing 2,500 colonists. The following year, 1676, saw the tide turn as Puritan militia destroyed their enemies' food supplies and sold hundreds of captives into slavery, including Metacom's wife and child. Perhaps five thousand Indians starved or died in battle, including Metacom himself.

King Philip's War Last major war between Indians and New England settlers; reduced Indian population by nearly 40 percent; ended Indian resistance

King Philip's War reduced southern New England's Indian population by almost 40 percent and eliminated open Indian resistance to white expansion. It also deepened whites' hostility toward all Native Americans, even the Christian Indians who had fought against King Philip. In 1677 ten praying towns were disbanded, and all Indians were restricted to the remaining four. Missionary work ceased.

Salem Witchcraft, 1691–1693

Nowhere in New England did the conflicts dividing white New Englanders converge more forcefully than in Salem, Massachusetts. Trade made Salem prosperous but destroyed the relatively equal society of the first generation. Such divisions were especially sharp in Salem Village, an economically stagnant district north of Salem Town; those who lived in the eastern section farmed richer soils and benefited from Salem Town's commercial expansion, whereas those in the less fertile western half did not share this prosperity and lost the political influence that they had once held.

In late 1691 several Salem Village girls encouraged an African slave woman, Tituba (TEE-too-bah), to tell fortunes and talk to them about sorcery. When the girls began behaving strangely, villagers assumed that they were victims of witchcraft. Pressed to identify their tormenters, they named two local white women and Tituba.

To this point the incident was not unusual; witchcraft beliefs remained strong in seventeenth-century Europe and its colonies. Generally, witches were women whose greed, pride, envy, or discontent supposedly drove them to sign pacts with the devil and use his supernatural power of evil to torment neighbors by causing illness, destroying property, or "possessing" their victims' minds and bodies. Witnesses also usually accused these women of unfeminine behavior. A disproportionate number of the accused witches in New England were women who had inherited or stood to inherit more property than the usual one-third of a husband's estate. In other words, most accused witches were assertive women who had or might have had more economic power and independence than many men. To New Englanders, who felt it necessary to limit both female independence and economic individualism, they were dangerous. In most earlier witchcraft accusations, there was only one defendant, and the case never went to trial. However, the **Salem witchcraft trials** would lead to a colonywide panic.

Salem witchcraft trials
Hysteria that delivered final blow to New England Way, revealing social divisions

By April 1692 the girls had denounced two prosperous farm wives long considered saints in the local church and identified the village's former minister as a wizard (male witch). Fear of witchcraft soon overrode doubts about the girls' credibility and led local judges to ignore legal bans on "spectral evidence," testimony that a spirit resembling the accused had been seen tormenting a victim. Thereafter, charges multiplied until the jails overflowed with 342 accused witches.

The pattern of hysteria and accusations reflected Salem Village's internal divisions. Most charges came from the western side of the village and were lodged against people from the eastern village and in Salem Town. Two-thirds of all accusers were girls aged eleven to twenty, and more than half of them had lost one or both parents in conflicts between Indians and settlers in Maine. They and other survivors had fled to Massachusetts, where most worked as servants in other families' households. They most frequently named as witches middle-aged wives and widows—women who had escaped the poverty and uncertainty that they themselves faced.

Those found guilty of witchcraft tried to stave off death by implicating others. As the pandemonium spread, fear dissolved ties of friendship and family. A minister was condemned by his granddaughter, a mother by her seven-year-old daughter, and a husband and father by his wife and daughter. Fifty saved themselves by confessing, but twenty were condemned and executed.

By late 1692, doubts about the charges were surfacing. Clergymen objected to the emphasis on spectral evidence, which was crucial to most convictions. By accepting such evidence in court, minister Increase Mather warned, the Puritans had fallen victim to a deadly game of "blind man's buffet" set up by Satan and were "hotly and madly mauling one another in the dark." In October, Governor William Phips forbade any further imprisonments for witchcraft. One hundred were still in jail, and two hundred more stood accused. In early 1693 Phips ended the terror by pardoning all those who were convicted or suspected of practicing witchcraft.

CHECKING IN

- John Winthrop proclaimed that Puritans would build "a city upon a hill" in the New World, a godly community that would be an example to the world.
- Threats to Puritan orthodoxy, the "New England Way," included religious dissenters Roger Williams and Anne Hutchinson and the growth of a market economy.
- White expansion steadily displaced New England's Native Americans; New Englanders celebrated the massacre of the Pequots, and later resistance, culminating in the bitter and costly King Philip's War, proved futile.
- The Half-Way Covenant relaxed standards for church membership and marked the beginning of the end of the New England Way.
- The Salem witchcraft hysteria delivered the final blow to the New England Way, revealing deep social divisions.

The witchcraft hysteria marked the end of Puritan New England. Colonists reaching maturity after 1692 would reject the ideals of earlier generations and become "Yankees" who shrewdly pursued material gain. True to their Puritan roots, they would retain their forceful convictions and self-discipline, giving New England a distinctive regional identity that would endure.

THE SPREAD OF SLAVERY: THE CARIBBEAN AND CAROLINA

Why and how did plantation agriculture shape slavery in the Caribbean and Carolina?

As European colonies expanded on the mainland, an even larger wave of settlement swept the West Indies. Between 1630 and 1642 nearly two-thirds of the English who emigrated to the Americas went to the Caribbean. Beginning in the 1640s both the French and the English followed the Spanish, Portuguese, and Dutch in using slave labor to produce sugar on large plantations. After 1670 large numbers of English islanders migrated to the Chesapeake and to Carolina; large-scale plantation slavery traveled with them.

Sugar and Slaves: The West Indies

Initially, the English West Indies developed along lines similar to Virginia, with tobacco the dominant crop. Because a single worker could tend only three acres of tobacco, tobacco farming demanded a large population. By 1640 more colonists lived on England's five West Indian islands than in all of Virginia.

Tobacco, requiring little equipment beyond a curing shed, was cheap to raise, and tobacco cultivation gave individuals with little money a chance at upward mobility. Through the 1630s the West Indies remained a society with a large percentage of independent landowners, an overwhelmingly white population, and no extreme inequality of wealth.

Sugar cane soon changed that, revolutionizing the islands' economy and society. Encouraged by Dutch merchants, wealthy English planters began to raise this enormously lucrative crop. The demand for labor soared because sugar required triple the labor force of tobacco. African slaves soon replaced indentured white servants in the fields. Most planters preferred black slaves to white servants because they could be driven harder and maintained more cheaply. Also, African slaves could better withstand the tropical diseases of the Caribbean, they had no rights under contract, and they toiled until they died. Although slaves initially cost two to four times more than indentured servants, they were an economical long-term investment. Some English immigrants to the Caribbean copied the example already set by the Spanish and enslaved both Indians and Africans.

By 1670 the sugar revolution had transformed the British West Indies into a predominantly black and slave society. In 1713 slaves outnumbered whites by four to one; the slave population leaped from 40,000 in 1670 to 130,000 in 1713, with the white population remaining stable at 33,000. Declining demand for white labor in the West Indies diverted the flow of England migration from the islands to mainland North America. Driven from the Indies by high land prices, thousands of English settlers went north to the mainland, settling in Carolina. By 1700 more than 30,000 left the islands.

Rice and Slaves: Carolina

In 1663 Charles II bestowed the swampy coast between Virginia and Spanish Florida on several English supporters, making it the first of several Restoration colonies. The proprietors named their colony Carolina in honor of Charles (*Carolus* in Latin).

Settlers from New England and the West Indies had established outposts along the northern Carolina coast in the 1650s; the proprietors organized them into a separate district with a bicameral legislature. In 1669 one of the proprietors, Anthony Ashley Cooper, accelerated settlement by offering immigrants fifty-acre headright grants for every family member, indentured servant, or slave they brought in. The next year, two hundred white Barbadians and their slaves began the settlement of

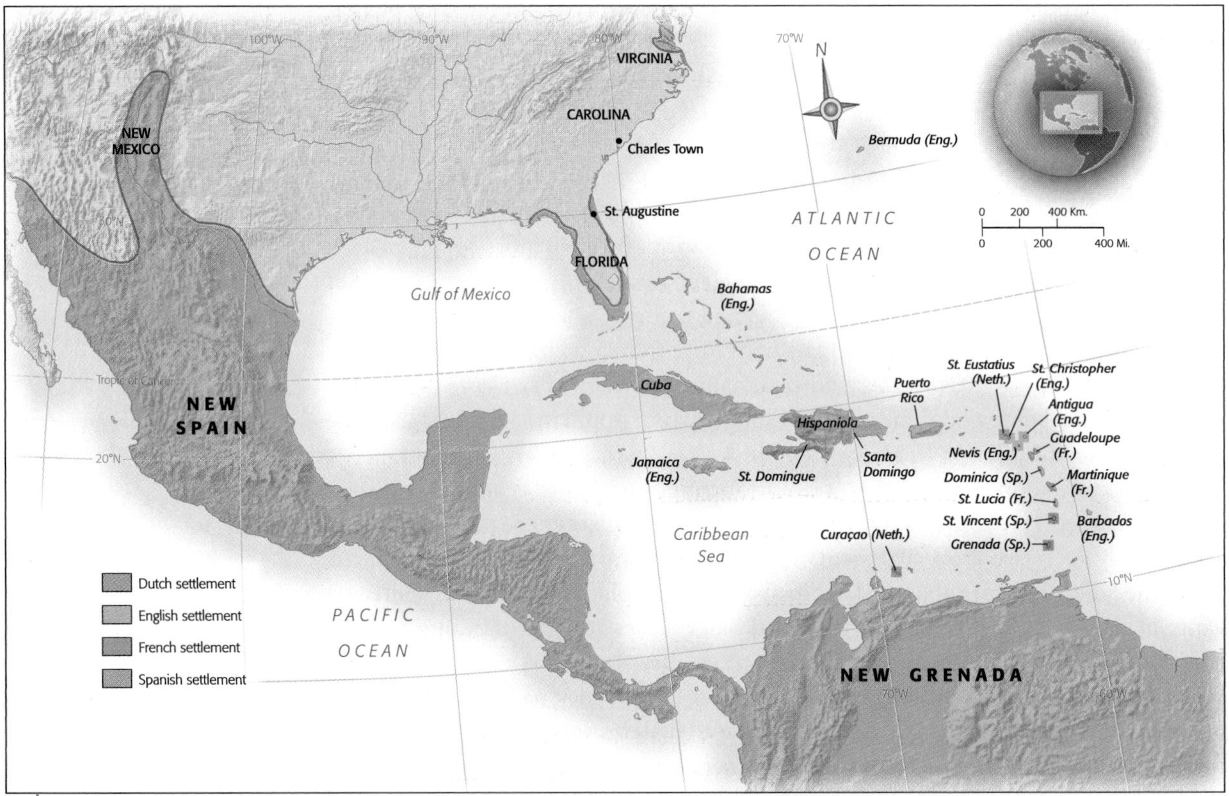

Map 3.3 The Caribbean Colonies, 1670

By 1660, nearly every West Indian island had been colonized by Europeans and was producing sugar with slave labor. Ten years later English colonists from Barbados were settling the new mainland colony of Carolina.

Interactive Map

southern Carolina near modern Charleston, "in the very chops of the Spanish." In the settlement they called Charles Town, they formed the colony's nucleus, with a bicameral legislature distinct from that of the northern district.

Cooper and his secretary, John Locke, devised an intricate plan for Carolina's settlement and government. Their Fundamental Constitutions of Carolina attempted to ensure the colony's stability by decreeing that political power and social rank should accurately reflect settlers' landed wealth. Thus, they invented a three-tiered nobility that would hold two-fifths of all land, make laws through a council of nobles, and dispense justice through manorial courts.

In the early years, Carolina's population consisted mainly of small landowners who saw little reason to follow the complex system drawn up on the other side of the Atlantic. Southern Carolinians raised livestock, and colonists in northern Carolina exported tobacco, lumber, and pitch. In neither north nor south did the people realize enough profit to maintain slaves, so self-sufficient white families predominated. However, southern Carolinians eagerly sought a cash crop. In the early 1690s they found it—rice. Rice cultivation enriched the few settlers with enough capital to acquire the dikes, dams, and slaves necessary to grow it. By earning annual profits of 25 percent, successful rice planters within a generation became the only colonial mainland elite whose wealth rivaled that of the Caribbean sugar planters.

Treated inhumanely, white indentured servants did not survive in the humid rice paddies swarming with malaria-carrying mosquitoes. Thus, planters imported an ever-growing force of African slaves, who possessed two major advantages. First, some had cultivated rice in Africa and possessed expertise vital to teaching whites how to raise the unfamiliar crop. Second, many Africans were immune to malaria and yellow fever, which were endemic in coastal regions of West Africa, and which they carried to North America. (Tragically, the antibody against malaria also tended to produce the sickle-cell trait, an often-fatal genetic condition.) These two factors made commercial rice production possible in Carolina.

The typical rice planter, with 130 acres in cultivation, needed sixty-five slaves. Demand drove the proportion of slaves in southern Carolina's population from 17 percent in 1680 to 67 percent in 1720, when the region officially became South Carolina. By 1776 the colony, with at least 100,000 slaves, would have more bondsmen than any other mainland colony in the eighteenth century. It would be Britain's only eighteenth-century mainland colony with a black majority.

As the black majority increased, whites relied on force and fear to control their slaves. In 1696 Carolina adopted the galling restrictions and gruesome punishments of the Barbados slave code. Bondage in the mainland colony grew as cruel and harsh as in the West Indies.

White Carolinians' attitudes toward Native Americans likewise hardened. The most vicious result was the trade in Indian slaves. White Carolinians armed allied Indians, encouraged them to raid and capture unarmed Indians to the south and west, and sold the captives to the West Indies during the 1670s and 1680s. A recent study estimates that the Carolina traders enslaved tens of thousands of Indians. Once shipped to the West Indies, most Native Americans died because they lacked immunities to European and tropical diseases.

CHECKING IN

- The English Caribbean colonies became dependent on sugar, which required a large labor force.
- Plantations appeared in the Caribbean, and slavery spread.
- South Carolina became wedded to a cash crop (rice), plantations, and slavery.
- Northern Carolinians exported tobacco, lumber, and pitch.

THE MIDDLE COLONIES

How did diversity distinguish the Middle Colonies?

The Dutch and the Swedish established small commercial outposts between the Chesapeake and New England. The Dutch took over New Sweden, and in turn England seized New Netherland in 1664; by 1681 England had used this territory as the basis for New York, New Jersey, and Pennsylvania, creating a fourth colonial region, the Middle Colonies.

Precursors: New Netherland and New Sweden

New Netherland became North America's first multiethnic society. Barely half the settlers were Dutch; most of the rest comprised Germans, French, Scandinavians, and Africans, both free and slave. In 1643 the population included Protestants, Catholics, Jews, and Muslims, speaking eighteen European and African languages. Religion counted for little (in 1642 the colony had seventeen taverns but not a single place of worship). The trading company that had established the settlement struggled to control the settlers, whose get-rich-quick attitude sapped company profits as private individuals traded illegally in furs. Eventually, the company legalized the private trade.

Privatization rapidly increased the number of guns in the hands of New Netherland's Iroquois allies, giving them a distinct advantage over other tribes. As overhunting depleted local fur supplies and smallpox epidemics raged, the Iroquois encroached on Huron territory for pelts and captives (who were adopted into Iroquois families to replace the dead). After 1648 the Dutch-armed Iroquois attacked French settlements along the St. Lawrence.

Although the Dutch had allied with the inland Iroquois, relations with the nearer Indian neighbors were terrible. With greedy settlers and military weakness, New Netherland largely had itself to blame. In 1643 an all-out war erupted when Governor Willem Kiefft ordered the massacre of previously friendly Indians. By 1645 the Dutch had temporarily prevailed, but only by enlisting English help and inflicting atrocities. The fighting cut New Netherland's Indian population from sixteen hundred to seven hundred.

Another European challenger, Sweden, distracted the Dutch in their war with the Native Americans. In 1638 Sweden had planted a small fur-trading colony in the lower Delaware Valley that was diverting furs from New Netherland. In 1655 the Dutch colony's stern soldier-governor, Peter Stuyvesant (STY-vuh-sant), marched against New Sweden, whose four hundred residents peacefully accepted Dutch annexation. But New Netherland paid dearly for its victory.

Although tiny, the Dutch and Swedish colonies were significant. Above all, they bequeathed a religious and ethnic diversity that would continue in England's Middle Colonies.

English Conquests: New York and New Jersey

Like the Carolinas, New York and New Jersey originated with Restoration-era proprietors hoping to grow rich from rents collected from settlers within a hierarchical society. New York marginally achieved this dream, but New Jersey did not.

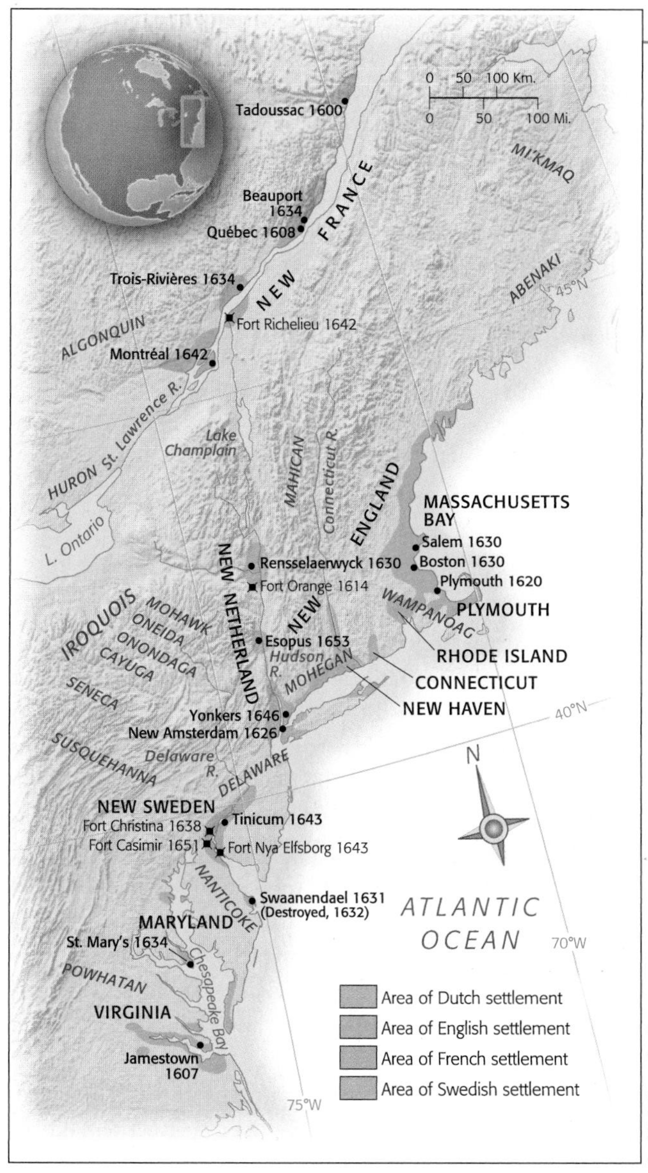

Map 3.4 European Colonization in the Middle and North Atlantic, c. 1650

North of Spanish Florida, four European powers competed for territory and trade with Native Americans in the early seventeenth century. Swedish and Dutch colonization was the foundation upon which England's Middle Colonies were built.

Interactive Map

In 1664, at war with the Dutch Republic, Charles II attacked the Dutch colony of New Netherland. Four hundred poorly armed Dutch civilians under Governor Peter Stuyvesant surrendered peacefully. Charles II made his brother James, Duke of York, proprietor of the new English colony and renamed it New York. With James's ascension to the throne in 1685, he converted New York into a royal colony. By 1700 immigration had swelled the population to twenty thousand, of whom just 44 percent were descended from the original Dutch settlers.

New York's governors rewarded their influential political supporters with large land grants. By 1703 five families held 1.75 million acres, which they carved into manors and rented to tenants. By 1750 the enormous income they earned from rents had made the New York estate owners a landed elite second in wealth only to the Carolina rice planters.

However, ambitious plans collided with American realities in New Jersey, which was also carved out of New Netherland. In 1664 the Duke of York awarded a group of supporters New Jersey, at the time inhabited by a few hundred Dutch and Swedes and several thousand Delaware Indians. Within a decade thousands of troublesome New England Puritans settled in New Jersey, and the proprietors sold the region to Quakers, who split the territory into East and West Jersey.

The Jerseys' Quakers, Anglicans, Puritans, Scottish Presbyterians, and Dutch Calvinists quarreled with one another and got along even worse with the proprietors. The governments collapsed between 1698 and 1701, and in 1702 the disillusioned proprietors surrendered their political powers to the crown, which then created the royal colony of New Jersey.

Quaker Pennsylvania

William Penn Quaker who tried to establish Pennsylvania as a "peaceable kingdom" that reflected Quaker ideals of tolerance

In 1681 Charles II paid off a huge debt by appointing a supporter's son, **William Penn,** as proprietor of the last unallocated tract of American territory at the king's disposal. Penn, a Quaker, thus founded the colony as a "holy experiment" based on the teachings of the English preacher George Fox. Penn also hoped for financial gain.

Quakers in late-seventeenth-century England stood well beyond the fringe of respectability. Challenging conventional foundations of social order, they appealed to those at the bottom of the economic ladder. But they also attracted some well-educated, well-to-do individuals disillusioned by the quarreling of rival religious faiths, including significant numbers of merchants. The members of this radical religious sect, which had been born in war-torn England during the 1640s and 1650s, called themselves the Society of Friends, but most others dubbed them Quakers.

At the heart of their founder George Fox's theology was the belief that the Holy Spirit, or "Inner Light," could inspire every soul. Mainstream Christians found this claim highly suspicious. In their religious services ("meetings"), Quakers sat silently until the Inner Light prompted one of them to speak. Quakers believed that the Inner Light could "speak in the female as well as the male," and they thus accorded women unprecedented equality.

Quaker behavior often seemed disrespectful to government and to the social elite, and thus aroused hostility. For example, Quakers refused to tip their hat to their social betters, insisting that spiritual state, not wealth or status, deserved recognition. Their refusal to bear arms appeared unpatriotic and cowardly, yet they faced persecution, imprisonment, and even death with courage.

Care and planning made the Quaker migration to Pennsylvania one of the most successful initial transplantations of Europeans in any North American colony. After sending an advance party, Penn arrived in 1682. He named his new capital Philadelphia, the "City of Brotherly Love." Within five years, eight thousand English Quakers had joined him. Quakers migrated in family groups, and their high birthrate led to rapid population growth. (Pennsylvania's religious toleration attracted not only Quakers but also many other religious groups: Presbyterians, Baptists, Anglicans, and Catholics from England, and Lutherans and radical sectarians from Germany.)

A victim of persecution, Penn hated intolerance and arbitrary governance. He offered Quakers the opportunity to make laws according to their ideals. His Frame of Government (constitution) featured a strong executive branch (a governor and governor's council) and a lower chamber (the assembly) with limited power. Friends, a majority in the colony, dominated the assembly, and Penn generally named Quakers to other positions. To prevent wrangling and to achieve an orderly disposition of property, Penn personally oversaw land sales. He also designed a grid plan for Philadelphia, reserving park areas to keep it a "greene country towne." Penn sought peace with Native Americans by reassuring the Indians that the Quakers wished "to live together as Neighbours and Friends" and by buying land from them fairly.

Pennsylvania seemed an ideal colony—intelligently organized, well financed, tolerant, open to all industrious settlers, and at peace with the Indians. Rich lands and a lengthy growing season produced bumper crops. West Indian demand for grain generated widespread prosperity. By 1700 Philadelphia had become a major port. In 1704 counties along the lower Delaware River, where Swedes and Dutch had settled long before Penn, gained the right to elect their own legislature and became the colony of Delaware.

However, by this time Penn's "peaceable kingdom" had bogged down in human bickering. In 1684 Penn returned to England, and during his fifteen-year absence the settlers quarreled incessantly. Struggles between pro- and anti-Penn forces deadlocked the government. Penn's return in 1699 restored some order, but before leaving again in 1701, he made the legislature unicameral (one chamber) and allowed it to initiate measures.

Despite Penn's hopes, conflict among Quakers shook Pennsylvania in the 1690s, prompting some Friends to join the Church of England. Their departure began a major decline in the Quaker share of Pennsylvania's population, which fell even further after 1710 as Quakers stopped migrating in large numbers.

The Middle Colonies demonstrated that English America could benefit by encouraging pluralism. New York and New Jersey successfully integrated Dutch and Swedish populations; Pennsylvania, New Jersey, and Delaware refused to require residents to support any official church. However, the virtual completion of English claim-staking along the Atlantic Coast set England on a collision course with France and Spain, which were also vying for American territory.

Checking In

- The Dutch established New Netherland (later called New York) and took over Swedish colonies to the south.
- The Dutch colonies, seized by England in 1664, brought a tradition of religious and ethnic diversity and tolerance to the English empire.
- William Penn established the Pennsylvania colony as a refuge for Quakers, who suffered persecution.
- Penn tried to create a "peaceable kingdom" in Pennsylvania, encouraging good relations with Indians and religious tolerance.

Rivals for North America: France and Spain

How did the French and Spanish empires develop in the seventeenth century?

Unlike England, with its compact seacoast colonial settlements in North America, France and Spain had cast enormous nets of widely separated trading posts and missions across the interior. The two Catholic nations had converted many Indians to Christianity and made them trading partners and allies. By 1720, scattered missionaries, fur traders, and merchants had spread French and Spanish influence across two-thirds of today's United States.

France Claims a Continent

After briefly losing Canada to England (1629–1632), France resumed and extended its colonization there. Initially a privately held company, the Company of New France issued extensive tracts to large landlords, who in turn imported indentured servants or rented out small tracts. Nonetheless, Canada's harsh winters and short growing season sharply limited their numbers.

More successful were the traders and missionaries who spread beyond the settlements and relied on stable relations with the Indians to succeed. The lucrative opportunities offered by trade converted many would-be farmers into traders.

Jesuit missionaries followed the traders into the interior, spreading French influence westward to the Great Lakes. Ursuline nuns ministered to Native American women and girls nearer Quebec, ensuring that Catholic piety and morality reached all members of Indian families.

Under King Louis XIV (personally reigned 1661–1715), France sought to subordinate its American colony to French interests, following the doctrine of *mercantilism*. According to this doctrine, colonies should serve as sources of raw materials and as markets for manufactured goods so that the colonial power did not have to depend on rival nations for trade. The French hoped that New France would increase the fur trade, provide agricultural surpluses to ship to France's West Indies colonies, and export timber for those colonies and for the French navy. To achieve this, the French government transformed New France into a royal colony, confronted and sought to stifle the Iroquois, and encouraged French immigration to Canada.

The Iroquois had long limited French colonial profits by intercepting convoys of fur pelts. In the 1660s Louis XIV dispatched French troops to New France, where the French army burned Mohawk villages. Sobered by the destruction, the Iroquois Confederacy made a peace that permitted New France's rapid expansion of fur exports.

The French crown energetically built up New France's population, primarily by sending indentured servants to New France; army members stationed there were encouraged to stay, become farmers, and marry the "king's girls," female orphans shipped over with dowries. After 1673, however, immigration dwindled. Colonists who returned to France—more than two-thirds of the immigrants—told horrifying tales of disease, Canada's hard winter, and "savage" Indians. Natural increase would replace immigration as the chief source of population growth, guaranteeing slow development for New France.

Even male immigrants who stayed did not always fulfill the French vision of sturdy farmers. Many of them struck out westward from the St. Lawrence Valley, becoming ***coureurs de bois*** (koo-RUHR duh BWAH), independent and sometimes disreputable fur traders. These French traders obtained furs from the Indians in exchange for European goods, including guns. The coureurs lived and married among the Indians, forging for France a precarious empire based on alliances with Canadian and Great Lakes Indians. Alarmed by the rapid expansion of England's colonies, France sought to contain the English colonies and prevent Spain from linking Florida with New Mexico by dominating the North American heartland.

coureurs de bois French fur traders who spread throughout the French empire in North America

As early as 1672, fur trader Louis Jolliet and Jesuit missionary Jacques Marquette became the first Europeans known to have reached the upper Mississippi; they later paddled twelve hundred miles downstream to the Mississippi's junction with the Arkansas. Ten years later, the Sieur de La Salle, an ambitious dreamer and adventurer, descended the entire Mississippi to the Gulf of Mexico, ultimately claiming the entire Mississippi basin—half the territory of the present-day United States—for Louis XIV.

Having asserted title to Louisiana, as La Salle christened this empire, the French began settling its southern gateway. The first colonizers arrived on the Gulf Coast in 1698; within a year, the French had erected a fort near modern Biloxi, Mississippi; in 1702 the French founded a trading post where De Soto had faltered and called it Mobile. But Louisiana's growth would be delayed for another decade.

New Mexico: The Pueblo Revolt

Lying at the northerly margin of Spain's empire, New Mexico and Florida remained small and weak through the seventeenth century. Their security depended on friendly relations with Native Americans, but Spanish policies made that nearly impossible.

The Spanish sought to rule New Mexico by subordinating the Pueblo Indians to their authority. Franciscan missionaries established churches in the native communities (pueblos) and tried to force the Indians to attend Mass and observe Catholic rituals and morality. Spanish landowners received *encomiendas* that allowed them to exploit Indian labor. Finally, the Spanish drove a wedge between the Pueblo Indians and their nonfarming trade partners, the Apaches (uh-PATCH-ees) and the Navajos (NAV-uh-hoes). Corn once used for trade was now claimed as tribute by the Spanish. In response, the Apaches raided both pueblos and Spanish settlements, driving most of the pueblo dwellers to stronger ties with the Spanish.

Spanish rule began to chafe, especially after 1660. Drought withered Pueblo crops, leaving populations vulnerable to disease and starvation. The Pueblo population plummeted from eighty thousand in 1600 to barely seventeen thousand by the 1670s. Compounding the misery, Apaches riding horses stolen from the Spanish raided and plundered the pueblos. Desperate Indians turned to traditional beliefs and ceremonies to restore the spiritual balance and bring rainfall and peace. Determined to suppress this "witchcraft," Franciscan missionaries entered sacred kivas, destroyed religious objects, and publicly whipped native religious leaders and their followers.

In 1675 Governor Juan Francisco Treviño ordered the kivas sacked and religious leaders arrested. Three leaders went to the gallows; a fourth hanged himself; forty-three others were jailed, whipped, and sentenced to be sold as slaves.

Indian resentment against the Spanish blazed, and Pueblo leaders began planning to overthrow the Spanish. At the head of the revolt was **Popé** (poe-PAY), who had been arrested in 1675. Other leaders included disillusioned Christian converts and individuals of mixed Pueblo-Spanish ancestry. Most had tried to reconcile Christianity and Spanish rule with their Indian identity, but the deteriorating conditions and Spanish intolerance turned them against Catholicism.

Popé Leader of the Pueblo Revolt against the Spanish in 1680

The Pueblo Revolt began in August 1680 as Popé and cohorts attacked Spanish colonists residing near Taos and killed sixty-eight of the seventy who lived there. Joined by Indians from neighboring pueblos, they laid siege to New Mexico's capital, Santa Fe. The rebels destroyed the churches and killed nearly four hundred colonists and missionaries. The Spanish fled, not to return for twelve years. They left behind them large numbers of livestock and horses, around which many Native Americans would build new ways of life.

New Mexico History Museum

Taos Pueblo, New Mexico
Although this photo was taken in 1880, Taos's appearance had changed little during the two centuries since the Pueblo Revolt.

Led by a new governor, Diego de Vargas, the Spanish returned in 1692, using both violence and threats of violence to reestablish their rule. Spanish control of New Mexico remained limited as the Europeans abolished the *encomiendas* and reined in the Franciscans. Pueblo suspicion of the Spanish remained, but there were no more revolts. Instead, the Indians accepted the limited Spanish control and sustained their cultural identity within the boundaries of colonial rule.

CHECKING IN

- France created a New World empire that encompassed North America from the Appalachians to the Rockies.
- The French empire rested primarily on trade with Native Americans rather than on conquest and displacement.
- Spanish policies led to the Pueblo Revolt in 1680, but the Spanish reestablished control by 1700.
- The Spanish tried to establish frontiers in Texas and Florida, but their presence there was weak and scattered.

Florida and Texas

The Spanish fared no better in Florida. Periodic rebellions swept the Spanish settlements; beginning in the 1680s, Indian slave raiders, allied with the English, killed or captured thousands of Florida natives and sold them to English slave traders. Even before a new round of warfare erupted in Europe at the turn of the century, Spain was ill prepared to defend its beleaguered North American empire.

English expansion threatened Florida, while the French establishment of Louisiana dashed Spanish hopes of linking Florida to New Mexico. To offset the French, Spanish authorities proclaimed the province of Tejas (Texas) in 1691, but no permanent Spanish settlements appeared there until 1716.

Chapter Summary

How did tobacco shape the Chesapeake colonies? (page 40)

Unlike New England with its diversified economy, the Chesapeake colonies relied on a single cash crop, tobacco. Tobacco shaped the Chesapeake region by leading to the plantation system and dependence on African slavery, which developed gradually in the seventeenth century.

What was the "New England Way," and what challenges did it endure? (page 46)

Puritans established "a city upon a hill" in Massachusetts Bay to serve as a model to the world. The "New England Way"—a society based on religion—was threatened by dissenters Roger Williams and Anne Hutchinson and by the rise of a market economy. White expansion steadily displaced New England's Native Americans, and from the Pequot War to the bitter and costly King Philip's War resistance was crushed. The Half-Way Covenant marked the beginning of the end for the New England Way by relaxing standards for church membership, and the Salem witchcraft hysteria delivered the final blow, revealing deep social divisions.

Why and how did plantation agriculture shape slavery in the Caribbean and Carolina? (page 55)

Dependent on sugar cane, the Caribbean colonies evolved a harsh form of plantation slavery, while rice created a similarly harsh system in southern Carolina, which became the only mainland colony with a black majority population. Carolinians also enslaved tens of thousands of Indians.

How did diversity distinguish the Middle Colonies? (page 58)

The Middle Colonies followed yet another path of development. The Dutch New Netherland colony, conquered and incorporated by the English, contributed a strong history of religious and ethnic diversity. William Penn's "holy experiment" in Pennsylvania flourished, although it gradually moved away from some of its founder's ideals. Nonetheless, it, too, maintained both religious and economic diversity.

KEY TERMS

Bacon's Rebellion *(p. 45)*
a city upon a hill *(p. 47)*
the "New England Way" *(p. 48)*
Old Deluder Act *(p. 48)*
Roger Williams *(p. 48)*
Anne Hutchinson *(p. 48)*
Half-Way Covenant *(p. 51)*
King Philip's War *(p. 53)*
Salem witchcraft trials *(p. 54)*
William Penn *(p. 60)*
coureurs de bois (p. 62)
Popé *(p. 63)*

How did the French and Spanish empires develop in the seventeenth century? (page 61)

In contrast to the fairly compact English settlements, the French empire became a far-flung web stretching from the Appalachians to the Rockies, dependent almost exclusively on trade and thus on good relations with Native Americans. After suppressing the Pueblo Revolt in the late seventeenth century, the Spanish tried to establish their imperial frontiers in Texas and Florida, but both remained only lightly settled.

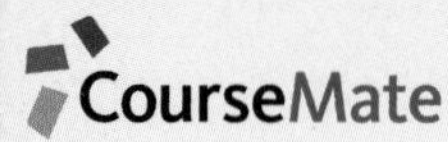

Go to the CourseMate website at **www.cengagebrain.com** for additional study tools and review materials—including audio and video clips—for this chapter.

CHAPTER 4

The Bonds of Empire

1660–1750

Courtesy, The Henry Francis du Pont Winterthur Museum

Mrs. Harme Gansevoort (Magdalena Bouw), by Pieter Vanderlyn, c. 1740

CHAPTER PREVIEW

Rebellion and War, 1660–1713
How did the Glorious Revolution shape relations between England and its North American colonies?

Colonial Economies and Societies, 1660–1750
What were the most important consequences of British mercantilism for the mainland colonies?

Competing for a Continent, 1713–1750
What factors explain the relative success of the British, French, and Spanish empires in North America?

Public Life in British America, 1689–1750
How did politics, the Enlightenment, and religious movements shape public life in the colonies?

Two men, George Whitefield and Benjamin Franklin, exemplified the major cultural currents that swept across the Atlantic from Europe to the colonies in the mid-eighteenth century. The embodiment of the powerful revival of piety that reinvigorated Protestantism on both sides of the ocean, Whitefield also demonstrated and reinforced the close ties that bound England and the colonies. Franklin, considered the leading American scientist of his time, personified the faith in reason known as the Enlightenment.

Born on opposite sides of the Atlantic, both men moved easily in English and colonial society, leaving behind provincialism for careers that brought them renown on both sides of the Atlantic. Their lives illustrate the increasingly close ties between England and her mainland colonies, ties that strengthened as the political and economic bonds of the empire grew tighter.

This new imperial relationship enabled the Anglo-American colonies to achieve a level of growth and prosperity unequalled elsewhere in the Americas.

REBELLION AND WAR, 1660–1713

How did the Glorious Revolution shape relations between England and its North American colonies?

After the Restoration (1660), England undertook a concerted effort to expand overseas trade and to subordinate its colonies to English commercial interests and political authority. The fall of the Stuart dynasty in 1689 and a succession of international wars hindered but did not halt this effort. By the time peace was restored in 1713, the colonists had become closely tied to a new, powerful British empire.

Royal Centralization, 1660–1688

The sons of a king executed by Parliament, the last Stuart monarchs, Charles II and James II, disliked representative government. Beginning in the mid-1670s, they tried to rule England as much as possible without Parliament and eyed American colonial assemblies suspiciously.

As Duke of York during his brother Charles's rule, James showed his disdain for colonial assemblies almost as soon as he became the proprietor of New York. Calling elected assemblies "of dangerous consequence," he forbade legislatures to meet from 1664 to 1682. In Charles's twenty-five-year reign, more than 90 percent of the governors whom he appointed were army officers, a serious violation of the English tradition of holding the military accountable to civilian authority. When James became king, he continued the policy.

Ever resentful of outside meddling, New Englanders resisted such centralization of power. In 1661 the Massachusetts assembly declared its citizens exempt from all English laws and royal decrees except declarations of war.

Provoked, Charles moved to break the Puritan establishment's power. In 1679 he carved a new royal territory, New Hampshire, from Massachusetts. In 1684 he declared Massachusetts a royal colony and revoked its charter, the very foundation of the Puritan city upon a hill.

James II went further. In 1686 the new king merged five separate colonies—Massachusetts, New Hampshire, Connecticut, Rhode Island, and Plymouth—into the **Dominion of New England,** later adding New York and the Jerseys. Under the new system, these colonies' legislatures ceased to exist. Sir Edmund Andros, a former army officer, became governor of the new supercolony.

Dominion of New England James II's attempt to tighten royal control of colonies by creating a new political entity

Andros's arbitrary actions ignited burning hatred in Massachusetts. He limited towns to one annual meeting and jailed prominent citizens to crush protests. He forced a Boston Puritan congregation to share its meetinghouse with an Anglican minister. Confronted by outraged colonists, he snapped "You have no more privileges left you than not to be sold for slaves."

Tensions also ran high in New York, where Catholics held high political and military posts under the Duke of York's rule. Anxious colonists feared that these

Chronology

1651–1733	England enacts the Navigation Acts
1660	Restoration of the English monarchy
1686–1689	Dominion of New England
1688–1689	Glorious Revolution in England
1689	Uprisings in Massachusetts, New York, and Maryland; royal authority established English Bill of Rights
1689–1697	King William's War (in Europe, War of the League of Augsburg)
1690	John Locke, *Essay Concerning Human Understanding*
1701	Iroquois Confederacy agrees to remain neutral in future wars between England and France
1702–1713	Queen Anne's War (in Europe, War of the Spanish Succession)
1715–1716	Yamasee War in Carolina
1716	San Antonio de Bexar founded
1718	New Orleans founded
1732	Georgia founded
1735	John Peter Zenger acquitted of seditious libel in New York; Jonathan Edwards leads revival in Northampton, Massachusetts
1739	Great Awakening begins with George Whitefield's arrival in British colonies; Stono Rebellion in South Carolina
1739–1740	Anglo-Spanish War
1739–1748	King George's War (in Europe, the War of the Austrian Succession)
1743	Benjamin Franklin founds American Philosophical Society
1750	Slavery legalized in Georgia

Catholic officials would betray the colony to France. When Andros's local deputy allowed harbor forts to deteriorate, New Yorkers suspected the worst.

The Glorious Revolution in England and America, 1688–1689

The Protestant majority in England also worriedly monitored Stuart displays of pro-Catholic sympathies. The Duke of York himself became a Catholic in 1676, and Charles II converted on his deathbed. Both rulers violated English law by allowing Catholics to hold high office and to worship openly.

In 1688 James's second wife bore a son, who would be raised—and perhaps would rule—as a Catholic. Aghast at the idea, English political leaders asked James's Protestant daughter Mary and her husband, William of Orange (the Dutch Republic's leader), to intervene. When William and Mary led a small army to England in November 1688, royal troops defected to them, and James II fled to France.

This nearly bloodless coup, the **"Glorious Revolution,"** created a "limited monarchy" as defined by England's **Bill of Rights** of 1689. The monarchs promised to summon Parliament annually, to sign its bills, and to respect civil liberties. Neither the English nor Anglo-Americans would ever forget this vindication of

"Glorious Revolution" Overthrow of James II in favor of William and Mary

Bill of Rights Drastically limited kingly power; vindicated limited representative government

Courtesy of the City of New Rochelle

Jacob Leisler

Leisler led an ill-fated uprising in New York following the Glorious Revolution, and was executed for his efforts. Nevertheless, his followers remained politically forceful in New York for a generation after his death.

limited representative government. News of the Glorious Revolution electrified Massachusetts Puritans, who arrested Andros and his councilors. Acting in the name of William and Mary, the Massachusetts elite resumed its own government. The new monarchs allowed Connecticut and Rhode Island to resume election of their own governors and permitted Massachusetts to absorb the Plymouth colony. But Massachusetts enjoyed only a partial victory. The colony's new royal charter of 1691 reserved to the crown the appointment of the governor. Moreover, property ownership replaced church membership as the criterion for voting. Worst of all, the Puritan colony had to tolerate Anglicans and all other Protestants, who were proliferating in the port towns.

New York's counterpart to the anti-Stuart uprising was Leisler's Rebellion. In May 1689 the city militia, under Captain Jacob Leisler (LIES-luhr), seized the harbor's main fort and called elections for an assembly. In 1691 Leisler, still riding high, denied newly arrived English troops entry to key forts for fear that they were loyal to James II. But after a brief skirmish, Leisler was arrested and charged with treason. Elite New Yorkers, many of whom Leisler had arrested, packed the jury, and both he and his son-in-law were convicted and hanged.

Arbitrary government and fears of Catholic plots had also brought turmoil to Maryland by 1689, where the Protestant-dominated lower house and the Catholic upper chamber were feuding. When the Glorious Revolution toppled James II, Lord Baltimore, away in England, dispatched a courier to Maryland, commanding obedience to William and Mary. However, the courier died en route.

Protestant rebel John Coode organized the Protestant Association to secure Maryland for William and Mary. In July 1689 Coode and his coconspirators seized the capital, removed Catholics from office, and requested that the crown take over the colony. Maryland became a royal province in 1691 and made the Church of England its established religion in 1692. Catholics, making up less than one-fourth of the population, lost the right to vote and to worship in public. In 1715 the fourth Lord Baltimore joined the Church of England and regained his proprietorship.

The revolutionary events of 1688–1689 reestablished the colonies' legislative government and ensured Protestant religious freedom. William and Mary allowed colonial elites to reassert local control and encouraged Americans to identify their interests with England, laying the foundation for an empire based on voluntary allegiance, not raw force.

A Generation of War, 1689–1713

The Glorious Revolution ushered in a quarter-century of war that convulsed both England and the colonies. In 1689 England joined a European coalition against France's Louis XIV and plunged into the War of the League of Augsburg (which Anglo-Americans called **King William's War**).

King William's War European war that spilled over into North America (1689–1697)

In 1690 the war spread to North America, as New Yorkers and New Englanders launched an invasion of England's enemy, New France. The invasion deteriorated into cruel but inconclusive border raids by both sides. The Iroquois, allied to the English, bore the brunt of the war. French forces, enlisting the aid of virtually every other tribe from Maine to the Great Lakes, played havoc with Iroquois land and peoples. By 1700 one-fourth of the Iroquois warriors had been killed or taken prisoner, or had fled to Canada. The total Iroquois population declined 20 percent, to fewer than seven thousand. (By comparison, Europeans suffered about 1,300 casualties.) In 1701 the Iroquois agreed to let Canada's governor settle their disputes with other Indians and to remain neutral in future Anglo-French wars. Thereafter, playing French and English off against each other, the Iroquois maintained control of their lands, rebuilt their population, and held the balance of power along the Great Lakes.

Queen Anne's War European war that spilled over into North America

In 1702 a new European war pitted England against France and Spain. During what the colonists called **Queen Anne's War,** Anglo-Americans became painfully aware of their own military weakness. French and Indian raiders from Canada destroyed New England towns, while the Spanish invaded southern Carolina and nearly took Charles Town in 1706. Colonial vessels fell to French and Spanish warships. English forces, however, gained control of the Hudson Bay region, Newfoundland, and Acadia (henceforth called Nova Scotia). The peace signed in 1713 allowed Britain to keep these lands but left the French and Indians in control of their interior.

These wars had a profound political consequence. Anglo-Americans, realizing how much they needed the protection of the Royal Navy and identifying with England's leadership in the Protestant cause, became more loyal than ever to the English crown.

CHECKING IN

- After the Restoration, Britain attempted to tighten control over the colonies.
- The Glorious Revolution drove James II from the throne in 1688.
- The colonies regained their legislative rights.
- Protestant religious freedom was ensured.
- European wars from 1689 to 1713 played out in part in North America and strengthened colonial ties to England.

COLONIAL ECONOMIES AND SOCIETIES, 1660–1750

What were the most important consequences of British mercantilism for the mainland colonies?

The arrival of peace in 1713 shifted the competition among England, France, and Spain from the military to the economic. Britain and France sought to integrate their colonies into single colonial empires; Spain also attempted to do so but found its power north of Mexico and the Caribbean severely limited.

Mercantilist Empires in America

A set of political-economic assumptions known as **mercantilism** supplied the framework for the new imperial economies. The term refers to European policies aimed at guaranteeing prosperity by making the European country (England, France, or Spain) as self-sufficient as possible by eliminating its dependence on

mercantilism Political/economic theory that self-sufficiency was the way to national prosperity; tied colonial economies to the mother country foreign suppliers, damaging its foreign competitors' commerce, and increasing the national stock of gold and silver by selling more goods abroad than it bought. Colonies would supply raw materials, but the home countries would do most of the manufacturing.

Navigation Acts Series of laws meant to make colonies conform to the ideas of mercantilism

A series of **Navigation Acts** governing commerce between Britain and its colonies embodied mercantilism. In 1651 the English Parliament passed the first Navigation Act to exclude the Dutch from English trade. During the Restoration, Parliament enacted the Navigation Acts of 1660 and 1663; they barred colonial merchants from exporting such commodities as sugar and tobacco to anywhere but England and from importing goods on non-English ships. Another major measure, the Molasses Act of 1733, sought to integrate Caribbean sugar growers into the imperial economy by slapping heavy import taxes on non-British imports and thus creating in effect a protective tariff.

By 1750 a long series of Navigation Acts was affecting the colonial economy in four major ways. First, the laws limited imperial trade to British-owned ships whose crews were three-quarters British (broadly defined to include all colonists, even slaves). This new shipping restriction helped Britain to become Europe's foremost shipping nation and laid the foundations for an American merchant marine. By the 1750s Americans owned one-third of all imperial vessels. The swift growth of the merchant marine diversified the colonial economy and made it more self-sufficient. The expansion of colonial shipping hastened urbanization. By 1770 New York, Philadelphia, Boston, and Charleston had become major ports.

Second, the Navigation Acts barred the colonies' export of "enumerated goods" unless they first passed through England or Scotland. Among these were tobacco, rice, furs, indigo, and naval stores (masts, hemp, tar, and turpentine). Parliament did not restrict grain, livestock, fish, lumber, or rum, which constituted 60 percent of colonial exports. To sweeten the deal, Parliament gave American tobacco a monopoly in British markets; it also eased the burden of customs duties on both tobacco and rice. Despite the restrictive laws, planters' profits dropped only 3 percent.

Third, the navigation system encouraged economic diversification. Parliament paid modest bounties to Americans producing silk, iron, dyes, hemp, lumber, and other products that Britain would otherwise have had to import from foreign countries. Parliament also erected protective tariffs against foreign goods. In addition, the trade laws forbade Anglo-Americans from competing with British manufacturing of certain products, especially clothing. There were no restrictions on the production of iron, and by the eve of the Revolution, 250 ironworks were in production.

Finally, the Navigation Acts made the colonies a protected market for low-priced consumer goods from Britain. As a result, the share of British exports bound for America rose from just 5 percent in 1700 to almost 40 percent by 1760. Mercantilism gave rise to a "consumer revolution" in British America.

Britain's fellow mercantilists in France and Spain enjoyed no such growth or prosperity. France's Canadian colonies had few materials other than furs to export, and they imported primarily wine and brandy. The French government actually lost money in the fur trade by sending sizable amounts of cloth, firearms, and other manufactured commodities to its Indian allies; the large army that France kept stationed in North America was also a drain on the French treasury. French Canada continued to lack the private investment, commercial infrastructure, consumer market, and manufacturing capacity that British North America was rapidly developing. The French did achieve some economic success in the West Indies, however, where sugar planters (in defiance of mercantilist principles) turned their cane into molasses and then sold much of the molasses to New England merchants. Louisiana remained unprofitable, a drain on French resources.

Spain's economic record was even more dismal. The revival of the Spanish and Latin American economies during the eighteenth century did not extend north of Mexico, where many Spanish colonists turned to smuggling goods to and from Spain's rivals as a source of income. These economic successes and failures mirrored what was happening in the European mother countries. In both France and Spain, most wealth was in the form of land held by the nobility and the Catholic Church; there was almost no liquidity. In contrast, England's economy was a commercial-mercantile one. More and more wealth was in the hands of merchants, who used it as capital to invest in commercial enterprises, trade, and manufacturing. Britain's navy protected that trade, while the Bank of England ensured a stable money supply. Great Britain was well on the way to becoming the world's first industrial nation, and its colonies benefited accordingly; indeed, the colonies' per capita income from 1650 to 1770 rose twice as fast as that of Britain.

Population Growth and Diversity

Demographic differences reinforced Britain's economic advantages. By 1750 the British North American colonies boasted more than 1.1 million inhabitants; the French colonies, 60,000; and the Spanish colonies, an almost negligible 19,000.

Potential Spanish immigrants generally chose the wealthier Latin American colonies as their destination. Spain saw its settlements north of Mexico primarily as a buffer against French or English expansion and consequently maintained a heavy military presence there.

Poverty kept most French people from immigrating, and tales of harsh Canadian winters and wretched Louisiana conditions often deterred those who might otherwise have tried their luck in the New World. French Canada's population growth was primarily the result of natural increase; to populate Louisiana, the French government dispatched paupers and criminals and encouraged the large-scale importation of slaves. By 1732 two-thirds of lower Louisiana's 5,800 people were slaves.

Unlike their French and Spanish rivals, the British colonies could offer potential immigrants ample farmland and a healthy imperial economy. Equally important, the British willingly accepted non-British immigrants—as long as they were not Catholics—including a handful of Jews. Thus, British North America had a much deeper pool of potential immigrants.

Natural increase fueled population growth. After 1700, when life expectancy and family size in the South rose to parallel those of the North, Anglo-America's growth far outpaced Britain's. In 1700 England's population outnumbered the colonies' by twenty to one; by 1775 the ratio would be only three to one. Nevertheless, continuing immigration contributed significantly to colonial population growth. In the forty years after Queen Anne's War, 350,000 newcomers had reached the colonies.

Between 1630 and 1700 approximately two thousand English settlers arrived in the colonies annually, constituting 90 percent of all European immigrants. After

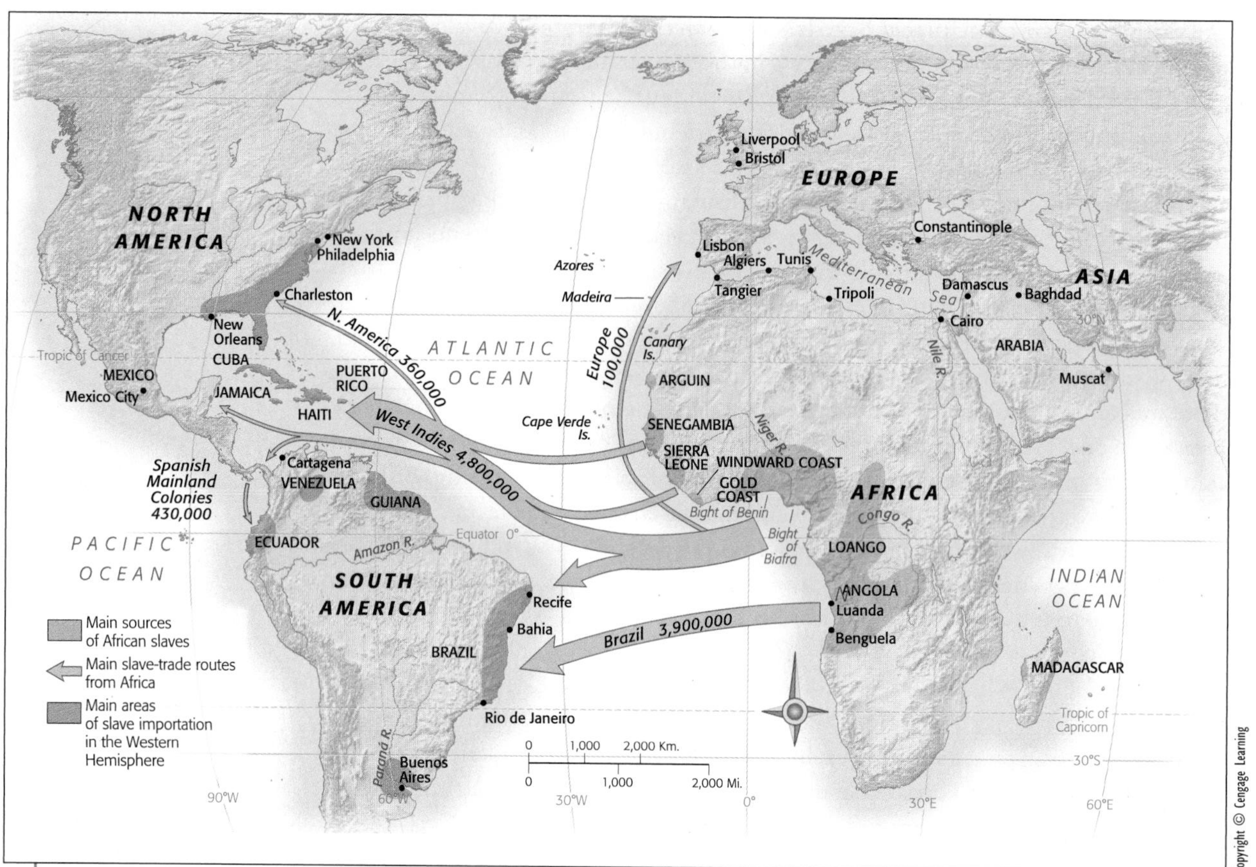

Map 4.1 Main Sources of African Slaves, ca. 1500–1800

The vast majority of enslaved Africans were taken to plantation colonies between Chesapeake Bay and the Brazilian coast.

Interactive Map

1713 the flood slowed to a trickle of five hundred English immigrants a year. Rising employment and wages in England made emigration less attractive, but economic hardships elsewhere in the British Isles and on the Continent guaranteed a steady stream of immigrants, greatly increasing ethnic diversity among white North Americans.

More than 100,000 newcomers in this era were from Ireland. Two-thirds of these were "Scots-Irish," the descendants of sixteenth-century Scottish Presbyterian settlers of northern Ireland. The Scots-Irish generally immigrated as complete families.

German-speaking lands in central Europe contributed some 125,000 settlers, the majority seeking escape from desperate poverty. One-third were "redemptioners" who had sold themselves or their children as indentured servants. Lutherans and Calvinists predominated, but a significant minority belonged to small, pacifist sects that desired above all to be left alone.

Indentured servants had to work one to four years for a master who might exploit them cruelly. Servants could be sold or rented out, beaten, kept from marrying, and sexually harassed; attempted escape usually meant an extension of service.

At the end of their term, most collected "freedom dues," which helped them to marry and acquire land.

The piedmont, a broad, rolling upland stretching along the eastern slope of the Appalachians, drew many immigrants seeking open land. Upper New York, Pennsylvania, and Maryland attracted large numbers of Germans and Scots-Irish. Charles Town became a popular gateway for immigrants who later moved westward to the Carolina piedmont to become small farmers. In 1713 few Anglo-Americans lived more than fifty miles from the Atlantic, but by 1750 one-third of the colonists resided in the piedmont.

Not all of the white immigrants came voluntarily. Between 1718 and 1783 some thirty thousand English convicts arrived in North America; some were murderers, but most were poor petty criminals. They were sold as servants. Relatively few committed crimes in the colonies, and some established themselves as successful backcountry farmers.

Benjamin Franklin reflected the attitude of many colonists when he asked, "Why should Pennsylvania, founded by the English, become a colony of aliens, who will shortly be so numerous as the Germanize us instead of us Anglicizing them, and will never adopt our language or customs any more than they can acquire our complexions?" Franklin also suggested that the colonists send rattlesnakes to Britain in exchange for its convict laborers.

There were no volunteers among the 140,000 enslaved Africans who constituted the largest single group of newcomers. Most were from Africa's west coast, and all had survived a sea crossing of sickening brutality known as the **Middle Passage.** Ship captains closely calculated how many slaves they could jam into their vessels. Kept below deck in near-darkness, surrounded by filth and stench, numbed by depression, the Africans frequently fell victim to disease. Slaves who refused to eat or otherwise defied shipboard authority were flogged. Open rebellions erupted on about 10 percent of the ships; shippers responded by hiring full-time guards and installing barricades to confine slaves even further.

By mid-century blacks constituted 20 percent of the North American colonies' population. Although slavery remained primarily a southern institution, 15 percent of all slaves lived north of Maryland; by 1750 one in seven New Yorkers was a slave.

West Indian and Brazilian slave buyers outbid Anglo-Americans, who of necessity not only bought a higher proportion of female slaves but also protected their investments by maintaining slaves' health. As a result, slaves in British mainland colonies, more often than their Caribbean or Brazilian

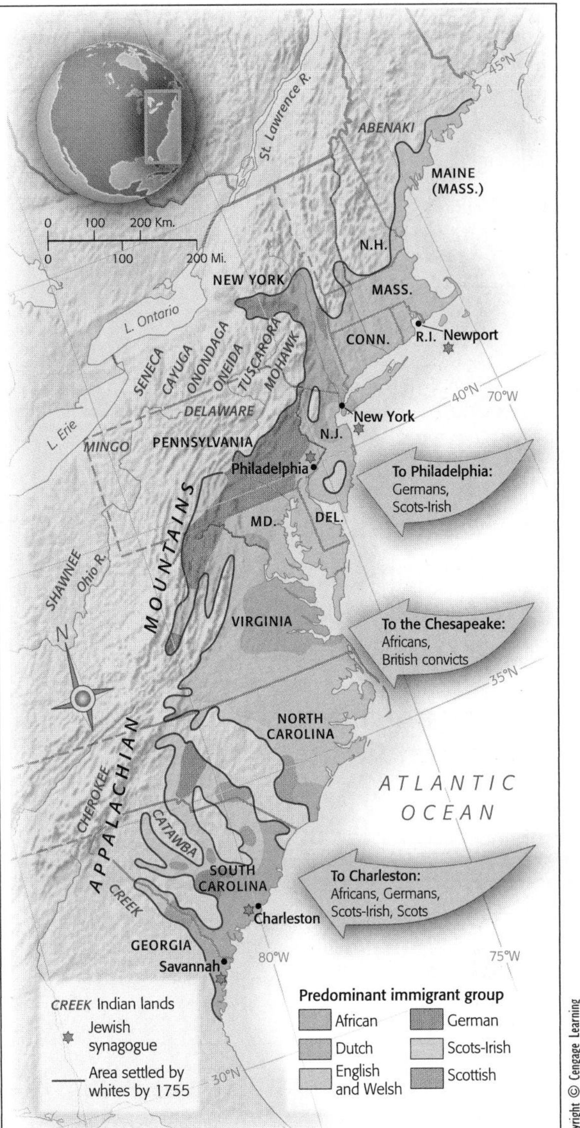

Map 4.2 Immigration and British Colonial Expansion, to 1755

Black majorities emerged in much of the Chesapeake tidewater and the Carolina-Georgia low country. Immigrants from Germany, Ireland, and Scotland predominated among the settlers in the Piedmont. A significant Jewish population emerged in the seaports.

Interactive Map

Middle Passage Brutal and often fatal slave journey from Africa to the Americas

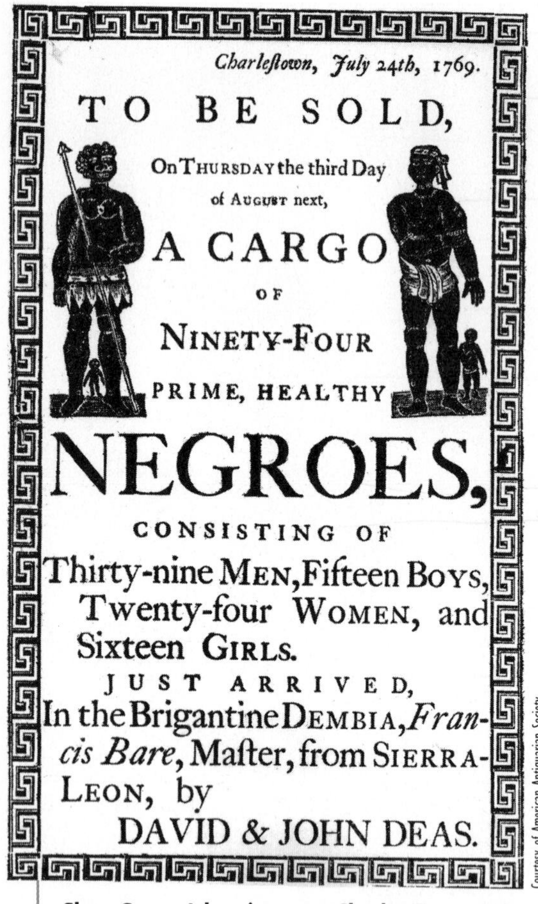
Charlestown, July 24th, 1769.

TO BE SOLD,

On THURSDAY the third Day of AUGUST next,

A CARGO OF NINETY-FOUR PRIME, HEALTHY

NEGROES,

CONSISTING OF

Thirty-nine MEN, Fifteen BOYS, Twenty-four WOMEN, and Sixteen GIRLS.

JUST ARRIVED,

In the Brigantine DEMBIA, *Francis Bare*, Master, from SIERRA-LEON, by

DAVID & JOHN DEAS.

Courtesy of American Antiquarian Society

Slave Cargo Advertisement, Charles Town, 1769
"Slavers," as the shippers of enslaved Africans were known, sought buyers for their "cargo" upon reaching an American port.

counterparts, formed families and lived longer. Natural increase among African-Americans almost equaled that of whites, and in some places American-born slaves outnumbered those born in Africa.

Rural White Men and Women

Because the vast majority of colonial landowners had just enough acreage for a working farm, most could not provide land for their children when they married. Moreover, with longevity increasing, children often did not receive their inheritances until middle age or later, and because families were large, a farmer's wealth was typically divided into small portions. Under these circumstances, a young man typically worked from about age sixteen to age twenty-three as a field hand to save money just to buy farm equipment, and a young husband generally had to rent land until he reached his mid-thirties.

The payment of mortgages was slow. A farmer could expect to earn 6 percent cash income per year, which barely equaled mortgage interest. After making a down payment of one-third, a husband and wife generally paid the next third through their inheritances. The final third would be paid when the children reached their teens and helped to double the regular farm income. Most colonial parents found themselves free of debt only as they reached their late fifties.

Rural families depended somewhat on barter and much more on what wives and daughters manufactured: soap, preserved food, knitted goods, yarn, and the products of dairy, orchard, and garden. However, legal constraints bound colonial women. A woman's most independent decision was her choice of a husband. Once married, she lost control of any goods or money she brought into the marriage. Nevertheless, widows controlled substantial property—an estimated 8 to 10 percent of all property in eighteenth-century Anglo-America—and a few ran large estates or plantations.

Colonial Farmers and the Environment

As English settlement expanded, the environment east of the Appalachians changed rapidly. Eighteenth-century settlers cleared forest land to plant crops in its fertile soil. New England farmers also cleared from their land innumerable large rocks, debris from the last Ice Age. The felled trees provided timber to construct houses, barns, and fences and were burned as fuel for cooking and heating. Urban dwellers bought their firewood and construction timber from farmers and planters.

deforestation Removal of trees that had a devastating ecological impact

Removal of trees **(deforestation)** deprived large forest creatures, such as bears, panthers, and wild turkeys, of their habitat, while the planted land provided free lunch for rabbits, mice, and possums. Deforestation removed protection from wind and sun, producing warmer summers and harsher winters, and, ironically, reinforcing the demand for firewood. By hastening the runoff of spring waters, deforestation led to heavier flooding and, where water could not escape, to larger swamps. Volatile temperatures and water levels rapidly reduced the number of fish in colonial streams and lakes.

Deforestation also dried and hardened the soil; colonial crops had even more drastic effects. Native Americans rotated their crops to protect against soil depletion, but many colonial farmers lacked enough land to do so—and many more were unwilling to sacrifice short-term profits for long-term benefits. Tobacco yields in the Chesapeake region declined in fields planted for only three or four consecutive years. As Chesapeake tobacco growers abandoned tidewater fields and moved to the piedmont, they hastened erosion. By 1750, to remain productive, many shifted from tobacco to wheat.

Well-to-do Europeans had already turned to conservation and "scientific farming." North American colonists, however, ignored such techniques. Some could not afford to implement them, and virtually all believed that America's vast lands, including those still held by Indians, would sustain them and future generations indefinitely.

Historic St. Mary's City

Poor Farmer's House
Many poor Chesapeake farmers lived in a single room with a dirt floor, no interior walls, an unglazed window, and minimal furnishings.

The Urban Paradox

Cities were colonial America's economic paradox. Although they shipped the livestock, grain, and lumber that enriched the countryside, at the same time they were caught in a downward spiral of declining opportunity.

After 1740 many among the 4 percent of colonists in cities found economic success elusive. Philadelphia, New York, and Boston faced escalating poverty. The cities' poor rolls, moreover, always bulged with the survivors of mariners lost at sea; unskilled, landless men; and women (often widows) and children from the countryside. High population density and poor sanitation left colonial cities vulnerable to the rapid spread of contagious diseases. As a result, half of all city children died before age twenty-one, and urban adults averaged ten fewer years of life than rural residents.

Even the able-bodied found cities economically treacherous. Traditionally, artisans trained apprentices and employed them as journeymen until they could open their own shops. After 1750, however, more employers released their workers when business slowed. And from 1720 onward, recessions hit frequently, creating longer spells of unemployment.

After 1700 urban poverty became a major problem. In Boston, for example, the proportion of the population too poor to pay taxes climbed steadily. New York did not build its first poorhouse until 1736, but 4 percent of its population needed public assistance by 1772. The percentage of Philadelphia families listed as poor jumped from 3 percent in 1720 to 11 percent by 1760.

Wealth remained highly concentrated. New York's wealthiest 10 percent (mostly merchants) owned about 45 percent of the property throughout the eighteenth century; Boston and Philadelphia followed similar patterns.

In the South, most cities were little more than large towns, although Charles Town was North America's fourth-largest city. South Carolina's capital offered gracious living to wealthy planters during the months of heat and insect infestations on their plantations. But shanties on the city's outskirts sheltered a growing crowd of destitute whites. Like their counterparts in northern port cities, Charles Town's poor whites competed for work with urban slaves whose masters rented out their labor. Racial tensions simmered.

Middle-class urban women faced less manual drudgery than their rural counterparts. Nonetheless, they managed complex households, often including servants and other nonfamily members. Although they sewed, knitted, and raised poultry and vegetables, urban women generally purchased their cloth and most of their food. Household servants, usually young single women or widows, helped with cooking, cleaning, and laundering. Wives also worked in family businesses, usually located in the owner's home.

Widows and less affluent wives took in boarders and often spun and wove cloth for local merchants. As grim conditions in Boston forced many widows with children to look to the community for relief, more prosperous Bostonians scorned them. A leading minister lamented "thye swarms of children . . . that are continually strolling and playing about the streets of our metropolis, clothed in rags and brought up in idleness and ignorance." Another clergyman warned that charity for widows and their children was money "worse than lost."

Slavery

Masters could usually afford to keep slaves healthy, but they rarely made their human chattels comfortable. Slave upkeep generally cost 60 percent less than the maintenance of indentured servants. White servants ate two hundred pounds of beef or pork a year; slaves, fifty pounds. A master would spend as much providing beer and hard cider for a servant as food and clothing for a slave. Adult slaves received eight quarts of corn and one pound of pork weekly and were expected to grow vegetables and raise poultry.

Slaves worked for a longer portion of their lives than whites. Slave children worked part time from the age of seven and full time as early as eleven. African-American women performed hard work alongside men and tended tobacco and rice crops even when pregnant. Most slaves toiled until they died, although those in their sixties rarely did hard labor.

As the number of Creole (American-born) slaves grew, sharp differences between them and African-born blacks arose. Creoles enjoyed the advantage of knowing the English language, the local environment, and the ways of their masters. They often translated this advantage into greater autonomy. Wealthier planters in particular used African-born slaves as field hands while training Creoles to perform household duties, such as repairing and driving carriages, preparing and serving meals, sewing, and caring for their children.

Both Africans and Creoles maximized opportunities within this harsh system. House slaves demanded that guests tip them for shining shoes and stabling horses; they also expected gifts on holidays. In the Carolina and Georgia rice country, the task system gave slaves some control of their work. Under tasking, each slave spent half a day caring for one-quarter acre, after which his or her duties ended. Ambitious slaves used the rest of the day to keep hogs or to grow vegetables for sale in Charles Town.

The gang system used on tobacco plantations gave Chesapeake slaves less free time than their counterparts in Carolina. However, despite Carolina slaves' greater autonomy, racial tensions ran high, especially as blacks began to outnumber whites. For example, a law of 1735 imposed severe restrictions on slave clothing. Of far greater concern were large gatherings of blacks uncontrolled by whites. In 1721 Charles Town enacted a 9:00 p.m. curfew for blacks. Slaves responded with increased instances of arson, theft, flight, and violence.

By mid-century, slaves constituted 20 percent of New York City's population and formed a majority in Charles Town and Savannah. Skilled urban slaves hired themselves out and kept part of their wages. By 1770 one-tenth of Savannah's slaves were living in rented rooms away from their owners. Despite substantial personal freedom, they remained slaves.

Tensions erupted in 1739 when a slave uprising known as the **Stono Rebellion** jolted South Carolina. Stealing guns and ammunition from a store at the Stono River Bridge, one hundred slaves headed for Florida crying, "Liberty!" Along the way they burned seven plantations and killed twenty whites. Within a day, however, mounted militiamen surrounded the runaways, cut them down, and spiked a rebel head on every milepost back to Charles Town. Whites expressed their fears in a new slave code stipulating constant surveillance and discipline for slaves, and requiring legislative approval for manumission (the freeing of individual slaves). The Stono Rebellion thus accelerated South Carolina's emergence as a racist and fear-ridden society.

Stono Rebellion Failed South Carolina slave uprising

Racial tensions wracked cities as well as plantations. In 1712 rebellious slaves in New York City killed nine whites; as a result, thirteen slaves were hanged, one was starved to death, three were burned at the stake, one was broken on the wheel, and six committed suicide. In 1741 a wave of thefts and fires attributed to slaves in New York led to the torture and hanging of thirteen slaves, the burning of thirteen more, and the sale of seventy to the West Indies.

The Rise of the Colonial Elites

A few colonists benefited disproportionately from the growing wealth of Britain and its colonies. Most elite colonists derived their wealth the old-fashioned way, by birth and by marriage. Elite males were generally large planters or farmers, or attorneys, clergy, and other professionals who catered to fellow elites.

Before 1700 class structure in the colonies was relatively invisible; the rural elite spent its resources on land, servants, and slaves instead of on conspicuous luxuries.

A traveler visiting one of Virginia's richest planters noted that his host owned only "good beds but no curtains and instead of cane chairs . . . stools made of wood." After 1720, however, the display of wealth became more ostentatious. The greater gentry—the richest 2 percent of the population—built splendid estate homes. The lesser gentry, or the second-wealthiest 2 to 10 percent, lived in more modest field-stone or wood-frame houses, and middle-class farmers typically inhabited one-story wooden buildings with four small rooms.

The gentry also exhibited their wealth after 1720 by imitating European "refinements." They wore costly English fashions, drove carriages, and bought expensive china, books, and furniture. They pursued a gracious life by studying foreign languages, learning formal dances, and cultivating polite manners. Men were to be gentlemen: dignified, responsible, generous, kind to their dogs and horses, and community leaders. Wives were to be ladies: skillful household managers and refined, respectful hostesses.

CHECKING IN

- After 1713, competition for North America shifted from the military to the economic realm as Britain embraced mercantilism.
- Prosperity boomed in the English colonies.
- The English colonies saw rapid population growth, in part from immigration.
- The differences between rural and urban life sharpened, and the number of colonial elites rose.
- Slavery became more important both economically and socially.

COMPETING FOR A CONTINENT, 1713–1750

What factors explain the relative success of the British, French, and Spanish empires in North America?

Europeans transformed North America in the first half of the eighteenth century as they expanded their territorial claims, opened new areas for settlement, and engaged in more intensive trade and warfare with Native Americans. In turn, Native Americans often welcomed trade but resisted Europeans who tried to settle nearby.

France and the American Heartland

Louisiana became a principal focus of France's imperial efforts. New Orleans, established in 1718, became the colony's capital and port. France hoped to use the Choctaw Indians as allies, but by the 1730s the tribe had become bitterly divided between pro-English and pro-French factions.

Louisiana's sluggish export economy forced settlers and slaves to find other means of support. Like the Indians, they hunted, fished, gathered wild plants, and cultivated gardens. And Indian, white, and black Louisianans traded with one another. Indians provided corn, tallow, and, above all, deerskins to merchants in return for blankets, axes, chickens, guns, and alcohol. Indians from west of the Mississippi brought horses and cattle, usually stolen from Spanish ranches in Texas. West African slaves, familiar with cattle from their homelands, managed many of Louisiana's herds; some became rustlers and illicit traders of beef.

French settlements in Upper Louisiana, usually referred to as Illinois (but also including parts of Missouri), were somewhat better off. Wheat became Illinois's major export, a more stable and profitable crop than the plantation commodities grown farther south. However, the colony's remote location limited exports and attracted few whites. It continued to depend on Native American allies to defend it from Indian enemies.

French attention also turned to the Ohio Valley, which, thanks to Iroquois neutrality, had become a refuge for dislocated Native American tribes, such as the Kickapoos, Shawnees, and Delawares. To counter growing English influence and to secure commercial and diplomatic ties with the Indians, the French expanded their trade. Several French posts, including Detroit, ballooned into sizable villages of Indian, French, and mixed-ancestry residents. Although the French were generally more successful than the English among the Indians, they never won over the Carolina-backed Chickasaws, and waged brutal warfare against the Mesquakies at Detroit and the Natchez in Louisiana. The French sold captives seized in these wars as slaves in their mainland colonies and in the West Indies. By 1744 French traders had explored as far west as North Dakota and Colorado, buying beaver pelts and Indian slaves on the Great Plains. These traders and their competitors spread trade goods, including guns, to Native Americans throughout central Canada and the Plains. Meanwhile, Indians in the southern Plains and the Great Basin acquired horses from the thousands left behind by fleeing Spaniards after the Pueblo Revolt of 1680. Horses and guns enabled tribes such as the Lakota Sioux and the Comanche to move onto the Plains and build a new, highly mobile way of life based on the pursuit of the buffalo. By 1750, France claimed an immense territory but its domain was precariously dependent on relations with Native Americans.

Native Americans and British Expansion

The depopulation and dislocation of Native Americans made possible the colonies' rapid expansion. Epidemic diseases, environmental changes, war, and political pressure opened new land for Europeans. In Carolina, imperial wars and the trade in Indian slaves soon produced violence. Between 1711 and 1713, clashes between the Tuscaroras and white settlers led to the death or enslavement of about one-fifth of the tribe; most survivors migrated northward to upstate New York to become the sixth nation of the Iroquois Confederacy. Settler abuses against Indians continued, leading the Yamasees and several allied nations to attack English settlements in 1715 and 1716. Only by relying on the aid of the Cherokees and by arming four hundred slaves did the colony crush the uprising.

The defeat of the Yamasees in turn left their Catawba allies wedged uncomfortably between the English to the south and the Iroquois to the north. They turned to the English for help. In return for land and promises to defend the colony against other Indians, the Catawbas received guns, food, and clothing. Although this gave the Catawbas at least temporary security, the rapidly increasing white population and the competition for resources sharply limited Catawba autonomy.

To the north, the Iroquois tried to accommodate the English and consolidate their own power. Late in the seventeenth century, the Iroquois entered into a series of agreements, known as the **Covenant Chain**, to relocate Indians whose lands the colonists desired. These tribes were moved to areas of New York and Pennsylvania, on the periphery of the Iroquois homeland, where they served as buffers against English expansion. In that way, and by incorporating the Tuscaroras into their confederacy, the Iroquois created a center of Native American power distinct from, but cooperative with, the British.

Covenant Chain Treaties by which Iroquois agreed to relocate displaced tribes to the periphery of Iroquois lands

In similar fashion, Pennsylvania coerced the Delawares into selling more than fifty thousand acres between 1729 and 1734. Then the colony's leaders produced a fraudulent treaty, dated to 1686, that required the Delawares to cede twelve hundred square miles of land. The Iroquois forced the Delawares to move to the upper Ohio Valley while the proprietors made a huge profit by selling the Delawares' land. Indians elsewhere along the westward-moving frontier faced pressure from settlers on one side and the Iroquois on the other.

British Expansion in the South: Georgia

In 1732 Parliament chartered a new colony, Georgia. It was designed to be a refuge for debtors, whose settlement would buffer South Carolina against attacks from Spanish Florida. Further, the new English colony would export expensive commodities, such as wine and silk.

James Oglethorpe Founder of Georgia colony

James Oglethorpe, who dominated the provincial board of trustees, shaped Georgia's early years. He established the port of entry, Savannah, in 1733. By 1740

Map 4.3 European Occupation of North America, to 1750

Spanish and French occupation depended on ties with Native Americans. By contrast, British colonists had dispossessed Native peoples and densely settled the eastern seaboard.

Interactive Map

nearly three thousand colonists resided in Georgia. Almost half were non-English immigrants from Germany, Switzerland, and Scotland, and most had their overseas passage paid by the government. A small number of Jews were among the early settlers. Thus, Georgia began as the last English colony.

Idealism and concerns about security led Oglethorpe to ban slavery from Georgia. Oglethorpe thought that slavery degraded blacks, made whites lazy, and presented a terrible risk. Parliament thus made Georgia the only colony where slavery was forbidden.

Oglethorpe's well-intentioned plans failed. Few debtors arrived because of Parliament's restrictions on their release from prison. Limitations that Oglethorpe had secured on settlers' rights to enlarge or sell their holdings discouraged immigrants, as did the ban on slavery. Georgia exported neither wine nor silk; only rice proved profitable. After a decade of struggle against economic reality, Oglethorpe yielded. In 1750 slavery became legal, and restrictions on landholdings ended. Within 10 years, 6,500 whites and 3,500 black slaves made Georgia even more prosperous.

Spain's Borderlands

While trying to maintain an empire in the face of Native American, French, and British adversaries, Spain spread its language and culture over much of North America, especially the Southwest. To repopulate New Mexico with settlers after the Pueblo Revolt (see Chapter 3), Spain handed out huge land grants and constructed fortifications, primarily for defense against, first, the Apaches and, later, the Comanches (cuh-MAN-cheese). Livestock-raising *ranchos* (ranches) monopolized vast amounts of land along the Rio Grande and blocked the establishment of further towns. On these ranchos, mounted herders of cattle and sheep (*vaqueros*) (vah-CARE-ohs) created the way of life later adopted by the American cowboy, featuring lariat and roping skills, cattle drives, and roundups.

By 1750 New Mexico's population numbered about 14,000, more than half of them Pueblos. Integrated into New Mexico society, most Pueblos practiced both Catholicism and their traditional religion and helped to defend the colony. Most Apaches had fled to Mexico or made peace with the Spanish to gain support against raids by Utes (yoots) and Comanches from the north.

To counter growing French influence among the Comanches and other Native Americans on the southern plains, Spain colonized Texas. In 1716 the Spanish established four missions. The most successful of the missions was at San Antonio de Bexar (day beh-HAR), where friars constructed a fortified building known as the Alamo. The Spanish presence in Texas remained light, however; by mid-century only 1,200 Spaniards lived there, and they were under constant threat of Indian raids.

Spain's position in Florida was only slightly less precarious. As early as 1700, when 3,800 English had settled in the Carolinas, only 1,500 Spanish were in Florida, a discrepancy that would continue to widen. To some extent, trade with the Creeks helped offset this numerical difference. But Florida's trade profits remained slim because it lacked cheap, desirable trade goods.

Florida gained more at English expense through its recruitment of escaped slaves from Carolina. In 1693 the Spanish monarch, Charles II, decreed that any

English-owned slaves who reached Florida and became Catholic would be freed. Word of this spread back to the Carolinas, prompting more slaves to flee to Florida. Eventually the Spanish would recruit an all-black militia unit and build a fortified village for the former slaves and their families.

By 1750 the French and Spanish empires had reached their limits in North America. Spain controlled much of the Southeast and Southwest, and France claimed the Mississippi, Ohio, and Missouri river valleys. Spain also maintained a precarious hold on Florida. Both empires, spread thin, depended heavily on Indian goodwill. In contrast, British North America, compact and wealthy, was densely populated by whites and was generally antagonistic toward Native Americans.

CHECKING IN

- The French remained lightly scattered over their North American empire and dependent on maintaining good relations with the Indians.
- British expansion continued to push Indians westward.
- Spain extended its control in the Southwest and established a light presence in Texas.
- Early in the eighteenth century, continental European wars again spread to North America.

The Return of War, 1739–1748

From 1713 to 1739 peace and prosperity prevailed, but in 1739 war again erupted; Spanish authorities cut off the ear of Robert Jenkins, a British smuggler, and Britain launched the "War of Jenkins' Ear" against Spain. James Oglethorpe led a massive but unsuccessful assault on St. Augustine in 1740; Spanish troops and refugee slaves from South Carolina likewise failed in a counterattack on Georgia two years later. By then, the Anglo-Spanish War had merged with one in Europe, the War of the Austrian Succession (1739–1748), known as King George's War to the colonists. In this conflict, four thousand New Englanders besieged the French fortress at Louisbourg, at the mouth of the St. Lawrence, and captured it after seven intense weeks of fighting. The war was inconclusive, and in 1748 Britain returned Louisbourg to the French under terms of the peace treaty ending the conflict.

PUBLIC LIFE IN BRITISH AMERICA, 1689–1750

How did politics, the Enlightenment, and religious movements shape public life in the colonies?

During the early and middle eighteenth century, the ties linking Britain and its colonies extended far beyond the movement of goods and peoples. England's new Bill of Rights was the foundation of government and politics in the colonies. English thinkers inspired the Enlightenment, and English preacher George Whitefield (WHIT-field) sparked a generation of colonists to transform the practice of Protestantism in British America. Significantly, these developments involved many more colonists than before as active participants in politics, in intellectual discussions, and in new religious movements. This wider participation signaled the emergence of a broad Anglo-American "public."

Colonial Politics

The most important political development after 1700 was the rise of the assembly as the dominant force in colonial government. In most colonies, the crown or proprietors chose colonial governors, who in turn named a council, or upper legislative house. Only in the lower house, or assembly, could members of the gentry assert their interests. Until 1689 governors and councils drafted laws, and the assemblies generally followed passively. Thereafter, assemblies assumed a more central role in politics, as colonial leaders argued that their legislatures should exercise the same rights as Parliament's House of Commons, which represented the people, defended their rights, and enjoyed the exclusive right to originate money-raising measures. Parliament's victory in the Glorious Revolution convinced Americans that their governors should defer to the assemblies.

The lower houses refused to permit meddling in their procedures, took control over taxes and budgets, and kept a tight rein on the salaries of governors who received no salary from Britain and remained vulnerable to such financial pressure. This power of the purse often forced governors to sign laws opposed by the crown.

Moreover, Britain's lack of interest in colonial politics allowed the assemblies to take considerable power. The Board of Trade, established by Parliament in 1696 to monitor American affairs, did not have the staff, the energy, or the vision to maintain royal authority by supporting embattled governors. This political vacuum allowed the colonies to become self-governing in most respects except for regulating trade, printing money, and declaring war. Colonial autonomy, reinforced by self-assertive assemblies, would haunt British authorities when they attempted to exercise more direct rule after 1763 (see Chapter 5).

Elites, wealthy landowners, merchants, and attorneys dominated politics as well as society. Governors appointed members of the greater gentry to serve on councils and as judges in the highest courts. The upper gentry, along with militia majors and colonels, also dominated among the representatives elected to the legislatures' lower houses (the assemblies). Members of the lesser gentry sat less often in the legislatures, but they commonly served as justices of the peace in the county courts.

Outside New England, property restrictions barred 80 percent of white men from running for the assembly. In any case, few ordinary citizens could have afforded the high costs of elective office. Assemblymen received meager living expenses, which did not cover the cost of staying at the capital, much less make up for six to ten weeks of missed work. Consequently, political leadership fell to a small number of wealthy families with a tradition of public service.

The colonies generally set liberal qualifications for male voters, but all excluded women, blacks, and Indians from voting. In seven colonies, voters had to own land (usually forty to fifty acres), and in the others they had to have enough property to furnish a house and to work a farm. Most white males in Anglo-America could vote by age forty, whereas across the Atlantic, two-thirds of all Englishmen and 90 percent of Irishmen could never vote.

Rural voting participation was low, averaging 45 percent. Governors called elections randomly so that after years without an election, one could be called on short notice. Voters in isolated areas often did not know of an upcoming election. Voting took place at the county seat, and many voters did not risk traveling long distances over poor roads to reach the voting place. In many colonies voters stated their preference publicly, often face to face with the candidates, a practice that discouraged dissenters. There were no political parties to stimulate popular interest or to mobilize voters. Candidates nominated themselves and ran on their reputation, not on the issues.

In view of these factors, political indifference was widespread. For example, to avoid paying legislators' expenses, many Massachusetts towns refused to elect assemblymen. From 1731 to 1760, one-third of South Carolina's elected assemblymen neglected to take their seats. Apathy might have been even greater had candidates not plied voters with alcohol. For example, George Washington dispensed almost two quarts of liquor for each voter when he was first elected to Virginia's assembly in 1758.

Competitive politics first developed in the northern seaports. Wealthy colonists aligned themselves with or against royal and proprietary governors. To gain advantage over rivals, some factions courted artisans and small shopkeepers whose fortunes had stagnated or declined as the distribution of wealth favored the rich.

John Peter Zenger Central figure in a trial that opened the way for freedom of the press

In 1735 New York became the site of a celebrated trial. Newspaper printer **John Peter Zenger** was charged with seditiously libeling the colony's governor. Zenger's acquittal on the charge broadened political discussion and participation beyond a small circle of elites. It also established truth as a defense against the charge of libel, opening the way toward greater freedom of the press in the future.

The Enlightenment

If property and wealth were keys to political participation and office-holding, literacy and education enabled Anglo-Americans to participate in the transatlantic world of ideas and beliefs. Eighteenth-century Anglo-America was probably the world's most literate society. Ninety percent of New England's adult white males and 40 percent of its women could write well enough to sign documents. In other colonies the literacy rate varied from 35 to 50 percent. (In England it stood at just over 30 percent.) Nevertheless, ordinary Americans' reading encompassed only a few books: an almanac, a psalter, and the Bible.

Members of the gentry, well-to-do merchants, and educated ministers lived in a world of print culture. Although costly, books and writing paper opened eighteenth-century European civilization to men and women of these classes who could read. And a rich, exciting world it was. Great advances in natural science seemed to explain the laws of nature, human intelligence appeared poised to triumph over ignorance and prejudice, and life itself would surely become more pleasant. For those with time to read and think, an age of optimism and boundless progress had dawned: the **Enlightenment.**

Enlightenment Intellectual revolution that elevated reason, science, and logic

Sir Isaac Newton British scientist whose ideas lay at the heart of the Enlightenment

Enlightenment ideals combined confidence in reason with skepticism about beliefs not based on science or logic. Enlightenment thought drew on the work of the English physicist **Sir Isaac Newton** (1642–1727), who explained how gravitation ruled the universe. Newton's work demonstrated the harmony of natural laws and stimulated others to search for rational principles in medicine, law, psychology, and government.

Benjamin Franklin American who embodied Enlightenment ideas

No American more embodied the Enlightenment spirit than **Benjamin Franklin** (1706–1790). Born in Boston, Franklin migrated to Philadelphia at age seventeen, bringing considerable assets: skill as a printer, ambition, and insatiable curiosity. In 1732 Franklin began publishing *Poor Richard's Almanack,* a collection of maxims and proverbs that made him famous—and rich. By age forty-two he had saved enough money to retire from printing and devote himself to science and community service.

To Franklin, science and community service were intertwined; true science would make everyone's life more comfortable. For example, his experiments in flying a kite during a thunderstorm proved that lightning was electricity and led to the invention of the lightning rod. In 1743 Franklin organized the American Philosophical Society to encourage "all philosophical experiments that let light into the nature of things, tend to increase the power of man over matter, and multiply the conveniences and pleasures of life." By 1769 the society had blossomed into an intercolonial network of amateur scientists.

Benjamin Franklin
This earliest known portrait of Franklin dates to about 1740, when he was a rising leader in bustling Philadelphia.

Although some plantation owners, among them Thomas Jefferson, championed the Enlightenment, it flourished primarily in the seaboard cities, where the latest ideas from Europe circulated and gentlemen and artisans met in small societies to investigate nature. To these individuals, the Royal Society in London, the foremost learned society in the English-speaking world, represented the ideal. The Enlightenment thus initially strengthened ties between British and colonial elites. Its adherents envisioned progress as gradual and proceeding from the top down. Just as Newton inspired the scientific bent of Enlightenment intellectuals, the *Essay Concerning Human Understanding* by English philosopher **John Locke** (1690) led many to embrace "reasonable" or "rational" religion. Locke contended that ideas are not inborn but are acquired by investigation of, and reflection on, experience. Enlightenment intellectuals believed that the study of the harmony and order of nature provided the best argument for God, a rational Creator. A handful insisted that where the Bible conflicted with reason, one should follow reason. Those—including Franklin and Jefferson—who took the argument furthest were called **Deists.** They concluded that God, having created a perfect universe, did not miraculously intervene in its workings but instead left it alone to operate according to natural law.

John Locke British philosopher who explained how reason functions

Deists Rationalists who insisted that the universe operates by natural law

Most colonists influenced by the Enlightenment considered themselves Christians but feared Christianity's excesses, particularly persecution in the name of religion and "enthusiasts" who emphasized emotion over reason. Mindful of Locke's caution that no human can be absolutely certain of anything but his or her own existence, they distrusted zealots and sectarians, and believed that religion's value lay in the encouragement of virtue and morality, not in theological hair splitting.

In 1750 the Enlightenment's greatest contributions to American life lay in the future, when Anglo-Americans would draw on the Enlightenment's revolutionary ideas as they declared independence and created a new nation. In the meantime, a series of religious revivals known as the Great Awakening would challenge the Enlightenment's most basic assumptions.

The Great Awakening

Rationalists viewed the world as orderly and predictable. Many Americans, however, did not enjoy orderly and predictable lives. The result was a spiritual longing that neither traditional religion nor Enlightenment philosophy could satisfy.

"Great Awakening" Protestant revival movement that emphasized each person's urgent need for salvation by God

A quickening of religious fervor in scattered places in the 1730s became passionate revivalism throughout Anglo-America in 1739. This **"Great Awakening"** cut across lines of class, status, and education. Above all, the Great Awakening represented an unleashing among ordinary people of anxiety about sin and longing for assurances of salvation. Some revivalists were steeped in Enlightenment ideas; for all, however, religion was primarily a matter of emotional commitment.

Jonathan Edwards Revivalist preacher whose sermon "Sinners in the Hands of an Angry God" summarized Great Awakening beliefs

In contrast to rationalists, who stressed the human potential for betterment, the ministers of the Great Awakening emphasized the corruption of human nature, the fury of divine wrath, and the need for immediate repentance. Congregationalist minister **Jonathan Edwards** of Northampton, Massachusetts, drove home this message with breathtaking clarity. During a 1735 revival Edwards preached his great sermon "Sinners in the Hands of an Angry God." "The God that holds you over the pit of Hell, much as one holds a spider or other loathsome insect over the fire, abhors you," Edwards intoned. "His wrath toward you burns like fire; He looks upon you as worthy of nothing else but to be cast into the fire."

George Whitefield English preacher who toured the colonies and played a major role in the Great Awakening

Other colonial ministers—Presbyterian William Tennent and Dutch Reformed Theodore Frelinghuysen—had anticipated Edwards's themes. Pulling the diverse threads of revival together was the arrival in 1739 of the charismatic English cleric **George Whitefield.** A man of overpowering presence and a booming voice, Whitefield attracted some crowds exceeding 20,000. On a tour through the colonies, Whitefield inspired thousands, mainly young adults, to seek salvation.

Whitefield's powerful allure awed even his critics. However, divisions over the revivals developed in Whitefield's wake. For example, after leaving Boston in October 1740, Whitefield invited Gilbert Tennent (William's son) to follow "in order to blow up the divine flame lately kindled there." Denouncing Boston's established clergy as "dead Drones" and lashing out at elites, Tennent built a following among the poor and downtrodden.

Exposing colonial society's divisions, Tennent and other radicals corroded support for revivals among established ministers and officials. Increasingly, lines hardened between the revivalists, the "New Lights," and the rationalist clergymen, or "Old Lights," who dominated the Anglican, Presbyterian, and Congregational churches. In 1740 Gilbert Tennent hinted that most Presbyterian ministers lacked saving grace and were bound for hell, and he urged parishioners to abandon them for the New Lights. By sowing doubts about ministers, Tennent undermined one of the foundations of the social order: if people could not trust their ministers, whom *could* they trust? Old Light rationalists fired back. In 1742 Charles Chauncy, a Boston Congregationalist, condemned revivals as an epidemic of the "enthusiasm" that enlightened intellectuals so hated. Chauncy especially blasted enthusiasts who mistook the ravings of their overheated imagination for direct communications from God.

The Great Awakening thus split American Protestantism. In 1741 Old and New Light Presbyterians formed rival branches that reunited in 1758 when the revivalists emerged victorious. The Anglican church lost many members to New Light Presbyterians and Baptists. Congregationalists also splintered badly; by 1760 New Lights had seceded from one-third of all churches and formed separate parishes.

The Great Awakening peaked in New England in 1742, but New Lights made steady gains into the 1770s, and the revival's long-term effects far exceeded its immediate impact. First, the revival started a decline in the influence of older sects, such as the Quakers, Anglicans, and Congregationalists. In turn, the number of Presbyterians and Baptists increased after 1740, and that of Methodists rose steadily after 1770. These churches have since dominated American Protestantism. Second, the Great Awakening stimulated the founding of new colleges unscarred by religious wars. The College of New Jersey (Princeton, 1746), King's College (Columbia, 1754), the College of Rhode Island (Brown, 1764), Queen's College (Rutgers, 1766), and Dartmouth (1769) trace their roots to this era. Third, the revival drew many African-Americans and Native Americans to Protestantism for the first time. Its oral and communal nature, and its emphasis on piety rather than learning, incorporated aspects of both groups' traditional cultures. The Great Awakening marked the emergence of black Protestantism as New Lights reached out to slaves. Meanwhile, a few New Light preachers, Indian as well as white, became missionaries to Indians. Still, nonwhites faced discrimination, even among New Lights.

The Great Awakening, moreover, gave women added prominence in colonial religion. For several decades, ministers had praised women—the majority of church members—as the embodiment of Christian piety. Now some New Light sects, mainly Baptist and Congregationalist, granted women the right to speak and vote in church meetings. Some women, like Anne Hutchinson a century earlier, presided over prayer meetings that included women, men, and sometimes even slaves. Although some of these women's activities were suppressed, none was prosecuted, as Hutchinson had been. The Great Awakening also fostered religious tolerance by blurring theological differences among New Lights. Indeed, revivalism's emphasis on inner experience, rather than on doctrinal fine points, emphasized Protestants' common experiences and promoted the coexistence of denominations.

Historians disagree about whether the Great Awakening had political effects. Although New Lights flayed the wealthy, they neither advocated a social revolution nor developed a political ideology. Yet, by empowering ordinary people to criticize those in authority, the revivals helped to lay the groundwork for political revolutionaries in this generation.

CHECKING IN

- Elected assemblies, dominated by colonial elites, became increasingly powerful.
- Political participation and competition were more evident in cities than in the countryside.
- The Enlightenment, with its optimism and strong emphasis on rationality, spread widely among colonial elites.
- At the same time, the Great Awakening expressed widespread religious longings, and new Protestant denominations challenged older ones.

Chapter Summary

How did the Glorious Revolution shape relations between England and its North American colonies? (page 68)

After the Restoration of the Stuart kings to England's throne, the British government attempted to tighten control over the colonies with measures such as the Navigation Acts and the Dominion of New England. When the Glorious Revolution drove James II from England, the colonies regained control of

KEY TERMS

Dominion of New England *(p. 68)*

"Glorious Revolution" *(p. 69)*

Bill of Rights *(p. 69)*

their own legislatures. England's wars on the continent of Europe spread to the New World, raising colonists' recognition of their own military weakness and strengthening their bonds to England.

What were the most important consequences of British mercantilism for the mainland colonies? (page 71)

The Navigation Acts, passed in response to a quickening sense of mercantilism in England, sought to control colonial trade. The primary effect was to increase colonial prosperity. Britain's colonies welcomed immigrants, and their population soared. Slavery became increasingly widespread, as did fears of slave rebellion. Population growth was a major factor in deforestation, which in turn stimulated westward movement away from depleted soils. Increased prosperity also contributed to the rise of colonial elites, but the poverty rate rose among ordinary city dwellers.

What factors explain the relative success of the British, French, and Spanish empires in North America? (page 80)

The first half of the eighteenth century saw renewed competition among the French, the British, and the Spanish for control of North America. France and Spain maintained sparse settlement and relied on good relations with Indians. English expansion created renewed problems for Native Americans.

How did politics, the Enlightenment, and religious movements shape public life in the colonies? (page 84)

The same time frame saw an explosion of colonial interest in politics and other elements of public life, such as intellectual discussion and new religious movements. Politics was far more an urban than a rural phenomenon; its chief feature was the rise of the colonial assembly. The Enlightenment brought the growth of rationalism and the religious movement known as Deism. At the same time, Protestant ministers, such as Jonathan Edwards, sought to restore religious enthusiasm. New denominations, such as Unitarians, Baptists, and Methodists, appeared. Women played a larger role in religion, and the questioning of authority was encouraged.

KEY TERMS continued

King William's War *(p. 71)*
Queen Anne's War *(p. 71)*
mercantilism *(p. 71)*
Navigation Acts *(p. 72)*
Middle Passage *(p. 75)*
deforestation *(p. 76)*
Stono Rebellion *(p. 79)*
Covenant Chain *(p. 81)*
James Oglethorpe *(p. 82)*
John Peter Zenger *(p. 86)*
Enlightenment *(p. 86)*
Sir Isaac Newton *(p. 86)*
Benjamin Franklin *(p. 86)*
John Locke *(p. 87)*
Deists *(p. 87)*
"Great Awakening" *(p. 88)*
Jonathan Edwards *(p. 88)*
George Whitefield *(p. 88)*

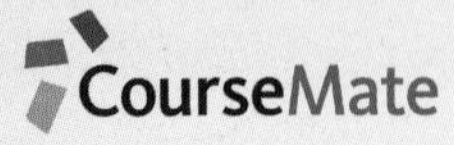

Go to the CourseMate website at **www.cengagebrain.com** for additional study tools and review materials—including audio and video clips—for this chapter.

CHAPTER 5

Roads to Revolution 1750–1776

Library of Congress

The Boston Massacre, 1770, Engraving, by Paul Revere

CHAPTER PREVIEW

- **Triumph and Tensions: The British Empire, 1750–1763**
  How did Britain and its colonies view their joint victory over France in the Seven Years' War?

- **Imperial Authority, Colonial Opposition, 1760–1766**
  What was imperial reorganization, and how did it change relations between Britain and the North American colonies?

- **Resistance Resumes, 1766–1770**
  In what ways did resistance to the Townshend duties differ from earlier colonial resistance efforts?

- **The Deepening Crisis, 1770–1774**
  In what ways did colonists' views of parliamentary authority change after 1770?

- **Toward Independence, 1774–1776**
  What led most colonists in 1776 to abandon their loyalty to Britain and choose national independence?

By 1763 Britain had defeated France, its chief competitor for preeminence in North America, and stood at the height of eighteenth-century imperial power. British rule ran undisputed from the Atlantic seacoast to the Mississippi River and from northernmost Canada to the Florida straits. Ironically, this greatest of British triumphs would turn into one of the greatest of British defeats.

The imperial reorganization that occurred after 1763 as a result of war and conquest radically altered Britain's relationship with its American colonies. Conflict arose between Britain and the colonies when Parliament, as it searched for ways to pay off the enormous debt accumulated during the war, attempted to tighten control over colonial affairs. The colonists, accustomed to legislating for themselves, resisted this effort to centralize decision making in London. American leaders interpreted Britain's clampdown as calculated antagonism, intended to deprive them of both prosperity and relative independence.

Conflict spilled out beyond constitutional issues. In port cities, crowds of poor and working people engaged in direct, often violent demonstrations against British authority. Settlers in the backcountry invoked the ideas of urban radicals when resisting large landowners and distant colonial governments dominated by elites. These movements reflected political and economic tensions within the colonies as well as growing defiance of elites by ordinary colonists. The growing participation of white women reflected impatience with restraints imposed by traditional gender norms. Nonwhites, both African-American and Native American, often perceived the colonists as greater threats to their liberty than the British. Within Britain itself many opposed the government's colonial policies.

Colonial resistance to British policies also reflected democratic stirrings in America and throughout the North Atlantic world. Among the products of this democratic surge were both the American Revolution, which erupted in 1776, and the French Revolution, which began in 1789 and sparked unrest over much of Europe and the Americas.

Despite their apprehension, colonial politicians expressed their opposition peacefully from 1763 to 1775 through legislative resolutions and commercial boycotts. Even after fighting erupted, the colonists agonized for more than a year about whether to sever their political relationship with Britain—which even native-born Americans sometimes referred to affectionately as "home." Of all the world's colonial peoples, none became rebels more reluctantly than Anglo-Americans did in 1776.

Triumph and Tensions: The British Empire, 1750–1763

How did Britain and its colonies view their joint victory over France in the Seven Years' War?

King George's War (see Chapter 4) did nothing to avert a showdown between Britain and France. The conflict resumed in 1756 and ended in 1763. Known as the **Seven Years' War,** it was a major turning point in both American and European history.

Seven Years' War Major French-British conflict known in North America as the French and Indian War

A Fragile Peace, 1750–1754

Because neither Britain nor France emerged from King George's War as the dominant power in North America, each prepared for another war. The Ohio Valley became the tinderbox for conflict. When France started building a chain of forts to regain control of the Virginia and Pennsylvania Indian trade, Virginia sent a twenty-one-year-old surveyor, George Washington, to demand that the French abandon their forts. In 1754 French troops drove the Virginians back to their homes.

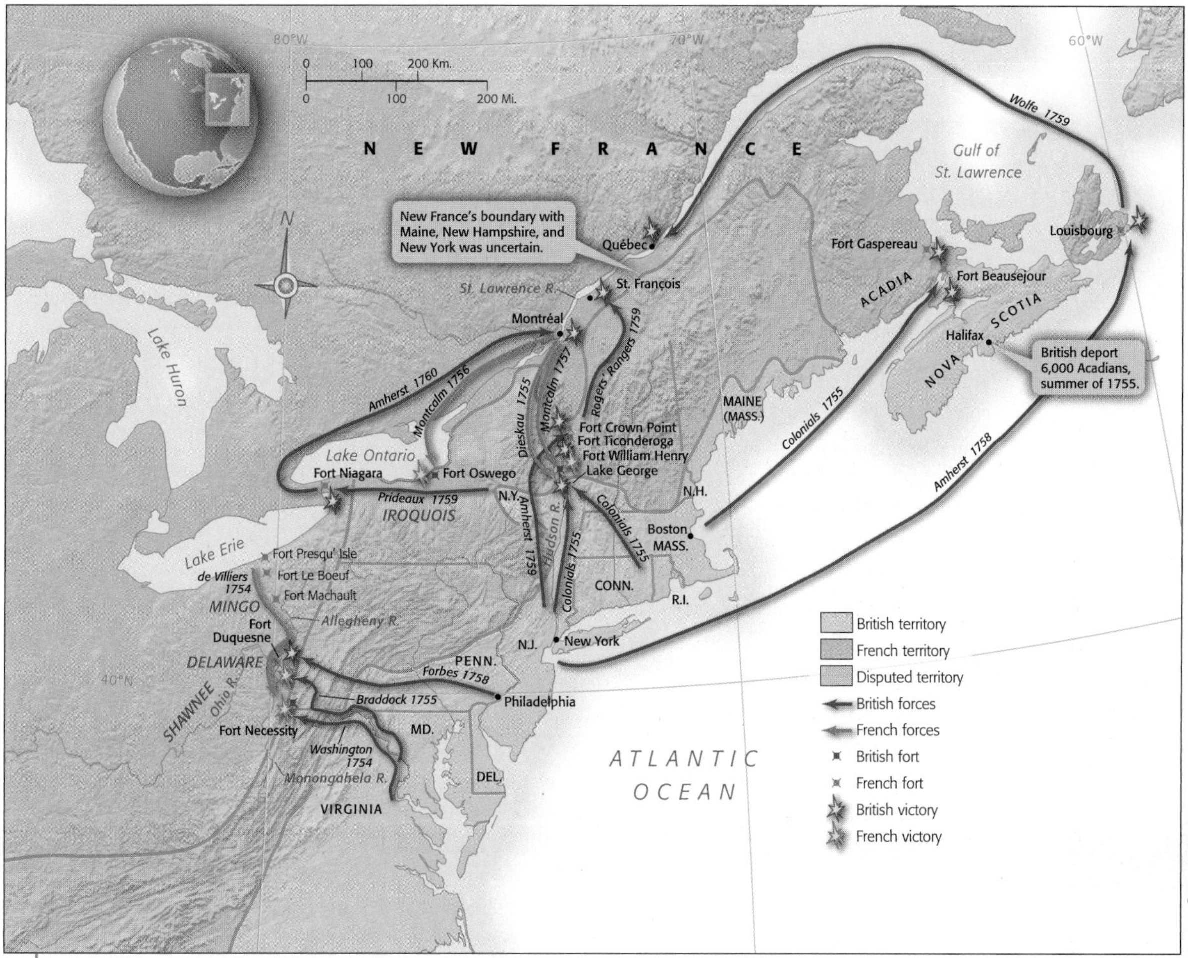

Map 5.1 The Seven Years' War in North America, 1754–1760

After experiencing major defeats early in the war, Anglo-American forces turned the tide against the French in 1758 by taking Fort Duquesne and Louisbourg. After Canada fell in 1760, the fighting shifted to Spain's Caribbean colonies.

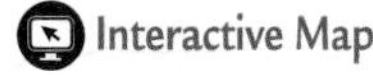

In mid-1754 seven colonies sent delegates to Albany, New York, to coordinate their mutual defense with British officials. The Albany Congress persuaded the wary Iroquois to support the British and endorsed a plan for a colonial confederation, the Albany Plan of Union, often seen as a predecessor to the federal system under the Constitution. However, the plan collapsed because no colonial legislature would surrender control over its powers of taxation.

The Seven Years' War in America, 1754–1760

Although France and Britain remained at peace in Europe until 1756, Washington's clash with the French had created a virtual state of war in North America. In 1754 Britain dispatched General Edward Braddock and one thousand regulars to take Fort Duquesne (doo-KAIN) at the headwaters of the Ohio River.

Chronology

1740–1748	King George's War
1754	Albany Congress
1756–1763	Seven Years' War
1760	George III becomes king of Great Britain; writ of assistance
1763	Proclamation of 1763; Treaty of Paris divides France's North American empire between Britain and Spain
1763	Pontiac leads Indian uprising in Ohio Valley and Great Lakes
1764	Sugar Act
1765	Stamp Act followed by colonial resistance; First Quartering Act
1766	Stamp Act repealed; Declaratory Act
1767	Revenue Act (Townshend duties); American Board of Customs Commissioners created
1768	Massachusetts circular letters; John Hancock's ship *Liberty* seized by Boston customs commissioner; St. George's Fields massacre in London; First Treaty of Fort Stanwix
1770	Townshend duties, except tea tax, repealed; Boston Massacre
1772	Somerset decision in Britain
1772–1774	Committees of correspondence formed
1773	Tea Act and Boston Tea Party
1774	Coercive Acts and Quebec Act (Intolerable Acts); First Continental Congress meets in Philadelphia and adopts Suffolk Resolves
1775	Battles of Lexington and Concord; Lord Dunmore offers freedom to Virginia slaves joining British forces; Olive Branch Petition; battles at Breed's Hill and Bunker Hill; King and Parliament declare colonies to be in rebellion
1776	Thomas Paine, *Common Sense*; Declaration of Independence

Scornful of colonial soldiers and friendly Native Americans, Braddock expected his disciplined regulars to make short work of the French. On July 9, 1755, about 850 French and Indians ambushed Braddock's 2,200 Britons and Virginians near Fort Duquesne. After three hours of steady fire, the British regulars broke and retreated, leaving Washington's Virginians to cover the withdrawal. Nine hundred regular soldiers and colonists died, including Braddock.

In 1756–1757 New France's daring commanding general, Louis Joseph de Montcalm, maintained the offensive. Anglo-Americans outnumbered Canadians twenty to one, but Montcalm benefited from large numbers of French regulars, Indian support, and full-scale mobilization of the Canadian population. The Anglo-American colonies supported the war grudgingly, providing few and usually poorly trained troops. French-armed Shawnees, Delawares, and Mingos struck hard at settlers in Western Pennsylvania, Maryland, and Virginia. These attacks halted British expansion and prevented the three colonies from joining the war against France for three years.

However, 1758 proved a turning point for the British. First, Indian support for the French evaporated. (Preferring competitive trade to warfare, most Indians hoped that neither European power would drive out the other.) Indian withdrawal enabled

Britain to capture Fort Duquesne and win control of the Ohio Valley. Second, British minister William Pitt took over Britain's military affairs. The imaginative and single-minded Pitt reinvigorated the military campaign, strengthened patriotism on both sides of the Atlantic, and became a popular hero in the colonies. Hard pressed in Europe by France and its allies (which after 1761 included Spain), Pitt believed that mobilizing colonial forces was the key to crushing New France. Keeping fewer than 4,000 British regulars in North America, he promised that Parliament would bear the cost of maintaining colonial troops.

Pitt's offer to free Americans from the war's financial burden generated unprecedented support. In 1758, and again in 1759, the colonies organized 40,000 troops. As a result, Britain took the offensive and captured Louisbourg and Fort Duquesne in 1758, followed by Quebec in September 1759. In 1760, with Montreal's surrender, French resistance in the New World ended.

The End of French North America, 1760–1763

In the **Treaty of Paris of 1763,** France ceded all its territories on the North American mainland. Several thousand French colonists, scattered from Quebec to Louisiana, became British or Spanish citizens. However, one group, the Acadians (uh-KAY-dee-uns) of Nova Scotia, suffered tremendous dislocation. The British deported the Acadians, nearly 5 percent of Canada's French population, to more southerly colonies, such as Pennsylvania and Maryland. Impoverished and facing intense anti-French, anti-Catholic prejudice, most fled to Louisiana, where they became known as the "Cajuns."

Treaty of Paris of 1763 Treaty by which France ceded virtually its entire North American empire to Britain and Spain

Under the Treaty of Paris, Britain received all French lands east of the Mississippi; Spain acquired the port of New Orleans and all French lands west of the Mississippi. Spain traded Florida to Britain in return for Cuba. Thus, Spain's New World empire actually increased in size, but France's virtually vanished, shrinking to a handful of islands. In contrast, Britain's North American empire quadrupled in size.

The effects of King George's War and the Seven Years' War were mixed. On one hand, shedding their blood in a common cause led British citizens and Americans to rely on each other as never before. However, the conclusion of both wars planted the seeds of mutual misunderstanding and suspicion.

Anglo-American Friction

During the war, British officers complained that colonial troops not only fought poorly but also tended to return home, even in the midst of campaigns, when their term was up or when their pay lagged. In turn, colonial soldiers complained that British officers treated their troops "little better than slaves."

Tensions flared as well between British officers and colonial civilians. Officers groused about colonial unwillingness to provide food or shelter, whereas colonists resented the officers' arrogance. Moreover, Pitt's promise to reimburse the colonies for their military expenses enraged Britons. Wartime spending had brought substantial profits to colonial farmers, artisans, and merchants. In addition, some merchants had continued their illicit trade with the French West Indies, simultaneously violating the Navigation Acts *and* trading with the enemy. Britain's national

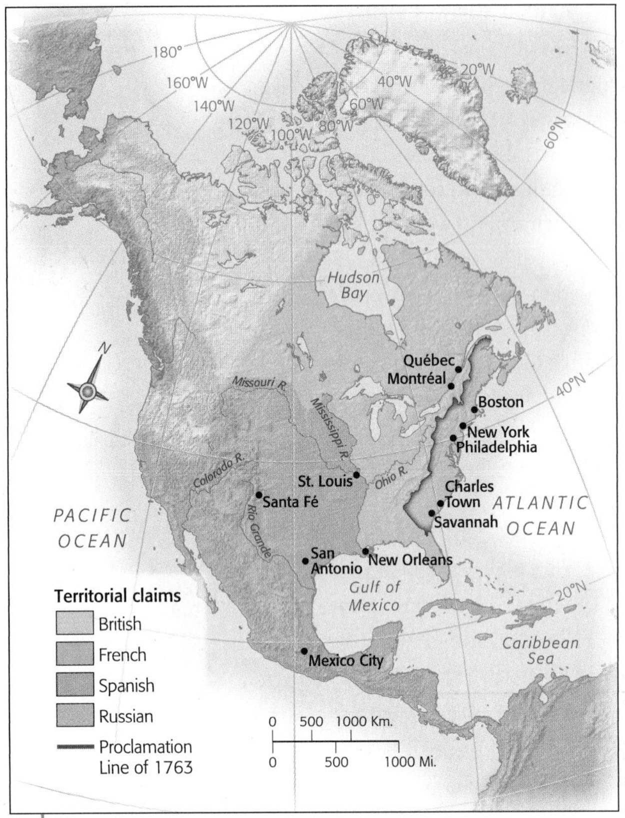

Map 5.2 European Territorial Claims, 1763

The treaties of San Ildefonso (1762) and Paris (1763) divided France's North American empire between Britain and Spain. In 1763 Britain established direct imperial authority west of the proclamation line.

Interactive Map

debt had nearly doubled during the war, to more than £132 million. In contrast, the total colonial debt amounted to less than £2 million. Staggering under debt and taxes, the British thought it outrageous to repay the Americans for defending themselves.

Colonists felt equally burdened. Wartime profits had gone to pay for British goods, accelerating the "consumer revolution" that had been under way for several decades (see Chapter 4). The wartime boom ended when peace returned. Now accustomed to a new middle-class lifestyle, colonists went into debt, and British creditors obliged by extending repayment terms from six months to a full year. Newly prosperous colonists began to suspect Britain of plotting to "enslave" the colonies to protect its own merchants and manufacturers.

The new revenue measures followed the ascension to the British throne of George III (reigned 1760–1820). The new king was determined to play a major role in government, but he proved ill suited to the task of building political coalitions or pursuing consistent policies. Until 1774, George III's frequent abrupt changes in government leadership destabilized politics in Britain and exacerbated relations with the colonies.

Frontier Tensions

Worse, Britain's victory over the French generated new Anglo-Indian conflicts that drove the British debt even higher. No longer able to play the two imperial powers off against each other, Indians feared the consequences. They were right. To cut costs after the war, the British stopped distributing food and ammunition to their Indian allies. Meanwhile, colonial squatters were moving onto Indian lands, raising both fears and tensions.

Pontiac Ottawa chief who created short-lived anti-British coalition among Native Americans

In early 1763 the Delaware Indian religious prophet Neolin called for Indians to repudiate European culture, goods, and alliances. **Pontiac,** an Ottawa Indian, and other leaders forged an anti-British coalition that sacked eight British forts and besieged British positions at Detroit and Pittsburgh. Short on food and ammunition, suffering a smallpox epidemic (deliberately spread by the British), and recognizing that the French would not return, the Indians surrendered in early fall.

Proclamation of 1763 An attempt to end Indian problems by preventing westward movement by colonists

However, the British victory was indecisive. Hoping to end the frontier fighting, George III issued the **Proclamation of 1763,** which asserted royal control of land transactions, settlements, and trade of non-Indians west of the Appalachians, and recognized existing Indian land titles everywhere west of the "proclamation line," which ran down the crest of the Appalachian Mountains. Although the policy calmed Indian fears, it angered the colonies by subordinating their western land claims to imperial authority and slowing colonial expansion.

Pontiac's rebellion also led the British government to station ten thousand regular troops in North America to occupy the western lands that France had ceded and to intimidate the Indians. The cost of administering British North America reached almost £440,000 yearly. Britons believed it perfectly reasonable for the colonists to help offset this expense. The colonists, however, struggling with their own postwar economic recession, saw it as none of their responsibility.

Although partially offsetting the colonies' unfavorable balance of payments with Britain, these troops raised fears of a peacetime "standing army" that could threaten American liberty. With the French menace gone, increasing numbers of colonists viewed Indian lands to the west as the key to future prosperity. The British troops that enforced the Proclamation Act of 1763, rather than being protectors, became threats to that future.

CHECKING IN

- In 1754 the colonies considered and rejected the Albany Plan of Union.
- The European Seven Years' War pitted the French and their Indian allies against the British in North America.
- The Treaty of Paris of 1763 ended the French empire in North America and enormously enlarged Britain's North American holdings.
- Victory brought mixed consequences: closer ties between Britain and the colonies but also the seeds of friction.

IMPERIAL AUTHORITY, COLONIAL OPPOSITION, 1760–1766

What was imperial reorganization, and how did it change relations between Britain and the North American colonies?

Even as the Seven Years' War wound down, tensions developed between Britain and its colonies, largely as the result of Britain's plans to finance its greatly enlarged empire by a series of revenue measures whose enforcement bypassed local authorities and seemed a dangerous extension of Parliamentary powers. The success of protest and opposition movements after the Stamp Act revealed a widening gulf between British and colonial ideas about the proper relationship between the empire and its colonies.

The Writ of Assistance, 1760–1761

To halt American trade with the enemy in the French West Indies during the Seven Years' War, Britain cracked down on colonial smuggling. In 1760 the royal governor of Massachusetts authorized the use of the **writ of assistance** to seize illegally imported goods. A general search warrant, the writ permitted customs officials to enter any ship or building where smuggled goods might be hidden. Because it required no evidence of probable cause for suspicion, the writ was considered unconstitutional by most British legal authorities.

writ of assistance A general search warrant of dubious legality

The writ of assistance proved a powerful weapon against smuggling. Merchants in Boston, the colonies' smuggling capital, hired James Otis to challenge the device's constitutionality. The former prosecuting attorney for Boston's vice-admiralty court, Otis had resigned to protest the use of the writ. Before Massachusetts' highest court in 1761, he argued that "an act against the Constitution is void"—even an act of Parliament. But the court, noting the use of an identical writ of assistance in Britain, ruled against the merchants.

Despite losing his case, Otis had stated with clarity the colonial conception of Parliament's role under the British constitution. Most British politicians assumed that Parliament's laws themselves were part of the unwritten constitution and that Parliament could in effect alter the constitution at will. But, like most colonists, Otis believed that Parliament had no authority to violate the traditional "rights of Englishmen" by authorizing illegal searches and seizures in private homes.

Sugar Act Act passed by British Parliament that placed new taxes and restrictions on colonists' trade

The Sugar Act, 1764

In 1764, three years after Otis's court challenge, Parliament passed the **Sugar Act** to offset part of Britain's North American military expenses. In ending the long-standing exemption of colonial trade from revenue-raising measures, the Sugar Act triggered new tension between Britain and the colonies. The Navigation Acts, in contrast, had been intended not to raise revenue but to benefit the imperial economy by controlling trade.

The Sugar Act amended the Molasses Act of 1733, which constituted a 6-pence-per-gallon tariff on French-produced molasses. Colonists commonly bribed customs inspectors 1½ pence per gallon to look the other way when they unloaded smuggled molasses. In designing the Sugar Act, British officials, well aware of the widespread bribery, wrongly assumed that the colonists would willingly pay a lower, 3-pence-per-gallon tax.

Colonists found other features of the Sugar Act equally objectionable. The act stipulated that the colonists had to export certain raw commodities *through Britain* instead of going directly to foreign ports, as they had been doing. It also complicated the requirements for shipping colonial goods. A captain had to fill out a confusing series of documents certifying the legality of his trade. The absence of any document left his cargo liable to seizure. The law's petty regulations made it virtually impossible for many colonial shippers to avoid committing technical violations of the act.

Finally, the Sugar Act discarded many traditional British protections for a fair trial. First, the law allowed customs officials to transfer smuggling cases from the colonial courts, in which juries decided the outcome, to vice-admiralty courts, in which a judge delivered the verdict. Because the act awarded vice-admiralty judges 5 percent of any confiscated cargo, it gave them a financial incentive to find defendants guilty. Second, until 1767 the law required all cases to be heard in the vice-admiralty court at Halifax, Nova Scotia. The law also reversed normal procedure by presuming the guilt of the accused and requiring the defendant to prove innocence.

The Sugar Act was no idle threat—the navy enforced it vigorously. A Boston resident complained that "no vessel hardly comes in or goes out but they find some pretence to seize and detain her."

Americans continued to smuggle molasses rather than pay the three-pence tax until 1766, when the British lowered the duty to a penny, making it cheaper to pay the tax than to smuggle. After that, the tax brought in about £30,000 a year.

Generally, opposition to the Sugar Act remained fragmented; the act provoked the most opposition in the most heavily affected colonies—Massachusetts, New York, and Pennsylvania. Other colonies that were unaffected protested very little. Although its immediate impact was slight, the Sugar Act heightened colonists' sensitivities to the new direction of imperial policies.

The Stamp Act Crisis, 1765–1766

Revenues raised by the Sugar Act did little to ease Britain's financial crisis. Britons groaned under the second-highest tax rates in Europe and looked resentfully at the lightly taxed colonists, who paid an average of one shilling per person compared to their twenty-six shillings per person.

In March 1765, to force colonists to shoulder a larger share of imperial expenses, Parliament passed the **Stamp Act.** The law obliged Americans to purchase and use specially marked or stamped paper for newspapers, customs documents, wills, contracts, and other public legal documents. Violators faced prosecution in vice-admiralty courts, without juries. Unlike the Sugar Act, which was an *external* tax levied on imports, the Stamp Act was an *internal* tax levied directly on property, goods, and services in the colonies. External taxes regulated trade and fell primarily on merchants and ship captains, but internal taxes were designed to raise revenue and affected most people, at least occasionally. William Pitt and others objected to such an internal tax, arguing that the colonies taxed themselves through their elected assemblies. But to Grenville and his supporters, the tax seemed a small price for the benefits of empire, especially because Britons had paid a similar tax since 1695. Grenville agreed with Stamp Act opponents that Parliament could not tax British subjects unless they enjoyed representation in that body. He contended, however, that the colonists, like many other British adult males who did not vote for members of Parliament, were *virtually* represented. According to the theory of virtual representation, every member of Parliament considered the welfare of *all* subjects, not just his constituents, in deciding issues. Whether or not they voted in parliamentary elections, all imperial subjects, including Americans, could depend on each member of Parliament to protect their well-being.

Stamp Act Revenue measure that provoked open opposition by colonists

Grenville and his supporters also held that the colonial assemblies were local governments, with no powers other than those Parliament allowed them. This view clashed directly with the stance of the many colonists who had argued for decades that their assemblies exercised legislative power equivalent to that of Britain's House of Commons.

The Stamp Act caused many colonists to believe that they had to confront parliamentary taxation head on or surrender any claim to meaningful self-government. However much they admired Parliament, few Americans thought that it represented them. Although virtual representation might apply to Britain and Scotland, they argued, it certainly did not extend across the Atlantic. In the American view, unless a lawmaker shared his constituents' interests, he would have no personal stake in opposing bills contrary to their welfare. Thus, the colonists favored *actual*, rather than virtual, representation.

The Colonial Williamsburg Foundation

Anti-Stamp Act Teapot

Some colonists signaled their opposition to the Stamp Act on the pots from which they drank tea (ironically, purchased from British merchants). Less than a decade later, they would protest a British tax on tea itself.

To the colonists, the Stamp Act demonstrated both Parliament's indifference to their interests and the shallowness of virtual representation. Nonetheless, they conceded that Parliament possessed limited powers of legislation, and they accepted the parliamentary regulation of imperial trade.

In a speech opposing the Sugar Act, James Otis expressed Americans' basic argument: "that by [the British] Constitution, every man in the dominions is a free man; that no parts of His Majesty's dominions can be taxed without consent; that every part has a right to be represented in the supreme or some subordinate legislature." In essence, the colonists saw the empire as a loose federation (union) in which their legislatures possessed considerable autonomy.

Patrick Henry, a twenty-nine-year-old Virginia lawyer with a gift for fiery oratory, expressed the rising spirit of resistance in late May 1765. He persuaded Virginia's House of Burgesses to adopt four relatively mild resolutions denying Parliament's power to tax the colonies, but the House rejected three stronger ones. Garbled accounts of Henry's resolutions and speeches—he probably never said, "Give me liberty or give me death"—electrified other colonists.

Meanwhile, active resistance took shape outside elite political circles. In Boston by late summer, middle-class artisans and businessmen had created the Loyal Nine to fight the Stamp Act. They recognized that the stamp distributors, who alone could sell the specially watermarked paper, represented the law's weak link. If public pressure could force them to resign before the tax went into effect on November 1, the Stamp Act would not work.

Boston's preeminence in opposing Parliament was no accident. Bostonians lived primarily by trade and distilling, and in 1765 they were not living well. The heavy tax on molasses burdened rum producers, and the Sugar Act's trade restrictions dried up the wine import business and interfered with the direct export of New England products to profitable overseas markets. Moreover, its shipbuilding and fishing industries were declining; taxes, unemployment, and poverty had skyrocketed; and the city was recovering from a disastrous fire that had left every tenth family homeless.

This widespread economic distress produced an explosive situation. It was easy to blame British policy for hard times. Furthermore, poor and working-class Bostonians were accustomed to gathering in large crowds to express themselves politically. The morning of August 14, 1765, a likeness of Boston's stamp distributor, Andrew Oliver, was found swinging from a tree. Oliver did not take the hint to resign, so at dusk several hundred Bostonians demolished a new building of his at the dock. The mob then surged toward Oliver's house and vandalized it. Surveying his devastated home the next morning, Oliver announced his resignation.

Anger against the Stamp Act unleashed spontaneous, contagious violence. For example, in late August, rioting Bostonians demolished the elegant home of Lieutenant Governor and Chief Justice Thomas Hutchinson.

Sons of Liberty Groups formed to resist Stamp Act; formed by elites in an attempt to curb violence

At the same time, groups calling themselves **Sons of Liberty** were forming throughout the colonies. Elite leaders of these groups sought to curb violence, fearful that attacks on one set of elites could lead to attacks on all elites. The Sons of Liberty focused their actions against property and carefully left avenues of escape for their victims; they forbade their members to carry weapons in order to avoid harming royal soldiers or officials.

Stamp Act Congress Assembly where representatives from nine colonies met to discuss resistance to the Stamp Act

In October 1765 representatives from nine colonies met in New York City in the **Stamp Act Congress.** There the colonies agreed on, and boldly articulated, the principle that Parliament had no authority to levy taxes outside Britain or to deny any person a jury trial. The united front of the Stamp Act Congress was far more effective than the one earlier intercolonial meeting, the Albany Congress of 1754. Although they emboldened and unified the colonies, declarations of principle like the

Stamp Act Congress resolutions did little to sway Parliament. By late 1765 most stamp distributors had resigned or fled, and without the watermarked paper required by law, most customs officials and court officers refused to perform their duties. In response, legislators compelled them to resume operations by threatening to withhold their pay. At the same time, merchants obtained sailing clearances by insisting that they would sue if their cargoes spoiled while delayed in port. By late December the colonial courts and harbors were again functioning.

In these ways colonial elites assumed control of the public outcry against the Stamp Act. Respectable gentlemen kept an explosive situation under control by taking over leadership of local Sons of Liberty, by coordinating protest through the Stamp Act Congress, and by having colonial legislatures resume normal business. But the Stamp Act remained in effect. To force its repeal, New York's merchants agreed on October 31, 1765, to boycott all British goods. Others followed. Because the colonies purchased 40 percent of Britain's manufactures, this nonimportation strategy triggered panic within Britain's business community.

Parliamentary support for repeal gradually grew—the result of practicality, not principle. In March 1766 Parliament revoked the Stamp Act. Simultaneously, however, Parliament passed the **Declaratory Act,** affirming parliamentary power to legislate for the colonies "in all cases whatsoever."

Declaratory Act Parliamentary assertion of right to legislate for the colonies

Because Americans interpreted the Declaratory Act as merely a face-saving measure on Parliament's part, they ignored it. In truth, however, the House of Commons intended that the colonists take the Declaratory Act literally to mean that they were not exempt from *any* parliamentary statute, including a tax law. The Stamp Act crisis thus ended in a fundamental disagreement between Britain and America over the colonists' political rights.

Ideology, Religion, and Resistance

The Stamp Act crisis had revealed a chasm between the colonies and Great Britain. For the first time, some Anglo-Americans saw a sinister quality in the imperial relationship with Britain. To put their concerns into perspective, educated colonists turned to philosophers, historians, and political writers. Many more looked to religion.

Educated colonists were familiar with John Locke and other Enlightenment political thinkers. Locke argued that, in a state of nature, people enjoyed the "natural rights" of life, liberty, and property. To form governments to protect these rights, people entered into a "social contract." A government that encroached on natural rights broke its contract with the people. In such cases the people could resist their government. To many colonial readers, Locke's concept of natural rights justified opposition to Parliament's arbitrary legislation.

Colonists also read European writers who portrayed concentrations of executive power as threats to liberty. Some balanced Locke's emphasis on the rights of the individual with an emphasis on subordinating individual interests to the good of the people as a whole. Looking to the Greeks and Romans, these "republican" theorists admired the sense of civic duty of the Roman republic. Like the early Romans, they maintained that a free people had to practice "public virtue." An elected leader of a republic would command obedience "more by the virtue of the people than by the terror of his power."

The political writers read most widely in the colonies included a group known as the oppositionists. According to John Trenchard and Thomas Gordon, among others, Parliament—the freely elected representatives of the people—formed the foundation of Britain's unique political liberties and protected them against the inherent corruption and tyranny of executive power. Most members of Parliament, they held, no longer represented the true interests of their constituents; instead, they had sold their souls for financial gain and joined a "conspiracy against liberty."

Influenced by such ideas, a number of colonists believed they detected a diabolical conspiracy underlying British policy. Joseph Warren of Massachusetts observed that the Stamp Act "induced some to imagine that the minister designed by this to force the colonies into a rebellion, and from thence to take occasion to treat them with severity and, by military power, to reduce them to servitude."

Beginning with the Stamp Act crisis, many Protestant clergymen summoned their flock to stand up for God and liberty. Clergymen who exalted the cause of liberty exerted an enormous influence on popular opinion. Far more Americans heard or read sermons than had access to newspapers or pamphlets. A popular theme was how God sent the people woes only to strengthen and sustain them until victory. Moreover, protest leaders' calls to boycott British luxuries meshed neatly with ministers' traditional warnings against frivolity and wastefulness.

CHECKING IN

- The young British king George III was ill suited to the job.
- War and imperial expansion left Britain with staggering debt, and the British concluded that colonists should pay their fair share.
- Parliament passed a series of laws to rationalize control over the colonies, such as the Proclamation of 1763 and the Sugar Act, which colonists found distasteful.
- The Stamp Act, clearly intended to raise revenues, instead raised open resistance.
- Colonists welcomed repeal of the Stamp Act and unwisely ignored the Declaratory Act.

RESISTANCE RESUMES, 1766–1770

In what ways did resistance to the Townshend duties differ from earlier colonial resistance efforts?

Repeal of the Stamp Act temporarily quieted colonial protests, but Britain's search for new revenue soon revived them. Most colonists became convinced that the Stamp Act had been not an isolated mistake, but part of a deliberate design to undermine colonial self-government. Meanwhile growing numbers of British people likewise protested their government's policies.

Opposing the Quartering Act, 1766–1767

In August 1766 George III dismissed the government and summoned William Pitt, an opponent of taxing the colonies, to form a cabinet. However, Pitt's health collapsed in March 1767, and Charles Townshend, the chancellor of the exchequer (treasurer), became the effective leader.

Quartering Act Required colonial legislatures to provide supplies to British troops

Just as Townshend took office, a conflict arose with the New York legislature over the **Quartering Act** of 1765, which ordered colonial legislatures to pay for certain goods used by British soldiers stationed within their borders—candles, window-panes, mattress straw, and a small liquor ration. The law aroused resentment because it constituted an *indirect* tax. In other words, although it did not empower royal officials to collect money directly from the colonists, it obligated assemblies to raise revenue by whatever means they considered appropriate. The act fell lightly on all the colonies except New York, where more soldiers were stationed than in any other province. New York refused to grant the supplies.

New York's resistance unleashed a torrent of anti-American feeling in Parliament, which was still bitter after revoking the Stamp Act. Townshend responded by drafting the New York Suspending Act, which threatened to nullify all laws passed by the colony after October 1, 1767, if it refused to provide the supplies. By the time George III signed the measure, New York had already appropriated the funds. Nonetheless, the conflict over the Quartering Act demonstrated that British leaders would not hesitate to defend Parliament's authority through the most drastic of all steps: interfering with American claims to self-government.

Crisis over the Townshend Duties, 1767–1770

This new wave of British resentment toward the colonies coincided with an outpouring of frustration over the government's failure to cut taxes from wartime levels. Townshend sought to tax the colonists by exploiting a loophole in their arguments against the Stamp Tax. Americans had emphasized their opposition to internal taxes but had said nothing about external taxes—Parliament's right to tax imports as they entered the colonies. Townshend interpreted this silence as evidence that the colonists accepted Britain's right to impose external taxes. Parliament passed Townshend's Revenue Act of 1767 (popularly called the **Townshend duties**) in the summer. The new law taxed glass, paint, lead, paper, and tea imported into the colonies.

Townshend duties More Parliamentary attempts to raise revenues from the colonies

Superficially, this measure seemed to adhere to colonial principles, but fundamentally the Townshend duties differed significantly from what Americans considered a legitimate way of regulating trade through taxation. To the colonists, charging a duty was a lawful way for British authorities to control trade only if it excluded foreign goods by making them prohibitively expensive. The Revenue Act of 1767, however, set moderate rates that did not price goods out of the colonial market; clearly, its purpose was to collect money for the treasury. Thus, from the colonial standpoint, Townshend's duties were taxes just like the Stamp Act duties.

The Revenue Act never yielded the income that Townshend had anticipated. Of all the items taxed, only tea produced any significant revenue—£20,000 of the £37,000 expected. And because the measure would serve its purpose only if the colonists could afford British tea, Townshend eliminated £60,000 in import fees paid on East Indian tea entering Britain before transshipment to America. On balance, the Revenue Act *worsened* the British treasury's deficit by £23,000. By 1767, Parliament had grown less concerned with raising revenues than with asserting its authority over the colonies.

The Colonists' Reaction, 1767–1769

Resistance to the Revenue Act remained weak until December 1767, when John Dickinson published *Letters from a Farmer in Pennsylvania.* These twelve essays stated that no tax designed to produce revenue could be considered constitutional unless a people's elected representatives voted for it. Dickinson's writings convinced Americans that their arguments against the Stamp Act also applied to the Revenue Act.

In early 1768 the Massachusetts assembly asked Samuel Adams, who had helped organize the Sons of Liberty in Boston, to draft a "circular letter" to other legislatures. Adams's circular letter denounced taxation without representation but acknowledged Parliament as the "supreme legislative Power over the whole Empire" and advocated no illegal activities.

Virginia's assembly warmly approved Adams's eloquent measure and sent out a more strongly worded letter of its own, urging all the colonies to oppose imperial policies that would "have an immediate tendency to enslave them." But most colonial legislatures reacted indifferently to these letters. In fact, resistance might have disintegrated had not the British government overreacted.

Parliamentary leaders saw even the mild Massachusetts letter as "little better than an incentive to Rebellion." Disorganized because of Townshend's sudden death in 1767, the king's Privy (PRIH-vee) Council (advisers) directed Lord Hillsborough, the first appointee to the new post of secretary of state for the colonies, to express the government's displeasure. Adopting a "no more Mr. Nice Guy" approach, Hillsborough ordered the Massachusetts assembly to disown its letter, forbade all overseas assemblies to endorse it, and commanded royal governors to dissolve any legislature that violated his instructions.

The tactic backfired. Protesting Hillsborough's bullying, many legislatures previously indifferent to the Massachusetts letter adopted it enthusiastically. Royal governors responded by dismissing legislatures in Massachusetts and elsewhere, playing into the hands of Samuel Adams and others who wished to ignite widespread opposition to the Townshend duties.

Increasingly outraged, the colonists still needed an effective means of pressuring Parliament for repeal. Nonimportation seemed especially promising because it offered an alternative to violence and would distress Britain's economy. Thus, in August 1768 Boston's merchants adopted a nonimportation agreement, and the tactic spread southward. "Save your money, and you save your country!" trumpeted the Sons of Liberty, who reorganized after two years of inactivity. However, not all colonists supported nonimportation. Many merchants continued to import British goods until early 1769. The boycott probably kept out about 40 percent of British imports, while encouraging colonists to resist British policies more actively.

In 1770 yet another new prime minister, Lord North, assumed office. At his urging, Parliament eliminated most of the Townshend duties—but kept the tea tax as a symbol of its authority. Colonial leaders faced a dilemma: It was intolerable that taxes remained on tea, but should they boycott all British goods or only tea? Ultimately the nonimportation movement collapsed, but colonists agreed not to drink British tea. Colonial resistance leaders derived little pleasure from forcing Parliament to compromise; the tea duty remained a galling reminder that Parliament refused to abandon its broad interpretation of the Declaratory Act.

Board of Customs Commissioners Officials sent to oversee the collection of taxes; their corruption was a target for colonial anger

Customs "Racketeering," 1767–1770

Townshend also sought to increase revenues by tightening enforcement of existing customs laws. In 1767 he induced Parliament to create the American **Board of Customs Commissioners** to strictly enforce the Navigation Acts.

The new law increased the number of port officials, funded a colonial coast guard to catch smugglers, and provided money for secret informers.

The act also included new provisions that awarded an informer one-third of the value of all goods and ships appropriated through a conviction of smuggling. The fact that fines could be tripled under certain circumstances provided an even greater incentive to seize illegal cargoes. Smuggling cases were heard in vice-admiralty courts where the probability of conviction was extremely high. However, the law quickly drew protests because of the ways it was enforced and because it reversed the traditional legal process by assuming the accused to be guilty until proven otherwise.

Revenue agents commonly perverted the law by filing charges for technical violations of the Sugar Act, even when no evidence existed of intent to conduct illegal trade. They most often exploited the provision that declared any cargo illegal unless it had been loaded or unloaded with a customs officer's written authorization.

Customs commissioners also fanned anger by invading sailors' traditional rights. Long-standing maritime custom allowed crews to supplement their income by making small sales between ports. Anything stored in a sailor's chest was considered private property, exempt from the Navigation Acts. But after 1767, revenue agents treated such belongings as cargo, thus establishing an excuse to seize the entire ship. Under this policy, crewmen saw arrogant inspectors break open their trunks and then lost trading stock worth several months' wages. In these ways the commissioners embarked on a program of "customs racketeering" that constituted legalized piracy. This program fed an upsurge in popular violence, as sailors waited for chances to get even. Above all, customs commissioners' use of informers provoked retaliation. The *Pennsylvania Journal* in 1769 scorned these agents as "dogs of prey, thirsting after the fortunes of worthy and wealthy men."

Nowhere were customs agents and informers more detested than in Boston, where citizens retaliated in June 1768. When customs agents seized colonial merchant John Hancock's sloop *Liberty* on a technicality, a crowd tried to prevent the towing of Hancock's ship and then began assaulting customs officials. Swelling to several hundred, the mob drove all revenue inspectors from the city. To appease angry colonists momentarily, British officials dropped the charges against Hancock. At the same time, to make it clear they conceded nothing to the colonists, they dispatched four thousand troops to Boston, a warning that they would not tolerate further violence in defiance of their authority.

Wilkes and Liberty, 1768–1770

By no means did all Britons support Parliament. Their protests became part of a larger movement in the 1760s against the policies of George III and a Parliament dominated by wealthy landowners. **John Wilkes,** a fiery London editor whose newspaper regularly and irreverently denounced the king, became both leader and focal point of the protest. A member of Parliament, Wilkes was tried for seditious libel and acquitted, to great popular acclaim. George III's government then shut down his newspaper and persuaded members of the House of Commons to deny Wilkes his seat. After publishing another slashing attack on the king, Wilkes fled to Paris.

John Wilkes British opponent of King George III who became a hero to American colonists

William L. Clements Library

John Wilkes, by William Hogarth, 1763
Detesting Wilkes and all he stood for, Hogarth depicted the radical leader as menacing and untrustworthy.

In 1768 Wilkes returned to Britain, defying an arrest warrant, and again ran for Parliament. By then, government policies, including the Townshend Acts, had unleashed a flood of protests against the "obnoxious" government ministers. Manufacturers, merchants, and artisans all rallied around the cry "Wilkes and Liberty."

When the newly elected Wilkes was once again arrested, twenty to forty thousand angry "Wilkesites" massed on St. George's Fields, outside the prison where he was being held. Soldiers and police opened fire on rock-throwing demonstrators, killing eleven. The "massacre of St. George's Fields" furnished martyrs to the protesters, and Wilkes received enormous outpourings of public support from the North American colonies as well as from Britain. From his prison cell, Wilkes maintained a regular correspondence with Boston's Sons of Liberty, and Bostonians cheered his release from prison in April 1770 with a massive celebration.

The Wilkes furor sharpened the political ideas of government opponents on both sides of the Atlantic. British voters sent petitions to Parliament proclaiming that its refusal to seat Wilkes was an affront to the electorate's will and calling "virtual representation" a sham. Emboldened by the "Wilkes and Liberty" movement, William Pitt and others forcefully denounced the government's colonial policies. The colonists themselves concluded that Parliament and the government represented a small but powerful minority whose authority they could legitimately question.

CHECKING IN

- The Quartering Act showed colonists that Parliament was willing to interfere with their self-government.
- The Townshend duties failed to raise revenues, but their intent to do so angered colonists even more.
- Colonial reaction to Parliament united in the protests of John Dickinson, the Massachusetts circular letter, and nonimportation agreements; women played an important public role in implementing nonimportation.
- The Board of Customs Commissioners sent to Boston to oversee collection of taxes were often corrupt and became a target for colonial anger.
- John Wilkes became a symbol of the dangers posed by a too-powerful government.

Women and Colonial Resistance

Colonial boycotts of British goods provided a unique opportunity for white women, whose participation in public affairs had been widening slowly for several decades, to join the resistance to British policies. By the 1760s, upper-class female patriots had played a part in defeating the Stamp Act, some by attending political rallies and many more through expressing their opposition in discussions and correspondence with family and friends.

In early 1770, urged on by American leaders convinced that women could exert a persuasive moral influence on public opinion, women calling themselves Daughters of Liberty assumed a more prominent role in protests against the tax on tea. In early 1770 more than three hundred "mistresses of families" in Boston denounced the consumption of the beverage. In some ways nonconsumption was more effective than nonimportation, for the colonists' refusal to consume imports would chill merchants' economic incentive to import British goods.

Nonconsumption agreements therefore became popular and were extended to include other goods, mainly clothes. Again, women played a vital role, because the boycott would fail unless the colonists replaced British imports with apparel of their own making. Responding to leaders' pleas for an expansion of domestic cloth production, women of all social ranks organized spinning bees. These attracted intense publicity as evidence of American determination to fight parliamentary taxation. Spinning bees not only helped to undermine the masculine prejudice that women had no place in public life, but also endowed spinning and weaving, previously considered routine tasks, with political virtue. Female activities such as spinning bees and tea boycotts dramatically demonstrated that American protests extended beyond a few male merchants and crowds of angry men, into the heart of American households and congregations. Women's participation showed that colonial protests reached into the heart of American households and were leading to broader popular participation in politics.

THE DEEPENING CRISIS, 1770–1774

In what ways did colonists' views of parliamentary authority change after 1770?

After 1770 the imperial crisis took on ominous new dimensions. Colonists and British troops clashed on the streets of Boston. Resistance leaders in the colonies developed ways to systematically coordinate their actions and policies. After the defiance manifested in the Boston Tea Party, Britain was determined to subordinate the colonies once and for all. Adding to the general tension were several violent conflicts that erupted in the western backcountry.

The Boston Massacre, 1770

British authorities responded to the violence directed at customs commissioners by dispatching four thousand British troops to Boston in 1768. However, the violence only escalated, intersecting with intracolonial tensions and extending the crisis beyond the port cities.

Crackling with tension, Boston took on the atmosphere of an occupied city. Armed soldiers and resentful civilians traded insults, and off-duty soldiers undercut local laborers by working for lower wages. Many of the soldiers were Irish Catholics, which was especially galling to the mainly Protestant Bostonians.

Bostonians' resentment of British authority boiled over on February 22, 1770, when a customs informer fired birdshot at several children throwing rocks at his house and killed an eleven-year-old boy. Samuel Adams organized a burial procession to maximize the horror over a child's death, relying on grief to unite the community in opposition to British policies. "My Eyes never beheld such a funeral," wrote his cousin John Adams. "A vast Number of Boys walked before the Coffin, a vast Number of Women and Men after it. . . . This Shows there are many more Lives to spend if wanted in the Service of their country."

Although the army had played no part in the shooting, it became a target for Bostonians' rage. A week after the funeral, tension erupted at the guard post protecting the customs office. When an officer tried to disperse a crowd led by Crispus Attucks, a seaman of African and Native American ancestry, the mob responded with a barrage of flying objects. One soldier, knocked down by a block of ice, fired, and then the others opened fire. Their volley killed five people, including Attucks.

Royal authorities moved quickly to defuse the crisis by isolating the army on a fortified island in the harbor and putting soldiers who had fired on trial. Patriot leader John Adams defended the accused British troops by claiming that they had been provoked by a "motley rabble," an accusation that resonated with Boston's "respectable" middle- and upper-class elites. Only two soldiers were found guilty; they received the relatively mild punishment of branding on their thumbs.

Boston Massacre
Confrontation between colonists and British troops in which five colonists were shot and killed

Burning hatred underlay the **Boston Massacre**—a name designed to invoke the St. George's Fields massacre two years earlier. For the first time colonists had to confront the stark possibility that a tyrannical British government was determined to coerce and suppress them through armed force.

The Committees of Correspondence, 1772–1773

In the fall of 1772 Lord North prepared to implement Townshend's goal of paying royal governors from customs revenues, freeing them from the control of the colonial assemblies. With representative government deeply threatened, Samuel Adams persuaded Boston's town meeting to request that every Massachusetts community appoint people to exchange information and coordinate measures to defend colonial rights. Within a year, most Massachusetts communities had established **committees of correspondence,** and the idea spread throughout New England.

committees of correspondence
Local committees established throughout colonies to coordinate anti-British actions

The committees of correspondence, the resistance leaders' first attempt to maintain close political cooperation over a wide area, allowed Samuel Adams to conduct a campaign of political education for all New England. He sent messages for each local committee to read at its town meeting, which debated the issues and adopted formal resolutions. The system made tens of thousands of citizens consider evidence that their rights were being endangered and committed them to take a stand. Adams's most successful venture in whipping up public alarm came in June 1773, when he published letters from the governor of Massachusetts, Thomas Hutchinson, obtained by Benjamin Franklin, advocating "an abridgement of what are called British liberties" and "a great restraint of natural liberty." The Hutchinson correspondence confirmed Americans' suspicions that a plot was afoot to destroy their basic freedoms.

Patrick Henry, Thomas Jefferson, and Richard Henry Lee had proposed in March 1773 that Virginia establish committees of correspondence, and by early 1774 a communications web linked leaders from all the colonies.

Conflicts in the Backcountry

Although most of the turbulence between 1763 and 1775 swirled through coastal seaports, rapid expansion led to violence in the West as well. There, numerous clashes involving Native Americans, colonists, and colonial governments flared in the Appalachian backcountry.

Tension then flared into violence in Pennsylvania's backcountry. Settlers in and around the town of Paxton blamed the Pennsylvania assembly, which was

The Granger Collection, NYC

Boys Expedition

Militia units organize in Philadelphia, ready to march against the Paxton Boys if necessary.

dominated by Quakers, for failing to provide military protection and for denying them equal representation in the assembly. The "Paxton Boys," as they were known, believed all Native Americans were their racial enemies. After laying waste to two villages of peaceful Conestoga Indians, killing and scalping men, women, and children, in February 1764 about 200 Paxton Boys headed for Philadelphia with plans to kill Christian Indian refugees there. A government delegation headed by Benjamin Franklin met the armed mob on the outskirts of the city and promised that the assembly would consider their grievances. Appeased, the Paxton Boys returned home.

Land pressures and the lack of adequate revenue from the colonies left the British government helpless to enforce the Proclamation of 1763. Speculators, squatters, hunters, and thieves trespassed on Native American lands, often leading Indians to respond violently, while the British withdrew troops that might have maintained order.

Under such pressures, Britain and the Iroquois, in the Treaty of Fort Stanwix (1768), turned land along the Ohio River that was occupied by the Shawnees, Delawares, and Cherokees over to the Virginia and Pennsylvania governments, resolving the two colonies' overlapping land claims in Ohio at the Indians' expense. The Shawnees assumed leadership among the Ohio Indians, who, with the Cherokees, were convinced that appeasement would not stop colonial expansion.

The treaty heightened rather than eased frontier tensions, especially in the Ohio country. Colonists moving westward into what they called Kentucky collided with Shawnee and Mingo Indians, and in 1774 Virginia launched Lord Dunmore's War.

After Virginia's victory at Point Pleasant, Virginia gained uncontested rights to all land south of the Ohio River in exchange for giving up all claims north of the river. Resentment continued to fester on both sides, and fighting would resume when war broke out between Britain and the colonies.

Other frontier disputes led to conflict among the colonists themselves. Settlers in western Massachusetts in the early 1760s, for example, found their titles challenged by New Yorker landlords. In 1766, threatened with eviction, the New Englanders staged an armed uprising. And in 1769 New Hampshire settlers calling themselves the Green Mountain Boys began guerrilla warfare against other New York landlords. The independent government they formed ultimately became that of Vermont.

Expansion also provoked conflict between frontier settlers and their own colonial governments. In North Carolina, westerners, who were underrepresented in the assembly, found themselves exploited by dishonest officeholders appointed by eastern politicians. Twenty-five hundred armed westerners, known as Regulators, clashed with thirteen hundred North Carolina militia on May 16, 1771, at the battle of Alamance Creek. Although the Regulators' uprising disintegrated, it crippled the colony's subsequent ability to resist British authority. A Regulator movement also arose in South Carolina, in this case to counter the government's unwillingness to prosecute bandits who terrorized the settlers. Fearful that the colony's slave population might revolt if the militia was dispatched, South Carolina's government yielded to the Regulators by establishing new courts and allowing jury trials in recently settled areas.

Although unrelated, these episodes reflected the tensions generated by a land-hungry white population willing to use violence against Native Americans, other colonists, and British officials.

The Tea Act, 1773

Smuggling and nonconsumption had taken a heavy toll on Britain's East India Company, the holder of the legal monopoly on importing tea into the British Empire. By 1773, as tons of tea rotted in warehouses, the East India Company was teetering on the brink of bankruptcy. But Lord North could not let the company fail because, by maintaining British authority in India at its own expense, the East India Company had become a vital component in the British imperial structure.

Tea Act Attempt to bail out the East India Company that heightened tensions between Britain and colonists

In May 1773, to save the beleaguered East India Company, Parliament passed the **Tea Act,** which eliminated all import duties on tea entering Britain and thus lowered the selling price to consumers. To reduce the price further, the Tea Act also permitted the company to sell tea directly to consumers rather than through wholesalers. These provisions reduced the cost of East India Company tea in the colonies to well below the price of smuggled tea. Parliament expected economic self-interest to overcome American scruples about buying taxed tea.

But the Tea Act alarmed many Americans, who recognized that the revenues raised by the law would place royal governors' purses beyond the reach of the colonial assemblies. The law also threatened to seduce Americans into accepting parliamentary taxation in return for a frivolous luxury. The committees of correspondence decided to resist the importation of tea by pressuring the East India Company's agents to refuse acceptance or by preventing the landing of East India Company cargoes.

In Boston on November 28, 1773, the first ship came under jurisdiction of the customhouse, to which duties would have to be paid within twenty days, or the cargo would be seized from the captain and the tea would be claimed by the company's agents and placed on sale. When Samuel Adams, John Hancock, and others asked customs officers to issue a special clearance for the ship's departure (to avoid the seizure and sale), Governor Hutchinson refused.

On the evening of December 16, 1773, Samuel Adams convened a meeting in the Old South Church, at which he told five thousand citizens about Hutchinson's insistence on landing the tea, warned them that the grace period would expire in a few hours, and proclaimed that "this meeting can do no more to save the country." About fifty young men disguised as Indians and armed with "tomahawks" headed for the wharf, followed by the crowd. Thousands lined the waterfront to watch them heave forty-five tons of tea overboard; for an hour the only sounds echoing through the crisp, moonlit night were the steady chop of hatchets breaking open wooden chests and the soft splash of tea on the water. Their work finished, the participants left quietly. The town lapsed into a profound hush—"never more still and calm," according to one observer.

CHECKING IN

- After the Boston Massacre, colonists confronted the possibility that Britain would use armed force against them.
- Lord North attempted partial conciliation by repealing most of the Townshend duties, but insisted on retaining the tax on tea.
- Under Sam Adams's leadership, the colonies formed committees of correspondence to coordinate intercolonial actions.
- The Tea Act of 1773 was intended primarily to aid British imperialism in India but aroused colonial opposition.
- Colonists applauded the Boston Tea Party, but it fanned enormous anger in Britain.

TOWARD INDEPENDENCE, 1774–1776

What led most colonists in 1776 to abandon their loyalty to Britain and choose national independence?

The calm that followed the Boston Tea Party was the calm before the storm. Furious at the colonists' actions, the British government became more determined than ever to quash colonial insubordination. Colonial leaders were equally determined to defend their self-government and liberty. The empire and its American colonies were on a collision course, but the colonists hesitated at a declaration of independence. In the meantime, African-Americans, both free and slave, pondered how to realize their own freedom.

Liberty for African-Americans

Throughout the imperial crisis, African-American slaves quickly responded to calls for liberty and equality. In 1772 a British court decision electrified much of the black population. A Massachusetts slave, James Somerset, whose master had taken him to Britain, sued for his freedom; Lord Chief Justice William Mansfield ruled that Parliament had never explicitly established slavery and that therefore no court could compel a slave to obey an order depriving him of his liberty.

Although the decision applied only in Britain, Massachusetts slaves petitioned the legislature to apply it in their colony as well. In the Chesapeake area, dozens of slaves ran away from their masters and sought passage on ships bound for Britain. As Anglo-American tensions mounted in 1774, many slaves began to anticipate the arrival of British troops as their path to liberation. White Chesapeake colonists began to fear that war would lead to slave rebellion.

Lord Dunmore Royal governor of Virginia who promised freedom to slaves who fought to restore royal authority

Bearing out such fears in 1775, Virginia's royal governor, **Lord Dunmore,** promised freedom to any slave who enlisted in the cause of restoring royal authority. Nearly a thousand slaves responded to Dunmore's proclamation before angry colonists forced him to flee the colony. Perhaps more important, both whites and blacks began to see a clear link between British forces and slave liberation.

The "Intolerable Acts"

Boston's "Tea Party" enraged the British, prompting them to once more adopt a "no more Mr. Nice Guy" policy. Only "New England fanatics" could imagine that cheap tea oppressed them, fumed Lord North. A Welsh member of Parliament declared that "the town of Boston ought to be knocked about by the ears, and destroy'd." The great orator Edmund Burke pled in vain for the one action that could end the crisis: "Leave America . . . to tax herself." But the British government swiftly asserted its authority through the passage of four Coercive Acts that, along with the Quebec Act, became known to many colonists as the **"Intolerable Acts."**

Intolerable Acts Laws intended to punish Massachusetts for the Boston Tea Party and strengthen royal authority

The first Coercive Act, the Boston Port Bill, was passed on April 1, 1774. It ordered the navy to close Boston Harbor unless the town arranged to pay for the ruined tea by June 1. The impossibly short deadline was meant to ensure the harbor's closing, which would plunge Boston into economic distress. The second Coercive Act, the Massachusetts Government Act, revoked the Massachusetts charter and made the colony's government less democratic. The upper house would be appointed for life by the crown, not elected annually by the assembly. The royal governor gained absolute control over the appointment of judges and sheriffs. Finally, the new charter limited town meetings to one a year. Although these changes brought Massachusetts government into line with that of other colonies, the colonists interpreted them as assaults on representative government.

The final two Coercive Acts—the Administration of Justice Act and a new Quartering Act—rubbed salt into the wounds. The first of these permitted any person charged with murder while enforcing royal authority in Massachusetts to be tried in Britain or in another colony. To colonists, this seemed like a declaration of open season upon them. The second went beyond the Quartering Act of 1765 by allowing the governor to requisition *empty* private buildings for quartering, or housing, troops. Americans learned of the unrelated Quebec Act at the same time as the Coercive Acts. Intended to cement loyalty to Britain among conquered French-Canadian Catholics, the law established Roman Catholicism as Quebec's official religion. Protestant Anglo-Americans, who associated Catholicism with arbitrary government, took alarm. Furthermore, the Quebec Act gave Canada's governor sweeping powers but established no legislature. The law extended Quebec's territorial claims south to the Ohio River and west to the Mississippi, a vast area populated by Indians and some French, and claimed by several colonies.

The Intolerable Acts, coupled with the appointment of General Thomas Gage, Britain's military commander in North America, convinced New Englanders that the crown planned to abolish traditional British liberties throughout North America.

Once the Coercive Acts destroyed these liberties in Massachusetts—many believed—the Quebec Act would serve as a blueprint for extinguishing representative government in other colonies. Parliament would replace all colonial governments with ones like Quebec's. Elected assemblies, freedom of religion for Protestants, and jury trials would vanish.

Intended only to punish Massachusetts, the Coercive Acts thus pushed most colonies to the brink of revolution. Repeal of these laws became the colonists' nonnegotiable demand. The Declaration of Independence would refer to these laws six times in listing colonial grievances justifying the break with Britain.

The First Continental Congress

In response to the Intolerable Acts, the committees of correspondence of every colony but Georgia sent delegates to a **Continental Congress** in Philadelphia. The fifty-six delegates who assembled on September 5, 1774, included the colonies' most prominent politicians: Samuel and John Adams of Massachusetts; John Jay of New York; Joseph Galloway and John Dickinson of Pennsylvania; and Patrick Henry, Richard Henry Lee, and George Washington of Virginia.

Continental Congress Major step toward resistance to Britain and unity among colonies

The Continental Congress endorsed the Suffolk (SUFF-uk) Resolves, extreme statements of principle that proclaimed that the colonies owed no obedience to the Coercive Acts, advocated a provisional government until restoration of the Massachusetts charter, and vowed that defensive measures should follow any attack by royal troops. The Continental Congress also voted to boycott British goods after December 1, 1774, and to stop exporting goods to Britain and its West Indies possessions after September 1775. This agreement, called the Continental Association, would be enforced by locally elected committees of "observation" or "safety." But not all the delegates embraced such bold defiance. Jay, Dickinson, Galloway, and other moderates who dominated the contingent from the Middle Colonies feared that a confrontation with Britain would spawn internal colonial turmoil. They vainly opposed nonimportation and unsuccessfully sought support of a plan for an American legislature that would share with Parliament the authority to tax and govern the colonies.

Finally, the delegates summarized their principles and demands in a petition to George III. They conceded to Parliament the power to regulate colonial commerce but argued that parliamentary efforts to impose taxes, enforce laws through admiralty courts, suspend assemblies, and revoke charters were unconstitutional. By addressing the king rather than Parliament, Congress was imploring George III to end the crisis by dismissing the ministers responsible for passing the Coercive Acts.

From Resistance to Rebellion

Most Americans hoped that resistance would jolt Parliament into renouncing its claims of authority over the colonies. But tensions between American radicals and moderates ran high.

To solidify defiance, American resistance leaders used coercion against waverers and loyalists ("Tories"). Committees elected to enforce the Continental Association became vigilantes, compelling merchants to burn British imports, browbeating clergymen who preached pro-British sermons, and pressuring Americans to free themselves of dependence on British imports by adopting simpler diets and homespun clothing. In colony after colony, moreover, the committees assumed governmental functions by organizing volunteer military companies and extralegal legislatures. By spring 1775 colonial patriots had established provincial "congresses" that paralleled existing royal governments.

In April 1775 armed conflict erupted in Massachusetts. Citizens had collected arms and organized militia units ("minutemen") to respond instantly in an emergency. The British government ordered Massachusetts's Governor Thomas Gage to quell the "rude rabble" and to arrest the patriot leaders. Aware that most of these had fled Boston, Gage, on April 19, 1775, sent seven hundred British soldiers to seize colonial military supplies stored at **Concord.** Two couriers, William Dawes and Paul Revere, alerted nearby towns of the British troop movements. At **Lexington** on the road to Concord, about seventy minutemen faced the British on the town green. After a confused skirmish in which eight minutemen died and a single redcoat was wounded, the British marched to Concord. They found few munitions but encountered a swarm of armed Yankees. When some minutemen mistakenly concluded that the town was being burned, they exchanged fire with British regulars and touched off a running battle that continued most of the sixteen miles back to Boston. By day's end the redcoats had lost 273 men. These engagements awakened the countryside. Within a day, some 20,000 New Englanders were besieging the British garrison in Boston.

Concord Skirmish between colonists and British troops

Lexington One of the first armed conflicts between Britain and the colonists

Three weeks later, the Continental Congress reconvened in Philadelphia. Most delegates still opposed independence and agreed to send a "loyal message" to George III. The resulting Olive Branch Petition presented three demands: a cease-fire in Boston, repeal of the Coercive Acts, and negotiations to establish guarantees of American rights. Yet the same delegates who pleaded for peace voted to establish an "American continental army" and to appoint George Washington as commander, measures that the British could only see as rebellious.

The Olive Branch Petition reached London along with news of the Continental Army's formation and of the battles of Breed's Hill and Bunker Hill just outside Boston. Although the British dislodged the Americans in the clashes, they suffered 2,200 casualties, a 50 percent casualty rate, compared to colonial losses of only 311. After Bunker Hill the British public wanted retaliation, not reconciliation. In August, George III proclaimed New England to be in a state of rebellion; in December, Parliament declared all of the colonies rebellious, outlawing all British trade with them and subjecting their ships to seizure.

Common Sense

Many Americans still clung to hopes of reconciliation. Even John Adams, who believed separation inevitable, said that he was "fond of reconciliation, if we could reasonably entertain Hopes of it on a constitutional basis." The majority of Americans who resisted independence blamed evil ministers, rather than the king, for unconstitutional measures and expected saner heads to rise to power in Britain. On both counts they were wrong.

Americans' sentimental attachment to the king, the last emotional barrier to independence, crumbled in January 1776 with the publication of Thomas Paine's

Common Sense. Paine had immigrated to the colonies from Britain in 1774 with a penchant for radical politics and a gift for plain and pungent prose. Paine told Americans what they had been unable to bring themselves to say: Monarchy was an institution rooted in superstition, dangerous to liberty, and inappropriate for Americans. The King himself was "the royal brute," a "hardened, sullen-tempered Pharoah." Further, America did not need its British connection. "The commerce by which she [America] hath enriched herself are the necessaries of life, and will always have a market while eating is the custom in Europe," Paine argued. And, he pointed out, the events of the preceding six months had made independence a reality. Finally, Paine linked America's awakening nationalism with a sense of religious mission: "We have it in our power to begin the world over again. A situation, similar to the present, hath not happened since the days of Noah until now." America, Paine wrote, would be a new *kind* of nation, a model republic free of oppressive European beliefs and corrupt institutions.

Common Sense Brilliant pamphlet by Thomas Paine that summarized pro-independence arguments

Common Sense, "a landflood that sweeps all before it," sold more than 100,000 copies in three months, one copy for every fourth or fifth adult male in the colonies. By spring 1776 Paine's pamphlet had dissolved lingering allegiance to George III and removed the last psychological barrier to independence.

Declaring Independence

Even as colonists absorbed Paine's views, the military conflict between Britain and the colonies escalated, further diminishing the prospects of reconciliation. In May 1775 colonial troops captured Fort Ticonderoga and Crown Point on the key route connecting New York and Canada. Six months later Washington ordered Colonel Henry Knox, in civilian life a book seller and in war the army's senior artillery officer, to bring the cannons captured at Ticonderoga to reinforce the siege of Boston. Using crude sleds, Knox and his men hauled fifty-nine cannons through dense forest and over snow-covered mountains, one of the Revolution's great feats of endurance. The Ticonderoga cannon forced the British to evacuate Boston on March 17, 1776.

Regrouping, the British planned an assault on New York to drive a wedge between New England and the other colonies. Washington countered by moving his forces there in April 1776. Other military moves quickened the drift toward all-out war. A two-pronged assault on Canada by the colonists failed, as did a British offensive in the southern colonies.

Stimulated by Paine's soaring rhetoric, local gatherings throughout the colonies, ranging from town meetings to militia musters, passed resolutions favoring American independence.

Art Gallery, Williams Center, Lafayette College

Thomas Paine

Having arrived in the colonies less than two years earlier, Paine became a best-selling author with the publication of *Common Sense* (1776).

Most of New England was already in rebellion, and Rhode Island declared itself independent in May 1776. The Middle Colonies hesitated to support revolution because they feared, correctly, that the war would largely be fought over control of Philadelphia and New York. The South began to press for separation. In April, North Carolina authorized its congressional delegates to vote for independence, and in June, Virginia followed suit. On July 2 the Continental Congress formally adopted the Virginia resolution and created the United States of America.

The drafting of a statement to justify the colonies' separation from Britain fell to Virginia's Thomas Jefferson. Congress made two important changes to Jefferson's first draft: It inserted the phrase "pursuit of happiness" instead of "property" in the document's most famous sentence, and it deleted a condemnation of George III for forcing the slave trade on unwilling colonists. Congress then approved Jefferson's manuscript on July 4, 1776. Even though parliamentary authority had been the focal point of dispute since 1765, the **Declaration of Independence** never mentioned Parliament by name because Congress was unwilling to imply that Parliament held any authority over America. Jefferson instead focused on George III, citing "repeated injuries and usurpations" against the colonies.

Declaration of Independence Document drafted primarily by Thomas Jefferson presenting the American Revolution as a struggle for universal principles

Like Paine, Jefferson elevated colonial grievances to a struggle of universal dimensions. In the tradition of Enlightenment thought, Jefferson argued that Britain had violated its contract with the colonists, giving them the right to replace it with a government of their own. His emphasis on the equality of all individuals and their natural entitlement to justice, liberty, and self-fulfillment expressed the Enlightenment's deep longing for government that rested on neither legal privilege nor the exploitation of the majority by the few—and deliberately ignored the existence of slavery.

Jefferson addressed the Declaration of Independence as much to Americans uncertain about the wisdom of independence as to world opinion. Above all, he wanted to convince his fellow Americans that social and political progress was impossible within the British empire. However, the declaration did not address the status of blacks, poor white men, and women. All thirteen of the new states countenanced slavery, severely restricted the rights of free blacks, used property qualifications to determine voting rights, and relegated women to second-class status. Jefferson also put Indians beyond the pale when he accused the king of having unleashed "the merciless Indian savages" on innocent colonists.

Thus, the declaration expressed the sentiments of a minority of colonists at the same time that it set out the hopes of thousands upon thousands more. The struggle for independence from Britain had merged with a quest for equality and personal independence that would eventually transcend class, race, and gender. The declaration never claimed that perfect justice and equal opportunity existed; instead, it challenged the revolutionary generation and all who followed to bring this ideal closer to reality.

CHECKING IN

- The Coercive (or Intolerable) Acts pushed the colonies to the brink of war.
- Members of the First Continental Congress proclaimed that parliamentary taxation of the colonies was unconstitutional but stopped short of declaring independence.
- The battles of Lexington and Concord transformed colonial resistance from words into an armed struggle.
- Thomas Paine's *Common Sense* universalized American ideals and prodded colonies toward independence.
- In the Declaration of Independence, Thomas Jefferson proclaimed the colonies to be defending universal natural rights.

Chapter Summary

How did Britain and its colonies view their joint victory over France in the Seven Years' War? (page 92)

Great Britain emerged victorious in the Seven Years' War against France; in 1763 France ceded almost all of her North American empire to Britain, quadrupling the size of the British empire in North America. Ironically, this triumph would also provide the framework for friction between Britain and its colonies.

What was imperial reorganization, and how did it change relations between Britain and the North American colonies? (page 97)

Attempts at imperial reorganization in the early 1760s were intended to help defray the enormous costs of Britain's victory by increasing revenues from the colonies, but the attempts succeeded primarily in alienating the colonists. After open resistance boiled over in the Stamp Act crisis, Parliament backed down a bit but insisted that it had complete authority over the colonies.

In what ways did resistance to the Townshend duties differ from earlier colonial resistance efforts? (page 102)

Controversy between Britain and the colonies continued with measures such as the Quartering Act and the Townshend duties. Colonial protests found shape in the work of John Dickinson and a hero in the person of John Wilkes. In an attempt to increase tax revenues, Britain created a Board of Customs Commissioners, but many of the commissioners were corrupt, and the board became the target of colonial anger.

In what ways did colonists' views of parliamentary authority change after 1770? (page 107)

The Boston Massacre brought a temporary lull in conflict between Britain and the colonies, but Lord North's attempt to aid the East India Company led to the Boston Tea Party. Colonists defied Britain's continued revenue-raising measures.

KEY TERMS

Seven Years' War *(p. 92)*
Treaty of Paris of 1763 *(p. 95)*
Pontiac *(p. 96)*
Proclamation of 1763 *(p. 96)*
writ of assistance *(p. 97)*
Sugar Act *(p. 98)*
Stamp Act *(p. 99)*
Sons of Liberty *(p. 100)*
Stamp Act Congress *(p. 100)*
Declaratory Act *(p. 101)*
Quartering Act *(p. 102)*
Townshend duties *(p. 103)*
Board of Customs Commissioners *(p. 104)*
John Wilkes *(p. 105)*
Boston Massacre *(p. 108)*
committees of correspondence *(p. 108)*
Tea Act *(p. 110)*
Lord Dunmore *(p. 112)*
Intolerable Acts *(p. 112)*
Continental Congress *(p. 113)*
Concord *(p. 114)*
Lexington *(p. 114)*
Common Sense (p. 115)
Declaration of Independence *(p. 116)*

What led most colonists in 1776 to abandon their loyalty to Britain and choose national independence? *(page 111)*

In response to the Tea Party, Parliament passed a series of Coercive Acts—known to the colonists as the Intolerable Acts—which spawned the First Continental Congress and the beginning of fully coordinated colonial resistance. In 1775 the battles of Lexington and Concord transformed the friction between Britain and the colonies into armed conflict. Thomas Paine's *Common Sense* ridiculed the arguments against independence and portrayed the colonial struggle as one of universal principles on which Thomas Jefferson elaborated in the Declaration of Independence.

CHAPTER 6

Securing Independence, Defining Nationhood

1776–1788

Image copyright © The Metropolitan Museum of Art / Art Resource, NY

Trumbull, "George Washington"

CHAPTER PREVIEW

On May 1, 1777, eighteen-year-old Agrippa Hull, a free African-American man from Stockbridge, Massachusetts, enlisted in the Continental Army. Like most black recruits, Hull enlisted for the duration of the Revolutionary War. He spent four years as an orderly for General Thaddeus Kósciuszko, a Polish republican and abolitionist who had volunteered for the American cause.

Upon discharge, Hull returned to Stockbridge, where he was welcomed as a hero and became a New England celebrity until his death at age eighty-nine. A gifted storyteller, Hull regaled locals and visitors with accounts of his wartime experiences—of horrors such as assisting surgeons in performing amputations, and of lighter moments such as Kósciuszko's finding him entertaining his black friends in the general's uniform. When Kósciuszko made a return visit to the United States in 1797, Hull and the Polish patriot reunited in New York to public acclaim.

For victorious patriots like Hull, military service strengthened a new national identity. In July 1776, the thirteen colonies had jointly declared their independence from Britain and formed a loosely knit confederation of states, later formalized with the adoption of the Articles of Confederation. Shaped by the collective hardships experienced during eight years of terrible fighting, the former colonists shifted from seeing themselves primarily as military allies to accepting one another as fellow citizens. But divisions remained, erupting in the national contest over replacing the Articles of Confederation. The ratification of the Constitution in 1787 marked a triumph for those favoring more centralization of power at the national level. It also left most of Agrippa Hull's fellow African-Americans in slavery.

THE PROSPECTS OF WAR

What factors enabled the Americans to defeat the British in the American Revolution?

The Revolution was both a collective struggle that pitted the independent states against Britain and a civil war among American peoples. American opponents of independence constituted one of several factors working in Britain's favor as war began. Others included Britain's larger population and its superior military resources and preparation. America, on the other hand, was located far from Britain and enjoyed the intense commitment to independence from patriots and the Continental Army.

Loyalists and Other British Sympathizers

Even after the Declaration of Independence, some Americans remained opposed to secession from Britain, including about 20 percent of all whites. Although these internal enemies of the Revolution called themselves **loyalists,** they were "Tories" to their patriot, or Whig, opponents.

loyalist Colonist who supported the British

Loyalists, like Whigs, typically opposed parliamentary taxation of the colonies. Many loyalists thus found themselves fighting for a cause with which they did not entirely agree; as a result, many switched sides during the war. But loyalists believed that separation was illegal and was not necessary to preserve the colonists' constitutional rights. Above all, they retained a profound reverence for the crown and believed that if they failed to defend their king, they would sacrifice their personal honor.

The mutual hatred between Whigs and Tories was intense. Each side saw its cause as sacred, and those who opposed it as traitors. The worst atrocities of the war were committed by Americans against each other.

The most important factor in determining loyalist strength in any area was the political power of local Whigs and their success in convincing their neighbors that Britain threatened their liberty. For several years, colonial resistance leaders in New England, Virginia, and South Carolina had vigorously pursued a program of political education and popular mobilization. As a result, probably no more than 5 percent of whites in these areas were committed loyalists in 1776. Loyalist strength was greatest in New York and New Jersey, where elites were especially reluctant to declare their allegiance to either side. Those two states eventually furnished about half of the twenty-one thousand Americans who fought as loyalists.

A second major factor in loyalist strength was the geographic distribution of recent British immigrants, who identified closely with their homeland. These newcomers included thousands of British veterans of the French and Indian War who had remained in the colonies, usually in New York. The 125,000 British immigrants who arrived between 1763 and 1775 formed major centers of loyalist sympathy. In New York, Georgia, and the Carolina piedmont, where these newcomers clustered, loyalists probably constituted 25 to 40 percent of the white population in 1776.

Quebec's religious and secular elites comprised another significant white minority with pro-British sympathies. When Continental forces invaded Quebec in 1775–1776, they found widespread support among non-elite French as well as British Canadians. After British forces repulsed the invasion, Britain's military, supported by local elites, retained control of Canada throughout the war.

Black slaves and Native Americans also widely supported the British. As in Virginia, hundreds of South Carolina slaves sought refuge on British ships before the outbreak of war. During the war itself, about twenty thousand slaves escaped their owners. Most were recaptured or died, especially from epidemics, but a small minority achieved freedom, often after serving as laborers or soldiers in the Royal Army. Meanwhile, about five thousand enslaved and free African-Americans, mostly from New England, calculated that supporting the rebels would hasten their own emancipation and equality.

Finally, most Indians, recognizing the threat that expansion-minded colonists posed, likewise supported the British. In the Ohio country, most Shawnees, Delawares, and other Indians continued to resent settlers' incursions, but a few communities initially supported the Americans. Most tribes of the Six Nations Iroquois confederacy followed the lead of the Mohawk chief **Joseph Brant** in supporting Britain. But the Oneidas (oh-NIE-duhs) and Tuscaroras (tuss-kuh-ROR-uhs), influenced by a New England missionary, actively sided with the rebels against other Iroquois. Meanwhile, Cherokee ranks were split between anti-American militants and those who thought that the Cherokees' best hope was to steer clear of the Anglo-American conflict.

Joseph Brant Mohawk chief (Thayendagea) and obstinate foe of American military and expansion

The Opposing Sides

Britain entered the war with two major advantages. First, Britain's 11 million people greatly outnumbered the 2.5 million colonists, one-third of whom were either slaves or loyalists. Second, Britain possessed the world's largest navy and one of its best armies. During the war, the army's size more than doubled, from 48,000 to 111,000 men. In addition, Britain hired 30,000 German mercenaries known as Hessians (HESH-uns) and enlisted 21,000 loyalists to supplement its own fighting force.

However, Britain's ability to crush the rebellion was weakened by the decline in its sea power, a result of budget cuts after 1763. Midway through the war, half of Britain's ships languished in dry dock awaiting major repairs. In addition, during the war U.S. Navy ships and privateers would capture more than 2,000 British merchant vessels and 16,000 crewmen. Seriously overextended, the navy barely kept the army supplied and never effectively blockaded American ports. Maintaining public support presented another serious problem for Britain. The war more than doubled the British national debt, adding to the burdens of a people already paying record taxes.

The United States faced different but equally severe problems. Besides the fact that many colonists, slaves, and Native Americans favored the British, the patriots faced a formidable military challenge. Although militias often performed well in hit-and-run guerrilla skirmishes, they were not trained to fight against professional armies like Britain's. Congress recognized that independence would never be secured if the new nation relied on guerrilla tactics, avoided major battles, and ceded its cities to the enemy. Moreover, potential European allies would recognize that dependence on guerrilla warfare meant the rebels could not drive out the British army.

The Continental Army would thus have to fight in European fashion, relying on precision movements of mass formations of troops and rapid maneuvers to crush an enemy's undefended flank or rear. After advancing within musket range, opposing troops would stand upright and fire at each other until one line weakened. Discipline, training, and nerve would be essential if soldiers were to hold their line as comrades fell around them.

In 1775, Britain possessed a well-trained army with a strong tradition of discipline and bravery under fire. In contrast, the Continental Army had neither an inspirational heritage nor experienced officers. Although the United States mobilized about 220,000 troops, compared to the 162,000 who served the British, most served short terms. Most whites and blacks who did sign up for longer terms were poor.

Chronology

1776	British force American troops from New York City
1777	Congress approves Articles of Confederation; American victory at Saratoga
1777–1778	British troops occupy Philadelphia; Continental Army winters at Valley Forge
1778	France formally recognizes the United States; declares war on Britain
1779	Spain declares war on Britain; John Sullivan leads American raids in Iroquois country
1780	British seize Charles Town Articles of Confederation ratified; Battle of Yorktown
1781	British General Cornwallis surrenders
1783	Treaty of Paris
1784	Spain closes New Orleans to American trade; economic depression begins in New England
1785	Ordinance of 1785; Treaty of Fort McIntosh
1786	Congress rejects Jay-Gardoqui Treaty
1786–1787	Shays's Rebellion in Massachusetts
1787	Northwest Ordinance; Philadelphia convention frames federal Constitution
1787–1788	Alexander Hamilton, James Madison, and John Jay, *The Federalist*
1788	Constitution ratified

Such men joined not out of patriotism but because, as one of them, a jailed debtor named Ezekiel Brown, put it, they had "little or nothing to lose."

The Americans experienced a succession of heartbreaking defeats in the war's early years. Yet, to win the war, the Continentals did not have to destroy the British army but only prolong the rebellion until Britain's taxpayers lost patience with the struggle. Until then, American victory would depend on the ability of one man to keep his army fighting. That man was George Washington.

After resigning his commission in 1758, Washington served in the Virginia House of Burgesses, where his influence grew, not because he thrust himself into every issue but because others respected him and sought his opinion. Having emerged as an early, though not outspoken, opponent of parliamentary taxation, he later sat in the Continental Congress. Washington was the logical choice to head the Continental Army.

The young Washington's mistakes and defeats in the Ohio Valley (see Chapter 5) taught him about the dangers of overconfidence and the need for determination in the face of defeat. He also learned that American soldiers fought best when led by example and treated with respect.

Checking In

- At the war's start, the British enjoyed major advantages in population, economic development, and military preparedness.
- However, British supply lines were long and popular support for the war short-lived.
- Americans had no trained army when the war began.
- Americans did not have to defeat the British; they just had to prolong the rebellion.
- Washington kept his army fighting despite defeats; this experience taught him the need for determination and earned him enormous respect among Americans.

War and Peace, 1776–1783

How did the war unfold?

Each side initially won important victories in the North. West of the Appalachians, revolutionary forces prevailed over the British and their Indian allies. However, it was the American and French victory at Yorktown in 1781 that decided the war and gained British recognition of American independence.

Shifting Fortunes in the North, 1776–1778

During the second half of 1776, the two sides focused on New York. Under two brothers—General William Howe and Admiral Lord Richard Howe—130 British warships carrying 32,000 royal troops landed at New York in the summer of 1776. Defending the city were 18,000 poorly trained soldiers under George Washington. By the end of the year, William Howe's men had killed or captured one-quarter of Washington's troops and had forced the survivors to retreat from New York across New Jersey and the Delaware River into Pennsylvania.

With the British nearing Philadelphia, Washington decided to seize the offensive before the morale of his army and country collapsed completely. On Christmas night 1776, his troops returned to New Jersey and attacked a Hessian garrison at Trenton. At the **Battle of Trenton,** Washington captured 918 Germans and lost only four Continentals. Washington's men then attacked twelve hundred British at Princeton on January 3, 1777, and killed or captured one-third of them while sustaining only forty casualties.

Battle of Trenton New Jersey battle where Washington took more than 900 Hessian prisoners on Christmas Night, 1776; vital victory to improve national morale

The American victories at Trenton and Princeton boosted civilian and military morale and drove a wedge between New Jersey's five thousand loyalists and the British army. Washington's victories forced the British to remove virtually all their New Jersey garrisons to New York early in 1777. Once the British were gone, New Jersey's militia disarmed known loyalists and jailed their leaders. Bowing to the inevitable, most remaining loyalists swore allegiance to the Continental Congress.

After the Battle of Princeton, the Marquis de Lafayette (mar-KEE deh lah-fay-ETT), a young French aristocrat, joined Washington's staff. Given Lafayette's close connections with the French court, his presence indicated that France might recognize American independence and declare war on Britain. Before recognizing the new nation, however, King Louis XVI wanted proof that the Americans could win a major battle.

Louis did not have to wait long. In the summer of 1777, the British planned a two-pronged assault intended to crush American resistance in New York State and thereby isolate New England. Pushing off from Montreal, a force under Lieutenant Colonel Barry St. Leger would invade central New York from the west. At the same time, General John Burgoyne would lead the main British force south from Quebec and link up with St. Leger near Albany (see Map 6.1).

However, nothing went according to British plans. St. Leger's force encountered a Continental force holding a chokepoint at Fort Stanwix. Unable to take the post after three weeks, St. Leger retreated in late August 1777. Burgoyne's campaign appeared more promising after his force of eighty-three hundred British and Hessians recaptured Fort Ticonderoga, but nearly seven thousand American troops under General Horatio Gates challenged him near Saratoga. In two battles in the fall, the British suffered twelve hundred casualties. Surrounded and hopelessly outnumbered, Burgoyne surrendered on October 17, 1777.

Battle of Saratoga American victory in 1777 that convinced the French to support the revolutionaries

The **Battle of Saratoga** would prove to be the war's turning point. The victory convinced France that the Americans could win the war. In February 1778, France formally recognized the United States. Four months later, it went to war with Britain. Spain and Holland ultimately joined the war as French allies.

In late August 1777, British General Howe landed eighteen thousand troops near Philadelphia. With Washington at their head and Lafayette at his side, sixteen thousand Continentals occupied the imperiled city. The two armies collided on September 11, 1777, at Brandywine Creek, Pennsylvania. After the Continentals crumbled in the face of superior British discipline, Congress fled Philadelphia, allowing Howe to occupy it. Howe again defeated Washington at Germantown on October 4. In one month's bloody fighting, 20 percent of the Continentals were killed, wounded, or captured.

While the British army wintered comfortably in Philadelphia, the Continentals huddled eighteen miles away in the bleak hills of Valley Forge. "The greatest part were not only shirtless and barefoot," wrote a seventeen-year-old Massachusetts recruit, "but destitute of all other clothing, especially blankets." Shortages of provisions, especially food, would continue to undermine morale and, on some occasions, discipline among American forces.

The army also lacked training. At Saratoga, the Americans' overwhelming numbers more than their skill had forced Burgoyne to surrender. Indeed, when Washington's men had met Howe's forces on equal terms, they lost badly. The Continental Army received a desperately needed boost in February 1778, when

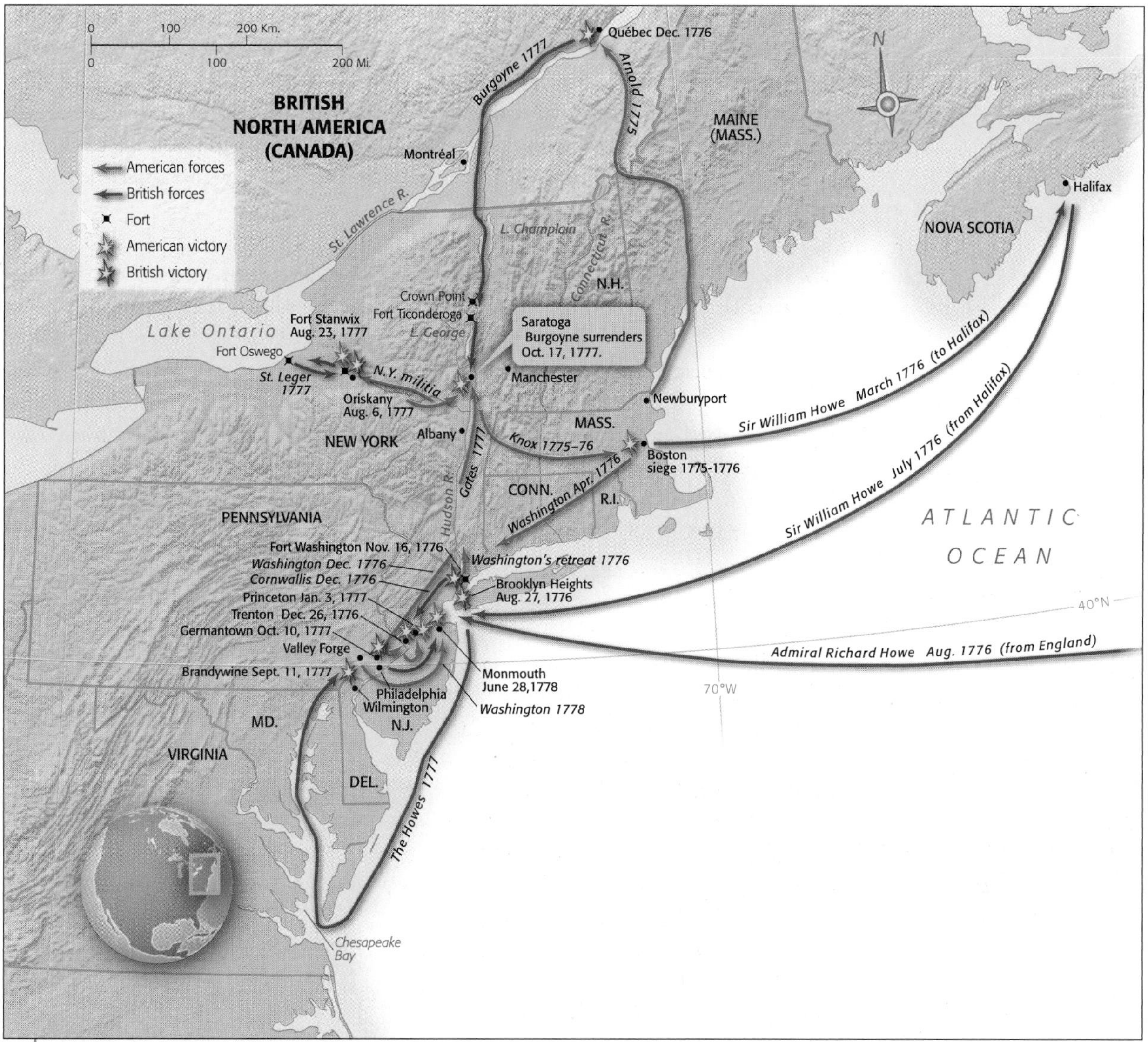

Map 6.1 The War in the North, 1775–1778

During the early years of the war, most of the fighting took place from Philadelphia northward.

Interactive Map

a German soldier of fortune, Friedrich von Steuben, arrived at Valley Forge. This earthy German instinctively liked Americans and had a talent for motivating men (and for swearing forcefully in several languages). An administrative genius and immensely popular individual, Steuben almost single-handedly turned the army into a formidable fighting force in a mere four months.

The Continental Army got its first opportunity to demonstrate Steuben's training at Monmouth, New Jersey, on June 28, 1778, when it met a force led by General Henry Clinton, the new commander-in-chief in North America. The battle raged for six hours in one-hundred-degree heat, with the Continentals throwing back

Britain's finest troops. The British finally broke off contact and slipped away under cover of darkness. Never again would they win easy victories against the Continental Army.

The Battle of Monmouth ended the contest for the North. Clinton occupied New York, which the Royal Navy made safe from attack. Washington kept his army on watch nearby, while Whig militia hunted down the last few Tory guerrillas.

The War in the West, 1776–1782

A different kind of war developed west of the Appalachians, consisting of small-scale skirmishes, often sparked by long-standing frontier tensions, rather than major battles involving thousands of troops. The war in the West erupted in 1776 when Cherokees began attacking settlers from North Carolina and nearby colonies who had encroached on their homelands (see Map 6.2). After suffering heavy losses, the

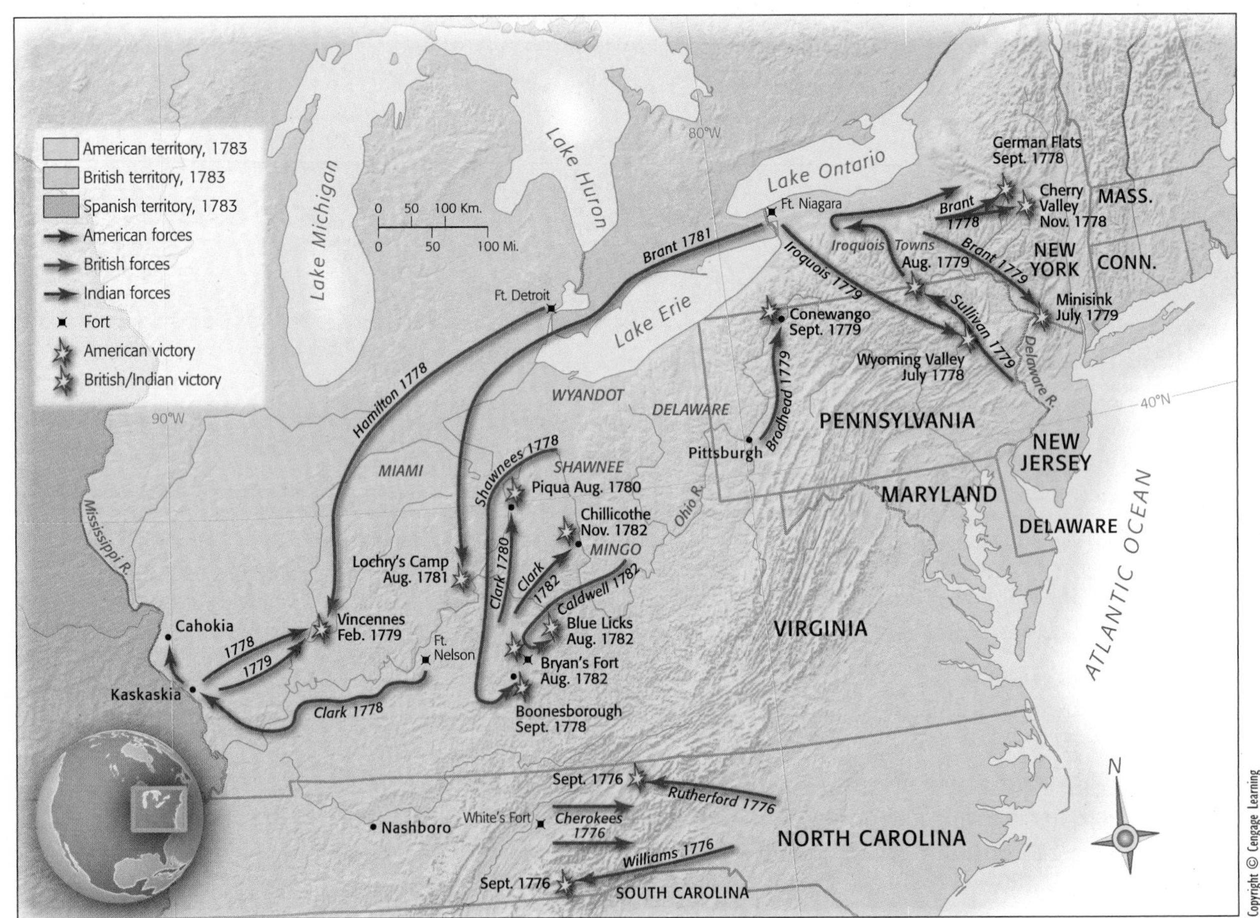

Map 6.2 The War in the West, 1776–1782

The war's western front was closely tied to Native Americans' defense of their homelands against expansionist settlers.

Interactive Map

colonies recovered and organized retaliatory expeditions. Within a year, these expeditions had burned most Cherokee towns, forcing the Cherokees to sign treaties that ceded most of their land in the Carolinas and Tennessee.

The intense fighting lasted longer in the Northwest. Ohio Indians and white settlers fought for two years in Kentucky, with neither side gaining a clear advantage. But after British troops occupied French settlements in what is now Illinois and Indiana, Colonel George Rogers Clark led 175 Kentucky militiamen north of the Ohio River and took Vincennes by February 1779. Most Ohio Indians continued to resist the Americans until the war's end.

In the East, pro-British Iroquois under the gifted Mohawk leader Joseph Brant devastated the New York and Pennsylvania frontiers in 1778. General John Sullivan led a Continental force, with Tuscarora and Oneida allies, against the Iroquois. Victorious at what is now Elmira, New York, in 1779, Sullivan and his forces burned two dozen Iroquois villages and destroyed a million bushels of corn. The Iroquois fled north to Canada, and untold hundreds starved to death. Sullivan's campaign devastated the pro-British Iroquois.

Fighting continued in the West until 1782. Despite their intensity, the western campaigns did not determine the outcome of the war itself. Nevertheless, they would have a significant impact on the future shape of the United States.

American Victory in the South, 1778–1781

In 1778, the war's focus shifted to the South. By securing southern ports, Britain expected to acquire the flexibility needed to move its forces back and forth between the West Indies—where they faced French and Spanish opposition—and the mainland, as necessity dictated. In addition, the South looked like a relatively easy target. General Clinton expected to seize key southern ports and, with the aid of loyalist militiamen, move back toward the North, pacifying one region after another.

The plan unfolded smoothly at first. In the spring of 1778, British troops from East Florida took control of Georgia. After a two-year delay caused by political bickering at home, Clinton sailed from New York with nine thousand troops and forced the surrender of Charles Town, South Carolina. He left the mopping-up operation to **Lord Charles Cornwallis.** However, the British quickly found that there were fewer loyalists than they had expected.

Lord Charles Cornwallis British general whose surrender at Yorktown in 1781 effectively ended the Revolutionary War

Southern loyalism had suffered several serious blows since the war began. When the Cherokees had attacked the Carolina frontier in 1776, they killed whites indiscriminately. Numerous Tories joined the rebel militia to defend their homes. In addition, the arrival of British troops sparked a renewed exodus of enslaved Africans from their plantations. About one-third of Georgia's blacks and one-fourth of South Carolina's fled to British lines in the quest of freedom. The British made every effort to return them to their owners. Nonetheless, fear of slave rebellion caused many former loyalists to abandon their British ties and welcome the rebels' return to power.

Meanwhile, battles between British troops and Continental regulars led to a string of Continental defeats. America's worst loss of the entire war came at Camden, South Carolina, in August 1780. General Horatio Gates's combined force of professionals and militiamen faced Cornwallis's army. The militiamen fled after the first volley, and the badly outnumbered Continentals were overrun. Washington sent

General Nathanael Greene to confront Cornwallis. Under Greene, the rebels lost three major battles in 1781 but won the campaign nonetheless by stretching British supply lines and inflicting heavy casualties. Greene's dogged resistance forced Cornwallis to abandon the Carolina backcountry and lead his battered troops into Virginia.

Cornwallis established a base at Yorktown, Virginia. Britain's undoing began on August 30, 1781, when a French fleet dropped anchor off the Virginia coast

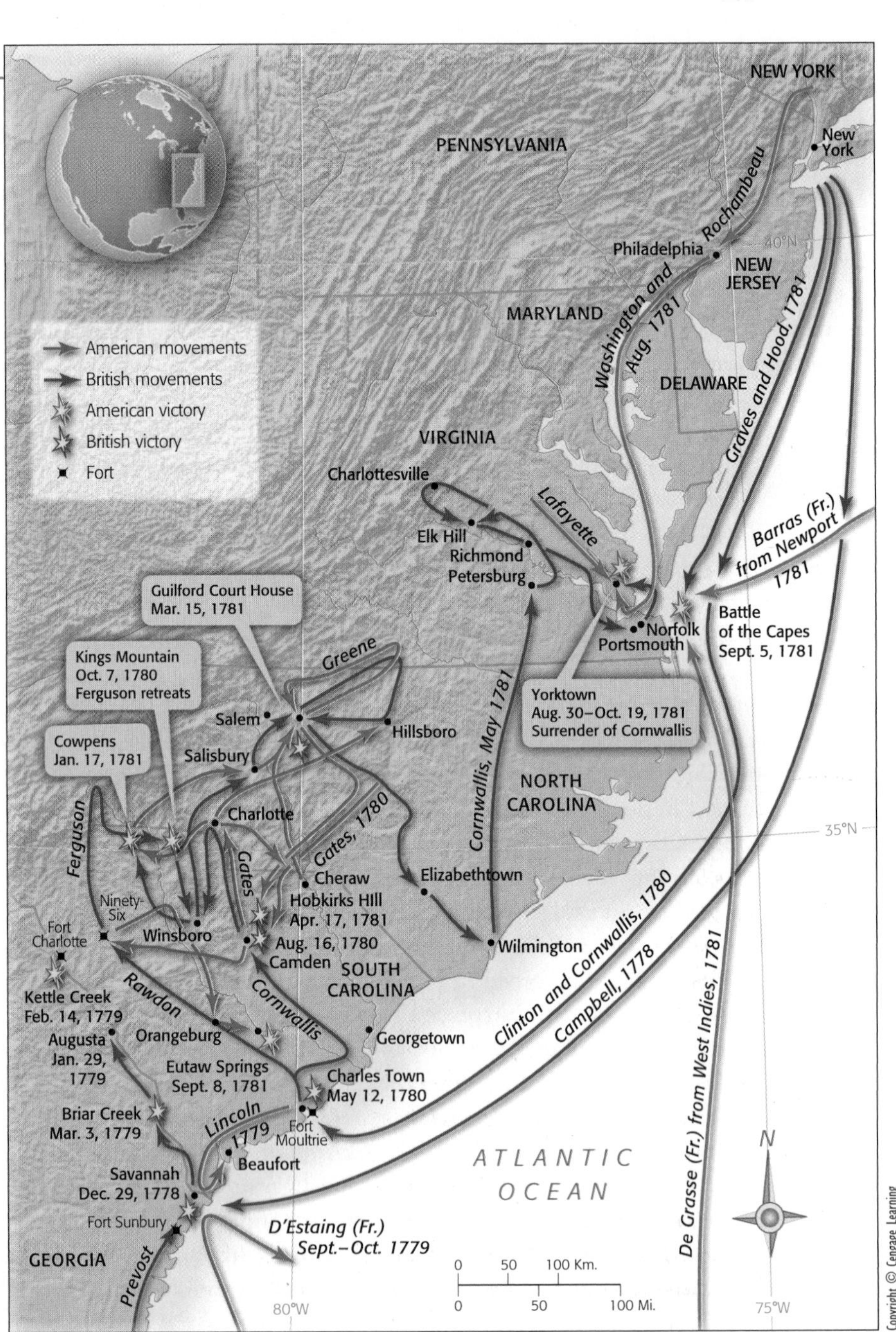

Map 6.3 The War in the South, 1778–1781

The South was the setting for the final, decisive phase of the war, culminating in the British surrender at Yorktown in October 1781.

Interactive Map

and landed troops near Yorktown. Lafayette and a small force of Continentals from nearby joined the French while Washington arrived with his army from New York. In the Battle of Yorktown, six thousand trapped British troops stood off eighty-eight hundred Americans and seventy-eight hundred French for three weeks before surrendering with military honors on October 19, 1781.

Peace at Last, 1782–1783

"Oh God!" Lord North exclaimed on hearing of Yorktown. "It's all over." Cornwallis's surrender had extinguished the will of Britain's overtaxed people to fight and forced the government to negotiate for peace. John Adams, Benjamin Franklin, and John Jay were America's principal delegates to the peace talks in Paris, which began in June 1782.

Military realities largely influenced the terms of the Treaty of Paris (1783). Britain recognized American independence and agreed to withdraw all royal troops from the new nation's soil. The British had little choice but to award the Confederation all lands east of the Mississippi. Twenty thousand Anglo-Americans now lived west of the Appalachians. Moreover, Clark's victories had given Americans control of the Northwest, while Spain had kept Britain out of the Southwest.

On the whole, the settlement was highly favorable to the United States, but it left some disputes unresolved. Under a separate treaty, Britain returned East and West Florida to Spain, but the boundaries designated by this treaty were ambiguous. Further, although the United States promised to urge state legislatures to compensate loyalists for property losses, several states would later refuse to comply. Completely left out of the treaty—and on their own—were the Native Americans who had supported the British. Indian leaders were outraged; many did not acknowledge the new nation's sovereignty over their territory.

Independence carried a heavy price. At least 5 percent of all free males between the ages of sixteen and forty-five—white, black, and Native American—died fighting the British. Furthermore, the war drove perhaps one of every six loyalists, several thousand slaves, and several thousand Native Americans into exile. And the peace left two important issues unsettled: what kind of society the United States would become and what sort of government it would possess.

CHECKING IN

- Initial rounds of the war were fought mainly in the North, with mixed results.
- The American victory at Saratoga represented a major turning point, because it drew the French into the war on the Americans' side.
- Success in the West allowed the revolutionaries to claim the Mississippi as their western boundary.
- In 1778 the focus of the war shifted to the South. Here, the British won inconclusive victories and were then forced to surrender at Yorktown.
- The Treaty of Paris of 1783 ended the war and confirmed the independence of the colonies.

THE REVOLUTION AND SOCIAL CHANGE

How did the war affect relationships among Americans of different classes, races, and genders?

Two forces shaped the Revolution's social effects: the principles articulated in the Declaration of Independence and the dislocations caused by the war. These factors combined to force questions of class, gender, and race into public discussion. Popular attitudes about the rights of non-elite white men and of white women, and the future of slavery, shifted somewhat. Although the resulting changes were not substantive, the discussions ensured that these issues would continue to be debated in the United States. For Native Americans, however, the Revolution was a step backward.

Egalitarianism Among White Men

Between 1700 and 1760 social relations between elites and common people had grown more formal, distant, and restrained. Members of the colonial gentry lived sumptuously to emphasize their position. By the late 1760s, however, many in the upper class were wearing homespun clothing in support of boycotts of British goods. When the Virginia planters organized militia companies in 1775, they put aside their expensive officers' uniforms and dressed in buckskin or homespun hunting shirts of a sort that even the poorest farmer could afford. Elites maintained the appearance, if not the substance, of equality.

The war accelerated the erosion of class differences by forcing gentry officers to respect ordinary men serving as privates. Indeed, the soldiers demanded to be treated with consideration, especially in light of the ringing statement of the Declaration of Independence that "all men are created equal."

After returning to civilian life, the soldiers retained their sense of self-esteem and insisted on respectful treatment by elites. As these feelings of personal pride gradually translated into political behavior and beliefs, many candidates took care not to scorn the common people. The war thus subtly democratized Americans' political assumptions.

Many elites who considered themselves republicans did not welcome the apparent trend toward democracy. These men continued to insist that each social class had its own particular virtues and that a chief virtue of the lower classes was deference to those possessing the wealth and education necessary to govern. "A popular government is the worse Curse," wrote John Adams in 1776, concluding that "despotism is better."

Nevertheless, most Americans from the Revolutionary War generation came to insist that virtue and sacrifice defined a citizen's worth independently of his wealth. Voters still elected the wealthy to office, but not if they flaunted their money or were condescending toward common people. The new emphasis on equality did not extend to males, women, and nonwhites without property, but it undermined the tendency to believe that wealth or distinguished family background conferred a special claim to public office.

Although many whites became more egalitarian in their attitudes, the Revolution left the actual distribution of wealth in the nation unchanged. The war had been directed at British imperial rule and not at the structure of American society. The exodus of loyalists did not affect the class structure because the 3 percent who fled the United States represented a cross-section of society. Overall, the American upper class seemed to own about as much of the national wealth in 1783 as it did in 1776.

White Women in Wartime

White women broadened their involvement in the anti-British cause, creating a wide range of activities during the war. Female "camp followers," many of them soldiers' wives, cooked, laundered, and nursed the wounded for both sides. A few women actually disguised themselves as men and joined the fighting. Women who remained at home managed families, households, farms, and businesses on their own. Despite—and because of—enormous struggles, women gained confidence in their ability to think and act on matters traditionally reserved for men. Although women's public roles and visibility increased during the Revolution, the question was to what extent the new nation would make these gains permanent.

As in all wars, women's public roles and visibility heightened during the Revolution. In 1779, a number of women, including Franklin's daughter Sally Franklin Bache, organized a campaign to raise money for the troops. They likened their role to Joan of Arc and other female heroes who had saved their people, and they proclaimed that American women were "born for liberty" and would never "bear the irons of a tyrannic government."

Abigail Adams Wife of John Adams, who issued the most direct challenge to established gender relations

The most direct challenge to established gender relations came from **Abigail Adams.** "In the new Code of Laws..." she wrote to her husband John in 1776, "I desire that you would Remember the Ladies." Otherwise, she continued, "we are determined to foment a Rebellion and will not hold ourselves bound by any Laws in which we have no voice, or Representation." Abigail made it clear that women saw that the arguments against arbitrary British rule also applied to gender relations. Despite his high regard for his wife's intellect, John Adams dismissed her plea as an effort to extend rights and power to the unworthy. The assumption that women were naturally dependent continued to dominate discussions of the female role. For that reason, married women's property remained, in Abigail's bitter words, "subject to the control and disposal of our partners, to whom the law have given a sovereign authority."

A Revolution for Black Americans

The wartime condition of African-Americans contradicted the ideals of equality and justice for which Americans fought. About a half million blacks—20 percent of the total population—inhabited the United States in 1776, all but about twenty-five thousand of whom were enslaved. Free blacks could not vote, lived under curfews, and lacked the guarantees of equal justice afforded to even the poorest white criminal.

The war nevertheless presented new opportunities to African-Americans. Early fighting in New England drew several hundred blacks into the militia and Continental units. Some slaves ran off and posed as free persons. A 1775 ban on black soldiers was collapsing by 1777, when Washington agreed to Rhode Island's plea that it be allowed to raise a nonwhite

Phillis Wheatley, African-American Poet

Though a slave, Wheatley was the best-known poet in America at the time of the Revolution. Despite her fame, she died in poverty in 1784.

regiment. The regiment of African-Americans and Native Americans distinguished itself in several battles, including at Yorktown. Yet Washington was wary of arming slaves. When Congress urged Georgia and South Carolina to arm three thousand slaves against advancing British troops in 1779, Washington vetoed the plan.

Until the mid-eighteenth century, few Europeans and white Americans had criticized slavery at all. But in the decade before the Revolution, American opposition to slavery had swelled, especially as resistance leaders increasingly compared the colonies' relationship with Britain to that between slaves and a master. The earliest organized initiatives against slavery originated among Quakers. The yearly meeting of the New England Friends abolished slavery among its members in 1770. By 1779, Quaker slave owners had freed 80 percent of their slaves, and some activists were broadening their condemnations to include slavery everywhere.

antislavery movement Opposition to slavery that began slowly during the revolutionary period

Discussions of liberty, equality, and natural rights, particularly in the Declaration of Independence, also spurred the beginnings of the **antislavery movement.** Between 1777 and 1784, Vermont, Pennsylvania, Massachusetts, Rhode Island, and Connecticut began phasing out slavery. New York did not do so until 1799, and New Jersey until 1804. Most state abolition laws provided for gradual emancipation, typically declaring all children born of a slave woman after a certain date—often July 4—free. In addition, most northern states granted some civil rights to free blacks after the Revolution. Many repealed or stopped enforcing curfews and other colonial laws restricting free African-Americans' freedom of movement and access to the courts.

No state south of Pennsylvania abolished slavery. Nevertheless, all states except South Carolina and Georgia ended slave imports and all but North Carolina passed laws making it easy for masters to manumit (set free) slaves. However, these "free persons of color" faced a future of destitution and second-class citizenship. Most had used up their cash savings to purchase their freedom and were past their physical prime. They found few whites willing to hire them. Most free blacks remained poor laborers or tenant farmers, although a few became landowners or skilled artisans. Phillis Wheatley, a slave in a Boston merchant family, gained her freedom in 1773, the same year her poems were published to acclaim in Britain. Several of these poems linked the liberty sought by white Americans with a plea for the liberty of slaves.

One of the most prominent free blacks to emerge during the Revolutionary War period was Prince Hall of Boston. After gaining his freedom in 1770, Hall took a leading role among Boston blacks protesting slavery. During the war he formed a separate black Masonic lodge, initiating a movement that spread to other northern communities. In 1786 he petitioned the Massachusetts legislature for support of a plan that would enable interested blacks "to return to Africa, our native country… where we shall live among our equals and be more comfortable and happy than we can be in our present situation." Later activists would echo his call for blacks to "return to Africa."

The Revolution neither ended slavery nor brought equality to free blacks. Most wartime opportunities for black men grew out of the army's need for personnel rather than a white commitment to equal justice. However, the war did begin a process by which slavery eventually might have been extinguished. In half the nation, the end of human bondage seemed to be in sight. Many white southerners viewed slavery as a necessary evil rather than as a positive good. Slavery had begun to crack, and free blacks had made some gains. However, events in the 1790s would reverse the tentative move toward egalitarianism (as discussed in Chapter 7).

Native Americans and the Revolution

Revolutionary ideology held out at least abstract hope for African-Americans and women, but it made no provisions for the many Indians who sought to maintain political and cultural independence. Moreover, in an overwhelmingly agrarian society, the Revolution's promise of equal economic opportunity for all set the stage for territorial expansion beyond settled areas, thereby threatening Indian lands. Even where Indians retained land, the influx of settlers posed dangers in the form of deadly diseases, farming practices hostile to Indian subsistence, and alcohol. Indians were all the more vulnerable because during the wars between 1754 and 1783, their population east of the Mississippi had fallen by about half, and many villages had been uprooted.

In the face of these uncertainties, Native Americans continued to incorporate aspects of European culture into their lives. From the early colonial period, they had adopted European-made goods of cloth, metal, and glass while retaining some of their traditional clothing, tools, and weapons. Indians also participated in the American economy by occasionally working for wages or selling food, craft items, and other products.

Thus, Native Americans did not hold stubbornly to traditional ways, but they did insist on retaining control of their communities and ways of life. In the Revolution's aftermath, it remained doubtful that the new nation would accommodate Native Americans on these terms.

CHECKING IN

- Egalitarianism among white males increased as a result of the war.
- The war offered free blacks some gains in opportunities and rights, but most still faced a future of uncertainty and second-class citizenship.
- Northern states provided for the eventual end of slavery, and an antislavery movement began.
- Women built on their contributions during the war to play a larger public role.
- Native Americans were left in an ambiguous and threatened position.

FORGING NEW GOVERNMENTS, 1776–1787

What political concerns were reflected in the first state constitutions and Articles of Confederation?

In establishing new political institutions, revolutionary Americans endeavored to guarantee liberty at the state level by minimizing executive power and by subjecting all officeholders to frequent scrutiny by voters. In turn, the new national government was subordinate, under the Articles of Confederation, to the thirteen states. However, challenges facing the Confederation made clear to many elites the need for more centralized authority at the national level.

From Colonies to States

Before 1776, colonists had regarded their popularly elected assemblies as the bulwark of their liberties against encroachments by governors wielding executive power. Thereafter, the legislatures retained that role even when voters, rather than the British crown, chose governors.

In keeping with colonial practice, eleven states maintained bicameral (two-chamber) legislatures. Colonial legislatures had consisted of an elected lower house (or assembly) and an upper house (or council) appointed by the governor or chosen by the assembly. These two-part legislatures mirrored Parliament's division into the House of Commons and House of Lords, symbolizing the assumption that a government should have separate representation by the upper class and the common people. Likewise, few questioned the long-standing practice of setting property requirements for voters and elected officials. Property ownership, most people argued, enabled voters and officeholders to think and act independently. Nine of the thirteen states slightly reduced property requirements for voting, but none abolished such qualifications entirely.

Another colonial practice that persisted beyond independence was the equal (or nearly equal) division of legislative seats among all counties or towns, regardless of differences in population. As a result, a minority of voters usually elected a majority of assemblymen. Only the most radical constitution, Pennsylvania's, sought to avoid such outcomes by attempting to ensure that election districts would be roughly equal in population.

Despite the holdover of certain colonial-era practices, the state constitutions in other respects departed radically from the past. Above all, they were written documents that usually required popular ratification and could be amended only by the voters. In short, Americans jettisoned the British conception of a constitution as a body of customary arrangements and practices, insisting instead that constitutions were written compacts that defined and limited the powers of rulers and established the rights of citizens. By 1784, all state constitutions included explicit bills of rights that outlined certain freedoms that lay beyond the control of any government.

The earliest state constitutions strengthened legislatures at governors' expense. In most states, the governor became an elected official, and elections themselves occurred far more frequently. In most states, the power of appointments was transferred from the governor to the legislature. Legislatures usually appointed judges and could reduce their salaries, and legislatures could impeach both judges and governors (try them for wrongdoing). By relieving governors of most appointive powers, the constitutions gave governors little to do. Pennsylvania went further, simply eliminating the office of governor.

As the new state constitutions weakened the executive branch and vested more power in the legislatures, they also made the legislatures more responsive to the will of the voters. Nowhere could the governor appoint the upper chamber. Eight constitutions written before 1780 allowed voters to select both houses of the legislature. Pennsylvania and Georgia abolished the upper house altogether. States' weakening of the executive branch and enhancement of legislative and popular authority reflected Americans' fears of centralized authority, rooted in bitter memories of royal governors who had acted arbitrarily.

Despite their high regard for popularly elected legislatures, revolutionary leaders described themselves as republicans rather than democrats. These words had different connotations in the eighteenth century than they do today. To many elites, democracy suggested mob rule or, at least, the concentration of power in the hands of an uneducated multitude. In contrast, **republicanism** presumed that government would be entrusted to virtuous leaders elected for their superior talents and commitment to the public good. For most republicans, the ideal government would delicately balance the interests of different classes to prevent any one group from

republicanism Ideal of early revolutionaries that government should be entrusted to leaders chosen for wisdom gaining absolute power. A few, including John Adams, thought that a republic could include a monarchy if needed to counterbalance democratic tendencies. But having rid themselves of one king, even most elites did not wish to enthrone another.

In the first flush of revolutionary enthusiasm, elites had to be content with state governments dominated by popularly elected legislatures. Gradually, however, wealthier landowners, bankers, merchants, and lawyers reasserted the prerogatives of wealth. In Massachusetts, an elite-dominated convention in 1780 pushed through a constitution largely authored by John Adams. The document stipulated stiff property qualifications for voting and holding office and a governor with considerable powers. The Massachusetts constitution signaled a general trend. Georgia and Pennsylvania substituted bicameral for unicameral legislatures by 1790. Other states raised property qualifications for members of the upper chamber in a bid to encourage the "senatorial element" and to make room for men of "Wisdom, remarkable integrity, or that Weight which arises from property."

Formalizing a Confederation, 1776–1781

Americans' first national government reflected their fears of centralized authority. In 1776, John Dickinson drafted a proposal for a national government, and in 1777, Congress sent a weakened version of this document, the **Articles of Confederation,** to the states for ratification. However, not until February 1781—six months before the American victory at Yorktown—did the last state, Maryland, agree to ratification.

Articles of Confederation First American national government; all power held by states

The Articles of Confederation explicitly reserved to each state—and not to the national government—"its sovereignty, freedom and independence." The "United States of America" was no more than "a firm league of friendship" among sovereign states, much like today's European Union. As John Adams later explained, Congress never thought of "consolidating this vast Continent under one national Government" but instead erected "a Confederacy of States, each of which must have a separate government."

Under the Articles, the national government consisted of a single-chamber Congress, elected by the state legislatures, in which each state had one vote. Congress could request funds from the states but could not tax without every state's approval, nor could it regulate interstate or overseas commerce. The Articles provided for no executive branch. Rather, congressional committees oversaw financial, diplomatic, and military affairs. Nor was there a judicial system by which the national government could compel allegiance to its laws. The Articles did eliminate all barriers to interstate travel and trade, and guaranteed that all states would recognize one another's judicial decisions.

Finance, Trade, and the Economy, 1781–1786

Perhaps the greatest challenge facing the Confederation was putting the nation on a sound financial footing. Winning the war cost $160 million, far more than taxation could raise. The government borrowed from abroad and printed paper money, called continentals. But from 1776 to 1781 lack of public faith in the government destroyed 98 percent of the continentals' value, creating an inflationary disaster. Congress turned to Robert Morris, a wealthy Philadelphia merchant who became the nation's superintendent of finance in 1781. Morris proposed a national import duty of 5 percent to finance the congressional budget and to guarantee interest payments on the war debt, but the duty failed to pass because one state, Rhode Island, rejected it.

Meanwhile, seeing themselves as sovereign, most states had assumed some responsibility for the war debt and begun compensating veterans and creditors within their borders. But Morris and other nationally minded elites insisted that the United States needed sources of revenue independent of the states. Hoping to panic the country into seeing things their way, Morris and New York congressman Alexander Hamilton engineered a dangerous gamble known later as the **Newburgh Conspiracy.** In 1783, the two men secretly persuaded some army officers, encamped at Newburgh, New York, to threaten a coup d'état unless the treasury obtained the taxation authority necessary to raise funds for their pay, which was months late. George Washington forestalled the conspiracy by appealing to his officers' honor.

Newburgh Conspiracy Threatened mutiny that showed how deeply some were concerned about the weakness of the national government

When peace came in 1783, Morris found it impossible to fund the government adequately. After New York blocked another congressional tax measure sent to the states, state contributions to Congress fell steadily. By the late 1780s the states lagged 80 percent behind in providing the funds that Congress requested.

Nor did the Confederation succeed in prying trade concessions from Britain. The continuation after the war of British trade prohibitions contributed to an economic depression that gripped New England beginning in 1784. A short growing season and poor soil kept yields so low, even in the best of times, that farmers barely produced enough grain for local consumption. New Englanders also faced high taxes to repay the money borrowed to finance the Revolution. Economic depression and overpopulation only aggravated the region's miseries.

Meanwhile, southern planters faced frustration at the failure of their principal crops, tobacco and rice, to return to prewar export levels. Whereas nearly two-thirds of American exports originated in the South in 1770, less than half were produced by southern states in 1790. As a result they were left with thousands of underemployed slave laborers. The mid-Atlantic states, on the other hand, were less dependent on British-controlled markets for their exports. As famine stalked Europe, farmers in Pennsylvania and New York prospered from climbing export prices. By 1788, the region had largely recovered from the Revolution's ravages.

The Confederation and the West, 1785–1787

The postwar settlement and administration of western lands posed another formidable challenge to the new government. Settlers and speculators were determined to possess these lands, and Native Americans were equally determined to keep them out. At the same time, Britain and Spain sought to contain the new nation's territorial expansion.

After the states surrendered claims to more than 160 million acres north of the Ohio River, Congress established procedures for surveying this land in the Ordinance of 1785. Subsequently, in the **Northwest Ordinance** (1787), Congress defined the steps for the creation and admission of new states. This law designated

Northwest Ordinance Law that provided for creating new states the area north of the Ohio River as the Northwest Territory and provided for its later division into states. It forbade slavery while the region remained a territory, although the citizens could legalize the institution after statehood.

The Northwest Ordinance outlined three stages for admitting states into the Union. First, during the initial years of settlement, Congress would appoint a territorial governor and judges. Second, as soon as five thousand adult males lived in a territory, voters would approve a territorial constitution and elect a legislature. Third, when the total population reached sixty thousand, voters would ratify a state constitution, which Congress would have to approve before granting statehood.

The most significant achievements of the Confederation, the Ordinance of 1785 and Northwest Ordinance, had lasting effects. Besides laying out procedures for settling and establishing governments in the Northwest, they later served as models for organizing territories farther west. The Northwest Ordinance also established a significant precedent for banning slavery from certain territories.

The Northwest Territory seemed to offer enough land to guarantee property to American citizens for centuries. This fact satisfied republicans like Thomas Jefferson who feared that the rapidly growing white population would quickly exhaust available land east of the Appalachians and so create a large class of landless poor who could not vote.

However, the realization of these expansionist dreams was by no means inevitable. Most "available" territory from the Appalachians to the Mississippi River belonged to those peoples whom the Declaration of Independence had condemned as "merciless Indian savages." Divided into more than eighty tribes and numbering perhaps 150,000 people in 1789, Native Americans were struggling to preserve their own independence.

At postwar treaty negotiations, U.S. commissioners told Native Americans, "You are a subdued people. . . . We claim the country by conquest." Under threat of continued warfare, some Indian leaders initially yielded. Through treaties the Iroquois lost about half their land in New York and Pennsylvania, and the Delawares and Shawnees were obliged to recognize American sovereignty over their lands. But most Indians repudiated the treaties, denying that their negotiators had the authority to give up their nations' lands.

The Indians' resistance also stemmed from their confidence that the British would provide the arms necessary to defy the Americans. Britain had refused to abandon seven forts along the nation's northwestern frontier, ostensibly because Tories remained uncompensated for property losses. In April 1784 the British colonial office secretly ordered Canada's governor to hold onto the forts, hoping to reestablish Britain's claim to the Northwest Territory.

The Mohawk Joseph Brant initially sought to lead Indian resistance to white settlements. Courageous, skilled in

Fenimore Art Museum, Cooperstown, New York

Joseph Brant, by Gilbert Stuart, 1786

The youthful Mohawk leader was a staunch ally of the British during the Revolutionary War, and thereafter resisted U.S. expansion in the Northwest.

diplomacy, and well educated, he organized the northwestern Indians into a military alliance in 1786 to keep out white settlers. But Brant and his followers, who had relocated beyond American reach in Canada, could not win support from Native Americans on U.S. soil. Militia raids launched by Kentuckians and others gradually forced the Indian evacuation of southern Indiana and Ohio. In spring 1788, some fifty New Englanders sailed down the Ohio River in a bulletproof barge named the *Mayflower* to found the town of Marietta. A few months later a second group of latter-day pilgrims established a settlement on the Ohio at the site of modern Cincinnati.

Alexander McGillivray Creek leader determined to retain his people's territory

The Confederation faced similar problems in the Southeast, where Spain and its Indian allies worked to block American encroachment on their land. The Spanish found an ally in the shrewd Creek leader **Alexander McGillivray,** who was determined to regain Creek territory held by Georgia. McGillivray negotiated a secret treaty with Spain that promised the Creeks weapons to protect themselves "from the Bears and other fierce Animals." In 1786, after Creeks expelled occupants of the disputed lands, Georgia quickly accepted McGillivray's offer of a cease-fire.

Spain also attempted to prevent American infiltration by denying western settlers permission to ship crops down the Mississippi River to New Orleans. In 1784, the Spanish closed New Orleans to American commerce. Spain and the United States negotiated the Jay-Gardoqui Treaty (1786), which opened Spanish markets to American merchants and renounced Spanish claims to disputed lands—at the cost, however, of postponing American exporters' access to New Orleans for another twenty years. Westerners and southerners charged that the treaty sacrificed their interests to benefit northern commerce, and Congress rejected it.

Unable to prevent American settlers from occupying territory it claimed in the Southeast, Spain sought to win the newcomers' allegiance through bribes and offers of citizenship. Some settlers began talking openly of secession. As young Andrew Jackson (the future president) concluded in 1789, making some arrangements with the Spanish seemed "the only immediate way to obtain peace with the Savage [Indians]."

CHECKING IN

- Individual states, in drafting their state constitutions, served as workshops for the creation of new republican forms of government.
- Americans made their first national government under the Articles of Confederation deliberately weak, leaving most power to the states.
- National finances remained shaky, but prosperity returned quickly to the mid-Atlantic.
- The Ordinance of 1785 and Northwest Ordinance represented the new government's major accomplishments.
- Indian resistance and Spain's closing of the port of New Orleans hampered Americans' movement westward.

TOWARD A NEW CONSTITUTION, 1786–1788

What were the principal issues dividing proponents and opponents of the new federal Constitution?

Despite the United States' enormous strides in establishing itself as an independent nation, impatience with the national government's limitations continued to grow among those seeking to establish the republic on a more solid economic and military footing. Impatience became anxiety when protesting Massachusetts farmers defied local authorities and threatened to march on Boston. A national convention called to consider amendments to the Articles of Confederation instead created a radical new frame of government, the Constitution. In 1788, the states ratified the Constitution, setting a bold new course for America.

Shays's Rebellion, 1786–1787

The depression that had begun in 1784 persisted in New England, which had never recovered from the loss of its prime export market in the British West Indies. With farmers already squeezed financially, the state legislature, dominated by commercially minded elites, voted early in 1786 to pay off its Revolutionary War debt in three years. This ill-considered policy necessitated a huge tax hike. Meanwhile, the state's unfavorable balance of payments with Britain had produced a shortage of specie (gold and silver coin) because British creditors refused any other currency. Lowest in this cycle of debt were thousands of small family farmers.

The plight of small farmers was especially severe in western Massachusetts, where agriculture was least profitable. Facing demands that they pay their debts and taxes in hard currency, which few of them had, farmers held public meetings in which they denounced their own "tyrannical government." Farmers led by Daniel Shays in 1786 shut down the courts in five counties. Then in January 1787, they marched on a federal arsenal at Springfield, Massachusetts. But troops, funded by Boston elites to quell the uprising, reached the arsenal first and beat back the rebels. Thereafter, the troops scattered or routed bands of insurgents. Although the movement was defeated militarily, sympathizers of Shays won control of the Massachusetts legislature in elections later that year. They went on to cut taxes and secured a pardon for their leader.

Although **Shays's Rebellion** caused little bloodshed and never raised a serious threat of anarchy, critics of the Confederation painted it and similar, less radical movements elsewhere as a taste of the disorder to come under the weak national government. By threatening to seize weapons from a federal arsenal, the Shaysites unintentionally enabled nationalists to argue that the United States had become vulnerable to "mobocracy."

Shays's Rebellion Uprising by Massachusetts farmers that convinced many Americans their government was too weak

Instead of igniting an uprising from below, as Washington feared, Shays's Rebellion sparked elite nationalists into action from above. Shortly before the outbreak of the rebellion, delegates from five states had assembled at Annapolis, Maryland. They had intended to discuss means of promoting interstate commerce but instead called for a general convention to propose amendments to the Articles of Confederation. Accepting their suggestion, Congress asked the states to appoint delegations to meet in Philadelphia.

The Philadelphia Convention, 1787

In May 1787, fifty-five delegates, coming from every state but Rhode Island, began gathering at the Pennsylvania State House in Philadelphia, later known as Independence Hall. Among them were established figures like George Washington and Benjamin Franklin, as well as talented newcomers such as Alexander Hamilton and James Madison. Most were wealthy and in their thirties or forties, and nineteen owned slaves. More than half had legal training.

The convention immediately closed its sessions to the press and the public, kept no official journal, and even monitored the aged and talkative Franklin at dinner parties lest he disclose details of its discussions. Although these measures opened the convention to charges of being undemocratic, the delegates preferred secrecy to minimize public pressure on their debates.

Picture Research Consultants & Archives

Independence Hall, Philadelphia, 1776
While the Continental Congress deliberated inside on the grave issues of the day, city residents outside carried on with their everyday lives.

The delegates shared a "nationalist" perspective, instilled through their extended involvement with the national government. Thirty-nine had sat in Congress, where they had seen the Confederation's limitations firsthand. In the postwar years, they had become convinced that unless the national government was freed from the control of state legislatures, the country would disintegrate. Most were prepared to replace the Articles altogether with a new constitution that gave more power to the national government.

Virginia Plan Madison's blueprint for a new national government; favored large states

The first debate among the delegates concerned the conflicting interests of large and small states. James Madison's **Virginia Plan** boldly called for a national government rather than a confederation of states. It gave Congress virtually unrestricted powers to legislate, levy taxes, veto state laws, and authorize military force against the states. The Virginia Plan specified a bicameral legislature and made representation in both houses of Congress proportional to each state's population. The houses would jointly name the country's president and judges. But opposition to Madison's plan surfaced immediately, particularly to his call for proportional representation, which favored Virginia, the largest state. On June 15, William Paterson of New Jersey offered a counterproposal, the **New Jersey Plan.** It featured a unicameral legislature in which each state had one vote, just as under the Articles.

New Jersey Plan Counterproposal to Virginia Plan that favored small states

The two plans exposed the convention's great stumbling block: the question of representation. The Virginia Plan gave the four largest states—Virginia, Massachusetts, New York, and Pennsylvania—a majority in both houses. The New Jersey Plan allowed the seven smallest states, with only 25 percent of the U.S. population, to control Congress. By early July the convention was stalemated. To end the impasse, the delegates appointed a "grand committee" dedicated to compromise. This panel adopted a proposal by the Connecticut delegation: an equal vote for each state in the upper house and proportional representation in the lower house. The convention accepted the compromise on July 17 and in two months overcame the remaining hurdles.

As finally approved on September 17, 1787, the Constitution of the United States was an extraordinary document. In addition to reconciling the interests of large and small states, it balanced the delegates' desire for a strong national government against their fear of tyranny and interference with the states' sovereignty. It increased national authority in several ways. It vested in Congress the authority to levy and collect taxes, to regulate interstate commerce, and to conduct diplomacy. Under the Constitution, all acts and treaties of the United States would become "the supreme law of the land." State officials would have to uphold the Constitution, even against acts of their own state. The national government could use military force against any state.

The Constitution's Framers restrained the new national government in two key ways. First, they established a **separation of powers** among the three distinct branches within the government—the legislative, the executive, and the judicial. Second, they designed a system of checks and balances to prevent one branch from dominating the others. States' equal representation in the Senate offset proportional representation by population in the House, and each chamber could block measures passed by the other. Further, the president could veto acts of Congress, but to prevent capricious use of the presidential veto, a two-thirds majority in each house could override a veto. The president would conduct diplomacy, but only the Senate could ratify treaties. The president appointed his cabinet, but only with Senate approval. Congress could, by joint vote, remove the president and his appointees from office, but only for "high crimes," not for political disagreements.

separation of powers The establishment of three distinct branches of government

To further guarantee the independence of each branch, the Constitution provided that the members of one branch would not choose those of another, except judges, whose independence was protected by lifetime appointments. For example, the president was to be selected by electors, whom the states would select as their legislatures saw fit. The number of electors in each state would equal the number of its senators and representatives. State legislatures would also elect senators, whereas popular vote would determine delegates to the House of Representatives.

In addition to checks and balances, the Constitution embodied a form of federalism—a system of shared power and dual lawmaking by the state and national governments—to limit central authority. Not only did the state legislatures have a key role in electing the president and senators, but the Constitution could be amended by the votes of three-fourths of the state legislatures. Federalism assumed that the national government would limit its activities to foreign affairs, national defense, regulation of commerce, and coining of money. Most other political matters were left to the states. The states could otherwise act autonomously on purely internal matters, including slavery.

The dilemma confronting the Philadelphia convention centered not on whether slavery would be allowed but only on the much narrower question of whether slaves should be counted as persons when it came to determining a state's representation at the national level. For most legal purposes, slaves were regarded not as persons but rather as the chattel property of their owners. But southern states saw their large numbers of slaves as a means of augmenting their numbers in the House of Representatives and in the Electoral College. So strengthened, they hoped to prevent northerners from ever abolishing slavery.

"three-fifths clause" Provided that three-fifths of slaves were to be counted in determining congressional representation

Representing states that had begun ending slavery, northern delegates opposed giving southern states a political advantage. But after Georgia and South Carolina threatened to secede if their demands were not met, northerners agreed to the **"three-fifths clause,"** allowing three-fifths of all slaves to be counted for congressional representation and, thereby, in the Electoral College. The Constitution also reinforced slavery in other ways. It forbade citizens of any state, even those that had abolished slavery, to prevent the return of escaped slaves to another state. And it prohibited Congress from banning the importation of slaves until 1808. The Constitution limited slavery only in one respect—it maintained Congress's earlier ban on slavery in the Northwest Territory.

ratification Approval by state conventions of new federal Constitution

Although leaving much authority to the states, the Constitution established a national government clearly superior to the states in several spheres and abandoned the notion of a confederation of virtually independent states. Having thus strengthened national authority, the convention faced the issue of **ratification.** Two factors argued against submitting the Constitution to the state legislatures for ratification. First, the state legislatures would probably reject the Constitution, which shrank their power relative to that of the national government. Second, most of the Framers believed that the government had to rest on the consent of the American people themselves. The Constitution's opening words—"We the people of the United States"—embodied this view. In the end, the Philadelphia Convention provided for ratification by special state conventions composed of delegates elected by the people. Approval by nine such conventions would enable the new government to operate.

Under the Constitution, the Framers expected the nation's elites to continue exercising political leadership. Seeking to rein in the democratic currents set in motion by the Revolution, they curtailed what they considered the excessive power of popularly elected state legislatures. And while they located sovereignty in the people rather than in the states, they provided for an Electoral College that would actually elect the president. The Framers did provide for one crucial democratic element in the new government—the House of Representatives. Moreover, by making the Constitution amendable, and by dividing political power among competing branches of government, the Framers made it possible for the national government to be slowly democratized, in ways unforeseen in 1787.

The Struggle over Ratification, 1787–1788

At first the Constitution had little national support. Many Americans hesitated to accept the idea of a radically restructured government. To quiet fears of centralized national authority, the Constitution's supporters shrewdly dubbed themselves **Federalists,** a term implying that the Constitution successfully balanced the relationship between state and national governments.

Federalists Name supporters of the new Constitution gave themselves during the ratification struggle

The Constitution's opponents became known as Antifederalists. This negative-sounding title probably hurt them, for it did not convey the crux of their argument against the Constitution—that it was not "federalist" at all since it failed to balance the power of the national and state governments. By augmenting national authority, Antifederalists maintained, the Constitution would ultimately doom the states and the people's liberty.

Antifederalist arguments reflected the deep-seated Anglo-American suspicion of any concentration of power, a suspicion that had driven events from the Stamp Act Congress through the War of Independence and the early years of the new republic. Unquestionably, the Constitution gave the national government unprecedented authority in an age when most writers on politics agreed that the sole means of preventing despotism was restraining the power of government officials. Distant from the people, especially in an era when news traveled slowly, the national government would be far less responsive to the popular will than state governments would be. Furthermore, no one could be sure that the untried scheme of checks and balances would work. And the Constitution contained no guarantees that the new government would protect the liberties of individuals or the states. The absence of a bill of rights prompted Madison's nationalist ally and fellow Virginian George Mason, the author of the first state bill of rights in 1776, to oppose the Constitution.

The Antifederalists confronted several major disadvantages. While Antifederalist ranks included some prominent figures, none had the stature of George Washington or Benjamin Franklin. In addition, most newspapers were Federalist and did not hesitate to bias their reporting in favor of ratification. Finally, the Antifederalists, largely drawn from state and local leaders, lacked their opponents' contacts and experience at the national level. Ultimately, however, Federalist superiority in funds and political organizing proved decisive. The Antifederalists failed to create a sense of urgency among their supporters, assuming incorrectly that a large majority would rally to them. Only one-quarter of the voters turned out to elect delegates to the state ratifying conventions, and most had been mobilized by Federalists.

The Constitution became the law of the land when the ninth state, New Hampshire, ratified it on June 21, 1788. Federalist delegates prevailed in seven of the first nine state conventions by margins of at least two-thirds. Such lopsided votes reflected the Federalists' organizational skills rather than the degree of popular support for the Constitution. The Constitution's advocates rammed through approval in some states "before it can be digested or deliberately considered," in the words of a Pennsylvania Antifederalist.

However, unless the large states of Virginia and New York ratified, the new government would be unworkable. Antifederalism ran high in both states, especially among small farmers, who believed that the Constitution favored city dwellers and moneyed interests. Prominent Antifederalists included New York's Governor George Clinton and Virginia's Richard Henry Lee, George Mason, Patrick Henry, and future president James Monroe.

At Virginia's convention, Federalists won crucial support from the representatives of the western counties who wanted a strong national government capable

Map 6.4 Federalist and Antifederalist Strongholds, 1787–1790

Federalists drew their primary backing from densely populated areas, whereas Antifederalist support was strongest among small farmers in interior regions. However, some westerners advocated a strong central government that would push back Native Americans.

Interactive Map

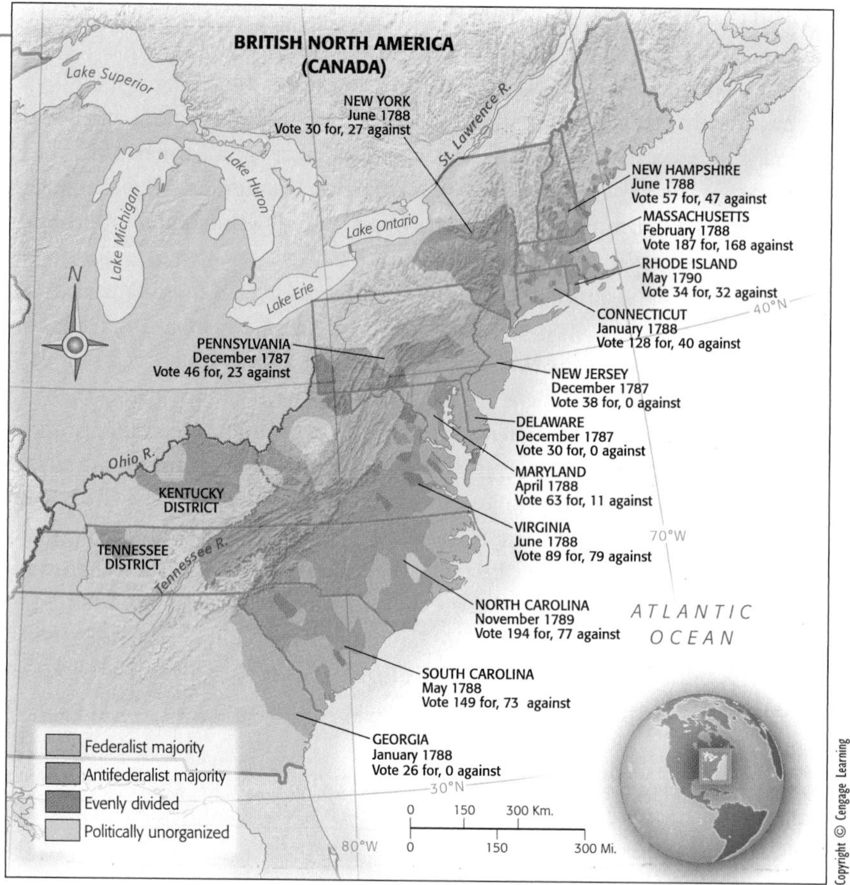

CHECKING IN

- For many, Shays's Rebellion catalyzed fears that the national government was too weak.
- The delegates to the Philadelphia Convention struggled to balance the interests of the large and small states while creating a sufficiently strong national government.
- The Constitution created a new framework, federalism, allowing shared power between state and national governments, and embodied the separation of powers and checks and balances as ways to protect against tyranny.
- Ratification of the Constitution was won, but not automatically, with Antifederalists voicing loud opposition.
- The ratification struggle left an important legacy in *The Federalist* papers, which helped shape the American philosophy of government.

of ending Indian raids. Western Virginians' votes, combined with James Madison's leadership among tidewater planters, proved too much for Henry's spellbinding oratory. On June 25, the Virginia delegates ratified by a narrow 53 percent majority. The struggle was even hotter in New York. Antifederalists controlled the state convention and probably would have voted down the Constitution had not news arrived of New Hampshire's and Virginia's ratification. Federalist leaders Alexander Hamilton and John Jay spread rumors that if the convention failed to ratify, pro-Federalist New York City and adjacent counties would secede from the state and join the Union alone, leaving upstate New York a landlocked enclave. Alarmed, several Antifederalist delegates switched sides, and on July 26 New York ratified by a 30-to-27 vote.

In the end, the Antifederalists went down in defeat, and they did not survive as a political movement. Yet their influence was lasting. At their insistence, the Virginia, New York, and Massachusetts conventions approved the Constitution with the accompanying request that it be amended to include a bill of rights protecting Americans' basic freedoms.

Antifederalists' objections in New York also stimulated a response in the form of one of the great classics of political thought, ***The Federalist,*** a series of eighty-five newspaper essays penned by Alexander Hamilton, James Madison, and John Jay. Although *The Federalist* papers, as they are commonly termed, did little to influence the New York vote, they provided a glimpse of the Framers' intentions in designing the Constitution and thus powerfully shaped the American philosophy of government. The Constitution, insisted *The Federalist's* authors, had two main purposes: to defend minority rights against majority tyranny and to prevent a stubborn minority from blocking measures necessary for the national interest. In the most profound essay in the series, Federalist No. 10, Madison argued that the nation's size and diversity would neutralize the attempts of factions to steer unwise laws through Congress.

The Federalist Series of essays, known commonly as the Federalist Papers, designed to explain the new Constitution and convince people to support it

Madison's analysis was far too optimistic, however. The Constitution afforded enormous scope for special interests to influence government. The great challenge for Madison's generation would be maintaining a government that provided equal benefits to all, but special privileges to none.

Chapter Summary

What factors enabled the Americans to defeat the British in the American Revolution? (page 120)

Although the British enjoyed huge advantages in military preparedness and manpower at the war's start, their supply lines were long and their population was tax-weary. The colonists eventually forged a professional army and defeated them. The most important key to American victory was George Washington's leadership, especially his determination to continue to fight.

How did the war unfold? (page 123)

Initially, the Continental Army suffered several defeats. Saratoga was the turning point of the war, because the colonial victory there convinced the French to support the Revolution with money, men, and ships. Once other nations joined the anti-British cause, making the Revolution an international war, the tide turned. Now fatally overextended, Britain was defeated by American-French forces at Yorktown and obliged to surrender.

How did the war affect relationships among Americans of different classes, races, and genders? (page 129)

Most wars bring major social changes; the Revolution was no exception. By war's end, white males enjoyed considerably more equality, slavery was clearly being rejected in the northern states, and women had played a significant public role. However, the war only worsened the position of Native Americans.

Key Terms

loyalist *(p. 120)*
Joseph Brant *(p. 121)*
Battle of Trenton *(p. 123)*
Battle of Saratoga *(p. 124)*
Lord Charles Cornwallis *(p. 127)*
Abigail Adams *(p. 131)*
antislavery movement *(p. 132)*
republicanism *(p. 134)*
Articles of Confederation *(p. 135)*
Newburgh Conspiracy *(p. 136)*
Northwest Ordinance *(p. 136)*
Alexander McGillivray *(p. 138)*
Shays's Rebellion *(p. 139)*
Virginia Plan *(p. 140)*
New Jersey Plan *(p. 141)*
separation of powers *(p. 141)*
"three-fifths clause" *(p. 142)*
ratification *(p. 142)*
Federalists *(p. 143)*
The Federalist *(p. 145)*

What political concerns were reflected in the first state constitutions and Articles of Confederation? (page 133)

In creating their constitutions, the new states served as workshops for experimenting with various forms of republican government. At the national level the Articles of Confederation created a weak government that almost immediately faced tremendous economic and diplomatic problems. Over time, elites favoring stronger executive power gained support for a plan to replace the Articles of Confederation with the new federal Constitution. A failed experiment in general, the Articles succeeded in formulating the Northwest Ordinance, a blueprint for future expansion.

What were the principal issues dividing proponents and opponents of the new federal Constitution? (page 138)

The new Constitution represented the triumph of nationalism and provided a strong central government, although its framework of federalism seemed to leave considerable power in the hands of the states. Its ratification was far from assured, but it enjoyed the support of respected men such as Franklin, Jefferson, and Washington; in the end, the Federalists achieved ratification. An important legacy of the struggle for ratification was *The Federalist* papers, which laid a foundation for an American philosophy of government.

Go to the CourseMate website at **www.cengagebrain.com** for additional study tools and review materials—including audio and video clips—for this chapter.

CHAPTER 7

Launching the New Republic 1788–1800

Terra Foundation for American Art, Chicago / Art Resource, NY

Judith Sargent Stevens (Murray) by John Singleton Copley, circa 1770

CHAPTER PREVIEW

Constitutional Government Takes Shape, 1788–1796
What role did George Washington play in translating the Constitution from words into government?

Hamilton's Domestic Policies, 1789–1794
Which points in Hamilton's economic program were most controversial and why?

The United States in a Wider World, 1789–1796
How did the new nation deal with France, Spain, and Britain?

Parties and Politics, 1793–1800
What principal issues divided Federalists and Republicans in the election of 1800?

Economic and Social Change
On what basis were some Americans denied full equality by 1800?

For most Americans, the 1790s was a decade marked by political and economic transformation. But Nancy Ward, a Cherokee Indian, had less reason to be optimistic. Born in about 1738, she became a "War Woman" in 1755 when, after attacking Creeks killed her husband, she picked up his gun and helped drive them off. As a War Woman, Ward not only participated in combat but conducted diplomacy and occasionally released war captives.

When the American Revolution broke out, the Cherokees were hopelessly divided. Ward and other leaders urged the Cherokees to avoid war and negotiate. Ward helped persuade the Americans not to take additional Cherokee land. But after the war ended,

U.S. treaty commissioners pressured the Cherokees in 1783 and 1785 to cede another eight thousand square miles. However, Ward continued to urge Cherokee resisters to make peace—not because she embraced the new republic, but because she recognized that resistance to its military power was futile.

Since the 1750s, the Cherokees had lost nearly half of their population and more than half of their land. During the same period, the former colonies had grown from just under 2 million people to over 5 million, 90 percent of whom lived and worked on the land. These farmers equated the ownership of land with liberty and political rights, and considered Native Americans like Ward an obstacle.

Besides holding common attitudes toward Native Americans, whites in 1789 successfully launched a new constitutional republic. But over the next decade, they became increasingly divided over the political and diplomatic course the United States should take. By 1798, voters had formed two parties, each viewing the other as a threat to liberty. Only when the election of 1800 had been settled—by the narrowest of margins—did it seem certain that the United States would endure.

CONSTITUTIONAL GOVERNMENT TAKES SHAPE, 1788–1796

What role did George Washington play in translating the Constitution from words into government?

Given the social and political divisions among Americans, compounded by their fears of centralized authority, success at implementing the new Constitution was anything but guaranteed. Would Americans accept the results of a national election? Would the three branches of the new government function effectively? Would a Bill of Rights, which several states had made a condition of ratification, amend the Constitution?

Implementing Government

The first order of business in putting the new government into practice was the election of a president and Congress. These first elections, in the fall of 1788, swept the Federalists into power with eighteen of twenty seats in the Senate and fifty-four of fifty-nine in the House. The Electoral College unanimously chose George Washington as the first president and John Adams as the vice president.

The choice of Washington was hardly a surprise. His leadership during the Revolutionary War and the Constitutional Convention had earned him a reputation as a national hero. Given his reputation, Washington was able to calm Americans' fears of presidential power.

Traveling slowly over the new nation's miserable roads, the men entrusted with launching the federal experiment assembled in New York, the new national capital, in March 1789. Washington did not arrive until April 23 and took his oath of office a week later.

The Constitution was vague about the executive departments, mentioning only in passing that the president must obtain the Senate's "advice and consent" to his nominees to head these bureaus. Otherwise, Congress was free to determine the organization and accountability of what became known as the cabinet, consisting of the secretaries of state, treasury, and war, as well as the attorney general and postmaster general. The Senate narrowly defeated a proposal to forbid the president from dismissing cabinet officers without its approval. This outcome strengthened the president's authority to make and carry out policy independently of congressional oversight, beyond what the Constitution required.

The Federal Judiciary and the Bill of Rights

The Constitution authorized Congress to establish federal courts below the level of the Supreme Court but provided no plan for their structure. In 1789 many citizens feared that federal courts would ride roughshod over local customs. In passing the **Judiciary Act** of 1789, Congress quieted popular apprehensions by establishing in each state a federal district court that operated according to local procedures. As the Constitution stipulated, the Supreme Court exercised final jurisdiction. Congress's compromise respected state traditions while offering wide access to federal justice.

Judiciary Act Established federal court system in 1789

The Constitution offered some protection of citizens' individual rights. It barred Congress from passing *ex post facto* laws (criminalizing previously legal actions) and bills of attainder (punishment without a trial). Nevertheless, the absence of a comprehensive bill of rights had prompted several delegates at Philadelphia to refuse to

Chronology

1788	First elections under the Constitution
1789	First Congress convenes in New York; George Washington sworn in as first president; Judiciary Act; French Revolution begins
1790	Alexander Hamilton submits his Reports on Public Credit and National Bank to Congress; Treaty of New York
1791	Bank of the United States granted a twenty-year charter; Bill of Rights ratified; slave uprising begins in French colony of Saint-Domingue
1792	Washington reelected president
1793	Fugitive Slave Law; France at war with Britain and Spain; Citizen Genêt arrives in the United States; first Democratic societies established
1794	Whiskey Rebellion; Battle of Fallen Timbers
1795	Treaty of Greenville; Jay's Treaty
1796	Treaty of San Lorenzo; Washington's Farewell Address; John Adams elected president
1798	XYZ Affair; Alien and Sedition Acts; Eleventh Amendment to the Constitution ratified
1798–1799	Virginia and Kentucky Resolutions
1798–1800	Quasi-War between United States and France
1800	Gabriel's rebellion in Virginia; Thomas Jefferson elected president

CHECKING IN

- Americans remained suspicious of executive power, and thus of the presidency.
- George Washington was unanimously chosen president by the first Electoral College.
- Although the Constitution did not spell out the organization of the executive branch, Washington named five department heads who formed his first cabinet.
- The Judiciary Act of 1789 helped allay state fears concerning federal courts.
- The Bill of Rights guaranteed personal liberties.

sign the Constitution. From the House of Representatives, James Madison led the drafting of the ten amendments that became known as the **Bill of Rights.**

The First Amendment safeguarded the most fundamental freedoms of expression—religion, speech, press, and political activity. The Second Amendment ensured that "a well-regulated militia" would preserve the nation's security by guaranteeing "the right of the people to bear arms." Like the Third Amendment, it sought to protect citizens from what Americans saw as the most sinister embodiment of tyranny: standing armies. The Fourth through Eighth Amendments limited the police powers of the states by guaranteeing individuals fair treatment in legal and judicial proceedings. The Ninth and Tenth Amendments reserved to the people or to the states powers not allocated to the federal government. In general, the Bill of Rights imposed no serious check on the Framers' nationalist objectives. The ten amendments were submitted to the states and ratified by December 1791.

Bill of Rights First ten amendments to the Constitution; guaranteed personal liberties

HAMILTON'S DOMESTIC POLICIES, 1789–1794

Which points in Hamilton's economic program were most controversial and why?

Alexander Hamilton Washington's chief adviser; architect of major plans for American future

Washington's reluctance to become involved with legislation enabled Secretary of the Treasury **Alexander Hamilton** to set domestic priorities. Hamilton emerged as an imaginative and dynamic statesman by formulating a sweeping program to strengthen the federal government and promote national economic development. While Hamilton succeeded in pushing his proposals through Congress, the controversies surrounding them undermined popular support for Federalist policies.

Establishing the Nation's Credit

In Hamilton's mind, the most immediate danger facing the United States concerned the possibility of war with Britain, Spain, or both. The republic could finance a major war only by borrowing heavily, but because Congress under the Confederation had not assumed responsibility for the Revolutionary War debt, the nation's credit was weakened abroad and at home.

Reports on the Public Credit Hamilton's plan to ensure support for the new government by maintaining permanent debt

Responding to a request from Congress, Hamilton in January 1790 issued the first of two **Reports on the Public Credit.** It outlined a plan to strengthen the country's credit, enable it to defer paying its debt, and entice wealthy investors to place their capital at its service. The report listed $54 million in U.S. debt, $42 million of which was owed to Americans, and the rest to Europeans.

Hamilton recommended first that the federal government "fund" the $54 million national debt by selling an equal sum in new government bonds. Purchasers of these securities would choose from several combinations of federal "stock" and western lands. Those who wished could retain their original bonds and earn 4 percent interest. His report also proposed that the federal government pay off the $25 million in state debts remaining from the Revolution in the same manner.

George Washington's Inaugural Journey Through Trenton, 1789
Washington received a warm welcome in Trenton, site of his first victory during the Revolutionary War.

Hamilton exhorted the government to use the money earned by selling federal lands in the West to pay off the $12 million owed to Europeans as quickly as possible. In his Second Report on the Public Credit, submitted to Congress in December 1790, he argued that the Treasury could accumulate the interest owed on the remaining $42 million by collecting customs duties on imports and an excise tax (a tax on products made, sold, or transported within a nation's borders) on whiskey. In addition, Hamilton urged that the government not attempt to repay the $42 million principal but instead keep paying interest to bondholders. Under Hamilton's plan, the government could uphold the national credit at minimal expense, without ever paying off the debt itself.

Hamilton advocated a perpetual debt as a lasting means of uniting the economic fortunes of the nation's creditors to the United States. In an age when financial investments were notoriously risky, the federal government would protect the savings of wealthy bondholders while offering an interest rate competitive with the Bank of England's. Few other investments would entail so little risk.

Hamilton's recommendations provoked immediate controversy. Although no one in Congress doubted that they would enhance the country's fiscal reputation, many objected that those least deserving of reward would gain the most. The original owners of more than three-fifths of the debt certificates issued by the Continental

Congress were Revolutionary War patriots of modest means who had long before sold their certificates for a fraction of their promised value, usually out of dire financial need. Foreseeing that the government would fund the debt, wealthy speculators had bought the certificates and now stood to reap huge gains at the expense of the original owners.

To Hamilton's surprise, Madison—his longtime ally—emerged as a leading opponent of funding. Facing opposition to the plan in his home state of Virginia, Madison tried but failed to obtain compensation for original owners who had sold their certificates. Opposition to Hamilton's proposal that the federal government assume states' war debts also ran high. Only Massachusetts, Connecticut, and South Carolina had failed to make effective provisions for satisfying their creditors. The issue stirred the fiercest indignation in the South, which except for South Carolina had already paid off 83 percent of its debt. Madison and others maintained that to allow residents of the laggard states to escape heavy taxes was to reward irresponsibility.

Southern hostility almost defeated assumption. In the end, however, Hamilton saved his proposal by enlisting Secretary of State Thomas Jefferson's help. Jefferson and other Virginians favored moving the capital to the Potomac River, hoping to preserve Virginia's position as the largest, most influential state. In return for the northern votes necessary to transfer the capital, Hamilton secured enough Virginians' support to win the battle for assumption. Despite this concession, the debate over state debts confirmed many southerners' suspicions that northern commercial interests would benefit from Hamilton's policies at southerners' expense.

Congressional enactment in 1790 of Hamilton's recommendations dramatically reversed the nation's fiscal standing. European investors grew so enthusiastic about U.S. bonds that by 1792 some securities were selling at 10 percent above face value.

Creating a National Bank

Having significantly expanded the stock of capital available for investment, Hamilton intended to direct that money toward projects that would diversify the national economy through a federally chartered bank. Accordingly, in December 1790 he presented Congress with the **Report on a National Bank.**

Report on a National Bank Hamilton's proposal to create the Bank of the United States

The proposed Bank of the United States would raise $10 million through a public stock offering. Private investors could purchase shares by paying for three-quarters of their value in government bonds. In this way the bank would capture a substantial portion of the recently funded debt and make it available for loans; it would also receive steady interest payments from the treasury. Shareholders would profit handsomely.

Hamilton argued that the bank would cost taxpayers nothing and greatly benefit the nation. It would provide a safe place for federal deposits, make inexpensive loans to the government when taxes fell short, and relieve the scarcity of hard cash by issuing paper notes. Further, the bank would regulate the business of state banks and, above all, provide much-needed credit for economic expansion.

Hamilton's critics denounced the national bank as a dangerous scheme that gave a small elite special power to influence the government. These critics believed that the Bank of England had undermined the integrity of the government in Britain. Shareholders of the Bank of the United States could just as easily become tools of unscrupulous politicians. Members of Congress who owned bank stock would likely vote in support of the bank even at the cost of the national good.

Madison led the opposition to the bank in Congress, arguing that it was unconstitutional. Unless Congress closely followed the Constitution, he argued, the central government might oppress the states and trample on individual liberties, just as Parliament had done to the colonies. Strictly limiting federal power seemed the surest way of preventing the United States from degenerating into a corrupt despotism.

Congress approved the bank by only a thin margin. Dubious about its constitutionality, Washington asked Jefferson and Hamilton for advice. Like many southern planters whose investments in slaves left them short of capital and often in debt, Jefferson distrusted banking and did not want to extend government power beyond the letter of the Constitution. But Hamilton urged Washington to sign the bill. Because Article I, Section 8, of the Constitution specified that Congress could enact all measures "necessary and proper," Hamilton contended that the only unconstitutional activities were those *forbidden* to the national government. Washington accepted Hamilton's argument, and in February 1791 the Bank of the United States obtained a twenty-year charter. Washington's acceptance of a "loose interpretation" of the Constitution marked an important victory for advocates of an active, assertive national government. But the split between Jefferson and Hamilton, and Washington's siding with the latter, signaled a deepening political divide within the administration.

Emerging Partisanship

Hamilton built a political base by appealing to people's economic self-interest. His "rescue" of the national credit provided huge gains for speculators, merchants, and other urban "moneyed men" who by 1790 held most of the revolutionary debt. As holders of bank stock, these same groups had reason to use their prestige on behalf of national authority. Moreover, federal assumption of state debts liberated taxpayers from crushing burdens in New England, New Jersey, and South Carolina, while Hamilton's promotion of industry, commerce, and shipping won favor with the Northeast's budding entrepreneurs and hard-pressed artisans.

Opposition to Hamilton's program was strongest in sections of the country where it offered few benefits. Hamilton's plan offered little to the West and was especially detested in the South. Southern states had generally paid off their revolutionary debts, and few southerners still held revolutionary certificates. Moreover, the Bank of the United States had few southern stockholders. Resentment against eastern "moneyed men" and Yankees who refused to pay their debts united westerners, southerners, and some mid-Atlantic citizens into a political coalition. Challenging the Federalists, these opponents called for a return to true Republicanism.

With Hamilton presenting his measures as "Federalist," Jefferson, Madison, and their supporters began calling themselves "Republicans." They reached out to former Antifederalists whose ranks had been fatally weakened after the election of 1788. In 1791 they supported the establishment of an opposition newspaper, *The National Gazette.* The paper's editor, Philip Freneau, attacked Hamilton relentlessly, accusing him of trying to create an aristocracy and a monarchy in America.

Whiskey Rebellion, 1794

Rebels in Washington County, Pennsylvania, tar and feather a federal tax collector.

In response Hamilton, using pseudonyms, attacked Jefferson as an enemy of President Washington.

Although partisanship intensified as the election of 1792 approached, there was no organized political campaigning. Most voters saw organized factions, or parties, as inherently corrupt. The Constitution's Framers had neither wanted nor planned for political parties. In addition, Washington, by appearing to be above partisan disputes, remained supremely popular. Washington was unanimously chosen for a second term; by a fairly close margin, John Adams was again chosen vice president.

The Whiskey Rebellion

Whiskey Rebellion Tax protest by western farmers that gave Washington and Hamilton the opportunity to assert the power of national government

Hamilton's program not only sparked an angry congressional debate but also helped to ignite a civil insurrection in 1794 called the **Whiskey Rebellion.** Severely testing federal authority, this uprising posed the young republic's first serious crisis.

To augment national revenue, Hamilton had proposed an excise tax on domestically produced whiskey. He maintained that such a tax would not only distribute the expense of financing the national debt evenly but also improve morals by inducing Americans to drink less liquor. Although Congress passed Hamilton's program in March 1791, many doubted that Americans, who drank an average of six gallons of hard liquor per adult per year, would submit tamely to sobriety. James Jackson of Georgia, for example, warned the administration that his constituents "have long been in the habit of getting drunk and that they will get drunk in defiance of . . . all the excise duties which Congress might be weak or wicked enough to pass."

The validity of such doubts became apparent in September 1791 when a crowd tarred and feathered an excise tax agent near Pittsburgh. Western Pennsylvanians found the new tax especially burdensome. Unable to export crops through New Orleans, most local farmers distilled their rye or corn into alcohol, which could be carried across the Appalachians at a fraction of the price charged for bulkier grain.

Hamilton's excise tax equaled 25 percent of whiskey's retail value, enough to wipe out a farmer's profit.

The law also stipulated that trials for evading the tax would be conducted in federal courts. Any western Pennsylvanian indicted for noncompliance would have to travel three hundred miles to Philadelphia. Besides facing a jury of unsympathetic easterners, the accused would have to bear the cost of the long journey and lost earnings while at court, in addition to fines and other penalties if found guilty.

In a scene reminiscent of colonial protests against Britain, large-scale resistance erupted in July 1794. Roving bands torched buildings, assaulted tax collectors, and raised a flag symbolizing an independent country that they hoped to create from six western counties.

Echoing elites' denunciation of colonial protests, Hamilton blasted the rebellion as simple lawlessness. Washington concluded that a federal failure to respond strongly would encourage outbreaks in other frontier areas. The president accordingly mustered 12,900 militiamen to march west under his command, but opposition evaporated once the troops reached the Appalachians. The president left Hamilton in charge of making arrests. Of about 150 suspects seized, Hamilton sent twenty in irons to Philadelphia. Two men received death sentences, but Washington eventually pardoned them both.

The Whiskey Rebellion was a milestone in determining the limits of public opposition to federal policies. In the early 1790s, many Americans assumed that it was still legitimate to protest unpopular laws by using the methods that they had employed against British policies. By firmly suppressing the first major challenge to national authority, Washington served notice that citizens who resorted to violent means of political action would feel the full force of federal authority. In this way, he gave substance to elites' fears of "mobocracy," now resurfacing in reaction to the French Revolution.

CHECKING IN

- Alexander Hamilton proposed that the federal government assume and make permanent national and state debt from the revolutionary period.
- Hamilton proposed and achieved a national bank over the objections of Jefferson and Madison.
- Hamilton's opponents charged that his policies benefited eastern bankers and commercial interests at the expense of southern and western farmers.
- The Whiskey Rebellion gave Washington and Hamilton an opportunity to reinforce national authority.

THE UNITED STATES IN A WIDER WORLD, 1789–1796

How did the new nation deal with France, Spain, and Britain?

By 1793 disagreements over foreign affairs had become the primary source of friction in American public life. The division created by controversy over Hamilton's economic program hardened into ideologically oriented factions that disagreed vehemently over whether American foreign policy should favor industrial and mercantile interests or those of farmers, planters, and small businessmen. Complicating American policy making was the French Revolution, which had electrified all of Europe in 1789 and touched off a series of wars between France and its neighbors that would last until 1815.

As part of the Atlantic world, the United States could not avoid entanglement in these wars, despite the desire of most Americans to remain uninvolved. Thus, differences over foreign policy fused with differences over domestic affairs, further intensifying partisanship in American politics.

Spanish Power in Western North America

Spain enjoyed a brief resurgence of imperial success in the late eighteenth century. Stimulated by its acquisition of Louisiana, the Spanish built new presidios in northern Mexico, New Mexico, and Texas at which they stationed more troops and coordinated the actions of civilian and military authorities. By 1800 the Apaches, Navajos, and Comanches had agreed to cease their raids in New Mexico and Texas, but the success of the truce depended on Spain's ability to strengthen and broaden its imperial position in North America.

Spain's efforts in New Mexico and Texas were part of its larger effort to counter rivals for North American territory and influence. Russian fur traders had made substantial inroads along the Northwest Coast as early as the 1740s, and British and American traders followed in the 1780s. All three nations used American furs in the rapidly burgeoning and hugely profitable China trade, and their mounting influence threatened Spain's northwestern frontier.

"Alta California" Spanish colony on the Pacific coast, donated by missions

To counter these threats, Spain flung colonists and missionaries northward along the Pacific coast. However, efforts to encourage large-scale Mexican immigration to **"Alta California"** failed. The colony became a chain of religious missions, several presidios, and a few large ranches. Franciscan missionaries tried to convert coastal Indians to Catholicism and "civilize" them by imposing harsh discipline and putting them to work in vineyards and other enterprises. However, epidemic and venereal diseases carried by the Spanish raged among the native coastal tribes; between 1769 and 1830 the Indian population plummeted from about 72,000 to about 18,000.

Between New Mexico and California, Spain attempted to make alliances with Indians in the area later known as Arizona. In this way, Spain hoped to dominate North America between the Pacific and the Mississippi River. But resistance from the Hopi (HOE-pee), Yuma (YOU-muh), and other Native Americans thwarted these hopes.

Challenging American Expansion, 1789–1792

East of the Mississippi River, on the trans-Appalachian frontier, rivalries also multiplied. Spain, Britain, the United States, and Native Americans jockeyed for advantage in an area that all considered central to their interests.

Realizing that the United States was in no position to dictate developments immediately in the West, President Washington pursued a course of patient diplomacy that was intended "to preserve the country in peace if I can, and to be prepared for war if I cannot." The prospect of peace improved in 1789 when Spain unexpectedly opened New Orleans to American commerce. As a result, secessionist sentiment subsided.

In the 1790s the Spanish bribed many well-known political figures in Tennessee and Kentucky, including James Wilkinson, one of Washington's former generals. The admission of Vermont (1791), Kentucky (1792), and Tennessee (1796) as states was meant in part to strengthen their flickering loyalty to the Union.

Washington then moved to weaken Spanish influence in the West by neutralizing Spain's most important ally, the Creek Indians. The Creeks numbered more than twenty thousand, including perhaps five thousand warriors, and were fiercely hostile toward Georgian settlers, whom they called "the greedy people who want our lands." Under the terms of the 1790 Treaty of New York, American settlers could occupy the Georgia piedmont but not other Creek territory. Washington insisted that Georgia restore to the Chickasaws and Choctaws, Creek allies, a vast area along the Mississippi River that Georgia had already begun selling off to land speculators.

Washington adopted a harsher policy toward Native Americans who resisted efforts by American citizens to occupy the Ohio Valley. But two military campaigns, in 1790 and 1791, failed to force peace and cost the United States eleven hundred men. Matters worsened in 1792 when Spain persuaded the Creeks to renounce the Treaty of New York and resume hostilities. The damage done to U.S. prestige by these setbacks convinced many Americans that the combined strength of Britain, Spain, and the Native Americans could be counterbalanced only by an alliance with France.

France and Factional Politics, 1793

One of the most momentous events in history, the French Revolution, began in 1789. Many Americans watched sympathetically as the French abolished nobles' privileges, wrote a constitution, and repelled invading armies. In 1793, after becoming a republic, France proclaimed a war of all peoples against all kings and unleashed a "Reign of Terror," executing not only the king but also dissenting revolutionaries.

Americans were bitterly divided in their views of the French Revolution and how the United States should respond to it. Republicans such as Jefferson supported it as an assault on monarchy and tyranny. In contrast, Federalists like Hamilton denounced France as a "mobocracy" and supported Great Britain in resisting efforts to sow revolution abroad.

White southern slave owners were among France's fiercest supporters. In 1791 slaves in the French colony of Saint-Domingue (san doh-MIN-geh) rebelled against slavery and against French rule, a bloody uprising that took a heavy death toll among French planters and sent thousands fleeing to the United States. Fearful southern whites believed that the British had intentionally sparked the bloodshed and would do the same in the American South.

Many northerners, on the other hand, were more repelled by the bloodshed in revolutionary France. The revolution was "an open hell," thundered Massachusetts's Fisher Ames, "still smoking with sufferings and crimes." New England Protestants detested the French for worshiping Reason instead of God. Less religious Federalists condemned French leaders as evil radicals who incited the poor against the rich. Northern and southern reactions to the French Revolution also diverged for economic reasons. Merchants, shippers, and ordinary sailors in New England, Philadelphia, and New York feared that an alliance with France would provoke British retaliation against American commerce. They argued that the United States could win valuable concessions by demonstrating friendly intentions toward Britain.

Southerners had no such reasons to favor Britain. They perceived American reliance on British commerce as a menace to national self-determination, and they wished to divert most U.S. trade to France. Jefferson and Madison advocated reducing British imports through the imposition of steep duties. These recommendations threatened ties with Britain, which sold more manufactured goods to the

United States than to any other country. If Congress adopted trade retaliation, Hamilton predicted, "an open war between the United States and Great Britain" would result.

Pro-French feelings were also high in the western states, especially after France went to war against Spain and Great Britain in 1793. Westerners hoped that a French victory would remove Spanish and British roadblocks to expansion, put an end to Indian wars, and open the Mississippi for navigation.

After declaring war with Spain and Britain in 1793, France sought to embroil the United States in the conflict. France dispatched Edmond Genêt (zhe-NAY) as minister to the United States with orders to mobilize Republican sentiment in support of France and to enlist American mercenaries to conquer Spanish territories and attack British shipping. Much to France's disgust, President Washington issued a proclamation of neutrality on April 22, 1793.

Citizen Genêt French minister to the United States who ignored U.S. neutrality and recruited Americans to fight the British and Spanish

Meanwhile, defying Washington's proclamation, **Citizen Genêt** (as he was known in French revolutionary style) recruited volunteers for his American Foreign Legion. Making generals of George Rogers Clark of Kentucky and Elisha Clarke, Genêt ordered them to seize Spanish garrisons at New Orleans and St. Augustine. Genêt also contracted with American privateers. By the summer of 1793, almost a thousand Americans were at sea in a dozen ships flying the French flag. These privateers seized more than eighty British vessels. Refusing Secretary of State Jefferson's patient requests that he desist, Genêt threatened to urge Americans to defy their own government.

Diplomacy and War, 1793–1796

Although Washington swiftly closed the nation's harbors to Genêt's buccaneers, the episode provoked an Anglo-American crisis. Britain decided that only a massive show of force would deter American aggression. Thus, on November 6, 1793, Britain's Privy Council issued orders confiscating foreign ships trading with the French islands in the Caribbean. The orders were kept secret until most U.S. ships carrying winter provisions to the Caribbean left port so that their captains would not know that they were sailing into a war zone. The Royal Navy ultimately seized more than 250 U.S. ships.

Meanwhile, the U.S. merchant marine suffered another galling indignity—the drafting of its crewmen into the Royal Navy. Thousands of British sailors had fled to American ships looking for an easier life than the tough, poorly paying British system. In late 1793 British naval officers began inspecting American crews for British subjects, whom they then impressed (forcibly enlisted) as the king's sailors. Overzealous commanders sometimes exceeded orders by taking U.S. citizens—and in any case Britain did not recognize its former subjects' right to adopt American citizenship. Impressment struck a raw nerve in most Americans.

The British, along with the Spanish and Native Americans, also challenged the United States for control of the West. In February 1794, Canada's governor denied U.S. claims north of the Ohio River and urged Indians to destroy every white settlement in the Northwest. Britain soon erected an eighth garrison on U.S. soil, Fort Miami, near present-day Toledo, Ohio. That same year, Spain encroached on U.S. territory by building Fort San Fernando at what is now Memphis, Tennessee.

Hoping to halt the drift toward war, Washington launched a desperate diplomatic initiative, sending Chief Justice John Jay to Great Britain and Thomas

Pinckney to Spain. The president also authorized General Anthony Wayne to negotiate a treaty with the Indians of the Ohio Valley.

The Indians scoffed at Washington's peace offer until "Mad Anthony" Wayne led three thousand regulars and militiamen deep into their homeland, ravaging every village in reach. On August 20, 1794, Wayne's troops routed four hundred Shawnees at the Battle of Fallen Timbers, two miles from Britain's Fort Miami. In August 1795 Wayne compelled twelve Ohio Valley tribes to sign the Treaty of Greenville, which opened most of modern-day Ohio and a portion of Indiana to white settlement and temporarily ended Indian hostilities.

Wayne's success allowed John Jay a major diplomatic victory in London: a British promise to withdraw troops from American soil. Jay also gained American access to West Indian markets, but only by bargaining away U.S. rights to load cargoes of sugar, molasses, and coffee from the Caribbean.

Aside from fellow Federalists, few Americans would interpret **Jay's Treaty** as preserving peace with honor. Jay's Treaty left Britain free to violate American neutrality and to restrict U.S. trade with France. Moreover, Jay did not succeed in ending impressment and failed to gain compensation for slaves taken by the British during the Revolution. After the Senate barely ratified the treaty in 1795, Jay nervously joked that he could find his way across the country at night by the fires of rallies burning him in effigy.

Despite its unpopularity, Jay's Treaty prevented war with Britain and finally ended British occupation of U.S. territory. The treaty also helped stimulate an expansion of American trade. Upon its ratification, Britain permitted Americans to trade with its West Indian colonies and with India. American exports to the British Empire shot up 300 percent.

On the heels of Jay's Treaty came an unqualified diplomatic triumph engineered by Thomas Pinckney. Ratified in 1796, the 1795 **Treaty of San Lorenzo** (also called Pinckney's Treaty) with Spain gave westerners unrestricted, duty-free access to world markets via the Mississippi River. Spain also promised to recognize the thirty-first parallel as the United States' southern boundary, to dismantle all fortifications on American soil, and to discourage Indian attacks against western settlers.

By 1796 the Washington administration had defended the nation's territorial integrity, restored peace to the frontier, opened the Mississippi for western exports, reopened British markets to U.S. shipping, and kept the nation out of a European war. However, as the outcry over Jay's Treaty showed, foreign policy had left Americans far more divided in 1796 than in 1789.

Jay's Treaty Agreement that opened some British markets to Americans but otherwise accomplished little

Treaty of San Lorenzo Agreement that gave Americans access to the Mississippi and to the Gulf of Mexico via New Orleans

Checking In

- Spanish power enjoyed a brief resurgence in the 1790s, and Spain strengthened its position in the West and the Southeast.
- Washington countered Spanish expansion by neutralizing its Indian allies and making peace with other tribes.
- The French Revolution produced a deep split in American opinion.
- Citizen Genêt tried to embroil the United States in war against the British.
- Jay's Treaty stimulated American trade with the British Empire, and Pinckney's Treaty resolved many tensions with Spain.

Parties and Politics, 1793–1800

What principal issues divided Federalists and Republicans in the election of 1800?

By the time of Washington's reelection, controversies over domestic and foreign policy had led to the formation of two distinct political factions. During the president's second term, these factions became formal political parties, Federalists and Republicans, which waged a bitter battle culminating in the election of 1800.

Ideological Confrontation, 1793–1794

Conflicting attitudes about events in France, federal power, and democracy accelerated the polarization of American politics. Linking the French Revolution and the Whiskey Rebellion, Federalists trembled at the thought of guillotines and "mob rule." Citizen Genêt had openly encouraged opposition to the Washington administration, and had found hundreds of Americans willing to fight for France. Federalists worried that all of this was just the tip of a revolutionary iceberg.

By the mid-1790s Federalists' worst fears of democracy seemed to have been confirmed. The people, they believed, were undependable and vulnerable to rabble rousers such as Genêt. Federalists saw democracy as "government by the passions of the multitude" and argued that personal merits, not policy, should decide elections. Elected officials, they maintained, should rule in the people's name but be independent of direct popular influence.

Republicans offered a very different perspective on government and politics. They stressed the corruption inherent in a powerful government dominated by a highly visible few, and insisted that liberty would be safe only if power were widely diffused among white male property owners.

It might at first glance seem contradictory for southern slave owners to support a radical ideology like Republicanism, with its emphasis on liberty and equality. A few southern Republicans advocated abolishing slavery gradually, but most did not trouble themselves over their ownership of human beings. The liberty and equality they advocated were intended for white men only.

Political ambition drove men like Jefferson and Madison to rouse ordinary citizens' concerns about civic affairs. The awe in which Washington was held precluded open criticism of him or his policies. However, Jefferson, Madison, and other Republicans hoped to hold the Federalists accountable to a public that could remove them from office for misguided or unpopular policies.

Jefferson's increasing frustration prompted him to resign from Washington's cabinet in 1793, widening the political split. Each side saw itself as the guardian of republican virtue and the other as an illegitimate "cabal" or "faction." In 1793–1794 opponents of Federalist policies began organizing Democratic societies. They drew into their ranks planters, small farmers and merchants, artisans, distillers, and sailors; conspicuously absent were big businessmen, the clergy, the poor, nonwhites, and women.

The Republican Party, 1794–1796

In 1794, party development reached a decisive stage after Washington openly identified himself with Federalist policies. Republicans attacked the Federalists' pro-British leanings in many local elections and won a slight majority in the House of Representatives. The election signaled the Republicans' transformation from a coalition of officeholders and local societies to a broad-based party capable of coordinating local political campaigns throughout the nation.

Federalists and Republicans alike used the press to mold public opinion. American journalism came of age in the 1790s as the number of newspapers multiplied from 92 to 242. By 1800, newspapers had about 140,000 paid subscribers (roughly one-fifth of the eligible voters), and their secondhand readership probably exceeded 300,000. Newspapers of both camps cheerfully engaged in fear mongering and character assassination. Federalists accused Republicans of plotting a reign of terror and of conspiring to turn the nation over to France. Republicans charged Federalists with favoring a royal dynasty that would form when John Adams's daughter married George III. Despite the extreme rhetoric, newspaper warfare stimulated citizens to become politically active.

Washington grew impatient with the nation's growing polarization into openly hostile parties, and he deeply resented Republican charges that he secretly supported alleged Federalist plots to establish a monarchy. Lonely and surrounded by mediocre advisers after Hamilton returned to private life, Washington decided in the spring of 1796 to retire after two terms. Washington recalled Hamilton to write his Farewell Address.

The heart of Washington's message was a vigorous condemnation of political parties. Partisan alignments, he insisted, endangered the republic's survival, especially if they became entangled in foreign policy disputes. Aside from fulfilling existing treaty obligations and maintaining foreign commerce, the United States had to avoid "political connection" with Europe and its wars. If the United States gathered its strength under "an efficient government," it could defy any foreign challenge; but if it was drawn into Europe's quarrels and corruption, the republican experiment would be doomed. Washington and Hamilton thus turned the central argument of Republicanism against their Republican critics. They also evoked a vision of a United States virtuously isolated from foreign intrigue and power politics, an ideal that would remain a potent inspiration for long thereafter.

Washington left the presidency in 1797 and died in 1799. Like many later presidents, he went out amid a barrage of partisan criticism.

The Election of 1796

As the election of 1796 approached, the Republicans cultivated a large, loyal body of voters, marking the first time since the Revolution that the political elite had effectively mobilized ordinary Americans to participate in politics. The Republican constituency included the Democratic societies, workingmen's clubs, and immigrant-aid associations.

Immigrants became a prime target for Republican recruiters. During the 1790s the United States absorbed twenty thousand French refugees from Saint-Domingue and sixty thousand Irish. Although few immigrants could vote, the Irish exerted critical influence in Pennsylvania and New York, where public opinion was so closely divided that a few hundred voters could tip the balance.

In 1796 the presidential candidates were Vice President John Adams, whom the Federalists supported, and the Republicans' Jefferson. Republican strength in the South offset Federalist strength in New England, leaving Pennsylvania and New York as crucial swing states where the Irish vote might tip the scales. In the end, the Republicans took Pennsylvania but not New York, so that Jefferson lost the presidency by just three electoral votes. As the second-highest vote-getter in the Electoral College, he became vice president. The Federalists narrowly regained control of the House and maintained their firm grip on the Senate.

Adams's intellect and devotion to principle have rarely been equaled among American presidents. But the new president was more comfortable with ideas than with people, especially non-elites. He inspired trust and often admiration but could not command personal loyalty or inspire the public. Adams's stubborn personality and disdain for ordinary people left him ill-suited to govern, and he ultimately proved unable to unify the country.

The French Crisis, 1798–1799

Even before the election, the French had recognized that Jay's Treaty was a Federalist-sponsored attempt to assist Britain in its war against France. On learning of Jefferson's defeat, France began seizing American ships carrying goods to British ports and within a year had plundered more than three hundred vessels. The French also directed that every American captured on a British naval ship (even those involuntarily impressed) should be hanged. Hoping to avoid war, Adams dispatched a peace commission to Paris. The French foreign minister, Charles de Talleyrand (sharl duh TAL-ee-rahn), refused to meet with the Americans, instead promising through three unnamed agents ("X, Y, and Z") that talks could begin after he received $250,000 and France obtained a $12 million loan. This barefaced demand for a bribe became known as the **XYZ Affair.** Outraged Americans adopted the battle cry "Millions for defense, not one cent for tribute."

XYZ Affair French demand for bribes from American negotiators; triggered great anger

The XYZ Affair discredited Republican foreign policy views. The party's leaders compounded the damage by refusing to condemn French aggression and opposing Adams's call for military preparedness. While Republicans tried to excuse French behavior, the Federalists rode a wave of militant patriotism to an enormous victory in the 1798 congressional elections.

Congress responded to the XYZ Affair by arming fifty-four ships to protect U.S. commerce. The new warships joined what became known as the Quasi (KWAH-zee)-War—an undeclared Franco-American naval conflict in the Caribbean from 1798 to 1800, during which U.S. forces seized ninety-three French privateers while losing just one ship. By early 1799 the French no longer posed a serious threat at sea.

Meanwhile, the Federalist-controlled Congress tripled the regular army to ten thousand men in 1798, with an automatic expansion of land forces to fifty thousand in case of war. But the risk of a land war with France was minimal. What Federalists actually wanted was a strong military force ready in case of a civil war, for the crisis had produced near-hysterical fears that French and Irish malcontents were hatching treasonous conspiracies.

The Alien and Sedition Acts, 1798

The Federalists insisted that the possibility of war with France demanded stringent legislation to protect national security. In 1798 the Federalist Congress passed four measures known collectively as the **Alien and Sedition Acts.** Although President Adams neither requested nor wanted the laws, he deferred to Congress and signed them.

Alien and Sedition Acts Federalist-supported measures to suppress Republican supporters of Jefferson

The least controversial of the four laws, the Alien Enemies Act, was designed to prevent wartime espionage or sabotage. It outlined procedures for determining

The Library of Congress

"Preparation for War to Defend Commerce" (1800) by William Birch
Birch's engraving depicts the building of the frigate *Philadelphia* during the Quasi-War.

whether a hostile country's citizens, when staying in America, posed a threat to the United States; if so, they would be deported or jailed. It also established principles to respect the rights of enemy citizens. This law would not be used until the War of 1812.

The second of the laws, the Alien Friends Act, authorized the president to expel foreign residents whose activities he considered dangerous. It required no proof of guilt. Republicans maintained that the law's real purpose was to deport immigrants critical of Federalist policies. Republicans also denounced the third law, the Naturalization Act. This measure increased the residency requirement for U.S. citizenship from five to fourteen years (the last five continuously in one state) to reduce Irish voting.

Finally came the Sedition Act, the only one of these measures enforceable against U.S. citizens. Although its alleged purpose was to punish attempts to encourage the violation of federal laws or to seed a revolution, the act defined criminal activity so broadly that it blurred distinctions between sedition and legitimate political discussion. Thus, it forbade an individual or a group "to oppose any measure or measures of the United States"—wording that could be interpreted to ban any criticism of the party in power. Another clause made it illegal to speak, write, or print any statement that would bring the president "into contempt or disrepute." A newspaper editor could therefore face imprisonment for criticizing Adams or his cabinet. However one regarded it, the Sedition Act interfered with free speech. The Federalists wrote the law to expire in 1801 so that it could not be used against them if they lost the next election.

A principal target of Federalist repression was the opposition press. Four of the five largest Republican newspapers were charged with sedition just as the election campaign of 1800 was getting under way. The attorney general used the Alien Friends Act to drive Irish journalists underground, and Scottish editor Thomas Callender went to prison for criticizing the president.

Federalist leaders never intended to fill the jails with Republican martyrs. Rather, they hoped to use a few highly visible prosecutions to silence Republican journalists and candidates during the election of 1800. The attorney general charged seventeen persons with sedition and won ten convictions. Among the victims was Republican congressman Matthew Lyon of Vermont, who spent four months in prison for publishing a blast against Adams.

In 1788, opponents of the Constitution had warned that giving the national government extensive powers would eventually endanger freedom. Ten years later, their prediction seemed to have come true. Shocked Republicans realized that because the Federalists controlled all three branches of the government, neither the Bill of Rights nor the system of checks and balances reliably protected individual liberties. In this context, they advanced the doctrine of states' rights as a means of preventing the national government from violating basic freedoms.

Virginia and Kentucky Resolutions Jefferson's and Madison's resolutions stressing states' rights and the power of nullification in response to the Alien and Sedition Acts

Recognizing that opponents of federal power would never prevail in the Supreme Court, which was still dominated by Federalists, Madison and Jefferson anonymously wrote manifestos on states' rights known as the **Virginia and Kentucky Resolutions,** adopted respectively by the legislatures of those states in 1798. Madison in the Virginia Resolutions declared that state legislatures retained both their right to judge the constitutionality of federal actions and an authority called *interposition,* which enabled them to protect the liberties of their citizens. Jefferson's resolution for Kentucky went further by declaring that states could "nullify"—declare invalid—objectionable federal laws. Although Kentucky's legislature deleted the term "nullify" before approving the resolution, the intention of both resolutions was to invalidate any federal law in a state that had deemed the law unconstitutional.

Although most states did not endorse the resolutions, their passage demonstrated the potential for disunion in the late 1790s. So did several near-violent confrontations between Federalist and Republican crowds in Philadelphia and New York City. National leaders acted as if a crisis were imminent. Vice President Jefferson hinted that events might push the southern states into secession from the Union; President Adams hid guns in his home. A tense atmosphere hung over the republic as the election of 1800 neared.

The Election of 1800

In the election campaign, the parties once again rallied around the Federalist Adams and the Republican Jefferson. Moderate leadership in both parties ensured that the nation would survive the tumultuous election. Jefferson and Madison discouraged radical activity, while Adams rejected demands by extreme "High Federalists" that he ensure victory by deliberately sparking an insurrection or asking Congress to declare war on France.

"Nothing but an open war can save us," declared a High (extreme) Federalist. But when the president discovered the French willing to seek peace in 1799, he proposed a special diplomatic mission. Adams obtained Senate approval for his envoys only by threatening to resign and thus making Jefferson president. Outraged High Federalists tried to dump Adams, but their ill-considered maneuver rallied most New Englanders around the stubborn, upright president.

Adams's negotiations with France did not achieve a settlement until 1801, but the expectation of normal relations prevented Federalists from exploiting charges of Republican sympathy for the enemy. With the immediate threat of war removed, voters grew resentful that, in just two years, taxes had soared 33 percent to support an army that had done virtually nothing. As the danger of war receded, voters gave Federalists less credit for standing up to France and more blame for adding $10 million to the national debt.

While High Federalists spitefully withheld the backing that Adams needed to win, Republicans redoubled their efforts to elect Jefferson. As a result of Republicans' mobilization of voters, popular interest in politics rose sharply. Voter turnout in 1800 leaped to more than double that of 1788, rising from about 15 percent to almost 40 percent; in hotly contested Pennsylvania and New York, more than half the eligible voters participated.

Adams lost the presidency by just eight electoral votes out of 138. But Adams's loss did not ensure Jefferson's election. Because all 73 Republican electors voted for both Jefferson and his running mate, New York's Aaron Burr, the Electoral College deadlocked in a tie between them. The choice of president devolved upon the House of Representatives, where thirty-five ballots over six days produced no result. Aware that Republican voters and electors wanted Jefferson to be president, the wily Burr cast about for Federalist support. But after Hamilton—Burr's bitter rival in New York politics—declared his preference for Jefferson as "by far not so dangerous a man," a Federalist representative abandoned Burr and gave Jefferson the presidency by history's narrowest margin.

CHECKING IN

- Federalists viewed the French Revolution with alarm, but Jefferson and his supporters initially viewed it optimistically.
- The XYZ Affair alienated many Americans and hardened party lines between Federalists and Republicans.
- Jefferson's supporters became the Republican Party by the mid-1790s; the election of 1796 was the first party-based election.
- In the Alien and Sedition Acts, the Federalists attempted to suppress the Republican Party.
- Jefferson's victory in the election of 1800 showed that the party system was firmly entrenched.

ECONOMIC AND SOCIAL CHANGE

On what basis were some Americans denied full equality by 1800?

During the nation's first twelve years under the Constitution, the spread of economic production for markets, even by family farms, transformed the lives of many Americans. These transformations marked the United States' first small steps toward industrial capitalism.

Meanwhile, some Americans rethought questions of gender and race in American society during the 1790s. Even so, legal and political barriers to gender and racial equality actually became more entrenched.

Producing for Markets

For centuries most economic production in European societies and their colonial offshoots took place in household settings. At the core of each household was a patriarchal nuclear family—the male head, his wife, and their unmarried children. Many households included additional people—relatives; boarders; apprentices and journeymen in artisan shops; servants and slaves in well-off urban households; and slaves, "hired hands," and tenant farmers in rural settings. Unlike in our modern world, before the nineteenth century most people except mariners worked at what was temporarily or permanently "home." The notion of "going to work" would have struck them as odd.

Although households varied greatly in the late eighteenth century, most were on small farms and consisted of only an owner and his family. By 1800, such farm families typically included seven children whose labor contributed to production. Husbands and older sons worked in the fields; wives and daughters maintained the barns and gardens; wives, of course, bore and reared the children as well. Most farm families produced food and other products largely for their own consumption.

After the American Revolution, this began to change in heavily settled regions of the Northeast. Prosperous farmers began to sell their surplus—produce, meat, and dairy products—to urban customers. Accordingly, men introduced clover into their pastures, expanded acreage devoted to hay, and built barns to shelter their cows in cold weather and to store the hay. Consequently, dairy production rose as mid-Atlantic farmwomen, or "dairymaids," by 1800 milked an average of six animals twice a day. Farmwomen turned much of the milk into butter for sale to urban consumers.

Poorer farmers found other ways to produce for commercial markets. Young men and young couples moved west, while unmarried daughters frequently remained at home and spun and wove cloth. Enterprising merchants began catering to an emerging urban market for cloth as well as selling to southerners who wanted the cheapest possible material for slave clothing. Merchants would supply raw flax (for linen), wool, and cotton to mothers and daughters in farm households, returning in a few weeks to pay the women cash for their handiwork. A similar system emerged in the shoe industry, where prosperous shoemakers began supplying leather to others and paying them for the finished product. Numerous other enterprises emerged, employing both men and women to satisfy needs, such as making nails, that self-contained households could not have met.

Behind the new industries was an ambitious class of risk-taking entrepreneurs. The country's first private banks were founded in the 1780s. Philadelphia merchants created the Pennsylvania Society for the Encouragement of Manufactures and the Useful Arts in 1787. This organization promoted the immigration of British artisans familiar with the latest industrial technology, including Samuel Slater, who helped establish a cotton-spinning mill at Pawtucket, Rhode Island, in 1790 (see Chapter 9). In 1791, investors from New York and Philadelphia started the Society for the Encouragement of Useful Manufactures, which attempted to demonstrate the potential of large-scale industrial enterprises by building a factory town at Paterson, New Jersey. That same year, the first formal association for trading government bonds appeared in New York; it ultimately became the New York Stock Exchange.

For many Americans, the choice between manufacturing and farming was moral as well as economic. Hamilton's support of industrialization was consistent with his larger vision for America and contradicted that of Jefferson. As outlined in his Report on the Subject of Manufactures (1791), Hamilton admired efficiently run factories in which a few managers supervised large numbers of workers. Manufacturing would provide employment opportunities, promote emigration, and expand the applications of technology. Jefferson, on the other hand, idealized white, landowning family farmers as bulwarks of republican liberty and virtue. "Those who labour in the earth are the chosen people," he wrote in 1784, whereas the dependency of European factory workers "begets subservience and venality." Hamilton embraced capital, technology, and managerial discipline; Jefferson envisioned land as the key to prosperity and liberty for all. The argument over these competing ideals would remain a constant in American politics until the twentieth century.

Library Company of Philadelphia

Advocating Women's Rights, 1792

In this illustration from an American magazine for women, the "Genius of the Ladies Magazine" and the "Genius of Emulation" present Liberty with a petition based on British feminist Mary Wollstonecraft's *Vindication of the Rights of Woman.*

White Women in the Republic

Along with the growing importance of women's economic roles, discussions of Republicanism raised larger questions of women's rights and equality. Neither the Revolution nor republican state constitutions had substantially altered the legal position of white women. Some states made it easier for women to obtain divorces, but only New Jersey allowed women to vote. In 1807, however, New Jersey disfranchised both women and free blacks.

Throughout American life, social change and republican ideology combined to challenge traditional attitudes toward women's rights. Americans increasingly recognized the right of a woman to choose her husband. In the Northeast, young women increasingly became pregnant as a way to force their father's consent to marriage. Pregnancy and marriage allowed young women to gain economic support in a region where the westward exodus of young men was increasingly leaving a growing number of women single.

White women also had fewer children than their mothers and grandmothers. Both declining farm sizes and urbanization contributed to the shrinkage; in one

Massachusetts town, for example, the average number of children a woman bore declined from nine per marriage in 1750 to six by 1800. Some women were clearly finding relief from the nearly endless cycle of pregnancy and nursing that had consumed their grandmothers.

As white women's roles expanded, so too did republican notions of male-female relations. "I object to the word 'obey' in the marriage-service," wrote a female author calling herself Matrimonial Republican. "The obedience between man and wife is, or ought to be mutual." Divorce petitions filed by women increasingly cited lack of mutuality as the cause for divorce. A few women also challenged the double standard that allowed men to engage in extramarital affairs while condemning their female partners. Writing in 1784, an author calling herself "Daphne" called on her "sister Americans" to "stand by and support the dignity of our own sex" by publicly condemning seducers rather than their victims.

Judith Sargent Murray Poet and foremost advocate of women's rights at the end of the eighteenth century

republican motherhood As virtuous wives and mothers, educated white women would strengthen the new nation

Gradually, the subordination of women became the subject of debate. In "On the Equality of the Sexes" (1790), essayist and poet **Judith Sargent Murray** (see page 147) contended that the genders had equal intellectual ability and deserved equal education. Murray hoped that "sensible and informed" women would improve their minds rather than rush into marriage (as she had at eighteen).

Like many of her contemporaries, Murray supported the idea of **republican motherhood.** Advocates of republican motherhood emphasized the importance of educating white women in the values of liberty and independence to strengthen virtue in the new nation. It was the republican duty of mothers to inculcate these values in their sons—the nation's future leaders—as well as their daughters. John Adams reminded his daughter that she would be "responsible for a great share of the duty and opportunity of educating a rising family, from whom much will be expected." Before the 1780s, only a few women had acquired an advanced education through private tutors. Thereafter, urban elites broadened such opportunities by founding numerous private schools, or academies, for girls; in 1789, Massachusetts forbade any town to exclude girls from its elementary schools.

Republican assertions of male and female moral and intellectual equality provoked scattered calls for political equality. However, the great struggle for women's political rights would begin only in the next century. Prohibitions against married women's ownership of property went virtually unchallenged. Women could indeed be virtuous wives and mothers, but the world outside their home offered them few opportunities to apply their education.

Land and Culture: Native Americans

Native Americans occupied the most tenuous position in American society. By 1800, Indians east of the Mississippi had suffered severe losses of population, territory, and political and cultural self-determination. Thousands of deaths had resulted from battle, famine, and disease during successive wars and from poverty, losses of land, and discrimination during peacetime (see Map 7.1). Settlers, liquor dealers, and criminals trespassed on Indian lands, often defrauding or inflicting violence on Native Americans and provoking them to retaliate. Indians who worked for whites were often paid in the unfamiliar medium of cash and then found little to spend it on in their isolated communities, except alcohol.

While employing military force against Native Americans who resisted U.S. authority, Washington recognized that American citizens' actions often contributed to Indians' resentment. Accordingly, they pursued a policy similar to Britain's under the Proclamation of 1763 (see Chapter 5) in which the federal government sought to regulate relations between Indians and non-Indians. Congress enacted the new policy gradually in a series of **Indian Trade and Intercourse Acts** (1790–1796). The acts prohibited transfers of tribal lands to outsiders except as authorized in formal treaties or by Congress. Other provisions regulated the conduct of non-Indians on lands still under tribal control. The legislation also authorized the federal government to establish programs that would "promote civilization" among Native Americans as a replacement for traditional culture. By "civilization," Knox and his supporters meant Anglo-American culture. But before 1800, the Indian Trade and Intercourse Acts went largely unenforced.

Indian Trade and Intercourse Acts Series of laws designed to promote better relations between Indians and whites

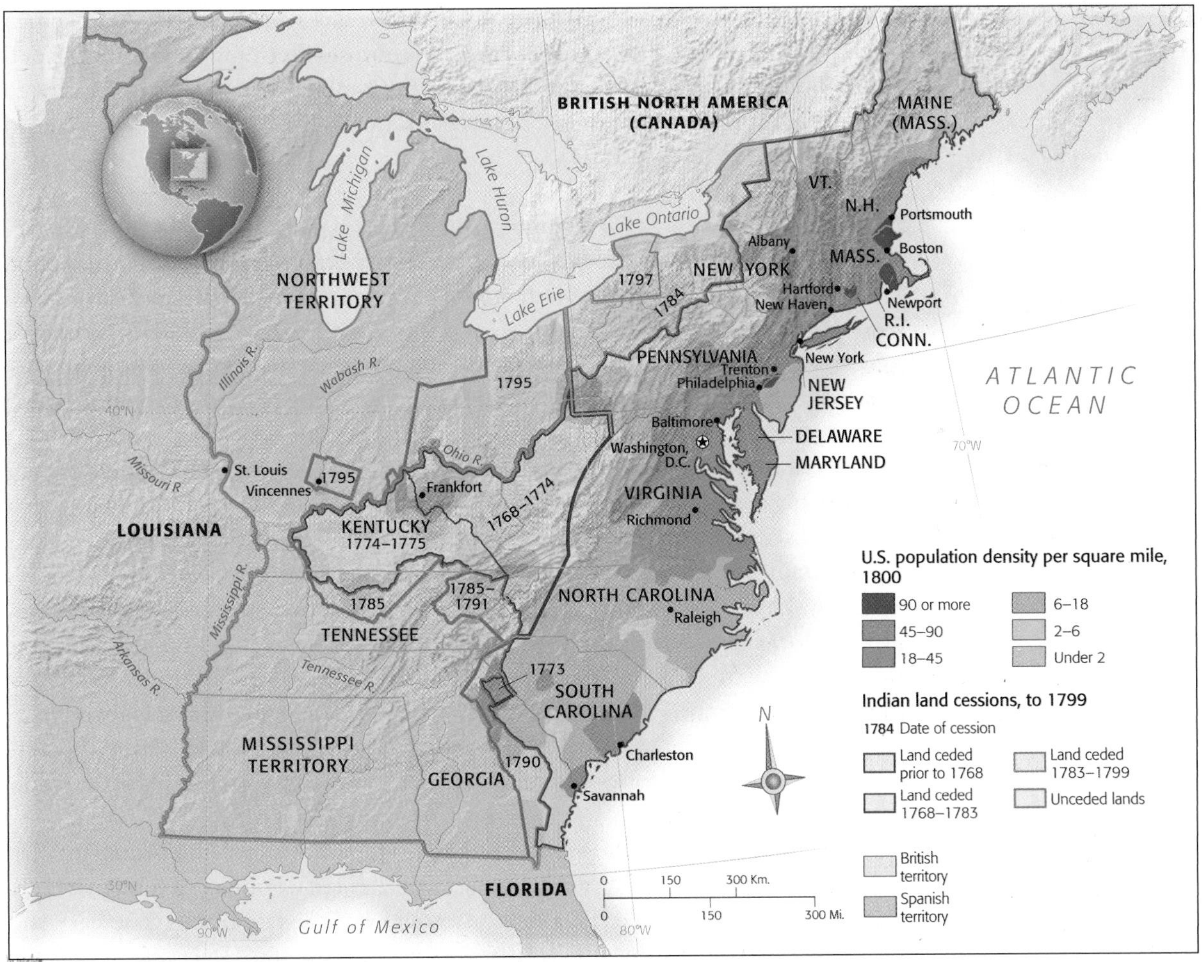

Map 7.1 Indian Land Cessions, 1768–1799

During the last third of the eighteenth century, Native Americans were forced to give up extensive homelands throughout the eastern backcountry and further west in the Ohio and Tennessee River valleys.

 Interactive Map

Among the most devastated Native Americans in the 1790s were the Seneca Iroquois of western New York and Pennsylvania. Most surviving Iroquois had moved to Canada after the Revolution, and those like the Seneca who stayed behind were isolated from one another on tiny reservations. Unable to hunt, trade, or wage mourning wars, Seneca men frequently resorted to heavy drinking, often becoming violent.

In 1799, a Seneca prophet, Handsome Lake, emerged and led his people in a remarkable spiritual revival. Severely ill, alcoholic, and near death, he experienced a series of visions. Handsome Lake preached against alcoholism and sought to revive self-confidence among the Seneca. But whereas many Indian visionary prophets rejected all white ways, Handsome Lake welcomed civilization, as introduced by Quaker missionaries supported by federal aid. In particular, he urged a radical shift in gender roles, with Seneca men displacing women not only in farming but also as heads of their families. However, the most traditional Senecas rejected Handsome Lake's message that Native American men should work like white farmers. And women often resisted because they stood to lose their control of farming and their considerable political influence. After 1800, missionaries would expect Native Americans to convert to Christianity as well as adopt "civilization."

African-American Struggles

The republic's first years marked the high tide of African-Americans' revolutionary-era success in bettering their lot. Although racism persisted, Jefferson's eloquent words "all men are created equal" awakened many white consciences. In 1790, 8 percent of African-Americans enjoyed freedom. By 1800, 11 percent were free. State reforms, meanwhile, attempted to improve slaves' conditions. In 1791 the North Carolina legislature declared that the "distinction of criminality between the murder of a white person and one who is equally an human creature, but merely of a different complexion, is disgraceful to humanity" and authorized the execution of whites who murdered slaves. By 1794 most states had outlawed the Atlantic slave trade.

Hesitant measures to ensure free blacks' legal equality appeared in the 1780s and early 1790s. Most states dropped restrictions on their freedom of movement, protected their property, and allowed them to enroll in the militia. All but three states either permitted free blacks to vote or made no specific attempts to exclude them. But before the 1790s ended, the trend toward lessening the social and legal distances between the races ended. Abolitionist sentiment ebbed, slavery became more entrenched, and whites demonstrated reluctance to accept free blacks as fellow citizens.

Federal law led the way in restricting the rights of African-Americans. In 1790 congressional procedures for naturalizing aliens limited eligibility to foreign whites. The federal militia law of 1792 allowed states to exclude free blacks. The navy and marine corps forbade nonwhite enlistments in 1798. By 1807 Delaware, Maryland, Kentucky, and New Jersey had stripped free blacks of the vote. Although free blacks enjoyed rights in some areas, the number of places treating them as the political equals of whites dropped sharply in the early 1800s.

Some free blacks rose above these disadvantages, and a few of them gained recognition among whites. One of the best-known was Benjamin Banneker of Maryland, a self-taught mathematician and astronomer. Banneker was one of three surveyors who laid out the new national capital in Washington, DC, and after 1791 he published a series of widely read almanacs. Sending a copy of one to Thomas Jefferson, Banneker chided the future president for holding views of black inferiority that contradicted his ringing words in the Declaration of Independence.

Faced with growing constriction of their freedom and opportunities, free African-Americans turned to one another for support, especially through religious channels. During the 1780s Richard Allen and Absalom Jones formed the Free African Society of Philadelphia, whose members pooled their resources to aid one another and other blacks in need. When the white-dominated Methodist church they attended restricted black worshippers to the gallery, Allen and Jones and their followers formed their own congregation. Comparable developments in other northern communities would lead to the establishment of the African Methodist Episcopal Church (see Chapter 9).

In 1793 a yellow fever epidemic swept Philadelphia, leaving about four thousand dead. Most affluent whites fled the area. Allen and Jones organized a relief effort in which African-Americans tended to the sick and buried the dead of both races. Their only reward was a vicious publicity campaign wrongly accusing blacks of profiting at whites' expense.

An especially revealing symptom of changing attitudes occurred in 1793 when Congress passed the **Fugitive Slave Law**. The law required judges to award possession of a runaway slave on a formal request by a master or his representative. Accused runaways were denied jury trials and sometimes were refused permission to present evidence. Slaves' legal status as property disqualified them from claiming these constitutional privileges, but the Fugitive Slave Law denied even *free* blacks the legal protections guaranteed to them under the Bill of Rights. White Americans clearly found it easy to forget that the Constitution had not limited citizenship to their race.

Fugitive Slave Law Required return of runaway slaves; denied blacks any constitutional protections

The bloody slave revolt on Saint-Domingue (which victorious blacks would rename Haiti in 1802) undermined the trend toward abolition and reinforced the kinds of fears that spawned racism. Reports of the slaughter of French slaveholders made white Americans more reluctant to criticize slavery and helped to transform the image of blacks from that of victims of injustice to one of potential menaces. In August 1800 a planned insurrection of more than one thousand slaves in Richmond, Virginia, kindled smoldering white fears. The militia put down the conspiracy and executed thirty-five slaves, including the leader, Gabriel. **Gabriel's rebellion** fanned fears of future revolts. Isolated uprisings occurred in the United States for years after, and rumors persisted that a massive revolt was brewing. Antislavery sentiment diminished rapidly. The antislavery movement would not recover from the damage inflicted by the Saint-Domingue revolt until the early 1830s.

Gabriel's rebellion Failed slave rebellion in Virginia

A technological development also strengthened slavery. During the 1790s, demand in the British textile industry stimulated the cultivation of cotton in coastal South Carolina and Georgia. Here the soil and climate were ideal for growing long-staple cotton, whose fibers could be separated easily from its seed. In the South's upland and interior regions, however, only short-staple cotton thrived. Its seed clung tenaciously to the fibers and defied cleaning. In 1793 a New Englander, Eli Whitney, invented a

CHECKING IN

- By 1800 the market economy was beginning to challenge traditional household economies.
- White women gained educational but few other opportunities.
- The status of Native Americans continued to decline.
- The early republic moved slowly toward ending slavery, but the slave revolt on Saint-Domingue and Gabriel's rebellion in Virginia halted progress.
- The invention of the cotton gin in 1793 transformed southern agriculture and entrenched slavery firmly in the South.

cotton gin Invention that made cleaning of southern cotton fast and cheap

cotton gin that efficiently cleaned short-staple cotton. Improved by others, Whitney's machine removed a major obstacle to cotton cultivation, gave plantation slavery a new lease on life, and undermined the doubts of those who considered slavery economically outmoded.

By 1800, free blacks had suffered noticeable erosion of their post-Revolutionary War gains, and southern slaves were farther from freedom than a decade earlier. By arrangement with her late husband, Martha Washington freed the family's slaves a year after George died. But many of the freed blacks remained impoverished and dependent on the Washington estate because Virginia law prohibited the education of blacks. Meanwhile, across the Potomac, enslaved blacks were performing most of the labor on the new national capital that would bear the first president's name. African-Americans were manifestly losing ground.

Chapter Summary

What role did George Washington play in translating the Constitution from words into government? (page 148)

As president, Washington worked hard to lessen fears of the government by balancing his cabinet among competing sectional interests. He also established the precedent of serving only two terms. The Judiciary Act of 1789, which left room for state practice, and the Bill of Rights, which guaranteed personal liberties, underscored his commitment to the ideals of the Revolution.

Which points in Hamilton's economic program were most controversial and why? (page 150)

Alexander Hamilton, as Washington's treasury secretary, pushed through a series of controversial measures that strengthened federal and executive authority as well as northeastern commercial interests. Among other things, Hamilton advocated the assumption of revolutionary-era debt, establishment of a national bank, and strong support for industrial development. Jefferson, Madison, and others opposed these measures, arguing that they favored a few Americans at the expense of the rest and that they threatened liberty.

How did the new nation deal with France, Spain, and Britain? (page 155)

Spain attempted to expand its North American holdings, but Washington countered by neutralizing its Indian allies. The French Revolution proved a source of contention in the United States, especially with the arrival of Citizen Genêt and his scheme to enlist Americans to fight on France's behalf. To try to relieve tensions, Americans undertook diplomatic missions. Jay's Treaty solved few problems but stimulated the American economy by opening American trade with the British Empire. Pinckney's Treaty resolved tensions with Spain.

KEY TERMS

Judiciary Act *(p. 149)*
Bill of Rights *(p. 150)*
Alexander Hamilton *(p. 150)*
Reports on the Public Credit *(p. 150)*
Report on a National Bank *(p. 152)*
Whiskey Rebellion *(p. 154)*
"Alta California" *(p. 156)*
Citizen Genêt *(p. 158)*
Jay's Treaty *(p. 159)*
Treaty of San Lorenzo *(p. 159)*
XYZ Affair *(p. 162)*
Alien and Sedition Acts *(p. 162)*
Virginia and Kentucky Resolutions *(p. 164)*
Judith Sargent Murray *(p. 168)*
republican motherhood *(p. 168)*
Indian Trade and Intercourse Acts *(p. 169)*
Fugitive Slave Law *(p. 171)*
Gabriel's rebellion *(p. 171)*
cotton gin *(p. 172)*

What principal issues divided Federalists and Republicans in the election of 1800? (page 159)

During the mid-1790s, elites formed two rival political parties—the Federalists and the Republicans. The emergence of political parties clarified and intensified debate over the shape of the nation's future. Frightened by Jefferson's Republican supporters, the Federalists supported the Alien and Sedition Acts. The split over the French Revolution was only one of a series of major issues on which the two parties disagreed.

On what basis were some Americans denied full equality by 1800? (page 165)

The market economy began to transform society. While educated white women defined a public if subservient role for themselves as "republican mothers," Native Americans saw their condition continue to deteriorate. There were some moves toward ending slavery, especially in the northern states, but a series of events essentially put a halt to this—namely, the revolution in Saint-Domingue, Gabriel's rebellion in Virginia, and the invention of the cotton gin.

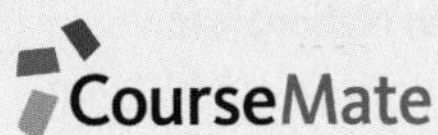

Go to the CourseMate website at **www.cengagebrain.com** for additional study tools and review materials—including audio and video clips—for this chapter.

Chapter 8

America at War and Peace

1801–1824

War of 1812 Scene

Chapter Review

The Age of Jefferson
How did Jefferson's philosophy shape policy toward public expenditures, the judiciary, and Louisiana?

The Gathering Storm
How did the United States slide into war with Great Britain?

The War of 1812
How did the War of 1812 influence American domestic politics?

The Awakening of American Nationalism
To what extent did Jefferson's legacy persist into the so-called Era of Good Feelings?

Jefferson's triumph in the election of 1800 left a bitter taste. Nevertheless, in his inaugural address, Jefferson struck a conciliatory note. He traced the political convulsions of the 1790s to different responses to the French Revolution, an external event whose fury had passed. What Americans needed to recognize was that they agreed on essentials, that "we are all republicans, we are all federalists."

However, foreign affairs continued to agitate American politics. A month before Jefferson's inauguration, Tripoli, an Islamic state in North Africa, declared war on the United States. Since 1785, the "Barbary pirates" from North Africa had been seizing American vessels and enslaving their crews. With its tiny navy, the United States had no choice but to pay exorbitant ransoms and bribes. Tripoli warred on the United States because its ruler wanted a bigger bribe. Instead, Jefferson authorized hostilities. The ensuing Tripolitan War (1801–1805) ended favorably for the United States.

American naval success also depended on European events over which it had no control. Starting in 1805, Britain renewed its seizure of American merchant ships bound for ports controlled by the French emperor Napoleon. Jefferson's answer was the Embargo Act of 1807, a self-blockade in which the United States sought to influence Britain and France by denying American trade to each. This policy of "peaceable coercion" failed, and in 1812 the United States went to war with Britain.

The treaty ending the War of 1812 did not guarantee neutral rights. But fortunately for the United States, the treaty coincided with Napoleon's decline. With peace in Europe, American trading ships enjoyed freedom of the seas for the next century. The American navy returned to the Mediterranean in 1815 and forced all the Barbary states to abandon forever their claims for tribute from the United States.

These developments fed American pride. However, the harmony for which Jefferson longed proved elusive. Between 1801 and 1824, the Federalist Party collapsed as a force in national politics. Yet the Federalists' decline opened the way to intensified factionalism within the Republican Party, especially during Jefferson's second term (1805–1809) and during the mistakenly named "Era of Good Feelings" (1817–1824). Most ominously, between 1819 and 1821, northern and southern Republicans split over the extension of slavery into Missouri.

THE AGE OF JEFFERSON

How did Jefferson's philosophy shape policy toward public expenditures, the judiciary, and Louisiana?

Narrowly elected, Jefferson saw his popularity rise in his first term as he scaled down seemingly unnecessary government expenditures. Increasingly confident of public support, he worked to loosen the Federalist grip on appointed offices, especially in the judiciary, and purchased Louisiana. Both political calculation and his philosophy of government, known as Jeffersonianism, guided his moves.

Jefferson and Jeffersonianism

A man of extraordinary attainments, Jefferson spoke fluent French, read Latin and Greek, and studied several Native American languages. For more than twenty years he was president of America's foremost scientific society, the American Philosophical Society. He designed Monticello (mon-te-CHELL-oh), his mountaintop mansion in Virginia, and spent forty years overseeing its construction. Fascinated by gadgets, he invented a device for duplicating his letters and a revolving book stand. His personal library of seven thousand books was the foundation of the Library of Congress. His public career was luminous: principal author of the Declaration of Independence, governor of Virginia, ambassador to France, secretary of state, vice president, and ultimately president.

Yet Jefferson was, and remains, a controversial figure. His critics, pointing to his doubts about some Christian doctrines and his early support for the French Revolution, portrayed him as an infidel and radical. In 1802 a former supporter, James Callender, wrote a newspaper account in which he named **Sally Hemings,** a house slave at Monticello, as Jefferson's mistress. Drawing on the DNA of Sally's male descendents and linking the timing of Jefferson's visits to Monticello with the

Sally Hemings Jefferson's slave rumored to be his mistress and mother of several of his children

Alexia Ouyoumjian

start of Sally's pregnancies, most scholars now view it as very likely that Jefferson, a widower, was the father of at least one of her four surviving children.

Callender's story did little damage to Jefferson's reputation in Virginia. Jefferson acted according to the rules of white Virginia gentlemen by never acknowledging any of Sally's children as his own. Although he freed two of her children (the other two ran away), he never freed Sally, nor did he ever mention her in his correspondence. Yet the story of Sally fed the charge that Jefferson was a hypocrite, for throughout his career he condemned the "race mixing" that he seems to have practiced.

Jefferson did not believe that blacks and whites could live permanently side by side, and he greatly feared a race war so vicious that it could be suppressed only by a dictator. Only by colonizing blacks in Africa, he believed, could America avert revolution and chaos.

Jefferson worried that high taxes, standing armies, and corruption could destroy American liberty by turning government into the master rather than the servant of the people. To prevent tyranny, Jefferson advocated that state governments retain great authority because they were immediately responsive to popular will.

He also believed that popular liberty required popular virtue. For republican theorists like Jefferson, virtue consisted of a decision to place public good above private interest and to exercise vigilance in keeping government under control. To Jefferson, the most vigilant and virtuous people were educated farmers who were accustomed to acting and thinking with sturdy independence. Jefferson regarded cities as breeding grounds for mobs and as menaces to liberty. When the people "get piled upon one another in large cities, as in Europe," he wrote, "they will become corrupt as in Europe."

Jefferson's "Revolution"

Jefferson described his election as a revolution. However, the revolution he actually sought was to restore the liberty and tranquility that he thought the United States had enjoyed in its earliest years and to reverse what he saw as a drift into despotism. The $10 million growth in the national debt under the Federalists alarmed Jefferson and his secretary of the treasury, Albert Gallatin. They rejected Alexander Hamilton's argument that debt strengthened the government by giving creditors a stake in its health. Just paying interest on the debt would require taxes, which would suck money from industrious farmers, the backbone of the republic. Increased tax revenues might also tempt the government to establish a standing army, which was always a threat to liberty.

Jefferson and Gallatin secured the repeal of many taxes, and they slashed expenditures by closing some embassies overseas and reducing the army. A lull in the war between Britain and France persuaded Jefferson that minimal military preparedness was a sound policy. This may have been wishful thinking, but it rested on a sound economic calculation, for the vast territory of the United States could not be secured from attack without astronomical expense.

Jefferson and the Judiciary

Jefferson hoped to conciliate the moderate Federalists, but conflicts over the judiciary derailed this objective. Washington and Adams had appointed only Federalists to the bench, including the new chief justice, John Marshall. The Federalist-sponsored Judiciary Act of 1801 reduced the number of Supreme Court justices from six to five and created sixteen new federal judgeships, which outgoing president John Adams had filled by last-minute ("midnight") appointments of Federalists. To Jefferson, this was proof that the Federalists intended to use the judiciary as a stronghold from which "all the works of Republicanism are to be beaten down and erased." In 1802, he won congressional repeal of the Judiciary Act of 1801.

Jefferson's troubles with the judiciary were not over. On his last day in office, Adams had appointed a Federalist, William Marbury, as justice of the peace in the District of Columbia. When Jefferson's secretary of state, James Madison, refused to send him notice of the appointment, Marbury petitioned the Supreme Court to issue a writ compelling delivery. In ***Marbury* v. *Madison*** (1803), Chief Justice John Marshall ruled that he was under no legal obligation to do so because Congress had exceeded its constitutional authority in writing the Judiciary Act of 1789.

Marbury* v. *Madison Supreme Court decision that set the framework for judicial review

For the first time, the Supreme Court had asserted its authority to void an act of Congress on the grounds that it was "repugnant" to the Constitution—thus firmly establishing the doctrine of **judicial review.**

judicial review Principle that Supreme Court can review and reject measures passed by Congress

While the *Marbury* decision was brewing, the Republicans took the offensive against the judiciary by moving to impeach (charge with wrongdoing) two Federalist judges, John Pickering and Samuel Chase. Pickering, an insane alcoholic, was quickly removed from office, but Chase presented difficulties. He was a partisan Federalist notorious for jailing several Republican editors under the Sedition Act of 1798. Nonetheless, the Constitution specified that judges could be impeached only for treason, bribery, and "high Crimes and Misdemeanors." Was impeachment

Chronology

1801	Thomas Jefferson's inauguration; start of Tripolitan War (1801–1805)
1802	Repeal of the Judiciary Act of 1801; Yazoo land compromise
1803	*Marbury* v. *Madison*; conclusion of the Louisiana Purchase
1804	Aaron Burr kills Alexander Hamilton in a duel; Jefferson elected to a second term
1804–1806	Lewis and Clark expedition
1807	*Chesapeake* affair; Embargo Act passed
1808	James Madison elected president
1809	Non-Intercourse Act passed; Embargo Act repealed
1812	United States declares war on Britain; Madison reelected to a second term
1814	British burn Washington, DC; Hartford Convention; Treaty of Ghent signed
1815	Battle of New Orleans
1816	James Monroe elected president; Second Bank of the United States chartered
1818	British-American Convention of 1818 sets U.S.-Canada border in West; Andrew Jackson invades West Florida
1819	Adams-Onís (Transcontinental) Treaty; *Dartmouth College* v. *Woodward*; *McCulloch* v. *Maryland*
1820–1821	Missouri Compromise
1823	Monroe Doctrine

appropriate because a judge was excessively partisan? Moderate Republicans came to doubt it, and partly for that reason, the Senate narrowly failed to convict Chase.

Chase's acquittal ended Jefferson's skirmishes with the judiciary. Unlike his radical followers, Jefferson objected neither to judicial review nor to an appointed judiciary; he merely challenged Federalist use of judicial power for political goals. Federalists never tried to use their domination of the courts to undo Jefferson's "revolution" of 1800. The Marshall Court upheld the constitutionality of the repeal of the Judiciary Act of 1801. And for his part, Jefferson never proposed to impeach Marshall.

Extending the Land: The Louisiana Purchase, 1803

Jefferson's goal of avoiding foreign entanglements would remain beyond reach as long as European powers held large territories in North America. In the Treaty of San Ildefonso (san eel-duh-FON-soh) (1800), a weakened Spain returned the vast Louisiana Territory to France, which, under Napoleon Bonaparte, was emerging as Europe's strongest military power. Jefferson was appalled. The president had long imagined that the inevitable expansion of a free and

The Mariners Museum, Newport News, Virginia

Burning of the *Philadelphia*

The American frigate *Philadelphia* ran aground in the shallow waters guarding Tripoli harbor. Both the ship and its crew were captured. To prevent the enemy from using it, on February 16, 1804, a small American force led by Lt. Stephen Decatur slipped into Tripoli harbor and boarded and burned the *Philadelphia*.

virtuous American people would create an "empire of liberty." Spain was no obstacle, but Jefferson knew that Bonaparte's capacity for mischief was boundless. Bonaparte dreamed of re-creating a French New World empire bordering the Caribbean and the Gulf of Mexico. The island of Saint-Domingue (modern Haiti and the Dominican Republic) would be the fulcrum of the empire, and Louisiana its breadbasket. Before this dream could become reality, however, the French would have to subdue Santo Domingo, where a bloody slave rebellion had led to the creation of a government under the black statesman Toussaint L'Ouverture (too-SAN loo-ver-TOOR). Napoleon accordingly dispatched an army to reassert French control and to reestablish slavery, but yellow fever and fierce resistance by the former slaves doomed the French forces.

In the short run, Jefferson worried most about New Orleans, the only port for the $3 million in annual produce of farmers along the Mississippi and Ohio river systems. Spain had temporarily granted Americans the right to park their produce there while awaiting transfer to seagoing vessels. But in 1802, the Spanish colonial administrator in New Orleans issued an order revoking this right. The order had originated in Spain, but most Americans assumed it had come from Bonaparte who, although he now owned Louisiana, had yet to take possession of it. "The day that France takes possession of N. Orleans," Jefferson wrote, "we must marry ourselves to the British fleet and nation."

The combination of France's failure to subdue Saint-Domingue and the termination of American rights to deposit produce in New Orleans led to the American purchase of Louisiana. Jefferson dispatched James Monroe and Robert R. Livingston to Paris to buy New Orleans from France. Meanwhile, Bonaparte concluded that his Caribbean empire was not worth the cost. In addition, he planned to resume war in Europe and needed cash. So he decided to sell *all* of Louisiana. The American commissioners and the French government settled on a price of $15 million. Thus, the United States gained an immense, uncharted territory between the Mississippi River and the Rocky Mountains (see Map 8.1). Although no one knew its exact size, the **Louisiana Purchase** virtually doubled the area of the United States at a cost, omitting interest, of thirteen and one-half cents an acre.

Louisiana Purchase
Jefferson's purchase of the interior of North America from France; virtually doubled the size of the United States

Jefferson found himself caught between ideals and reality. He believed in strict construction—the doctrine that the Constitution should be interpreted according to its letter—but recognized that doubling the size of the republic would guarantee land for American farmers, the backbone of the nation and the true guardians of liberty. Strict construction was not an end in itself but a means to promote republican liberty. If that end could be achieved in some way other than by strict construction, so be it. Political considerations also figured in Jefferson's calculations. Federalists generally opposed the Louisiana Purchase because it would decrease the relative importance of their strongholds on the eastern seaboard. As the leader of the Republican Party, the president saw no reason to hand the Federalists an issue by dallying over ratification of the treaty.

The Election of 1804

Jefferson's acquisition of Louisiana left the Federalists dispirited. As the election of 1804 approached, the main threat to Jefferson was not the Federalist Party but his

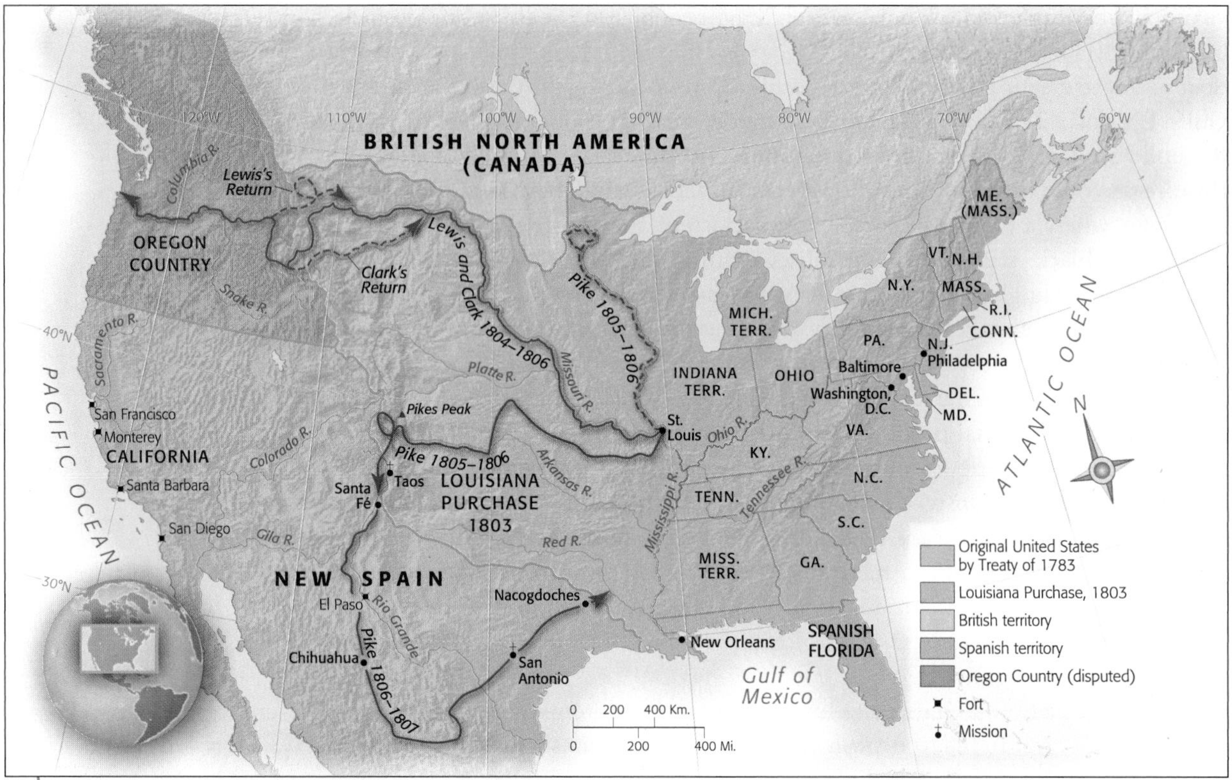

Map 8.1 The Louisiana Purchase and the Exploration of the West

The explorations of Lewis and Clark demonstrated the vast extent of the area purchased from France.

own vice president, Aaron Burr. In 1800, Burr had tried to take advantage of a tie in the Electoral College to gain the presidency. The Twelfth Amendment had clarified the electoral process but had not eliminated Burr's conniving; he spent much of his vice presidency in intrigues with the Federalists. The Republicans dumped him from the ticket in 1804 in favor of George Clinton. In the election, the Federalist nominees Charles C. Pinckney and Rufus King carried only two states. Jefferson's overwhelming victory brought his first term to a fitting close. Between 1801 and 1804 the United States had doubled its territory and started to pay off its debt. President Jefferson basked in the sun of success.

Exploring the Land: The Lewis and Clark Expedition

Louisiana dazzled Jefferson's imagination. Americans knew virtually nothing about the immense territory, not even its western boundary. A case could be made for the Pacific Ocean, but Jefferson was content to claim that Louisiana extended at least to the mountains west of the Mississippi, mountains that few Americans had seen. Thus, the Louisiana Purchase was both a bargain and a surprise package.

Even before the purchase, Jefferson had planned an exploratory expedition; picked its leader, his personal secretary and fellow Virginian Lieutenant Meriwether

Lewis; and sent him to Philadelphia for a crash course in zoology, astronomy, and botany. Jefferson instructed Lewis to trace the Missouri River to its source, cross the western highlands, and follow the best water route to the Pacific. Although Jefferson stressed commercial possibilities in requesting congressional funding for the expedition, his instructions to Lewis cited the need to learn about Indian customs, climate, plants, birds, and insects. Above all, Jefferson hoped the **Lewis and Clark expedition** would find a water route across the continent.

Lewis and Clark expedition Two-year exploration of newly acquired territory; a scientific treasure trove

Setting forth from St. Louis in May 1804, Lewis, his second-in-command, William Clark, and about fifty others followed the Missouri and then the Snake and Columbia rivers. In the Dakota Country they hired a French-Canadian fur trader, Toussaint Charbonneau (SHAR-bun-noh), as guide and interpreter. Slow-witted and inclined to panic in crises, Charbonneau proved to be a mixed blessing, but his wife, **Sacajawea** (sock-a-ja-WAYah) made up for his failings. A sixteen-year-old Shoshone (show-SHOW-nee), Sacajawea had been stolen by a rival tribe and then claimed by Charbonneau. When first encountered by Lewis and Clark, she had just given birth to a son; indeed, the infant's presence helped reassure Native American tribes of the expedition's peaceful intent.

Sacajawea Shoshone Indian, wife of Charbonneau, who assisted Lewis and Clark on their expedition

Even with their peaceful intent established, Lewis and Clark faced obstacles. The expedition brought them into contact with numerous tribes, each with a history of warring on other tribes and carrying on its own internal feuds. Reliant on Indians for guides, packers, and interpreters, Lewis and Clark had to become instant diplomats. Jefferson had instructed them to assert American sovereignty over the Purchase. They distributed medals and uniforms to chiefs ready to support American authority and staged military parades and displays of their weapons, which included cannons. But no tribe had a single chief, and Lewis and Clark sometimes miscalculated, thinking a minor chief to be head of an entire tribe. Yet their diplomacy was generally successful, less because they were sophisticated ethnographers than because they avoided violence.

The group finally reached the Pacific Ocean in November 1805 and then returned to St. Louis, but not before collecting a mass of scientific information, including the disturbing fact that more than three hundred miles of mountains separated the Missouri from the Columbia. The expedition also produced a sprinkling of tall tales, many of which Jefferson believed, about gigantic Indians, soil too rich to grow trees, and a mountain composed of salt. Finally, the expedition's drawings of the geography of the region led to more accurate maps and heightened interest in the West.

CHECKING IN

- President Jefferson feared too strong a central government and saw educated farmers as the backbone of Republicanism.
- The Jefferson administration rejected the Hamiltonian idea of a permanent national debt and downplayed military preparedness.
- Despite qualms about its constitutionality, Jefferson eagerly carried out the Louisiana Purchase.
- With apparent success in both domestic and foreign policy, Jefferson easily won reelection in 1804.
- The Lewis and Clark expedition collected large amounts of scientific data and sparked interest in the West.

THE GATHERING STORM

How did the United States slide into war with Great Britain?

In gaining Louisiana, the United States benefited from the European powers' preoccupation with their own struggles. But between 1803 and 1814, the Napoleonic Wars turned the United States into a pawn in a chess game played by others and made Jefferson's second term far less successful than his first.

Europe was not Jefferson's only problem. He had to deal with a plot to dismantle the United States, hatched in the inventive and perverse mind of Aaron Burr, as well as face down challenges from within his own party.

Challenges on the Home Front

Aaron Burr suffered a string of reverses in 1804. After being denied re-nomination as vice president, he began to scheme with a faction of extreme (or "High") Federalists who were plotting to form a "Northern Confederacy" that would include Nova Scotia, New England, New York, and even Pennsylvania. To advance their plot, the Federalists helped Burr to gain the Federalist nomination for governor of New York. Alexander Hamilton, who had thwarted Burr's grab for the presidency in 1800 by supporting Jefferson, now foiled Burr a second time by allowing publication of his "despicable opinion" of Burr. After his defeat in the New York election, Burr challenged Hamilton to a duel and mortally wounded him at Weehawken, New Jersey, on July 11, 1804.

Indicted in two states for murdering Hamilton, Burr—still vice president—now hatched a scheme so audacious that not even his opponents could believe that he was capable of such treachery. Burr allied himself with General James Wilkinson, the unsavory military governor of the Louisiana Territory, who had been on Spain's payroll intermittently as a secret agent since the 1780s. Their plot had several dimensions: They would create an independent confederacy of western states, conquer Mexico, and invade West Florida. The scheming duo presented the plot imaginatively. To westerners they said that it had the covert support of the Jefferson administration; to the British, that it was a way to attack Spanish lands; and to the Spanish, that it would open the way to dividing up the United States.

In the fall of 1806, Burr and some sixty followers made their way down the Ohio and Mississippi rivers to join Wilkinson at Natchez (NATCH-ezz). In October, Jefferson denounced the conspiracy. Wilkinson abandoned the plot and proclaimed himself the most loyal of Jefferson's followers. Burr was captured and brought back to Richmond, where he was put on trial for treason. Chief Justice Marshall presided at the trial and instructed the jury that the prosecution had to prove actual treasonable acts—an impossible task because the conspiracy had never reached fruition. The jury returned a verdict of not proved, which Marshall entered as "not guilty." Still under indictment for his murder of Hamilton, Burr fled to Europe where he tried to interest Napoleon in making peace with Britain as a prelude to a proposed Anglo-French invasion of the United States and Mexico.

Besides the Burr conspiracy, Jefferson also faced a challenge from a group of Republicans led by fellow Virginian John Randolph, an eccentric man of acerbic wit. Randolph believed that governments always menaced popular liberty. Jefferson had originally shared this view, but he recognized it as an ideology of opposition, not power; once in office, he compromised. In contrast, Randolph remained frozen in the 1770s, denouncing every government action as decline and proclaiming that he would throw all politicians to the dogs except that he had too much respect for dogs.

Randolph turned on Jefferson, most notably, for backing a compromise in the Yazoo land scandal. In 1795, the Georgia legislature had sold the huge Yazoo tract

(35 million acres composing most of present-day Alabama and Mississippi) for a fraction of its value to land companies that had bribed virtually the entire legislature. The next legislature canceled the sale, but many investors had already bought land. In 1803, a federal commission compromised with an award of 5 million acres to the Yazoo investors. For Randolph, the compromise was further evidence of the decay of republican virtue.

The Suppression of American Trade and Impressment

Burr's acquittal and Randolph's taunts shattered the aura of invincibility that had surrounded Jefferson. Now foreign affairs posed even sharper challenges. As Britain and France resumed their war, the United States prospered at Britain's expense by carrying sugar and coffee from the French and Spanish Caribbean colonies to Europe. This trade not only provided Napoleon with supplies but also drove down the price of sugar and coffee from British colonies by adding to the glut of these commodities on the world market. The British concluded that their economic problems stemmed from American prosperity.

Fueling this boom was the re-export trade, which created conflicts with Britain. According to the British Rule of 1756, any trade closed during peacetime could not be opened during war. For example, France usually restricted the sugar trade to French ships during peacetime and thus could not open it to American ships during war. The U.S. response to the Rule of 1756 was the "broken voyage," by which U.S. ships would carry French sugar or coffee to American ports, unload it, pass it through customs, and then re-export it as *American* produce. Britain tolerated this dodge for nearly a decade but in 1805 initiated a policy of total war toward France, including the strangulation of French trade. In 1805, a British court declared broken voyages illegal.

Next came a series of British trade decrees ("Orders in Council"), through which Britain intended to blockade part of continental Europe and thus staunch the flow of any products that might aid the French war effort. French counter-decrees followed, proclaiming that ships obeying British regulations would be subject to seizure by France. In effect, this Anglo-French war of decrees outlawed virtually all U.S. trade; if an American ship complied with British regulations, it became a French target, and vice versa. In total war, however, there was no room for neutrality, so both Britain and France seized U.S. ships. British warships hovered just beyond the American coast, searching virtually every U.S. ship it encountered.

Although less damaging to the American economy than the seizure of ships, **impressments** were equally galling. Even American-born seamen, six thousand between 1803 and 1812, were impressed into the Royal Navy. British arrogance peaked in June 1807. A British warship, HMS *Leopard*, patrolling off Virginia, attacked an unsuspecting American frigate, USS *Chesapeake,* and forced it to surrender. The British then boarded the vessel and seized four supposed deserters. One, a genuine deserter, was later hanged; the other three, former Britons, had "deserted" only from impressments and were now American citizens. The so-called *Chesapeake-Leopard* Affair enraged the country. Jefferson remarked that he had not seen so belligerent a spirit in America since 1775.

impressment British practice of taking deserters and others from American ships for service in the Royal Navy

Boarding and Taking of the American Ship *Chesapeake*

The loss of the frigate *Chesapeake* to HMS *Leopard* in 1807 and the dying words of its commander, James Lawrence, inspired the motto "Don't Give Up the Ship," which was emblazoned on the battle flag of Captain Oliver Hazard Perry.

The Embargo Act of 1807

Yet while making some preparations for war, Jefferson adopted "peaceable coercion" by suspending trade with Britain and France to gain respect for neutral rights. By far the most controversial legislation of Jefferson's presidency, the **Embargo Act of 1807** prohibited vessels from leaving American harbors for foreign ports. Technically, it prohibited only exports, but its practical effect was to stop imports as well, for few foreign ships would venture into American ports if they had to leave without cargo. Amazed by the boldness of the act, a British newspaper described the embargo as "little short of an absolute secession from the rest of the civilized world."

Embargo Act of 1807 Jefferson's attempt at "peaceable coercion" by suspending American trade with France and Britain

The embargo did not have the intended effect. Although British sales to the United States dropped 50 percent between 1807 and 1808, the British quickly found new markets in South America. Furthermore, the Embargo Act contained some loopholes. For example, it allowed American ships blown off course to put in at European ports if necessary; suddenly, many captains were reporting that adverse winds had forced them across the Atlantic. Treating the embargo as a joke, Napoleon seized any

American ships he could lay hands on and then informed the United States that he was only helping to enforce the embargo.

The United States itself felt the harshest effects of the embargo. Some thirty thousand American seamen found themselves out of work. Hundreds of merchants went into bankruptcy, and jails swelled with debtors. Farmers were devastated. Unable to export their produce or sell it at a decent price to hard-pressed urban dwellers, many farmers could not pay their debts. New England suffered most; in Massachusetts, which accounted for a third of foreign trade, the embargo was a calamity.

The situation was not entirely bleak, however. The embargo forced a diversion of merchants' capital into manufacturing. Before 1808, the United States had only fifteen cotton textile mills; by the end of 1809, an additional eighty-seven mills had been constructed (see Chapter 9). But none of this comforted merchants who were already ruined or mariners driven to soup kitchens. Nor could New Englanders forget that the source of their misery was a policy initiated by one of the "Virginia lordlings," "Mad Tom" Jefferson, who knew little about New England and loathed cities, the very foundations of New England's prosperity.

James Madison and the Failure of Peaceable Coercion

With Jefferson's blessing, the Republicans nominated James Madison and George Clinton for the presidency and vice presidency in 1808. The Federalists re-nominated Charles C. Pinckney and Rufus King, the same ticket that had failed in 1804. In 1808 the Federalists staged a modest comeback, but Madison handily won the presidency, and the Republicans continued to control Congress.

The Federalists' revival, modest as it was, rested on two factors. First, the Embargo Act gave them the national issue that they had long lacked. Second, younger Federalists had abandoned their elders' gentlemanly disdain for campaigning and deliberately imitated such vote-winning techniques as barbecues and mass meetings, which had worked for the Republicans.

To some contemporaries, "Little Jemmy" Madison, five feet four inches tall, seemed a weak figure compared to Jefferson. In fact, Madison's intelligence and capacity for systematic thought equaled Jefferson's. He had the added advantage of being married to Dolley Madison. A striking figure in her turbans and colorful dresses, Dolley arranged receptions at the White House in which she charmed Republicans, and even some Federalists, into sympathy with her husband's policies.

Madison continued the embargo with minor changes. Like Jefferson, he reasoned that Britain was "more vulnerable in her commerce than in her armies." The American embargo, however, was coercing no one, and on March 1, 1809, Congress replaced the Embargo Act with the weaker, face-saving Non-Intercourse Act. This act opened trade to all nations except Britain and France and then authorized the president to restore trade with either of those nations if it stopped violating neutral rights. However, neither nation complied. In May 1810, Congress substituted a new measure, Macon's Bill No. 2, which opened trade with Britain and France and offered each a clumsy bribe: If either nation repealed its restrictions on neutral shipping, the United States would halt trade with the other.

None of these steps had the desired effect. While Jefferson and Madison lashed out at France and Britain as moral demons ("The one is a den of robbers and the other of pirates," snapped Jefferson), the belligerents saw the world as composed of a few great powers and many weak ones. When great powers went to war, there were no neutrals. Weak nations like the United States should stop babbling about moral ideals and seek the protection of a great power.

"war hawks" Members of Congress elected from western states in 1810 who wanted war with Britain

As peaceable coercion became a fiasco, Madison came under fire from militant Republicans, known as **"war hawks,"** who demanded more aggressive policies. Coming mainly from the South and West, regions where "honor" was a sacred word, the militants were infuriated by insults to the American flag. In addition, economic recession between 1808 and 1810 had convinced the firebrands that British policies were wrecking their regions' economies. The election of 1810 brought several war hawks to Congress. Led by Henry Clay of Kentucky, the war hawks included John C. Calhoun of South Carolina, Richard M. Johnson of Kentucky, and William King of North Carolina, all future vice presidents. Clay was elected Speaker of the House.

Tecumseh and the Prophet

More emotional and pugnaciously nationalistic than Jefferson or Madison, the war hawks called for the expulsion of the British from Canada and the Spanish from the Florida region. Their demands merged with westerners' fears that the British in Canada were recruiting Indians to halt the march of U.S. settlement. In reality, American policy, not British meddling, was the source of bloodshed on the frontier.

Jefferson believed that Indians and whites could live peacefully together if the Indians abandoned their hunting and nomadic ways and took up farming. If they farmed, they would need less land. However, the march of white settlement was steadily shrinking Indian hunting grounds, and some Indians were willing to sign away land in return for blankets, guns, and liquor.

No American was more eager to acquire Indian lands than William Henry Harrison, governor of the Indiana Territory. Harrison realized that Indiana would not become a state without more residents, and the best way to attract more residents was to offer them Indian land. Disregarding instructions from Washington, Harrison rounded up a delegation of half-starved Indians, none of whom lived on the rich lands along the Wabash (WAH-bash) River that he craved. By the Treaty of Fort Wayne in September 1809, these Indians ceded millions of acres along the Wabash at a price of two cents an acre.

Tecumseh Shawnee leader who tried to build a coalition of several western tribes; allied with British in War of 1812

This treaty outraged the numerous tribes that had not been party to it. Among the angriest were **Tecumseh** (tuh-CUM-suh), the Shawnee chief, and his brother Lalawéthica (la-la-WAY-thuh-kuh). In 1805, Lalawéthica had had a frightening dream, a vision of drunken Indians who were tormented for eternity. Overnight he was transformed from a drunken misfit into a preacher. He gave up liquor and began beseeching surrounding tribes to return to the old ways and avoid contact with whites. Now known as the Prophet, he took a new name, Tenskwatawa (tens-KWAH-tah-wah), the "open door" through which Indians could achieve salvation. Shawnees responded to his message.

In the meantime, Tecumseh had tried to build a coalition of several tribes to stem the tide of white settlement. He insisted that Indian lands belonged collectively

Cincinnati Museum Center

Tecumseh and William Henry Harrison at Vincennes, August 1810

This portrait of a personal duel between Tecumseh and Indiana governor William Henry Harrison is fanciful. But the confrontation between the two at Vincennes nearly erupted into violence. Tecumseh told Harrison that Indians could never trust whites because "when Jesus Christ came upon the earth you kill'd him and nail'd him on a cross."

to all the tribes and could not be sold by splinter groups. Failing to reach a settlement with Tecumseh or the Prophet, Harrison concluded that it was time to attack the Indians. His target was a Shawnee encampment near the mouth of the Tippecanoe (TIP-pee-cun-oo) River. With Tecumseh absent and recruiting more followers, the Prophet launched an attack on Harrison's forces in November 1811. Outnumbered two to one and short of ammunition, Tenskwatawa's force was beaten off after inflicting heavy casualties.

Although a small engagement, the Battle of Tippecanoe had far-reaching effects. Harrison became a national hero and ultimately rode his reputation to the White House. The Prophet was discredited, but his brother Tecumseh became recognized as a leader among the western tribes. Finally, Tecumseh concluded that an alliance with the British was the only way to stop the spread of American settlement.

Congress Votes for War

By spring 1812, President Madison had concluded that war was inevitable, and he sent a war message to Congress on June 1. Ironically, an economic slump prompted Britain to repeal its Orders in Council on June 23, but by then Congress had declared war. Neither the war hawks nor westerners held the key to the vote in favor of war; the votes of Republicans in states like Pennsylvania, Maryland, and Virginia were the decisive force in propelling the declaration of war through Congress. Opposition came mainly from Federalist strongholds in New England and New York.

Madison, in his war message, listed impressment, the presence of British ships in U.S. waters, and British violation of neutral rights as wrongs that justified war. None of these complaints fully explains why America declared war in 1812. Neither do continuing Indian problems (blamed on the British) along the frontier. A more important underlying cause for the war was the economic recession that affected the South and West after 1808. Finally, it was critical that Madison, rather than Jefferson, was president in 1812. Jefferson had believed that Britain was motivated primarily by its desire to defeat Napoleon, and that once the war in Europe ended, the provocations would stop. Madison held that Britain's real motive was to strangle American trade and thus to eliminate the United States as a trading rival.

CHECKING IN

- In his second term, Jefferson faced challenges from Aaron Burr and John Randolph.
- Impressment became a major issue between the United States and Great Britain.
- Jefferson tried "peaceable coercion" through the Embargo Act; however, it was a failure.
- "War hawks" from the southern and western states demanded more aggressive policies.
- James Madison ultimately asked Congress for a declaration of war because he saw Great Britain as a long-term threat to the United States.

THE WAR OF 1812

How did the War of 1812 influence American domestic politics?

Although American warships would win a few sensational duels with British men-of-war, the U.S. Navy simply could not challenge the Royal Navy on the high seas, or even prevent a British blockade of the American coast. Madison thus shifted his sights to Canada, whose small population made it seem an easy mark. Jefferson, for example, saw the conquest of Canada as "a mere matter of marching."

Little justified such optimism. Although the British remained preoccupied with the Napoleonic wars in Europe, they enlisted Native Americans as their allies—and used fear of these "uncontrollable savages" to force American surrenders. American militias were often Sunday soldiers who "hollered for water half the time, and whiskey the other." Few understood what the war was about, and fewer still cared.

On to Canada

From the summer of 1812 to the spring of 1814, the Americans launched a series of unsuccessful attacks on Canada (see Map 8.2). In July 1812, General William Hull led an American army from Detroit into Canada, quickly returned when Tecumseh cut his supply line, and surrendered Detroit and two thousand men to thirteen hundred British and Indian troops. In the fall of 1812, the British and their Mohawk allies crushed a force of American regulars at the Battle of Queenston, near Niagara Falls. A third American offensive in 1812, a projected attack on Montreal via Lake Champlain, fell apart when the militia again refused to advance into Canada.

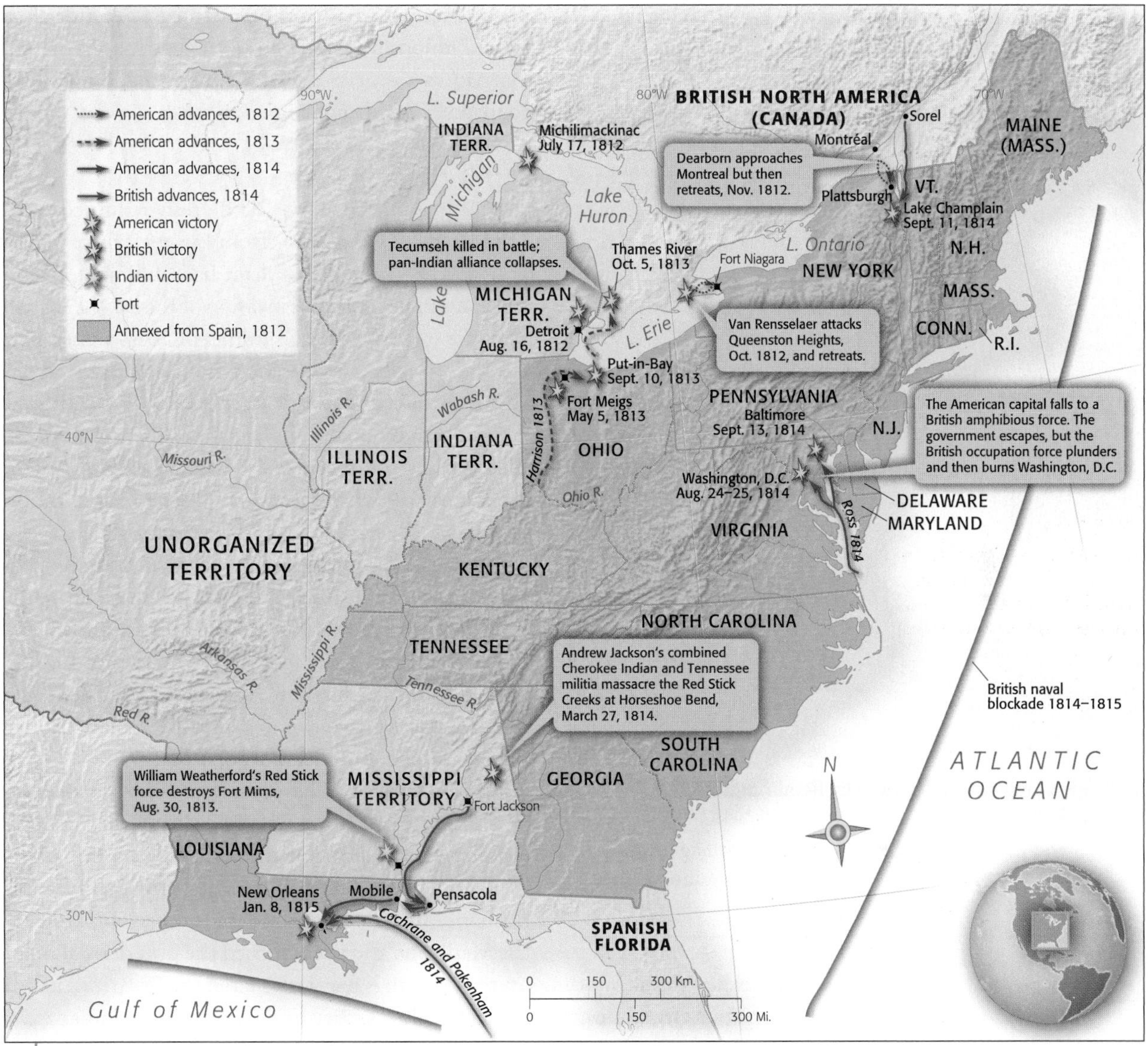

Map 8.2 Major Battles of the War of 1812

Most of the war's major engagements occurred on or near the United States' northern frontier, but the Royal Navy blockaded the entire Atlantic coast, and the British army penetrated as far south as Washington and New Orleans.

 Interactive Map

Renewed U.S. offensives and subsequent reverses in 1813 convinced the Americans that they could not retake Detroit while the British controlled Lake Erie. During the winter of 1812–1813, U.S. captain Oliver Hazard Perry built ships and outfitted them with captured cannons, and on September 10, 1813, the homemade American fleet destroyed a British squadron at Put-in-Bay on the western end of Lake Erie. "We have met the enemy, and they are ours," Perry triumphantly reported. The British then pulled out of Detroit, but American forces under General William Henry Harrison overtook and defeated a combined British-Indian force at the Battle

Bettmann/CORBIS

First Lady Dolley Madison by Rembrandt Peale, c. 1809

Friendly, tactful, and blessed with an unfailing memory for names and events, First Lady Dolley Madison earned a reputation as an elegant hostess.

of the Thames (thaymes) on October 5. Tecumseh, a legend among whites, died in the battle. Perry's and Harrison's victories cheered Americans, but efforts to invade Canada continued to falter.

The British Offensive

With fresh reinforcements from Europe, where Napoleon had abdicated as emperor after his disastrous invasion of Russia, the British took the offensive in the summer of 1814. General Sir George Prevost led a force of ten thousand British veterans in an offensive meant to split New England from the rest of the country. The British advanced down Lake Champlain until meeting the well-entrenched American forces at Plattsburgh. After his fleet met defeat on September 11, Prevost abandoned the campaign.

Ironically, Britain's most spectacular success began as a diversion from Prevost's offensive. In 1814, a British army landed near Washington and met a larger American force, composed mainly of militia, at Bladensburg, Maryland, on August 24. The Battle of Bladensburg deteriorated into the "Bladensburg Races" as the American troops fled, almost without firing a shot. The British then descended on Washington. Madison, who had witnessed the Bladensburg fiasco, escaped into the Virginia hills. His wife, Dolley, loaded her carriage before joining her husband. British troops ate the supper prepared for the Madisons and then burned the presidential mansion and other public buildings in the capital. A few weeks later, the British attacked Baltimore, but after failing to crack its defenses, they broke off the operation.

The Treaty of Ghent, 1814

Treaty of Ghent Treaty that ended War of 1812, restoring *status quo ante bellum*

Napoleon's abdication made Britain's primary goal a lasting European peace, and thus the British had little to gain by prolonging a minor war in America. The **Treaty of Ghent,** signed on Christmas Eve, 1814, restored the *status quo ante bellum*:* The United States neither gained nor lost territory. The fixing of the Canadian-American border was referred to a joint commission for future settlement. Impressment was left hanging, but the end of the European war made neutral rights a dead issue.

Ironically, America's most dramatic victory came on January 8, 1815, two weeks after the treaty had been signed but before word of it reached America. A British force had descended on New Orleans. U.S. troops commanded by General Andrew ("Old Hickory") Jackson, legendary as a fierce Indian fighter, shredded the line of

* *Status quo ante bellum:* Latin for "the state of affairs before the war"

advancing redcoats, inflicting more than two thousand casualties while suffering only thirteen of their own.

The Hartford Convention

Although it meant nothing in terms of the war, the Battle of New Orleans had a devastating effect on the Federalist Party. The Federalist comeback had continued into the election of 1812, when their candidate, DeWitt Clinton, an antiwar Republican, carried all of New England except Vermont, along with New York and New Jersey. American military setbacks had intensified Federalist disdain for Madison. He seemed to epitomize a decade of Republican misrule at New England's expense. The Louisiana Purchase, while constitutionally dubious, had reduced the importance of New England, the Embargo Act had nearly destroyed the region's commerce, and "Mr. Madison's War" had brought fresh misery in the form of the British blockade. A few Federalists began to talk of New England's secession from the Union.

In late 1814, a special Federalist convention met in Hartford, Connecticut. Although some supported secession, moderates took control and passed a series of resolutions expressing New England's grievances. Convinced that New England was becoming a permanent minority in a nation dominated by southern Republicans who failed to understand the region's commercial interests, the **Hartford Convention** leaders proposed a series of constitutional amendments: to abolish the three-fifths clause, which allowed southerners to count slaves as a basis for representation; to require a two-thirds vote of Congress to declare war and to admit new states into the Union; to limit the president to a single term; to prohibit the election of two successive presidents from the same state; and to bar embargoes lasting more than sixty days.

These proposals were as bold as their timing was disastrous. News of the peace and of Jackson's victory at New Orleans dashed Federalist hopes of gaining popular support, while the states' rights emphasis of the convention smelled of treason to many delegates. The restoration of peace stripped the Federalists of their primary grievance. In the presidential election of 1816, James Monroe, Madison's hand-picked successor and another Virginia Republican, swept the nation over negligible Federalist opposition. He would win reelection in 1820 with only a single dissenting electoral vote. As a force in national politics, the Federalists were finished.

Hartford Convention Federalist meeting that showed seeming disloyalty in time of war; began downfall of the party

CHECKING IN

- The United States failed in its attempts to invade Canada.
- When the war in Europe ended, Britain launched a major offensive in the United States, which included the ransacking of Washington, DC.
- The Treaty of Ghent ended the war with a restoration of the *status quo ante bellum.*
- At the Hartford Convention, dissatisfied Federalists toyed with the idea of secession, a move ultimately fatal to them as a political party.
- The war produced a hero in Andrew Jackson and a renewed sense of nationalism and confidence throughout the nation.

THE AWAKENING OF AMERICAN NATIONALISM

To what extent did Jefferson's legacy persist into the so-called Era of Good Feelings?

The United States emerged from the War of 1812 bruised but intact. In its first major war since independence, the American republic had demonstrated that it could fight on even terms against a major power and that republics could conduct wars without becoming despotisms. The war also produced several major symbols of American nationalism: the presidential mansion, whitewashed to hide smoke damage, became the White House; Britain's failed attack on Fort McHenry in Baltimore Harbor inspired Francis Scott Key's "Star-Spangled Banner"; and the Battle of New Orleans made Andrew Jackson a national hero and reinforced legends about the prowess of American frontier people and their marksmanship with a rifle. Much of the legend spun around the Battle of New Orleans was untrue, but Americans loved it nonetheless, especially because it confirmed their conviction that amateur soldiers and militiamen could outfight a professional army.

Madison's Nationalism and the "Era of Good Feelings," 1817–1824

The War of 1812 had three major political consequences. First, it eliminated the Federalists as a national political force. Second, it went far toward convincing the Republicans that the nation was strong and resilient, capable of fighting a war while maintaining liberty. Third, with political rivals removed, the Republicans began to embrace some Federalist ideas.

Both President Madison and Henry Clay became advocates of federal support for internal improvements, tariff protection for new industries, and the creation of a new national bank; Clay christened these ideas the American System and proclaimed that they would make the nation economically self-sufficient. In 1816 Congress chartered the Second Bank of the United States and enacted a moderate tariff, but federally supported internal improvements were more difficult. Madison vetoed an internal improvements bill in 1817, believing that a constitutional amendment was necessary to authorize such improvements.

"Era of Good Feelings" Somewhat misleading label given to the period of one-party politics during the administration of James Monroe

As Republicans adopted positions they had once disdained, an **"Era of Good Feelings"** dawned on American politics. A Boston newspaper, impressed by the warm reception accorded President James Monroe while touring New England, coined the phrase in 1817. It has stuck as a description of Monroe's two administrations from 1817 to 1825.

However, the good feelings were paper-thin. Madison's 1817 veto of the internal-improvements bill revealed the persistence of disagreements about the federal government's role under the Constitution. Furthermore, the continuation of slavery was arousing sectional animosities that a journalist's phrase about good feelings could not dispel. Not surprisingly, the postwar consensus began to unravel almost as soon as Americans recognized its existence.

John Marshall and the Supreme Court

In 1819, Jefferson's old antagonist John Marshall, who was still chief justice, issued two opinions that stunned Republicans. The first case, *Dartmouth College* v. *Woodward,* focused on New Hampshire's attempt to transform a private corporation, Dartmouth College, into a state university. Marshall concluded that Dartmouth's original charter was a contract and thus was protected under the constitutional prohibition against state interference in contracts. Marshall's ruling had enormous implications. In effect, Marshall said that, once a state had chartered a college or business, that state surrendered its power to alter the charter and, in large measure, its authority to regulate the beneficiary.

A few weeks later, the chief justice handed down an even more momentous decision in ***McCulloch* v. *Maryland*.** At issue was whether the state of Maryland had the power to tax a national corporation—specifically, the Baltimore branch of the Second Bank of the United States. Marshall focused on two issues. First, did Congress have the power to charter a national bank? The Constitution, Marshall conceded, did not explicitly grant this power, but the broad sweep of enumerated powers implied the power to charter a bank. This was a clear enunciation of a broad, or "loose," construction (interpretation) of the Constitution. The second issue revolved around whether a state could tax an agency of the federal government that was located within its borders. Marshall argued that any power of the national government, enumerated or implied, was supreme within its sphere. States could not interfere with the exercise of federal power; thus, Maryland's attempt to tax the bank was plainly unconstitutional.

McCulloch* v. *Maryland
Supreme Court decision that bolstered broad construction; restated national supremacy over states

The *McCulloch* decision dismayed many Republicans. The bank, initially supported by Madison and Monroe, had triggered the Panic of 1819 by tightening credit. Distressed western farmers angrily blamed the bank for their dilemmas. And now Marshall's decision placed the hated bank beyond the reach of any state government. The Constitution, Marshall said, was the creation not of state governments but of the people of *all* the states and thus overrode state laws. The decision was as much an attack on state sovereignty as a defense of the bank itself.

Like Jefferson, most Republicans considered the Union a compact among states and saw state governments as the guarantors of popular liberty. In Republican eyes, the *Dartmouth* and *McCulloch* cases stripped state governments of the power to impose the will of their people on corporations and thus threatened liberty.

The Missouri Compromise, 1820–1821

The controversy over statehood for Missouri highlighted the fragility of the so-called Era of Good Feelings. Carved from the Louisiana Purchase, Missouri had attracted many southerners who expected to use slaves to grow cotton and hemp. By 1819, slaves made up 16 percent of the territory's inhabitants.

In February 1819, the House of Representatives considered a bill to admit Missouri as a slave state. A New York Republican offered an amendment that prohibited the further introduction of slaves into Missouri and provided for the emancipation, at age twenty-five, of all slave offspring born after Missouri joined the Union. Following rancorous debate, the House accepted the amendment and the Senate rejected it. Both chambers voted along sectional lines.

Before 1819, slavery had not been a major source of the nation's sectional divisions, which tended to pit New England against the South and West. But the Missouri question, which Jefferson called "a fire bell in the night [which] awakened me and filled me with terror," thrust slavery into the center of long-standing sectional divisions.

Several factors drove the slavery issue to the forefront. In 1819, the Union had eleven free and eleven slave states. The admission of Missouri as a slave state would upset this balance to the advantage of the South. Equally important, Missouri was on the same latitude as the free states of Ohio, Indiana, and Illinois, and northerners worried that admitting Missouri as a slave state would set a precedent for the

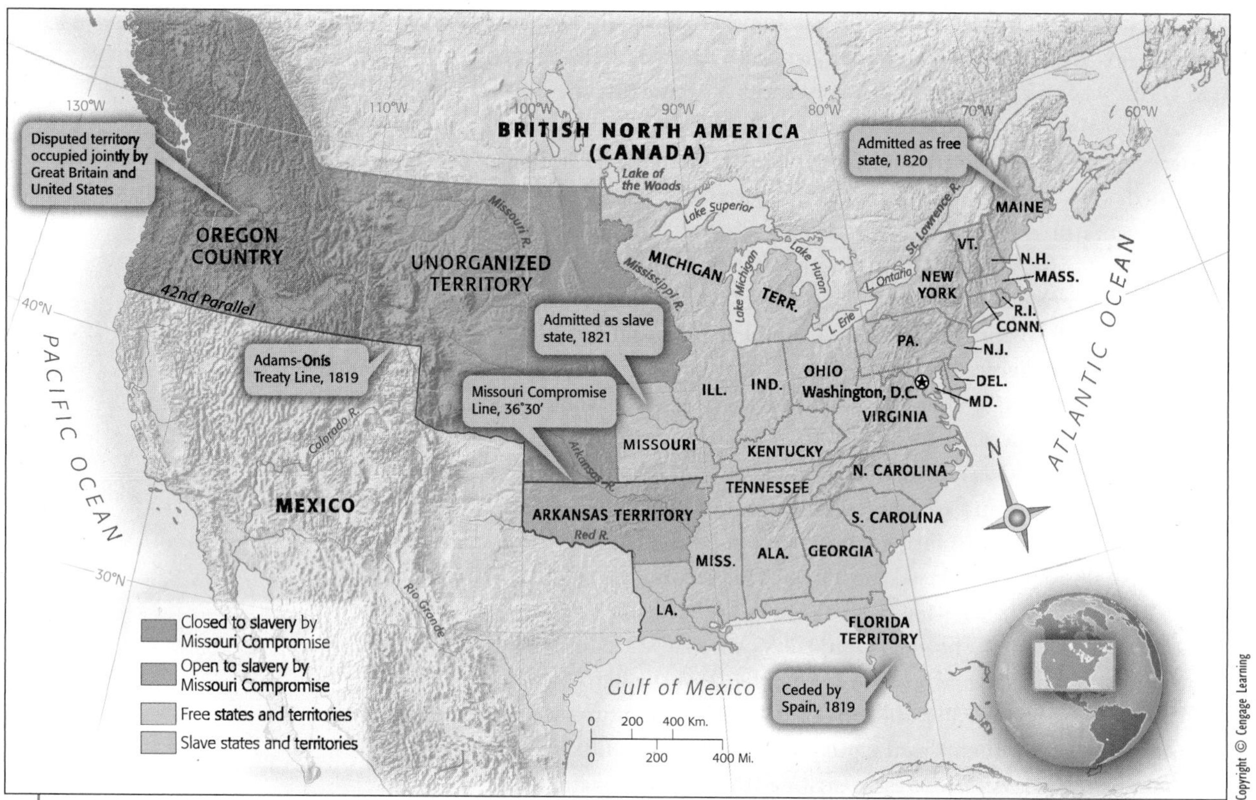

Map 8.3 The Missouri Compromise, 1820–1821

The Missouri Compromise temporarily quelled controversy over slavery by admitting Maine as a free state and Missouri as a slave state and by prohibiting slavery in the remainder of the Louisiana Purchase north of 36°30′.

Interactive Map

extension of slavery into the northern part of the Purchase. Finally, the disintegration of the Federalists as a national force reduced the need for unity among Republicans, and they increasingly heeded sectional pressures more than calls for party loyalty.

Virtually every issue that would wrack the Union in the next forty years was present in the Missouri controversy: southern charges that the North was conspiring to destroy the Union and to end slavery; northern accusations that southerners were conspiring to extend slavery. For a while, leaders doubted that the Union would survive the crisis; the words "disunion" and "civil war" were freely uttered, Henry Clay wrote.

Missouri Compromise An attempt to end slavery controversy by bringing Missouri and Maine into the Union, drawing a line limiting slavery across the Louisiana Purchase

A series of congressional agreements known collectively as the **Missouri Compromise** resolved the crisis. To balance the number of slave states and free states, Congress in 1820 admitted Maine as a free state and Missouri as a slave state; to forestall a further crisis, it also prohibited slavery in the remainder of the Louisiana Purchase north of 36°30′, Missouri's southern border.

The Missouri Compromise was widely viewed as a southern victory. The South had gained admission of Missouri, whose acceptance of slavery was controversial, while the North had merely gained Maine, whose rejection of slavery sparked no controversy. But at the same time, the South had allowed slavery to be banned from a vast territory north of 36°30′, an area that would not long remain a wilderness. The Missouri Compromise also reinforced the principle that Congress could prohibit slavery in some territories. Southerners had implicitly agreed that slaves were not like other forms of property that could be moved from place to place at will.

Foreign Policy Under Monroe

American foreign policy between 1816 and 1824 reflected more consensus than conflict. The end of the Napoleonic Wars and the signing of the Treaty of Ghent had removed most of the foreign-policy disagreements between Federalists and Republicans. Moreover, President Monroe had as his secretary of state an extraordinary diplomat, John Quincy Adams. The son of the last Federalist president, Adams had been the only Federalist in the Senate to support the Louisiana Purchase, and he later became an ardent Republican. Adams was a tough negotiator and a fervent nationalist.

Adams moved quickly to strengthen the peace with Great Britain. During his term the Rush-Bagot Treaty of 1817 demilitarized the Great Lakes, and the British-American Convention of 1818 fixed the Canadian-American boundary and restored U.S. fishing rights off Newfoundland. With its northern border secure, the United States could turn its attention southward and westward.

The nation now turned its attention to dealing with Spain, who still owned East Florida and claimed West Florida. It had never been clear whether the Louisiana Purchase included West Florida. Acting as if it did, the United States in 1812 simply added a slice of West Florida to the state of Louisiana and another piece to the Mississippi Territory. Using the pretext that it was a base for Seminole Indian raids and a refuge for fugitive slaves, Andrew Jackson, now a military commander in the South, invaded West Florida in 1818, hanged two British subjects, and captured Spanish forts. Although Jackson had acted without explicit orders, Adams supported the raid, guessing correctly that it would panic the Spanish into further concessions. In 1819, Spain agreed to the **Adams-Onís (Transcontinental) Treaty,** ceding East Florida to the United States, renouncing all claims to West Florida, and agreeing to a southern border of the United States west of the Mississippi, while Spain agreed to a northern limit to its claims to the West Coast (see Map 8.3). It thereby left the United States free to pursue its interests in Oregon.

Adams-Onís (Transcontinental) Treaty An 1819 treaty by which Spain conceded Florida to the United States; established boundary lines in the West

The Monroe Doctrine, 1823

John Quincy Adams believed that God and nature had ordained that the United States would eventually span the entire continent of North America. While negotiating the purchase of Florida, he made it clear to Spain that the United States might seize what it could not purchase—including Texas and Mexico. Besides, Spain was concerned with larger issues than American encroachment. Its primary objective was to suppress the revolutions against Spanish rule that had broken out in South America. Britain's foreign minister, George Canning, proposed a joint U.S.-British statement opposing European interference in South America and pledging that neither nation would annex any part of Spain's empire in the New World.

Monroe Doctrine Statement that proclaimed U.S. primacy in the New World

While sharing Canning's opposition to European intervention in the New World, Adams preferred that the United States make a declaration of policy on its own rather than "come in as a cock-boat in the wake of the British man-of-war." Adams flatly rejected Canning's insistence on a joint pledge never to annex Spain's former territories, for Adams wanted the freedom to annex Texas or Cuba.

This was the background of the **Monroe Doctrine,** as President Monroe's message to Congress on December 2, 1823, later came to be called. Written largely by Adams, the message announced three key principles: that U.S. policy was to avoid European wars unless American interests were involved; that the "American continents" were not "subjects for future colonization by any European power"; and that the United States would construe any attempt at European colonization in the New World as an "unfriendly act."

Europeans widely derided the Monroe Doctrine as an empty pronouncement. With hindsight, however, the Europeans might have taken the doctrine more seriously, for it had important implications. First, by pledging itself not to interfere in European wars, the United States was excluding the possibility that it would support revolutionary movements in Europe. Second, by keeping open its options to annex territory in the Americas, the United States was using the Monroe Doctrine to claim a preeminent position in the New World.

CHECKING IN

- As the Federalist Party faded as a national force, Monroe's years in the White House became known as the Era of Good Feelings.
- John Marshall's Supreme Court strengthened the power of the central government with critical rulings on the use of implied powers and the limits of state power.
- The Missouri Compromise showed how dangerous the issue of slavery was.
- Through a series of treaties, the United States consolidated its northern and southern borders.
- Although derided by other nations, the Monroe Doctrine represented a major step toward American domination of the Western Hemisphere.

Chapter Summary

How did Jefferson's philosophy shape policy toward public expenditures, the judiciary, and Louisiana? (page 175)

Jefferson brought with him to the White House a well-defined set of ideas about the necessity for tightly controlled central government, payment of the national debt, and downsizing the American military. Nonetheless, when offered the chance to buy Louisiana, an action not specified in the Constitution, Jefferson eagerly jumped at the chance to rid the New World of France. His sponsorship of the Lewis and Clark expedition exemplified his interest in science and his hope for practical results from science.

How did the United States slide into war with Great Britain? (page 181)

Despite the success of his first term, Jefferson struggled throughout his second term. He faced challenges from within his own party, notably from the mischief of Aaron Burr and from old Republicans like John Randolph, who charged that Jefferson was abandoning pure Republican doctrines. Relations with Great Britain steadily worsened. His attempts at "peaceable coercion" were fruitless, and "war hawks" from the western states became increasingly vocal

KEY TERMS

Sally Hemings *(p. 175)*
Marbury v. *Madison (p. 177)*
judicial review *(p. 177)*
Louisiana Purchase *(p. 179)*
Lewis and Clark expedition *(p. 181)*
Sacajawea *(p. 181)*
impressment *(p. 183)*
Embargo Act of 1807 *(p. 184)*
"war hawks" *(p. 186)*
Tecumseh *(p. 186)*
Treaty of Ghent *(p. 190)*
Hartford Convention *(p. 191)*
"Era of Good Feelings" *(p. 192)*
McCulloch v. *Maryland (p. 193)*

and powerful. James Madison, Jefferson's successor, saw Britain as a continuing threat to the United States; his declaration of war was based much more on that long-term fear than on short-term problems such as impressment.

KEY TERMS continued

Missouri Compromise *(p. 194)*

Adams-Onís (Transcontinental) Treaty *(p. 195)*

Monroe Doctrine *(p. 196)*

How did the War of 1812 influence American domestic politics? (page 188)

The War of 1812 saw few American successes, but in the Treaty of Ghent, Great Britain essentially restored the *status quo ante bellum.* Nonetheless, the war destroyed the Federalists, who committed political suicide at the Hartford Convention. It also produced at least one major hero, Andrew Jackson, and spawned a renewed sense of confidence and nationalism. With the Federalist Party evaporating as a political force, the nation entered what one observer dubbed an Era of Good Feelings. But despite the appearance of harmony, conflict was never far below the surface. In the absence of Federalist opposition, Republicans began to fragment into sectional factions.

To what extent did Jefferson's legacy persist into the so-called Era of Good Feelings? (page 191)

During the Monroe administration, the United States consolidated its northern and southern borders, saw a broad interpretation of the Constitution put in place by the Marshall court, and confronted and then dodged the issue of slavery with the Missouri Compromise. Finally, the Monroe Doctrine represented a major step toward American domination of the Western Hemisphere.

Go to the CourseMate website at **www.cengagebrain.com** for additional study tools and review materials—including audio and video clips—for this chapter.

CHAPTER 9

The Transformation of American Society

1815–1840

American Textile History Museum

Middlesex Company, Woolen Mills, Lowell, Massachusetts, c. 1840

CHAPTER PREVIEW

Westward Expansion
What caused the surge of westward migration after the War of 1812?

The Growth of the Market Economy
What changes were linked to the rise of the market economy?

Industrial Beginnings
What caused the rise of industrialization?

Equality and Inequality
What caused urban poverty in this period?

The Revolution in Social Relationships
How did the rise of the market economy and industrialization change relationships within families and communities?

The life of Harriet Jane Hanson Robinson (1825–1911) intersected several developments that left a distinct imprint on America between 1820 and the Civil War. She directly experienced early industrialization as one of the "operatives" in the Lowell, Massachusetts, textile mills. Harriet entered factory work at the age of ten but managed to acquire an education in a public high school. Her literary refinement, along with her handsome features and lively wit, attracted her future husband, William Stevens Robinson. Like William, Harriet supported the antislavery movement and the Whig political party. Later, she embraced women's suffrage.

Harriet's experiences serve as a window on her times. By 1820, New England's small, rock-strewn farms could no longer support its rural population. Many of its young men moved west, while young women sought work in the new textile mills. In 1830, more than 70 percent of the female workers in Lowell were between the ages of fifteen and nineteen. When she was eleven, Harriet led her young coworkers in a "turn-out" (strike) to protest a reduction in wages. But native-born, Protestant girls like Harriet did not see themselves as part of a permanent working class—most left factory work when they married.

Rather, the mill girls sought "betterment." Between 1839 and 1845, the girls edited their own literary monthly, the *Lowell Offering,* which gained international repute. These upwardly mobile farm girls became part of the "middling classes" in antebellum America. They came to see themselves as individuals who could control their lives and bodies. Harriet's maternal grandfather had sired fifteen children; Harriet gave birth to only four.

The world Harriet knew in the mills was passing by the time of her marriage in 1848. A new generation of mill workers, many of them Irish immigrants, was forming a permanent factory working class. Founded as a pastoral "mill village," Lowell was turning into a city with sharpening tensions between the native-born and the Irish, Protestants and Catholics, rich and poor. As such, it was becoming a mirror of a changing America.

Westward Expansion

What caused the surge of westward migration after the War of 1812?

In 1790, the vast majority of the non-Indian population of the United States lived east of the Appalachian Mountains; by 1840, one-third were living between the Appalachians and the Mississippi River, defined as the West. These Americans rapidly developed a distinctive western culture.

Most Americans came west dreaming of a better version of the life they had known in the East. Several factors fed this dream: the growing power of the federal government; its often-ruthless removal of Indians from the path of white settlements; and a boom in the prices of agricultural commodities.

The Sweep West

This westward movement occurred in several thrusts. Americans leapfrogged the Appalachians after 1791 to bring four new states into the Union by 1803: Vermont, Kentucky, Tennessee, and Ohio. From 1816 to 1821, momentum carried settlers farther west, even across the Mississippi River, and six more states entered: Indiana, Mississippi, Illinois, Alabama, Maine, and Missouri. Ohio's population jumped from 45,000 in 1800 to 1,519,000 by 1840; Michigan's rose from 5,000 in 1810 to 212,000 by 1840.

Seeking security, pioneers usually migrated as families. To reach markets with their produce, most settlers clustered near the navigable rivers of the West, especially the magnificent water system created by the Ohio and Mississippi rivers. Only with the spread of canals in the 1820s and 1830s, and later of railroads, did westerners feel free to venture far from rivers.

Western Society and Customs

Migrants to the West brought with them values and customs peculiar to the regions they had left behind. For example, migrants who hailed from New England or upstate New York settled the northern areas of Ohio, Indiana, and Illinois, where they primarily grew wheat, supplemented by dairying and fruit orchards. Emigrants from the Upland South settled the southern parts of Ohio, Indiana, and Illinois, where they raised corn and hogs.

Regardless of their origins, most westerners craved sociability. Rural families joined their neighbors for sports and festivities. Men met for games that tested strength and agility: wrestling, lifting weights, pole jumping (for distance, not height), and hammer throwing. Women usually combined work and play in quilting and sewing bees, carpet tackings, and even goose and chicken pluckings. At "hoe-downs" and "frolics," the settlers danced to a fiddler's tune.

The West developed a character of its own. Eastern elegance yielded to western lack of refinement, making westerners easy targets for easterners' contemptuous jibes. Westerners responded that at least they were honest democrats, not soft would-be aristocrats. Pretension got short shrift. A sojourner at a tavern who hung a blanket to cover his bed from public gaze might find it ripped down. A politician who rode to a public meeting in a buggy instead of on horseback lost votes.

Chronology

1790	Samuel Slater opens his first Rhode Island mill
1793	Eli Whitney invents the cotton gin
1807	Robert R. Livingston and Robert Fulton introduce the steamboat *Clermont* on the Hudson River
1811	Construction of the National Road begins at Cumberland, Maryland
1813	Establishment of the Boston Manufacturing Company
1816	Second Bank of the United States chartered
1817	Construction of the Erie Canal started; Mississippi enters the Union
1819	Economic panic, ushering in four-year depression; Alabama enters the Union
1820s	Expansion of New England textile mills
1824	*Gibbons* v. *Ogden*
1828	Baltimore and Ohio Railroad chartered
1830	Indian Removal Act passed by Congress
1831	*Cherokee Nation* v. *Georgia*
1832	*Worcester* v. *Georgia*
1834	First strike at the Lowell mills
1835–1838	Trail of Tears
1837	Economic panic begins a depression that lasts until 1843
1840	System of production by interchangeable parts perfected

The Far West

Exploration carried some Americans even farther west. Zebulon Pike explored the Spanish Southwest in 1806. By 1811, in the wake of Lewis and Clark, the New York merchant John Jacob Astor founded a fur-trading post at the mouth of the Columbia River in the Oregon Country. At first, whites relied on the Native Americans for furs, but in the 1820s such "mountain men" as Kit Carson and Jedediah Smith penetrated deep beyond the Rockies.

Jedediah Smith was representative of these men. Born in the Susquehanna Valley of New York in 1799, Smith moved west with his family to Pennsylvania and Illinois and signed on with an expedition bound for the upper Missouri River in 1822. In the course of this and subsequent explorations, he was almost killed by a grizzly bear in South Dakota, learned from the Native Americans to trap beaver and kill buffalo, explored California's San Joaquin Valley, and hiked back across the Sierras to the Great Salt Lake, a forbidding trip. The exploits of Smith and the other mountain men were popularized in biographies, and they became legends in their own day.

The Federal Government and the West

The federal government's growing strength spurred westward expansion. Under the Articles of Confederation, several states had ceded western lands to the national government, creating a bountiful public domain. The Louisiana Purchase brought the entire Mississippi River under American control. Six million acres of public land had been promised to volunteers during the War of 1812. The **National Road,** a highway begun in 1811 in Cumberland, Maryland, stretched farther westward, reaching Wheeling, Virginia, in 1818 and Vandalia, Illinois, by 1838. Soon settlers thronged the road.

National Road Federally sponsored highway that crossed the Appalachians and opened the way for families to move west

The same government strength that aided whites brought misery to the Indians. Virtually all the foreign-policy successes during the Jefferson, Madison, and Monroe administrations worked to Native Americans' disadvantage. In the wake of the Louisiana Purchase, Lewis and Clark bluntly told the Indians that they must "shut their ears to the counsels of bad birds" and listen henceforth only to the "Great Father" in Washington. The outcome of the War of 1812 also worked against the Native Americans. Early in the negotiations leading to the Treaty of Ghent, the British had insisted on the creation of an Indian buffer state in the Old Northwest. But the British eventually dropped the demand and essentially abandoned the Indians to the Americans.

The Removal of the Indians

Westward-moving white settlers found sizable numbers of Native Americans in their paths, particularly in the South, home to the so-called **"Five Civilized Tribes":** the Cherokees, Choctaws, Creeks, Chickasaws, and Seminoles. Years of commercial dealings and intermarriage with whites had created in these tribes an influential minority of mixed-bloods who embraced Christianity, practiced agriculture, built gristmills, and even owned slaves. Cherokees had a written form of their language and their own bilingual newspaper, the *Cherokee Phoenix.*

"Five Civilized Tribes" Once-powerful southeastern Indians "removed" in the 1830s to make way for white settlement

The "civilization" of the southern Indians impressed New England missionaries more than southern whites, who viewed the Civilized Tribes with contempt and their land with envy. A handful of tribes had sold their lands to the federal government and accepted removal west of the Mississippi River by 1830, but most clung to their land and customs. When the Creek mixed-blood chief William McIntosh sold all Creek lands in Georgia and two-thirds of Creek lands in Alabama to the government in 1825, the tribal council executed him.

In the 1820s, white squatters moved onto tribal lands; southern legislatures, loath to restrain white settlers, moved to expropriate Indian lands. State laws extended state jurisdiction over the tribes and excluded Indians from serving as witnesses in court cases involving whites, which effectively made it virtually impossible for Indians to collect debts owed them by whites.

These measures delighted President Andrew Jackson. Himself a frontiersman contemptuous of Native Americans, Jackson believed it was ridiculous to treat the

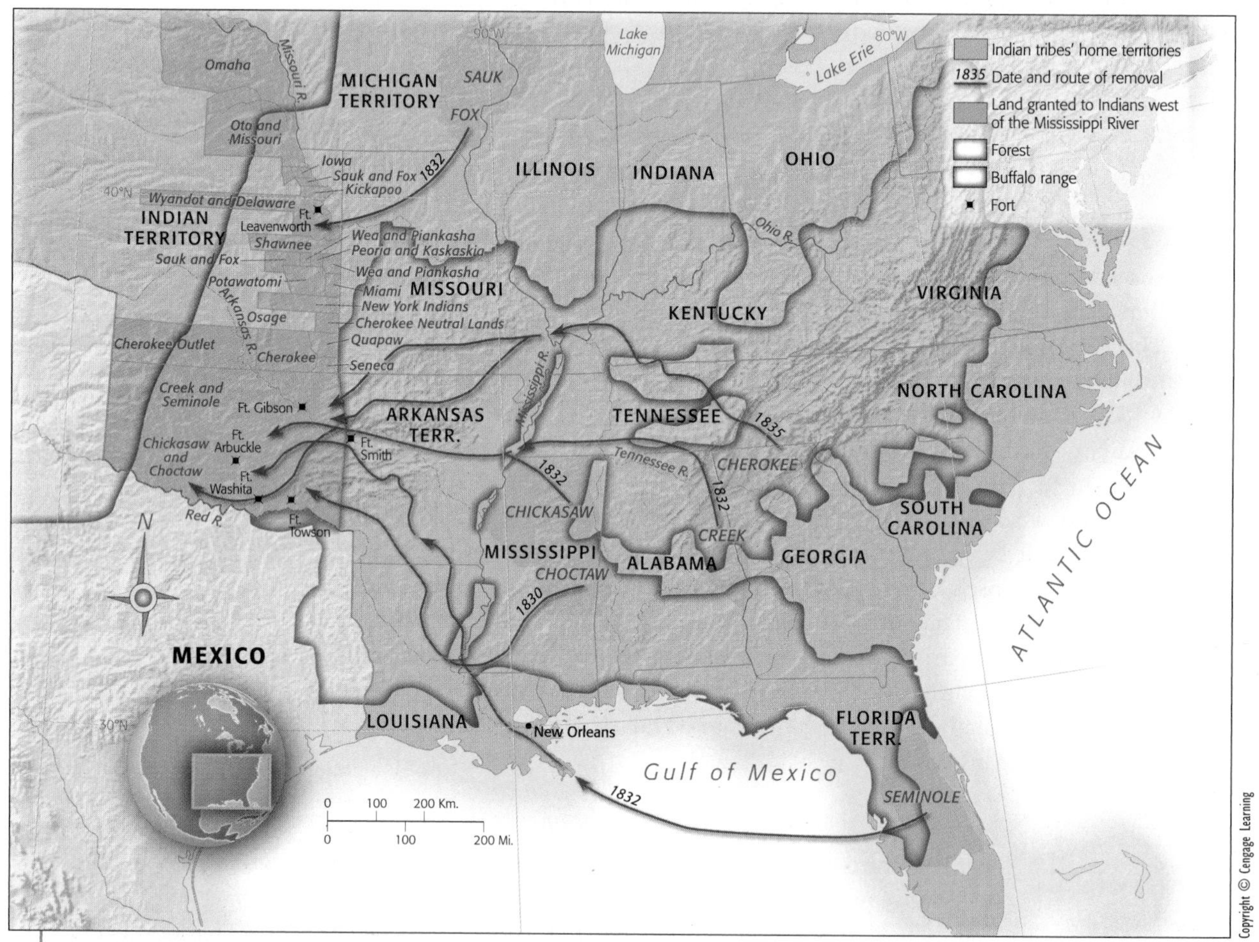

Map 9.1 The Removal of the Native Americans to the West, 1820–1840

The so-called Trail of Tears, followed by the Cherokees, was one of several routes along which various tribes migrated on their forced removal to reservations west of the Mississippi.

Interactive Map

Indians as independent nations; rather, he felt they should be subject to the laws of the states where they lived. This position spelled doom for the Indians, who could not vote or hold state office. In 1834, Cherokee chief John Ross got a taste of what state jurisdiction meant: Georgia, without consulting him, put his house up as a prize in the state lottery.

In 1830, President Jackson secured passage of the Indian Removal Act, which authorized him to exchange public lands in the West for Indian territories in the East. During Jackson's eight years in office, the federal government forced Indians to exchange 100 million acres of their lands for 32 million acres of public lands. The Choctaws, Creeks, and Chickasaws began their "voluntary" migration in the late 1820s. In 1836, Creeks who clung to their homes were forcibly removed, many in chains. Most Seminoles were removed from Florida, but only after a bitter war between 1835 and 1842 that cost the federal government $20 million (see Map 9.1).

Ironically, the Cherokees, often considered the "most civilized" tribe, suffered the worst fate. Pursuing their claims before the Supreme Court, they won two favorable decisions from Chief Justice John Marshall. In ***Cherokee Nation* v. *Georgia*** (1831), Marshall recognized the Cherokees as a "domestic dependent nation" with a legitimate claim to their lands in Georgia. A year later, in ***Worcester* v. *Georgia*,** Marshall declared them a "distinct" political community entitled to federal protection from Georgia's claims.

Cherokee Nation* v. *Georgia Supreme Court decision recognizing Cherokees' claim to their lands; ignored by President Jackson

Worcester* v. *Georgia Court decision declaring that Cherokees were entitled to federal protection; ignored by President Jackson

President Andrew Jackson reportedly sneered, "John Marshall has made his decision; now let him enforce it" and ignored the ruling. Next, federal agents persuaded some minor Cherokee chiefs to sign the Treaty of New Echota (1835), which ceded all Cherokee lands in the United States for $5.6 million and free passage west. Congress ratified this treaty, but the vast majority of Cherokees denounced it. In 1839, a Cherokee party took revenge by murdering its three principal signers.

The end of the story was simple and tragic. In 1838, the Cherokees were forcibly removed to the new Indian Territory along what became known as the **Trail of Tears.** Perhaps as many as eight thousand Cherokees, more than one-third of the entire nation, died during and just after the removal.

Trail of Tears The death of one-third or more of the Cherokee tribe upon their "removal" to the West

Indians in the Northwest Territory fared no better after they signed land-cession treaties. Two uprisings marked their westward removal. The first was quickly crushed, but the second, led by a Sac and Fox chief, Black Hawk, raged along the Illinois

***Trail of Tears*, by Robert Lindneux**

Forced by Andrew Jackson's removal policy to give up their lands east of the Mississippi and migrate to an area in present-day Oklahoma, the Cherokee people suffered disease, hunger, and exhaustion on what they remembered as the "Trail of Tears."

frontier until federal troops and state militiamen virtually annihilated the Indians in 1832. Black Hawk's downfall persuaded the other Old Northwest tribes to cede their lands. Between 1832 and 1837, the United States acquired nearly 190 million acres of Indian land in the Northwest for $70 million.

Working the Land: The Agricultural Boom

After the War of 1812, the rising prices of agricultural commodities sharpened white land hunger. Several factors accounted for rising farm prices. With the conclusion of the Napoleonic Wars, American farmers found brisk demand for their wheat and corn in Britain and France. In addition, demand within the United States for western farm commodities intensified after 1815 with the quickening pace of industrialization and urbanization in the East. Finally, the West's splendid river systems made it possible for farmers to ship wheat and corn downriver to New Orleans. Just as government policies made farming in the West possible, high prices for foodstuffs made it attractive.

Cotton, and Eli Whitney's cotton gin, provided the impetus for settlement of the Old Southwest, especially Alabama and Mississippi. Indeed, the explosive westward thrust of southern farmers and planters after the War of 1812 resembled a gold rush. By 1817, "Alabama fever" gripped the South; settlers bid the price of good land up to thirty to fifty dollars an acre. Accounting for less than a quarter of all American exports between 1802 and 1807, cotton comprised nearly two-thirds by 1836.

Checking In

- The War of 1812 opened the way for several thrusts of westward migration that carried the American population across the Mississippi River.
- Western society evolved its own set of values and prided itself on its democratic nature.
- Expansion multiplied the problems of Native Americans, culminating in the "removal" of tribes in the Southeast and the Old Northwest.
- An agricultural boom fueled the drive west.
- In the South, the cotton gin combined with rich western lands to create a huge surge in cotton production and export.

The Growth of the Market Economy

What changes were linked to the rise of the market economy?

The high prices of agricultural commodities, such as wheat and cotton, tempted a growing number of farmers to add a cash crop, thus venturing into commercial agriculture or the **market economy.** In the South, the sale of slaves from older states to the new Cotton Belt accelerated rapidly after 1815. However, farmers often launched into the market economy without weighing the risks. The new commercial farmers encountered wildly fluctuating markets and long intervals between harvest and the sale of crops, sending many deeply into debt. Meanwhile, the federal government struggled to devise an effective policy for transferring the public domain directly into the hands of small farmers.

market economy Newly developing commercial economy that depended on goods and crops produced for sale rather than consumption

Federal Land Policy

Partisan and sectional pressures buffeted federal land policy like a kite in a March wind. The result was a succession of land laws passed between 1796 and 1820, each of which sought to undo the damage caused by its predecessors.

At the root of early federal land policy lay a preference for the orderly settlement of the public domain. To this end, the Ordinance of 1785 divided public lands into sections of 640 acres. Ordinary farmers could not afford such large purchases, but it was assumed that they would pool their money to buy sections. Federalists, with their political base in the East, were reluctant to encourage western settlement but were eager to sell land to raise revenue for the government. They reconciled their conflicting goals by encouraging the sale of huge tracts of land to speculators who waited for its value to rise and then sold off parcels to farmers.

Sure that the small farmer was the backbone of the republic, Jefferson and the Republicans took a different tactic. The land law of 1800 dropped the minimum purchase to 320 acres and allowed up to four years for full payment. By 1832, the minimum purchase had shrunk to 40 acres.

Although Congress steadily liberalized land policy, speculators always remained one step ahead. With agricultural prices soaring, speculators were willing to bid high on new land, which they resold to farmers at hefty profits. The growing availability of credit after the War of 1812 fed speculation. The chartering of the Second Bank of the United States in 1816 increased the amount of money in circulation and stimulated the growth of state banks. Between 1812 and 1817, bank notes in circulation soared from $45 million to $100 million. The result was an orgy of speculation; by 1819, the dollar value of sales of public lands was more than 1,000 percent greater than the average from 1800 to 1814.

The Speculator and the Squatter

Despite these problems, most of the public domain found its way into the hands of small farmers. The desire to recoup investments led speculators to sell quickly, as did the proliferation of squatters.

Squatters had long helped themselves to western land. George Washington himself had been unable to drive squatters off lands he owned in the West. Proud and independent, they hated land speculators and pressured Congress to allow "preemption" rights—that is, the right to purchase at the minimum price the land that they already lived on and had improved. After passing a series of limited preemption laws, Congress acknowledged a general right of preemption in 1841.

Preemption laws were of no use to farmers who arrived after speculators had already bought up land. These settlers had to buy land from speculators on credit at interest rates that were as high as 40 percent. Many western farmers, drowning in debt and forced to raise cash crops in a hurry, worked their acreage to exhaustion and thus had to keep moving in search of new land. The phrase "the moving frontier" refers not only to the obvious fact that the line of settlement shifted farther west with each passing decade, but also to the fact that the same people kept moving, chasing their elusive dreams. Typical was Abraham Lincoln's family, who migrated from the East through several farms in Kentucky and then on to Indiana.

The Panic of 1819

In 1819, the land boom collapsed, the victim of a financial panic caused in large part by state banks that issued their own bank notes, which were little more than a promise to pay the bearer a certain amount of specie (gold and silver coin) on demand. These plentiful notes had helped fuel the land boom after 1815. Farmers also borrowed to buy more land and plant more crops. But even as they did so, bumper crops in Europe combined with an economic slump in Britain to trim foreign demand for U.S. crops.

The result was a cascade of economic catastrophes. In the summer of 1819, the Bank of the United States, holding large amounts of state bank paper, began to insist that the state banks redeem this paper in specie. To pay these debts, state banks demanded that farmers and land speculators repay their loans. Credit contracted sharply throughout the nation, particularly in the West. Prices for commodities like wheat, corn, cotton, and tobacco sank by 50 percent or more. Hard-pressed farmers could not pay their debts, speculators could not collect their money, and land values collapsed from nearly $70 an acre to barely $2.

The Panic left a bitter taste about banks, particularly the Bank of the United States, which was widely blamed for the hard times. The Panic also demonstrated how dependent farmers had become on distant markets. This in turn accelerated the search for better, cheaper ways to get crops to market.

The Transportation Revolution: Steamboats, Canals, and Railroads

The transportation system linking Americans in 1820 had severe weaknesses. The great rivers west of the Appalachians flowed north to south and hence could not by themselves connect western farmers to eastern markets. Roads were expensive to maintain, and horse-drawn wagons had limited capacity. After 1820 investment shifted to improving transportation on waterways, thus initiating the **transportation revolution.**

transportation revolution Rapid expansion of canals, steamships, and railroads

Clermont First of the steamboats that revolutionized river travel

In 1807, Robert R. Livingston and Robert Fulton introduced the steamboat ***Clermont*** on the Hudson River. They soon gained a monopoly from the New York legislature to run a New York–New Jersey ferry service. Competitors filed suit to break the Livingston-Fulton monopoly. After a long court battle, the Supreme Court decided against the monopoly in 1824 in the famous case of *Gibbons* v. *Ogden.* Chief Justice John Marshall ruled that Congress's constitutional power to regulate interstate commerce prevailed over New York's power to license the Livingston-Fulton monopoly. In the aftermath of this decision, other state-granted monopolies collapsed, and steamboat traffic increased rapidly. The number of steamboats operating on western rivers jumped from seventeen in 1817 to 727 by 1855.

Steamboats assumed a vital role along the Mississippi-Ohio river system. It took a keelboat (a covered flatboat pushed by oars or poles) three or four months to complete the 1,350-mile voyage from New Orleans to Louisville; in 1817, a steamboat could make the trip in twenty-five days. The development of long, shallow hulls permitted navigation of the Mississippi-Ohio river system even when hot, dry summers lowered the river level. Steamboats became more ornate as well as more practical, offering luxurious cabins and lounges, called saloons. The saloon of the *Eclipse,* a Mississippi River steamboat, was the length of a football field and featured skylights, chandeliers, a ceiling crisscrossed with Gothic arches, and velvet upholstered mahogany furniture.

While steamboats proved their value, canals replaced roads and turnpikes as the focus of popular enthusiasm and financial speculation. Although the cost of canal construction was mind-boggling—Jefferson dismissed the idea of canals as "little short of madness"—canals offered the possibility of connecting the Mississippi-Ohio river system with the Great Lakes and even the East Coast.

A canal boom followed the completion in 1825 of the **Erie Canal,** which stretched 363 miles from Buffalo to Albany. Ohio built a network of canals that enabled farmers to ship wheat by water to Lake Erie; the wheat was then shipped to Rochester for milling and finally traveled via the Erie Canal and the Hudson River to New York City. Shipping costs via the canal network were 10 percent of costs via road (see Map 9.2).

Erie Canal Major canal that linked the Great Lakes to New York City, opening the upper Midwest to wider development

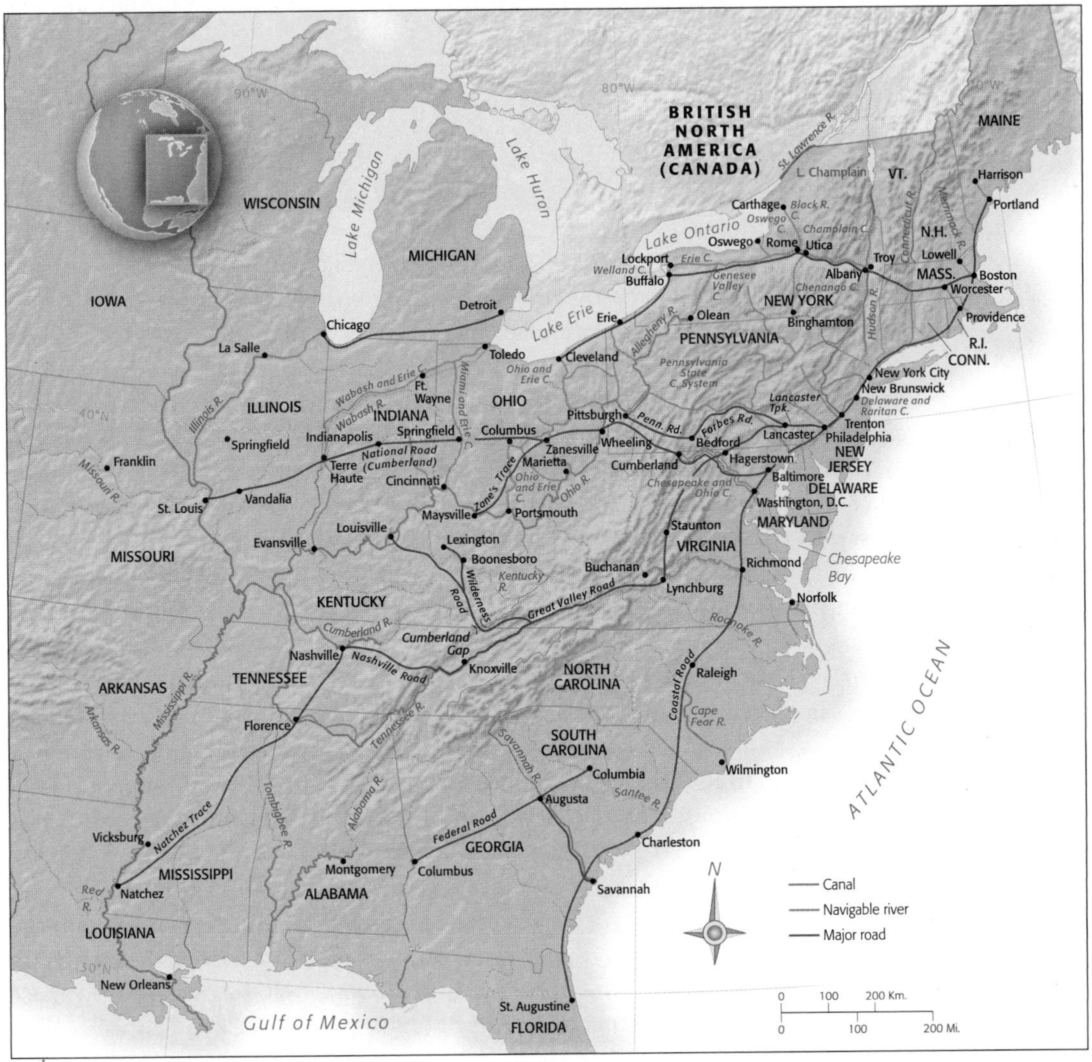

Map 9.2 Major Rivers, Roads, and Canals, 1825–1860

Railroads and canals increasingly tied the economy of the Midwest to that of the Northeast.

 Interactive Map

***Erie Canal*, by John William Hill, 1831**
Construction of the Erie Canal was a remarkable feat, all the more so because the United States did not have any engineering school at the time. The project's heroes were lawyers and merchants who taught themselves engineering and brawny workmen, often Irish immigrants, who hacked a waterway through the forests and valleys of New York.

When another economic depression hit in the late 1830s, states found themselves overcommitted to costly canal projects and ultimately scrapped many. As the canal boom was ending, the railroad, an entirely new form of transportation, was being introduced. In 1825, the world's first commercial railroad began operation in Britain, and by 1840 some three thousand miles of track had been laid in America, about the same as the total canal mileage.

Since they were cheaper to build, faster, and able to reach more places, railroads had obvious advantages over canals. But railroads' potential was only slowly realized. Most early railroads ran between cities in the East, rather than from east to west, and carried more passengers than freight. Not until 1849 did freight revenues exceed passenger revenues, and not until 1850 was the East Coast connected by rail to the Great Lakes.

There were two main reasons for this slow pace of development. First, unlike canals, most railroads were built by private companies that tended to skimp on costs, and as a result they produced lines requiring constant repair. In contrast, canals needed little maintenance. Second, shipping bulky commodities, such as iron, coal, and grain, was cheaper by canal than by rail.

CHECKING IN

- For farmers, the market economy was alluring but risky.
- Federal land policy was aimed at small farmers but helped feed a speculative boom.
- When the speculative bubble burst, the Panic of 1819 created economic havoc and intensified the American distrust of banks.
- The transportation revolution—steamboats, canals, and railroads—played a major role in westward expansion.
- Western cities mushroomed, first along rivers and then on the Great Lakes.

The Growth of the Cities

The transportation revolution accelerated the growth of towns and cities. Indeed, the forty years before the Civil War, 1820 to 1860, saw the most rapid urbanization in U.S. history. By 1860, New York City's population had rocketed from 124,000 to 800,000. Even more spectacular was the transformation of sleepy villages into bustling towns.

City and town growth was particularly fast in the West. The War of 1812 stimulated manufacturing and transformed villages into towns, as did the agricultural boom and the introduction of steamboats after 1815. Virtually all the major western cities were river ports. Of these, Pittsburgh, Cincinnati, Louisville, and New Orleans were the most prominent. Pittsburgh was a manufacturing center, but the others were commercial hubs flooded by people eager to make money.

What the transportation revolution gave, it could also take away. The completion of the Erie Canal shifted the center of western economic activity toward the Great Lakes. The result was a gradual decline in the importance of river cities and a rise in the importance of lake cities such as Buffalo, Cleveland, Detroit, Chicago, and Milwaukee. In 1830, nearly 75 percent of all western city-dwellers lived in the river ports of New Orleans, Louisville, Cincinnati, and Pittsburgh; by 1840 the proportion had dropped to 20 percent.

Industrial Beginnings

What caused the rise of industrialization?

Industrialization gave an added boost to the growth of cities and towns. In any way possible, Americans sought to counter Britain's full-generation lead in building factories; Britain in turn banned the emigration of its skilled mechanics. However, one of those mechanics, **Samuel Slater,** was able to reach the United States in 1789. He helped design and build the first cotton mill in the United States the following year. The mill's work force mushroomed from nine to one hundred, and his mills multiplied. The pace of industrialization quickened in the 1810s and 1820s, especially in cotton textiles and shoes.

Samuel Slater British "mechanic" who carried plans for a textile mill to the United States; began the American textile industry

Industrialization was uneven. There was little in the South, where planters preferred to invest in land and slaves, and much in New England, where poor soil made agriculture an even poorer investment. Generally, industrialization involved three steps: the subdivision of tasks, the gathering of workers in large factories, and the use of high-speed machines to replace handwork.

Industrialization changed lives. Many benefited from industrialization as former luxury goods became cheaper. And while cheap machine-made goods brought luxuries within the reach of working people, they also undermined skilled artisans. Most early factory workers were recruited from farms, where they had set their own pace and took breaks as tasks were completed. In contrast, machines and the clock dictated the factory worker's pace. Finally, industrialization led to specialization; farmers could now concentrate on farming and buy clothes, shoes, and other products they had previously made.

Causes of Industrialization

A host of factors stimulated industrialization. Merchants barred from foreign trade by the Embargo Act of 1807 redirected their capital into factories. After the War of 1812, acceptance of tariffs was widespread. Protected from foreign competition, New England's textile output rose from 4 million yards in 1817 to 323 million yards by 1840. New England's farm families were deserting worn-out soils for full-time manufacturing. And the transportation revolution gave manufacturers easier access to markets in the South and West.

Technology played a major role. Lacking craft organizations that tied artisans to a single trade, Americans could freely experiment with machines outside their own craft. Americans also improved on foreign ideas and techniques. For example, in 1798 Eli Whitney, inventor of the cotton gin, gained a government contract to produce ten thousand muskets within a two-year period by using interchangeable parts, an idea originally developed in France. Although Whitney missed his deadline by more than a decade, his idea captured the imagination of many American leaders and foreshadowed the rise of a full-scale industrial economy.

Textile Towns in New England

Lowell, Waltham Massachusetts towns where two large textile mills were established as early experiments in factory manufacturing

New England became America's first industrial region. The trade wars leading up to the War of 1812 had devastated the Northeast's traditional economy and stimulated capital investment in manufacturing. New England's many swift-flowing rivers were ideal sources of waterpower for mills. The westward migration of New England's young men, unable to wrest a living from rocky soil, left a surplus of young women who supplied cheap industrial labor. The establishment of the Boston Manufacturing Company in 1813 opened a new chapter in U.S. manufacturing. Backed by ample capital, the Boston Company built textile mills in the Massachusetts towns of **Lowell** and **Waltham;** by 1836 the company employed more than six thousand workers.

Jack Naylor Collection/Picture Research Consultants & Archives

Mill Girl Around 1850

This girl most likely worked in a Massachusetts textile mill, at either Lowell or Waltham. Her swollen and rough hands suggest that she was a "warper," one of the jobs usually given to children. Warpers were responsible for constantly straightening out the strands of cotton or wool as they entered the loom.

Unlike Slater's mills, the Waltham and Lowell factories turned out more finished products, thus elbowing aside Slater's cottage industry. Slater had tried to preserve tradition by hiring entire families to work at his mills—the men to raise crops, the women and children to toil in the mills. In contrast, 80 percent of the workers in the Lowell and Waltham mills were unmarried women who were fifteen to thirty years old. Hired managers and company regulations, rather than families, provided discipline. Workers had to live in company boarding houses or approved private homes, attend Sabbath services, observe a 10:00 p.m. curfew, and accept the company's "moral police." These regulations were designed to give mills a good reputation so that families would continue to send their daughters to work there.

Conditions in the mills were dreadful. To provide the humidity necessary to keep the threads from snapping, overseers nailed factory windows shut and sprayed the air with water. Operatives also had to contend with flying dust and the deafening roar of the machines. Keener competition and a worsening economy in the late 1830s led mill owners to reduce wages and speed up work schedules.

Owners rarely visited factories; their agents, all men, gave orders to the workers, mainly women. In 1834 and again in 1836, women at the Lowell mills quit work to protest low wages. The largest strikes in American history to that point, they not only pitted workers against management but also women against men.

The Waltham and Lowell mills were much larger than most factories; as late as 1860, the average industrial establishment employed only eight workers. Outside of textiles, many industries continued to depend on industrial "outwork." For example, before the introduction of the sewing machine led to the concentration of all aspects of shoe manufacture in large factories in the 1850s, women often sewed parts of shoes at home and sent the piecework to factories for finishing.

Artisans and Workers in Mid-Atlantic Cities

The skilled artisans of New York City and Philadelphia tried to protect their interests by forming trade unions and "workingmen's" political parties. Initially, they sought to restore privileges and working conditions that artisans had once enjoyed, but gradually they joined forces with unskilled workers. When coal heavers in Philadelphia struck for a ten-hour day in 1835, carpenters, cigar makers, leather workers, and other artisans joined in what became the first general strike in the United States. The emergence of organized worker protests underscored the mixed blessings of economic development. Whereas some people prospered, others found their economic position deteriorating. By 1830 many Americans were questioning whether their nation was truly a land of equality.

Checking In

- Multiple factors stimulated industrialization, including protective tariffs, available capital, and advances in technology.
- Textile mills made New England America's first industrial region.
- Mills like those at Waltham and Lowell relied heavily on the labor of young women.
- "Outwork" dominated early industrialization outside the textile industry.
- Industrialization brought mixed results; as many workers' economic position deteriorated, new questions arose about equality in the United States.

Equality and Inequality

What caused urban poverty in this period?

The idea that one (white) man was as good as another became the national creed in antebellum America. For example, servants insisted on being viewed as neighbors invited to assist in running the household rather than as permanent subordinates. Politicians never lost an opportunity to celebrate artisans and farmers as the equal of lawyers and bankers. A French visitor observed that the wealthiest Americans pretended to respect equality by riding in public in ordinary rather than luxurious carriages.

The market and transportation revolutions, however, were placing new pressure on the ideal of equality between 1815 and 1840. At the same time that improved transportation enabled some eastern farmers to migrate to the richer soils of the West, it became difficult for those left behind to compete with the cheaper grain carried east by canals and railroads. Many eastern farmers now had to move to cities to take whatever work they could find, often as casual day laborers on the docks or in small workshops.

Urban Inequality: The Rich and the Poor

The gap between rich and poor widened in the first half of the nineteenth century. In cities, a small fraction of the people owned a huge share of the wealth. For example, in New York City, the richest 4 percent owned nearly half the wealth in 1828 and more than two-thirds by 1845. Splendid residences and social clubs set the rich apart. In

1828, over half of the five hundred wealthiest families in New York City lived on just eight of its more than 250 streets. By the late 1820s, the city had a club so exclusive that it was called simply The Club.

Although commentators celebrated the self-made man and his rise "from rags to riches," few actually fit this pattern. Less than 5 percent of the wealthy had started life poor; almost 90 percent of well-off people had been born rich. Clearly, the old-fashioned way to wealth was to inherit it, to marry more of it, and to invest it wisely. Occasional rags-to-riches stories like that of John Jacob Astor and his fur-trading empire sustained the myth, but it was mainly a myth.

At the opposite end of the social ladder were the poor. By today's standards, most antebellum Americans were poor. They lived close to the edge of misery and depended heavily on their children's labor to meet expenses. But when antebellum Americans spoke of poverty, they were referring to "pauperism," a state of dependency or inability to fend for oneself. Epidemics of yellow fever and cholera could devastate families. A frozen canal, river, or harbor spelled unemployment for boatmen and dock workers. The absence of health insurance and old-age pensions condemned many infirm and aged people to pauperism.

Contemporaries usually classified all such people as the "deserving" poor and contrasted them with the "undeserving" poor, such as indolent loafers and drunkards whose poverty was seen as self-willed. Most moralists assumed that since pauperism resulted either from circumstances beyond anyone's control, or from voluntary decisions to squander money on liquor, it would not pass from generation to generation.

This assumption was comforting but also misleading. A class of people who could not escape poverty was emerging in the major cities during the first half of the nineteenth century. One source was immigration. As early as 1801, a New York newspaper called attention to the arrival of boatloads of immigrants with large families, without money or health, and "expiring from the want of sustenance."

The poorest white immigrants were from Ireland, where British landlords had evicted peasants from the land and converted it to commercial use. Severed from the land, the Irish increasingly became a nation of wanderers. By the early 1830s, the great majority of canal workers in the North were Irish immigrants. Without their backbreaking labor, the Erie Canal would never have been built. Other Irish congregated in New York's infamous Five Points district.

The Irish were not only poor but were also Catholics, a faith despised by the Protestant majority in the United States. But even the Protestant poor came in for rough treatment in the years between 1815 and 1840. The more that Americans convinced themselves that success was within everyone's grasp, the more they were inclined to hold the poor responsible for their own misery. Ironically, even as many Americans blamed the poor for being poor, they practiced discrimination that kept some groups mired in enduring poverty. Nowhere was this more true than in the case of northern free blacks.

Free Blacks in the North

Prejudice against blacks was deeply ingrained in white society throughout the nation. Although slavery had largely disappeared in the North by 1820, discriminatory laws remained. The voting rights of African-Americans were severely restricted; for example, New York eliminated property requirements for whites but kept them for blacks. There were attempts to bar free blacks from migrating. And segregation prevailed in northern schools, jails, and hospitals. By 1850, blacks could vote on equal terms with whites in only one city, Boston.

Of all restrictions on free blacks, the most damaging was the social pressure that forced them into the least-skilled and lowest-paying occupations. Although a few free blacks accumulated moderate wealth, free blacks in general were only half as likely as other city-dwellers to own real estate.

One important response of African-Americans to discrimination was the establishment of their own churches. When a group of free blacks was ejected from a Philadelphia church, they ultimately established the first black-run Protestant denomination, the **African Methodist Episcopal Church,** in 1816. The A.M.E. rapidly expanded to encompass a territory bounded by Washington, DC, Pittsburgh, and New York City. Its members campaigned against slavery, provided education for black children, and formed mutual-aid societies.

African Methodist Episcopal Church First American denomination established by and for African-Americans

Just as northern African-Americans left white churches to form their own, free blacks gradually acquired some control over the education of their children. Northern city governments made little provision for the education of free persons of color, at first leaving northern blacks dependent on the philanthropy of sympathetic whites to educate their children. But the 1820s and 1830s witnessed an explosion of black self-hope societies devoted to encouraging black education and run by graduates of the African Free School.

The "Middling Classes"

Most antebellum Americans were neither fabulously rich nor grindingly poor, but instead were part of the **"middling classes."** Even though the wealthy owned an increasing proportion of wealth, per capita income grew at 1.5 percent annually between 1840 and 1860, and the standard of living generally rose after 1800.

"middling classes" Americans who were neither fabulously rich nor grindingly poor

Americans applied the term "middling classes" to families headed by professionals, small merchants, landowning farmers, and self-employed artisans. Commentators portrayed these people as living stable and secure lives. In reality, life in the middle often was unpredictable. The economy of antebellum America created greater opportunities for success and for failure. An enterprising import merchant, Allan Melville, the father of novelist Herman Melville, did well until the late 1820s, when his business sagged. By 1830, he was "destitute of resources and without a shilling." In 1832 he died, broken in spirit and nearly insane.

Artisans shared the perils of life in the middling classes. During the colonial period, many had attained the ideal of self-employment, owning their tools, taking orders, making their products, and training their children and apprentices in the craft. By 1840, in contrast, artisans had entered a new world of economic relationships. Some carpenters and shoemakers, usually those with access to capital, became contractors and small manufacturers. In effect, the old class of artisans was splitting into two new groupings. On one side were artisans who had become entrepreneurs; on the other, journeymen with little prospect of self-employment.

CHECKING IN

- The gap between rich and poor widened, especially in cities.
- Americans generally blamed the poor for being poor.
- Free blacks saw their rights and economic position erode even further.
- The "middling classes" increased, but many did not achieve stability.
- More than ever, transience characterized American society.

An additional characteristic of the middling classes, one they shared with the poor, was a high degree of transience, or spatial mobility. The transportation revolution made it easier for Americans to purchase services as well as goods and spurred many young men to abandon farming for the professions. The itinerant clergyman riding an old nag to conduct revivals became a familiar figure in newly settled areas. Even well-established lawyers and judges spent part of each year riding from one county courthouse to another.

Transience affected the lives of most Americans. Farmers exhausted their land by intensive cultivation of cash crops and then moved on. City-dwellers moved frequently as they changed jobs—public transportation lagged far behind the spread of the cities. A survey on September 6, 1851, found that on that day 41,729 entered the city of Boston while 42,313 left. Most of these were searching for work, a frequent necessity for the middling classes as well as the poor.

THE REVOLUTION IN SOCIAL RELATIONSHIPS

How did the rise of the market economy and industrialization change relationships within families and communities?

Following the War of 1812, the growth of interregional trade, commercial agriculture, and manufacturing disrupted traditional social relationships and forged new ones. Two broad changes took place. First, Americans began to question traditional forms of authority and to embrace individualism; once the term had meant nothing more than selfishness, but now it connoted positive qualities such as self-reliance and the ability of each person to judge his or her own best interests. Wealth, education, and social position no longer received automatic deference. Second, Americans created new foundations for authority. For example, women developed the idea that they possessed a "separate sphere" of authority in the home, and individuals formed voluntary associations to influence the direction of society.

The Attack on the Professions

Intense criticism of lawyers, physicians, and ministers exemplified the assault on, and erosion of, traditional authority. Between 1800 and 1840, the wave of religious revivals known as the Second Great Awakening (see Chapter 10) sparked fierce attacks on the professions. Revivalists blasted the clergy for creating complex theologies, drinking expensive wines, and fleecing the people. One revivalist accused physicians of inventing fancy Latin and Greek names for diseases to disguise their inability to cure them.

These jabs at the learned professions peaked between 1820 and 1850. Samuel Thomson led a successful movement to eliminate all barriers to entry into the medical profession, including educational requirements. By 1845, every state had repealed laws requiring licenses or education to practice medicine. In religion, ministers found little job security as finicky congregations dismissed clergymen whose theology displeased them. In turn, ministers became more ambitious and more inclined to leave poor, small churches for large, wealthy ones.

The increasing commercialization of the economy led to both more professionals and more attacks on them. In 1765, America had one medical school; by 1860 there were sixty-five. The newly minted doctors and lawyers had neither deep roots in the towns where they practiced nor convincing claims to social superiority. "Men dropped down into their places as from clouds," one critic wrote. "Nobody knew who or what they were, except as they claimed."

This questioning of authority was particularly sharp on the frontier. Easterners sneered that every man in the West claimed to be a "judge," "general," "colonel," or "squire." Where neither law nor custom sanctioned claims of superiority, would-be gentlemen substituted an exaggerated sense of personal honor. Obsessed with their fragile status, many reacted testily to the slightest insult. Dueling became a widespread frontier practice. At a Kentucky militia parade in 1819, for example, an officer's dog jogged onto the field and sat at his master's knee. Enraged by this breach of military decorum, another officer ran the dog through with his sword. A week later, the two men met with pistols at ten paces. One was killed, the other maimed for life.

The Challenge to Family Authority

Meanwhile, children quietly questioned parental authority. The era's economic change forced many young people to choose between staying at home to help their parents and venturing out on their own. This desire for independence fueled westward migration as well. Restless single men led the way. Two young men from Virginia put it succinctly: "All the promise of life now seemed to us to be at the other end of the rainbow—somewhere else—anywhere else but on the farm."

As young antebellum Americans tried to escape close parental supervision, courtship and marriage patterns also changed. No longer dependent on parents for land, young people wanted to choose their own mate. Romantic love, rather than parental preference, increasingly determined marital decisions.

Courtesy Childs Gallery, Boston

The Country Parson Disturbed at Breakfast

This young couple's decision to wed seems to have been made on the spur of the moment. As young men and women became more independent of parental control, they gave their impulses freer play.

One sign of young people's growing control over courtship and marriage was the declining likelihood that the young women of a family would marry in their birth order. Traditionally, fathers wanted their daughters to marry in the order of their birth to avoid any suspicion that there was something wrong with one or more of them. By the end of the eighteenth century, daughters were making their own decisions about marriage, and the custom of birth order vanished. Another mark of the times was the growing popularity of long engagements; young women were reluctant to tie the knot, fearing that marriage would snuff out their independence. Equally striking was the increasing number of young women who chose not to marry.

Thus, young people lived more and more in a world of their own. Moralists reacted with alarm and flooded the country with books of advice to youth, which stressed the same message: newly independent young people should develop self-control and "character." The self-made adult began with the self-made youth.

Wives and Husbands

Another class of advice books counseled wives and husbands about their rights and duties. These books were a sign that relations between spouses were also changing. Young men and women accustomed to making their own decisions would understandably approach marriage as a compact among equals. Although inequalities within marriage remained—especially the legal tradition that married women could not own property—the trend was toward a form of equality.

separate spheres Popular doctrine that emphasized women's morality and authoritative role within the home

One source of this change was the rise of the doctrine of **separate spheres.** Traditionally, women had been viewed as subordinate to men in all spheres of life. Now middle-class men and women developed a kind of separate-but-equal doctrine that portrayed men as superior in making money and governing the world, and women as superior for their moral influence on family members.

Most important was the shift of responsibility for child rearing from fathers to mothers. During the eighteenth century, church sermons reminded fathers of their duty to govern the family; by the 1830s, child-rearing manuals were addressed to mothers rather than fathers. Advice books instructed mothers to discipline children by withdrawing love rather than using corporal punishment. A whipped child might obey but would remain sullen and bitter; gentler methods would penetrate the child's heart, making the child want to do the right thing.

The idea of a separate women's sphere blended with the image of family and home as secluded refuges from a disorderly society. Popular culture painted an alluring portrait of the pleasures of home in such sentimental songs as "Home, Sweet Home" and such poems as "A Visit from St. Nicholas." Even the physical appearance of houses changed. The prominent architect Andrew Jackson Downing published plans for peaceful single-family homes to offset the hurly-burly of daily life. "There must be nooks about it," he wrote, "where one would love to linger; windows, where one can enjoy the quiet landscape at his leisure; cozy rooms, where all fireside joys are invited to dwell."

But reality diverged far from this ideal. Ownership of a quiet single-family home lay beyond the reach of most Americans, even much of the middle class. Farm homes, far from tranquil, were beehives of activity, and city-dwellers often had to sacrifice privacy by taking in boarders to supplement family income.

The decline of cottage industry and the growing number of men (merchants, lawyers, brokers) who worked outside the home gave women more time to lavish attention on children. Married women found these ideals sources of power. A subtle implication of the doctrine of separate spheres was that women should control not only the discipline of children but also the number they would bear.

In 1800, the United States had one of the highest birthrates ever recorded. The average American woman bore 7.04 children. Children were valuable for the labor they provided and for the relief from the burdens of survival that they could bring to aging parents. The more children, the better, most couples assumed. However, the growth of the market economy raised questions about children's economic value. Unlike a farmer, a merchant or lawyer could not send his children to work at the age of seven or eight. The average woman was bearing only 5.02 children by 1850, and 3.98 by 1900. The birthrate remained high among blacks and many immigrant groups, but it fell drastically among native-born whites, particularly in towns and cities.

Abstinence, *coitus interruptus* (the withdrawal of the penis before ejaculation), and abortion were common birth-control methods. Remedies for "female irregularity"—unwanted pregnancy—were widely advertised. The rubber condom and the vaginal diaphragm were familiar to many Americans by 1865. Whatever the method, husbands and wives jointly decided to limit family size. Husbands could note that the economic value of children was declining; wives, meanwhile, noted that having fewer children would give them more time to nurture each one and thereby to carry out their domestic duties.

Supporters of the ideal of separate spheres did not advocate full legal equality for women. Indeed, the ideal of separate spheres was an explicit alternative to legal equality. But the concept enhanced women's power within marriage by giving them influence in such vital issues as child rearing and the frequency of pregnancies.

Horizontal Allegiances and the Rise of Voluntary Associations

As some forms of authority weakened, Americans devised new ways by which individuals could extend their influence over others. The antebellum era witnessed the widespread substitution of *horizontal* allegiances for *vertical* allegiances. In vertical allegiances, authority flowed from the top down. Subordinates identified their interests with those of superiors rather than with others in the same subordinate roles. The traditional patriarchal family was an example of vertical allegiance, as was the traditional apprentice system.

Although vertical relationships did not disappear, they became less important in people's lives. Increasingly, relationships were more likely to be marked by horizontal allegiances that linked those in a similar position. For example, in large textile mills, operatives discovered they had more in common with one another than with their managers and overseers. Similarly, married women formed maternal associations to exchange advice about child rearing, and young men developed associations with other young men. Maternal and debating societies exemplified the American zeal for **voluntary associations**—associations that arose apart

voluntary association
Horizontal allegiance (as opposed to superior-subordinate relationship) of individuals with similar interests or circumstances

CHECKING IN

- As the market economy took hold, American society placed greater emphasis on individualism.
- As part of a general questioning of authority, most Americans viewed professions such as law and medicine with increasing skepticism.
- Young people increasingly rebelled against family authority.
- The doctrine of "separate spheres" appeared as part of a transformation of ideas about gender roles.
- Voluntary associations flourished.

Alexis de Tocqueville Young Frenchman whose *Democracy in America* provides rich insight into the United States in the 1830s

from government and sought to accomplish some goal of value to their members. **Alexis de Tocqueville,** a brilliant French observer, described them as "public associations in civil life."

Voluntary associations encouraged sociability as transients and newcomers came together, usually in associations based on gender or race. These associations served as vehicles for members to assert their influence. Temperance societies fought to abolish alcohol, while moral-reform societies combated prostitution. Just as strikes in Lowell in the 1830s were a form of collective action by working women, moral-reform societies represented collective action by middle-class women to increase their influence in society.

Chapter Summary

What caused the surge of westward migration after the War of 1812? (page 199)

An agricultural boom lured people west, as did the swelling demand for cotton created by the cotton gin. Westward movement carried the American population across the Mississippi River by 1820, raising both hopes and problems. A new society was rising in the West, one that viewed itself as more democratic and more egalitarian than the East. Native Americans were ruthlessly pushed aside or "relocated" to make room for white settlers.

What changes were linked to the rise of the market economy? (page 204)

Western farmers soon entered the market economy, which was both lucrative and volatile. They began to plant cash crops and to purchase manufactures. Although federal land policy was meant to sell parcels to small farmers, speculators snapped up much of the land. The speculative boom collapsed in the Panic of 1819, but the movement westward continued, with the transportation revolution opening the way for settlers and products. And cities mushroomed, especially in the Great Lakes area.

What caused the rise of industrialization? (page 209)

Protective tariffs, technology, and the ready availability of capital stimulated industrial development, especially in New England, where the textile industry led the way. Young women formed the primary work force at many New England mills, but elsewhere a piecemeal system of work predominated. Results of this early industrialization were uneven, particularly in terms of equality and inequality.

What caused urban poverty in this period? (page 211)

In America's cities, the gap between rich and poor widened; most people held the poor responsible for their poverty. While the "middling classes" increased, free blacks saw even more of their rights slip away.

KEY TERMS

National Road *(p. 201)*
"Five Civilized Tribes" *(p. 201)*
Cherokee Nation v. *Georgia* *(p. 203)*
Worcester v. *Georgia* *(p. 203)*
Trail of Tears *(p. 203)*
market economy *(p. 204)*
transportation revolution *(p. 206)*
Clermont *(p. 206)*
Erie Canal *(p. 207)*
Samuel Slater *(p. 209)*
Lowell, Waltham *(p. 210)*
African Methodist Episcopal Church *(p. 213)*
"middling classes" *(p. 213)*
separate spheres *(p. 216)*
voluntary association *(p. 217)*
Alexis de Tocqueville *(p. 218)*

How did the rise of the market economy and industrialization change relationships within families and communities? (page 214)

Individualism increasingly characterized American society, while most Americans questioned authority in general and viewed the professions with skepticism. Young people more and more defied or ignored familial authority. Women both benefited from and were harmed by the doctrine of "separate spheres." Voluntary, horizontal organizations thrived.

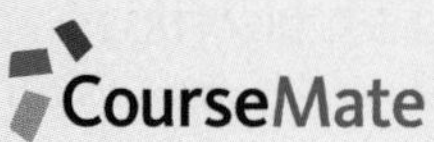

Go to the CourseMate website at **www.cengagebrain.com** for additional study tools and review materials—including audio and video clips—for this chapter.

CHAPTER 10

Democratic Politics, Religious Revival, and Reform

1824–1840

Detroit Institute of Arts, USA/Gift of Mrs Samuel T. Carson/The Bridgeman Art Library

First State Election in Michigan

CHAPTER PREVIEW

The Rise of Democratic Politics, 1824–1832
How did the democratization of American politics contribute to the rise of Andrew Jackson?

The Bank Controversy and the Second Party System, 1833–1840
What were the major factors in the rise of the second party system?

The Rise of Popular Religion
What new assumptions about human nature lay behind the religious movements of the period?

The Age of Reform
Did the reform movements aim primarily at making Americans more free or more orderly?

One cold Sunday in March 1841, schoolteacher Dorothea Dix was teaching a religious class for women prisoners in the House of Corrections at East Cambridge, Massachusetts. After class, she was shocked to discover a number of insane inmates shivering in unheated cells. When she confronted the jailer, he explained that providing stoves for "lunatics" was not only dangerous but unnecessary, because they did not suffer from cold. The outraged Dix went to court and successfully petitioned to have stoves provided for the jail's insane inmates.

For two years, Dix traveled the state documenting the conditions of the mentally ill. In 1843, she presented to the legislature a report or "memorial" describing the insane confined "in cages, closets, cellars, stalls, pens! Chained, naked, beaten with rods, and lashed into obedience." The Massachusetts legislature responded by funding an expansion of the state's mental hospital. Encouraged by her success, Dix spent the next fifteen years traveling throughout the nation, documenting abuses and presenting her memorials. By the time of the Civil War, twenty-eight states, four cities, and the federal government had constructed public mental institutions.

What drove this sickly woman to endure dangerous travel, confront the terrible living conditions of the mentally ill, and endure the ridicule of those who found her crusade "unladylike"? Dorothea Dix's reform impulse drew from a deep well of religious conviction. She embraced theological perfectionism: the belief in the innate moral capacities of all men and women and their ability to strive toward spiritual perfection. Even the raving lunatic, in Dix's eyes, carried a spark of inner divinity that should be nurtured.

Dorothea Dix's perfectionist faith was shared by other reformers who regarded asylums—such as penitentiaries, almshouses, and orphan homes—as the solution for many of society's ills. If humankind was fundamentally good, they reasoned, then poor environments must be at fault when people went wrong. The solution was to place deviants in specially designed environments that imposed strict order on their disorderly lives and minds.

Spread primarily by the wave of religious revivals known as the Second Great Awakening, theological perfectionism shaped a host of reforms that swept the United States after 1820, including temperance, antislavery, education, women's rights, and utopian communitarianism. Most of these movements, like Dix's crusade for the mentally ill, raised fundamental questions about the proper balance of order and freedom in the new American democracy. Such questions also lay at the heart of the new two-party system that would reshape American political life during the presidential terms of Andrew Jackson.

THE RISE OF DEMOCRATIC POLITICS, 1824–1832

How did the democratization of American politics contribute to the rise of Andrew Jackson?

In 1824, Andrew Jackson and John Quincy Adams were both members of Jefferson's Republican Party; by 1834, Jackson was a Democrat and Adams, a Whig. Tensions spawned by industrialization, the rise of the Cotton South, and westward expansion split Jefferson's old party. Generally, supporters of states' rights joined the **Democrats,** and advocates of national support for economic development became **Whigs.**

Democrats Members of the political party that emerged from Jefferson's Republican Party; one of two dominant parties in the second party system

Whigs Initially called National Republicans; members of the other dominant party

Democrat or Whig, leaders had to adapt to the rising notion that politics should be an expression of the will of the common people rather than an activity that gentlemen conducted on the people's behalf. Americans still looked up to their leaders, but the leaders could no longer look down on the people.

Democratic Ferment

Political democratization took several forms. One of the most common was the abolition of the requirement that voters own property; no western states had such a requirement, and eastern states gradually liberalized their laws. Moreover, written

Chronology

1824	John Quincy Adams elected president by the House of Representatives
1826	American Temperance Society organized
1828	Andrew Jackson elected president; "Tariff of Abominations"; John Calhoun anonymously writes *South Carolina Exposition and Protest*
1830	Jackson's Maysville Road Bill veto; Indian Removal Act
1830–1831	Charles G. Finney's Rochester revival
1831	William Lloyd Garrison starts *The Liberator*
1832	Jackson vetoes recharter of the Bank of the United States; Jackson reelected president; South Carolina Nullification Proclamation
1833	Force Bill; Compromise Tariff; American Anti-Slavery Society founded; South Carolina nullifies the Force Bill
1834	Whig party organized
1836	Specie Circular; Martin Van Buren elected president
1837	Elijah Lovejoy murdered by proslavery mob; Grimké sisters set out on lecture tour of New England
1838	Sarah Grimké's *Letters on the Condition of Women and the Equality of the Sexes* released
1840	Independent Treasury Act passed; William Henry Harrison elected president; first Washington Temperance Society started
1841	Dorothea Dix begins exposé of prison conditions
1844	Brook Farm community founded; Joseph Smith murdered by anti-Mormon mob
1848	Seneca Falls Convention

ballots replaced the custom of voting aloud, which had enabled elites to influence their subordinates at the polls. Appointive offices became elective. Though the Electoral College survived, the choice of presidential electors by state legislatures gave way to direct election by the voters. By 1832, only South Carolina followed the old custom.

The fierce tug of war between Republicans and Federalists that began in the 1790s had taught both parties to court voters. At grand party-run barbecues in the North and South, potential voters washed down free clams and oysters with free beer and whiskey.

Political democratization had its limitations. The parties were still run from the top down as late as 1820, with candidates nominated by caucus (a conference of party members in the legislature). And political democracy did not extend to allowing either women or free blacks the right to vote.

The Election of 1824 and the Adams Presidency

In 1824, sectional tensions ended the Era of Good Feelings when five Republican candidates vied for the presidency. John Quincy Adams emerged as New England's favorite. John C. Calhoun and William Crawford fought for southern support. Out of the West marched the ambitious Henry Clay of Kentucky, confident that his American System of protective tariffs and internal improvements would win votes from both eastern manufacturing interests and western

TABLE 10.1 THE ELECTION OF 1824

CANDIDATE	PARTY	ELECTORAL VOTE	POPULAR VOTE	PERCENTAGE OF POPULAR VOTE
John Quincy Adams	Democratic-Republican	84	108,740	30.5
Andrew Jackson	Democratic-Republican	99	153,544	43.1
William H. Crawford	Democratic-Republican	41	46,618	13.1
Henry Clay	Democratic-Republican	37	47,136	13.2

agriculturalists. Opposing Henry Clay was the popular war hero, Andrew Jackson of Tennessee.

A paralyzing stroke soon removed Crawford from the race. Calhoun assessed Jackson's support and prudently decided to run unopposed for the vice presidency. In the election, Jackson won more popular and electoral votes than any other candidate but failed to gain the majority required by the Constitution. Therefore, the election was thrown into the House of Representatives. Clay threw his support to New Englander John Quincy Adams, who won the election. When the new president appointed Clay his secretary of state, Jackson's supporters accused Adams of stealing victory by entering a "corrupt bargain" with Clay, an allegation that formed a dark cloud over Adams's presidency.

The guiding principle of the Adams presidency was social improvement. In his First Annual Message to Congress, he laid out his plans to improve public education, expand commerce, and fund internal improvements. But Adams's ambitions met with growing political opposition. Strict constructionists opposed internal improvements on constitutional grounds. Southerners protested Adams's plan to participate in a pan-American conference because it required association with regimes that had abolished slavery, including the black republic of Haiti. Instead of building new bases of support, Adams clung to the increasingly obsolete view of the president as custodian of the public good, aloof from partisan politics. Idealistic though his view was, it guaranteed him a single-term presidency.

The Rise of Andrew Jackson and the Election of 1828

As President Adams's popularity declined, Andrew Jackson's rose. While seasoned politicians distrusted his notoriously hot temper and his penchant for duels, Jackson was still a popular hero for his victory over the British in the Battle of New Orleans. And because he had fought in the American Revolution as a boy, Jackson seemed to many Americans a living link to a more virtuous past.

The presidential campaign of 1828 began almost as soon as Adams was inaugurated. Jackson's supporters began to put together a modern political machine based on local committees, partisan newspapers, and public rallies. By 1826, towns and villages across the country buzzed with political activity. Because supporters of Jackson, Adams, and Clay all still called themselves Republicans, few realized that a new political system was being born. The man most alert to the new currents was Martin Van Buren, who would be Jackson's vice president and then president.

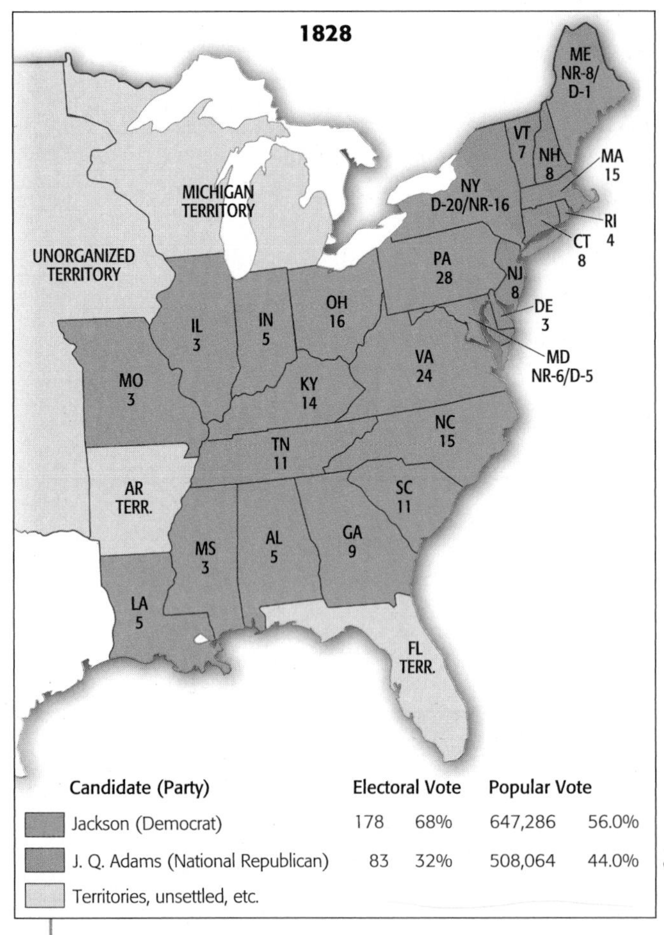

Map 10.1 The Election of 1828

Interactive Map

Van Buren exemplified a new breed of politician. A tavern keeper's son, he had worked his way up through New York politics and created a powerful statewide machine, the Albany Regency, composed of men like himself from the middling and lower ranks. His archrival, DeWitt Clinton, was everything Van Buren was not—tall, handsome, and aristocratic. But Van Buren's geniality put ordinary people at ease.

The election of 1824 had convinced Van Buren of the need for two-party competition. Without the discipline imposed by party competition, the Republicans had splintered into sectional factions. The country would be better served, he thought, by reducing the shades of opinion in the country to just two so that parties could clash and a clear winner would emerge. Jackson was the logical leader, and the presidential nominee, of one new party, which would become known as the Democratic Party; its opponents, calling themselves National Republicans, nominated Adams. The second American party system was taking shape.

The 1828 campaign was a vicious, mud-slinging affair. The National Republicans called Jackson a murderer for killing several men in duels and military executions. They charged him with adultery for living with Rachel Robards when she was still married to another man. Jackson's supporters responded by accusing Adams of wearing silk underwear, spending public funds on a billiard table for the White House, and offering a beautiful American prostitute to the Russian tsar.

Although both sides slung mud, Jackson's men had better aim. Charges by Adams's supporters that Jackson was an illiterate backwoodsman backfired, increasing his popularity by casting him as a common man. Jackson's supporters presented him as the common man incarnate—his mind unclouded by learning, his morals simple and true, his will fierce and resolute. Adams, in contrast, was an aristocrat, a scholar whose learning obscured the truth, a writer rather than a fighter.

The election swept Jackson into office with twice Adams's electoral votes. The popular vote, which was much closer, reflected the strong sectional bases of the new parties. Adams doubled Jackson's vote in New England, while Jackson doubled Adams's vote in the South and nearly tripled it in the Southwest.

Jackson in Office

Jackson rode to the presidency on a wave of opposition to corruption and privilege. One of his first moves was to institute "rotation in office"—the removal of officeholders of the rival party. Nearly half of the higher-ranking civil servants were summarily fired. Although his opponents called it the **"spoils system,"** Jackson defended rotation in office on the basis of democracy: The duties of most officeholders were so simple that as many plain people as possible should have the chance to work for the government.

"spoils system" Practice of rewarding political supporters with public office

Jackson's positions on internal improvements and tariffs sparked even more intense controversy. He did not oppose all federal aid for internal improvements. However, Jackson suspected that public officials used such aid to win political support by handing out favors. To end such corruption, he flatly rejected federal support for roads within states. In 1830, when a bill came before him that would have provided federal money for a road between Maysville and Lexington, Kentucky, Jackson vetoed it.

The tariff issue tested Jackson's support even in the South, where the Indian Removal Act of 1830 (see Chapter 9) enhanced his popularity. In 1828, while Adams was still president, some of Jackson's supporters in Congress had helped pass a high protective tariff favorable to western agriculture and New England manufacturing. Jackson's supporters had calculated that southerners would blame the Adams administration for this **"Tariff of Abominations."** Instead, they leveled their fury at Jackson.

"Tariff of Abominations" Protective tariff of 1828 that infuriated southerners; spawned the Nullification Crisis

Nullification

The 1828 tariff opened a major rift between Jackson and his vice president, John C. Calhoun. Although he had entered Congress as a "war hawk" and had championed nationalism early in his career, Calhoun had gradually become a states' rights sectionalist. He had supported the tariff of 1816 but would fiercely oppose that of 1828.

Calhoun also burned with ambition to be president. Since Jackson had stated that he would serve only one term, Calhoun, as vice president, assumed that he would succeed Jackson. To do so, he needed to maintain the support of the South, which was increasingly taking an antitariff stance. Calhoun's own state, South Carolina, had suffered economic decline throughout the 1820s; its citizens blamed protective tariffs. Tariffs, according to Calhoun's constituents, not only drove up the price of manufactured goods; they also threatened to damage the American market for British textiles and thus reduce British demand for southern cotton.

Calhoun also opposed the tariff on constitutional grounds. He embraced the view, set forth in the Virginia and Kentucky Resolutions of 1798–1799, that the Union was a compact by which the states had conferred limited and specified powers on the federal government. He insisted that the only constitutional tariff was one that raised money for

Memphis Brooks Museum of Art, Memphis, TN, Memphis Park Commission Purchase

***Andrew Jackson*, by Ralph Earl**
Jackson during the Nullification Crisis, looking serene in the uniform of a major-general and determined to face down the greatest challenge to his presidency.

National Portrait Gallery, Smithsonian Institution/Art Resource, NY

***John C. Calhoun,* by Charles Bird King, c. 1825**
The magnetic Calhoun, Jackson's vice president, broke with Jackson over nullification and the Peggy Eaton affair, and resigned the vice presidency in 1832.

the common national defense. Calhoun expressed these views anonymously in the widely circulated *South Carolina Exposition and Protest* (1828), which argued that aggrieved states had the right to nullify that tariff within their borders.

Like Calhoun, Jackson was strong-willed and proud. Unlike Calhoun, he already was president and the leader of a national party that included supporters of the tariff. To retain key northern support while soothing the South, Jackson devised two policies. First, he distributed surplus federal revenue, derived largely from the tariff duties, to the states, hoping to remove the taint of sectional injustice from the tariff. Second, he tried to ease tariffs down from the sky-high 1828 rates, and Congress passed slight reductions in 1832. But these measures did little to satisfy Calhoun and the South Carolinians.

Meanwhile, two personal issues further damaged relations between Calhoun and Jackson. In 1829, Jackson's secretary of war, John H. Eaton, married the widowed daughter of a Washington tavern keeper. The newlyweds were snubbed socially by Calhoun's wife and his friends in the cabinet. To make matters worse, in 1830 Jackson received conclusive evidence supporting his long-time suspicion that in 1818, then-secretary of war Calhoun had urged that Jackson be punished for his unauthorized raid into Spanish Florida. This confirmation combined with the Eaton affair to convince Jackson that he had to "destroy [Calhoun] regardless of what injury it might do me or my administration." At a Jefferson Day dinner in April 1830, when Jackson proposed the toast, "Our Union: It must be preserved," Calhoun pointedly responded, "The Union next to Liberty the most dear. May we always remember that it can only be preserved by distributing equally the benefits and burdens of the Union."

Nullification Crisis
Controversy over nullification that pitted Jackson against Calhoun and led to talk of secession by southerners

The stage was set for the **Nullification Crisis.** In November 1832, a South Carolina convention, citing Calhoun's states' rights doctrine, nullified the tariffs of 1828 and 1832 and forbade the collection of customs duties within the state. Jackson reacted quickly. He labeled nullification an "abominable doctrine" that would reduce the government to anarchy, and denounced the nullifiers as "unprincipled men who would rather rule in hell, than be subordinate in heaven." He sent arms to Unionists in South Carolina and issued a proclamation that lambasted nullification as unconstitutional. The Constitution, he emphasized, had established "a single nation," not a league of states.

The crisis eased in March 1833 when Jackson signed into law two measures, called by one historian "the olive branch and the sword." The olive branch was the Compromise Tariff of 1833, which provided for a gradual reduction of duties between 1833 and 1842. The sword was the Force Bill, authorizing the president to use arms to collect customs duties in South Carolina. Although South Carolina promptly nullified the Force Bill, it construed the Compromise Tariff as a concession and rescinded its nullification of the tariffs of 1828 and 1832.

This so-called Compromise of 1833 mixed partisanship with statesmanship. Its chief architect was Henry Clay of Kentucky, who had long favored high tariffs. Clay supported tariff reduction because he feared that without some concessions to South Carolina, the Force Bill would produce civil war. Clay preferred to take responsibility for lowering tariffs himself, rather than pass the responsibility to the Jacksonians. The nullifiers, recognizing that no other states had supported them, preferred that Clay, not Jackson, be the hero of the hour. So they supported Clay's Compromise Tariff. Everywhere Americans hailed Clay as the Great Compromiser. Even Martin Van Buren acknowledged that Clay had "saved the country."

The Bank Veto and the Election of 1832

Jackson recognized that the gap between rich and poor was widening. Although he did not object to wealth earned by hard work, he believed that the wealthy too often enjoyed privileges granted by corrupt legislatures. Additionally, disastrous speculation early in his life had led him to distrust all banks, paper money, and monopolies. The **Bank of the United States** was guilty on all counts.

Bank of the United States National Bank created by Alexander Hamilton

The Second Bank of the United States had received a twenty-year charter from Congress in 1816. As a creditor to state banks, with the option of demanding repayment in specie (gold or silver coinage), the Bank of the United States held the power to restrain the state banks from excessive printing and lending of money. Such power provoked hostility. Many Americans blamed the bank for precipitating the Panic of 1819. Further, as the official depository for federal revenue, the bank's capital of $35 million was more than double the annual expenditures of the federal government. Yet this powerful institution was only distantly controlled by the government. Its stockholders were private citizens and its directors enjoyed considerable independence. Its president, the aristocratic Nicholas Biddle, viewed himself as a public servant, duty-bound to keep the bank above politics.

Encouraged by Henry Clay, who hoped that supporting the bank would help carry him to the White House in 1832, Biddle secured congressional passage of a bill to recharter the bank. Jackson vetoed it, denouncing the bank as a private and privileged monopoly that drained the West of specie, eluded state taxation, and made "the rich richer and the potent more powerful."

By 1832, Jackson had made his views on major issues clear. He was simultaneously a strong defender of states' rights *and* a staunch Unionist. Although he cherished the Union, Jackson believed the states were far too diverse to accept strong direction from the federal government. Throwing aside earlier promises to retire, Jackson ran for the presidency again in 1832, with Martin Van Buren as his running mate. Henry Clay ran on the National Republican ticket, stressing his American System of protective tariffs, national banking, and federal support for internal improvements. Jackson won. Secure in office for another four years, he was ready to finish dismantling the Bank of the United States.

CHECKING IN

- During the 1820s politics became increasingly democratic, and voter participation increased dramatically.
- Andrew Jackson emerged as "the common man."
- As president, Jackson opposed the use of federal funds for internal improvements.
- The Nullification Crisis of 1828–1833 exposed deep divisions between the North and the South.
- Jackson saw his veto of the charter of the Bank of the United States as a victory for the common man.

THE BANK CONTROVERSY AND THE SECOND PARTY SYSTEM, 1833–1840

What were the major factors in the rise of the second party system?

Jackson's bank veto ignited a searing controversy that threatened to engulf all banks. One major problem was that the United States had no paper currency of its own. Instead, private bankers issued paper notes, which they promised to redeem in specie. These IOUs fueled economic development by making credit easy. But if a bank note depreciated, wage earners paid in paper would suffer. Further, paper money encouraged speculation, which multiplied both profit and risk. For example, farmers could now buy land on credit in the belief that its value would rise; if it did, they could sell the land at a profit, but if its value fell, the farmers became mired in debt. Would the United States embrace swift economic development at the price of allowing some people to get rich quickly while others languished? Or would the nation undergo more modest growth in traditional molds, anchored by "honest" manual work and frugality?

The War on the Bank

Jackson could have allowed the bank to die quietly when its charter ran out in 1836. But Jackson and some of his followers feared the bank's power too much to wait. When Biddle, anticipating further attacks, began to call in the bank's loans and contract credit during the winter of 1832–1833, Jacksonians saw their darkest fears confirmed. The bank, Jackson assured Van Buren, "is trying to kill me, but I will kill it." Jackson then began to remove federal deposits from the Bank of the United States and place them in state banks, called "pet banks" by their critics because they were usually selected for loyalty to the Democratic Party.

However, Jackson's redistribution of federal deposits backfired. He himself opposed paper money and easy credit. But as state banks became depositories for federal revenue, they were able to print more paper money and extend more loans to farmers and speculators eager to buy public lands in the West. Government land sales rose from $6 million in 1834 to $25 million in 1836. Jackson's policy was producing exactly the kind of economy he wanted to suppress.

Jackson was caught between crosswinds. Western Democrats resented the Bank of the United States because it periodically contracted credit and restricted lending by state banks. Advocating "soft" or paper money, these Democrats in 1836 pressured a reluctant Jackson to sign the Deposit Act, which increased the number of deposit banks and loosened federal control over them. But Jackson continued to believe that paper money sapped "public virtue" and "robbed honest labour of its earnings to make knaves rich, powerful and dangerous." Seeking to reverse the damaging effects of the Deposit Act, Jackson issued a proclamation in 1836 called the Specie Circular, which provided that only specie could be accepted in payment for public lands.

Meanwhile, the hard-money (specie) view was advocated within Jackson's inner circle and by a faction of the New York Democratic Party called the Locofocos.

The Locofocos grew out of several different "workingmen's" parties that called for free public education, the abolition of imprisonment for debt, and a ten-hour workday.

The Rise of Whig Opposition

During Jackson's second term, the opposition National Republican Party gave way to the new Whig party. Jackson's magnetic personality had swept him to victory in 1828 and 1832. As Jackson's policies became clearer and sharper, the opposition attracted people alienated by his positions.

For example, Jackson's crushing of nullification led some southerners to the Whigs, as did his war against the bank and opposition to federal aid for internal improvements. Although most of the South remained Democratic, the Whigs made substantial inroads. And supporters of Henry Clay's American System joined advocates of public education and temperance in seeking a more activist, interventionist national government.

Northern social reformers were attracted to the Whigs. Just as Clay hoped to use government to promote economic development, these reformers wanted government to improve American society by ending slavery and liquor consumption, improving public education, and elevating public morality. The reformers, overwhelmingly Protestant, distrusted immigrants, especially Irish Catholics, who viewed drinking as a normal recreation and opposed public schools because they promoted Protestantism. The reform agitation and its association with the Whigs drove the Irish into the Democratic Party. In turn, many native-born Protestant workers, contemptuous of the Irish, turned Whig.

The most remarkable source of Whig strength was Anti-Masonry. Freemasonry had long provided prominent men, including George Washington, with fellowship and exotic rituals. The spark that ignited the Anti-Masonic crusade was the abduction and disappearance in 1826 of William Morgan, a Mason who had threatened to expose the order's secrets. Efforts to solve the mystery of Morgan's disappearance failed because local officials were themselves Masons, seemingly determined to thwart the investigation. Rumors spread that Masonry was a powerful anti-Christian conspiracy of the rich in order to suppress popular liberty and an exclusive retreat for drunkards. Anti-Masonry brought many northeastern small farmers and artisans into the Whig party.

By 1836, the Whigs had become a national party with widespread appeal. Whigs everywhere assailed Andrew Jackson as an imperious dictator, "King Andrew I," and the name "Whigs" evoked memories of the American patriots who had opposed King George III in 1776.

The Election of 1836

Andrew Jackson was a hard act to follow. Democrats nominated Martin Van Buren, proclaiming that he and the Democratic Party were Jackson's heirs, the perfect embodiment of the popular will. The Whigs ran three candidates from different sections of the country. The Democrats accused the Whigs of attempting to split the vote and throw the election into the House, where they could wheel and deal as in 1824. In reality, the Whigs were simply divided, and Van Buren won a clear majority.

But there were signs of trouble ahead for the Democrats. The popular vote was close. In the South, where four years earlier the Democrats had won two-thirds of the votes, they now won barely half.

The Panic of 1837

Jackson left office in 1837 in a burst of glory. Yet he bequeathed to his successor a severe depression.

In the speculative boom of 1835 and 1836, born of Jackson's policy of placing federal funds in state banks, the total number of banks doubled, the value of bank notes in circulation nearly tripled, and both commodity and land prices soared skyward. But the overheated economy began to cool rapidly in May 1837. Prices tumbled as bank after bank suspended specie payments.

The ensuing depression had multiple roots. Domestically, Jackson's Specie Circular of July 1836—declaring that only specie, not paper money, could be used to purchase public lands—dried up credit. Global events played a major role as well. In the 1820s, Americans had used freshly mined silver imported from Mexico to buy tea, silks, and other goods in China. By the early 1830s, the Chinese were using increasing amounts of this silver to pay for opium grown in India and peddled by British merchants. In turn, large amounts of silver flowed out of British coffers to invest in canals and other American projects. Worried that British investors were overextended, in 1836 the Bank of England drastically raised interest rates.

Making a bad situation much worse, the price paid for American cotton by British merchants plummeted in the late 1830s because of bumper cotton harvests in the United States. But crop prices remained high; to pay for imported foodstuffs, the Bank of England raised money by raising interest rates again. This dried up the source of investment in American canals, leaving the American landscape littered with half-finished canals to nowhere.

The depression was far more severe and prolonged than the Panic of 1819. Wages fell by one-third between 1836 and 1842. In despair, many workers turned to the teachings of William Miller, a New England religious enthusiast convinced that the end of the world was imminent. Miller's followers roamed urban sidewalks and rural villages in search of converts. Many sold their possessions and purchased white robes to ascend into heaven on October 22, 1843, the day the world was supposed to end.

"Little Magician" Martin Van Buren needed all his political skills to confront the depression that was damaging not only ordinary citizens but the Democratic Party itself. To seize the initiative, Van Buren called for the creation of an independent Treasury. The idea was simple: The federal government, instead of depositing its money in banks, which would use it as the basis for speculative loans, would hold onto its revenues and keep them from the grasp of corporations. When Van Buren finally signed the Independent Treasury Bill into law on July 4, 1840, his supporters hailed it as a second Declaration of Independence.

The Whigs, who blamed the depression on Jackson's Specie Circular rather than on the banks, continued to encourage bank charters as a way to spur economic development. But the independent Treasury reflected the deep Jacksonian suspicion of an alliance between government and banking. In Louisiana and Arkansas, Democrats prohibited banks altogether, and elsewhere they imposed severe restrictions—banning, for example, the issuing of paper money in small denominations. After 1837, the Democrats became an antibank, hard-money party.

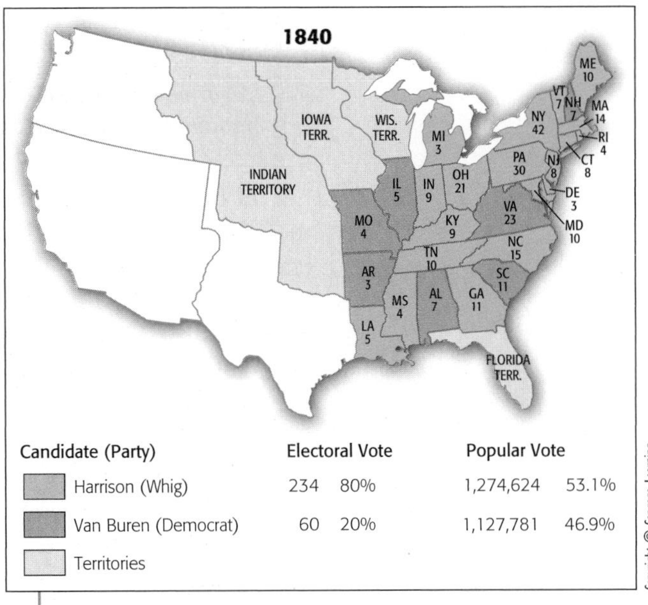

Map 10.2 The Election of 1840

Interactive Map

Log Cabins, Hard Cider, and a Maturing Second Party System

Despite the depression, the Democrats renominated Van Buren. Avoiding the mistake of 1836, the Whigs nominated a single candidate, Ohio's William Henry Harrison, and ran John Tyler of Virginia for vice president.

Early in the campaign the Democrats made a fatal mistake, ridiculing Harrison as "Old Granny," who desired only to spend his declining years in a **log cabin** sipping cider. In so doing, they handed the Whigs the most famous campaign symbol in American history. The Whigs saluted Harrison as a rugged frontiersman, the hero of the Battle of Tippecanoe (tip-pee-cuh-NOO), and a defender of all those people who lived in log cabins. Disdaining a platform, the Whigs ran a "hurrah" campaign using log cabins for headquarters, singing log cabin songs, and ladling out log cabin cider. Instead of a platform, they trumpeted, "Tippecanoe and Tyler, too!" and attacked Van Buren as an aristocrat who lived in "regal splendor."

log cabin Symbol of the Whig party in the 1840 "hurrah" campaign for the presidency

Harrison was elected in a clear victory. The depression would have made it difficult for any Democrat to win, but many of Van Buren's problems stemmed from his style of campaign. While the Whigs ran a rousing race aimed directly at the "common man," Van Buren quietly wrote letters of encouragement to key supporters. Ironically, the Whigs beat the master politician at his own game.

The strong contrasts between the two parties and the sharp choices they presented jolted the American electorate. Nearly 2.4 million people voted in 1840, up an astonishing 60 percent from 1836. Prior to 1840 the proportion of white males who voted had ranged from 55 to 58 percent; in 1840 it rose to 80 percent.

Both the depression and the frenzied log cabin campaign brought voters to the polls in 1840, but voter turnouts stayed high even after prosperity returned. The second party system reached a high plateau in 1840 and remained there for over a decade. The gradual hardening of the line between the two parties stimulated popular interest in politics. Another major current feeding partisan political passion in American life was reform. Yet the social and moral reform movements that burst onto the national scene in the 1830s originated not in politics, but in religion.

CHECKING IN

- Jackson's "war" on the bank intensified the differences between the Democrats and the Whigs.
- The new Whig party included reformers and opponents of Jackson.
- The Panic of 1837 exploded during the administration of Martin Van Buren and greatly strengthened the Whigs.
- The election of 1840, the first real "hurrah" campaign, gave the Whigs the White House for the first time.
- After 1840 the second party system was firmly in place.

THE RISE OF POPULAR RELIGION

What new assumptions about human nature lay behind the religious movements of the period?

In *Democracy in America,* Alexis de Tocqueville called religion "the foremost of the political institutions" in the United States. Tocqueville was referring to the way religious impulses reinforced democracy and liberty. Just as Americans demanded that politics be accessible to average people, they insisted that ministers preach doctrines that appealed to ordinary men and women. Successful ministers used plain language to move the heart, not theological complexity to dazzle the intellect. Increasingly, Americans put individuals in charge of their own religious destiny, thrusting aside Calvinist predestination in favor of the belief that anyone could attain heaven. A series of religious revivals known as the Second Great Awakening contributed to the growing harmony between religion and politics and to the growing conviction that heaven itself was democratic.

Second Great Awakening Religious revival that swept the country and fed into reform movements

The Second Great Awakening

The **Second Great Awakening** ignited in Connecticut during the 1790s. At first, educated Congregationalists and Presbyterians such as Yale president Timothy Dwight dominated the revivals. But as they spread to frontier states like Tennessee and Kentucky, revivals underwent striking changes that were typified by the rise of camp meetings. These were gigantic, prolonged revivals in which members of several denominations gathered into sprawling open-air camps to hear revivalists proclaim that the time for repentance was now.

The most famous camp meeting occurred at Cane Ridge, Kentucky, in August 1801, when a huge crowd assembled to hear thunderous sermons, sing hymns, and experience the influx of divine grace. Among the more extreme features of frontier revivals was the "exercises" in which men and women rolled around like logs, jerked their heads furiously, and barked like dogs. The most successful revivalists were not college graduates but ordinary farmers and artisans who had themselves experienced powerful religious conversions and regarded learned ministers with contempt for their dry expositions of orthodox theology.

Methodists Arose out of revivalism to become the largest American Protestant denomination

No religious denomination proved more successful on the frontier than the **Methodists.** The Methodists became America's largest Protestant denomination by 1844, claiming over a million members. In contrast to New England Congregationalists and Presbyterians, Methodists emphasized that religion was primarily a matter of the heart rather than the head. The frontier Methodists disdained "settled" ministers tied to fixed parishes. They preferred itinerant circuit riders—young, often unmarried men who traveled from place to place on horseback and preached in houses, open fields, and wherever listeners gathered.

Although the frontier revivals disrupted religious custom, they also promoted social and moral order on the frontier. After Methodist circuit riders left an area, their converts formed weekly "classes" that served as the grassroots structure for Methodist churches. The classes established a Methodist code of behavior, called the Discipline, which reinforced family and community values amidst the social disorder of frontier life. Class members reprimanded one another for drunkenness, fighting, fornication, gossiping, and even sharp business practices.

Eastern Revivals

By the 1820s, the Second Great Awakening had begun to shift back to the East. The hottest revival fires blazed in an area of western New York known as the Burned-Over District. No longer a frontier, western New York teemed with people drawn by the hope of wealth after the completion of the Erie Canal. It was a fertile field of high expectations and bitter discontent. The man who harnessed these anxieties to religion was **Charles Grandison Finney,** a lawyer-turned-Presbyterian minister. His greatest "harvest" came in the thriving canal city of Rochester in 1830–1831.

Charles Grandison Finney One of the most important revivalists; stressed individual responsibility

Finney's innovations at the Rochester revival justified his reputation as the "father of modern revivalism." First, it was a citywide revival in which all denominations participated. Finney was a pioneer of cooperation among Protestant denominations. Second, in Rochester and elsewhere, Finney introduced new devices for speeding conversions, such as the "anxious seat," where those ready for conversion were led so they could be made objects of special prayer, and the "protracted meeting," which went on nightly for up to a week.

Although a Presbyterian, Finney rejected the Calvinist doctrine of total depravity, humankind's irresistible inclination to sin. Instead, he proclaimed, sin was a voluntary act, and those who willed themselves to sin could just as readily will themselves not to sin. In theory, men and women could live perfect lives, free of sin. Those converted by Finney or other evangelists (ee-VAN-juh-lists) believed that they were cleansed of past guilt and were beginning a new life. "I have been born again," a young convert wrote. "I am three days old when I write this letter."

Originally controversial, Finney's ideas came to dominate "evangelical" (eh-van-JELL-ih-cull) Protestantism, which focused on the need for an emotional religious conversion. He succeeded because he told people what they wanted to hear: that their destiny was in their own hands. A society that celebrated the self-made individual embraced Finney's assertion that, even in religion, people could make of themselves what they chose. Finney multiplied his success by emphasizing the role of women, who outnumbered male converts nearly two to one. Finney encouraged women to give public testimonials of their conversion, and he often converted men by first winning over their wives and daughters.

Critics of Revivals: The Unitarians

Although some praised revivals for saving souls, others doubted their lasting effects. The **Unitarians** were a small, but influential group of critics. Although their basic doctrine—that Jesus Christ was less than fully divine—gained acceptance among religious liberals in the eighteenth century, Unitarianism became a formal denomination only in the early nineteenth century. Unitarians won few converts outside New England, but their tendency to attract the wealthy and educated gave them influence beyond their numbers.

Unitarians Denomination of generally educated, wealthy New Englanders upset by the emotionalism of revivals

Unitarians criticized revivals as uncouth emotional exhibitions and argued that "character building" was more effective than sudden emotional conversion. Yet they and the revivalists agreed in rejecting the Calvinist emphasis on human wickedness. Christianity had only one purpose, a Unitarian leader proclaimed: "the perfection of human nature, the elevation of men into nobler beings."

The Rise of Mormonism

Joseph Smith Founder of the Mormon Church, the first major denomination founded in the United States

Far more controversial than the Unitarians were the Mormons and their church, another new denomination of the 1820s named the Church of Jesus Christ of Latter-day Saints. **Joseph Smith,** its founder, grew up in the heart of the Burned-Over District. Conflict among the various religious denominations that thrived in the region—Methodists, Presbyterians, Baptists—left Smith confused. He wondered who was right and who was wrong or whether they were "all wrong together."

Smith's religious perplexity was common in the Burned-Over District, but his path to resolving the confusion was unique. An angel named Moroni, he reported, led him to a buried book of revelation and special seer stones to help with its translation, which he completed in 1827. The Book of Mormon tells the story of an ancient Hebrew prophet, Lehi, whose descendants migrated to America and created a prosperous civilization. Jesus had appeared and performed miracles in the New World, but Lehi's descendants had departed from the Lord's ways and quarreled among themselves. God had cursed some of these defectors with dark skin; these were the American Indians, who had long since forgotten their history.

Smith quickly gathered followers. For some believers, the Book of Mormon resolved the turmoil created by conflicting Protestant interpretations of the Bible. But Smith's claim to a new revelation guaranteed a hostile response from many American Protestants, who believed he had undermined the authority of their Scripture. To escape persecution, and move closer to the Indians whose conversion was one of their goals, Smith and his followers began relocating west from New York. In Illinois, they built a model city called Nauvoo and a magnificent temple supported by thirty huge pillars. However, in 1844 a group of dissident Mormons accused Smith and his inner circle of practicing plural marriage. When Smith destroyed the group's newspaper press, militias moved in to restore law and order. They arrested Smith and his brother Hirum and threw them into jail in Carthage, Illinois, where a lynch mob killed them both.

Joseph Smith had once hoped that Americans would fully embrace Mormonism. But ongoing persecution had gradually convinced the Mormons' prophet that their survival lay in separation from American society. In removing from the larger society of "Gentiles," the Mormons mirrored the efforts of many other religious communities during the 1830s and 1840s. One in particular, the Shakers, has held an enduring fascination for Americans.

The Shakers

Shakers Sect that stressed withdrawal from society; known for craftsmanship

The founder of the **Shakers** (who derived their name from a convulsive religious dance that was part of their ceremony) was Mother Ann Lee, the illiterate daughter of an British blacksmith. Lee and her followers established a series of tightly knit agricultural-artisan communities in America after her arrival in 1774. Shaker artisanship, particularly in furniture, quickly gained renown for its simple lines, beauty, and strength. Shaker advances in the development of new farm tools and seed varieties were a boon to the growing market economy.

For all their achievements as artisans, the Shakers were fundamentally otherworldly. Mother Ann, who had lost four infant children, had a religious vision in which God expelled Adam and Eve from the Garden of Eden for their sin of sexual intercourse. Shaker communities practiced celibacy and carefully separated the sleeping and working quarters of men and women to discourage contact between them. To maintain their membership, Shakers relied on new converts and the adoption of orphans. As part of their pursuit of religious perfection, they practiced a form of Christian socialism, pooling their land and implements to create remarkably prosperous villages.

While the Shakers chose to separate themselves from the competitive individualism of the larger society, the message of most evangelical Protestants, including Charles G. Finney, was that religion and economic self-advancement were compatible. Most revivalists taught that the pursuit of wealth was acceptable as long as people were honest, temperate, and bound by conscience. But many of them recognized that the world was in serious need of improvement, and they believed that converts had a religious responsibility to pursue moral and social reform.

CHECKING IN

- The "democratization" process reached religion as well as politics.
- The Second Great Awakening emphasized the emotional aspects of religion.
- Methodism emerged as a major Protestant denomination.
- The Mormon Church and the Shakers were born amid the fever of revivalism, but their members lived apart from society.
- Despite such new sects, revivalists generally encouraged involvement in society and were a powerful stimulus to reform movements.

THE AGE OF REFORM

Did the reform movements aim primarily at making Americans more free or more orderly?

At the heart of religious revival was the democratic belief that individual men and women could take charge of their own spiritual destinies and strive toward perfection. For many converts, similar expectations applied to the society around them. Saved souls, they believed, could band together to stamp out the many evils that plagued the American republic. The abolition of slavery, the rights of women, temperance, the humane treatment of criminals and the insane, and public education were high on reformers' agendas. Carrying the moralism of revival into their reform activities, they tended to view all social problems as clashes between good and evil.

Not all reformers were converts of revivalism. Many school reformers and women's rights advocates were either hostile or indifferent to revivals. Abolitionists openly criticized the churches for condoning slavery. However, by portraying slaveholding as a sin that called for immediate repentance, even religiously liberal abolitionists borrowed their language and their psychological appeal from revivalism. Whatever a reformer's personal relationship to the revivals of the Second Great Awakening, the Age of Reform drew much of its fuel from that evangelical movement.

The War on Liquor

Early nineteenth-century Americans were very heavy drinkers. In 1825, the average adult male drank about seven gallons of alcohol annually, in contrast to less than two gallons in our own time. One reason for this heavy consumption was the state of western agriculture. Before the transportation revolution, western farmers could not make a profit by shipping grain in bulk to eastern markets. But they could profit by condensing their corn and rye into whiskey. Drunkenness pervaded all social classes and occupations.

temperance Abstinence from alcohol; name of the movement against alcohol

Before 1825, **temperance** (TEM-per-enss) reformers advocated moderation in consuming alcohol. But in that year, Connecticut revivalist Lyman Beecher delivered six widely acclaimed lectures that condemned all use of alcoholic beverages. A year later, evangelical Protestants created the American Temperance Society, the first national temperance organization. By 1834, some five thousand state and local temperance societies were affiliated with it.

The primary strategy of the American Temperance Society was to use "moral suasion" to persuade people to "take the pledge"–the promise never to consume any alcoholic beverage. Among the main targets of evangelical temperance reformers were the laboring classes. In the small workshops of the pre-industrial era, passing the jug every few hours throughout the workday was a time-honored practice. But early factories demanded a more disciplined, sober work force, so industrial employers were quick to embrace temperance reform. Industrial employers in Rochester, New York, invited Charles G. Finney to preach up a revival in their city as part of an effort to convince their workers to abstain from alcohol.

Workers themselves initially showed little interest in temperance. But after the Panic of 1837, some grew convinced that their economic survival depended on a commitment to sobriety. In 1840, in Baltimore, they formed the Washington Temperance Society. Many members were themselves reformed drunkards. Take care of temperance, one Washingtonian assured his Baltimore audience, and the Lord will take care of the economy. The Washington Societies spread farther and faster than any other antebellum temperance organization.

As the temperance movement won new supporters, some crusaders began to demand legal prohibition–the banning of liquor traffic at the local and state level. In 1838, Massachusetts prohibited the sale of distilled spirits in amounts less than fifteen gallons. In 1851, Maine banned the manufacture and sale of all intoxicating beverages. Taken together, the two central strategies of the temperance movement–moral suasion and legal prohibition–scored remarkable success. Per capita consumption of distilled spirits began to fall during the 1830s. By the 1840s, consumption had dropped to less than half its peak rate in the 1820s.

Public-School Reform

Like temperance crusaders, school reformers worked to encourage orderliness and thrift in the common people. Rural "district" schools were a main target. Here students ranging in age from three to twenty crowded into a single room and learned to read and count, but little more.

Horace Mann Important public-school reformer

District schools enjoyed considerable support from rural parents. However, reformers insisted that schools had to equip children for the emerging competitive and industrial economy. In 1837, **Horace Mann** of Massachusetts became the first secretary of his state's newly created board of education. He presided over sweeping reforms to transform schools from loose organizations into highly structured institutions that occupied most of a child's time and energy. Mann's goals included shifting financial support of schools from parents to the state, compelling attendance, extending the school term, introducing standardized textbooks, and dividing students into grades based on their age and achievements.

School reformers sought to spread industrial values as well as combat ignorance. Requiring students to arrive on time would teach punctuality, and matching children against their peers would stimulate competitiveness. The McGuffey readers, which sold 50 million copies between 1836 and 1870, preached industry, honesty, sobriety, and patriotism.

Success did not come easily. Educational reformers faced challenges from farmers who were satisfied with the district school, from Catholics objecting to anti-Catholic and anti-Irish barbs in the textbooks, and from the working poor, who widely saw compulsory education as a menace to families dependent on children's wages. Mann and other school reformers prevailed in part because their opponents could not cooperate with one another and in part because the reformers attracted influential allies, including urban workers, manufacturers, and women. Reformers predicted that school reform would make teaching a suitable profession for women, and they were right. By 1900, about 70 percent of the nation's schoolteachers were women.

School reform also appealed to native-born Americans alarmed by the influx of immigrant foreigners. The public school was coming to be seen as the best mechanism for creating a common American culture out of an increasingly diverse society. As one reformer observed, "We must decompose and cleanse the impurities which rush into our midst" through the "one infallible filter—the SCHOOL." Very few educational reformers, however, called for the integration of black and white children. When black children did enter public schools, they encountered open hostility and sometimes violence.

Abolition

Antislavery sentiment had flourished among whites during the revolutionary era but faded in the early nineteenth century. The American Colonization Society, founded in 1817, was the main antislavery organization of this period. It proposed gradual emancipation, compensation for slave owners when slaves became free, and the shipment to Africa of freed blacks. Although these proposals attracted some support from slave owners in the Upper South, they were unrealizable. The growing cotton economy had made slavery more attractive than ever to most southerners, and few owners were unwilling to free their slaves, even if compensated. Between 1820 and 1830—a period when the slave population nearly doubled in size—only 1,400 blacks migrated to Liberia, and most of them were already free blacks.

Most African-Americans opposed colonization. As native-born Americans, they asked, how could they be sent back to a continent they had never known? "We are natives of this country," one black pastor proclaimed. "We only ask that we be treated as well as foreigners." In opposition to colonization, blacks formed their own abolition societies. One free black, David Walker of Boston, urged slaves to rise up and murder their masters if slavery were not abolished.

In 1821, Benjamin Lundy, a white Quaker, began a newspaper, the *Genius of Universal Emancipation,* that trumpeted repeal of the Constitution's three-fifths

William Lloyd Garrison Outspoken radical opponent of slavery

clause, the outlawing of the internal slave trade, and the abolition of slavery in U.S. territories. Seven years later Lundy hired a young New Englander, **William Lloyd Garrison,** as an editorial assistant. The prematurely bald, bespectacled Garrison would become a potent force in the antislavery movement.

In 1831, Garrison launched a newspaper, *The Liberator,* to spread his radical antislavery message. "I am in earnest," he wrote. "I will not equivocate—I will not excuse—I will not retreat a single inch—AND I WILL BE HEARD." His battle cry was "immediate emancipation"; his demand, civil and legal equality for African-Americans. However, even Garrison did not believe that all slaves could be freed overnight. People first had to realize that slavery was sinful and its continued existence intolerable.

Frederick Douglass Escaped slave who became a major figure in the antislavery movement

Black abolitionists supported Garrison; in its early years three-fourths of *The Liberator's* subscribers were African-American. Other blacks were also emerging as powerful writers and speakers. **Frederick Douglass,** an escaped slave, could rivet an audience with an opening line: "I appear before the immense assembly this evening as a thief and a robber. I stole this head, these limbs, this body from my master, and ran off with them."

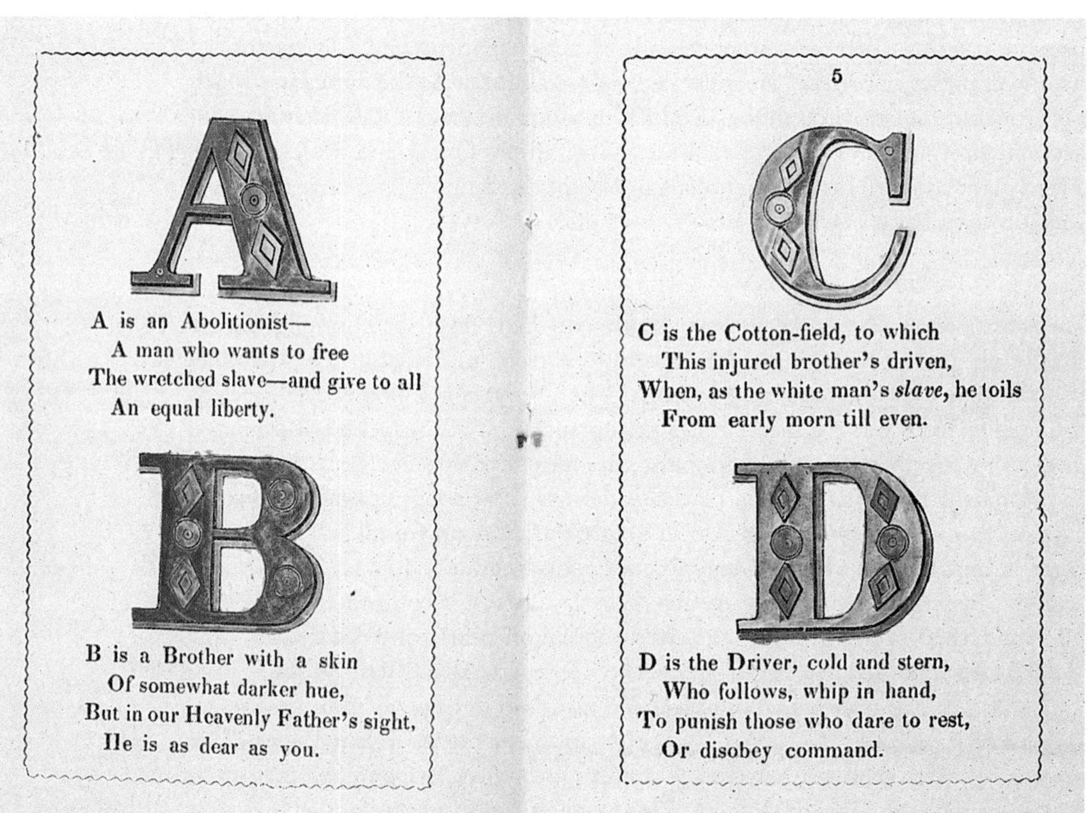

The Alphabet

Viewing children as morally pure and hence as natural opponents of slavery, abolitionists produced antislavery toys, games, and, as we see here, alphabet books.

Relations between white and black abolitionists were not always harmonious. Many white abolitionists called for legal, but not civil and social, racial equality; preferred light-skinned to dark-skinned blacks; and hesitated to admit African-Americans to antislavery societies. And widespread white prejudice made the life of any abolitionist precarious. Mobs attacked abolitionists often. In 1837, a mob in Alton, Illinois, destroyed the printing press of antislavery editor Elijah P. Lovejoy, then shot him dead and dragged his mutilated corpse through the streets.

Furthermore, Protestant churches did not rally solidly behind abolition. Lyman Beecher roared against the evils of strong drink but merely whispered about those of slavery.

Even as the obstacles mounted, issues of strategy and tactics divided abolitionists during the 1830s. Some believed that the legal and political arena presented the best opportunities for ending slavery. But Garrison and his followers were beginning to reject all participation not only in party politics, but in government itself. In 1838, they founded the New England Non-Resistance Society, based on Garrison's radical new doctrine of nonresistance. According to that doctrine, the fundamental evil of slavery was its reliance on force, the opposite of Christian love. And just like slavery, government itself ultimately rested on coercion. True Christians, Garrison concluded, should refuse to vote, hold office, or have anything to do with government.

Another major issue dividing abolitionists was the role of women in the movement. In 1837, **Angelina and Sarah Grimké** (GRIM-kee), the daughters of a South Carolina slaveholder, made an antislavery lecture tour of New England. The Grimké sisters were controversial because they spoke to audiences of both men and women at a time when it was thought indelicate for women to address male audiences. Clergymen chastised the Grimké sisters for lecturing men rather than obeying them.

Angelina and Sarah Grimké Sisters who were powerful antislavery speakers; later leaders of women's rights movement

The Grimkés responded in 1838 by writing two classics of American feminism: Sarah Grimké's *Letters on the Condition of Women and the Equality of the Sexes,* and Angelina Grimké's *Letters to Catharine E. Beecher* (who opposed female equality). Some abolitionists dismissed their efforts: Women's grievances, said poet John Greenleaf Whittier, were "paltry" compared to the injustices of slavery. Garrison, welcoming the controversy, promptly espoused women's rights and urged equal treatment for women in the American Anti-Slavery Society. In 1840, the election of Abby Kelley to a previously all-male committee split the society, with many profeminists splintering off to form their own groups.

However, the break-up of the American Anti-Slavery Society did not significantly damage the larger movement. By 1840, there were more than fifteen hundred local antislavery societies circulating abolitionist tracts, newspapers, and even chocolates wrapped in antislavery messages. Local societies pursued a grassroots campaign to flood Congress with petitions calling for an end to slavery in the District of Columbia. When exasperated southerners in 1836 adopted a "gag rule" automatically tabling these petitions without discussion, they triggered a debate that shifted public attention from abolitionism to the constitutional rights of free expression—a debate that further served the antislavery cause. The less secure southerners felt, the more they blundered into clumsy overreactions like the gag rule.

Women's Rights

When Sarah and Angelina Grimké took up the cause of women's rights in 1838, they were not merely defending their right to participate in the antislavery movement. They were responding to perceived similarities between the conditions of slaves and women. Early issues of *The Liberator* contained a "Ladies' Department" illustrated with a kneeling slave woman imploring, "Am I Not a Woman and a Sister?" When abolitionists such as Lucretia (loo-CREE-shuh) Mott, Lucy Stone, and Abby Kelley embraced women's rights, they were acknowledging a sisterhood in oppression with female slaves.

Seneca Falls, New York Site of first women's rights convention in 1848

Women occupied a paradoxical position in the 1830s. They could not vote and, if married, had no right to own property or to keep their own wages. Divorced women could not gain custody of their children; domestic violence went virtually unchallenged. At the same time, reform movements gave women unprecedented opportunities to work in public without openly defying the dictate that their proper sphere was the home. When women left their homes to distribute religious tracts, battle intemperance, or work for peace, they could claim they were transforming wretched homes into nurseries of happiness.

Miriam and Ira D. Wallach Division of Art, Prints and Photographs, The New York Public Library, Astor, Lenox and Tilden Foundations

Sojourner Truth, 1864

Born into slavery in New York, the woman who named herself Sojourner Truth became a religious perfectionist, a powerful evangelical preacher, and one of the most influential abolitionists and feminists of her time.

The argument that women were natural guardians of family life was double-edged. It justified reform activities on behalf of the family but undercut women's demands for legal equality. However, the experiences acquired in a range of reform activities provided invaluable skills for women to take up the cause of their own rights. And the women's rights movement, at its most radical, openly challenged gender-based double standards. "Men and women," Sarah Grimké wrote, "are CREATED EQUAL! They are both moral and accountable beings, and whatever is right for man to do, is right for woman."

Although feminism first emerged within abolitionism, the discrimination encountered by women in the antislavery movement drove them to make women's rights a separate cause. In the 1840s, Lucy Stone became the first abolitionist to give a lecture devoted entirely to women's rights. When Lucretia Mott arrived at the World's Anti-Slavery Convention in London in 1840, and was seated in a screened-off section for women, her own allegiance to women's rights was sealed. The incident made a deep impression on Mott and Elizabeth Cady Stanton. In 1848, Mott and Stanton together organized the Seneca Falls Convention for women's rights at **Seneca** (SEN-ih-cuh) **Falls, New York.** That convention's Declaration of Sentiments, modeled on the Declaration of Independence, began with the assertion that "all men and women are created equal." The participants passed a series of resolutions, including a call for the right of women to vote, which would become the centerpiece of women's rights activity after the Civil War.

Women's rights advocates won a few notable victories. In 1860, Stanton's lobbying helped secure passage of a New York law allowing married women to own property. But women's rights had less impact than many other reforms, including temperance, school reform, and abolitionism. Women would not secure the national right to vote until 1920, fifty-five years after the Thirteenth Amendment abolished slavery. Nineteenth-century feminists had to content themselves with piecemeal gains.

Penitentiaries and Asylums

Beginning in the 1820s, reformers began to combat poverty, crime, and insanity by establishing new model institutions based on innovative theories about the roots of deviancy. As urban poverty and crime grew increasingly visible, investigators concluded that such problems arose not from innate sinfulness, but from poor home environments. Both religious and secular reformers believed that human nature could be improved through placement in the proper moral environment. For paupers, criminals, and the mentally ill, that place was the asylum, an institution that would remove deviants from corrupting influences and provide them with moral supervision and disciplined work.

The colonial jail had been merely a temporary holding cell for offenders awaiting trial; early American criminals were punished by flogging, branding, or hanging rather than extended prison terms. By contrast, the nineteenth-century penitentiary (pen-ih-TEN-char-ee) was an asylum designed to lead criminals to "penitential" reformation by isolating them and encouraging them to contemplate their guilt. Two different models for the penitentiary emerged in the antebellum era. New York's "Auburn (AW-burn) system" forbade prisoners to speak to one another and confined them in individual, windowless cells by night. Under the more extreme "Pennsylvania" or "separate system," each prisoner was confined day and night in a single cell with a walled courtyard for exercise, deprived of human contact within the prison, and permitted visits from the outside.

Antebellum reformers also designed special asylums for the poor and the mentally ill. The prevailing colonial practice of poor relief was "outdoor relief," supporting the poor by placing them in other people's households. The new "indoor relief" confined the infirm poor in almshouses (AHMS-houses) and the able-bodied poor in workhouses. A parallel movement shaped new approaches to treating the mentally ill, as illuminated in the work of humanitarian reformer **Dorothea Dix.** Instead of imprisoning the insane in jails and sheds, she argued, society should house them in orderly hospitals where they should receive proper medical and moral care.

Dorothea Dix Leader of the crusade to improve conditions for the insane

Penitentiaries, almshouses and workhouses, and insane asylums all reflected the same optimistic belief that the solution for deviancy lay in proper moral environments. From one point of view, such efforts were humanitarian. But from another point of view, the asylum reformers were practicing extreme forms of social control. Convinced that criminals, the poor, and the insane required regimentation, they confined them in prison-like conditions, policed their social interaction, and controlled their every move.

Utopian Communities

The reformist belief in the possibility of human perfection assumed purest expression in the utopian (yoo-TOH-pee-ehn) communities that first began to surface in the 1820s. Most of these, founded by intellectuals, were meant to be alternatives to the prevailing competitive economy and models whose success would inspire others.

New Harmony One of the most important utopian communities, founded in Indiana by Robert Owen

In 1825, British industrialist Robert Owen founded the **New Harmony** community in Indiana. As a mill owner, Owen had improved his workers' living conditions and educational opportunities; he was convinced that the problems of the early industrial age were social, not political. Vice and misery would vanish if social arrangements were perfected, he thought. The key was the creation of small, planned communities—"Villages of Unity and Mutual Cooperation"—with a perfect balance of occupational, religious, and social groups.

Upon founding New Harmony, Owen confidently predicted that northerners would embrace its principles within two years. Instead, the community became a magnet for idlers and fanatics, and failed within two years. Nonetheless, Owen's ideas survived the wreckage of New Harmony. His insistence that human character was formed by environment and that cooperation was superior to competition had an enduring impact on urban workers, who took up his cause of educational reform in the years to come.

transcendentalists American religious philosophers who believed in the capacity of the human spirit; included many renowned writers

Experimental communities multiplied rapidly during the economic crises of the late 1830s and 1840s. Brook Farm, near Boston, was the creation of a group of religious philosophers called **transcendentalists** (tran-sen-DEN-tuh-lists), who sought to revitalize Christianity by proclaiming the infinite spiritual capacities of ordinary men and women. Convinced that the competitive commercial life of the cities was unnatural, Brook Farmers spent their days milking cows and mowing hay, and their evenings contemplating philosophy. This utopian community attracted several renowned writers, including Ralph Waldo Emerson and Nathaniel Hawthorne, and its literary magazine, *The Dial*, became an important forum for transcendentalist ideas (as discussed further in Chapter 11). But its life-span was brief.

The most controversial utopian experiment was the Oneida (oh-NYE-duh) Community, established in 1848 in New York by John Humphrey Noyes (noise). A convert of Charles Finney, Noyes also became a theological perfectionist. At Oneida, he advocated a form of Christian communism. The Oneidans renounced private property, put men to work in kitchens, and adopted the radical new bloomer costume for women. But what most upset their critics was the application of communism to marriage. Noyes advocated "complex marriage," in which every member of the community was married to every other member of the other sex. Oneida did not promote sexual free-for-all, however: Couplings were arranged through an intermediary, in part to track paternity.

Contemporaries dismissed Noyes as a licentious crackpot. Yet Oneida achieved considerable economic prosperity and was attracting new members long after other, less radical utopias had failed. Despite the ridicule of many of their contemporaries, utopian communities exemplified the idealism and hopefulness that permeated nearly all reform movements in the antebellum period.

CHECKING IN

- Reform movements, invigorated by revivalism, swept over the North and West, but had little impact in the South.
- The temperance movement targeted workers and enjoyed considerable success.
- Educational reform aimed both to prepare children for life in an industrializing economy and to reinforce Protestant American culture; reformers also established new institutions to deal with the poor, criminals, and the insane.
- The antislavery movement gained momentum but was split by disagreements.
- The struggle for women's rights emerged from women's participation in the antislavery movement and other reform efforts.
- Reformers established a variety of utopian communities (usually unsuccessful), which sought to create a model for ideal society.

Chapter Summary

How did the democratization of American politics contribute to the rise of Andrew Jackson? (page 221)

Starting in the 1820s, restrictions on voting for white males dwindled, and politics became increasingly inclusive. Andrew Jackson, seen as the incarnation of democratic politics, won the White House for two terms and fought for what he saw as the causes of the common man, especially in his crusade against the Bank of the United States. However, the Nullification Crisis revealed sharp differences between North and South.

What were the major factors in the rise of the second party system? (page 228)

In waging his "war" against the bank, Jackson intensified differences between the Democrats and the Whigs. This war helped to solidify the second party system but led to the Panic of 1837. The resulting depression engulfed and destroyed the presidency of Martin Van Buren and handed the White House to the Whigs in 1840, putting the second party system firmly in place. New styles of campaigning emerged with the "log cabin" campaign of 1840, and voter participation soared.

What new assumptions about human nature lay behind the religious movements of the period? (page 232)

Revivalism dominated religion for many Americans during the Second Great Awakening, bringing changes of both style (emotionalism) and substance (an emphasis on personal responsibility and a growing belief in the capacity of all people to achieve moral and spiritual perfection). The Mormon Church, the first American-born religion, rose amid the fervor of revivalism. Revivalists generally emphasized the need for involvement in society and thus became a powerful stimulus to reform movements.

KEY TERMS

Democrats *(p. 221)*
Whigs *(p. 221)*
"spoils system" *(p. 225)*
"Tariff of Abominations" *(p. 225)*
Nullification Crisis *(p. 226)*
Bank of the United States *(p. 227)*
log cabin *(p. 231)*
Second Great Awakening *(p. 232)*
Methodists *(p. 232)*
Charles Grandison Finney *(p. 233)*
Unitarians *(p. 233)*
Joseph Smith *(p. 234)*
Shakers *(p. 234)*
temperance *(p. 236)*
Horace Mann *(p. 236)*
William Lloyd Garrison *(p. 238)*
Frederick Douglass *(p. 238)*
Angelina and Sarah Grimké *(p. 239)*
Seneca Falls, New York *(p. 240)*
Dorothea Dix *(p. 241)*
New Harmony *(p. 242)*
transcendentalists *(p. 242)*

Did the reform movements aim primarily at making Americans more free or more orderly? (page 235)

Reform movements targeted a wide range of social issues, including alcohol consumption, education, the treatment of the mentally ill, prisons, slavery, and women's rights. Reformers sought the radical improvement of human nature through a combination of individual and institutional efforts. Yet for all their optimism, many reformers proved willing to coerce people into change by such measures as prohibiting liquor sales, requiring school attendance, and placing prisoners in solitary confinement. One movement frequently led to another, as antislavery spawned the drive for women's rights. Utopian communities appeared; most collapsed. But the search for social and political alternatives continued.

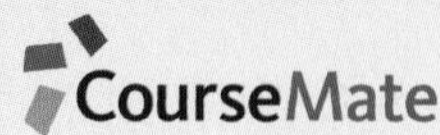

Go to the CourseMate website at **www.cengagebrain.com** for additional study tools and review materials—including audio and video clips—for this chapter.

Chapter 11

Technology, Culture, and Everyday Life

1840–1860

Steam Locomotive Crossing the Niagara Railway Suspension Bridge

William B. Becker Collection/American Museum of Photography

Chapter Preview

Technology and Economic Growth
What technological improvements brought about American economic growth between 1840 and 1860?

The Quality of Life
In what ways did technology transform the lives of ordinary Americans?

Democratic Pastimes
In what new ways did Americans pass their free time during this period?

The Quest for Nationality in Literature and Art
How did the work of American writers and artists become distinctly American?

In 1850, Isaac M. Singer's life was not going well. Thirty-nine and often penniless, he had been an unsuccessful actor, carpenter, and inventor. His early inventions had been clever, but not commercially successful. Having deserted his wife and children, he lured Mary Ann Sponslor into living with him by promising marriage. Sponslor nursed him when he was sick, but instead of marrying her, Singer beat her and had affairs with other women. But in 1850, Singer made significant improvements on a sewing machine similar to one patented in 1846 by Elias Howe, Jr., and within ten years, he was a wealthy man.

Here was a machine everyone wanted. Contemporaries could not praise sewing machines enough. The *New York Tribune* predicted that, with the spread of sewing machines, people "will dress better, change oftener, and altogether grow better looking." This optimistic response to technological change was typical of the 1850s. Many Americans believed that **technology** was God's chosen instrument of progress. For New Englander Edward Everett in 1852, the locomotive was "a miracle of science, art, and capital, a magic power."

technology The practical application of science to improving life

Yet progress had a darker side. Ralph Waldo Emerson said bluntly, "Machinery is dangerous. The weaver becomes the web, the machinist the machine. If you do not use the tools, they use you." The newly invented revolver was useless for hunting, but excellent for violently settling private scores. Philosophers and artists began to worry about the despoliation of the landscape by the factories that made guns and sewing machines, and conservationists launched efforts to preserve natural enclaves as retreats from the evils of progress.

Technology and Economic Growth

What technological improvements brought about American economic growth between 1840 and 1860?

Widely hailed as democratic, technology drew praise from all sides. Conservative statesman Daniel Webster, for example, praised machines for doing the work of people without consuming food or clothing.

The technological improvements that transformed life in antebellum America included the steam engine, the cotton gin, the reaper, the sewing machine, and the telegraph. Some of these originated in Europe, but Americans had a flair for investing in others' inventions and perfecting their own. Sadly, these advances did not benefit everyone. The cotton gin, for example, riveted slavery firmly in place by intensifying southern dependence on cotton. Nonetheless, the improved transportation and increased productivity that technology made possible raised the living standard of many free Americans between 1840 and 1860.

Agricultural Advancement

After 1830, American settlers were edging westward from the woodlands of Ohio and Kentucky into parts of Indiana, Michigan, Illinois, and Missouri, where the flat grasslands of the prairie alternated with forests. Prairie soil, though richly fertile, was root-matted and difficult to break. But in 1837, **John Deere** invented a steel-tipped plow that cut in half the labor required to till for planting. Timber for houses and fencing was available in nearby woods, and settlements spread rapidly.

John Deere Inventor of the steel plow

Wheat became to midwestern farmers what cotton was to the South. Technological advances sped the harvesting as well as the planting of wheat. The traditional hand sickle consumed huge amounts of time and labor, and the cut wheat also had to be picked up and bound by hand. But in 1834, **Cyrus McCormick** of Virginia patented a horse-drawn mechanical reaper that harvested grain seven times faster with half the work force. In 1847, he opened a factory in Chicago, and by 1860 he had sold 80,000 reapers. The mechanical reaper guaranteed that wheat would dominate the midwestern prairies.

Cyrus McCormick Inventor of the mechanical reaper

Ironically, just as Connecticut Yankee Eli Whitney's cotton gin had created the Old South's economy, an invention by Cyrus McCormick, a pro-slavery Democrat,

Chronology

1823	Philadelphia completes the first urban water-supply system; James Fenimore Cooper, *The Pioneers*
1826	Cooper, *The Last of the Mohicans*
1833	The *New York Sun,* the first penny newspaper, is established
1834	Cyrus McCormick patents the mechanical reaper
1835	James Gordon Bennett establishes the *New York Herald*
1837	Ralph Waldo Emerson, "The American Scholar"
1839	Edgar Allen Poe, "The Fall of the House of Usher"
1841	P. T. Barnum opens the American Museum
1844	Samuel F. B. Morse patents the telegraph; Poe, "The Raven"
1846	William T. G. Morton successfully uses anesthesia; Elias Howe, Jr., patents the sewing machine
1849	Second major cholera epidemic
1850	Nathaniel Hawthorne, *The Scarlet Letter*
1851	Hawthorne, *The House of the Seven Gables;* Herman Melville, *Moby-Dick;* Erie Railroad completes its line to the West
1853	Ten small railroads are consolidated into the New York Central Railroad
1854	Henry David Thoreau, *Walden*
1855	Walt Whitman, *Leaves of Grass*
1856	Illinois Central completed between Chicago and Cairo, Illinois
1858	Frederick Law Olmsted is appointed architect-in-chief for Central Park

would help the Union win the Civil War. Northern agriculture took advantage of his reaper and copies of it to raise agricultural production; southerners, reliant on slave labor, had little reason to mechanize. The reaper would keep northern agricultural production high despite the mobilization of hundreds of thousands of northern men.

Although Americans generally remained wasteful farmers—abundant cheap land made it more "practical" to move west than to try to improve played-out soil—a movement for more efficient cultivation developed before the Civil War, primarily in the East. By feeding their cows better and improving dairy processing, New York dairy farmers produced a superior butter that commanded more than double the price of ordinary butter. Other eastern farmers turned to soil improvement. By fertilizing their fields with plaster left over from canal construction, Virginia wheat growers raised their average yield from six bushels per acre in 1800 to fifteen bushels by the 1850s. American cotton planters in the Southeast began to import guano (sea bird droppings) from Peru to fertilize their fields in an effort to compete successfully with the fertile soil of the Old Southwest.

Technology and Industrial Progress

Industrial advances between 1840 and 1860 owed an immense debt to the development of effective machine tools. By the 1840s, machine tools had greatly reduced the need to hand file parts to make them fit, and they were applied to the manufacture of firearms, clocks, and sewing machines. After mid-century, Europeans began to call this system of manufacturing **interchangeable parts** the "American System of Manufacturing." After touring American factories in 1854, a British engineer concluded that Americans "universally and willingly" resorted to machines as a substitute for manual labor.

interchangeable parts
Identical components made by machine tools, speeding the manufacturing process; pioneered by Eli Whitney

The American manufacturing system had several distinct advantages. Traditionally, damage to any part of a mechanical contrivance had rendered the whole thing useless, because no new part would fit. The perfection of interchangeable parts made replacement parts possible. In addition, improved machine tools enabled entrepreneurs to push inventions into mass production with a speed that attracted investors. Sophisticated machine tools, according to one manufacturer, increased production "by confining a worker to one particular limb of a pistol until he had made two thousand."

After Samuel F. B. Morse transmitted the first telegraph message, Americans eagerly seized on the telegraph's promise to eliminate the constraints of time and place. They formed telegraph companies and strung lines with stunning speed. By 1852, more than fifteen thousand miles of line connected cities as distant as Quebec, New Orleans, and St. Louis. The first transcontinental line was completed in 1860. A later historian would christen the telegraph the "Victorian Internet" because of the ways it changed business and personal communication.

The Railroad Boom

Even more than the telegraph, the railroad dramatized technology's democratic promise. In 1790, even European royalty could travel no faster than fourteen miles an hour and then only with frequent changes of horses. By 1850, an ordinary American could travel three times as fast—by train.

Americans loved railroads, reported one Frenchman, "as a lover loves his mistress." Their love of early railroad travel had a great deal to overcome. Sparks from locomotives showered passengers riding in open cars, and discouraged passengers in closed coaches from opening the windows. In the absence of brakes, passengers on trains often had to get off to help stop them. Trains rarely ran at night because they lacked lights. Before the introduction of standard time zones in 1883, scheduling was a nightmare and delays were frequent. Individual railroads used different gauge track, making frequent train changes necessary; even in the 1850s, a journey from Charleston to Philadelphia required eight transfers.

Yet nothing slowed the advance of railroads or cured Americans' mania for them. In 1851, the editor of the *American Railroad Journal* wrote that in the previous twenty years, the locomotive had become "the great agent of civilization and progress, the most powerful instrument for good the world has yet reached." Between 1840 and 1860, the size of the rail network and the power and convenience of trains underwent a stunning transformation. Railroads extended track mileage from three thousand to thirty thousand miles; closed coaches replaced open cars; kerosene lamps made night travel possible; and increasingly powerful engines enabled trains to climb steep hills. By 1860, the United States had more track than all the rest of the world combined.

Railroads represented the second major phase of the transportation revolution. Canals remained in use—the Erie Canal did not reach its peak volume until

1880—but the railroads gradually overtook them, first in passengers and then in freight. By 1860, the value of goods transported by railroads greatly surpassed that carried by canals.

By 1860, railroads had spread like vast spider webs east of the Mississippi River (see Map 11.1). They transformed southern cities like Atlanta and Chattanooga into thriving commercial hubs. Most important, the railroads linked the East and the Midwest. New York City was joined with Buffalo while Philadelphia was linked to Pittsburgh. Intense construction in Ohio, Indiana, and Illinois created trunk lines that tied these routes to cities farther west.

Chicago's growth illustrates the impact of these rail links. In 1849, it was a village of a few hundred people with virtually no rail service. By 1860, it had become a metropolis of 100,000, served by eleven railroads. Farmers in the upper Midwest no longer had to send their grain, livestock, and dairy products down the Mississippi to New Orleans; they could now ship their products directly east. Chicago supplanted New Orleans as the interior's main commercial hub.

Rail lines stimulated the settlement of the Midwest. By 1860, Illinois, Indiana, and Wisconsin had replaced Ohio, Pennsylvania, and New York as the leading wheat-growing states. Railroads increased the value of farmland and promoted additional settlement. In turn, population growth stimulated industrial development in cities such as Chicago and Minneapolis, for the new settlers needed lumber for fences and houses, as well as mills to grind wheat into flour.

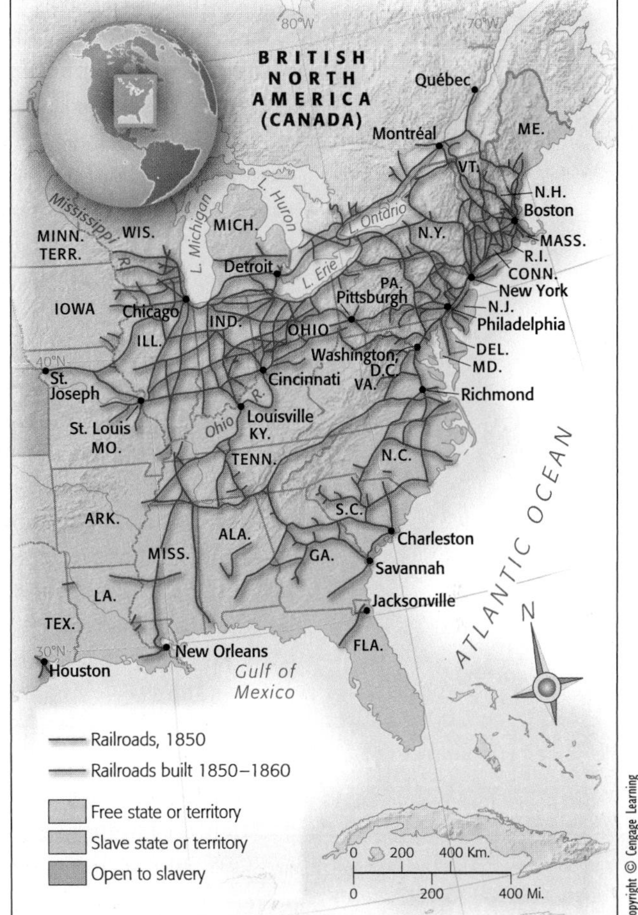

Map 11.1 Railroad Growth, 1850–1860
Rail ties between the East and the Midwest greatly increased during the railroad boom of the 1850s.

Interactive Map

Railroads also spurred the growth of small towns along their routes. The Illinois Central Railroad, which had more track than any other railroad in 1855, made money not only from its traffic but from real estate speculation. Purchasing land along its path, the Illinois Central laid out entire towns around its stations. The railroad used a template for all such towns, laying them out on a grid with east-west streets named after trees and north-south streets numbered. By the Civil War, few thought of the railroad-linked Midwest as a frontier region.

As the nation's first big business, the railroads transformed the way business was conducted. During the early 1830s railroads, like canals, depended on state funding. With the onset of a financial depression in the late 1830s, however, state governments scrapped many railroad projects. Convinced that railroads burdened them with high taxes and blasted hopes, voters in several states amended their constitutions to bar state funding for railroads and canals. Federal aid would not become widely available until the Civil War. However, the large railroads of the 1850s needed more capital than small investors alone could generate.

Gradually, the center of railroad financing shifted to New York City, where the railroad boom of the 1850s helped make Wall Street the nation's greatest capital market. The securities of all the leading railroads were traded on the floor of the New York Stock Exchange. Investment firms evaluated the securities of railroads and found purchasers for these securities in New York and Philadelphia, Paris and London, and Hamburg. Investment bankers soon began to exert influence over the railroads' internal affairs. A Wall Street analyst noted that railroad men seeking financing "must remember that money is power, and that the [financier] can dictate to a great extent his own terms."

Rising Prosperity

Technology also improved life by lowering prices. Clocks that cost $50 to make by hand in 1800 could be made by machine for 50¢ by 1850. Widespread use of steam power led to a 25 percent rise in the average worker's real income (purchasing power) between 1840 and 1860; unlike water wheels, steam engines could run in all seasons, so workers did not have to face long winter layoffs. Although cotton textile workers saw little gain in hourly wages, their average annual wages rose from $160 to $201 between 1830 and 1859.

The growth of towns and cities also contributed to the upward trend in average annual wages. In contrast to rural farming areas, with their heavily seasonal labor, urban settings offered jobs year-round. Towns and cities also provided women and children—who seldom were paid for farm labor—new opportunities for paid work. Children's wages played an important role in family finances for working-class families. An average New York or Philadelphia working-class family spent $500 to $600 per year on food, rent, clothing, and fuel. However, an average male head of household earned $300 a year. Clearly, the survival of many families depended on the wages of children and wives.

The average urban worker was marginally better off than the average rural worker, primarily because of seasonal fluctuations in agricultural work. Most antebellum Americans continued to see farming as the ideal occupation, but comparatively few could raise the $500 or so in cash necessary to purchase, clear, and stock a farm and then wait three to five years for any reward. The economic advantages of urban living help explain why so many Americans were moving to cities. During the 1840s and 1850s, American cities provided their residents with an unprecedented range of comforts and conveniences.

CHECKING IN

- Technology, such as the steel plow, the mechanical reaper, and the cotton gin, revolutionized American agriculture.
- The American system of manufacturing, based on interchangeable parts, grew rapidly.
- The amount of railroad track multiplied tenfold, linking major cities and transforming villages into cities.
- Railroads, America's first big business, revolutionized not only transportation but also financial systems.
- Prices fell and prosperity increased for most white Americans.

THE QUALITY OF LIFE

In what ways did technology transform the lives of ordinary Americans?

"Think of the numberless contrivances and inventions for our comfort and luxury," exclaimed poet Walt Whitman, "and you will bless your star that Fate has cast your lot in the year of Our Lord 1857." Improvements in the quality of life affected such mundane activities as eating, drinking, and washing. Machine-made furniture began to transform the interiors of houses. Stoves revolutionized heating and cooking.

However, change occurred unevenly. Technology made it possible for the middle class to enjoy luxuries formerly reserved for the rich, yet it widened the gulf between middle class and poor. As middle-class homes became increasingly lavish, the urban poor crowded into cramped tenements. And some critical elements—medicine, for example—lagged far behind in the technological explosion.

Dwellings

During the early 1800s, the randomly sited wood frame houses that had dotted colonial cities began to yield to more orderly brick row houses. Row houses, which were practical responses to rising land values (as much as 750 percent in Manhattan between 1785 and 1815), drew criticism for their "extreme uniformity." But they were not all alike. Middle-class row houses were larger and more elaborate than working-class row houses and less likely to be subdivided for occupancy by several families. The worst of the subdivided row houses, called tenements, were often inhabited by Irish immigrants and free blacks.

Home furnishings also revealed the widening gap between the prosperous and the poor. Middle- and upper-class families decorated their houses with fine furniture in the ornate, rococo style, along with wool carpeting, wallpaper, pianos, pictures, and gilt-framed mirrors. The mass-production of furniture reduced prices and tended to level taste between the middle and upper classes, while still setting those classes off from everyone else.

In rural areas, the quality of housing depended largely on the age of the settlement. In new settlements, the standard dwelling was a rude log cabin with planked floors, clay chimneys, and windows covered by oiled paper or cloth. As rural communities matured, log cabins gave way to insulated balloon-frame houses of two or more rooms. The balloon-frame—built with a skeleton of two-by-fours spaced at eighteen-inch intervals—was lighter and stronger than the older post-and-beam method. The simplicity and cheapness of such houses endeared them to western builders.

Conveniences and Inconveniences

By today's standards, everyday life in the 1840s and 1850s was primitive. But contemporaries were struck by how much better it was becoming. Stoves made it possible to cook several dishes at once, and railroads brought fresh vegetables to the city, an unobtainable luxury in the 1830s. Urban waterworks carried fresh water from rivers and reservoirs to hydrants. In 1823, Philadelphia completed the first urban water-supply system; by 1860, sixty-eight public water systems were operating in the United States.

Despite these improvements, home comforts remained limited. Coal burned longer and hotter than wood, but left a dirty residue that polluted the air. Only the rich could afford fruit out of season, since they alone could afford the sugar to preserve it. Home iceboxes were rare before 1860, so salt remained the most widely used preservative. (One reason antebellum Americans ate more pork than beef was that salt pork didn't taste quite as bad as salt beef.) Although public waterworks were engineering marvels, their impact is easily exaggerated. Only a fraction of the urban population lived near water hydrants, so most houses still had no running water. Taking a bath still required heating the water, pot by pot, on a stove. A New England physician reported that not one in five of his patients took even one bath a year.

Infrequent bathing added pungent body odors to the many strong smells of urban life. In the absence of municipal sanitation, street cleaning was done by private contractors with a reputation for slack performance. Hogs were allowed to roam freely and scavenge. Mounds of stable manure and outdoor privies added to the stench. Flush toilets were rare, and sewer systems lagged behind water-supply systems. Boston—which boasted more flush toilets than most other cities—had only five thousand for a population of 178,000 in 1860. Conveniences like running water and flush toilets became one more way for progress to set off the upper and middle classes from the poor. Conveniences also sharpened gender differences. Freed from making articles for home consumption, women were now expected to achieve fulfillment by obsessively making every house a "glorious temple" of spotless floors and gleaming furniture.

Disease and Health

epidemic diseases Diseases, such as cholera and yellow fever, that spread rapidly and were difficult to control

Despite the slowly rising living standard, Americans remained vulnerable to disease. **Epidemic diseases** swept through antebellum American cities and felled thousands. Yellow fever and cholera (CAH-luh-rah) killed one-fifth of New Orleans's population in 1832–1833, and cholera alone carried off 10 percent of St. Louis's population in 1849.

The transportation revolution increased the danger of epidemic diseases. The cholera epidemic of 1832, which was the first truly national epidemic, followed transportation networks out of New York City: one disease route ran up the Hudson River across the Erie Canal to Ohio and down the Ohio and Mississippi rivers to New Orleans; the other route followed shipping lines up and down the East Coast.

The failure of physicians to explain epidemic diseases reinforced hostility toward their profession. No one understood that bacteria caused cholera and yellow fever. Physicians clashed over whether epidemic diseases were spread by human touch or by "miasmas" (MY-az-muz), gases arising from rotten vegetation or dead animals. Neither theory worked. Quarantines failed to prevent the spread of epidemics (an argument against the contagion theory), and many residents of swampy areas contracted neither yellow fever nor cholera (a refutation of the miasma theory). Understandably, municipal leaders declined to delegate more than advisory powers to boards of health, which were dominated by physicians.

Although epidemic diseases baffled antebellum physicians, the discovery of anesthesia opened the way for advances in surgery. Laughing gas (nitrous oxide) had long provided partygoers who inhaled it with enjoyable sensations of giddiness and painlessness, but it was difficult to handle. Then in 1842, Crawford Long, a Georgia physician who had attended laughing gas frolics in his youth, employed sulfuric ether (a liquid with the same properties as nitrous oxide) during surgery. Dr. Long did not follow up his discovery, but four years later William T. G. Morton, a dentist, successfully employed sulfuric ether during an operation at Massachusetts General Hospital. Within a few years, ether came into wide surgical use.

The discovery of anesthesia improved the public image of surgeons, long viewed as brutes who tortured their patients. It also permitted longer and thus more careful operations. However, the failure of most surgeons to recognize the importance of clean hands and sterilized instruments partially offset the value of anesthesia. As early as 1843, Oliver Wendell Holmes, Sr., a poet and physician, published a paper on how unclean hands spread puerperal (poo-ER-puh-rul) fever among women giving birth, but disinfection was accepted only gradually. Operations remained as dangerous as the conditions they tried to heal. The mortality rate for amputations hovered around 40 percent.

Popular Health Movements

Suspicious of orthodox medicine, antebellum Americans turned to various alternative therapies that promised longer and healthier lives. Hydropathy (high-DRAW-puh-thee), the "water cure," offered "an abundance of water of dewy softness and crystal transparency, to cleanse, renovate, and rejuvenate the disease-worn and dilapidated system." The water cure held a special attraction for women: hydropathy promised to relieve the pain associated with childbirth and menstruation, and sanatoriums proved to be congenial gathering places for middle-class women.

In contrast to the relatively expensive water cure, Sylvester Graham, a former temperance reformer, propounded a health system that anyone could afford. In response to the 1832 cholera epidemic, Graham urged Americans to eat vegetables, fruits, and whole-grain bread (called Graham bread), and abstain from meat, spices, coffee, and tea as well as alcohol. Soon he added to his list of forbidden indulgences "sexual excess"—which for married couples meant having intercourse more than once a month. Just as temperance reformers blamed the craving for alcohol and abolitionists blamed the craving for illicit power, Graham blamed the craving for meat, stimulants, and sex.

Graham was dismissed by Ralph Waldo Emerson as "the prophet of bran bread and pumpkins." But Graham's doctrines attracted a broad audience. Boarding houses began to set Grahamite tables in their dining rooms. Graham's books sold well, and his public lectures were thronged. His regime

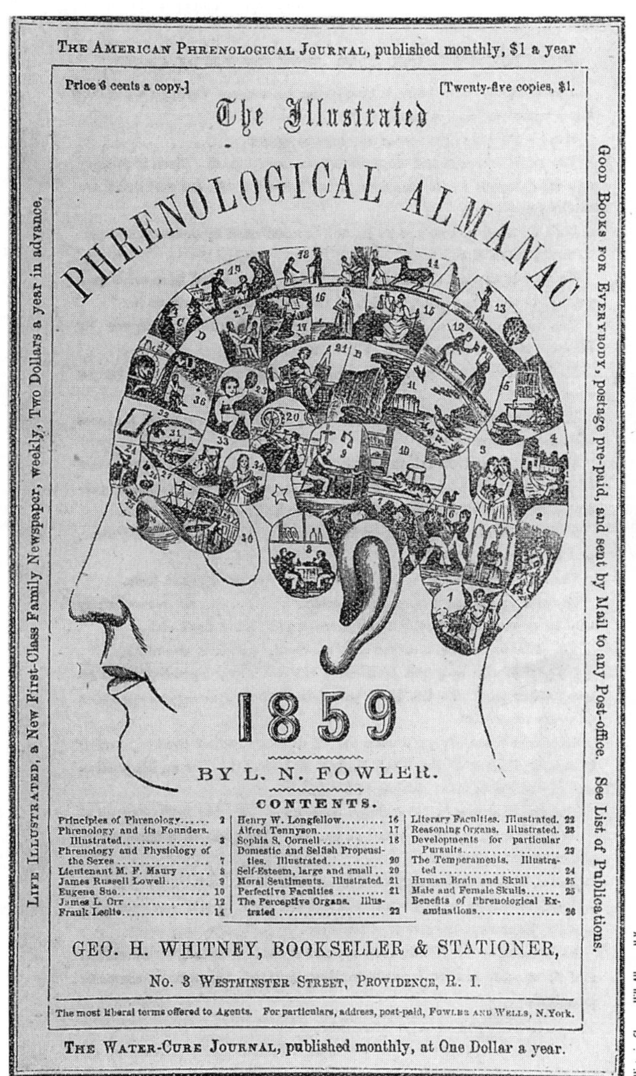

THE AMERICAN PHRENOLOGICAL JOURNAL, published monthly, $1 a year

Price 6 cents a copy.] [Twenty-five copies, $1.

The Illustrated

PHRENOLOGICAL ALMANAC

1859

BY L. N. FOWLER.

CONTENTS.

Principles of Phrenology...... 2
Phrenology and its Founders. Illustrated........ 3
Phrenology and Physiology of the Sexes........ 7
Lieutenant M. F. Maury...... 8
James Russell Lowell........ 9
Eugene Sue........ 10
James L. Orr........ 12
Frank Leslie........ 14
Henry W. Longfellow........ 16
Alfred Tennyson........ 17
Sophia S. Cornell........ 18
Domestic and Selfish Propensities. Illustrated........ 20
Self-Esteem, large and small.. 20
Moral Sentiments. Illustrated. 21
Perfective Faculties........ 21
The Perceptive Organs. Illustrated........ 22
Literary Faculties. Illustrated. 22
Reasoning Organs. Illustrated. 23
Developments for particular Pursuits........ 23
The Temperaments. Illustrated........ 24
Human Brain and Skull...... 25
Male and Female Skulls...... 25
Benefits of Phrenological Examinations........ 26

GEO. H. WHITNEY, BOOKSELLER & STATIONER,

No. 3 WESTMINSTER STREET, PROVIDENCE, R. I.

The most liberal terms offered to Agents. For particulars, address, post-paid, FOWLER AND WELLS, N. York.

THE WATER-CURE JOURNAL, published monthly, at One Dollar a year.

LIFE ILLUSTRATED, a New First-Class Family Newspaper, weekly, Two Dollars a year in advance.

GOOD BOOKS FOR EVERYBODY, postage pre-paid, and sent by Mail to any Post-office. See List of Publications.

"The Illustrated Phrenological Almanac, 1859"

By dividing the brain into a large number of "faculties," phrenologists like Lorenzo Fowler, editor of the *Phrenological Almanac* for 1859, made the point that each person, regardless of whether born high or low, had an abundance of improvable talents.

addressed the popular desire for better health at a time when orthodox medicine seemed to do more damage than good.

Phrenology

The belief that each person was master of his or her own destiny underlay not only evangelical religion and health movements but also the most popular of the antebellum scientific fads: **phrenology** (free-NAHL-uh-jee). Phrenology rested on the idea that the human mind comprised thirty-seven distinct faculties, or "organs," each localized in a different part of the brain. Phrenologists thought that the degree of each organ's development determined skull shape, so that they could accurately analyze an individual's character by examining the bumps and depressions of the skull.

phrenology Belief that one can read a person's character by examining bumps on the skull

In the United States two brothers, Orson and Lorenzo Fowler, became the chief promoters of phrenology in the 1840s. Orson opened a publishing house in New York City (Fowlers and Wells) that marketed phrenology books on the subject. The Fowlers met criticisms that phrenology was godless by pointing out a huge organ called "Veneration" to prove that people were naturally religious, and they answered charges that phrenology was pessimistic by claiming that exercise could improve every desirable mental organ. Lorenzo proudly reported that several of his own skull bumps had been grown.

Americans were drawn to the practicality of phrenology. In a mobile, individualistic society, it promised a quick assessment of others. Some merchants used phrenological charts to pick suitable clerks, and some women asked their fiancés to undergo phrenological analysis before the wedding. Easily understood and practiced, and filled with the promise of universal improvement, phrenology was ideal for antebellum Americans. Just as they had invented machines to better their lives, they invented "sciences" that promised personal improvement.

CHECKING IN

- Housing generally improved in the mid-nineteenth century, but class distinctions became more pronounced.
- Improvements in urban living conditions, such as stoves and water systems, were somewhat offset by increased pollution.
- Epidemic diseases still flourished, but anesthesia came into use, and interest in antisepsis stirred.
- Health fads like hydropathy proliferated.
- Phrenology became a popular phenomenon.

DEMOCRATIC PASTIMES

In what new ways did Americans pass their free time during this period?

Between 1830 and 1860, technology transformed leisure by making Americans more dependent on recreation methods that were manufactured and sold. People purchased entertainment in the form of cheap newspapers and novels as well as affordable tickets to plays, museums, and lectures. Men like James Gordon Bennett, one of the founders of the **penny press** in America, and P. T. Barnum, the greatest showman of the nineteenth century, amassed fortunes by making the public want whatever they had to sell.

penny press Cheap newspapers developed by James Gordon Bennett

Technology also began the process by which individuals became spectators rather than creators of their own amusements. Americans had also found ways to enjoy themselves—even the gloomiest Puritans had enjoyed games and sports. After 1830, however, the provision of entertainment began to shift from individuals to the entrepreneurs who supplied ways to entertain the public. Commercial entertainment encouraged the passivity of those who consumed it.

Newspapers

In 1830, the typical American newspaper was four pages long, with the front and back pages filled almost completely with advertisements. The interior pages contained editorials, details of ship arrivals and cargoes, reprints of political speeches, and notices of political events. Such papers relied financially not on circulation, but on subsidies from the political groups with which they allied. In this way, they could profit without offering the exciting news stories and eye-catching illustrations that later generations of newspaper readers would take for granted.

The 1830s witnessed the beginnings of a stunning transformation in the American newspaper. Cheaper paper and steam-driven presses drastically lowered production costs, and enterprising journalists, among them James Gordon Bennett, saw the implications: slash prices, boost circulation, and reap vast profits. In 1833, New York's eleven daily newspapers had a combined daily circulation of only 26,500. Two years later, the combined circulation of the three largest "penny" newspapers had soared to 44,000. From 1830 to 1840, the combined daily circulation of American newspapers rose from roughly 78,000 to 300,000, and the number of weekly newspapers more than doubled.

The penny press also revolutionized the marketing and format of newspapers. Newsboys hawked the penny papers on busy street corners, and reporters filled the papers with gripping news stories designed to attract readers. The penny papers subordinated political and commercial coverage to human-interest stories of robberies, murders, rapes, and abandoned children. They dispatched reporters to police courts and printed transcripts of sensational trials. Charles Dickens parodied such coverage by naming one fictional American newspaper the *New York Stabber.*

But despite such limitations, as sociologist Michael Schudson observes, "The penny press invented the modern concept of 'news.'" Penny newspapers also invented modern news reporting, employing their own correspondents and using the telegraph to speed the communications process. The best penny papers, such as Bennett's *New York Herald* and Horace Greeley's *New York Tribune,* pioneered modern financial and political reporting. The *Herald* featured a daily "money article" that analyzed and interpreted financial events. "The spirit, pith, and philosophy of commercial affairs is what men of business want," Bennett wrote.

The Theater

Like newspapers, theaters increasingly appealed to a mass audience. Antebellum theaters were large and crowded; cheap seats drew a democratic throng of lawyers, merchants, and their wives; artisans and clerks; sailors and noisy boys; and a sizable body of prostitutes.

The presence of prostitutes in the audience was only one of many factors that made theaters vaguely disreputable. Theater audiences were notoriously ill-behaved: they stamped their feet, hooted at villains, and threw potatoes and garbage at the stage when they disliked the characters or the acting. Contributing to such rowdiness was the animosity between the fan bases of different theatrical stars. In 1849, a long-running feud between the leading American actor Edwin Forrest and popular British actor William Macready culminated in the Astor Place riot in New York City, which left twenty-two people dead.

The most popular plays were emotionally charged melodramas in which virtue was rewarded, vice punished, and the hero won the beautiful heroine. Melodramas offered sensational features such as volcanic eruptions, staged battles, even live horses on stage. Yet the single most popular dramatist was William Shakespeare. In 1835, Philadelphia audiences witnessed sixty-five performances of his plays. However, Shakespeare might not have recognized some of these performances, adapted as they were for popular audiences. Theatrical managers highlighted sword fights and assassinations, cut long speeches, and occasionally substituted happy endings for sad ones. And they entertained audiences between acts with jugglers and acrobats, impersonations of Tecumseh or Aaron Burr, or the exhibition of a three-year-old child who weighed one hundred pounds.

minstrel show Blackface show of "Negro" song and dance

National Portrait Gallery, Smithsonian Institution/Art Resource, NY

P. T. Barnum and Tom Thumb

When P. T. Barnum posed with his protégée—whose real name was Charles Sherwood Stratton—sometime around 1850, the twelve-year-old "human curiosity" stood a little over two feet in height. Barnum and Stratton enjoyed a long partnership which brought considerable wealth to both of them.

Minstrel Shows

The popular **minstrel shows** of the 1840s and 1850s forged enduring racial stereotypes that buttressed white Americans' sense of superiority by diminishing black Americans.

Minstrel shows featured white performers in burnt-cork blackface who entertained their audiences with songs, dances, and humorous sketches that pretended to mimic black culture. But while minstrelsy did borrow a few elements of African-American culture, most of its contents were white inventions. The shows' images of African-Americans both expressed and reinforced the prejudices of the working-class whites who dominated the audience. Minstrel troupes depicted blacks as stupid, clumsy, and absurdly musical, and parodied Africanness by naming their performances the "Nubian Jungle Dance" and the "African Fling." Minstrel shows used stock characters to capture white expectations about black behavior. These included Uncle Ned, the tattered and docile slave, and Zip Coon, the arrogant urban freeman who paraded around in high hat and long-tailed coat and lived off his girlfriends.

By the 1850s, major cities from New York to San Francisco had several minstrel theaters. Touring professionals and local amateurs brought minstrelsy to small towns and villages. Author Mark Twain recalled how minstrelsy had burst upon Hannibal, Missouri, in the early 1840s as "a glad and stunning surprise." Minstrel troupes even entertained a succession of presidents in the antebellum White House.

P. T. Barnum

No one understood better than **P. T. Barnum** how to turn the public's craving for entertainment into a profitable business. He was simultaneously a hustler who cheated his customers before they could cheat him, and an idealist who founded a newspaper to attack wrongdoing and who thought of himself as a public benefactor.

P. T. Barnum Showman who exhibited "natural wonders," real and otherwise

After moving to New York City in 1834, Barnum launched his career as an entertainment entrepreneur. He got his start exhibiting a black woman named Joice Heth, whom he billed as the 169-year-old former slave nurse of George Washington. In fact, she was probably around eighty, but Barnum neither knew nor cared, so long as people paid to see her. He was playing a game with the public, and the public played right back.

In 1841 Barnum purchased a run-down museum in New York City, rechristened it the American Museum, and opened a new chapter in the history of popular entertainment. Avoiding the educational slant of other museums, Barnum concentrated on curiosities and faked exhibits; he wanted to interest people, not to educate them. The American Museum included ventriloquists, magicians, albinos, a twenty-five-inch-tall five-year-old whom Barnum named General Tom Thumb, and the "Feejee Mermaid," billed by Barnum as "positively asserted by its owner to have been taken alive in the Feejee Islands." By 1850, the American Museum had become the best-known museum in the nation.

Blessed with a genius for publicity, Barnum recognized that newspapers could invent as well as report news. One of his favorite tactics was to puff his own exhibits by writing letters to newspapers (under various names) hinting that the scientific world was agog over some astonishing curiosity that the public could soon view at the American Museum. At a time when each year brought new technological marvels, Americans would believe in anything, even the Feejee Mermaid. But Barnum did not rely solely on curiosities and clever marketing. To secure that his museum had a reputation for providing safe family entertainment, he provided regular lectures on the evils of alcohol and the benefits of Christian religion—thus wrapping the exotic and sensational in a sheen of respectability.

CHECKING IN

- Between 1830 and 1860, entrepreneurs found new business opportunities with popular entertainment.
- James Gordon Bennett revolutionized the newspaper world with the penny press.
- Theater became a major source of entertainment for diverse and often rowdy audiences.
- Blackface minstrel shows provided popular entertainment while reinforcing negative stereotypes of African-Americans.
- P. T. Barnum introduced Americans to the wonders of the Feejee Mermaid and other oddities.

THE QUEST FOR NATIONALITY IN LITERATURE AND ART

How did the work of American writers and artists become distinctly American?

Europeans paid no attention to American poetry or fiction before the 1820s. Although Americans could point with pride to Washington Irving's tales of Sleepy Hollow and Rip Van Winkle, they also had to admit that Irving had done most of his work while living in Britain.

After 1820, the United States experienced a literary flowering known as the **American Renaissance.** Leading figures of this burst of creativity included James Fenimore Cooper, Ralph Waldo Emerson, Henry David Thoreau (theh-ROW), Margaret Fuller, Walt Whitman, Nathaniel Hawthorne, Herman Melville, and

American Renaissance Literary movement that flourished after 1820

Edgar Allan Poe. In 1830, 40 percent of books published in the United States were written by Americans; by 1850, this number had increased to 75 percent.

American writers often sought to depict the national features of the United States—its land and its people—in their work. The quest for a distinctively American literature shaped the writings of Cooper, Emerson, and Whitman. It also revealed itself in the majestic paintings of the Hudson River School, the first home-grown movement in art, and in the landscape architecture of Frederick Law Olmsted.

Roots of the American Renaissance

Two broad movements, one economic and the other philosophical, contributed to this development. First, the transportation revolution created a national market for books, especially fiction. First to benefit from this new market was Sir Walter Scott, a British author whose historical novels became wildly popular in the United States and showed that there was a huge market for fiction. Scott became a model for many American authors, including James Fenimore Cooper.

Second, a new philosophical movement, romanticism, saturated the American Renaissance. Romantics emphasized emotion and inner feelings, focusing on the individual and his or her unique response to nature and emotion. This new emphasis on emotion created a more democratic literature, accessible to virtually everyone (unlike earlier classicism, which demanded knowledge of ancient history and mythology). Women entered the fiction market in large numbers; although barred from higher education and the classics, they could easily access their emotions and tweak the emotions of their readers. Harriet Beecher Stowe's massive bestseller, *Uncle Tom's Cabin,* illustrates how successful women authors were in tugging at their readers' heartstrings. Novels also possessed a subversive quality, a freedom of plot and character not available to the essayist. Authors could create unconventional characters, situations, and outcomes, and left more room for interpretation by the reader, who was far more likely to focus on plot and characters than moral sentiments.

Cooper, Emerson, Thoreau, Fuller, and Whitman

James Fenimore Cooper was a trailblazer in the development of a national literature with distinctively American themes. In his frontiersman Natty Bumppo, "Leatherstocking," Cooper created an American archetype. Natty first appears in *The Pioneers* (1823) as an old man, a former hunter, who blames the farmers for wantonly destroying upstate New York's game and turning the silent and majestic forests into deserts of tree stumps. As a spokesman for nature against the march of civilization, Natty became a highly popular figure, and his life unfolded in several other enormously popular novels, such as *The Last of the Mohicans* (1826), *The Pathfinder* (1840), and *The Deerslayer* (1841).

During the 1830s, Ralph Waldo Emerson emerged as the most influential spokesman for those who sought a national literature and art. Emerson, who served briefly as a Unitarian minister and then became a popular lecturer, voiced American intellectual ambitions in his 1837 address "The American Scholar," which called on American writers to break free of European standards.

As the leader of transcendentalism, the American offshoot of romanticism, Emerson contended that ideas of God and freedom were innate, not the result of reason. Knowledge was like sight—an instantaneous and direct perception of truth. Anyone, whether a learned university professor or a common farmer, could glimpse truth by following the promptings of his heart. Thus, the United States, young and democratic, could produce as noble a literature and art as any tradition-bound European nation. "Our day of independence, our long apprenticeship to the learning of other lands draws to a close," he proclaimed. Let "the single man plant himself indomitably on his instincts and . . . the huge world will come around to him."

Although he admired Cooper's fiction, Emerson expressed his own version of literary nationalism in essays characterized by a homely reliance on the individual as well as an interest in broad philosophical questions. The true scholar, he stressed, must be independent. Emerson did not present systematic arguments backed by evidence to prove his point. Rather, he relied on a sequence of vivid if unconnected assertions whose truth the reader was supposed to see instantly. (One reader complained that she might have understood Emerson better if she had stood on her head.)

Emerson had a magnetic attraction for young intellectuals who were ill at ease in conventional society. Henry David Thoreau, born in 1817, typified the younger Emersonians. Unlike Emerson, whose adventurousness was largely intellectual, Thoreau was both a thinker and a doer. At one point he went to jail rather than pay poll taxes that would support the Mexican War, a conflict that he saw as part of a southern conspiracy to extend slavery. The experience of jail led Thoreau to write *Civil Disobedience* (1849), in which he defended disobedience of unjust laws.

On July 4, 1845, in a personal declaration of independence, Thoreau moved a few miles from Concord Center to the woods near Walden Pond. He spent two years there living in a small cabin he constructed on land owned by Emerson and providing for his own wants as simply as possible. His purpose in retreating to Walden was to write an account of a canoe trip he took with his brother in 1839. But he wrote a more important book, *Walden* (1854), which was filled with day-to-day descriptions of hawks and the pond, his invention of raisin bread, and his trapping of the woodchucks that ravaged his vegetable garden. But Walden had a larger transcendentalist message. Thoreau's retreat taught him that anyone could satisfy his material wants with only a few weeks' work each year and preserve the remainder of his time for examining life's purpose. The problem with Americans, he said, was that they turned themselves into "mere machines" to acquire pointless wealth.

One of the most remarkable figures in Emerson's circle was Margaret Fuller, an intellectual whose status distanced her from conventional society. Her father, although disappointed that she was not a boy, gave her the sort of education a young man might have received at Harvard; she read Latin and Greek, the modern German romantics, and the British literary classics. Transcendentalism, with its emphasis on the free life of the spirit and the need for each person to discover truth on his or her own, opened a new world for Fuller. For five years she supported herself by presiding over "conversations" by Boston's elite men and women. Transcendentalism also reinforced her feminist ideas; in *Women in the Nineteenth Century* (1845) she cast aside the doctrine of "separate spheres" and contended that no woman could achieve

Constance Fuller Threinen/Picture Research Consultants and Archive

Margaret Fuller

In 1846, Margaret Fuller was sent by Horace Greeley to Europe as the *Tribune's* foreign correspondent. There she met artists and writers, observed the Revolutions of 1848, and married an Italian nobleman. On her return to America in 1850, she, her husband, and her infant son died in a shipwreck off Long Island.

personal fulfillment without developing her intellectual abilities and overcoming her fear of being called masculine.

One of Emerson's qualities was an ability to sympathize with such dissimilar people as the prickly Thoreau, the scholarly Fuller, and the outgoing and earthy **Walt Whitman.** The self-educated Whitman had left school at age eleven and worked his way up from printer's apprentice to journalist and then newspaper editor. A familiar figure at Democratic Party functions, he marched in party parades and put his pen to the service of its antislavery wing.

Leaves of Grass shattered existing poetic conventions. Whitman composed in free verse, and his blunt, often lusty words assailed "delicacy." He wrote of "the scent of these armpits finer than prayer" and "winds whose soft-tickling genitals rub against me."

To some contemporary critics, *Leaves of Grass* seemed the work of an escaped lunatic. One derided it as a "heterogeneous mass of bombast, egotism, vulgarity, and nonsense." Emerson and a few others, however, reacted enthusiastically. Emerson had long awaited the appearance of "the poet of America" and knew immediately that Whitman was that poet.

Hawthorne, Melville, and Poe

Three major writers of the 1840s and 1850s strayed far from Emerson's ideals. Nathaniel Hawthorne, Herman Melville, and Edgar Allan Poe wrote fiction that paid little heed to Emerson's call for a literature treating the everyday experiences of ordinary Americans. Hawthorne, for example, set *The Scarlet Letter* (1850) in New England's Puritan past, *The House of the Seven Gables* (1851) in a mansion haunted by memories of the past, and *The Marble Faun* (1859) in Rome. Poe set several of his short stories in Europe; and Melville's novels *Typee* (1846), *Omoo* (1847), and *Mardi* (1849) took place in the exotic South Seas, whereas his masterpiece, *Moby-Dick* (1851), was set aboard a whaler. If the only surviving documents from the 1840s and 1850s were its major novels, historians would face an impossible task in trying to understand daily life in antebellum America.

Walt Whitman Protégé of Emerson and author of daringly original poetry

In part, these three writers felt that American life lacked the materials for great fiction. Hawthorne bemoaned the difficulty of writing about a country "where there is no shadow, no antiquity, no mystery, no picturesque and gloomy wrong, nor anything but a commonplace prosperity in broad and simple daylight." Psychology, not society, fascinated these writers. Each probed the depths of the human mind rather than the intricacies of social relationships. Their work displayed an underlying pessimism about the human condition and the fundamental irrationality of human nature.

Pessimism led these authors to create characters obsessed by pride, guilt, a desire for revenge, or a quest for perfection and then to set their stories along the byways of society, where they could explore the complexities of human motivation without the jarring intrusions of everyday life. For example, in *The Scarlet Letter* Hawthorne returned to the Puritan era to examine the psychological and moral consequences of the adultery committed by Hester Prynne (prin) and the minister Arthur Dimmesdale, although he devoted little attention to depicting the Puritan village in which the action takes place. Melville, in *Moby-Dick,* created the frightening Captain Ahab (AY-hab), whose relentless pursuit of a white whale fails to fill the chasm in his soul and brings death to all his crew except the narrator. Poe, in his short story "The Fall of the House of Usher" (1839), interwove the symbol of a crumbling mansion to convey the moral agony of a decaying, incestuous family.

Although these three authors ignored Emerson's call to write about the ordinary life of their fellow Americans, they fashioned a distinctively American fiction. Their works, preoccupied with analysis of moral dilemmas and psychological states, fulfilled Tocqueville's prediction that writers in democratic nations, while rejecting traditional sources of fiction, would explore the abstract and universal questions of human nature.

Literature in the Marketplace

The suspicion that commercialism would corrupt art did not entirely vanish in nineteenth-century America, but it certainly withered. The brilliant poet Emily Dickinson made little or no attempt to publish her work at all. But other authors, hard strapped for cash, entered the marketplace. Poe, for example, scratched out a meager living writing short stories for popular magazines. Thoreau craved recognition and tried to market his poems in New York City; failing that, he turned to detailed narratives of nature that sold very well.

Emerson, too, wanted to reach a broader public. After abandoning his first vocation as a Unitarian minister, he reached for a new sort of audience and a new source of income: the lyceum. Lyceums—local organizations for sponsoring lectures—spread throughout the northern tier of states after the late 1820s to meet popular demands for entertainment and self-improvement. Thanks to newly built railroads and the cheap newspapers that publicized lyceum programs, other speakers followed in Emerson's path. As Herman Melville pledged, "If they will pay my expenses and give a reasonable fee, I am ready to lecture in Labrador or on the Isle of Desolation off Patagonia."

The age offered women few opportunities for public speaking, and most lyceum lecturers were men. But women were tapping into the growing market for literature. Fiction-writing became the most lucrative occupation open to women before the Civil War. Novelist Susan Warner's *The Wide, Wide World,* published in 1850, went through fourteen editions by 1852. Harriet Beecher Stowe's *Uncle Tom's Cabin,* published in 1852, exceeded all previous sales by selling 100,000 copies in just five months. Nathaniel Hawthorne, whose own works sold modestly, bitterly condemned what he called the "d—d mob of scribbling women" who were outselling and outearning him.

The most popular form of fiction in the 1840s and 1850s was the sentimental or domestic novel, written mostly by women for women. In a typical novel, a female orphan or a spoiled rich girl was thrown into hard times by a drunken father and learned to prevail. The moral was clear: Women could overcome trials and improve their lives. Another popular genre in the antebellum reading market was sensationalist fiction, which drew on such dark romantic themes as criminality, mystery, and horror.

Therefore, authors such as Hawthorne, Poe, and Melville had to compete with the popular culture of the story newspapers, sentimental fiction, and sensationalism. The philosopher Emerson shared the lecture circuit with the showman P. T. Barnum. By and large, however, the major writers of the American Renaissance were successful. But the writers most likely to achieve commercial success were those who best met certain popular expectations, such as moral and spiritual uplift, horror and mystery, or love stories and happy endings.

Thomas Cole, The Last of the Mohicans, Cora Kneeling at the Feet of Tamenund, 1827

One year after James Fenimore Cooper's novel *The Last of the Mohicans* was published, Thomas Cole painted the white captive Cora pleading with Tamenund, Chief of the Delaware, not to be forced into marriage with an evil Indian warrior. In Cole's painting, this human drama is dwarfed by the sublime beauty of the American wilderness.

American Landscape Painting

At the same time as American writers were trying to create a distinctly American literature, American painters were searching for a national style in art. Lacking a mythic past of gods and goddesses, they subordinated historical and figure painting to landscape painting. The American landscape, though barren of the "poetry of decay" that Europe's ruined castles and crumbling temples provided, was fresh and relatively unencumbered by the human imprint. These conditions posed a challenge to the painters of the **Hudson River School,** which flourished from the 1820s to the 1870s. Its best-known representatives–Thomas Cole, Asher Durand, and Frederic Church–painted scenes of the unspoiled region around the Hudson River.

Hudson River School
Landscape painting that emphasized grandeur, emotion

Although all three men compared the majesty of the Hudson to that of the Rhine, none was exclusively a landscapist. Some of Cole's most popular paintings were allegories, such as *The Course of Empire,* a sequence of five canvases depicting the rise and fall of an ancient city; it implied that luxury doomed republican virtue.

The works of Washington Irving and the opening of the Erie Canal had piqued interest in the Hudson during the 1820s. Then, after 1830, Emerson and Thoreau lauded primitive nature; "in wildness is the preservation of the world," Thoreau wrote. By this time, much of the original American forest had already fallen to pioneer axes, and one writer urgently concluded that "it behooves our artists to rescue from [civilization's] grasp the little that is left before it is too late."

The Hudson River painters did more than preserve a passing wilderness; they also emphasized emotional effect. Cole's rich colors; billowing clouds; massive, gnarled trees; towering peaks; and deep chasms so heightened the dramatic impact of his paintings that poet William Cullen Bryant compared them to "acts of religion." Similar motifs marked Frederick Church's paintings of the Andes Mountains, which used erupting volcanoes and thunderstorms to evoke dread and a sense of majesty. In powerful, evocative canvases, American artists aimed to capture the natural grandeur of their land.

Frederick Law Olmsted
Prominent landscape architect and co-designer, with Calvert Vaux, of New York City's Central Park

Like Cole, George Catlin tried to preserve a vanishing America through his art. His goal was to paint as many Native Americans as possible in their pure and "savage" state. By 1837, he had created 437 oil paintings and thousands of sketches of faces and customs from nearly fifty tribes. Catlin's romantic view of the Indians as noble savages was a double-edged sword. His admirers delighted in his dignified portrayals of Indians but shared his foreboding that the march of progress had already doomed these noble creatures to oblivion.

Landscape architects tried to create small enclaves of nature to provide spiritual refreshment to harried city-dwellers. "Rural" cemeteries with pastoral names like Harmony Grove, placed near major cities, became tourist attractions, designed as much for the living as for the dead. On a grander scale **Frederick Law Olmsted** and Calvert Vaux (voh) designed New York City's Central Park to look like undisturbed countryside. Drainage pipes carried water to man-made lakes, and trees screened out the surrounding buildings. Central Park became an idealized version of nature, meant to remind visitors of landscapes that they had seen in pictures. Thus, nature was made to mirror art.

CHECKING IN

- Romanticism combined with the technological revolution to produce an American Renaissance.
- American literature took on nationalistic themes with James Fenimore Cooper and his tales of the frontier.
- Ralph Waldo Emerson was the center of the transcendentalist movement, which included Henry David Thoreau and Margaret Fuller.
- American writers such as Poe, Hawthorne, and Melville plumbed the depths of the human psyche.
- The Hudson River School of painting romanticized the American landscape and drenched it in emotion.

Chapter Summary

What technological improvements brought about American economic growth between 1840 and 1860? (page 246)

Rapid technological growth revolutionized agriculture and greatly increased productivity in the manufacturing sector as well. Railroads played a vital role, linking cities, spawning new cities, creating markets, and providing a new business model. Prices fell, and prosperity rose.

In what ways did technology transform the lives of ordinary Americans? (page 250)

As cities grew, housing and living conditions improved for better-off residents, but squalor and pollution persisted, and class distinctions sharpened. The inability to control epidemic disease fed such popular fads as hydropathy and phrenology.

In what new ways did Americans pass their free time during this period? (page 254)

Popular entertainment became the realm of entrepreneurs such as James Bennett Gordon with his "penny press" and P. T. Barnum with his stable of wonders. Theater flourished, drawing diverse and rowdy audiences, and black-face minstrel shows reinforced negative stereotypes.

How did the work of American writers and artists become distinctly American? (page 257)

The disappearing frontier elicited a distinctly American literature from James Fenimore Cooper. An American Renaissance produced such democratic writers as Whitman and Emerson, as well as those fascinated by the darker side of human nature, such as Poe, Hawthorne, and Melville. The Hudson River School emphasized the grandeur and emotion of the American landscape.

KEY TERMS

technology *(p. 246)*
John Deere *(p. 246)*
Cyrus McCormick *(p. 246)*
interchangeable parts *(p. 248)*
epidemic diseases *(p. 252)*
phrenology *(p. 254)*
penny press *(p. 254)*
minstrel show *(p. 256)*
P. T. Barnum *(p. 257)*
American Renaissance *(p. 257)*
Walt Whitman *(p. 260)*
Hudson River School *(p. 263)*
Frederick Law Olmsted *(p. 263)*

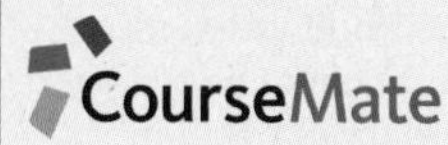

Go to the CourseMate website at **www.cengagebrain.com** for additional study tools and review materials—including audio and video clips—for this chapter.

CHAPTER 12

The Old South and Slavery

1830–1860

Courtesy of George Eastman House, International Museum of Photography and Film

Family Group
The African-American woman shown here probably was a slave mammy who substituted for the absent mother of the children.

CHAPTER PREVIEW

King Cotton
How did the rise of cotton cultivation affect the South?

The Social Groups of the White South
What major social divisions segmented the white South?

Social Relations in the White South
How did slavery affect social relations in the South?

Life Under Slavery
How did slaves and free blacks respond to their circumstances?

The Emergence of African-American Culture
What were the distinctive features of African-American society and culture in the South?

Nat Turner Leader of the largest slave rebellion in U.S. history

Slipping through the swampy woodlands of Southampton County, Virginia, in the early morning of August 22, 1831, a band of slaves led by **Nat Turner** embarked on a grisly campaign of liberation. As the death count rose, so did the number of slaves following Turner; by noon more than sixty slaves had taken up axes, hatchets, and muskets, and more than sixty whites had been shot, clubbed, or hacked to death.

Despite Southampton County's isolation, word of the slave uprising soon reached the capital, Richmond, and neighboring North Carolina counties, and thousands of militia and vigilantes poured into the area. Shocking destruction greeted them; dismembered bodies and fresh blood testified to the rage unleashed by the rebels. In turn, the slaves would fall victim to white rage, as scores of blacks were killed, whether or not they had actually been involved. Most of Turner's followers were either shot on sight or jailed, tried, and hanged. Turner himself eluded capture until late October; after a trial he, too, was hanged.

The Granger Collection, New York

Nat Turner

By noon Turner's army, which had grown to sixty or seventy followers, had murdered about sixty whites. As word of trouble spread, militia and vigilantes, thousands strong, poured into Southampton from across the border in North Carolina and from other countries in Virginia.

Revenge was one thing, but understanding was another. In his subsequently published "Confessions" (recorded by his court-appointed lawyer), Turner did not claim that he had been mistreated by his owners. What they did reveal was an intelligent and deeply religious man who had somehow learned to read and write as a boy, and who claimed to have seen heavenly visions of white and black spirits fighting each other. Christianity was supposed to make slaves more docile, but Nat Turner's ability to read had enabled him to find passages in the Bible that threatened death to him who "stealeth" a man, a fair description of slavery. Asked by his lawyer if he now found himself mistaken, Turner replied, "Was not Christ crucified?" Small wonder that a niece of George Washington concluded that she and all other white Virginians were now living on a "smothered volcano."

In the wake of Turner's insurrection, many Virginians, especially nonslaveholding whites in the western part of the state, urged that Virginia follow the lead of northern states and emancipate its slaves. During the winter of 1831–1832, the Virginia legislature wrangled over emancipation proposals. The narrow defeat of these proposals marked a turning point; thereafter, opposition to slavery steadily weakened not only in Virginia but throughout the region known to history as the Old South.

As late as the Revolution, *south* referred more to a direction than to a place. But as one northern state after another embraced emancipation, slavery became the "peculiar institution" that distinguished the Old South from other sections.

Upper South Virginia, North Carolina, Tennessee, and Arkansas; a more economically diverse region

Lower (Deep) South South Carolina, Georgia, Florida, Alabama, Mississippi, Louisiana, and Texas

A rift of sorts split the Old South into the **Upper South** and the **Lower (Deep) South.** With its diversified economy, the Upper South relied far less than the Lower South on slavery and cotton, and in 1861 it approached secession more reluctantly than its sister states. Yet in the final analysis, slavery forged a single Old South where it scarred all social relationships. Without slavery, there never would have been an Old South.

KING COTTON

How did the rise of cotton cultivation affect the South?

In 1790, the South was essentially stagnant. Tobacco, its primary cash crop, had lost its economic vitality even as it had depleted the once-rich southern soils, and neither rice nor cotton could replace tobacco's economic importance. Three out of four southerners still lived along the Atlantic seaboard, specifically in the Chesapeake and the Carolinas. One of three resided in Virginia alone.

Chronology

1790s	Methodists and Baptists start to make major strides in converting slaves to Christianity
1800	Gabriel Prosser plans a slave rebellion in Virginia
1808	Congress prohibits external slave trade
1816–1819	Boom in cotton prices stimulates settlement of the Southwest
1820–1821	Missouri Compromise
1822	Denmark Vesey's conspiracy is uncovered in South Carolina
1831	Nat Turner leads a slave rebellion in Virginia
1832	Virginia legislature narrowly defeats a proposal for gradual emancipation
1844–1845	Methodist and Baptist churches split over slavery into northern and southern wings
1849	Sugar production in Louisiana reaches its peak
1849–1860	Period of high cotton prices

The contrast between that South and the dynamic South of 1850 was stunning. By 1850, southerners had moved south and west—now only one out of seven southerners lived in Virginia—and cotton reigned as king, shaping this new South. The growth of the British textile industry had created a huge demand for cotton, while Indian removal had made way for southern expansion into the "Cotton Kingdom," a broad swath of land that stretched from South Carolina, Georgia, and northern Florida in the East through Alabama, Mississippi, central and western Tennessee, and Louisiana, and from there on to Arkansas and Texas.

The Lure of Cotton

Southerners extolled **King Cotton.** A warm climate, wet springs and summers, and relatively dry autumns made the Lower South the ideal location for cultivating cotton. A cotton farmer did not need slaves, cotton gins, or the capital required for sugar cultivation. Perhaps 50 percent of farmers in the "Cotton Belt" owned no slaves, and to process their harvest they could turn to the widely available commercial gins. Cotton promised to make poor men prosperous and rich men kings.

King Cotton Term expressing the southern belief that U.S. and British economies depended on cotton

Yet large-scale cotton cultivation and slavery grew together as the southern slave population nearly doubled between 1810 and 1830 (Figures 12.1 and 12.2).

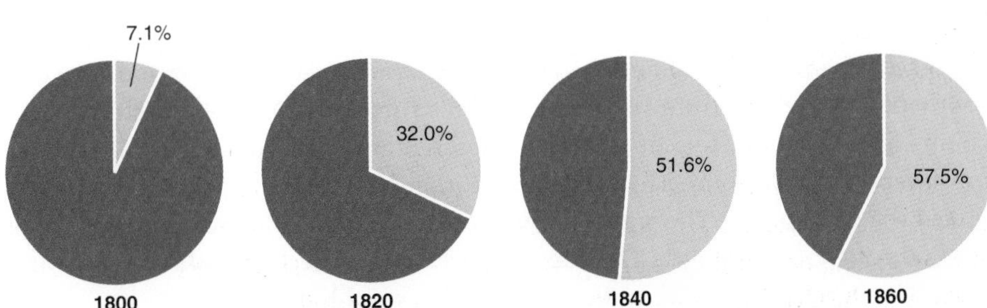

Figure 12.1 Value of Cotton Exports as a Percentage of All U.S. Exports, 1800–1860

By 1840 cotton accounted for more than half of all U.S. exports.

Figure 12.2 Growth of Cotton Production and the Slave Population, 1790–1860

Cotton and slavery rose together in the Old South.

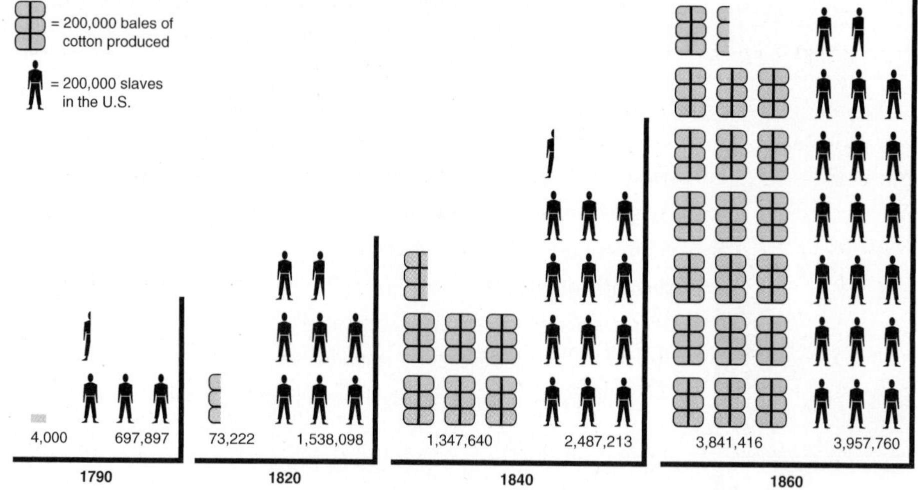

Three-fourths of all southern slaves worked in the cotton economy in 1830. Owning slaves enabled a planter to harvest vast fields of cotton speedily, a crucial advantage because a sudden rainstorm at harvest time could pelt cotton to the ground and soil it.

Cotton was also compatible with corn production. Corn could be planted either earlier or later than cotton and harvested before or after. Because the cost of owning a slave remained the same regardless of whether he or she was working, corn production allowed slaveholders to shift slave labor between corn and cotton. By 1860 the acreage devoted to corn in the Old South actually *exceeded* that devoted to cotton. Economically, corn and cotton gave the South the best of two worlds. Intense demand in Britain and New England kept cotton prices high and money flowing into the South. Because of southern self-sufficiency in growing corn and raising hogs that thrived on the corn, money did not drain away to pay for food. In 1860 the twelve wealthiest counties in the United States were all in the South.

Ties Between the Lower and Upper South

Two giant cash crops, sugar and cotton, dominated agriculture in the Lower South. The Upper South, a region of tobacco, vegetable, hemp, and wheat growers, depended far less on the great cash crops. Nevertheless, a common dependence on slavery unified the Upper and the Lower South, and made the Upper South identify more with the Lower South than with the nation's free states.

A range of social, political, and psychological factors promoted this unity. First, many settlers in the Lower South had come from the Upper South. Second, all white southerners benefited from the Constitution's three-fifths clause, which let them count slaves as a basis for congressional representation. Third, abolitionist attacks on slavery stung all southerners and bound them together. Fourth, economic ties linked the two Souths. The profitability of cotton and sugar increased the value of slaves throughout the South. The sale of slaves from the declining **plantation** states of the Upper South to the booming Lower South was a huge business.

plantation Large landholding devoted to a cash crop, such as cotton or tobacco

The North and South Diverge

However, the changes responsible for the dynamic growth of the South widened the distance between it and the North. The South remained predominantly rural, whereas the North became more and more urban.

Lack of industry kept the South rural; by 1860, it had one-third of the U.S. population but accounted for only one-tenth of the nation's manufacturing. The industrial output of the entire South in 1850 was less than one-third that of Massachusetts alone.

A few southerners advocated industrialization to reduce the South's dependency on northern manufactured products. After touring northern textile mills, South Carolina's William Gregg established a company town for textiles at Graniteville in 1845. By 1860, Richmond boasted the nation's fourth-largest producer of iron products, the Tredegar (TREH-du-gur) Iron Works. But these were exceptions.

Compared to factories in the North, most southern factories were small, produced for nearby markets, and were closely tied to agriculture. The leading northern factories turned hides into tanned leather and leather into shoes, or cotton into threads and threads into suits. In contrast, southern factories turned grain into flour, corn into meal, and logs into lumber.

Slavery posed a major obstacle to southern industrialization, but not because slaves were unfit for factories; the Tredegar Iron Works, for example, was among many factories that employed slaves. However, industrial slavery troubled slaveholders. Away from the strict discipline and supervision possible on a plantation, slaves sometimes behaved as if they were free, shifting jobs, working overtime, and even negotiating better working conditions. But the chief brake on southern industrialization was money, not labor. To raise the capital needed to build factories, planters would have had to sell their slaves. They had little incentive to do so. Cash crops like cotton and sugar were proven winners, whereas the benefits of industrialization were remote and doubtful. As long as southerners believed that an economy founded on cash crops would remain profitable, they had little reason to leap into the uncertainties of industrialization.

As in industry, the South lagged behind the North in education. Whereas northerners recognized the benefits of an educated work force for their growing manufacturing economy, agriculturally oriented southerners rejected compulsory education and were reluctant to tax property to support schools. They abhorred the thought of educating slaves, and southern lawmakers made it a crime to teach slaves to read. For most whites, the only available schools were private. White illiteracy thus remained high in the South as it declined in the North. Before the Civil War, for example, nearly 60 percent of North Carolinians who enlisted in the U.S. Army were illiterate, compared to 30 percent for northern enlistees.

Agricultural, self-sufficient, and independent, the middling and poor whites of the South remained unconvinced of the need for public education. They had little dependence on the printed word, few complex commercial transactions, and infrequent dealings with urban people. Planters did not need an orderly and disciplined white work force; they already had a black one that they were determined to keep illiterate lest it acquire ideas about freedom.

Because the South diverged so sharply from the North, outsiders often dismissed it as backward. A northern journalist wrote of white southerners in the 1850s,

Map 12.1 Distribution of Slaves, 1820 and 1860

In 1790 the majority of slaves resided along the southeastern seaboard. By 1860, however, slavery had spread throughout the South, and slaves were most heavily concentrated in the Deep South states.

(Ordeal by Fire: The Civil War and Reconstruction *by James M. McPherson. Copyright 1982 by Alfred A. Knopf, Inc.*)

Interactive Map

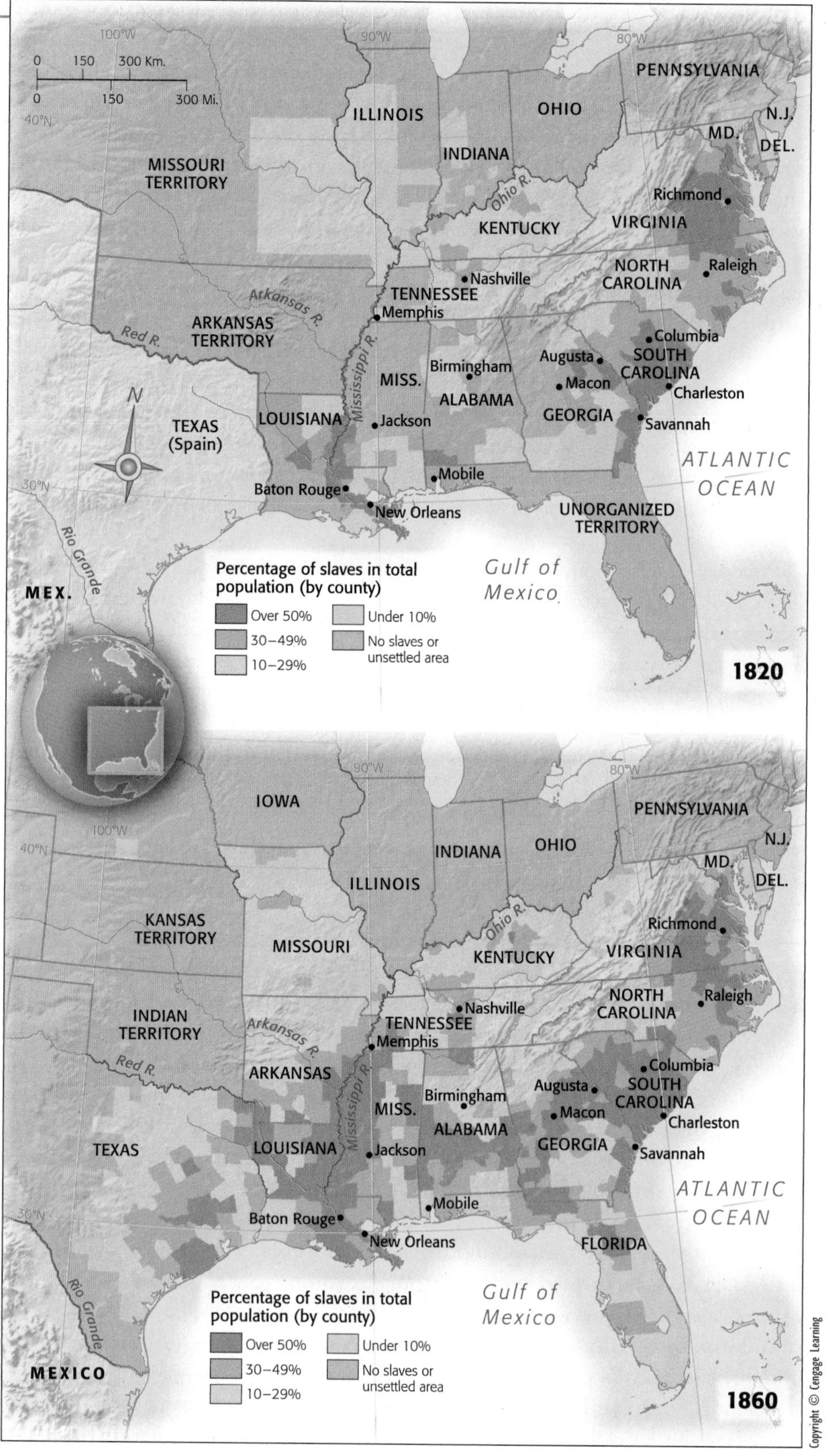

"They work little, and that little, badly; they earn little, they sell little; they buy little, and have little—very little—of the common comforts and consolations of civilized life."

Yet the South did not lack progressive features. By 1860, white per capita income in the South exceeded the national average. Like northerners, white southerners were restless, eager to make money, and skillful at managing complex commercial enterprises. Thus, the white South was not economically backward—it was merely different. Cotton was a wonderful crop, and southerners could hardly be blamed for making it their ruler. As a southern senator wrote in 1858, "You dare not make war upon cotton; no power on earth dares to make war upon it. Cotton is king."

CHECKING IN

- By 1830, the cotton economy dominated the South.
- Although cotton production flourished primarily in the Lower South, the Upper South benefited as well.
- "King Cotton" brought great prosperity to the South, but it also made slavery seem ever more vital to white southerners.
- The South nevertheless lagged far behind the North in industrialization and education.

THE SOCIAL GROUPS OF THE WHITE SOUTH

What major social divisions segmented the white South?

There was wide diversity within and between the South's slaveholding and nonslaveholding classes. Although some planters owned hundreds of slaves and lived lavishly, most lived more modestly. In 1860 one-fourth of all white families in the South owned slaves; nearly half of those owned fewer than five slaves, and three-fourths had fewer than ten slaves. Only 12 percent owned twenty or more slaves, and only 1 percent owned a hundred or more. Nonslaveholders were equally diverse. Most owned farms and drew on the labor of family members, but other whites squatted on land in the pine barrens or piney woods and scratched out a living by raising livestock, hunting, fishing, and planting a few acres of corn, oats, or sweet potatoes.

Planters, small slaveholders, family farmers, and pine-barrens folk composed the South's four main white groups. Lawyers, physicians, merchants, and artisans did not fall into any of these groups, but they tended to identify their interests with one or another of the agricultural groups.

Planters and Plantation Mistresses

The plantation, with its porticoed mansion and fields teeming with slaves, stands at the center of the popular image of the Old South. This romanticized view, reinforced by novels and movies like *Gone with the Wind,* is not entirely false, for the South did contain plantations that travelers found "superb beyond description." Abundant slaves, the division of labor they afforded, and plentiful land allowed large plantations to generate incomes of $20,000 or more a year, an immense sum in those years.

In the eighteenth century during the initial flush of settlement in the piedmont and trans-Appalachian South, even well-off planters generally had lived in humble log cabins. After 1810, however, elite planters vied with one another to build stately mansions. Yet most planters counted their wealth not in grand mansions and elegant furnishings but in the value of their slaves. A field hand was worth as much as $1,700 in the 1850s, and few planters sold their slaves to buy furniture and silver plates.

In their constant worry about profit, planters enjoyed neither repose nor security. High fixed costs—housing and feeding slaves, maintaining cotton gins, hiring overseers—led them to search for more and better land, higher efficiency, and greater self-sufficiency. Because cotton prices tended to fluctuate seasonally, planters often assigned their cotton to commercial agents in cities who held the cotton until the price was right. The agents extended credit so that the planters could pay their bills before the cotton was sold. Indebtedness became part of the plantation economy and intensified the planters' quest for profitability. Psychological strains compounded economic worries. Frequent moves disrupted circles of friends and relatives, particularly as migration to the Southwest (Alabama and Mississippi) carried families into less settled, more desolate areas. Until 1850, this area was still the frontier (see Map 12.1).

Migration to the Southwest often deeply unsettled plantation women. They suddenly found themselves in frontier conditions surrounded by slaves and without friends, neighbors, or relatives nearby. Frequent absences by husbands, regardless if they were looking for new land, supervising outlying plantations, or conducting business in the city, intensified wives' loneliness.

Planters and their wives found various ways of coping with their isolation. Employing overseers to run the plantation, some lived in cities; in 1850 half the planters in the Mississippi Delta lived in New Orleans or Natchez. Most planters acted as their own overseers, however, and dealt with harsh living conditions by opening their home to visitors. The responsibility for such hospitality fell heavily on wives, who might have to entertain as many as fifteen people for breakfast and attend to the needs of visitors who stayed for days. Plantation wives also bore the burdens of raising their children, supervising house slaves, making clothing and carpets, looking after smokehouses and dairies, planting gardens, and, often, keeping the plantation accounts.

Among the heaviest sorrows of some plantation mistresses was the presence of mulatto (moo-LOT-oh) children, who stood as daily reminders of their husbands' infidelities. Mary Boykin Chesnut, an astute Charleston woman and famous diarist, commented, "Any lady is ready to tell you who is the father of all the mulatto children in everybody's household but her own. These, she seems to think, drop from clouds." Insisting on sexual purity for white women, southern men followed a looser standard for themselves. Richard M. Johnson of Kentucky was elected vice president of the United States in 1836 despite having lived openly for years with his black mistress.

The Small Slaveholders

In 1860, 88 percent of all slaveholders owned fewer than twenty slaves, and most possessed fewer than ten. One out of every five slaveholders worked outside of agriculture, as a lawyer, physician, merchant, or artisan.

yeoman Independent small farmer, usually nonslaveholding

Small slaveholders experienced conflicting loyalties and ambitions. In upland regions they absorbed the outlook of the more numerous **yeomen** (YO-men), who owned only a few slaves and rarely aspired to become large planters. In contrast, in the plantation-dominated low country and delta regions, small slaveholders often aspired to planter status. There someone with ten slaves could realistically look forward to owning thirty. And ambitious, acquisitive individuals equated success with owning more slaves. The logic of slavery remained the same: The only way to justify the investment in slaves was to set them to work on profitable crops. Such crops demanded more and better land, and both the planters and the small slaveholders of the deltas were restless and footloose.

The social structure of the deltas was fluid. In the early antebellum period, large planters had been reluctant to risk transporting their hundreds of valuable slaves in a still-turbulent region. It was small slaveholders who led the initial westward push into the Cotton Belt in the 1810s and 1820s. Gradually, large planters, too, moved westward, buying up the land that the small slave owners had developed and turning the region from Vicksburg to Natchez into large plantations. Small slave owners took the profits from selling their land, bought more slaves, and moved on. They gradually transformed the region from Vicksburg to Tuscaloosa (tusk-uh-LOO-suh), Alabama, into a belt of medium-sized farms with a dozen or so slaves on each.

The Yeomen

Nonslaveholding family farmers, or yeomen, composed the largest single group of southern whites. Most owned land, and many hired slaves to help at harvest. In areas of poor soil, such as eastern Tennessee, yeomen were typically subsistence farmers, although most yeomen grew some cash crops. Their landholdings were comparatively small, ranging from fifty to two hundred acres. Yeomen generally inhabited uplands, such as the piedmont of the East or the hilly upcountry of the Southwest, far from the rich coastal plains and deltas.

Above all, the yeomen valued self-sufficiency. Unlike planters, who were driven to acquire more land and to plant more cash crops, the yeomen devoted much of their acreage to subsistence crops, such as corn, sweet potatoes, and oats. The planter's ideal was profit with modest self-sufficiency; in contrast, the yeoman's goal was self-sufficiency with modest profit.

Yeomen living in planter-dominated regions were often dismissed as "poor white trash." However, in the upland regions that they dominated, the yeomen were highly respected. Upland slaveholders tended to own only a few slaves; like the yeomen, they were essentially family farmers.

Unlike southern planters, yeomen marketed their cash crops locally, trading cotton, wheat, and tobacco for goods and services from nearby artisans and merchants. In some areas yeomen sold their surplus corn to drovers and herdsmen who specialized in raising hogs. Along the French Broad River in eastern Tennessee, for example, twenty thousand to thirty thousand hogs a year were fattened for market. At peak season a traveler would see one thousand hogs a mile. The hogs were penned at night in huge stock stands—veritable hog hotels—and fed with corn supplied by the local yeomen.

The People of the Pine Barrens

Independent whites of the wooded "pine barrens" were among the most controversial groups in the Old South. Making up about 10 percent of southern whites, they usually squatted on the land; put up crude cabins; cleared some acreage, where they planted corn between tree

CHECKING IN

- The white South consisted of four main social groups: plantation owners, small slaveholders, yeomen, and the people of the pine barrens.
- Plantation owners, who owned most of the slaves, were at the top of the social structure.
- Small slaveholders, including professionals as well as farmers, most often owned fewer than ten slaves.
- Yeomen farmers, who generally owned no slaves, were the largest segment of the white population.
- The fiercely proud and independent people of the pine barrens composed 10 percent of the white population.

stumps; and grazed hogs and cattle in the woods. They neither raised cash crops nor engaged in the daily routine of orderly work that characterized family farmers. With their ramshackle houses and handfuls of stump-strewn acres, they appeared lazy and shiftless.

Abolitionists cited the pine-barrens people as proof that slavery degraded whites, but southerners responded that, although the pine-barrens folk were poor, they could at least feed themselves, unlike the paupers of northern cities. In general, the people of the pine barrens were both self-sufficient and fiercely independent. Pine-barrens men were reluctant to hire themselves out as laborers to do "slave" tasks, and the women refused to become servants.

Social Relations in the White South

How did slavery affect social relations in the South?

Northerners often charged that slavery twisted the entire social structure of the South out of shape. The enslavement of blacks, they alleged, robbed lower-class whites of the incentive to work, reduced them to shiftless misery, and rendered the South a throwback in an otherwise progressive age. The behavior of individual southerners also struck northerners as running to extremes. One minute, southerners were hospitable and gracious; the next, savagely violent. The practice of dueling intensified in the Old South at a time when it was dying in the North.

In reality, a curious mix of aristocratic and democratic, premodern and modern features marked social relations in the white South. Although it contained considerable class inequality, property ownership was widespread. Rich planters occupied seats in state legislatures out of proportion to their numbers in the population, but they did not necessarily get their way, nor did their political agenda always differ from that of other whites.

Conflict and Consensus in the White South

Planters tangled with yeomen on several issues. With extensive economic dealings and the need for credit, planters inclined toward the Whig party, which generally supported economic development. The independent yeomen, cherishing their self-sufficiency, tended to be Democrats.

Yet few conflicts arose between these groups. An underlying political unity reigned in the South. Geography was in part responsible: Planters, small slaveholders, yeomen, and pine-barrens folk tended to cluster in different regions, each independent of the others. There was somewhat more geographical intermingling of groups in the Upper South. With widespread land ownership and few factories, the Old South was not a place where whites worked for other whites, and this tended to minimize friction.

The white South's political structure was sufficiently democratic to prevent any one group from gaining exclusive control over politics. Planters dominated state legislatures, but they owed their election to the popular vote. And the democratic currents that swept northern politics between 1815 and 1860 affected the South as well; newer southern states entered the Union with democratic constitutions that included universal white manhood suffrage—the right of all adult white males to vote.

Although yeomen often voted for planters, the nonslaveholders did not give their elected representatives a blank check to govern as they pleased. During the 1830s and 1840s, Whig planters who favored banks faced intense and often successful opposition from Democratic yeomen. The nonslaveholders got their way often enough to nurture their belief that they, not the slaveholders, controlled politics.

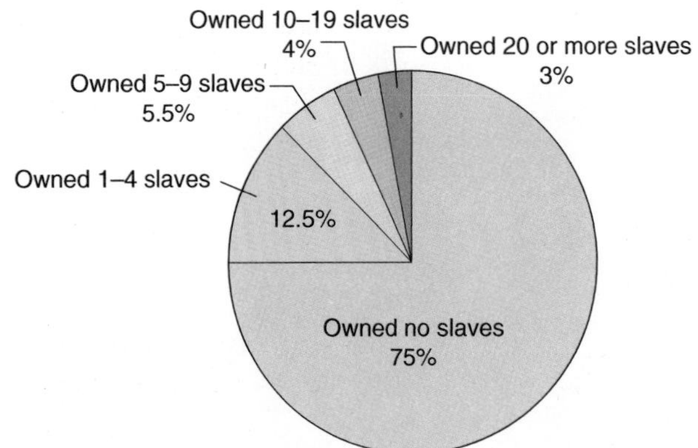

Figure 12.3 Slave Ownership, 1860

In combination with the impact of Hinton R. Helper's *The Impending Crisis of the South* (1857), which called on nonslaveholders to abolish the institution of slavery in their own interest, this decline left slaveholders worried about the loyalty of nonslaveholders to slavery.

Conflict over Slavery

Nevertheless, considerable *potential* existed for conflict between slaveholders and nonslaveholders. The southern white carpenter who complained in 1849 that "unjust, oppressive, and degrading" competition from slave labor depressed his wages surely had a point. Between 1830 and 1860 the slaveholding class shrank in size in relation to the total white population, but its share of total wealth increased. As a Louisiana editor wrote in 1858, "The present tendency of supply and demand is to concentrate all the slaves in the hands of the few, and thus excite the envy rather than cultivate the sympathy of the people."

Yet although pockets of opposition dotted the South, slavery did not create profound or lasting divisions between slaveholders and nonslaveholders (Figure 12.3). For example, antagonism to slavery flourished in parts of Virginia up to 1860, but proposals for emancipating the slaves dropped from the state's political agenda after 1832. Kentucky had a history of antislavery activity dating back to the 1790s, but after calls for emancipation suffered a crushing defeat in an 1849 referendum, slavery ceased to be a political issue there.

The rise and fall of pro-emancipation sentiment in the South raises a key question: As most white southerners were nonslaveholders, why didn't they attack slavery more consistently? To look ahead, why were so many southerners willing to fight ferociously and to die bravely during the Civil War in defense of an institution in which they apparently had no real stake? There are several reasons. First, some nonslaveholders hoped to become slaveholders. Second, most southerners accepted the racist assumptions on which slavery rested; they dreaded the likelihood that emancipation would encourage "impudent" blacks to entertain ideas of social equality with whites. Third, no one knew where the slaves, if freed, would go or what they would do. Colonizing freed blacks in Africa was unrealistic, southerners concluded, but they also believed that, without colonization, emancipation would lead to a race war.

The Proslavery Argument

Between 1830 and 1860, southerners constructed a defense of slavery as a **positive good** rather than a necessary evil. St. Paul's injunction that servants obey their

positive good Southern argument that slavery benefited both black and white

The Negro in His Own Country and the Negro in America
Proslavery propagandists contrasted what they believed to be the black's African savagery with the blessings of civilization on an American plantation.

masters became a biblical justification for some. Others looked to the classical past to argue that slavery was both an ancient and a classical institution; the slave society of Athens, they said, had produced Aristotle (AIR-iss-taht-ul) and Plato (PLAY-toh), and Roman slaveholders had laid the foundations of Western civilization. George Fitzhugh of Virginia contrasted the plight of the northern "wage slaves," callously discarded when they became too ill or too old to work, with the lot of southern slaves, cared for by masters who attended to their health, their clothing, and their discipline.

At the same time, southerners increasingly suppressed any open discussion of slavery within the South. Proslavery writers warned that abolitionists wanted to destroy the family as well as slavery by undermining the "natural" submission of children to parents, wives to husbands, and slaves to masters. In the 1830s, proslavery southerners seized abolitionist literature from the southern mail and burned it. Although Kentucky abolitionist Cassius Marcellus Clay protected his press with two cannons, in 1845 a mob dismantled it anyway.

The rise of the proslavery argument coincided with a shift in southern churches' position on slavery. During the 1790s and early 1800s, some Protestant ministers had assailed slavery as immoral, but by the 1830s, most clergymen had convinced themselves that slavery was both compatible with Christianity and necessary for the proper exercise of Christian religion. Slavery, they proclaimed, displayed Christian responsibility toward one's inferiors, and it helped African-Americans to develop Christian virtues, such as humility and self-control. Southerners increasingly attacked antislavery evangelicals in the North for disrupting the "superior" social arrangement of the South. In 1837, southerners and conservative northerners had combined forces to drive antislavery New School Presbyterians out of that denomination's main body; in 1844, the Methodist Episcopal Church split into northern and southern wings; and in 1845, Baptists formed a separate Southern Convention.

In effect, southern evangelicals seceded from national church organizations long before the South seceded from the Union.

Violence, Honor, and Dueling in the Old South

Throughout the colonial and antebellum periods, violence deeply colored the daily lives of white southerners. In the 1760s, a minister described backcountry Virginians "biting one anothers Lips and Noses off, and gowging one another—that is, thrusting out anothers Eyes, and kicking one another on the Cods [genitals], to the great damage of many a Poor Woman." Gouging out eyes became a specialty of sorts among poor southern whites. On one occasion a South Carolina judge entered his court to find a plaintiff, a juror, and two witnesses all missing one eye. Stories of eye gougings and ear bitings became part of Old South folklore. Mike Fink, a legendary southern fighter and hunter, boasted that he was so mean in infancy that he refused his mother's milk and howled for whiskey. Yet beneath the folklore lay the reality of violence that gave the Old South a murder rate as much as ten times higher than that of the North.

At the root of most violence in the white South lay intensified feelings of personal pride that reflected the inescapable presence of slaves. White southerners saw slaves degraded, insulted, and powerless to resist. In turn, whites reacted violently to even trivial insults to demonstrate that they had nothing in common with slaves.

Among gentlemen this exaggerated pride took the form of a code of honor, with honor defined as an extraordinary sensitivity to one's reputation. Northern moralists celebrated a rival idea—character—the quality that enabled an individual to behave in steady fashion regardless of how others acted toward him or her. In the honor culture of the Old South, however, even the slightest insult, as long as it was perceived as intentional, could become the basis for a duel.

Formalized by French and British officers during the Revolutionary War, **dueling** gained a secure niche in the Old South as a means by which gentlemen dealt with affronts to their honor. Seemingly trivial incidents—a harmless brushing against the side of someone at a public event, a hostile glance—could trigger a duel. Yet dueling did not necessarily lead to violence. Gentlemen viewed dueling as a refined alternative to the random violence of lower-class life. Instead of leaping at his antagonist's throat, a gentleman remained cool, settled on a weapon with his opponent, and agreed to a meeting place. In the interval, friends of the parties negotiated to clear up the "misunderstanding" that had provoked the challenge. Most confrontations ended peaceably rather than on the field of honor at dawn.

dueling Formal man-to-man fight over a matter of honor

Nonetheless, many ended violently. Many southerners saw recourse to the law as a way to settle personal disputes involving honor as cowardly and shameless. Andrew Jackson's mother told the future president, "The law affords no remedy that can satisfy the feelings of a true man."

Dueling rested on the assumption that gentlemen could recognize each other and know when to respond to a challenge. Nothing in the code of honor compelled a person to duel with someone who was not a gentleman, for such a person's opinion hardly mattered. An insolent porter who insulted a gentleman might get a whipping but did not merit a duel. Yet it was often difficult to determine who was a gentleman. Indeed, the Old South teemed with would-be gentlemen.

The Southern Evangelicals and White Values

With its emphasis on the personal redress of grievances and its inclination toward violence, the ideal of honor conflicted with the values preached by the southern evangelical churches, notably the Baptists, Methodists, and Presbyterians. These denominations stressed humility and self-restraint, virtues that sharply contrasted with the culture of display that buttressed the extravagance and violence of the Old South.

By the 1830s, however, southern evangelicals had begun to change. They no longer made an effort to reach out to women, blacks, and the poor; instead, women were now expected to remain silent in church, while urban blacks increasingly formed their own churches. Both Methodists and Baptists began to attract the well-to-do, a tendency that increased with the opening of colleges such as Randolph-Macon and Wake Forest. More and more, southern gentry and evangelicals shared values, including a prickly regard for their honor and reputation. By the 1860s the South counted many gentlemen like the Bible-quoting Presbyterian general Thomas J. "Stonewall" Jackson, fierce in a righteous war but a sworn opponent of strong drink, gambling, and dueling.

CHECKING IN

- Southern politics became more democratic.
- White southerners, even those who owned no slaves, united in support of slavery.
- The defense of slavery as a "positive good" emerged after 1830.
- White "gentlemen" had an exaggerated sense of honor, which often led to duels.
- Southern evangelicals became supporters of existing systems, including slavery.

LIFE UNDER SLAVERY

How did slaves and free blacks respond to their circumstances?

Slavery, the institution at the root of the code of honor and other distinctive features of the Old South, has long inspired controversy among historians. Some have seen slavery as a benevolent institution in which African-Americans lived contentedly under kindly masters; others, as a brutal system that drove slaves into constant rebellion. Neither view is accurate, but both contain a germ of truth. There were kind masters, and some slaves developed genuine affection for their owners. Yet slavery inherently oppressed its African-American victims by forcibly appropriating their life and labor. Even kind masters exploited blacks in order to earn profits. And kindness was a double-edged sword; the benevolent master expected grateful affection from his slaves and interpreted that affection as loyalty to slavery itself. When northern troops descended on the plantations during the Civil War, masters were genuinely surprised and dismayed to find many of their most trusted slaves deserting to Union lines.

The kindness or cruelty of masters was important, but three other factors primarily determined slaves' experience: the kind of agriculture in which they worked, whether they resided in rural or urban areas, and what century they lived in. The experiences of slaves working on cotton plantations in the 1830s differed radically from those of slaves in 1700, for reasons unrelated to the kindness or brutality of masters.

The Maturing of the Plantation System

Slavery changed significantly between 1700 and 1830. In 1700, the typical slave was a man in his twenties, recently arrived from Africa or the Caribbean, who worked on an isolated small farm. Drawn from different regions of Africa, few slaves spoke the same language. Because slave ships carried twice as many men as women, and because slaves were widely scattered, blacks had difficulties finding partners and creating a semblance of family life. Severe malnutrition sharply limited the number of children slave women bore. Without continuing importations, the number of slaves in North America would have declined between 1710 and 1730.

Collection of the New-York Historical Society

Black Women and Men on a Trek Home, South Carolina
Here African-American women loaded down with cotton join their men on the march home after a day in the fields.

In contrast, by 1830 the typical North American slave was as likely to be female as male, had been born in America, spoke English, and worked beside numerous other slaves on a plantation. The rise of plantation agriculture in the eighteenth century was at the heart of the change. Plantation slaves found mates more easily than slaves on scattered farms. The ratio between slave men and women fell into balance, and marriage between slaves on the same or nearby plantations increased. The native-born slave population soared after 1750. The importation of African slaves declined, and in 1808 Congress banned it.

Work and Discipline of Plantation Slaves

In 1850, the typical slave worked on a large farm or plantation with at least ten fellow bond servants. Almost three-quarters of all slaves that year were owned by masters with ten or more slaves, and slightly over one-half lived in units of twenty or more slaves. In smaller units, slaves usually worked under the task system. Each slave had a daily or weekly quota of tasks to complete. On large cotton and sugar plantations, slaves would occasionally work under the task system; however, more closely supervised and regimented gang labor prevailed.

An hour before sunrise, a horn or bell awakened the slaves. After a sparse breakfast, they marched to the fields, where slave men and women worked side by side. Those female slaves who did not labor in the fields remained busy. A former slave, John Curry, described how his mother milked cows, cared for children whose mothers worked in the fields, cooked for field hands, washed and ironed for her master's household, and looked after her own seven children. Plantations never lacked tasks for slaves of either gender, and in any season the slave's day stretched from dawn to dusk. When darkness made fieldwork impossible, slaves toted cotton bales to the ginhouse, gathered wood for supper fires, and fed the mules. Weary from their labors, they slept in log cabins on wooden planks.

Although virtually all antebellum Americans worked long hours, no others experienced the combination of long hours and harsh discipline that slave field hands endured. Northern factory workers did not live in fear of drivers walking among them with a whip. Repulsive brutality pervaded American slavery. For example, pregnant slave women were sometimes forced to lie in depressions in the ground and endure whipping on their backs, a practice that supposedly protected the fetus while abusing the mother. Masters often delegated discipline and punishment to white overseers and black drivers. The barbaric discipline meted out by others twinged the conscience of many masters, but most justified it as their Christian duty to ensure the slaves' proper "submissiveness."

Despite the system's brutality, some slaves advanced—not to freedom but to semiskilled or skilled indoor work. Some became blacksmiths, carpenters, or gin operators, and others served as cooks, butlers, and dining room attendants. These house slaves became legendary for their disdain of field hands and poor whites. Slave artisans and house slaves generally enjoyed higher status than the field hands.

The Slave Family

Masters thought of slaves as naturally promiscuous and flattered themselves into thinking that they alone held slave marriages together. Masters had powerful incentives to encourage slave marriages: bringing new slaves into the world and discouraging slaves from running away. Some masters baked wedding cakes for slaves and even arbitrated marital disputes. Still, the keenest challenge to the slave family came not from the slaves themselves but from slavery. The law did not recognize or protect slave families. Although some slaveholders were reluctant to break apart slave marriages by sale, economic hardships might force their hand. The reality, one historian calculated, was that in a lifetime, on average, a slave would witness the sale of eleven family members.

Inevitably, the commonplace buying and selling of slaves disrupted attempts to create a stable family life. Poignant testimony to the effects of sale on slave families appeared in advertisements for runaway slaves. An 1851 North Carolina advertisement said that a particular fugitive was probably "lurking in the neighborhood of E. D. Walker's, at Moore's Creek, who owns most of his relatives, or Nathan Bonham's who owns his mother; or perhaps, near Fletcher Bell's, at Long Creek, who owns his father." Small wonder that a slave preacher pronounced a couple married "until death or *distance* do you part."

Other factors disrupted slave marriages. The marriage of a slave woman did not protect her against the sexual demands of her master or, indeed, of any white person. Slave children of white masters sometimes became targets for the wrath of white mistresses. Field work kept slave mothers from their children, who were cared for by the elderly or by the mothers of other children.

Despite these enormous obstacles, relationships within slave families were often intimate and, where possible, long lasting. Lacking legal protection, slaves developed their own standards of family morality. A southern white woman observed that slaves "did not consider it wrong for a girl to have a child before she married, but afterwards were extremely severe upon anything like infidelity on her part." Given the opportunity, slaves solemnized their marriages before members of the clergy. White clergymen who accompanied Union armies into Mississippi and Louisiana

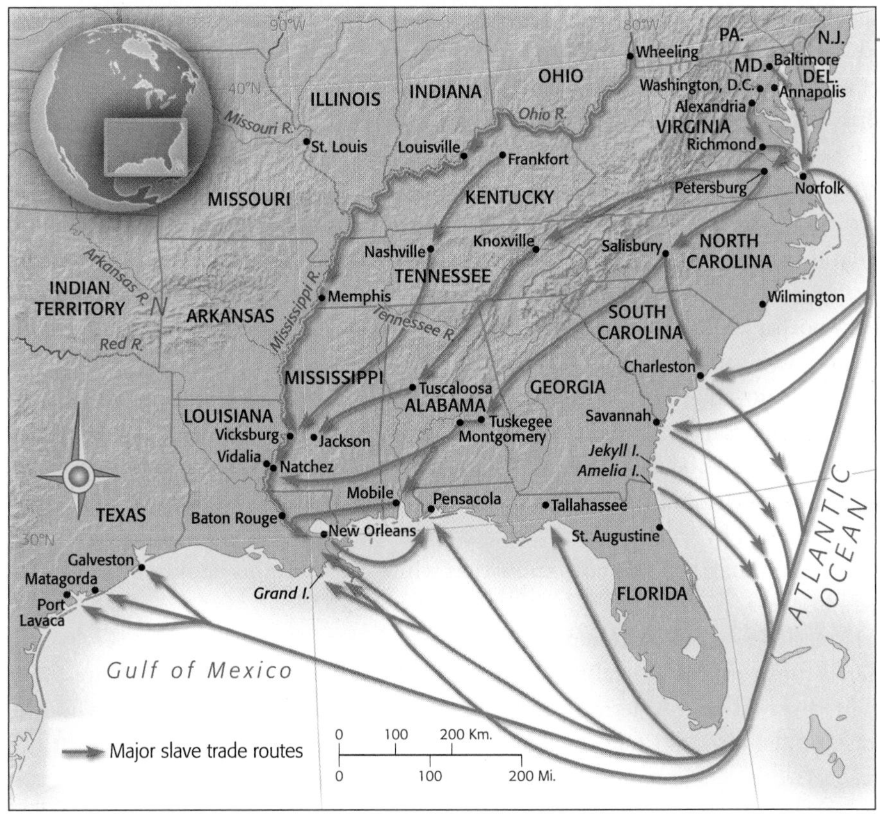

Map 12.2 Internal Slave Trade, 1810–1860

An internal slave trade developed after the slave trade with Africa ended in 1808. With the growth of cotton production, farmers in the Upper South found it profitable to sell their slaves to planters in the Lower South.

Interactive Map

during the Civil War conducted thousands of marriage rites for slaves who had long viewed themselves as married and desired a formal ceremony and registration.

On balance, slave families differed profoundly from white families. Many planters divided their holdings into several farms and distributed slaves among them without regard to marriage ties. Conditions on small farms and new plantations discouraged the formation of families. Spouses were always vulnerable to being sold.

Broad kinship patterns—close ties between children and grandparents, aunts, and uncles, as well as parents—had marked West African cultures, and they were reinforced by the separation of children and parents that routinely occurred under slavery. Frederick Douglass never knew his father and saw his mother rarely, but he vividly remembered his grandmother. In addition, slaves often created "fictive" kin networks, naming friends as their uncles, aunts, brothers, or sisters. In this way they helped to protect themselves against the disruption of family ties and established a broader community of obligation. When plantation slaves greeted each other as "brother," they were making a statement not about actual kinship, but about obligations to each other.

The Longevity, Health, and Diet of Slaves

Of the 10 million to 12 million Africans imported to the New World between the fifteenth and nineteenth centuries, North America received only 550,000 of them (about 5 percent), whereas Brazil received 3.5 million (nearly 33 percent). Yet by 1825, 36 percent of all slaves in the Western Hemisphere lived in the United States, and only 31 percent in Brazil. The reason for this difference is that slaves in the United States reproduced faster and lived longer than those in Brazil and elsewhere in the Western Hemisphere.

Several factors account for U.S. slaves' longer lives and higher rates of reproduction. First, with the gender ratio among slaves equalizing more rapidly in North America, slaves there married earlier and had more children. Second, because raising corn and livestock was compatible with growing cotton, the Old South produced plentiful food. Slaves generally received a peck of cornmeal and three to four pounds of fatty pork a week, which they often supplemented with vegetables grown on small plots and with catfish and game.

Slaves enjoyed greater immunity from malaria and yellow fever than whites but suffered more from cholera, dysentery, and diarrhea. Lacking privies, slaves usually relieved themselves behind bushes; consequently, urine and feces contaminated the sources of their drinking water. Slave remedies for stomach ailments, although commonly ridiculed by whites, often worked. For example, slaves ate white clay to cure dysentery and diarrhea. We now know that white clay contains kaolin, a remedy for these disorders.

Nonetheless, slaves suffered a higher mortality rate than whites. The very young suffered most; infant mortality among slaves was double that among whites, and one in three African-American children died before age ten. Plantations in the disease-ridden lowlands had the worst overall mortality rates, but even in healthier areas overworked field hands often miscarried or bore weakened infants.

Away from the Plantation: Slaves in Town and Free Blacks

Greater freedom from supervision and greater opportunities awaited slaves who worked off plantations in towns and cities. Most southern whites succumbed to the lure of cotton and established small farms; the resulting shortage of white labor created a steady demand for slaves outside the plantation economy. Driving wagons, working as stevedores on the docks, manning river barges, and toiling in mining and lumbering gave slaves an opportunity to work somewhere other than the cotton fields. Other African-Americans served as engineers for sawmills or artisans for ironworks. African-American women and children constituted the main labor force for the South's fledgling textile industry.

The draining of potential white laborers from southern cities also provided the opportunity for slaves to become skilled artisans. Slave or free, blacks found it easier to pursue skilled occupations in southern cities than in northern ones, where immigrant laborers competed with blacks for work.

Despite slavery's stranglehold, urban African-Americans in the South enjoyed opportunities denied to their counterparts in the North. Generally, slaves who worked in factories, mining, or lumbering were hired out by their masters rather than owned by their employers. If working conditions for hired-out slaves deteriorated badly, masters would refuse to provide employers with more slaves. Consequently, working conditions for slaves off the plantation generally stayed at a tolerable level.

Even more likely than southern blacks in general to live in cities were free blacks. In 1860, one-third of the free blacks in the Upper South and more than half in the

Lower South were urban. The relatively specialized economies of the cities provided free people of color with opportunities to become carpenters, barrel makers, barbers, and even small traders. Most of the meat, fish, and produce in an antebellum southern market was prepared for sale by free blacks. Urban free blacks formed their own fraternal orders and churches; in New Orleans free blacks also had their own opera and literary journals. In Natchez, a free black barber, William Tiler Johnson, invested the profits of his shop in real estate, rented it out, bought slaves and a plantation, and hired a white overseer.

As Johnson's career suggests, some free blacks were highly successful. They continued to increase in absolute numbers (a little more than 250,000 free people of color lived in the South in 1860), but the rate of growth of the free black population slowed radically after 1810. Fewer masters freed their slaves after that time, and following the Nat Turner rebellion in 1831, states legally restricted the liberties of free blacks. By the mid-1830s most southern states made it a felony to teach blacks to read and write. Every southern state forbade free blacks to enter, and in 1859, Arkansas ordered all free blacks to leave.

Although a free-black culture flourished in certain cities, that culture did not reflect the conditions under which the majority of blacks lived. Most free blacks dwelled in rural areas, where whites lumped them together with slaves, and a much higher percentage of blacks were free in the Upper South than in the Lower South.

Many free blacks were mulattos, the product of white masters and black women, and looked down on "darky" field hands and laborers. But as discrimination against free people of color intensified during the late antebellum period, many free blacks realized that whatever future they had was as blacks, not whites. Feelings of racial solidarity increased during the 1850s, and after the Civil War, the leaders of the ex-slaves were usually blacks who had been free before the war.

Slave Resistance

Ever-present fears of slave insurrection haunted the Old South. In the delta areas of the Lower South where blacks outnumbered whites, slaves experienced continuous forced labor on plantations. In the cities, free blacks could have provided leadership for rebellions. Rumors of slave conspiracies flew within the southern white community, and all whites knew of the massive black revolt that had destroyed French rule in Saint-Domingue.

Yet Nat Turner's revolt remained the only slave rebellion that actually resulted in white deaths. Most slave rebellions were conspiracies that never materialized. For example, in 1800 a Virginia slave named Gabriel Prosser plotted an uprising but was betrayed by other slaves and executed. In 1822, **Denmark Vesey** (VEE-see) and his followers planned to attack Charleston, South Carolina, and seize the city's arms and ammunition, but other slaves informed the authorities, and the conspirators were executed.

Denmark Vesey Free black who planned a slave uprising in 1822; conspiracy was thwarted and Vesey executed

The Old South experienced far fewer rebellions than the Caribbean region or South America. Several factors explain this apparent tranquility. First, although slaves formed a majority in South Carolina and a few other areas, they did not constitute a *large* majority in any state. Second, unlike Caribbean slave owners, most southern masters lived on their plantations; they possessed armed force and were willing to use it. Third, family ties among U.S. slaves made them reluctant to risk death and thereby to orphan their children. Finally, slaves who ran away or plotted rebellion had no allies. Southern Indians routinely captured runaway slaves and claimed rewards for them; some Indians even owned slaves.

Unable to rebel, many slaves tried to escape to freedom in the North. Some light mulattos who passed as whites succeeded. More often, however, slaves borrowed, stole, or forged passes from plantations or obtained papers describing them as free. For example, Frederick Douglass borrowed a sailor's papers to make his escape from Baltimore to New York City. Some former slaves, including Harriet Tubman and Josiah Henson, returned to the South to help others escape. Despite legends of an "underground railroad" of abolitionists helping slaves to freedom, fugitive slaves owed little to abolitionists. The "safe houses" of white sympathizers in border states were better known to slave catchers than to runaways.

Escape to freedom was a dream rather than a realistic alternative for most blacks. Out of millions of slaves, probably fewer than a thousand actually escaped to the North. Often, slaves ran away from masters not to escape to freedom but to visit spouses or avoid punishment. Most runaways remained in the South; some sought only to return to kinder former masters. During the eighteenth century, African slaves had often run away in groups and tried to create the sort of villages they had known in Africa. But the American acquisition of Florida deprived potential runaways of their major haven, leaving them few uninhabited places to which they could flee.

Despite poor prospects for permanent escape, slaves could disappear for prolonged periods into the free-black communities of southern cities. Slaves enjoyed a fair degree of practical freedom to drive wagons to market and to come and go when they were off plantations. Slaves sent to a city might overstay their leave and pass themselves off as free. This kind of practical freedom did not change slavery's underlying oppressiveness, but it did give slaves a sense of having certain rights, and it helped to channel slave resistance into activities that were furtive and relatively harmless, rather than open and violent. Theft, for example, was so common that planters kept tools, smokehouses, and closets under lock and key. Overworked field hands might leave tools out to rust, feign illness, or simply refuse to work. Slaves could not be fired for such malingering or negligence. And Frederick Law Olmsted even found masters afraid to punish a slave "lest [he or she] should abscond, or take a sulky fit and not work, or poison some of the family, or set fire to the dwelling, or have recourse to any other mode of avenging himself."

Olmsted's reference to arson and poisoning is a reminder that not all furtive resistance was peaceful. Arson and poisoning, both common forms of vengeance in African culture, flourished in the Old South. So did fear. Masters afflicted by dysentery never knew for sure that they had not been poisoned.

Arson, poisoning, theft, work stoppage, and negligence acted as alternatives to violent rebellion, but their goal was not freedom. Their object was merely to make slavery bearable. Most slaves would have preferred freedom but settled for less. "White folks do as they please," an ex-slave said, "and the darkies do as they can."

CHECKING IN

- Plantation field hands often labored under brutal conditions, whereas "house slaves" fared better.
- Nuclear slave families were precarious, but the slave culture of extended families offset this to some extent.
- Although slaves in the United States generally lived longer than slaves elsewhere in the Western Hemisphere, the mortality rate of slave children under the age of ten was 35 percent.
- Free blacks had opportunities but also faced stifling restrictions.
- Although the Nat Turner rebellion was a notable exception, slave resistance generally was subtle, furtive, and widespread.

THE EMERGENCE OF AFRICAN-AMERICAN CULTURE

What were the distinctive features of African-American society and culture in the South?

Enslaved blacks combined elements of African and American cultures to create a distinctive culture of their own, giving a distinctive twist to both the African and American components of slave culture.

The Language of Slaves

Before slaves could develop a common culture, they needed a common language. During the colonial period, African-born slaves, speaking a variety of languages, had developed a **"pidgin"** (PID-jin)—that is, a language that has no native speakers but in which people with different native languages can communicate. Many African-born slaves spoke English pidgin poorly, but their American-born descendants used it as their primary language.

"pidgin" Common language spoken by slaves who spoke many different tongues

Like all pidgins, English pidgin was a simplified language. Slaves often dropped the verb *to be* (which had no equivalent in African tongues) and ignored or confused genders. Instead of saying "Mary is in the cabin," they typically said, "Mary, he in cabin." They substituted *no* for *not,* as in "He no wicked." Some African words, among them *banjo,* moved from pidgin to standard English, and others, such as *goober* ("peanut"), entered southern white slang. Although many whites ridiculed pidgin and black house servants struggled to speak standard English, pidgin proved indispensable for communication among slaves.

African-American Religion

Religion played an equally important role in forging an African-American culture. Africa contained rich and diverse religious customs and beliefs. Despite the presence of a few Muslims and Christians in the early slave population, most of the slaves brought from Africa followed one of many native African religions. Most of these religions drew little distinction between the spiritual and natural worlds—storms, illnesses, and earthquakes were all assumed to stem from supernatural forces.

For these reasons, African religions did not unify blacks in America. Yet remnants of African religion remained. Dimly remembered African beliefs such as the reverence for water may have predisposed slaves to accept Christianity when they were finally urged to do so, because water has a symbolic significance for Christians, too, in the sacrament of baptism. Evangelical Christianity also resembled African religions in that it also drew few distinctions between the sacred and the secular. Just as Africans believed that droughts and plagues resulted from supernatural forces, the early revivalists knew in their hearts that every drunkard who fell off his horse and every Sabbath-breaker struck by lightning had experienced a deliberate and direct punishment from God.

By the 1790s, African-Americans formed about one-quarter of the membership of the Methodist and Baptist denominations. The fact that converted slaves played significant roles in the South's three slave rebellions reinforced whites' fears that a

Slave Handicraft

These two musical instruments, a banjo and a gourd fiddle, were made by slaves in Virginia.

Christian slave would be a rebellious slave. These slave uprisings, especially the Nat Turner rebellion, spurred Protestant missionaries to intensify their efforts among slaves. They pointed to the self-taught Turner as proof that slaves could learn about Christianity and claimed that only organized efforts at conversion would ensure that the slaves were taught correct versions of Christianity.

The experiences of Christianized blacks in the Old South illustrate the contradictions of life under slavery. Urban blacks often had their own churches, but rural blacks and slaves worshipped in the same churches as whites. Although African-Americans sat in segregated sections, they heard the same service as whites. Churches became the most interracial institutions in the Old South, and biracial churches sometimes disciplined whites for abusing black Christian members. But Christianity was not a route to black liberation. Ministers went out of their way to remind slaves that spiritual equality was not the same as civil equality.

However, slaves listening to the same sermons as whites often came to different conclusions. For example, slaves drew parallels between their captivity and that of the Jews, the Chosen People. Like the Jews, slaves concluded, they were "de people of de Lord." If they kept the faith, they would reach the Promised Land.

A listener could interpret a phrase like "the Promised Land" in several ways; it could refer to Israel, to heaven, or to freedom. From the perspective of whites, the only permissible interpretations were Israel and heaven, but some blacks, like Denmark Vesey, thought of freedom as well. Many plantations had black preachers, slaves trained by white ministers to spread Christianity among blacks. In the presence of masters or ministers, African-American preachers repeated the familiar biblical command "Obey your master." Often, however, slaves met for services apart from whites, and then the message changed.

Some slaves privately interpreted Christianity as a religion of liberation, but most recognized that their prospects for freedom were slight. Generally, Christianity neither turned blacks into revolutionaries nor made them model slaves. It did, however, provide slaves with a view of slavery different from their masters' outlook. Masters argued that slavery was a benign and divinely ordained institution, but Christianity told slaves that the institution was an affliction, a terrible and unjust system that God had allowed in order to test their faith. For having endured slavery, he would reward slaves. For having created it, he would punish masters.

Black Music and Dance

African-American culture expressed blacks' feelings. Long after white rituals had grown sober and sedate, the congregation in African-American religious services shouted

"Amen" and let their body movements reflect their feelings. Slaves also expressed their emotions in music and dance. Southern law forbade them to own "drums, horns, or other loud instruments, which may call together or give sign or notice to one another of their wicked designs and intentions." Instead, slaves made rhythmic clapping, called "patting juba" (JOO-buh), an indispensable accompaniment to dancing. Slaves also played an African instrument, the banjo, and beat tin buckets as substitutes for drums. Slave music was tied to bodily movement; slaves expressed themselves in a dance that was African in origin, emphasizing shuffling steps and bodily contortions rather than quick footwork and erect backs as in whites' dances.

spiritual Slave religious song that stressed liberation from difficult situations

Whether at work or prayer, slaves liked to sing. Work songs usually consisted of a leader's chant and a choral response. Masters encouraged such songs, believing that singing induced slaves to work harder and that the innocent content of work songs proved that slaves were happy. However, Frederick Douglass, recalling his own past, observed that "slaves sing most when they are most unhappy. The songs of the slave represent the sorrows of his heart; and he is relieved by them, only as an aching heart is relieved by its tears."

Blacks also sang religious songs, later known as **spirituals,** which reflected the powerful emphasis that slave religion placed on deliverance from earthly travails. Whites took a dim view of spirituals and tried to make slaves sing "good psalms and hymns" instead of "the extravagant and nonsensical chants, and catches, and hallelujah songs of their own composing." But enslaved blacks clung to their spirituals, drawing hope from them that "we will soon be free, when the Lord will call us home," as one spiritual promised.

CHECKING IN

- Slaves developed "pidgin" as a way of communicating.
- After 1800 most slaves were Christian.
- Masters tried to use Christianity to encourage submissiveness, but slaves saw it as a faith that promised rewards for them and punishment for their masters.
- Slave music and dance incorporated many African elements.
- Spirituals reflected the slaves' desire for deliverance.

Chapter Summary

How did the rise of cotton cultivation affect the South? (page 266)

By the 1830s cotton production dominated the South, and southerners spoke proudly of "King Cotton." Although it brought great prosperity, the cotton economy also slowed down the development of industry and education. And it made slavery seem more vital than ever.

What major social divisions segmented the white South? (page 271)

Geography and economics divided white southerners into four distinct groups: plantation owners, small slave owners, yeomen, and the people of the pine barrens. Yeomen, the largest group, generally owned no slaves, nor did the people of the pine barrens.

KEY TERMS

Nat Turner *(p. 265)*
Upper South *(p. 266)*
Lower (Deep) South *(p. 266)*
King Cotton *(p. 267)*
plantation *(p. 268)*
yeoman *(p. 272)*
positive good *(p. 275)*
dueling *(p. 277)*
Denmark Vesey *(p. 283)*
"pidgin" *(p. 285)*
spiritual *(p. 287)*

How did slavery affect social relations in the South? (page 274)

Whites, although divided politically, were united in defense of slavery, which gave all whites an automatically superior position. They defended slavery as a "positive good," and southern churches became supporters and defenders of slavery as well.

How did slaves and free blacks respond to their circumstances? (page 278)

Field hands labored under harsh conditions. Nuclear families were always threatened, but the tradition of extended families somewhat offset this. Free blacks faced a life bounded by severe restrictions. Rebellion against slavery, despite the spectacular example of Nat Turner, was usually subtle, emerging in the form of pretended illness, carelessness, or feigned stupidity.

What were the distinctive features of African-American society and culture in the South? (page 285)

Whites tried to use Christianity to preach submission and obedience, but slaves saw it as a faith of hope and liberation. Slave music and dance frequently incorporated African elements, and spirituals expressed the slave desire for deliverance.

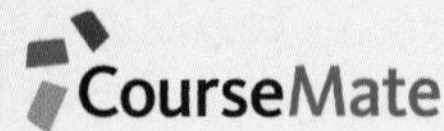

Go to the CourseMate website at **www.cengagebrain.com** for additional study tools and review materials—including audio and video clips—for this chapter.

Chapter 13

Immigration, Expansion, and Sectional Conflict

1840–1848

Unknown maker, American. Gold Miners with Sluice, ca 1850 Nelson-Atkins Museum of Art, Kansas City, Missouri. Gift of Hallmark Cards, Inc., 2005.27.116

Gold Miners

Chapter Preview

Newcomers and Natives
How did immigration in the 1840s influence the balance of power between the Whig and Democratic parties?

The West and Beyond
What economic and political forces fed westward expansion during the 1840s?

The Politics of Expansion, 1840–1846
How did "Manifest Destiny" influence American politics?

The Mexican-American War and Its Aftermath, 1846–1848
How did the outcome of the Mexican-American War intensify intersectional conflict?

Visitors to Texas will find a thoroughfare named after José Antonio Navarro in his native San Antonio, an official Navarro Day, and Navarro County. As one of the two native Texans to have signed the state of Coahuila-Texas's Declaration of Independence from Mexico in 1836, and later a member of the Congress of the independent Republic of Texas, Navarro is justly remembered as a founder of Texas.

However, Navarro's **Tejano** identity placed him uncomfortably between two nations vying for control over Texas. Captured by Mexican troops and jailed in 1841, he was offered freedom and wealth if he would renounce his allegiance to Texas. "I will never forsake Texas and her cause," Navarro replied. "I am her son."

Tejano A native Texan of Mexican descent

Navarro escaped and returned to San Antonio, only to find that the now-dominant Anglos were forsaking people like him.

"The continuation of greasers [Mexicans] among us," a resolution drafted by Anglos in Goliad proclaimed, "is an intolerable nuisance." Navarro was starting to realize that the Texas he knew, a place where Anglos and Tejanos lived in harmony, was being swallowed by the relentless expansion of the United States. Navarro never held public office again.

"Americans regard this continent as their birthright," thundered Sam Houston, the first president of the Republic of Texas, in 1847. Indians and Mexicans had to make way for "our mighty march." This was not idle talk. In barely a thousand days during James K. Polk's administration (1845–1849), the United States expanded by 50 percent. It annexed Texas, gained half of the vast Oregon territory through negotiations with Britain, and claimed California and New Mexico after deliberately provoking war. At the same time, Brigham Young led the main body of Mormons on a trek from Illinois to the Great Salt Lake Valley, in search of a better life beyond the constraints of eastern settlements. And immigrants poured into the United States, largely from Europe.

Immigration and territorial expansion were linked, with most immigrants gravitating to the expansionist Democratic Party. The immigrant vote helped tip the election of 1844 to Polk, an ardent expansionist. But tensions flared between immigrants and the native-born. Influential Democrats concluded that the best solution to intensifying class and ethnic conflicts lay in expanding the national boundaries, bringing more land under cultivation, and recapturing the ideal of America as a nation of self-sufficient farmers.

Democrats also saw expansion as a way to reduce strife between the sections. Oregon would gratify the North; Texas, the South; and California, everyone. In reality, expansion brought sectional antagonisms to the boiling point, split the Democratic Party in the late 1840s, and set the nation on the path to Civil War.

NEWCOMERS AND NATIVES

How did immigration in the 1840s influence the balance of power between the Whig and Democratic parties?

Between 1815 and 1860, 5 million European immigrants reached the United States. Of these, 4.2 million arrived between 1840 and 1860, and 3 million crowded in from 1845 to 1854 alone, the largest immigration relative to population in U.S. history. The Irish and the Germans dominated this wave of newcomers; by 1860 three-fourths of foreign-born Americans were Irish or German (see Figure 13.1).

Expectations and Realities

Although a desire for religious freedom drew some immigrants to U.S. shores, hopes of economic betterment lured the majority. Travelers' accounts and relatives' letters assured Europeans that America was an ideal world, a utopia. Yet, typically, immigrants faced hard times.

Their problems began at ports of embarkation. Because ships sailed irregularly, many spent precious savings in waterfront slums while awaiting departure. Squalid

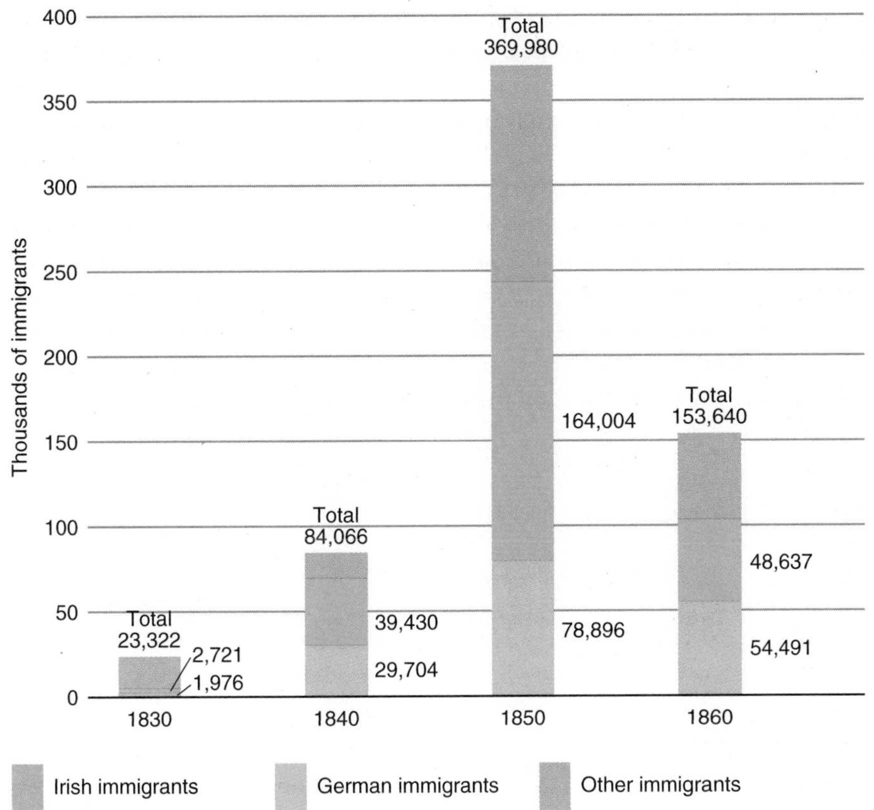

Figure 13.1 German, Irish, and Total Immigration, 1830–1860

Irish and German immigrants led the more than tenfold growth of immigration between 1830 and 1860.

Source: U.S. Bureau of the Census, Historical Statistics of the United States, Colonial Times to 1970, *Bicentennial Edition I (Washington, DC, 1975)*

cargo ships carried most of the emigrants, who endured quarters almost as crowded as on slave ships.

For many, the greatest shock came after landing. Immigrants quickly discovered that farming in America was a perilous prospect, radically different from what they had known in Europe. Unlike the compact farming communities of Europe, American agricultural areas featured scattered farms, and Americans' individualism led them to speculate in land and to move frequently.

Clear patterns emerged amid the shocks and dislocations of immigration. For example, most Irish immigrants lacked the capital to purchase land and consequently crowded into urban areas of New England, New York, New Jersey, and Pennsylvania, where they could find jobs. German immigrants often arrived at southern ports, but slavery, climate, and lack of economic opportunity gradually drove them north to settle in Illinois, Ohio, Wisconsin, and Missouri.

Cities, rather than farms, attracted most antebellum immigrants. By 1860, **German and Irish immigrants** formed more than 60 percent of the population of St. Louis and nearly half the population of New York City, Chicago, Cincinnati, Milwaukee, Detroit, and San Francisco. These fast-growing cities needed people with strong backs who were willing to work for low wages. In addition to jobs, cities provided immigrants with the community life lacking in farming areas.

German and Irish immigrants Largest contingents of migrants seeking opportunity in the United States before 1860

Chronology

1822	Stephen F. Austin founds the first American community in Texas
1830	Mexico closes Texas to further American immigration
1835	Santa Anna invades Texas
1836	Texas declares its independence from Mexico; fall of the Alamo; Goliad massacre; Battle of San Jacinto
1840	William Henry Harrison elected president
1841	Harrison dies; John Tyler becomes president
1842	Webster-Ashburton Treaty
1844	James K. Polk elected president
1845	Congress votes by joint resolution to annex Texas; Mexico rejects Slidell mission
1846	The United States declares war on Mexico; John C. Frémont proclaims the Bear Flag Republic in California; Congress votes to accept a settlement of the Oregon boundary issue with Britain; Tariff of 1846; Wilmot Proviso introduced
1847	Mexico City falls to Scott; Lewis Cass's principle of "squatter sovereignty"
1848	Gold discovered in California; Treaty of Guadalupe-Hidalgo signed; Zachary Taylor elected president

The Germans

In 1860, there was no German nation, only a collection of principalities and small kingdoms. Immigrants from this area thought of themselves as Bavarians, Westphalians, or Saxons, rather than Germans.

German immigrants spanned a wide spectrum of class and occupation. Most were farmers, but professionals, artisans, and tradespeople made up a sizable minority. For example, Levi Strauss, a Jewish tailor from Bavaria, reached the United States in 1847. When gold was discovered in California the next year, Strauss gathered rolls of cloth and sailed for San Francisco. There he fashioned tough work overalls from canvas. Demand soared, and Strauss opened a factory to produce his cheap overalls, later known as blue jeans or Levi's.

A common language transcended the differences among German immigrants and bound them together. They clustered in the same neighborhoods, formed their own militia and fire companies, and established German-language parochial schools and newspapers. The diversity of the German-speaking population further fostered solidarity. Because Germans supplied their own lawyers, doctors, teachers, and merchants from their midst, they had no need to go outside their neighborhoods. Native-born Americans simultaneously admired German industriousness and resented German self-sufficiency, which they interpreted as clannishness. The Germans responded by becoming even more clannish. Their separateness made it difficult for the Germans to be as politically influential as the Irish immigrants.

The Irish

There were three waves of Irish immigration. Between 1815 and the mid-1820s, most Irish immigrants were Protestants, small landowners, and tradespeople drawn by enthusiastic veterans of the War of 1812 who reported that America was a paradise where "all a man needed was a gun and sufficient ammunition to be able to live like a prince." From the mid-1820s to the mid-1840s, Irish immigration became both more Catholic and poorer, comprised primarily of tenant farmers evicted by Protestant landlords. Rich or poor, Protestant or Catholic, nearly a million Irish crossed the Atlantic to the United States between 1815 and 1845.

Then, between 1845 and the early 1850s, the character of Irish immigration changed dramatically. In Ireland, blight destroyed harvest after harvest of potatoes, virtually the only food of the peasantry, and triggered one of the most gruesome famines in history. The Great Famine killed a million people. Those who survived, a landlord wrote, were "famished and ghastly skeletons." To escape suffering and death, 1.8 million Irish emigrated to the United States in the decade after 1845.

Overwhelmingly poor and Catholic, these newest Irish immigrants entered the work force at the bottom. While Irish men dug streets, canals, and railroads, Irish women worked as maids and textile workers. Poverty drove women to work at early ages, and the outdoor, all-season labor performed by their husbands turned many of them into working widows. Because the Irish usually married late, almost half the Irish immigrants were single adult women, many of whom never married.

It sometimes seemed that, no matter what the Irish did, they clashed with other Americans. The poorer Irish who dug canals, took in laundry, or worked as domestics competed with equally poor free blacks. This competition stirred up Irish animosity toward blacks and a hatred of abolitionists. At the same time, the Irish who secured skilled or semiskilled jobs clashed with native-born white workers.

Anti-Catholicism, Nativism, and Labor Protest

The surge of Irish immigration revived anti-Catholic fever, long a latent impulse among American Protestants. A groundswell of anti-Catholic publications climaxed in 1836 with Maria Monk's best-selling *Awful Disclosures of the Hotel Dieu Nunnery in Montreal,* which vividly described wild sexual relations between nuns and priests. Although she claimed to be a former nun, Maria Monk was actually a former prostitute.

The surge of Catholic immigration in the 1840s also had political ramifications fueled by **nativism.** Protestants formed anti-immigrant societies with names like the American Republicans and the United Order of Americans. One such secret society, the Order of the Star-Spangled Banner, would become the **"Know-Nothing" party,** or American Party, which was a major political force in the 1850s. In the 1840s, nativist parties prospered during flare-ups over local issues, such as whether the Protestant or Catholic version of the Bible should be used in predominantly Catholic schools. In 1844, for example, the "Bible Riots" in Philadelphia, spurred on by the electoral success of American Republican Party candidates, led to the deaths of sixteen people and the destruction of thirty buildings at the hands of Protestant mobs.

nativism Reaction against immigrants of different ethnic and/or religious backgrounds

"Know-Nothing" party Also "Order of the Star-Spangled Banner" or American Party; expression of nativism

Nativism fed on an explosive mixture of fears and discontents. Protestants thought that their doctrine that each individual could interpret the Bible was more democratic than Catholicism, which made doctrine the province of the pope and bishops. In addition, at a time when the wages of native-born artisans and journeymen were depressed in the aftermath of the Panic of 1837 (see Chapter 10), many Protestant workers concluded that poor Catholic immigrants were threats to their jobs.

Many Irish immigrants, refugees from an agricultural society, believed that they could gain more through unions and strikes than through farming. Even women workers organized unions in these years; the leader of a seamstresses' union proclaimed, "Too long have we been bound down by tyrant employers."

Probably the most important development for workers in the 1840s was a state court decision. In *Commonwealth v. Hunt* (1842), the Massachusetts Supreme Court ruled that labor unions were not illegal monopolies that restrained trade. However, because less than 1 percent of the work force at that time belonged to a union, their impact was sharply limited. Thus, Massachusetts employers easily brushed aside the *Commonwealth* decision, firing union agitators and replacing them with cheap immigrant labor.

Ethnic and religious tensions also split the antebellum working class during the 1830s and 1840s. Friction between native-born and immigrant workers inevitably became intertwined with the political divisions of the second party system.

Immigrant Politics

Few immigrants had voted before reaching America, and even fewer had fled political persecution. Political upheavals had erupted in Austria and some German states in the turbulent year of 1848, but among the million German immigrants to the United States, only about 10,000 were political refugees, or "Forty-Eighters."

Once settled in the United States, however, many immigrants became politically active. They discovered that urban political organizations could help them find housing and jobs—in return for votes. Both the Irish and the Germans identified overwhelmingly with the Democratic Party. By 1820, the Irish controlled Tammany Hall, the New York City Democratic organization; Germans became staunch Democrats in cities like Milwaukee and St. Louis.

Immigrants' fears about jobs partly explained their widespread Democratic support. Former president Andrew Jackson had given the Democratic Party an antiaristocratic coloration, making the Democrats seem more sympathetic than the Whigs to the common people. In addition, antislavery was linked to the Whig party, and the Irish loathed abolitionism because they feared that freed slaves would become their economic competitors. Moreover, the Whigs' moral and religious values seemed to threaten those of the Irish and Germans. Hearty-drinking Irish and German immigrants shunned temperance-crusading Whigs, many of whom were also rabid anti-Catholics. Even public-school reform, championed by the Whigs, was perceived as a menace to the Catholicism of Irish children and as a threat to the integrity of German language and culture.

Although liquor regulations and school laws were city or state concerns rather than federal responsibilities, the Democratic Party schooled immigrants in broad, national principles. It taught them to venerate George Washington and Thomas Jefferson, and to view "monied capitalists" as parasites who would tremble when the people spoke. It introduced immigrants to Democratic newspapers, Democratic picnics, and Democratic parades. The Democrats helped give immigrants a sense of themselves as Americans.

CHECKING IN

- Immigrants often found American realities far less attractive than their utopian dreams.
- German immigrants tended to cluster together, cutting off their access to political power.
- Irish immigrants, poor and usually Catholic, triggered an ethnic and religious backlash known as nativism.
- Immigrants often spearheaded early union movements.
- German and Irish immigrants generally became Democrats; most nativists were Whigs.

By the same token, the Democratic Party introduced immigrants to national issues. It redirected political loyalties that often had been forged on local issues into the arena of national politics. During the 1830s, the party had persuaded immigrants that national measures that were seemingly remote from their daily lives, like banking reform and the tariff, were vital to them. Now, in the 1840s, the Democrats would try to convince immigrants that national expansion likewise advanced their interests.

THE WEST AND BEYOND

What economic and political forces fed westward expansion during the 1840s?

As late as 1840, the American West meant the area between the Appalachian Mountains and the Mississippi River or just beyond. West of that lay the inhospitable Great Plains. A semiarid, treeless plateau, the Plains sustained huge buffalo herds and the nomadic Indians who lived off the buffalo. Because the Great Plains presented would-be farmers with formidable obstacles, public interest shifted toward the Far West, the fertile region beyond the Rockies.

The Far West

By the Transcontinental (or Adams-Onís) Treaty of 1819, the United States had relinquished to Spain its claims to Texas west of the Sabine River, and in return Spain renounced its claims to the Oregon country north of California. Two years later, the Mexican Revolution brought Mexico independence from Spain and possession of all North American territory claimed by Spain—Texas, California, and the southwest quadrant of the continent. In 1824 and 1825, Russia yielded its claims to Oregon south of Alaska. In 1827, the United States and Great Britain revived an earlier agreement for the joint occupation of the Oregon Territory. Texas, New Mexico, California, and Oregon stretched over an area larger than Britain, France, and Germany combined. Although this vast region should have tempted them, in the 1820s Mexico, the United States, and Britain all viewed the Far West as a remote and shadowy frontier. The American line of settlement reached only to Missouri, a 2,000-mile trek (allowing for mountains) from the West Coast.

Far Western Trade

After sailing around South America and up the Pacific coastline, early merchants established American and British outposts on the West Coast. Between the late 1790s and the 1820s, for example, Boston merchants built a thriving trade, exchanging goods from the eastern United States for western sea-otter fur, cattle, hides, and tallow (rendered from cattle fat and used for making candles and soap). The British Hudson's Bay Company developed a similar trade in Oregon and northern California. The California trade generated little friction with Mexico. Californians were as eager to buy as the traders were to sell. Traders who settled in California, like the Swiss-born John Sutter, learned to speak Spanish and became assimilated into Mexican culture.

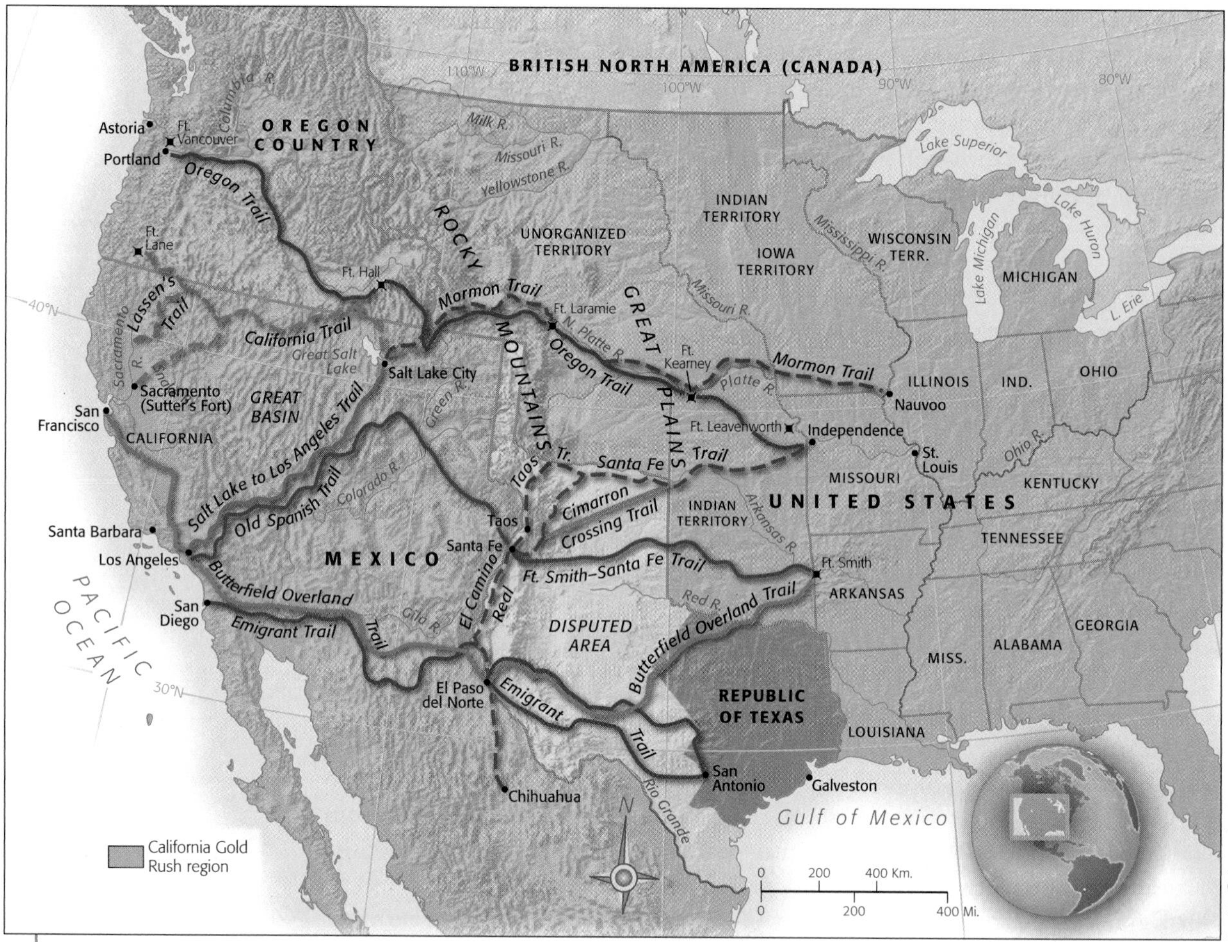

Map 13.1 Trails to the West, 1840

By 1840 several trails carried pioneers from Missouri and Illinois to the West.

 Interactive Map

Also during the 1820s, trading links developed between St. Louis and Santa Fe. Each spring, midwesterners loaded wagon trains with tools, clothing, and household sundries and rumbled westward to Santa Fe, where they traded their goods for mules and silver (see Map 13.1). Mexico welcomed this trade. By the 1830s, more than half the goods trucked west along the Santa Fe Trail trickled into the mineral-rich Mexican provinces of Chihuahua and Sonora, and were exchanged for Mexican silver pesos, which became the principal medium of exchange in Missouri.

Some Americans ventured north from Santa Fe to trap beaver in what is today western Colorado and eastern Utah. Americans from St. Louis soon found themselves competing with both the Santa Fe traders and the agents of the Hudson's Bay Company for lucrative beaver pelts. Gradually, the St. Louis traders wrested the beaver trade from their Santa Fe competitors. Although silk hats were overtaking beaver ones in popularity by 1854, more than half a million beaver pelts were auctioned off in London that year.

Although the relations between Mexicans and Americans were mutually beneficial during the 1820s, the potential for conflict was always present. Spanish-speaking,

Roman Catholic, and accustomed to a more hierarchical society, the Mexicans formed a striking contrast to the largely Protestant, individualistic Americans. Further, American traders returned with glowing reports of the climate and fertility of Mexico's northern provinces. By the 1820s, American settlers were already moving into eastern Texas. At the same time, the ties that bound the central government of Mexico to its northern frontier provinces were starting to fray.

Mexican Government in the Far West

Spain, and later Mexico, recognized that the key to controlling the frontier provinces lay in promoting their settlement by civilized Hispanic people—Spaniards, Mexicans, and Indians who had embraced Catholicism and agriculture. The key instruments of Spain's expansion on the frontier had long been the Spanish missions. Protected by forts, or presidios, the Franciscan priests who staffed the missions endeavored to convert Native Americans and settle them as farmers on mission lands. San Francisco was the site of a mission and a presidio founded in 1776, and did not develop as a town until the 1830s.

Dealt a blow by the successful struggle for Mexican independence, Spain's system of missions began to decline in the late 1820s. The Mexican government gradually "secularized" the missions by distributing their lands to ambitious government officials and private ranchers who turned the mission Indians into forced laborers. As many Native Americans fled the missions and returned to their nomadic ways, lawlessness surged on the Mexican frontier.

To bring in settlers and to gain protection against Indian attacks, in 1824 the Mexican government began to encourage Americans to settle in the eastern part of the Mexican state known as Coahuila-Texas (koh-uh-WHEEL-uh TAY-has) by bestowing generous land grants on agents known as *empresarios* (em-pre-SAR-ee-ohs) to recruit American settlers. Initially, most Americans, like the *empresario* **Stephen F. Austin,** were content to live in Texas as naturalized Mexican citizens. But trouble brewed quickly. Most of the American settlers were southern farmers, often slaveholders. Having emancipated its own slaves in 1829, Mexico closed Texas to further American immigration in 1830 and forbade the introduction of more slaves. But the Americans, white and black, kept coming, and in 1834 Austin secured repeal of the 1830 prohibition on American immigration. By 1836, Texas contained some thirty thousand white Americans, five thousand black slaves, and four thousand Mexicans.

Stephen F. Austin *Empresario* who led first Americans into Texas

As American immigration swelled, Mexican politics (which Austin compared to the country's volcanic geology) grew increasingly unstable. In 1834, Mexican president Antonio López de **Santa Anna** instituted a policy of restricting the powers of the regimes in Coahuila-Texas and other Mexican states. His actions ignited a series of rebellions in those regions, the most important of which became known as the Texas Revolution.

Santa Anna Mexican dictator who helped provoke Texas Revolution

The Texas Revolution, 1836

Santa Anna's brutality in crushing most of the rebellions alarmed the initially moderate Austin and others. When Santa Anna invaded Texas in the fall of 1835, Austin cast his lot with the more radical Americans who wanted independence.

Alamo Site of the famed defeat of Texans during the Texas Revolution

Sam Houston Military and political leader of Texas during and after the Texas Revolution

Santa Anna's army initially met with success. In February 1836, four thousand of his men laid siege to San Antonio, where two hundred rebels had retreated into an abandoned mission, the **Alamo.** On March 6—four days after Texas had declared its independence, although they did not know about it—the defenders of the Alamo were overwhelmed by Mexican troops. Under Santa Anna's orders, the Mexican army killed all the Alamo's defenders, including the wounded. A few weeks later, Mexican troops massacred some 350 prisoners taken from an American settlement at Goliad (GO-lee-add).

Meanwhile, the Texans formed an army, with **Sam Houston** at its head. A giant man who wore leopard-skin vests, Houston retreated east to pick up recruits (mostly Americans who crossed the border to fight Santa Anna). Once reinforced, Houston turned and surprised the complacent Mexicans at San Jacinto (juh-SIN-toh), just east of what is now the city of Houston. Shouting "Remember the Alamo!" Houston's army of eight hundred tore through the Mexican lines, killing nearly half of Santa Anna's men in fifteen minutes and taking Santa Anna himself prisoner. Houston then forced Santa Anna to sign a treaty (which the Mexican government never ratified) recognizing the independence of Texas (see Map 13.2).

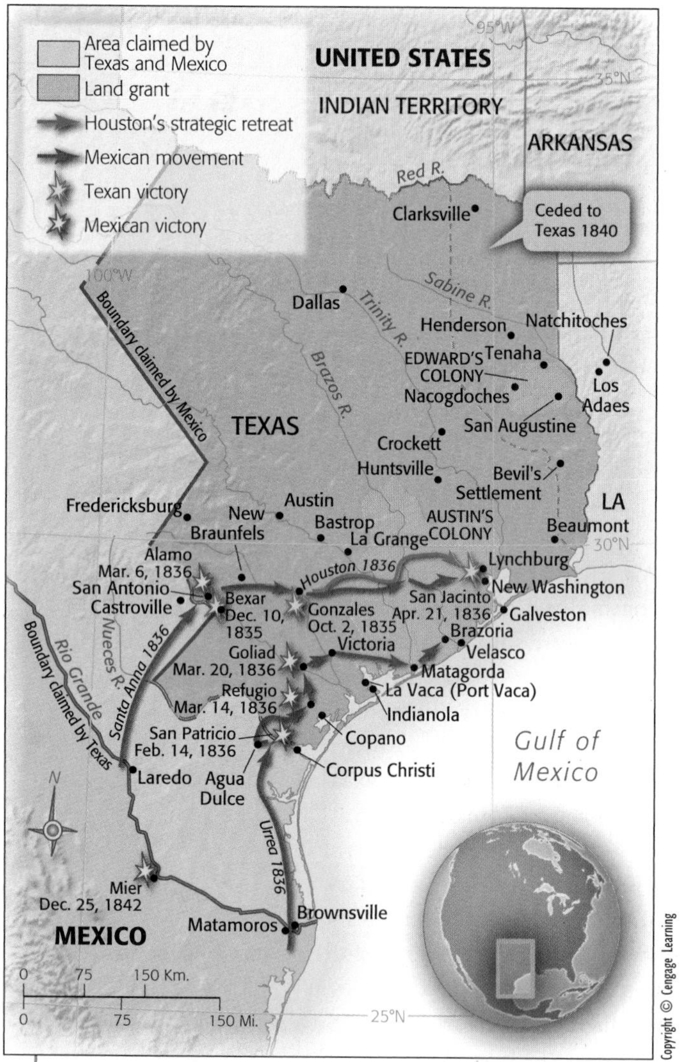

Map 13.2 Major Battles in the Texas Revolution, 1835–1836
Sam Houston's victory at San Jacinto was the decisive action of the war and avenged the massacres at the Alamo and Goliad.

Interactive Map

American Settlements in California, New Mexico, and Oregon

Before 1840, California and New Mexico, which were both less accessible than Texas, exerted no more than a mild attraction for American settlers. Only a few hundred Americans resided in New Mexico in 1840 and perhaps four hundred lived in California. A contemporary observed that the Americans living in California and New Mexico "are scattered throughout the whole Mexican population, and most of them have Spanish wives. . . . They live in every respect like the Spanish."

Yet the beginnings of change were evident. During the 1840s, Americans streamed into the Sacramento Valley, lured by favorable reports of the region and welcomed by the Hispanic population as a way to encourage economic development. To the north, Oregon's abundant farmland beckoned settlers from the Mississippi Valley. By 1840, some five hundred Americans had settled there, in what was described as a "pioneer's paradise" where "the pigs are running around under the great acorn trees, round and fat and already cooked, with knives and forks sticking in them so that you can cut off a slice whenever you are hungry."

The Huntington Library & Art Collections, San Marino, California

Crossing the River Platte
In the absence of bridges, pioneers had to bet on shallow river bottoms to cross rivers.

The Overland Trails

Whether bound for California or Oregon, Americans faced a four-month ordeal crossing terrain little known in reality but vividly depicted in fiction as an Indian killing ground. Cautious pioneers stocked up on enough guns to equip an army in jump-off towns such as Independence and St. Joseph, Missouri. In fact, they were more likely to shoot one another than to be shot by the usually cooperative Indians, and much more likely to be scalped by the inflated prices charged by merchants in Independence or "St. Joe."

overland trails Routes westward to Oregon and California followed by thousands of Americans

Once embarked, the emigrants faced new hardships and hazards: kicks from mules, oxen that collapsed from thirst, and overloaded wagons that broke down. Trails were difficult to follow—at least until they became littered by the debris of broken wagons and by the bleached bones of oxen. Guidebooks were more like guessbooks. The Donner party lost so much time following the advice of one such book that its members became snowbound in the High Sierras and reached California only after its survivors had turned to cannibalism. Emigrants met the challenges of the **overland trails** by close cooperation with one another, traveling in huge wagon trains rather than alone. Men yoked and unyoked the oxen, drove the wagons and stock, and hunted. Women packed, cooked, and assisted in childbirths.

Between 1840 and 1848, an estimated 11,500 pioneers followed an overland trail to Oregon, and some 2,700 reached California. Such small numbers made a difference, for the British did not settle Oregon at all, and the Mexican population of California was small and scattered. By 1845, California was clinging to Mexico by the thinnest of threads. The territory's Hispanic population, the *californios,* felt little allegiance to Mexico, which they contemptuously called "the other shore." Some of them wanted

CHECKING IN

- By the 1820s Americans were deeply involved in trade along Mexico's northern frontiers.
- In the 1820s the Mexican government invited Americans to settle in Texas as a buffer against Indians; within a decade more than thirty thousand Americans lived in Texas.
- Texans rebelled against Mexico in 1836 and won their independence.
- In the 1840s, Americans began streaming into Oregon and California.
- More than fourteen thousand Americans followed the overland trails west.

independence from Mexico, whereas others contemplated British or French rule. But these *californios,* with their tenuous allegiances, faced a growing number of American settlers with definite political sympathies.

THE POLITICS OF EXPANSION, 1840–1846

How did "Manifest Destiny" influence American politics?

Westward expansion raised the question of whether the United States should annex the independent Texas republic. In the mid-1840s, the Texas-annexation issue sparked political passions and became entangled with equally unsettling issues relating to California, New Mexico, and Oregon. Between 1846 and 1848, a war with Mexico and a dramatic confrontation with Britain settled all these questions on terms favorable to the United States.

At the start of the 1840s, western issues received little attention in a nation concerned primarily with issues relating to economic recovery—tariffs, banking, and internal improvements. Only after politicians failed to address the economic problems coherently did opportunistic leaders thrust expansion-related issues to the top of the political agenda.

The Whig Ascendancy

The election of 1840 brought Whig candidate William Henry Harrison to the presidency and installed Whig majorities in both houses of Congress. The Whigs proposed to replace Van Buren's Independent Treasury (see Chapter 10) with some sort of national fiscal agency, like the defunct Bank of the United States. The Whig party also favored a revised tariff that would increase government revenues but remain low enough to permit the importation of foreign goods. According to the Whig plan, the states would then receive tariff-generated revenues for internal improvements.

The Whig agenda might have breezed into law, but Harrison died after only one month in office. His successor, Vice President John Tyler, an upper-crust Virginian put on the ticket in 1840 for his southern appeal, then assumed the presidency. A former Democrat and a supporter of states' rights, he repeatedly vetoed Whig proposals, including a bill to create a new national bank.

Tyler also played havoc with the Whig tariff policy. The Compromise Tariff of 1833 had provided for a gradual scaling down of tariff duties to 20 percent. Amid the depression of the early 1840s, however, the tariff appeared too low to generate the revenue Whigs needed to distribute among the states for internal improvements. In response, Whigs passed two bills in the summer of 1842 that simultaneously postponed the final reduction of tariffs to 20 percent and ordered distribution to the states to proceed. Tyler promptly vetoed both bills, infuriating Whig leadership. Some Whigs spoke of impeachment. Finally, in August, Tyler signed a new bill that maintained some tariffs above 20 percent but abandoned distribution to the states.

Tyler's erratic course confounded and disrupted his party. By maintaining some tariffs above 20 percent, the tariff of 1842 satisfied northern manufacturers, but by abandoning distribution, it infuriated many southerners and westerners. In the congressional elections of 1842, the Whigs paid a heavy price for failing to enact their program. Although retaining a slim majority in the Senate, they lost control of the House to the Democrats. Now the nation had one party in control of the Senate, its rival in control of the House, and a president who appeared to belong to neither party.

Tyler and the Annexation of Texas

Although disowned by his party, Tyler ardently desired a second term as president. Domestic issues offered him little hope of building a popular following, but foreign policy was another matter. In 1842, Tyler's secretary of state, Daniel Webster, concluded the Webster-Ashburton Treaty with Great Britain, settling a long-festering dispute over the Maine-Canada border. Tyler reasoned that if he could follow the treaty, which was highly popular in the North, with the annexation of Texas, he could build a national following.

The issue of slavery, however, clouded every discussion of Texas. Antislavery northerners saw proposals to annex Texas as part of a southern conspiracy to extend slavery, because Texas would certainly enter the Union as a slave state. In fact, some southerners dreamed of creating four or five slave states from Texas's vast area.

Nevertheless, in summer 1843, Tyler launched a propaganda campaign for Texas annexation. He alleged that Britain had designs on Texas, which Americans would be prudent to forestall. In spring 1844, Tyler and John C. Calhoun, who became secretary of state in 1844, submitted to the Senate a treaty annexing Texas. Accompanying the treaty was a letter from Calhoun to the British minister in Washington, defending slavery as beneficial to African-Americans, the only way to protect them from "vice and pauperism." Abolitionists now had evidence that the annexation of Texas was linked to a conspiracy to extend slavery. Consequently, both Whig and Democratic leaders came out in opposition to the annexation of Texas, and the treaty went down to crushing defeat in the Senate. However, this vote only postponed the final decision on annexation to the upcoming election of 1844.

The Election of 1844

Tyler's ineptitude turned the presidential campaign into a free-for-all. Unable to gather support as an independent, he dropped out of the race. Henry Clay had a secure grip on the Whig nomination, but Martin Van Buren's apparently clear path to the head of the Democratic ticket vanished as the issue of annexation split his party. A deadlocked Democratic Party finally turned to James K. Polk of Tennessee, the first "dark horse" nominee in American history and a supporter of immediate annexation.

Jeering "Who is James K. Polk?" the Whigs derided the nomination. Polk was little known outside the South. Yet he persuaded many northerners that annexation of Texas would benefit them. Conjuring an imaginative scenario, Polk and his supporters argued that if Britain succeeded in abolishing slavery in Texas, slavery would not be able to move westward; racial tensions in existing slave states would intensify; and the chances of a race war would increase. However far-fetched, this argument played effectively on northern racial phobias and helped Polk detach annexation from Calhoun's narrow, prosouthern defense of it.

In contrast to the Democrats, whose position was clear, Clay kept muddying the waters. After several shifts, Clay finally came out against annexation, but not until September. His wavering alienated his southern supporters and prompted some of his northern supporters to bolt the Whigs for the antislavery Liberty party, formed in 1840. The Whigs also infuriated Catholic immigrant voters by nominating Theodore Frelinghuysen (fray-ling-HIGH-zun) for the vice presidency. A supporter of temperance and an assortment of other causes, Frelinghuysen confirmed fears that the Whigs were the orthodox Protestant party. Catholic immigrants turned out in large numbers to vote for the Democrats.

On the eve of the election in New York City, so many Irish marched to the courthouse to be qualified for voting that the windows had to be opened to allow people to enter and leave. Polk won the electoral vote 170 to 105, but his margin in the popular vote was only 38,000 out of 2.6 million votes cast. A shift of 6,000 votes in New York, where the immigrant vote and Whig defections to the Liberty party had hurt Clay, would have given Clay the state and the presidency.

Manifest Destiny, 1845

The election of 1844 demonstrated the strength of national support for the annexation of Texas. The surging popular sentiment for expansion reflected a growing conviction that America's natural destiny was to expand into Texas and all the way to the Pacific Ocean.

Expansionists emphasized extending the "area of freedom" and talked of "repelling the contaminating proximity of monarchies upon the soil that we have consecrated to the rights of man." Americans needed only a phrase to capture this ebullient spirit. In 1845, John L. O'Sullivan, a New York Democratic journalist, supplied that phrase when he wrote of "our manifest destiny to overspread and to possess the whole of the continent which Providence has given us for the development of the great experiment of liberty and federated self-government entrusted to us."

Manifest Destiny Phrase coined to describe beliefs of ardent expansionists

Advocates of **Manifest Destiny** used lofty language and invoked God and Nature to sanction expansion. Northern Whigs frequently dismissed Manifest Destiny as a smoke screen aimed at concealing the evil intent of expanding slavery. In reality, many expansionists were neither supporters of slavery nor zealous annexationists. Most had their eyes not on Texas but on Oregon and California. Blaming the post-1837 depression on the failure of Americans to find markets for their agricultural surplus, they saw California and Oregon as solutions. An Alabama Democrat praised California's "safe and capacious harbors," which "invite to their bosoms the rich commerce of the East."

However, more than trade was at stake. At the heart of their thinking lay an impulse to preserve the predominantly agricultural character of the American people and thereby to safeguard democracy. Fundamentally Jeffersonian, expansionists equated industrialization and urbanization with social stratification and class strife. To avoid the "bloated wealth" and "terrible misery" that afflicted Britain, the United States *had* to expand.

Democrats saw expansion as a logical complement to their support of low tariffs and their opposition to centralized banking. High tariffs and banks tended to "favor and foster the factory system," but expansion would provide farmers with land as well as access to foreign markets. Americans would continue to be farmers, and the foundations of the republic would remain secure.

This message, trumpeted by the penny press, made sense to the working poor, many of them Irish immigrants. Expansion would open economic opportunity for the common people and thwart British plans to free American slaves, whom the poor viewed as potential competition for already-scarce jobs.

Expansionism drew on the ideas of Thomas Jefferson, John Quincy Adams, and other leaders of the early republic who had proclaimed the American people's right to displace any people, uncivilized or European, from their westward path. Early expansionists had feared that overexpansion might create an ungovernable empire, but their successors had no such qualms. Although they pointed with alarm to the negative effects of industrialization, the expansionists also relied on the technology of industrialization. The railroad and the telegraph, they said, had annihilated the problem of distance and made expansion safe.

James K. Polk

Lacking charm, Polk bored even his friends, but few presidents could match his record of acquiring land for the United States.

Polk and Oregon

The growing spirit of Manifest Destiny intensified the Oregon issue. To soften northern criticism of the pending annexation of Texas, the Democrats included in their 1844 platform the assertion that American title "to the whole of the Territory of Oregon is clear and unquestionable." Taken literally, this statement, which Polk later repeated, pressed an American claim to the entire Oregon Territory between California and 54°40', the southern boundary of Alaska, a claim never before advanced.

Polk's objectives in Oregon were more subtle than his language. He knew that the United States could never obtain all of Oregon without a war with Britain, and he wanted to avoid that. He hoped the belligerent language would persuade the British to accept what they had previously rejected, a division of Oregon at the forty-ninth parallel. This settlement would give the United States the superb deep-water harbor of Puget Sound and the southern tip of Vancouver Island. The British had long held out for a division along the Columbia River, which entered the Pacific Ocean far south of the forty-ninth parallel.

CHECKING IN

- The death of William Henry Harrison threw Whig control of the national government into turmoil.
- Attempts to bring Texas into the Union raised the volatile issue of slavery.
- Dark horse candidate and expansionist James K. Polk won the 1844 election.
- "Manifest Destiny" became the slogan of expansionists.
- Polk won a treaty dividing the Oregon Territory with Great Britain, giving the United States its first Pacific boundary.

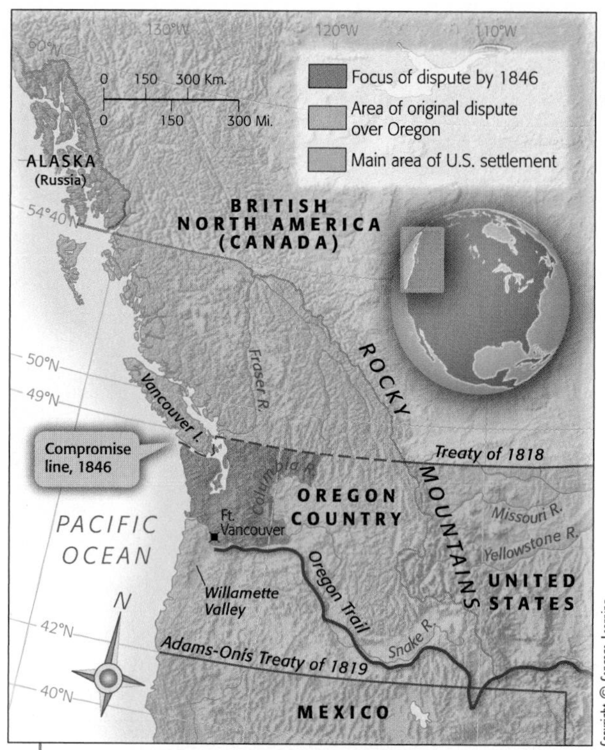

Map 13.3 Oregon Boundary Dispute
Although demanding that Britain cede the entire Oregon Territory south of 54°40', the United States settled for a compromise at the forty-ninth parallel.

Interactive Map

Polk's position roused furious interest in acquisition of the entire territory. Mass meetings adopted such resolutions as "The Whole or None!" and "Fifty-four Forty or Fight!" Each year brought new American settlers into Oregon. John Quincy Adams, although no supporter of the annexation of Texas or the 54°40' boundary for Oregon, believed that American settlements gave the United States a stronger claim than discovery and exploration had given the British. The United States, Adams preached, was the nation bound "to make the wilderness blossom as the rose, to establish laws, to increase, multiply, and subdue the earth," all "at the first behest of God Almighty."

In April 1846, Polk forced the issue by notifying Britain that the United States was terminating the joint British-American occupation of Oregon. In effect, this message was that the British could either go to war over the American claims to 54°40'—or negotiate. Britain chose to negotiate. Although the British raged against "that ill-regulated, overbearing, and aggressive spirit of American democracy," they had too many other problems to wage war over "a few miles of pine swamp." The ensuing treaty divided Oregon at the forty-ninth parallel, although Britain retained all of Vancouver Island and temporary navigation rights on the Columbia River (see Map 13.3). On June 15, 1846, the Senate ratified the treaty.

THE MEXICAN-AMERICAN WAR AND ITS AFTERMATH, 1846–1848

How did the outcome of the Mexican-American War intensify intersectional conflict?

Between 1846 and 1848, the United States successfully fought a war that cost Mexico its claims to Texas and the provinces of New Mexico and California. Many Americans rejoiced in the stunning victory. But some recognized that deep divisions over the status of slavery in New Mexico and California boded ill for their nation's future.

The Origins of the Mexican-American War

While Polk was challenging Britain over Oregon, the United States and Mexico moved toward war. The impending conflict had both remote and immediate causes. One long-standing grievance lay in the Mexican government's failure to pay some $2 million in debts owed to American citizens. Bitter memories of the Alamo and the Goliad massacre reinforced American loathing of Mexico. Above all, the issue of Texas poisoned relations between the two nations. Beset by internal strife—Mexico's presidency changed hands twenty times between 1829 and 1844—Mexico feared that, once in control of Texas, the "Colossus of the North" might seize other provinces, perhaps even Mexico itself, and treat Mexicans much as it treated its slaves.

Polk's election increased the strength of the pro-annexationists, as his campaign had persuaded many northerners that Texas's annexation would bring national benefits. In February 1845, both houses of Congress responded to popular sentiment by passing a resolution annexing Texas. However, Texans balked, in part because some feared that union with the United States would provoke a Mexican invasion and war on Texas soil.

Polk moved rapidly. To sweeten the pot for Texans, he supported their claim that the Rio Grande (REE-oh GRAN-day) constituted Texas's southern border, despite Mexico's contention that the Nueces (NOO-ay-sess) River, one hundred miles farther north, bounded Texas. Because the Rio Grande meandered west and north nearly two thousand miles, it encompassed a huge territory, including part of modern New Mexico. The Texas that Polk proposed to annex was thus far larger than the Texas that had gained independence from Mexico. On July 4, 1845, reassured by Polk's support, Texas voted to accept annexation. Under Polk's orders, American troops under General Zachary Taylor deployed at Corpus Christi, south of the Nueces River, in territory still claimed by Mexico.

California and its fine harbors influenced Polk's actions, for he had entered the White House with the firm intention of extending American control over that province, too. If Mexico went to war with the United States over Texas, Polk's supporters claimed, "the road to California will be open to us." Reports from American agents convinced Polk that the way lay open for California to join the United States as Texas would—by revolution and then annexation.

Continued turmoil in Mexican politics further complicated this complex situation. In early 1845, a new Mexican government agreed to negotiate with the United States, and Polk decided to give negotiations a chance. In November 1845, he dispatched John Slidell to Mexico City with instructions to gain Mexican recognition of the annexation of Texas with the Rio Grande border. In exchange, the U.S. government would assume the debt owed by Mexico to American citizens. Polk also authorized Slidell to offer up to $25 million for California and New Mexico. However, by the time Slidell reached Mexico City, the government there had become too weak to make concessions and refused to negotiate. Polk then ordered Taylor to move southward to the Rio Grande, hoping to provoke a Mexican attack and unite the American people behind war.

The Mexican government dawdled. Polk was about to send a war message to Congress when word finally arrived that Mexican forces had crossed the Rio Grande and attacked the U.S. army. *"American blood has been shed on American soil!"* one of Polk's followers jubilantly proclaimed. On May 11, 1846, Polk informed Congress that war "exists by the act of Mexico herself" and called for $10 million to fight the war.

Polk's disarming assertion that the United States was already at war provoked furious opposition in Congress. For one thing, the Mexican attack on Taylor's troops had taken place on land never before claimed by the United States. By announcing that war already existed, moreover, Polk seemed to be undercutting Congress's power to declare war and using a mere border incident as a pretext to acquire more slave territory. But Polk had maneuvered the Whigs into a corner. They could not afford to appear unpatriotic—they remembered vividly what opposition to the War of 1812 had cost the Federalists—so they swallowed their outrage and supported war.

Polk's single-minded pursuit of his goals had prevailed. As a humorless, austere man who banned dancing and liquor from the White House, he inspired little personal warmth. But he triumphed over all opposition, in part because of his opponents' fragmentation, in part because of expansion's popular appeal, and in part because of his foreign antagonists' weakness. Reluctant to fight over Oregon, Britain had negotiated. Too weak to negotiate, Mexico chose to fight over territory that it had already lost (Texas) and where its hold was feeble (California and New Mexico).

The Mexican-American War

Most European observers expected Mexico to win the war. Its army was four times the size of the American forces, and it was fighting on home ground. Having botched its one previous attempt to invade a neighbor, Canada, in 1812, the United States now had to sustain offensive operations in an area remote from American settlements. American expansionists, however, hardly expected the Mexicans to fight at all. Racism and arrogance convinced many Americans that the Mexican people, degraded by their mixed Spanish and Indian population, were "as sure to melt away at the approach of [American] energy and enterprise as snow before a southern sun."

In fact, the Mexicans fought bravely and stubbornly, although unsuccessfully. In May 1846, Taylor, "Old Rough and Ready," routed the Mexican army in Texas and pursued it across the Rio Grande, eventually capturing the major city of Monterrey (mon-ter-RAY). War enthusiasm surged in the United States. Recruiting posters blared, "Here's to old Zach! Glorious Times! Roast Beef, Ice Cream, and Three Months' advance." Taylor's conspicuously ordinary manner—he went into battle wearing a straw hat and a plain brown coat—endeared him to the public, which kicked up its heels in celebration to the "Rough and Ready Polka" and the "General Taylor Quick Step."

After taking Monterrey, Taylor, starved for supplies, halted and granted Mexico an eight-week armistice. Eager to undercut Taylor's popularity—the Whigs were already touting him as a presidential candidate—Polk stripped him of half his forces and reassigned them to General Winfield Scott. Scott was to mount an amphibious attack on Vera Cruz (VEHR-uh-krooz) and proceed to Mexico City, following the path of Cortés and his conquistadors. Events outstripped Polk's scheme, however, when Taylor defeated a far larger Mexican army at the Battle of Buena Vista (BWAY-nuh VEES-tuh), on February 22–23, 1847.

Farther north, American forces took advantage of the shakiness of Mexican rule to strip away New Mexico and California. In spring 1846, Colonel Stephen Kearny led an army from Fort Leavenworth, Kansas, toward Santa Fe. Reaching New Mexico, Kearny took the territory by a combination of bluff, bluster, and perhaps bribery, all without firing a shot. The Mexican governor, following his own advice that "it is better to be thought brave than to be so," fled at Kearny's approach. Once he had suppressed a brief rebellion by Mexicans and Indians, Kearny controlled New Mexico securely enough that he could dispatch part of his army south into Mexico to support Taylor at Buena Vista.

California also fell easily into American hands. In 1845, Polk had ordered the Pacific Squadron under Commodore John D. Sloat to occupy California's ports in the event of war. The president had also dispatched a courier overland with secret orders for the colorful **John C. Frémont**. A Georgia-born adventurer, Frémont took advantage of his marriage to the daughter of a powerful senator to have accounts of his explorations in the Northwest published as official government documents, and then basked in glory as "the Great Pathfinder." Polk's courier caught up with Frémont in Oregon. Instructed to proceed to California and "watch over the interests of the United States," Frémont interpreted his orders liberally. In June 1846, he rounded up some American insurgents, seized the town of Sonoma (suh-NOH-muh), and proclaimed the independent "Bear Flag Republic." The combined efforts of Frémont, Sloat, and Kearny (who arrived in California after capturing New Mexico) established U.S. control over California.

John C. Frémont Adventurer who played a role in California rebellion against Mexico; later a force in national politics

The final and most important campaign of the war saw the conquest of Mexico City itself. In March 1847, Winfield Scott landed near Vera Cruz and quickly pounded that city into submission. Moving inland, Scott encountered Santa Anna at the seemingly impregnable pass of Cerro Gordo (SERR-oh GORD-oh), but a young captain in Scott's command, Robert E. Lee, helped find a trail that led around the Mexican flank to a small peak overlooking the pass. There Scott planted howitzers and, on April 18, stormed the pass and routed the Mexicans. Scott now moved directly on Mexico City. Taking the key fortresses of Churubusco and Chapultepec (where another young captain, Ulysses S. Grant, was cited for bravery), Scott took the city on September 13, 1847 (see Map 13.4).

Although the Mexican army outnumbered the Americans in virtually every battle, they could not match the superior artillery or the logistics and organization of the "barbarians of the North." The Americans died like flies from yellow fever, and they carried into battle the agonies of venereal disease, which they picked up (and left) in many of the Mexican towns they took. But the Americans benefited from the unprecedented quality of their weapons, supplies, and organization.

By the **Treaty of Guadalupe-Hidalgo** (gwah-duh-LOO-pay ee-DOLL-go) (February 2, 1848), Mexico ceded Texas with the Rio Grande boundary, New Mexico, and California to the United States; from the Mexican cession would come the states of New Mexico, California, Nevada, and Utah, most of Arizona, and parts of Colorado and Wyoming. In turn, the United States assumed the claims of U.S. citizens against the Mexican government and paid Mexico $15 million. Although some rabid expansionists denounced the treaty because it failed to include all of Mexico, Polk, like most Americans, was satisfied. Empty territory was fine, but few Americans wanted to annex the mixed Spanish and Indian population of Mexico itself and incorporate into the United States "ignorant and indolent half-civilized Indians," in one writer's words. The virulent racism of American leaders allowed the Mexicans to retain part of their nation. On March 10, 1848, the Senate ratified the treaty by a vote of 38 to 10.

Treaty of Guadalupe Hidalgo Agreement ending the Mexican-American War; ceded vast amounts of land to the United States

The War's Effects on Sectional Conflict

Despite wartime patriotic enthusiasm, sectional conflict sharpened between 1846 and 1848. Territorial expansion sparked the Polk administration's major battles. To Polk, it mattered little whether new territories were slave or free. Expansion would serve the

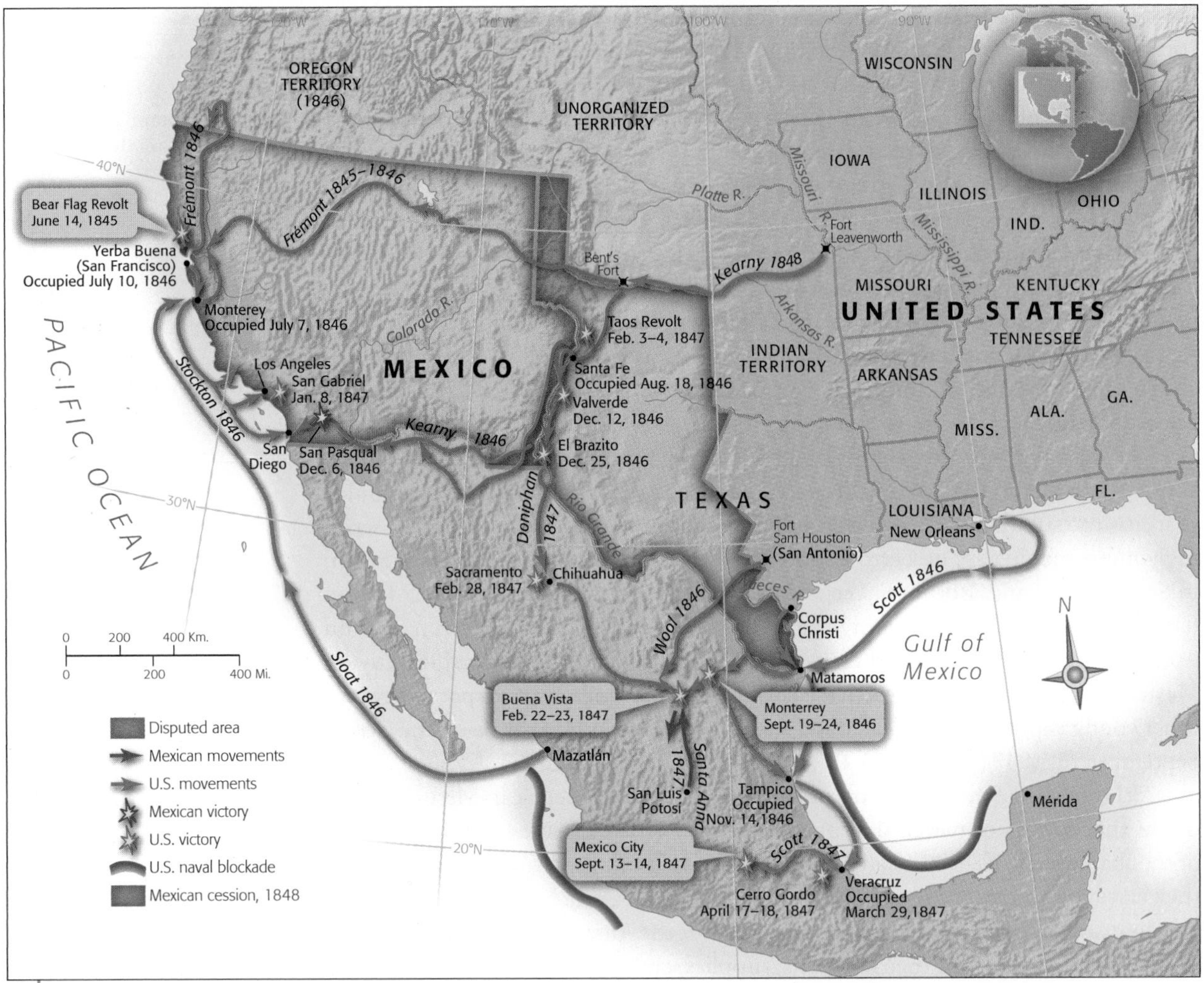

Map 13.4 Major Battles of the Mexican-American War

The Mexican-American War's decisive campaign began with General Winfield Scott's capture of Vera Cruz and ended with his conquest of Mexico City.

Interactive Map

nation's interests by dispersing population and retaining its agricultural and democratic character. Focusing attention on slavery in the territories struck him as "not only unwise but wicked." The Missouri Compromise, prohibiting slavery north of 36°30', impressed him as a simple and permanent solution to the problem of territorial slavery.

However, many northerners were coming to see slavery in the territories as a profoundly disruptive issue that neither could nor should be solved simply by extending the 36°30' line westward. Amounting to a small minority, abolitionists, who opposed any extension of slavery on moral grounds, posed a minor threat to Polk. More important were northern Democrats who feared that expansion of slavery into California and New Mexico (parts of each lay south of 36°30') would deter free laborers from settling those territories. These Democrats argued that competition with slaves degraded free labor, that the westward extension of slavery would check the westward migration of free labor, and that such a barrier would aggravate the social problems already beginning to plague the East: class strife, social stratification, and labor protest.

The Wilmot Proviso

A young Democratic congressman from Pennsylvania, David Wilmot, became the spokesman for these disaffected northern Democrats. In August 1846, he introduced an amendment to an appropriations bill. This amendment, which became known as the **Wilmot Proviso,** stipulated that slavery must be prohibited in any territory acquired by the war with Mexico. Neither an abolitionist nor a critic of Polk on tariff policy, Wilmot spoke for those loyal Democrats who had supported the annexation of Texas on the assumption that Texas would be the last slave state. Wilmot's intention was not to split his party along sectional lines but instead to hold Polk to what Wilmot and other northern Democrats took as an implicit understanding: Texas for the slaveholders, California and New Mexico for free labor.

Wilmot Proviso Attempt to ban slavery from any territory acquired from Mexico

With strong northern support, the proviso passed in the House but stalled in the Senate. Polk refused to endorse it, and most southern Democrats opposed any barrier to the expansion of slavery south of the Missouri Compromise line. They believed that the westward extension of slavery would reduce the concentration of slaves in the older regions of the South and thus lessen the chances of a slave revolt.

The proviso raised unsettling constitutional questions. Calhoun and other southerners contended that, because slaves were property, the Constitution protected slaveholders' right to carry their slaves wherever they chose. This position led to the conclusion that the Missouri Compromise was unconstitutional. On the other side, many northerners cited the Northwest Ordinance of 1787, the Missouri Compromise, and the Constitution itself, which gave Congress the power to "make all needful rules and regulations respecting the territory or other property belonging to the United States," as justification for congressional legislation over slavery in the territories. With the election of 1848 approaching, politicians of both sides, eager to hold their parties together and avert civil war, frantically searched for a middle ground.

The Election of 1848

The Whigs watched in dismay as prosperity returned under Polk's program of an independent treasury and low tariffs. Never before had Henry Clay's American System of national banking and high tariffs seemed so irrelevant. But the Wilmot Proviso gave the Whigs a political windfall; originating in the Democratic Party, it allowed the Whigs to portray themselves as the South's only dependable friends.

These considerations inclined the majority of Whigs toward Zachary Taylor. As a Louisiana slaveholder, he had obvious appeal to the South. As a political newcomer, he had no loyalty to a discredited American System. And as a war hero, he had broad national appeal. Nominating Taylor as their presidential candidate in 1848, the Whigs presented him as an ideal man "without regard to creeds or principles" and ran him without any platform.

The Democrats faced a greater challenge because David Wilmot was one of their own. They could not ignore the issue of slavery in the territories, but if they embraced the positions of either Wilmot or Calhoun, the party would split along sectional lines. When Polk declined to run for reelection, the Democrats nominated Lewis Cass of Michigan, who had formulated the doctrine of "squatter sovereignty," or **popular sovereignty,** as it was later called. Cass argued that Congress should let the question of slavery in the territories be decided by the people who settled there. Squatter sovereignty appealed to many because of its arresting simplicity and vagueness; it neatly dodged the explosive question of whether Congress actually possessed the power to prohibit territorial slavery.

popular sovereignty Proposal that settlers in new territories should decide the issue of slavery for themselves

In the campaign, both parties tried to avoid the issue of slavery in the territories, but neither succeeded. A pro-Wilmot faction of the Democratic Party linked up with the abolitionist Liberty party and antislavery "Conscience" Whigs to form the Free-Soil party. Declaring their dedication to "Free Trade, Free Labor, Free Speech, and Free Men," the Free-Soilers nominated Martin Van Buren on a platform opposing any extension of slavery.

Zachary Taylor benefited from the opposition's alienation of key northern states over the tariff issue, from Democratic disunity over the Wilmot Proviso, and from his war-hero stature. He captured a majority of electoral votes in both the North and the South. Although it failed to carry any state, the Free-Soil party ran well enough in the North to demonstrate the grassroots popularity of opposition to the extension of slavery. By showing that opposition to the spread of slavery had far more appeal than outright abolitionism, the Free-Soilers sent both Whigs and Democrats a message that they would be unable to ignore in future elections.

"Union" Woodcut by Thomas W. Strong, 1848
This 1848 campaign poster for Zachary Taylor reminded Americans of his military victories, unmilitary bearing (note the civilian dress and straw hat), and deliberately vague promises.

The California Gold Rush

When Wilmot introduced his proviso, the issue of slavery in the West was more abstract than immediate, for Mexico had not yet ceded any territory. The picture quickly changed when an American carpenter discovered gold while building a sawmill in the foothills of California's Sierra Nevada only nine days before the Treaty of Guadalupe-Hidalgo was signed. A frantic gold rush erupted. A San Francisco paper complained that all California "resounds with the sordid cry to *GOLD, GOLD, GOLD!* while the field is left half-planted, the house half-built, and every thing neglected but the manufacture of shovels and pickaxes."

By December 1848, pamphlets with titles like *The Emigrant's Guide to the Gold Mines* hit the streets of New York City, and the gold rush was on. Overland emigrants to California increased from 400 in 1848 to 44,000 in 1850. Arriving by land as well as by sea, gold-rushers swelled California's population from 15,000 in the summer of 1848 to 250,000 by 1852. They came from every corner of the world; one journalist reported that, when she walked through a miners' camp, she heard English,

Italian, French, Spanish, German, and Hawaiian. Clashes between Anglo-Americans and Hispanics were frequent. Anglo-Americans particularly resented the Chinese who flooded into California in the 1850s as contract laborers. Rampant prejudice did not stop Americans from hiring Chinese workers, however.

Within a decade, the gold rush turned the sleepy Hispanic town of Yerba Buena (YAIR-buh BWAY-nah), with 150 people in 1846, into "a pandemonium of a city" of 50,000 known as San Francisco. No other American city boasted people from more parts of the world. The ethnic and racial tensions of the gold fields spilled over into the city. In 1851, San Francisco's merchants organized the first of several Committees of Vigilance, which patrolled the streets, deported undesirables, and tried and hanged alleged thieves and murderers.

The gold rush made the issue of slavery in the West an immediate, practical concern. The newcomers to California included free blacks and slaves brought by planters from the South. White prospectors loathed the idea of competing with these groups and wanted to drive them from the gold fields. Violence mounted, and demands grew for a strong civilian government to replace the ineffective military government left over from the war. Polk began to fear that without a satisfactory congressional solution to the slavery issue, Californians might organize a government independent of the United States. The gold rush guaranteed that the question of slavery in the Mexican cession would be the first item on the agenda for Polk's successor and the nation.

CHECKING IN

- The United States entered into the Mexican-American War by choice rather than by necessity.
- After losing the war, Mexico ceded to the United States the Southwest quadrant of the present United States and recognized Texas's independence.
- Victory in the war again raised the question of the expansion of slavery.
- The election of 1848 revealed the growing strength of opposition to the expansion of slavery.
- The discovery of gold in California guaranteed that, despite politicians' wishes to sidestep the issue, the expansion of slavery would rise to the top of the national agenda.

Chapter Summary

How did immigration in the 1840s influence the balance of power between the Whig and Democratic parties? (page 290)

The massive immigration of the 1840s changed the face of American politics. Angered by Whig nativism and anti-Catholicism, the new German and Irish immigrants swelled the ranks of the Democratic Party. Meanwhile, the Whigs were unraveling. The untimely death of President Harrison brought John Tyler, a Democrat in Whig's clothing, to the White House. Tyler's vetoes of key Whig measures left the Whig party in disarray.

What economic and political forces fed westward expansion during the 1840s? (page 295)

Americans had begun trading along Mexico's northern frontiers early in the nineteenth century. In the 1820s, Mexico invited Americans to settle in Texas as a buffer against hostile Native Americans. But Texans rebelled against Mexico in 1836 and won their independence. In the following decade, thousands of people followed the overland trails to California and Oregon.

KEY TERMS

Tejano *(p. 289)*
German and Irish immigrants *(p. 291)*
nativism *(p. 293)*
"Know-Nothing" party *(p. 293)*
Stephen F. Austin *(p. 297)*
Santa Anna *(p. 297)*
Alamo *(p. 298)*
Sam Houston *(p. 298)*
overland trails *(p. 299)*
Manifest Destiny *(p. 302)*
John C. Frémont *(p. 307)*
Treaty of Guadalupe Hidalgo *(p. 307)*
Wilmot Proviso *(p. 309)*
popular sovereignty *(p. 310)*

How did "Manifest Destiny" influence American politics? (page 300)

The issue of annexation of Texas stalled because it raised the vexatious issue of the expansion of slavery. But the pro-expansion sentiment known as Manifest Destiny helped bring ardent expansionist James K. Polk to the White House in 1844 and fueled support for Texas annexation despite the slavery question. Polk and his followers ingeniously argued that national expansion was in the interests of northern working-class voters, many of them immigrants.

How did the outcome of the Mexican-American War intensify intersectional conflict? (page 304)

In the Treaty of Guadalupe-Hidalgo, the United States gained one-fourth of its present territory, and Mexico recognized Texas's independence. However, once again the question of the expansion of slavery came to the forefront of American politics. The Wilmot Proviso exposed deep sectional divisions that had only been papered over by the ideal of Manifest Destiny. Victorious over Mexico and enriched by the discovery of gold in California, Americans counted the blessings of expansion but began to fear its costs.

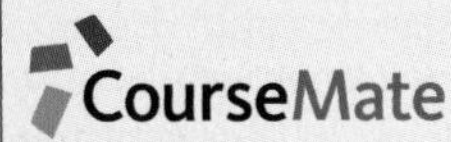

Go to the CourseMate website at **www.cengagebrain.com** for additional study tools and review materials—including audio and video clips—for this chapter.

CHAPTER 14

From Compromise to Secession 1850–1861

Kansas State Historical Society

Southern Rights Flag
Proslavery forces carried this flag while attacking the antislavery stronghold of Lawrence in the Kansas Territory.

CHAPTER PREVIEW

On April 12, 1861, Edmund Ruffin, a sixty-seven-year-old agricultural reformer and political pundit who had joined the Palmetto Guards, a volunteer military company, stood by a cannon on Morris Island in the bay of Charleston, South Carolina. With flowing white hair that dropped below his shoulders, he cut a striking figure among the Guards. Although young enough to be his grandchildren, many of the volunteers knew him as a champion of secession. The only way to save the South's civilization, he had argued for decades, was for the southern states to leave the United States and start a new nation.

Led by South Carolina, seven states in the Lower South had already done so, and in February 1861, they had formed the Confederate States of America. Now, the question became who would commit the first hostile act, Union or Confederacy? President Abraham Lincoln had vowed to defend federal property in the seceding states, including Fort Sumter in Charleston Bay. Impatient Confederate leaders demanded its immediate surrender; the fort's commander refused. At 4:30 A.M., Ruffin pulled the cannon's lanyard and commenced the bombardment that compelled the fort's surrender the next day. Lincoln responded by calling for 75,000 volunteers to suppress the rebellion. The Civil War had begun.

Just over four years later and back in his native Virginia, Ruffin breakfasted with his family and then went to his room to compose a farewell message: "I hereby declare my unmitigated hatred to Yankee rule—to all political, social, and business connections with Yankees—& to the Yankee race. Would that I could impress these thoughts on every living southerner, & bequeath them to everyone yet to be born!" Putting his pen down, Ruffin then put the muzzle of a rifle inside his mouth and used a forked stick to pull the trigger.

Irony marked Ruffin's dramatic suicide in the name of the "South." Before 1860, few listened to his ranting. The Republican Party, formed in the 1850s, dedicated itself to stopping the extension of slavery into the territories, but the party's leaders insisted that they lacked constitutional authority to interfere with slavery in the southern states. Most white southerners trusted their influence in national institutions, especially the Democratic Party, to secure slavery.

John Brown Self-appointed agent of God sent to destroy slavery; responsible for the Pottawatomie Massacre as well as the Harpers Ferry raid

However, sectional conflicts over slavery extension during the 1850s eroded the appeal of national parties. Then, in October 1859, a fanatical abolitionist named **John Brown** led a small band in seizing the federal arsenal at Harpers Ferry, Virginia, in the hope of igniting a slave insurrection. An abject failure, Brown's raid nevertheless brought to the surface all the white South's doubts about the "real" intentions of the North. Ruffin, long the prophet without honor in his own country, became the man of the hour and secession became a bright star on the horizon.

THE COMPROMISE OF 1850

How did the Fugitive Slave Act lead to the undoing of the Compromise of 1850?

Ralph Waldo Emerson's grim prediction that a U.S. victory in the Mexican War would be like swallowing arsenic proved disturbingly accurate. When the war ended in 1848, the United States contained an equal number (fifteen each) of free and slave states, but the vast territory gained by the war threatened to upset this balance. Any solution to the question of slavery in the Mexican cession—a free-soil policy, extension of the Missouri Compromise line, or popular sovereignty—ensured controversy. The prospect of free soil angered southerners, whereas extension of the Missouri Compromise line antagonized free-soil northerners as well as southern extremists who proclaimed that Congress could not bar slavery's expansion. Popular sovereignty offered the greatest hope for compromise by taking the question of slavery out of national politics and handing it to each territory, but this notion pleased neither free-soil nor proslavery extremists.

As the rhetoric escalated, events plunged the nation into crisis. Utah and then California, both acquired from Mexico, sought admission to the Union as free states. Texas, admitted to the Union as a slave state in 1845, aggravated matters by claiming the eastern half of New Mexico, thus potentially opening the door to slavery's extension into other newly acquired territory.

Chronology

1848	Zachary Taylor elected president
1849	California seeks admission to the Union as a free state
1850	Nashville convention assembles to discuss the South's grievances; Compromise of 1850
1852	Harriet Beecher Stowe, *Uncle Tom's Cabin;* Franklin Pierce elected president
1853	Gadsden Purchase
1854	Ostend Manifesto; Kansas-Nebraska Act
1854–1855	Know-Nothing and Republican parties rise
1855	Proslavery forces steal the election for a territorial legislature in Kansas, establish a government in Lecompton; free-soil government established in Topeka, Kansas
1856	The "sack" of Lawrence, Kansas; John Brown's Pottawatomie Massacre; James Buchanan elected president
1857	*Dred Scott* decision; President Buchanan endorses the Lecompton constitution in Kansas
1858	Congress refuses to admit Kansas to the Union under the Lecompton constitution; Lincoln-Douglas debates
1859	John Brown's raid on Harpers Ferry
1860	Abraham Lincoln elected president; South Carolina secedes from the Union
1861	The remaining Lower South states secede; Confederate States of America established; Crittenden compromise plan collapses; Lincoln takes office; firing on Fort Sumter; Civil War begins; Upper South secedes

By 1850 other issues had become intertwined with territorial questions. Northerners had grown increasingly unhappy with slavery in the District of Columbia, within the shadow of the Capitol; southerners, meanwhile, complained about lax enforcement of the Fugitive Slave Act of 1793. Any broad compromise would have to take both matters into account.

Zachary Taylor's Strategy

President Zachary Taylor believed that the South must not kindle the issue of slavery in the territories, because neither New Mexico nor California was suited for slavery. Taylor's position differed significantly from the thinking behind the still-controversial Wilmot Proviso, which proposed that Congress bar slavery in the territories ceded by Mexico. Taylor's plan, in contrast, left the decision to the states. He prompted California to apply for admission as a free state, bypassing the territorial stage, and hinted that he expected New Mexico (where the Mexican government had abolished slavery) to do the same. This strategy appeared to offer a quick, practical solution to the problem of extending slavery. The North would gain two new free states, and the South would gain acceptance of each individual state's right to bar or permit slavery as it chose.

But southerners rejected Taylor's plan. Not only would it yield the Wilmot Proviso's goal—the banning of slavery from the lands acquired from Mexico—but it rested on the shaky assumption that slavery could never take root in California or New Mexico. Southerners also protested the addition of two new free states. "If we are to be reduced to a mere handful . . . wo, wo, I say to this Union," John C. Calhoun warned. Disillusioned with Taylor, a slaveholder from whom they had expected better, nine southern states agreed to send delegates to a convention to meet in Nashville in June 1850.

Henry Clay Proposes a Compromise

Had Taylor held a stronger position in the Whig party, he might have blunted mounting southern opposition. But many leading Whigs had never accepted this political novice, and in early 1850 Kentucky senator Henry Clay challenged Taylor's leadership by forging a compromise bill to resolve the whole range of contentious issues. Clay proposed (1) the admission of California as a free state; (2) the division of the remainder of the Mexican cession into two territories, New Mexico and Utah, without federal restrictions on slavery; (3) the settlement of the Texas–New Mexico boundary dispute on terms favorable to New Mexico; (4) as an incentive for Texas, an agreement that the federal government would assume the state's large public debt; (5) continuation of slavery in the District of Columbia but abolition of the slave trade there; and (6) a more effective fugitive slave law.

Clay rolled all these proposals into a single "omnibus" bill. The debates over the compromise bill during late winter and early spring 1850 marked the last major appearance on the public stage of Clay, Calhoun, and Webster—the trio of distinguished senators whose lives had mirrored every public event of note since the War of 1812. Clay, ever the conciliator, warned the South against the evils of secession and assured the North that nature would check the spread of slavery. Gaunt and gloomy, the dying Calhoun listened as another senator read Calhoun's address for him, a repetition of his warnings that only if the North treated the South as an equal could the Union survive. Webster spoke vividly in favor of compromise, "not as a Massachusetts man, nor as a Northern man, but as an American," and chided the North for trying to "reenact the will of God" by excluding slavery from the Mexican cession.

However eloquent, the conciliatory voices of Clay and Webster made few converts. Strident voices countered these attempts at conciliation. The antislavery Whig William Seward (SOO-urd) of New York enraged southerners by talking of a "higher law than the Constitution"—namely, the will of God—against the extension of slavery. Clay's compromise faltered as Clay broke with President Taylor, who attacked Clay as a glory-hunter.

As the Union faced its worst crisis since 1789, events in the summer of 1850 eased the way toward resolution. When the Nashville convention met in June, only nine of the fifteen slave states, primarily in the Lower South, sent delegates. Despite the reckless pronouncements of the "fire-eaters" (extreme advocates of "southern rights"), moderates dominated. Then Zachary Taylor celebrated too extravagantly on July 4 and died five days later of a stomach ailment. His successor, Millard Fillmore of New York, supported Clay's compromise. Finally, Senator Stephen A. Douglas of Illinois took over stewardship of the compromise. He broke the omnibus into a series of individual measures; to secure Democratic support, Douglas proposed that popular sovereignty settle the slavery issue in New Mexico and Utah. These

Map 14.1 The Compromise of 1850

The Compromise of 1850 admitted California as a free state. Utah and New Mexico were left open to slavery or freedom according to the principle of popular sovereignty.

Interactive Map

tactics worked. By summer's end the **Compromise of 1850** had become reality (see Map 14.1).

Compromise of 1850 Last-ditch attempt to paper over the issue of slavery expansion; ultimately a failure

Assessing the Compromise

Although President Fillmore hailed the compromise as a final settlement of sectional issues, it failed to bridge the underlying differences between the North and the South. Southerners had voted against the admission of California and northerners against the Fugitive Slave Act.

Each section both gained and lost from the Compromise of 1850. The North won California as a free state, New Mexico and Utah as likely future free states, a favorable settlement of the Texas–New Mexico boundary, and the abolition of the slave trade in the District of Columbia. The South's benefits were cloudier. By stipulating popular sovereignty for New Mexico and Utah, the compromise, to most southerners' relief, had buried the Wilmot Proviso's insistence that Congress formally prohibit slavery in these territories. But to southerners' dismay, the compromise left open the question of whether Congress could prohibit slavery in territories outside of the Mexican cession.

The one clear advantage gained by the South, a more stringent fugitive slave law, quickly proved a mixed blessing. Because few slaves had been taken into the Mexican cession, the question of slavery there had a hypothetical quality. However, the new fugitive slave law authorized real southerners to pursue real fugitives on northern soil. Here was a concrete issue to which the average northerner, who may never have seen a slave and who cared little about slavery a thousand miles away, would respond with fury.

Fugitive Slave Act Harsh measure allowing recapture of escaped slaves; part of the Compromise of 1850; alienated northerners and southerners alike

Enforcement of the Fugitive Slave Act

Northern moderates accepted the **Fugitive Slave Act** of 1850 as the price of saving the Union, but the law outraged antislavery northerners. It denied alleged fugitives the right of trial by jury, forbade them to testify at their own trials, permitted their return to slavery merely on the testimony of a claimant, and enabled court-appointed commissioners to collect ten dollars if they ruled for the slaveholder but only five if they ruled for the fugitive. As one commentator noted, the law threatened to turn the North into "one vast hunting ground." It targeted *all* runaways, putting at risk even fugitives who had lived as free blacks for thirty years or more. Above all, the law brought home to northerners the uncomfortable truth of their own complicity in slavery's continuation. By legalizing the activities of slave-catchers on northern soil, the law reminded northerners that slavery was a national problem, not merely a southern institution.

Efforts to catch and return runaways inflamed emotions in both the North and the South. In 1854, a Boston mob, aroused by antislavery speeches, killed a courthouse guard in an abortive effort to rescue fugitive slave Anthony Burns. Determined to enforce the law, President Franklin Pierce sent federal troops to escort Burns to the harbor, where a ship carried him back to slavery. As five platoons of troops marched Burns to the ship, fifty thousand people lined the streets. The Burns incident shattered the complacency of conservative supporters of the Compromise of 1850. "We went to bed one night old fashioned conservative Compromise Union Whigs," textile manufacturer Amos A. Lawrence wrote, "and waked up stark mad Abolitionists."

Northerners devised ways to interfere with the enforcement of the Fugitive Slave Act. "Vigilance" committees spirited endangered blacks to Canada, lawyers dragged out hearings to raise slave-catchers' expenses, and "personal liberty laws" hindered state officials' enforcement of the law. These obstructionist tactics convinced southerners that the "victory" represented by the passage of the Fugitive Slave Act was increasingly illusory.

Uncle Tom's Cabin Harriet Beecher Stowe's classic novel about slavery; had enormous political impact

Uncle Tom's Cabin

Harriet Beecher Stowe's novel ***Uncle Tom's Cabin*** (1852) drummed up wide northern support for fugitive slaves. Stowe, the daughter of famed evangelical Lyman Beecher, greeted the Fugitive Slave Act with horror. In one of the novel's most memorable scenes, she depicted the slave Eliza, clutching her infant son, bounding to freedom across ice floes on the Ohio River. Slavery itself was Stowe's main target. Much of her novel's power derived from its view that good intentions mean little in the face of so

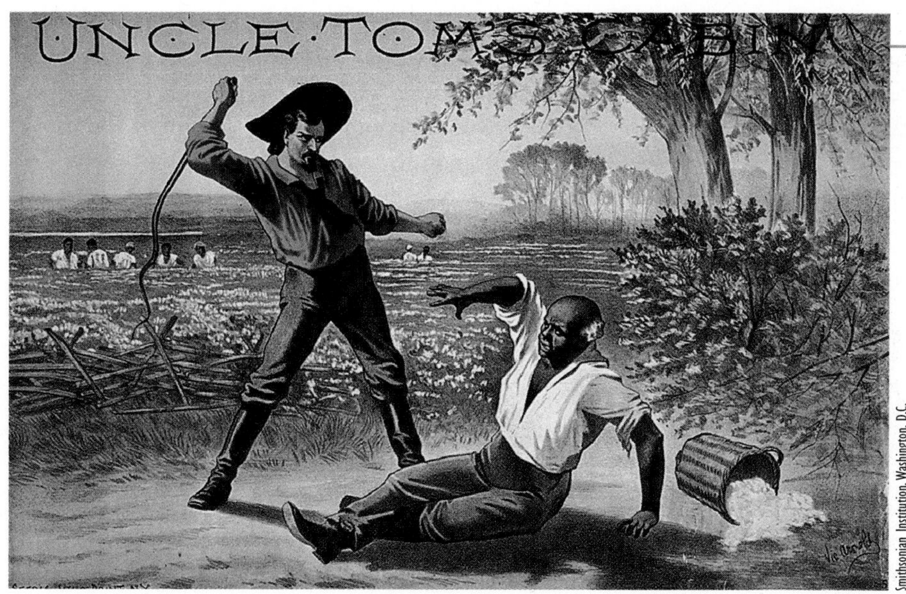

Smithsonian Institution, Washington, D.C.

***Uncle Tom's Cabin* Theater Poster**

With its vivid imagery of slavery, Harriet Beecher Stowe's *Uncle Tom's Cabin* translated well to the stage. Scenes of Eliza crossing the ice of the Ohio River with bloodhounds in pursuit and the evil Simon Legree whipping Uncle Tom outraged northern audiences and turned many against slavery. Southerners, however, damned Mrs. Stowe as a "vile wretch in petticoats."

evil an institution. The good intentions of a kindly slave owner die with him, and Uncle Tom is sold to the vicious Yankee Simon Legree, who whips Tom to death.

Three hundred thousand copies of *Uncle Tom's Cabin* were sold in 1852, and 1.2 million by summer 1853. Stage dramatizations reached perhaps fifty times more people than the novel did. As a play, *Uncle Tom's Cabin* enthralled working-class audiences who were normally indifferent or hostile to abolitionism. A reviewer of one stage performance observed that the gallery was filled with men "in red woollen shirts." Astonished by the silence that fell over these men at the point when Eliza escapes across the river, the reviewer turned to discover that many of them were in tears.

Although *Uncle Tom's Cabin* hardly lived up to a proslavery lawyer's prediction that it would convert 2 million people to abolitionism, it did push many waverers to an aggressive antislavery stance. Indeed, fear of its effect inspired a host of southerners to pen anti-*Uncle Tom* novels. As historian David Potter concluded, the northern attitude toward slavery "was never quite the same after *Uncle Tom's Cabin*."

Library of Congress

Sojourner Truth

Sojourner Truth was born into slavery in upstate New York and named Isabella by her Dutch owner. She was illiterate and a mystic given to hearing messages from God, including one in 1843 that told her to change her name to Sojourner Truth. By then she had joined William Lloyd Garrison's band of abolitionists. In the 1840s and 1850s she traveled from New England to Indiana preaching against slavery. In one notable instance, when hecklers questioned her femininity, she bared her breasts to silence them.

Checking In

- The Compromise of 1850 brought California into the Union and attempted to postpone any further dealing with the expansion of slavery.
- The compromise was passed by a series of coalitions, not a united Congress.
- The compromise did not resolve deep divisions, and the new, stringent Fugitive Slave Act worsened North-South relations.
- *Uncle Tom's Cabin* had an enormous impact on northern popular opinion against slavery.
- The Whig party fragmented over the compromise and lost the election of 1852 by a wide margin.

The Election of 1852

The Fugitive Slave Act fragmented the Whig party. Northern Whigs took the lead in defying the law, and southern Whigs had a difficult time explaining away the power of vocal free-soil Whigs.

In 1852, the Whigs' nomination of Mexican-American War hero General Winfield Scott as their presidential candidate widened the sectional split in the party. Although a Virginian, Scott owed his nomination to the northern free-soil Whigs. His single, feeble statement endorsing the Compromise of 1850 undercut southern Whigs who were trying to portray the Democrats as the party of disunion and themselves as the party of both slavery and the Union.

The Democrats bridged their own sectional division by nominating Franklin Pierce of New Hampshire, a dark-horse candidate whose chief attraction was that no faction of the party strongly opposed him. Northern and southern Democrats alike rallied behind the Compromise of 1850 and behind the ideal of popular sovereignty, and Pierce won a smashing victory. In the most one-sided election since 1820, he carried twenty-seven of the thirty-one states and collected 254 of 296 electoral votes. The Whigs were devastated in the South; one Whig stalwart lamented "the decisive breaking-up of our party."

The Collapse of the Second Party System, 1853–1856

Why did the Whig party disintegrate, and what were the consequences?

Franklin Pierce was the last presidential candidate to carry the popular and electoral vote in both the North and the South until Franklin D. Roosevelt swept into office in 1932. Pierce also became the last president to hold office under the second party system—Whigs against Democrats. Within four years of Pierce's election, the Whig party would disintegrate, to be replaced by two newcomers: the American (Know-Nothing) party and the **Republican Party.**

Republican Party Party, opposed to slavery expansion, that emerged after the Whig party's disintegration; strong in the North, nonexistent in the South

Unlike the Whigs, the Republican Party was a purely sectional, northern party, drawing its support from both former Whigs and discontented Democrats. The Democrats survived as a national party, but with a base so shrunken in the North that the newborn Republican Party captured two-thirds of the free states in 1856.

For decades the second party system had kept the conflict over slavery in check by providing Americans with other issues to argue about—banking, internal improvements, tariffs, and temperance. By the 1850s the debate over slavery extension overshadowed such issues and exposed raw divisions in each party. Whigs, with their larger, more aggressive free-soil wing, were much more vulnerable to disruption than the Democrats. Thus, when Stephen A. Douglas put forth a proposal in 1854 to organize the vast Nebraska Territory with no restrictions on slavery, he ignited a firestorm that consumed the Whig party.

The Kansas-Nebraska Act

Signed in late May 1854, the **Kansas-Nebraska Act** shattered the already weakened second party system and triggered renewed sectional strife. The bill's roots lay in the seemingly uncontroversial desire of farmers to organize the large territory west of Iowa and Missouri. Railroad enthusiasts who dreamed of a rail line linking the Midwest to the Pacific also wanted the territory organized.

Kansas-Nebraska Act Attempt to allow popular sovereignty in newly organizing territories

In January 1854, Democratic senator Stephen A. Douglas of Illinois proposed a bill to organize Nebraska as a territory. Douglas believed that a railroad to the Pacific would bring national benefits, including a continuous line of settlement, and he thought that a railroad-based western expansion would unite the splintering Democratic factions.

Two sources of potential conflict loomed. First, some southerners advocated a southern-based Pacific route rather than a midwestern one. Second, Nebraska lay north of the Missouri Compromise line in the Louisiana Purchase, a region closed to slavery. Under Douglas's bill, the South would lose the Pacific rail route *and* face the possibility of more free territory in the Union. To placate southerners and win their votes, Douglas made two concessions. He stated publicly that the Nebraska bill "superseded" the Missouri Compromise and rendered it "void." Next, he agreed to a division of Nebraska into two territories: Nebraska to the west of Iowa, and Kansas to the west of Missouri. Because Missouri was a slave state, most congressmen assumed that the division aimed to secure Kansas for slavery and Nebraska for free soil.

These modifications to Douglas's original bill set off a storm of protest. Despite Douglas's belief that national expansion was the critical issue, most attention focused on the extension of slavery. Antislavery northerners assailed the bill as "an atrocious plot" to violate the "sacred pledge" of the Missouri Compromise and to turn Kansas into a "dreary region of despotism, inhabited by masters and slaves." Their anger provoked an equal response among southerners and added the issue of sectional pride to the already-volatile mix of expansion and slavery.

Despite the uproar, Douglas successfully guided the Kansas-Nebraska bill through the Senate. In the House, where the bill passed by little more than a whisker, 113 to 100, the true dimensions of the conflict became apparent. Not a single northern Whig representative in the House voted for the bill, whereas the northern Democrats split evenly.

The Surge of Free Soil

Amid the clamor over his bill, Douglas ruefully observed that he could now travel to Chicago by the light of his own burning effigies. Neither a fool nor a political novice, he was the victim of a political bombshell—**free soil**—that exploded under his feet.

free soil Movement opposed to any expansion of slavery

Support for free soil united many who agreed on little else. Many free-soilers were racists who opposed allowing any African-Americans, slave or free, into the West. Others repudiated slavery on moral grounds and rejected blatantly racist legislation. Although split over the morality of slavery, most free-soilers agreed that slavery impeded whites' progress. Because a slave worked for nothing, free-soilers claimed, no free laborer could compete with a slave. If slavery secured a toehold in Kansas, free-soilers warned, Minnesota would fall to slavery as well.

To free-soilers, the Kansas-Nebraska Act, with its erasure of the Missouri Compromise, was the last straw, for it revealed, one wrote, "a continuous movement by slaveholders to spread slavery over the entire North." Free-soilers saw southern planters, southern politicians, and their northern dupes, such as Stephen A. Douglas, entangled in a gigantic conspiracy to extend slavery.

The Ebbing of Manifest Destiny

The uproar over the Kansas-Nebraska Act embarrassed the Pierce administration. It also doomed Manifest Destiny, the one issue that had held the Democrats together in the 1840s.

Franklin Pierce had come to office championing Manifest Destiny, but increasing sectional rivalries sidetracked his efforts. In 1853 his emissary, James Gadsden, negotiated the purchase of a strip of land south of the Gila River (now southern Arizona and part of southern New Mexico), an acquisition favored by advocates of a southern railroad route to the Pacific. Fierce opposition to the Gadsden Purchase revealed mounting free-soilers' suspicions of expansion, and the Senate approved the treaty only after slashing nine thousand square miles from the purchase. The sectional rivalries beginning to engulf the Nebraska bill clearly threatened any proposal to gain new territory.

Cuba provided even more vivid proof of the change in public attitudes toward expansion. In 1854 a former Mississippi governor, John A. Quitman, planned a filibuster (an unofficial military expedition) to seize Cuba from Spain. Pierce wanted to acquire Cuba and may first have encouraged Quitman's plans, but the president backed down in the face of northern opposition. Northerners saw the filibuster as another manifestation of the Slave Power—the conspiracy of slaveholders and their northern dupes to grab more territory for slavery.

Events, however, slipped out of Pierce's control. In October 1854, the American ambassadors to Great Britain, France, and Spain, two of them southerners, met in Belgium and issued the unofficial Ostend Manifesto, calling on the United States to acquire Cuba by any means, including force.

Despite the Pierce administration's disavowal of the Ostend Manifesto, the idea of expansion into the Caribbean continued to attract southerners, including the Tennessee-born adventurer William Walker. Between 1853 and 1860, the year a firing squad in Honduras (hahn-DURE-uss) executed him, Walker led a succession of filibustering expeditions into Mexico and Nicaragua (nee-ka-RAH-gwa). Taking advantage of civil chaos in Nicaragua, he made himself the chief political force there, reinstituted slavery, and talked of making Nicaragua a U.S. colony.

Although some southerners were against expansion—among them the Louisiana sugar planters who opposed acquiring Cuba because Cuban sugar would compete with their product—southern expansionists stirred up enough commotion to worry antislavery northerners that the South aspired to establish a Caribbean slave empire. Like a card in a poker game, the threat of expansion southward was all the more menacing for not being played. As long as the debate on the extension of slavery focused on the continental United States, prospects for expansion were limited. However, adding the wild card of Caribbean territory changed all calculations.

The Whigs Disintegrate, 1854–1855

While straining Democratic unity, the Kansas-Nebraska Act wrecked the Whig party. Although Democrats lost ground in the 1854 congressional elections, the Whigs failed to benefit. No matter how furious the free-soil Democrats were at Douglas for introducing the act, they could not forget that southern Whigs had supported him. Northern Whigs split into two camps: antislavery "Conscience" Whigs, led by Senator William Seward of New York, and conservatives, led by former president Millard Fillmore. The conservatives believed that the Whig party had to adhere to the Compromise of 1850 to maintain itself as a national party.

This deep division within the Whig party repelled antislavery Democrats and prompted antislavery Whigs to look for an alternative party. By 1856 the new Republican Party would become home for these antislavery refugees; however, in 1854 and 1855 the American, or Know-Nothing, party emerged as the principal alternative to the faltering established parties.

The Rise and Fall of the Know-Nothings, 1853–1856

One of a number of nativist societies that mushroomed in opposition to the massive immigration of the 1840s, the **Know-Nothings** originated in the secret Order of the Star-Spangled Banner. The party's popular name derived from the standard response of its members to inquiries about its activities: "I know nothing." The Know-Nothings' core purpose was to rid the United States of immigrant and Catholic political influence. To this end, they pressured the existing parties to elevate only native-born Protestants to office and advocated an extension of the naturalization period before immigrants could vote.

Know-Nothings Nativist party that enjoyed a brief surge of power in the early 1850s

Throughout the 1840s, nativists usually voted Whig, but their allegiance to the Whigs started to buckle during Winfield Scott's campaign for the presidency in 1852. In an attempt to revitalize his party, Scott had courted the traditionally Democratic Catholic vote. But Scott's tactic backfired. Most Catholics voted for Franklin Pierce, while many nativists bailed out of the Whig party. The Kansas-Nebraska Act cemented nativist allegiance to the Know-Nothings. The Know-Nothings, unified by an obsessive fear of conspiracies, simultaneously denounced a papal conspiracy against the American republic and a Slave Power conspiracy reaching its tentacles throughout the United States. The Know-Nothings' surge was truly stunning. In 1854, they captured the governorship, all the congressional seats, and almost all the seats in the state legislature in Massachusetts.

After rising spectacularly between 1853 and 1855, the star of Know-Nothingism plummeted and gradually disappeared below the horizon after 1856. The Know-Nothings proved as vulnerable as the Whigs to sectional conflicts over slavery. Although primarily a force in the North, the Know-Nothings had a southern wing, comprised mainly of former Whigs who loathed both the antislavery northerners who were abandoning the Whig party and the southern Democrats, whom they viewed as disunionist firebrands. In 1855, these southern Know-Nothings combined with northern conservatives to make acceptance of the Kansas-Nebraska Act part of the Know-Nothing platform. Thus, they blurred the attraction of Know-Nothingism to those northern voters who were more antislavery than anti-Catholic.

One Whig refugee, Illinois congressman Abraham Lincoln, asked pointedly, "How can anyone who abhors the oppression of negroes be in favor of degrading classes of white people?" "We began by declaring," Lincoln continued, "that 'all men are created equal.' We now practically read it 'all men are created equal except negroes.' When the Know-Nothings get control, it will read 'all men are created equal, except Negroes and Foreigners and Catholics.'" Even most Know-Nothings concluded that "neither the Pope nor the foreigners ever can govern the country or endanger its liberties, but the slavebreeders and slavetraders do govern it, and threaten to put an end to all government but theirs." Consequently, the Know-Nothings proved vulnerable to the challenge posed by the emerging Republican Party, which did not officially embrace nativism and had no southern wing to placate.

The Republican Party and the Crisis in Kansas, 1855–1856

Born in the chaotic aftermath of the Kansas-Nebraska Act, the Republican Party would become the main opposition to the Democratic Party by 1856 and would win each presidential election from 1860 until 1884. In 1855, however, few would have predicted such a bright future. While united by opposition to the Kansas-Nebraska Act, the Republicans held various shades of opinion in uneasy balance. At one extreme were conservatives who merely wanted to restore the Missouri Compromise; at the other was a small faction of former Liberty Party abolitionists; and the middle held a sizable body of free-soilers.

Faced with these diverse constituencies, Republican leaders became political jugglers. To maintain internal harmony, the party's leaders avoided potentially divisive national issues such as the tariff and banking. Even so, Republican leaders recognized that they and the Know-Nothings were competing for many of the same voters. Republicans had clearer antislavery credentials than the Know-Nothings, but this fact alone did not guarantee that voters would respond more to antislavery than to anti-Catholicism or temperance. The Republicans needed a development that would make voters worry more about the Slave Power than about rum or Catholicism. Violence in Kansas united the party around its free-soil center and boosted Republican fortunes.

In the wake of the Kansas-Nebraska Act, Boston-based abolitionists sent antislavery settlers into Kansas. The abolitionists' aim was to stifle efforts to turn Kansas into a slave state. But the bulk of the territory's early settlers came from Missouri or elsewhere in the Midwest. Very few of these early settlers opposed slavery on moral grounds. Some, in fact, favored slavery; others simply wanted to keep all blacks, whether slave or free, out of Kansas.

Despite most settlers' racist leanings and utter hatred of abolitionists, Kansas became a battleground between proslavery and antislavery forces. In March 1855, thousands of proslavery Missourian "border ruffians," led by Senator David R. Atchison, crossed into Kansas to vote illegally in the first election for a territorial legislature. By stealing the election, the proslavery forces committed a grave tactical blunder. A cloud of fraudulence thereafter hung over the proslavery legislature subsequently established at Lecompton, Kansas. This legislature then further darkened its image by passing a succession of outrageous laws, limiting officeholding to individuals who would swear allegiance to slavery, punishing the harboring of fugitive

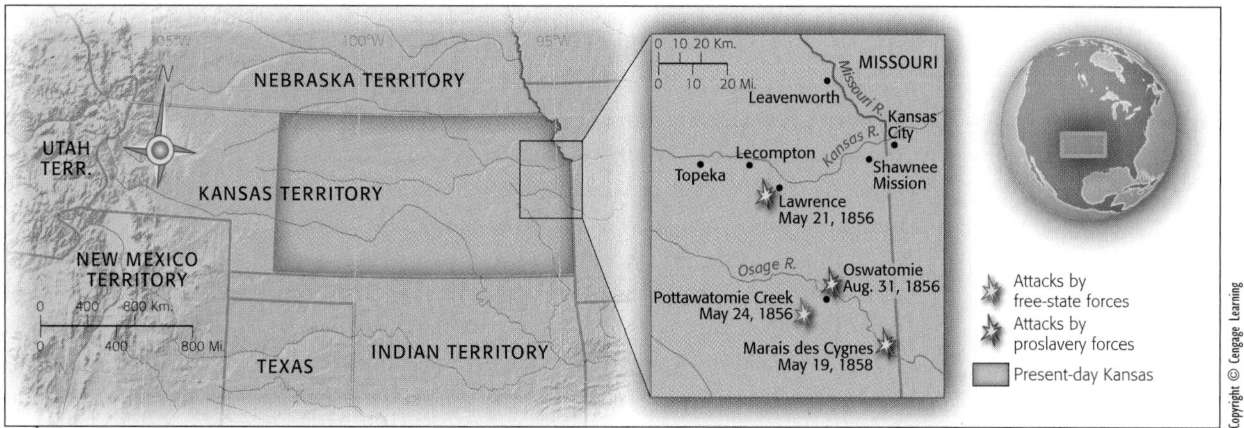

Map 14.2 Bleeding Kansas

Kansas became a battleground between free-state and slave-state factions in the 1850s.

Interactive Map

slaves by ten years' imprisonment, and making the circulation of abolitionist literature a capital offense.

The territorial legislature's actions set off a chain reaction. Free-staters organized a rival government at Topeka in the summer and fall of 1855. In response, the Lecompton government in May 1856 dispatched a posse to Lawrence, where free-staters had taken up arms. Bearing banners emblazoned with slogans such as "Southern Rights" and "Let Yankees Tremble and Abolitionists Fall," the proslavery posse tore through Lawrence, burning several buildings and destroying two free-state presses. There were no deaths, but Republicans immediately dubbed the incident "the sack of Lawrence."

The next move was made by John Brown. The sack of Lawrence convinced Brown that God now beckoned him "to break the jaws of the wicked." In late May, Brown led seven men, including his four sons and his son-in-law, toward the Pottawatomie (pot-uh-WATT-uh-mee) Creek near Lawrence. Setting upon five men associated with the Lecompton government, they shot one to death and hacked the others to pieces with broadswords. Brown's "Pottawatomie Massacre" struck terror into the hearts of southerners and completed the transformation of Bleeding Kansas into a battleground between the South and the North (see Map 14.2).

Popular sovereignty had failed in Kansas. Instead of resolving the issue of slavery extension, popular sovereignty merely institutionalized the division over slavery by creating rival governments in Lecompton and Topeka. The Pierce administration then shot itself in the foot by denouncing the Topeka government and recognizing only its Lecompton rival. Pierce had forced northern Democrats into the awkward position of appearing to ally with the South in support of the "Bogus Legislature" at Lecompton.

Nor did popular sovereignty keep the slavery issue out of national politics. On the day before the sack of Lawrence, Republican senator Charles Sumner of Massachusetts delivered a bombastic and wrathful speech, "The Crime Against

Kansas." Sumner singled out Senator Andrew Butler of South Carolina for making "the harlot, slavery" his mistress and for the "loose expectoration" of his speech (a nasty reference to the aging Butler's tendency to drool). Two days later, a relative of Butler, Democratic representative Preston Brooks of South Carolina, strode into the Senate chamber, found Sumner at his desk, and struck him repeatedly with a cane. The hollow cane broke after five or six blows, but Sumner required stitches, experienced shock, and did not return to the Senate for three years. Brooks became an instant hero in the South, and the fragments of his weapon were "begged as sacred relics." A new cane, presented to Brooks by the city of Charleston, bore the inscription "Hit him again."

Now Bleeding Kansas and Bleeding Sumner united the North. The sack of Lawrence, Pierce's recognition of the proslavery Lecompton government, and Brooks's actions seemed to clinch the Republican argument that an aggressive "slaveocracy" held white northerners in contempt. Abolitionists remained unpopular in northern opinion, but southerners were becoming even less popular. By denouncing the Slave Power more than slavery itself, Republican propagandists sidestepped the issue of slavery's morality, which divided their followers, and focused on portraying southern planters as arrogant aristocrats and the natural enemies of the laboring people of the North.

The Election of 1856

The presidential race of 1856 revealed the scope of the political realignment of the preceding few years. The Republicans, in their first presidential contest, nominated John C. Frémont, the "pathfinder" of California "Bear State" fame. Northern Know-Nothings also endorsed Frémont, while southern Know-Nothings nominated Millard Fillmore, the last Whig president. The Democrats dumped the battered Pierce for James Buchanan (byoo-CAN-un) of Pennsylvania, who had had the luck to be out of the country (as minister to Great Britain) during the Kansas-Nebraska furor. A signer of the Ostend Manifesto, Buchanan was popular in the South; virtually all of his close friends in Washington were southerners.

The campaign became two separate races: Frémont versus Buchanan in the free states and Fillmore versus Buchanan in the slave states. Buchanan was in effect the only national candidate. Although Frémont attracted wide support in the North and Fillmore equal support in the South, Buchanan carried enough votes in both the North and South to win the presidency.

The election yielded three clear conclusions. First, the American party was finished as a major national force. Having worked for the Republican Frémont, most northern Know-Nothings joined that party. Fillmore's dismal showing in the South convinced southern Know-Nothings to abandon their party and seek a new political affiliation. Second, although in existence for barely a year, lacking any base in the South, and running a political novice, the Republican Party did very well. A purely sectional party had nearly captured the presidency. Third, as long as the Democrats could unite behind a single national candidate, they would be hard to defeat. To achieve unity, however, the Democrats would have to find more James Buchanans—"doughface" moderates acceptable to southerners and northerners alike.

Checking In

- The Kansas-Nebraska Act set off a firestorm of controversy.
- The free-soil movement strengthened as the Whigs splintered over the act.
- The Know-Nothings briefly flourished as an alternative to the Whigs.
- "Bleeding Kansas" boosted the sectional Republican Party, which was emerging in the North with former free-soilers, Whigs, and Know-Nothings.
- The election of 1856 showed that the Whigs had vanished as a political force and that the Republicans were on the rise.

THE CRISIS OF THE UNION, 1857–1860

What major issues dominated American politics from 1857 to 1860?

No one ever accused James Buchanan of impulsiveness or fanaticism. Although a moderate who wished to avoid controversy, Buchanan would preside over one of the most controversy-ridden administrations in American history. A Supreme Court decision concerning Dred Scott, a Missouri slave who had resided in free territory for several years; the creation of the proslavery Lecompton constitution in Kansas; the raid by John Brown on Harpers Ferry, Virginia; and secession itself would wrack Buchanan's administration. The forces driving the nation apart were spinning out of control by 1856, and Buchanan could not stop them. By his inauguration, southerners saw creeping abolitionism in the guise of free soil, and northerners detected an ever more insatiable Slave Power. Once these potent images took hold in the minds of the American people, politicians could do little to erase them.

The *Dred Scott* Case, 1857

Pledged to congressional "noninterference" with slavery in the territories, Buchanan looked to the courts for resolution of the vexatious issue of slavery's extension. A case that appeared to promise a solution had been winding its way through the courts for years; on March 6, 1857, two days after Buchanan's inauguration, the Supreme Court handed down its decision in *Dred Scott v. Sandford.*

During the 1830s, Dred Scott, a slave, had been taken by his master from the slave state of Missouri into Illinois and the Wisconsin Territory, which were both closed to slavery. After his master's death, Scott sued for his freedom on the grounds of his residence in free territory.

The Court faced two key questions. Did Scott's residence in free territory during the 1830s make him free? Did Scott, again enslaved in Missouri, have the right to sue in the federal courts? The Supreme Court could have neatly sidestepped controversy by ruling that Scott had no right to sue, but it chose not to do so.

Instead, Chief Justice Roger B. Taney, a seventy-nine-year-old Marylander, handed down a sweeping decision that touched off another firestorm. First, Taney wrote, Scott, a slave, could not sue for his freedom. Further, no black, whether a slave or a free descendant of slaves, could become a U.S. citizen. Continuing his incendiary opinion, Taney ruled that even had Scott been entitled to sue, his residence in free territory did not make him free, because the Missouri Compromise, whose provisions prohibited slavery in the Wisconsin Territory, was itself unconstitutional. The compromise, declared Taney, violated the Fifth Amendment's protection of property (including slaves).

The ***Dred Scott* decision,** instead of settling the issue of the expansion of slavery, touched off another blast of controversy. The antislavery press flayed it as "willful perversion" filled with "gross historical falsehoods." Republicans saw the decision as further evidence that the fiendish Slave Power gripped the nation. Five of the six justices in the majority were from slave states.

***Dred Scott* decision** Judicial decision that threw out the Missouri Compromise, creating political turmoil

Like Stephen A. Douglas after the Kansas-Nebraska Act, James Buchanan now appeared as another northern dupe of the "slaveocracy." Republicans restrained themselves from open defiance of the decision only by insisting that it did not bind the nation; Taney's comments on the constitutionality of the Missouri Compromise, they contended, were opinions unnecessary to settling the case and therefore technically not binding.

Reactions to the decision provided more proof that no "judicious" or nonpartisan solution to slavery extension was possible. Anyone who still doubted this needed only to read the fast-breaking news from Kansas.

The Lecompton Constitution, 1857

In Kansas, the free-state government at Topeka and the officially recognized proslavery government at Lecompton regarded each other with profound distrust. Buchanan's plan for Kansas looked simple: An elected territorial convention would draw up a constitution that would either prohibit or permit slavery; Buchanan would submit the constitution to Congress; Congress would then admit Kansas as a state.

Unfortunately, the plan exploded in Buchanan's face. Popular sovereignty, the essence of the plan, demanded fair play, a scarce commodity in Kansas. The territory's history of fraudulent elections left both sides reluctant to commit their fortunes to the polls. In June 1857, an election for a constitutional convention took place, but free-staters, by now a majority in Kansas, boycotted the election on grounds that the proslavery forces would rig it. A constitutional convention dominated by proslavery delegates then met and drew up the **Lecompton constitution,** which protected the rights of slaveholders already residing in Kansas and provided for a referendum to decide whether to allow more slaves into the territory.

Lecompton constitution
Advanced by proslavery advocates in Kansas; would have protected rights of slaveholders; endorsed by Buchanan

Buchanan faced a dilemma. As a supporter of popular sovereignty, he had favored letting Kansas voters decide the slavery issue. But now he confronted a constitution drawn up by a convention chosen by less than 10 percent of the eligible voters. However, there were compelling reasons to accept the Lecompton constitution. The South, which had provided Buchanan's winning margin in the 1856 election, supported it. To Buchanan, the wrangling over slavery in Kansas was a case of extremists' turning minor issues into major ones, especially because only about two hundred slaves resided in Kansas and because prospects for slavery in the remaining territories were slight. The admission of Kansas to the Union as free or slave seemed the quickest way to end the commotion. Therefore, in December 1857, Buchanan endorsed the Lecompton constitution.

Stephen A. Douglas and other northern Democrats broke with Buchanan. To them, the Lecompton constitution, in allowing voters to decide only whether more slaves could enter Kansas, violated the spirit of popular sovereignty. "I care not whether [slavery] is voted down or voted up," Douglas declared. However, he felt that refusing to allow a vote on the constitution itself, with its protection of existing slave property, smacked of a "system of trickery and jugglery to defeat the fair expression of the will of the people."

Meanwhile, in Kansas, the newly elected territorial legislature called for a referendum on the Lecompton constitution and thus on slavery itself. Two elections followed. In December 1857, the referendum called by the constitutional convention took place. Free-staters boycotted it, and the Lecompton constitution passed overwhelmingly. Two weeks later, the election called by the territorial legislature took place. This time proslavery forces boycotted, and the constitution went down to crushing defeat. Buchanan tried to ignore this second election, but when he attempted to bring Kansas into the Union under the Lecompton constitution, Congress blocked him and forced yet another referendum. This time, Kansas could accept or reject the entire constitution, with the proviso that rejection would delay statehood. Despite the proviso, Kansans voted down the Lecompton constitution.

Buchanan had simultaneously failed to tranquilize Kansas and alienated northerners in his own party, who now more than ever believed that the southern Slave Power pulled all the important strings in the Democratic Party. Douglas emerged as a hero for northern Democrats but saw his cherished formula of popular sovereignty become a prescription for strife rather than harmony.

The Lincoln-Douglas Debates, 1858

Despite the acclaim that he received for his stand against the Lecompton constitution, Douglas faced a stiff challenge in the 1858 Illinois senatorial election. Of his Republican opponent, Abraham Lincoln, Douglas remarked, "I shall have my hands full. He is the strong man of his party—full of wit, facts, and dates—and the best stump speaker with his droll ways and dry jokes, in the West."

Physically and ideologically, the two candidates presented a striking contrast. Tall (6'4") and gangling, Lincoln possessed energy, ambition, and a passion for self-education that had carried him from the Kentucky log cabin where he was born into law and politics in his adopted Illinois. First elected as a Whig, he joined the Republican Party in 1856. The New England–born Douglas stood a foot shorter than Lincoln, but to the small farmers of southern origin who populated the Illinois flatlands, he was the "little giant," the personification of the Democratic Party in the West. The campaign quickly became more than just another Senate race, for it pitted the Republican Party's rising star against the Senate's leading Democrat, and, thanks to the railroad and the telegraph, it received unprecedented national attention.

Opening his campaign with his famous "House Divided" speech ("this government cannot endure permanently half *slave* and half *free*"), Lincoln stressed the gulf between his free-soil position and Douglas's popular sovereignty. Douglas dismissed the house-divided doctrine as an invitation to secession. What mattered to him was not slavery but the continued expansion of white settlement. Douglas believed popular sovereignty was the surest way to attain this goal without disrupting the Union.

The high point of the campaign came in a series of seven debates held from August to October 1858. Douglas used the debates to portray Lincoln as a virtual abolitionist and advocate of racial equality. Lincoln replied that Congress had no constitutional authority to abolish slavery in the South. He also asserted that "I am not, nor ever have been in favor of bringing about the social and political equality of the white and black man."

In the debate at Freeport, Illinois, Lincoln tried to make Douglas squirm by asking how popular sovereignty could be reconciled with the *Dred Scott* decision. Lincoln maintained that if Congress had no authority to exclude slavery from a territory, then it seemingly followed that a territorial legislature created by Congress also lacked the power to do so. Douglas responded that, although the Supreme Court

Stephen A. Douglas

Douglas's politics were founded on his unflinching conviction that most Americans favored national expansion and would support popular sovereignty as the fastest and least controversial way to achieve it. However, Douglas's self-assurance blinded him to rising northern sentiment for free soil.

Abraham Lincoln

Clean-shaven at the time of his famous debates with Douglas, Lincoln would soon grow a beard to give himself a more distinguished appearance.

had ruled that Congress could not exclude slavery from the territories, the voters in a territory could do so by refusing to enact laws that gave legal protection to slave property. This "Freeport doctrine" salvaged popular sovereignty but did nothing for Douglas's reputation among southerners, who preferred the guarantees of *Dred Scott* to the uncertainties of popular sovereignty. Trying to move beyond debates on free soil and popular sovereignty, Lincoln shifted in the closing debates to attacks on slavery as "a moral, social, and political evil." He argued that Douglas's view of slavery as merely an eccentric and unsavory southern custom would dull the nation's conscience and facilitate the legalization of slavery everywhere. At the same time, however, Lincoln compromised his own position by rejecting both abolition and equality for blacks.

Neither man scored a clear victory in the debates, and the senatorial election, which Douglas won, settled no major issues. Nonetheless, the candidates' contest was crucial. It solidified the sectional split in the Democratic Party and made Lincoln famous in the North—and infamous in the South.

The Legacy of Harpers Ferry

Although Lincoln explicitly rejected abolitionism, he called free soil a step toward the "ultimate extinction" of slavery. Many southerners ignored the differences between free soil and abolitionism and saw the entire North locked in the grip of demented leaders bent on civil war.

Nothing did more to freeze this southern image of the North than the evidence of northern complicity in John Brown's raid on the federal arsenal at **Harpers Ferry,** Virginia, on October 16, 1859. Brown and his followers were quickly overpowered; Brown himself was tried, convicted, and hanged. Lincoln and Seward condemned the raid, but some northerners turned Brown into a martyr; Ralph Waldo Emerson exulted that Brown's execution would "make the gallows as glorious as the cross." Further, captured correspondence disclosed that Brown had received financial support from northern abolitionists. His objective, to inspire an armed slave insurrection, rekindled the deepest fears of white southerners.

Harpers Ferry Federal arsenal in Virginia; site of John Brown's abortive attempt to fuel a slave uprising in the South

In the wake of Brown's raid, rumors flew around the South, and vigilantes turned out to battle conspiracies that existed only in their minds. Volunteers, for example, mobilized to defend northeastern Texas against thousands of abolitionists supposedly on their way to pillage Dallas and its environs. Elsewhere, vigilantes rounded up thousands of slaves, tortured some into confessing to nonexistent plots, and then lynched them. The hysteria generated by such rumors played into the hands of the extremists known as fire-eaters, who encouraged the witch-hunts in order to gain political support.

More and more southerners concluded that the Republican Party itself directed abolitionism and deserved blame for John Brown's raid. After all, had not influential Republicans assailed slavery, unconstitutionally tried to ban it, and spoken of an "irrepressible conflict" between slavery and freedom?

The South Contemplates Secession

A pamphlet published in 1860 embodied a growing southern conviction: *The South Alone Should Govern the South.* Most southerners, however, reached this conclusion gradually and reluctantly. In 1850, insulated from the main tide of immigration, southerners thought themselves the most American of Americans. The events of the 1850s led growing numbers of southerners to conclude that the North had deserted the principles of the Union and had virtually declared war on the South by using such headline-grabbing phrases as "irrepressible conflict" and "a higher law." To southerners, the North, not slavery, was the problem.

Viewed as a practical tactic to secure concrete goals, secession did not make a great deal of sense. Some southerners contended that secession would make it easier for the South to acquire more territory for slavery in the Caribbean; yet the South was scarcely united in desiring additional slave territory in Mexico, Cuba, or Central America. Furthermore, if the South were to secede, the remaining continental territories would belong exclusively to the North. Nor would secession stop future John Browns from infiltrating the South to provoke slave insurrections.

Yet to dwell on the impracticality of secession as a choice for the South is to miss the point. Talk of secession was less a tactic with clear goals than an expression of the South's outrage at the Republicans. Southerners believed that the North was treating the South as its inferior, as no more than a slave. They bitterly dismissed Republican portrayals of the South as a region of arrogant planters and degraded white common folk. Submission to the Republicans, declared Democratic senator Jefferson Davis of Mississippi, "would be intolerable to a proud people."

CHECKING IN

- In the *Dred Scott* decision, which nullified the Missouri Compromise, the Supreme Court tossed a bombshell into American politics.
- Turmoil and bloodshed continued in Kansas.
- Although he lost the 1858 senatorial election in Illinois, his campaign debates with Stephen Douglas made Abraham Lincoln a national figure.
- John Brown's raid on Harpers Ferry intensified the deep divisions between North and South.
- By 1860 many southerners seriously contemplated secession.

THE COLLAPSE OF THE UNION, 1860–1861

Why did southerners conclude that the North was bent on extinguishing slavery in southern states?

As long as the pliant James Buchanan occupied the White House, southerners only talked of secession. However, once Buchanan declined to seek reelection, they anxiously awaited the next presidential election. By 1860, voters were deciding not just an election but also the fate of the Union. Lincoln's election began the parade out of the Union by southern states. Initially only the Lower South seceded, encouraging moderates to search frantically for a compromise to save the Union. But the time for compromise had passed.

The Election of 1860

As a single-issue, free-soil party, the Republicans had done well in the election of 1856. To win in 1860, however, they would have to broaden their appeal. Republican leaders needed an economic program to complement their advocacy of free soil. A severe economic slump following the Panic of 1857 provided them an opening. The depression shattered a decade of prosperity and thrust economic concerns to the fore. In response, the Republicans developed an economic program based on support for a protective tariff, federal aid for internal improvements, and grants to settlers of free 160-acre homesteads carved from public lands.

To broaden their appeal, the Republicans chose Abraham Lincoln as their presidential candidate over the better-known William H. Seward. Lincoln offered a stronger possibility of carrying such key states as Pennsylvania and his home state of Illinois, and projected a more moderate image than Seward, whose penchant for phrases like "irrepressible conflict" and "higher law" made him appear radical. In contrast, Lincoln had repeatedly said that Congress had no constitutional right to interfere with slavery in the South and had rejected the "higher law" doctrine.

The Democrats, still clinging to national party status, had to bridge their own sectional divisions. The *Dred Scott* decision and the conflict over the Lecompton constitution had weakened northern Democrats and strengthened southern Democrats. While Douglas still desperately defended popular sovereignty, southern Democrats stretched *Dred Scott* to conclude that Congress now had to protect slavery in the territories.

The Democratic Party's internal turmoil boiled over at its Charleston convention in the spring of 1860. Failing to win a platform guaranteeing the federal protection of slavery in the territories, delegates from the Lower South stormed out. The convention adjourned to Baltimore, where a new fight erupted over whether to seat the pro-Douglas delegates hastily chosen to replace the absent delegates from the Lower South. When the convention voted to seat these new delegates, representatives from Virginia and the Upper South walked out. What remained of the original Democratic convention nominated Douglas, but the seceders marched off to yet another hall in Baltimore and nominated Buchanan's vice president, John C. Breckinridge of Kentucky, on a platform calling for the congressional protection of slavery in the territories. The spectacle of two different Democratic candidates for the presidency signaled the complete disruption of the party.

The South still contained a sizable number of moderates, often former Whigs. In 1860, these southern moderates joined former northern Whigs in the new Constitutional Union party. They nominated John Bell of Tennessee, a slaveholder who had opposed the Kansas-Nebraska Act and the Lecompton constitution. Calling for the Union's preservation, the new party took no stand on slavery's extension.

The four candidates presented a relatively clear choice. At one end of the spectrum, Lincoln conceded that the South had the constitutional right to preserve slavery, but he demanded that Congress prohibit its extension. At the other end, Breckinridge insisted that Congress had to protect slavery anywhere it existed. In the middle were Bell and Douglas, the latter still trying to salvage popular sovereignty. In the end, Lincoln won 180 electoral votes; his three opponents, only 123. However, Lincoln's popular votes, 39 percent of the total, came almost completely from the North. Douglas, the only candidate to run in both sections, ran second in the popular vote but carried only Missouri. Bell won most of the Upper South, and Breckinridge took Maryland and the Lower South.

The Movement for Secession

Lincoln's election struck most of the white South as a calculated northern insult. The North, a South Carolina planter told a visitor from Britain, "has got so far toward being abolitionized as to elect a man avowedly hostile to our institutions."

Few southerners believed that Lincoln would fulfill his promise to protect slavery in the South; most feared that he would act as a mere front man for more John Browns. "Now that the black radical Republicans have the power I suppose they will Brown us all," a South Carolinian lamented.

Some southerners had threatened secession at the prospect of Lincoln's election, and now the moment of decision had arrived. On December 20, 1860, a South Carolina convention voted unanimously for secession; in short order Alabama,

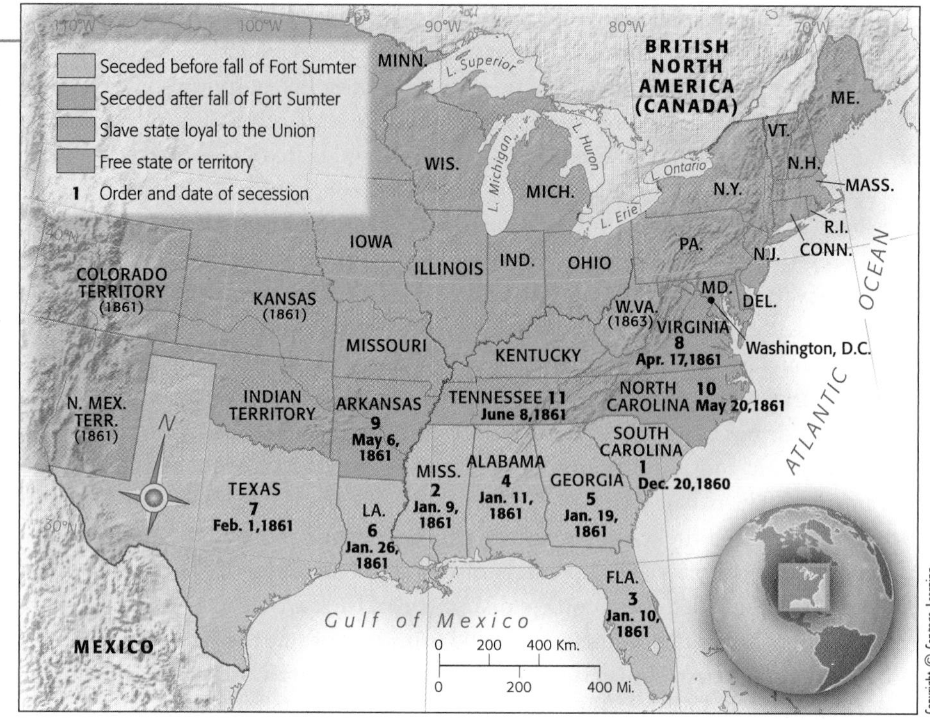

Map 14.3 Secession

Four key states—Virginia, Arkansas, Tennessee, and North Carolina—did not secede until after the fall of Fort Sumter. The border slave states of Maryland, Delaware, Kentucky, and Missouri stayed in the Union.

Interactive Map

Mississippi, Florida, Georgia, Louisiana, and Texas followed. On February 4, 1861, delegates from these seven states met in Montgomery, Alabama, and established the Confederate States of America. But uncertainty colored the secession movement. Many southerners, even in the Deep South, had resisted the fire-eaters' call to leave the Union. Jefferson Davis, inaugurated in February 1861 as president of the Confederacy, was a reluctant secessionist who had remained in the Senate two weeks after his own state of Mississippi had seceded.

At first, the Upper South rejected secession completely. More economically dependent on the North, it had proportionately fewer slaves and more nonslaveholders, whose loyalty in case of secession was dubious. Finally, if secession precipitated a war, the Upper South was the likely battleground. Consequently, the secession movement that South Carolina had begun so boldly in December 1860 seemed to be falling apart by March 1861.

The Search for Compromise

The lack of southern unity confirmed the view of most Republicans that the secessionists were more bluster than substance. Seward described secession as the work of "a relatively few hotheads," and Lincoln believed that the loyal majority of southerners would soon wrest control from the fire-eating minority.

This perception stiffened Republican resolve to resist compromise. Moderate John J. Crittenden of Kentucky suggested compensation for owners of runaway slaves, repeal of northern personal-liberty laws, a constitutional amendment to prohibit the federal government from interfering with slavery in southern states, and another amendment to restore the Missouri Compromise line. But in the face of adamant Republican opposition, the **Crittenden plan** collapsed.

Crittenden plan Attempt to find a compromise that would prevent the Union from splitting

Lincoln's faith in a "loyal majority" of southerners exaggerated both their numbers and their dedication to the Union. Many southern opponents of the fire-eating secessionists sat on the fence, waiting for major concessions from the North; their allegiance to the Union was conditional. But compromise would have meant the abandonment of free soil, a basic principle of the Republican Party, and Lincoln, who misread southern opinion, resisted.

Beyond the issue of compromise, the precipitous secession of the Lower South had changed the question that Lincoln faced. The issue no longer revolved around slavery's extension but around secession. The Lower South had left the Union in the face of losing a fair election. For Lincoln to cave in to such pressure would violate majority rule, the sacred principle on which the nation had been founded.

The Coming of War

By the time Lincoln took office in March 1861, only a spark was needed to set off a war. Lincoln had pledged in his inaugural address to "hold, occupy, and possess" federal property in the states that had seceded, a statement that committed him to the defense of Fort Pickens in Florida and **Fort Sumter** in the harbor of Charleston, South Carolina. Accordingly, the president informed South Carolina's governor of his intention to supply Fort Sumter with provisions but neither reinforcements nor ammunition. Shortly before dawn on April 12, 1861, Confederate shore batteries bombarded the fort, which surrendered the next day.

Fort Sumter Federal fort in Charleston, South Carolina, harbor, where the first shots of the Civil War were fired when the Union attempted to resupply troops

Proclaiming an insurrection in the Lower South, Lincoln called for 75,000 volunteers to suppress the rebellion. The outbreak of hostilities ended fence-sitting in the Upper South. "I am a Union man," one southerner wrote, "but when they [the Lincoln administration] send men south it will change my notions. I can do nothing against my own people." In quick succession Virginia, North Carolina, Arkansas, and Tennessee joined the Confederacy. Acknowledging that "I am one of those dull creatures that cannot see the good of secession," Robert E. Lee resigned from the U.S. Army rather than lead troops against his native Virginia.

The North, too, was ready for a fight, less to abolish slavery than to punish secession. Stephen Douglas, exhausted by his efforts to find a peaceable solution to the issue of slavery extension, assaulted "the new system of resistance by the sword and bayonet to the results of the ballot-box" and affirmed, "I deprecate war, but if it must come I am with my country, under all circumstances, and in every contingency."

CHECKING IN

- Lincoln's victory in the 1860 presidential election brought matters to a head.
- Fearing they were now at the mercy of abolitionists, states in the Lower South began to secede.
- Moderates sought a compromise, but Republicans resisted.
- An attempt to resupply Fort Sumter, a federal fort in Charleston harbor in South Carolina, met with armed resistance.
- When President Lincoln called for militia to suppress an insurrection, the states of the Upper South seceded.

Chapter Summary

How did the Fugitive Slave Act lead to the undoing of the Compromise of 1850? (page 314)

Unlike the Compromise of 1820, the Compromise of 1850 was a medley of different bills supported by shifting coalitions. It temporarily averted disunion, but it failed to resolve underlying divisions between the North and the South. In particular, the new Fugitive Slave Act alienated the North because of its harshness and the South because of northern resistance.

Why did the Whig party disintegrate, and what were the consequences? (page 320)

The surprising strength of the Know-Nothings and the free-soil movement both undercut the Whigs, who were already battered into sectional fragments by the Compromise of 1850; the Kansas-Nebraska Act delivered the final blow. Temporarily the Democrats were the only major political party, and when the Republicans emerged as a counterpart, they were a sectional rather than a national party.

What major issues dominated American politics from 1857 to 1860? (page 327)

The last years of the 1850s saw several tumultuous political issues emerge: the *Dred Scott* decision, Bleeding Kansas, and John Brown's raid on Harpers Ferry. Each one dramatized the failures of popular sovereignty, frayed the political fabric of the nation a bit further, and galvanized northern opposition to the southern "slavocracy."

Why did southerners conclude that the North was bent on extinguishing slavery in southern states? (page 332)

Southerners, already feeling besieged, did not believe Abraham Lincoln's promise to leave slavery untouched in the South. They saw his election as a sign that they had lost all influence at the national level. Lower South states seceded quickly, but the Upper South remained in the Union until Lincoln ordered the resupplying of Fort Sumter, a federal fort in the harbor of Charleston, South Carolina, and shooting erupted. Emotion, as much as reason, dictated these moves.

KEY TERMS

John Brown *(p. 314)*
Compromise of 1850 *(p. 317)*
Fugitive Slave Act *(p. 318)*
Uncle Tom's Cabin *(p. 318)*
Republican Party *(p. 320)*
Kansas-Nebraska Act *(p. 321)*
free soil *(p. 321)*
Know-Nothings *(p. 323)*
Dred Scott decision *(p. 327)*
Lecompton constitution *(p. 328)*
Harpers Ferry *(p. 331)*
Crittenden plan *(p. 335)*
Fort Sumter *(p. 335)*

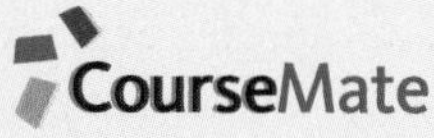

Go to the CourseMate website at **www.cengagebrain.com** for additional study tools and review materials—including audio and video clips—for this chapter.

Chapter 15

Crucible of Freedom: Civil War

1861–1865

National Library of Medicine

Union Soldiers

Chapter Preview

Mobilizing for War
What major advantages did each side possess at the start of the Civil War?

In Battle, 1861–1862
How was the war fought in its early years?

Emancipation Transforms the War, 1863
How did the issue of emancipation transform the war?

War and Society, North and South
In what ways did the Civil War affect the two sides?

The Union Victorious, 1864–1865
How did the Union finally win the war?

"Events transcending in importance anything that has ever happened within the recollection of any living person in our country, have occurred since I have written last in my journal," wrote Georgia matron Gertrude Clanton Thomas in July 1861. "War has been declared."

At her marriage in 1852, Gertrude Thomas had become mistress of a small estate, Belmont, about six miles south of Augusta, Georgia. Slavery was the basis of Gertrude Thomas's wealth and social position; she disliked it not because it oppressed the enslaved but because it posed problems for the slave-owning elite. When war began, Gertrude fervently supported the newborn Confederacy. Her husband, Jefferson Thomas, enlisted in a cavalry company and served until 1862. "We claim nothing of the North but—to be let alone."

As war raged on, Gertrude Thomas longed for its end. But the Civil War's end brought hardship to the Thomas family, which lost fifteen thousand dollars in Confederate bonds and ninety slaves. One by one, the former slaves left the Belmont estate, never to return. "As to the emancipated Negroes," Gertrude Thomas told her journal in May 1865, "while there is of course a natural dislike to the loss of so much property, in my inmost soul, I cannot regret it."

In their determination, militance, and false expectations, the Thomases were not alone. Few volunteers or even politicians anticipated a protracted war. Most northern estimates ranged from one month to a year; rebels, too, counted on a speedy victory. Neither side anticipated the carnage that war would bring; one out of every five soldiers who fought in the Civil War died in it. Once it became clear that war would extend beyond a few battles, leaders on both sides considered strategies once unpalatable or even unthinkable. By the war's end, the Confederacy was ready to arm its slaves in an ironically desperate effort to save a society founded on slavery. The North, which began the war with the limited objective of overcoming secession and explicitly disclaimed any intention of interfering with slavery, found that in order to win, it had to shred the fabric of southern society by destroying slavery.

MOBILIZING FOR WAR

What major advantages did each side possess at the start of the Civil War?

Neither the North nor the South was prepared for war. In April 1861, most of the Union's small army, a scant sixteen thousand men, was scattered across the West. One-third of its officers had resigned to join the Confederacy. The nation had not had a strong president since James K. Polk in the 1840s, and many viewed the new president, Abraham Lincoln, as a yokel. It seemed doubtful that such a government could marshal its people for war. The Confederacy was even less prepared. It had no tax structure, no navy, only two tiny gunpowder factories, and poorly equipped, unconnected railroad lines.

During the first two years of war, both sides would have to overcome these deficiencies, raise and supply large armies, and finance the war. In each region, mobilization would expand the powers of the central government to a degree that few had anticipated.

Recruitment and Conscription

The Civil War armies were the largest organizations ever created in America; by the end of the war, more than 2 million men had served in the Union army and 800,000 in the Confederate army.

At first the raising of armies was a local, rather than a national or state, effort. Regiments usually consisted of volunteers from the same locale. Southern cavalrymen provided their own horses, and uniforms were left to local option. In both armies the troops themselves elected officers up to the rank of colonel. This informal, democratic way of raising and organizing soldiers reflected the nation's political traditions but could not long withstand the stresses of the Civil War. As early as July 1861, the Union began examinations for officers. With casualties mounting, moreover, military demand exceeded the supply of volunteers. The Confederacy felt the pinch first and in April 1862 enacted the first **conscription** law in American history, requiring all able-bodied white men aged eighteen to thirty-five to serve in the military. (By war's end the limits would be seventeen and fifty.) The Confederacy's Conscription Act aroused little enthusiasm. A later amendment exempting owners or overseers of twenty or more slaves evoked complaints about "a rich man's war but a poor man's fight."

conscription Drafting men to serve in the army

Despite opposition, the Confederate draft became increasingly difficult to evade; this fact stimulated volunteering. Seventy to eighty percent of eligible white southerners served in the Confederate army. Only one soldier in five was a draftee. The requirement that soldiers serve for at least three years ensured that a high proportion of Confederate soldiers would be battle-hardened veterans.

Once the Confederacy raised the army, it needed supplies. At first, the South imported arms and ammunition from Europe to supplement weapons taken from federal arsenals and guns captured on the battlefield. Gradually, the Confederacy assigned contracts to privately owned factories, such as the Tredegar Iron Works in Richmond; provided loans to establish new plants; and created government-owned industries, such as the giant Augusta Powder Works in Georgia. The South lost few, if any, battles for want of munitions.

Supplying troops with clothing and food proved more difficult. When the South invaded Maryland in 1862, thousands of Confederate soldiers remained behind because they could not march barefoot on Maryland's gravel-surfaced roads. Late in the war, Robert E. Lee's Army of Northern Virginia ran out of food but never out of ammunition. Supply problems had several sources: railroads that fell into disrepair or were captured, an economy that grew more cotton and tobacco than food, and Union capture of the livestock and grain-raising districts of central Tennessee and Virginia. Close to desperation, the Confederate Congress in 1863 passed the Impressment Act, authorizing army officers to take food from reluctant farmers at prescribed prices and to impress slaves into labor for the army.

The industrial North had fewer supply problems, but recruitment was another matter. When the initial tide of enthusiasm for enlistment ebbed, Congress followed the Confederacy's example and turned to conscription with the Enrollment Act of March 1863. Every able-bodied white male citizen aged twenty to forty-five faced the draft.

Like the Confederate conscription law of 1862, the Enrollment Act provided some exemptions and offered two ways of escaping the draft: substitution, or paying another man to serve; and commutation, or paying a $300 fee to the government. Democrats denounced conscription as a violation of individual liberties and states' rights, and ordinary citizens resented the substitution and commutation privileges, leveling their own "poor man's fight" charges. Nevertheless, as in the Confederacy, the law stimulated volunteering. Only 8 percent of all Union soldiers were draftees or substitutes.

Chronology

1861	President Abraham Lincoln calls for volunteers to suppress the rebellion (April); Virginia, Arkansas, Tennessee, and North Carolina join the Confederacy (April–May); Lincoln imposes a naval blockade on the South (April); First Battle of Bull Run (July); First Confiscation Act (August)
1862	Legal Tender Act (February); George B. McClellan's Peninsula Campaign (March–July); Battle of Shiloh (April); Confederate Congress passes the Conscription Act (April); David G. Farragut captures New Orleans (April); Homestead Act (May); Seven Days' Battles (June–July); Morrill Land Grant Act (July); Second Battle of Bull Run (August); Battle of Antietam (September); Battle of Fredericksburg (December)
1863	Emancipation Proclamation issued (January); Lincoln suspends writ of *habeas corpus* nationwide (January); National Bank Act (February); Congress passes the Enrollment Act (March); Battle of Gettysburg (July); Surrender of Vicksburg (July); New York City draft riots (July)
1864	Ulysses S. Grant given command of all Union armies (March); Battle of the Wilderness (May); surrender of Atlanta (September); Lincoln reelected (November); William Tecumseh Sherman's march to the sea (November–December)
1865	Congress passes the Thirteenth Amendment (January); Sherman moves through South Carolina (January–March); Grant takes Richmond (April); Robert E. Lee surrenders at Appomattox (April); Lincoln dies (April)

Financing the War

The recruitment and supply of huge armies lay far beyond the capacity of American public finance at the start of the war. During the 1840s and 1850s, the federal government met its meager revenue needs from tariff duties and income from the sale of public lands. During the war, however, annual federal expenditures gradually rose, and the need for new sources of revenue became urgent. Yet neither Union nor Confederacy initially wished to impose taxes, to which Americans were unaccustomed.

Both sides therefore turned to war bonds; that is, to loans from citizens to be repaid by future generations. However, many hoarded their gold rather than spend it on bonds. Grasping the limits of taxes and of bond issues, both sides began to print paper money. Early in 1862, President Lincoln signed into law the Legal Tender Act, authorizing the issue of $150 million in paper **"greenbacks."** Although the North's financial officials distrusted paper money, they came around to the idea as funds dwindled. However, unlike gold and silver, which had established market values, the value of paper money depended on the public's confidence in the government that issued it. To bolster that confidence, Union officials made the greenbacks legal tender (that is, acceptable in payment of most public and private debts).

"greenbacks" Paper money used by the Union to help finance war

In contrast, the Confederacy never made its paper money legal tender; suspicions arose that the southern government lacked confidence in it. To compound the problem, the Confederacy raised less than 5 percent of its wartime revenue from taxes (compared to 21 percent in the North). The Confederacy did enact a comprehensive tax measure in 1863, but Union invasions and poor internal transportation made tax collection a hit-or-miss proposition.

Confidence in the Confederacy's paper money quickly evaporated, and the value of paper money in relation to gold plunged. The Confederate response—printing more paper money, a billion dollars by 1865—merely accelerated inflation. Whereas prices in the North rose about 80 percent during the war, the Confederacy suffered an inflation rate of over 9,000 percent.

By raising taxes, floating bonds, and printing paper money, both the North and the South broke with the hard-money, minimal-government traditions of American public finance. In the North, Republicans took advantage of the departure of southern Democrats to push through Congress a measure that they and their Whig predecessors had long advocated: a national banking system. Passed in February 1863, the National Bank Act allowed banks to obtain federal charters and to issue national bank notes (backed by the federal government). The North's ability to revolutionize its system of public finance reflected both its long experience with complex financial transactions and its political cohesion.

Library of Congress

Abraham Lincoln

A portrait of Lincoln made in the Washington, DC, studio of photographer Alexander Gardner in November 1863, eleven days before the president gave the Gettysburg Address.

Political Leadership in Wartime

The Civil War pitted rival political systems as well as armies and economies against each other. The South entered the war with several apparent political advantages. Lincoln's call for militiamen to suppress the rebellion had transformed southern waverers into tenacious secessionists. Southerners also had a strong leader in Jefferson Davis, the president of the Confederacy, who possessed experience, honesty, courage, and what one officer called "a jaw sawed in *steel*."

In contrast, the Union's list of political liabilities appeared lengthy. Loyal but contentious northern Democrats disliked conscription, the National Bank Act, and the abolition of slavery. Among Republicans, Lincoln, with little national experience, had trouble commanding respect. A small but vocal group of Republicans known as the Radicals—including Secretary of the Treasury Salmon P. Chase, Senator Charles Sumner of Massachusetts, and Representative Thaddeus Stevens of Pennsylvania—vigorously criticized Lincoln. They assailed him early in the war for failing to make emancipation a war goal and later for being too eager to readmit the conquered rebel states into the Union.

Lincoln's style of leadership both encouraged and disarmed opposition among Republicans. Self-contained until ready to act, he met criticism with homespun anecdotes that threw his opponents off guard. Caught between Radicals and conservatives, Lincoln used his cautious reserve to maintain open communications with both wings of the party and to fragment his opposition. He also co-opted some members of the opposition, including Chase, by bringing them into his cabinet.

In contrast, Jefferson Davis had a knack for making enemies. A West Pointer, he would rather have led the army than the government. Davis's cabinet suffered frequent resignations; the Confederacy had five secretaries of war in four years. Relations between Davis and his vice president, Alexander Stephens of Georgia, verged on disastrous. Leaving Richmond, the Confederate capital, in 1862, Stephens spent most of the war in Georgia, where he sniped at Davis as "weak and vacillating, timid, petulant, peevish, obstinate."

The clash between Davis and Stephens involved not just personalities but also the ideological divisions that lay at the heart of the Confederacy. The Confederate Constitution explicitly guaranteed the sovereignty of the Confederate states and prohibited the government from enacting protective tariffs or supporting internal improvements. For Stephens and other influential Confederate leaders, the Confederacy existed to protect slavery and to enshrine states' rights. In contrast, Davis's main objective was to secure the independence of the South from the North, even at the expense of states' rights, if necessary.

This difference between Davis and Stephens somewhat resembled the discord between Lincoln and the northern Democrats. Like Davis, Lincoln believed that victory demanded a strong central government; like Stephens, northern Democrats resisted centralization. But Lincoln could control his opponents more effectively than Davis controlled his. By temperament Lincoln was more suited to reconciliation than Davis was, and the different nature of party politics in the two sections favored him as well.

In the South, the Democrats and the remaining Whigs agreed to suspend party politics for the war's duration. Although intended to encourage unity, this decision led to discord. As southern politics disintegrated along personal and factional lines, Davis found himself without organized political support. In contrast, in the Union, northern Democrats' opposition to Lincoln tended to unify the Republicans. After Democrats won control of five states in the election of 1862, Republicans swallowed a bitter lesson: No matter how much they disdained Lincoln, they had to rally behind him or risk being driven from office. Ultimately, the Union developed more political cohesion than the Confederacy, not because it had fewer divisions but because it managed those divisions more effectively.

Securing the Union's Borders

Even before large-scale fighting began, Lincoln moved to safeguard Washington, which was bordered by two slave states (Virginia and Maryland) and filled with Confederate sympathizers. A week after Fort Sumter's fall, a Baltimore mob attacked a Massachusetts regiment bound for Washington, but enough troops slipped through to protect the capital. Lincoln then dispatched federal troops to Maryland and suspended the writ of *habeas corpus** (HAY-bee-uss CORE-puss); federal troops could now arrest prosecession Marylanders without formally charging them with specific offenses. Both Maryland and Delaware, another border slave state, voted down secession.

Next, Lincoln authorized the arming of Union sympathizers in Kentucky, a slave state with a Unionist legislature, a secessionist governor, and a thin chance of staying

* *Habeas corpus:* a court order requiring that the detainer of a prisoner bring the person in custody to court and show cause for his or her detention.

neutral. Lincoln also stationed troops just across the Ohio River from Kentucky, in Illinois; when a Confederate army invaded Kentucky early in 1862, those troops drove it out. Officially, at least, Kentucky became the third slave state to declare for the Union. Four years of murderous fighting ravaged the fourth, Missouri, as Union and Confederate armies and bands of guerrillas clashed. Despite the savage fighting and the divided loyalties of its people, Missouri stayed in the Union. West Virginia was formed in 1861 when thirty-five counties in the primarily nonslaveholding regions west of the Shenandoah Valley refused to secede; it became a state in 1863.

By holding the border slave states in the Union, Lincoln kept open his lines to the free states and gained access to the river systems in Kentucky and Missouri that led into the heart of the Confederacy. Lincoln's firmness, particularly in the case of Maryland, scotched charges that he was weak-willed. The crisis also forced the president to exercise long-dormant powers. In *Ex parte Merryman* (1861), Chief Justice Roger B. Taney ruled that Lincoln had exceeded his authority in suspending the writ of *habeas corpus* in Maryland. Lincoln, citing the Constitution's authorization of the writ's suspension in "Cases of Rebellion" (Article I, Section 9), insisted that he would determine whether a rebellion existed, and simply ignored Taney's ruling.

Checking In

- The North enjoyed enormous manpower and industrial advantages.
- Both sides resorted to conscription, although most soldiers were volunteers.
- The Union was far more successful than the Confederacy in raising money to finance the war.
- The Union could rely on established political, military, and economic systems; the Confederacy suffered from political divisions and conflicting views of the Confederate government's role.
- Abraham Lincoln proved to be a far better leader than Jefferson Davis.

In Battle, 1861–1862

How was the war fought in its early years?

The Civil War was the first war in which both sides relied extensively on railroads, the telegraph, mass-produced weapons, joint army-navy tactics, iron-plated warships, rifled guns and artillery, and trench warfare. Thus, there is some justification for its description as the first modern war. But to its participants slogging through muddy swamps and weighed down with equipment, the war hardly seemed modern.

Armies, Weapons, and Strategies

The Confederacy had 9 million people, one-third of them slaves, in 1861. By comparison, the Union had 22 million people at that time. The North also enjoyed 3.5 times as many white men of military age, 90 percent of all U.S. industrial capacity, and two-thirds of its railroad track (see Figure 15.1). Nonetheless, the North faced a daunting challenge: to force the South back into the Union. The South, in contrast, fought only for independence. To subdue the Confederacy, the North would have to sustain offensive operations over a vast area.

Measured against this challenge, the North's advantages in population and technology shrank. The North had more men but needed them to defend long supply lines and to occupy captured areas. Consequently, a smaller proportion of its overall force was available to commit to combat. The South, relying on slaves for labor, could assign a higher proportion of its white male population to combat. And

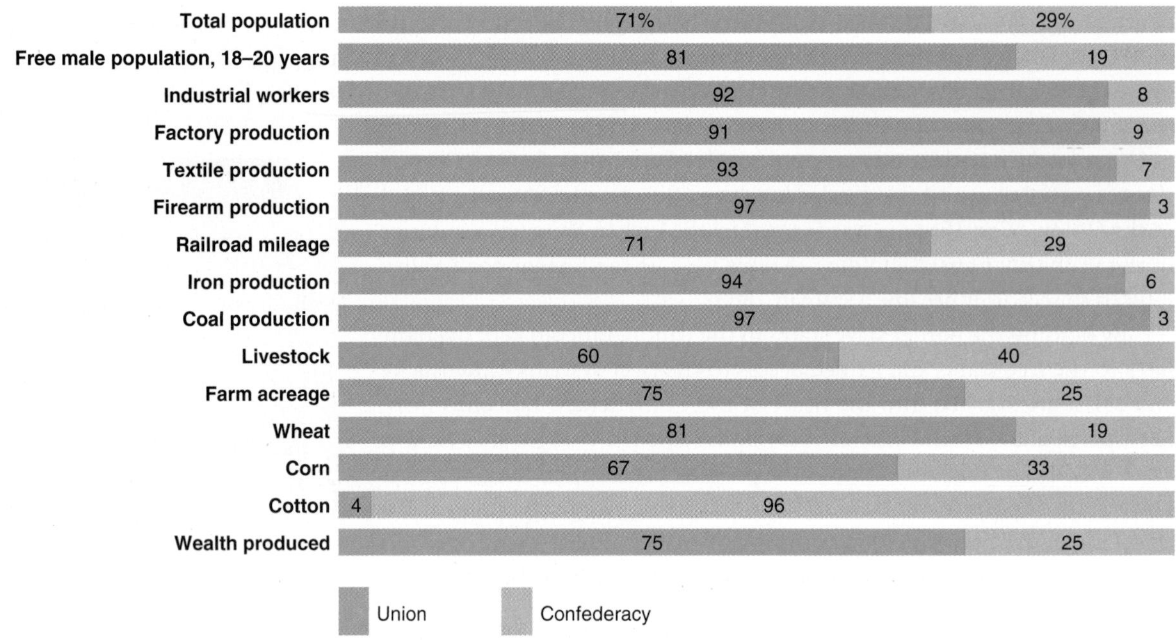

Figure 15.1 Comparative Population and Economic Resources of the Union and Confederacy, 1861

At the start of the war, the Union enjoyed huge advantages in population, industry, railroad mileage, and wealth, and—as it would soon prove—a superior ability to mobilize its vast resources. The Confederacy, however, enjoyed the many advantages of fighting a defensive war.

although the Union had superior railroads, it had to move its troops and supplies huge distances, whereas the Confederacy could shift its troops relatively short distances within its defense area without railroads. Finally, southerners had an edge in morale, for Confederate troops usually fought on home ground.

The Civil War witnessed experiments with a variety of new weapons, including the submarine, the repeating rifle, and the multibarreled Gatling gun, the predecessor of the machine gun. Whereas smooth-bore muskets had an effective range of 80 yards, the Springfield or Enfield rifles widely in use by 1863 were accurate at 400 yards. However, the rifle's development posed a challenge to long-accepted military tactics, which stressed the mass infantry charge. Armed with muskets, defenders could fire only a round or two before being overwhelmed. Armed with rifles, however, defenders could fire several rounds before closing with the enemy. Attackers would have far greater difficulty getting close enough to thrust bayonets; fewer than 1 percent of the casualties in the Civil War resulted from bayonet wounds.

As the fighting wore on, both sides recognized the value of trenches, which offered defenders protection against withering rifle fire. In addition, the rifle forced generals to depend less on cavalry. Traditionally, cavalry had been among the most prestigious components of an army, in part because cavalry charges were often devastatingly effective and in part because the cavalry helped to maintain class distinctions within the army. More accurate rifles reduced cavalry effectiveness by increasing the firepower of foot soldiers. Thus, both sides relegated cavalry to reconnaissance (reh-CAHN-nuh-sense) missions and raids on supply trains.

Still, the introduction of the rifle did not totally invalidate traditional tactics. An attacking army still had a good chance of success if it surprised its enemy, and the lush forests of the South offered abundant opportunities for surprise. In contrast, lack of the element of surprise could doom an attacking army. At the Battle of Fredericksburg in December 1862, Confederate forces virtually annihilated Union forces charging uphill over open terrain. Likewise, at Gettysburg in July 1863, Union riflemen and artillery shredded charging southerners.

Much like previous wars, the Civil War was basically fought in a succession of battles during which exposed infantry traded volleys, charged, and countercharged. The side that withdrew first from the battlefield was considered the loser, even though it frequently sustained lighter casualties than the supposed victor. The defeated army usually moved back a few miles to lick its wounds; the winners stayed in place to lick theirs. Politicians on both sides berated generals for not pursuing a beaten foe, but it was almost impossible for a mangled victor to gather horses, mules, supply trains, and exhausted soldiers for a new attack. Not surprisingly, for much of the war, generals on both sides concluded that the best defense was a good offense.

SCOTT'S GREAT SNAKE.

Library of Congress

"Scott's Great Snake," 1861

General Winfield Scott's scheme to surround the South and await a seizure of power by southern Unionists drew scorn from critics who called it the Anaconda plan. In this lithograph, the "great snake" prepares to push down the Mississippi, seal off the Confederacy, and crush it.

What passed for long-range Union strategy in 1861 was the **Anaconda plan,** which called for the Union to blockade the southern coast and to thrust, like a huge snake, down the Mississippi River. In theory, sealing off and severing the Confederacy would make the South recognize the futility of secession and end the war quickly. However, the lack of adequate ships and men to seize the Mississippi in 1861 prevented the implementation of this ambitious plan.

Anaconda plan Early Union strategy to split the Confederacy down the Mississippi and force its surrender

Early in the war, the need to secure the border slave states, especially Kentucky and Missouri, dictated Union strategy in the West, sending northern armies plunging southward from Kentucky into Tennessee. The Appalachian Mountains tended to separate this western theater from the eastern theater, where major clashes took place in 1861.

Stalemate in the East

The Confederacy's decision in May 1861 to move its capital from Montgomery, Alabama, to Richmond, Virginia, shaped Union strategy. "Forward to Richmond!" became the Union's first war cry. But before Union troops could reach Richmond, one hundred miles southwest of Washington, they would have to dislodge a Confederate army brazenly encamped at Manassas (muh-NASS-suss) Junction, Virginia, only twenty-five miles from the Union capital. Lincoln ordered General Irvin McDowell

Map 15.1 The War in the East, 1861–1862

Union advances on Richmond were turned back at Fredericksburg and the Seven Days' Battles, and the Confederacy's invasion of Union territory was stopped at Antietam.

Interactive Map

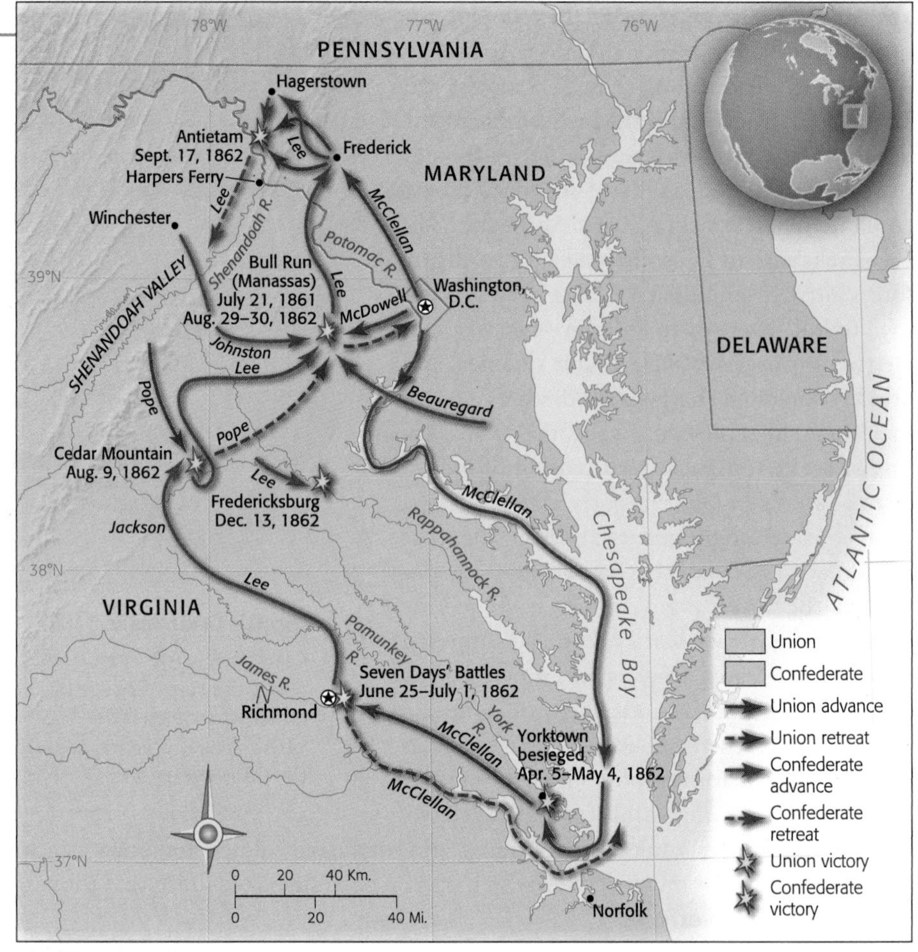

First Battle of Bull Run The war's first full battle, also called First Manassas; fiasco that showed war would be longer and harder than first thought

George B. McClellan Union general who was very popular with troops; Lincoln thought he had the "slows" and replaced him

to attack the rebel force. In the resulting **First Battle of Bull Run** (or First Manassas), amateur armies clashed in bloody chaos under a blistering July sun. Well-dressed, picnicking Washington dignitaries witnessed the carnage, as the Confederates routed the larger Union army.

After Bull Run, Lincoln appointed General **George B. McClellan** to replace McDowell as commander of the Army of the Potomac, the Union's main fighting force in the east. McClellan, a master of administration and training, transformed a ragtag mob into a disciplined fighting force. His soldiers adored him, but Lincoln became disenchanted. To the president, the key to victory lay in launching simultaneous attacks on several fronts so that the North could exploit its advantages in manpower and communications. McClellan, a proslavery Democrat, hoped for a relatively bloodless southern defeat, followed by readmission of the Confederate states with slavery intact.

In the spring of 1862, McClellan got a chance to demonstrate the value of his strategy. After Bull Run, the Confederates pulled back behind the Rappahannock River to block a Union march toward Richmond. McClellan decided to go around the southerners by transporting his troops down the Chesapeake Bay to the tip of the peninsula formed by the York and James rivers and then to attack Richmond from the rear.

At first, McClellan's Peninsula Campaign unfolded smoothly. By late May, McClellan was within five miles of Richmond. But then he hesitated. Overestimating Confederate strength, he refused to launch a final attack without further reinforcements, which were turned back by Confederate general Thomas "Stonewall" Jackson in the Shenandoah Valley. As McClellan delayed, General **Robert E. Lee** assumed command of the Confederacy's Army of Northern Virginia. A foe of secession and so courteous that at times he seemed too gentle, Lee possessed the qualities that McClellan most lacked: boldness and a willingness to accept casualties.

Robert E. Lee Bold and resourceful commander of the Army of Northern Virginia

Seizing the initiative, Lee attacked McClellan in late June 1862. The ensuing Seven Days' Battles, fought in the forests east of Richmond, cost the South nearly twice as many men as the North and ended in a virtual slaughter of Confederates. Unnerved by mounting casualties, McClellan sent increasingly panicky reports to Washington. Lincoln, who cared little for McClellan's Peninsula Campaign, ordered McClellan to call off the campaign and return to Washington.

With McClellan out of the picture, Lee and his lieutenant, Stonewall Jackson, pushed north, routing a Union army at the Second Battle of Bull Run (Second Manassas) in August 1862. Lee's next stroke was even bolder. Crossing the Potomac River in early September 1862, he invaded western Maryland, where the forthcoming harvest could feed his troops. Lee could now threaten Washington, indirectly relieve pressure on Richmond, improve the prospects of peace candidates in the North's fall elections, and possibly induce Britain and France to recognize Confederate independence. But McClellan met Lee at the Battle of **Antietam** (or Sharpsburg) on September 17. A tactical draw, Antietam proved a strategic victory for the North: Lee subsequently canceled his invasion and retreated south of the Potomac.

Antietam Union victory in August 1862 that gave Lincoln the opportunity to announce the Emancipation Proclamation

Heartened by the success of Union forces, Lincoln then issued the **Emancipation Proclamation,** a war measure that freed all slaves under rebel control. Lincoln complained that McClellan had "the slows" and faulted him for not pursuing Lee after Antietam. McClellan's replacement, General Ambrose Burnside, thought himself unfit for high command. He was right. In December 1862, he led 122,000 federal troops against 78,500 Confederates at the Battle of Fredericksburg (Virginia). Burnside captured the town but then sacrificed his army in futile charges up the heights west of the town. Even Lee shuddered at the carnage. "It is well that war is so terrible, or we should grow too fond of it," he told an aide during the battle. Richmond remained, in the words of a southern song, "a hard road to travel." The war in the East had become a stalemate.

Emancipation Proclamation Declaration that freed all slaves in Confederate-held territory; changed the nature of the Civil War

The War in the West

The Union fared better in the West. There, the war ranged over a vast terrain that provided access to rivers leading directly into the South. The West also spawned new leadership in the person of an obscure Union general, **Ulysses S. Grant.** A West Point graduate with a reputation for heavy drinking, and a failed farmer and businessman, Grant soon proved to be one of the Union's best leaders.

Ulysses S. Grant Lincoln-appointed head of the Army of the Potomac; ultimately defeated Lee

In 1861–1862, Grant stabilized control of Missouri and Kentucky and then moved south to attack Corinth (CORE-inth), Mississippi, a major rail junction.

Antietam National Battlefield, Sharpsburg, MD

Library of Congress

Scenes of Antietam

A painting of the Antietam battlefield by James Pope, a Union soldier of the Second Vermont Infantry, shows three brigades of Union troops advancing under Confederate fire. In the photograph of Antietam, dead rebel gunners lie next to the wreckage of their battery. The building in both the painting and photograph, a church, was the scene of furious fighting.

In early April 1862, Confederate forces staged a surprise attack on Grant's army, encamped at Shiloh (SHY-loe) Church in southern Tennessee. Driven back on the first day, Union forces counterattacked on the second day and drove the Confederate army from the field. Of 77,000 men who fought at Shiloh, 23,000 were killed or wounded. Defeated at Shiloh, the Confederates evacuated Corinth.

To attack Grant at Shiloh, the Confederacy had stripped the defenses of its largest city, New Orleans. A combined Union land-sea force under General Benjamin Butler and Admiral David G. Farragut (FAIR-uh-gut) seized the opportunity. Farragut took New Orleans in late April and soon conquered Baton Rouge and Natchez as well. When a Union flotilla moved down the river in June and took Memphis, the North controlled the great river except for a 200-mile stretch between Port Hudson, Louisiana, and Vicksburg, Mississippi.

Union and Confederate forces also clashed in 1862 in the trans-Mississippi West. On the banks of the Rio Grande, Union volunteers and Mexican-American companies drove a Confederate army from Texas out of New Mexico. A thousand miles to the east, opposing armies battled for control of the crucial Missouri River. In Pea Ridge, Arkansas, in March 1862, northern troops scattered a Confederate force of 16,000.

These Union victories changed the trans-Mississippi war. As the rebel threat faded, western volunteers who had mobilized to crush Confederates turned to fighting Indians. After 1865, federal troops moved west to complete the rout of the Indians that had begun during the Civil War.

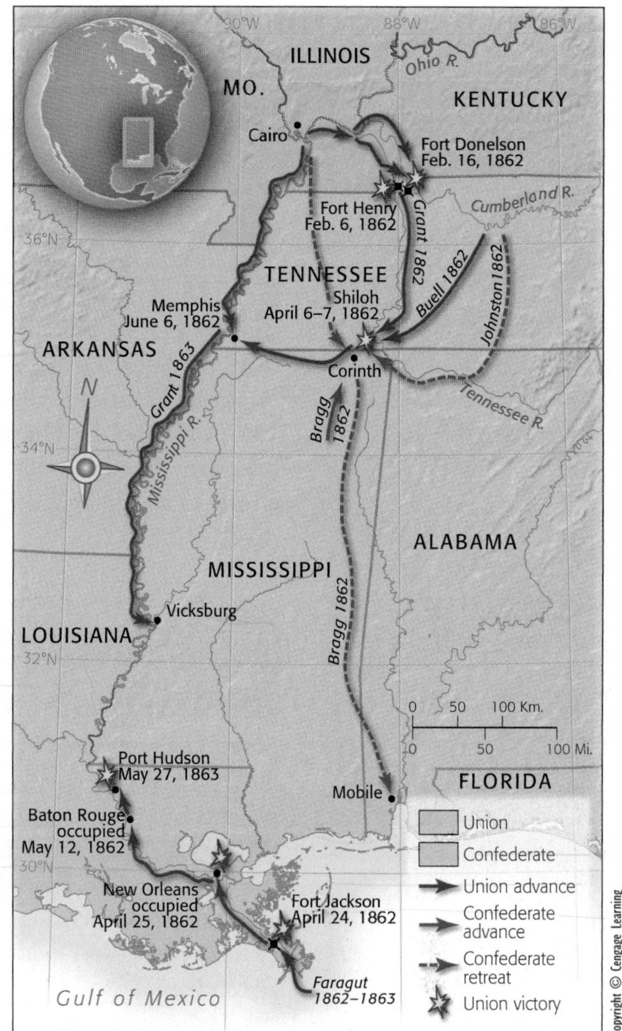

Map 15.2 The War in the West, 1861–1862

By the end of 1862 the North held New Orleans and the entire Mississippi River except for the stretch between Vicksburg and Port Hudson.

Interactive Map

The Soldiers' War

Civil War soldiers were typically volunteers from farms and small towns who joined companies of recruits from their area. Local loyalties spurred enrollment, especially in the South, as did ideals of honor and valor. Soldiers on both sides saw military life as a transforming experience in which citizens became warriors and boys became men. Exultant after a victory, an Alabama volunteer told his father, "With your first shot you become a new man."

Recruits were meshed into regiments and then sent to training camps. Training was meager, and much of army life was tedious and uncomfortable. Union troops ate beans, bacon, salt pork, pickled beef, and hardtack—biscuits that were almost impossible to crack. Confederate forces ate bacon and cornmeal, and they often ran out of food, blankets, shoes, socks, and clothes. Both sides suffered from a multitude of lice, fleas, ticks, flies, and rats, as well as from the diseases they carried.

Dreams of military glory faded swiftly. Soldiers quickly learned to inure themselves to the stench of death. "Soldier," a Confederate chaplain told his troops in 1863, "your business is to die." The deadly cost of battle fell most heavily on the

infantry, in which at least three out of four soldiers served. A combination of inexperience, inadequate training, and barriers of terrain curbed their impact. Large masses of soldiers faced one another at close range for long periods of time, exchanging fire until one side or the other gave up and fell back. Armies gained in efficiency in battle through experience, and only late in the war.

In their voluminous letters home (Civil War armies were the most literate armies that had ever existed), volunteers discussed their motives as soldiers. Some Confederates joined to defend slavery, which they paired with liberty. As the war ground on, more and more Union soldiers came to see emancipation as their goal, sometimes for humanitarian reasons. "Since I am down here I have learned and seen more of what the horrors of slavery was than I ever knew before," an Ohio officer wrote from Louisiana. Others had more practical goals. By the summer of 1862, Union soldiers in the South had become agents of liberation. Many who had once damned the "abolitionist war" now endorsed emancipation as part of the war effort. As an Indiana soldier said, "Every negro we get strengthens us and weakens the rebels."

Ironclads and Cruisers: The Naval War

By plunging the navy into the Confederacy like a dagger, the Union exploited a clear-cut advantage. The North began the war with more than forty active warships—the South had none—and by 1865 northern industrial advantages had given the United States the largest navy in the world. Steamships could penetrate the South's river systems from any direction.

Yet the Union navy faced an extraordinary challenge in its efforts to blockade the South's 3,500 miles of coastline. Sleek Confederate blockade runners darted in and out of southern harbors with little chance of capture early in the war. Their chances of success gradually diminished, however, as the North tightened the blockade and began to capture key southern ports. In 1861, almost 90 percent of blockade runners made it through; by 1865, the rate had sunk to 50 percent. Union seizure of rebel ports and coastal areas shrank the South's foreign trade even more. In daring amphibious assaults in 1861 and 1862, the Union captured the excellent harbor of Port Royal, South Carolina; the coastal islands off South Carolina; and most of North Carolina's river outlets. Naval patrols and amphibious operations shrank the South's ocean trade to one-third its prewar level.

Despite meager resources, the South made impressive efforts to offset the North's naval advantage. Early in the war the Confederates raised a scuttled Union frigate, the *Merrimac;* sheathed its sides in iron; rechristened it the *Virginia;* and deployed it to attack wooden Union ships at Hampton Roads, Virginia. The *Virginia* met its match on March 9, 1862, when it tangled with the hastily built Union ironclad *Monitor.* This battle, the first ever fought between ironclads, ended in a draw.

The South constructed other ironclads and even the first submarine, which dragged a mine through the water to sink a Union ship off Charleston in 1864. Unfortunately, the "fish" failed to surface and went down with its prey. However, the South never built enough ironclads to overcome northern supremacy in home waters. Nor did Confederate success on the high seas—where wooden, steam-driven raiders wreaked havoc on the Union's merchant marine—tip the balance of war in the South's favor: the North, unlike its foe, did not depend on imports for war materials. The South would go on to lose the naval war.

The Diplomatic War

While armies and navies clashed in 1861–1862, conflict developed on a third front: diplomacy. At the war's start southerners had confidently opened a campaign to gain swift diplomatic recognition for the Confederacy. They were sure of the support of Britain's and France's upper classes and even more certain that Britain, dependent on the South for four-fifths of its cotton, would have to break the Union blockade.

In 1861, Confederate diplomats James Mason and John Slidell sailed for Europe to lobby for recognition of an independent South, but their ship, the *Trent,* fell into Union hands. When the pair ended up as prisoners in Boston, British tempers exploded. Considering one war at a time quite enough, President Lincoln ordered Mason and Slidell released.

Settling the *Trent* affair did not eliminate friction between the United States and Britain, however. Union diplomats protested the construction in British shipyards of the Confederate commerce raiders *Alabama* and *Florida.* In 1863, the U.S. minister to London, Charles Francis Adams (son of President John Quincy Adams and grandson of President John Adams), threatened war if two British-built ironclads commissioned by the Confederacy were turned over to the South. Britain capitulated to Adams's protests and purchased the ships for its own navy.

The South fell far short of its diplomatic objectives. Neither Britain nor France ever recognized the Confederacy as a nation. Southerners overestimated the power of its vaunted "cotton diplomacy." Forces beyond southern control had weakened British demand. Bumper cotton crops in the late 1850s had glutted the British market by the start of the war and Britain had found new suppliers in Egypt and India. Gradually, too, the North's tightened blockade restricted southern exports. The South's share of the British cotton market slumped from 77 percent in 1860 to only 10 percent in 1865.

The South had also exaggerated Britain's stake in helping the Confederacy. As a naval power that had frequently blockaded its own enemies, Britain's diplomatic interest lay in supporting the Union blockade in principle; from Britain's standpoint, to help the South break the blockade would set a precedent that could easily boomerang. Finally, although France and Britain often considered recognizing the Confederacy, the timing never seemed quite right. Union success at Antietam in 1862 and Lincoln's subsequent issuance of the Emancipation Proclamation dampened Europe's enthusiasm for recognition at a crucial juncture. The Emancipation Proclamation stirred pro-Union feelings in antislavery Britain. The proclamation, declared Henry Adams (diplomat Charles Francis Adams's son) from London, "has done more for us here than all of our former victories and all our diplomacy."

Checking In

- Despite new weapons, such as the rifle, the Civil War was basically fought as a traditional war, with mass infantry charges and large battles.
- In the early years of the conflict, the war in the East was a stalemate.
- The South found a brilliant leader in Robert E. Lee, but Lincoln continued to search fruitlessly for a comparable Union general.
- Union forces established superiority west of the Mississippi early in the war.
- Despite hopes based on the British textile industry's need for cotton, the Confederacy never succeeded in enlisting Great Britain and France as allies.

EMANCIPATION TRANSFORMS THE WAR, 1863

How did the issue of emancipation transform the war?

"I hear old John Brown knocking on the lid of his coffin and shouting 'Let me out! Let me out!'" abolitionist Henry Stanton wrote to his wife after the fall of Fort Sumter. "The Doom of Slavery is at hand." In 1861, this prediction seemed wildly premature. In his inaugural address Lincoln had stated bluntly, "I have no purpose, directly or indirectly, to interfere with the institution of slavery in the states where it exists." Yet within two years both necessity and ideology made emancipation a primary northern goal.

The rise of emancipation as a war goal reflected the changing character of the conflict itself. As the fighting raged on, demands for the prosecution of a "total war" intensified in the North, and many people who were unconcerned about the morality of slavery started to recognize the military value of emancipation as a tactic to cripple the South.

From Confiscation to Emancipation

The Union's policy on emancipation developed in several stages. As soon as northern troops invaded the South, questions arose about captured rebel property, including slaves. Generally, slaves who fled behind Union lines were considered "contraband"—enemy property liable to seizure—and were put to work for the Union army. In August 1861, Congress passed the first Confiscation Act, which authorized the seizure of all property, including slaves, used in military aid of the rebellion. However, nothing in the act actually freed these individuals, nor did the law apply to fugitive slaves who had not worked for the Confederate military.

Several factors underlay the Union's cautious approach. Officially maintaining that the South could not legally secede, Lincoln argued that southerners were still entitled to the Constitution's protection of property. The president also had practical reasons to walk softly. He did not want to alienate slaveholders in the border states or proslavery Democrats in the North. Aware of such fears, Lincoln assured Congress in December 1861 that the war would not become a "remorseless revolutionary struggle."

From the start of the war, however, Radical Republicans pushed Lincoln to adopt a policy of emancipation. Radicals agreed with black abolitionist Frederick Douglass that "to fight against slaveholders without fighting against slavery, is but a half-hearted business." Each Union defeat, moreover, reminded northerners that the Confederacy, with a slave labor force in place, could commit a higher proportion of its white men to battle. The idea of emancipation as a military measure thus gained increasing favor in the North, and in July 1862 Congress passed the second Confiscation Act. This law authorized the seizure of the property of all persons in rebellion and stipulated that slaves who came within Union lines "shall be forever free." The law also authorized the president to employ blacks as soldiers.

Nevertheless, Lincoln continued to stall. "My paramount object in this struggle is to save the Union, and is not either to save or destroy slavery," Lincoln averred. "If I could save the Union without freeing *any* slave, I would do it, and if I could save it by freeing *all* the slaves, I would do it; and if I could save it by freeing some and leaving others alone, I would also do that." Yet Lincoln had always loathed slavery, and by the spring of 1862, he had accepted the Radical position that the war must lead to its abolition. Reluctant to push the issue while Union armies reeled in defeat, he drafted a proclamation of emancipation and waited for the right moment to announce it. After the Union victory at Antietam, Lincoln issued the Preliminary Emancipation Proclamation (September 1862), which declared all slaves under rebel control free as of January 1, 1863. The final Emancipation Proclamation, issued on January 1, 1863, declared "forever free" all slaves in areas in rebellion.

The proclamation had limited practical impact, however. It applied only to areas in which it could not be enforced, those still in rebellion, and did not touch slavery in the border states. But the Emancipation Proclamation was a brilliant political stroke. By making it a military measure, Lincoln pacified northern conservatives, and by issuing the proclamation himself, he stole the initiative from the Radicals in Congress. Through the proclamation, moreover, Lincoln mobilized support for the Union among European liberals, pushed the border states toward emancipation (both Missouri and Maryland abolished slavery before the war's end), and increased slaves' incentives to escape as Union troops neared.

The Emancipation Proclamation did not end slavery everywhere or free "*all* the slaves," but it changed the war. From 1863 on, the war for the Union was also a war against slavery.

Crossing Union Lines

The attacks and counterattacks of the opposing armies turned many slaves into pawns of the war: free when Union troops overran their area, slaves again if the Confederates regained control. One North Carolina slave celebrated his liberation twelve different times. By 1865, about half a million former slaves were in Union hands.

Although in the first year of the war masters could retrieve slaves from Union armies, after 1862 slaves who crossed Union lines were considered free. Many freed slaves served in army camps as cooks, teamsters, and laborers. Some worked for pay on abandoned plantations or were leased out to planters who swore allegiance to the Union. Whether in camps or on plantations, freedmen questioned the value of liberation. Deductions for clothing and food ate up most of their earnings, and labor contracts bound them for long periods of time. Moreover, the freedmen encountered fierce prejudice among Yankee soldiers, who widely feared that emancipation would propel blacks northward after the war. The best solution to the widespread "question of what to do with the darkies," wrote one Union soldier, "would be to shoot them."

But this was not the whole story. Fugitive slaves who aided the Union as spies and scouts helped to break down bigotry. "The sooner we get rid of our foolish prejudice the better for us," a Massachusetts soldier wrote home. In March 1865, Congress established the Freedmen's Bureau to provide relief, education, and work for the former slaves. The same law also provided that forty acres of abandoned or confiscated land could be leased to each freedman or southern Unionist, with an option to buy after three years. This was the first and only time that Congress provided for the redistribution of confiscated Confederate property.

Black Soldiers in the Union Army

During the first year of the war, the Union had rejected African-American soldiers. Only after the Emancipation Proclamation did the large-scale enlistment of blacks begin. Prominent African-Americans, including Frederick Douglass, worked as recruiting agents in northern cities. Douglass clearly saw the link between military service and citizenship. "Once let the black man get upon his person the brass letters, U.S.; let him get an eagle on his button, and a musket on his shoulder and bullets in his pocket, and there is no power on earth which can deny that he has earned the right to citizenship." By the war's end, 186,000 African-Americans had served in the Union army, making up one-tenth of all Union soldiers. Half of them came from the Confederate states.

White Union soldiers commonly objected to the new recruits on racial grounds. But some, including Colonel Thomas Wentworth Higginson, a liberal minister and former John Brown supporter who led a black regiment, welcomed the black soldiers. "There is a fierce energy about them [in battle]," he exulted, "beyond anything of which I have ever read, except it be the French Zouaves [(zoo-AHVZ), troops in North Africa]." Even Union soldiers who held blacks in contempt came to approve of "anything that will kill a rebel." All blacks served in segregated regiments under white officers. Colonel Robert Gould Shaw of the 54th Massachusetts Infantry, an elite black regiment, died in combat—as did half his troops—in an attack on Fort Wagner in Charleston harbor in July 1863.

Black soldiers suffered a far higher mortality rate than whites. Seldom committed to combat, they were far more likely to die of disease in bacteria-ridden garrisons. The Confederacy refused to treat captured black Union soldiers as prisoners of war; instead, they were sent back to the states from which they had come to be re-enslaved or executed. In an especially gruesome incident, when Confederate troops under General Nathan Bedford Forrest captured Fort Pillow, Tennessee, in 1864, they massacred 262 blacks—an act that provoked outcries but no retaliation from the North.

Black soldiers also faced inequities in pay. Not until June 1864 did Congress belatedly equalize the earnings of black and white soldiers. Although fraught with inequities and hardships, military service symbolized citizenship for blacks. It proved that "black men can give blows as well as take them," Frederick Douglass declared. "Liberty won by white men would lose half its luster." Above all, the use of black soldiers, especially former slaves, struck a telling blow against the Confederacy. "They will make good soldiers," General Grant wrote to Lincoln in 1863, "and taking them from the enemy weakens him in the same proportion they strengthen us."

Slavery in Wartime

Anxious white southerners on the home front felt as if they were perched on a volcano. "We should be practically helpless should the negroes rise," declared a Louisiana planter's daughter, "since there are so few men left at home." To control 3 million slaves, they tightened slave patrols, spread scare stories among slaves, and sometimes even moved entire plantations to relative safety in Texas.

Some slaves remained faithful to their owners, hiding treasured belongings from marauding Union soldiers. Others wavered between loyalty and hunger for freedom: one slave accompanied his master to war, rescued him when he was wounded, and then escaped on his master's horse. Slaves who were given the chance to flee to Union lines usually did.

Most slaves, however, lacked the means of escape and remained under their owners' nominal control. Despite the fears of southern whites, no general slave uprising occurred, and the Confederate war effort continued to utilize slave labor. Thousands of slaves worked in war plants, toiled as teamsters and cooks in army camps, and served as nurses in field hospitals.

But even slaves with no chance of flight were alert to the opportunity that war provided and swiftly tested the limits of enforced labor. Moreover, wartime conditions reduced the slaves' productivity. With most of the white men off at war, the master-slave relationship weakened and the women and boys who remained on plantations complained of difficulty in controlling slaves. Many refused to work, did their work inefficiently, or destroyed property.

Whether slaves fled to freedom or merely stopped working, they effectively undermined the plantation system. Slavery disintegrated even as the Confederacy fought to preserve it. By 1864, a desperate Confederate Congress considered impressing slaves into the army in exchange for their freedom at the war's end. Although Robert E. Lee himself favored making slaves into soldiers, others were adamantly opposed. "If slaves will make good soldiers," a Georgia general argued, "our whole theory of slavery is wrong." In March 1865, however, the Confederate Congress passed a bill to arm 300,000 slave soldiers, although it omitted any mention of emancipation. Since the war ended a few weeks later, however, the plan was never put into effect.

Although the Confederacy's decision to arm the slaves came too late to affect the war, the debate over arming them hurt southern morale. By then, the South's military position had started to deteriorate.

The Turning Point of 1863

In summer and fall 1863, Union fortunes improved dramatically in every theater of the war. Yet the year began badly, as General Joseph "Fighting Joe" Hooker, a windbag fond of issuing pompous proclamations to his troops, suffered a crushing defeat at Chancellorsville, Virginia, in May 1863. Although Chancellorsville cost the South dearly—Stonewall Jackson was accidentally killed by his own troops—it humiliated the North, whose forces had outnumbered the Confederate troops two to one. Reports from the West brought no better news: Grant was still unable to take Vicksburg, and the rebels clung to a vital two-hundred-mile stretch of the Mississippi.

Union fortunes rose after Chancellorsville when Lee decided to invade the North. Lee needed supplies that war-racked Virginia could no longer provide; he also hoped that Lincoln would move troops from Vicksburg back into the eastern theater. Lee envisioned a major Confederate victory on northern soil that would increase the sway of pro-peace Democrats and gain European recognition of the Confederacy. Lee led his 75,000 men into Maryland and then pressed forward into southern Pennsylvania. Lincoln, rejecting Hooker's plan to attack a virtually unprotected Richmond, replaced him with the more reliable General George G. Meade.

Early in July 1863, Lee's offensive ground to a halt at a Pennsylvania road junction, **Gettysburg.** Confederates foraging for shoes in the town stumbled into Union cavalry, and both sides called for reinforcements. Thus began the war's greatest

Gettysburg Union victory that halted the Confederate invasion of Pennsylvania; turning point in the war in the East

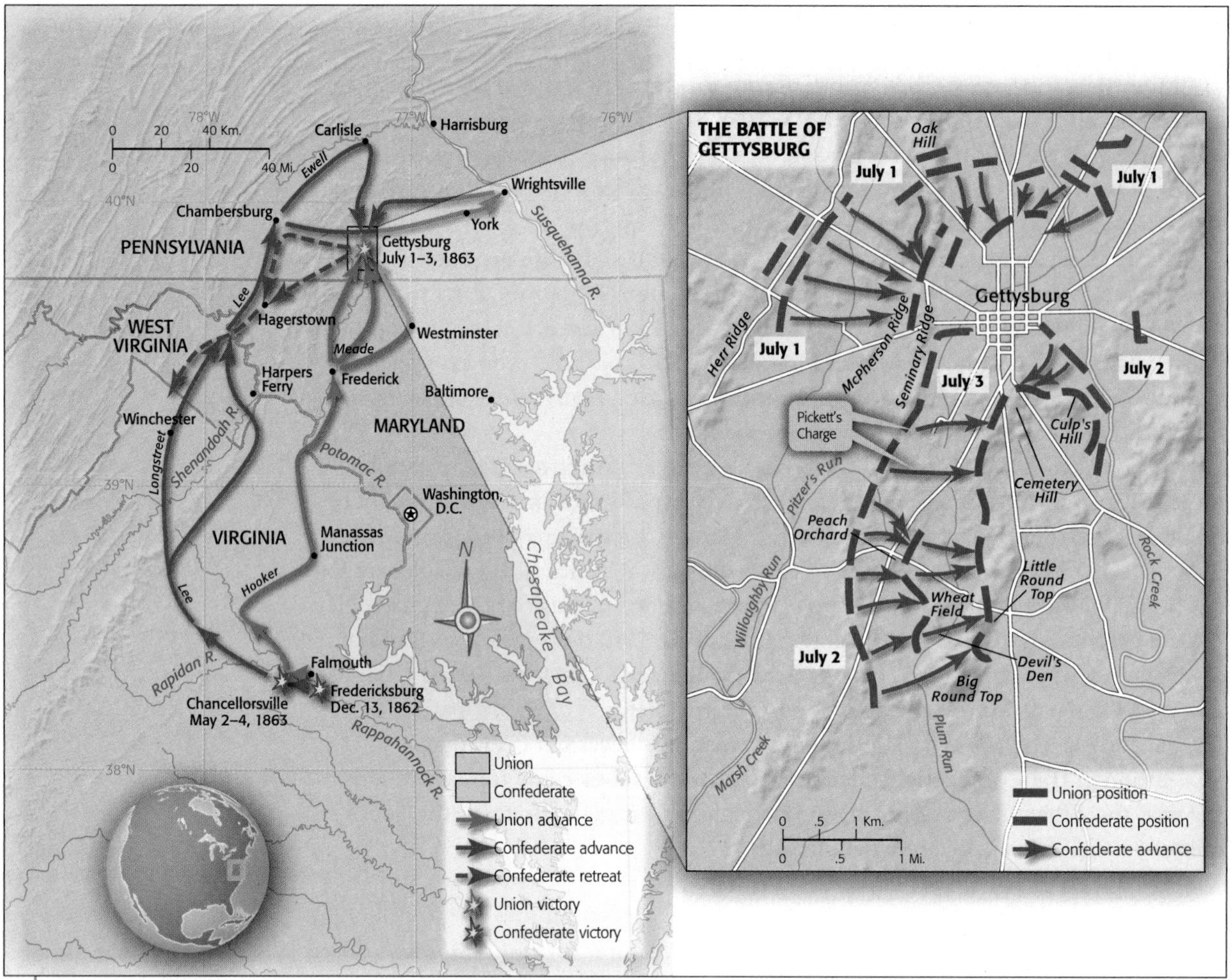

Map 15.3 Gettysburg, 1863

The failure of Pickett's charge against the Union center on July 3 was the decisive action in the war's greatest battle.

battle. The Union fielded 90,000 troops against Lee's 75,000, and the struggle raged for the first three days of July. On July 2, Lee rejected advice to plant his army in a defensive position between Meade's force and Washington and instead attacked the Union flanks. But because Confederate assaults were uncoordinated, and some southern generals disregarded orders and struck where they chose, the Union was able to move in reinforcements and regain its earlier losses.

On the afternoon of the third day, Lee ordered a direct frontal assault on the Union lines, and 15,000 men under General George E. Pickett charged across the open field, flags bright in the brilliant sunshine. Union rifles poured volley after volley into the onrushing Confederates, whose line wavered and then broke. More than half of Pickett's force lay dead, wounded, or captured. When Lee withdrew to Virginia on July 4, he had lost seventeen generals and more than one-third of his army. Total Union and Confederate casualties numbered 50,000. Although Meade failed to pursue the retreating rebels, he had halted Lee's foray into the North; the Union rejoiced.

Almost simultaneously, the North won a strategically vital battle in the West, at **Vicksburg.** After arduous maneuvering, Grant had besieged Vicksburg, the key to the Mississippi. After a six-week siege, during which southern soldiers and civilians alike survived by eating mules and even rats, the Confederate commander surrendered his 30,000-man garrison to Grant on July 4, the day that Lee began his withdrawal from Pennsylvania. Port Hudson, the last Confederate stronghold on the Mississippi, soon surrendered. "The Father of Waters flows unvexed to the sea," Lincoln proclaimed.

Vicksburg Union victory that gave the North complete control of the Mississippi River

A second crucial Union victory in the West soon followed, as Union reinforcements broke a Confederate siege on the forces of General William S. Rosecrans, who had been bottled up in Chattanooga, Tennessee. With Chattanooga secure, the way lay open for a Union strike into Georgia.

Union successes in the second half of 1863 stiffened the North's will to continue fighting and plunged some Confederate leaders into despair. Hearing of Vicksburg's fall, Confederate ordnance chief Josiah Gorgas lamented, "Yesterday we rode the pinnacle of success—today absolute ruin seems our portion. The Confederacy totters to its destruction."

Totter it might, but the South was far from beaten. Lee defended Virginia and Richmond. Although the loss of Vicksburg had cut the Confederacy in half, southern states west of the Mississippi could still provide soldiers. And the heart of the Confederacy—the Carolinas, Georgia, Florida, Mississippi, and Virginia—remained in southern hands. Few thought the fate of the Confederacy was sealed.

Checking In

- The Emancipation Proclamation made the war a conflict about slavery, but it only freed slaves in rebel-held territory.
- The proclamation kept Britain and France from recognizing the Confederacy.
- Confederate slaves posed a refugee problem for Union armies; the refugees suffered discrimination but performed valuable tasks for the federal troops.
- Despite early reluctance to enlist black soldiers, 186,000 African-Americans served in Union armies; the South ultimately authorized the use of black troops, but too late to take effect.
- Union victories at Gettysburg and Vicksburg in early July 1863 were the turning point of the war.

War and Society, North and South

In what ways did the Civil War affect the two sides?

The Civil War, engulfing two economies and societies, extended far beyond the battlefields. By 1863, the contrasts between North and South were stark. Superior resources enabled the Union to meet wartime demand as the imperiled Confederacy could not. But both sides confronted similar problems: labor shortages, inflation, and disunity and dissent. Families were disrupted and dislocated, especially in the South. Women on both sides took on new roles at home, in the workplace, and in relief efforts.

The War's Economic Impact: The North

War affected the Union's economy unevenly. Some industries fared poorly; for example, the cotton-textile industry, deprived of raw cotton, went into a tailspin. But northern industries directly related to the war effort, such as the manufacture of arms and uniforms, benefited from huge government contracts. Railroads flourished. Some privately owned lines, which had overbuilt before the war, doubled their volume of traffic.

Pacific Railroad Act Legislation that gave cash and land subsidies to those building the transcontinental railroad

Republicans in Congress, now a big majority, actively promoted business growth. Congress hiked the tariff in 1862 and again in 1864 to protect domestic industries. In July 1862, it passed the **Pacific Railroad Act** to build a transcontinental railroad. With the South out of the picture and unable to demand a southern route, Congress chose a northern route from Omaha to San Francisco. The government chartered the Union Pacific and Central Pacific corporations and gave each large land grants and generous loans: more than 60 million acres and $20 million. Issuance of greenbacks and the creation of a national banking system brought a measure of uniformity to the nation's financial system.

Homestead Act Measure that provided free land on the Great Plains to those willing to live there and develop it

Morrill Land Grant Act Law that established funding for agricultural and mechanical colleges, not traditional liberal arts colleges

Republicans designed these measures to help all social classes, and partially succeeded. The **Homestead Act,** passed in May 1862, embodied the party's ideal of "free soil, free labor, free men." It granted 160 acres of public land to settlers after five years of residence on the land. By 1865, twenty thousand homesteaders occupied new land in the West under the Homestead Act. Republicans also sponsored the **Morrill Land Grant Act** of 1862, which gave states proceeds from public land sales to establish universities emphasizing "such branches of learning as are related to agriculture and mechanic arts [engineering]." The law spurred the growth of large state universities, mainly in the Midwest and West, including Michigan State, Iowa State, and Purdue, among many others.

In general, however, the war benefited wealthy citizens more than others. Corrupt contractors grew rich by selling the government substandard merchandise, such as the notorious "shoddy" clothing made from compressed rags, which quickly disintegrated. Speculators made millions in the gold market, profiting more from Union defeats than from Union victories. Dealers with access to scarce commodities reaped astonishing profits. Manpower shortages in agricultural areas stimulated demand for Cyrus McCormick's mechanical reaper. McCormick redoubled his profits by investing in pig iron and watching as wartime demand almost doubled its price.

However, ordinary Americans suffered. Higher protective tariffs, wartime excise taxes, and inflation bloated the price of finished goods, while wages lagged 20 percent or more behind cost increases. As boys and women poured into government offices and factories to replace men serving in the army, they drew lower pay, and the threat that employers could hire more youths and females undercut the bargaining power of the men who remained in the labor force.

Many workers decried low wages, and some, such as cigar makers and locomotive engineers, formed national unions. Employers denounced worker complaints as unpatriotic hindrances to the war effort, and in 1864, the government diverted troops from combat to put down protests in war industries.

The War's Economic Impact: The South

The war shattered the South's economy. In fact, if both regions are considered together, the war retarded *American* economic growth. For example, American commodity output, which had increased 51 percent and 62 percent in the 1840s and 1850s, respectively, rose only 22 percent during the 1860s. Even this modest gain depended wholly on the North, for during that same decade commodity output in the South *declined* 39 percent.

Multiple factors offset the South's substantial wartime industrial growth. War destroyed the South's railroads. Cotton production plunged from 4 million bales in 1861 to 300,000 in 1865. Southern food production also declined because of Union occupation and a shortage of manpower. In areas under Confederate control, the yields per acre of crops like wheat and corn contracted; scarcities abounded. Agricultural shortages compounded the South's already severe inflation. By 1860, salt selling for $1.25 a sack in New York City cost $60 in the South, and food riots erupted in Mobile, Atlanta, and Richmond.

Part of the blame for the South's food shortage rested with planters. Despite government pleas to grow more food, many planters continued to raise cotton. To feed its hungry armies, the Confederacy impressed food from civilians. Farms and plantations run by the wives of active soldiers provided the easiest targets for food-impressment agents, and the women sent desperate pleas to their husbands to return home. By late 1864, half the Confederacy's soldiers were absent from their units.

The manpower drain that hampered food production reshaped the lives of southern white women. With three of every four white men in the military during the war, southern women faced new challenges and chronic shortages. With manufactured goods in short supply, women wove cloth and improvised replacements for unavailable goods, such as ink, dye, coffee, shoes, and candles. The war made refugees of many women; Texas became an appealing haven for those who sought to preserve their slave property.

In one respect, the persistence of cotton growing aided the South, as cotton became the basis for the Confederacy's flourishing trade with the enemy. In July 1861, the U.S. Congress virtually legalized this trade by allowing northern commerce with southerners loyal to the Union. In practice, it proved impossible to tell loyalists from rebels, and northern traders happily swapped bacon, salt, blankets, and other products for southern cotton. By 1864, traffic through the lines provided enough food for Lee's Army of Northern Virginia. A northern congressman lamented that it seemed the Union's policy was "to feed an army and fight it at the same time."

Dealing with Dissent

Both wartime governments faced mounting dissent and disloyalty. Within the Confederacy, dissent assumed two basic forms. First, a vocal group of states' rights supporters persistently attacked Jefferson Davis's government as despotic. Second, pro-Union sentiment flourished among the nonslaveholding small farmers who lived in the Appalachian region. To these people, the Confederate rebellion was a slaveowners' conspiracy. An Alabama farmer complained of the planters, "All they want is to get you pupt up and to fight for their infurnal negroes and after you do there fighting you may kiss there hine parts for o they care." On the whole, the South responded mildly to such popular disaffection. In 1862, the Confederate Congress gave President Davis the power to suspend the writ of *habeas corpus*, but he used it sparingly.

Lincoln faced similar challenges in the North, where the Democratic minority opposed both emancipation and the wartime growth of centralized power. One faction, the "Peace Democrats" (called **Copperheads** by their opponents, to suggest a resemblance to a species of easily concealed poisonous snakes), demanded a truce

Copperheads Northern "Peace Democrats" who opposed war

and a peace conference. They charged that the administration's war policy would "exterminate the South," make reconciliation impossible, and spark "terrible social change and revolution."

Strongest in the border states, the Midwest, and northeastern cities, the Democrats mobilized farmers of southern background and the urban working class, especially recent immigrants, who feared losing their jobs to free blacks. In 1863, this volatile mix of political, ethnic, racial, and class antagonisms exploded into antidraft protests in several cities. By far the most violent eruption occurred in July 1863 in New York City, where mobs of Irish working-class men and women roamed the streets for four days until federal troops suppressed them. The Irish loathed the idea of being drafted to fight a war on behalf of slaves who, once freed, might compete with them for jobs. They also bitterly resented the provision of the draft law that allowed the rich to purchase substitutes. The rioters lynched at least a dozen blacks, injured hundreds more, and burned draft offices, the homes of wealthy Republicans, and the Colored Orphan Asylum.

President Lincoln's dispatch of federal troops to quash these riots typified his forceful response to dissent. Lincoln imposed martial law with far less hesitancy than Davis; he suspended the writ of *habeas corpus* nationwide in 1863 and authorized the arrest of rebels, draft resisters, and anyone engaged in "any disloyal practice." The responses of Davis and Lincoln to dissent underscored the differences between the two regions' wartime political systems. Davis lacked the institutionalization of dissent provided by party conflict and had to tread warily, lest his foes brand him a despot. In contrast, Lincoln and other Republicans used dissent to rally patriotic fervor against the Democrats.

Yet Lincoln did not unleash a reign of terror against dissent. In general, the North preserved freedom of the press, speech, and assembly. Of some fifteen thousand civilians arrested during the war, most were quickly released. A few cases aroused concern, however. In 1864, a military commission sentenced an Indiana man to be hanged for an alleged plot to free Confederate prisoners. The Supreme Court reversed his conviction two years later; it ruled that civilians could not be tried by military courts when the civil courts were open (*Ex parte Milligan,* 1866). Of more concern were arrests of politicians, notably Clement L. Vallandigham, an Ohio Peace Democrat, who in 1863 was sentenced to jail by a military commission. When Ohio Democrats nominated him for governor, Lincoln banished him from the country.

The Medical War

U.S. Sanitary Commission
Major source of medical aid for soldiers

Wartime patriotism impelled civilians in both the North and the South, especially women, to work tirelessly to aid soldiers. The **U.S. Sanitary Commission,** organized in June 1861 to assist the Union's medical bureau, depended on women volunteers. The commission raised funds, bought and distributed supplies, and ran special kitchens to supplement army rations. The legendary "Mother" Mary Ann Bickerdyke served sick and wounded Union soldiers as both nurse and surrogate mother. When a doctor asked her by what authority she demanded supplies for the wounded, she shot back, "From the Lord God Almighty. Do you have anything that ranks higher than that?"

Women also reached out to aid the battlefront through the nursing corps. Some 3,200 women nurses served the Union and the Confederacy. Dorothea Dix, famed for her campaigns on behalf of the insane, became head of the Union's nursing corps. **Clara Barton,** an obscure clerk in the Patent Office, found ingenious ways of channeling medicine to the sick and wounded. Learning of Union movements before Antietam, she showed up at the battlefield on the eve of the clash with a wagonload of supplies. When army surgeons ran out of bandages and started to dress wounds with corn husks, she raced forward with lint and bandages. In 1881, she founded the American Red Cross.

Clara Barton Nurse who worked for the Sanitary Commission; later founded the Red Cross

The Confederacy, too, had legendary nurses. Belle Boyd, both a nurse and a spy, once dashed through a field to give Stonewall Jackson information. However, danger stalked nurses even in hospitals far from the front. Louisa May Alcott, a nurse at the Union Hotel Hospital in Washington, DC, contracted typhoid. Wherever they worked, nurses witnessed haunting, nightmarish scenes. "About the amputating table," one wrote, "lay large piles of human flesh—legs, arms, feet, and hands . . . the stiffened membranes seemed to be clutching oftentimes at our clothing."

Pioneered by British reformer Florence Nightingale in the 1850s, nursing was a new vocation for women and, to critics, a brazen departure from women's proper sphere. Male doctors were unsure about how to react to women in the wards. Some saw a potential for mischief in women's presence in male hospital wards. Other physicians, however, viewed nursing and sanitary work as useful. The miasm theory of disease (see Chapter 11) won wide respect among physicians and stimulated valuable sanitary measures. In partial consequence, the ratio of disease to battle deaths was much lower in the Civil War than in the Mexican-American War. Nonetheless, for every soldier killed during the Civil War, two died of disease. The germ theory of disease was unknown, and arm and leg wounds often led to gangrene (GAN-green) or tetanus (TET-uh-nuss). Typhoid, malaria, diarrhea, and dysentery raged through army camps.

Prison camps posed a special problem. The two sides had far more prisoners than they could handle, and prisoners on both sides suffered gravely. The worst conditions plagued the southern camps. Squalor and insufficient rations turned the Confederate prison camp at Andersonville, Georgia, into a virtual death camp; 3,000 prisoners a month (out of a total of 32,000) were dying there by August 1864. After the war an outraged northern public demanded, and got, the execution of Andersonville's commandant.

Checking In

- During the war, northern Republicans pushed several economic development measures through Congress—tariffs, railroad subsidies, national banking, and homestead legislation—and industrialization thrived.
- The Confederate economy, in contrast, crumpled under wartime pressure, and civilians suffered shortages and hardship.
- Lincoln was much quicker than Davis to suppress dissent.
- The war stimulated the use of women as nurses and led to advances in anesthesia and sanitary conditions.
- Women like Elizabeth Cady Stanton pointed to women's wartime service to promote women's rights; however, in the end, the war did not bring acceptance of women's political or economic equality.

The War and Women's Rights

Nurses and Sanitary Commission workers were not the only women to serve society in wartime. In the North and South alike, thousands of women took over jobs vacated by men. In rural areas, where manpower shortages were most acute, women often plowed, planted, and harvested.

Northern women's rights advocates hoped that the war would yield equality for women as well as freedom for slaves. A grateful North, they contended, should reward women for their wartime service and recognize the link between black rights and women's rights. In 1863, feminists Elizabeth Cady Stanton and Susan B. Anthony organized the National Woman's Loyal League. The league gathered four hundred thousand signatures on a petition calling for a constitutional amendment to abolish slavery, but Stanton and Anthony used the organization to promote woman suffrage as well.

Despite high expectations, the war did not bring women significantly closer to economic or political equality. Nor did it much change the prevailing definition of women's sphere. Men continued to dominate the medical profession, and for the rest of the century the census classified nurses as domestic help. The keenest disappointment of women's rights advocates lay in their failure to capitalize on rising abolitionist sentiment to secure the vote for women. Northern politicians saw little value in woman suffrage. The *New York Herald,* which supported the Loyal League's attack on slavery, dismissed its call for woman suffrage as "nonsense and tomfoolery." Stanton wrote bitterly, a few years later, "Women's cause is in deep water."

The Union Victorious, 1864–1865

How did the Union finally win the war?

Successes at Gettysburg and Vicksburg in 1863 notwithstanding, the Union stood no closer to taking Richmond at the start of 1864 than in 1861, and most of the Lower South remained under Confederate control. The North's persistent inability to destroy the main Confederate armies eroded the Union's will to attack. War weariness strengthened the Democrats and jeopardized Lincoln's reelection in 1864.

The year 1864 was crucial for the North. A Union army under General William Tecumseh Sherman captured Atlanta in September, boosting northern morale and helping to reelect Lincoln. Sherman then marched unimpeded across Georgia and into South Carolina and devastated the states. In Virginia, Grant backed Lee into trenches around Petersburg and Richmond and forced the evacuation of both cities—and ultimately the Confederacy's collapse.

The Eastern Theater in 1864

Early in 1864, Lincoln made Grant the commander of all Union armies and promoted him to lieutenant general. At first glance, the stony-faced, cigar-puffing Grant seemed an unlikely candidate for so exalted a rank, held previously only by George Washington. Grant's only distinguishing characteristics were his ever-present cigar and a penchant for whittling sticks into chips. "There is no glitter, no parade about him," a contemporary noted. But Grant's successes in the West had made him the Union's most popular general. He moved his headquarters to the Army of the Potomac in the East and mapped a strategy for final victory.

Grant shared Lincoln's belief that the Union had to coordinate its attacks on all fronts to exploit its numerical advantage. He planned a sustained offensive against Lee in the East while ordering Sherman to attack the rebel army in Georgia. Sherman's mission was "to break it [the Confederate army] up, and to get into the interior of the enemy's country . . . inflicting all the damage you can."

The war's pace quickened dramatically. In early May 1864, Grant led 118,000 men against Lee's 64,000 in a forested area near Fredericksburg, Virginia, called the Wilderness. The Union army fought the Army of Northern Virginia in a series of bloody engagements in May and June. These battles ranked among the war's fiercest; at Cold Harbor, Grant lost 7,000 men in one hour. Instead of recoiling from such an immense "butcher's bill," Grant pressed on, forcing Lee to pull back to trenches guarding Petersburg and Richmond.

Once entrenched, Lee could not threaten the Union rear with rapid moves, as he had done for three years. Lee sent General Jubal A. Early on raids down the Shenandoah (sheh-nan-DOH-uh) Valley, which served the Confederacy as a granary as well as an indirect way to menace Washington. Grant countered by ordering General Philip Sheridan to march down the valley from the north and "lay it waste." By September 1864, Sheridan controlled the Shenandoah Valley.

While Grant and Lee grappled in the Wilderness, Sherman led 98,000 men into Georgia. Opposing him with 53,000 men (later reinforced to 65,000), General Joseph Johnston slowly retreated toward Atlanta, conserving his strength for a defense of the city and forcing Sherman to elongate his supply lines. Dismayed by this defensive strategy, President Davis replaced Johnston with the adventurous John B. Hood. He gave Davis what he wanted, a series of attacks on Sherman, but Sherman pressed relentlessly forward against Hood's increasingly depleted army. Unable to defend Atlanta, Hood evacuated the city, which fell to Sherman on September 2, 1864.

The Election of 1864

Atlanta's fall came at a timely moment for Lincoln, who was in the thick of a tough campaign for reelection. Radical Republicans opposed his re-nomination, largely because of his desire to restore occupied parts of the Confederacy to the Union, and rallied around Secretary of the Treasury Salmon P. Chase. The Democrats, meanwhile, had not forgiven Lincoln for making emancipation a war goal, and now the Copperheads demanded an immediate armistice followed by negotiations.

Lincoln, however, benefited from his own resourcefulness and his foes' problems. Chase's challenge failed, and by the time of the Republican convention, Lincoln's managers controlled the nomination. To isolate the Peace Democrats, the Republicans formed a temporary organization, the National Union party, and chose a southern Unionist, Democratic senator Andrew Johnson of Tennessee, for the vice presidency. The Democrats nominated George B. McClellan, former commander of the Army of the Potomac, who advocated military victory and tried to distance himself from the Democratic platform, which called for peace without victory.

Lincoln doubted that he would be reelected and even arranged furloughs so that Union soldiers, most of whom supported him, would be able to vote in states lacking absentee ballots. The fall of Atlanta provided an enormous boost and saved Lincoln's presidency. With 55 percent of the popular vote and 212 out of 233 electoral votes, he swept to victory.

The convention that nominated Lincoln also endorsed a constitutional amendment to abolish slavery, which Congress passed early in 1865. The **Thirteenth Amendment** would be ratified by the end of the year.

Thirteenth Amendment
Ended slavery in all U.S. territory

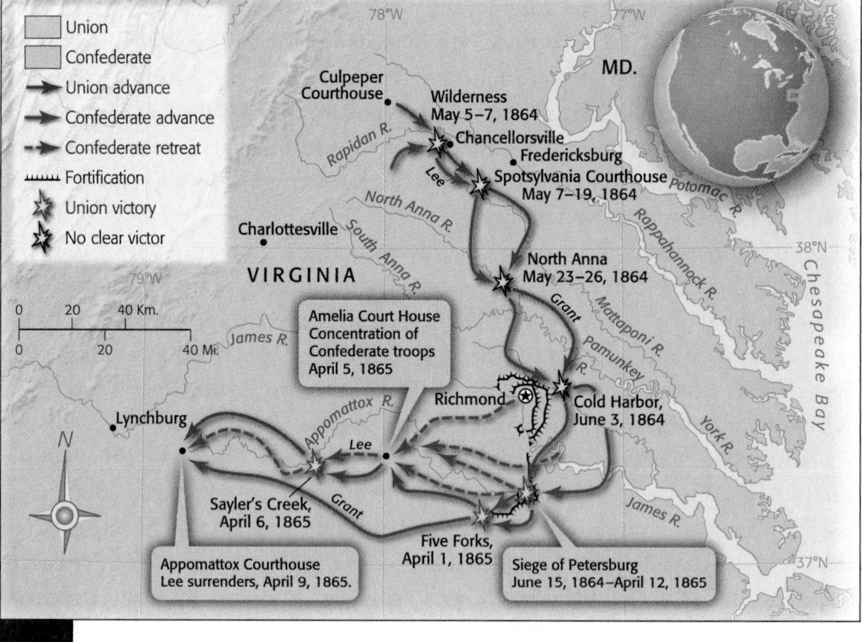

Map 15.4 The Final Virginia Campaign, 1864–1865

Refusing to abandon his campaign in the face of enormous casualties, Grant finally pushed Lee (below) into defensive fortifications around Petersburg, whose fall doomed Richmond. When Lee tried to escape to the west, Grant cut him off and forced his surrender.

Interactive Map

Sherman's March Through Georgia

Meanwhile, Sherman gave the South a lesson in total war. Refusing to chase Hood back into Tennessee, he decided to abandon his own supply lines, to march his army across Georgia to Savannah (suh-VAN-uh), and to live off the countryside. He would break the South's will to fight, terrify its people, and "make war so terrible . . . that generations would pass before they could appeal again to it."

Sherman began by burning much of Atlanta and forcing the evacuation of its civilian population. This harsh measure freed him of the need to feed and garrison the city. Then he led the bulk of his army, 62,000 men, out of Atlanta toward Savannah. Four columns of infantry, augmented by cavalry squads and followed by thousands of jubilant slaves, moved on a front sixty miles wide and at a pace of ten miles a day, destroying everything that could aid the Confederacy—arsenals, railroads, munitions plants, cotton gins, crops, and livestock. This ruin far exceeded Sherman's orders. Although told not to destroy civilian property, foragers ransacked and demolished homes. Indeed, havoc seemed a vital part of Sherman's strategy. By the time he occupied Savannah, he estimated that his army had destroyed $100 million worth of property.

After taking Savannah in December 1864, Sherman's army wheeled north toward South Carolina, the first state to secede and, in his view, one "that deserves all that seems in store for her." Sherman's columns advanced unimpeded to Columbia, where fires set by looters, slaves, soldiers of both sides, and liberated Union prisoners razed the city. Sherman then headed for North Carolina. By spring 1865, his army had left behind four hundred miles of ruin. Other Union armies controlled the entire Confederacy, except Texas and Florida, and destroyed its wealth. "War is cruelty and you cannot refine it," Sherman wrote. "Those who brought war into our country deserve all the curses and maledictions a people can pour out."

Toward Appomattox

While Sherman headed north, Grant renewed his assault on the entrenched Army of Northern Virginia. His main objective was Petersburg, a railroad hub south of Richmond. The fall of Atlanta and the devastation wrought by Sherman's army took a heavy toll on Confederate morale. Desertions reached epidemic proportions. Late in March 1865, Grant, reinforced by Sheridan, swung his army around the western flank of the Petersburg defenders. Lee could not stop him. On April 2, a courier brought the grim news to Jefferson Davis, attending church in Richmond: "General Lee telegraphs that he can hold his position no longer."

Davis left his pew, gathered his government, and fled. On the morning of April 3, Union troops entered Richmond, pulled down the Confederate flag, and raised the Stars and Stripes over the capital. Explosions set by retreating Confederates left the city "a sea of flames." Union troops liberated the jail, which held slaves awaiting sale, and its rejoicing inmates poured into the streets. On April 4, Lincoln toured the city and for a few minutes sat at Davis's desk with a dreamy expression on his face.

Appomattox Courthouse Site of Lee's surrender to Grant

Lee led a last-ditch effort to escape westward to Lynchburg and its rail connections. But Grant and Sheridan choked off the route, and on April 9 Lee bowed to the inevitable. He asked for terms of surrender and met Grant in a private home in the village of **Appomattox** (app-oh-MAT-tux) **Courthouse,** east of Lynchburg. As stunned troops gathered outside, Lee appeared in full dress uniform, complete with sword. Grant entered in his customary disarray, smoking a cigar. The final surrender came four days later, as Lee's troops laid down their arms between federal ranks. "On our part," wrote a Union officer, "not a sound of trumpet . . . nor roll of drum; not a cheer . . . but an awed stillness rather." Grant paroled Lee's 26,000 men and sent them home with the horses and mules "to work their little farms." Within a month the remnants of Confederate resistance collapsed. Johnston surrendered to Sherman on April 18, and Davis was captured in Georgia on May 10.

National Archives

Grant in 1864

Exuding determination and competence, General Ulysses S. Grant posed in front of his tent in 1864. Within a year, Grant's final assault on Petersburg and the Union army's triumphant march into Richmond would bring the war to an end.

Grant headed back to a jubilant Washington. On April 14, he turned down a theater date with the Lincolns; his wife found Mrs. Lincoln overbearing. That night at Ford's Theater an unemployed pro-Confederate actor, John Wilkes Booth, entered Lincoln's box and shot him in the head. Shouting the

Virginia state motto, *"Sic Semper Tyrannis"* ("Such is always the fate of tyrants"), Booth leaped onto the stage and fled. Assassination attempts on the secretary of state and vice president failed, and Booth escaped. Within two weeks Union troops hunted him down and shot him to death. Four accused accomplices were hanged, and four more were imprisoned. On April 15, Lincoln died, and Andrew Johnson became president. Six days later, Lincoln's funeral train left Washington on its mournful journey to Springfield, Illinois. Crowds of thousands gathered at stations to weep as the black-draped train passed.

The Impact of the War

The Civil War took a larger human toll than any other war in American history. More than 620,000 soldiers died during the tragic four years of war, nearly equal the number of American soldiers killed in all the nation's earlier and later wars. The death count stood at 360,000 Union soldiers and 260,000 Confederates. Most families in the nation suffered losses. Vivid reminders remained well into the twentieth century. For many years, armless and legless veterans gathered at regimental reunions, and thousands of communities built monuments to the dead.

The war's costs were staggering, but only the southern economy was destroyed. By war's end the North had most of the nation's wealth and industrial capacity. Spurring economic modernization, the war provided opportunities for industrial development and capital investment. No longer the largest slave-owning power in the world, the United States would become a major industrial nation.

The war had political ramifications as well. States never regained their antebellum range of powers. The national banking system gradually supplanted state banks, and greenbacks provided a national currency. The war also promoted large-scale organization in both the business world and public life.

Finally, the Civil War fulfilled abolitionists' prophecies as well as Union goals, producing the very sort of radical upheaval within southern society that Lincoln had tried to avoid. Beaten Confederates wondered whether blacks and Yankees would permanently take over the South. "Hello, massa," an African-American Union soldier called out when he spotted his former owner among Confederate prisoners whom he was guarding. "Bottom rail top dis time." The nation now shifted its attention to the reconstruction of the conquered South and the fate of 3.5 million newly freed slaves.

CHECKING IN

- Lincoln finally found the general he needed in Ulysses S. Grant, who realized that the South could not withstand the enormous casualties of relentless combat.
- Sherman brought total war to the South with his march through Georgia and the Carolinas.
- Lincoln's triumph in the 1864 election reflected increasing Union confidence in victory.
- Forced to leave Richmond undefended, Lee surrendered in April 1865, effectively ending major combat.
- In the final months of the war, Congress passed the Thirteenth Amendment, abolishing slavery, but the assassination of Lincoln left the postwar future in limbo.

Chapter Summary

What major advantages did each side possess at the start of the Civil War? (page 338)

The Union had enormous manpower advantages, as well as a strong industrial base. However, to sustain Confederate independence, the South had to fight a defensive war, whereas the northern armies had to invade and occupy a vast region. As war dragged on, both regions faced political and economic problems. The North weathered these problems somewhat better than the South, where political rifts appeared over the role of national government in the Confederacy. Lincoln was a far better political leader than Davis.

How was the war fought in its early years? (page 343)

Although new weapons, such as the rifle, appeared, the Civil War was basically fought as a traditional war, with mass infantry charges and large battles. The war in the East quickly became a stalemate, but the Union established supremacy west of the Mississippi early in the war. Many Confederate leaders assumed that the British textile industry's need for southern cotton would force Britain to become an ally, but the British remained aloof.

How did the issue of emancipation transform the war? (page 352)

The Emancipation Proclamation transformed the Civil War from a conflict over secession into a war about slavery, and it effectively prevented Great Britain from openly supporting the Confederacy. Whenever possible, slaves strove to escape from slavery. Slave refugees posed problems for Union armies but also performed valuable tasks for federal troops. Nearly 190,000 African-Americans fought in Union armies, and manpower shortages drove the Confederacy to authorize the use of black troops as well.

In what ways did the Civil War affect the two sides? (page 357)

During the war, the federal Congress passed major bills promoting economic development: tariffs, railroad subsidies, national banking laws, and legislation to encourage homesteading. However, the war devastated the South's economy, with resulting shortages and hardships for civilians. Women assumed new roles as nurses and hoped that their service would advance the cause of women's rights.

Key Terms

conscription *(p. 339)*
"greenbacks" *(p. 340)*
Anaconda plan *(p. 345)*
First Battle of Bull Run *(p. 346)*
George B. McClellan *(p. 346)*
Robert E. Lee *(p. 347)*
Antietam *(p. 347)*
Emancipation Proclamation *(p. 347)*
Ulysses S. Grant *(p. 347)*
Gettysburg *(p. 355)*
Vicksburg *(p. 357)*
Pacific Railroad Act *(p. 358)*
Homestead Act *(p. 358)*
Morrill Land Grant Act *(p. 358)*
Copperheads *(p. 359)*
U.S. Sanitary Commission *(p. 360)*
Clara Barton *(p. 361)*
Thirteenth Amendment *(p. 363)*
Appomattox Courthouse *(p. 365)*

How did the Union finally win the war? (page 362)

Lincoln found the general he had been searching for in Ulysses S. Grant, who was willing to absorb enormous casualties to inflict the losses he knew the South could not afford. Sherman's capture of Atlanta guaranteed Lincoln's reelection in 1864 and boosted northern determination. By April 1865, Lee was forced to abandon the defense of Richmond and surrendered at Appomattox Courthouse. The Thirteenth Amendment, passed in the final months of the war, ended slavery. However, Lincoln's assassination left the postwar future in limbo.

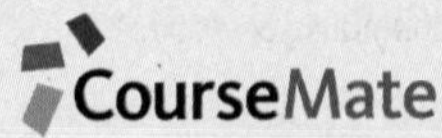

Go to the CourseMate website at **www.cengagebrain.com** for additional study tools and review materials—including audio and video clips—for this chapter.

Chapter 16

The Crisis of Reconstruction

1865–1877

Louisiana and Lower Mississippi Valley Collection, C-31LSU Libraries, Louisiana State University

The Devastated South

Chapter Preview

Reconstruction Politics, 1865–1868
How did Radical Republicans gain control of Reconstruction politics?

Reconstruction Governments
What impact did federal Reconstruction policy have on the former Confederacy and ex-Confederates?

The Impact of Emancipation
How did the newly freed slaves reshape their lives after emancipation?

New Concerns in the North, 1868–1876
Why did northern concern about Reconstruction begin to wane?

Reconstruction Abandoned, 1876–1877
What factors contributed to the end of Reconstruction in 1877?

"I never forget de day we was set free," former slave Katie Rowe recalled. "Dat morning we all go to de cotton field early. After a while de old horn blow up at de overseer's house, and we all stop and listen, 'cause it de wrong time of day for de horn." Later that day, after several more blasts of the horn, a stranger, apparently a Yankee, addressed the slaves. "'Today you is free, just lak I is,' de man say," Katie Rowe declared. "'You is your own bosses now.'" The date was June 4, 1865. Rowe called it the day "that I begins to live."

Emancipation in June 1865 brought an era of transition for the former slaves. "None of us know whar to go," Katie Rowe remembered. The plantation overseer charged the former slaves "half de crop for de quarter and all de mules and tools and grub." His replacement offered better arrangements: "[W]e all got something left over after dat first go-out." But new changes occurred. The next year the former owner's heirs sold the plantation, "and we scatter off." Katie eventually married a Cherokee man and moved to Oklahoma.

For the nation, as for Katie Rowe, the end of the Civil War was an instant of uncharted possibilities and a time of unresolved conflicts. While former slaves exulted over their freedom, their former owners were often as grim as the wasted southern landscape. Several thousand fled to Brazil, Mexico, or Europe, but most remained.

In most armed conflicts, the morale of the vanquished rarely concerns the victors. However, the Civil War was a special case, for the Union had sought not merely military triumph but the return of national unity. Therefore, the federal government in 1865 faced unprecedented questions. How could the Union be restored and the South reintegrated? Who would control the process—Congress or the president? Should Confederate leaders be tried for treason? Most important, what would happen to the 3.5 million former slaves? The freedmen's future was *the* crucial issue of the postwar era, for emancipation had set in motion a profound upheaval. Before the war, slavery had determined the South's social, economic, and political structure. What would replace it? The end of the Civil War, in short, posed two huge challenges that had to be solved simultaneously: how to readmit the South to the Union and how to define the status of free blacks in American society.

Between 1865 and 1877, the nation met these challenges, but not without discord and turmoil. Conflict prevailed in the halls of Congress, in the former Confederacy, and in the industrializing postwar North. The crises of Reconstruction—the restoration of the former Confederate states and the fate of the former slaves—reshaped the legacy of the Civil War.

RECONSTRUCTION POLITICS, 1865–1868

How did Radical Republicans gain control of Reconstruction politics?

The end of the Civil War offered multiple possibilities for chaos and vengeance. The federal government could have imprisoned or executed Confederate leaders, demobilized Confederate soldiers might have continued armed resistance, and freed slaves might have taken revenge on former masters. However, none of this occurred. Instead, intense *political* conflict dominated the immediate postwar period. National politics produced new constitutional amendments, a presidential impeachment, and some of the most ambitious domestic legislation ever enacted by Congress: the Reconstruction Acts of 1867–1868. It culminated in something that few expected: the enfranchisement of African-American men.

Radical Republicans Faction in Congress, led by Thaddeus Stevens and Charles Sumner, that called for full civil rights for freedmen without compromise

In 1865 only a handful of **Radical Republicans** advocated African-American suffrage. But in the complex political battles of Reconstruction, the Radicals won broad support for their program, including African-American male enfranchisement. Just as the Civil War had led to emancipation, Reconstruction led to African-American suffrage.

Lincoln's Plan

Conflict over Reconstruction began even before the war ended. In December 1863, President Abraham Lincoln issued the Proclamation of Amnesty and Reconstruction, which enabled southern states to rejoin the Union if at least 10 percent of those who had voted in the 1860 elections swore an oath of allegiance to the Union and accepted emancipation. This plan excluded most Confederate officials and military officers, who would have had to apply for presidential pardons, as well as African-Americans, who had not voted in 1860. Through these requirements, Lincoln hoped both to undermine the Confederacy and to build a southern Republican Party.

Radical Republicans in Congress, however, envisioned a slower readmission process that would bar even more ex-Confederates from political life. The Wade-Davis Bill, passed by Congress in July 1864, provided that a military governor would rule each former Confederate state; after at least half the eligible voters took an oath of allegiance to the Union, delegates could be elected to a state convention that would repeal secession and abolish slavery. To qualify as a voter or a delegate, a southerner would have to take a second, "ironclad" oath, swearing that he had never voluntarily supported the Confederacy. The Wade-Davis Bill would have delayed readmission of southern states almost indefinitely.

Chronology

1863	Abraham Lincoln issues the Proclamation of Amnesty and Reconstruction
1864	Wade-Davis Bill passed by Congress and pocket-vetoed by Lincoln
1865	Freedmen's Bureau established; Civil War ends; Lincoln assassinated; Andrew Johnson becomes president; Johnson issues his Proclamation of Amnesty and Reconstruction; ex-Confederate states hold constitutional conventions; Thirteenth Amendment added to the Constitution
1866	Civil Rights Act of 1866 and the Supplementary Freedmen's Bureau Act passed over Johnson's vetoes; Ku Klux Klan founded in Tennessee; race riots occur in southern cities; Republicans win congressional elections
1867	Reconstruction Act of 1867; William Seward negotiates the purchase of Alaska; constitutional conventions meet in the ex-Confederate states
1868	Andrew Johnson impeached, tried, and acquitted; Fourteenth Amendment added to the Constitution; Ulysses S. Grant elected president
1869	Transcontinental railroad completed
1870	Congress readmits the four remaining southern states to the Union; Fifteenth Amendment added to the Constitution; Enforcement Act of 1870
1871	Second Enforcement Act; Ku Klux Klan Act
1872	Liberal Republican party formed; Amnesty Act; *Alabama* claims settled; Grant reelected president
1873	Panic of 1873 begins, setting off five-year depression
1874	Democrats gain control of the House of Representatives
1875	Civil Rights Act of 1875; Specie Resumption Act
1876	Disputed presidential election: Rutherford B. Hayes versus Samuel J. Tilden
1877	Electoral commission decides election in favor of Hayes; the last Republican-controlled state governments fall
1879	"Exodus" movement spreads through several southern states

Lincoln pocket-vetoed* the Wade-Davis Bill, and an impasse followed. Arkansas, Louisiana, Tennessee, and parts of Virginia moved toward readmission under variants of Lincoln's plan, but Congress refused to seat their delegates. What Lincoln's ultimate policy would have been remains unknown. But after his assassination, on April 14, 1865, Radical Republicans turned with hope toward his successor, Andrew Johnson of Tennessee.

Andrew Johnson Former slave owner and senator from Tennessee; as Lincoln's successor and seventeenth president, he lost control over Reconstruction policy and barely survived impeachment in 1868

Presidential Reconstruction Under Johnson

At first glance, **Andrew Johnson** seemed a likely ally for the Radicals. The only southern senator to remain in Congress when his state seceded, Andrew Johnson served as military governor of Tennessee from 1862 to 1864. Defying the Confederate stand, he declared that "treason is a crime and must be made odious." Self-educated, of humble origins, a foe of the planter class, a supporter of emancipation—Johnson carried impeccable credentials. However, as a lifelong Democrat he had his own political agenda, which was sharply different from that of the Radicals. He neither adopted abolitionist ideals nor challenged racist sentiments. He hoped mainly that the fall of slavery would cripple southern aristocrats.

In May 1865, with Congress out of session, Johnson shocked Republicans by announcing his own program, A Proclamation of Amnesty and Reconstruction, to bring back into the Union the seven southern states still without Reconstruction governments—Alabama, Florida, Georgia, Mississippi, North Carolina, South Carolina, and Texas. Almost all southerners who took an oath of allegiance would receive a pardon and amnesty; all their property except slaves would be restored. Oath takers could elect delegates to state conventions, which would call regular elections, proclaim secession illegal, repudiate debts incurred under the Confederacy, and ratify the Thirteenth Amendment, which abolished slavery. As under Lincoln's plan, Confederate civil and military officers would still be disqualified, as would well-off ex-Confederates (those with taxable property worth $20,000 or more). This purge of the plantation aristocracy, Johnson said, would benefit "humble men, the peasantry of the South, who have been decoyed . . . into rebellion." Poorer whites would now be in control.

Presidential Reconstruction Andrew Johnson's plan to pardon ex-Confederate leaders and readmit former Confederate states to the union on lenient terms

Presidential Reconstruction began in the summer of 1865, but developed unforeseen consequences. Johnson handed out pardons liberally (some thirteen thousand) and dropped his plans to punish treason. By the end of 1865 all seven states had created new civil governments that in effect restored the status quo from before the war. Confederate officers and large planters resumed state offices. Former Confederate congressmen and officials—including Alexander Stephens of Georgia, the former Confederate vice president—won election to Congress. Some states even refused to ratify the Thirteenth Amendment or to repudiate their Confederate debts.

"black codes" Laws passed by southern states to limit the rights of freedmen

Most infuriating to the Radicals, all seven states passed **"black codes"** intended to ensure a landless, dependent black labor force. These codes, which replaced earlier slave codes, guaranteed the freedmen some basic rights—to marry, own property, make contracts, and testify in court against other blacks—but also harshly restricted freedmen's behavior. Some states established segregation; most prohibited racial

* Pocket-vetoed: failed to sign the bill within ten days of Congress's adjournment.

intermarriage, jury service by blacks, and court testimony by blacks against whites. All codes included provisions that effectively barred former slaves from leaving the plantations, usually through labor contracts stipulating that anyone who had not signed a labor contract was a vagrant and subject to arrest.

As a result of the black codes, freedmen were no longer slaves but not really liberated either. In practice, many clauses in the codes never took effect: the Freedmen's Bureau suspended the enforcement of the racially discriminatory provisions of the new laws. Nonetheless, the black codes revealed white southern intentions and showed what "home rule" would have been like without federal intervention.

Many northerners denounced what they saw as southern defiance. When Congress convened in December 1865, it refused to seat delegates of ex-Confederate states and prepared to dismantle the black codes and to lock ex-Confederates out of power.

Congress Versus Johnson

Southern blacks' status became the major issue in Congress. With Congress split into four blocs—Radical, moderate, and conservative Republicans, as well as Democrats—a politically adroit president could have protected his program. Ineptly, Johnson alienated a majority of the moderates and pushed them into the Radicals' arms.

In late 1865 Congress voted to extend the life of the Freedmen's Bureau for three more years. This federal agency, headed by former Union general O. O. Howard and staffed mainly by army officers, provided relief, rations, and medical care; built schools for freed blacks; put them to work on abandoned or confiscated lands; and tried to protect their rights as laborers. To strengthen the bureau, Congress gave it new power to run special military courts, to settle labor disputes, and to invalidate labor contracts forced on freedmen by the black codes. In February 1866, Johnson vetoed the bill. The Constitution, he declared, did not sanction military trials of civilians in peacetime, nor did it support a system to care for "indigent persons." Then in March 1866 Congress passed the **Civil Rights Act of 1866,** which made African-Americans U.S. citizens with the same civil rights as other citizens and authorized federal intervention to ensure black rights in court. Johnson vetoed this measure as well, arguing that it would "operate in favor of the colored and against the white race." In April Congress overrode his veto, and in July it enacted the Supplementary Freedmen's Bureau Act over another presidential veto.

Civil Rights Act of 1866 Made blacks U.S. citizens; first major law ever passed over a presidential veto

These vetoes puzzled many Republicans because the new laws did not undercut presidential Reconstruction. Although the vetoes gained support for Johnson among northern Democrats, they cost him dearly among moderate Republicans, who now joined Radicals to oppose him. Was Johnson a political incompetent, or was he merely trying, unsuccessfully, to forge a centrist coalition? Whatever the case, he drove moderate and Radical Republicans together toward their next step: the passage of a constitutional amendment to protect the new Civil Rights Act.

The Fourteenth Amendment, 1866

In April 1866, Congress adopted the **Fourteenth Amendment,** its most ambitious attempt to deal with the problems of Reconstruction. In the first clause, the

Fourteenth Amendment Defined citizenship and guaranteed equal protection under the law amendment proclaimed that all persons born or naturalized in the United States were citizens and that no state could abridge their rights without due process of law or deny them equal protection under the law. This section nullified the *Dred Scott* decision of 1857, which had declared that blacks were not citizens. Second, the amendment guaranteed that, if a state denied suffrage to any male citizen, its representation in Congress would be proportionally reduced. Third, the amendment disqualified from state and national offices *all* prewar officeholders who had supported the Confederacy. In so providing, Congress intended to invalidate most of the pardons that President Johnson had ladled out. Finally, the amendment repudiated the Confederate debt and maintained the validity of the federal debt.

The amendment's passage created a firestorm. Abolitionists decried it as a "swindle" because it did not explicitly ensure black suffrage, southerners blasted it as vengeful, and President Johnson denounced it. His defiance solidified the new alliance between moderate and Radical Republicans, and transformed the congressional elections of 1866 into a referendum on the Fourteenth Amendment.

Over the summer, Johnson set off on a whistle-stop train tour from Washington to St. Louis and Chicago and back. But this innovative campaign tactic—the "swing around the circle," as Johnson called it—failed. Humorless and defensive, the president made fresh enemies and doomed his hope of sinking the Fourteenth Amendment, which moderate and Radical Republicans defended.

Republicans carried the congressional elections of 1866 in a landslide, winning almost two-thirds of the House and four-fifths of the Senate. They had secured a mandate for the Fourteenth Amendment and their own Reconstruction program.

Congressional Reconstruction, 1866–1867

Congressional debate over reconstructing the South began in December 1866 and lasted three months. Radical leaders called for black suffrage, federal support for public schools, confiscation of Confederate estates, and extended military occupation of the South. Moderate Republicans accepted parts of this plan. In February 1867, after complex legislative maneuvers, Congress passed the Reconstruction Act of 1867. Johnson vetoed the law, and on March 2, Congress passed it over his veto. Three more Reconstruction acts—passed in 1867 and 1868 over presidential vetoes—refined and enforced the first act.

Reconstruction Act of 1867 Imposed military rule on ten southern states and required them to ratify the Fourteenth Amendment

The **Reconstruction Act of 1867** invalidated the state governments formed under the Lincoln and Johnson plans. Only Tennessee, which had already ratified the Fourteenth Amendment and had been readmitted to the Union, escaped further Reconstruction. The new law divided the other ten former Confederate states into five temporary military districts, each run by a Union general (see Map 16.1). Voters—all black men, plus whites not disqualified by the Fourteenth Amendment—could elect delegates to a state convention that would write a new state constitution granting black suffrage. Once Congress approved the state constitution, and once the state legislature ratified the Fourteenth Amendment, Congress would readmit the state into the Union. The Reconstruction Act of 1867 was far more radical than the Johnson program because it enfranchised blacks and disfranchised many ex-Confederates. Even then, however, it provided only temporary military rule, made no provisions to prosecute Confederate leaders for treason, and neither confiscated nor redistributed property.

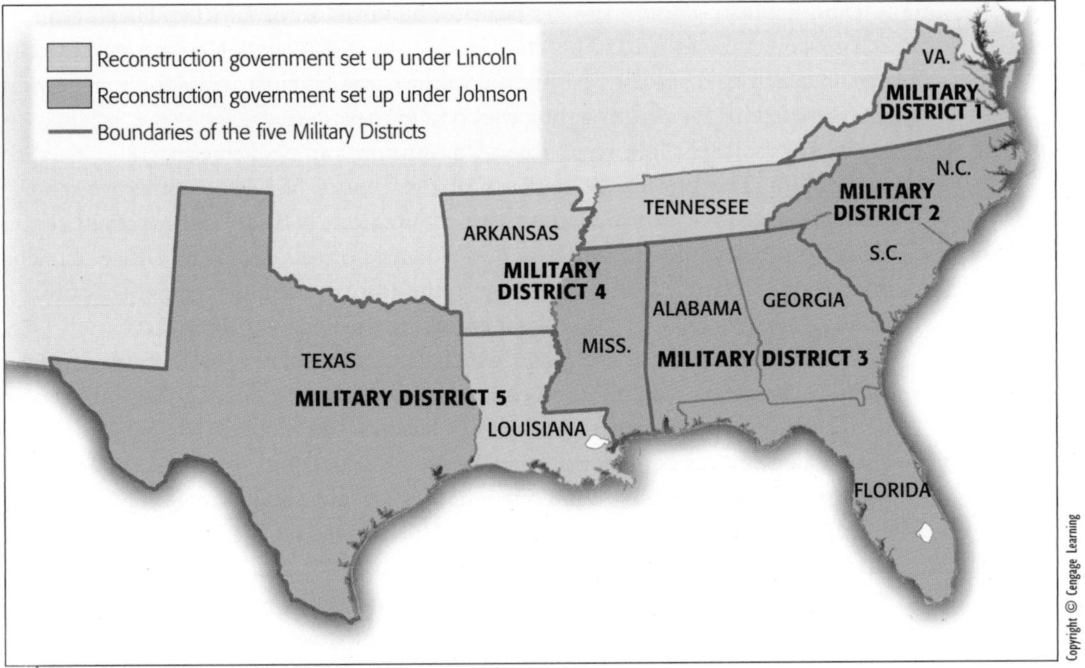

Map 16.1 The Reconstruction of the South

The Reconstruction Act of 1867 divided the former Confederate states, except Tennessee, into five military districts and set forth the steps by which new state governments could be created.

During the congressional debates, Radical Republican congressman Thaddeus Stevens had argued for the confiscation of large Confederate estates to "humble the proud traitors" and to provide for former slaves. He had proposed subdividing such confiscated property into forty-acre tracts to be distributed among the freedmen and selling the rest to pay off war debts. Stevens's land-reform bill won Radical support but never made progress; most Republicans held property rights sacred. Tampering with such rights, they feared, would endanger the rest of Reconstruction. Thus, land reform never came about. The "radical" Reconstruction acts were a compromise.

Congressional Reconstruction took effect in spring 1867, but Johnson impeded its enforcement by replacing pro-Radical military officers with conservative ones. Republicans seethed. More suspicious than ever, congressional moderates and Radicals again joined forces to block Johnson from further hampering Reconstruction.

The Impeachment Crisis, 1867–1868

In March 1867, Republicans in Congress passed two laws to curb presidential power. The **Tenure of Office Act** prohibited the president from removing civil officers without Senate consent. Its purpose was to bar Johnson from dismissing Secretary of War Edwin M. Stanton, a Radical ally. The other law barred the president from issuing military orders except through the commanding general, Ulysses S. Grant, who could not be removed without the Senate's consent.

Tenure of Office Act Law requiring the president to seek Senate consent before removing civil officers

The Radicals' enmity toward Johnson, however, went further: They began to seek grounds on which to impeach him. The House Judiciary Committee, aided by private detectives, could at first find no valid charges against Johnson. But Johnson again rescued his foes by providing the charges they needed.

In August 1867, Johnson suspended Stanton and, in February 1868, tried to remove him. The president's defiance of the Tenure of Office Act drove moderate Republicans back into alliance with the Radicals. The House approved eleven charges of impeachment, nine based on violation of the Tenure of Office Act. The other charges accused Johnson of being "unmindful of the high duties of the office," seeking to disgrace Congress, and not enforcing the Reconstruction acts.

Johnson's trial by the Senate, which began in March 1868, riveted public attention for eleven weeks. Seven congressmen, including leading Radicals, served as prosecutors, or "managers." Johnson's lawyers maintained that he was merely seeking a court test by violating the Tenure of Office Act, which he thought was unconstitutional. They also contended that the law did not protect Stanton, because Lincoln, not Johnson, had appointed him. Finally, they asserted, Johnson was guilty of no crime indictable in a regular court.

Congressional "managers" countered that impeachment was a political process, not a criminal trial, and that Johnson's "abuse of discretionary power" constituted an impeachable offense. Some Senate Republicans wavered, fearful that the removal of a president would destroy the balance of power within the federal government. They also distrusted Radical Republican Benjamin Wade, the president pro tempore of the Senate. Because there was no vice president, Wade would become president if Johnson were thrown out.

Ultimately, despite intense pressure, seven Republicans risked political suicide by voting with the Democrats against removal, and the Senate failed by one vote to convict Johnson. In so doing, they set a precedent: Their vote discouraged impeachment on political grounds for decades to come. But the anti-Johnson forces had also achieved their goal: Andrew Johnson had no future as president. Republicans in Congress, meanwhile, pursued their last major Reconstruction objective: to guarantee black male suffrage.

The Fifteenth Amendment and the Question of Woman Suffrage, 1869–1870

Black suffrage was the linchpin of congressional Reconstruction, since only with the black vote could Republicans secure control of the ex-Confederate states. The Reconstruction Act of 1867 had forced southern states to enfranchise black men in order to reenter the Union, but much of the North rejected black suffrage. The **Fifteenth Amendment,** proposed by Congress in 1869, sought to protect black suffrage in the South, and to enfranchise northern and border-state blacks, who would presumably vote Republican. The amendment prohibited the denial of suffrage by the states to any citizen on account of "race, color, or previous condition of servitude."

Fifteenth Amendment Prevented states from denying the vote to any citizen on account of "race, color, or previous condition of servitude"

Democrats opposed the amendment on the grounds that it violated states' rights, but they did not control enough states to defeat the amendment, and it was ratified in 1870 (see Table 16.1). Some southerners appreciated the amendment's omissions: as a Richmond newspaper pointed out, it had "loopholes through which

TABLE 16.1 THE RECONSTRUCTION AMENDMENTS

AMENDMENT AND DATE OF CONGRESSIONAL PASSAGE	PROVISIONS	RATIFICATION
Thirteenth (January 1865)	Prohibited slavery in the United States	December 1865
Fourteenth (June 1866)	Defined citizenship to include all persons born or naturalized in the United States Provided proportional loss of congressional representation for any state that denied suffrage to any of its male citizens Disqualified prewar officeholders who supported the Confederacy from state or national office Repudiated the Confederate debt	July 1868, after Congress made ratification a prerequisite for readmission of ex-Confederate states to the Union
Fifteenth (February 1869)	Prohibited the denial of suffrage because of race, color, or previous condition of servitude	March 1870; ratification required of Virginia, Texas, Mississippi, and Georgia for readmission to the Union

a coach and four horses can be driven." For example, the Fifteenth Amendment neither guaranteed black officeholding nor prohibited voting restrictions such as property requirements and literacy tests. Such restrictions ultimately were used to deny blacks the vote.

The debate over black suffrage drew new participants into the fray. Women's rights advocates tried to promote both black suffrage and woman suffrage, but Radical Republicans rejected any linkage between the two, preferring to concentrate on black suffrage. Supporters of women's rights were themselves divided. Frederick Douglass argued that black suffrage had to receive priority. "If the elective franchise is not extended to the Negro, he is dead," explained Douglass. "Woman has a thousand ways by which she can attach herself to the ruling power of the land that we have not." But women's rights leaders Elizabeth Cady Stanton and **Susan B. Anthony** disagreed. In their view, the Fourteenth Amendment had disabled women by including the word "male." If the Fifteenth Amendment did not include women, they emphasized, it would increase women's disadvantages.

The battle over black suffrage and the Fifteenth Amendment split women's rights advocates into two rival suffrage associations, both formed in 1869. The Boston-based American Woman Suffrage Association sought state-by-state suffrage, whereas the more radical National Woman Suffrage Association, based in New York and led by Stanton and Anthony, promoted a constitutional amendment for woman suffrage.

Throughout the 1870s, the rival woman suffrage associations vied for constituents. In 1869 and 1870, independent of the suffrage movement, two territories, Wyoming and Utah, enfranchised women. But suffragists failed to sway legislators elsewhere. When Susan B. Anthony mobilized

Susan B. Anthony Women's rights advocate whose National Woman Suffrage Association called for a federal women suffrage amendment

CHECKING IN

- Lincoln's somewhat lenient plan for Reconstruction died with him.
- President Johnson's even more tolerant plan for Reconstruction infuriated Radical Republicans.
- Congress overrode presidential vetoes of Reconstruction measures such as the Freedmen's Bureau and passed its own harsher version of Reconstruction legislation.
- The Fourteenth Amendment defined citizenship and guaranteed equal protection under the law, and the Fifteenth Amendment guaranteed the right of freedmen, but not of women, to vote.
- The attempt to impeach Johnson on political grounds failed by a narrow margin.

about seventy women to try to vote nationwide in 1872, she was indicted, convicted, and fined. In 1875 the Supreme Court ruled that a state could deny women the right to vote. Divided and rebuffed, woman suffrage advocates braced for a long struggle.

By 1870, when the Fifteenth Amendment was ratified, Congress could look back on five years of achievement. Since the start of 1865, three constitutional amendments had broadened the scope of American democracy by abolishing slavery, expanding civil rights, and prohibiting the denial of suffrage on the basis of race. Congress had also readmitted the former Confederate states into the Union. But after 1868, congressional momentum slowed, and the theater of action shifted to the South, where tumultuous change occurred.

RECONSTRUCTION GOVERNMENTS

What impact did federal Reconstruction policy have on the former Confederacy and ex-Confederates?

During the unstable years of presidential Reconstruction, 1865–1867, the southern states had to create new governments, revive the war-torn economy, and face the impact of emancipation. Crises abounded. Cities and factories lay in rubble, plantation labor systems disintegrated, and racial tensions flared as freedmen organized to protest ill treatment and demand equal rights. Race riots erupted in major southern cities. In May 1866, white crowds attacked black veterans in Memphis and rampaged through black neighborhoods, killing forty-six people.

Congressional Reconstruction, supervised by federal troops, took effect in the spring of 1867. The Johnson regimes were dismantled and voters elected new state governments, which Republicans dominated. By 1868 most former Confederate states had rejoined the Union, and within two years the process was complete.

But Republican rule did not long endure in the South. Opposition from southern Democrats, the landowning elite, vigilantes, and most white voters proved insurmountable. Nevertheless, the governments formed under congressional Reconstruction were unique because black men, including former slaves, participated in them. Slavery had ended in other societies, too, but only in the United States had freedmen gained democratic political rights.

A New Electorate

The Reconstruction laws of 1867–1868 transformed the southern electorate by temporarily disfranchising 10 to 15 percent of potential white voters and by enfranchising more than 700,000 freed slaves. Black voters outnumbered whites by 100,000 overall and held voting majorities in five states.

This new electorate provided a base for the Republican Party, which had never existed in the South. To scornful Democrats, the Republicans comprised three types of scoundrels: northern "carpetbaggers" who had come south for wealth and power; southern "scalawags," poor and ignorant whites, who sought to profit from Republican rule; and hordes of uneducated freedmen, who were easily manipulated.

Crossing class and racial lines, the hastily established Republican Party was in fact a loose coalition of diverse factions with often contradictory goals.

To northerners who moved south after the war, the former Confederacy was an undeveloped region, ripe with possibility. The carpetbaggers included many former Union soldiers who hoped to buy land, open factories, build railroads, or simply enjoy the warmer climate. Holding almost one in three state offices, they wielded disproportionate political power.

Although a handful of scalawags were old Whigs, most were small farmers from the mountain regions of North Carolina, Georgia, Alabama, and Arkansas. As former Unionists who had owned no slaves and felt no loyalty to the landowning elite, they sought to improve their economic position and lacked commitment to black rights. Most came from regions with small black populations and cared little whether blacks voted or not. Scalawags held the most political offices during Reconstruction, but they proved the least stable element of the southern Republican coalition; eventually, many drifted back to the Democratic fold.

Republicans in the South Carolina Legislature, ca. 1868

Only in South Carolina did blacks comprise a dominant majority in the legislature. This photographic collage of "Radical" legislators, black and white, suggests the extent of black representation. In 1874, blacks won the majority of seats in South Carolina's state senate as well.

Freedmen, the backbone of southern Republicanism, provided eight out of ten Republican votes. They sought land, education, civil rights, and political equality, and remained loyal Republicans. Although Reconstruction governments depended on African-American votes, freedmen held at most one in five political offices and constituted a legislative majority only in South Carolina, whose population was more than 60 percent black. A mere 6 percent of southern members of the House were African-American, and almost 50 percent came from South Carolina. No blacks became governor, and only two served in the U.S. Senate—the same number as served during the twentieth century.

Black officeholders on the state level formed a political elite. They often differed from black voters in background, education, and wealth. Many were literate blacks who had been free before the Civil War. In the South Carolina legislature, most black members came from large towns and cities; many had spent time in the North; and some were well-off property owners or even former slave owners. Color differences were evident as well: 43 percent of South Carolina's black legislators were of mixed race, compared to just 7 percent of the state's black population.

Black officials and black voters often had different priorities. Most freedmen cared mainly about their economic future, especially about acquiring land; black officeholders cared most about attaining equal rights. Still, both groups shared high expectations and prized enfranchisement. "We'd walk fifteen miles in wartime to find out about the battle," a Georgia freedman declared. "We can walk fifteen miles and more to find how to vote."

Republican Rule

Large numbers of African-Americans participated in government for the first time in the state constitutional conventions of 1867–1868. The South Carolina convention had a black majority, and in Louisiana half the delegates were freedmen. These conventions forged democratic changes. Delegates abolished property qualifications for officeholding, made many appointive offices elective, and established universal manhood suffrage.

However, no state instituted land reform. When proposals for land confiscation and redistribution arose at the state conventions, they fell to defeat, as they had in Congress. Hoping to attract northern investment, southern Republicans hesitated to threaten property rights or to adopt land-reform measures that northern Republicans had rejected. South Carolina did set up a commission to buy land and make it available to freedmen, and several states changed their tax structures to force uncultivated land onto the market, but in no case was ex-Confederate land confiscated.

Once civil power shifted to the new state governments, Republican administrations began ambitious programs of public works. They built roads and bridges, approved railroad bonds, and funded institutions to care for orphans, the insane, and the disabled. They also expanded state bureaucracies and formed state militias in which blacks often were heavily represented. Finally, they created public-school systems, which were almost nonexistent in the South until then. These reforms cost millions, and taxes skyrocketed. Although northern tax rates still exceeded southern tax rates, southerners, particularly landowners, resented the new levies.

To Reconstruction's foes, Republican rule was wasteful and corrupt, the "most stupendous system of organized robbery in history." Indeed, corruption did permeate some state governments, as in Louisiana and South Carolina. The main profiteers were government officials who accepted bribes and railroad promoters who doled them out. But neither group was exclusively Republican. In fact, corruption increasingly characterized government *nationally* in these years and was both more flagrant and more lucrative in the North.

Counterattacks

Ex-Confederates spoke with dread about black enfranchisement and the "horror of Negro domination." As soon as congressional Reconstruction took effect, former Confederates campaigned to undermine it. Democratic newspapers called Louisiana's constitution "the work of ignorant Negroes cooperating with a gang of white adventurers."

Democrats delayed mobilization until the southern states were readmitted to the Union, and then swung into action. At first, they pursued African-American votes; however, when that failed they tried other tactics. In every southern state the Democrats contested elections, backed dissident Republican factions, elected some Democratic legislators, and lured scalawags away from the Republican Party.

Vigilante efforts to reduce black votes bolstered Democratic campaigns to win white ones. Antagonism toward free blacks, long a motif in southern life, resurged after the war. In 1865, Freedmen's Bureau agents itemized a variety of outrages against blacks, including shooting, murder, rape, arson, roasting, and "inhuman beating." Vigilante groups sprang up in all parts of the former Confederacy, but one organization rose to dominance. In the spring of 1866, six young Confederate war veterans in Tennessee formed a social club, the **Ku Klux Klan,** distinguished by elaborate rituals, hooded costumes, and secret passwords. New Klan dens spread rapidly. By the election of 1868, the Klan had become a terrorist movement directed against potential African-American voters.

Ku Klux Klan Organization that used terrorism to prevent freedmen from voting and to reestablish white supremacy

The Klan sought to suppress black voting, reestablish white supremacy, and topple the Reconstruction governments. It attacked Freedmen's Bureau officials, white Republicans, black militia units, economically successful blacks, and black voters. Concentrated in areas where white and black populations were most evenly balanced and racial tensions were greatest, Klan dens adapted their tactics to local

Tennessee State Archives

The Ku Klux Klan

Disguised in long white robes and hoods, Ku Klux Klansmen sometimes claimed to be the ghosts of Confederate soldiers. The Klan, which spread rapidly after 1867, sought to end Republican rule, restore white supremacy, and obliterate, in one southern editor's words, "the preposterous and wicked dogma of Negro equality."

Enforcement Acts Series of laws to protect black voters passed in 1870 and 1871; banned the Klan and similar groups

conditions. In Mississippi, the Klan targeted black schools; in Alabama, it concentrated on Republican officeholders. Some Democrats denounced Klan members as "cutthroats and riff-raff." But Klansmen included prominent ex-Confederates, among them General Nathan Bedford Forrest, the leader of the 1864 Fort Pillow massacre (see p. 354). Vigilantism united southern whites of different social classes; in areas where the Klan was inactive, other vigilante groups took its place.

CHECKING IN

- The Republican Party, with a large bloc of freedmen, temporarily dominated the South.
- Reconstruction governments instituted such reforms as public-school systems.
- To many southern whites, such reforms seemed a costly waste of money, aggravated by government corruption.
- The Ku Klux Klan and other groups used terrorism against freedmen and their white supporters in an effort to prevent black voting and restore white supremacy.
- The federal government passed laws against such activities but left too few troops in place to protect freedmen.

Republican legislatures passed laws to outlaw vigilantism. However, when state militias could not enforce the laws, state officials turned to the federal government for help. Between May 1870 and February 1871 Congress passed three **Enforcement Acts,** each progressively more stringent. The First Enforcement Act protected black voters. The Second Enforcement Act provided for federal supervision of southern elections, and the Third Enforcement Act, or Ku Klux Klan Act, authorized the use of federal troops and the suspension of *habeas corpus* (HAY-bee-us KORP-us), the requirement that cause for detaining a prisoner be shown in court. Although thousands were arrested under the Enforcement Acts, most terrorists escaped conviction.

By 1872 the federal government had effectively suppressed the Klan, but vigilantism had served its purpose. A large military presence in the South could have protected black rights, but instead federal troop levels fell steadily. Congress allowed the Freedmen's Bureau to die in 1869; the Enforcement Acts thus became dead letters. The battle over Reconstruction was in essence a battle over the implications of emancipation, and it had begun as soon as the war ended.

THE IMPACT OF EMANCIPATION

How did the newly freed slaves reshape their lives after emancipation?

"The master he says we are all free," a South Carolina slave declared in 1865. "But it don't mean we is white. And it don't mean we is equal." Yet despite the daunting handicaps they faced—illiteracy, lack of property, meager skills—most former slaves found the exhilaration of freedom overwhelming. Emancipation gave them the right to their own labor and a new sense of autonomy. Under Reconstruction, they sought to cast off white control and shed the vestiges of slavery.

Confronting Freedom

For former slaves, liberty meant mobility. Some moved out of the slave quarters; others fled the plantation completely. "The moment they see an opportunity to improve themselves, they will move on," diarist Mary Chesnut observed.

Emancipation stirred waves of migration within the former Confederacy. Some slaves headed to the Deep South, where desperate planters paid higher wages for labor, but more moved to towns and cities. Urban black populations doubled or tripled after emancipation. The desire to find lost family members prompted much of the movement. Parents sought children who had been sold; husbands and wives who had been separated reunited; and families reclaimed youngsters from masters' homes. The Freedmen's Bureau helped former slaves to get information about missing relatives and to travel to find them. Bureau agents also tried to resolve conflicts that arose when spouses who had been separated under slavery married other people.

However, reunification efforts often failed. Some fugitive slaves had died during the war or were untraceable. Still, success stories abounded. Once reunited, freed blacks quickly legalized unions formed under slavery, sometimes in mass ceremonies of up to seventy couples. Legal marriage had a tangible impact on family life. Men asserted themselves as household heads; wives of able-bodied men often withdrew from the work force to care for homes and families. "When I married my wife, I married her to wait on me and she has got all she can do right here for me and the children," a Tennessee freedman explained.

Severe labor shortages followed immediately after the war because women had made up half of all field workers. Still, by Reconstruction's end, many black women had returned to agricultural work as part of sharecropper families. Others took work in cities as laundresses, cooks, and domestic servants. (White women often sought employment as well, for the war had reduced the supply of future husbands and left families destitute.) However, former slaves continued to view stable, independent domestic life, especially the right to rear their own children, as a major blessing of freedom.

African-American Institutions

The freed blacks' desire for independence also led to the growth of black churches. The African Methodist Episcopal Church, founded by Philadelphia blacks in the 1790s, gained thousands of new southern members. Negro Baptist churches, their roots often in plantation "praise meetings" organized by slaves, sprouted everywhere.

Black churches offered a fervent, participatory experience. They also provided relief, raised funds for schools, and supported Republican policies. Black ministers assumed leading political roles until Reconstruction's end and then remained the main pillars of authority within African-American communities.

Schools, too, played a crucial role for freedmen as the ex-slaves sought literacy for themselves and, above all, for their children. At emancipation, blacks organized their own schools, which the Freedmen's Bureau soon supervised. Northern philanthropic societies paid the wages of instructors, about half of them women. In 1869, the bureau reported more than four thousand black schools were established in the former Confederacy. Within three years, each southern state had a public-school system, at least in principle, generally with separate schools for blacks and whites. The Freedmen's Bureau helped to establish Howard, Atlanta, and Fisk universities (1866–1867) and Hampton Institute (1868).

However, black education remained limited. Few rural blacks could reach the freedmen's schools located in towns. Underfunded black public schools held classes only for short seasons and sometimes drew vigilante attacks. At the end of Reconstruction, more than 80 percent of the black population was still illiterate, though literacy rose steadily among youngsters.

Archival and Museum Collection/Hampton University

Hampton Institute

Founded in 1868, Hampton Institute in southeastern Virginia welcomed newly freed African-Americans to vocational programs in agriculture, teacher training, and homemaking. These students, photographed at the school's entrance around 1870, were among Hampton's first classes.

Civil Rights Act of 1875 Called for the desegregation of transportation facilities, juries, and public accommodations; invalidated by the Supreme Court in 1883

School segregation and other forms of racial separation were taken for granted. Even after the invalidation of the black codes, segregation continued on streetcars, steamboats, and trains as well as in churches, theaters, and restaurants. In honor of the late Republican senator Charles Sumner, Congress passed the **Civil Rights Act of 1875,** banning segregation except in schools. But in the 1883 *Civil Rights Cases,* the Supreme Court threw the law out. The Fourteenth Amendment did not prohibit discrimination by individuals, the Court ruled, only that perpetrated by the state.

White southerners rejected the prospect of racial integration, which they insisted would lead to racial amalgamation. "If we have social equality, we shall have intermarriage," one white southerner contended, "and if we have intermarriage, we shall degenerate." Urban blacks sometimes challenged segregation practices, but most freed blacks were less interested in "social equality" than in black liberty and community. Moreover, the new postwar elite—teachers, ministers, and politicians—served

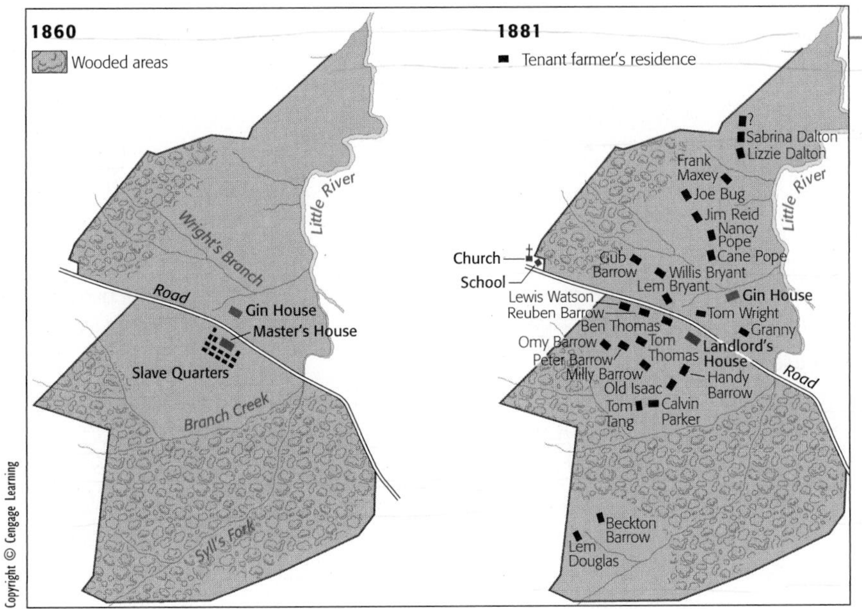

Map 16.2 The Barrow Plantation, 1860 and 1881

The transformation of the Barrow plantation in Oglethorpe County, Georgia, illustrates the striking changes in southern agriculture during Reconstruction. After the war, the former slaves signed labor contracts with owner David Crenshaw Barrow and worked in squads under a hired foreman. But the freedman disliked the arrangement. By 1881, the old plantation had been subdivided into tenant farms of around thirty acres each. One out of four families was named Barrow.

Interactive Map

black constituencies and thus had a vested interest in separate black institutions. Rural blacks, too, widely preferred all-black institutions, as they had little desire to mix with whites. In fact, they sought freedom from white control. Above all, they wanted to secure personal independence by acquiring land.

Land, Labor, and Sharecropping

"The sole ambition of the freedman," a New Englander wrote from South Carolina in 1865, "appears to be to become the owner of a little piece of land, there to erect a humble home, and to dwell in peace and security, at his own free will and pleasure." Indeed, to freed blacks everywhere, "forty acres and a mule" (a phrase that originated during the war as General William T. Sherman set aside land on the South Carolina Sea Islands for black settlement) promised emancipation from plantation labor, white domination, and cotton, the "slave crop."

However, the freedmen's visions of landownership failed to materialize, for, as we have seen, large-scale land reform never occurred. Some freedmen obtained land with the help of the Freedmen's Bureau or sometimes by pooling resources (see Map 16.2). In 1866, Congress passed the Southern Homestead Act, which set aside 44 million acres of public land in five southern states for freedmen and loyal whites. About four thousand blacks resettled on homesteads under the law. But the soil was poor and few former slaves had the resources to survive until their first harvest (poor whites fared little better). By Reconstruction's end, only a small minority of former slaves owned working farms. In Georgia in 1876, for example, blacks controlled a mere 1.3 percent of total acreage. Without large-scale land reform, obstacles to black landownership remained overwhelming.

What were these obstacles? First, freedmen lacked capital to buy land or tools. Furthermore, white southerners generally opposed selling land to blacks. Most important, planters sought to preserve a black labor force and took steps to ensure that black labor would remain available on the plantations.

During presidential Reconstruction, southern state legislatures tried to curb black mobility and preserve a captive labor force through the black codes. Under labor contracts in effect in 1865–1866, freedmen received wages, housing, food, and clothing in exchange for field work. With cash scarce, wages usually took the form of a very small share of the crop, often one-eighth or less, divided among the entire plantation work force. Freedmen's Bureau agents promoted the new labor system, seeing wage labor as a step toward economic independence. "You must begin at the bottom of the ladder and climb up," Freedmen's Bureau head O. O. Howard exhorted a group of Louisiana freedmen in 1865.

Problems arose immediately. Freedmen disliked the new wage system, especially the use of gang labor, which resembled the work pattern under slavery. Moreover, postwar planters had to compete for labor even as many scorned African-American workers as lazy or inefficient. One landowner estimated that workers accomplished only "two-fifths of what they did under the old system." As productivity fell, so did land values. Plummeting cotton prices and poor harvests compounded planters' woes. By 1867, an agricultural impasse had been reached: Landowners lacked labor, and freedmen lacked land.

sharecropping System in which a tenant farmer paid a share of the crop as rent to the landowner

Southerners began experimenting with new labor schemes, including the division of plantations into small tenancies. **Sharecropping,** the most widespread arrangement, evolved as a compromise. Under this system, landowners subdivided large plantations into farms of thirty to fifty acres, which they rented to freedmen under annual leases for a share of the crop, usually half. Freedmen preferred sharecropping to wage labor because it represented a step toward independence. Planters, meanwhile, retained control of their land. The most productive land thus remained in the hands of a small group of owners; in effect, sharecropping helped to preserve the planter elite.

Although the wage system continued on sugar and rice plantations, by 1870 the plantation tradition had yielded to sharecropping in the Cotton South (see Map 16.3). A severe depression in 1873 drove many blacks and independent white farmers into sharecropping. By 1880, 80 percent of the land in the cotton-producing states had been subdivided into tenancies, most of it farmed by sharecroppers, both white and black. In fact, white sharecroppers outnumbered black, although a higher proportion of southern blacks, about 75 percent, were involved in the system. Changes in marketing and finance, meanwhile, made the sharecroppers' lot increasingly precarious.

Toward a Crop-Lien Economy

The postwar South's hundreds of thousands of tenant farmers and sharecroppers needed a local credit system to see them through the growing season until they could harvest their crops. Rural merchants advanced supplies to tenants and sharecroppers on credit and sold their crops to wholesalers. Because renters had no property to use as collateral, merchants secured their loans with a lien (leen), or claim, on each farmer's next crop. Exorbitant interest rates of 50 percent or more quickly forced many tenants and sharecroppers into a cycle of indebtedness. The sharecropper

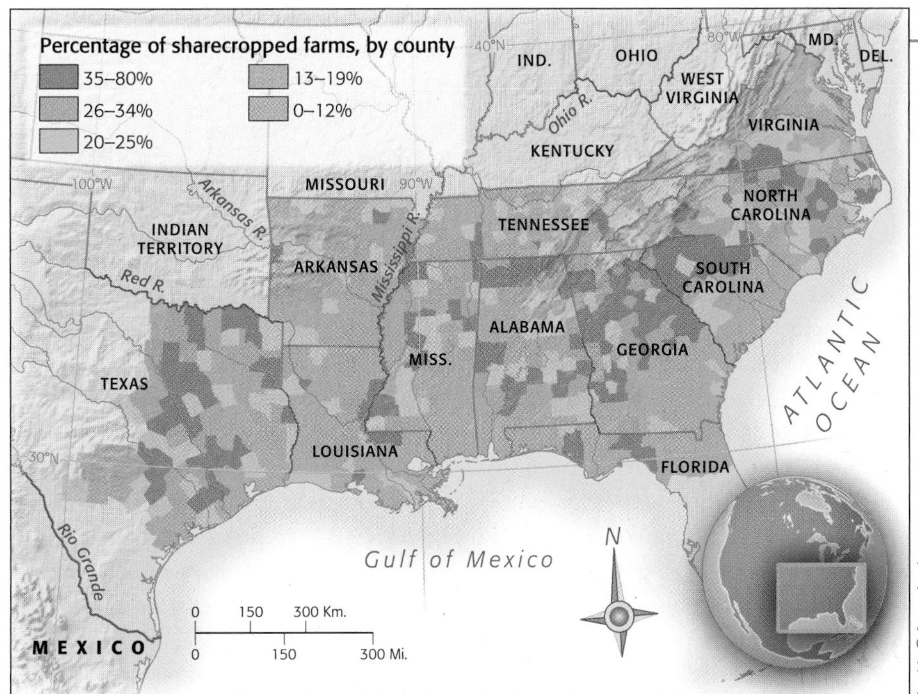

Map 16.3 Southern Sharecropping, 1880

The depressed economy of the late 1870s caused poverty and debt, increased tenancy among white farmers, and forced many renters, black and white, into sharecropping. By 1880, the sharecropping system pervaded most southern counties, with highest concentrations in the Cotton Belt from South Carolina to eastern Texas.

Interactive Map

might well owe part of his crop to the landowner and another part (the rest of his crop, or more) to the merchant. Illiterate tenants who lost track of their financial arrangements often fell prey to unscrupulous merchants. Once a tenant's real or alleged debts exceeded the value of his crop, he was tied to the land, to cotton, and to sharecropping.

By Reconstruction's end, sharecropping and crop liens had bound the South to staple crops, such as cotton, and prevented crop diversification. Plunging prices, soil depletion, land erosion, and outmoded equipment soon locked much of the South into a cycle of poverty. Trapped in perpetual debt, tenant farmers became the chief victims of the new agricultural order. Cotton remained the only survival route open to poor farmers, regardless of race, but low income from cotton locked them into sharecropping and crop liens. African-American tenants saw their political rights dwindle as rapidly as their hopes for economic freedom. When Reconstruction ended, neither state governments nor the national government offered them protection, for northern politicians were preoccupied with their own problems.

Checking In

- Tens of thousands of freedmen sought missing family members, and former slaves hastened to legalize the marriages they had made under slavery.
- Blacks formed their own communities, churches, and schools as segregation became firmly established in the South.
- Few former slaves achieved land ownership, and sharecropping became the dominant form of agricultural labor for blacks and many poor whites.
- Without economic status, blacks quickly saw their political rights erode.

New Concerns in the North, 1868–1876

Why did northern concern about Reconstruction begin to wane?

The nomination of Ulysses S. Grant for president in 1868 launched a chaotic era in national politics. Grant's two terms in office saw political scandals, a party revolt, a massive depression, and a steady retreat from Reconstruction. By the mid-1870s, northern voters cared more about unemployment, labor unrest, and currency problems than about the "southern question." Responsive to the shift in popular mood, Republicans turned their backs on the freedmen.

Grantism

Republicans had good reason to nominate General Grant. A war hero, he was endorsed by veterans and admired throughout the North. To oppose Grant, the Democrats nominated New York Governor Horatio Seymour, arch-critic of the Lincoln administration in wartime and now a foe of Reconstruction. Grant ran on personal popularity more than issues. Although he carried all but eight states, the popular vote was close; in the South, newly enfranchised freedmen provided Grant's margin of victory.

A strong leader in war, Grant proved to be a passive president with little political skill. Many of his cabinet appointees were mediocre if not unscrupulous; scandals plagued his administration. In 1869 financier Jay Gould and his partner Jim Fisk tried to corner the gold market with the help of Grant's brother-in-law. When gold prices tumbled, investors were ruined and Grant's reputation suffered. Near the end of Grant's first term, his vice president, Schuyler Colfax, got caught up in the Crédit Mobilier (CRAY-dee MOH-bill-yay) scandal, a fraudulent scheme to skim off the profits of the Union Pacific Railroad. In 1875, Grant's personal secretary, Orville Babcock, was found guilty of accepting bribes from the "whiskey ring," distillers who bribed federal agents to avoid paying millions in taxes. And in 1876, voters learned that Grant's secretary of war, William E. Belknap, had taken bribes to sell lucrative Indian trading posts in Oklahoma.

Boss Tweed

Thomas Nast's cartoons in *Harper's Weekly* helped topple New York Democratic boss William M. Tweed, who, with his associates, embodied corruption on a large scale. The Tweed Ring had granted lucrative franchises to companies they controlled, padded construction bills, practiced graft and extortion, and exploited every opportunity to plunder the city's funds.

Brown Brothers

Harper's Weekly, 1871

Although uninvolved in the scandals, Grant defended his subordinates. To his critics, "Grantism" came to stand for fraud, bribery, and political corruption—evils that spread far beyond Washington. The New York City press revealed in 1872 that Democratic boss William M. Tweed, the leader of Tammany Hall, led a ring that had looted the city treasury and collected millions in kickbacks and payoffs. When Mark Twain and Charles Dudley Warner published their satiric novel *The Gilded Age* in 1873, readers recognized the book's speculators, self-promoters, and opportunists as familiar figures in public life. (The term "Gilded Age" has subsequently been used to refer to the decades from the 1870s to the 1890s.)

Grant did enjoy some foreign-policy successes. In 1872, his administration engineered the settlement of the *Alabama* claims with Britain. To compensate for damage done by Confederate-owned but British-built ships, an international tribunal awarded the United States $15.5 million. But Grant's administration faltered when it tried to add non-adjacent territory to the United States. In 1867, Johnson's secretary of state, William H. Seward, had negotiated a treaty to buy Alaska from Russia at the bargain price of $7.2 million. The purchase had rekindled expansionists' hopes, and in 1870, Grant decided to annex the eastern half of the Caribbean island of Santo Domingo (today called the Dominican Republic). Annexation, Grant believed, would promote Caribbean trade and provide a haven for persecuted southern blacks. Despite speculators' hopes for windfall profits, the Senate rejected the annexation treaty and further diminished Grant's reputation.

As the election of 1872 approached, dissident Republicans feared that "Grantism" would ruin the party. Former Radicals and other Republicans left out of Grant's "Great Barbecue" formed their own party, the **Liberal Republicans.**

Liberal Republicans Dissident political faction that opposed Grant and called for civil service reform and an end to congressional Reconstruction in the South

The Liberals' Revolt

The Liberal Republican revolt split the party and undermined Reconstruction. (The label "liberal" at the time meant support for economic doctrines such as free trade, the gold standard, and the law of supply and demand.) Liberals demanded civil service reform to bring the "best men" into government. They demanded an end to "bayonet rule" in the South and argued that blacks, now enfranchised, could fend for themselves. Corruption in government posed a greater threat than Confederate resurgence, the Liberals claimed, and they demanded that the "best men" in the South, ex-Confederates barred from holding office, be returned to government.

For president, the new party nominated *New York Tribune* editor Horace Greeley, who had inconsistently supported both a stringent Reconstruction policy and leniency toward former rebels. The Democrats endorsed Greeley as well; their campaign slogan was "Anything to Beat Grant." Horace Greeley campaigned so diligently that he worked himself to death making speeches from the back of a train, and died a few weeks after the election.

Grant carried 56 percent of the popular vote and won the electoral vote handily. But division among Republicans affected Reconstruction. To deprive the Liberals of a campaign issue, Grant Republicans in Congress passed the Amnesty Act, which allowed all but a few hundred ex-Confederate officials to hold office. In Grant's second term, Republican desires to discard the "southern question" mounted as depression gripped the nation.

The Panic of 1873

The postwar years brought accelerated industrialization, rapid economic growth, and frantic speculation as investors rushed to take advantage of seemingly boundless opportunities. Railroads led the speculative boom. The transcontinental line reached completion in 1869 (see Chapter 17). By 1873, almost four hundred railroads crisscrossed the Northeast. In addition to transforming the economy, the railroad boom led entrepreneurs to overspeculate, with drastic results.

In 1869 Philadelphia banker Jay Cooke took over a new transcontinental line, the Northern Pacific. Northern Pacific securities sold briskly for several years, but in 1873 construction costs outran bond sales. In September, Cooke defaulted on his obligations, and his bank, the largest in the nation, shut down. A financial panic began; other firms collapsed, as did the stock market. The Panic of 1873 plunged the nation into a five-year depression. Within two years, eighteen thousand businesses went bankrupt; 3 million people were unemployed by 1878. Wage cuts struck those still employed; labor protests mounted; and industrial violence spread. The depression of the 1870s revealed that conflicts born of industrialization had replaced sectional divisions.

The depression also fed a dispute over currency that had begun in 1865. During the Civil War, Americans had used greenbacks, a paper currency not backed by a specific weight in gold. "Sound money" supporters demanded the withdrawal of greenbacks from circulation as a means of stabilizing the currency. Their opponents, such as farmers and manufacturers dependent on easy credit who were known as "easy money" advocates, wanted to expand the currency by issuing additional greenbacks. The deepening depression created even more demand for easy money. The issue divided both major parties and was compounded by another one: how to repay the federal debt.

In wartime, the Union government had borrowed astronomical sums through the sale of war bonds. Bondholders wanted repayment in "coin," gold or silver, even though many of them had paid for the bonds in greenbacks. The Public Credit Act of 1869 promised payment in coin. Senator John Sherman, the author of the Public Credit Act, guided legislation through Congress that defined "coin" as gold only and swapped old short-term bonds for new ones payable over the next generation. Sherman's Specie Resumption Act of 1875 promised to put the nation back on the gold standard by 1879. His measures preserved the public credit, the currency, and Republican unity.

However, Sherman's measures did not satisfy the Democrats, who gained control of the House in 1875. Many Democrats and some Republicans demanded the restoration of the silver dollar in order to expand the currency and relieve the depression. The Bland-Allison Act of 1878 partially restored silver coinage by requiring the government to buy and coin several million dollars' worth of silver each month. In 1876, other expansionists formed the **Greenback Party,** which adopted the debtors' cause and fought to keep greenbacks in circulation, though with little success. As the depression receded in 1879, the clamor for "easy money" subsided, only to return in the 1890s (see Chapter 20). The controversial, but unresolved, "money question" of the 1870s gave politicians and voters another reason to forget about the South.

Greenback Party "Easy money" advocates who favored continued issuance of greenbacks and the free coinage of silver

Reconstruction and the Constitution

The Supreme Court of the 1870s also played a role in weakening northern support for Reconstruction as new constitutional questions surfaced. First, would the Court support laws to protect freedmen's rights? The decision in *Ex Parte Milligan* (1866) had suggested not. In *Milligan,* the Court had ruled that a military commission could not try civilians in areas where civilian courts were functioning. Thus, special military courts to enforce the Supplementary Freedmen's Bureau Act were doomed. Second, would the Court sabotage the congressional Reconstruction plan, as Republicans feared? In *Texas v. White* (1869), the Court had let Reconstruction stand, ruling that Congress had the power to ensure each state a republican form of government.

However, in the 1870s, the Court backed away from Reconstruction. In the *Slaughterhouse* case of 1873, the Court considered whether Louisiana had violated the constitutional rights of butchers excluded from a slaughterhouse monopoly established by the state in 1869. In ruling against the butchers, the Court ruled that the Fourteenth Amendment protected only the rights of *national* citizenship, such as the right to interstate travel, but not those rights that fell to citizens through *state* citizenship. The *Slaughterhouse* decision vitiated the intent of the Fourteenth Amendment—to secure freedmen's rights against state encroachment.

The Supreme Court again backed away from Reconstruction in two cases in 1876 involving the Enforcement Act of 1870, which were enacted to protect black suffrage. In *United States v. Reese* and *United States v. Cruikshank,* the Supreme Court undercut the act's effectiveness. Continuing its retreat from Reconstruction, the Supreme Court in 1883 invalidated both the Civil Rights Act of 1875 and the Ku Klux Klan Act of 1871. These decisions cumulatively dismantled the Reconstruction policies that Republicans had sponsored after the war and confirmed rising northern sentiment that Reconstruction's egalitarian goals could not be enforced.

Republicans in Retreat

The Republicans gradually disengaged from Reconstruction, beginning with the election of Grant as president in 1868. Grant believed in decentralized government and hesitated to assert federal authority in local and state affairs.

In the 1870s, Republican idealism waned. The Liberal Republican revolt of 1872 eroded what remained of radicalism. Commercial and industrial interests now dominated both wings of the party, and few Republicans wished to rekindle sectional strife. After the Democrats won the House in 1874, support for Reconstruction became a political liability.

By 1875, the Radical Republicans, so prominent in the 1860s, had vanished. Thaddeus Stevens and Charles Sumner were dead. Other Radicals had lost office or conviction. Republican leaders reported that voters were "sick of carpetbag government" and tiring of both the "southern question" and the "Negro question." It seemed pointless to continue the unpopular and expensive policy of military intervention in the South. Finally, Republican leaders and voters generally agreed that blacks, although worthy of freedom, were inferior to whites. The Republicans' retreat from Reconstruction set the stage for its demise in 1877.

Checking In

- Grant's administration was riddled by corruption, mirroring politics in much of the country.
- The Panic of 1873 devastated the northern economy, plunging the nation into a deep depression.
- Through the 1870s the Supreme Court struck down basic legislation protecting freedmen's rights.
- Most Radical Republican leaders had died by the early 1870s, and commercial and industrial interests began to dominate the Republican Party.

RECONSTRUCTION ABANDONED, 1876–1877

What factors contributed to the end of Reconstruction in 1877?

"We are in a very hot political contest just now," a Mississippi planter wrote his daughter in 1875, "with a good prospect of turning out the carpetbag thieves by whom we have been robbed for the past six to ten years." Similar contests raged through the South in the 1870s, as the white resentment grew and Democratic influence surged. By 1876 Republican rule survived in only three southern states—South Carolina, Florida, and Louisiana. Democratic victories in state elections that year and political bargaining in Washington in 1877 ended what little remained of Reconstruction.

"Redeeming" the South

Republican collapse in the South accelerated after 1872. Congressional amnesty enabled virtually all ex-Confederate officials to regain office; divisions among the Republicans weakened their party's grip on the southern electorate; and attrition diminished Republican ranks. Carpetbaggers returned north or became Democrats. Scalawags deserted in even larger numbers. Tired of northern interference and seeing the possibility of "home rule," scalawags concluded that staying Republican meant going down with a sinking ship. Unable to win new white votes or retain the old ones, the fragile Republican coalition crumbled.

Meanwhile, Democrats mobilized once-apathetic white voters. The resurrected southern Democratic Party was divided. Businessmen who envisioned an industrialized "New South" opposed an agrarian faction called the Bourbons—the old planter elite. But Democrats shared one goal: to oust Republicans from office (see Table 16.2).

TABLE 16.2 THE DURATION OF REPUBLICAN RULE IN THE EX-CONFEDERATE STATES

FORMER CONFEDERATE STATES	READMISSION TO THE UNION UNDER CONGRESSIONAL RECONSTRUCTION	DEMOCRATS (CONSERVATIVES) GAIN CONTROL	DURATION OF REPUBLICAN RULE
Alabama	June 25, 1868	November 14, 1874	6½ years
Arkansas	June 22, 1868	November 10, 1874	6½ years
Florida	June 25, 1868	January 2, 1877	8½ years
Georgia	July 15, 1870	November 1, 1871	1 year
Louisiana	June 25, 1868	January 2, 1877	8½ years
Mississippi	February 23, 1870	November 3, 1875	5½ years
North Carolina	June 25, 1868	November 3, 1870	2 years
South Carolina	June 25, 1868	November 12, 1876	8 years
Tennessee	July 24, 1866*	October 4, 1869	3 years
Texas	March 30, 1870	January 14, 1873	3 years
Virginia	January 26, 1870	October 5, 1869†	0 years

Source: Reprinted by permission from John Hope Franklin, *Reconstruction After the Civil War* (Chicago: University of Chicago Press, 1962), 231.

*Admitted before the start of congressional Reconstruction.

†Democrats gained control before readmission.

Tactics varied by state. In several Deep South states Democrats resorted to violence. In Vicksburg, Mississippi, in 1874, rampaging whites slaughtered about three hundred blacks and terrorized thousands of potential voters. The "Mississippi plan" took effect in 1875; local Democratic clubs armed their members, who broke up Republican meetings, patrolled voter-registration locations, and marched through black areas. "The Republicans are paralyzed through fear and will not act," the anguished carpetbag governor of Mississippi wrote to his wife. "Why should I fight a hopeless battle?" In 1876, South Carolina's "Rifle Clubs" and "Red Shirts," armed groups that threatened Republicans, continued the scare tactics that had worked so well in Mississippi.

Terrorism did not completely squelch black voting, but it did deprive Republicans of enough black votes to win state elections. Throughout the South, economic pressures reinforced intimidation; labor contracts included clauses barring attendance at political meetings, and planters used eviction threats to keep sharecroppers in line. Together, intimidation and economic pressure succeeded.

"Redemption," the word that Democrats used to describe their return to power, brought sweeping changes. States rewrote constitutions, cut expenses, lowered taxes, eliminated social programs, limited the rights of tenants and sharecroppers, and shaped laws to ensure a stable black labor force. Legislatures restored vagrancy laws, strengthened crop-lien statutes, and rewrote criminal law. Local ordinances in heavily black counties often restricted hunting, fishing, gun carrying, and even dog ownership, drastically curtailing the ability of freedmen to live off the land. States passed severe laws against trespassing and theft; for example, stealing livestock or wrongly taking part of a crop became grand larceny with a penalty of up to five years at hard labor. By Reconstruction's end, black convict labor was commonplace.

For the freedmen, whose aspirations rose under Republican rule, redemption was devastating. The new laws, Tennessee blacks contended at an 1875 convention, would impose "a condition of servitude scarcely less degrading than that endured before the late civil war." In the late 1870s, as the political climate grew more oppressive, an "exodus" movement spread through the Deep South. Nearly fifteen thousand **"exodusters"** from the Deep South moved to Kansas and set up homesteads. But scarce resources left most of the freed slaves stranded. Mass movement of southern blacks to the North and Midwest would not gain momentum until the twentieth century.

"exodusters" Thousands of blacks who left the Deep South for homesteads in Kansas in the 1870s

The Election of 1876

By the autumn of 1876, with redemption almost complete, both parties moved to discard the animosity left by the war and Reconstruction. Republicans nominated Rutherford B. Hayes, three times Ohio's governor, for president. Untainted by the Grant-era scandals and popular with all factions in his party, Hayes presented himself as a "moderate" on southern policy. He favored "home rule" in the South and a guarantee of civil and political rights for all—two contradictory goals. The Democrats nominated Governor Samuel J. Tilden of New York, a political reformer known for his assaults on the Tweed Ring that had plundered New York City's treasury. Both candidates favored sound money, endorsed civil service reform, and decried corruption.

Tilden won the popular vote by a 3 percent margin and seemed destined to capture the 185 electoral votes needed for victory. But the Republicans challenged pro-Tilden returns from South Carolina, Florida, and Louisiana, and the Democrats challenged (on a technicality) one electoral vote from Oregon. Southern Republicans managed to throw out enough Democratic ballots in the contested states to proclaim Hayes the winner.

The nation now faced an unprecedented dilemma. Each party claimed victory, and each accused the other of fraud. In fact, both sets of southern votes were fraudulent: Republicans had discarded legitimate Democratic ballots, and Democrats had illegally prevented freedmen from voting. In January 1877, Congress created a special electoral commission—seven Democrats, seven Republicans, and one independent—to resolve the conflict. When the independent resigned, Congress replaced him with a Republican, and the commission gave Hayes the election by a vote of 8 to 7.

Congress now had to certify the new electoral vote. However, Democrats controlled the House, and some threatened to delay approval of the electoral vote. For many southern Democrats, regaining control of their states was far more important than preventing the election of a Republican president—*if* the new Republican administration would leave the South alone. Republican leaders, although sure of eventual triumph, were willing to bargain as well, for candidate Hayes desired not merely victory but southern approval. Informal negotiations followed, with both parties exchanging promises. Ohio Republicans and southern Democrats agreed that if Hayes won the election, he would remove federal troops from South Carolina and Louisiana, and Democrats could gain control of those states. Other negotiations led to the understanding that southerners would receive federal patronage, federal aid to railroads, and federal support for internal improvements. In turn, southerners promised to accept Hayes as president and to treat the freedmen fairly.

Compromise of 1877 Deal that gave Republicans the presidency and restored Democrats to power in the South, ending Reconstruction

CHECKING IN

- The Republican collapse in the South accelerated after 1872.
- Democrats regained control of southern states.
- "Redeemers" ended reforms and limited or eliminated black rights.
- The election of 1876 resulted in challenges to some electoral votes and charges of fraud on both sides.
- The price of Republican victory in the election was the end of Reconstruction and the virtual abandonment of the freedmen.

Congress thus ratified Hayes's election. Once in office, Hayes fulfilled some of the promises his Republican colleagues had made. He appointed a former Confederate as postmaster general and ordered federal troops who guarded the South Carolina and Louisiana statehouses back to their barracks. Republican rule toppled in Louisiana, South Carolina, and Florida. But some of the bargains struck in the **Compromise of 1877,** such as Democratic promises to treat southern blacks fairly, were forgotten, as were Hayes's pledges to ensure freedmen's rights. "When you turned us loose, you turned us loose to the sky, to the storm, to the whirlwind, and worst of all . . . to the wrath of our infuriated masters," Frederick Douglass charged at the 1876 Republican convention. "The question now is, do you mean to make good to us the promises in your Constitution?" By 1877 the answer was clear: "No."

Chapter Summary

How did Radical Republicans gain control of Reconstruction politics? (page 370)

Radical Republicans saw Johnson as too lenient on Reconstruction and passed a stringent congressional Reconstruction program over his veto. They even attempted to impeach the president for political reasons, but failed. The Fourteenth and Fifteenth Amendments, which Johnson opposed, were major triumphs for the Radicals.

KEY TERMS

Radical Republicans *(p. 370)*
Andrew Johnson *(p. 372)*
Presidential Reconstruction *(p. 372)*

What impact did federal Reconstruction policy have on the former Confederacy and ex-Confederates? (page 378)

Democrats and ex-Confederates were largely excluded from political power in the South, which fell to Republicans and freedmen. The Reconstruction governments passed costly reform measures, most of which were later abandoned or scaled back. Terrorist organizations such as the Ku Klux Klan flourished briefly. They were outlawed by the federal government but had already intimidated freedmen.

How did the newly freed slaves reshape their lives after emancipation? (page 382)

Former slaves sought missing family members, legalized marriages made under slavery, and created schools and churches in large numbers. However, without land reform most remained poor and ultimately were caught in the pernicious sharecropping system; their rights were soon eroded.

Why did northern concern about Reconstruction begin to wane? (page 387)

Other concerns soon began to preoccupy Republicans. Corruption, epitomized by the Grant administration, permeated the nation. The Panic of 1873 led to a major depression. The Supreme Court threw out important measures intended to protect freedmen's rights. Finally, with most Radical Republican leaders gone by the early 1870s, commercial and industrial interests began to dominate the Republican Party.

What factors contributed to the end of Reconstruction in 1877? (page 392)

Republican control of the South began to collapse in the early 1870s. As Democrats "redeemed" southern states, they curtailed reforms and eliminated black rights. The price of the Republican victory in the disputed presidential election of 1876 was the end of Reconstruction and the return of the South to Democratic control.

KEY TERMS continued

"black codes" *(p. 372)*
Civil Rights Act of 1866 *(p. 373)*
Fourteenth Amendment *(p. 373)*
Reconstruction Act of 1867 *(p. 374)*
Tenure of Office Act *(p. 375)*
Fifteenth Amendment *(p. 376)*
Susan B. Anthony *(p. 377)*
Ku Klux Klan *(p. 381)*
Enforcement Acts *(p. 382)*
Civil Rights Act of 1875 *(p. 384)*
sharecropping *(p. 386)*
Liberal Republicans *(p. 389)*
Greenback Party *(p. 390)*
"exodusters" *(p. 393)*
Compromise of 1877 *(p. 394)*

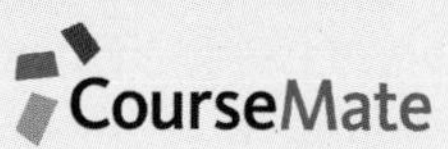

Go to the CourseMate website at **www.cengagebrain.com** for additional study tools and review materials—including audio and video clips—for this chapter.

The Transformation of the Trans-Mississippi West

Chapter 17

1860–1900

Fire Canoe at Fort Berthold, by William de la Montagne Cary

Chapter Preview

Native Americans and the Trans-Mississippi West
How was Indian life on the Great Plains transformed in the second half of the nineteenth century?

Settling the West
What roles did the federal government, the army, and the railroads play in the settlement of the West?

Southwestern Borderlands
How did ranchers and settlers displace Spanish-speaking Americans in the Southwest?

Exploiting the Western Landscape
How did mining, ranching, and farming shape the West?

The West of Life and Legend
How was the Wild West image of cowboys and Indians created, and what developments prompted the establishment of national parks?

"The buffaloes and the black-tail deer are gone, and our Indian ways are almost gone," reminisced Maxidiwiac (mah-chee-dee-WEE-ahsh), or Buffalo Bird Woman, in 1920. A Hidatsa Indian born about 1843 in present-day North Dakota, she found the changes overwhelming. "Sometimes I find it hard to believe I ever lived them [her Indian ways]," she continued. "My little son grew up in the white man's school. He can read books, and he owns cattle and has a farm. . . . But for me, I cannot forget our old ways." In her own lifetime, Buffalo Bird Woman had moved from a traditional native existence into the modern world.

President Jefferson's emissaries Meriwether Lewis and William Clark had wintered among the Hidatsas in 1804 and had been impressed by their horsemanship and hunting ability. The Hidatsas in the 1840s had joined with two neighboring tribes to build a new village called Like-A-Fishhook. Initially the new settlement prospered. But, after the Civil War, as white settlers crowded onto their lands, Buffalo Bird Woman and her tribe were pressured by a nearby military garrison into signing away more and more of their territory and forced to scatter onto small farms. Buffalo Bird Woman and her tribe abandoned their village in 1885.

Buffalo Bird Woman's experience was all too common. The settlement of the trans-Mississippi West began with the removal of native peoples. This peaceful or, more commonly, brutal relocation of the Indians onto reservations opened up vast tracts of land for settlement and development. Miners, farmers, land speculators, and railroad developers in the 1850s flooded onto the fertile prairies of Iowa, Minnesota, and Kansas, carving the land into farms and communities. Then, in the 1860s, drawn by the earlier discovery of gold in the Rocky Mountains, these same settlers swarmed onto the Great Plains and the semiarid regions beyond them. Scarcely a decade later, the trans-Mississippi West became a contested terrain as native peoples fought to protect their homeland from these newcomers.

The transformation of the West left a mixed legacy. Although many white families prospered on the High Plains, the rapid development of the land and its resources threatened not only the Native Americans, but also the environment and sometimes the settlers themselves. Unscrupulous westerners exploited white, Native American, Chinese, and Mexican laborers alike. Hunters slaughtered millions of bison for their hides, miners skinned the mountainsides in search of minerals, and farmers plowed up the prairie sod to build farms. Although westerners attributed their economic achievements to American self-reliance, the development of the trans-Mississippi West depended heavily on the federal government. The government sent troops to subjugate the Indians, promoted the acquisition of farm land through the Homestead Act (1862), and subsidized the transcontinental railroad lines. In their scramble for new economic opportunities, many Americans chose to view the destruction of the Indian ways of life as the necessary price of civilization and progress.

Native Americans and the Trans-Mississippi West

How was Indian life on the Great Plains transformed in the second half of the nineteenth century?

No aspect of the transformation of the West was more visible and dramatic than the assault on the traditional Indian way of life. Caught between a stampede of miners and settlers who took their land and the federal government that sought to force them onto reservations, Native Americans fought back. By the 1890s confinement on reservations had become the fate of almost every Indian nation. Undaunted, Native Americans struggled to preserve their customs and rebuild their numbers.

Chronology

1862	Homestead Act; Morrill Anti-Bigamy Act; Pacific Railroad Act
1864	Nevada admitted to the Union; massacre of Cheyennes at Sand Creek, Colorado; George Perkins Marsh, *Man and Nature*
1867	Joseph McCoy organizes cattle drives to Abilene, Kansas; Medicine Lodge Treaty
1868	Fort Laramie Treaty
1869	Board of Indian Commissioners established; Wyoming gives women the vote
1872	Yellowstone National Park established
1873	Timber Culture Act; biggest strike on Nevada's Comstock Lode
1874	Invention of barbed wire; gold discovered in the Black Hills of South Dakota; Red River War
1875	John Wesley Powell, *The Exploration of the Colorado River*
1876	Colorado admitted to the Union; Little Bighorn massacre
1877	Desert Land Act
1878	John Wesley Powell, *Report on the Lands of the Arid Regions of the United States*
1881	Helen Hunt Jackson, *A Century of Dishonor*
1883	Women's National Indian Rights Association founded; William ("Buffalo Bill") Cody organizes the Wild West Show
1887	Dawes Severalty Act; Edmunds-Tucker Act
1888	White Caps raid ranches in northern New Mexico
1889	Oklahoma Territory opened for settlement
1890	Ghost Dance movement spreads to the Black Hills; massacre of Teton Sioux at Wounded Knee, South Dakota
1892	John Muir organizes Sierra Club
1898	Curtis Act

The Plains Indians

The Indians of the Great Plains inhabited three major subregions. The northern Plains, from the Dakotas and Montana southward to Nebraska, were home to several large tribes, most notably the Lakota as well as Flatheads, Blackfeet, Assiniboins (ah-SIN-ih-bwans), northern Cheyennes (shy-ANNS), Arapahos (a-RAP-a-hose), Crows, Hidatsas, and Mandans. Some of these were allies, but others were bitter enemies. In the Central Plains, the so-called Five Civilized Tribes, driven there from the Southeast in the 1830s, pursued an agricultural life in the Indian Territory (present-day Oklahoma). Farther west, the Pawnees of Nebraska maintained the older, more settled tradition characteristic of Plains river valley culture. On the southern Plains of western Kansas, Colorado, eastern New Mexico, and Texas, the Comanches, Kiowas, Cheyennes, southern Arapahos, and Apaches still maintained a migratory life appropriate to the arid environment.

Considerable diversity flourished among the Plains peoples, and customs varied even within subdivisions of the same tribe. For example, the Dakota Sioux (soo) of Minnesota led a semisedentary life based on small-scale agriculture and bison hunting. In contrast, many Plains tribes—the Lakota Sioux, Blackfeet, Crows, and

Cheyennes—using horses obtained from the Spanish, roamed the High Plains to the west and followed the bison migrations.

For all the **Plains Indians,** life revolved around extended family ties and tribal cooperation. Families and clans joined forces to hunt and farm, and reached decisions by consensus. Sioux religion, which provided the cement for village and camp life, was complex. The Lakota Sioux thought of life as a series of circles. Living within the daily cycles of the sun and moon, Lakotas were born into a circle of relatives, which broadened to the band, the tribe, the Sioux Nation, and on to animals and plants. The Lakotas also believed in a hierarchy of spirits whose help could be invoked in ceremonies like the Sun Dance. On the semiarid High Plains, where rainfall averaged less than twenty inches a year, both the bison and the native peoples adapted to the environment. The huge bison herds, which at their peak contained an estimated 30 million animals, broke into small groups in the winter and dispersed into river valleys. In the summer, they returned to the High Plains in vast herds to mate and feed on the nutritious short grasses. Like the bison, the Indians dispersed across the landscape to minimize their impact on any one place, wintering in the river valleys and returning to the High Plains in summer.

Plains Indians Diverse Native American societies inhabiting the region from the Dakotas to Texas

The movement of miners and settlers onto the eastern High Plains in the 1850s threatened the Native American way of life. In the 1860s, the whites began systematically to hunt the animals to supply the eastern market with carriage robes and industrial belting. **William F. "Buffalo Bill" Cody,** a famous scout and Indian fighter, killed nearly forty-three hundred bison in 1867–1868 to feed construction crews building the Union Pacific Railroad. Army commanders also encouraged the slaughter of buffalo to undermine Indian resistance. The carnage that resulted was almost inconceivable in its scale. Between 1872 and 1875, hunters killed 9 million buffalo, taking only the skin and leaving the carcasses to rot. By the 1880s, the once-thundering herds had been reduced to a few thousand animals, and the Native American way of life dependent on the buffalo had been ruined.

William F. "Buffalo Bill" Cody Renowned scout, Indian fighter, and showman who symbolized the "Wild West" mythos

The Assault on Nomadic Indian Life

In the 1850s, Indians who felt pressure from the declining bison herds and deteriorating grasslands faced the onslaught of thousands of pioneers lured by the discovery of gold and silver in the Rocky Mountains. The federal government's response was to reexamine its Indian policies. Abandoning the previous position, which had treated much of the West as a vast Indian reserve, the federal government sought to introduce a system of smaller tribal reservations where the Indians were to be concentrated, by force if necessary.

Some Native Americans peacefully adjusted to their new life. Others, among them the Navajos (NAH-vuh-hohs) of Arizona and New Mexico and the eastern Dakota Sioux, opposed the new policy to no avail. By 1860, eight western reservations had been established. Significant segments of the remaining tribes on the Great Plains, more than a hundred thousand people, fought against removal. Between 1860 and 1890, the western Sioux, Cheyennes, Arapahos, Kiowas, and Comanches on the Great Plains; the Nez Percés (nez per-SAY) and Bannocks in the northern Rockies; and the Apaches in the Southwest faced the U.S. Army, toughened by its experiences in the Civil War, in a series of final battles for the West (see Map 17.1).

Indian Mother and Son, c. 1890s

Indian children were taught to ride horses at an early age. Horses were a form of wealth for migratory Plains peoples and made hunting buffalo (depicted on the tipi) considerably easier.

Misunderstandings, unfulfilled promises, brutality, and butchery marked the conflict. Near Sand Creek, Colorado, in 1864, soldiers from the local militia who had replaced regular army troops fighting in the Civil War destroyed Cheyenne and Arapaho camps. The Indians retaliated with a flurry of attacks on travelers. The governor, in a panic, authorized Colorado's white citizenry to kill hostile Indians on sight. He then activated a regiment of troops under Colonel John M. Chivington, a Methodist minister. At dawn on November 29, Chivington's troops massacred a peaceful band of Indians, including terrified women and children, camped at Sand Creek.

This massacre and others that followed rekindled public debate over federal Indian policy. In response, in 1867 Congress sent a peace commission to end the fighting and set aside two large land reserves, one north of Nebraska, the other south of Kansas. Behind the federal government's persuasion lay the threat of force. Any Native Americans who refused to relocate, warned Commissioner of Indian Affairs Ely S. Parker, himself a Seneca Indian, "would be . . . treated as friendly or hostile as circumstances might justify." At first the plan appeared to work. Representatives of sixty-eight thousand southern Kiowas, Comanches, Cheyennes, and Arapahos signed the Medicine Lodge Treaty of 1867 and pledged to live on land in present-day Oklahoma. The following year, scattered bands of Sioux, representing nearly fifty-four thousand northern Plains Indians, signed the **Fort Laramie Treaty** and agreed to move to reservations in what is now South Dakota in return for money and provisions.

Fort Laramie Treaty
Agreement that moved thousands of Plains Indians to reservations in South Dakota in 1867

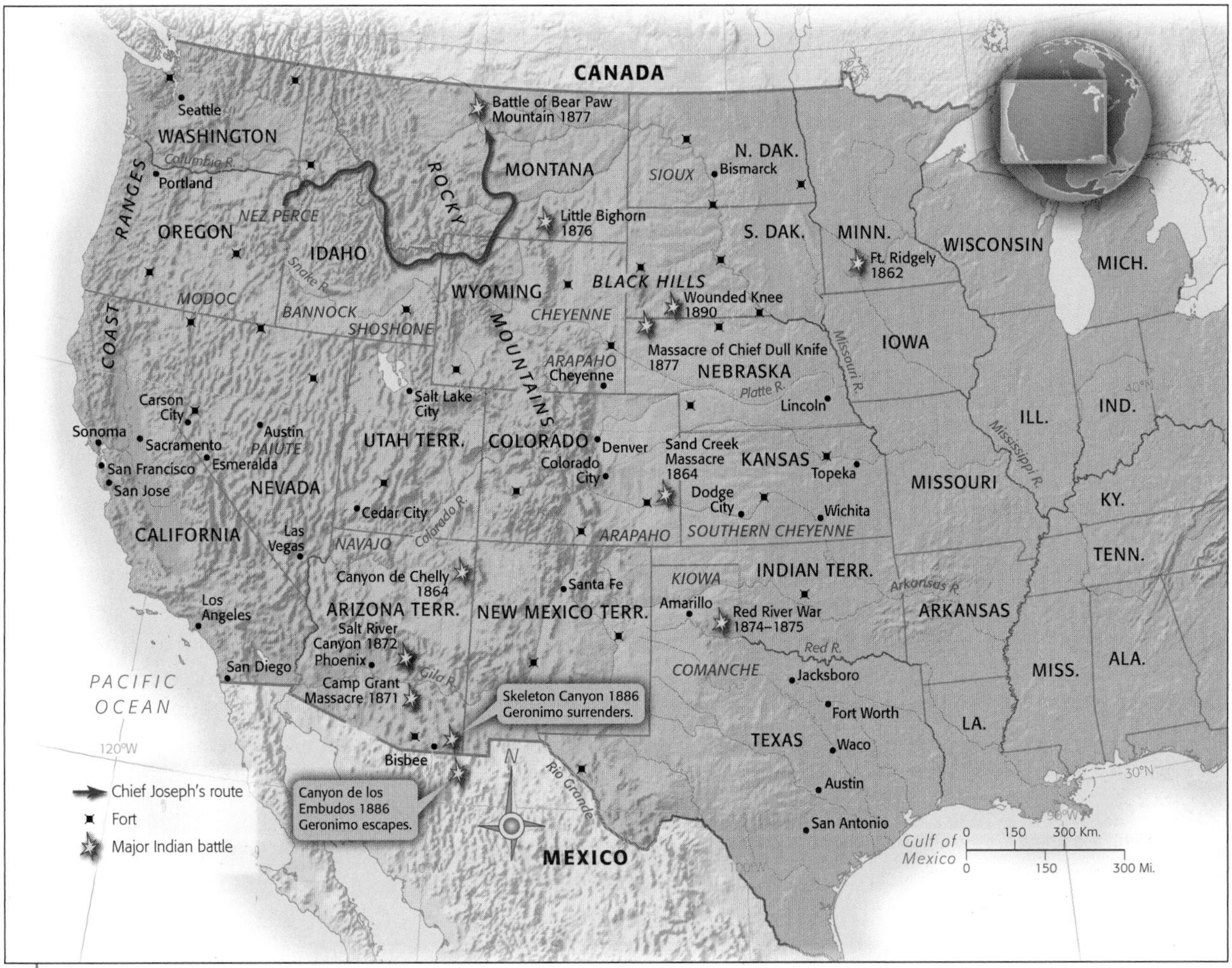

Map 17.1 Major Indian-White Clashes in the West

Although never recognized as such in the popular press, the battles between Native Americans and the U.S. Army on the Great Plains amounted to a major undeclared war.

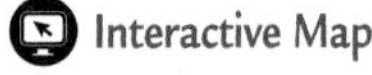

Indian dissatisfaction with the treaties ran deep. In August 1868, war parties of defiant Cheyennes, Arapahos, and Sioux raided frontier settlements in Kansas and Colorado, burning homes and killing whites. In retaliation, army troops attacked Indians, even peaceful ones, who refused confinement. That autumn, Lieutenant Colonel George Armstrong Custer's raiding party attacked a sleeping Cheyenne village, killing more than one hundred warriors. Other Cheyennes and Arapahos were pursued, captured, and returned to reservations.

In 1869, spurred on by Christian reformers, Congress established a Board of Indian Commissioners to reform abuses on the reservations by Indian agents. But the new and inexperienced church-appointed Indian agents quickly encountered problems. Indians left the reservations in large numbers and agents were unable to restrain scheming whites who fraudulently purchased reservation lands from those who remained. Frustrated by the manipulation of Indian treaties and irritated by the ineptness of the Indian agents, Congress in 1871 abolished treaty making and replaced treaties with executive orders and acts of Congress. In the 1880s, the federal government ignored the churches' nominations for Indian agents and made its own appointments.

Caught in the sticky web of an ambiguous and deceptive federal policy, defiant Native Americans struck back in the 1870s. On the southern Plains, Kiowa, Comanche, and Cheyenne raids in the Texas Panhandle in 1874 set off the so-called Red River War. In a fierce winter campaign, regular army troops slaughtered a hundred Cheyenne fugitives in Kansas. The exile of seventy-four "ringleaders" to reservations in Florida thus ended Native American independence on the southern Plains. In the Southwest, the Apaches fought an intermittent guerrilla war until their leader, Geronimo (jer-RON-eh-moe), surrendered in 1886.

Custer's Last Stand, 1876

Of all the acts of Indian resistance against the new reservation policy, none aroused more passion or caused more bloodshed than the battles waged by the western Sioux tribes in the Dakotas, Montana, and Wyoming. The 1868 Treaty of Fort Laramie had set aside the Great Sioux Reserve "in perpetuity." However, not all the Sioux bands had fought in the war or signed the treaty.

By 1873, Chief Red Cloud's Oglala band and Chief Spotted Tail's Brulé (BROO-lay) band had managed to remain on their traditional lands. To protect their hunting grounds, they raided encroaching non-Indian settlements in Nebraska and Wyoming, intimidated federal agents, and harassed anyone who ventured onto their lands.

Sitting Bull Leader of the Sioux warriors who wiped out George Armstrong Custer's force at Little Bighorn in 1876

Non-treaty Sioux found a powerful leader in the Lakota Sioux chief and holy man **Sitting Bull.** Broad-shouldered and powerfully built, Sitting Bull led by example and had considerable fighting experience. In 1874, General William Tecumseh Sherman sent a force under Colonel George Armstrong Custer into the Black Hills of South Dakota, near the western edge of the Great Sioux Reserve. Lean and mustachioed, the thirty-four-year-old Custer had been a celebrity since his days as an impetuous young Civil War officer.

Custer's mission was to extract concessions from the Sioux. In November 1875, negotiations to buy the Black Hills had broken down because the Indians' asking price was deemed too high. Custer now sought to drive the Indians out of the Black Hills. In June 1876, leading six hundred troops of the Seventh Cavalry, Custer proceeded to the Little Bighorn River area of present-day Montana, a hub of Indian resistance. On the morning of June 25, underestimating the Indian enemy and unwisely dividing his force, Custer, with 209 men, recklessly advanced against a large company of Cheyenne and Sioux warriors led by Chief Sitting Bull, who had encamped along the Little Bighorn. Custer and his outnumbered troops were wiped out.

Americans reeled from this unexpected Indian victory. Newspaper columnists groped to assess the meaning of "Custer's Last Stand." Some questioned the wisdom of current federal policy toward the Indians. Others worried that an outraged public would demand retaliation. Most, however, endorsed the federal government's determination to quash the Native American rebellion.

Defeat at Little Bighorn made the army more determined. In Montana, troops harassed various Sioux bands for more than five years, attacking Indian camps in the dead of winter and destroying all supplies. Even Sitting Bull, who had led his band to Canada to escape the army, surrendered in 1881 for lack of provisions. The slaughter of the buffalo had wiped out his tribe's major food source.

Similar measures were used elsewhere in the West. Chief Dull Knife of the northern Cheyennes led the remnants of his tribe north to join the Sioux in September 1878. But the army chased them down and imprisoned them in Fort Robinson, Nebraska. On a frigid night in January 1879, Dull Knife and his followers shot the guards and broke for freedom. Soldiers fired and gunned down half of them in the snow, including women and children as well as Dull Knife himself. Although sporadic Indian resistance continued until the end of the century, these brutal tactics sapped the Indians' will to resist.

"Saving" the Indians

Growing numbers of Americans were outraged by the federal government's flagrant violation of its Indian treaties. The Women's National Indian Rights Association, founded in 1883, and other groups took up the cause. **Helen Hunt Jackson** of Colorado published *A Century of Dishonor* in 1881 to rally public opinion against the government's record of broken treaty obligations. "It makes little difference . . . where one opens the record of the history of the Indians," she wrote; "every page and every year has its dark stain."

Helen Hunt Jackson Humanitarian and author who popularized wrongs done to Indians

To encourage Indians to abandon nomadic life, reformers like Jackson advocated the creation of Indian boarding schools. Richard Henry Pratt, a retired military officer, opened such a school in Carlisle, Pennsylvania, in 1879. Pratt believed that the Indians' customs and languages had halted their progress toward white civilization. His motto therefore became "Kill the Indian and save the man." Modeled after Carlisle, other Indian boarding schools taught farming, carpentry, dressmaking, and nursing. Despite the reformers' best efforts, the attempt to stamp out Indian identity in the boarding schools often backfired. Forming friendships with Indians from many different tribes, boarding school students forged their own sense of Indian identity.

In addition to their advocacy of boarding schools, well-intentioned humanitarians concluded that the Indians' interests would be best served by breaking up the reservations, ending recognition of tribal governments, and gradually giving them the rights of citizens. In short, they proposed to eliminate the "Indian problem" by eliminating the Indians as a culturally distinct entity. Inspired by this vision, they supported the **Dawes Severalty Act,** which was passed in 1887.

Dawes Severalty Act Law intended to "civilize" Indians by distributing tribal lands to individuals

The Dawes Severalty Act sought to turn Indians into landowners and farmers. The law emphasized severalty, or the treatment of Indians as individuals rather than as tribal members, and called for the distribution of 160 acres of reservation land to each head of an Indian family who accepted the law's provisions. The remaining reservation lands were to be sold to speculators and settlers. To prevent unscrupulous people from taking the lands granted to individual Indians, the government would hold each tribal member's property in trust for twenty-five years and make them U.S. citizens.

The Dawes Act proved to be a boon to speculators, who commonly evaded its safeguards and obtained the Indians' best land. By 1934, the act had slashed Indian acreage by 65 percent. Much of what remained in Indian hands was too dry and gravelly for farming. Although some Native Americans who received land under the Dawes Act prospered enough to expand their holdings, countless others struggled just to survive. Alcoholism, a continuing problem exacerbated by the prevalence of whiskey as a trade item, became more prevalent as Native Americans strove to adapt to the constraints of reservation life.

The Ghost Dance and the End of Indian Resistance on the Great Plains, 1890

Living conditions for the Sioux worsened in the late 1880s. The federal government reduced their meat rations and restricted hunting. When disease killed a third of their cattle, they became desperate. The Sioux turned to Wovoka, a new visionary prophet popular among the Great Basin Indians in Nevada. Wovoka foresaw a catastrophic event that would bring the return of dead relatives, the restoration of the bison herds, and the renewal of traditional life. Some versions of his vision included the destruction of European-Americans. To bring on this new day, the prophet preached a return to traditional ethics, and taught his followers a cycle of ritual songs and dance steps known as the **Ghost Dance.**

Ghost Dance Ritual that the prophet Wovoka promised would restore Indians to control of their lands

In the fall of 1890, as the Ghost Dance movement spread among the Sioux in the Dakota Territory, Indian officials grew alarmed. The local reservation agent decided that Chief Sitting Bull, whose cabin on the reservation had become a rallying point for the Ghost Dance movement, must be arrested. When two policemen pulled

Denver Public Library

Wounded Knee, Pine Ridge Reservation, South Dakota, 1890

Thrown into an open trench, the frozen bodies of the Sioux slaughtered at Wounded Knee were a grim reminder that the U.S. Army would brook no opposition to its control of Indian reservations.

the chief from his cabin, shots rang out, and Sitting Bull was mortally wounded. As bullets whizzed by, Sitting Bull's horse began to perform the tricks it remembered from its days in the Wild West show. Observers were terrified, convinced that the spirit of the dead chief had entered his horse.

Two weeks later, one of the bloodiest episodes of Indian-white strife on the Plains occurred. On December 29, as the Seventh Cavalry was rounding up 340 starving and freezing Sioux at **Wounded Knee,** South Dakota, a shot was fired. The soldiers retaliated with cannon fire. Within minutes three hundred Indians, including seven infants, were slaughtered. As the frozen corpses at Wounded Knee were dumped into mass graves, a generation of Indian-white conflict on the Great Plains shuddered to a close.

Wounded Knee Massacre of three hundred Indians by the U.S. Army in 1890; the last chapter of the battle for the Great Plains

Many Native Americans did try to adapt to non-Indian ways, and some succeeded fully. Goodbird, the son of Buffalo Bird Woman, became a Congregational minister, a prosperous farmer, and a leader of the Hidatsa tribe. Others struggled with poverty. Driven onto reservations, many Indians became dependent on governmental support. By 1900, the Plains Indian population had shrunk from nearly a quarter-million to just over a hundred thousand. Nevertheless, the population began to increase slowly after 1900. Against overwhelming odds, the pride, religious traditions, and cultural identities of the Plains Indians survived all efforts at eradication.

Unlike the nomadic western Sioux, the more settled Navajos of the Southwest adjusted more successfully to the reservation system, preserving traditional ways while incorporating elements of the new order. By 1900, the Navajos had tripled their reservation land, dramatically increased their numbers and their herds, and carved out for themselves a distinct place in Arizona and New Mexico.

In the name of civilization and progress, whites after the Civil War had forced Indians off their lands in an effort that involved a mixture of sincere (if misguided) benevolence, coercion wrapped in an aura of legality, and outbursts of naked violence. Many white Americans felt only contempt for Indians and greed for their land. Others had tried to uplift and Christianize the natives. Both groups, however, were blind to the value of Native American life and traditions. And both were unsuccessful in their attempts to shatter proud peoples and their ancient cultures.

Checking In

- The destruction of the Great Plains buffalo herds opened the way for the destruction of the Plains Indians.
- The battle for control of the Plains pitted nomadic Indians who rejected reservation life against the U.S. Army.
- Custer's Last Stand, in which Indians wiped out 209 cavalry troops, infuriated Americans and increased support for violence against the Plains tribes.
- The Dawes Severalty Act sought to "civilize" Plains Indians by dissolving tribal bonds and distributing tribal lands among individual Indians and speculators.
- The massacre of 300 starving Indians at Wounded Knee signaled the end of armed conflict on the Great Plains.

Settling the West

What roles did the federal government, the army, and the railroads play in the settlement of the West?

The successive defeats of the Native Americans opened a vast territory for settlement. After 1870, railroad expansion made the overland trip from the East to Oregon and California—previously a six- to eight-month trip in ox-drawn wagons—faster and easier than ever before. In the next three decades, more land was parceled out into farms than in the previous 250 years of American history combined, and agricultural production doubled.

The First Transcontinental Railroad

Passed in 1862, the Pacific Railroad Act authorized the construction of a new transcontinental link. The act provided grants of land and other subsidies to the railroads for each mile of track laid, which made them the largest landholders in the West. More than any other factor, the expansion of these railroads accelerated the transformation of everyday life west of the Mississippi.

Building the railroad took backbreaking work. Searching for inexpensive labor, the railroads turned to immigrants. For example, the Central Pacific employed Chinese workers to chip and blast rail bed out of solid rock in the Sierra Nevada (see Table 17.1). Nearly twelve thousand Chinese graded the roadbed while Irish, Mexican-American, and black workers put down the track.

On May 10, 1869, Americans celebrated the completion of the first railroad spanning North America. As the two sets of tracks—the Union Pacific's, stretching westward from Omaha, Nebraska, and the Central Pacific's, reaching eastward from Sacramento, California—met at Promontory Point, Utah, beaming officials drove in a final ceremonial golden spike. The nation's vast midsection was now far more accessible than it had ever been.

TABLE 17.1 THE AFRICAN-AMERICAN AND CHINESE POPULATION IN WESTERN STATES AND TERRITORIES, 1880–1900

STATE OR TERRITORY	BLACKS		CHINESE	
Arizona Terr.	155	1,846	1,630	1,419
California	6,018	11,045	75,132	45,753
Colorado	2,435	8,570	612	599
Idaho	53	293	3,379	1,467
Kansas	43,107	52,003	19	39
Montana	346	1,523	1,765	1,739
Nebraska	2,385	6,269	18	180
Nevada	488	134	5,416	1,352
New Mexico Terr.	1,015	1,610	57	341
North Dakota	113	286	NA	32
Oklahoma Indian Terr.	NA	56,684*	NA	31
Oregon	487	1,105	9,510	10,397
South Dakota	288	465	NA	165
Texas	393,384	620,722	136	836
Utah	232	672	510	572
Washington	325	2,514	3,186	3,629

Source: U.S. Bureau of the Census, Negro Population in the United States, 1790–1915 (Washington, DC: U.S. Government Printing Office, 1918), 43, 44; Michael Doran, "Population Statistics of Nineteenth Century Indian Territory," *Chronicles of Oklahoma* 53 No. 4 (Winter 1975), 501; and *The Tenth Census, 1880, Population, and Twelfth Census, 1900, Population* (Washington, DC: U.S. Government Printing Office, 1883 & 1901).

*Combined total for Indian and Oklahoma territories.

The railroads sped up western development. In the battles against Native Americans, the army shipped horses and men west in the dead of winter to attack the Indians when they were most vulnerable. From the same trains, hunters gained quick access to the bison ranges and increased their harvest of the animals. Once Indian resistance had been broken, the railroads hastened the arrival of new settlers and provided access for the shipment of cattle and grain to eastern urban markets.

Settlers and the Railroad

During the decade after the passage of the Pacific Railroad Act, Congress awarded the railroads 170 million acres, worth over half a billion dollars. By 1893, Minnesota and Washington had also deeded to railroad companies a quarter of their state lands. As mighty landowners, the railroads had a unique opportunity to shape settlement in the region—and to reap enormous profits (see Map 17.2).

The railroads set up land sales offices and sent agents to the East Coast and Europe to recruit settlers. The land bureaus offered prospective buyers long-term

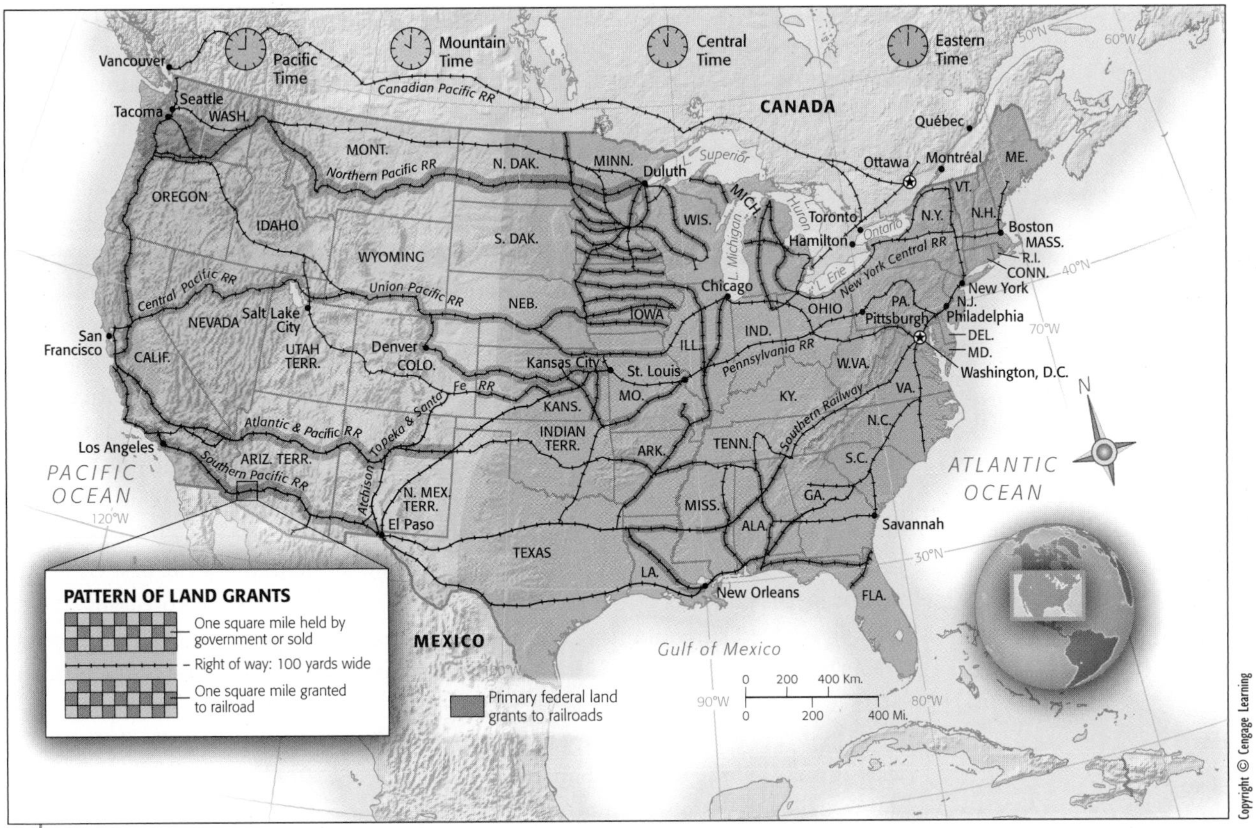

Map 17.2 Transcontinental Railroads and Federal Land Grants, 1850–1900

Despite the laissez-faire ideology that argued against government interference in business, Congress heavily subsidized American railroads and gave them millions of acres of land. As illustrated in the box, belts of land were reserved on either side of a railroad's right of way. Until the railroad claimed the exact one-mile-square sections it chose to possess, all such sections within the belt remained closed to settlement.

Interactive Map

loans and free transportation. Acknowledging that life on the Great Plains could be lonely, the promoters advised young men to bring their wives (because "maidens are scarce") and to emigrate as entire families and with friends. The railroads also helped bring nearly 2.2 million foreign-born settlers to the trans-Mississippi West between 1870 and 1900. Some agents recruited whole villages of Germans and eastern Europeans to relocate to the North Dakota plains.

The railroads influenced agriculture as well. To ensure repayment of money owed to them, the railroads urged new immigrants to specialize in cash crops—wheat on the northern Plains, corn in Iowa and Kansas, cotton in Texas. Although these crops initially brought in high revenues, many farmers grew dependent on income from a single crop and became vulnerable to fluctuating market forces.

Homesteading on the Great Plains

Liberalized land laws pulled settlers westward. The 1862 Homestead Act reflected the Republican Party's belief that free land would promote economic opportunity. It offered 160 acres of land to anyone who would pay a ten-dollar registration fee, live on the land for five years, and cultivate it. Although nearly four hundred thousand families claimed land under its provisions between 1860 and 1900, the law did not function as Congress had envisioned. Unscrupulous speculators filed false claims for the choicest locations, and railroads acquired huge landholdings. Only one acre in every nine went to the pioneers for whom it was intended.

The 160-acre limit specified by the Homestead Act created a second problem. On the rich soils of Iowa, a 160-acre farm was ample, but in the drier areas west of the hundredth meridian, a farmer needed more land. In 1873, to rectify this problem, Congress passed the Timber Culture Act, which gave homesteaders an additional 160 acres if they planted trees on 40 acres. For states with little rainfall, Congress enacted the Desert Land Act in 1877, which made 640 acres available at $1.25 an acre. However, this act was abused by grasping speculators, lumber-company representatives, and cattle ranchers. Even though families did not receive as much land as Congress had intended, federal laws kept alive the dream of the West as a place for new beginnings.

In addition to problems caused by insufficient rainfall in many regions, almost all settlers faced difficult psychological adjustments to frontier life. The first years of settlement were the most difficult. Toiling to build a house, plant the first crop, and dig a well, the pioneers put in an average of sixty-eight hours of backbreaking work a week in isolated surroundings. For blacks who emigrated from the South to Kansas and other parts of the Plains after the Civil War, prejudice compounded the burdens of adjusting to a different life (see Chapter 16).

Many women found adaptation to Plains frontier life especially difficult. At least initially, some were enchanted by the landscape. But far more were struck by the "horrible tribes of Mosquitoes" and the crude sod huts that served as their early homes because of the scarcity of timber. One woman burst into tears upon first seeing her new sod house. The young bride angrily informed her husband that her father had built a better house for his hogs.

The high transience rate on the Great Plains in these years reflected the difficulty that newcomers faced in adjusting. Nearly half of those who staked homestead claims in Kansas between 1862 and 1890 gave up and moved on. Those who stayed eventually came to identify deeply with the land. Within a decade, the typical Plains family that had "stuck it out" had moved into a new wood-framed house and had fixed up the front parlor. There were just enough of these success stories to sustain the popular ideal of the West as a place of hope and opportunity.

New Farms, New Markets

Farmers on the Plains took advantage of advances in farm mechanization and the development of improved strains of wheat and corn to boost production dramatically. Efficient steel plows; specially designed wheat planters; and improved grain binders, threshers, and windmills all allowed the typical Great Plains farmer of the late nineteenth century to increase the land's yield tenfold.

Barbed wire, patented in 1874, was another crucial invention that permitted farmers to keep roving livestock out of their crops. But fencing the land touched off violent clashes between farmers and cattle ranchers, who demanded the right to let their herds roam freely until the roundup. Generally the farmers won.

The invention of labor-saving machinery together with increased demand for wheat, milk, and other farm products created the impression that farming was entering a period of unparalleled prosperity. But few fully understood the perils of pursuing agriculture as a livelihood. Faced with huge start-up costs and substantial mortgage payments, many farmers had to specialize in a crop such as wheat or corn that would fetch high prices. This specialization made them dependent on the railroads for shipping and put them at the mercy of the international grain market's shifting prices. High demand could bring prosperity, but when world overproduction forced grain prices down, the heavily indebted grower faced ruin. Confronted with these realities, many Plains farmers quickly abandoned the illusion of frontier independence and easy wealth.

Unpredictable rainfall and weather conditions further exacerbated homesteaders' difficulties west of the hundredth meridian, where rainfall averaged less than twenty inches a year. Farmers in such places used specialized "dry farming" techniques, built windmills, and diverted creeks for irrigation. But the onset of unusually dry years in the 1870s, together with grasshopper infestations and the major economic depression that struck the United States between 1873 and 1878 (see Chapter 16), made the plight of some midwesterners desperate.

Building a Society and Achieving Statehood

Despite the hardships, many remote farm settlements blossomed into thriving communities. Churches and Sunday schools became humming centers of social activity as well as of worship. Neighbors readily lent a hand to the farmer whose barn had burned or whose family was sick. Cooperation was a practical necessity and a form of insurance in a rugged environment where everyone was vulnerable to instant misfortune or even disaster.

When the population increased, local boosters lobbied to turn the territory into a state. Kansas entered the Union in 1861, followed by Nevada in 1864, Nebraska in 1867, and Colorado in 1876. Not until 1889 did North Dakota, South Dakota, Montana, and Washington gain statehood. Wyoming and Idaho followed the next year, and Utah in 1896. Oklahoma's admission in 1907 and Arizona's and New Mexico's in 1912 completed the process of creating states in the trans-Mississippi West.

Although generally socially conservative, the new state governments supported woman suffrage. As territories became states, pioneer women battled for the vote. Success came first in the Wyoming Territory, where men outnumbered women 6 to 1. The tiny legislature enfranchised women in 1869 in the hope that it would attract women, families, and economic growth. The Utah Territory followed in 1870. Nebraska in 1867 and Colorado in 1876 permitted women to vote in school elections. Although these successes were significant, by 1910 only four states—Idaho, Wyoming, Utah, and Colorado—had granted women full voting rights.

Edmunds-Tucker Act Federal confiscation of Mormon church property to pressure it to abandon the practice of polygamy

The Spread of Mormonism

Persecuted in Illinois, members of the Church of Jesus Christ of Latter-day Saints, known as Mormons, moved to the Great Salt Lake Valley in 1847. Led by Brigham Young, their prophet-president, they sought to create the independent country of Deseret. Their faith emphasized self-sufficiency and commitment to family. In the next two decades, recruitment boosted their numbers to more than 100,000. These Mormon communities increasingly clashed with non-Mormons and with the U.S. government, which disapproved of the church's involvement in politics, its communal business practices, and its support of polygamy or plural marriage.

The Mormons sought at first to be economically independent. In 1869, they developed their own railroad lines out of Salt Lake City and set up Zion's Cooperative Mercantile Institution to control wholesale and retail activities. But a series of federal acts and court decisions, starting with the Morrill Anti-Bigamy Act in 1862, challenged the authority of their church and their practice of polygamy. In *United States v. Reynolds* (1879), the Supreme Court declared plural marriages unlawful. Then, in 1887, the **Edmunds-Tucker Act** dissolved the church corporation, abolished women's right to vote, and put its properties and funds into receivership (control by the courts).

In response, in 1890 the church president publicly announced the official end of polygamy. The church supported the application for statehood (Utah), which was granted in 1896. Confiscated church properties were returned, voting rights were restored, and jailed polygamists were pardoned, but the balance between sacred and secular had permanently shifted. Mormon settlements would continue in the twentieth century to draw new members and to influence development in western communities.

CHECKING IN

- The completion of the first transcontinental railroad in 1869 opened the Great Plains for white settlement.
- Railroad companies encouraged the settlement of the Plains, recruiting settlers and offering loans and free transportation.
- The Homestead Act, offering free land to people who would farm it, lured tens of thousands of would-be settlers to the Plains.
- Homesteaders persevered in the face of such major obstacles as isolation, drought, and the perils of the commercial market.
- The Mormons, persecuted elsewhere, found a home in the West and helped Utah achieve statehood. By 1912 all western territories had been brought into the Union as states.

SOUTHWESTERN BORDERLANDS

How did ranchers and settlers displace Spanish-speaking Americans in the Southwest?

The treaty that ended the Mexican-American War in 1848 ceded to the United States an immense territory, part of which became Texas, California, Arizona, and New Mexico. At the time, Mexicans controlled vast expanses of the Southwest. They built their own churches, maintained large ranching operations, and traded with the Indians. Although the United States had pledged to protect the liberty and property of Mexicans who remained on American soil, over the next three decades American ranchers and settlers took control of the territorial governments and forced much of the Spanish-speaking population off the land. Mexicans who stayed in the region adapted to the new Anglo society with varying degrees of success.

In Texas, the struggle for independence from Mexico left a legacy of bitterness and misunderstanding. After 1848, Texas cotton planters confiscated Mexican lands and began a racist campaign that labeled Mexicans as nonwhite. Mexican bandits retaliated by raiding American communities. Tensions peaked in 1859 when Juan Cortina, a Mexican rancher, attacked the Anglo border community of Brownsville, Texas. Cortina battled the U.S. Army for years until the Mexican government, fearing a U.S. invasion, imprisoned him in 1875.

Mexican-Americans in California in the 1850s and 1860s faced similar pressures. A cycle of flood and drought, together with a slumping cattle industry, ruined many of the large southern California ranches owned by the *californios,* Spanish-speaking descendants of the original Spanish settlers. The collapse of the ranch economy forced many of them to retreat into segregated urban neighborhoods called barrios. Spanish-surnamed citizens made up nearly half the 2,640 residents of Santa Barbara, California, in 1870; ten years later, after an influx of new settlers, they comprised barely a quarter of the population.

In many western states, Mexicans, Native Americans, and Chinese experienced similar patterns of racial discrimination, manipulation, and exclusion. At first, the number of new "Anglos" was small. As the number of whites increased, they identified minority racial, cultural, and language differences as marks of inferiority. White state legislators passed laws that made ownership of property difficult for non-Anglos. Relegated to a migratory labor force, non-Anglos were tagged as shiftless and irresponsible. Yet their labor made possible increased prosperity for the farmers, railroads, and households that hired them.

The cultural adaptation of Spanish-speaking Americans to Anglo society initially unfolded more smoothly in Arizona and New Mexico, where Spanish settlement had been sparse and a small class of wealthy Mexican landowners had long dominated a poor, illiterate peasantry. Moreover, since the 1820s, well-to-do Mexicans in Tucson, Arizona, had educated their children in the United States and had formed trading partnerships and business alliances with Americans.

Examples of successful cooperation between Hispanic and white Americans helped moderate American settlers' antagonistic attitudes. So, too, did the work of popular writers like Helen Hunt Jackson, who sentimentalized the colonial Spanish past. Jackson's 1884 romance *Ramona,* a tale of the doomed love of a Hispanicized mixed-blood (Irish-Indian) woman set on a California ranch overwhelmed by the onrushing tide of Anglo civilization, was enormously popular.

Still, conflicts over property persisted in Arizona and New Mexico. In the 1880s, Mexican-American ranchers organized themselves into a self-protection vigilante group called Las Gorras Blancas (the **White Caps**). In 1888, they tore up railroad tracks and attacked both Anglo newcomers and those upper-class Hispanics who had fenced acreage in northern New Mexico that had previously been considered public grazing land. However, this vigilante action did not stop the

White Caps Mexican-American vigilante group in northern New Mexico that protested the enclosure of grazing lands

Museum of New Mexico

Santa Fe Plaza, New Mexico, in the 1880s, by Francis X. Grosshenney

After the railroad went through in 1878, Santa Fe became a popular tourist attraction known for its historic adobe buildings.

Anglo-dominated corporate ranchers from steadily increasing their land holdings. Meanwhile, the Spanish-speaking population living in the cities became more impoverished. In Tucson, 80 percent of the Mexican-Americans in the work force were laborers in 1880, taking jobs as butchers, barbers, cowboys, and railroad workers.

As increasing numbers of Mexican-American men were forced to search for seasonal migrant work, women took responsibility for holding families and communities together. Women managed the households when their husbands were away and maintained traditional customs, kinship ties, and allegiance to the Catholic church. They tended garden plots and traded food and produce with other women, generally stabilizing the community in times of drought or persecution by Anglos.

Violence and discrimination against Spanish-speaking citizens of the Southwest escalated in the 1890s, a time of rising racism in the United States. Rioters in Beeville and Laredo, Texas, in 1894 and 1899 attacked and beat up Mexican-Americans. Whites increasingly labeled Mexican-Americans as violent and lazy. For Spanish-speaking citizens, the battle for fair treatment and respect would continue into the twentieth century.

CHECKING IN

- Violence frequently flared between Anglos and Mexicans in Texas and California.
- In California, thousands of Mexicans, deprived of their land, ended up in urban barrios.
- The Spanish-speaking population adapted more smoothly in New Mexico and Arizona, where their numbers were smaller.
- After losing their land, many Mexican-Americans became laborers.
- Women often held Mexican-American communities together, emphasizing culture and kinship.

EXPLOITING THE WESTERN LANDSCAPE

How did mining, ranching, and farming shape the West?

The displacement of Mexican-American and native peoples from their lands opened the way for the exploitation of the natural environment in the trans-Mississippi West. Between 1860 and 1900, a generation of Americans sought to strike it rich by joining the ranks of those convinced of the region's boundless opportunity. Although the mining, ranching, and farming "bonanzas" promised unheard-of wealth, they set in motion a boom-and-bust economy in which some succeeded but others went bankrupt or barely survived.

The Mining Frontier

In the half-century that began with the California gold rush in 1849, a series of mining booms swept from the Southwest northward into Canada and Alaska. In 1853, Henry Comstock, an illiterate prospector, stumbled on the rich **Comstock Lode** along Nevada's Carson River. Later in the same decade, prospectors uncovered deep veins of gold and silver near present-day Denver. Over the next five decades, gold was discovered in Idaho, Montana, Wyoming, South Dakota, and, in 1896, in the Canadian Klondike. By 1900 more than a billion dollars' worth of gold had been mined in California alone.

Comstock Lode Fabulously rich silver discovery that opened mining bonanza in the West

The early discoveries of "placer" gold, panned from streams, attracted a young male population thirsting for wealth and reinforced the myth of mining country as "a poor man's paradise." In contrast to the Great Plains, where ethnic groups recreated their own ethnic enclaves, western mining camps became ethnic melting pots. In the California census of 1860, more than thirty-three thousand Irish and thirty-four thousand Chinese had staked out early claims.

Although a few prospectors became fabulously wealthy, the experience of Henry Comstock, who sold out one claim for eleven thousand dollars and another for two mules, was more typical. Because the larger gold and silver deposits lay embedded in veins of quartz deep within the earth, extracting them required huge investments in workers and expensive equipment. No sooner had the major discoveries been made, therefore, than large mining companies backed by eastern or British capital bought them out and took them over.

Life in the new mining towns was vibrant but unpredictable. During the heyday of the Comstock Lode in the 1860s and 1870s, Virginia City, Nevada, erupted in an orgy of speculation and building. Men outnumbered women three to one. Money quickly earned was even more rapidly lost. The gold rush mania also spurred the growth of settlement in Alaska. Small strikes were made there in 1869, two years after the United States had purchased the territory from Russia. But it was the discovery of gold in the Canadian Klondike in 1897 that brought thousands of prospectors into the area and eventually enabled Alaska to establish its own territorial government in 1912.

Word of new ore deposits like the ones in Alaska lured transient populations salivating to get rich. Miners who worked deep within the earth for large corporations typically earned about $2,000 a year at a time when teachers made $450 to $650 and domestic help $250 to $350. But most prospectors at best earned only enough to go elsewhere, perhaps buy some land, and try again. And the work was dangerous. One out of eighty miners died annually in the 1870s.

Progress came at a high cost to the environment. Hydraulic mining turned creeks brown and flushed millions of tons of silt into valleys. The scarred landscape that remained was littered with rock and gravel filled with traces of mercury and cyanide, and nothing would grow on it. Smelters spewed dense smoke containing lead, arsenic, and other carcinogenic chemicals, often making those who lived nearby sick. The devastation is still evident today.

Cowboys and the Cattle Frontier

The feverish growth of open-range cattle ranching paralleled the expansion of the mining frontier during the 1860s and 1870s. In this case, astute businessmen and railroad entrepreneurs, eager to fund their new investments in miles of track, promoted cattle herding as the new route to fame and fortune. The cowboy, once scorned as a ne'er-do-well and drifter, was now glorified as a man of rough-hewn integrity and self-reliant strength.

In 1868, Joseph G. McCoy, a young cattle dealer from Springfield, Illinois, shrewdly transformed the cattle industry into a new money-maker. With the forced relocation of the Plains Indians onto reservations and the extension of the railroads into Kansas, McCoy realized that cattle dealers could now amass enormous fortunes by raising steers cheaply in Texas and bringing them north for shipment to eastern urban markets.

McCoy built a new stockyard in Abilene, Kansas. To make the overland cattle drives from Texas to Abilene easier, McCoy also helped survey and shorten the Chisholm Trail in Kansas. At the end of his first year in business, thirty-five thousand steers were sold in Abilene; the following year the number more than doubled. The great **cattle drives** of the 1860s and 1870s turned into a bonanza for herd owners. Steers purchased in Texas at nine dollars a head could be sold in Abilene for twenty-eight dollars. But the cattlemen, like the grain growers farther north on the Great Plains, lived at the mercy of high interest rates and an unstable market. During the financial panic of 1873, cattle drovers fell into bankruptcy by the hundreds.

cattle drives Millions of head of cattle moved from Texas grazing lands to the railroad terminals in Kansas in the 1870s and 1880s

Little of the money made by the large-scale cattle ranchers found its way into the pockets of the cowboys themselves. The typical cowpuncher endured long hours, low pay, and hazardous work, all for a mere thirty dollars a month, about the same as common laborers. They also braved the gangs of cattle thieves—most notably William H. Bonney, better known as Billy the Kid—that operated along the trails. Most cowboys were men in their teens and twenties who worked for a year or two and then pursued different livelihoods. Of the estimated 35,000 to 55,000 men who rode the trails in these years, nearly one-fifth were black or Mexican. Barred by discrimination from many other trades, blacks enjoyed the freedom of life on the trail.

The cattle bonanza, which peaked between 1880 and 1885, produced more than 4.5 million head of cattle for eastern markets. Prices began to sag as early as 1882, however, and many ranchers plunged heavily into debt. In 1885 and 1886, two of the coldest winters on record combined with summer droughts and Texas fever to destroy nearly 90 percent of the cattle in some regions, pushing thousands of ranchers into bankruptcy. The cattle industry lived on, but railroad expansion brought the days of the open range and the great cattle drives to an end.

Cattle Towns and Prostitutes

One legacy of the cattle boom was the growth of cities like Abilene, Kansas, which shipped steers to Chicago and eastern markets. Like other cattle towns, Abilene went through an early period of violence that saw cowboys pulling down the walls of the jail as it was being built. But the town quickly established a police force to maintain law and order. City ordinances—enforced by the legendary town marshal James B. "Wild Bill" Hickok—forbade carrying firearms and regulated saloons, gambling, and prostitution. Transient, unruly types certainly gave a distinctive flavor to cattle towns like Abilene, Wichita, and Dodge City, but the overall homicide rates there were not unusually high.

If cattle towns were neither as violent nor as lawless as legend would have it, they did still experience a lively business in prostitution. Given the large numbers of unattached young men and numerous saloons, prostitution thrived. Some became prostitutes as an escape from domestic violence or because of economic hardship. Others, like the Chinese, were forced into the trade. But whatever the reasons for entering the business, prostitutes faced a number of risks: venereal disease, physical abuse, and drug and alcohol addiction. As western towns became more settled, the numbers of women in other occupations increased.

Bonanza Farms

Like the gold rushes and cattle bonanzas, the wheat boom of the 1870s and 1880s started small but rapidly attracted large capital investments that produced the nation's first agribusinesses. The boom in the Dakota Territory began during the Panic of 1873, when the Northern Pacific Railroad began exchanging land for its depreciated bonds. Speculators purchased more than three hundred thousand acres in the fertile Red River valley of North Dakota for between fifty cents and a dollar an acre.

Operating singly or in groups, the speculators established factory-like ten-thousand-acre farms, each run by a hired manager, and invested heavily in labor and equipment. On the Cass-Cheney-Dalrymple farm near Fargo, North Dakota, fifty or sixty plows rumbled across the flat landscape on a typical spring day. Cass's first harvest earned a huge profit. The publicity generated by the tremendous success of a few large investors like Cass and Oliver Dalrymple led to an unprecedented wheat boom. North Dakota's population tripled in the 1880s, and wheat production skyrocketed. However, the profits soon evaporated. By 1890, some Red River valley farmers were destitute.

The wheat boom collapsed for a variety of reasons. Overproduction, high investment costs, too little or too much rain, excessive reliance on one crop, and depressed grain prices on the international market all undercut farmers' earnings. Large-scale farmers who had invested in hopes of getting rich felt lucky just to survive.

Large-scale farms proved most successful in California's Central Valley. Using canals and other irrigation systems to water their crops, farmers by the mid-1880s were growing higher-priced specialty crops and had created new cooperative marketing associations for cherries, apricots, grapes, and oranges. By 1900, led by the California Citrus Growers' Association, which used the "Sunkist" trademark for their oranges, large-scale agribusinesses in California were shipping a variety of fruits and vegetables in refrigerated train cars to midwestern and eastern markets.

The Oklahoma Land Rush, 1889

As farmers in the Dakotas and Minnesota endured hard times, would-be homesteaders greedily eyed the Indian Territory, as present-day Oklahoma was then known. The federal government, considering much of this land virtually worthless, had reserved it for the Five Civilized Tribes since the 1830s. These tribes (except for some Cherokees) had sided with the Confederacy during the Civil War. Although Washington had already punished them by settling other tribes on lands in the western part of the territory, land-hungry whites demanded even more land.

Curtis Act Dissolved the Indian Territory and abolished tribal governments in 1898

In 1889, over the Native Americans' protests, Congress transferred to the federally owned public domain nearly 2 million acres in the central part of the Oklahoma Territory that had not been specifically assigned to any Indian tribe. At noon on April 22, 1889, thousands of men, women, and children in buggies and wagons stampeded into the new lands to stake out homesteads. (Other settlers, the so-called Sooners, had illegally arrived earlier and were already plowing the fields.) Nine weeks later, six thousand homestead claims had been filed. In the next decade, the Dawes Severalty Act broke up the Indian reservations into individual allotments and opened the surplus to non-Indian settlement (see Map 17.3). The **Curtis Act** in 1898 dissolved the Indian Territory and abolished tribal governments.

The Oklahoma land rush demonstrated the continuing power of the frontier myth, which tied "free" land to the ideal of economic opportunity. Still, within two generations a combination of exploitative farming, poor land management, and sporadic drought would place Oklahoma at the desolate center of what in the 1930s would be called the dust bowl (see Chapter 24).

Checking In

- Mining booms periodically flared in the West, producing a boom-and-bust cycle that enriched a few.
- The fabled era of the great cattle drives lasted a scant twenty years.
- The real-life low pay and hazardous work of cowboys and the settled monotony of cow towns were much less exciting than the fictionalized and romanticized version.
- Wheat farming became "agribusiness" in North Dakota, but weather and market forces deflated the boom in factory farms.
- The Oklahoma land rush, in which homesteaders staked claims to 2 million acres of free land, epitomized the power of the frontier myth.

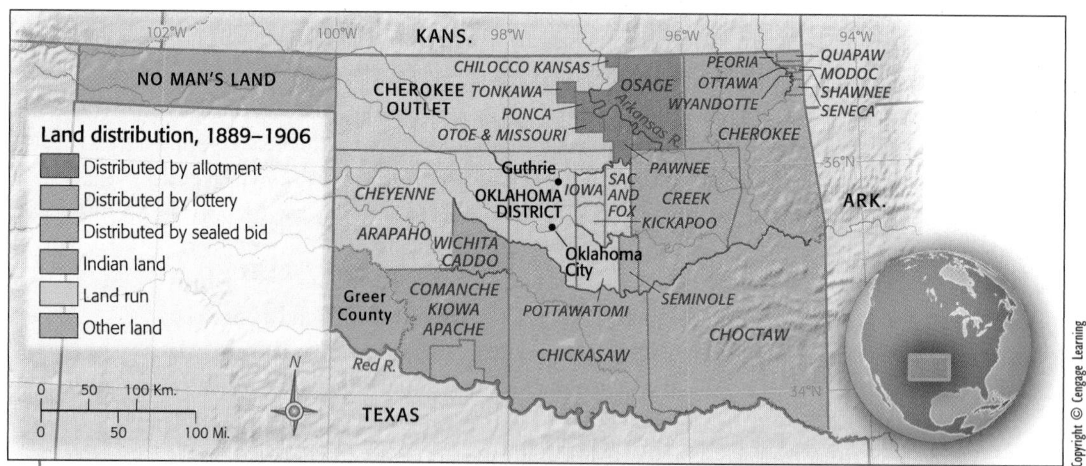

Map 17.3 The Oklahoma Land Rush, 1889–1906

Lands in Oklahoma not settled by "Sooners" were sold by lotteries, allotments, and sealed-bid auctions. By 1907, the major reservations had been broken up, and each Native American family had been given a small farm.

Interactive Map

THE WEST OF LIFE AND LEGEND

How was the Wild West image of cowboys and Indians created, and what developments prompted the establishment of national parks?

In 1893, a young Wisconsin historian, Frederick Jackson Turner, delivered a lecture entitled "The Significance of the Frontier in American History." "[T]he frontier has gone," declared Turner, "and with its going has closed the first period of American history." Although Turner's assertion that the frontier was closed was based on a Census Bureau announcement, it was inaccurate (more western land would be settled in the twentieth century than in the nineteenth). But his linking of economic opportunity with the transformation of the trans-Mississippi West caught the popular imagination and launched a new school of historical inquiry into the effects of the frontier on U.S. history.

Scholars now recognize that many parts of Turner's "frontier thesis," particularly its ethnocentric omission of Native Americans' claims to the land, were inaccurate. Yet his idealized view of the West did reflect ideas popular among his contemporaries in the 1890s. A legendary West had taken deep root in the American imagination. In the nineteenth century, this mythic West was a product of novels, songs, and paintings. In the twentieth century, it would be perpetuated by movies, radio programs, and television shows. The legend merits attention, for its evolution is fascinating and its influence has been far-reaching.

The American Adam and the Dime-Novel Hero

Late-nineteenth-century writers presented the frontiersman as a kind of mythic American Adam—simple, virtuous, and innocent—untainted by a corrupt social order. For example, at the end of Mark Twain's *Huckleberry Finn,* Huck rejects the constraints of settled society as represented by Aunt Sally and heads west with the declaration, "I reckon I got to light out for the territory ahead of the rest, because Aunt Sally she's going to adopt me and sivilize me, and I can't stand it. I been there before." In this version of the legend, the West is a place of adventure where one can escape from society and its pressures.

But even as this conception of the myth was being popularized, another powerful theme had emerged as well. The authors of the dime novels of the 1860s and 1870s offered the image of the western frontiersman as a new masculine ideal, the tough guy who fights for truth and honor. In *Buffalo Bill: King of the Border Men* (1869), a dime novel loosely based on real-life William F. "Buffalo Bill" Cody, Edward Judson (pen-named Ned Buntline) created an idealized hero who is a powerful moral force as he drives off treacherous Indians and rounds up villainous cattle rustlers.

Cody himself, playing upon the public fascination with cowboys, organized his own **Wild West Show** in 1883. In the show, which toured the East Coast and Europe, cowboys engaged in mock battles with Indians, reinforcing the dime-novel image of the West as an arena of moral encounter where virtue always triumphed.

Wild West Show William F. "Buffalo Bill" Cody's extravagant Western-themed traveling show

Revitalizing the Frontier Legend

Eastern writers and artists eagerly embraced both versions of the myth—the West as a place of escape from society and the West as a stage on which the moral conflicts confronting society were played out. Three young members of the eastern establishment, Theodore Roosevelt, Frederic Remington, and Owen Wister, spent much time in the West in the 1880s, and each was intensely affected by the adventure.

Each man found precisely what he was looking for. The frontier that Roosevelt glorified in such books as *The Winning of the West* (four volumes, 1889–1896), and that Remington portrayed in his statues and paintings, was a stark physical and moral environment that stripped away all social artifice and tested each individual's character. Roosevelt and Remington exalted the disappearing frontier as the proving ground for a new kind of virile manhood and the last outpost of an honest and true social order.

Owen Wister Author of *The Virginian,* which portrayed the cowboy as a moral force

This version of the frontier myth reached its apogee in the enormously popular novel *The Virginian* (1902) by **Owen Wister.** In Wister's tale, the environment of the Great Plains produces individuals like his unnamed cowboy hero, "the Virginian." The Virginian is one of nature's aristocrats—ill-educated and unsophisticated but tough, steady, and deeply moral. The Virginian sums up his own moral code in describing his view of God's justice: "He plays a square game with us." For Wister, as for Roosevelt and Remington, the cowboy was the Christian knight on the Plains, indifferent to material gain as he upheld justice and attacked evil.

Needless to say, the western myth was far removed from the reality of the West. The idealized version of the West also glossed over the darker underside of frontier

Chasm of the Colorado, 1873–1874, by Thomas Moran

Dazzled by the monumental beauty of the West, painters portrayed natural wonders such as the Grand Canyon as one of God's works. In the process, they stimulated a new popular interest in preserving the spectacular features of the land.

expansion—the hard physical labor of the cattle range, the forced removal of the Indians to reservations, the racist discrimination against Mexican-Americans and blacks, and the boom-and-bust mentality rooted in the selfish exploitation of natural resources.

Further, the myth obscured the complex links between the settlement of the frontier and the emergence of the United States as a major industrialized nation increasingly tied to a global economy. Eastern and foreign capitalists controlled large-scale mining, cattle, and agricultural operations in the West. Without the railroad—the brainchild of well-financed inventors, not rough-and-tumble cowboys—the transformation of the West would have been far slower.

Beginning a National Parks Movement

Despite its one-sided and idealized vision, Owen Wister's celebration of the western experience reinforced a growing recognition that many unique features of the western landscape were being threatened by overeager entrepreneurs. One important by-product of the western legend was a surge of public support for creating national parks and the beginning of an organized conservation movement.

Those who went west in the 1860s and 1870s to map the rugged terrain were often awed by the natural beauty of the landscape. Major **John Wesley Powell,** the one-armed veteran of the Civil War who charted the Colorado River through the Grand Canyon in 1869, waxed euphoric about its towering rock formations and powerful cataracts. "On coming nearer," he wrote, "we find fountains bursting from the rock, high overhead, and the spray in the sunshine forms the gems which bedeck the way." In his important study, *Report on the Lands of the Arid Regions of the United States* (1878), Powell called for public ownership and governmental control of watersheds, irrigation, and public lands, a request that went largely unheeded.

John Wesley Powell Explorer who wrote eloquently about the beauty of the West, which was a necessity for environmental conservation

Around the time Powell was educating Congress about the arid nature of the far West, a group of adventurers led by General Henry D. Washburn visited the hot springs and geysers near the Yellowstone River in northwestern Wyoming and eastern Montana. Overwhelmed by the view, the Washburn explorers abandoned their plan to claim the area for the Northern Pacific Railroad and instead petitioned Congress to protect it from settlement, occupancy, and sale. Congress responded in 1872 by creating **Yellowstone National Park** to "provide for the preservation . . . for all time, [of] mineral deposits, natural curiosities, or wonders within said park . . . in their natural condition." In doing so, they excluded the Native Americans who had long considered the area a prime hunting range.

Yellowstone National Park First national park founded as a result of the conservation movement

These first steps to conserve a few of the West's unique natural sites reflected the beginning of a changed awareness of the environment. In his influential study *Man and Nature* in 1864, **George Perkins Marsh,** an architect and politician from Vermont, attacked the view that nature existed to be tamed and conquered. "Man," he wrote, "is every where a disturbing agent. Wherever he plants his foot, the harmonies of nature are turned to discords."

George Perkins Marsh Architect and politician from Vermont who challenged the notion that nature existed merely to be exploited

Marsh's plea for conservation found its most eloquent support in the work of **John Muir,** a Scottish immigrant who had grown up in Wisconsin. In 1869, Muir traveled to San Francisco and quickly fell in love with the redwood forests. For the next forty years, he tramped the rugged mountains of the West and campaigned for

John Muir Conservationist who played a major role in wilderness preservation their preservation. A romantic at heart, he yearned to experience the wilderness at its most elemental level. Once trekking high in the Rockies during a summer storm, he climbed the tallest pine he could find and swayed back and forth in the raging wind.

Muir became the late nineteenth century's most articulate publicist for wilderness protection. "Climb the mountains and get their good tidings," he advised city-dwellers. "Nature's peace will flow into you as the sunshine into the trees." Muir's spirited campaign to protect the wilderness contributed strongly to the establishment of Yosemite National Park in 1890. Two years later, the Sierra Club, an organization created to encourage the enjoyment and protection of the wilderness in the mountain regions of the Pacific coast, made Muir its first president.

Ironically, despite the crusades of Muir, Powell, and Marsh to educate the public about conservation, the campaign for wilderness preservation re-affirmed the image of the West as a unique region whose magnificent landscape produced tough individuals of superior ability. Overlooking the senseless violence and ruthless exploitation of the land, contemporary writers proclaimed that the settlement of the final frontier marked a new stage in the history of civilization, and they kept alive the legend of the western frontier as a seedbed of American virtues.

CHECKING IN

- Historian Frederick Jackson Turner linked the frontier to economic opportunity but ignored the land's native occupants.
- Dime novels and Wild West shows reinforced the myth of the West as a moral arena where virtue always triumphed.
- Writers like Theodore Roosevelt and Owen Wister exalted the cowboy as a Christian knight on a pinto pony.
- John Wesley Powell led the way in extolling the western landscape, while stressing the need to conserve its resources.
- John Muir played a major role in encouraging preservation of the western wilderness and the creation of national parks.

Chapter Summary

How was Indian life on the Great Plains transformed in the second half of the nineteenth century? (page 397)

After the Civil War, the Great Plains became a battleground between the nomadic Plains Indians and the U.S. Army. Under the banner of economic opportunity and individual achievement, Americans used the army to subdue the Indians, undermine their traditional way of life, and drive them onto reservations. Well-intentioned whites tried to "civilize" the Indians through measures such as the Dawes Act, but it was the massacre at Wounded Knee that finally marked the end of conflict on the Plains.

What roles did the federal government, the army, and the railroads play in the settlement of the West? (page 405)

Aided by federal subsidies and the protection of the U.S. Army, the transcontinental railroad was completed in 1869. The railroad companies actively recruited settlers. Homesteaders faced obstacles they had not foreseen—isolation, drought, the perils of the commercial agricultural market—but many persevered. The Mormons, persecuted elsewhere, found a home in the West and helped Utah achieve statehood in 1896. By 1912 all of the western lands had been brought into the Union.

KEY TERMS

Plains Indians *(p. 399)*
William F. "Buffalo Bill" Cody *(p. 399)*
Fort Laramie Treaty *(p. 400)*
Sitting Bull *(p. 402)*
Helen Hunt Jackson *(p. 403)*
Dawes Severalty Act *(p. 403)*
Ghost Dance *(p. 404)*
Wounded Knee *(p. 405)*
Edmunds-Tucker Act *(p. 410)*
White Caps *(p. 411)*
Comstock Lode *(p. 413)*
cattle drives *(p. 414)*
Curtis Act *(p. 416)*
Wild West Show *(p. 417)*
Owen Wister *(p. 418)*

How did ranchers and settlers displace Spanish-speaking Americans in the Southwest? (page 410)

In California and Texas there were frequent clashes between Anglo and Mexican populations as the Mexicans gradually lost control of their lands; many Spanish-speakers ended up in urban barrios. In New Mexico and Arizona, adaptation went somewhat more smoothly. Nonetheless, Mexicans gradually lost status, and most became laborers.

How did mining, ranching, and farming shape the West? (page 413)

All three of these sectors of the economy enjoyed periodic booms in the West, from the Comstock Lode to the great cattle drives to the bonanza wheat farms of North Dakota. However, these booms often led to busts, and they did serious harm to the environment.

How was the Wild West image of cowboys and Indians created, and what developments prompted the establishment of national parks? (page 417)

Dime novels and Wild West shows reinforced the idea of the West as a moral arena in which good triumphed; Theodore Roosevelt, Owen Wister, and other writers portrayed the cowboy as a heroic figure. John Wesley Powell and John Muir powerfully described the western landscape and urged its conservation, leading to the creation of a national park system.

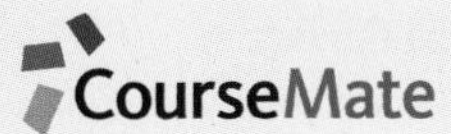

Go to the CourseMate website at **www.cengagebrain.com** for additional study tools and review materials—including audio and video clips—for this chapter.

KEY TERMS continued

John Wesley Powell *(p. 419)*
Yellowstone National Park *(p. 419)*
George Perkins Marsh *(p. 419)*
John Muir *(p. 419)*

Chapter 18

The Rise of Industrial America 1865–1900

The Granger Collection, NYC

Court of Honor, World's Columbian Exposition, 1893

Chapter Preview

The Rise of Corporate America
How did Carnegie, Rockefeller, and other corporate leaders consolidate control over their industries?

Stimulating Economic Growth
What innovations in technology and business drove increases in industrial production after 1865?

The New South
Why did the South's experience with industrialization differ from that of the North and the Midwest?

Factories and the Work Force
How did the changing nature of work affect factory workers' lives, and how did they respond?

Labor Unions and Industrial Conflict
How did corporate executives undercut labor's bargaining power in the 1890s?

On October 21, 1892, before two hundred thousand onlookers, presidential candidate Grover Cleveland proudly opened the World's Columbian Exposition in Chicago. The Chicago world's fair represented the triumph of fifty years of industrial development. The country's largest corporations displayed their newest products, including Westinghouse Company's dynamos, American Bell Telephone's connections to the East Coast, and Thomas A. Edison's phonograph. The fair dazzled its more than 25 million visitors.

Many late-nineteenth-century Americans found themselves both exhilarated and unsettled as the nation was transformed by industrialization. At midcentury, the United States had played a minor role in the world economy. Five decades later, the country now produced 35 percent of the world's manufactured goods—more than England, Germany, and France combined. It had become one of the world's greatest industrial powers. By 1900, new enterprises both large and small, supported by investment bankers and using a nationwide railroad distribution system, offered a vast array of goods.

This stunning industrial growth came at a high cost. New manufacturing processes transformed the nature of work, undercut skilled labor, and created mind-numbing assembly-line routines. Large-scale manufacturing companies often polluted the environment. The challenges of new business practices made the American economy difficult to control. Rather than smoothly rolling forward, it lurched between booms and busts in business cycles that produced labor unrest and crippling depressions in 1873–1879 and 1893–1897.

THE RISE OF CORPORATE AMERICA

How did Carnegie, Rockefeller, and other corporate leaders consolidate control over their industries?

In the early nineteenth century, the corporate form of business organization had been used to raise large amounts of start-up capital for transportation enterprises such as turnpikes and canals. By selling stocks and bonds to raise money, the corporation separated the company's managers, who guided its day-to-day operation, from its owners. After the Civil War, American business leaders pioneered new forms of corporate organization that combined innovative technologies, creative management structures, and limited liability should the enterprise fail. The rise of the giant corporation is a story of risk-taking and innovation as well as of conspiracy and corruption.

The Character of Industrial Change

Six features dominated the world of large-scale manufacturing after the Civil War: (1) the exploitation of immense coal deposits as a source of cheap energy; (2) the rapid spread of technological innovation in transportation, communication, and factory systems; (3) the demand for workers who could be carefully controlled; (4) the constant pressure on firms to compete tooth-and-nail by cutting costs and prices; (5) the relentless drop in prices; and (6) the failure of the money supply to keep pace with productivity.

All six factors were closely related. The great coal deposits in Pennsylvania, West Virginia, and Kentucky provided cheap energy to fuel railroad and factory growth. New technologies stimulated productivity and catalyzed breathtaking industrial expansion. Technology also enabled manufacturers to cut costs and hire cheap unskilled or semiskilled labor. Cost cutting enabled firms to undersell one another, destroy weaker competitors, and consolidate themselves into stronger, more efficient, and more ruthless firms. Cheap energy, cost reduction, new technology, and fierce competition forced down overall price levels.

Frank & Marie-Therese Wood Print Collections, Alexandria, VA

Abusive Monopoly Power

This Puck cartoon depicts financiers Jay Gould (left) and Cornelius Vanderbilt (right) and suggests that their manipulation of markets and their ownership of railroads, telegraph companies, and newspapers is powerful enough to strangle Uncle Sam.

Out of the new industrial system poured clouds of haze and soot, as well as the first tantalizing trickle of what would become an avalanche of consumer goods. In turn, mounting demands for consumer goods stimulated heavy industry's production of capital goods—machines to boost farm and factory output—even further. Together with the railroads, the corporations that manufactured capital goods, refined petroleum, and made steel became driving forces in the nation's economic growth.

Railroad Innovations

Competition among the aggressive and innovative capitalists who headed American heavy industry was intense, especially among the nation's railroads. By 1900, 193,000 miles of railroad track crisscrossed the United States—more than in all of Europe including Russia. These rail lines connected every state in the Union and opened up an immense new internal market.

Railroad entrepreneurs such as Collis P. Huntington of the Central Pacific Railroad and **Jay Gould** of the Union Pacific faced enormous financial and organizational problems. To raise the staggering sums necessary for laying track and building engines, railroads obtained generous land and loan subsidies from the government and borrowed money from the public (in the form of stocks and bonds). By 1900, the yearly interest repayments required by the combined debt of all U.S. railroads (which stood at an astounding $5.1 billion—nearly five times that of the federal government) cut heavily into their earnings.

In addition to developing ways to raise large amounts of capital, the railroads created new systems for collecting and using information. Railroads relied heavily on the magnetic telegraph, a device invented in 1837. To improve efficiency, they set up clearly defined, hierarchical organizational structures and used elaborate accounting systems. Railroad officials could set rates and accurately predict profits as early as the 1860s, a time when most businesses had no idea of their total profit until they closed their books at year's end. Railroad management innovations thus became a model for many other businesses seeking a national market.

Jay Gould Captain of industry and owner of the Union Pacific Railroad

Consolidating the Railroad Industry

The expansion and consolidation of railroading reflected both the ingenuity and the dishonesty flourishing on the corporate management scene. Despite advances in

Chronology

1859	First oil well drilled in Titusville, Pennsylvania
1866	National Labor Union founded
1869	Transcontinental railroad completed; Knights of Labor organized
1870	John D. Rockefeller establishes Standard Oil Company
1873	Panic of 1873 triggers a depression lasting until 1879
1876	Alexander Graham Bell patents the telephone
1877	Edison invents phonograph; railway workers stage first nationwide strike
1879	Henry George, *Progress and Poverty;* Edison perfects incandescent lamp
1882	Standard Oil Trust established; Edison opens first electric power station in New York City; Chinese Exclusion Act
1883	William Graham Sumner, *What Social Classes Owe to Each Other;* Lester Frank Ward, *Dynamic Sociology*
1886	American Federation of Labor (AFL) formed; Haymarket riot in Chicago
1887	Interstate Commerce Act establishes Interstate Commerce Commission
1888	Edward Bellamy, *Looking Backward*
1889	Andrew Carnegie, "The Gospel of Wealth"
1890	Sherman Anti-Trust Act; United Mine Workers formed
1892	Standard Oil of New Jersey and General Electric formed; Homestead Strike; Columbian Exposition in Chicago
1893	Panic of 1893 triggers a depression lasting until 1897
1894	Pullman Palace Car workers strike
1901	J. Pierpont Morgan organizes United States Steel

organizational technique, the industry remained chaotic in the 1870s. Hundreds of small companies used different standards for track width and engine size. Huntington, Gould, and others devoured these smaller lines to create large, integrated track networks. West of the Mississippi, five companies controlled most of the track by 1893.

Huntington, Gould, and the other corporate leaders who expanded the railroad industry in the 1870s and 1880s often were depicted by their contemporaries as villains and robber barons who manipulated stock markets to line their own pockets. Recent historians, however, have pointed out that the great industrialists were a diverse group. Some were ironfisted pirates; others managed their companies with daring and innovation. Indeed, some of their ideas were startling in their originality and inventiveness.

The massive systems created by these entrepreneurs became the largest business enterprises in the world. They standardized all basic equipment and facilities. In 1883, independently of the federal government, the railroads corrected scheduling problems by dividing the country into four time zones. In May 1886, all railroads shifted simultaneously to the new standard 4′ 8½″ gauge track. Finally, cooperative billing arrangements enabled the railroads to ship cars from other roads at uniform rates nationwide.

However, the systemization and consolidation of the railroads had its costs. Heavy indebtedness, overextended systems, and crooked business practices forced the railroads to compete recklessly with each other for traffic. Competition and expansion drove some overbuilt lines into bankruptcy.

Stung by exorbitant rates and secret kickbacks, farmers turned to state governments for help. In the 1870s, midwestern state legislatures responded by outlawing rate discrimination. Initially upheld by the Supreme Court, these and other decisions were negated in the 1880s when the Court ruled that states could not regulate interstate commerce. In response to this situation, Congress passed the **Interstate Commerce Act** in 1887. A five-member Interstate Commerce Commission (ICC) was established to oversee the practices of interstate railroads. Although the law was supposed to ban monopolistic activity, it went largely unenforced until the Progressive Era of the early twentieth century (see Chapter 21).

Interstate Commerce Act First federal attempt to control unfair practices by railroads

The railroads' vicious competition weakened in 1893 when a national depression forced a number of roads into the hands of **J. Pierpont Morgan** and other investment bankers. Morgan took over the weakened systems, reorganized their administration, refinanced their debts, and built intersystem alliances. By 1906, under the bankers' centralized management, seven giant networks controlled two-thirds of the nation's rail mileage.

J. Pierpont Morgan Investment banker who helped create U.S. Steel, as well as other huge corporations

Applying the Lessons of the Railroads to Steel

The close connections between railroad expansion and the growth of corporate organization and management are well illustrated in the career of **Andrew Carnegie** (CAR-neh-gee). Born in Scotland, Carnegie immigrated to America in 1848 at the age of twelve. His first job as a bobbin boy in a Pittsburgh textile mill paid only $1.20 a week. The following year, Carnegie became a Western Union messenger boy. Taking over when the telegraph operators wanted a break, he soon became the city's fastest telegraph operator. The job gave Carnegie an insider's view of railroad operations.

Andrew Carnegie Scottish immigrant who built an enormous steel company

Carnegie's big break came in 1852 when Tom Scott, superintendent of the Pennsylvania Railroad's western division, hired him as his secretary and personal telegrapher. Later promoted to division chief, Carnegie cut costs while doubling the road's mileage. By 1868, Carnegie was earning more than $56,000 a year from his investments, a substantial fortune in that era.

In the early 1870s, Carnegie decided to build his own steel mill. Carnegie's philosophy was deceptively simple: "Watch the costs, and the profits will take care of themselves." Using rigorous cost accounting and limiting wage increases to his workers, he lowered his production costs and prices below those of his competitors. His adoption of a new production technique named after its English inventor, Henry Bessemer, ensured a high-quality product.

vertical integration Technique of controlling all phases of production, extracting maximum profit

As output climbed, Carnegie discovered the benefits of **vertical integration**—that is, controlling all aspects of manufacturing, from extracting raw materials to selling the finished product. By 1900, Carnegie Steel had become the world's largest industrial corporation. Carnegie's competitors, worried about his domination of the market, decided to buy him out. In 1901, J. Pierpont Morgan purchased Carnegie's companies and set up the United States Steel Corporation, the first business capitalized at more than $1 billion (see Figure 18.1).

A systematic self-publicist, Carnegie consistently portrayed his success as the result of self-discipline and hard work. He also cultivated a reputation as a philanthropist, giving away more than $300 million to libraries, universities, and international-peace causes. However, the full story was more complex. Carnegie's success came not just from his work ethic, but also from his opportunistic temperament and callousness in keeping wages for his workers as low as possible. To a public unaware of corporate management techniques, however, Carnegie's success leant credence to the idea that anyone might rise from rags to riches.

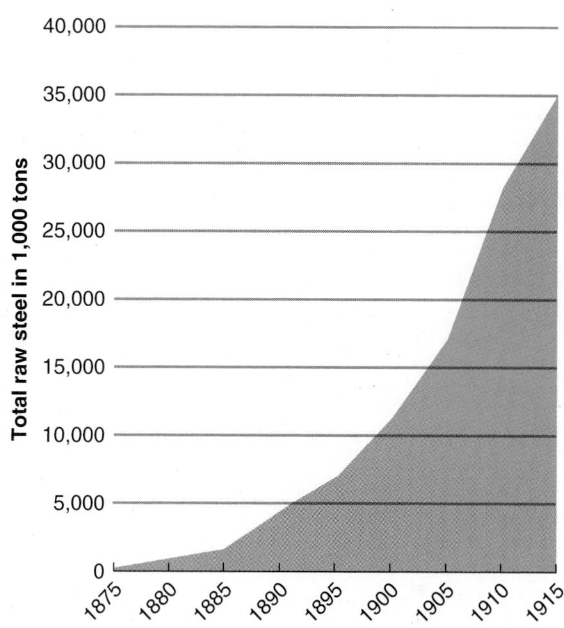

Figure 18.1 Iron and Steel Production, 1875–1915

New technologies, improved plant organization, economies of scale, and the vertical integration of production brought a dramatic spurt in iron and steel production.

Note: short ton = 2,000 pounds.

Historical Statistics of the United States.

The Trust: Creating New Forms of Corporate Organization

Between 1870 and 1900, the same fierce competition that had stimulated consolidation in the railroad and steel industries also swept the oil, salt, sugar, tobacco, and meatpacking industries. The evolution of the oil industry illustrates the process by which new corporate structures evolved. After Edwin L. Drake drilled the first successful petroleum (or "crude-oil") well in 1859 near Titusville, Pennsylvania, competitors rushed into the business. Petroleum was distilled into oil, which soon replaced animal tallow as the major lubricant, and into kerosene, which became the leading fuel for household and public lighting.

By the 1870s the landscape near Pittsburgh and Cleveland was littered with rickety drilling rigs, assorted collection tanks, and ramshackle refineries. In this rush for riches, **John D. Rockefeller,** a young Cleveland merchant, gradually achieved dominance. Rockefeller opened his first refinery in 1863. Like Carnegie, the solemn Rockefeller had a passion for cost cutting and understood the benefits of vertical integration. In 1872, he purchased his own tanker cars and obtained not only a 10 percent rebate from the railroads for hauling his oil but also a kickback on his competitors' shipments. When new pipeline technology became available, Rockefeller set up his own massive interregional pipeline network.

John D. Rockefeller Creator of Standard Oil and master of the use of pools and trusts to monopolize an industry

Like Carnegie, Rockefeller aggressively forced out his competitors. If local refineries rejected his offers to buy them out, he priced his products below cost and strangled their businesses. When rival firms teamed up against him, Rockefeller set up a pool—an agreement among several companies—that established production quotas and fixed prices. By 1879, Rockefeller had seized control of 90 percent of the country's oil-refining capacity.

Worried about competition, Rockefeller in 1882 decided to eliminate it by establishing a new form of corporate organization, the **Standard Oil Trust.** In place of the pool, a verbal agreement among companies that lacked legal status, the trust

Standard Oil Trust An umbrella organization of forty companies that controlled the U.S. oil industry created an umbrella corporation that ran them all. Within three years the Standard Oil Trust had consolidated crude-oil buying throughout its member firms and slashed the number of refineries in half. In this way Rockefeller integrated the petroleum industry both *vertically* and *horizontally,* by merging the competing oil companies into one giant system.

Sherman Anti-Trust Act Law against trusts; initially unsuccessful

Taking a page from Rockefeller's book, companies in the tobacco, copper, sugar, whiskey, lead, and other industries established their own trust arrangements. But their unscrupulous tactics, semimonopolistic control, and sky-high earnings provoked a public outcry. Both major political parties denounced them in the presidential election of 1888.

Fearful that the trusts would stamp out all competition, Congress passed the **Sherman Anti-Trust Act** in 1890. The Sherman Act outlawed trusts and any other monopolies that fixed prices in restraint of trade and slapped violators with fines of up to $5,000 and a year in jail. But the act failed to define clearly either *trust* or *restraint of trade.* When Standard Oil's structure was challenged in 1892, its lawyers simply reorganized the trust as a giant holding company, which simply owned a controlling share of the stock of one or more firms. The new board of directors for Standard Oil (New Jersey), the new holding company, made more money than ever.

The Supreme Court further hamstrung congressional antitrust efforts by interpreting the Sherman Act in ways sympathetic to big business. In 1895, for example, the federal government brought suit against the sugar trust in *United States v. E. C. Knight Company*—and lost. Thus vindicated, corporate mergers and consolidations surged ahead. By 1900, these mammoth firms accounted for nearly two-fifths of the capital invested in the nation's manufacturing sector.

CHECKING IN

- Immense coal deposits, rapid technological innovation, and the spread of the factory system combined with other factors to give birth to modern industrial America.
- Railroads, consolidated into enormous trunk lines, were symbols of industrial progress and laboratories for new business techniques and organization.
- Andrew Carnegie was the first to transfer lessons learned from the railroads to another industry, steel, and to use vertical integration on a large scale.
- John D. Rockefeller led the way in developing new forms of business organization, especially the trust.
- By the end of the nineteenth century, consolidation had resulted in the formation of huge corporations.

STIMULATING ECONOMIC GROWTH

What innovations in technology and business drove increases in industrial production after 1865?

Large-scale corporate enterprise was not the only cause of the colossal growth of the U.S. economy. Other factors proved equally important, including new inventions, specialty production, and innovations in advertising and marketing.

The Triumph of Technology

New inventions did more than streamline the manufacture of traditional products; they also stimulated consumer demand by creating entirely new product lines. The development of a safe, practical way to generate electricity, for example, made possible a vast number of electrical motors, household appliances, and lighting systems.

Many of the major inventions that stimulated industrial output in these years were largely hidden from public view. Few Americans had heard of the improved technologies that facilitated bottle making, canning, flour milling, and petroleum refining.

The inventions people did see were the ones that changed the patterns of everyday life: the sewing machine, mass-produced by the Singer Sewing Machine Company beginning in the 1860s; the telephone, developed by Alexander Graham Bell in 1876; and the light bulb, perfected by **Thomas A. Edison** in 1879.

Thomas A. Edison Inventor; founder of the first industrial research laboratory

These new inventions eased household drudgery and reshaped social interactions. The sewing machine, which relieved the tedium of sewing apparel by hand, expanded personal wardrobes. The spread of telephones not only transformed communication but also undermined social conventions for polite behavior that had been premised on face-to-face or written exchanges. The light bulb, by freeing people from dependence on daylight, made it possible to shop after work.

In the eyes of many, Thomas A. Edison epitomized the inventive impulse. Born in 1847 in Milan, Ohio, Edison, like Andrew Carnegie, had little formal education and got his start in the telegraphic industry. A born salesman and self-promoter, Edison shared Carnegie's vision of a large, interconnected industrial system resting on a foundation of technological innovation.

Edison's first major invention, a stock-quotation printer, in 1868, earned enough money to set up his first "invention factory" in Newark, New Jersey, a research facility that he moved to nearby Menlo Park in 1876. Edison boastfully predicted "a minor invention every ten days, and a big one every six months."

Buoyed by the success and popularity of his 1877 invention of a phonograph, or "sound writer" (*phono:* "sound"; *graph:* "writer"), Edison set out to develop a new filament for incandescent (in-can-DESS-ent) light bulbs. Edison realized that practical

U.S. Department of the Interior/National Park Service/Edison National Historic Site

Thomas Edison's Laboratories in Menlo Park, New Jersey, c. 1881

Always a self-promoter, Edison used this depiction of his "invention factory" to suggest that his development of a durable light bulb in 1879 would have an impact on life around the globe.

electrical lighting had to be part of a complete system containing generators, meters, and wiring. In 1882, the Edison Illuminating Company opened a power plant in the heart of New York City's financial district, furnishing lighting for eighty-five buildings.

In the following years, Edison and his researchers pumped out invention after invention, including the mimeograph machine, the microphone, the motion picture camera and film, and the storage battery. By the time of his death in 1931, he had patented 1,093 inventions and amassed an estate worth more than $6 million. Edison's Menlo Park laboratory demonstrated that the systematic use of science in support of industrial technology paid large dividends. Invention had become big business.

Specialized Production

Along with inventors, manufacturers of custom and specialized products such as machinery, jewelry, furniture, and women's clothes dramatically expanded economic output. Keenly attuned to innovations in technology and design, they constantly created new products tailored to the needs of individual buyers.

Until the turn of the twentieth century, when ready-to-wear clothes came to dominate the market, most women's apparel was custom produced in small shops run by women proprietors. Unlike the tenement sweatshops that produced men's shirts and pants, dressmakers and milliners paid good wages to highly skilled seamstresses. The small size of the shops together with the skill of the workers enabled them to shift styles quickly to follow the latest fashions.

Thus, alongside of the increasingly rationalized and bureaucratic big businesses like steel and oil in the late nineteenth century, American productivity was also stimulated by small producers who provided a variety of goods that supplemented the bulk-manufactured staples of everyday life.

Advertising and Marketing

As small and large factories alike spewed out an amazing array of new products, business leaders often discovered that their output exceeded what the market could absorb. Strategies for whetting consumer demand and for differentiating one product from another represented a critical component of industrial expansion in the post–Civil War era.

The growth of the flour industry illustrates both the spread of mass production and the emergence of new marketing concepts. In the 1870s, the nation's flour mills installed continuous-process machines that graded, cleaned, hulled, ground, and packaged the product in one rapid operation. These companies, however, soon produced more flour than they could sell. To unload this excess, the mills thought up new products such as cake flours and breakfast cereals and sold them using easy-to-remember brand names like Quaker Oats.

Through the use of brand names, slogans, endorsements, and other gimmicks, manufacturers built demand for their products and won enduring consumer loyalty. For instance, Americans bought Ivory Soap, first made in 1879 by Procter and Gamble of Cincinnati, because of the absurdly precise but impressive pledge that it was "99 and 44/100ths percent pure."

In the 1880s, George Eastman developed a paper-based photographic film as an alternative to the bulky, fragile glass plates then in use and sold this film loaded into an inexpensive camera. Consumers returned the camera to his Rochester factory where, for a charge of ten dollars, the film was developed and printed, the camera reloaded, and everything shipped back. In this manner, Eastman revolutionized an industry and democratized a visual medium previously confined to a few.

Bettmann/CORBIS

Industrial Pollution

Although some Americans celebrated factory smoke as a sign of industrial growth, those who lived downwind, such as the longshoreman in this Thomas Nast cartoon, often suffered from respiratory diseases and other ailments. For him as well as for other Americans, the price of industrial progress was often pollution.

Social and Environmental Costs and Benefits

By 1900, the chaos of early industrial competition, when thousands of companies had struggled to enter a national market, had given way to the most productive economy in the world. An industrial transformation that had originated in railroading and expanded to steel and petroleum had spread to every nook and cranny of American business.

The vast expansion of economic output brought social benefits, in the form of labor-saving products, lower prices, and advances in transportation and communications. However, the benefits and liabilities sometimes seemed inextricably interconnected. The sewing machine, for example, created thousands of new factory jobs and eased the lives of millions of housewives. At the same time, it encouraged avaricious entrepreneurs to operate sweatshops in which the immigrant poor toiled long hours for pitifully low wages (see Chapter 21).

For those who fell by the wayside, the cost could be measured in bankrupted companies and shattered dreams. John D. Rockefeller put things with characteristic bluntness when he said he wanted "only the big ones, only those who have already proved they can do a big business" in the Standard Oil Trust. "As for the others, unfortunately they will have to die." The cost was high, too, for millions of American workers, immigrant and native-born alike. The vast expansion of new products was built on the backs of an army of laborers who were paid subsistence wages and who could be fired on a moment's notice.

Industrial growth often devastated the environment as well. Rivers fouled by oil or chemical waste, skies filled with clouds of soot, and a landscape littered with reeking garbage and toxic materials bore mute witness to the relentless drive for efficiency and profit.

Whatever the final balance sheet of social gains and costs, one thing was clear: The United States had muscled its way onto the world stage as an industrial titan. The ambition and drive of countless inventors, financiers, managerial innovators, and marketing wizards had combined to lay the groundwork for a new social and economic order in the twentieth century.

Checking In

- Technology created new ways of manufacturing and new products that stimulated demand.
- Many inventions, such as the telephone and electric light, changed daily life.
- Edison established the first major research laboratory at Menlo Park, New Jersey, calling it "an invention factory."
- Companies developed brand-name products and marketed them heavily.
- Rapid economic growth, with both negative and positive effects, propelled the United States to the forefront of the global economy.

THE NEW SOUTH

Why did the South's experience with industrialization differ from that of the North and the Midwest?

The South entered the industrial era far more slowly than the Northeast. As late as 1900, total southern cotton-mill output, for example, remained little more than half that of the mills within a thirty-mile radius of Providence, Rhode Island.

The reasons for the South's late economic blossoming are not hard to discern. The Civil War's physical devastation, racism, the scarcity of southern towns and cities, lack of capital, illiteracy, northern control of financial markets, and a low rate of technological innovation crippled efforts by southern business leaders to promote industrialization. Economic progress was also impeded by the myth of the Lost Cause, which, through its nostalgic portrayal of pre–Civil War society, perpetuated an image of the South as traditional and unchanging. As a result, southern industrialization inched forward haltingly and was shaped in distinctive ways.

Obstacles to Economic Development

Much of the South's difficulty in industrializing arose from its lack of capital. For example, the federal government required anyone wishing to start a bank to have fifty thousand dollars in capital. Few southerners could meet this standard. With banks in short supply, country merchants loaned supplies rather than cash to local farmers in return for a lien, or mortgage, on their crops (see Chapter 16). The burden of paying these liens trapped farmers on their own land and created a shortage of the labor needed for industrial expansion.

The South's chronic shortage of funds also limited the resources available for education. During Reconstruction, northern philanthropists together with various relief agencies had begun a modest expansion of public schooling for both blacks and whites. But Georgia and many other southern states operated segregated schools and refused to tax property for school support until 1889. As a result, school attendance remained low, severely limiting the number of educated people able to staff technical and managerial positions in business and industry.

Southern states, like those in the North, often contributed the modest funds they had to war veterans' pensions. In this way, southern state governments built a white patronage system for Confederate veterans. As late as 1911, veterans' pensions in Georgia ate up 22 percent of the state's entire budget, leaving little for economic or educational development.

Henry W. Grady Editor of the *Atlanta Constitution* and tireless booster of his city and region

The New South Creed and Southern Industrialization

Despite these obstacles, energetic southern newspaper editors such as **Henry W. Grady** of the *Atlanta Constitution* championed the doctrine that became known as the New South creed. The South's rich coal and timber resources and cheap labor, they proclaimed in their papers, made it a natural site for industrial development.

The movement to industrialize the South gained momentum in the 1880s. To attract northern capital, southern states offered tax exemptions for new businesses, set up industrial and agricultural expositions, and leased prison convicts to serve as cheap labor. Florida, Texas, and other states gave huge tracts of lands to railroads, which expanded dramatically throughout the South and in turn stimulated the birth of new towns and villages.

Following the lead of their northern counterparts, the southern iron and steel industries expanded as well. Birmingham, Alabama, was founded in 1871 in the heart of a region blessed with rich deposits of coal, limestone, and iron ore. In less than three decades, it grew into a bustling city with noisy railroad yards and roaring blast furnaces. By 1900 it was the nation's largest pig-iron shipper.

As large-scale recruiters of black workers, the southern iron and steel mills contributed to the migration of blacks to the cities. By 1900, 20 percent of the southern black population was urban. Southern industry reflected the patterns of racial segregation in southern life. Tobacco companies used black workers, particularly women, to clean the tobacco leaves while white women, at a different location, ran the machines that made cigarettes. The burgeoning textile mills were lilywhite. In the iron and steel industry, blacks, who comprised 60 percent of the unskilled work force by 1900, had practically no chance of advancement.

Black miners were also recruited by the West Virginia coal industry that lured them with free transportation, high wages, and company housing. In good times, wages for black workers in the lumbering industry could be better than those offered to farm laborers. Still, economic opportunities for blacks remained severely limited. During economic downturns workers were laid off or confined to work camps by vagrancy laws and armed guards.

The Southern Mill Economy

Unlike the urban-based southern iron and steel industry, the textile mills that mushroomed in the southern countryside in the 1880s often became catalysts for the formation of new towns and villages. In the mill towns, country ways and values suffused the new industrial workplace.

The cotton-mill economy grew largely in the Piedmont, the highland country of central Virginia and northern Georgia and Alabama. The Piedmont had long been the South's backcountry. But postwar railroad construction opened the region to textile-mill expansion. By 1920, the South was the nation's leading textile-mill center. Augusta, Georgia, with 2,800 mill workers, became known as the Lowell of the South, named after the mill town in Massachusetts where industrialization had flourished earlier.

Sharecroppers and tenant farmers at first hailed the new cotton mills as a way out of rural poverty. But appearances were deceptive. The chief cotton-mill promoters were drawn from the same ranks of merchants, lawyers, doctors, and bankers who had profited from the commercialization of southern agriculture. Cotton-mill entrepreneurs shamelessly exploited their workers, paying just seven to eleven cents an hour, 30 percent to 50 percent less than what comparable mill workers in New England were paid.

The mills dominated most Piedmont textile communities. The mill operator not only built and owned the workers' housing and the company store but also supported the village church, financed the local elementary school, and pried into the morals and behavior of the mill hands. Because they were often paid in scrip—a certificate redeemable only in goods from the company store—workers frequently were drawn into a cycle of indebtedness like that faced by sharecroppers.

To help make ends meet, mill workers kept their own garden patches and raised chickens, cows, and pigs. Southern mill hands thus brought communal farm values, long associated with large farm families and nurtured through cooperative planting and harvesting, into the mills themselves. This helped ease the shift from rural to village-industrial life.

As northern cotton mills did before the Civil War, southern textile companies exploited the cheap rural labor around them, settling transplanted farm people in paternalistic company-run villages. Using these tactics, the industry underwent a period of steady growth.

The Southern Industrial Lag

Industrialization occurred on a smaller scale and at a slower rate in the South than in the North and also depended far more on outside financing, technology, and expertise. The late-nineteenth-century southern economy remained essentially in a colonial status, subject to domination by northern industries and financial syndicates.

An array of factors thus combined to retard industrialization in the South. Banking regulations requiring large reserves, scarce capital, absentee ownership, wartime debts, lack of industrial experience, a segregated labor force, discrimination against blacks, and control by profit-hungry northern enterprises all hampered the region's economic development. Dragged down by a poorly educated white population as well as a largely unskilled black population, southern industry languished.

As in the North, industrialization brought significant environmental damage, including polluted rivers and streams, decimated forests, grimy coal-mining towns, and soot-infested cities. Although Henry Grady's vision of a New South may have inspired many southerners to work toward industrialization, economic growth in the South, limited as it was by outside forces, progressed in its own distinctly regional way.

CHECKING IN

- Lack of capital proved to be a major obstacle to southern industrialization.
- An underfunded, poorly attended public education system became another impediment to the industrialization of the South.
- Proponents of the New South creed urged industrialization, with some success.
- Cotton textile mills blossomed across the South from the 1880s onward.
- Despite such advances, the South lagged far behind the rest of the nation in industrialization and economic development.

FACTORIES AND THE WORK FORCE

How did the changing nature of work affect factory workers' lives, and how did they respond?

Industrialization proceeded unevenly nationwide, and most late-nineteenth-century Americans still worked in small shops. But as the century unfolded, large factories with armies of workers sprang onto the industrial scene in more and more locales. The pattern of change was evident. Between 1860 and 1900, the number of industrial workers jumped from 885,000 to 3.2 million, and the trend toward large-scale production became unmistakable.

From Workshop to Factory

The transition to a factory economy came not as an earthquake but rather as a series of seismic jolts varying in strength and duration. Changes in factory production had a profound impact on artisans and unskilled laborers alike. The impact of these changes can be seen by examining the shoe industry. As late as the 1840s, almost every shoe was custom-made by a skilled artisan who worked in a small, independent shop. Shoemakers were aristocrats in the world of labor. They took pride in their work and controlled the quality of their products.

A distinctive working-class culture subdivided along ethnic lines evolved among these shoemakers. Foreign-born English, German, and Irish workers set up ethnic trade organizations and joined affiliated benevolent associations. Bound together by religious and ethnic ties, they observed weddings and funerals according to old-country traditions and relaxed together at the local saloon after work.

As early as the 1850s, changes in the ready-made shoe trade had eroded the status of skilled labor. The manufacturing process was broken down into a sequence of repetitive, easily mastered tasks. Thus, instead of crafting a pair of shoes from start to finish, each team member specialized in only one part of the process, such as attaching the heel or polishing the leather.

In the 1880s, shoe factories became larger and more mechanized, and traditional skills largely vanished. Shoe companies replaced skilled operatives with lower-paid, less-skilled women and children. By 1890, women made up more than 35 percent of the work force. Like the laborer whose machine nailed heels on 4,800 shoes a day, even "skilled" workers in the new factories found themselves performing numbingly repetitive tasks.

The Hardships of Industrial Labor

The expansion of the factory system spawned an unprecedented demand for unskilled labor. By the 1880s nearly one-third of the 750,000 workers employed in the railroad and steel industries, for example, were common laborers. In the construction trades and the garment-making industries, the services of unskilled laborers were procured under the so-called contract system. Large companies negotiated an agreement with a subcontractor who supervised gangs of unskilled day laborers; these laborers were hired in times of need and laid off in slack periods.

Notoriously transient, unskilled laborers drifted from city to city and from industry to industry. In the late 1870s unskilled laborers earned $1.30 a day, while bricklayers and blacksmiths earned more than $3. Only unskilled southern mill workers, whose wages averaged a meager eighty-four cents a day, earned less.

Unskilled and skilled workers alike not only worked up to twelve-hour shifts but also faced grave hazards to their health and safety. Children were the most vulnerable. In the coal mines and cotton mills, child laborers typically entered the work force at age eight or nine. In the cotton mills, children could be injured by the unprotected pulley belts that powered the machines. In the coal industry, where children were commonly employed to remove pieces of slate from the conveyor belts, the cloud of coal dust that swirled around them gave them black lung disease—a disorder that led to emphysema and heart failure.

Library of Congress

Textile Workers

Young children like this one often were used in the textile mills because their small fingers could tie together broken threads more easily than those of adults.

For adult workers, the railroad industry was one of the most perilous. In 1889, the first year that the Interstate Commerce Commission compiled reliable statistics, almost two thousand rail workers were killed on the job and more than twenty thousand injured. Disabled workers and widows received minimal financial aid from employers. When a worker was killed or maimed in an accident, the family depended on minimal payouts from their fraternal organizations—or more commonly, the kindness of relatives or friends—for support.

Immigrant Labor

As we shall see in more detail in Chapter 19, factory owners turned to unskilled immigrant workers for the muscle they needed. Despite the hazardous conditions they found in the factories, those immigrants who were disposed to work an eighty-four-hour week could save fifteen dollars a month, far more than they could have earned in their homeland.

Although most immigrants worked hard, few adjusted easily to the fast pace of the factory. Peasants from southern and eastern Europe found it difficult to abandon their seasonal work habits for rigid factory schedules. Factory operations were relentless, dictated by the unvarying speed of the machines. Employers used a variety of tactics to enforce discipline. Some sponsored temperance societies and Sunday schools to teach punctuality and sobriety. Others cut wages and put workers on the piecework system, paying them only for the items produced. Employers sometimes also provided low-cost housing to gain leverage against work stoppages; if workers went on strike, the boss could simply evict them.

In the case of immigrants from southern Europe whose skin colors were often darker than northern Europeans', employers asserted that the workers were non-white and thus did not deserve the same compensation as native-born Americans. Rather than being a fixed category based on biological differences, the concept of "whiteness" was thus used to justify the harsh treatment of foreign-born labor.

Women and Work in Industrial America

Women's work experiences, like those of men, were shaped by marital status, social class, and race. Upper-class white married women widely accepted an ideology of "separate spheres" (see Chapter 19) and remained at home, raised children, and looked after the household. The well-to-do hired maids and cooks to ease their burdens.

Working-class married women, in contrast, also often had to contribute to the financial support of the family. In fact, working for wages at home by sewing, button-making, taking in boarders, or doing laundry had predated industrialization. In the late nineteenth century, unscrupulous urban entrepreneurs exploited this captive work force. In the clothing industry, manufacturers hired out finishing tasks to lower-class married women and their children, who labored long hours in crowded apartments.

Young, working-class single women often viewed factory work as an opportunity. In 1870, 13 percent of all women worked outside the home, the majority as cooks, maids, cleaning ladies, and laundresses. But most working women intensely disliked the long hours, low pay, and social stigma of being a "servant." Between 1870 and 1900, the number of women working outside the home nearly tripled.

A variety of factors propelled the rise in the employment of single women. Changes in agriculture prompted many young farm women to seek employment in the industrial sector. Plant managers welcomed young immigrant women as a ready source of inexpensive unskilled labor. But factory owners treated them as temporary help and kept their wages low. In 1890, young women operating sewing machines earned as little as four dollars for seventy hours of work while their male counterparts made eight. Far from fostering economic independence, therefore, industrial work tied women more deeply to a family economy that depended on their earnings.

When the typewriter and the telephone came into general use in the 1890s, office work provided new employment opportunities. Women were attracted by the clean, safe working conditions and relatively good pay. First-rate typists could earn six to eight dollars a week, which compared favorably with factory wages. Office work carried higher prestige and was generally steadier than work in the factory or shop.

Despite the growing number of women workers, the late-nineteenth-century popular press portrayed women's work outside the home as temporary. Few people even considered the possibility that a woman could attain prominence in the emerging corporate order.

Hard Work and the Gospel of Success

Although women were generally excluded from the equation, influential opinion molders in these years preached that any man could achieve success in the new industrial era. In *Ragged Dick* (1867) and scores of later tales, **Horatio Alger,** a Unitarian minister turned dime novelist, recounted the adventures of poor but honest lads who rose through initiative and self-discipline. The career of Andrew Carnegie was often offered as proof that the United States remained the land of opportunity and "rags to riches."

Horatio Alger Author of more than one hundred "rags to riches" books for boys

Some critics did not accept this belief. In an 1871 essay, Mark Twain chided the public for its naïveté and suggested that business success was more likely to come to those who lied and cheated. What are the facts? Carnegie's rise from abject poverty to colossal wealth was the rare exception, as studies of nearly two hundred of the largest corporations reveal. Ninety-five percent of the industrial leaders came from middle- and upper-class backgrounds. The best chance of success for immigrants and native-born working-class Americans was in mastering a skill and rising to the top of a small company. Although only a few reaped immense fortunes, many improved their standard of living.

Thus, while some skilled workers became owners of their own companies, the opportunities for advancement for unskilled immigrant workers were considerably more limited. Some did move to semiskilled or skilled positions; yet, most immigrants, particularly the Irish, Italians, and Chinese, moved far more slowly than the sons of middle- and upper-class Americans who began with greater educational advantages and family financial backing. The upward mobility possible for such unskilled workers was generally mobility within the working class. Immigrants who got ahead in the late nineteenth century went from rags to respectability, not rags to riches.

One positive economic trend in these years was the rise in real wages, representing gains in actual buying power. Average real wages climbed 31 percent for unskilled workers and 74 percent for skilled workers between 1860 and 1900. Overall gains in purchasing power, however, were often undercut by injuries and unemployment during slack times or economic slumps. During the depressions of the 1870s and 1890s, wage cuts, extended layoffs, and irregular employment pushed those at the bottom of the industrial work force to the brink of starvation.

Thus, the overall picture of late-nineteenth-century economic mobility was complex. At the top of the scale, a mere 10 percent of American families owned 73 percent of the nation's wealth in 1890, while less than half of industrial laborers earned more than the five-hundred-dollar poverty

CHECKING IN

- Factory work was a numbing routine with no place for skilled workers.
- Unskilled workers received low pay for long hours and labored under hazardous conditions; children as young as eight worked in coal mines and cotton mills.
- Immigrants, the mainstay of the industrial labor force, answered the need for unskilled labor and were often paid less than native-born workers.
- Women entered the industrial work force through the longstanding practice of working at home for wages; many single women moved into the factory work force and then into office jobs.
- Reality often contradicted the "rags to riches" mythology, as most industrial laborers frequently confronted poverty.

line annually. In between the very rich and the very poor, skilled immigrants and small shopkeepers improved their economic position significantly. So although the standard of living for millions of Americans rose, the gap between the poor and the well-off remained a yawning abyss.

LABOR UNIONS AND INDUSTRIAL CONFLICT

How did corporate executives undercut labor's bargaining power in the 1890s?

Aware that the growth of large corporations gave industrial leaders unprecedented power to control the workplace, labor leaders searched for ways to protect their members. But the drive to create a nationwide labor movement faced many problems. Employers deliberately accentuated ethnic and racial divisions within the work force. Skilled crafts workers, moreover, felt little kinship with low-paid common laborers. Thus, unionization efforts moved forward slowly and experienced setbacks.

Two groups, the National Labor Union and the Knights of Labor, struggled to build a mass labor movement that would unite skilled and unskilled workers. After impressive initial growth, however, both efforts collapsed. Far more effective was the American Federation of Labor (AFL), which represented skilled workers in powerful independent craft unions. The AFL survived and grew, but it represented only a small portion of the total labor force.

With unions weak, labor unrest during economic downturns reached crisis proportions. When pay rates were cut or working conditions became intolerable, laborers walked off the job without union authorization. These actions, called **wildcat strikes,** often exploded into violence. The bloody labor clashes of the 1890s would increase the demand for state regulation and eventually contribute to a movement for progressive reform.

wildcat strikes Spontaneous strikes not authorized by a labor union; some turned violent

Organizing Workers

From the eighteenth century on, skilled workers had organized trade unions to fight wage reductions and provide benefits for their members in times of illness or accident. But the effectiveness of these organizations was limited. The challenge that labor leaders faced in the postwar period was how to boost the unions' clout. Some believed that this goal could be achieved by forming one big association that would transcend craft lines and pull in the mass of unskilled workers.

In 1866, Philadelphia labor leader William H. Sylvis called a convention in Baltimore to form a new organization, the **National Labor Union (NLU).** The NLU endorsed the eight-hour-day movement, which insisted that labor deserved eight hours for work, eight hours for sleep, and eight hours for personal affairs. It also endorsed immigration restriction, especially of Chinese migrants, whom native-born workers blamed for undercutting prevailing wage levels. The NLU supported the cause of working women and urged black workers to organize as well, though in racially separate unions.

National Labor Union (NLU) Early attempt to establish a single national union

When Sylvis's own union failed to win a strike in 1867 to improve wages, Sylvis turned to national political reform. He invited a number of reformers to the 1868 NLU convention, including woman suffrage advocates Susan B. Anthony and Elizabeth Cady Stanton. But when Sylvis suddenly died in 1869, the NLU faded quickly.

Knights of Labor Organization that took up where the NLU left off; enjoyed considerable success for a while

The dream of a labor movement that combined skilled and unskilled workers lived on in a new organization, the **Knights of Labor,** which was founded in 1869. Led by Uriah H. Stephens of Philadelphia, the Knights welcomed all wage earners. The Knights demanded equal pay for women, an end to child labor and convict labor, and the cooperative employer-employee ownership of factories, mines, and other businesses. At a time when no federal income tax existed, they called for a progressive tax on all earnings, graduated so that higher-income earners would pay more.

The Knights grew slowly at first. But membership rocketed in the 1880s after the eloquent Terence V. Powderly replaced Stephens as the organization's head. In the early 1880s, the Knights of Labor reflected both its idealistic origins and Powderly's collaborative vision. Powderly opposed strikes and urged temperance upon the membership. Powderly advocated the admission of blacks into local Knights of Labor assemblies, although he allowed southern local assemblies to be segregated. The Knights welcomed women members; by 1886, women made up an estimated 10 percent of the union's membership.

Powderly supported restrictions on immigration and a total ban on Chinese immigration. In 1877, San Francisco workers demonstrating for an eight-hour work day destroyed twenty-five Chinese-run laundries. In 1880, both major party platforms included anti-Chinese immigration plans. Two years later, Congress passed the Chinese Exclusion Act, placing a ten-year moratorium on Chinese immigration. The ban was extended in 1902 and not repealed until 1943.

Powderly's greatest triumph came in 1885. In that year, Jay Gould tried to get rid of the Knights of Labor on his Wabash railroad by firing active union members. Powderly instructed all Knights on the Wabash line to walk off the job and those on other lines to refuse to handle Wabash cars. This action crippled Wabash's operations. To the nation's amazement, Gould met with Powderly and canceled his campaign against the Knights of Labor.

Membership in the Knights of Labor soared. By 1886, more than seven hundred thousand workers were organized in nearly six thousand locals. The Knights mounted campaigns in nearly two hundred towns and cities nationwide that fall, electing several mayors and judges. Business executives warned that the Knights could cripple the economy and take over the country if they chose.

However, the organization's strength soon waned. Workers became disillusioned when a series of unauthorized strikes failed in 1886. By the late 1880s, the Knights of Labor was a shadow of its former self. Nevertheless, the organization had awakened in thousands of workers a sense of group solidarity and potential strength.

As the Knights of Labor declined, another national labor organization, pursuing more immediate and practical goals, was gaining strength. The skilled craft unions had long been uncomfortable with labor organizations like the Knights that welcomed skilled and unskilled alike. They were also concerned that the Knights' broad reform goals would undercut the interests of their particular crafts. The break came in May 1886 when the craft unions left the Knights of Labor to form the **American Federation of Labor (AFL).**

American Federation of Labor (AFL) Skilled craft unions united under the leadership of Samuel Gompers

The AFL replaced the Knights' grand visions with practical tactics aimed at bread-and-butter issues. **Samuel Gompers,** the immigrant cigar maker who became head of the AFL in 1886 and led it until his death in 1924, believed in "trade unionism, pure and simple." Gompers argued that if labor were to stand up to the corporations, it would have to harness the bargaining power of skilled workers and concentrate on the practical goals of raising wages and reducing hours.

To persuade workers from the various trades to join forces without violating their sense of craft autonomy, Gompers organized the AFL as a federation of trade unions, each retaining control of its own members but all linked by an executive council that coordinated strategy during boycotts and strike actions.

Gompers at first sidestepped divisive political issues. The new organization's platform did, however, demand an eight-hour workday, employers' liability for workers' injuries, and mine safety laws. The AFL did little to recruit women workers after 1894 because Gompers and others believed that women workers undercut men's wages. By 1904, the AFL had grown to more than 1.6 million strong.

Library of Congress

Ethnic and Racial Hatred
Conservative business owners used racist advertising, such as this trade card stigmatizing Chinese laundry workers, to promote their own products and to associate their company with patriotism.

Despite these advances, labor organizations before 1900 remained weak. Less than 5 percent of the work force joined union ranks. Split between skilled artisans and common laborers, separated along ethnic and religious lines, and divided over tactics, the unions battled with only occasional effectiveness against the growing power of corporate enterprise. They typically watched from the sidelines when unorganized workers launched wildcat strikes that sometimes turned violent.

Samuel Gompers AFL leader who focused on practical goals like wages, hours, and working conditions

Strikes and Labor Violence

Americans had lived with a high level of violence from the nation's beginnings. Terrible labor clashes toward the end of the century were part of this continuing pattern, but they nevertheless shocked and dismayed contemporaries. From 1881 to 1905, close to 37,000 strikes erupted, in which nearly 7 million workers participated.

The first major wave of strikes began in 1873 when a Wall Street crash triggered a major depression. The tension turned deadly in 1877 during a wildcat railroad strike. Ignited by a wage reduction on the Baltimore and Ohio Railroad in July, the strike spread across the country. Rioters in Pittsburgh torched Union Depot. By the time troops could arrive to quell the strike two weeks later, nearly one hundred people had died, and two-thirds of the nation's railroads stood idle.

The railroad strike stunned middle-class America. The same Americans who worried about Jay Gould and the corporate abuse of power grew terrified of mob violence. Employers capitalized on the public hysteria to crack down on labor. Many required their workers to sign "yellow dog" contracts in which they promised not to strike or join a union. Some hired Pinkerton agents, a private police force, to defend their factories and turned to the U.S. Army to suppress labor unrest.

Although the economy recovered, more strikes and violence followed in the 1880s. On May 1, 1886, 340,000 workers walked off their jobs in support of the campaign for an eight-hour workday. Three days later, Chicago police shot and killed four strikers at the McCormick Harvester plant. At a protest rally the next evening in the city's Haymarket Square, someone threw a bomb from a nearby building, killing or fatally wounding seven policemen. In response, the police fired wildly into the crowd and killed four demonstrators.

Public reaction was immediate. Business leaders and middle-class citizens lashed out at labor activists and particularly at the sponsors of the Haymarket meeting, most of whom were associated with a German-language anarchist newspaper. Eight men were arrested. Although no evidence connected them directly to the bomb throwing, all were convicted of murder, and four were executed. In Haymarket's aftermath, animosity toward labor unions intensified.

The events of 1892 amplified this trend. In one incident along Idaho's Coeur d'Alene (coor dah-LEEN) River, miners blew up a mill and captured the guards sent to defend it. Back east that same year, armed conflict broke out during the **Homestead Strike** at the Carnegie Steel Company plant in Homestead, Pennsylvania. To destroy the union, managers cut wages and locked out the workers. When workers fired on the armed men from the Pinkerton Detective Agency who came to protect the plant, a battle broke out. Seven union members and three Pinkertons died. A week later the governor sent National Guardsmen to restore order. With the union crushed, the mills resumed full operation a month later.

Homestead Strike Company lock-out that sparked a strike and violence at a Carnegie steel plant in 1892

The most systematic use of troops to smash union power came in 1894 during a strike against the Pullman Palace Car Company. In 1880 railroad car manufacturer George Pullman had constructed a factory and town, called Pullman, ten miles south of Chicago. When the depression of 1893 hit, he slashed workers' wages without reducing their rents. In reaction, thousands of workers joined the newly formed American Railway Union and went on strike. Led by their fiery young organizer, **Eugene V. Debs,** union members working for the nation's largest railroads refused to switch Pullman cars, paralyzing rail traffic in and out of Chicago.

Eugene V. Debs Union organizer, arrested as leader of the striking National Railway Union; would become a Socialist leader

In response, top railroad executives set out to break the union. They brought in strikebreakers and asked U.S. attorney general Richard Olney, who sat on the board of directors of three major railroad networks, for a federal injunction (court order) against the strikers for allegedly refusing to move railroad cars carrying U.S. mail. Olney, citing the Sherman Anti-Trust Act, secured an injunction against the union, arrested Debs, and sent federal troops in. During the ensuing riot, workers burned seven hundred freight cars, resulting in the deaths of thirteen people. By July 18 the strike had been crushed. In 1895, the U.S. Supreme Court upheld Debs's prison sentence and legalized the use of injunctions against labor unions (*In re Debs*).

Yet organizers persisted. In 1897, the feisty Irish-born Mary Harris Jones, known as Mother Jones, persuaded coal miners in Pennsylvania to join the United Mine

Workers of America. By 1900, their numbers had climbed to 300,000. However, despite the achievements of the United Mine Workers, the successive attempts by the National Labor Union, Knights of Labor, American Federation of Labor, and American Railway Union to build a national working-class labor movement achieved only limited success. Ineffective in the political arena, blocked by state officials, divided by ethnic differences, harassed by employers, and frustrated by court decisions, American unions failed to expand their base of support. Post–Civil War labor turmoil had given it a negative public image that it would not shed until the 1930s.

Social Thinkers Probe for Alternatives

Widespread violence sparked a new debate over the social meaning of the new industrial order. At stake was a larger issue: Should government become the mechanism for helping the poor and regulating big business?

Defenders of capitalism preached the laissez-faire (LESS-ay fare), or "hands-off," argument, insisting that government should never attempt to control business. In his essay "The Gospel of Wealth" (1889), Andrew Carnegie justified laissez-faire by applying the evolutionary theories of British social scientist Herbert Spencer to human society. "The law of competition," Carnegie argued, "may be sometimes hard for the individual, [but] it is best for the race, because it insures the survival of the fittest in every department."

Yale professor **William Graham Sumner** shared Carnegie's disapproval of government interference. His combative book *What Social Classes Owe to Each Other* (1883) applied the evolutionary theories of British naturalist Charles Darwin to human society. In an early statement of what became known as **Social Darwinism,** Sumner asserted that inexorable natural laws controlled the social order. The state, declared Sumner, owed its citizens nothing but law, order, and basic political rights. As to the question of whether society should help the less fortunate, Sumner wrote famously: "A drunkard in the gutter is just where he ought to be."

William Graham Sumner Tough-minded Yale professor and theorist of Social Darwinism

Social Darwinism Theory that "survival of the fittest" competition benefits society by weeding out the unfit

Sumner's argument did not go unchallenged. In *Dynamic Sociology* (1883), Lester Frank Ward, a geologist, argued that contrary to Sumner's claim, the supposed "laws" of nature could be circumvented by human will. Just as scientists had applied their knowledge to breeding superior livestock, government experts could use the power of the state to protect society's weaker members and prevent the heedless exploitation of natural resources.

Other social theorists offered more utopian solutions to the problems of poverty and social unrest. Henry George, a self-taught San Francisco newspaper editor and economic theorist, proposed to solve the nation's uneven distribution of wealth through what he called the single tax. In *Progress and Poverty* (1879), he argued that land should be taxed and the funds used to ameliorate the misery caused by industrialization. George's program was so popular that he only narrowly missed being elected mayor of New York in 1886.

The vision of a harmonious industrialized society was vividly expressed in the utopian novel *Looking Backward* (1888) by the Massachusetts newspaper editor Edward Bellamy. Cast as a glimpse into the future, Bellamy's novel envisioned a completely centralized, state-run economy and a prosperous society in which everyone works for the common welfare. Bellamy's vision so inspired middle-class Americans fearful of corporate power and working-class violence that nearly five hundred local Bellamyite organizations, called Nationalist clubs, sprang up to try to turn his dream into reality.

Ward, George, and Bellamy did not deny the benefits of the existing industrial order; they simply sought to humanize it. These utopian reformers envisioned a harmonious society whose members all worked together.

Marxism Belief that capitalism would inevitably destroy itself in a violent class struggle, thus paving the way for classless, communist utopia

Marxist socialists advanced a different view. Elaborated by the German philosopher and radical agitator Karl Marx (1818–1883) in *Das Kapital* (dass cop-ee-TALL) (1867) and other works, **Marxism** rested on the labor theory of value: a proposition that the labor required to produce a commodity was the only true measure of that commodity's value. Any profit made by the capitalist employer was "surplus value" appropriated from the exploited workers. The essence of modern history, according to Marx, was the class struggle between the bourgeoisie (capitalists) and the impoverished proletariat (the workers). The eventual victors of this revolutionary struggle, according to Marx, would be the workers. Their triumph would usher in a classless, communist utopia in which the state would "wither away" and all exploitation would cease.

Despite Marx's keen interest in the United States, Marxism proved to have little appeal in late-nineteenth-century America other than for a tiny group of primarily German-born immigrants. More alarming to the public at large was the handful of anarchists, again mostly immigrants, who rejected Marxist discipline and preached the destruction of capitalism, the violent overthrow of the state, and the immediate introduction of a stateless utopia. In 1892 an anarchist attempted to assassinate Henry Clay Frick, the manager of Andrew Carnegie's Homestead Steel Works. His act confirmed the business stereotype of "labor agitators" as lawless and violent.

CHECKING IN

- Early organizers attempted to create all-encompassing unions, such as the National Labor Union, with grand political aims.
- The Knights of Labor, which welcomed all workers, enjoyed considerable success but eventually fizzled.
- The more tightly focused craft union movement under AFL leader Samuel Gompers prospered by concentrating on lunchbox issues like wages.
- Violence, such as the Haymarket Square riot, turned many Americans against labor unions and made the use of violence against them seem acceptable.
- Ideas like Social Darwinism and the Gospel of Wealth clashed with the beliefs of those who criticized industrial society's excesses.

Chapter Summary

How did Carnegie, Rockefeller, and other corporate leaders consolidate control over their industries? (page 423)

Abundant resources and technological innovation combined with other factors to fuel industrial growth. Railroads pioneered new business techniques; Carnegie, Rockefeller, and others successfully transferred these techniques to other industries, such as steel and oil. Pools were created to limit competition but were replaced by more efficient trusts and, ultimately, holding companies, leading to huge corporations.

KEY TERMS

Jay Gould *(p. 424)*
Interstate Commerce Act *(p. 426)*
J. Pierpont Morgan *(p. 426)*
Andrew Carnegie *(p. 426)*
vertical integration *(p. 426)*
John D. Rockefeller *(p. 427)*
Standard Oil Trust *(p. 427)*

What innovations in technology and business drove increases in industrial production after 1865? (page 428)

Technology contributed new ways of manufacturing as well as new products to stimulate growth. Many inventions, such as the telephone and electric light bulb, changed daily life. Advertising and marketing stimulated demand for the growing output of products.

Why did the South's experience with industrialization differ from that of the North and the Midwest? (page 432)

Lack of capital and a poor education system hamstrung southern development. Major growth came with the establishment of cotton textile mills and a handful of heavy industries, such as steel, but the South lagged far behind the rest of the nation.

How did the changing nature of work affect factory workers' lives, and how did they respond? (page 434)

Factory work depended on unskilled workers who performed mind-numbing routine tasks, often hazardous, for low pay. Immigrants became the mainstay of the industrial work force, but children as young as eight worked in coal mines and cotton mills. Women worked out of their homes and entered both the factory and the office work force.

How did corporate executives undercut labor's bargaining power in the 1890s? (page 439)

Workers tried to create all-encompassing structures, such as the National Labor Union and the Knights of Labor, to protect workers' rights, but these attempts failed. The American Federation of Labor, focusing on skilled workers and practical issues, was far more successful. Violence flared when used by strikers and strikebreakers alike; governments generally were also willing to use violence against strikes. Social Darwinism and the Gospel of Wealth were attempts to explain and justify the harshness of the new industrial order, although a number of utopian thinkers, notably Marxists and anarchists, protested.

KEY TERMS continued

Sherman Anti-Trust Act *(p. 428)*
Thomas A. Edison *(p. 429)*
Henry W. Grady *(p. 432)*
Horatio Alger *(p. 438)*
wildcat strikes *(p. 439)*
National Labor Union (NLU) *(p. 439)*
Knights of Labor *(p. 440)*
American Federation of Labor (AFL) *(p. 440)*
Samuel Gompers *(p. 441)*
Homestead Strike *(p. 442)*
Eugene V. Debs *(p. 442)*
William Graham Sumner *(p. 443)*
Social Darwinism *(p. 443)*
Marxism *(p. 444)*

Go to the CourseMate website at **www.cengagebrain.com** for additional study tools and review materials—including audio and video clips—for this chapter.

Chapter 19

Immigration, Urbanization, and Everyday Life

1860–1900

Courtesy of George Eastman House, International Museum of Photography and Film

Backyard Baseball, Boston, 1906, by Lewis Hine

Chapter Preview

The New American City
How did the influx of immigrants before 1900 create an awareness of ethnic and class differences?

Middle- and Upper-Class Society and Culture
How did Victorian morality shape middle-class society and culture?

Reforming the Working Class
How did social and religious reformers address urban poverty?

Working-Class Leisure in the Immigrant City
How did the urban working class change attitudes toward leisure and recreation by 1900?

Cultures in Conflict
How did writers, artists, and educational reformers address issues of cultural conflict?

On a sweltering day in August 1899, **Scott Joplin,** a young black pianist, signed an unusual contract with his music publisher. Instead of receiving the usual one-time fee for his new composition, "Maple Leaf Rag," Joplin would earn one cent for every copy sold. The contract signaled a new era in the popular music industry. Over the next two decades, "Maple Leaf Rag" would sell more than half a million copies a year and make Joplin the king of ragtime, the syncopated dance music that had become a national sensation.

Scott Joplin Black composer who gained great popularity with a playful new musical style called ragtime

Joplin published more than seventy-five songs or piano rags before 1917. But his success was undercut by white competitors who stereotyped his compositions as "Negro music" and "Coon songs." His publishers refused to accept his classical compositions, including his opera *Treemonisha.* Opera was considered a high art form for the upper classes; blacks could not enter the field. As Joplin's experience revealed, racial discrimination could reinforce the barriers of social class.

Joplin's thwarted dreams were similar to those of countless others who tried to move up the economic ladder. American society was slowly shifting from a rural producer economy that stressed work and thrift to an urban consumer economy in which new forms of entertainment, leisure activities, and material possessions were becoming the hallmarks of personal identity. These changes, together with the expansion of salaried, white-collar occupations such as teaching and accounting, fostered growing class awareness.

Nowhere were class divisions more visible than in the cities crowded with immigrants, where the working class created its own vigorous culture of dance halls, saloons, vaudeville theaters, social clubs, and amusement parks. Middle-class reformers who strove to remake this working-class culture into their own image of propriety were soon frustrated. In the long run, the culture of the masses would prove more influential in shaping modern America.

THE NEW AMERICAN CITY

How did the influx of immigrants before 1900 create an awareness of ethnic and class differences?

Everyday life was transformed most dramatically and visibly in cities. Between 1870 and 1900 New Orleans's population nearly doubled, Buffalo's tripled, and Chicago's increased more than fivefold. By 1900, Philadelphia, New York, and Chicago all had more than a million residents, and 40 percent of all Americans lived in cities (see Table 19.1).

This spectacular urban growth, fueled by migration from the countryside and the arrival of nearly 11 million immigrants between 1870 and 1900, stimulated economic development. Like the frontier, the city symbolized opportunity for all comers.

The city's unprecedented scale and diversity threatened traditional expectations of community life and social stability. Rural America had been a place of face-to-face personal relations. In contrast, the city was a seething caldron where immigrant groups contended with one another and with native-born Americans for jobs, power, and influence. Moreover, rapid growth strained city services, generating terrible housing and sanitation problems.

Native-born American city-dwellers complained about the noise, stench, and congestion of this transformed cityscape. They fretted about the newcomers' squalid tenements, fondness for drink, and strange social customs. When native-born reformers set about cleaning up the city, they sought not only to improve the physical environment but also to destroy the distinctive customs that made immigrant cultures different from their own. The late nineteenth century thus witnessed an intense struggle to control the city and to benefit from its economic and cultural potential.

TABLE 19.1 URBAN GROWTH: 1870–1900

CITY	1870 POPULATION	1900 POPULATION	PERCENT INCREASE
Boston	250,525	560,892	123.88
Chicago	298,977	1,698,575	468.12
Los Angeles	5,728	102,479	1,689.08
Milwaukee	71,440	285,315	299.37
New Orleans	191,418	287,104	49.98
New York	1,478,103	3,437,202	132.54
Philadelphia	647,022	1,293,697	99.94
Pittsburgh	86,076	321,616	273.64
Portland	8,293	90,426	990.38
Richmond	51,038	85,050	66.64
San Francisco	149,473	342,782	129.32
Seattle	1,107	237,194	21,326.73

Source: Thirteenth Census of the United States (Washington, DC: U.S. Government Printing Office, 1913).

Migrants and Immigrants

The concentration of industries in urban settings produced demands for thousands of new workers. The promise of good wages and a broad range of jobs drew men and women from the countryside. So great was the migration from rural areas, especially New England, that some farm communities vanished from the map.

Young farmwomen led the exodus to the cities. With the growing mechanization of farming in the late nineteenth century, farming was increasingly male work. Rising sales of factory-produced goods through nationally distributed mail-order catalogs reduced the need for rural women's labor. Therefore, young farmwomen flocked to the cities, where they competed for jobs with immigrant, black, and city-born white women.

From 1860 to 1890, the prospect of a better life also attracted nearly 10 million northern European immigrants to American cities. Their numbers included 3 million Germans; 2 million English, Scottish, and Welsh; and 1.5 million Irish. By 1900, more than 800,000 French-Canadians had entered the New England mills, and close to a million Scandinavian newcomers had put down roots in the rich farmlands of Wisconsin and Minnesota.

new immigrants Wave of immigrants after 1880 coming mainly from southern and eastern Europe

In the 1890s, these earlier immigrants from northern and western Europe were joined by swelling numbers of **"new immigrants"**—Italians, Slavs, Greeks, and Jews from southern and eastern Europe, Armenians from the Middle East, and, in Hawaii, Japanese from Asia. In the next three decades, these new immigrants, many from peasant backgrounds, would boost America's foreign-born population by more than 18 million.

The overwhelming majority of both old and new immigrants settled in cities in the northeastern and north-central states. The effect of their numbers was

Chronology

1865	Vassar College founded
1869	First intercollegiate football game
1872	Anthony Comstock founds New York Society for the Suppression of Vice
1873	John Wanamaker opens his Philadelphia department store
1876	National League of baseball organized
1880	William Booth's followers establish an American branch of the Salvation Army
1881	Josephine Shaw Lowell founds New York Charity Organization Society (COS)
1884	Mark Twain, *Huckleberry Finn*
1889	Jane Addams and Ellen Gates Starr open Hull House
1891	University of Chicago founded; basketball invented at Springfield College, Massachusetts
1892	Ellis Island Immigration Center opened; General Federation of Women's Clubs organized
1895	Coney Island amusement parks open in Brooklyn, New York
1899	Scott Joplin, "Maple Leaf Rag"; Kate Chopin, *The Awakening;* Thorstein Veblen, *The Theory of the Leisure Class*
1900	Theodore Dreiser, *Sister Carrie;* National Association of Colored Women's Clubs organized
1910	Angel Island Immigration Center opens in San Francisco

staggering. In 1890 New York City contained twice as many Irish as Dublin, as many Germans as Hamburg, half as many Italians as Naples, and two and a half times the Jewish population of Warsaw. Four out of five people in New York City had been born abroad or were children of foreign-born parents (see Map 19.1).

Overpopulation, crop failure, famine, religious persecution, or industrial depression had driven some of these immigrants from their homelands. At the same time, the promise of high wages lured more than 100,000 Japanese to work on Hawaiian sugar plantations. Many people, especially single young men, immigrated in the belief that the United States held a better future than their homeland. Wives and children waited in the old country until the family breadwinner had secured a job and saved enough money to pay for their passage to America.

The transatlantic journey, cramped and often stormy, featured poor food, little privacy, and rudimentary sanitary facilities. Immigrants arrived tired, fearful, and in some cases sick. Then customs officials examined them for physical handicaps and contagious diseases. After 1892, those with "loathsome" infections such as leprosy or a sexually transmitted disease were refused admittance and deported. Immigrants who passed the physical examination had their names recorded. If a customs official had difficulty pronouncing a foreign name, he often Anglicized it. One German Jew became flustered when asked for his name and mumbled, "Schoyn vergessen [I forget]." The inspector, who did not know Yiddish, wrote, "Sean Ferguson."

In 1892, the federal government built a new immigration facility on **Ellis Island** in New York harbor. Angel Island in San Francisco Bay on the West Coast served a similar purpose after 1910. At the immigrant processing centers, America's newest residents exchanged foreign currency for U.S. dollars, purchased railroad tickets, and

Ellis Island Immigrant processing center in New York City harbor through which millions passed

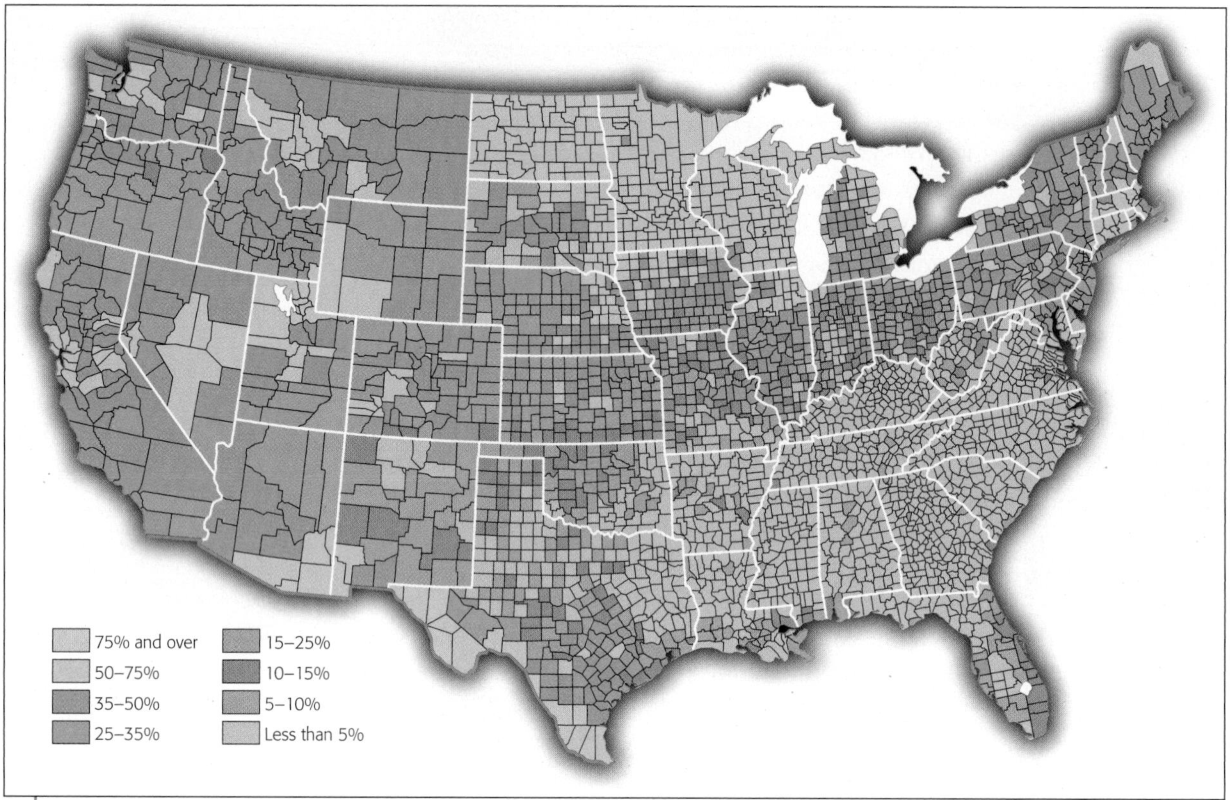

75% and over
50–75%
35–50%
25–35%
15–25%
10–15%
5–10%
Less than 5%

Map 19.1 Percent of Foreign-Born Whites and Native Whites of Foreign or Mixed Parentage in Total Population, by Counties, 1910

As this map indicates, new immigrants rarely settled in the South.

arranged lodgings. Those who arrived with enough cash, including many Germans and Scandinavians, commonly traveled west to Chicago, Milwaukee, and the rolling prairies beyond. Most of the Irish, and later the Italians, remained in eastern cities like Boston, New York, and Philadelphia.

Adjusting to an Urban Society

In the cities, immigrants tended to cluster together to ease the transition to life in a new society. In 1890 a reporter observed that, if a map of New York City's streets were colored in by nationality, it "would show more stripes than on the skin of a zebra, and more colors than any rainbow."

Some immigrant groups adjusted more easily than others. Skilled workers and those familiar with Anglo-American customs had relatively few problems. Ethnic groups that formed a substantial percentage of a city's population also had a major advantage. The Irish of Boston, New York, and Chicago, as well as the Germans of Milwaukee, dominated Democratic Party politics and controlled the hierarchy of the

Catholic church. Because of their success, upwardly mobile Irish became known as "lace curtain" Irish, a reference to their adoption of middle-class ideals.

The domination of urban institutions by one immigrant group, however, often made adjustment to American society more difficult for others. English and German dominance of the building trades, for example, enabled those nationalities to limit the numbers of Italians hired. Also, not all immigrants intended to remain in the United States. Expecting only a brief stay, some made little effort to learn English or understand American customs. Of the Italians who immigrated to New York before 1914, nearly 50 percent went back to Italy.

However, most immigrants stayed. As the number of foreigners in U.S. cities ballooned toward the turn of the century, all immigrant groups faced increasing hostility from white native-born Americans who disliked the newcomers' social customs and worried about their growing influence. Fearing the loss of the privileges and status that were associated with their white skin color, native-born whites often stigmatized immigrants as racially different and inferior. Only gradually, and with much effort, did Irish, Jews, Slavs, and Italians come to be considered "white."

Slums and Ghettos

Every major city had run-down, overcrowded slum neighborhoods, created when landlords subdivided old buildings and packed in too many residents. The poorer the renters, the worse the slums. Slums became ghettos when laws, prejudice, and community pressure prevented inhabitants from moving out. During the 1890s, Italians in New York City, blacks in Philadelphia and Chicago, Mexicans in Los Angeles, and Chinese in San Francisco increasingly became locked into segregated ghettos.

Life in the slums was particularly difficult for children. Juvenile diseases, such as whooping cough, measles, and scarlet fever, took a fearful toll, and infant mortality was high. In one immigrant ward in Chicago in 1900, 20 percent of infants died in their first year.

Because tenements often bordered industrial districts, residents had to put up with the noise, pollution, and foul odors of foundries, factories, and packing houses. Coal-fired steam engines and apartment house furnaces produced vast quantities of soot and dust that tinged the atmosphere a hazy gray and coated buildings with a grimy patina.

Most immigrants stayed in the shabbiest tenements only until they could afford better housing. Blacks, in contrast, were trapped in segregated districts. Driven out of the skilled trades and excluded from most factory work, blacks took menial jobs whose low pay left them little income for housing. Racist city-dwellers used high rents, real-estate covenants (agreements not to rent or sell to blacks), and neighborhood pressure to exclude them from areas inhabited by whites. Nevertheless, as **W. E. B. Du Bois,** a black sociologist, pointed out in *The Philadelphia Negro* (1899), wealthy black entrepreneurs within these neighborhoods built their own churches, ran successful businesses, and established charitable organizations to help their people.

W. E. B. Du Bois Black sociologist, later one of the founders of the NAACP

Fashionable Avenues and Suburbs

The same cities that harbored slums, suffering, and violence also boasted neighborhoods of dazzling opulence. The wealthy built monumental residences on exclusive thoroughfares just outside the downtown, among them Fifth Avenue in New York, Commonwealth Avenue in Boston, and Euclid (YOO-clid) Avenue in Cleveland.

In the 1870s and 1880s, those who could afford it began moving to nearby suburbs. Promoters of the suburban ideal contrasted the rolling lawns and stately houses on the city's periphery with the teeming streets, noisy saloons, and mounds of garbage and horse excrement downtown. Soon, many major cities could boast of their own stylish suburbs.

Middle-class city-dwellers followed the precedents set by the wealthy. Skilled artisans, shopkeepers, clerks, accountants, and sales personnel moved either to new developments at the city's edge or to outlying suburban communities. Lawyers, doctors, small businessmen, and other professionals moved farther out along the main thoroughfares served by the street railway and purchased homes with large lots.

A pattern of informal residential segregation by income took shape in the cities and suburbs. Built for families of a particular income level, certain city neighborhoods and suburbs developed remarkably similar internal standards for lot size and house design. Commuters who rode the new street railways out from the city center could identify the changing neighborhoods along the way as readily as a geologist might distinguish different strata on a washed-out riverbank. And with the physical change in American cities came a new awareness of class and cultural disparities.

CHECKING IN

- From 1870 to 1900, 11 million immigrants flooded into American cities.
- Native-born Americans disliked and feared these "new immigrants."
- The majority of immigrants crammed into tenements and slums.
- Wealthy city-dwellers created fashionable avenues as havens, while the middle class moved to the suburbs.
- These physical changes in cities created a new awareness of cultural and class differences.

MIDDLE- AND UPPER-CLASS SOCIETY AND CULTURE

How did Victorian morality shape middle-class society and culture?

Spared the struggle for survival that confronted most Americans, society's middle and upper ranks faced a different challenge: how to rationalize their enjoyment of the products of the emerging consumer society. To justify the position of society's wealthiest members, ministers and advice-book writers appealed to **Victorian morality,** a set of social ideas influential among the privileged classes of England and America during the reign (1837–1901) of Britain's Queen Victoria.

Victorian morality Strict code of gentility that permeated late-nineteenth-century society

Proponents of Victorian morality argued that the success of the middle and upper classes rested on their superior talent, intelligence, morality, and self-control. Women were identified as the driving force for moral improvement. While men were expected to engage in self-disciplined, "manly" dedication to the new industrial order, women would provide the gentle, elevating influence that would lead society in its upward march.

Manners and Morals

Several fundamental assumptions shaped the Victorian worldview. First, human nature was malleable; people could improve themselves. Second, work had social value: Working hard not only developed self-discipline but also helped advance the progress of the nation. Finally, good manners and the cultivation of literature and art ennobled society. Although these genteel assumptions were sometimes ignored, they were held up as universal standards.

Victorian morality stressed the importance of manners and social rituals. Behavior as well as income defined social standing. Good manners, including knowledge of dining and entertaining etiquette, and good posture became important marks of status. Meals became important rituals that differentiated the social classes. Meals presented occasions for displaying a family's proper manners and elaborate silver and china, regarded as symbols of refinement and sophistication.

The Victorian code—with its emphasis on morals, manners, and proper behavior—thus heightened the sense of class differences and created visible distinctions among social groups. Victorian Americans made bold claims about their interest in helping others improve themselves. More often than not, however, their self-righteous, intensely moralistic outlook simply widened the gap that income disparities had already opened.

The Cult of Domesticity

Victorian views on morality and culture, coupled with the need to make decisions about a mountain of domestic products, had a subtle but important impact on middle-class expectations about a woman's role within the home. From the 1840s onward, the home had been idealized as "the woman's sphere," a protected retreat where she could express her special maternal gifts, including a sensitivity toward children and an aptitude for religion.

During the 1880s and 1890s, Victorian advocates of the cult of domesticity added a new obligation to foster an artistic environment that would nurture her family's cultural improvement. Houses became statements of cultural aspiration with front parlors cluttered with artwork and curiosities. Excluded from the world of business and commerce, women directed their energy to transforming their homes into "a place of repose, a refuge from the excitement and distractions of outside . . . , provided with every attainable means of rest and recreation."

Not all middle-class women pursued this domestic ideal, however. For some, the drudgery of housework and of running the family overwhelmed any concern for artistic accomplishment. For others, the artistic ideal itself was not to their taste. In the 1880s and 1890s,

JUST BEFORE THE CHRISTMAS HOLIDAYS—SATURDAY AFTERNOON ON SIXTH AVENUE, IN THE HEART OF THE WEST-SIDE SHOPPING DISTRICT, NEW YORK CITY.

New-York Historical Society

Saturday on Sixth Avenue, 1897

Large department stores, located on fashionable city avenues, turned shopping into a social activity that telegraphed one's social status. To return home, the wealthy took horse-drawn cabs rather than the elevated trains.

as women sought other outlets for their creative energies in settlement-house work, social reform, and women's club activities, the older domestic ideal began to unravel.

Department Stores

Although Victorian thought justified the privileges of the well-to-do, many people found it difficult to shake the thriftiness of their early years and accept the new preoccupation with accumulation and display. In the 1880s merchandisers encouraged Americans to loosen their purse strings and enjoy prosperity by emphasizing the high quality and low cost of their goods.

department store Emporium dedicated to convincing middle- and upper-class women that consumption was attractive and respectable

Department stores set the standard for consumption. In the final quarter of the nineteenth century, entrepreneurs like Roland Macy, John Wanamaker, and Marshall Field built giant department stores that transformed the shopping experience for their middle- and upper-class patrons. The merchants overcame reluctance to spend by advertising "rock-bottom" prices and by making shopping an exciting activity. Rapid turnover of merchandise created a sense of constant novelty. With stained-glass skylights, marble staircases, sparkling chandeliers, and plush carpets, the large urban department store functioned as a social club for comfortably fixed women. For those who could afford it, shopping became an adventure, a form of entertainment, and a way to affirm their place in society.

The Transformation of Higher Education

At a time when relatively few Americans possessed even a high-school education, colleges and universities represented another stronghold of the business and professional elite. Wealthy capitalists gained stature and a measure of immortality by endowing colleges and universities. Leland Stanford and his wife, Jane Lathrop Stanford, launched Stanford University in 1885 with a bequest of $24 million; John D. Rockefeller donated $34 million to the University of Chicago in 1891. Industrialists and businessmen dominated the boards of trustees of most educational institutions.

Courtesy, The Winterthur Library: The John and Carolyn Grossman Collection

Cigar-Box Label, c. 1910

Vassar College, founded in 1865, promoted the new image of womanhood by stressing the interconnections among education, athletics, and ethics.

The athletic field as well as the classroom prepared affluent young men for business and the professions. Football, adapted from English rugby, became an elite sport played by college teams. But the game, initially played without pads or helmets, was marred by violence. In 1905, eighteen students died of playing-field injuries. Many college presidents dismissed football as a dangerous waste of time and money, but eager alumni and coaches strongly defended the new sport. Some praised it as a character-building activity that could function as a surrogate frontier experience in an increasingly urbanized society. By 1900, collegiate football had become a popular fall ritual, and team captains were campus heroes.

More than 150 new public, private, and religiously affiliated colleges and universities appeared between 1880 and 1900, and enrollments more than doubled. Coeducational private colleges and public universities enrolled increasing numbers of women. Some colleges—for instance, Vassar (1865) and Bryn Mawr (1884)—were founded solely for women. At these institutions, women developed the self-confidence to break with the Victorian ideal of passive womanhood and to compete with men by displaying strength, aggressiveness, and intelligence—popularly considered male attributes. By the turn of the century, women made up more than one-third of the total college-student population.

research university New type of school offering a wide variety of subjects, encouraging research

Innovative presidents such as Cornell's Andrew D. White and Harvard's Charles W. Eliot sought to change the focus of higher education. The change was most evident in medical education. Using the experimental method developed by German scientists, American medical professors insisted that all medical students be trained in biology, chemistry, and physics, including working in a laboratory. New educational and professional standards, similarly, were established for architects, engineers, and lawyers.

These changes were part of a larger transformation in higher education that produced a new institution, the **research university.** Unlike antebellum colleges, which focused on teaching Latin and Greek, theology, logic, and mathematics, the new research universities offered courses in a wide variety of subjects, established professional schools, and encouraged faculty members to pursue basic research. At Cornell, the University of Wisconsin at Madison, Johns Hopkins, Harvard, and other institutions, this conception of higher education laid the groundwork for the central role that U.S. universities would play in the intellectual, cultural, and scientific life of the twentieth century.

Checking In

- The middle class adopted upper-class Victorian attitudes that focused on morality and social convention.
- The "cult of domesticity" shaped the lives of middle-class women, who were expected to focus on the home and its cultural refinement.
- Department stores catered to the middle and upper classes, and made shopping attractive and respectable.
- Football became the dominant college sport because it was thought to build character.
- Higher education flourished; new coeducational policies allowed women to acquire college education as never before; the research university emerged.

Reforming the Working Class

How did social and religious reformers address urban poverty?

The contrast between the affluent world of the college-educated middle and upper classes and the gritty lives of the working class was graphically displayed in the nation's growing urban centers. If department stores furnished new social spaces for the middle and upper classes, saloons became the poor man's club, and dance halls became single women's home away from home. The rich and the well-born looked askance at lower-class recreational activities and sought to force the poor to change their ways. But working-class Americans fought to preserve their own way of life. Indeed, the late nineteenth century witnessed an ongoing battle to eradicate social drinking and curb lower-class recreational activities.

Battling Poverty

Stunned by the levels of poverty and suffering in the expanding industrial cities, middle-class city leaders sought comprehensive solutions. Jacob Riis and the first generation of reformers believed that immigrants' lack of self-discipline and their unsanitary living conditions caused their problems. Only later would Jane Addams, Florence Kelley, and other settlement-house workers examine the crippling impact of low wages and dangerous working conditions. Humanitarians often turned their campaigns to help the destitute into missions to Americanize the immigrants and eliminate customs that they perceived as offensive and self-destructive.

Poverty relief workers first targeted their efforts at the young, who were considered the most malleable. Early Protestant social reformers started charitable societies to help transient youths and street waifs. In 1843 Robert M. Hartley founded the New York Association for Improving the Condition of the Poor to help poor families. Hartley's voluntaristic approach was supplemented by the more coercive tactics of Charles Loring Brace, who founded the New York Children's Aid Society in 1853. Worried that they might join the city's "dangerous classes," Brace swept orphaned children off the streets, shipped them to the country, and placed them with families to work as farm hands.

Whereas Brace gave adolescents an alternative to living in the slums, the Young Men's Christian Association (YMCA) and Young Women's Christian Association (YWCA) provided housing and wholesome recreation for country boys and young women who had migrated to the city. Both organizations subjected their members to curfews and expelled them for drinking and other forbidden behavior. By 1900, more than fifteen hundred YMCAs and YWCAs served as havens for nearly a quarter-million young men and women. But YMCA and YWCA leaders reached only a small portion of the young adult population. The strategy was too narrowly focused to stem the rising tide of urban problems.

New Approaches to Social Reform

Salvation Army Religious group established to aid the poor

The inability of relief organizations to cope with the explosive growth of the urban poor in the 1870s and 1880s convinced reformers to search for new allies. One effective agency was the **Salvation Army.** A church established along pseudomilitary lines in England in 1865 by Methodist minister "General" William Booth, the Salvation Army sent its uniformed volunteers to the United States in 1880 to provide food, shelter, and temporary employment for families. The army's strategy was simple. Attract the poor with marching bands and lively preaching; follow up with offers of food, assistance, and employment; and then teach them the solid, middle-class virtues of temperance, hard work, and self-discipline.

New York's Charity Organization Society (COS), founded in 1882 by Josephine Shaw Lowell, implemented a similar approach to poor relief. The society sent "friendly visitors," who were trained, salaried women, into the tenements to counsel families on how to improve their lives. Convinced that moral deficiencies lay at the root of poverty, and that the "promiscuous charity" of overlapping welfare agencies undermined the desire to work, the COS tried to foster self-sufficiency in its charges.

Critics justly accused the COS and similar groups of seeking more to control than to help the poor. One of the manuals, for example, stressed the importance of introducing "messy housekeepers" to the "pleasures of a cheery, well-ordered home." Unable to see slum problems from the vantage point of the poor, they failed, for the most part, in their underlying objective: to convert the poor to their own standards of morality and decorum.

The Moral Purity Campaign

Other reformers pushed for tougher measures against sin and immorality. In 1872 **Anthony Comstock,** a pious young dry-goods clerk, founded the New York Society for the Suppression of Vice. The organization demanded that municipal authorities close down gambling and lottery operations and censor obscene publications.

Anthony Comstock Leader of the moral purity crusade against urban vice and corruption

Nothing symbolized the contested terrain between middle- and lower-class culture better than the fight over prostitution, considered socially degenerate to some and a source of recreation to others. After the Civil War, the number of brothels expanded rapidly. In the 1880s, saloons and cabarets hired prostitutes of their own. Even though immigrant women do not appear to have made up the majority of big-city prostitutes, reformers often labeled them as the major source of the problem.

In 1892, New York Presbyterian minister Charles Parkhurst founded the City Vigilance League to clean up prostitution, gambling dens, and saloons. Parkhurst blamed the "slimy, oozy soil of Tammany Hall" (the Democratic organization that dominated New York City politics, discussed in the next chapter) and the New York City police for the city's rampant evil. He pressured city officials to enforce the laws against prostitution, gambling, and Sunday liquor sales.

However, the purity campaign quickly fell apart. New York's population was too large and its ethnic constituencies too diverse for the middle and upper classes to curb all the illegal activities flourishing within the sprawling metropolis.

The Social Gospel

In the 1870s and 1880s, a handful of Protestant ministers who were appalled by slum conditions took a different approach to helping impoverished city-dwellers. These ministers argued that the rich and the well-born had a Christian responsibility to do something about urban poverty.

William S. Rainsford, the Irish-born minister of New York City's St. George's Episcopal Church, pioneered the so-called institutional church movement. Large downtown churches in once-elite districts that had been overrun by immigrants would provide their new neighbors with social services as well as a place to worship. With the financial help of J. Pierpont Morgan, a warden of his church, Rainsford organized a boys' club, built recreational facilities on the Lower East Side, and established an industrial training program.

Other Protestant ministers, led by Washington Gladden, a Congregational clergyman in Columbus, Ohio, launched the **Social Gospel** movement in the 1870s. Gladden insisted that true Christianity commits men and women to fight social injustice. Walter Rauschenbusch, a minister in New York City's notorious Hell's Kitchen neighborhood, refined this nostrum into a coherent philosophy. Educated in Germany, Rauschenbusch argued that a truly Christian society would unite all churches, reorganize the industrial system, and work for international peace. Although the Social Gospel attracted only a handful of Protestants, their earnest voices blended with a growing chorus of critics bemoaning the nation's urban woes.

Social Gospel Protestant doctrine that wealthy must aid the poor

Chicago Historical Society

Garbage Box, First Ward, Chicago, c. 1900

Lacking space for recreation, immigrant children play atop garbage boxes in crowded alleys. Concerned for their health, Jane Addams wrote that "this slaughter of innocents, this infliction of suffering on the new-born, is so gratuitous and so unfair, that it is only a question of time until an outraged sense of justice shall be aroused on behalf of these children."

Jane Addams Leader in settlement-house movement; later won the Nobel Peace Prize

The Settlement-House Movement

In the 1880s, a younger generation of charity workers led by **Jane Addams** developed a new weapon against destitution: the settlement house. Like the Social Gospelers, these reformers recognized that the hardships of slum life were often beyond the individual's control. Living in the poor neighborhoods where they worked, they could see firsthand "the struggle for existence, which is so much harsher among people near the edge of pauperism."

The youngest daughter of a successful Illinois businessman, Jane Addams purchased a dilapidated mansion in Chicago in 1889 and opened it as Hull House, the first experiment in the settlement-house approach. Putting the middle-class ideal of true womanhood into action, Addams and her colleague Ellen Gates Starr turned Hull House into a social center for recent immigrants. She invited them to plays; sponsored art projects; held classes in English, civics, cooking, and dressmaking; and encouraged them to preserve their traditional crafts. She set up a kindergarten, a laundry, an employment bureau, and a day nursery for working mothers. Addams and her coworkers made studies of city housing conditions and pressured politicians to enforce sanitation regulations.

By 1895, at least fifty settlement houses had opened around the nation. Settlement-house leaders trained a generation of young college students, mostly women, many of whom would later serve as state and local government officials. Florence Kelley, for example, who had worked at Hull House, became the chief factory inspector for Illinois in 1893. Through their sympathetic attitudes toward the immigrants and their systematic publication of data about slum conditions, settlement-house workers gave Americans new hope that the cities' problems could be overcome.

But in their attempt to promote class cooperation and social harmony, settlement houses had mixed success. Although immigrants appreciated the settlement houses' resources and activity, they widely felt that the reformers cared little for increasing immigrant political power. "They're like the rest," complained one immigrant, "a bunch of people planning for us and deciding what is good for us without consulting us or taking us into their confidence."

CHECKING IN

- The first generation of urban reformers blamed weak moral discipline for the plight of the poor; with this focus, reformers ignored the issues of low wages and dangerous working conditions.
- The Salvation Army and other reform groups provided needed aid and tried to improve moral character by instilling middle-class values.
- The Social Gospel taught the responsibility of the rich and well-born to help the poor and fight injustice.
- Settlement houses brought middle-class women into the slums to provide services and attack urban problems.

WORKING-CLASS LEISURE IN THE IMMIGRANT CITY

How did the urban working class change attitudes toward leisure and recreation by 1900?

In colonial America, preachers had warned against leisure and idleness as temptations to sin. In the rural culture of the early nineteenth century, the unremitting routines of farm labor had left little time for relaxation. Family picnics, horse races, county fairs, revivals, and holidays like the Fourth of July and Christmas had provided permissible diversion. But most Americans continued to view leisure activities skeptically.

As urban populations and factories multiplied after the Civil War, new patterns of leisure and amusement emerged, especially among the urban working class. After long hours in factories and mills or behind department store counters, working-class Americans craved relaxation and diversion. They thronged the streets, patronized saloons and dance halls, cheered at boxing matches and baseball games, and organized boisterous group picnics and holiday celebrations. Amusement parks, vaudeville theaters, sporting clubs, and racetracks provided further entertainment for workers, and mass leisure became a big business.

Streets and Saloons

No segment of the populace had a greater need for recreation than the urban working class. Hours of tedious, highly disciplined, and physically exhausting labor left workers tired but thirsty for excitement and escape from their cramped living quarters. In 1889 a banner carried by a carpenters' union summed up their wishes: "eight hours for work, eight hours for rest, and eight hours for what we will."

City streets provided recreation that anyone could afford. Relaxing after a day's work, shop girls and laborers clustered on busy corners, watching shouting pushcart peddlers and listening to organ grinders play familiar melodies. For a penny or a nickel, they could buy a bagel, a baked potato, or a soda. In the summer, when the heat and humidity within the tenements reached unbearable levels, the streets became a hive of neighborhood social life.

The streets were open to all, but other leisure institutions drew mainly a male clientele. Saloons offered men companionship, conviviality, and five-cent beer, often with a free lunch thrown in. By 1900, New York City had an estimated ten thousand saloons. As neighborhood gathering places, saloons reinforced group identity and became centers for immigrant politics. Saloonkeepers often doubled as local ward bosses who performed small services for their patrons. With rich mahogany bars, shiny brass rails, and elegant mirrors, saloons provided patrons with a taste of high-toned luxury.

However, it would be a mistake to view the old-time saloon through a haze of sentimental nostalgia. Prostitution and crime flourished in the rougher saloons. Drunken husbands sometimes beat their wives and children, squandered their meager paychecks, and lost their jobs. The pervasiveness of alcoholism was devastating. Temperance reformers, in their attack on saloons, targeted a real and widespread social problem.

The Rise of Professional Sports

As an English game called rounders, baseball had existed since the seventeenth century. If Americans did not create baseball, they did turn it into a major professional sport. In 1845, the first organized baseball team, the New York Knickerbockers, was formed. In the 1860s, rules were codified and the sport assumed its modern form. Overhand pitches replaced underhand tosses. Fielders wore gloves, games were standardized at nine innings, and bases were spaced ninety feet apart.

In 1869, the Cincinnati Red Stockings, the first team to put its players under contract for the whole season, toured the country and ended the season with fifty-seven wins and no losses. Team owners organized the National League in 1876, took control from the players by requiring them to sign exclusive contracts, and limited each city to one professional team. Soon the owners were filling baseball parks with crowds of ten to twelve thousand fans and earning enormous profits. By the 1890s, baseball had become big business.

The working class in particular took the sport to heart. The most profitable teams were those in industrial cities with a large working-class population. However, if baseball helped build solidarity among some ethnic groups, it also fostered discrimination against blacks. At least fifty-five blacks played on integrated teams between 1883 and 1898. Increasingly thereafter, blacks were banned from playing on professional teams and banished to their own league.

Although no other organized sport attracted as large a following as baseball, horse racing and boxing also drew large crowds of spectators and bettors. Louisville's Kentucky Derby became an important social event for the rich, but professional boxing aroused more passionate devotion among laborers. Bare-knuckled prizefighting became a testing ground where men could demonstrate their toughness and physical prowess.

John L. Sullivan Heavyweight boxing champion

For many working-class Americans, heavyweight fighter **John L. Sullivan** personified these traits. Of Irish immigrant stock, Sullivan began boxing in 1877 at age nineteen. With his massive physique, handlebar mustache, and arrogant swagger, Sullivan was enormously popular among immigrants. Barnstorming across the country, he vanquished a succession of local strong men, invariably wearing his trademark green tights with an American flag wrapped around his middle. Yet, Sullivan refused to fight blacks, supposedly in deference to the wishes of his fans. This policy conveniently allowed him to avoid facing the finest boxer of the 1880s, the Australian black, Peter Jackson.

Vaudeville, Amusement Parks, and Dance Halls

In contrast to the male preserve of saloons and prizefights, the world of vaudeville shows, amusement parks, and neighborhood dance halls welcomed all comers regardless of gender. Some of them proved particularly congenial to working-class women.

Vaudeville (VAWD-vill) evolved out of antebellum minstrel shows that featured white comedians made up as blacks. The vaudeville show typically opened with an animal act or a dance number, followed by a musical interlude. Comic skits then ridiculed the trials of urban life, satirized police and municipal ineptitude, and poked fun at immigrant accents, mining a rich vein of ethnic humor and stereotypes. Blackface skits were sometimes included, thus reinforcing prejudice against blacks. After a highbrow operatic aria and acts by ventriloquists and magicians, the program ended with a "flash" finale featuring flying-trapeze artists or the like. By the 1880s vaudeville was drawing larger crowds than any other form of theater.

Whereas vaudeville offered psychological release from the stresses of working-class life, amusement parks provided physical escape. New York's Coney Island evolved into an oceanfront resort for the masses in the 1870s. At Coney Island, young couples went dancing, rode through the dark Tunnel of Love, and sped down the dizzying roller coaster in Steeplechase Park. Customers were encouraged to surrender to the spirit of play and lose themselves in fantasy.

By the end of the nineteenth century, New York City had well over three hundred thousand female wage earners. For this army of low-paid young working women, amusement parks exerted a powerful lure. Here they could meet friends, spend time with young men beyond the watchful eyes of their parents, show off their new dresses, and try out the latest dance steps. For such women, the exciting music and the spell of a warm summer night could seem a magical release from the drudgery of daily life.

Ragtime

Nothing illustrated more sharply the differences between middle- and working-class culture than the contrasting styles of popular music they favored. Whereas the middle class preferred hymns or songs that conveyed a moral lesson, the working class delighted in ragtime, the product of black musicians in the saloons and brothels of the South.

Ragtime developed out of the rich tradition of songs through which black Americans had eased the burdens of their lives. Like spirituals, ragtime used

CHECKING IN

- Saloons became political as well as social centers for immigrant men.
- Professional sports, particularly baseball, appealed strongly to urban immigrants.
- Boxing produced manly heroes like John L. Sullivan, the "Boston Strong Boy."
- Vaudeville and dance halls provided cheap popular entertainment, and urban amusement parks like Coney Island attracted huge crowds.
- Ragtime brought black music into white communities even as it confirmed racial stereotypes.

syncopated rhythms and complex harmonies, but it blended them with marching-band musical structures to create a distinctive style. A favorite of "honky-tonk" piano players, ragtime was introduced to the broader public in the 1890s and became a national sensation.

The reasons for the sudden ragtime craze were complex. Inventive, playful, with catchy syncopations and an infectious rhythm in the bass clef, the music displayed an originality that had an appeal all its own. Part of ragtime's popularity also came from its origin in brothels and its association with blacks, who were widely stereotyped in the 1890s as sexual, sensual, and uninhibited by the rigid Victorian social conventions that restricted whites. Hence, ragtime's great popularity proved a mixed blessing for blacks. While it helped break down the barriers faced by blacks in the music industry, it also confirmed some whites' stereotype of blacks as primitive and sensual, a bias that underlay the racism of the period and helped justify segregation and discrimination.

CULTURES IN CONFLICT

How did writers, artists, and educational reformers address issues of cultural conflict?

Even within the elite and middle classes, Victorian morality and genteel cultural standards were never totally accepted. As the century ended, increasing numbers of people questioned these beliefs. Women stood at the center of the era's cultural turbulence. Thwarted by a restrictive code of feminine propriety, they made their dissatisfactions heard. The rise of women's clubs, the growth of women's colleges, and even the 1890s bicycle fad testified to the emergence of what some began to call the "new woman."

In no period of American history have class conflicts been as open and raw. As middle-class leaders nervously eyed the sometimes disorderly culture of city streets, saloons, boxing clubs, dance halls, and amusement parks, they saw a challenge to their own cultural and social values. Some middle-class reformers promoted public schools as a means to impose middle-class values on the urban masses. Others battled urban "vice" and "immorality." But ultimately it was the polite mores of the middle class, not urban working-class culture, that proved more vulnerable. By 1900 the Victorian social and moral ethos was crumbling on every front.

The Genteel Tradition and Its Critics

What was this genteel culture that aroused such opposition? In the 1870s and 1880s, a group of upper-class writers and editors, led by Charles Eliot Norton of Harvard and E. L. Godkin of *The Nation*, codified Victorian standards for literature and the arts with the goal of creating a coherent national artistic culture. Joining forces with editors and writers in Boston and New York, these elites lectured the middle class about the value of high culture and the insights to be gained from painting and music. They censored their own publications to remove all sexual allusions, disrespectful treatments of Christianity, and unhappy endings.

Although these genteel magazines provided an important forum for new authors, their editors' strident elitism and imperialistic desire to control national literary standards bred opposition. Samuel Langhorne Clemens, better known as **Mark Twain,** spoke for many young writers when he declared that he was through with "literature and all that bosh." Attacking aristocratic literary conventions, Twain and others who shared his concerns explored new forms of fiction and worked to broaden literature's appeal to the general public.

Mark Twain Writer, humorist, and critic of genteel tradition

These efforts to chart new directions for American literature rested on fundamental changes taking place within the publishing industry. New magazines like *Ladies' Home Journal, Cosmopolitan,* and *McClure's* competed with the elite publications. The new magazines slashed their prices and tripled their circulation. Supported by advertising rather than subscriptions, they provided an outlet for writers who could provide accurate depictions of the "whirlpool of real life."

Some of these writers have been called regionalists because they captured the distinctive dialects and details of their featured locale. Others, among them William Dean Howells, have been called realists because of their focus on the truthful depiction of the commonplace. Still others have been categorized as naturalists because their stories deny free will and stress the ways in which life's outcomes are determined by economic and psychological forces. Stephen Crane's *Maggie: A Girl of the Streets* (1892), a bleak story of an innocent girl's exploitation and ultimate suicide in an urban slum, generally is considered the first naturalistic American novel. Labels aside, all these writers shared a skepticism about literary conventions and an intense desire to understand the society around them.

The careers of Mark Twain and Theodore Dreiser highlight the changes in the publishing industry and the evolution of new forms of writing. Both were products of the Midwest, outsiders to the East Coast literary establishment—Twain from Missouri and Dreiser from Indiana. As young men, both worked as newspaper reporters and traveled widely.

Drawing on their own experiences, Twain and Dreiser wrote about the human impact of the wrenching social changes taking place around them: the flow of people to the expanding cities and the relentless scramble for power, wealth, and fame. In *Adventures of Huckleberry Finn* (1884), Twain uses the river journey of two runaways, the rebellious Huck and the slave Jim, to explore the nature of contemporary American society by contrasting the idyllic life on the raft with the tawdry, fraudulent world of the small riverfront towns. Dreiser's *Sister Carrie* (1900) traces the journey of Carrie Meeber, an innocent and

North Wind Picture Archives

Mark Twain

Twain not only broke from highbred literary standards but also created a unique personal style through his studied prose and distinctive attire.

attractive girl, from her Wisconsin farm home to Chicago. Seduced by a traveling salesman, Carrie moves in with the married proprietor of a fancy saloon. Driven by her desire for expensive department-store clothes and lavish entertainment, Carrie follows her married lover to New York, abandons him when his money runs out, and pursues her own career in the theater.

Twain and Dreiser broke sharply with the genteel tradition's emphasis on manners and decorum. As evidence, *Century* magazine readers complained that *Huckleberry Finn* was "destitute of a single redeeming quality." The publisher of *Sister Carrie* was so repelled by Dreiser's novel that he printed only a thousand copies (to fulfill the legal terms of his contract) and then stored them in a warehouse.

Growing numbers of scholars and critics challenged the certitudes of Victorian mores, including assumptions that moral worth and economic standing were closely linked and that the status quo represented a social order decreed by God and nature alike. Economist Thorstein Veblen's *The Theory of the Leisure Class* (1899) caustically critiqued the lifestyles of the new capitalist elite. Raised in a poor Norwegian farm community in Minnesota, Veblen looked at the captains of industry and their families with a jaundiced eye. He documented their "conspicuous consumption" and lamented the widening economic gap between "those who worked without profit" and "those who profited without working."

Within the new discipline of sociology, Annie MacLean exposed the exploitation of department-store clerks, Walter Wyckoff uncovered the hand-to-mouth existence of unskilled laborers, and W. E. B. Du Bois documented the hardships faced by blacks in Philadelphia. The publication of these writings, coupled with the economic depression and seething labor agitation of the 1890s, made it increasingly difficult for turn-of-the-century middle-class Americans to accept the smug, self-satisfied belief in progress and genteel culture that had been a hallmark of the Victorian outlook.

Modernism in Architecture and Painting

The challenge to the genteel tradition also found support among architects and painters. Architects followed the lead of Louis Sullivan, who argued that a building's form should follow its function. In this view, banks, for example, should look like financial institutions, not Greek temples. Striving to create functional American design standards, the Chicago architects looked for inspiration to the future—to **modernism**—not to the past.

modernism Trend in early twentieth-century thought and aesthetics that rejected Victorian formalism in favor of new modes of experience and expression

Frank Lloyd Wright Architect who rejected Victorian fussiness

The Chicago architect **Frank Lloyd Wright** designed "prairie-school" houses that represented a typical modernist break with past styles. Wright scorned the three-story Victorian house with its large attic and basement. His designs, which featured broad, sheltering roofs and horizontal silhouettes, used interconnecting rooms to create a sense of spaciousness. Modernism's rejection of Victorian refinement influenced late-nineteenth-century painting as well. Winslow Homer's watercolors pictured nature as brutally tough and unsentimental; in his grim, elemental seascapes, lone men struggle against overwhelming waves. Thomas Eakins's canvases of swimmers, boxers, and rowers captured moments of vigorous physical exertion. While Mary Cassatt shared Eakins's interest in everyday life, she often took as her subject the bond between mother and child, as in her painting *The Bath* (c. 1891).

The revolt by architects' and painters against Victorian standards was symptomatic of a larger shift in middle-class thought that resulted from fundamental economic changes. As one minister observed in 1898, the transition from muscle to mechanical power had "separated, as by an impassable gulf, the simple, homespun, individualistic world of the . . . past, from the complex, closely associated life of the present." Victorian platitudes about proper manners and graceful arts seemed out of place in the big, glittering, electrified cities of iron and glass.

Distrusting idealistic Victorian assumptions about social progress, the middle class nevertheless remained divided over how to replace them. Not until the Progressive Era would social reformers draw on new expertise in social research with an enlarged conception of the federal government's regulatory power to break sharply with their Victorian predecessors' social outlook.

From Victorian Lady to New Woman

The role of middle-class women in the revolt against Victorian refinement was complex and ambiguous. Dissatisfaction with the cult of domesticity did not necessarily lead to their open rebellion. Although they chafed against the constraints of the genteel code and the assumption that they should limit their activities to the home, many women remained committed to playing a nurturing role within the family. In fact, early advocates of a "widened sphere" for women often fused the traditional Victorian ideal of womanhood with a firm commitment to political action.

The career of temperance leader **Frances Willard** illustrates how the cult of domesticity could evolve into a broader view of women's social and political responsibilities. Willard believed that by nature women were compassionate, nurturing, and sensitive to others; she was equally convinced that drinking encouraged men to squander their earnings and profoundly threatened family life. In 1874, Willard resigned her positions as dean of women and professor of English at Northwestern University to devote her energies completely to the temperance cause. Five years later, she was elected president of the recently formed Woman's Christian Temperance Union (WCTU).

Frances Willard Activist in temperance and women's issues

Willard took the traditional belief that women had unique moral virtues and transformed it into a rationale for political action. The domestication of politics, she asserted, would protect the family and improve public morality. She launched a crusade in 1880 to win the franchise for women so that they could outlaw liquor. Willard soon expanded the WCTU's activities to include welfare work, prison reform, labor arbitration, and public health. By 1890, the WCTU, with a membership of 150,000, had become the nation's first mass organization of women. Through it, women gained experience as lobbyists, organizers, and lecturers, in the process undercutting the assumption of "separate spheres."

An expanding network of women's clubs offered another means by which middle- and upper-class women could hone their skills in civic affairs, public speaking, and intellectual analysis. Club women became involved in social-welfare projects, public-library expansion, and tenement reform. By 1892, the General Federation of Women's Clubs boasted 495 affiliates and a hundred thousand members. Middle-class black women, excluded from many white clubs, formed their own National Association of Colored Women's Clubs in 1900.

Bicycling and Courtship: Sheet Music, 1896

The bicycling fad not only allowed women to get outdoor exercise, but it also became a way for young women and men to meet away from the watchful eyes of parents.

Younger women challenged social conventions by joining the bicycling craze that swept urban America at the turn of the century. The fascination with bicycle riding developed as part of a new interest in health and physical fitness. Middle- and upper-class Americans explored various ways to improve their vigor. Some used health products such as cod-liver oil and sarsaparilla for "weak blood." Others played basketball, invented in 1891 by a physical education instructor at Springfield College in Massachusetts to keep students in shape during the winter months.

Bicycling especially appealed to young women who had chafed under the restrictive Victorian attitudes about female exercise, which held that proper young ladies must never sweat and that the female body must be fully covered at all times. By pedaling along in a shirtwaist or "split" skirt, a woman bicyclist made an implicit feminist statement suggesting that she had broken with genteel conventions.

Changing attitudes about women's proper role also found expression in gradually shifting ideas about marriage. Charlotte Perkins Gilman, a suffrage advocate and speaker for women's rights, asserted that women would make an effective contribution to society only when they won economic independence from men. One tangible indicator of women's changing relationship to men was the substantial rise in the divorce rate. In 1880, one in every twenty-one marriages ended in divorce. By 1900, the rate had climbed to one in twelve. Women who brought suit for divorce increasingly cited their husbands' failure to act responsibly and to respect their autonomy.

Kate Chopin Feminist author; plotlines of her novel *The Awakening* violated social conventions

Women writers generally welcomed the new female commitment to independence and self-sufficiency. Mary Wilkins Freeman's short stories, for example, compare women's expanding role to the frontier ideal of freedom. Her characters fight for their beliefs without concern for society's reaction. Feminist **Kate Chopin** pushed the debate to the extreme by having the married heroine of her 1899 novel *The Awakening* violate social conventions by falling in love with another man and then taking her life when his ideas about women prove as narrow and traditional as those of her husband.

Nonetheless, attitudes changed slowly. The enlarged concept of women's role in society exerted its greatest influence on college-educated, middle-class women who had leisure time and could hope for success in journalism, social work, or nursing. For shop girls who worked sixty hours a week to make ends meet, the ideal remained a more distant goal.

Public Education as an Arena of Class Conflict

Controversy over the scope and function of public education engaged Americans of all socioeconomic levels and highlighted class and cultural divisions in late-nineteenth-century society. Viewing public schools as an instrument for indoctrinating and controlling the lower ranks, middle-class educators and civic leaders campaigned to expand and centralize public schooling. Not surprisingly, the reformers' efforts aroused considerable opposition from ethnic and religious groups whose outlook and interests differed sharply from theirs.

Thanks to the crusade for universal public education started by Horace Mann, most northern states had public-school systems by the time of the Civil War. More than half the nation's children received some formal education, but most attended only a few years, and few went to high school. In the 1870s, middle-class activists, concerned that many Americans lacked sufficient knowledge to participate wisely in public affairs or function effectively in the labor force, worked to increase the number of years spent in school.

One such reformer was federal commissioner of education William Torrey Harris. Harris urged teachers to instill in their students a sense of order, decorum, self-discipline, and civic loyalty. Believing that modern industrial society depended on citizens' conforming to the timetables of the factory and the train, he envisioned the schools as models of precise scheduling: "The pupil must have his lessons ready at the appointed time, must rise at the tap of the bell, move to the line, return; in short, go through all the evolutions with equal precision."

To achieve these goals and to wrest control of schools from neighborhood leaders and ward politicians, reform-minded educators like Harris stressed punctuality, compulsory-attendance laws, and a tenure system to insulate teachers from political favoritism and parental pressure. By 1900, thirty-one states required all children from eight to fourteen years of age to attend school. But the steamroller methods of Harris and others to systematize public education prompted protests. New York pediatrician Joseph Mayer Rice, after interviewing twelve hundred teachers, scornfully criticized the schools' reliance on singsong memorization and prisonlike discipline.

Rice overlooked real advances; for example, the national illiteracy rate dropped from 17 percent in 1880 to 13 percent by 1900, despite the influx of immigrants. He was on target, however, in assailing many teachers' rigid emphasis on silence, docility, and unquestioning obedience to rules.

By the 1880s, several different groups were opposing the centralized urban public-school bureaucracies. Working-class families that depended on their children's meager wages for survival, for example, resisted attempts to force their sons and daughters to attend school past the elementary grades. Although some immigrant families made great sacrifices to give their children an education, many withdrew their offspring from school as soon as they had learned the rudiments of reading and writing, and sent them to work.

Furthermore, Catholic immigrants objected to the overwhelmingly Protestant orientation of the public schools. Catholics set up separate parochial systems and denounced federal aid to public schools as a ploy to "form one homogeneous American people after the New England Evangelical type." Meanwhile, upper-class parents who did not wish to send their children to immigrant-thronged public schools enrolled them in private seminaries and boarding schools, like St. Paul's in Concord, New Hampshire. The proliferation of private and parochial schools, together with the controversies over compulsory education, school funding, and classroom decorum, reveals the extent to which public education had become mired in ethnic and class differences.

Unlike Germany and Japan, which centralized their national educational systems in the nineteenth century, the United States created a diverse system of locally run public and private institutions, a system that allowed each segment of society some influence over its schools. Amid the disputes, school enrollments dramatically expanded. In 1870, fewer than 72,000 students attended the nation's 1,026 high schools. By 1900, the number of high schools had jumped to more than 5,000 and the number of students to more than 500,000.

CHECKING IN

- Cultural conflict pitted Victorian gentility against rowdier immigrant life.
- Mark Twain and Theodore Dreiser led the attack on Victorian literature.
- Louis Sullivan, Frank Lloyd Wright, and other architects and artists created "modernism."
- Through new forms of political, creative, and physical expression, the "new woman" struggled to free herself from the bonds of genteel tradition.
- Public schools were increasingly seen as a way to inculcate middle-class values, although Catholics resisted.

Chapter Summary

How did the influx of immigrants before 1900 create an awareness of ethnic and class differences? (page 447)

A flood of immigrants jostled against native-born Americans who feared and disliked them; the immigrants were crowded into ghettos. The wealthy created fashionable enclaves, the middle class moved to the suburbs, and the physical changes in cities sharpened class awareness. To further distinguish themselves from these newcomers, native-born Americans stressed their commitment to Victorian morality.

How did Victorian morality shape middle-class society and culture? (page 452)

Victorian morality and its emphasis on gentility, manners, decorum, and self-control shaped the middle class. The cult of domesticity demanded that women maintain culturally refined homes. Lavish department stores and artistically designed houses reflected the middle- and upper-class faith that the consumption of material goods indicated good taste. To raise standards, the prosperous classes expanded the number of high schools and created a new research university system for training educators, lawyers, doctors, and other professionals.

KEY TERMS

Scott Joplin *(p. 446)*
new immigrants *(p. 448)*
Ellis Island *(p. 449)*
W. E. B. Du Bois *(p. 451)*
Victorian morality *(p. 452)*
department store *(p. 454)*
research university *(p. 455)*
Salvation Army *(p. 456)*
Anthony Comstock *(p. 457)*
Social Gospel *(p. 457)*
Jane Addams *(p. 458)*
John L. Sullivan *(p. 460)*
Mark Twain *(p. 463)*
modernism *(p. 464)*
Frank Lloyd Wright *(p. 464)*
Frances Willard *(p. 465)*
Kate Chopin *(p. 466)*

How did social and religious reformers address urban poverty? (page 455)

While Jacob Riis, Jane Addams, and other reformers worked to improve overcrowded housing and dangerous working conditions, Anthony Comstock and other less sympathetic reformers attacked immigrant values and cultures in an effort to uplift and Americanize them.

How did the urban working class change attitudes toward leisure and recreation by 1900? (page 459)

Urban immigrants thronged saloons, dance halls, vaudeville theaters, and amusement parks. They listened avidly to ragtime and cheered on professional baseball teams and sports heroes such as boxer John L. Sullivan. The elite vision of sport as a vehicle for instilling self-discipline was transformed into a new commitment to sports as spectacle and entertainment. Sports had become big business and an important part of the new consumerism. As Victorian morality eroded, undermined by dissension from within and opposition from without, new standards of behavior and creative expression emerged.

How did writers, artists, and educational reformers address issues of cultural conflict? (page 462)

Genteel Victorianism found itself pitted against—and losing out to—immigrant rowdiness and spirit. Mark Twain and others challenged the "genteel tradition" in literature, while architects like Louis Sullivan and Frank Lloyd Wright reshaped the urban landscape. Women struggled to escape the bonds of Victorian gentility. Public schools were seen as a place to inculcate middle-class values and overthrow immigrant culture. Despite these efforts, the raucous working-class culture of the late-nineteenth-century city can be seen as the seedbed of twentieth-century mass culture.

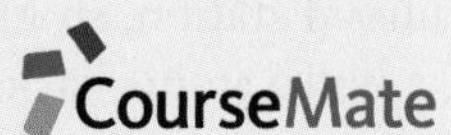

Go to the CourseMate website at **www.cengagebrain.com** for additional study tools and review materials—including audio and video clips—for this chapter.

Chapter 20

Politics and Expansion in an Industrializing Age

1877–1900

Frank & Marie-Therese Wood Print Collections, Alexandria, VA

The Politics of Industrialization

Chapter Preview

Party Politics in an Era of Upheaval, 1877–1884
How did political parties build coalitions out of their diverse ethnic and regional constituencies?

Politics of Privilege, Politics of Exclusion, 1884–1892
What factors prompted the rise of the Grange and the Farmers' Alliance movements?

The 1890s: Politics in a Depression Decade
Why did William Jennings Bryan fail to win the presidency in 1896?

Expansionist Stirrings and War with Spain, 1878–1901
Why did the United States go to war with Spain and become an imperial power?

July 2, 1881, was a muggy summer day in Washington, DC, and President James A. Garfield was leaving town for a visit to western Massachusetts. At 9:30 A.M., as he strolled through the railroad station, shots rang out. Garfield fell, a bullet in his back. The shooter, Charles Guiteau, immediately surrendered. At first, doctors thought the president would recover. But as the doctors probed the wound with bare hands and unsterilized instruments, blood poisoning set in. On September 19, Garfield died.

The nation mourned. Garfield embodied the American dream of the self-made man. Born in a log cabin in Ohio, he fought in the Civil War, went to Congress in 1863, and was elected president in 1880.

Garfield also embodied a political generation that seemed more preoccupied with the spoils of office than with the problems of ordinary people. In Congress, Garfield had been tainted by the 1872 Crédit Mobilier scandal and other corruption charges (see Chapter 16). The obscure Guiteau, a loyal party member who had supported Garfield, expected to be rewarded with a high diplomatic post. When this failed to materialize, his delusionary mental state worsened. Viewing Garfield's death as "a political necessity," he believed that the public would hail him as a hero. The jury rejected Guiteau's insanity plea, and in June 1882 he was hanged.

While contemporary critics viewed Garfield's assassination as an example of the absurdity of late-nineteenth-century politics, historians today see it as a sign of how closely contested political battles were. The expansion of large corporations, the settlement of the trans-Mississippi West, and the surge in urban growth put intense pressure on the political process. At stake was the government's proper role in the stimulation and regulation of America's explosive industrial growth.

This debate involved nothing less than contending visions of how industrial growth should or should not be regulated and who should benefit financially. The struggle to control economic expansion reached its peak in the 1890s when a new third party, the Populists, joined with the Democrats to challenge corporate control of the economy. In contrast, the Republican Party remained committed to encouraging the growth of large corporations, to freeing industry to expand without regulation, and to developing new markets.

From the mid-1870s to the mid-1890s, no party was able to control the political process. But in 1896, the election of President William F. McKinley ushered in a generation of Republican domination of national politics. Elected in a campaign focused on the restoration of prosperity, McKinley stumbled into war with Spain, substantially increased U.S. territory, and established new outposts from which American corporations could gain access to overseas markets.

PARTY POLITICS IN AN ERA OF UPHEAVAL, 1877–1884

How did political parties build coalitions out of their diverse ethnic and regional constituencies?

Between 1877 and 1894, four presidents squeezed into office by the narrowest of margins; control of the House of Representatives changed hands five times; and seven new western states were admitted into the Union. Amid intense competition, no party could muster a working majority. While the Democrats rebuilt their strength in the South, Republicans struggled to maintain the loyalties of the working class and to increase their support from business. At the municipal level, political machines worked to attract loyalty among immigrants and other newcomers in the rapidly expanding cities.

Contested Political Visions

In the late nineteenth century, more than 80 percent of eligible white males often voted. At the same time that voter turnout shot up, however, political parties sidestepped

Chronology

1869	Boss William M. Tweed gains control of Tammany Hall
1878	Congress requires U.S. Treasury to purchase silver
1880	James Garfield elected president
1881	Assassination of Garfield; Chester A. Arthur becomes president
1883	Pendleton Civil Service Act
1884	Grover Cleveland elected president
1886	*Wabash v. Illinois*
1887	Interstate Commerce Act
1888	Benjamin Harrison elected president
1889	National Farmers' Alliance formed
1890	Sherman Silver Purchase Act; Sherman Anti-Trust Act; McKinley Tariff
1893	Panic of 1893; repeal of the Sherman Silver Purchase Act
1894	Coxey's "army" marches on Washington; Pullman strike
1895	Supreme Court declares federal income tax unconstitutional
1896	Democratic Party nominates William Jennings Bryan; William McKinley elected president
1898	Acquisition of Hawai'i; Spanish-American War
1898	Guerrilla uprising in Philippines, lasted until 1902
1900	Currency Act officially places United States on gold standard
1901	Platt Amendment retains U.S. role in Cuba

many of the issues created by industrialization, such as taxation of corporations, support for those injured in factory accidents, and poverty relief. Except for the Interstate Commerce Act of 1887 and the largely symbolic Sherman Anti-Trust Act of 1890, Washington generally ignored the social consequences of industrialization and focused instead on encouraging economic growth.

How can we explain this refusal and, at the same time, account for the enormous popular support for parties? The answer lies in the political ideology of the period and the three major symbolic and economic issues that preoccupied lawmakers nationally: the tariff, the money supply, and civil-service reform.

Political parties in the late nineteenth century energized voters not only by appealing to economic self-interest, as in support for industrialization and pensions for Civil War veterans, but also by linking their programs to deeply held beliefs about the nature of the family and the proper role of government. Republicans justified their support for the tariff and defended their commitment to Union widows' pensions as a protection for the family home. Democrats countered, using metaphors of the seduction and rape of white women by outsiders and labeling Republican programs as classic examples of the perils of excessive government force. High tariffs endangered the family and threatened economic disaster. With respect to both parties, men, in particular, associated loyalty to party with a sense of masculinity.

Despite their differences, neither Republicans nor Democrats believed that the national government had any right to regulate corporations or to protect the social welfare of workers. Neither party therefore courted the labor union vote. Many members of both parties embraced the doctrine of **laissez-faire**—the belief that unregulated competition represented the best path to progress. According to this view, the federal government should promote economic development but not regulate industry.

laissez-faire Belief that government should not interfere with the workings of the free market

Grand Army of the Republic (GAR) Union veterans' group that sought to broaden pensions and exercised political power by "waving the bloody shirt"

Rather than looking to Washington, people turned to local or state authorities. On the Great Plains, angry farmers demanded that their state legislatures regulate railroad rates. In the cities, immigrant groups competed for political power while native-born reformers periodically attempted to oust the political machines and clean up corruption. Meanwhile, city and state governments vied with each other for control. When Chicago wanted to issue permits to street popcorn vendors, for example, the Illinois legislature had to pass a special act.

Both parties, in the North and the South, practiced fraud by rigging elections, throwing out opposition votes, and paying for "floaters" who moved from precinct to precinct to vote. Each expressed moral outrage at the other's illegal behavior.

By linking economic policy to family values, both parties encouraged the participation of women in the political process, although most could not vote. Frances Willard and her followers in the Woman's Christian Temperance Union (WCTU), for example, helped create a Prohibition and Home Protection Party in the 1880s. A decade later, western women Populists won full suffrage in Colorado, Idaho, and Utah.

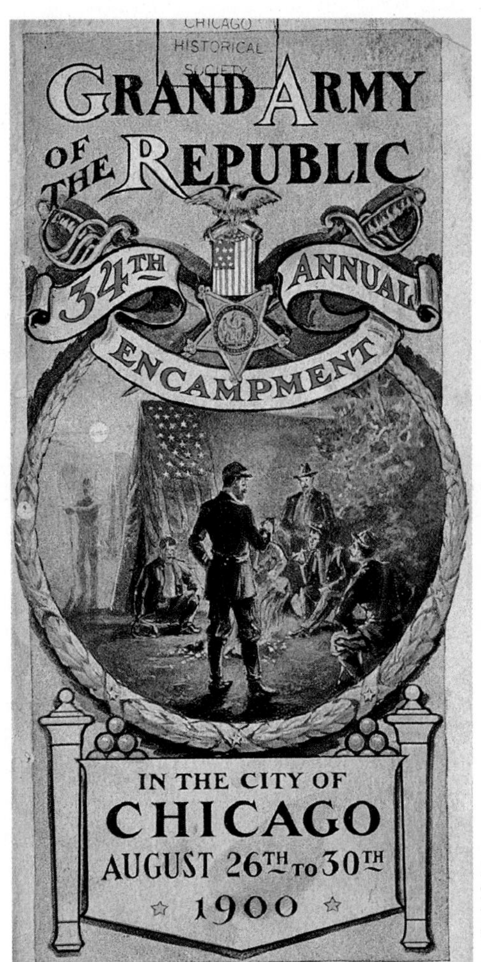

Chicago Historical Society

Poster Announcing GAR Encampment, Chicago, 1900

In addition to their nostalgic annual reunions, Union army veterans, organized as the Grand Army of the Republic, were a potent force in Republican Party politics by lobbying for pensions and other benefits.

Patterns of Party Strength

In the 1870s and 1880s, each party had its own ideological appeal and centers of regional strength. The Democrats ruled the South, southern sections of border states like Ohio, and northern cities with large immigrant populations. They opposed tariff increases and attacked "governmental interference in the economy." In addition, Democrats staunchly defended their immigrant followers. On state and local levels, they fiercely opposed prohibition, supported parochial schools, and rejected attempts to require English-only schooling.

The Republicans reigned in rural and small-town New England, Pennsylvania, and the upper Midwest, and drew support from the **Grand Army of the Republic (GAR),** a social and political organization of northern Civil War veterans. Republicans often "waved the bloody shirt," reminding voters that their party had led the nation during the Civil War. The Republicans ran a series of former Union army generals for president and voted for generous veterans' benefits.

Although issues of governmental authority dominated on the federal level, family tradition, ethnic ties, religious affiliation, and local issues often determined an individual's vote. Outside the South, ethnicity and religion were the most reliable predictors of party affiliation. Catholics and Americans of German ancestry tended to vote Democratic. Old-stock Protestant northerners and immigrants from northern Europe, in contrast, voted Republican, as did blacks in both the North and the South. Political battles often centered on cultural differences, most notably prohibition. Irish whiskey drinkers, German beer drinkers, and Italian wine drinkers were equally outraged by antiliquor legislation.

Political Bosses and Machine Politics

political machine Urban political organization that controlled patronage and manipulated immigrants

The swelling numbers of urban dwellers gave rise to a new kind of politician, the "boss," who presided over the city's **political machine**—an unofficial political organization designed to keep a particular party or faction in office. Whether officially serving as mayor or not, the boss, assisted by local ward or precinct captains, wielded enormous influence in city government.

For better or worse, the political machine was America's unique contribution to municipal government in an era of pell-mell urban growth. Typified by Tammany Hall, the Democratic organization that dominated New York City politics from the 1830s to the 1930s, machines emerged in a host of cities after the Civil War.

By the turn of the century, many cities had experienced machine rule. Working through the local ward captains to turn out voters, the machine rode herd on the tangle of municipal bureaucracies, controlling who was hired for the police and fire departments. It rewarded its friends and punished its enemies through its control of taxes, licenses, and inspections.

At the neighborhood level, the ward boss often acted as a welfare agent, helping the needy and protecting the troubled. Spending three dollars to pay a fine for a juvenile offense meant a lot to the poor, but it was small change to a boss who raked in millions from public-utility contracts and land deals. While the machine helped alleviate some suffering, it entangled urban social services with corrupt politics and often prevented city government from responding to the real problems of the city's neediest inhabitants.

William "Magear" Tweed Corrupt boss of the Tammany Hall organization that ran New York City

Under New York City's boss **William "Magear" Tweed,** the Tammany Hall machine sank to new depths of corruption. Between 1869 and 1871, Tweed dispensed sixty thousand patronage positions and pumped up the city's debt by $70 million through graft and inflated contracts.

By the turn of the century, the bosses were facing well-organized assaults on their power, led by an urban elite whose members sought to restore "good government." In this atmosphere the bosses increasingly forged alliances with civic organizations and reform leagues. The results paved the way for new sewage and transportation systems, expanded parklands, and improved public services—a record of considerable accomplishment, given the magnitude of the problems created by urban growth.

Regulating the Money Supply

In the 1870s, politicians confronted a tough problem of economic policy: how to create a money supply adequate for a growing economy without producing inflation. Americans' almost superstitious reverence for gold and silver created problems of its own. Many believed that only gold or silver, or certificates exchangeable for these metals, were trustworthy. All antebellum federal currency consisted of gold or silver coins or U.S. Treasury notes redeemable in gold or silver. During the Civil War, the federal government issued "greenbacks," paper money not backed by either precious metal.

Bankers and creditors also believed that economic stability required a strictly limited currency supply. Debtors, in contrast, favored expanding the money supply to make it easier for them to pay off their debts. The monetary debate thus focused on a specific question: Should the Civil War paper "greenbacks" still in circulation be retained or eliminated, leaving only a currency backed by gold? The hard times associated with the Panic of 1873 sharpened this dispute.

The Greenback Party (founded in 1877) called for an expanded money supply, as well as other measures to benefit workers and farmers. In the 1878 midterm elections, Greenback candidates received more than 1 million votes and won fourteen seats in Congress (see Chapter 16).

As prosperity returned, the Greenback Party faded, but the money issue did not. An even longer-lasting controversy surged over the coinage of silver. In 1873, Congress instructed the U.S. mint to cease making silver coins, thus "demonetizing" silver. But new discoveries in Nevada (see Chapter 17) soon increased the silver supply, leading debtor groups to demand that the government resume the coinage of silver.

Enthusiastically backed by the silver-mine owners, silver forces won a partial victory in 1878, when Congress required the treasury to buy and mint up to $4 million worth of silver each month. But the treasury, dominated by monetary conservatives, sabotaged the law's intent by refusing to circulate the silver dollars that it minted.

Frustrated silver advocates tried a new approach in the **Sherman Silver Purchase Act** of 1890. This measure instructed the treasury to buy 4.5 million ounces of silver monthly and issue treasury notes, redeemable in gold or silver, equivalent to the cost of these purchases. The money supply increased, but only slightly. Thus, the controversy over silver dragged on.

Sherman Silver Purchase Act Law passed in 1890 in response to farmers' calls for inflationary monetary policies

Civil-Service Reform

For decades, successful candidates had rewarded supporters and contributors with jobs ranging from cabinet seats to lowly municipal posts. Defenders called the system "rotation in office" and claimed that it was a democratic way of filling government positions. Critics, however, dubbed it the spoils system after the old expression, "To the victor belong the spoils."

For years, a small but influential group of reformers had campaigned for a professional civil service based on merit. Well-educated and wealthy, these reformers favored a government staffed by "gentlemen." The reformers had a point. A professional civil service was needed as government grew more complex. Cautiously embracing

"Where Is the Difference?"

By equating criminal payoffs to the police with corporate contributions to senators, this cartoon in *Puck* magazine suggests that corruption pervades society and needs to be stopped.

The Granger Collection, NYC

the civil-service cause, President Hayes in 1877 launched an investigation of the corrupt New York City customs office and fired two high officials. One, Chester A. Arthur, had played a key role in passing out jobs.

When Congressman James A. Garfield won the 1880 Republican presidential nomination, the delegates, to appease the opposing New York faction, chose Chester A. Arthur, the loyalist Hayes had recently fired, as Garfield's running mate. Since Garfield enjoyed excellent health, the choice of the totally unqualified Arthur seemed safe. The Democrats nominated a career army officer, Winfield Scott Hancock, and the Greenbackers gave the nod to Congressman James B. Weaver of Iowa. Garfield edged out Hancock by a razor-thin margin; Weaver trailed far behind.

Pendleton Civil Service Act
Attempt to end spoils system and create a professional civil service

Garfield's assassination in 1881 by the crazed office-seeker Charles Guiteau brought Vice President Arthur, the very symbol of patronage corruption, to the White House. Civil-service reformers then portrayed the fallen president as a spoils-system martyr. In 1883, Congress enacted the **Pendleton Civil Service Act,** which set up a commission to prepare competitive examinations and establish standards of merit for a variety of federal jobs. It also forbade political candidates from soliciting contributions from government workers.

The creation of a professional civil service helped bring the federal government in step with the modernizing trends transforming society. As for Chester A. Arthur, his performance surprised those who had expected him to be an utter disaster. Arthur supported civil-service reform and proved quite independent. Fed up with the feuding Republicans, in 1882 the voters gave the Democrats a strong majority in the House of Representatives. In 1884, for the first time since 1856, they would put a Democrat in the White House: Grover Cleveland.

CHECKING IN

- Republicans stressed probusiness measures, such as the tariff, and claimed they were protecting American families.
- Democrats decried government interference, such as the tariff, and said they were the ones protecting families.
- Republicans flourished in New England and the Midwest, whereas Democrats dominated the South and urban areas.
- Battles over greenbacks and the coinage of silver played a major role in national politics.
- Civil-service reform became a major issue, especially after Garfield's death at the hands of a deranged office-seeker.

Politics of Privilege, Politics of Exclusion, 1884–1892

What factors prompted the rise of the Grange and the Farmers' Alliance movements?

The stalemate between the two major parties in their battle to establish the standards for economic growth continued under President Cleveland, a Democrat, and President Harrison, a Republican. Both challenged powerful interests and faced stiff opposition. Cleveland alienated strong lobbies by calling for cuts in the tariff and in veterans' pensions. In 1888, one of the most corrupt elections in American history put Benjamin Harrison of Indiana in the White House, thus restoring big business and the veterans' lobby to the driver's seat. Simultaneously, debt-ridden farmers mounted protests and began to organize. And in the South, the white majority consolidated their political power by denying the region's black citizens their most basic rights.

A Democrat in the White House: Grover Cleveland, 1885–1889

At a tumultuous Chicago convention in 1884, the Republicans nominated their best-known leader, James G. Blaine. Blaine was a gifted orator; however, his name had been stained by the revelation that he, as Speaker of the House, had offered political favors to a railroad company in exchange for stock. For reformers, Blaine epitomized the hated patronage system. To E. L. Godkin, he "wallowed in spoils like a rhinoceros in an African pool."

Sensing Blaine's vulnerability, the Democrats chose a sharply contrasting nominee, Grover Cleveland of New York. In a meteoric rise from reform mayor of Buffalo to governor, Cleveland had fought the bosses and spoils men. The shrewdness of the Democrats' choice became apparent when Godkin, Carl Schurz, and other Republican reformers bolted to Cleveland. They were promptly nicknamed **Mugwumps,** an Algonquian term for a renegade chief.

Mugwumps Reformers, including E. L. Godkin and Carl Schurz, who switched from the Republican to the Democratic Party in 1884

Unfortunately, as a young man Cleveland had fathered an illegitimate child. He admitted the indiscretion, but the Republicans still jeered at rallies: "Ma, Ma, where's my pa?" Facing opposition from the New York City Democratic machine that he had fought as governor, Cleveland risked losing his own state. But in October, a New York City clergyman publicly denounced the Democrats as the party of "Rum, Romanism, and Rebellion." Blaine failed to immediately repudiate the remark. This blunder and the Mugwumps' defection allowed Cleveland to carry New York State by twelve hundred votes, and with it the election.

Once in office, Cleveland embraced the belief that government must not meddle in the economy and opposed any public regulation of corporations. He also rejected providing any governmental help for those in need. In vetoing a bill that would have provided seeds to drought-stricken farmers in Texas, he warned that people should not expect the government to solve their problems.

One matter did arouse Cleveland, however: the tariff. Since it was a major source of revenue in the era before a federal income tax, the tariff functioned as a protection for special interests and a source of government income. But questions remained regarding which imported goods should be subject to duties, and how much?

Opinions differed radically. Producers of commodities like coal, timber, and wool demanded tariff protection against foreign competition, as did many manufacturers. Other businesses, however, while seeking protection for their finished products, wanted low tariffs on the raw materials they required. Most farmers, in contrast, hated all tariffs for making it hard to sell American farm products abroad.

Cleveland's call for lower tariffs arose from his concern that high tariffs created huge federal budget surpluses, which tempted legislators to spend more money on pet projects in their home districts. With his distaste for paternalistic government, Cleveland viewed the budget surplus as a corrupting influence. Although the Democratic campaign of 1888 gave little attention to the issue, corporate leaders found Cleveland's talk of lower tariffs threatening.

Cleveland stirred up another hornet's nest by opposing the routine payment of veterans' disability pensions. No one opposed pensions for the deserving, but fraudulent claims proliferated. Unlike his predecessors, Cleveland investigated these claims and rejected many. He also vetoed a bill that would have pensioned all disabled veterans whether or not the disability occurred in military service. The pension roll should be an honor roll, he stressed, not a refuge for fraud.

Big Business Strikes Back: Benjamin Harrison, 1889–1893

By 1888 some influential groups had concluded that Cleveland must go. Republicans turned to Benjamin Harrison of Indiana. A corporation lawyer and former senator, Harrison was so aloof that some ridiculed him as the human iceberg. To avoid alienating voters, his campaign managers brought delegations to his Indiana home, where he hammered at the tariff issue. Harrison warned that only a high tariff could ensure business prosperity, decent wages, and a healthy home market for farmers.

The Republicans amassed a $4 million campaign fund from worried business leaders to purchase posters, buttons, and votes. Despite voter fraud, Cleveland received almost one hundred thousand more votes than Harrison. But Harrison won the key states of New York and Indiana and won the electoral vote. Once in office, Harrison swiftly rewarded his supporters. He appointed as commissioner of pensions a GAR official who, on taking office, declared "God help the surplus!" The pension rolls soon ballooned from 676,000 to nearly a million. This massive pension system became America's first large public-welfare program. In 1890, the triumphant Republicans also passed the McKinley Tariff, which pushed rates to an all-time high.

Rarely has the federal government been so subservient to entrenched economic interests and so out of touch with the plight of the disadvantaged as during the 1880s. But inaction bred discontent. In the election of 1890, the Democrats gained sixty-six congressional seats and won control of the House of Representatives. Farmers, too, turned to politics and swung into action.

Agrarian Protest and the Rise of the People's Party

Plains farming had long been a risky venture (see Chapter 17). Between 1873 and 1877, terrible grasshopper infestations consumed half the midwestern wheat crop. As production recovered, prices fell. Wheat tumbled from

$2.95 a bushel in 1866 to $1.06 in 1880. Indebted farmers went bankrupt or barely survived. One struggling Minnesota farmer wrote the governor in 1874, "[W]e can see nothing but starvation in the future if relief does not come."

In 1867, midwestern farmers formed the **Grange,** or "Patrons of Husbandry." Membership climbed to more than 1.5 million by the early 1870s. Offering information, emotional support, and fellowship, the Grange urged farmers to "buy less and produce more, in order to make our farms more self-sustaining." They negotiated special discounts with farm-machinery dealers and set up "cash-only" cooperative stores and grain-storage elevators to cut out the "middlemen"—the bankers, grain brokers, and merchants who made money at the farmers' expense.

Grange First major farmers' political movement

Grangers focused their wrath on railroads, which gave discounts to large shippers, bribed state legislators, and charged higher rates for short runs than for long hauls. Midwestern Grangers successfully lobbied state legislatures in 1874 to pass laws fixing maximum rates for freight shipments. The railroads appealed these "Granger laws" to the Supreme Court. But in *Munn v. Illinois* (1877), the Court ruled against the railroads and upheld an Illinois law setting maximum grain storage rates.

When the Court reversed itself in *Wabash v. Illinois* (1886), Congress passed the Interstate Commerce Act (1887), reaffirming the federal government's power to oversee railroad activities and establishing a new agency, the Interstate Commerce Commission (ICC), to do just that. Although the commission failed to curb the railroads' monopolistic practices, it did establish the principle of federal regulation of interstate transportation.

Despite promising beginnings, the Grange movement soon faltered. By 1878, through lobbying at the state level, railroads had won repeal of most state regulations. In addition, the cash-only cooperatives failed, because most farmers had little cash. The Grange ideal of financial independence proved unrealistic because conditions prevailing on the Plains made it impossible to farm without borrowing money. When the prices of corn, wheat, and cotton briefly revived after 1878, many farmers deserted the movement.

The problems that drove farmers to form the Grange prompted southern and midwestern farmers to form the alliance movement. The **Farmers' Alliance** began in Texas in the 1870s as small planters, trapped by the crop lien system, mortgaged future harvests to cover current expenses. Mired in debt, about a third of southern farmers gave up their land and became tenants or sharecroppers by 1900.

Farmers' Alliance Successful farm protest movement, organized regionally; spawned the Populist Party

In 1887, Texan Charles W. Macune assumed leadership of the Alliance movement. By 1889, Macune had merged several regional groups into the National Farmers' Alliance and Industrial Union, or the Southern Alliance. A parallel black organization, the National Colored Farmers' Alliance, emerged in Arkansas and spread to other southern states.

As they attended alliance rallies, read the alliance newspaper, and listened to alliance speakers, hard-hit farm families became increasingly aware of their political potential. An Arkansas member wrote in 1889, "Reform never begins with the leaders, it comes from the people." By 1890, the Southern Alliance boasted 3 million members and its black counterpart another 1.2 million.

Meanwhile, alliance fever had spread to the Great Plains. Alliances sprang up in Kansas, Nebraska, Iowa, and Minnesota. Hit hard by drought and insect infestations, Western Kansas lost 50 percent of its population between 1888 and 1892.

"In God we trusted, in Kansas we busted," some scrawled on their wagons. Others hung on, and the Kansas Alliance grew to 130,000 members by 1890. What had begun as a desperate attempt to save their farms had now turned into a massive political campaign.

Reformers at first tried to create a biracial movement. Southern Alliance leaders Tom Watson of Georgia and Leonidas Polk of North Carolina urged southern farmers, black and white, to act together. For a time, this message of racial cooperation in the interest of reform offered promise. Women were involved in the movement as well. Mary E. Lease, a Wichita lawyer, burst on the scene in 1890 as a fiery alliance orator. Other women rallied to the new cause, founding the National Women's Alliance (NWA) in 1891.

As the movement swelled, the opposition turned nasty. When Jerry Simpson, an alliance rancher from Kansas, mentioned the silk stockings of a conservative politician in his district and noted that he had no such finery, a hostile newspaper editor labeled him "Sockless Jerry" Simpson, the nickname he carried to his grave. When Mary Lease advised Kansans to "raise less corn and more hell," a conservative newspaper sneered, "[Kansas] has started to raise hell, as Mrs. Lease advised, and [the state] seems to have an overproduction."

All this activity helped shape a new political agenda. In 1889, the Southern and Northwestern Alliances loosely merged and lined up candidates in the 1890 midterm elections. Alliance candidates focused on government action on behalf of farmers and workers, including tariff reduction, a graduated income tax, public ownership of the railroads, a ban on landownership by aliens, and "the free and unlimited coinage of silver."

The 1890 elections revealed the strength of agrarian protest. Southern Democrats who endorsed alliance goals won four governorships and control of eight state legislatures. On the Great Plains, alliance-endorsed candidates controlled the Kansas and Nebraska legislatures and gained the balance of power in Minnesota and South Dakota. Three alliance-backed senators and fifty congressmen went to Washington in 1890 as angry winds from the hinterlands buffeted the political system.

Regional differences, which threatened to divide the movement, were soon overcome by shared economic grievance. In February 1892, alliance leaders organized the People's Party of the United States, generally called the **Populist Party.** At the party convention in Omaha, Nebraska, that August, cheering delegates nominated for president the former Civil War general James B. Weaver of Iowa. The Populist platform called for the direct popular election of senators and other electoral reforms. It also endorsed a **subtreasury plan** by which farmers could store their nonperishable commodities in government warehouses and then sell the stored commodities when market prices rose. Ignatius Donnelly's ringing preamble called for a return of the government "to the hands of 'the plain people' with which class it originated."

Populist Party Agrarian-based third-party challenge to Republicans and Democrats

subtreasury plan Charles Macune's plan to bring government aid to struggling farmers

African-Americans After Reconstruction

As the Populists organized, a group of citizens with profound grievances suffered renewed oppression. As discussed in Chapter 16, with the end of Reconstruction in 1877 and the restoration of power to white elites, southern whites sought an end to "Negro rule" and tried to suppress the black vote. Initially, whites relied on intimidation, terror, and fraud to limit black voting rights, but in 1890 Mississippi amended its state constitution to exclude most black voters, and other southern states followed suit.

Because the Fifteenth Amendment (1870) had guaranteed all male citizens' right to vote, white southerners used indirect means, such as literacy tests, poll taxes, and property requirements, to disfranchise blacks. To protect illiterate whites, the so-called grandfather clause exempted from these electoral requirements anyone with an ancestor who had voted in 1860. Black disfranchisement proceeded erratically, but by the early twentieth century it was essentially complete.

Disfranchisement was only one part of the system of white supremacy. In a parallel development, state after state passed laws imposing strict racial segregation in many realms of life (see Chapter 21). African-American caterers, barbers, contractors, bricklayers, carpenters, and other artisans lost their white clientele. Blacks who went to prison—sometimes for minor offenses—faced the convict-lease system, which cotton planters, railroad builders, and other employers used to "lease" prison gangs and force them to work under slave-labor conditions. Thousands died under the brutal convict-labor system, which survived into the early decades of the twentieth century.

Lynching became the ultimate enforcer of white supremacy. Through the 1880s and 1890s, about a hundred blacks were lynched annually in the United States, mainly in the South. The stated reasons for lynching, often the rape of a white woman, frequently arose from rumor and unsubstantiated accusations. The charge of "attempted rape" could cover a wide range of behaviors unacceptable to whites, such as questioning authority or talking back.

lynching Vigilante hanging of those accused of crimes; used primarily against blacks

The lynch mob demonstrated whites' absolute power. In the South, more than 80 percent of the lynchings involved black victims. Lynchings most commonly occurred in the Cotton Belt, and they tended to rise at times of economic distress. Not surprisingly, lynching reached its highest point in 1892 as many poor blacks joined the agrarian protest and rallied to the Populist Party banner.

The relationship between southern agrarian protest and white racism was complex. Some Populists, like Georgia's Tom Watson, sought to build an interracial movement. Watson denounced lynching and the convict-lease system. When a black Populist leader pursued by a lynch mob took refuge in his house during the 1892 campaign, Watson summoned two thousand armed white Populists to defend him. However, most white Populists clung to racism.

On balance, the rise of southern agrarian protest deepened racial hatred and worsened blacks' situation. Meanwhile, the federal government stood aside. A generation of northern politicians paid lip service to egalitarian principles but failed to apply them to African-Americans.

The Supreme Court similarly abandoned African-Americans. The Court ripped gaping holes in the Fourteenth Amendment, which guaranteed blacks citizenship and equal protection of the law, and the Civil Rights Act of 1875, which outlawed racial discrimination. In the *Civil Rights Cases* (1883), the Court declared the Civil Rights Act of 1875 unconstitutional. According to the justices, the Fourteenth Amendment prevented governments, but not individuals, from infringing on civil rights. In ***Plessy* v. *Ferguson*** (1896), the Court upheld a Louisiana law requiring segregated railroad cars. Racial segregation was constitutional, the justices ruled, if equal facilities were made available to each race. With the Supreme Court's blessing,

Plessy* v. *Ferguson Supreme Court ruling validating "separate but equal"

the South also segregated its public schools, ignoring the caveat that separate facilities must be equal. White children studied in nicer buildings, used newer equipment, and were taught by better-paid teachers. Not until 1954 did the Court overturn the "separate but equal" doctrine. Rounding out a dismal record, the justices in 1898 upheld the poll tax and literacy tests by which southern states had disfranchised blacks.

Few northerners protested the South's white supremacist society. However, the restoration of sectional harmony came at a high price: acquiescence by the North of the utter debasement of the South's black citizenry. Further, the separatist principle endorsed in *Plessy* had a pervasive impact, affecting blacks nationwide, Mexicans in Texas, Asians in California, and other groups.

Booker T. Washington
Leading black figure of the late nineteenth century; stressed vocational education and accommodation

Blacks responded to their plight in various ways. The nation's foremost black leader from the 1890s until his death in 1915 was **Booker T. Washington.** Born into slavery in Virginia in 1856, Washington enrolled at a freedman's school in Hampton, Virginia, and in 1881 organized a black state vocational school in Alabama that eventually became Tuskegee (tuss-KEE-ghee) University. Washington attained prominence in 1895 when he gave an address in Atlanta insisting that the first task of blacks must be to acquire vocational skills. Once blacks proved their economic value, he predicted, racism would fade; meanwhile, they must patiently accept their lot. Washington lectured widely, and his autobiography, *Up from Slavery* (1901), recounted his rise from poverty thanks to honesty, hard work, and kindly patrons—themes familiar from Horatio Alger's self-help books.

Other blacks responded resourcefully to racism. Black churches provided emotional support, as did black fraternal lodges. In addition, a handful of blacks established banks and successful businesses, such as insurance companies and barbershops.

Meanwhile, voices of black protest never wholly died out. Frederick Douglass urged that blacks press on for full equality. Blacks should meet violence with violence, insisted militant New York black leader T. Thomas Fortune. But for others, the solution was to leave the South. In 1879, several thousand "exodusters" moved to Kansas (see Chapter 16). Some ten thousand migrated to Chicago between 1870 and 1890. Blacks who moved north, however, soon found that public opinion sanctioned many forms of de facto discrimination.

The rise of the so-called solid South had important political implications. For one thing, it made a mockery of the two-party system. For years, the only meaningful election south of the Potomac was the Democratic primary. The large bloc of southern Democrats elected to Congress each year, accumulating seniority and power, exerted a great and often reactionary influence on public policy. Finally, southern Democrats wielded enormous clout in the national party. No Democratic contender for national office who was unacceptable to them stood a chance.

Above all, the rigid caste system of the post-Reconstruction South shaped the consciousness of those caught up in it, white and black alike. Describing her girlhood in the turn-of-the-century South, white novelist Lillian Smith wrote, "I learned it is possible to pray at night and ride a Jim Crow car the next morning; . . . to glow when the word democracy was used, and to practice slavery from morning to night."

CHECKING IN

- Grover Cleveland attempted tariff reforms and tried to gain control of the pension system.
- Big business and the GAR combined to defeat Cleveland in 1888.
- The Grange movement rose as an attempt by farmers to reassert control over their lives, which seemed to be at the mercy of railroads, middlemen, and bankers.
- The Alliance superseded the Grange and ultimately organized the Populist Party in 1892.
- Blacks were increasingly shut out of political life; they turned to accommodationist leaders like Booker T. Washington.

THE 1890S: POLITICS IN A DEPRESSION DECADE

Why did William Jennings Bryan fail to win the presidency in 1896?

In the 1890s, smoldering discontent with the major parties burst into flames. As banks failed and railroads went bankrupt, the nation slid into a grinding depression. The crises of the 1890s laid bare the paralysis of the federal government—dominated by a business elite—when confronted by the new social realities of factories, urban slums, immigrant workers, and desperate farmers. In response, irate farmers, laborers, and their supporters joined a new party, the Populists, to challenge the system.

1892: Populists Challenge the Status Quo

The Populist Party platform adopted in July 1892 offered a broad vision of national reform. That same month, thirteen people died in a gun battle between strikers and strike-breakers at the Homestead steel plant near Pittsburgh, and President Harrison sent federal troops to Idaho, where a silver-mine strike had turned violent. Events seemed to justify the Populists' warnings of chaos ahead.

The 1892 campaign for the White House was a replay of 1888, Harrison versus Cleveland, but this time Cleveland won by more than 360,000 votes, a decisive margin in an era of close elections. A public reaction against labor violence and the McKinley Tariff hurt Harrison. Meanwhile, a solid showing by Populist candidates sparked great hopes for the future. James B. Weaver got more than 1 million votes, 8.5 percent of the total, and the Populists elected five senators, ten congressmen, and three governors. But the party's strength was spotty. It made no dent in New England, the urban East, or the traditionally Republican farm regions of the Midwest.

In the South, racism, Democratic loyalty, distaste for the former Union general Weaver, and widespread voter fraud kept the Populist tally under 25 percent. This failure killed the prospects for interracial agrarian reform. After 1892, southern politicians seeking to appeal to poor whites—including a disillusioned Tom Watson—stayed within the Democratic fold and laced their populism with racism.

Capitalism in Crisis: The Depression of 1893–1897

Cleveland soon confronted a major crisis: an economic collapse in the railroad industry that quickly spread. The first hint of trouble flared up in February 1893 when the Philadelphia and Reading Railroad failed. This bankruptcy came at a moment of weakened confidence in the government's ability to redeem paper money with gold on demand. Economic problems in London in 1890 had forced British investors to unload millions of dollars in American stocks, draining U.S. gold reserves. Moreover, the Sherman Silver Purchase's requirement that the government pay for its monthly silver purchases with treasury certificates redeemable for either silver or gold further drained gold reserves.

Between January 1892 and March 1893, the gold reserve had fallen to $100 million, the minimum considered necessary to support the dollar. This decline alarmed those who viewed the gold standard as the only sure evidence of the government's financial stability.

Panic of 1893 Wall Street collapse that touched off a nationwide economic depression

The railroad's collapse thus triggered the **Panic of 1893.** Fear fed on itself as alarmed investors converted their stock holdings to gold. Stock prices plunged; the gold reserve sank; by the end of the year, seventy-four railroads and more than fifteen thousand commercial institutions, including six hundred banks, had failed. The Panic of 1893 started a full-scale depression and set off four years of hard times.

The crisis took a heavy human toll. Industrial unemployment soared to as much as 25 percent. Millions of factory workers had no money to buy food or heat their homes, and jobless men tramped the streets looking for work. Unusually harsh winters in 1893 and 1894 aggravated the misery, especially in major cities. In New York City, where the crisis quickly swamped local relief agencies, a minister reported actual starvation. Rural America, already hard hit by declining agricultural prices, faced ruin. Corn plummeted from 50¢ to 21¢ a bushel. Cotton fell to 5¢ a pound.

Some desperate Americans turned to protest. In Massillon, Ohio, self-taught monetary expert Jacob Coxey proposed as a solution to unemployment a $500 million public-works program funded with paper money. Coxey organized a march on Washington to lobby for his scheme. Thousands joined him en route, and several hundred actually reached Washington in late April 1894. However, police arrested Coxey and other leaders when they attempted to enter the Capitol grounds, and his "army" broke up. Although some considered Coxey eccentric, his proposal closely resembled programs that the government would adopt during the depression of the 1930s.

As unrest intensified, fear clutched middle-class Americans. A church magazine demanded that troops put "a pitiless stop" to outbreaks of unrest. To some observers, a bloody upheaval seemed imminent.

Business Leaders Respond

In the face of suffering and turmoil, Cleveland refused to intervene. Boom-and-bust economic cycles were inevitable, he insisted. Government could do nothing. Missing the larger picture, Cleveland focused on a single issue, the gold standard. In August 1893, he persuaded Congress to repeal the Sherman Silver Purchase Act, which he blamed for the run on gold.

Nevertheless, the gold drain continued. In early 1895, with the gold reserve down to $41 million, Cleveland turned to Wall Street. Bankers J. P. Morgan and August Belmont agreed to lend the government $62 million in exchange for discounted U.S. bonds. The government then purchased gold to replenish the reserve. Meanwhile, Morgan and Belmont resold their bonds for a substantial profit. The deal helped to restore confidence in the government's economic stability. However, Cleveland's gambit confirmed radicals' suspicions of an unholy alliance between Washington and Wall Street.

As the tariff battle made clear, corporate interests held the whip hand. Although Cleveland favored tariff reform, the Congress of 1893–1895—despite its Democratic majorities—generally yielded to high-tariff lobbyists. The Wilson-Gorman Tariff of 1894 made so many concessions to special interests that Cleveland disgustedly allowed it to become law without his signature.

Hinting at changes ahead, the Wilson-Gorman Tariff imposed a modest income tax of 2 percent on all income over $4,000 (about $40,000 in purchasing power today). But in 1895 the Supreme Court declared the tax unconstitutional. Thus, whether one looked at the executive, the legislature, or the judiciary, Washington's subordination to financial interests seemed absolute.

The depression also helped reorient social thought. Middle-class charitable workers, long convinced that individual character flaws caused poverty, now realized that even sober and hard-working people could succumb to economic forces beyond their control. Laissez-faire ideology weakened too, as depression-worn Americans adopted a broader conception of government's proper role in dealing with the social consequences of industrialization. The depression, in short, not only brought suffering; it also taught lessons.

Silver Advocates Capture the Democratic Party

Republican gains in the 1894 midterm elections revealed the depth of revulsion against Cleveland and the Democrats, who were blamed for the hard times. Republicans gained control of Congress and several key states. Populist candidates won nearly 1.5 million votes, 40 percent over their 1892 total. Most of the Populist gains came in the South.

The serious economic conflict that split Americans focused on a symbolic issue: free silver. Cleveland's rigid defense of the gold standard forced his opponents into an exaggerated obsession with silver, obscuring the genuine issues dividing rich and poor, creditor and debtor, and farmer and city-dweller. Conservatives tirelessly upheld the gold standard, and agrarian radicals extolled silver as a universal cure-all.

Each side had a point. Gold advocates recognized that uncontrolled inflation could be catastrophic. The silver advocates knew from experience how tight-money policies depressed prices and devastated farmers. Unfortunately, these underlying realities were rarely expressed clearly.

At the 1896 Democratic convention in Chicago, western and southern delegates adopted a platform demanding the free and unlimited coinage of silver at the ratio to gold of sixteen to one—in effect, repudiating the Cleveland administration. **William Jennings Bryan** of Nebraska, an ardent advocate of free silver, captured the nomination. Only thirty-six years old, the young lawyer had already served two terms in Congress championing western agrarian interests.

William Jennings Bryan
Orator, champion of farm interests, anti-imperialist, three-time Democratic presidential candidate

Joining Christian imagery with economic analysis, Bryan delivered his major convention speech during the debate over the platform. With his booming voice carrying his words to the upper gallery of the convention hall, Bryan praised farmers as the nation's bedrock. The wildly cheering delegates had identified their candidate even before he reached his rousing conclusion—"You shall not press down upon the brow of labor this crown of thorns, you shall not crucify mankind upon a cross of gold!"

The silverites' capture of the Democratic Party left the Populists with a dilemma. They, too, advocated free silver, but only as one reform among many. To back Bryan would be to abandon the broad Populist program. But a separate Populist ticket would likely siphon votes from Bryan and ensure a Republican victory. Reluctantly, the Populists endorsed Bryan. The Republicans, meanwhile, nominated former Ohio governor William McKinley on a platform endorsing the high protective tariff and the gold standard.

1896: Republicans Triumphant

Bryan did his best to sustain the momentum of the Chicago convention, crisscrossing the country by train to deliver his free-silver campaign speech. One skeptical editor compared him to Nebraska's notoriously shallow Platte River: six inches deep and a mile wide at the mouth.

Mark Hanna, a Cleveland industrialist, managed McKinley's campaign. Dignified and aloof, McKinley could not match Bryan's popular touch. Accordingly, Hanna built the campaign not around the candidate but around posters, pamphlets, and newspaper editorials. These publications warned of the dangers of free silver, caricatured Bryan as a radical, and portrayed McKinley and the gold standard as twin pillars of prosperity.

Drawing on a war chest possibly as large as $7 million, Hanna spent lavishly. J. P. Morgan and John D. Rockefeller together contributed $500,000 to the McKinley campaign, far more than Bryan's total campaign contributions. McKinley himself stayed home in Canton, Ohio, emerging from time to time to read speeches to visiting delegations. All told, some 750,000 people trekked to Canton to take part in McKinley's cleverly organized "front-porch campaign."

David J. Frent/Historical/Corbis

Women Bryan Supporters

Although women could not vote in national elections in the 1890s, they actively participated in political campaigns. These women worked to turn out the vote for William Jennings Bryan.

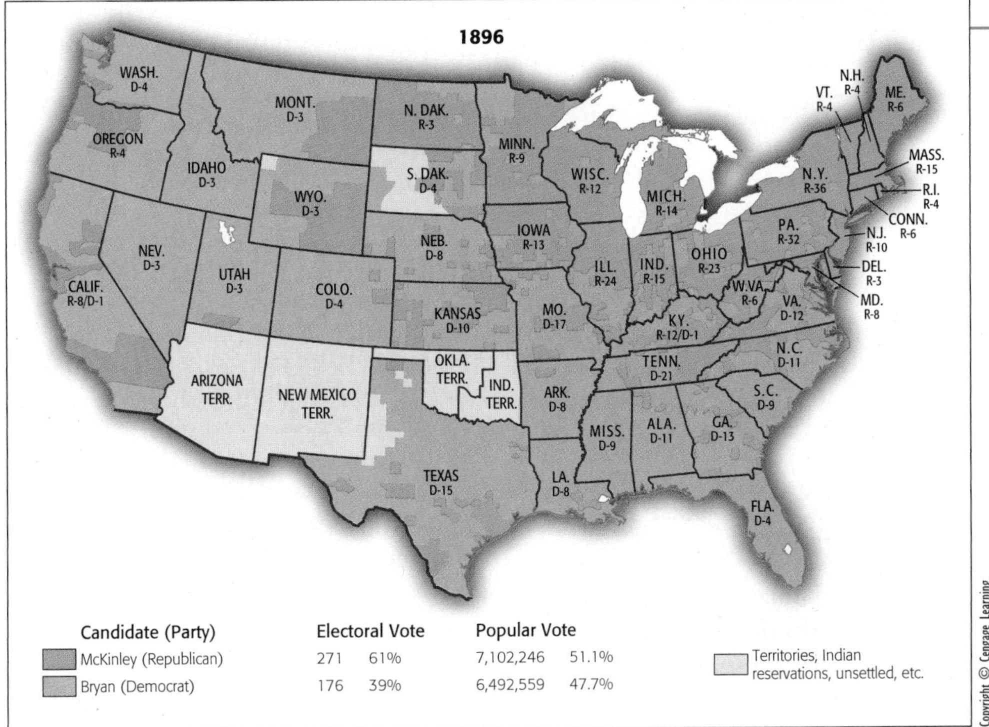

Map 20.1
The Election of 1896

Interactive Map

On election day, McKinley beat Bryan by over six hundred thousand votes (see Map 20.1). He swept the Northeast and the Midwest and even carried three farm states beyond the Mississippi as well as California and Oregon. Bryan's strength was limited to the South and the Great Plains and mountain states.

Why did Bryan lose despite protest spirit abroad in the land? His core constituency, while passionately loyal, was limited. Seduced by free silver and Bryan's oratory, the Democrats upheld a platform and a candidate with little appeal for factory workers. Urban voters, realizing that higher farm prices also meant higher food prices, went heavily for McKinley. Bryan's weakness in urban America reflected cultural differences as well. To urban Catholics and Jews, this moralistic, teetotaling Nebraskan thundering like a Protestant revival preacher seemed utterly alien.

The McKinley administration translated its conservative platform into law. The Dingley Tariff (1897) pushed rates to all-time highs, and the Currency Act of 1900 committed the United States to the gold standard. Because of returning prosperity, rising farm prices, and the discovery of gold in Alaska, these measures roused little opposition, and McKinley easily defeated Bryan again in 1900.

The elections of 1894 and 1896 produced a Republican majority that, except for Woodrow Wilson's presidency (1913–1921), would dominate national politics until the election of Franklin D. Roosevelt in 1932. Populism collapsed, but an emerging new reform movement, progressivism, would bring many of the Populists' proposals to fruition.

CHECKING IN

- Populists won more than a million votes in the 1892 presidential election.
- The Panic of 1893 hardened into a deep depression; want and suffering were widespread.
- Coxey's army showed the depth of discontent with the political system; nevertheless, corporate interests continued to dominate national politics.
- The midterm elections of 1894 showed revulsion against the Democrats, whom voters blamed for the depression following the Panic of 1893.
- In 1896, the Democrats bowed to free-silver interests and nominated the eloquent William Jennings Bryan, who was defeated by Republican William McKinley.
- Populism collapsed, paving the way for a Republican majority that would dominate national politics for the next fifteen years.

EXPANSIONIST STIRRINGS AND WAR WITH SPAIN, 1878–1901

Why did the United States go to war with Spain and become an imperial power?

The same corporate elite that dominated late-nineteenth-century domestic politics influenced U.S. foreign policy as well, contributing to surging expansionist pressures. Business leaders, politicians, statesmen, and editorial writers insisted that national greatness required that America match Europe's imperial expansion. Fanned by sensationalistic newspaper coverage of a Cuban struggle for independence, war between the United States and Spain broke out in 1898.

Roots of Expansionist Sentiment

Ever since the first European settlers had colonized North America's Atlantic coast, the newcomers had been an expansionist people. By the 1840s, the push westward had acquired a name: Manifest Destiny. Directed inward after 1865 toward the settlement of the trans-Mississippi West (see Chapter 17), this impulse turned outward in the 1880s as Americans followed the imperial example set by Great Britain, France, Belgium, Italy, Germany, and Japan. National greatness, it appeared, demanded an empire.

Many business leaders believed that continued domestic prosperity required overseas markets. Foreign markets offered a safety valve for potentially explosive pressures in the U.S. economy. Proponents of a strong navy further fueled the expansionist mood. In *The Influence of Sea Power upon History* (1890), **Alfred Thayer Mahan** equated sea power with national greatness and urged a rapid U.S. naval buildup, which required overseas bases. Meanwhile, some religious leaders proclaimed America's mission was to spread Christianity, an argument with racist tinges. One minister averred that "God is training the Anglo-Saxon race for its mission"—a mission of bringing Christianity and civilization to the world's "weaker races."

Alfred Thayer Mahan Leading proponent of imperialism and sea power

A group of Republican expansionists, led by Senator Henry Cabot Lodge, diplomat John Hay, and Theodore Roosevelt of New York, preached imperial greatness and military might. "I should welcome almost any war," declared Roosevelt in 1897; ". . . this country needs one." Such advocates of expansionism built upon Social Darwinist rhetoric of the day and argued that war, as a vehicle for natural selection, would test and refurbish American manhood, restore honor, and create a new generation of civic-minded Americans. This gendered appeal both counterbalanced concerns about women's political activism and helped forge the disparate arguments for expansionism into a simple, visceral plea that had a broad appeal.

A series of diplomatic skirmishes in the mid-1890s revealed the newly assertive American mood. In the mid-1880s, quarrels between the United States and Great Britain had flared over fishing rights in the North Atlantic and North Pacific, reawakening latent anti-British feelings and the old dream of acquiring Canada.

In 1898, a compromise settled the fishing rights dispute, but by then attention had shifted to Latin America. In 1891, tensions had flared between the United States and Chile after a mob in Valparaiso (val-puh-RYE-zoh) killed two American sailors on shore leave. War fever subsided only when Chile apologized and paid an indemnity of $75,000.

Another Latin American conflict arose from a boundary dispute between Venezuela and British Guiana (ghee-AHN-uh) in 1895. When the British condescendingly rejected a U.S. arbitration offer, a livid Grover Cleveland asked Congress to set up a commission to settle the dispute even without Britain's approval. As patriotic fervor pulsed through the nation, the British in 1897 accepted the commission's findings.

Pacific Expansion

Meanwhile, the U.S. Navy focused on the Samoan (suh-MOH-un) Islands in the South Pacific, where it sought the port of Pago Pago (PON-go PON-go) as a refueling station. In March 1889, the United States narrowly avoided a naval clash with Germany over the islands when a timely hurricane wrecked both fleets. Ultimately,

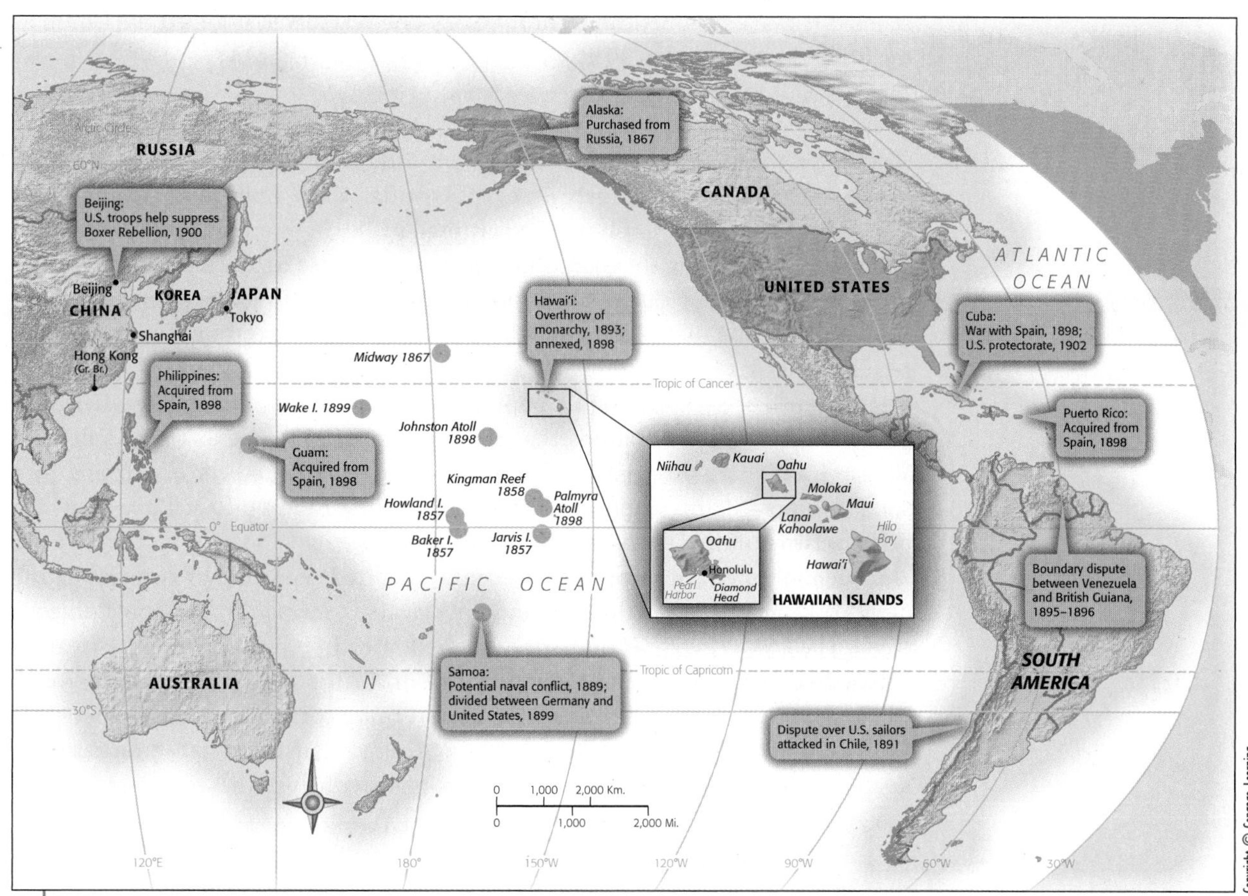

Map 20.2 U.S. Territorial Expansion in the Late Nineteenth Century

The major period of U.S. territorial expansion abroad came in a short burst of activity in the late 1890s, when newspapers and some politicians beat the drums for empire.

Interactive Map

America established a three-way protectorate over the islands with Germany and Great Britain.

Hawaiian Islands Independent island nation in the Pacific Ocean annexed by the United States in 1898

The **Hawaiian Islands,** with their economic and strategic significance, also beckoned U.S. imperialists. American missionaries and merchants had been active in the islands since the end of the eighteenth century. American-owned sugar plantations worked by Chinese and Japanese laborers dominated the Hawaiian economy. Under an 1887 treaty, the United States built a naval base at Pearl Harbor, near Honolulu. Then in 1891, angered by American economic domination, islanders welcomed Liliuokalani (lil-ee-oo-oh-ka-LAW-nee) to the Hawaiian throne. Strong-willed and hostile toward Americans, she became queen amid a crisis set off by a U.S. decision in 1890 to tax Hawaiian sugar. Hawaiian sugar prices plunged 40 percent as a result. Facing ruin, the planters deposed the queen in January 1893, proclaimed the independent Republic of Hawai'i, and requested U.S. annexation.

The grab for Hawai'i troubled Cleveland, especially when an emissary whom he sent cast doubt on whether the Hawaiians desired annexation. But when McKinley succeeded Cleveland, annexation moved rapidly forward, and in 1898 Congress proclaimed Hawai'i an American territory. Sixty-one years later, it joined the Union as the fiftieth state (see Map 20.2).

Crisis over Cuba

In 1898 American attention shifted to Cuba, a nation ninety miles off Florida, where a rebellion against Spanish rule had erupted in 1895. American businessmen had $50 million invested in the island and annually imported $100 million in sugar and other products from Cuba. Revolutionary turmoil would jeopardize these interests. Neither the Cleveland nor the McKinley administration supported the rebellion.

But the rebels' cause aroused popular sympathy in the United States. This support increased with revelations that the Spanish commander in Cuba, Valeriano Weyler (vah-lair-ee-AH-no WAY-ler), was herding vast numbers of Cubans into squalid camps. Malnutrition and disease turned these camps into hellholes in which perhaps two hundred thousand Cubans died.

Fueling American anger was the sensationalized reporting of two competing New York newspapers, William Randolph Hearst's *Journal* and Joseph Pulitzer's *World.* The *Journal's* color comic strip, "The Yellow Kid," provided a term for Hearst's debased editorial approach: yellow journalism. In the cutthroat battle for readers, both editors exploited the Cuban crisis, turning rumor into fact and detailing "Butcher" Weyler's atrocities. When a young Cuban woman was jailed for resisting a rape attempt by a Spanish officer, a Hearst reporter helped the woman escape and brought her triumphantly to New York.

In 1897 a new, more liberal Spanish government sought a peaceful solution to the Cuban crisis. However, Hearst and Pulitzer continued to inflame public opinion. On February 8, 1898, Hearst's *Journal* published a private letter from a Spanish diplomat describing McKinley as "weak." Irritation turned to outrage on February 15, 1898, when an explosion rocked the battleship *Maine* in Havana harbor, killing 226 American crewmen. Scholarly opinion about what caused the explosion is still divided, but a careful review of the evidence in 1998 concluded that a mine most likely set off the ammunition explosion that sank the ship. Newspaper headlines at the time blamed the same cause and war spirit flared high.

Despite further Spanish concessions, on April 11, McKinley sent a war message to Congress, and legislators passed a joint resolution recognizing Cuba's independence and authorizing force to expel the Spanish. The Teller Amendment, introduced by Senator Henry M. Teller of Colorado, renounced any U.S. interest in "sovereignty, jurisdiction, or control" in Cuba and pledged that America would leave the island alone once independence was assured.

The Spanish-American War, 1898

The war with Spain involved only a few days of actual combat. Action began on May 1, 1898, when a U.S. fleet under Admiral George Dewey steamed into Manila (muh-NILL-uh) Bay in the Philippines and destroyed or captured all ten Spanish ships anchored there, at the cost of 1 American and 381 Spanish lives. In mid-August, U.S. troops occupied the capital, Manila.

In Cuba, the war's only significant land engagement took place on July 1, when American troops seized three strongly defended Spanish garrisons overlooking Santiago (sahn-tee-AH-go) on El Caney Hill, Kettleman's Hill, and San Juan (sahn wahn) Hill, respectively. Leading the volunteer "Rough Riders" unit at San Juan Hill was Theodore Roosevelt, getting his taste of war—and abundant publicity—at last. Two days later, the Spanish fleet in the Santiago harbor made a gallant but doomed attempt to break through the American blockade to the open sea. The U.S. Navy fired and sank their archaic vessels, killing 474 Spaniards and ending four hundred years of Spanish empire in America.

John Hay thought that it had been "a splendid little war," but many who served in Cuba found it far from splendid. They went into summer combat wearing heavy wool uniforms, received abysmal medical care, and died in droves from yellow fever, food poisoning, and malaria. The United States lost more than five thousand men in Cuba, but only 379 of them in combat.

The thousands of black troops who fought in Cuba encountered Jim Crow racism at assembly points in Georgia and their embarkation port in Tampa, Florida. In Tampa, taunted by whites and refused service at restaurants and bars, some black troops exploded in riotous rage on June 6. White troops from Georgia restored order. The transport ships that carried troops to Cuba were segregated, with black troops often confined to the lowest quarters in stifling heat and denied permission to mingle on deck with other units. Despite such encounters with racism, African-American troops served with distinction in Cuba, playing key roles in the battles of San Juan Hill and El Caney Hill.

The Spanish sought an armistice on July 17. In the peace treaty signed that December in Paris, Spain recognized Cuba's independence and, after a U.S. payment of $20 million, ceded the Philippines, Puerto Rico, and the Pacific island of Guam to the United States. Americans now possessed an island empire stretching from the Caribbean to the Pacific.

From 1898 to 1902, the U.S. Army governed Cuba under the command of General Leonard Wood. Wood's administration improved public health, education, and sanitation but nevertheless violated the spirit of the 1898 Teller Amendment. The troops

National Archives

African-American Soldiers of the Tenth U.S. Cavalry in Cuba, July 1898
These men posed shortly after the capture of San Juan Hill. Black troops, known as buffalo soldiers, played an important role in the Spanish-American War, but they were subject to harassment and discrimination.

Platt Amendment Agreement to withdraw U.S. troops from Cuba; U.S. maintained a naval base

eventually withdrew, although the so-called **Platt Amendment** (1901), requested by the War Department, authorized the withdrawal only after Cuba agreed not to make any treaty with a foreign power limiting its independence and not to borrow beyond its means. The United States also reserved the right to intervene in Cuba and to establish a naval base there, Guantánamo (gwan-TAHN-uh-moh) Bay, near Santiago, which it still maintains. The Platt Amendment remained in force until 1934. U.S. investments in Cuba, some $50 million in 1898, soared to $500 million by 1920.

Critics of Empire

Some Americans had opposed imperialism for more than a decade, and the victories in Cuba and the Philippines did not bring universal praise. Although few in number, the critics were influential. Some of them, like Carl Schurz and E. L. Godkin, were former Mugwumps. Other anti-imperialists included William Jennings Bryan, settlement-house founder Jane Addams, novelist Mark Twain, and Harvard philosopher William James. Steel king Andrew Carnegie gave thousands of dollars to the cause. In 1898, these critics of empire formed the **Anti-Imperialist League.**

Anti-Imperialist League Small but influential group that opposed imperialism

For the United States to rule other peoples, the anti-imperialists believed, was to violate the principles of the Declaration of Independence and the Constitution. The military fever that accompanied expansionism also dismayed the anti-imperialists.

In February 1899, the anti-imperialists failed by one vote to prevent Senate ratification of the expansionist peace treaty with Spain. McKinley's overwhelming victory in 1900 over expansionist critic Bryan eroded the anti-imperialist cause. Nevertheless, at a time of jingoistic rhetoric and militaristic posturing, they had upheld an older and more traditional vision of America.

Guerrilla War in the Philippines, 1898–1902

Events in the Philippines confirmed the worst fears of the anti-imperialists. At the war's outset, few Americans knew much about the Philippines Islands. Without a map, McKinley later confessed, "I could not have told where those darn islands were within two thousand miles." American business, though, saw them as a steppingstone to the rich China market.

McKinley, reflecting the prevailing mood as always, reasoned that the Filipinos were unready for self-government and would be gobbled up if set adrift in a world of imperial rivalries. He further persuaded himself that American rule would enormously benefit a people he called "our little brown brothers." A devout Methodist, he explained that America's mission was "to educate the Filipinos, and to uplift and civilize and Christianize them." (In fact, most Filipinos were already Catholic, a legacy of centuries of Spanish rule.) Having prayerfully reached his decision, McKinley instructed the American peace negotiators in Paris to insist on U.S. acquisition of the Philippines.

"Uplifting" the Philippines proved difficult. In 1896 young **Emilio Aguinaldo** (eh-MEEL-ee-oh ah-gwin-ALL-doh) had organized a Filipino independence movement to drive out Spain. In the summer of 1898, with arms supplied by Admiral Dewey, Aguinaldo's forces captured most of Luzon (loo-ZAHN), the Philippines' main island. When the Spanish surrendered, Aguinaldo proclaimed Filipino independence and drafted a democratic constitution. In 1899, feeling betrayed when the peace treaty ceded his country to the United States, Aguinaldo ordered his rebel force to attack Manila, the American base of operations.

Emilio Aguinaldo Nationalist leader of the Filipino war against American occupation

These hostilities became the opening phase of a long guerrilla conflict. Before it ended, four thousand of the over 125,000 American men who served in the Philippines had been killed. In addition, as many as twenty thousand Filipino independence fighters died. As in the later Vietnam and Iraq wars, casualties and suffering ravaged the civilian population as well. Historians estimate that at least two hundred thousand civilians died in the conflict. Aguinaldo was captured in March 1901, but large-scale guerrilla fighting continued through the summer of 1902.

In 1902, a special Senate committee heard testimony from veterans of the Philippines war about the execution of prisoners, the torture of suspects, and the burning of villages. The humanitarian mood of 1898, when Americans had rushed to save Cuba from the cruel Spaniards, seemed remote indeed. In retrospect, the American troops' ambivalent attitudes toward the Filipinos, although deplorable, are not hard to understand. As American nationalism was reformulated in this cauldron of immigration, imperialism, and the "winning of the West," racist attitudes about native peoples and foreigners intermixed with rhetorical pleas for supervision and stewardship. In the process, as was evident in the treatment of American Indians (see Chapter 17), well-meaning paternalism often degenerated into deadly domination.

CHECKING IN

- Expansionist, and even warlike, sentiment flared in the 1890s.
- The United States took over Hawai'i after American planters deposed the rightful queen.
- The Spanish-American War was a popular assertion of rising American power.
- A small but vocal group criticized imperialism as a betrayal of American values.
- Acquisition of the Philippines from Spain led to a guerrilla war and the expansion of the American empire into the western Pacific.

The subjugation of the Philippines followed years of expansionism that proclaimed America's debut on the world stage. Nevertheless, most Americans remained ambivalent about the acquisition of territory. While anti-imperialist Mark Twain acidly condemned "the Blessings of Civilization Trust," labor leader Samuel Gompers warned that "an inundation of Mongolians" might steal jobs from white labor. White Americans recoiled from making the "barbarian peoples" of these territories a part of the United States. Deemed unfit to manage their own affairs, Filipinos were placed in a protective status that denied their independence but kept them under U.S. control.

Congress passed the Philippine Government Act in 1902, which vested authority in a governor general to be appointed by the president. The act also provided for an elected Filipino assembly and promised eventual self-government. Progress toward this goal inched forward, with intervals of semi-military rule. In 1946, nearly half a century after Admiral Dewey's guns had boomed in Manila Bay, independence finally came to the Philippines.

Chapter Summary

How did political parties build coalitions out of their diverse ethnic and regional constituencies? (page 471)

Both major national parties pursued centrist courses, with Republicans supporting big business and Democrats warning against government interference. Greenbacks and the coinage of silver were major issues, as was the patronage system and civil-service reform. As the parties struggled to achieve political dominance, they were forced to deal with ethnic, cultural, and racial issues that included prohibition, church schools, and segregation.

What factors prompted the rise of the Grange and the Farmers' Alliance movements? (page 477)

In the competition for new voters, the needs of rural Americans were often overlooked. Southern and western farmers struggled to overcome periodic droughts, falling prices, and a cycle of indebtedness. They created two regional organizations, the Grange and the Alliance, to try to reassert control over their lives. These movements led to the formation of the national Populist Party in 1892. Blacks were increasingly excluded from political life.

KEY TERMS

laissez-faire *(p. 473)*
Grand Army of the Republic (GAR) *(p. 473)*
political machine *(p. 474)*
William "Magear" Tweed *(p. 474)*
Sherman Silver Purchase Act *(p. 475)*
Pendleton Civil Service Act *(p. 476)*
Mugwumps *(p. 477)*
Grange *(p. 479)*
Farmers' Alliance *(p. 479)*
Populist Party *(p. 480)*
subtreasury plan *(p. 480)*
lynching *(p. 481)*
Plessy v. *Ferguson* *(p. 481)*

Why did William Jennings Bryan fail to win the presidency in 1896? (page 483)

Corporate interests continued to dominate politics. Populists won more than a million votes in the 1892 election. The Panic of 1893 and the subsequent depression devastated individuals and led to political unrest, such as Coxey's army. The victory of Republican William McKinley over William Jennings Bryan in the 1896 presidential election undermined Populism as an organized movement. However, many of the movement's ideas were incorporated into the two larger parties. The victorious Republican coalition would control national politics for the next fifteen years.

Why did the United States go to war with Spain and become an imperial power? (page 488)

The 1890s saw a surge of expansionist and warlike (jingoistic) sentiment. The Spanish-American War gave the United States control in the Caribbean and expanded American power far into the western Pacific with the acquisition of the Philippines. A bitter guerrilla war in the Philippines showed American determination to keep the new U.S. empire, despite criticism from a vocal group of anti-imperialists.

KEY TERMS continued

Booker T. Washington *(p. 482)*
Panic of 1893 *(p. 484)*
William Jennings Bryan *(p. 485)*
Alfred Thayer Mahan *(p. 488)*
Hawaiian Islands *(p. 490)*
Platt Amendment *(p. 492)*
Anti-Imperialist League *(p. 492)*
Emilio Aguinaldo *(p. 493)*

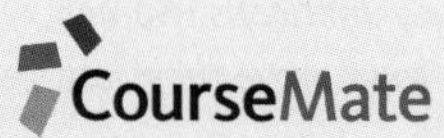

Go to the CourseMate website at **www.cengagebrain.com** for additional study tools and review materials—including audio and video clips—for this chapter.

CHAPTER 21

The Progressive Era 1900–1917

Library of Congress

Mulberry Street on New York City's Lower East Side, Around 1900

CHAPTER PREVIEW

Progressives and Their Ideas
How did intellectuals, novelists, and journalists inspire the progressive movement?

Grass-Roots Progressivism
How did state and local progressives seek to reform cities and the new industrial order?

Blacks, Women, and Workers Organize
How did progressives try to control morality, and how did they view immigrants and blacks?

National Progressivism Phase I: Roosevelt and Taft, 1901–1913
What strategies did African-Americans, women, and industrial workers use to improve their lot?

National Progressivism Phase II: Woodrow Wilson, 1913–1917
As progressivism became a national movement, what issues proved most important?

It was late Saturday afternoon on March 25, 1911. At the Triangle Shirtwaist factory in New York City, hundreds of young women and a few men remained at work at their clattering sewing machines. Suddenly fire broke out. Feeding on bolts of cloth, the fire soon turned the upper floors into an inferno. Panicked workers found some of the doors locked. Other doors that opened inward (a fire-law violation) were jammed shut by the crush of people trying to get out.

A few workers escaped. Young Pauline Grossman crawled to safety across a narrow alleyway when three male employees formed a human bridge. As others tried to cross, however, the weight became too great, and all fell to their deaths. Dozens of workers leaped from the windows to certain death below. Sunday's headlines summed up the grim count: 141 dead.

The horrifying Triangle fire underscored what many citizens had long recognized. Industrialization, for all its benefits, had taken a heavy toll on American life. Many factory workers and slum-dwellers endured a desperate cycle of poverty, exhausting labor, and early death. After the Triangle tragedy, New York passed a series of laws regulating factories and protecting workers.

Growing concerns about industrialization, urban growth, and the rise of great corporations prompted a wave of reform that came to be called the progressive movement. The progressive movement was a response to vast changes that had erased the familiar contours of an older America. In contrast to the rural Populists (see Chapter 20), progressives concentrated on the social effects of the new urban-industrial order.

Emerging in the 1890s at the city and state levels, an array of organizations, many led by women, pursued varied reform objectives. As journalists, novelists, religious leaders, social thinkers, and politicians joined in, these grass-roots efforts evolved into a national movement. By 1917, when reform gave way to war, America's political and social landscape had been transformed. New laws, organizations, and regulatory agencies had arisen to address the consequences of helter-skelter urbanization, industrial expansion, and corporate growth. The progressives could be maddeningly moralistic. They had their blind spots (especially on such subjects as immigration and race), and their reforms didn't always work as planned. But, on balance, their achievements left a powerful legacy.

Progressives and Their Ideas

How did intellectuals, novelists, and journalists inspire the progressive movement?

As the twentieth century dawned, groups across the nation grappled with the problems of the new urban-industrial order. Workers protested unsafe and exhausting jobs. Experts investigated social conditions. Women's clubs embraced reform. Intellectuals challenged the ideological foundations of a business-dominated social order, and journalists exposed municipal corruption and industrialism's human toll. Activists tried to make government more democratic, eradicate dangerous conditions in cities and factories, and curb corporate power.

Historians have grouped all these efforts under a single label: "the progressive movement." In fact, "progressivism" was less a single movement than a spirit of discontent with the status quo and an exciting sense of new social possibilities.

The Many Faces of Progressivism

Who were the progressives, and what reforms did they pursue? To answer this, we must examine the social changes of the era. Along with immigration, a growing middle class transformed U.S. cities. From the men and women of this class—most of them native born, white, and Protestant—came many of the progressive movement's leaders and supporters.

From 1900 to 1920, the white-collar work force jumped from 5.1 million to 10.5 million—more than double the growth rate of the labor force as a whole. This burgeoning white-collar class included corporate executives and small-business owners; secretaries, accountants, and sales clerks; civil engineers and people in advertising; and professionals such as lawyers, physicians, and teachers. Ambitious, well-educated, and valuing social stability, members of the new middle class were eager to make their influence felt.

For middle-class women, the city offered both opportunities and frustrations. Some became schoolteachers, secretaries, clerks, and telephone operators. The number of women in such white-collar jobs, as well as the ranks of college-educated women, more than tripled from 1900 to 1920. But for middle-class married women caring for homes and children, city life could bring stress and loneliness. The divorce rate rose from one in twelve marriages in 1900 to one in nine by 1916. As we shall see, middle-class women joined female white-collar workers and college graduates in leading a revived women's movement. Cultural commentators wrote nervously of the "New Woman."

Women Enter the Labor Force

Young female workers take an exercise break at the National Cash Register Company in Dayton, Ohio, around 1900. From schools and hospitals to corporate offices and crowded sweatshops, women poured into the work force in the early twentieth century.

Chronology

1900	International Ladies' Garment Workers' Union (ILGWU) founded; Carrie Chapman Catt becomes president of the National American Woman Suffrage Association (NAWSA)
1901	Assassination of McKinley; Theodore Roosevelt becomes president; J. P. Morgan forms United States Steel Company
1903	W. E. B. Du Bois, *The Souls of Black Folk;* Wright brothers' flight
1904	Theodore Roosevelt elected president in his own right; Lincoln Steffens, *The Shame of the Cities*
1905	Industrial Workers of the World (IWW) organized
1906	Upton Sinclair, *The Jungle*
1907	William James, *Pragmatism*
1908	William Howard Taft elected president; Model T Ford introduced
1909	Ballinger-Pinchot controversy; National Association for the Advancement of Colored People (NAACP) founded; Herbert Croly, *The Promise of American Life*
1910	Insurgents curb power of House Speaker Joseph Cannon
1911	Triangle Shirtwaist Company fire
1912	Republican Party split; Progressive (Bull Moose) Party founded; Woodrow Wilson elected president
1913	Sixteenth Amendment (Congress empowered to tax incomes); Seventeenth Amendment (direct election of U.S. senators)
1914	American Social Hygiene Association founded; Narcotics Act
1915	D. W. Griffith, *The Birth of a Nation*
1916	Margaret Sanger opens nation's first birth-control clinic; National Park Service created; Louis Brandeis appointed to Supreme Court
1919	Eighteenth Amendment (national prohibition)
1920	Nineteenth Amendment (woman suffrage)

This urban middle class rallied to the banner of reform. The initial reform impetus came not from political parties but from women's clubs, settlement houses, and private groups with names like the Playground Association of America and the American League for Civic Improvement.

However, the native-born middle class was not alone in promoting reform. On issues affecting factory workers and slum-dwellers, the urban-immigrant political machines—and workers themselves—often took the initiative. Some corporate leaders helped shape regulatory measures in ways to serve their interests.

What, then, was progressivism? Fundamentally, it was a broad-based response to industrialization and its social byproducts: immigration, urban growth, growing corporate power, and widening class divisions. In contrast to populism, progressivism's strength lay in the cities. Finally, most progressives were *reformers,* not radicals. They wished to make the new urban-industrial order more humane, not overturn it entirely.

But what specific remedies were required? Reaching different answers to this key question, progressive reformers spawned an array of activities that sometimes overlapped, sometimes diverged. Many demanded stricter business regulation, from local transit companies to the almighty trusts. Others focused on protecting workers and the urban poor. Still others championed reform of municipal government.

Some, fearful of urban disorder, favored immigration restriction or social-control strategies to regulate city-dwellers' behavior. All this contributed to the mosaic of progressive reform.

Progressives had a high regard for science and expert knowledge. Since scientific and technological expertise had produced the new industrial order, such expertise could surely also correct the social problems spawned by industrialism. Progressives marshaled research data, surveys, and statistics to support their various causes. Nevertheless, human emotion—whether indignation over child labor, suspicion of corporate power, or raw political ambition—helped to drive the movement forward.

Intellectuals Offer New Social Views

A group of innovative social thinkers provided progressivism's underlying ideas. As we have seen, some Gilded Age intellectuals had argued that Charles Darwin's theory of evolution justified unrestrained economic competition. In the 1880s and 1890s, sociologist Lester Ward, utopian novelist Edward Bellamy, and leaders of the Social Gospel movement had all attacked this harsh version of Social Darwinism (see Chapters 18 and 19). This attack intensified after 1900.

Economist Thorstein Veblen satirized America's newly rich capitalists in *The Theory of the Leisure Class* (1899). Dissecting their lifestyle the way an anthropologist might study an exotic tribe, he argued that they built mansions, threw elaborate parties, and otherwise engaged in "conspicuous consumption" to flaunt their wealth and assert their claims to superiority.

The Harvard philosopher William James argued in *Pragmatism* (1907) that truth emerges not from abstract theorizing but from the experience of coping with life's realities through practical action. James's philosophy of pragmatism deepened reformers' skepticism toward the older generation's entrenched ideas and strengthened their belief in the necessity of social change.

Herbert Croly shared this faith that new ideas could transform society. In *The Promise of American Life* (1909), he called for an activist government of the kind advocated by Alexander Hamilton, the first secretary of the treasury. But rather than serving the interests of the business class, as Hamilton had proposed, Croly argued that this activist government should promote the welfare of all. In 1914, Croly founded the *New Republic* magazine to promote progressive ideas.

The settlement-house leader Jane Addams also helped shape the ideology of the Progressive Era. In *Democracy and Social Ethics* (1902) and other books, Addams rejected the claim that unrestrained competition offered the best path to social progress. Instead, she argued, in a modern industrial society, each individual's well-being depends on the well-being of all. Teaching by example, Addams made her Chicago social settlement, Hull House, a center of social activism and legislative-reform initiatives.

With public-school enrollment growing from about 7 million in 1870 to more than 23 million in 1920, philosopher John Dewey saw schools as potent engines of social change. Banishing bolted-down chairs and desks from his model school at the University of Chicago, Dewey encouraged pupils to interact. The ideal school, he said in *Democracy and Education* (1916), would be an "embryonic community" where children would learn to live as members of a social group.

Oliver Wendell Holmes, Jr., of Harvard Law School focused on changing judicial thinking. In *The Common Law* (1881), Holmes criticized judges who interpreted the law rigidly to protect corporate interests and insisted that law must evolve as society changes. In a phrase much quoted by progressives, he declared, "The life of the law has not been logic; it has been experience." Appointed to the United States Supreme Court in 1902, Holmes often dissented from the conservative Court majority. As the new social thinking took hold, the courts slowly grew more open to reform legislation.

Novelists, Journalists, and Artists Spotlight Social Problems

While reform-minded intellectuals reoriented American social thought, novelists and journalists chronicled corporate wrongdoing, municipal corruption, slum conditions, and industrial abuses.

In his novel *The Octopus* (1901), Frank Norris of San Francisco portrayed the epic struggle between California railroad barons and the state's wheat growers. Theodore Dreiser's novel *The Financier* (1912) featured a hard-driving business tycoon utterly lacking a social conscience. Like Veblen's *Theory of the Leisure Class,* such works aroused sentiment against the industrial elite and in favor of tougher regulation of business.

"muckrakers" Journalists and novelists who wrote about urban corruption and wrongdoing

Mass magazines such as *McClure's* and *Collier's* stirred reform energies with articles exposing urban corruption and corporate wrongdoing. President Theodore Roosevelt criticized the authors as **"muckrakers"** obsessed with the seamier side of American life, but the name became a badge of honor. Journalist Lincoln Steffens began the exposé vogue in 1902 with a *McClure's* article documenting municipal corruption in St. Louis.

To gather material, some journalists worked as factory laborers or lived in slum tenements. The British immigrant John Spargo researched his 1906 book about child labor, *The Bitter Cry of the Children*, by visiting mines in Pennsylvania and West Virginia and attempting to do the work that young boys performed for ten hours a day, picking out slate and other refuse from coal in cramped workspaces filled with choking coal dust. Some magazine exposés later appeared in book form, including Lincoln Steffens's *The Shame of the Cities* (1904) and Ida Tarbell's damning *History of the Standard Oil Company* (1904).

Artists and photographers played a role as well. A group of New York painters dubbed the Ashcan School portrayed the harshness as well as the vitality of slum life. The photographer Lewis Hine, working for the National Child Labor Committee, captured haunting images of child workers with stunted bodies and worn expressions.

Checking In

- The new middle class was an important part of the progressive movement; so, too, were urban workers and, occasionally, political machines and corporate leaders.
- Progressivism was a response to the massive changes spawned by industrialization, urbanization, and immigration.
- The progressives were reformers who wanted to save, not to overthrow, the existing capitalist system.
- Intellectuals like William James, Herbert Croly, and John Dewey provided the foundation for progressive reforms, emphasizing the power of new ideas and purposeful effort in bettering society.
- Muckraking authors and journalists played a major role in unveiling problems and stirring the public to demand solutions.

Grass-Roots Progressivism

How did state and local progressives seek to reform cities and the new industrial order?

Middle-class readers also observed firsthand, in their own communities, the problems besetting urban-industrial America. In fact, the progressive movement began with grass-roots campaigns at the local level from New York to San Francisco. Eventually, these local efforts came together in a powerful national movement.

Reforming the Political Process

Beginning in the 1890s, native-born elites and middle-class reformers battled corrupt city governments (see Chapter 19). New York City experienced a succession of reform spasms in which Protestant clergy rallied against Tammany Hall, the city's entrenched Democratic organization. In Detroit, the reform mayor Hazen Pingree (served 1890–1897) brought honesty to city hall, lowered transit fares, and provided public baths and other services.

In San Francisco, a courageous newspaper editor led a 1907 crusade against the city's corrupt boss. When the original prosecutor was gunned down in court, attorney Hiram Johnson took his place, winning convictions against the boss and his cronies. Johnson rode his newly won fame to the California governorship and the U.S. Senate. In Toledo, Ohio, a colorful figure named Samuel M. ("Golden Rule") Jones led the reform crusade. A businessman converted to the Social Gospel, Jones introduced profit sharing in his factory, and as mayor he established playgrounds, free kindergartens, and lodging houses for homeless transients.

The political reformers soon moved beyond simply "throwing the rascals out" to probing the roots of urban misgovernment, including the private monopolies that ran municipal water, gas, electricity, and transit systems. Reformers passed laws regulating the rates that utilities could charge, taxing them more equitably, and curbing their political influence. Some advocated public ownership of utilities.

Reflecting the Progressive Era vogue of expertise and efficiency, a number of municipal reformers sought to substitute professional managers and administrators, chosen in citywide elections, for mayors and aldermen elected on a ward-by-ward basis. Supposedly above politics, these experts were to run the city like an efficient business.

Municipal reform attracted different groups depending on the issue. The native-born middle class provided the initial impetus for urban beautification and political reform. Business leaders often supported city-manager systems and citywide elections, which diminished the power of the ward bosses and increased that of the corporate elite. On practical matters, such as municipal services, immigrants and even political bosses supported reform.

The electoral-reform movement soon expanded to the state level. By 1910, all states had instituted secret ballots, making it much harder than before to rig elections. The direct primary, introduced in Wisconsin in 1903, enabled rank-and-file voters rather than party bosses to select their parties' candidates for public office. And some western states inaugurated the initiative, referendum, and recall. By an initiative, voters were able to instruct the legislature to consider a specific bill. In a referendum, citizens were actually able to enact a law or, in a *nonbinding* referendum, express their views on a measure. By a recall petition, voters were able to remove an official from office by gathering enough signatures.

While these reforms aimed to democratize voting, party leaders and interest groups soon learned to manipulate the new electoral machinery. Ironically, the new procedures may have weakened party loyalty and reduced voter interest. Voter-participation rates dropped steeply in these years, while political activity by organized interest groups increased.

Regulating Business and Protecting Workers

The corporate consolidation that produced giants like Carnegie Steel and Standard Oil (see Chapter 18) continued after 1900. Following the U.S. Steel pattern, J. P. Morgan in 1902 combined six competing companies into the International Harvester Company, which dominated the farm-implement business. The General Motors Company, formed in 1908 by William C. Durant, bought up various independent automobile manufacturers, from the inexpensive Chevrolet to the luxury Cadillac.

Many workers benefited from this corporate growth. Industrial workers' average annual real wages (defined in terms of actual purchasing power) rose from $487 in 1900 to $687 by 1915. In railroading and other unionized industries, wages climbed still higher. Still, such wages could barely support a family.

To survive, entire families went to work. Two-thirds of young immigrant women entered the labor force in the early 1900s, working in factories, laundries, or bakeries, or as domestics. Even children worked. In 1910, the nonfarm labor force included some 1.6 million children aged ten to fifteen employed in factories, mills, tenement sweatshops, and street trades such as shoe shining and newspaper vending.

Work was long and hazardous. Despite the eight-hour workday movement of the 1880s, in 1900 the average worker still toiled nine-and-a-half hours a day. Some southern textile mills required workdays of twelve or thirteen hours. In one typical year (1907), 4,534 railroad workers and more than three thousand miners were killed on the job. Few workers enjoyed vacations or retirement benefits.

Workers accustomed to the rhythms of farm labor faced the discipline of the factory. Efficiency experts used time-and-motion studies to increase production and make human workers as predictable as machines. In *Principles of Scientific Management* (1911), Frederick W. Taylor explained how to increase output by standardizing job routines and rewarding the fastest workers. "Efficiency" became a popular catchword, but workers resented the pressures to speed up.

Americans concerned about the social implications of industrialization deplored unregulated corporate power and the hazards facing industrial workers. The drive to regulate big business, inherited from the populists, became an important component of progressivism. Since corporations had benefited from government policies such as high protective tariffs and railroad subsidies, reformers reasoned, they should also be subject to government regulation.

Wisconsin, under Governor **Robert** ("Fighting Bob") **La Follette** (lah FALL-ett), took the lead in regulating railroads, mines, and other businesses. As a Republican congressman, La Follette had feuded with the state's conservative party leadership, and in 1900 he won the governorship as an independent. Challenging powerful corporate interests, La Follette and his administration adopted the direct-primary system, set up a railroad regulatory commission, increased corporate taxes, and limited campaign spending. Reflecting progressivism's faith in experts, La Follette consulted reform-minded professors at the University of Wisconsin and set up a legislative reference library to help lawmakers draft bills. La Follette's reforms gained national attention as the "Wisconsin Idea."

Robert La Follette Progressive politician; won Wisconsin governorship as independent and oversaw several reforms; later a U.S. senator

If electoral reform and corporate regulation represented the brain of progressivism, the impulse to improve conditions in factories and mills represented its

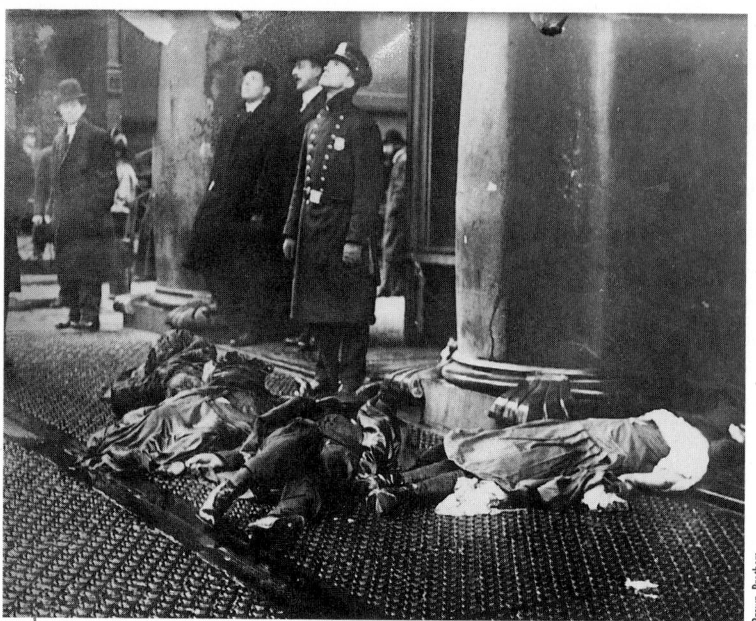

Brown Brothers

The Triangle Fire

The bodies of Triangle Shirtwaist factory workers who jumped from the burning building occupy the sidewalk.

heart. This movement, too, began at the local and state level. By 1907, for example, thirty states had outlawed child labor. A 1903 Oregon law limited women in industry to a ten-hour workday.

Campaigns for industrial safety and better working conditions won support from political bosses in the immigrant cities. State senator Robert F. Wagner, a leader of New York City's Democratic organization, headed the Triangle-fire investigation. Thanks to his committee's efforts, New York passed fifty-six worker-protection laws, including required fire-safety inspections. By 1914, twenty-five states had made employers liable for job-related injuries or deaths.

Florence Kelley of Hull House, the daughter of a conservative Republican congressman, spearheaded the drive to remedy industrial abuses. In 1893, Kelley persuaded the Illinois legislature to outlaw child labor and limit working hours for women. In 1899, she became head of the National Consumers' League, which mobilized consumer pressure for improved factory conditions. Campaigning for a federal child-labor law, Kelley asked, "Why are seals, bears, reindeer, fish, wild game in the national parks, buffalo, [and] migratory birds all found suitable for federal protection, but not children?"

Like many progressive reforms, the crusade for workplace safety relied on expert research. The bacteriologist Alice Hamilton, a pioneer in the new field of "industrial hygiene," reported on lead poisoning among industrial workers in 1910. Later, as an investigator for the U.S. Bureau of Labor, Hamilton publicized other work-related medical hazards.

Workers themselves, who well understood the hazards of their jobs, provided further pressure for reform. For example, when the granite industry introduced new power drills that created a fine dust that workers inhaled, the *Granite Cutters' Journal* called them "widow makers." Sure enough, investigators soon linked the dust to a deadly lung disease, silicosis.

Making Cities More Livable

By 1920, the urban population passed the 50 percent mark, and sixty-eight U.S. cities boasted more than a hundred thousand inhabitants. New York City grew by 2.2 million from 1900 to 1920, and Chicago by 1 million. America had become an urban nation.

Political corruption was only one of many urban problems. As manufacturing and businesses grew, a tide of immigrants and native-born newcomers engulfed the cities. Many cities became congested human warehouses, lacking adequate parks, public-health resources, and basic municipal services. As the reform spirit spread, the urban crisis loomed large.

Extending the achievements of Frederick Law Olmsted and others (see Chapter 11), reformers campaigned for parks, boulevards, and street lights, and proposed laws against billboards and unsightly overhead electrical wires. An influential voice for city planning and beautification was Daniel Burnham, chief architect of the 1893 Chicago world's fair. Burnham developed beautification plans for Washington, DC, Cleveland, San Francisco, and other cities. Many Progressive Era urban planners shared Burnham's faith that more beautiful cities and imposing public buildings would produce orderly, law-abiding citizens.

The municipal reform impulse also included such practical goals as decent housing and better garbage collection and street cleaning. Providing a model for other cities and states, the New York legislature imposed strict health and safety regulations on tenements in 1911. With the discovery in the 1880s that germs cause diseases like cholera and typhoid fever, municipal hygiene became a high priority. Reformers distributed public-health information, promoted school vaccination programs, and called for safer water and sewer systems and the regulation of food and milk suppliers. When Mary Mallon, an Irish-immigrant cook in New York, was found to be a healthy carrier of the typhoid bacillus in 1907, she was confined by the city health authorities and demonized in the press as "Typhoid Mary."

These efforts bore fruit. From 1900 to 1920, infant mortality (defined as death in the first year of life), as well as death rates from tuberculosis, typhoid fever, and other infectious or communicable diseases, all fell sharply.

Urban reformers shared the era's heightened environmental consciousness (see Chapter 17). Factory chimneys belching smoke had once inspired pride, but by the early 1900s physicians had linked factory smoke to respiratory problems, and civic reformers were deploring the soot and smoke spewing from coal-fueled factory steam boilers.

The antismoke campaign combined expertise with activism. Civil engineers formed the Smoke Prevention Association in 1906, and researchers at the University of Pittsburgh documented the hazards and costs of air pollution. As women's clubs and other civic groups embraced the cause, many cities passed smoke-abatement laws. But coal still provided 70 percent of the nation's energy as late as 1920, and railroads and corporations fought back in the courts and often won. Not until years later, with the shift to other energy sources, did municipal air pollution significantly diminish.

Moral Control in the Cities

Progressives' belief that they could improve society through research, legislation, and aroused public opinion sprang from their confidence that they knew what was best for other people. While municipal corruption, unsafe factories, and corporate abuses captured their attention, so, too, did issues of personal behavior, particularly the behavior of immigrants. The problems they addressed deserved attention, but their self-righteous rhetoric and the remedies they proposed also betrayed an impulse to impose their own moral standards by force of law.

Despite the slums, dangerous factories, and other problems, early-twentieth-century cities also offered fun and diversion. Department stores, vaudeville, music halls, and amusement parks (see Chapter 19) continued to flourish. Although some vaudeville owners sought respectability, bawdy routines typically full of sexual innuendo delighted working-class audiences. Amusement parks offered families escape from tenements, and gave female workers an opportunity to socialize with friends, meet young men, and show off new outfits. New York City's amusement park, Coney Island, attracted several million visitors a year by 1914.

With electrification, streetcar rides or evening strolls down well-lit downtown streets became leisure activities in themselves. Orville and Wilbur Wright's successful airplane flight in 1903, and the introduction of Henry Ford's Model T in 1908, transforming the automobile from a toy of the rich to a vehicle for the masses, foretold exciting changes ahead, with cities central to the action.

Jaunty music-hall songs added to the vibrancy of city life. The blues, rooted in the chants of southern black sharecroppers, reached a broader public with such songs as W. C. Handy's classic "St. Louis Blues" (1914). Ragtime, another import from the black South (see Chapter 19), enjoyed great popularity in early-twentieth-century urban America.

These years also brought a new entertainment medium—the movies. Initially a part of vaudeville shows, movies soon migrated to five-cent halls called "nickelodeons" in immigrant neighborhoods. At first featuring brief comic sequences like *The Sneeze* or *The Kiss*, movies began to tell stories with *The Great Train Robbery* (1903). *A Fool There Was* (1914), with its daring line, "Kiss me, my fool!," made Theda Bara the first female movie star. The British music-hall performer Charlie Chaplin immigrated to America and appeared in some sixty short comedies between 1914 and 1917. Like amusement parks, the movies allowed immigrant youth briefly to escape parental supervision.

The diversions that eased city life for the poor struck some middle-class reformers as moral traps. Fearful of immorality and social disorder, reformers campaigned to regulate amusement parks, dance halls, movies, and the darkened nickelodeons, which they saw as potential dens of vice. Several states and cities set up film censorship boards, and the Supreme Court upheld such measures in 1915.

Building on the moral purity crusade of the Woman's Christian Temperance Union (WCTU) and other groups (see Chapter 19), reformers also targeted prostitution, a major urban problem. Male procurers lured young women into prostitution and then took a share of their income. The paltry wages paid to women for factory work or domestic service diverted many to this more lucrative occupation. Why "get up at 6:30 . . . and work in a close stuffy room . . . until dark for $6 or $7 a week," reasoned one prostitute, when an afternoon with a man could bring in more.

As prostitution came to symbolize the larger moral dangers of cities, a "white slave" hysteria gripped the nation amid warnings of farm girls' being kidnapped and forced into urban brothels. In the usual progressive fashion, investigators gathered statistics on what they called "the social evil." The American Social Hygiene Association (1914), financed by John D. Rockefeller, Jr., sponsored medical research on sexually transmitted diseases, paid for "vice investigations" in various cities, and drafted antiprostitution laws. The federal Mann Act (1910) made it illegal to transport a woman across a state line "for immoral purposes." Amid much fanfare, reformers shut down the red-light districts of New Orleans, Chicago, and other cities.

In 1913, the African-American boxer Jack Johnson, the heavyweight champion, was convicted under the Mann Act; Johnson went abroad to escape imprisonment.

Battling Alcohol and Drugs

Temperance had long been part of the American reform agenda, but reformers' tactics and objectives changed in the Progressive Era. Most earlier campaigns had urged individuals to give up drink. The powerful **Anti-Saloon League (ASL),** founded in 1895, shifted the emphasis to legislating a ban on the sale of alcoholic beverages, and its presses produced propaganda touting prohibition. As churches and temperance groups worked for prohibition at the municipal, county, and state levels, the ASL moved to its larger goal: national prohibition.

Anti-Saloon League (ASL) Political advocacy group founded in 1895; signaled a new phase in the movement to ban the sale of alcohol

This was a heavy-drinking era, and alcohol abuse did indeed contribute to domestic abuse, health problems, and work injuries. But like the antiprostitution crusade, the prohibition campaign pitted native-born citizens against immigrants. Although it raised legitimate issues, the ASL also embodied Protestant America's impulse to control the immigrant city.

Reformers also targeted drug abuse—and for good reason. Physicians, patent-medicine peddlers, and legitimate drug companies freely prescribed or sold opium (derived from poppies) and its derivatives morphine and heroin. Cocaine, extracted from coca leaves, was an ingredient of Coca-Cola until about 1900.

Amid mounting reform pressure, Congress in 1914 passed the Harrison Act, banning the distribution of heroin, morphine, cocaine, and other addictive drugs except by licensed physicians or pharmacists. Like progressives' environmental concerns, this campaign anticipated an issue that remains important today. But this reform, too, had racist undertones. Antidrug crusaders luridly described Chinese "opium dens" (places where this addictive narcotic was smoked) and warned that "drug-crazed Negroes" imperiled white womanhood.

Immigration Restriction and Eugenics

Although many of the new city-dwellers came from farms and small towns, the main source of urban growth continued to be immigration. More than 17 million newcomers arrived from 1900 to 1917, and most settled in cities. As in the 1890s (see Chapter 19), the influx came mainly from southern and eastern Europe, but some 200,000 Japanese, 40,000 Chinese, and thousands of Mexicans also arrived between 1900 and 1920.

The obvious answer to the threats posed by the immigrant city, some reformers concluded, lay in excluding immigrants (see Figure 21.1). The many progressives who supported immigration restriction documented their case with alleged scientific expertise. For example, a 1911 congressional report allegedly proved the new immigrants' innate degeneracy. One prominent sociologist described the newcomers as "low-browed, big-faced persons of obviously low mentality." In 1896, 1913, and 1915, Congress passed literacy-test bills aimed at slowing immigration, but they fell victim to veto by a succession of presidents. These measures would have excluded immigrants over sixteen years old who could not read either English or their native language. In 1917, however, such a bill became law over President Wilson's veto.

Figure 21.1 Immigration to the United States, 1870–1930

With the end of the depression of the 1890s, immigrants from southern and eastern Europe poured into America's cities, spurring an immigration restriction movement, urban moral-control campaigns, and efforts to improve the physical and social conditions of immigrant life.

Sources: Statistical History of the United States from Colonial Times to the Present (Stamford, Conn.: Fairfield Publishers, 1965); and report presented by Senator William P. Dillingham, Senate document 742, 61st Congress, 3rd session, December 5, 1910: Abstracts of Reports to the Immigration Commission.

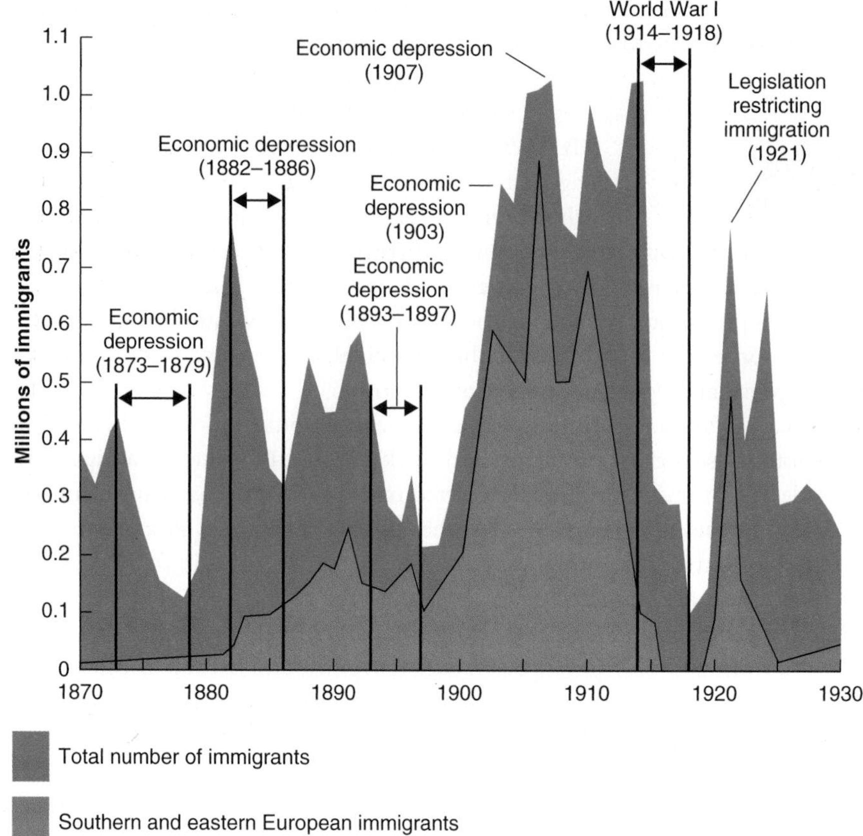

Anti-immigrant fears helped fuel the eugenics (you-JEN-icks) movement. Eugenics is the control of reproduction to alter a plant or animal species, and some U.S. eugenicists believed that human society could be improved by this means. Leading eugenicists urged immigration restriction to protect America from "inferior" genetic stock.

In *The Passing of the Great Race* (1916), Madison Grant, a prominent progressive and eugenics advocate, used bogus data to denounce immigrants from southern and eastern Europe, especially Jews. He also viewed African-Americans as inferior. Anticipating the program of Adolf Hitler in the 1930s (covered in Chapter 25), Grant called for racial segregation, immigration restriction, and the forced sterilization of the "unfit," including "worthless race types." The vogue of eugenics gave "scientific" respectability to racism and anti-immigrant sentiment. Inspired by eugenics, many states legalized the sterilization of criminals, sex offenders, and persons adjudged mentally deficient.

Racism and Progressivism

Progressivism arose at a time of intense racism in America as well of major African-American population movements. These racial realities are crucial to a full understanding of the movement.

In 1900, more than two-thirds of the nation's 10 million blacks lived in the South as sharecroppers and tenant farmers. By 1910, the cotton boll weevil and ruinous floods had driven 20 percent of these southern blacks into cities. Black men in the cities took jobs in factories, mines, docks, and railroads or became carpenters or bricklayers. Many black women became domestic servants, seamstresses, and laundry or tobacco workers. By 1910, 54 percent of America's black women held jobs.

Across the South, legally enforced racism peaked in the early twentieth century. Local "Jim Crow" laws segregated streetcars, schools, parks, and even cemeteries. The facilities for blacks, including the schools, were invariably inferior. Many southern cities imposed residential segregation by law until the Supreme Court restricted such measures in 1917. Most labor unions excluded black workers. Disfranchised and trapped in a cycle of poverty, poor education, and discrimination, southern blacks faced bleak prospects.

Fleeing such conditions, two hundred thousand blacks migrated north between 1890 and 1910. Wartime job opportunities drew still more blacks in 1917–1918 (as discussed in Chapter 22), and by 1920, 1.4 million African-Americans lived in the North, mostly in cities. Here, too, racism worsened after 1890 as hard times and immigration heightened social tensions. Segregation, though not imposed by law, was enforced by custom and sometimes by violence. Their ballots—usually cast for the party of Lincoln—brought little political influence. Blacks lived in run-down "colored districts," attended dilapidated schools, and worked at the lowest-paying jobs. Even the movies preached racism. D. W. Griffith's 1915 film classic *The Birth of a Nation* disparaged blacks and glorified the Ku Klux Klan.

Smoldering racism sometimes exploded in violence. White rioters in Atlanta in 1906 murdered twenty-five blacks and burned many black homes. From 1900 to 1920, an average of about seventy-five lynchings occurred yearly. Blacks whose assertive behavior or economic aspirations angered whites were especially vulnerable to lynch mobs. Some lynchings involved incredible sadism, with large crowds on hand, victims' bodies mutilated, and graphic photo postcards sold later. Authorities rarely intervened. At a 1916 lynching in Texas, the mayor warned the mob not to damage the hanging tree on city property.

In the face of such hostility, African-Americans developed strong institutions. Black religious life, centered in the African Methodist Episcopal church, provided a bulwark of support for many. Working African-American mothers, drawing on strategies dating to slavery days, relied on relatives and neighbors for child care. A handful of black higher-education institutions carried on against heavy odds. The urban black community included black-owned insurance companies and banks, and a small elite of entrepreneurs, teachers, and ministers. Although major-league baseball excluded blacks, a thriving Negro League attracted many African-American fans.

In this racist age, progressives compiled a mixed record on racial issues. Muckraker Ray Stannard Baker documented racism in *Following the Color Line* (1908). Settlement-house worker Mary White Ovington helped found the National Association for the Advancement of Colored People in 1909 and wrote *Half a Man* (1911) about racism's psychological toll.

But most progressives kept silent as blacks' rights were trampled. Viewing blacks as inferior, white progressives generally supported or tolerated segregation and the strict moral oversight of African-American communities, occasionally advocating,

CHECKING IN

- Progressives made significant progress in political reform at state and local levels, battling corruption and introducing electoral reform.
- At the state level, progressives achieved some success in the regulation of business and the reform of working conditions.
- Progressives also sought to improve urban conditions by beautifying cities and creating better public-health systems.
- At its worst, progressivism endeavored to impose middle-class morality on immigrants, as it did with the temperance movement.
- Many progressives supported immigration restrictions and tolerated racism.

at best, paternalistic efforts to "up-lift" this supposedly backward and childlike people. Viciously racist southern politicians like Governor James K. Vardaman of Mississippi and Senator Ben Tillman of South Carolina also supported progressive reforms.

At the national level, President Theodore Roosevelt's record on race was marginally better than that of other politicians. He appointed a black to head the Charleston customs house despite white opposition. And in a symbolically important gesture, he dined with Booker T. Washington at the White House. In 1906, however, he approved the dishonorable discharge of an entire regiment of black soldiers, including Congressional Medal of Honor winners, in Brownsville, Texas, because some members of the unit, goaded by racist taunts, had killed a local civilian. The "Brownsville Incident" incensed black Americans. (In 1972, after most of the men were dead, Congress reversed the dishonorable discharges.)

Under President Woodrow Wilson, racism became rampant in Washington. A southerner, Wilson displayed at best a patronizing attitude toward blacks, praised the racist movie *The Birth of a Nation,* appointed southerners to his cabinet, and allowed racial segregation in all levels of the government.

BLACKS, WOMEN, AND WORKERS ORGANIZE

How did progressives try to control morality, and how did they view immigrants and blacks?

The organizational strategy so central to progressivism generally also proved useful for groups facing discrimination or exploitation. African-Americans, middle-class women, and wage workers all organized to address their grievances and improve their situation.

African-American Leaders Organize Against Racism

With racism on the rise, Booker T. Washington's self-help message (see Chapter 20) seemed increasingly unrealistic, particularly to northern blacks. In 1902, one editor of a black newspaper called Washington's go-slow policies "a fatal blow . . . to the Negro's political rights and liberty." Another opponent was the black journalist and activist **Ida Wells-Barnett.** Moving to Chicago from Memphis in 1892 after a white mob destroyed her offices, Wells-Barnett mounted a national anti-lynching campaign, in contrast to Booker T. Washington's public silence on the subject.

Ida Wells-Barnett Eloquent speaker, writer, and civil rights activist who championed anti-lynching legislation

W. E. B. Du Bois African-American scholar and civil rights leader; author of *The Souls of Black Folk*

Washington's principal black critic was **W. E. B. Du Bois** (1868–1963). After earning a PhD in history from Harvard in 1895, Du Bois taught at Atlanta University. In *The Souls of Black Folk* (1903), Du Bois rejected Washington's emphasis on patience and manual skills. Instead, Du Bois demanded full racial equality, including equal educational opportunities, and urged resistance to all forms of racism.

In 1905, under Du Bois's leadership, blacks committed to battling racism held a conference at Niagara Falls. For the next few years, participants in the "Niagara Movement" met annually. In 1909, white reformers who had grown dissatisfied with

Washington's cautiousness joined with Du Bois and other blacks from the Niagara Movement to form the **National Association for the Advancement of Colored People (NAACP).** This new organization called for sustained activism, including legal challenges, to achieve political equality for blacks and full integration into American life. Attracting the urban black middle class, the NAACP by 1914 had six thousand members in fifty branches.

National Association for the Advancement of Colored People (NAACP) Major civil rights organization founded during the Progressive Era

Revival of the Woman-Suffrage Movement

As late as 1910, women could vote in only four western states: Wyoming, Utah, Colorado, and Idaho. But women's active role in progressive reform movements revitalized the suffrage cause. A vigorous suffrage movement in Great Britain reverberated in America as well. Like progressivism itself, this revived campaign had grass-roots origins. A 1915 suffrage campaign in New York State, though unsuccessful, underscored the new momentum.

Developments in California illustrated both the movement's new momentum and its limitations. By the early 1900s, California's women's clubs had evolved into a potent statewide organization active in municipal reform and public-school issues. This activism convinced many members that full citizenship meant the right to vote. While working with labor leaders and male progressives, the woman-suffrage strategists also insisted on the unique role of "organized womanhood" in building a better society. Success came in 1911 when California voters approved woman suffrage.

Carrie Chapman Catt Leader of women's movement; led the drive for woman suffrage in the early twentieth century

However, "organized womanhood" in California had its limits. Elite and middle-class women, mainly based in Los Angeles and San Francisco, led the campaign. Working-class and farm women played a small role, while African-American, Mexican-American, and Asian-American women were almost totally excluded.

New leaders translated the momentum in New York, California, and other states into a revitalized national movement. When Susan B. Anthony retired from the presidency of the National American Woman Suffrage Association (NAWSA) in 1900, **Carrie Chapman Catt** of Iowa succeeded her. Under Catt, NAWSA adopted the so-called Winning Plan: grass-roots organization with tight central coordination, focused on state-level campaigns.

Adopting techniques from the new urban consumer culture, suffragists ran newspaper ads, put up posters, waved banners with catchy slogans, organized parades in open cars, arranged photo opportunities for the media, and distributed fans and other items emblazoned with the suffrage message. Gradually, state after state fell into the suffrage column (see Map 21.1).

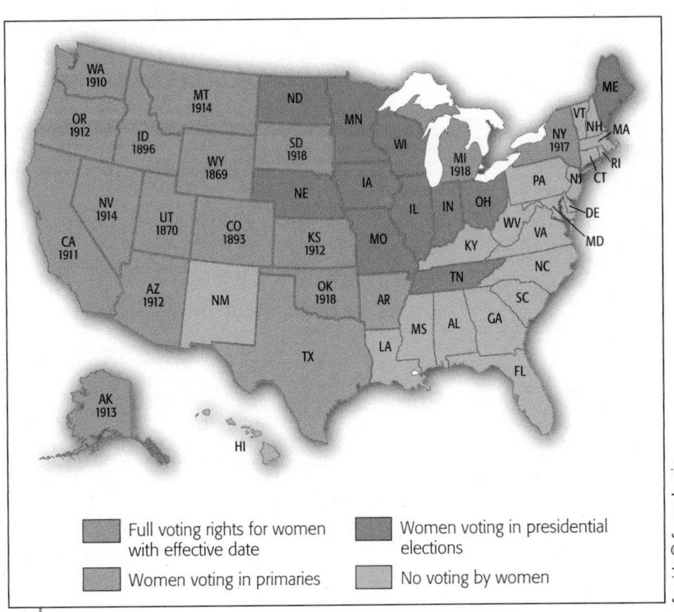

Map 21.1 Woman Suffrage Before the Nineteenth Amendment

Beginning with Wyoming in 1869, woman suffrage made steady gains in western states before 1920. Farther east, key victories came in New York (1917) and Michigan (1918). But much of the East remained an anti-woman suffrage bastion throughout the period.

Interactive Map

Library of Congress

Parading for Woman Suffrage

Suffrage leaders built support for the cause by using modern advertising and publicity techniques, including automobiles festooned with flags, banners, and—in this case—smiling little girls.

As in California (and like progressive organizations generally), NAWSA's membership remained largely white, native born, and middle class. Some upper-class women opposed the reform. Women already enjoyed behind-the-scenes influence, they argued; invading the male realm of electoral politics would tarnish their moral and spiritual role.

Not all suffragists accepted Catt's strategy. Alice Paul, influenced by the British suffragists' militant tactics, grew impatient with NAWSA's state-by-state approach. In 1913, Paul founded the Congressional Union for Woman Suffrage, renamed the National Woman's Party in 1917, to pressure Congress for a woman-suffrage amendment. In 1917–1918, with the United States at war, the suffrage cause prevailed in New York and Michigan and advanced toward final success (further discussed in Chapter 22).

Enlarging "Woman's Sphere"

The suffrage movement did not exhaust American women's talents or organizational energies. Women's club members, settlement-house leaders, and individual female activists joined in various campaigns: to bring playgrounds and day nurseries to the slums, to abolish child labor, to improve conditions for women workers, and to ban unsafe foods and quack remedies. As Jane Addams observed, women's concern for their own families' welfare could also draw them into political activism in an industrial age when hazards came from outside the home as well as inside.

Cultural assumptions about "woman's sphere" weakened as women invaded many fronts. Katherine Bement Davis served as New York City's commissioner of corrections. Emma Goldman crisscrossed the country delivering riveting lectures on politics, feminism, and modern drama while coediting a radical monthly, *Mother Earth*. A vanguard of pioneering women in higher education included Marion Talbot, first dean of women at the University of Chicago.

In *Women and Economics* (1898) and other works, feminist intellectual Charlotte Perkins Gilman explored the historical and cultural roots of female subordination, and linked women's inferior status to their economic dependence on men. Confining women to the domestic sphere, Gilman argued, was an evolutionary throwback that had become outdated and inefficient. She advocated economic independence for women through equality in the workplace, the collectivization of domestic chores, and state-run day-care centers.

Some Progressive Era reformers challenged federal and state laws banning the distribution of contraceptives and birth-control information. Although countless women, particularly the poor, suffered health problems from frequent pregnancies, artificial contraception was widely denounced as immoral. In 1914, **Margaret Sanger** of New York, whose mother had died after bearing eleven children, began her crusade for birth control, a term she coined. When the authorities proscribed her journal *The Woman Rebel* on obscenity charges, Sanger fled to Great Britain. Returning in 1916, she opened the nation's first birth-control clinic in Brooklyn and founded the American Birth Control League, forerunner of today's Planned Parenthood Federation.

Margaret Sanger Founder of the birth-control movement; leading feminist

Meanwhile, another New Yorker, Mary Ware Dennett, also emerged as an advocate of birth control and sex education. While Sanger championed direct action to promote the cause, Dennett urged lobbying efforts to change the law. Sanger insisted that only physicians should supply contraceptives; Dennett argued for widespread distribution. These differences, plus personal rivalries, produced divisions in the movement.

The birth-control and sex-education movements stand as important legacies of progressivism. At the time, however, conservatives bitterly opposed them. Dennett's frank 1919 informational pamphlet for youth, *The Sex Side of Life*, was long banned as obscene. Not until 1965 did the Supreme Court fully legalize the dissemination of contraceptive materials and information.

Workers Organize; Socialism Advances

In this age of organization, labor unions continued to expand. In 1900–1920, the American Federation of Labor (AFL) grew from 625,000 to 4 million members. This still represented only about 20 percent of the industrial work force. With immigrants hungry for jobs, union activities posed risks. The boss could always fire an "agitator" and hire a newcomer. Judicial hostility also retarded unionization. In the 1908 *Danbury Hatters* case, the Supreme Court ruled that boycotts in support of strikes violated the Sherman Anti-Trust Act. The AFL's strength remained in the skilled trades, not in the factories and mills where most immigrants and women worked.

A few unions did try to reach these laborers. The International Ladies' Garment Workers' Union (ILGWU), founded in 1900 by immigrant workers in New York City's needle trades, conducted successful strikes in 1909 and after the 1911 Triangle fire. Some picketers lost their jobs or endured police beatings, but the strikers did win higher wages and improved working conditions.

Another union that targeted the most exploited workers was the **Industrial Workers of the World (IWW),** or Wobblies, founded in Chicago in 1905. Led by the colorful William D. "Big Bill" Haywood, the IWW's membership peaked at around thirty thousand, mostly western miners, lumbermen, fruit pickers, and itinerant laborers. The IWW led some mass strikes of miners and timber workers, but its greatest success came in 1912 when it won a rancorous textile strike in Lawrence, Massachusetts. The victory owed much to Elizabeth Gurley Flynn, a fervent Irish-American orator who publicized the cause by

Industrial Workers of the World (IWW) Occasionally radical union discredited by use of violence sending strikers' children to sympathizers in New York City for temporary care. With an exaggerated reputation for violence, the IWW faced government harassment, especially during World War I, and by 1920 its strength was broken.

Other workers, along with some middle-class Americans, turned to socialism. Socialists advocated an end to capitalism and demanded public ownership of factories, utilities, railroads, and communications systems. But American workers generally rejected the revolutionary ideology of German social theorist Karl Marx in favor of democratic socialism achieved at the ballot box. In 1900 democratic socialists formed the Socialist Party of America (SPA). **Eugene V. Debs,** the Indiana labor leader, became the SPA's most popular spokesman and its candidate for president five times between 1900 and 1920.

The pinnacle of socialist strength came in 1912 when the SPA counted 118,000 members, Debs received over 900,000 (about 6 percent) of the votes for president, and the Socialists elected a congressman and many municipal officials. The party published over three hundred newspapers, including foreign-language papers targeting immigrants.

CHECKING IN

- In pursuit of political rights, some African-Americans, led by W. E. B. Du Bois, rejected Booker T. Washington's gradualism and became activists.
- The woman-suffrage movement emerged as a major component of progressivism.
- Women like Emma Goldman and Margaret Sanger pushed beyond the boundaries of the traditional "woman's sphere," promoting economic independence and birth control.
- The AFL grew larger and stronger but remained focused on the skilled trades; the more radical IWW blossomed, bloomed, and faded.
- Socialists gained strength, even among the middle class.

Eugene V. Debs Socialist labor leader whose surprising showing in the 1912 presidential election illustrated the growing frustrations of many workers

NATIONAL PROGRESSIVISM PHASE I: ROOSEVELT AND TAFT, 1901–1913

What strategies did African-Americans, women, and industrial workers use to improve their lot?

By 1905 localized reform movements had coalesced into a national effort. In 1906, Robert La Follette was elected a U.S. senator. Five years earlier, progressivism had found its first national leader, **Theodore Roosevelt,** nicknamed "TR."

Theodore Roosevelt Youthful successor to William McKinley in 1901; pushed an agenda of progressive reform

Self-righteous, jingoistic, verbose—but also brilliant, politically savvy, and endlessly interesting—Roosevelt became president in 1901 and made the White House a cauldron of political activism. Skillfully orchestrating public opinion, Roosevelt pursued his goals—labor mediation, consumer protection, corporate regulation, natural-resource conservation, and engagement abroad.

Roosevelt's activist approach permanently enlarged the powers of the presidency. His handpicked successor, **William Howard Taft,** proved politically inept, however, and controversy marked his administration. With the Republicans divided, the Democrat Woodrow Wilson, espousing a somewhat different reform vision, won the presidency in 1912.

William Howard Taft Roosevelt's hand-picked successor for president; later served as Supreme Court justice

Roosevelt's Path to the White House

On September 6, 1901, in Buffalo, an anarchist shot President William McKinley. On September 14 McKinley died, and forty-two-year-old Vice President Theodore Roosevelt became president. Many Republican leaders shuddered at the thought of what one called "that damned cowboy" in the White House. Roosevelt was the son of an aristocratic New York family and was sickly as a child, but he had used a body-building program and active summers in Wyoming to become a model of physical fitness. When his young wife died in 1884, he stoically carried on. Two years on a Dakota ranch deepened his enthusiasm for what he termed "the strenuous life."

Although his social peers scorned politics, Roosevelt served as a state assemblyman, New York City police commissioner, and U.S. civil-service commissioner. In 1898, fresh from his Cuban exploits, he was elected New York's governor. Two years later, the state's Republican boss, eager to be rid of him, arranged for Roosevelt's nomination as vice president.

Roosevelt enjoyed public life and loved the limelight. "When Theodore attends a wedding he wants to be the bride," his daughter observed, "and when he attends a funeral he wants to be the corpse." With his toothy grin, machine-gun speech, and amazing energy, he dominated the political landscape. When he refused to shoot a bear cub on a hunting trip, a shrewd toy maker marketed a cuddly new product, the Teddy Bear.

Labor Disputes, Trustbusting, and Railroad Regulation

The new president's political skills were quickly tested. In May 1902, the United Mine Workers Union (UMW) called a strike to gain higher wages, shorter hours, and recognition as a union. The mine owners refused to talk to UMW leaders. After five months, with coal reserves dwindling and winter looming, Roosevelt summoned the deadlocked parties to the White House. Threatening to take over the mines, he won reluctant acceptance of an arbitration commission to settle the dispute. In 1903, the commission granted miners a 10 percent wage hike and reduced their workday from ten to nine hours.

Roosevelt approached such labor disputes very differently from his predecessors, who had called out federal troops to break strikes. Although not consistently prolabor, he defended labor's right to organize and derided as "arrogant stupidity" business owners' resistance to arbitration.

With his elite background, Roosevelt neither feared nor much liked business tycoons. Conservative at heart, he had no desire to abolish big corporations, but he embraced the progressive philosophy that corporate behavior must be carefully regulated. A strict moralist, he believed that corporations, like individuals, must meet a high standard of virtue.

Another test came in 1901 when J. P. Morgan formed the United States Steel Company, the nation's first billion-dollar business. As public distrust of big corporations deepened, Roosevelt dashed to the head of the parade. His 1902 State of the Union message gave high priority to breaking up business monopolies, or "trustbusting." Roosevelt's attorney general soon filed suit against the Northern Securities Company, a mammoth holding company formed to control railroading in the Northwest, for violating the Sherman Anti-Trust Act. Roosevelt called for a "square deal" for all Americans and denounced special treatment for capitalists. "We don't wish to destroy corporations," he insisted, "but we do wish to make them serve the public good." In 1904, a divided Supreme Court ordered the Northern Securities Company dissolved.

The Roosevelt administration filed over forty antitrust lawsuits. In two key rulings in 1911, the Court ordered the breakup of the Standard Oil Company and the reorganization of the American Tobacco Company to make it less monopolistic.

As the 1904 presidential election approached, Roosevelt made peace with Morgan and other business magnates. When the convention that unanimously nominated Roosevelt adopted a probusiness platform, $2 million in corporate campaign contributions poured in. The Democrats, meanwhile, eager to erase the taint of radicalism lingering from the 1890s, embraced the gold standard and nominated a conservative New York judge.

Winning easily, Roosevelt turned to a major goal: railroad regulation. He now saw corporate regulation as more effective than trustbusting, and this shift underlay the 1906 **Hepburn Act**. This law empowered the Interstate Commerce Commission to set maximum railroad rates and to examine railroads' financial records. It also curtailed the railroads' practice of distributing free passes to ministers and other shapers of public opinion. Although failing to fully satisfy reformers, the Hepburn Act did expand the government's regulatory powers.

Hepburn Act Legislation that strengthened government power to regulate railroads

Consumer Protection

Of all progressive reforms, the campaign against unsafe food, drugs, and medicine proved especially popular. Upton Sinclair's *The Jungle* (1906) graphically described conditions in some meatpacking plants. Wrote Sinclair in one vivid passage, "[A] man could run his hand over these piles of meat and sweep off handfuls of dried dung of rats. These rats were nuisances, and the packers would put poisoned bread out for them, they would die, and then rats, bread, and meat would go into the hoppers together." Women's organizations and consumer groups rallied public opinion on this issue. Other muckrakers exposed useless or dangerous patent medicines laced with cocaine, opium, or alcohol. One tonic "for treatment of the alcohol habit" contained 26.5 percent alcohol. Peddlers of these nostrums freely claimed that they could cure cancer, grow hair, and restore sexual vigor.

Sensing the public mood, Roosevelt supported the Pure Food and Drug Act and the Meat Inspection Act, both passed in 1906. The former outlawed the sale of adulterated food and drugs, and required accurate ingredient labels; the latter imposed strict sanitary rules on meatpackers, set up a quality-rating system, and created a program of federal meat inspection.

Environmentalism Progressive-Style

In his first State of the Union message, Roosevelt singled out conservation as "the most vital internal question." By 1900 decades of urban-industrial growth and western expansion had taken a heavy toll on the land. In the West, land use disputes raged as mining and timber interests, farmers, ranchers, sheep growers, and preservationists advanced competing claims.

Western business interests and boosters preached exploitation of the region's resources, and farmers pushed for irrigation projects, but organizations like the Sierra Club battled to preserve large wild areas for their pristine beauty. Under a law passed in 1891, Presidents Harrison and Cleveland set aside some 35 million acres of public lands as national forests.

A wilderness vogue swept the United States in the early twentieth century. From congested cities and clanging factories, Americans looked to the wilderness for tranquility and spiritual solace. Popular writers evoked the lure of the primitive, and the Boy Scouts (1910) and Girl Scouts (1912) gave city children a taste of the outdoors.

Between the wilderness enthusiasts and the developers stood government professionals like Gifford Pinchot who saw the public domain as a resource to be managed wisely. Appointed by Roosevelt in 1905 to head the new U.S. Forest Service, Pinchot stressed not preservation but conservation—the planned use of forest lands for public and commercial purposes.

At heart Roosevelt was a preservationist. He once compared "the destruction of a species" to the loss of "all the works of some great writer." However, Roosevelt the politician backed the conservationists' call for planned development. He supported the **National Reclamation Act** of 1902, which earmarked the proceeds of public-land sales for water management in the arid western regions and established the Reclamation Service to plan dams and irrigation projects.

National Reclamation Act
Sold public land and used the revenues for water management and dam projects

This measure ranks with the Northwest Ordinance for promoting the development and productivity of a vast region of North America. Arizona's Roosevelt Dam

Yosemite National Park

President Theodore Roosevelt and Friends Commune with Nature, 1903

Dwarfed by an ancient sequoia, the Grizzly Giant, in the Mariposa Grove of California's Yosemite National Park, Roosevelt's party included California governor George Pardee (third from left), the naturalist and Sierra Club founder John Muir (fourth from right), and the presidents of Columbia University (third from right) and the University of California (far right). The Grizzly Giant still stands, and remains a favorite with tourists.

spurred the growth of Phoenix, and the Snake River project converted thousands of barren Idaho acres into fertile farmland. The law required those who benefited from reclamation projects to repay the government for construction costs, creating a federal fund for further projects. It made possible the transition of the West from a series of isolated "island settlements" into a thriving, interconnected region.

The competition for scarce water resources in the West sparked bitter political battles. The Los Angeles basin, for example, with 40 percent of California's population in 1900, found itself with only 2 percent of the state's surface water. In 1907, the City of Los Angeles derailed a Reclamation Service project intended for the farmers of California's Owens Valley, more than 230 miles to the north, and diverted the precious water to Los Angeles.

Meanwhile, President Roosevelt backed Pinchot's program of multiuse land management and set aside more than 200 million acres of public land as national forests, mineral reserves, and potential waterpower sites. But the national-forest provisions provoked corporate opposition, and in 1907 Congress revoked the president's authority to create national forests in six timber-rich western states. Before signing the bill, Roosevelt designated 16 million more acres in the six states as national forests. Roosevelt also created fifty-three wildlife reserves, sixteen national monuments, and five new national parks. Congress established the National Park Service in 1916 to manage them.

Gifford Pinchot organized a White House conservation conference for the nation's governors in 1908, but John Muir and other wilderness preservationists were not invited. However, preservationists won key victories in this era. For example, initiatives by private citizens saved a large grove of California's giant redwoods and a lovely stretch of the Maine coastline.

However, the Sierra Club lost a major battle to save the Hetch Hetchy Valley in Yosemite National Park when Congress in 1913 approved a dam on the Tuolumne River to provide water and hydroelectric power for San Francisco. The controversy focused attention on environmental issues, as Americans for the first time weighed the aesthetic implications of a major public-works project.

Taft in the White House, 1909–1913

Roosevelt had pledged not to run for a third term in 1908, and to the disappointment of millions, he kept his promise. The Republicans' most conservative leaders regained control. Although they nominated Roosevelt's choice, William Howard Taft, for president, they selected a conservative vice-presidential candidate and drafted a deeply conservative platform. The Democrats, meanwhile, nominated William Jennings Bryan for a third and final time. The Democratic platform called for a lower tariff, denounced the trusts, and embraced the cause of labor.

With Roosevelt's endorsement, Taft coasted to victory. However, the Democrats made gains, and progressive Republican state candidates outran the national ticket. Overall, the outcome suggested a lull in the reform movement, not its end. Taft differed markedly from Roosevelt. Whereas Roosevelt kept himself in fighting trim, Taft was obese. Roosevelt installed a boxing ring in the White House; Taft preferred golf. Roosevelt loved speechmaking and battling evildoers; Taft disliked controversy. His happiest days would come later, as chief justice of the United States.

Pledged to carry on Roosevelt's program, Taft supported the Mann-Elkins Act (1910), which strengthened the Interstate Commerce Commission's rate-setting powers and extended its authority to telephone and telegraph companies. Taft's administration actually prosecuted more antitrust cases than had Roosevelt's, but did so with little publicity. To the public, Roosevelt remained the mighty trustbuster.

The reform spotlight, meanwhile, shifted to Congress, where a group of reform-minded Republicans, nicknamed the Insurgents, including Senators La Follette and Albert Beveridge of Indiana and Congressman George Norris of Nebraska, challenged their party's conservative congressional leadership. In 1909, the Insurgents and Taft fought a bruising battle over the tariff. Taft first backed the Insurgents' call for a lower tariff. But when high-tariff advocates in Congress pushed through a measure raising duties on hundreds of items, Taft not only signed it but praised it extravagantly, infuriating the Insurgents.

The so-called Ballinger-Pinchot affair widened the rift. Richard A. Ballinger, Taft's secretary of the interior, was a Seattle lawyer who favored the unregulated private development of natural resources. Ballinger approved the sale of several million acres of coal-rich public lands in Alaska in 1909 to some Seattle businessmen, who promptly resold it to J. P. Morgan and other financiers. When a Department of Interior official protested, he was fired. In true muckraking style, he went public, blasting Ballinger in a *Collier's* magazine article. When Gifford Pinchot of the Forest Service also criticized Ballinger, he too got the ax. Roosevelt's supporters seethed.

Progressive Party National third party formed around Roosevelt's presidential candidacy in 1912

When Roosevelt returned to the United States from an African safari in June 1910, Pinchot met the boat. Openly breaking with Taft, Roosevelt campaigned for Insurgent candidates in that year's midterm elections. In a speech that alarmed conservatives, he endorsed the radical idea of reversing judicial rulings by popular vote. Borrowing a term from Herbert Croly's *The Promise of American Life*, Roosevelt proposed a "New Nationalism" that would powerfully engage the federal government in reform.

Democrats captured the House in 1910, and a coalition of Democrats and Insurgents controlled the Senate. As fervor for reform rose, Roosevelt sounded more and more like a presidential candidate.

The Four-Way Election of 1912

In February 1912, Roosevelt announced his candidacy for the Republican nomination. However, Taft wanted a second term. Although Roosevelt generally walloped Taft in the Republican state primaries and conventions, Taft controlled the party machinery, and the Republican convention in Chicago disqualified many of Roosevelt's hard-won delegates. Outraged, Roosevelt's backers walked out and formed the **Progressive Party.** What had been a general term for a broad reform movement now became the official name of a political party.

"I feel fit as a bull moose," Roosevelt trumpeted, thereby giving his organization its nickname, the Bull Moose Party. The party's convention platform endorsed most reform causes of the day, including lower

CHECKING IN

- Theodore Roosevelt's unprecedented presidential activism captivated the American people.
- Roosevelt became known as "the great trustbuster" for his vigorous enforcement of the Sherman Anti-Trust Act and stricter regulation of railroads.
- Protection of the public through such measures as the Pure Food and Drug Act and the Meat Inspection Act were cornerstones of Roosevelt's presidential progressivism.
- Roosevelt's administration set aside millions of acres for preservation but also promoted planned development of the West through the National Reclamation Act.
- Angered by what he saw as betrayal by his chosen successor, Taft, Roosevelt and his supporters formed the Bull Moose (Progressive) Party in 1912; with Republicans divided, the Democratic candidate, Woodrow Wilson, won the election.

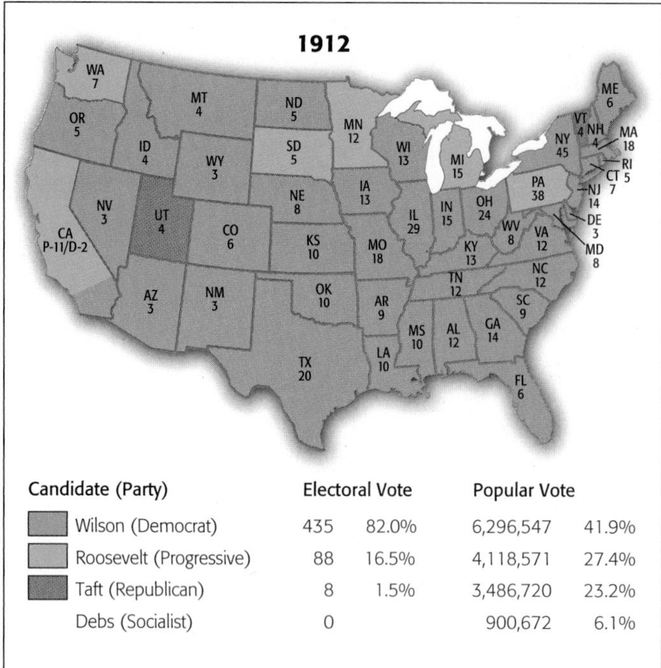

Candidate (Party)	Electoral Vote		Popular Vote	
Wilson (Democrat)	435	82.0%	6,296,547	41.9%
Roosevelt (Progressive)	88	16.5%	4,118,571	27.4%
Taft (Republican)	8	1.5%	3,486,720	23.2%
Debs (Socialist)	0		900,672	6.1%

Map 21.2 The Election of 1912

In the campaign, Taft more or less gave up, satisfied to have kept his party safe for conservatism. The Socialist candidate Eugene Debs proposed an end to capitalism. Roosevelt preached his New Nationalism: Corporations must be regulated in the public interest, the welfare of workers and consumers safeguarded, and the environment protected.

Interactive Map

tariffs, woman suffrage, business regulation, the abolition of child labor, the eight-hour workday, workers' compensation, the direct primary, and the popular election of senators. The new party attracted a diverse following, united mainly by affection for Roosevelt.

Meanwhile, the reform spirit also infused the Democratic Party. In New Jersey in 1910, voters elected a political novice, **Woodrow Wilson,** as governor. A "Wilson for President" boom soon arose, and when the Democrats assembled in Baltimore in June 1912, Wilson won the nomination, defeating several established party leaders.

Wilson called for a "New Freedom," evoking an earlier era of small government, small businesses, and free competition. The divided Republicans proved no match for the united Democrats. Wilson prevailed, and the Democrats took both houses of Congress (see Map 21.2). More than nine hundred thousand voters opted for Debs and socialism.

The 1912 election identified the triumphant Democrats with reform (except on the issue of race)—a link that Franklin D. Roosevelt would strengthen in the 1930s. In addition, Theodore Roosevelt's third-party campaign demonstrated the continued appeal of reform among many grass-roots Republicans.

Woodrow Wilson Democratic president whose election in 1912 ushered in a second wave of progressive reforms on the national level

National Progressivism Phase II: Woodrow Wilson, 1913–1917

As progressivism became a national movement, what issues proved most important?

The son and grandson of Presbyterian ministers, Wilson grew up in southern towns in a churchly atmosphere that shaped his oratory and moral outlook. Despite a learning disability (probably dyslexia), he graduated from Princeton and earned a PhD in political science from Johns Hopkins University. Joining Princeton's faculty, he became its president in 1902. A rigid unwillingness to compromise cost him faculty support, however, and in 1910 Wilson resigned to enter politics. Three years later, he was president of the United States.

Wilson was an eloquent orator who excelled at political deal making. But he could also retreat into a fortress of absolute certitude that tolerated no opposition. During his years as president, all these facets of his personality would come into play.

Wilson proved ready to use government to address the problems of the new corporate order, and the national progressive movement gained powerful new momentum.

Tariff and Banking Reform

Lowering tariff rates—long a goal of southern and agrarian Democrats—headed Wilson's agenda. A low-tariff bill passed the House but bogged down in the Senate. Showing his flair for drama, Wilson denounced tariff lobbyists, and his censure led to a Senate investigation of lobbyists and of senators who profited from high tariffs. Stung by the publicity, the Senate slashed tariff rates even more than the House had done. The Underwood-Simmons Tariff reduced rates an average of 15 percent.

In June 1913, Wilson called for banking and currency reform. The nation's totally decentralized banking system clearly needed overhauling. But no consensus existed on specifics. Many reformers wanted a publicly controlled central banking system, but the nation's bankers favored private control. Some opposed any central banking authority, public or private.

Wilson, who was no banking expert, insisted that the monetary system ultimately be publicly controlled. As the bargaining went on, Wilson played a crucial behind-the-scenes role. The result was the **Federal Reserve Act** (1913). A compromise measure, this law created twelve regional Federal Reserve banks under mixed public and private control. Each regional bank could issue U.S. dollars, called Federal Reserve notes, to the banks in its district to make loans. Overall control of the system was assigned to the heads of the twelve regional banks and the members of a Washington-based Federal Reserve Board (FRB), appointed by the president for fourteen-year terms.

Federal Reserve Act Major step toward establishing a solid national banking system

The Federal Reserve Act stands as Wilson's greatest legislative achievement. In time the FRB, nicknamed "the Fed," grew into the strong central monetary institution it remains today, setting interest rates and adopting fiscal policies to prevent financial panics, promote economic growth, and combat inflation.

Regulating Business; Aiding Workers and Farmers

In 1914, Wilson and his congressional allies turned to that perennial progressive cause, business regulation. The two laws that resulted sought a common goal, but embodied different approaches. The **Federal Trade Commission** Act (1914) reflected an administrative approach by creating a "watchdog" agency, the Federal Trade Commission (FTC), with power to investigate suspected violations, require regular reports from corporations, and issue cease-and-desist orders against unfair methods of competition. The Clayton Antitrust Act (1914) took a legal approach. It remedied the Sherman Anti-Trust Act's vagueness by spelling out a series of illegal practices, such as selling at a loss to undercut competitors. With the added clout of the Clayton Act, the Wilson administration filed antitrust suits against nearly a hundred corporations.

Federal Trade Commission Agency to ensure fair trade and practices

As he led a party long identified with workers, Wilson supported labor unions and workers' right to organize. He also endorsed a Clayton Act clause exempting strikes, boycotts, and picketing from the antitrust laws' prohibition of actions in restraint of trade. In 1916 (a campaign year), Wilson and congressional Democrats enacted three important worker-protection laws. The Keating-Owen Act barred from interstate commerce products manufactured by child labor (later declared unconstitutional). The Adamson Act established an eight-hour workday for interstate railway workers. The Workmen's Compensation Act provided accident and injury protection to federal workers.

Other 1916 laws helped farmers. The Federal Farm Loan Act and the Federal Warehouse Act enabled farmers, using land or crops as collateral, to get low-interest federal loans. The Federal Highway Act, providing funds for highway programs, benefited not only the new automobile industry but also farmers plagued by bad roads.

Progressivism and the Constitution

The probusiness bias of the courts moderated in the Progressive Era. In *Muller v. Oregon* (1908), the Supreme Court upheld an Oregon law limiting female laundry and factory workers to a ten-hour workday. To defend the constitutionality of the Oregon law, Boston attorney **Louis Brandeis** offered economic, medical, and sociological evidence of how long hours harmed women workers. The Court's acceptance of the "Brandeis brief" marked a breakthrough in the legal system's responsiveness to new social realities.

Louis Brandeis Jurist who pioneered the use of sociology and other social sciences in arguing legal cases

In 1916, Wilson nominated Brandeis to the Supreme Court. Many conservatives, including Republican leaders in Congress, disapproved of Brandeis's innovative approach to the law and protested. Anti-Semites opposed him because he was a Jew. But Wilson stood firm, and Brandeis won Senate confirmation.

These years also produced four constitutional amendments. The Sixteenth Amendment (ratified in 1913) granted Congress the authority to tax income. An earlier income tax measure had been declared unconstitutional, spurring advocates to campaign for an amendment. Quickly exercising its new authority, Congress in 1913 imposed a graduated federal income tax with a maximum rate of 7 percent on incomes in excess of $500,000. Income tax revenues helped pay for the government's regulatory activities under Progressive Era legislation. The Seventeenth Amendment (1913) completed a Populist crusade by mandating the direct popular election of U.S. senators. The Eighteenth Amendment (1919) established prohibition of "intoxicating liquors." The Nineteenth Amendment (1920) granted women the right to vote. This remarkable wave of amendments underscored the progressive movement's profound impact on the political landscape.

CHECKING IN

- Wilson achieved the long-sought Democratic goal of tariff reduction.
- The Federal Reserve Act, which gave the nation a central banking system, was Wilson's most important legislative achievement.
- The Clayton Anti-Trust Act strengthened government's regulatory powers.
- Wilson helped shepherd four constitutional amendments to ratification: direct popular election of senators, the income tax, prohibition, and woman suffrage.
- The outbreak of World War I curtailed and eventually ended the first great surge of progressivism.

1916: Wilson Edges Out Hughes

In 1916, Wilson easily won his party's nomination. The Republicans nominated Charles Evans Hughes, Supreme Court justice and former New York governor. Urged by Roosevelt, who was obsessed with drawing the United States into the war that had broken out in Europe in 1914 (see Chapter 22), the Progressive Party endorsed Hughes. With the Republicans more or less reunited, the election was extremely close. War-related issues loomed large. Wilson won the popular vote, but the Electoral College outcome remained in doubt for weeks as the California tally seesawed back and forth. Ultimately, Wilson carried the state by less than four thousand votes and, with it, the election.

The progressive movement lost momentum as attention turned from reform to war. Final success for the prohibition and woman-suffrage campaigns came in 1919–1920, and Congress enacted a few reform measures in the 1920s. But, overall, the movement faded as America marched to war in 1917.

Chapter Summary

How did intellectuals, novelists, and journalists inspire the progressive movement? (page 497)

The progressive movement began as preachers, novelists, journalists, photographers, and painters highlighted appalling conditions in America's cities and factories. Intellectuals offered ideas for reform through the creative use of government. Primarily middle class, progressives sought to improve urban life and working conditions, eliminate political corruption, and curb the excesses of the new urban, industrial society.

How did state and local progressives seek to reform cities and the new industrial order? (page 501)

At the local and state level, reformers like Mayor Hazen Pingree of Detroit and Wisconsin governor Robert M. La Follette, together with a host of reform organizations, worked to combat political corruption, make cities safer and more beautiful, regulate corporations, and improve conditions for workers.

How did progressives try to control morality, and how did they view immigrants and blacks? (page 510)

Progressivism had its coercive side. Some reformers concentrated on regulating urban amusements and banning alcohol consumption. Racism and hostility to immigrants comprised a part of the progressive legacy as well. Because of the refusal of progressive reformers to substantively address the problem of racial injustice, African-Americans became more politically active, founding the National Association for the Advancement of Colored People (NAACP).

What strategies did African-Americans, women, and industrial workers use to improve their lot? (page 514)

The women's movement focused on the achievement of suffrage. A handful of women, like birth-control advocate Margaret Sanger, pushed far beyond the accepted "woman's sphere." The labor movement grew stronger, especially the AFL; more radical movements like the IWW flared. Meanwhile, Roosevelt's

KEY TERMS

"muckrakers" *(p. 501)*
Robert La Follette *(p. 503)*
Anti-Saloon League (ASL) *(p. 507)*
Ida Wells-Barnett *(p. 510)*
W. E. B. Du Bois *(p. 510)*
National Association for the Advancement of Colored People (NAACP) *(p. 511)*
Carrie Chapman Catt *(p. 511)*
Margaret Sanger *(p. 513)*
Industrial Workers of the World (IWW) *(p. 513)*
Eugene V. Debs *(p. 514)*
Theodore Roosevelt *(p. 514)*
William Howard Taft *(p. 514)*
Hepburn Act *(p. 516)*
National Reclamation Act *(p. 517)*
Progressive Party *(p. 519)*
Woodrow Wilson *(p. 520)*
Federal Reserve Act *(p. 521)*
Federal Trade Commission *(p. 521)*
Louis Brandeis *(p. 522)*

activist presidency captivated the American public. Under Roosevelt, Congress strengthened railroad regulation, established the Food and Drug Administration, and enormously increased the amount of land set aside for conservation and preservation. Roosevelt became known as "the great trustbuster." However, President Taft alienated Roosevelt and progressive Republicans, who formed the Bull Moose (Progressive) Party. With Republicans divided, Democrat Woodrow Wilson won the presidency in 1912.

As progressivism became a national movement, what issues proved most important? (page 520)

Wilson's presidency saw enormous strides in increasing government's regulatory powers. For example, the Clayton Act strengthened antitrust law, and the Federal Reserve Act centralized banking. Four amendments to the Constitution embodied many progressive goals: direct popular election of senators, the income tax, prohibition, and woman suffrage. However, progressivism began to wane as attention turned to World War I. The next great reform movement, the New Deal of the 1930s, would draw on progressivism's legacy.

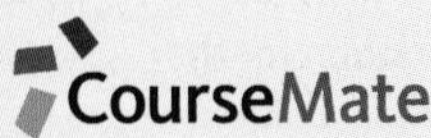

Go to the CourseMate website at **www.cengagebrain.com** for additional study tools and review materials—including audio and video clips—for this chapter.

CHAPTER 22

Global Involvements and World War I

1902–1920

Sow the seeds of Victory! plant & raise your own vegetables

Library of Congress

World War I Poster Urging Food Conservation, by the Illustrator James Montgomery Flagg

CHAPTER PREVIEW

Defining America's World Role, 1902–1914
What goals underlay America's early-twentieth-century involvements in Asia and Latin America?

War in Europe, 1914–1917
Considering both immediate and long-term factors, why did the United States go to war in 1917?

Mobilizing at Home, Fighting in France, 1917–1918
How did Washington mobilize the nation for war, and what role did U.S. troops play in the war?

Promoting the War and Suppressing Dissent
How did Americans respond to propaganda and suppression of dissent?

Economic and Social Trends in Wartime America
What was the war's economic, political, and social impact on the American home front?

Joyous Armistice, Bitter Aftermath, 1918–1920
How did the League of Nations begin, and why did the Senate reject U.S. membership in the League?

It was April 6, 1917, and Jane Addams was troubled. Congress had just supported President Woodrow Wilson's call for a declaration of war on Germany. Addams had deep patriotic roots, but she believed in peace and deplored her nation's decision for war. As the founder of Hull House, a Chicago settlement house, Addams had worked to overcome tensions among different ethnic groups. When war broke out in Europe in 1914, Addams worked to end the conflict. A founder of the Woman's Peace Party in 1915, she attended an International Congress of Women that called on the warring nations to submit their differences to arbitration. Addams also met with President Wilson in a futile effort to enlist his support for arbitration.

Now America had entered the war, and Addams had to take a stand. Many of her friends, including John Dewey, were lining up behind Wilson. Despite the pressures, Addams heeded her conscience and opposed the war. The reaction was swift. Editorial writers who had earlier praised her settlement-house work now criticized her. For years after, the American Legion and other patriotic organizations attacked Addams for her "disloyalty" in 1917.

Addams did not sit out the war on the sidelines, however. She gave speeches across America urging increased food production to aid refugees. In 1919, she was elected first president of the Women's International League for Peace and Freedom. In 1931, she won the Nobel Peace Prize.

Addams's experience underscores how deeply World War I affected American life. Beyond its immediate effects, the war had long-lasting social, economic, and political ramifications. In the late nineteenth century, America had become an industrial powerhouse seeking markets and raw materials, and these widening economic interests brought a new level of international engagement. This expanded world role, with important home-front ramifications, has continued to shape American history to the present. These broader involvements around the world, culminating in World War I, are the focus of this chapter.

DEFINING AMERICA'S WORLD ROLE, 1902–1914

What goals underlay America's early-twentieth-century involvements in Asia and Latin America?

As noted in Chapter 20, the annexation of Hawai'i, the Spanish-American War, the occupation of the Philippines, and other developments in the 1890s signaled America's growing involvement abroad. These foreign engagements reflected a desire to assert American power in an age of imperial expansion. This process of foreign engagement continued under Presidents Theodore Roosevelt, William Howard Taft, and Woodrow Wilson. America's dealings with Asian and Latin American nations in these years were shaped by both economic and ideological considerations.

The "Open Door": Competing for the China Market

As the campaign to suppress the Philippines insurrection dragged on (see Chapter 20), Americans shifted their focus to China. Their aim was not territorial but commercial. Proclaimed Indiana senator Albert J. Beveridge in 1898, "American factories are making more than the American people can use; American soil is producing more than they can consume. . . . [T]he trade of the world must and shall be ours." Textile producers dreamed of clothing China's millions; investors envisioned Chinese railroad construction. As China's 250-year-old Manchu Ch'ing empire grew weaker, U.S. businesspeople watched carefully.

But other nations—including Russia, Germany, and Great Britain—were also eyeing the China market. Some pressured the weak Manchu rulers to give them exclusive trading and development rights in designated regions, or "spheres of influence."

Chronology

1899	First U.S. Open Door note seeking access to China market; Boxer Rebellion erupts in China
1904	President Theodore Roosevelt proclaims "Roosevelt Corollary" to Monroe Doctrine
1905	Roosevelt mediates the end of the Russo-Japanese War
1906	San Francisco ends segregation of Asian schoolchildren; Panama Canal construction begins
1912	U.S. Marines occupy Nicaragua
1914	U.S. troops occupy Veracruz, Mexico; Panama Canal opens; World War I begins; President Wilson proclaims American neutrality
1915	U.S. Marines occupy Haiti and the Dominican Republic; Woman's Peace Party organized; British liner *Lusitania* sunk by German U-boat; Wilson permits U.S. bank loans to Allies
1916	U.S. punitive expedition invades Mexico, seeking Pancho Villa; Germany pledges not to attack merchant ships without warning; Wilson reelected
1917	U.S. troops withdraw from Mexico; Germany resumes unrestricted U-boat warfare; United States declares war; Selective Service Act sets up national draft; War Industries Board, Committee on Public Information, and Food Administration created; Espionage Act passed; NAACP march in New York City protests upsurge in lynchings; Bolsheviks seize power in Russia; U.S. government operates the nation's railroads
1918	Wilson outlines Fourteen Points; Sedition Amendment passed; global influenza pandemic takes heavy toll in United States; National War Labor Board created; American forces see action at Château-Thierry; Belleau Wood, St. Mihiel, and Meuse-Argonne campaign; armistice signed (November 11)
1919	Eighteenth Amendment added to the Constitution (prohibition); Peace treaty signed at Versailles; Supreme Court upholds silencing of war critics in *Schenck* v. *United States;* upsurge of lynchings; racial violence in Chicago; Wilson suffers paralyzing stroke; Versailles treaty, with League covenant, rejected by Senate
1920	"Red raids" organized by Justice Department; Nineteenth Amendment added to the Constitution (woman suffrage); Warren G. Harding elected president

In 1899, U.S. Secretary of State John Hay asked the major European powers to assure American trading rights in China by opening the ports in their spheres of influence to all countries. The nations gave noncommittal answers, but Hay blithely announced their acceptance of the principle of an "Open Door" to American business in China.

Hay's Open Door note showed how commercial considerations were increasingly influencing American foreign policy. It reflected a quest for what has been called "informal empire," in contrast to the formal acquisition of overseas territories.

As Hay pursued this effort, a more urgent threat emerged. In 1899, an antiforeign secret society known as the Harmonious Righteous Fists (called "Boxers" by Western journalists) killed thousands of foreigners and Chinese Christians. In June 1900, the Boxers occupied Beijing (BAY-jing), China's capital, and besieged the district housing the foreign legations. The United States contributed twenty-five hundred soldiers to an international army that marched on Beijing, quashed the **Boxer Rebellion,** and rescued the occupants of the threatened legations.

Boxer Rebellion Fanatical Chinese insurgency against Christians and foreigners, defeated by an international force

Open Door notes John Hay's statement of American policy to keep trade open in China

The Boxers' defeat further weakened China's government. Fearing that the regime's collapse would allow European powers to carve up China, John Hay issued a second, more important, series of **Open Door notes** in 1900. He reaffirmed the principle of open trade in China for all nations and announced America's determination to preserve China's territorial and administrative integrity. In general, China remained open to U.S. business interests and Christian missionaries. In the 1930s, when Japanese expansionism menaced China, Hay's policy helped shape the American response.

Along with U.S. economic expansion in China came missionary activity. American Protestant missionaries had come to Asia as early as the 1820s. By 1900, some five thousand U.S. missionaries were active in China, Africa, India, and elsewhere. As they preached their religious message, the missionaries also spread American influence globally and blazed the way for U.S. economic expansion.

The Panama Canal: Hardball Diplomacy

Dreams of a canal across the ribbon of land joining North and South America dated back to the Spanish conquest. Yellow fever and mismanagement brought a French company's late-nineteenth-century attempt to build a canal to disaster and left a half-completed waterway. To recoup some of the $400 million loss, the company offered to sell its assets, including a concession from Colombia, which then controlled the isthmus, to the United States for $109 million.

America was in an expansionist mood. In 1902, after the French lowered their price to $40 million, Congress authorized President Theodore Roosevelt to accept the offer. The United States negotiated an agreement with the Colombian diplomat for a ninety-nine-year lease on the proposed canal. But when the Colombian Senate rejected the deal, seeking a better offer, Roosevelt privately denounced the Colombians as "greedy little anthropoids."

Roosevelt found a willing collaborator in Philippe Bunau-Varilla (fih-LEEP boo-NAW vah-REE-yuh), an official of the bankrupt French company. Dismayed that his company might lose its $40 million, Bunau-Varilla organized a "revolution" in Panama from a New York hotel room. While his wife stitched a flag, he wrote a declaration of independence and a constitution for the new nation. On November 3, 1903, the "revolution" erupted on schedule, with a U.S. warship anchored offshore. In short order, Bunau-Varilla gained American recognition of the newly hatched nation and signed a treaty guaranteeing the United States a ten-mile-wide strip of land across Panama "in perpetuity" in return for $10 million and an annual payment of $250,000. Roosevelt later summarized the episode: "I took the Canal Zone, and let Congress debate, and while the debate goes on, the canal does also."

Before completing the canal, the United States first had to conquer yellow fever. After Dr. Walter Reed of the Army Medical Corps recognized the mosquito as its carrier, the army carried out a prodigious drainage project that eradicated the disease-bearing pest. Construction began in 1906, and in August 1914 the first ship sailed through the **Panama Canal.** The ill feeling generated by Theodore Roosevelt's actions, combined with other instances of U.S. interventionism, would long shadow U.S.-Latin American relations.

Panama Canal Waterway between the Pacific and Atlantic Oceans, completed by the United States in 1914

Roosevelt and Taft Assert U.S. Power in Latin America and Asia

While the Panama Canal remains this era's best-known foreign-policy achievement, other U.S. actions underscored Washington's growing determination to assert U.S. power and protect U.S. business interests in Latin America (see Map 22.1) and Asia. In 1904, when several European

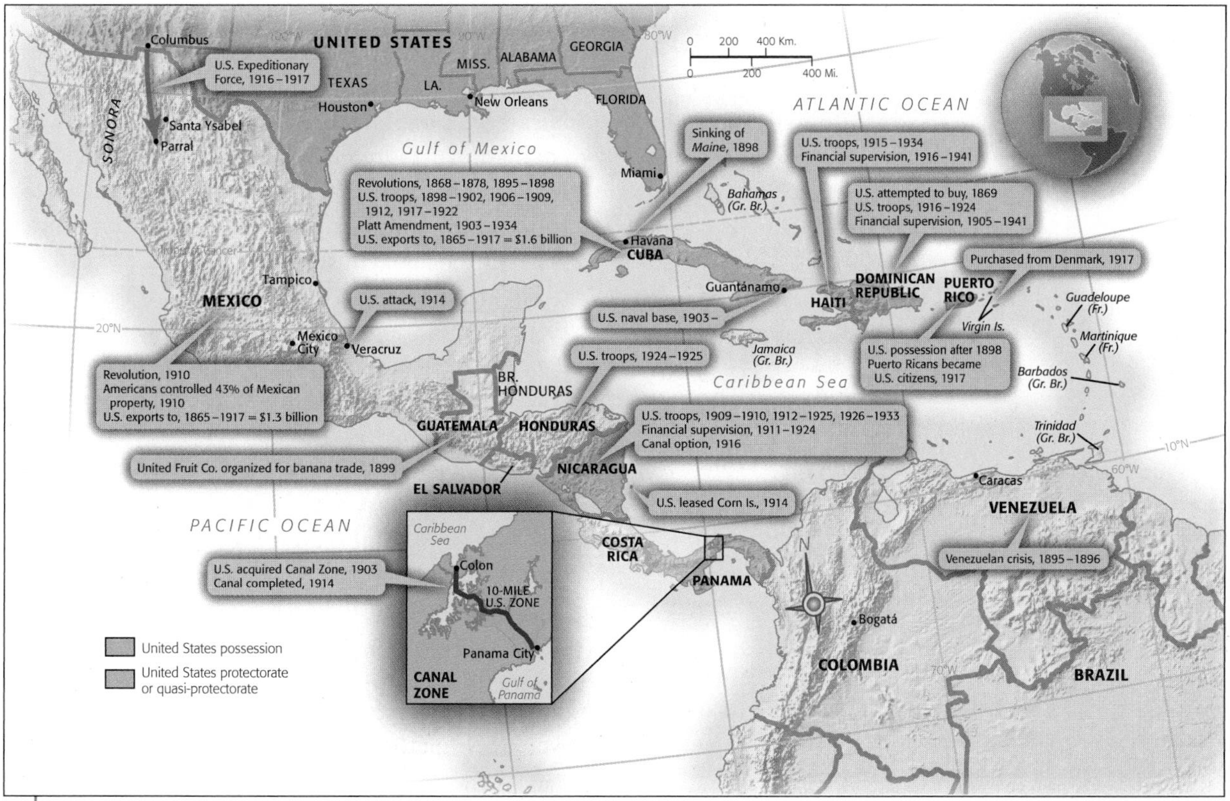

Map 22.1 U.S. Hegemony in the Caribbean and Latin America, 1900–1941

Through many interventions, territorial acquisitions, and robust economic expansion, the United States became the predominant power in Latin America in the early twentieth century. Acting on Theodore Roosevelt's assertion of a U.S. right to combat "wrongdoing" in Latin America and the Caribbean, the United States dispatched troops to the region, where they met nationalist opposition.

Interactive Map

nations threatened to invade the Dominican Republic, a small Caribbean island nation that had defaulted on its debts, Roosevelt reacted swiftly. If any nation intervened, he believed, it should be the United States. While denying territorial ambitions in the region, in December 1904 Roosevelt declared that "chronic wrongdoing" by any Latin American nation would justify U.S. intervention.

This pronouncement has been called "the Roosevelt Corollary" to the 1823 Monroe Doctrine, which had warned European powers against meddling in Latin America. Now Roosevelt asserted that "wrongdoing" (a word he left undefined) gave the United States the right to step in. Suiting actions to words, the Roosevelt administration took over the Dominican Republic's customs service for two years and managed its foreign debt. Roosevelt once summed up his foreign-policy approach by quoting what he said was an African proverb, "Speak softly and carry a big stick."

The foreign policy of the Taft administration (1909–1913) focused on advancing American commercial interests, a policy some called "dollar diplomacy." In 1911, a U.S.-supported revolution in Nicaragua brought to power Adolfo Díaz,

Woodrow Wilson, Schoolteacher

This 1914 cartoon captures the patronizing self-righteousness of Wilson's approach to Latin America that planted the seeds of long-term resentments.

an officer of an American-owned Nicaraguan mining property. U.S. bankers loaned the Díaz government $1.5 million in exchange for control of the Nicaraguan national bank, the customs service, and the national railroad. When a revolt against Díaz broke out in 1912, Taft sent in the marines to protect the bankers' investment. Except for one brief interval, they remained until 1933.

In Asia, too, both Roosevelt and Taft sought to project U.S. power and advance the interests of American business. In 1900, Russia exploited the chaos unleashed by the Boxer uprising by sending troops to occupy Manchuria (man-CHOO-ree-uh), China's northeastern province. In February 1904, a surprise Japanese attack destroyed Russian ships anchored at Port Arthur, Manchuria. Japan completely dominated in the Russo-Japanese War that followed. For the first time, an Asian power had checked European imperialist expansion.

Roosevelt, while pleased to see Russian expansionism challenged, believed that a Japanese victory would disrupt the Asian balance of power and threaten America's position in the Philippines. Accordingly, he invited Japan and Russia to a peace conference at Portsmouth, New Hampshire. In September 1905, the two rivals signed a peace treaty. Russia recognized Japan's rule in Korea and made other territorial concessions. After this outcome, curbing Japanese expansionism became America's major objective in Asia. For his role in ending the war, Roosevelt received the Nobel Peace Prize.

In 1906, U.S.-Japanese relations soured when the San Francisco school board, reflecting West Coast hostility to Asian immigrants, assigned all Asian children to segregated schools. Japan angrily protested this insult, and Roosevelt persuaded the school board to reverse this discriminatory policy. In return, in 1908 the administration negotiated a "gentlemen's agreement" with Japan by which Tokyo pledged to halt Japanese emigration to America. Racist attitudes and discriminatory laws against Japanese in California continued to poison U.S.-Japanese relations, however.

While Californians worried about the "yellow peril," Japanese journalists watching America's growing military strength wrote of a "white peril." In 1907, Roosevelt ordered sixteen gleaming white battleships on a "training operation" to Japan. Although officially treated as friendly, this "Great White Fleet" underscored America's growing naval might.

Under President Taft, U.S. foreign policy in Asia continued to focus on promoting U.S. commercial interests. A plan for a U.S.-financed railroad in Manchuria did not work out, however. Not only did U.S. bankers find the project too risky, but Russia and Japan signed a treaty carving up Manchuria for commercial purposes, freezing out the Americans.

Wilson and Latin America

Taking office in 1913, Woodrow Wilson criticized his Republican predecessors' expansionist policies. The United States, he pledged, would "never again seek one additional foot of territory by conquest." But he, too, intervened in Latin America. In 1915, after bloody upheavals in Haiti (HAY-tee) and the Dominican Republic, Wilson ordered in the marines. A Haitian (HAY-shun) constitution favorable to U.S. commercial interests was overwhelmingly ratified in a 1918 vote supervised by the marines. The marines occupied the Dominican Republic until 1924 and remained in Haiti until 1934.

Events in Mexico triggered Wilson's most serious crisis in Latin America. Mexico had won independence from Spain in 1820, but the nation remained divided between a landowning elite and an impoverished peasantry. In 1911, rebels led by the democratic reformer Francisco Madero ended the thirty-year rule of President Porfirio Díaz, a defender of the wealthy elite. Early in 1913, just as Wilson took office, Mexican troops loyal to General Victoriano Huerta, a full-blooded Indian, overthrew and murdered Madero.

Amid the chaos, Wilson tried to promote good government, protect U.S. investments, and safeguard U.S. citizens living in Mexico or along its border. Reversing the long-standing U.S. policy of recognizing all governments, Wilson refused to recognize Huerta's regime, which he called "a government of butchers." Wilson authorized arms sales to Venustiano Carranza (kuh-RON-zuh), a Huerta foe, and blockaded Vera Cruz (VAIR-uh krooz) to prevent weapons from reaching Huerta. Announced Wilson, "I am going to teach the South American republics to elect good men." In April 1914, seven thousand U.S. troops occupied Veracruz and engaged Huerta's forces. Sixty-five Americans and approximately five hundred Mexicans were killed or wounded. Bowing to U.S. might, Huerta abdicated, Carranza took power, and the U.S. troops withdrew.

But turmoil continued. In January 1916, a bandit chieftain in northern Mexico, Pancho Villa (PAN-choh VEE-yuh), murdered sixteen U.S. mining engineers. Villa's gang then burned the town of Columbus, New Mexico, and killed nineteen inhabitants. Sharing the public's outrage, Wilson sent into Mexico a punitive expedition that eventually totaled 12,000 U.S. troops. When Villa brazenly staged another raid into Texas, Wilson ordered 150,000 National Guardsmen to the border—a massive response that stirred anti-American feelings among Mexico's poor, for whom Villa was a folk hero. Villa ended his raids in 1920 when the Mexican government gave him a large land grant, but he was soon assassinated.

These involvements in Asia and Latin America illuminate the U.S. foreign-policy goal: to achieve a global order that would welcome both American political values and American business. They also illustrate the underlying worldview of the old-stock, upper-class men who directed U.S. foreign policy. Convinced of their ethnic, gender, and social superiority, they confidently promoted America's global interests while viewing with patronizing condescension the "backward" societies they sought to manipulate. The vision of a world order based on U.S. ideals would soon find expression in Woodrow Wilson's response to the crisis in Europe.

CHECKING IN

- The Open Door notes, asserting that trade with China must be open to all nations, represented an important part of the American quest for "informal empire."
- The Panama Canal was both a major accomplishment and a symbol of American imperialism.
- The Roosevelt Corollary, announcing that the United States would act as an international policeman in Latin America, was meant to guarantee American preeminence in the Caribbean.
- Wilson intervened in the Mexican Revolution to try to enforce American ideals.
- The Wilsonian view of a world based on American principles shaped American policy during and after World War I.

WAR IN EUROPE, 1914–1917

Considering both immediate and long-term factors, why did the United States go to war in 1917?

When war engulfed Europe in 1914, most Americans wished only to remain aloof. For nearly three years, the United States officially stayed neutral. But by April 1917 cultural ties to Britain and France, economic considerations, visions of a world remade in America's image, and German violations of Wilson's definition of neutral rights all combined to suck America into the maelstrom.

The Coming of War

Although Europe was at peace through much of the nineteenth century, a series of ominous developments raised warning flags. Germany had only achieved national unification in 1871. With many Germans convinced that Germany had lagged in the race for empire, Berlin's goal became modernization, expansion, and military power. Germany, Austria-Hungary, and Italy signed a mutual-defense treaty in 1882. In 1904 and 1907, Great Britain signed treaties with France and Russia. Meanwhile, the slow-motion collapse of the once-powerful Ottoman empire, centered in Turkey, left in its wake such newly independent nations as Romania, Bulgaria, and Serbia.

Serbian patriots dreamed of expanding their boundaries to include Serbs living in neighboring Bosnia-Herzegovina. Serbia's ally Russia supported these ambitions. The Austro-Hungarian empire, based in Vienna, also dreamed of expansion as Ottoman power faded. In 1908, Austria-Hungary annexed (took over) Bosnia-Herzegovina, alarming Russia and Serbia.

In this volatile atmosphere, Archduke Franz Ferdinand of Austria visited Bosnia in June 1914. As Ferdinand and his wife rode in an open car through Bosnia's capital, Sarajevo, a young Bosnian Serb gunned them down. In response, Austria declared war on Serbia. Russia, aligned with Serbia by a secret treaty, mobilized for war. Germany declared war on Russia and France. Great Britain, linked by treaty to the latter two powers, then declared war on Germany. An assassin's bullets had plunged Europe into war.

Thus began what contemporaries called the Great War, now known as World War I. On one side were Great Britain, Russia, and France, called the Allies. On the other side were the Central Powers: Germany and Austria-Hungary. (Italy, despite its alliance with the Central Powers, joined the Allies in 1915.)

The Perils of Neutrality

President Wilson urged Americans to remain neutral "in thought as well as in action." Most Americans fervently agreed. A popular song summed up the mood: "I Didn't Raise My Boy to Be a Soldier."

Neutrality proved difficult, however. Not only economic ties but also a common language, ancestry, and culture linked many Americans to Britain by strong emotional bonds. Many German-Americans, by contrast, sympathized with Germany, as did some Scandinavian immigrants. Irish-Americans speculated that a German victory might free Ireland from British rule. But most Americans saw staying out of the conflict as the chief goal.

Yet in 1917, America went to war. What caused this turnabout? Fundamentally, Wilson's vision of a peaceful, democratic, and capitalist world order conflicted with his neutrality. Such an international system would be impossible, he believed, if Germany won the war. To shape the peace, America must fight the war.

These underlying ideas influenced Wilson's handling of the war's most troubling immediate challenge: neutral nations' rights. When the war began, Britain intercepted U.S. merchant ships bound for Germany, insisting that their cargo might aid Germany's war effort. Wilson protested, especially when Britain, exploiting its naval advantage, declared the North Sea a war zone and planted it with explosive mines.

But Germany, not Britain, ultimately pushed the United States into war. If Britannia ruled the waves, Germany controlled the ocean depths with its torpedo-equipped submarines, or U-boats. In February 1915, Berlin proclaimed the waters around Great Britain a war zone and warned off all ships. Wilson responded: Germany would be held to "strict accountability" for any loss of U.S. ships or lives.

On May 1, 1915, in a small ad in U.S. newspapers, the German embassy cautioned Americans against travel on British or French vessels. Six days later, a U-boat

The Sinking of the Cunard Liner *Lusitania,* May 7, 1915, off the Irish Coast

The destruction of the *Lusitania* by a German U-boat, portrayed here in an illustration from a British newspaper, took nearly 1,200 lives including those of 128 Americans. This event outraged U.S. public opinion and led to the buildup in military preparedness. But as President Wilson pursued diplomatic exchanges with Germany, nearly two more years would pass before the United States entered the war.

sank the British liner *Lusitania* off Ireland, killing 1,198 passengers, including 128 Americans. (The *Lusitania,* historians later discovered, was secretly carrying munitions destined for Great Britain.) In three stern notes to Germany, Wilson demanded that Berlin stop unrestricted submarine warfare and pay reparations.

The *Lusitania* disaster exposed deep divisions in U.S. public opinion. Many Americans were ready for war. Theodore Roosevelt condemned Wilson—who had counseled patience after the attack—for "abject cowardice and weakness." The National Security League, a lobby of bankers and industrialists, promoted stepped-up U.S. arms production and organized "preparedness" parades in major cities. By late 1915, Wilson himself called for a military buildup. Lurid British propaganda (much of it false or exaggerated) screamed of atrocities committed by "the Huns" (a derogatory term for Germans).

Others, however, deplored the drift toward war. Some progressives warned that war fever was eroding support for reforms. Jane Addams, for example, lamented that the international movements to reduce infant mortality and improve care for the aged had been "scattered to the winds by the war." Divisions surfaced even within the Wilson administration. Secretary of State William Jennings Bryan, believing Wilson's *Lusitania* notes too hostile, resigned in June 1915. Early in 1916, Congress considered a bill to ban travel on belligerent ships, but President Wilson successfully opposed it, insisting that the principle of neutral rights must be upheld.

For a time, Wilson's conciliatory approach seemed to work. Germany ordered U-boats to spare passenger ships, and offered compensation for the Americans lost in the *Lusitania* sinking. In March 1916, however, a German submarine sank a French passenger ship, the *Sussex,* in the English Channel, injuring several Americans. Wilson threatened to break diplomatic relations, which was considered a step toward war. In response, Berlin pledged not to attack merchant vessels without warning, and the crisis eased.

Meanwhile, U.S. banks' support for the Allies eroded the principle of neutrality. In August 1915, Wilson's advisers urged him to allow Allies to purchase American munitions and farm products and to authorize substantial loans to Great Britain. Only these measures, they argued, could prevent serious financial problems in the United States. Swayed by such arguments and personally sympathetic to the Allies, Wilson permitted bank loans of $500 million to the British and French governments. By April 1917, U.S. banks had lent $2.3 billion to the Allies, in contrast to $27 million to Germany.

The land war, meanwhile, settled into a grim stalemate. A September 1914 German drive into France bogged down and the two sides dug in, constructing trenches across France from the English Channel to the Swiss border. For more than three years, this line scarcely changed. Occasional offensives devastated the countryside and took a horrendous cost in human life. Trench warfare was a nightmare of mud, lice, rats, artillery bursts, poison gas, and random death.

The war dominated the 1916 presidential election, which pitted Wilson against Republican Charles Evans Hughes, a former New York governor. Somewhat confusingly, Hughes criticized Wilson's lack of aggressiveness while rebuking him for policies that risked war. While Hughes did well among Irish-Americans and German-Americans, Wilson eked out a narrow victory, aided by women voters in western states that had adopted woman suffrage. The Democrats' winning campaign slogan, "He kept us out of war," revealed the strength of popular peace sentiment as late as November 1916.

The United States Enters the War

In January 1917, Germany resumed unrestricted submarine warfare. Germany's military leaders believed that even if the United States declared war as a result, full-scale U-boat warfare could bring victory before American troops reached the front.

Events now rushed forward. Wilson broke diplomatic relations on February 3. During February and March, U-boats sank five American ships. The British then intercepted a coded telegram from Arthur Zimmermann, the German foreign secretary, to Germany's ambassador to Mexico, promising that if Mexico declared war on the United States, Germany would help restore Mexico's "lost territories" of Texas, Arizona, and New Mexico. The "Zimmermann telegram" further inflamed the war spirit in America.

Events in distant Russia also helped create favorable conditions for America's entry into the war. In March 1917, liberal reformers and communist revolutionaries joined in an uprising that overthrew the repressive government of Tsar Nicholas II. A provisional government under the liberal Alexander Kerensky briefly seemed to promise a democratic Russia, making it easier for President Wilson to portray the war as a battle for democracy.

On April 2, Wilson appeared before a joint session of Congress and called for a declaration of war. Applause rang out as Wilson described his vision of America's role in creating a postwar international order to make the world "safe for democracy." After a short but bitter debate, the Senate voted 82 to 6 for war. The House agreed, 373 to 50. Three key factors—German attacks on American shipping, U.S. economic investment in the Allied cause, and American cultural links to the Allies, especially Britain—had propelled the United States into the war.

Checking In

- When World War I erupted, Wilson asked Americans to remain neutral in both thought and action.
- The question of neutral rights on the high seas was a point of dispute with both Great Britain and Germany.
- Americans loaned billions to the Allies, but only a few million to the Central Powers.
- Wilson was reelected in 1916 on the slogan "He kept us out of war."
- Renewed unrestricted submarine warfare and the Zimmermann telegram, suggesting a German-Mexican alliance, gave the United States the final push into World War I.

Mobilizing at Home, Fighting in France, 1917–1918

How did Washington mobilize the nation for war, and what role did U.S. troops play in the war?

Compared to its effects on Europe, the war only grazed the United States. Russia suffered heavily. France, Great Britain, and Germany fought for more than four years and their armed forces suffered casualties of 70 percent or more; the U.S. casualty rate was 8 percent. The fighting left parts of France and Belgium brutally scarred, whereas North America was physically untouched. Nevertheless, the war profoundly affected America.

Raising, Training, and Testing an Army

As Americans entered the war in April 1917, they found their military woefully unprepared. The regular army consisted of 120,000 men, only a few of whom had combat experience, and an aging officer corps. Ammunition reserves were paltry. The War Department was a jungle of jealous bureaucrats, one of whom hoarded thousands of typewriters as the war approached.

Selective Service Act Draft act to raise an army during World War I

Raising an army and imposing order on the War Department posed a daunting challenge. Wilson's secretary of war, Newton D. Baker, skillfully implemented the **Selective Service Act,** passed in May 1917. Baker cleverly made the first draft registration day a "festival and patriotic occasion." By war's end, more than 24 million men had registered, of whom nearly 3 million were drafted.

American Expeditionary Force (AEF) The three million American men drafted into a force to fight in Europe during World War I

The army's approach to military training echoed the Progressive Era's moral-control campaigns. The War Department closely monitored recruits' off-duty behavior. The Commission on Training Camp Activities presented films, lectures, and posters on the dangers of alcohol and prostitution. Beginning in December 1917, recruits also underwent intelligence testing. Psychologists eager to demonstrate the usefulness of their new field claimed that measuring recruits' "intelligence quotient" (IQ) could help win the war by identifying potential officers and those best suited to handle more specialized assignments. In fact, the tests mostly revealed that recruits lacked formal education and cultural sophistication, while reinforcing racial and ethnic stereotypes.

Library of Congress

A Recruitment Poster Targeting African-Americans

In this poster, Abraham Lincoln looks down approvingly as black soldiers battle the German foe. In reality, most black troops were restricted to noncombat roles.

Some twelve thousand Native Americans served in the **American Expeditionary Force (AEF).** While some reformers eager to preserve Indian culture argued for all-Indian units, military officials integrated Native Americans into the general army. Some observers predicted that the wartime experience would hasten the assimilation of Indians into mainstream American life. In addition, some 16,500 women served directly in the AEF as nurses, telephone operators, canteen workers, and secretaries.

Some blacks resisted the draft, especially in the South, but most followed W. E. B. Du Bois's advice urging African-Americans to "close ranks" and support the war. More than 260,000 blacks volunteered or were drafted, and some fifty thousand went to France. However, racism pervaded the military. The navy assigned blacks only to menial positions, and the marines excluded them altogether.

Black troops in some camps endured abuse. One racist senator from Mississippi warned that the sight of "arrogant, strutting" black soldiers would trigger race riots. Tensions reached the breaking point in Houston in August 1917, when some black soldiers, endlessly goaded by local whites, seized weapons from the armory and killed seventeen whites. After court-martial trials, nineteen black soldiers were hanged and sixty-one sentenced to life imprisonment.

Organizing the Economy for War

World War I helped shape modern America. The war advanced such key later developments as an expanded government role in the economy; the growth of new professional and managerial elites; and the spread of mass production, corporate consolidation, and product standardization.

The war led to unprecedented government economic oversight and corporate regulation, long advocated by Populists and progressives. The **War Industries Board (WIB)** was established in 1917 to coordinate military purchasing and ensure production efficiency. President Wilson reorganized the WIB in March 1918 and put the Wall Street financier Bernard Baruch (bah-ROOK) in charge. Under Baruch, the WIB allocated raw materials, established production priorities, and induced competing companies to standardize and coordinate their products and processes to save scarce commodities. Meanwhile, the Fuel Administration controlled coal output, regulated fuel prices and consumption, and in March 1918 introduced daylight savings time as a wartime conservation measure.

War Industries Board (WIB) Major federal agency created to regulate wartime production and allocation of materials

Baruch's counterpart on the agricultural front was Herbert Hoover, the head of the Food Administration. A mining engineer who had amassed a fortune in Asia, Hoover oversaw the production and allocation of wheat, meat, and sugar to ensure supplies for the army and the food-short Allies. Food Administration posters and ads urged Americans to conserve food. Housewives signed pledges to observe "Meatless Monday" and "Wheatless Wednesday."

In all, nearly five thousand government boards supervised home-front activities. These included the National War Labor Board, which resolved labor-management disputes that jeopardized production, and the Railroad Administration, headed by Treasury Secretary William McAdoo. When a railroad tie-up during the winter of 1917–1918 threatened the flow of supplies to Europe, the Railroad Administration stepped in and soon transformed the thousands of miles of track operated by competing companies into an efficient national system.

The war accelerated corporate consolidation and economic integration. In place of trustbusting, the government now encouraged cooperation among businesses. Overall, the war was good for business. Despite added taxes imposed by Congress, profits soared. After-tax profits in the copper industry, for example, jumped from 12 percent in 1913 to 24 percent in 1917.

The old laissez-faire suspicion of government, which was already eroded, now suffered further blows in 1917–1918. The wartime regulatory agencies disappeared quickly after the war, but their influence lingered. In the 1930s, when the nation faced a different kind of crisis, the government activism of World War I would be remembered.

The American Expeditionary Force in France

As the U.S. military mobilized for combat, Allied prospects looked bleak. German U-boats were battering Allied shipping. French troops mutinied in the spring of 1917 after suffering ghastly casualties. A British offensive along

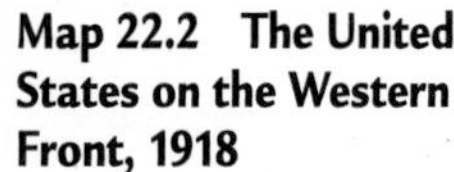

Map 22.2 The United States on the Western Front, 1918

American troops first saw action in the campaign to throw back Germany's spring 1918 offensive in the Somme and Aisne-Marne sectors. The next heavy American engagement came that autumn as part of the Allies' Meuse-Argonne offensive, which ended the war.

Interactive Map

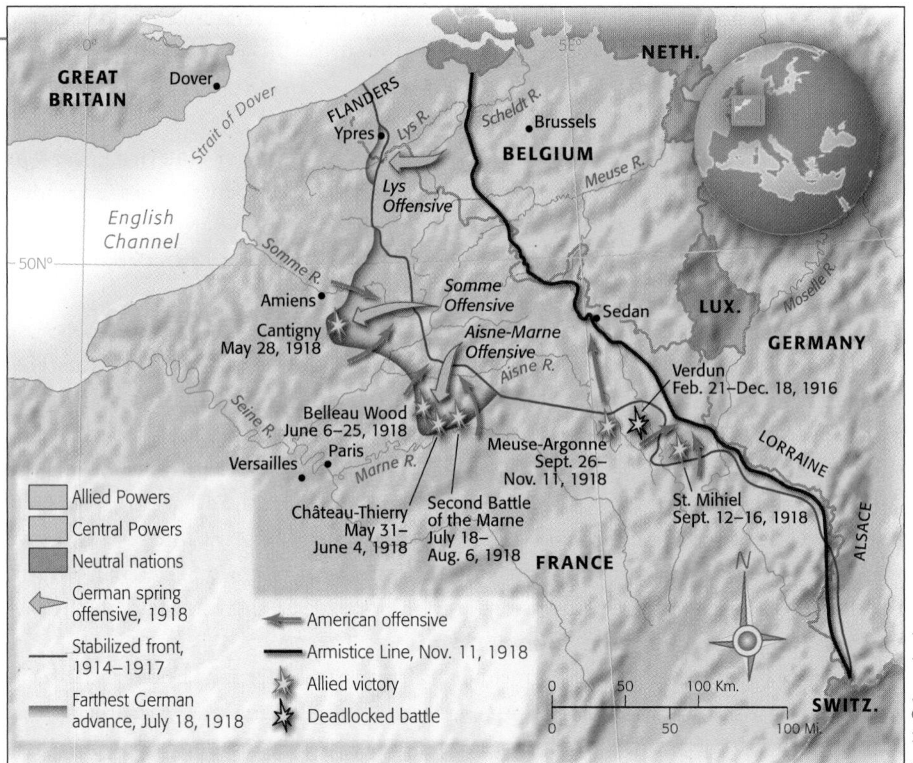

the French-Belgian border gained only four miles at a cost of many thousands killed and wounded.

Russia suffered serious setbacks, contributing to the revolutionary upheaval. The communist faction of the revolution, the Bolsheviks, gained strength when its top leaders, including Vladimir Lenin and Leon Trotsky, returned from exile abroad. On November 6, 1917, a Bolshevik coup overthrew Alexander Kerensky's provisional government and effectively removed Russia from the war. Early in 1918, the Bolsheviks signed an armistice with Germany, the Treaty of Brest-Litovsk, freeing thousands of German troops on the Russian front for fighting in France.

The first U.S. troops reached France in October 1917. Eventually about 2 million American soldiers served in France as members of the American Expeditionary Force (AEF) under General **John J. Pershing.** Most men of the AEF at first found the war a great adventure. Plucked from towns and farms, they sailed for Europe on crowded freighters; a lucky few traveled on captured German passenger liners.

John J. Pershing Commander of the American Expeditionary Force that fought in Europe

The African-Americans with the AEF in France worked mainly as mess-boys (mealtime aides), laborers, and stevedores (ship-cargo handlers). Although discriminatory, the latter assignments vitally aided the war effort. While most African-American troops served behind the front lines, regiments of the all-black 92nd and 93rd infantry divisions saw action under French command in the Second Battle of the Marne and the Meuse-Argonne campaign near the war's end. France awarded the Croix de Guerre, a military honor, to the entire 369th infantry regiment. Only in death was the AEF integrated, since graves in military cemeteries were not racially segregated.

In the air, a scant fifteen years after the Wright brothers' first flight, German and Allied planes dropped bombs, reported on troop movements, and engaged in deadly aerial dogfights. The U.S. Army's air corps was established early in 1918. America's output of planes lagged, however, despite pressure from Secretary of War Baker—a rare war-production failure.

American forces saw their first real combat in March 1918 when a German offensive threatened France's English Channel ports. The Allies created a unified command under French general Ferdinand Foch (fohsh), and American troops were thrown into the fighting around Amiens (AH-mee-ehn) and Armentières (are-men-TEE-air) that stemmed the German advance. The French and British wanted to continue the practice of absorbing the Americans into existing units. But for both military and political reasons (including assuring a strong U.S. voice at the peace table), Pershing and his superiors in Washington insisted that the AEF fight in "distinct and separate" units.

In May 1918, Germany launched the second phase of its spring offensive. By the end of the month, the Germans had broken through the Allied lines and had secured a nearly open road to Paris, only fifty miles away. At this critical moment, Americans spearheaded the forces that finally stopped the German advance at the town of Château-Thierry (shah-TOE tee-AIR-ee) and nearby Belleau (BELL-oh) Wood (see Map 22.2). Eighty-five thousand American troops helped to staunch the final German offensive of the war, a thrust at the ancient cathedral city of Rheims (reems). Germany's desperate attempt to take the offensive had failed. Now it was the Allies' turn.

Turning the Tide

On July 18, 1918, the Allies launched their counteroffensive, and the war's last great battle began on September 26 as 1.2 million Americans joined the struggle to drive the Germans from the Meuse River and the dense Argonne Forest north of Verdun. Poison gas hung in the air, and rats scurried through the mud, gorging on human remains. Americans now endured the filth, vermin, and dysentery familiar to veterans of the trenches. Some welcomed injuries as a ticket out of the battle zone. Others collapsed emotionally and were hospitalized for "shell shock."

The notion of war as a "great adventure" seemed remote indeed in the Meuse-Argonne campaign. Death came in many forms and without ceremony. Bodies, packs, rifles, photos, and letters from home sank indiscriminately into the all-consuming mud. Influenza killed thousands of AEF troops at the front and in training camps back home. Religious and ethical principles faded as men struggled to survive. "We are not men anymore, just savage beasts," wrote a young American. "Love of thy neighbor is forgotten," recalled another, with "all the falsities of a sheltered civilization." The war's brutality would shape the literature of the 1920s, as writers like Ernest Hemingway stripped away the illusions obscuring the reality of mass slaughter.

By early November, the AEF had fulfilled its assignment of cutting the Sedan-Mezières Railroad, a key German supply line. The successful Meuse-Argonne offensive ended the war. On November 11, 1918, Germany surrendered. By conservative estimates, World War I cost 10 million lives. Included in this toll were 112,000 American soldiers—forty-nine thousand in battle and sixty-three thousand from disease, mostly influenza.

Checking In

- The U.S. government instituted the draft to fill manpower needs.
- Government regulation of the economy, oversight of resources, and collaboration with business reached into American households and became accepted facts of life during the war.
- The Allied cause looked grim when America entered the war, but the 2 million American soldiers who served in France would play a key role in halting the last German offensive.
- American troops then spearheaded the Allied counteroffensive that led to the armistice in November 1918.

PROMOTING THE WAR AND SUPPRESSING DISSENT

How did Americans respond to propaganda and suppression of dissent?

In their own way, the war's domestic effects were as important as its battles. Spurred by government propaganda, patriotic fervor gripped America. The war fever, in turn, encouraged intellectual conformity and smothered dissent. Fueling the repressive spirit, government authorities and private vigilante groups hounded socialists, pacifists, and other dissidents, trampling citizens' constitutional rights.

Advertising the War

To President Wilson, selling the war at home was crucial to success in France. "It is not an army we must shape and train for war, it is a nation," he declared. The administration drew on the new professions of advertising and public relations to pursue this goal. Treasury Secretary McAdoo orchestrated a series of government bond drives, called Liberty Loans, that financed about two-thirds of the war's $35.5 billion cost.

Posters exhorted citizens to "Fight or Buy Bonds." Parades, rallies, and appearances by movie stars all aided the cause. Patriotic war songs reached a large public through phonograph recordings. Beneath the ballyhoo ran a note of coercion. Only "a friend of Germany," McAdoo warned, would refuse to buy bonds. The balance of the government's war costs came from taxes. Using the power granted it by the Sixteenth Amendment, Congress imposed wartime income taxes that reached 70 percent at the top level.

Committee on Public Information (CPI) Wartime propaganda agency established in April 1917; led by journalist George Creel

Journalist George Creel headed the key wartime propaganda agency, the **Committee on Public Information (CPI).** While claiming merely to combat rumors with facts, the Creel committee in reality publicized the government's version of events and discredited all who questioned that version. Posters, news releases, advertisements, and movies all trumpeted the government's sanitized version of events. The CPI poured foreign-language publications into the cities to ensure the loyalty of recent immigrants. Creel also organized the "four-minute men": a network of 75,000 speakers throughout the nation who gave patriotic talks to audiences of all kinds. Teachers, writers, religious leaders, and magazine editors overwhelmingly supported the war. These custodians of culture viewed the conflict as a struggle to defend threatened values and standards. Alan Seeger, a young Harvard graduate who volunteered to fight for France in 1916, wrote highly popular poems romanticizing the war. An artillery barrage became "the magnificent orchestra of war." The "sense of being the instrument of Destiny," wrote Seeger, represented the "supreme experience" of combat. He was killed in action in 1916.

Progressive reformers who had applauded Wilson's domestic program now cheered his war. Herbert Croly, Walter Lippmann, and other intellectuals associated with the *New Republic* magazine zealously backed the war. According to educator John Dewey, the war presented exciting "social possibilities." The government's wartime activism, he argued, could be channeled to reform purposes when peace returned. Internationally, America's participation in the war would transform an imperialistic struggle into a global democratic crusade.

Wartime Intolerance and Dissent

Responding to the propaganda, some Americans lashed out at all things German. Reports of sabotage by German agents, including mysterious fires at munitions plants in New Jersey and Pennsylvania, fanned the flames of fear. Libraries banished German books, and towns with German names changed them. An Iowa politician charged that "90 percent of all the men and women who teach the German language are traitors." Some restaurant menus replaced hamburgers with "liberty sandwiches." The Boston Symphony Orchestra dismissed its German-born conductor. A popular evangelist, Billy Sunday, proclaimed, "If you turn hell upside down you will find 'Made in Germany' stamped on the bottom."

The zealots also targeted American citizens suspected of pro-German or antiwar sentiments. Some were forced to kiss the flag or recite the Pledge of Allegiance. A Cincinnati mob horsewhipped a pacifist minister. Theodore Roosevelt branded antiwar Senator Robert La Follette "an unhung traitor." Columbia University fired two antiwar professors. In Collinsville, Illinois, in April 1918, a mob lynched a German-American coal miner, Robert Prager. When a jury freed the ringleaders, a jury member shouted, "Nobody can say we aren't loyal now."

Despite the persecution, many Americans persisted in opposing the war. Some were immigrants with ancestral ties to Germany. Others were religious pacifists, including Quakers, Mennonites, and Jehovah's Witnesses. Of some sixty-five thousand men who registered as conscientious objectors (COs), twenty-one thousand were drafted. The army assigned most to noncombat duty, such as cleaning latrines. Those who rejected this alternative were sent to military prisons.

Socialist leaders such as Eugene Debs denounced the war as a capitalist struggle for markets, with the soldiers as cannon fodder. The U.S. declaration of war, they insisted, mainly reflected Wall Street's desire to protect its loans to Great Britain and France. But other socialists supported the war, dividing the party. The war split the women's movement as well. While some leaders joined Jane Addams in opposition, others endorsed the war while keeping their own goals in view.

Draft resistance extended beyond the ranks of conscientious objectors. An estimated 2.4 to 3.6 million young men failed to register for the draft, and of those that did,

Milwaukee Socialist Leader Victor Berger Opposes War Profiteers and the Suppression of Free Speech

Elected to Congress in 1918, Berger was denied a seat because of his conviction under the wartime Espionage Act. The Supreme Court later reversed the conviction, and Berger served in Congress from 1923 to 1929.

about 12 percent did not appear when drafted or deserted from training camp. The rural South saw high levels of draft resistance, especially because the urban elites who ran draft boards were more likely to defer young men of their own class than poor farmers, white or black, fueling class resentment.

African-Americans had added reasons to oppose the draft. Of southern blacks who registered, one-third were drafted, compared to one-fourth of whites. White draft boards argued that low-income black families could more easily spare a male breadwinner. But the dynamics of race worked in complex ways: Some southern whites, fearful of arming black men even for military service, favored drafting only whites.

One war critic, Randolph Bourne, a young journalist, rejected John Dewey's argument that reformers could direct the war to their own purposes. "If the war is too strong for you to prevent," he asked, "how is it going to be weak enough for you to . . . mould to your liberal purposes?" Many prowar intellectuals eventually agreed. By 1919, Dewey conceded that the war, far from promoting reform, had encouraged reaction and intolerance.

Suppressing Dissent by Law

Espionage Act Criminalized virtually any antiwar activity

Sedition Amendment Curtailed First Amendment rights in criticizing war or government

Wartime intolerance also surfaced in federal laws and official actions. The **Espionage Act** of June 1917 set fines and prison sentences for a variety of loosely defined antiwar activities. The **Sedition Amendment** to the Espionage Act (May 1918) imposed stiff penalties on anyone convicted of using "disloyal, profane, scurrilous, or abusive language" about the government, the Constitution, the flag, or the military.

Wilson's wartime attorney general, Thomas W. Gregory, used these laws to suppress dissent. Opponents of the war should expect no mercy "from an outraged people and an avenging government," he said. Under this sweeping legislation and similar state laws, authorities arrested some fifteen hundred pacifists, socialists, IWW leaders, and other war critics. One socialist, Rose Pastor Stokes, received a ten-year prison sentence (later commuted) for telling an audience, "I am for the people, and the government is for the profiteers." Eugene Debs spent three years in prison for a speech discussing the economic causes of the war.

Under the Espionage Act, Postmaster General Albert S. Burleson banned socialist periodicals, including *The Masses.* In January 1919, Congressman-elect Victor Berger was convicted for publishing antiwar articles in his socialist newspaper, the *Milwaukee Leader.* (The Supreme Court reversed Berger's conviction in 1921.) Upton Sinclair protested to President Wilson that no one of Burleson's "childish ignorance" should wield such power. Still, Wilson did little to restrain the Postmaster General's excesses. The 1917 Bolshevik takeover in Russia sharpened the attacks on domestic radicals.

In 1919, the U.S. Supreme Court upheld Espionage Act convictions of war critics. In *Schenck* v. *United States,* Justice Oliver Wendell Holmes, Jr., writing for a unanimous court, justified such repression in cases where a person's speech posed a "clear and present danger" to the nation. When the war ended, Wilson vetoed a bill repealing the Espionage Act, increasing the likelihood that the miasma of conformity and suspicion would linger into the postwar era.

CHECKING IN

- The Wilson administration drew successfully on advertising techniques to popularize the war and to sell bonds.
- George Creel headed the effective propaganda campaign of the Wilson administration.
- Wartime emotion led to intolerance; virtually all things German became taboo.
- Although most progressives supported the war, there were a few critics, such as Randolph Bourne.
- The Espionage Act and the Sedition Amendment suppressed free speech and led to extreme reactions, as hundreds went to prison.

Economic and Social Trends in Wartime America

What was the war's economic, political, and social impact on the American home front?

In many diverse ways, the war affected the lives of millions of Americans, including industrial workers, farmers, women, and blacks. Another of the war's byproducts, a deadly influenza pandemic, took a grievous toll. Although some Progressive Era reforms advanced, overall the war weakened the reform movement.

Boom Times in Industry and Agriculture

World War I benefited the U.S. economy. From 1914 to 1918, factory output grew by more than one-third. Even with many men in uniform, the civilian work force expanded by 1.3 million between 1916 and 1918. Prices rose, but so did wages. Even unskilled workers enjoyed wartime wage increases averaging nearly 20 percent. Samuel Gompers, head of the American Federation of Labor, urged workers not to strike during the war. With the economy booming, most workers observed the no-strike request.

The war's social impact took many forms. Job seekers pouring into industrial centers strained housing, education, and municipal services. The consumption of cigarettes more than tripled. Reflecting wartime prosperity, automobile production jumped from 460,000 in 1914 to 1.8 million in 1917. Farmers profited, too. With European farm production disrupted, U.S. agricultural prices more than doubled between 1913 and 1918, and farmers' real income rose significantly.

This agricultural boom proved a mixed blessing. Farmers who borrowed heavily to expand production faced a credit squeeze when farm prices fell after the war. In the 1920s and 1930s, hard-pressed farmers would look back to the war years as a golden age of prosperity.

Blacks Migrate Northward

The war accelerated the exodus of southern blacks. An estimated half-million African-Americans moved north during the war, and most settled in cities. Chicago's black population swelled from 44,000 in 1910 to 110,000 in 1920 and Cleveland's expanded from 8,000 to 34,000.

With European immigration disrupted by the war, booming industries hired more black workers. Labor agents along with African-American newspapers like the *Chicago Defender* spread the word. One southern black, newly settled near Chicago, wrote home, "Nothing here but money, and it is not hard to get." Impoverished southern blacks welcomed the prospect of earning three dollars a day or more in a region where racism seemed less intense. By 1920, 1.5 million African-Americans were working in northern industry.

This vast population movement had widespread social ramifications. New city churches and storefront missions met the spiritual needs of deeply religious migrants from the South. The National Association for the Advancement of Colored

People (NAACP) grew from nine thousand members before the war to nearly one hundred thousand by the early 1920s. Heightened race consciousness and activism of the war years helped create the groundwork for the civil-rights movement that lay ahead. The concentration of blacks in New York City also prepared the way for the cultural flowering known as the Harlem Renaissance (see Chapter 23).

Still, African-American newcomers in northern cities faced severe challenges. White workers resented the labor competition, and white homeowners lashed out as jammed black neighborhoods spilled over into surrounding areas. Tensions sometimes sparked deadly riots. An outbreak on July 2, 1917, in East St. Louis, Illinois, led to the deaths of thirty-nine blacks. A few weeks later, an NAACP protest in New York City included one banner that echoed Wilson's phrase justifying U.S. involvement in the war: "Mr. President, Why Not Make AMERICA Safe for Democracy?"

Women in Wartime

The war affected women profoundly. Feminist leaders like Carrie Chapman Catt hoped that the war would lead to full equality and greater opportunity for women. For a time, these goals seemed attainable. In addition to the women in the AEF and in wartime volunteer agencies, about 1 million women worked in industry. Thousands more held other jobs, from streetcar conductors to bricklayers.

As the woman-suffrage movement gained momentum, a key victory came in November 1917 when New York voters amended the state constitution to permit women to vote. In Washington, Alice Paul and members of her National Woman's Party (see Chapter 21) picketed the White House. Several protesters were jailed and, when they went on a hunger strike, they were force-fed. Under growing pressure, Wilson declared that women's war service had earned them the right to vote. In 1919, the House and Senate overwhelmingly passed the **Nineteenth Amendment** granting women the right to vote. Ratification followed in 1920.

Nineteenth Amendment The amendment granting women the right to vote; ratified in 1920

Beyond this victory, however, the war did little to better women's status permanently. Relatively few women actually entered the work force for the first time in 1917–1918; most simply moved to better-paying jobs. As for the women in the AEF, the War Department refused their requests for military rank and benefits. At the war's end, many women lost their jobs to returning veterans. In 1920, the percentage of U.S. women in the paid labor force was actually slightly lower than it had been in 1910.

Public Health Crisis: The 1918 Influenza Pandemic

Amid battlefield casualties and home-front social changes, the nation in 1918 coped with a global outbreak of influenza, a highly contagious viral infection. The **influenza pandemic** killed an estimated 50 to 100 million people worldwide.

influenza pandemic Outbreak of illness in 1918 on the heels of the World War I devastation, in which more than a half million Americans died of influenza

Originating in Africa, the virus spread from battlefields in France to U.S. military camps, striking Fort Riley, Kansas, in March 1918 and quickly advancing to other bases and the urban population. The flu hit the cities hard. After a September Liberty Loan rally in Philadelphia, doctors reported 635 new influenza cases. Many cities forbade public gatherings. In the worst month, October, influenza killed 195,000 Americans. The total U.S. death toll reached about 550,000, over six times the number of AEF battle deaths in France.

Despite the development of a flu vaccine in the 1940s, flu pandemics remained a threat. In 2004, using tissue preserved from two U.S. soldiers who had died of influenza in 1918, scientists successfully synthesized the 1918 virus for research purposes.

The War and Progressivism

The war had mixed effects on Progressive Era reform movements. It strengthened the coercive, moral-control aspect of progressivism, including the drive for the prohibition of alcohol. When the **Eighteenth Amendment** establishing national prohibition passed Congress in December 1917, it was widely seen as a war measure. Ratified in 1919, it went into effect on January 1, 1920.

Eighteenth Amendment
Established national prohibition to encourage and regulate morality during wartime

Similarly, the war strengthened the Progressive Era antiprostitution campaign. The War Department closed red-light districts near military bases, including New Orleans's famed Storyville. (As Storyville's jazz musicians moved north, jazz reached a national audience.) Meanwhile, "protective bureaus" urged women to uphold standards of sexual morality. In Boston, female social workers hid in the Common after dark to apprehend young women dating soldiers from nearby bases.

Labor reforms advanced as well. The Railroad Administration and the **War Labor Board (WLB)** pressured factory owners to introduce the eight-hour workday and recognize unions' right to bargain with management. Under these favorable conditions, union membership rose from 2.7 million in 1916 to more than 5 million by 1920. In addition, the Bureau of War Risk Insurance (BWRI) provided direct aid to soldiers' families. By the war's end, over 2 million families were receiving regular BWRI checks.

War Labor Board (WLB)
Wartime agency that encouraged unionization and collective bargaining as a means of avoiding labor discord

Overall, however, the war weakened the progressive social-justice impulse. While the war brought increased regulation of the economy—a key progressive goal—business interests often dominated the regulatory agencies, and they were quickly dismantled after the war. The government's repression of radicals and antiwar dissenters fractured the progressive coalition and ushered in a decade of reaction. The 1918 midterm election signaled the shift: The Democrats lost both houses of Congress to a deeply conservative Republican Party.

Nevertheless, taking a longer view, reform energies, after diminishing in the 1920s, would reemerge in the depression decade of the 1930s. And as Franklin D. Roosevelt's New Deal took shape (see Chapter 24), the memory of such World War I agencies as the War Labor Board, the United States Housing Corporation, and the Bureau of War Risk Insurance provided ideas and inspiration.

Checking In

- The war produced boom times for farmers and manufacturers but left farmers in a credit squeeze later.
- Black migration to northern cities accelerated, but racial tensions also traveled north.
- Women advanced in the work force in large numbers but were seen only as temporary replacements for men.
- The war bolstered some progressive goals: greater government regulation of the economy, woman suffrage, and labor laws.
- In spite of the progressive advances, the war undermined the social-justice movement, as conservatives gained ground amid the wartime repression.

JOYOUS ARMISTICE, BITTER AFTERMATH, 1918–1920

How did the League of Nations begin, and why did the Senate reject U.S. membership in the League?

The euphoria that greeted the November 1918 armistice proved short lived. Having defined America's war aims in lofty terms, Woodrow Wilson dominated the 1919 peace conference but failed in his most cherished objective—American membership in the League of Nations. Amid a sour climate of racism and intolerance, the voters in 1920 repudiated Wilsonian idealism and internationalism and elected a conservative Republican as president.

Wilson's Fourteen Points; the Armistice

President Wilson planned to put his personal stamp on the peace. American involvement, he believed, could transform a sordid squabble for power into something higher and finer—a crusade for a new, more democratic world order.

Addressing Congress in January 1918, Wilson summed up U.S. war aims in fourteen points. Eight of these promised the subject peoples of the Austro-Hungarian and Ottoman empires the right of self-determination. A ninth point insisted that imperial disputes should consider the interests of the colonized peoples. The remaining five points offered Wilson's larger postwar vision: a world of free navigation, free trade, reduced armaments, openly negotiated treaties, and "a general association of nations" to resolve conflicts peacefully. The **Fourteen Points** helped solidify American support for the war, especially among liberals. They seemed proof that America was fighting for noble motives, not selfish aims.

Fourteen Points Wilson's blueprint for a better world; emphasized self-determination

In early October 1918, facing defeat, Germany proposed an armistice based on Wilson's Fourteen Points. The British and French hesitated, but when Wilson threatened to negotiate a separate peace, they agreed. Meanwhile, in Berlin, Kaiser Wilhelm II had abdicated and a German republic had been proclaimed.

In the early morning of November 11, 1918, the Allied commander Marshal Foch and his German counterparts signed an armistice ending hostilities at 11:00 A.M. Rockets burst over the front that night, not in anger but in relief and celebration. Back home, cheering throngs filled the streets. "Everything for which America has fought has been accomplished," Wilson proclaimed.

The Versailles Peace Conference, 1919

Unwisely, Wilson decided to lead the U.S. delegation to the peace conference himself. The strain of long bargaining sessions would take its toll on his frail nerves. Wilson compounded his mistake by naming only one Republican to the delegation, an elderly diplomat with little influence in the party. Selecting more prominent Republicans might have spared Wilson future grief. The Democrats' loss of Congress in 1918 offered a further ill omen.

Wilson received a hero's welcome in Europe. Shouts of "Voodrow Veelson" rang out in Paris, in Britain children spread flowers in his path, and in Italy an exuberant official compared him to Jesus Christ.

The euphoria faded, however, when the peace conference began on January 18, 1919, at the palace of Versailles (verh-SIGH) near Paris. A Council of Four officiated, comprising the heads of state of the Allied powers: Italy, France, Great Britain, and the United States. (Japan participated as well.) The French and British came to the **Versailles Peace Conference** determined to punish Germany for their nations' wartime losses. Their vindictive agenda bore little relation to Wilson's liberal vision. As French statesman Georges Clemenceau remarked, "God gave us the Ten Commandments and we broke them. Mr. Wilson has given us the Fourteen Points. We shall see."

Versailles Peace Conference Negotiations for a peace settlement in France; the resulting settlement harshly punished Germany, laying the seeds of future conflict

Differences surfaced quickly. Italy demanded a port on the eastern Adriatic Sea. Japan insisted on keeping the trading rights it had seized from Germany in China. Clemenceau and Lloyd George were obsessed with revenge. At one point, an appalled Wilson threatened to leave the conference.

Reflecting this toxic climate, the peace treaty signed by a sullen German delegation in June 1919 was harshly punitive. Germany was disarmed, stripped of its colonies, forced to admit sole blame for the war, and saddled with reparation payments of $56 billion. France regained the provinces of Alsace and Lorraine and took control for fifteen years of Germany's coal-rich Saar Basin. The treaty demilitarized Germany's western border and transferred a slice of eastern Germany to Poland. Italy received land, and Japan got the economic concessions it wanted. All told, the treaty cost Germany one-tenth of its population and one-eighth of its territory. These harsh terms, bitterly resented in Germany, planted the seeds of World War II.

However, some treaty provisions did reflect Wilson's themes of democracy and self-determination. The treaty recognized the independence of Poland and the Baltic states of Estonia, Latvia, and Lithuania. Separate treaties provided for the independence of Czechoslovakia and Yugoslavia, new nations carved from the Austro-Hungarian and Ottoman empires. Palestine, a part of Turkey's collapsed Ottoman empire, went to Great Britain under a mandate arrangement. In 1917, the British issued the Balfour Declaration supporting a Jewish "national home" in the region while also acknowledging the rights of the non-Jewish Palestinians.

But the statesmen of Versailles ignored the aspirations of colonized peoples in Asia and Africa. Nor did the peacemakers come to terms with revolutionary Russia. In August 1918 a fourteen-nation Allied army, including some seven thousand U.S. troops, landed at various Russian ports, ostensibly to secure them from German attack and to protect Allied war equipment. In fact, the aim was to overthrow the new Bolshevik regime, whose communist ideology terrified European and American leaders. Wilson and the other Allied leaders agreed to support a Russian military leader waging a last-ditch struggle against the Bolsheviks. Not until 1933 would the United States recognize the Soviet Union.

The Fight over the League of Nations

League of Nations Wilson's plan for an international deliberative body, viewed as necessary to keep the peace; rejected by the U.S. Senate; the United States never joined

Wilson focused on his one shining achievement at Versailles—the creation of a new international organization, the **League of Nations.** The agreement to establish the League, written into the treaty, embodied Wilson's vision of a new world order of peace and justice. But Wilson's League faced major hurdles. A warning shot came in February 1919 when thirty-nine Republican senators signed a letter rejecting the League in its present form.

When Wilson sent the treaty to the Senate for ratification in July 1919, Senator Henry Cabot Lodge bottled it up in the Foreign Relations Committee. To rally popular opinion, Wilson left Washington in September for a national speaking tour. Covering more than nine thousand miles by train, Wilson defended the League before large and friendly audiences. People wept as he described his visits to American war cemeteries in France and sketched his vision of a new world order. But the trip exhausted Wilson, and on October 2 he suffered a stroke that for a time left him near death. He spent the rest of his term mostly in bed or in a wheelchair, a reclusive invalid, his mind clouded, his fragile emotions betraying him into vindictive actions and tearful outbursts. He broke with close advisers and dismissed Secretary of State Lansing, accusing him of disloyalty. In January 1920, his physician advised him to resign, but Wilson refused.

Wilson's first wife, Ellen, had died in 1914. His strong-willed second wife, Edith Galt, played a crucial role behind the scenes during this crisis. She hid Wilson's condition from the public and decided who could see him. Cabinet members, diplomats, and congressional leaders were barred from the White House. Because the Twenty-fifth Amendment, dealing with issues of presidential disability, was not adopted until 1967, the impasse continued.

The League drama unfolded against this grim backdrop. On September 10, 1919, the Foreign Relations Committee at last sent the treaty to the Senate, but with a series of amendments. The Senate split into three groups. First were Democrats who supported the League covenant without changes. Second were Republican "Irreconcilables," who opposed the League absolutely. They feared that League membership would dangerously restrict U.S. freedom of action and entangle America with foreign powers they viewed as corrupt. Finally, a group of Republican "Reservationists," led by Lodge, demanded amendments as a condition of their support.

Had Wilson accepted compromise, the Senate would probably have ratified the Versailles treaty. But Wilson's illness aggravated his tendency toward rigidity. Isolated in the White House, he instructed Senate Democrats to vote against the treaty, which now included Lodge's reservations. Although international-law specialists argued that these reservations would not significantly weaken U.S. participation in the League, Wilson stood firm.

Despite Wilson's speaking tour, the public did not rally behind the League. On November 19, 1919, pro-League Democrats obeying Wilson's instructions and anti-League Irreconcilables joined forces to defeat the version of the Versailles treaty that included Lodge's reservations. A second vote in March 1920 produced the same result. The United States would not join the forty-four nations who in January 1920 launched the League of Nations, the forerunner of the United Nations. What might have been Wilson's crowning achievement had turned to ashes.

Racism and Red Scare, 1919–1920

The war's strident patriotism left a bitter aftertaste. The years 1919–1920 brought new racial violence and anti-radical hysteria. Seventy-six blacks were lynched in 1919, the worst toll in fifteen years. The victims included ten veterans, several still in uniform.

The worst violence exploded in Chicago, where simmering racial tension erupted on a hot afternoon in July 1919. When a black youth swimming at a Lake Michigan beach drowned after whites pelted him with stones, black neighborhoods erupted in fury. A thirteen-day reign of terror followed as white and black marauders engaged in random attacks and arson. The outbreak left fifteen whites and twenty-three blacks dead, over five hundred injured, and more than a thousand families, mostly black, homeless.

Wartime antiradicalism crested in the Red Scare of 1919–1920. (Communists were called "reds" because of the red flag favored by revolutionary organizations.) A rash of strikes in 1919 deepened overwrought fears of a communist takeover in America. When the IWW and other unions called a general strike in Seattle, the panicky mayor called for federal troops to maintain order. Anxiety crackled again in April, when various public officials received packages containing bombs. One severely injured a senator's maid; another damaged the home of Attorney General A. Mitchell Palmer.

Antiradical paranoia also infected politics. In 1919, the House of Representatives refused to seat Milwaukee socialist Victor Berger, recently indicted under the Espionage Act. Milwaukee voters promptly reelected him, but the House stood firm. The New York legislature expelled several socialist members. The Justice Department set up an antiradical division under young J. Edgar Hoover, future head of the Federal Bureau of Investigation, who ordered the arrest of hundreds of suspected communists and radicals. In December 1919, the government deported 249 Russian-born aliens, including Emma Goldman, a prominent lecturer and birth-control advocate.

On January 2, 1920, in a Justice Department dragnet, federal marshals and local police raided the homes of suspected radicals and the headquarters of radical organizations in thirty-two cities. Without search warrants or arrest warrants, they arrested more than four thousand persons (some 550 were eventually deported) and seized a horde of papers. Boston police paraded arrested persons through the streets in handcuffs and chains and jammed them into unsanitary cells without formal charges or the opportunity to post bail.

Palmer claimed that a "blaze of revolution was sweeping over every American institution of law and order . . . licking at the altars of the churches, leaping into the belfry of the school bell, crawling into the sacred corners of American homes . . . burning up the foundations of society." But the hysteria subsided as Palmer's irrational predictions failed to materialize. When a bomb exploded in New York City's financial district in September 1920, killing thirty-eight people, most Americans saw the deed as the work of an isolated fanatic, not evidence of approaching revolution.

The Election of 1920

As the 1920 election approached, the invalid Wilson, lost in fantasy, considered seeking a third term, but was dissuaded. Few heeded his call to make the election a "solemn referendum" on the League. When the Democrats convened in San

Warren G. Harding Elected in 1920; the well-meaning but undistinguished successor to Woodrow Wilson

Francisco, the delegates nominated James M. Cox, the mildly progressive governor of Ohio. As Cox's running mate they chose the young assistant secretary of the navy, Franklin D. Roosevelt, who possessed a potent political name.

The confident Republicans, meeting in Chicago, nominated Senator **Warren G. Harding** of Ohio, an amiable politician of little distinction. For vice president, they chose Massachusetts governor Calvin Coolidge, who had won attention in 1919 with his denunciation of a Boston policemen's strike. Harding's vacuous campaign speeches reminded one critic of "an army of pompous phrases moving over the landscape in search of an idea." But his reassuring promise of a return to "normalcy" resonated with many voters, and he won by a landslide. Nearly a million citizens defiantly voted for socialist Eugene Debs, still imprisoned for his earlier antiwar speeches.

The election dashed all hope for American entry into the League of Nations. Senator Lodge expressed grim satisfaction that the voters had ripped "Wilsonism" up by the roots. The sense of high purpose Wilson had evoked in April 1917 seemed remote indeed as Americans turned to a new president and a new era.

CHECKING IN

- Wilson saw the war as an opportunity to spread democracy globally.
- The Fourteen Points speech summed up Wilsonian ideals; however, European leaders were skeptical.
- Wilson was hailed by the European public but could not control the Versailles negotiations.
- Although it established the League of Nations, the Versailles treaty solved none of the problems that had led to World War I; instead, it laid the groundwork for World War II.
- The Senate ultimately refused to ratify the treaty, and the United States did not join the League.
- The election of 1920 was interpreted as a rejection of the crusading spirit, both at home and overseas.

Chapter Summary

What goals underlay America's early-twentieth-century involvements in Asia and Latin America? (page 526)

The early twentieth century saw intensifying U.S. involvement abroad. This new globalism arose from a desire to promote U.S. business interests internationally while exporting American values to other societies. Americans demanded an "Open Door" to the China trade. Theodore Roosevelt seized Panama and built the canal, then declared the Caribbean to be under American custodianship. Wilson intervened in the Mexican Revolution in an attempt to shoehorn Mexican politics into an American mold.

Considering both immediate and long-term factors, why did the United States go to war in 1917? (page 532)

Wilson attempted to maintain neutrality, but issues of neutral rights on the high seas and loans to the Allies made neutrality almost impossible to attain. The deaths of Americans on British ships, such as the *Lusitania,* poisoned U.S. relations with Germany, and the Zimmermann telegram, suggesting a German-Mexican alliance, ultimately pushed the United States into the war.

KEY TERMS

Boxer Rebellion *(p. 527)*
Open Door notes *(p. 527)*
Panama Canal *(p. 528)*
Selective Service Act *(p. 536)*
American Expeditionary Force (AEF) *(p. 536)*
War Industries Board (WIB) *(p. 537)*
John J. Pershing *(p. 538)*
Committee on Public Information (CPI) *(p. 540)*
Espionage Act *(p. 542)*
Sedition Amendment *(p. 542)*
Nineteenth Amendment *(p. 544)*
influenza pandemic *(p. 544)*

How did Washington mobilize the nation for war, and what role did U.S. troops play in the war? (page 535)

During the war, the federal government influenced the lives of Americans as never before. The United States initiated the draft and called 3 million men into service. Government regulation of the economy and the nation's resources, exemplified by the War Industries Board and the Food Administration, greatly increased, as did government-business collaboration. Two million Americans fought in France, arriving just in time to stop Germany's 1918 summer offensive and lead the Allies' counteroffensive.

How did Americans respond to propaganda and suppression of dissent? (page 540)

The Wilson administration drew successfully on the techniques of modern advertising to "sell" the war and conducted massive campaigns to sell war bonds. The all-too-effective anti-German propaganda led to intolerance and distrust of almost everything German. Some Americans criticized the war, but to do so was risky. The Espionage Act and the Sedition Amendment intensified the climate of intolerance and were used to jail hundreds of dissenters.

What was the war's economic, political, and social impact on the American home front? (page 543)

World War I had a profound impact on the United States. Farm production and prosperity soared, as did industry, but farmers faced a credit squeeze after the war. Large numbers of blacks left the South to live in northern cities; racism followed them. Women advanced in the work force in large numbers, but most lost their positions to returning troops. Some progressive goals benefited from the war—government regulation, woman suffrage, and labor laws—but the war ultimately revived conservative attitudes, sparked fear of radicalism, and extinguished the progressive spirit for a generation.

How did the League of Nations begin, and why did the Senate reject U.S. membership in the League? (page 546)

Wilson's goals, expressed in the Fourteen Points, included spreading democracy and reforming the international political system. Essentially, he wanted to Americanize the world. However, he never achieved most of these goals. Negotiations at Versailles were dominated by European leaders' thirst for vengeance, and the Versailles treaty guaranteed future conflict. Even participation in the League of Nations, which Wilson saw as the centerpiece of his new world order, eluded his grasp because of Republican opposition and the president's own stubbornness.

KEY TERMS continued

Eighteenth Amendment *(p. 545)*
War Labor Board (WLB) *(p. 545)*
Fourteen Points *(p. 546)*
Versailles Peace Conference *(p. 547)*
League of Nations *(p. 547)*
Warren G. Harding *(p. 550)*

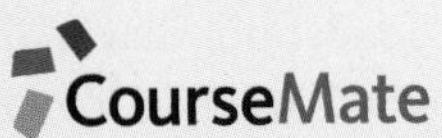

Go to the CourseMate website at **www.cengagebrain.com** for additional study tools and review materials—including audio and video clips—for this chapter.

CHAPTER 23

The 1920s: Coping with Change

1920–1929

A Pleasure-Mad Decade

CHAPTER PREVIEW

A New Economic Order
What economic innovations came in the 1920s, and what was their effect on different social groups?

Standpat Politics in a Decade of Change
What political and social ideas shaped the administrations of Presidents Harding and Coolidge?

Mass Society, Mass Culture
What developments underlay 1920s' mass culture, and how did they affect American life and leisure?

Cultural Ferment and Creativity
What social developments contributed to the cultural creativity of the 1920s?

A Society in Conflict
What events or movements revealed the major social and cultural conflicts of the 1920s?

Hoover at the Helm
How did Herbert Hoover's social and political thought differ from that of Harding and Coolidge?

Among the many immigrants arriving at Ellis Island in 1913 was the eighteen-year-old son of a veterinarian from a southern Italian village: Rodolfo Alfonso Raffaello Piero Filiberto Guglielmi di Valentina d'Antoguolla. After moving to Hollywood—and wisely shortening his name to "Rudolph Valentino"—he appeared in fifteen short films in 1919–1920. For the next six years, Valentino reigned as Hollywood's most popular male star. With his smoldering good looks and piercing dark eyes, he exuded sex appeal. In August 1926, at only thirty-one, Valentino died after surgery for a perforated ulcer. Lines of female fans stretched for blocks around the funeral home.

The popularity of the movies and their larger-than-life stars was only one novelty in a turbulent decade. These years also saw a torrent of new consumer goods, a flood of automobiles, and a babble of sound from millions of radios and phonographs. The decade also saw changing cultural values, creativity in the arts, and bitter social conflicts. With good reason, it soon acquired a nickname, "the Roaring Twenties." Many features of contemporary America may be traced to the 1920s. This chapter explores how different groups of Americans responded to technological, social, and cultural changes that could be both exciting and threatening.

A NEW ECONOMIC ORDER

What economic innovations came in the 1920s, and what was their effect on different social groups?

Fueled by new products and new ways of producing and selling goods, the economy surged in the 1920s. Not everyone benefited, however, and farmers suffered severe economic woes. Still, the overall picture appeared rosy. These economic changes influenced the decade's political, social, and cultural climate, as Americans confronted a changing society.

Booming Business, Ailing Agriculture

Recession struck in 1920 as Washington canceled wartime defense contracts and veterans reentered the job market. Recovery came by 1922, however, and for the next few years the nonfarm economy hummed. Unemployment fell to 3 percent, prices held steady, and the gross national product (GNP) grew by 43 percent from 1922 to 1929.

New consumer goods, including electrical products, fed the prosperity. By the mid-1920s, with more than 60 percent of the nation's homes electrified, new appliances, from refrigerators and vacuum cleaners to fans and razors, filled the stores. The manufacture of such appliances, as well as the construction of hydroelectric generating plants, provided a massive economic stimulus.

The automobile helped fuel the boom. Introduced before the war (see Chapter 21), the automobile came into its own in the 1920s. By 1930, some 60 percent of U.S. families owned cars. The Ford Motor Company led the market until mid-decade, when General Motors (GM) spurted ahead by touting greater comfort and a range of colors. GM's lowest-priced car, named for French automotive designer Louis Chevrolet, proved especially popular. In 1927, **Henry Ford** introduced the stylish Model A. By the end of the decade, the automobile industry accounted for about 9 percent of all wages in manufacturing and had stimulated such industries as rubber, gasoline and motor oil, advertising, and highway construction.

Henry Ford Innovator who perfected assembly-line manufacturing techniques and democratized the automobile

The business boom reverberated globally. To supply overseas markets, Ford, GM, and other corporations built production facilities abroad. U.S. meatpackers built plants in Argentina, Anaconda Copper acquired Chile's biggest copper mine, and

Getty Images

"Honey, Where Did You Park the Car?"
Hundreds of identical Fords jam Nantasket Beach near Boston on a Fourth of July in the early 1920s.

the mammoth United Fruit Company established plants across Latin America. But true economic globalization lay far ahead. Economic nationalism prevailed in the 1920s, as the industrialized nations, including the United States, erected high tariff barriers. The Fordney-McCumber Tariff (1922) and the Smoot-Hawley Tariff (1930) pushed U.S. tariffs to all-time highs, helping domestic manufacturers but stifling foreign trade.

While prosperity lifted overall wage rates, workers benefited unequally. The variation between North and South loomed largest. In 1928, unskilled laborers in New England earned an average of forty-seven cents an hour, in contrast to twenty-eight cents in the South. African-Americans, women workers, Mexican-Americans, and recent immigrants clustered at the bottom of the wage scale.

For farmers, wartime prosperity gave way to hard times. Grain prices plummeted when European agriculture revived and America's high tariffs depressed agricultural exports. As tractors and other new machinery boosted farm production, the resulting surpluses further weakened prices. Farmers who had bought land and equipment on credit during the war now felt the squeeze as payments came due.

New Modes of Producing, Managing, and Selling

Productivity increased dramatically in the 1920s. New assembly-line techniques boosted the per capita output of industrial workers by some 40 percent. At the Ford plants near Detroit, workers stood in place and performed repetitive tasks as chains conveyed the partly assembled vehicles past them.

Assembly-line labor did not foster the pride that came from farming or mastering a craft. To keep workers on task, managers discouraged initiative and forbade talking or laughter. As a result, job satisfaction diminished. Nevertheless, "Fordism" became a synonym worldwide for efficient assembly-line methods. In Russia, which purchased twenty-five thousand Ford tractors in the 1920s, people "ascribed a magical quality to the name of Ford," a visitor reported.

Business consolidation, spurred by the war, continued. By the late 1920s, over a thousand companies a year vanished through merger. Corporate giants dominated the major industries: Ford, GM, and Chrysler in automobiles; General Electric

Chronology

1920	Postwar recession; Warren G. Harding elected president; radio station KDKA, Pittsburgh, broadcasts election returns; Sinclair Lewis, *Main Street*
1921	Economic boom begins; agriculture remains depressed; Sheppard-Towner Act; *Shuffle Along,* all-black musical review
1921–1922	Washington Naval Arms Conference
1922	Supreme Court declares child-labor law unconstitutional; Fordney-McCumber Tariff restores high rates
1923	Harding dies; Calvin Coolidge becomes president; Teapot Dome scandals investigated; National Origins Act (immigration restriction)
1924	Calvin Coolidge elected president
1925	Scopes trial; Ku Klux Klan scandal in Indiana; Alain Locke, *The New Negro;* DuBose Heyward, *Porgy;* F. Scott Fitzgerald, *The Great Gatsby*
1926	National Broadcasting Company founded; Langston Hughes, *The Weary Blues*
1927	*The Jazz Singer,* first sound movie; Coolidge vetoes the McNary-Haugen farm bill; Henry Ford introduces the Model A; Ford apologizes for anti-Semitic publications; execution of Sacco and Vanzetti; Charles A. Lindbergh's transatlantic flight; Marcus Garvey deported; Mississippi River flood
1928	Herbert Hoover elected president
1929	Sheppard-Towner program terminated; Ernest Hemingway, *A Farewell to Arms;* Claude McKay, *Home to Harlem*

and Westinghouse in electricity; and so forth. Samuel Insull presided over a multi-billion-dollar empire of local and regional power companies and electric railroads. By 1930, one hundred corporations controlled nearly half the nation's businesses.

As U.S. capitalism matured, management structures evolved. Corporations set up separate divisions for product development, market research, economic forecasting, and employee relations. The shift to a consumer economy also affected wage policies. Rather than paying the lowest wages possible, business leaders realized that higher wages increased consumers' buying power. Henry Ford led the way in 1914 by paying his workers five dollars a day, well above the average for factory workers. Other companies soon followed suit.

New systems for distributing goods emerged. Automobiles, for example, reached consumers through dealer networks. By 1926, nearly ten thousand Ford dealerships dotted the nation. The A&P grocery chain boasted 17,500 stores by 1928. Chain stores accounted for about a quarter of all retail sales by 1930. Department stores grew more inviting, with remodeled interiors and attractive display windows. Air conditioning, a recent invention, made department stores (as well as movie theaters and restaurants) welcome havens on summer days.

Advertising and credit sales further stimulated the consumer economy. In 1929, corporations spent nearly $2 billion on radio, billboard, newspaper, and magazine ads, and advertising companies employed some six hundred thousand people. Advertisers used celebrity endorsements, promises of social success, and threats of social embarrassment. Beneath a picture of a sad young woman, a Listerine mouthwash ad suggested that young women failed to find husbands because of "halitosis," or bad breath. The remedy, of course, was Listerine, and lots of it.

Portraying a fantasy world of elegance, pleasure, and limitless abundance, ads aroused desires that the advertisers promised to fulfill. One critic in 1925 described the advertisers' "dream world":

> [S]hining teeth, schoolgirl complexions, cornless feet, perfect fitting [underwear], distinguished collars, wrinkleless pants, odorless breath, regularized bowels, . . . charging motors, punctureless tires, perfect busts, shimmering shanks, self-washing dishes, backs behind which the moon was meant to rise.

The advertisers defined America's essential meaning in terms of its abundance of material goods and consumers' "freedom of choice" in the marketplace. Buying more and more products, they claimed, fulfilled the "pursuit of happiness" promised in the Declaration of Independence, and was thus the duty of all good citizens. However, consumer freedom came at a price. Americans of the 1920s increasingly bought major purchases on credit. By 1929, credit purchases accounted for 75 percent of automobile sales.

Business values saturated 1920s' culture. "America stands for one idea: Business . . . ," proclaimed the *Independent* magazine in 1921; "Thru business, . . . the human race is finally to be redeemed." Presidents Harding and Coolidge praised business values and hobnobbed with corporate leaders. A 1923 opinion poll ranked Henry Ford as a leading presidential prospect. In *The Man Nobody Knows* (1925), ad man Bruce Barton described Jesus Christ as a managerial genius who "picked up twelve men from the bottom ranks of business and forged them into an organization that conquered the world."

business = Jesus, politics, life

Women in the New Economic Era

Although more women worked outside the home in the 1920s, their proportion of the total female population held steady at about 24 percent. Male workers dominated the auto plants and other assembly-line factories. Women who did enter the workplace faced wage discrimination. In 1929, for example, a male trimmer in the meatpacking industry received fifty-two cents an hour; a female trimmer, thirty-seven cents.

Most women workers held low-paying, unskilled positions. By 1930, however, some 2 million women were working in corporate offices as secretaries, typists, or filing clerks, although rarely at higher ranks.

Nearly fifty thousand women received college degrees in 1930, almost triple the 1920 figure. Of those who entered the workplace, most took clerical jobs or entered such traditional "women's professions" as nursing, librarianship, and school teaching. With medical schools limiting the number of women students to 5 percent, the number of women physicians actually declined from 1910 to 1930. A handful of women, however, following the lead of Progressive Era feminist trailblazers, pursued postgraduate education to become faculty members in colleges and universities.

Marginalized in the workplace, women were courted as consumers. In the decade's advertising, glamorous women smiled behind the steering wheel, swooned over new appliances, and smoked cigarettes in romantic settings. (One ad man promoted cigarettes for women as "torches of freedom.") In the advertisers' dream world, housework became an exciting challenge. As one ad put it, "Men are judged . . . according to their power to delegate work. Similarly the wise woman delegates to electricity all that electricity can do."

women's power = material

Struggling Labor Unions in a Business Age

Organized labor faced tough sledding in the 1920s. Union membership fell from 5 million in 1920 to 3.4 million in 1929. Several factors underlay this decline. For one thing, despite inequities and regional variations, overall wage rates rose in the decade, reducing the incentive to join a union. Further, the union movement's strength lay in older industries like printing, railroading, mining, and construction. These unions were ill suited to the new mass-production factories.

Management hostility further weakened organized labor. Henry Ford hired thugs to intimidate union organizers. In 1929, anti-union violence flared in North Carolina, where textile workers faced low wages, long hours, and appalling work conditions. In Marion, deputy sheriffs shot and killed six striking workers. In Gastonia, a sniper shot and killed strike leader and balladeer Ella May Wiggins en route to a union rally. In the end, these strikes failed, and the textile industry remained nonunion.

As the wartime antiradical mood continued, opponents of labor unions often smeared them with the "communist" label, whether accurate or not. The anti-union campaign took subtler forms as well. Manufacturers' associations renamed the nonunion shop the "open shop" and dubbed it the "American Plan" of labor relations. Some corporations provided cafeterias and recreational facilities for employees. Corporate publicists praised "welfare capitalism" (the term for this anti-union strategy) as evidence of employers' benevolent concern for their workers.

Black membership in labor unions stood at only about eighty-two thousand by 1929, mostly consisting of miners, dockworkers, and railroad porters. The American Federation of Labor officially prohibited racial discrimination, but most AFL unions in fact barred African-Americans. Corporations often hired jobless blacks as strikebreakers, increasing organized labor's hostility toward them.

CHECKING IN

- Automobiles were at the root of the economic boom in the 1920s; farmers were left out.
- Mass production and the assembly line came of age.
- Advertising played a major role in stimulating consumption.
- More women graduated from college and entered the office work force, but few were in high-wage industrial jobs.
- Labor unions struggled, in part because of general prosperity, and in part because of management measures to undermine them.

STANDPAT POLITICS IN A DECADE OF CHANGE

What political and social ideas shaped the administrations of Presidents Harding and Coolidge?

Politics in the 1920s reflected the decade's business orientation. Unsettled by rapid social change, voters turned to conservative candidates who seemed to represent stability and traditional values. In this climate, former progressives, would-be reformers, and exploited groups had few political options.

The Evolving Presidency: Scandals and Public-Relations Manipulation

While white southerners and urban immigrants remained heavily Democratic, the Republican Party continued to attract northern farmers, businesspeople, native-born white-collar workers and professionals, and some skilled blue-collar workers. The GOP also benefited from the antiradical mood that fueled the early postwar Red Scare (see Chapter 22) and the anti-union campaign.

With Republican progressives having bolted to Theodore Roosevelt in 1912, GOP conservatives controlled the 1920 convention and nominated Ohio senator Warren G. Harding for president. A genial backslapper, Harding enjoyed good liquor, a good poker game, and at least one long-term extramarital affair. In the election, Harding swamped his Democratic opponent James M. Cox. Harding made some notable cabinet selections: Charles Evans Hughes, former New York governor and 1916 presidential candidate, for secretary of state; Andrew Mellon, a Pittsburgh financier, for treasury secretary; and Herbert Hoover, the wartime food tsar, for secretary of commerce.

Harding also made some disastrous appointments, including a wartime draft dodger, Charles Forbes, as Veterans' Bureau head. Such men set the low ethical tone of Harding's presidency. By 1922, the Washington rumor mill hinted at corruption in high places. "I have no trouble with my enemies . . . ," Harding told an associate; "[b]ut . . . my goddamn friends . . . keep me walking the floor nights." In summer 1923, while vacationing in the West, Harding suffered a heart attack and died in a San Francisco hotel.

In 1924, a Senate investigation exposed the scandals. Charles Forbes, convicted of stealing Veterans' Bureau funds, evaded prison by fleeing abroad. The bureau's general counsel committed suicide, as did an aide to Attorney General Daugherty who was accused of influence peddling. Daugherty himself narrowly escaped conviction in two criminal trials. Interior Secretary Fall went to jail for leasing government oil reserves, including one in Teapot Dome, Wyoming, to oilmen in return for a $400,000 bribe. Like "Watergate" in the 1970s, **"Teapot Dome"** became a shorthand label for a tangle of scandals.

Teapot Dome Scandal of the Harding administration

Calvin Coolidge Former Massachusetts governor; soft-spoken, dour successor to Warren Harding

With Harding's death, Vice President **Calvin Coolidge,** on vacation in Vermont, took the presidential oath by lantern light from his father, a local magistrate. Elected Massachusetts governor in 1918, he secured the Republican vice-presidential nomination in 1920. Coolidge's image as "Silent Cal," a prim Yankee embodiment of old-fashioned virtues, was carefully crafted. The advertising executive Bruce Barton guided Coolidge's bid for national office in 1919–1920. Barton planted pro-Coolidge articles in magazines and in other ways marketed his candidate just as advertisers were marketing soap, socks, and cereal. Wrote an admirer of Barton: "No man is his equal in [analyzing] the middle-class mind and directing an appeal to it."

Republican Policy Making in a Probusiness Era

While Coolidge raised the ethical tone of the White House, the probusiness policies, symbolized by high tariffs, continued. Congress lowered income-tax rates for the wealthy from their high wartime levels and the Supreme Court overturned several progressive measures. In 1927, torrential spring rains caused severe flooding on the Mississippi River; hundreds died and hundreds of thousands more lost their homes. But Coolidge rejected a request for aid from flood victims with the reminder that government had no duty to protect citizens "against the hazards of the elements."

McNary-Haugen Bill Popular legislation to help farmers, vetoed by Coolidge

Another test of Coolidge's views came when hard-pressed farmers rallied behind the **McNary-Haugen Bill,** a price-support plan under which the government would annually purchase the surplus of basic farm commodities. Coolidge twice vetoed the McNary-Haugen Bill, in 1927 and 1928, warning of "the tyranny of bureaucratic regulation and control." These vetoes led many angry farmers to vote Democratic in 1928. In the 1930s, New Deal planners would draw upon the McNary-Haugen approach in shaping farm policy (as discussed in Chapter 24).

Independent Internationalism

Despite its refusal to join the League of Nations or the new World Court, the United States remained a world power. Republican presidents pursued what they saw as the national interest—an approach historians have called independent internationalism. Despite postwar Europe's battered economies, Washington demanded repayment of $22 billion in Allied war debts and German reparation payments. In addition, the Republican administrations worked to protect U.S. corporate interests in Mexico and Nicaragua, where President Coolidge in 1926 sent U.S. Marines to put down an insurrection against the country's president, Adolfo Diàz, who had close ties to a U.S.-owned gold-mining company.

Special Collections Research Center, University of Chicago Library

The 1927 Mississippi River Flood

A few of the 700,000 people displaced by the raging waters of the Mississippi await rescue, their partially submerged homes in the background. President Calvin Coolidge resisted calls for federal aid, insisting that the government had no obligation to help citizens suffering from "the hazards of the elements."

Washington Naval Arms Conference Attempt to limit weapons and arms spending among major nations

One notable diplomatic achievement was the **Washington Naval Arms Conference.** After the war ended, the United States, Great Britain, and Japan edged toward a dangerous (and costly) naval-arms race. In 1921, Secretary of State Hughes called for a conference in Washington and outlined a specific ratio of warships among the world's naval powers. Great Britain and Japan, together with Italy and France, accepted Hughes's plan and agreed to halt all battleship construction for ten years. Although this treaty ultimately failed to prevent war, it did represent an early arms-control effort.

Another U.S. peace initiative was mainly symbolic. In 1928, the United States and France, eventually joined by sixty other nations, signed the Kellogg-Briand Pact renouncing aggression and calling for the outlawing of war. Lacking enforcement mechanisms, this high-sounding document accomplished little.

Progressive Stirrings, Democratic Party Divisions

The reform spirit survived in Congress. The Sheppard-Towner Act (1921) funded rural prenatal and baby-care centers staffed by public-health nurses. In 1927, Congress created the Federal Radio Commission, extending the regulatory principle to this new industry. In the 1922 midterm election, labor and farm groups joined forces to defeat some conservative Republicans. In 1924, this alliance revived the Progressive Party and nominated Senator Robert La Follette—who also received the endorsement of the Socialist Party—for president.

Ku Klux Klan Anti-modern reactionary group; wielded substantial political power in the 1920s

Alfred E. Smith Former Tammany Hall machine politician; Democratic nominee for president in 1928

The 1924 Democratic convention in New York City split between urban and rural wings. By one vote, the delegates defeated a resolution condemning the **Ku Klux Klan.** While the party's Protestant southern wing favored former Treasury Secretary William G. McAdoo, the big-city delegates rallied behind New York's Catholic governor **Alfred E. Smith.** The Democratic split mirrored deep divisions in the nation. After 102 ballots, the exhausted delegates nominated an obscure New York corporation lawyer, John W. Davis.

Calvin Coolidge, aided by his media adviser Bruce Barton, easily won the Republican nomination. The GOP platform praised the high protective tariff and urged tax cuts and reduced government spending. Coolidge received nearly 16 million votes, about twice Davis's total. La Follette's 4.8 million votes cut into the Democratic total, contributing to the Coolidge landslide.

Women and Politics in the 1920s: Achievements and Setbacks

Reformers' hope that woman suffrage would transform politics survived briefly after the war. Polling places shifted from saloons to schools and churches. The 1920 major party platforms endorsed several measures proposed by the League of Women Voters. The Women's Joint Congressional Committee, a coalition of activist groups, backed the **Sheppard-Towner Act** and called for a constitutional amendment to ban child labor in 1924.

Sheppard-Towner Act Appropriated $1.2 million for rural prenatal and baby-care centers in 1921

As former suffrage advocates scattered across the political spectrum, however, the women's movement lost focus. The League of Women Voters, drawing middle-class and professional women, abandoned feminist activism and instead conducted nonpartisan studies of civic issues. Alice Paul's National Woman's Party proposed a constitutional amendment guaranteeing women equal rights, but other reformers argued it jeopardized laws protecting women workers. The proposed amendment got nowhere. Politically active African-American women battled racial discrimination rather than addressing feminist issues; Hispanic women in the Southwest put their energies into labor-union organizing.

The reactionary political climate intensified this retreat from feminism. Patriotic groups accused Jane Addams and other women's-rights leaders of communist sympathies. Younger women, bombarded by ads that defined liberation in terms of consumption, rejected the prewar feminists' civic idealism.

The reforms backed by women's groups proved short-lived. The Supreme Court struck down child-labor and women's-protective laws. The 1924 constitutional amendment banning child labor passed Congress, but few states ratified it. The Sheppard-Towner Act, denounced by the American Medical Association as a threat to physicians' monopoly of health care, expired in 1929.

Checking In

- Corruption damaged the Harding administration.
- The Coolidge administration remained staunchly probusiness.
- The United States remained fundamentally isolationist but pursued its national interest through "independent internationalism."
- The Democratic Party split between its urban and rural wings, and lost badly in 1924.
- Woman suffrage produced few changes as women splintered across the political spectrum.

Mass Society, Mass Culture

What developments underlay 1920s' mass culture, and how did they affect American life and leisure?

Amid this conservative political climate, major transformations were reshaping society. Assembly lines, advertising, new consumer products, and innovations in mass entertainment and corporate organization all fueled the ferment. While some welcomed these changes, others recoiled in fear.

Cities, Cars, and Consumer Goods

In the 1920 census, the urban population (defined as persons living in communities of twenty-five hundred or more) surpassed the rural (see Figure 23.1). The United States had become an urban nation.

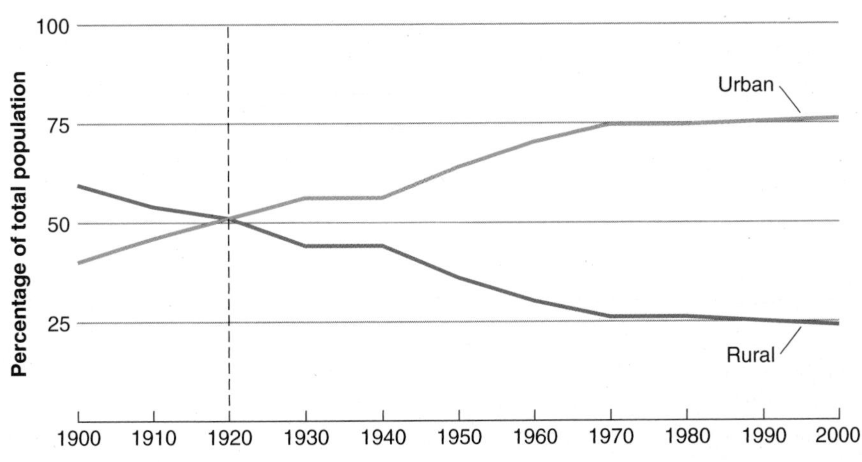

Figure 23.1 The Urban and Rural Population of the United States, 1900–2000

The urbanization of America in the twentieth century had profound political, economic, and social consequences.

Source: Census Bureau, Historical Statistics of the United States, *updated by relevant* Statistical Abstracts of the United States.

Urbanization affected different groups in different ways. African-Americans migrated cityward in massive numbers, especially after the 1927 Mississippi River floods. By 1930, more than 40 percent of the nation's 12 million blacks lived in cities. The first black congressman since Reconstruction, Oscar De Priest of Chicago, won election in 1928.

For many women, city life meant eased housework thanks to laborsaving appliances. Store-bought clothes replaced hand-sewn apparel. Home baking and canning declined as commercial bakeries arose and supermarkets proliferated. For social impact, however, nothing matched the automobile. In *Middletown* (1929), a study of Muncie, Indiana, Robert and Helen Lynd reported one resident's comment: "Why . . . do you need to study what's changing this country? I can tell you . . . in just four letters: A-U-T-O."

The A-U-T-O's social impact was decidedly mixed, as its convenience was tempered by traffic jams, parking problems, and highway fatalities (more than twenty-six thousand in 1924). In some ways, the automobile brought families together. As family vacations became more common, tourist cabins and roadside restaurants sprang up. But the automobile also eroded family cohesion and parental authority. Young people could borrow the car to go to the movies, attend a distant dance, or simply park in a secluded lovers' lane.

Middle- and upper-class women welcomed the automobile. They could now drive to work, attend meetings, visit friends, and gain a sense of independence. Stereotypes of feminine delicacy faded as women mastered this new technology. As the editor of an automotive magazine wrote in 1927, "[E]very time a woman learns to drive, . . . it is a threat to yesterday's order of things."

Automobiles offered farm families easier access to neighbors and to the city, lessening rural isolation. The automobile's country cousin, the tractor, proved instantly popular, with nearly a million in use in America by 1930. Yet increased productivity did not always mean increased profits. And as farmers bought tractors on credit, the rural debt crisis worsened.

Ads celebrated the freedom the automobile offered, in contrast to the fixed routes and schedules of trains and streetcars. Yet the automobile and other forms of motor transport in many ways further standardized American life. Buses carried children to consolidated schools. Neighborhood grocery stores declined as people drove to supermarkets served by trucks bringing commercial foods from distant facilities. With the automobile came the first suburban shopping center (in Kansas City), and the first fast-food chain (A&W Root Beer).

Even at $300 or $400, the automobile remained too expensive for many. The "automobile suburbs" that sprang up beyond the streetcar lines attracted mainly the well-to-do, widening class divisions in American society.

Soaring Energy Consumption and a Threatened Environment

Electrification and the spread of motorized vehicles impacted the nation's natural resources and the environment. As electrical use soared, power-generating plants consumed growing quantities of coal. In 1929, U.S. refineries used over a billion barrels of petroleum to meet the gasoline and oil demands of the nation's 20 million cars.

Rising gasoline consumption underlay Washington's efforts to ensure U.S. access to Mexican oil and triggered fevered activity in the oilfields of Texas and Oklahoma. In short, heavy fossil-fuel consumption, though small by later standards, already characterized America in the 1920s.

The wilderness that had inspired nineteenth-century artists and writers became more accessible as cars and improved roads gave vacationers easier access to the national parks and once-pristine regions. This development, too, had mixed effects. On one hand, it created a broader constituency for wilderness preservation. On the other hand, it subjected the nation's wilderness areas to heavy pressures as visitors expected good highways, service stations, restaurants, and hotels.

The Sierra Club and other groups worked to protect wilderness and wildlife. In 1923, a group of recreational fishermen persuaded Congress to halt a private-development scheme to drain a vast stretch of wetlands on the upper Mississippi. Instead, Congress declared this beautiful waterway a wildlife preserve. Aldo Leopold of the U.S. Forest Service warned of technology run amok. For too long, Leopold wrote in 1925, "a stump was our symbol of progress." However, few Americans in the expansive 1920s worried about the environmental issues that would occupy future generations.

Mass-Produced Entertainment

Prosperity and workplace drudgery stimulated leisure activities in the 1920s. In their free hours, Americans sought the fulfillment their jobs often failed to provide.

Mass-circulation magazines proliferated. By 1922, ten U.S. magazines boasted circulation of more than 2.5 million. The venerable *Saturday Evening Post,* with its Norman Rockwell covers, specialized in nostalgia. *Reader's Digest,* founded in 1921, offered condensed versions of articles first published elsewhere. A journalistic equivalent of the Model T, the *Digest* offered standardized fare for mass consumption.

Book publishers broadened their market by selling through department stores or directly to the public via the Book-of-the-Month Club, launched in 1926. While critics accused such mass-market ventures of debasing literary taste, they did help sustain a common national culture in an increasingly diverse society.

Radio and the movies similarly offered standardized cultural fare. The radio era began on November 2, 1920, when Pittsburgh station KDKA reported Warren Harding's election. In 1922, five hundred new stations began operations, as radio fever gripped America. The first

Collection of Hershenson-Allen Archives

The Romance of the Movies

The 1927 film *Wings,* starring twenty-two-year-old Clara Bow, told of two World War I flying aces in love with the same young woman. It won the first Academy Award for best picture.

radio network, the National Broadcasting Company (NBC), formed four years later; the Columbia Broadcasting System (CBS) followed in 1927. Testing popular taste through market research, the networks soon ruled broadcasting. Americans everywhere laughed at the same jokes, heard the same news, and absorbed the same commercials.

Some commentators advocated preserving radio as a public educational and cultural medium, free of advertising, but commercial sponsorship soon won out. The first network comedy show, *Amos 'n' Andy* (1928)—which included stereotyped caricatures of African-American life—enriched its sponsor, Pepsodent toothpaste.

Featuring stars like Valentino, the movies expanded from the nickelodeons of the immigrant wards into elegant uptown pleasure palaces with names like Majestic, Ritz, and Orpheum. In 1922, facing protests about sexually suggestive movies, industry moguls named Postmaster General Will Hays, a former head of the Republican National Committee, to police movie morals. Despite charges of immorality, movies often reinforced conservative values. For example, *The Ten Commandments* (1923), directed by Cecil B. De Mille (the son of an Episcopal clergyman), cautioned against breaking moral taboos.

Technical innovations kept moviegoers coming. Al Jolson's *The Jazz Singer* (1927) introduced sound. Walt Disney's cartoon *Steamboat Willy* (1928) not only introduced Mickey Mouse but also showed the potential of animation. Like advertising, the movies created a dream world only loosely tethered to reality. One ad promised "all the adventure, . . . romance, . . . [and] excitement you lack in your daily life." The movies also stimulated consumption with alluring images of the good life. Along with department stores, mass magazines, and advertising, they opened new vistas of consumer abundance.

For all its influence, the new mass culture penetrated society unevenly. It had less impact in rural America, and met resistance among evangelical Christians suspicious of worldly amusements. Mexican-Americans generally preferred traditional festivals and leisure activities. Local radio stations broadcast not only network shows, but also farm reports, local news, religious programs, community announcements, and ethnic or regional music. In short, despite the new mass culture, America still had room for diversity in the 1920s.

Celebrity Culture

Professional sports and media-promoted spectacles provided diversion as well. In 1921, Atlantic City promoters launched a bathing-beauty contest they grandly called the Miss America Pageant. Celebrities dominated professional sports. Few Americans were more famous than Babe Ruth of the New York Yankees or Ty Cobb, the Detroit Tigers' player/manager. Ruth was a heavy-drinking womanizer; Cobb, a foul-tempered racist. Yet the alchemy of publicity transformed them into heroes with contrived nicknames: "the Sultan of Swat" (Ruth) and "the Georgia Peach" (Cobb).

This celebrity culture illuminates the stresses facing ordinary Americans in these years of social change. For young women uncertain about society's shifting expectations, the beauty pageants offered one ideal to which they could aspire. For men grappling with unsettling developments from feminism to Fordism, the exploits of sports heroes like Ruth could help restore damaged self-esteem.

Celebrity worship crested in the response to **Charles Lindbergh,** a daredevil stunt pilot who flew solo across the Atlantic in his small single-engine plane, *The Spirit of St. Louis,* on May 20–21, 1927. His success gripped the public's imagination. In New York, thousands turned out for a ticker-tape parade. Radio, newspapers, magazines, and movie newsreels offered saturation coverage. An instant celebrity, Lindbergh became a blank screen onto which people projected their hopes, fears, and ideologies. President Coolidge praised the flight as a triumph of American business and corporate technology. Others saw Lindbergh as proof that despite mechanization, the individual still counted. To conservatives, Lindbergh's solid virtues proved that the old verities survived.

Charles Lindbergh
Celebrity hero; first to fly solo across the Atlantic

Overall, the new mass media had mixed social effects. Certainly, they promoted cultural standardization and uniformity of thought. But mass magazines, radio, and movies also introduced new viewpoints and ways of behaving. Implicitly, they conveyed a potent message: A person's immediate surroundings need not limit his or her horizons. If the larger world they opened for ordinary Americans was often superficial or tawdry, it could also be exciting and liberating.

CHECKING IN

- The automobile had a major impact in every sector of American life.
- Energy consumption soared, with little concern about environmental impact.
- The development of radio networks, large-circulation magazines, and national movie distribution created a shared mass culture.
- The 1920s were the first decade in which celebrity culture flourished; Babe Ruth and Charles Lindbergh were two noted celebrities of the time.
- Professional sports and athletes became highly popular.

CULTURAL FERMENT AND CREATIVITY

What social developments contributed to the cultural creativity of the 1920s?

American life in the 1920s involved more than politics, assembly lines, and celebrity worship. As writers, artists, and musicians contributed to the modernist spirit of cultural innovation, African-Americans created a cultural flowering known as the Harlem Renaissance.

The Jazz Age and the Postwar Crisis of Values

The war and its sour aftermath sharpened the cultural restlessness already bubbling in prewar America. The postwar crisis of values took many forms. Some young people—especially affluent college students—boisterously assailed middle-class standards of behavior. Seizing the freedom offered by the automobile, they threw parties, drank bootleg liquor, flocked to jazz clubs, and danced the Charleston. Young people also discussed sex more freely than their elders had. Sigmund Freud, the Viennese physician who explored the sexual aspects of human psychology, enjoyed a popular vogue in the 1920s.

Despite much talk about sex and charges of rampant immorality, however, the 1920s' "sexual revolution" was a hard concept to pin down. Premarital intercourse remained an exceptional occurrence and most people widely disapproved of the practice. What *was* documented were changing courtship patterns. "Courting" had once been a formal prelude to marriage. The 1920s brought the more casual practice of "dating," through which young people gained social confidence and a degree of sexual experience without necessarily contemplating marriage.

For women, these postwar changes in some ways proved liberating. Female sexuality was more openly acknowledged. Skirt lengths crept up, makeup became more acceptable, and the elaborate armor of petticoats and corsets fell away. The awesome matronly bosom mysteriously deflated as a more boyish figure became the fashion ideal. The so-called flapper, with her bobbed hair, defiant cigarette, lipstick, and short skirt, similarly epitomized youthful rejection of entrenched stereotypes.

But this image also objectified young women as decorative sexual objects. Further, the double standard, which held women to a stricter code of conduct, remained in force. Young men could boast of sexual exploits, but young women reputed to be "fast" risked damaged reputations. In some ways, 1920s' popular culture worked against full gender equality nearly as effectively as had the older Victorian stereotypes.

Around 1922, according to F. Scott Fitzgerald, adults embraced the rebelliousness of the young and "the orgy began." But such sweeping generalizations can mislead. During the years of Fitzgerald's alleged national orgy, the divorce rate remained constant, and many Americans adhered to traditional standards, rejecting alcohol and wild parties. Many farmers, industrial workers, blacks, Hispanics, and recent immigrants found economic concerns more pressing than the latest fads and fashions.

The "Jazz Age" was partially a media and literary creation. Fitzgerald's romanticized novel about affluent postwar youth, *This Side of Paradise* (1920), spawned many imitators. But if the Jazz Age stereotype obscured the complexity of the 1920s, it did capture a part of the postwar scene, especially the brassy new mass culture and the hedonism and materialism of the well-to-do as they basked in the era's prosperity.

Alienated Writers

Like Fitzgerald, many young writers found the decade's cultural turbulence energizing. Rejecting the old order's moralistic pieties, they also disliked the business pieties of the new order. In *Main Street* (1920), the novelist Sinclair Lewis satirized the smugness and cultural barrenness of Gopher Prairie, a fictional midwestern town based on his native Sauk Centre, Minnesota. In *Babbitt* (1922), Lewis skewered a mythic larger city, Zenith, and the title character George F. Babbitt, a real-estate agent trapped in middle-class conformity.

H. L. Mencken Master of satire; journalist who pilloried narrow-minded thinking

H. L. Mencken, a journalist, editor, and critic, in 1924 launched the iconoclastic *American Mercury* magazine, which was an instant success with the decade's alienated intellectuals and young people. Mencken championed writers like Lewis and Theodore Dreiser while ridiculing politicians, small-town America, Protestant fundamentalism, and the middle-class "Booboisie." Asked why he stayed in America, Mencken replied, "Why do people visit zoos?"

For the novelist Ernest Hemingway, who was seriously wounded in 1918 while serving as a Red Cross volunteer in northern Italy, World War I was a watershed experience. In 1926 Hemingway, now an expatriate in Paris, published *The Sun Also Rises,* portraying a group of American and British young people, variously damaged by the war, as they drift around Spain. His *A Farewell to Arms* (1929), loosely based on his own experiences, depicted the war's futility and politicians' empty rhetoric.

Although writers like Hemingway and Lewis blasted wartime hypocrisy and postwar vulgarity, they remained American at heart, striving to create a more authentic national culture. Even Fitzgerald, himself caught up in Jazz Age excesses, was fundamentally a moralist. His masterpiece, *The Great Gatsby* (1925), portrayed not only the party-filled lives of the decade's moneyed class, but also their superficiality, selfishness, and heedless disregard for the less fortunate.

Architects, Painters, and Musicians Celebrate Modern America

A burst of architectural activity transformed the urban skyline in the 1920s. By 1930, New York City boasted four buildings that were more than fifty stories tall. Work on the 102-story Empire State Building, long the world's tallest building, began that year.

The decade's leading painters took America—real or imagined—as their subject. While Thomas Hart Benton evoked a past of cowboys, pioneers, and riverboat gamblers, Edward Hopper portrayed faded towns and lonely cities of the present. Hopper's painting *Sunday* (1926), picturing a man slumped on the curb of an empty street of abandoned stores, conveyed both the bleakness and potential beauty of urban America. A similar fascination with the industrial city pervaded the work of artists Joseph Stella and Charles Sheeler. Wisconsin's Georgia O'Keeffe, who moved to New York City in 1918, evoked the allure of the metropolis in her paintings of the later 1920s.

The creative ferment of the 1920s inspired composers as well. Of all the musical innovations, jazz best captured the modernist spirit. The white bandleader Paul Whiteman offered watered-down "jazz" versions of standard tunes, and white composers embraced jazz as well. Aaron Copland's *Music for Theatre* (1925) and George Gershwin's *Rhapsody in Blue* (1924) and *An American in Paris* (1928) revealed strong jazz influences.

Meanwhile, black musicians preserved authentic jazz and explored its potential. The 1920s recordings of trumpeter Louis Armstrong decisively influenced the future of jazz. The composer and bandleader Duke Ellington performed to mesmerized audiences at Harlem's Cotton Club. Meanwhile, the piano's jazz potential was demonstrated by Fats Waller and Ferdinand "Jelly Roll" Morton. Although much of 1920s' popular culture faded quickly, jazz endured.

The Harlem Renaissance

Jazz was only one of many black contributions to 1920s' American culture. The social changes of these years energized African-American cultural life, especially in New York City's Harlem. An elite white suburb before World War I, Harlem attracted many African-Americans during and after the war, and by 1930 most of New York's 327,000 blacks lived within its boundaries. This concentration, plus the proximity of Broadway theaters, record companies, book publishers, and the NAACP's national headquarters, all contributed to the Harlem Renaissance.

This cultural flowering took varied forms. The Mississippi-born black composer William Grant Still, moving to Harlem in 1922, produced many works, including *Afro American Symphony* (1931). The painter Aaron Douglas and the sculptor Augusta Savage worked in the visual arts. The multitalented Paul Robeson gave vocal concerts, made films, and appeared on Broadway in Eugene O'Neill's *The Emperor Jones* and other plays.

Poet Langston Hughes incorporated African themes and southern black traditions in *The Weary Blues* (1926), and the Jamaican-born poet and novelist Claude McKay evoked Harlem's vibrant, sometimes sinister nightlife in *Home to Harlem* (1928). Nella Larsen, from the Danish West Indies, told of a mulatto woman's struggle with her mixed ethnicity in the 1928 novel *Quicksand.* In *The New Negro* (1925), Alain Locke, a philosophy professor at Howard University, assembled essays, poems, short stories, and reproductions of artworks to convey Harlem's rich cultural life.

The white cultural establishment took notice. Book publishers and magazine editors courted black writers. Broadway producers mounted black shows. Whites crowded Harlem's jazz clubs. DuBose Heyward's 1925 novel *Porgy* offered a sympathetic picture of Charleston's African-American community. George Gershwin's musical version, *Porgy and Bess,* premiered in 1935.

The Harlem Renaissance reached beyond America's borders. For example, jazz won fans in Europe. Langston Hughes and Claude McKay found readers in Africa, Latin America, and Europe. The dancer and singer Josephine Baker, after debuting in Harlem, moved to Paris in 1925, where her highly erotic performances created a sensation.

With white support came misunderstanding and attempts at control. Rebellious young whites romanticized Harlem nightlife, idealizing the spiritual or "primitive" qualities of black culture while ignoring the community's social problems. Nor did it bother them that the popular Cotton Club, controlled by gangsters, featured black performers but barred most blacks from the audience. When Langston Hughes's poems confronted the gritty realities of black life in America, his wealthy white patron angrily withdrew her support.

The exuberance of the Harlem Renaissance faded as hard times hit in the 1930s. Nevertheless, it stands as a memorable cultural achievement. Future black writers, artists, musicians, and performers would owe a great debt to their predecessors of the 1920s.

CHECKING IN

- The Jazz Age, symbolized by the bold behavior of "flaming youth" and the flamboyant sexuality of flappers, shocked traditionalists.
- Appalled by World War I, alienated writers criticized American society; many fled to Paris and elsewhere abroad.
- Architects and artists created a national visual culture; jazz, with its frenetic rhythms and sexual overtones, dominated the era's music among whites as well as blacks.
- The Harlem Renaissance was primarily a literary movement that ignored politics and racism.

A SOCIETY IN CONFLICT

What events or movements revealed the major social and cultural conflicts of the 1920s?

The social changes of the 1920s produced a fierce backlash. While Congress restricted immigration, highly publicized court cases in Massachusetts and Tennessee underscored the nation's social and cultural divisions. Millions of whites embraced the racist bigotry and moralistic rhetoric of a revived Ku Klux Klan, and many newly urbanized African-Americans rallied to Marcus Garvey, a magnetic black leader with a riveting message of racial pride. Prohibition stirred further controversy in this conflict-ridden decade.

Immigration Restriction

Fed by wartime efforts to enforce patriotism, the old impulse to remake America into a nation of like-minded, culturally homogeneous people revived in the 1920s.

The **National Origins Act** of 1924, a revision of the immigration law, restricted annual immigration from any foreign country to 2 percent of the number of persons of that "national origin" in the United States in 1890. Since the great influx of southern and eastern Europeans had come later, this provision clearly aimed to reduce immigration from these regions. As Calvin Coolidge observed on signing the law, "America must be kept American."

National Origins Act
Limitation of immigrants to keep out the "wrong sort"

This quota system, which survived to 1965, represented a strong counterattack by native-born Protestant America against the immigrant cities. Total immigration fell from 1.2 million in 1914 to 280,000 in 1929. The law excluded Asians and South Asians entirely. Court rulings underscored the nativist message. In *Ozawa v. United States* (1922), the U.S. Supreme Court denied citizenship to a Japanese-born university student. In 1923, the Supreme Court upheld a California law limiting Japanese immigrants' rights to own or lease farmland.

Needed Workers/ Unwelcome Aliens: Hispanic Newcomers

Although extremely restrictive otherwise, the 1924 law did not limit immigration from the Western Hemisphere. Accordingly, immigration from Latin America (as well as from French Canada) soared. Poverty and political turmoil propelled thousands of Mexicans northward. By 1930, at least 2 million Mexican-born immigrants lived in the United States, mostly in the Southwest. California's Mexican-American population surged from 90,000 to nearly 360,000 in the 1920s.

Many of these newcomers became migratory workers in large-scale agribusiness. Mexican labor sustained California's citrus industry. Cooperatives like the Southern California Fruit Growers Exchange (Sunkist) hired workers on a seasonal basis, provided substandard housing in isolated settlements, and fought the migrants' attempts to form labor unions.

Not all Mexican immigrants were migratory workers, however; many settled into U.S. communities. Although still emotionally linked to "México Lindo" ("Beautiful Mexico"), they formed local support networks and cultural institutions. However, Mexican-Americans found little support from the U.S. Catholic church. Earlier Catholic immigrants had attended ethnic parishes and worshipped in their own languages, but by the 1920s church policy had changed. In "Anglo" parishes with non-Hispanic priests, the Spanish-speaking newcomers faced discrimination and pressure to abandon their language and traditions.

In the larger society, Mexican immigrants faced ambivalent attitudes. Their labor was needed, but their presence angered nativists eager to preserve a "white" and Protestant nation. Would-be Mexican immigrants faced strict literacy and financial tests, and in 1929 Congress made it a criminal offense to cross the border without following required immigration procedures. Nevertheless, an estimated one hundred thousand illegal Mexican newcomers arrived annually to fill pressing demands in the U.S. labor market.

Nativism, Antiradicalism, and the Sacco-Vanzetti Case

The immigration-restriction movement reflected deep strains of ethnic, racial, and religious prejudice in 1920s' America. Anti-Semitic propaganda filled Henry Ford's weekly newspaper, the *Dearborn Independent,* which was distributed through Ford dealerships and mailed free to schools and libraries. Sued for defamation by a Jewish attorney, Ford in 1927 issued an evasive apology blaming subordinates.

Nativist, antiradical prejudices pervaded the Sacco-Vanzetti case, a Massachusetts murder case that began in April 1920, when robbers shot and killed the paymaster and guard of a shoe factory in South Braintree, Massachusetts. In 1921, a jury found two Italian immigrants, Nicola Sacco and Bartolomeo Vanzetti, guilty of the crime. After many appeals and a review by a commission of notable citizens, they were electrocuted on August 23, 1927.

Sacco and Vanzetti Anarchists accused and convicted of murder

These bare facts hardly convey the passions the case aroused. **Sacco and Vanzetti** were anarchists, and the prosecution harped on their radicalism. The judge barely concealed his hostility to the pair, whom he privately called "those anarchist bastards." While many conservatives supported the death sentence, liberals and socialists rallied to their cause.

Later research on Boston's anarchist community and ballistics tests on Sacco's gun pointed to their guilt. But the prejudices that tainted the trial remain indisputable, as does the case's symbolic importance in exposing the deep fault lines in 1920s' American society.

Fundamentalism and the Scopes Trial

Meanwhile, an equally celebrated case in Tennessee highlighted another front in the cultural wars of the 1920s: the growing prestige of science. While many Americans welcomed the advance of science, some religious believers found it threatening. Their fears deepened as scholars subjected the Bible to critical scrutiny, psychologists and sociologists studied supernatural belief systems as human social constructs and expressions of emotional needs, and biologists embraced Charles Darwin's naturalistic explanation for the variety of life forms on Earth advanced in *Origin of Species* (1859).

Fundamentalism Evangelical movement that taught literal interpretation of the Bible

While liberal Protestants generally accepted the findings of science, evangelical believers resisted. This gave rise to a movement called **Fundamentalism,** after *The Fundamentals,* a series of essays published in 1909–1914. Fundamentalists insisted on the Bible's literal truth, including the Genesis account of Creation.

In the early 1920s, fundamentalists targeted Darwin's theory of evolution. Many states considered legislation to bar public schools from teaching evolution, and several southern states enacted such laws. The former Democratic presidential candidate and secretary of state William Jennings Bryan, still widely admired in the American heartland, endorsed the antievolution cause.

When Tennessee's legislature barred the teaching of evolution in the state's public schools in 1925, the American Civil Liberties Union (ACLU) offered to defend any teacher willing to challenge this law. A high-school teacher in Dayton, Tennessee, John T. Scopes, encouraged by local businessmen eager to promote their town, accepted the offer. Scopes summarized Darwin's theory to a science class and was arrested. Famed criminal lawyer Clarence Darrow headed the defense, while Bryan assisted the prosecution. Journalists poured into Dayton, and a Chicago radio station broadcast the proceedings live. The **Scopes trial** became a media sensation.

Scopes trial Trial of John T. Scopes, the Tennessee teacher accused of violating the state's antievolution law

Cross-examined by Darrow, Bryan embraced the fundamentalist view of the Bible and dismissed evolutionary theory. Although the jury found Scopes guilty (in a decision later reversed on a technicality), the trial exposed Fundamentalism to ridicule. When Bryan died of a heart attack soon after, H. L. Mencken wrote a column mercilessly deriding him and his fundamentalist admirers.

Despite the setback in Dayton, Fundamentalism survived. Mainstream Protestant denominations grew more liberal, but many local congregations, radio preachers, Bible schools, new denominations, and flamboyant evangelists like Billy Sunday upheld the traditional faith. Southern and western states continued to pass antievolution laws, and textbook publishers deleted or modified their treatment of evolution to appease local school boards.

In Los Angeles, Aimee Semple McPherson, anticipating later TV evangelists, filled her cavernous Angelus Temple and reached thousands more by radio. The charismatic McPherson entranced audiences with theatrical sermons. She once used a gigantic electric scoreboard to illustrate the triumph of good over evil. Her followers, mainly transplanted midwesterners, embraced her fundamentalist theology while enjoying her mass-entertainment techniques. At her death in 1944, her International Church of the Foursquare Gospel had more than six hundred branches in the United States and abroad.

The Ku Klux Klan

The tensions gripping American society of the 1920s also bubbled up in the form of a resurrected Ku Klux Klan (KKK). The original Klan of the Reconstruction South eventually faded (see Chapter 16), but in 1915 hooded men gathered at Stone Mountain, Georgia, and revived it. D. W. Griffith's glorification of the original Klan in his 1915 movie *The Birth of a Nation* provided further inspiration.

Library of Congress

The Ku Klux Klan in Washington, DC

In a brazen display of power, the Ku Klux Klan organized a march in the nation's capital in 1926. By this time, however, the Klan was already in decline.

The movement remained obscure until 1920, when two Atlanta entrepreneurs organized a national membership drive to exploit the appeal of the Klan's ritual and its nativist, white-supremacist ideology. Their wildly successful scheme involved a ten-dollar membership fee divided among the salesman and their managers at the state and national level—with a rake-off to themselves. The sale of Klan robes, masks, horse blankets, and the bottled Chattahoochee River water used in initiation rites added to the take.

Preaching "100 percent Americanism," the Klan demonized blacks, Catholics, Jews, aliens, and, in some cases, women suspected of violating sexual taboos. Membership estimates for the KKK and its women's auxiliary in the early 1920s range as high as 5 million. From its southern base, the Klan spread through the Midwest and across the country from Long Island to the West Coast. Most of its members came from blue-collar ranks.

Although corrupt at the top and basically a money-making scam, the Klan was not a haven for criminals or fanatics. Observers commented on members' ordinariness. The Klan's litany of enemies and its promise to restore the nation's lost purity—racial, ethnic, religious, and moral—appealed to economically marginal Protestants disoriented by a new social order of giant corporations, mass media, rebellious youth, and immigrant-filled cities. The rituals, parades, and night-time cross burnings added a jolt of drama and a sense of camaraderie to lonely, unfulfilling lives.

But the Klan's menace as a mass movement was real. Some KKK groups employed threats, beatings, and lynching in their quest to purify America. In several states, the Klan won political power. For example, the Oregon Klan elected a governor and enacted legislation requiring all children to attend public school, which was an attempt to destroy the state's Catholic schools.

The Klan collapsed with shocking suddenness. In March 1925, Indiana's Grand Dragon, David Stephenson, brutally raped his young secretary, who swallowed poison and died several weeks later. In prison, Stephenson revealed sordid details of political corruption. Its moral pretensions in shreds, the KKK faded. When civil-rights activism surged in the 1950s, however, the Klan would again rear its head.

The Garvey Movement

Marcus Garvey Founder of the "Back to Africa" movement

Among African-Americans who fled southern rural poverty and racism only to experience discrimination and racism in the urban North, the decade's social strains produced a different kind of mass movement, led by the spellbinding **Marcus Garvey** and his Universal Negro Improvement Association (UNIA). Born in Jamaica in 1887, Garvey founded UNIA in 1914 and two years later moved to Harlem, which became the movement's headquarters. In a white-dominated society, Garvey glorified all things black. Urging black economic solidarity, he founded UNIA grocery stores and other businesses. He summoned blacks to return to "Motherland Africa" and established the Black Star Steamship Line to help them get there.

An estimated eighty thousand blacks joined UNIA, drawn by the appeal of the vision of economic self-sufficiency and a glorious future in Africa. Garvey's popularity unsettled the NAACP's middle-class leaders, who advocated racial integration rather than separation. W. E. B. Du Bois was among Garvey's sharpest critics.

In 1923, a federal court convicted Garvey of fraud in the management of his Black Star Steamship Line. In 1927, after two years' imprisonment, he was deported to Jamaica, and the UNIA collapsed. Nonetheless, this first mass movement in black America revealed both the social aspirations and the activist potential of African-Americans in the urban North. The NAACP, meanwhile, remained active even in a reactionary decade with racism rampant. In some three hundred branches nationwide, members kept the civil-rights cause alive and patiently laid the groundwork for legal challenges to segregation.

Prohibition: Cultures in Conflict

A bitter controversy over alcohol further exposed the fissures in American society. As noted in Chapter 21, the Progressive Era **prohibition** campaign was both a legitimate effort to address social problems associated with alcohol abuse and a weapon in the struggle of native-born Americans to control the immigrant cities. These tensions persisted in the 1920s. When the Eighteenth Amendment took effect in 1920, prohibitionists rejoiced. Saloons closed, liquor advertising vanished, and arrests for drunkenness declined. Yet prohibition gradually lost support, and in 1933 it ended.

prohibition Ban on alcohol consumption by the Eighteenth Amendment, effective 1920; after its failure, it was repealed in 1933

What went wrong? Essentially, prohibition's failure illustrates the difficulty in a democracy of enforcing a widely opposed law. The Volstead Act, the 1919 prohibition law, was underfunded and weakly enforced. Would-be drinkers grew bolder as enforcement faltered. For many young people, alcohol's illegality increased its appeal. Challenging the prohibition law, declared one college student, represented "the natural reaction of youth to rules and regulations."

Every city harbored speakeasies where customers could buy drinks. In addition, people concocted home brew and sacramental wine sales soared. By 1929, alcohol consumption reached about 70 percent of prewar levels.

Organized crime helped circumvent the law. Chicago, where rival gangs battled to control the liquor business, witnessed 550 gangland killings in the 1920s. Speakeasies controlled by Chicago gangster Al Capone generated annual profits of $60 million. Although not typical, Chicago's crime wave underscored prohibition's failure. A reform designed to improve the nation's morality was turning citizens into lawbreakers and mobsters into celebrities.

Thus prohibition, too, became a battleground in the decade's cultural wars and politics. The "drys"—usually native-born Protestants—praised it. The "wets"—liberals, Jazz Age rebels, big-city immigrants—condemned it as moralistic meddling. Prohibition also influenced the 1928 presidential campaign. While Democratic candidate Al Smith advocated repeal of the Eighteenth Amendment, Republican Herbert Hoover praised it as "a great social and economic experiment, noble in motive and far-reaching in purpose." When the Eighteenth Amendment was finally repealed in 1933, prohibition seemed little more than a relic of another age.

Checking In

- Many Americans found rapid change disorienting and frightening, which led to reaction and protest.
- Immigration restriction was an attempt to keep out the "wrong sort" of people.
- The Sacco-Vanzetti case highlighted a resurgence of nativism and the cultural divide between the country's conservatives and liberals.
- The Scopes trial showed the enormous gap between religious fundamentalists and Americans who accepted modern science.
- The Ku Klux Klan attracted millions of ill-educated, deeply religious, and economically marginal Americans, and functioned as an all-purpose hate group.
- Prohibition, although it failed, asserted traditional morality over urban, immigrant culture.

HOOVER AT THE HELM

How did Herbert Hoover's social and political thought differ from that of Harding and Coolidge?

Herbert Hoover, elected president in 1928, appeared well fitted to sustain the nation's prosperity. No standpat conservative like Harding and Coolidge, his social and political philosophy reflected his engineering background. Therefore, he seemed the ideal president for the new technological age.

The Election of 1928

A Hollywood casting agent could not have chosen two individuals who better personified America's divisions than the 1928 presidential candidates, Al Smith and Herbert Hoover. New York governor Al Smith easily won the Democratic nomination. A Catholic and a "wet," his brown derby perpetually askew, Smith exuded the flavor of immigrant New York. Originally a machine politician, he had impressed reformers by backing social-welfare measures.

Herbert Hoover won the Republican nomination after Coolidge chose not to run. However, some conservative party leaders mistrusted the brilliant but aloof Hoover, who had never held elective office and had spent much of his adult life abroad. An Iowan orphaned early in life, Hoover had put himself through Stanford University and made a fortune as a mining engineer in China and Australia. After his tour as wartime food administrator, he had served as secretary of commerce since 1921.

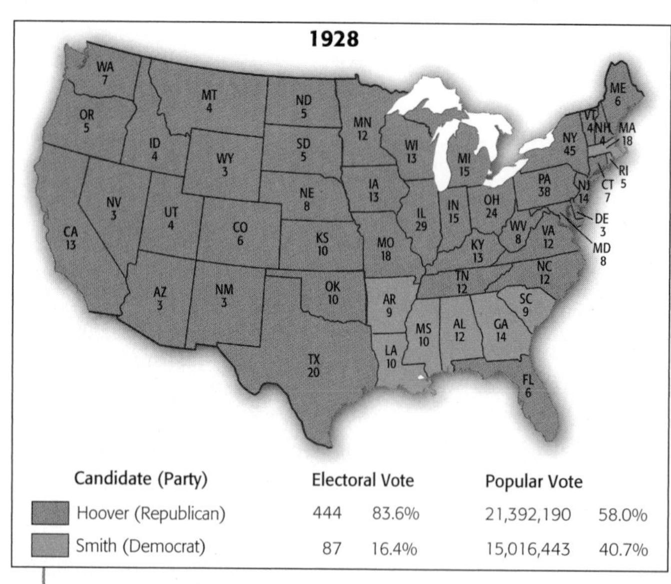

Map 23.1 The Election of 1928

Although Hoover won every state but Massachusetts and six Deep South states, Smith's 1928 vote in the midwestern farm belt and the nation's largest cities showed significant gains over 1924.

Interactive Map

Disdaining conventional campaigning, Hoover instead issued reports and read radio speeches in a droning monotone that obscured the originality of his ideas. Smith campaigned spiritedly throughout the country—a strategy that may have harmed him, for his big-city wisecracking and New York accent put off many voters.

The effect of Smith's Catholicism remains debatable. Hoover urged tolerance, and Smith denied any conflict between his faith and the duties of the presidency. Nonetheless, anti-Catholic prejudice played a role in the campaign. Rumors circulated that Smith would follow the Vatican's orders if he won. The decisive issue was probably not popery but prosperity. Republican orators pointed to the booming economy and warned of "soup kitchens instead of busy factories" if Smith won. In his nomination-acceptance speech, Hoover grandly predicted "the final triumph over poverty."

Hoover won in a landslide, grabbing 58 percent of the vote and even making deep inroads in the Democratic South (see Map 23.1).

However, the outcome also hinted at an emerging political realignment. Smith did well among hard-pressed midwestern farmers angered by Coolidge's insensitivity to their plight. In northern cities, Catholic and Jewish wards voted heavily Democratic. Smith carried the nation's twelve largest cities, all of which had gone Republican in 1924. Should prosperity falter, these portents suggested, the Republican Party faced trouble.

Herbert Hoover's Social Thought

Americans dubbed Hoover "the Great Engineer." Although a self-made man, he did not uncritically praise the capitalist system. His Quaker background, humanitarian activities, engineering experience, and Republican loyalties combined to produce a unique social outlook.

Like Theodore Roosevelt, Hoover opposed untrammeled free-market competition. Rational economic development, he insisted, demanded corporate cooperation in resource allocation, product standardization, and other areas. The economy, in short, should operate like an efficient machine. But above all, he advocated voluntarism. He felt the efficient, socially responsible economic order he envisioned must arise from the voluntary action of capitalist leaders, not government coercion.

As secretary of commerce, Hoover had convened more than 250 conferences with business leaders. He urged higher wages to increase consumer purchasing power. During the 1927 Mississippi River floods, as President Coolidge remained in Washington, Hoover had rushed to the stricken area to mobilize private relief efforts.

A conservationist, Secretary of Commerce Hoover had pushed for a number of environmental laws. In 1922, he negotiated a compact among western states for a division of Colorado River water. This agreement opened the way for a dam on the Colorado to provide hydroelectric power and water for irrigation. Construction began on Hoover Dam in 1930. (In an act of petty politics, Democrats changed the name to Boulder Dam in 1933, but Congress restored the original name in 1947.)

Hoover's ideology had limitations. He showed more enthusiasm for cooperation among capitalists than among consumers or workers. His belief that capitalists would voluntarily embrace enlightened labor policies overestimated the role of altruism in business decision making. And his opposition to government economic intervention brought him grief when such intervention became urgently necessary.

Still, Hoover's presidency began promisingly. Responding to the farm problem, he persuaded Congress to create a Federal Farm Board to promote cooperative marketing. This, he hoped, would raise farm prices while preserving the voluntarist principle. Meanwhile, however, an economic crisis was approaching that would overwhelm and ultimately destroy his presidency.

CHECKING IN

- The election of 1928 pitted urban immigrant champion Al Smith against self-made millionaire Herbert Hoover.
- Smith's Catholicism became a central issue in the campaign.
- Hoover's victory came with evidence of political realignment, as urban voters went heavily for Smith.
- Hoover believed strongly in voluntarism and welfare capitalism, but his ideas were limited by his opposition to direct government economic intervention.

Chapter Summary

What economic innovations came in the 1920s, and what was their effect on different social groups? (page 553)

The assembly line and mass production created the consumer economy with the automobile at its center. Advertising flourished. Farmers, however, were left out of the general prosperity. More women graduated from college, but few held high-wage industrial jobs. The labor union movement struggled.

What political and social ideas shaped the administrations of Presidents Harding and Coolidge? (page 557)

The Harding administration was stained by corruption. Both administrations were staunchly probusiness and wanted nothing to do with progressivism. Internationally, the United States followed an isolationist course but pursued its own national interest through independent internationalism. A split between rural and urban wings divided the Democratic Party, and the women's movement also splintered.

What developments underlay 1920s' mass culture, and how did they affect American life and leisure? (page 561)

The automobile had a major social as well as economic impact. Mass culture grew from the development of radio networks, large-circulation magazines, and movies. Celebrity culture celebrated heroes like Babe Ruth and Charles Lindbergh, and professional sports flourished. Skyscrapers, radio, the automobile, the movies, and electrical appliances—all familiar today—were exciting novelties in 1920s America.

What social developments contributed to the cultural creativity of the 1920s? (page 565)

The open sexuality of the Jazz Age, jazz music, and the flapper shocked many. Young people, freed from parental authority by the automobile, behaved in ways that seemed licentious to their elders. Alienated writers fled to Paris, and a literary renaissance among African-Americans flourished in Harlem.

What events or movements revealed the major social and cultural conflicts of the 1920s? (page 568)

Rapid change itself was disorienting. Immigration restrictions sought to keep out the "wrong sort" of people, the Sacco-Vanzetti case demonstrated the resurgence of nativism and the cultural divide in the nation, and the Ku Klux Klan functioned as an all-purpose hate group. Prohibition represented an unsuccessful attack on urban, immigrant culture. The Scopes trial reflected the fundamentalist rejection of modern science.

KEY TERMS

Henry Ford *(p. 553)*
Teapot Dome *(p. 558)*
Calvin Coolidge *(p. 558)*
McNary-Haugen Bill *(p. 558)*
Washington Naval Arms Conference *(p. 560)*
Ku Klux Klan *(p. 560)*
Alfred E. Smith *(p. 560)*
Sheppard-Towner Act *(p. 560)*
Charles Lindbergh *(p. 565)*
H. L. Mencken *(p. 566)*
National Origins Act *(p. 569)*
Sacco and Vanzetti *(p. 570)*
Fundamentalism *(p. 570)*
Scopes trial *(p. 570)*
Marcus Garvey *(p. 572)*
prohibition *(p. 573)*

How did Herbert Hoover's social and political thought differ from that of Harding and Coolidge? (page 574)

In many ways, the election summed up the conflicts of the 1920s. It pitted Al Smith, the epitome of urban immigrant culture, against Herbert Hoover, who seemed to be the embodiment of a Horatio Alger story. Smith's Catholicism dominated much of the political discussion. Hoover's victory represented a last hurrah for the rural traditionalism of the Republican Party and put into the White House a man whose political philosophy proved inadequate to the demands of the Great Depression.

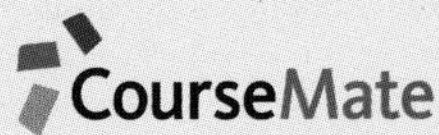

Go to the CourseMate website at **www.cengagebrain.com** for additional study tools and review materials—including audio and video clips—for this chapter.

The Great Depression and the New Deal

Chapter 24

1929–1939

FDR Library

President Franklin D. Roosevelt

Chapter Preview

Crash and Depression, 1929–1932
What caused the Great Depression, and how did President Hoover respond?

The New Deal Takes Shape, 1933–1935
What strategy guided the early New Deal, and what problems and challenges arose in 1934–1935?

The New Deal Changes Course, 1935–1936
What key measures and setbacks marked the course of the New Deal from 1935 on?

The New Deal's End Stage, 1937–1939
How did the New Deal end?

Social Change and Social Action in the 1930s
How did the depression and the New Deal affect specific social groups in the United States?

The American Cultural Scene in the 1930s
What key developments shaped American culture in the 1930s?

Franklin Delano Roosevelt seemed to have everything. Charming, handsome, and the scion of a well-to-do family, he had found life easy. Not yet forty, he had served as assistant secretary of the navy during World War I and had been the Democratic vice-presidential candidate in 1920. But while on vacation with his family in August 1921, Roosevelt was stricken with paralysis in his legs. He had suffered an attack of poliomyelitis. Except for a cumbersome shuffle with crutches and heavy metal braces, he would never walk again.

The illness could have marked the end of his career, but he endured endless therapy and gradually reentered politics. In 1928, laboriously mounting the podium at the Democratic National Convention, he nominated his friend Al Smith for president. That fall, he was elected governor of New York.

Roosevelt's disability profoundly shaped his personality. The ordeal changed him from a superficial, even arrogant, man into a person of greater compassion and far more understanding of the disadvantaged. "If you had spent two years in bed trying to wiggle your big toe," he once said, "after that every thing else would seem easy!"

Eleanor Roosevelt devoted herself to her husband's care, ultimately encouraging him to return to politics. At the same time, she joined the executive board of the New York Democratic Party and edited the women's division newsletter. Although painfully shy, she forced herself to make public speeches.

The Roosevelts would soon need these acquired characteristics. Elected president in 1932 amid the worst depression in U.S. history, Franklin Roosevelt dominated U.S. politics until his death in 1945. The early years of Roosevelt's long presidency spawned a dizzying array of laws, agencies, and programs. From 1933 to 1935, the first phase of the New Deal emphasized relief and recovery through a united national effort. In 1935, Roosevelt charted a more radical course. The so-called Second New Deal (1935 and after) placed less emphasis on unity and more on business regulation and on policies benefiting workers, small farmers, sharecroppers, migrant laborers, and others at the lower end of the scale.

This chapter develops two themes. The first is the New Deal's expansive view of the government's role in promoting economic and social welfare. The second is the American people's response to the Depression. From factory workers, urban blacks, and Hispanic migrant laborers to moviemakers, artists, and writers, diverse groups met the crisis with resourcefulness, creativity, and organized social action.

CRASH AND DEPRESSION, 1929–1932

What caused the Great Depression, and how did President Hoover respond?

The prosperity of the 1920s ended in October 1929 with the stock-market collapse. The Wall Street crash, and the deeper economic problems that underlay it, launched a depression that hit every household. President Hoover's commitment to private initiative and his distaste for direct federal intervention handcuffed him in providing a response. In November 1932, voters turned to the Democratic Party and its leader, Franklin Roosevelt. This election set the stage for a vast federal response to the crisis.

Black Thursday and the Onset of the Great Depression

Stock prices had risen through much of the 1920s, but 1928–1929 brought a frenzied upsurge as speculators plunged into the market. In 1925, the market value of all stocks stood at $27 billion; by October 1929 it had hit $87 billion. With stockbrokers lending buyers up to 75 percent of a stock's cost, credit or "margin" buying spread. The income-tax cuts promoted by Treasury

Chronology

1929	Stock market crash; onset of depression
1932	Reconstruction Finance Corporation; veterans' bonus march; Franklin D. Roosevelt elected president
1933	Repeal of Eighteenth Amendment; Civilian Conservation Corps (CCC); Federal Emergency Relief Act (FERA); Tennessee Valley Authority (TVA); Agricultural Adjustment Administration (AAA); National Recovery Administration (NRA); Public Works Administration (PWA)
1934	Securities and Exchange Commission (SEC); Taylor Grazing Act; Indian Reorganization Act
1934–1936	Strikes by Mexican-American agricultural workers in the West
1935	Supreme Court declares NIRA unconstitutional; Works Progress Administration (WPA); Resettlement Administration; National Labor Relations Act (Wagner Act); Social Security Act; NAACP campaign for federal anti-lynching law; Huey Long assassinated; Revenue Act raises taxes on corporations and the wealthy; Supreme Court reverses conviction of the "Scottsboro Boys"; Harlem riot
1935–1939	Era of the Popular Front
1936	Supreme Court declares AAA unconstitutional; Roosevelt wins landslide reelection victory; autoworkers' sit-down strike against General Motors begins (December)
1937	Roosevelt's "court-packing" plan defeated; Farm Security Administration; GM, U.S. Steel, and Chrysler sign union contracts
1937–1938	The "Roosevelt recession"
1938	Fair Labor Standards Act; Republicans gain heavily in midterm elections; Congress of Industrial Organizations (CIO) formed; Carnegie Hall concert by Benny Goodman Orchestra
1939	Hatch Act; Marian Anderson concert at Lincoln Memorial; John Steinbeck, *The Grapes of Wrath*
1940	Ernest Hemingway, *For Whom the Bell Tolls*

Secretary Andrew Mellon increased the flow of money into the market. Upbeat statements also fed the boom. In 1928–1929, construction declined by 25 percent, but few heeded the warning.

In 1928, and again in September 1929, the Federal Reserve Board tried to dampen speculation by increasing interest rates. But with speculators paying up to 20 percent interest to buy more stock, lending institutions continued to loan money freely—equivalent to dumping gasoline on a raging fire.

The collapse came on October 24, 1929—"Black Thursday." As prices fell, some stocks found no buyers at all: They had become worthless. In the ensuing weeks, feeble upswings alternated with further plunges. President Hoover, in the first of many optimistic statements, pronounced the economy "sound and prosperous." After a weak upswing early in 1930, the economy went into a long tailspin, producing a full-scale depression.

What caused the depression? Structural weaknesses in the American economy made the 1920s' prosperity unstable. Agriculture remained depressed throughout the decade. In the industrial sector, wage increases lagged behind factory output, reducing consumer purchasing power. At the same time, assembly-line methods encouraged overproduction. By summer 1929, not only housing, but also the automobile, textile, tire, and other major industries were seriously overextended. Further, key industries such as railroads, steel, textiles, and mining lagged technologically in the 1930s and could not attract the investment needed to stimulate recovery.

All analysts link the U.S. depression to a global economic crisis. European economies, struggling with war-debt payments and a severe trade imbalance with the United States, collapsed in 1931, crippling the U.S. export market.

The worsening depression devastated the U.S. economy. From 1929 to 1932, the gross national product dropped from $104 billion to $59 billion. Farm prices, already low, fell by nearly 60 percent. By early 1933, more than fifty-five hundred banks had closed, and unemployment stood at 25 percent, or nearly 13 million workers. In some cities, the jobless rate surged far higher. Many who still had jobs faced cuts in pay and hours.

Hoover's Response

Historically, Americans had viewed depressions as similar to natural disasters: Little could be done other than ride out the storm. President Hoover disagreed. Drawing upon his experience as U.S. food administrator in World War I and as secretary of commerce, Hoover initially responded boldly. However, his belief in private initiative limited his options.

Hoover urged business leaders to maintain wages and employment. Viewing unemployment as a local issue, he advised city and state officials to create public-works projects. In October 1930, he set up an Emergency Committee for Employment to coordinate voluntary relief efforts. In 1931, he persuaded the nation's largest banks to create a private lending agency to help smaller banks make business loans.

However, the crisis intensified, and public opinion turned against Hoover. In the 1930 midterm election, the Republicans lost the House of Representatives and gave up eight Senate seats. In 1931, dreading a budget deficit, Hoover called for a tax increase, further angering hard-pressed Americans. That same year, despite their pledges, U.S. Steel and other big corporations slashed wages. The crisis swamped private charities and local welfare agencies.

In 1932, a presidential election year, Hoover swallowed his principles and took a bold step. In January, at Hoover's recommendation, Congress set up a new agency, the **Reconstruction Finance Corporation (RFC),** to make loans to banks and other lending institutions. By July, the RFC had pumped $1.2 billion into the economy. The RFC also granted $2 billion to state and local governments for job-creating public-works programs.

Reconstruction Finance Corporation (RFC) Agency established by Hoover to provide funds to banks and insurance companies

Hoover supported these measures reluctantly, warning of "socialism and collectivism." He blamed global forces for the depression and argued that only international measures would help. His call for a moratorium on war-debt and reparations payments by European nations made sense, but seemed irrelevant to the plight of ordinary Americans. As Hoover urged self-help and local initiative and predicted recovery "just around the corner," his unpopularity deepened.

Mounting Discontent and Protest

An ominous mood spread as hordes of the jobless waited in breadlines, slept on park benches, trudged the streets, and rode freight trains seeking work. Americans reared on the ethic of hard work and self-reliance found chronic unemployment deeply demoralizing.

The *New York Times* described "Hoover Valley," a section of Central Park where jobless men lived in boxes and packing crates, keeping warm with layers of newspapers they bitterly called Hoover blankets. The suicide rate soared. Violence threatened to erupt in some cities when landlords evicted families unable to pay their rent.

Hard times battered the nation's farms, and many farmers lost their land because of tax delinquency. At some forced farm auctions, neighbors bought the foreclosed farm for a trivial sum and returned it to the evicted family. In 1931, midwestern farmers organized the Farmers' Holiday Association to force prices up by withholding grain and livestock from the market, and dairy farmers dumped thousands of gallons of milk.

The most alarming protest came from World War I veterans. In 1924, Congress had voted veterans a bonus stretched over a twenty-year period. In June 1932, some ten thousand veterans, many jobless, descended on Washington to lobby for immediate payment. When Congress refused, most of the "bonus marchers" went home, but about two thousand stayed on, building makeshift shelters on the outskirts of Washington. President Hoover called in the army.

On July 28, troops commanded by General Douglas MacArthur and armed with tear gas, tanks, and machine guns drove the veterans from their camp and burned it to the ground. As a journalist described the aftermath, veterans and their families "wandered from street to street or sat in ragged groups, the men exhausted, the women with wet handkerchiefs laid over their smarting eyes, the children waking from sleep to cough and whimper from the tear gas in their lungs." To many Americans, this action symbolized the administration's heartlessness.

American writers shared the despairing mood. In *The 42nd Parallel* (1930), John Dos Passos drew a dark panorama of twentieth-century America as money-mad, exploitive, and lacking spiritual meaning. As one character says, "Everything you've wanted crumbles in your fingers as you grasp it."

CHECKING IN

- A variety of economic problems, ranging from stock-market speculation to global economic problems, led to the crash and depression.
- Hoover turned to voluntarism to cope with the depression.
- The Reconstruction Finance Corporation was created to funnel money to banks and railroads, not directly to people.
- Americans grew increasingly angry at Hoover's failure to respond to their plight; the bonus march of 1932 illustrated the depth of despair.
- In the election of 1932, Americans rejected Hoover and gave the White House and Congress to Roosevelt and the Democrats.

The Election of 1932

Gloom pervaded the 1932 Republican convention that re-nominated Hoover. The Democrats, in contrast, sensed victory and drafted a platform to appeal to urban immigrants, farmers, and fiscal conservatives. Rejecting Al Smith, the party's 1928 candidate, the delegates nominated New York governor Franklin D. Roosevelt for president.

Breaking precedent, FDR flew to Chicago to accept the nomination in person, delivering a rousing speech promising "a new deal for the American people." But his campaign provided few specifics. He called for "bold, persistent experimentation" and promised more attention to "the forgotten man" while attacking Hoover's "reckless" spending.

Roosevelt exuded confidence, and above all he was not Hoover. On November 8, FDR and his running mate, John Nance Garner of Texas, received nearly 23 million votes, whereas Hoover received fewer than 16 million. Both houses of Congress went heavily Democratic.

THE NEW DEAL TAKES SHAPE, 1933–1935

What strategy guided the early New Deal, and what problems and challenges arose in 1934–1935?

The Roosevelt years began in a whirl of activity. An array of emergency measures proposed by Roosevelt and passed by Congress reflected three basic goals: industrial recovery through business-government cooperation and pump-priming federal spending; agricultural recovery through crop reduction; and short-term emergency relief distributed through state and local agencies when possible, but directly by the federal government if necessary. Presiding over this bustle, a confident FDR symbolized hope. By 1935, however, the New Deal faced problems, and opposition was building.

Roosevelt and His Circle

FDR's inaugural address exuded confidence and hope. "The only thing we have to fear," he intoned, "is fear itself." In an outpouring of support, half a million letters deluged the White House.

Roosevelt seemed an unlikely popular hero. Like his distant cousin Theodore, he was of the social elite, from a long line of merchants and landed aristocrats. His Harvard-Columbia background highlighted his social status. But as a state senator and governor of New York, he had allied with the Democratic Party's urban-immigrant wing, and when the depression hit, he had introduced such innovative measures as unemployment insurance and a public-works program. Intent on promoting recovery while preserving capitalism and democracy, Roosevelt encouraged competing proposals, compromised on (or papered over) differences, and then backed the measures he sensed that Congress and the public would support.

Roosevelt brought to Washington a circle of advisers nicknamed the brain trust, many of them from universities. It included Columbia University professor Rexford G. Tugwell and lawyer Adolph A. Berle. However, no single ideology or set of advisers controlled the New Deal, for FDR sought a broad range of opinions.

Eleanor Roosevelt played a key role. A niece of Theodore Roosevelt, she expressed her keen social conscience in settlement-house work and Florence Kelley's National Consumers' League. Through her, FDR met reformers, social workers, and advocates of minority rights. Mrs. Roosevelt traveled ceaselessly, observing depression America firsthand for her wheelchair-bound husband.

Eleanor Roosevelt Wife of FDR; redefined the role of First Lady and influenced social policy during the New Deal

Roosevelt's cabinet reflected the New Deal's diversity. Secretary of Labor **Frances Perkins,** the first woman cabinet member, had served as industrial commissioner of New York. Interior Secretary Harold Ickes had organized liberal Republicans for Roosevelt in 1932. Treasury Secretary Henry Morgenthau, Jr., FDR's neighbor and political ally, though a fiscal conservative, tolerated the spending necessary to finance New Deal anti-depression programs.

Frances Perkins Former Progressive reformer and first woman cabinet member; led the committee that wrote the Social Security Act

Newcomers poured into Washington in 1933—former progressives, liberal-minded professors, and bright young lawyers. They drafted bills, staffed government agencies, and debated recovery strategies. From this pressure-cooker environment emerged the laws, programs, and agencies gathered under a catch-all label: the New Deal.

Eleanor Roosevelt Visits a Nursery School in Des Moines Operated by the Works Progress Administration, June 1936

Intensely shy as a young woman, Mrs. Roosevelt played an active, influential, and highly visible role during her years as First Lady.

The Hundred Days

Between March and June, 1933, a period labeled the "Hundred Days," Congress enacted more than a dozen major bills (see Table 24.1). Drawing upon precedents from the Progressive Era, World War I, and the Hoover presidency, these measures expanded Washington's involvement in America's economic life.

FDR first addressed the banking crisis. As borrowers defaulted, depositors withdrew savings, and homeowners missed mortgage payments, thousands of banks failed, undermining confidence in the system. On March 5 he ordered all banks to close for four days. At the end of this so-called bank holiday, he proposed an Emergency Banking Act, which permitted healthy banks to reopen, set up procedures to manage failed banks, increased government oversight, and required that banks separate savings deposits from their investment funds. Congress also created the Federal Deposit Insurance Corporation (FDIC) to insure bank deposits up to

TABLE 24.1 MAJOR MEASURES ENACTED DURING THE "HUNDRED DAYS" (MARCH 9–JUNE 16, 1933)

March 9	Emergency Banking Relief Act
20	Economy Act
31	Unemployment Relief Act (Civilian Conservation Corps)
May 12	Agricultural Adjustment Act; Federal Emergency Relief Act
18	Tennessee Valley Authority
27	Federal Securities Act
June 13	Home Owners' Refinancing Act
16	Farm Credit Act; Banking Act of 1933 (Federal Deposit Insurance Corporation); National Industrial Recovery Act (National Recovery Administration; Public Works Administration)

$5,000. In the first of a series of radio talks dubbed "fireside chats," FDR assured Americans that they could again trust their banks.

Other measures addressed the urgent plight of Americans struggling to survive. Two new agencies assisted those who were losing their homes. The Home Owners Loan Corporation helped city-dwellers refinance their mortgages. The Farm Credit Administration provided loans to rural Americans to meet their farm payments.

Another early relief program, the **Civilian Conservation Corps (CCC),** employed jobless youths in environmentally friendly government projects such as reforestation, park maintenance, and erosion control. By 1935, half a million young men were earning thirty-five dollars a month in CCC camps—a godsend to desperate families. The principal relief measure of the Hundred Days, the **Federal Emergency Relief Act,** provided $500 million to fill the empty relief coffers of states and cities. To head this program, FDR chose Harry Hopkins, the relief administrator in New York State, who soon emerged as a powerful New Deal figure.

Civilian Conservation Corps (CCC) Agency that employed millions of young men

Federal Emergency Relief Act Keystone of the early New Deal that provided relief funds to cities and states

While supplying immediate relief, the early New Deal also faced the longer-term challenge of promoting agricultural and industrial recovery. Some New Dealers advocated reduced production as a means of raising farm prices. As a first step to cutting production, the government paid southern cotton planters to plow under much of their crop and midwestern farmers to slaughter some 6 million piglets and pregnant sows. However, destroying crops and killing pigs at a time of widespread hunger proved a public-relations nightmare. Pursuing the same goal more systematically, Congress passed the Agricultural Adjustment Act in May 1933. This law gave payments, called subsidies, to producers of the major farm commodities—including hogs, wheat, corn, cotton, and dairy products—in return for cutting production. A tax on food processors (a tax ultimately passed along to consumers) financed these subsidies. A new agency, the **Agricultural Adjustment Administration (AAA),** supervised the program.

Agricultural Adjustment Administration (AAA) Agency overseeing the effort to help farmers by reducing production and raising prices

The other key recovery measure of the Hundred Days, the National Industrial Recovery Act, appropriated $3.3 billion for heavy-duty government public-works programs to provide jobs and stimulate the economy. Interior Secretary Harold

Ickes headed the Public Works Administration (PWA), the agency that ran this program.

National Recovery Administration (NRA) Attempt to gain cooperation in recovery efforts among government, business, and labor leaders

This law also set up the **National Recovery Administration (NRA).** The NRA brought together business leaders to draft codes of "fair competition" for their industries. These codes set production limits, wages, and working conditions, and forbade price cutting and unfair competitive practices. The aim was to promote recovery by breaking the cycle of wage cuts, falling prices, and layoffs. However, some New Dealers had further goals. Under pressure from Labor Secretary Frances Perkins, the NRA's textile-industry code banned child labor. And thanks to Senator Robert Wagner of New York, Section 7a of the NIRA affirmed workers' rights to organize unions and to bargain collectively.

The NRA's success depended on voluntary support by both business and the public. NRA officials used parades, billboards, magazine ads, and celebrity events to persuade people to patronize only companies that subscribed to an NRA code and displayed the NRA symbol, a blue eagle, as well as its slogan, "We Do Our Part."

The Reconstruction Finance Corporation (RFC), dating from the Hoover years, remained active in the New Deal era. The RFC lent billions of dollars to banks, insurance companies, and even new business ventures. The early New Deal thus had a strong probusiness flavor.

A few measures adopted during the Hundred Days, however, took a tougher approach to business. The 1929 crash produced a strong antibusiness reaction. A Senate investigation of Wall Street discovered that none of the twenty partners of the Morgan Bank had paid any income tax in 1931 or 1932. People jeered when the president of the New York Stock Exchange told a Senate committee considering regulatory measures, "You gentlemen are making a big mistake. The Exchange is a perfect institution."

Reflecting the public mood, Congress in 1933 passed the Federal Securities Act requiring corporations to inform the government fully on all stock offerings. This law also made executives personally liable for any misrepresentation of securities their companies issued. In 1934 Congress created the Securities and Exchange Commission (SEC) to enforce the new regulations.

Tennessee Valley Authority (TVA) Ambitious plan of economic development; centered on dam building for the poor Appalachian area

The most innovative program of the Hundred Days was the **Tennessee Valley Authority (TVA).** This program advanced the economic and social development of the poverty-stricken Tennessee River valley. TVA dams brought electricity to the region, provided recreational facilities, and reduced flooding and soil erosion. Under director David Lilienthal, TVA proved one of the New Deal's most popular and enduring achievements.

The mind-boggling burst of laws and the "alphabet-soup" of new agencies during the Hundred Days symbolized both the dynamism and the confusion of the New Deal. How these new programs and agencies would work in practice remained to be seen.

Problems and Controversies Plague the Early New Deal

As the depression persisted, several early New Deal programs, including the NRA and the AAA, faltered. The NRA's problems related partly to the personality of its director, the hard-driving, hard-drinking Hugh Johnson, who left in 1934. But the trouble went deeper. Corporate America resisted NRA regulation. Code violations increased. Small businesses complained that the codes favored big corporations. Corporate trade associations used the codes to stifle competition and fix prices.

In May 1935, the Supreme Court unanimously declared the NRA unconstitutional. The Court ruled that the act gave the president regulatory powers that belonged to Congress and that it regulated commerce within states, violating the Constitution's limitation of federal regulation to commerce between or among states. Few mourned this ruling. As a recovery measure, the NRA had failed.

The AAA, too, proved controversial. Farm prices did rise as production fell, and from 1933 to 1937 overall farm income increased by 50 percent. But the AAA's crop-reduction payments actually hurt southern tenants and sharecroppers, who faced eviction as cotton planters removed acreage from production.

While some New Dealers focused on raising total agricultural income, others took a more class-based approach and urged attention to the poorest farmers. Their cause was strengthened as a parching drought centered in the Oklahoma panhandle region turned much of the Great Plains into a dust bowl (see Map 24.1). Each summer from 1934 through 1939, clouds of dust spread eastward, darkening the skies over coastal cities. As a dense dust cloud passed over Washington, DC, one legislator commented: "There goes Oklahoma."

Battered farmers abandoned the land in droves. Nearly 3.5 million people left the Great Plains in the 1930s. Some migrated to the cities; others packed their few belongings into old cars and headed west. Although from different states, they all bore the derisive nickname Okies.

Harry Hopkins A former administrator of New York State charitable organizations; emerged as one of the most powerful figures in the New Deal

Rivalries and policy differences also plagued New Deal relief. While Harold Ickes, head of the Public Works Administration, was super-cautious, **Harry Hopkins** was impatient to get money circulating. As unemployment continued, Hopkins

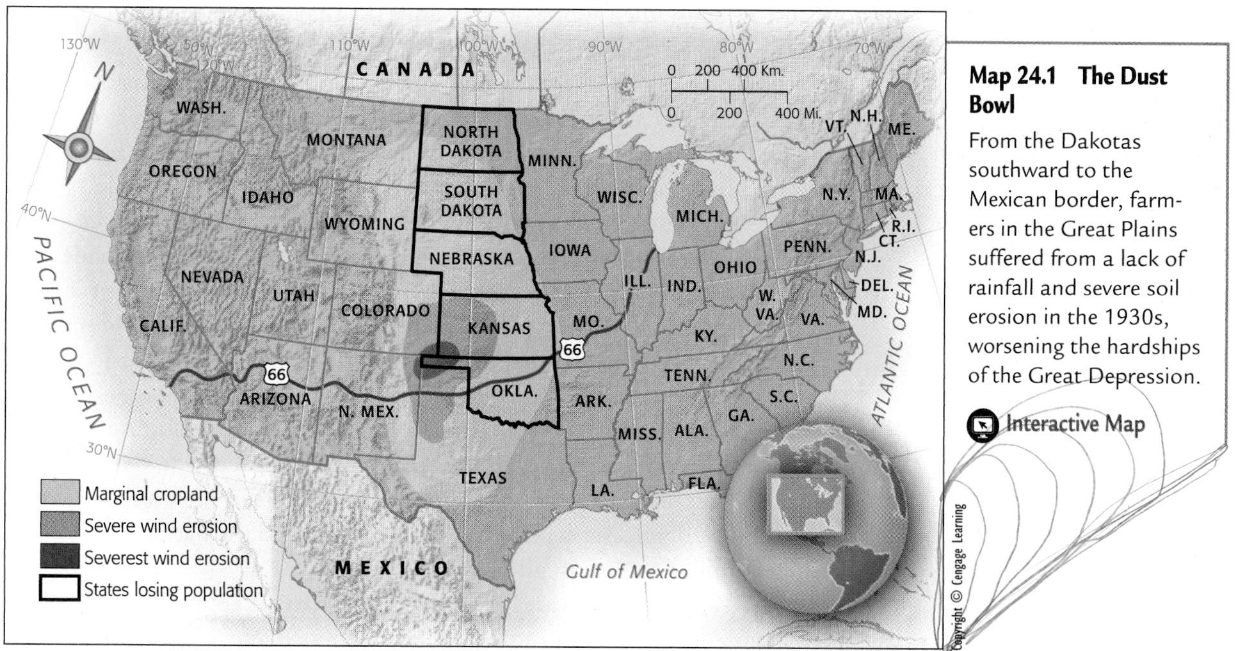

Map 24.1 The Dust Bowl

From the Dakotas southward to the Mexican border, farmers in the Great Plains suffered from a lack of rainfall and severe soil erosion in the 1930s, worsening the hardships of the Great Depression.

Interactive Map

convinced Roosevelt to support direct federal relief programs, rather than channeling funds through state and local agencies. Late in 1933, FDR named Hopkins to head a temporary public-works agency, the Civil Works Administration (CWA), which through the winter expended nearly a billion dollars on short-term work projects for the jobless. When warm weather returned, FDR abolished the CWA. Like his conservative critics, he feared creating a permanent underclass living on relief. But persistent unemployment that swamped local relief agencies made further federal programs inevitable.

1934–1935: Challenges from Right and Left

Despite the New Deal's brave beginnings, the depression persisted. In 1934 national income rose about 25 percent above 1933 levels but remained far below that of 1929. Millions had been jobless for three or four years. The rising frustration found expression in 1934 in nearly two thousand strikes, some of them communist-led. With the NRA under attack, conflict flaring over farm policy, and relief spending growing rather than declining, criticism mounted. Conservatives attacked the New Deal as socialistic. Anti-Roosevelt jokes circulated among the rich, many of whom denounced him as a traitor to his class.

But the New Deal remained popular, and FDR commanded the public stage. Pursuing the national-unity theme, he exhorted Americans to join the battle for economic recovery just as they had united for war in 1917. Although Republican newspaper publishers remained hostile, FDR enjoyed good relations with the working press, and journalists responded with favorable stories. FDR also savored public appearances and took naturally to radio. His easy mastery of radio provided a model for his successors in the television era.

The 1934 midterm election ratified the New Deal's popularity as the Democrats increased their majorities in the House and Senate. Kansas journalist William Allen White observed of FDR that "he's been all but crowned by the people."

Still, the political scene remained unstable. While conservatives criticized the New Deal for going too far, critics on the left attacked it for not going far enough and ridiculed Roosevelt's efforts to include big business in his "all-American team."

Demagogues peddled various nostrums. The Detroit Catholic priest and radio spellbinder Charles Coughlin viciously attacked FDR, made anti-Semitic allusions, and called for nationalization of the banks. For a time, Coughlin's National Union of Social Justice attracted considerable support, mainly from the lower middle class.

Meanwhile, California doctor Francis E. Townsend proposed that the government pay $200 monthly to all retired citizens, requiring them to spend it within thirty days. This plan, Townsend insisted, would help elderly Americans, stimulate the economy, and create jobs by encouraging retirement. Although the scheme would have bankrupted the nation, many older citizens rallied to Townsend's banner.

FDR's wiliest rival was Huey Long of Louisiana. A country lawyer elected governor in 1928, Long built highways, schools, and public housing. He

CHECKING IN

- FDR's own optimism, combined with his ability to convey it to the American people, was probably his single most important asset.
- The major goals of the New Deal were industrial recovery, agricultural recovery, and short-term relief.
- During the "Hundred Days," Congress rushed through major measures, such as the Federal Emergency Relief Act, the National Industrial Recovery Act, the Agricultural Adjustment Act, and the Civilian Conservation Corps.
- The New Deal also featured reforms, such as the establishment of the Securities and Exchange Commission and the Federal Deposit Insurance Corporation, and innovations, such as the Tennessee Valley Authority.
- Demagogues like Father Coughlin, Francis Townsend, and Huey Long peddled snake-oil alternatives to New Deal programs.

roared into Washington as a senator in 1933 and preached his "Share Our Wealth" program: a 100 percent tax on annual incomes exceeding $1 million and appropriation of all fortunes over $5 million. Once this money was redistributed, Long promised, every family could enjoy a comfortable income. "Every man a king," proclaimed Long. By 1935, he boasted 7.5 million supporters and clearly had his eye on the White House. Although an assassin's bullet cut him down that September, his organization survived.

THE NEW DEAL CHANGES COURSE, 1935–1936

What key measures and setbacks marked the course of the New Deal from 1935 on?

Roosevelt responded vigorously to his challengers. As the 1936 election neared, Roosevelt shelved the unity theme and championed the poor and the working class. His 1935 State of the Union address outlined six initiatives: expanded public-works programs, assistance to the rural poor, support for organized labor, benefits for retired workers, tougher business regulation, and heavier taxes on the well-to-do. These priorities translated into a bundle of reform measures some called "the Second New Deal." FDR's landslide victory in 1936 solidified a new Democratic coalition.

Expanding Federal Relief

With unemployment still high, Congress in April 1935 passed the Emergency Relief Appropriation Act. FDR swiftly established the **Works Progress Administration (WPA).** Like the CWA of the prior winter, the WPA funneled relief directly to individuals, and FDR insisted that the program provide work, not handouts. Over its eight-year life, the WPA employed more than 8 million Americans and constructed or improved vast numbers of bridges, roads, schools, post offices, and other public facilities.

Works Progress Administration (WPA) Massive public works program during the Second New Deal; included programs to employ artists, writers, and actors

The WPA also assisted writers, performers, and artists. The Federal Writers' Project employed out-of-work authors to produce state guides and histories of ethnic and immigrant groups. In the South they collected the reminiscences of ex-slaves. Under the Federal Music Project, unemployed musicians gave free concerts, often featuring American composers. By 1938 more than 30 million Americans had attended these events.

The Federal Theatre Project (FTP) employed actors. One FTP project, the Living Newspaper, dramatized contemporary social issues and was criticized as New Deal propaganda. Nonetheless, FTP drama companies touring small-town America gave many their first taste of theater. Artists working for the Federal Arts Project designed posters, offered school courses, and decorated post offices and courthouses with murals. Another 1935 agency, the National Youth Administration (NYA), provided job training for unemployed youth and part-time work to enable college students to remain in school. Eleanor Roosevelt, viewing young people as the hope of the future, took particular pride in the NYA.

Harold Ickes's Public Works Administration, after a slow start, eventually completed some thirty-four thousand major construction projects, from New York City's Lincoln Tunnel to the awesome Grand Coulee Dam on the Columbia River. The PWA employed thousands of jobless workers.

All this relief spending generated large federal budget deficits, cresting at $4.4 billion in 1936. According to British economist John Maynard Keynes, governments should deliberately use deficit spending during depressions to fund public-works programs, thereby increasing purchasing power and stimulating recovery. The New Deal approach, however, was not Keynesian. Because every dollar spent on relief programs was counterbalanced by taxation or government borrowing, the stimulus effect was nil.

Aiding Migrants, Supporting Unions, Regulating Business, Taxing the Wealthy

The second phase of the New Deal more frankly focused on the interests of workers, the poor, and the disadvantaged. Social-justice advocates like Frances Perkins and Eleanor Roosevelt helped shape this program, but so did hard-headed politics. Looking to 1936, FDR's political advisers feared that Coughlin, Townsend, and Long could siphon off enough votes to cost him the election. This worry underlay FDR's 1935 political agenda.

The Second New Deal's agricultural policy addressed the plight of sharecroppers (worsened by the AAA) and other poor farmers. The Resettlement Administration (1935) made loans to help tenant farmers buy their own farms and to enable sharecroppers, tenants, and dust-bowl migrants to move to more productive areas. The Rural Electrification Administration, also started in 1935, made low-interest loans to utility companies and farmers' cooperatives to extend electricity to the 90 percent of rural America that lacked it. By 1941, 40 percent of American farms enjoyed electricity.

The agricultural-recovery program suffered a setback in January 1936 when the Supreme Court declared the Agricultural Adjustment Act unconstitutional. The processing tax that funded the AAA's subsidies, the Court held, was an illegal use of the government's tax power. To replace the AAA, Congress passed a soil-conservation act that paid farmers to plant grasses and legumes instead of soil-depleting crops like wheat and cotton (which happened to be the major surplus commodities).

Organized labor won a key victory in 1935, again thanks to Senator Robert Wagner. Despite FDR's opposition during the New Deal's national-unity phase, Wagner built support for a prolabor law. In 1935, the Supreme Court ruled the NIRA unconstitutional, including Section 7a protecting union members' rights, and FDR called for a labor law that would survive court scrutiny. The **National Labor Relations Act** of July 1935 (the Wagner Act) guaranteed collective-bargaining rights, permitted closed shops (in which all employees must join a union), and outlawed such management tactics as blacklisting union organizers. The law created the National Labor Relations Board (NLRB) to supervise shop elections and deal with labor-law violations. A wave of unionization soon followed.

National Labor Relations Act Measure that furthered industrial unionization

The Second New Deal's more class-conscious thrust shaped other 1935 measures. The Banking Act strengthened the Federal Reserve Board's control over the nation's financial system. The Public Utilities Holding Company Act, targeting the public-utility empires of the 1920s, restricted gas and electric companies to one geographic region. Also in 1935, Roosevelt called for steeper taxes on the rich. With the Wealth Tax Act, Congress raised taxes on corporations and on the well-to-do to a maximum of 75 percent on incomes above $5 million. Although this law had many loopholes and was not quite the "soak the rich" measure some believed, it did express the Second New Deal's more radical spirit.

The Social Security Act of 1935: End of the Second New Deal

The **Social Security Act** of 1935 stands out among New Deal laws for its long-range significance. Drafted by a committee chaired by Frances Perkins, this measure established a mixed federal-state system of workers' pensions, survivors' benefits for victims of industrial accidents, unemployment insurance, and aid for disabled persons and dependent mothers and children. Taxes paid partly by employers and partly by workers (in the form of sums withheld from their paychecks) helped fund the program. This cut in take-home pay contributed to a recession in 1937, but it made sense politically because workers would resist any threat to a pension plan they had contributed to. As FDR put it, "With those taxes in there, no damned politician can ever scrap my social security program."

Social Security Act Measure to establish old-age pensions, unemployment benefits, and care for widows and orphans

The initial Social Security Act paid low benefits and bypassed farmers, domestic workers, and the self-employed. However, it established the principle of federal responsibility for social welfare and laid the foundation for vastly expanded future welfare programs.

As 1935 ended, the Second New Deal was complete. Without embracing the panaceas preached by Coughlin, Townsend, or Long, FDR had addressed the grievances they had exploited. Although conservatives called this phase of the New Deal "antibusiness," FDR always insisted that he had saved capitalism through prudent reform. Business interests remained influential in the 1930s, but the evolving New Deal also responded to other organized interest groups, including labor. And in 1935, with an election looming, New Deal strategists reached farther still, crafting legislation to aid sharecroppers, migrant workers, the disabled, the elderly, and others largely ignored by politicians of the past.

In the process, the New Deal enlarged the government's role in American life, as well as the power of the presidency. Americans began to expect presidents to offer programs and shape the terms of public debate. This decisively altered the power balance between the White House and Congress. Along with specific programs, the New Deal's importance thus also lay in how it enlarged the scope of the presidency and the social role of the state.

The 1936 Roosevelt Landslide and the New Democratic Coalition

FDR confidently faced the 1936 campaign. "There's one issue," he told an aide; "it's myself, and people must be either for me or against me."

The Republican candidate, Kansas governor Alfred Landon, a moderate fiscal conservative, proved an inept campaigner. FDR, by contrast, responded zestfully when Republicans lambasted his alleged dictatorial ambitions or charged that the social security law would require all workers to wear metal dog tags. The forces of "selfishness and greed . . . are united in their hatred for me," he declared at a tumultuous election-eve rally in New York City, "and I welcome their hatred."

In the greatest landslide since 1820, FDR carried every state but Maine and Vermont. The Democrats increased their majorities in Congress. Roosevelt also buried candidates of the Socialist and Communist Parties, as well as of the Union Party (a coalition of Coughlin, Townsend, and Share Our Wealth enthusiasts).

FDR's 1936 election announced the emergence of a new Democratic coalition. Since Reconstruction, the Democrats had counted on three bases of support: the white South, parts of the West, and urban white ethnic voters. FDR retained these centers of strength. He rarely challenged state or local party leaders who produced the votes, whether they supported the New Deal or not. FDR carried the nation's twelve largest cities in 1936. Aided by New Deal relief programs, many city-dwellers idolized Roosevelt. In filling New Deal positions, FDR often turned to the newer urban-immigrant groups, including Catholics and Jews.

Expanding the Democratic base, FDR also courted farmers and union members. Republican midwestern farmers, won over by the New Deal's agricultural program, voted accordingly. Union members, too, joined the Roosevelt bandwagon that year, and unions pumped money into Roosevelt's campaign chest (though far less than business gave the Republicans). FDR's reputation as a "friend of labor" proved unassailable.

African Americans came aboard as well. Although most southern blacks remained disfranchised, northern blacks could vote, and as late as 1932, two-thirds of them voted Republican, the party of Lincoln. The New Deal caused a historic shift in voting trends. In 1936, 76 percent of black voters supported FDR. In economic terms, this shift made sense. Owing mainly to racial discrimination, blacks' unemployment rates in the 1930s surpassed those of the work force as a whole. Thus, jobless blacks benefited heavily from New Deal relief programs.

On issues of racial justice, however, the New Deal's record was mixed at best. Some NRA codes included racially discriminatory clauses, causing black activists to deride the agency as "Negroes Ruined Again," and other New Deal agencies tolerated racial bias. Roosevelt kept aloof from an NAACP campaign

National Portrait Gallery, Smithsonian Museum, Washington, DC/Art Resource, NY

Marian Anderson at the Lincoln Memorial, Painting by Betsy Graves Reyneau

This painting portrays Marian Anderson at the Lincoln Memorial on Easter Sunday, 1939, where her concert drew an audience of seventy-five thousand and was broadcast nationally. Eleanor Roosevelt and Harold Ickes arranged the event after the Daughters of the American Revolution denied the use of Constitution Hall.

to make lynching a federal crime. In 1935 and 1938, he remained passive as anti-lynching bills were narrowly defeated in Congress.

In limited ways, FDR did address racial issues. He worked cautiously to rid New Deal agencies of blatant racism. He appointed more than one hundred African-Americans to policy-level and judicial positions, including educator Mary McLeod Bethune as director of minority affairs in the National Youth Administration. Bethune led the "black cabinet" that served as a link between the New Deal and black organizations. Roosevelt's Supreme Court appointees opposed racial discrimination in cases involving housing, voting rights, and other issues.

The New Deal also supported racial justice in symbolic ways. In 1938, when a meeting of an interracial welfare group in Birmingham, Alabama, was segregated in compliance with local statutes, Mrs. Roosevelt pointedly placed her chair halfway between the white and black delegates. In 1939, when the Daughters of the American Revolution barred a performance by black contralto Marian Anderson in Washington's Constitution Hall, Mrs. Roosevelt and Harold Ickes arranged for an Easter Sunday concert by Anderson at the Lincoln Memorial.

The Roosevelt administration also courted women voters. Molly Dewson led the effort as head of the Democratic Party's women's division. In 1936, fifteen thousand women volunteers distributed flyers describing New Deal programs. However, Dewson did not push a specifically feminist agenda. The New Deal's economic programs, she argued, benefited both sexes. FDR did, however, appoint the first woman cabinet member, the first woman ambassador, and a number of female federal judges. Through Dewson's efforts, the 1936 Democratic platform committee had a fifty-fifty gender balance.

Despite such symbolic gestures and FDR's appointment of a few blacks and women, racial and gender discrimination pervaded American society in the 1930s. Roosevelt, grappling with the depression, did relatively little to change things. That challenge would await a later time.

The Environment and the West

Environmental issues loomed large in the New Deal. While still in the New York Senate, FDR had sought logging regulation to protect wildlife. As president, for example, he strongly supported the Civilian Conservation Corps' program of planting trees, thinning forests, and building hiking trails.

Soil conservation emerged as a major priority. The 1930s dust storms resulted not only from drought, but also from overgrazing and poor farming practices. For decades settlers had used ever more powerful machines to cultivate more land on the Great Plains. They had plowed up the native grasses that anchored the soil, exposing the topsoil to parching winds when drought struck. By the 1930s erosion had destroyed 9 million acres of farmland, with more in jeopardy.

In response, the Department of Agriculture's Soil Conservation Service promoted contour plowing, crop rotation, and soil-strengthening grasses. The Taylor Grazing Act of 1934 restricted the grazing on public lands that had exacerbated the problem. In addition, TVA dams helped control the floods that worsened erosion in the Tennessee valley.

New Deal planners also promoted the national park movement. Washington state's Olympic, Virginia's Shenandoah, and California's Kings Canyon all became national parks in the 1930s. The administration also established some 160 new national wildlife refuges.

The wilderness-preservation movement gained momentum in the 1930s, supported by such groups as the Wilderness Society (1935), started by environmentalist Aldo Leopold and others, and the National Wildlife Federation (1936), funded by firearms makers eager to preserve hunting areas. Pressured by such groups, Congress began to set aside protected wilderness areas.

By later standards, the New Deal's environmental record was spotty. The decade's massive hydroelectric projects, while providing rural families with electricity, had serious ecological consequences. The Grand Coulee Dam, for example, destroyed salmon spawning on much of the Columbia River's tributary system. Other dams disrupted fragile ecosystems and the livelihoods of local residents, particularly Native American communities, who depended on them.

Viewed in context, however, the New Deal's environmental record remains impressive. While coping with a grave economic crisis, the Roosevelt administration focused on environmental issues in a way not seen since the Progressive Era, and not to be seen again for a generation.

The New Deal impact on the West was profound, especially because the federal government owned a third or more of the land in eleven western states. New Deal agencies and laws such as the Soil Conservation Service, the Taylor Grazing Act, and the Farm Security Administration (discussed shortly) set new rules for western agriculture, from prairie wheat fields and cattle ranges to California citrus groves and truck farms dependent on migrant labor.

The PWA and WPA built many large projects in the West, including thousands of public buildings, from courthouses and post offices to tourist facilities such as beautiful Timberline Lodge on Oregon's Mount Hood. Federal assistance also upgraded the highways linking the West to the rest of America, such as Route 66 from Chicago to Los Angeles.

Above all, the PWA in the West built dams—Grand Coulee (KOO-lee) and Bonneville (BAHN-eh-vill) on the Columbia, Shasta on the Sacramento, Glen Canyon on the Colorado, and others. Boulder (later Hoover) Dam on the Colorado, authorized by Congress in 1928, was completed by the PWA. Despite their ecological downside, these great undertakings—among the largest engineering projects in human history—supplied electric power to vast regions while also contributing to flood control, irrigation, and soil conservation. (Las Vegas owed its post–World War II emergence as a gambling and entertainment mecca to power from nearby Hoover Dam.)

A New Deal initiative particularly important to the West was Harold Ickes's National Resources Planning Board, established in 1934. This agency facilitated state and regional planning for such natural resources as water, soil, timber, and minerals. Despite the West's celebrated "rugged individualism," New Deal planning reshaped the public life of the region.

CHECKING IN

- The focus of the Second New Deal shifted to include social justice concerns and attacks on, rather than cooperation with, business.
- Enormous relief projects like those undertaken by the Works Progress Administration characterized the Second New Deal.
- Organized labor won a major victory with the passage of the National Labor Relations Act, which guaranteed collective bargaining and permitted closed shops.
- The Social Security Act set the framework for an expanded social-welfare state.
- In the 1936 election, a new Democratic coalition emerged that would dominate national politics for decades.
- FDR and Congress continued to drag their feet on racial matters, such as lynching, but they promoted conservation and reformed Indian policy.

THE NEW DEAL'S END STAGE, 1937–1939

How did the New Deal end?

Buoyed by his 1936 victory, Roosevelt proposed a controversial restructuring of the Supreme Court. After losing this fight, FDR confronted a stubborn recession and resurgent conservative opposition. With a few measures in 1937–1938, the New Deal ended.

FDR and the Supreme Court

In 1937, the Supreme Court comprised nine elderly men, four of them arch-conservatives who despised the New Deal. Joined by moderates, they had invalidated the NRA, the AAA, and progressive state laws. Roosevelt feared a similar fate for key measures of the Second New Deal, especially the Social Security Act.

In February 1937, FDR proposed a bill that would have allowed the president to appoint an additional Supreme Court member for each justice over age seventy, up to a total of six. Roosevelt blandly insisted that he was concerned about the heavy workload of aging justices, but his political motivation was obvious.

Congress and the public reacted with hostility. The Supreme Court's size (although unspecified in the Constitution) had become almost sacrosanct. Conservatives blasted FDR's "court-packing" scheme as a dangerous power grab. Even many Democrats disapproved. When the Senate voted down the scheme in July, FDR quietly dropped it.

But was it a defeat? Roosevelt's challenge to the Court, plus his 1936 electoral victory, sent powerful political signals that the justices heeded. In spring 1937, the Court upheld several New Deal measures, including the Wagner Act and a state minimum-wage law. Four conservative justices soon retired, enabling FDR to nominate successors of his choice and to create a judicial legacy that would long endure. In subsequent decades, the court proved much more receptive to business regulation and to the protection of individual rights as well as property rights.

The Roosevelt Recession

After showing signs of recovery, the economy dipped ominously in August 1937. Industrial production slumped, and soaring unemployment once again dominated the headlines. This "Roosevelt recession" resulted in part from federal policies that reduced consumer income. Social-security payroll taxes withdrew some $2 billion from circulation. The Federal Reserve Board raised interest rates to forestall inflation, further contracting the money supply. FDR, meanwhile, concerned about mounting deficits, cut back the New Deal relief programs.

Echoing Hoover, FDR assured his cabinet, "Everything will work out . . . if we just sit tight." Meanwhile, however, some advisers embraced John Maynard Keynes's advocacy of deficit spending as the key to recovery. They warned of a political backlash if conditions worsened. Convinced, FDR in April 1938 authorized new relief spending. By late 1938, unemployment declined and industrial output increased. As late as 1939, however, more than 17 percent of the labor force remained jobless.

The Library of Congress

A Camera's-Eye View of Depression-Era America

This 1937 image by Dorothea Lange, a photographer with the Farm Security Administration, pictures migrants from the Texas dust bowl gathered at a roadside camp near Calipatria in southern California.

Final Measures, Growing Opposition

Preoccupied by the Supreme Court fight, the recession, and menacing events abroad (covered in Chapter 25), FDR offered few domestic initiatives after 1936. Congress, however, enacted several significant measures. The Farm Tenancy Act of 1937 created the **Farm Security Administration (FSA)** to replace the Resettlement Administration. The FSA made low-interest loans to help tenant farmers and sharecroppers become farm owners. However, the FSA often rejected the poorest farmers' loan applications as too risky, weakening the program's impact.

Farm Security Administration (FSA) Made low-interest loans to help tenant farmers and sharecroppers become more self-sufficient

The FSA operated camps offering clean, sanitary shelter and medical services to impoverished migrant farm workers. The FSA also commissioned gifted photographers to record the lives of tenants, migrants, and uprooted dust-bowl families. These FSA photographs helped shape a gritty documentary style that pervaded 1930s popular culture.

Other measures set precedents for the future. For example, the Housing Act of 1937 appropriated $500 million for urban slum clearance and public housing. The

Fair Labor Standards Act of 1938 banned child labor and established a national minimum wage (initially 40 cents an hour) and a maximum workweek of forty hours. Despite many loopholes, the law improved conditions for some and underscored the government's role in regulating abusive workplace conditions.

Fair Labor Standards Act Federal regulation setting a national minimum wage and a maximum workweek

In a final stab at raising farm income, the Agricultural Adjustment Act of 1938 created a mechanism by which the government, in years of big harvests and low prices, would make loans to farmers and warehouse their surplus crops. When prices rose, farmers could sell these commodities and repay their loans. This complicated system set the framework of federal farm price support for decades. Overall, large-scale growers, not small family farms, benefited the most from subsidy payments.

The New Deal's slower pace after 1935 also reflected the rise of an anti-New Deal congressional coalition of Republicans and conservative southern Democrats. In 1937, this coalition rejected FDR's proposal to reorganize the executive branch. The conservative coalition also slashed relief appropriations, cut corporate taxes, and killed the Federal Theatre Project, a conservative target because of its alleged radicalism. Suspecting that FDR used WPA staff members for political purposes, conservatives in 1939 passed the Hatch Act, forbidding federal workers from participating in electoral campaigns.

Although FDR campaigned actively in 1938's midterm election, the Republicans gained heavily in the House and Senate, in addition to adding thirteen governorships. Roosevelt also tried to purge several prominent anti–New Deal Democratic senators in 1938, but his major targets all won reelection. Highlighting foreign affairs in his January 1939 State of the Union message, FDR proposed no new domestic measures and merely noted the need to "preserve our reforms." The New Deal was over.

CHECKING IN

- After reelection, FDR suffered a major setback in his "court-packing" scheme.
- An overconfident FDR reduced federal spending in 1937, leading to higher unemployment.
- A coalition of Republicans and conservative Democrats challenged the New Deal and blocked substantial measures.
- By 1939, the administration's focus had shifted to foreign affairs.

SOCIAL CHANGE AND SOCIAL ACTION IN THE 1930S

How did the depression and the New Deal affect specific social groups in the United States?

American life in the 1930s involved more than politics. The depression affected everyone, including the jobless and their families, working women, and all age groups. For industrial workers, African-Americans, a growing Hispanic community, and Native Americans, the crisis brought hard times but also encouraged organized resistance to exploitation and brought new legislative initiatives.

The Depression's Psychological and Social Impact

The depression brought untold human suffering. Unemployment never fell below about 14 percent, and for much of the decade it ran considerably higher. A quarter of all farm families sought public or private assistance during the 1930s. Those who were employed often had to take jobs below their qualifications. For example, college alumni pumped gas, business-school graduates sold furniture, and a retired navy captain might only find work as a movie theater usher.

Psychologists described "unemployment shock": jobless persons who walked the streets seeking work and then lay awake at night worrying. When their shoes wore out, cardboard or folded newspapers had to serve as replacements. Women's magazines described low-cost meals and other budget-trimming strategies. As Caroline Bird wrote in *The Invisible Scar* (1966), the depression for many boiled down to "a dull misery in the bones."

Senator Robert Wagner called the working woman in the depression years "the first orphan in the storm." Indeed, for the 25 percent of women employed in 1930, the depression brought hard times. The female jobless rate exceeded 20 percent for much of the decade. Working women often took lower-paying jobs. Laid-off factory workers became waitresses. Jobless men competed with women even for such traditional "women's work" as library posts and school teaching.

Married women workers endured harsh criticism. Although most worked out of economic necessity, they were accused of stealing men's jobs. Even Labor Secretary Frances Perkins urged married women to leave the labor market so more men could work. School boards sometimes fired married women teachers.

Women workers also faced wage discrimination. In 1939, women teachers earned nearly 20 percent less than male teachers with comparable experience. Some NRA codes authorized lower pay for women. The minimum-wage provision of the Fair Labor Standards Act did not include the more than 2 million women who worked for wages in private households.

The late 1930s' unionization drive had mixed effects on women workers. Some in the mass-production industries benefited, but the most heavily female sectors—textiles, clerical, service, and sales—resisted unionization. Despite the roadblocks, the percentage of wage-earning married women increased from under 12 percent to nearly 16 percent as married women took jobs to augment depressed family incomes.

The depression profoundly affected family life. The birthrate fell in the early 1930s as married couples postponed starting a family and birth-control devices became more readily available. The U.S. population in the 1930s grew by only 7 percent, in contrast to an average of 20 percent per decade from 1900 to 1930.

Family survival posed major challenges. Parents patched clothes, stretched food resources, and sought public assistance when necessary. In homes with a tradition of strong male authority, the husband's loss of a job could prove devastating. Desertions increased, and the divorce rate spiked, hitting a then all-time high by 1940.

The depression spared neither old nor young. For example, bank failures wiped out the savings of older Americans. By 1935, a million citizens over sixty-five were on relief. As for young people, one observer compared them to a team of runners waiting for a starting gun that never sounded. High-school enrollment increased as many youths, lacking job prospects, stayed in school. The marriage rate declined as anxious young people postponed this step. Depression-era children wrote sad letters to Eleanor Roosevelt. A thirteen-year-old Arkansas girl wrote, "I have to stay out of school because I have no books or clothes to ware."

Out of necessity, many families rediscovered traditional skills. They painted their own houses and repaired their own cars. Home baking and canning revived. Many would later recall the 1930s as a time of simple, inexpensive pleasures and neighborly sharing of scant resources.

For the neediest—among them blacks, Hispanics, and southern sharecroppers—the depression imposed added misery on poverty-blighted lives. In *Native Son* (1940), novelist Richard Wright vividly portrayed the desperate conditions of family life in Chicago's black slums. Yet hope survived. Emotional resilience, habits of mutual aid, and survival skills honed over the years helped poor families cope.

Industrial Workers Unionize

Of America's 7.7 million factory workers in 1930, most remained unorganized. Major industries such as steel, automobiles, and textiles resisted workers' attempts to unionize. The conservative mood of the 1920s further weakened the labor movement.

But hard times and a favorable government climate bred a new labor militancy in the 1930s. The Wagner Act's guarantee of workers' rights to organize energized some American Federation of Labor (AFL) leaders. In November 1935 John L. Lewis of the United Mine Workers (UMW) and Sidney Hillman of the Amalgamated Clothing Workers, chafing at the AFL's slowness in organizing factory workers, started the Committee for Industrial Organization (CIO) within the AFL. CIO activists preached unionization in Pittsburgh's steel mills, Detroit's auto plants, and southern textile factories. Unlike the narrowly exclusive AFL unions, CIO unions welcomed all workers in a particular industry, regardless of race, gender, or skill level.

In 1936, a CIO-sponsored organizing committee geared up for a major strike to unionize the steel industry. (In fact, Lewis had already secretly negotiated a settlement with the head of U.S. Steel.) In March 1937, U.S. Steel recognized the union, raised wages, and accepted a forty-hour workweek. Other big steel companies followed, and soon four hundred thousand steelworkers signed union cards.

Other CIO organizers targeted General Motors, an anti-union stronghold. Their leader was a redheaded young autoworker and labor activist, Walter Reuther (ROOther). In December 1936, employees at GM's two body plants in Flint, Michigan, stopped work and peacefully occupied the factories, paralyzing GM's production by their "sit-down strike." GM's management responded by calling in local police to harass the sit-down strikers, sending spies to union meetings, and threatening to fire strikers. A January 1937 showdown with the police at one of the body plants led to the formation of the Women's Emergency Brigade, whose members remained on twenty-four-hour alert for picket duty or to surround the plants in case of police raids.

GM asked the Roosevelt administration and Michigan's governor to send troops to expel the strikers by force. Both officials declined. Although FDR disapproved of the sit-down tactic, he refused to intervene. On February 11, GM signed a contract recognizing the United Automobile Workers (UAW). As Chrysler fell into line also, the UAW soon boasted more than four hundred thousand members. Unionization of the electrical and rubber industries advanced as well.

In 1938, the Committee for Industrial Organization left the AFL to become the **Congress of Industrial Organizations,** a 2-million-member association of industrial unions. In response, the AFL began to adapt to the changed nature of the labor force. Union membership shot up from under 3 million in 1933 to more than 8 million in 1941.

Congress of Industrial Organizations Counterpart of the AFL, but for unskilled industrial workers

Some big corporations resisted. Henry Ford hated unions, and his tough lieutenant Harry Bennett organized a squad of union-busting thugs to fight the UAW. In 1937, Bennett's men beat Walter Reuther and other UAW officials outside Ford's plant near Detroit. Not until 1941 did Ford yield to union pressure.

The Republic Steel Company, headed by a union hater named Tom Girdler, also dug in. Even after U.S. Steel signed with the CIO, Republic and other smaller companies, known collectively as "Little Steel," resisted. In May 1937, workers in twenty-seven Little Steel plants, including Republic's factory in South Chicago, walked off the job. On May 30, Memorial Day, strikers approached over 250 police officers guarding the plant. Someone threw a large stick at the police, who opened fire, killing four strikers and wounding scores. An investigative committee condemned the killings as "clearly avoidable." In 1941, under growing pressure, the Little Steel companies, including Republic, finally accepted the CIO union.

Another holdout was the textile industry, whose more than six hundred thousand workers, mostly in the South and 40 percent female, generally earned very low wages and had no recourse against autocratic bosses. In 1934, the AFL-affiliated United Textile Workers launched a new drive. Some four hundred thousand workers went on strike, but the mill owners fought back. Several strikers were killed and thousands arrested. The strike failed, and the 1930s ended with most textile workers still unorganized.

The union movement bypassed low-paid workers—domestics, farm workers, department store clerks, restaurant and laundry workers—who tended to be women, blacks, or recent immigrants. More than three-quarters of all nonfarm workers remained unorganized in 1940. Nonetheless, the unionization of many industrial workers represents one of the decade's most memorable achievements.

Labor Organizing, 1930s-Style

Walter Reuther (left) and Richard Frankensteen of the United Auto Workers appear here after their beating by Ford Motor Company security guards, Detroit, May 1937.

Archives of Labor and Urban Affairs / Wayne State University

Why did powerful corporations yield to unionization after years of resistance? Workers' militancy and union organizers' tactical skill were crucial, but so was a changed government climate. Corporations had once routinely called on the government to help break strikes. Although this still happened in the 1930s, as in the textile-industry strike, the Roosevelt administration and state officials generally refused to play the role of strikebreaker. New Deal labor laws made clear that Washington would no longer automatically back management in labor disputes. Once corporate managers realized this, unionization often followed.

Organized labor's successes in the later 1930s concealed some complex tensions. A core of activists, including communists and socialists, led the unionizing drive. Most rank-and-file workers were not political radicals; however, once the CIO's militant minority showed the effectiveness of picket lines and sit-down strikes, workers signed up by the thousands. As they did, the radical organizers lost influence, and the unions became more conservative.

Blacks and Hispanic Americans Resist Racism and Exploitation

The depression also stirred activism within the African-American and Hispanic communities. Although black migration northward slowed in the 1930s, four hundred thousand southern blacks moved to northern cities in the decade. By 1940, nearly one-quarter of America's 12 million blacks lived in the urban North. Rural or urban, life was hard. Black tenant farmers and sharecroppers often faced eviction. Although some black industrial workers benefited from the CIO's nondiscriminatory policy, workplace racism remained a fact of life.

Over one hundred blacks died by lynching in the 1930s, and other miscarriages of justice continued, especially in the South. In 1931 an all-white jury in Scottsboro, Alabama, sentenced eight black youths to death on highly dubious charges of rape. In 1935, after heavy publicity and an aggressive defense, the Supreme Court ordered a new trial for the "Scottsboro Boys" because they had been denied legal counsel and blacks had been excluded from the jury. Five of the group were again convicted, however, and served long prison terms.

However, rising activism signaled changes ahead. The NAACP battled in courts and legislatures for voting rights and against lynching and segregation. The Urban League campaigned with boycotts and picket lines against businesses in black neighborhoods that employed only whites. In March 1935, hostility toward white-owned businesses in Harlem, fueled by anger over racism and joblessness, ignited a riot that caused an estimated $200 million in damage and left three blacks dead.

The Communist Party publicized lynchings and racial discrimination, and supplied lawyers for the "Scottsboro Boys," as part of a depression-era recruitment effort in the black community. But despite a few notable recruits (including the novelist Richard Wright), few blacks joined the party.

Other minority groups also faced discrimination. For example, California continued to restrict land-ownership by Japanese-Americans. In 1934, Congress limited annual immigration from the Philippines (still a U.S. possession) to fifty—lower than that for any other nation. Congress also offered free travel "home" for Filipinos long settled in the United States.

The more than 2 million Hispanic-Americans faced trying times as well. Some were citizens with ancestral roots in the Southwest, but most were recent arrivals from Mexico or Caribbean islands, such as Cuba and Puerto Rico (a U.S. holding whose residents were and are American citizens). Whereas the Caribbean immigrants settled in East Coast cities, most Mexican newcomers worked as migratory agricultural laborers in the Southwest and elsewhere, or in midwestern steel or meatpacking plants.

As the depression deepened, Mexican-born residents faced mounting hostility. "Okies" fleeing the dust bowl competed for jobs with Hispanic farm workers. By 1937, over half of Arizona's cotton workers were out-of-staters who had supplanted Mexican-born laborers. With their migratory work patterns disrupted, Mexican-Americans poured into the barrios (Hispanic neighborhoods) of southwestern cities. Lacking work, half a million Mexicans returned to their native land in the 1930s. Although some did so voluntarily, immigration officials and local authorities expelled thousands. Mexican-American farm workers who remained faced appalling conditions and near-starvation wages. A labor organization called the Confederación de Uniones de Campesinos y Obreros Mexicanos (Confederation of Unions of Mexican Workers and Farm Laborers) emerged from a 1933 strike by grape workers. More strikes erupted in 1935–1936 on farms across the state.

Organizations like the citrus-growers' marketing cooperative Sunkist fought the unions, sometimes with violence. In October 1933, bullets ripped into a cotton pickers' union hall in Pixley, California, killing two men and wounding others. Resisting intimidation, the strikers won a 20 percent pay increase, and others achieved a few successes, too. These strikes awakened at least some Americans to the plight of one of the nation's most exploited groups.

A New Deal for Native Americans

The 1930s also revived attention to the nation's 330,000 Native Americans, most of whom endured poverty, scant education, and poor health care. The Dawes Severalty Act of 1887 (see Chapter 17) dissolved the tribes as legal entities, allocated some tribal lands to individuals, and sold the rest. By the early 1930s, whites owned about two-thirds of the land that Native Americans had possessed in 1887. Although Indians gained voting rights in 1924, this did little to improve their lot.

In the 1920s a reform movement arose. One reformer, John Collier, who had lived among the Pueblo Indians of New Mexico, founded the American Indian Defense Association in 1923 to reverse the Dawes Act approach and to revitalize traditional Indian life. Appointed commissioner of Indian affairs in 1933, Collier cadged funds from New Deal agencies to build schools, hospitals, and irrigation systems on Indian reservations and to preserve sites of cultural importance. The Civilian Conservation Corps employed twelve thousand Indian youths to work on projects on Indian lands.

Indian Reorganization Act Effort during the New Deal to restore the sovereignty and viability of Indian tribes

Pursuing his vision, Collier drafted a bill to halt tribal land sales and restore the remaining unallocated lands to tribal control. Collier's bill also envisioned tribal councils with broad governing powers and required Indian schools to teach Native American history and handicrafts. The bill sparked opposition. Some Indian leaders criticized it as a plan to transform the reservations into living museums and to treat Native Americans as exotic and backward. Successful Indian property owners and entrepreneurs rejected the bill's tribalist assumptions. The bill did, indeed, reflect the idealism of well-meaning outsiders rather than the views of the nation's diverse Native American groups.

The **Indian Reorganization Act** of 1934, a compromise measure, halted the sale of tribal lands and enabled tribes to regain title to unallocated lands. But Congress scaled back Collier's proposals for tribal self-government and dropped measures to renew tribal culture. A majority of tribes approved the law, as required for it to take effect, but opinion was divided. Still, the restoration of tribes as legal entities laid the groundwork for later tribal business ventures as well as tribal lawsuits seeking to enforce long-violated treaty rights.

CHECKING IN

- The depression profoundly, and negatively, affected women in the work force.
- Families struggled to cope economically and psychologically.
- Now under government protection, industrial unions like the United Auto Workers organized and grew strong.
- Blacks, often the last hired and first fired, continued to face discrimination, injustice, and even violence.
- Migrant workers were hard hit by the depression as well as by competition from "Okies" and other displaced farmers.

THE AMERICAN CULTURAL SCENE IN THE 1930S

What key developments shaped American culture in the 1930s?

Hard times and the New Deal shaped American cultural life in the 1930s. While radio and the movies offered escapist fare, novelists, artists, playwrights, and photographers responded to the crisis as well. As the decade wore on, a more positive and affirmative tone in cultural expressions reflected both the renewed hope of the New Deal and apprehension about events abroad.

Avenues of Escape: Radio and the Movies

The standardization of mass culture continued in the 1930s. Each evening millions of Americans gathered around their radios to listen to news, musical programs, and comedy shows. Radio humor flourished when the real world was grim.

So, too, did the fifteen-minute afternoon dramas known as soap operas (for the soap companies that sponsored them). Despite their assembly-line quality, these daily dollops of romance and melodrama won a devoted audience, mostly housewives. Identifying with the troubled radio heroines, female listeners gained at least temporary escape from their own difficulties. As one put it, "I can get through the day better when I hear they have sorrows, too."

The movies were also extremely popular, and most people could still afford the twenty-five-cent admission. In 1939, 65 percent of Americans went to the movies at least once a week. Films of the early 1930s like *I Am a Fugitive from a Chain Gang* (1932) captured the grimness of the early depression. The popular Marx Brothers movies reflected the uncertainty of the Hoover years. In comedies like *Animal Crackers* (1930) and *Duck Soup* (1933), these vaudeville troupers of German-Jewish immigrant origins ridiculed authority and satirized the established order.

After Roosevelt took office, Warner Brothers studio (with close ties to the administration) made several topical films that presented the New Deal in a favorable light. These included *Wild Boys of the Road* (1933), about unemployed youth; *Massacre* (1934), on the mistreatment of Indians; and *Black Fury* (1935), dealing with striking coal miners.

Early thirties' gangster movies, inspired by real-life criminals like Al Capone, presented a different style of film realism. Films like *Little Caesar* (1930) and *The Public Enemy* (1931) offered gritty images of depression America: menacing streets, forbidding industrial sites, and gunfights between rival gangs. When civic groups protested the glorification of crime, Hollywood made police and "G-men" (FBI agents) the heroes, while retaining the violence. The movie gangsters played by Edward G. Robinson and James Cagney, variants of the Horatio Alger hero battling adversity, appealed to depression-era moviegoers.

Above all, Hollywood offered escape from depression-era realities. Musicals such as *Gold Diggers* in 1933 (with its theme song, "We're in the Money") offered dancing, music, and cheerful plots involving the triumph of pluck over adversity. In Frank Capra's *Mr. Deeds Goes to Town* (1936) and *Mr. Smith Goes to Washington* (1939), virtuous heroes representing "the people" vanquish entrenched interests. When color movies arrived in the late 1930s, they seemed an omen of better times ahead.

African-Americans appeared in 1930s' movies, if at all, mostly as stereotypes: the scatterbrained maid in *Gone with the Wind* (1939), the indulgent house servant in *The Little Colonel* (1935), or the slow-witted "Stepin Fetchit" played in many movies by black actor Lincoln Perry, for example. In representing women, Hollywood offered mixed messages. While some 1930s' movie heroines found fulfillment in marriage and domesticity, other films challenged the stereotype. Katharine Hepburn portrayed independent-minded women in such films as *Spitfire* (1934) and *A Woman Rebels* (1936). Similarly, Mae West, brassy and openly sexual, mocked conventional stereotypes in *I'm No Angel* (1933) and other 1930s hits.

The Later 1930s: Opposing Fascism, Reaffirming Traditional Values

The 1930s ended on a cautiously upbeat note. America had survived the depression. The social fabric remained whole; revolution had not come. As other societies collapsed into dictatorships, U.S. democracy endured. Writers, composers, and other cultural creators reflected the changed mood.

Popular Front Coalition of liberal, communist elements against fascism

A movement known as the **Popular Front** influenced this shift. In 1935 Russian dictator Joseph Stalin (STAHL-in), fearing attack by Nazi (NAHT-zee) Germany, called for a worldwide alliance, or Popular Front, against Adolf Hitler and his Italian ally in fascism (FASH-ism), Benito Mussolini (ben-EE-toh moos-soh-LEE-nee). Parroting the new Soviet line, U.S. communists who in the early 1930s had attacked FDR and the New Deal now praised Roosevelt and summoned writers and intellectuals to the antifascist cause. Many noncommunists, alarmed by developments in Europe, responded.

The high-water mark of the Popular Front came during the Spanish Civil War of 1936–1939. In July 1936, Spanish fascist general Francisco Franco revolted against Spain's legally elected left-wing government. With military aid from Hitler and Mussolini, Franco won backing from Spanish monarchists, landowners, and industrialists, and from the Roman Catholic hierarchy.

In America, writers, artists, and intellectuals who backed the Popular Front rallied to support the anti-Franco Spanish Loyalists (those loyal to the elected government). The novelist Ernest Hemingway, who visited Spain in 1936–1937, expressed a newfound sense of worthwhile purpose in *For Whom the Bell Tolls* (1940), the story of a young American volunteer who dies while fighting with the Loyalists.

The Popular Front collapsed in August 1939 when the Soviet Union and Nazi Germany signed a nonaggression pact. Overnight, enthusiasm for joining with communists under the "antifascism" banner faded. But while it lasted, the Popular Front influenced U.S. culture and alerted Americans to threatening events abroad.

The New Deal's achievements also contributed to the cultural shift of the later 1930s. The satire and cynicism of the 1920s and early 1930s yielded to a more hopeful view of grass-roots America. In John Steinbeck's best-selling novel *The Grapes of Wrath* (1939), an uprooted dust-bowl family, the Joads, make their difficult way from Oklahoma to California, revealing the strength shown by ordinary people in depression America. As Ma Joad tells her son Tom, "They ain't gonna wipe us out. Why, we're the people—we go on."

In 1936 writer James Agee and photographer Walker Evans spent weeks living with Alabama sharecroppers to research a magazine article. The result was *Let Us Now Praise Famous Men* (1941). Enhanced by Evans's unforgettable photographs, Agee's masterpiece evoked the strength and decency of those living on society's margins.

On the stage, Thornton Wilder's *Our Town* (1938) lovingly portrayed early twentieth-century life in a New England town. Composers also reflected this spirit of cultural nationalism. In *Billy the Kid* (1938) and other compositions, Aaron Copland drew upon American legends and folk melodies. George Gershwin adapted a popular 1920s play about black street life in Charleston, South Carolina, for his opera *Porgy and Bess* (1935).

Jazz gained popularity thanks to swing, a danceable style popularized by the big bands of Benny Goodman, Count Basie, Duke Ellington, and others. White clarinetist Benny Goodman challenged the color line in jazz, including black musicians in his orchestra. A turning point in the acceptance of jazz came in 1938, when Goodman's band performed at New York's Carnegie Hall, a citadel of high culture.

The later 1930s also saw a heightened interest in regional literature, painting, and folk art. Zora Neale Hurston's novel *Their Eyes Were Watching God* (1937) portrayed a black woman's search for fulfillment in rural Florida. In addition, William Faulkner's *Absalom, Absalom!* (1936) continued the saga of his mythic Yoknapatawpha County in Mississippi. Painters Thomas Hart Benton of Missouri, John Steuart Curry of Kansas, and Iowa's Grant Wood explored traditional and regional themes in their work.

Galleries displayed folk paintings, Amish quilts, and New England weather vanes. A 1939 show at New York's Museum of Modern Art featured seventy-nine-year-old Anna "Grandma" Moses of Hoosick Falls, New York, whose memory paintings of her farm girlhood enjoyed great popularity.

The surge of cultural nationalism heightened interest in American history. Visitors flocked to historical re-creations such as Henry Ford's Greenfield Village near Detroit and Colonial Williamsburg in Virginia. Texans restored the Alamo in San Antonio, the "Cradle of Texas Liberty." Historical novels like Margaret Mitchell's Civil War epic *Gone with the Wind* (1936) became best sellers. These restorations and fictions often distorted history. Colonial Williamsburg and Mitchell's novel downplayed or romanticized slavery. And "Texas Liberty" resonated differently for the state's Hispanic, African-American, and Indian peoples than it did for the white patriotic organizations that venerated the Alamo.

Streamlining and a World's Fair: Corporate America's Utopian Vision

A design style called streamlining also shaped the visual culture of the late 1930s. This style originated in the 1920s when industrial designers, inspired by the airplane, introduced smoothly flowing curves into the design of commercial products. Streamlining appealed to consumers—a vital business consideration during the depression. When Sears Roebuck streamlined its Coldspot refrigerators, sales surged. As products ranging from house trailers to pencil sharpeners and cigarette lighters emerged in sleek new forms, streamlining helped corporate America rebuild its image and present itself as the benevolent shaper of a better future.

Under the theme "The World of Tomorrow," the 1939 New York World's Fair represented the high point of the streamlining vogue and corporate America's public-relations blitz. Inside the fair's hallmark Perisphere, a giant globe, visitors found "Democracity," a revolving diorama showing a harmonious city of the future.

"The World of Tomorrow" was also a technological utopia, filled with such wonders as televisions and automatic dishwashers. The hit of the fair was General

Motors' Futurama, which gave visitors a vision of the United States in the distant year 1960—a nation of complex multilane highways with stacked interchanges. A brilliant public-relations investment, Futurama built support for the interstate highway system that would soon become a reality. Forget the depression and the bitter auto-workers' strike, GM's exhibit seemed to whisper; behold the exciting future we are preparing for you.

The fair epitomized hopefulness stirring in America as the 1930s ended, but the hopefulness was tinged with fear, as danger loomed beyond the seas. The anxiety triggered by the menacing world situation surfaced on October 31, 1938, when CBS Radio aired an adaptation of H. G. Wells's science fiction story *War of the Worlds,* directed by Orson Welles. In realistic detail, the broadcast reported the landing of a spaceship in New Jersey and the advance of aliens with deadly ray guns toward New York. The show sparked a panic as horrified listeners believed the end was at hand. Beneath the terror lay a more rational fear: of approaching war. For a decade, as America battled the depression, the international situation steadily worsened. By October 1938, another European war loomed on the horizon.

The panic triggered by Orson Welles's Halloween prank quickly faded, but the anxieties aroused by the all-too-real dangers abroad only escalated. By the time the New York World's Fair offered its hopeful vision of the future, the actual world of 1939 looked bleak indeed.

CHECKING IN

- During the depression, radio and the movies offered escapist fare to millions of Americans.
- The Popular Front briefly linked noncommunist and communist intellectuals.
- A positive mood emerged by the late 1930s in works like *The Grapes of Wrath.*
- The success of the New Deal and looming international problems fed into a rising sense of cultural nationalism.
- By 1939, Americans looked to the future with optimism, embodied in the World's Fair, but their optimism was mixed with anxiety about world affairs.

Chapter Summary

What caused the Great Depression, and how did President Hoover respond? (page 579)

Hoover's emphasis on voluntarism proved inadequate to the magnitude of problems caused by the Great Depression, but he would not move beyond that to extend direct aid to people. Disenchanted Americans sneered at "Hoovervilles" and were appalled by the way the administration responded to the bonus march.

What strategy guided the early New Deal, and what problems and challenges arose in 1934–1935? (page 583)

Initially, Roosevelt welcomed big business in his depression-fighting coalition. The first hundred days of FDR's term saw passage of measures intended to achieve industrial recovery, agricultural recovery, and short-term relief: the Federal Emergency Relief Act, the National Industrial Recovery Act, the Agricultural Adjustment Act, the Tennessee Valley Authority, and the Civilian Conservation Corps. The New Deal also featured reform measures, such as the Securities and Exchange Commission and the Federal Deposit Insurance Corporation.

KEY TERMS

Reconstruction Finance Corporation (RFC) *(p. 581)*

Eleanor Roosevelt *(p. 583)*

Frances Perkins *(p. 583)*

Civilian Conservation Corps (CCC) *(p. 585)*

Federal Emergency Relief Act *(p. 585)*

Agricultural Adjustment Administration (AAA) *(p. 585)*

National Recovery Administration (NRA) *(p. 586)*

Tennessee Valley Authority (TVA) *(p. 586)*

Harry Hopkins *(p. 587)*

What key measures and setbacks marked the course of the New Deal from 1935 on? (page 589)

From 1935 on, during the so-called Second New Deal, federal policies became more concerned with social justice and less interested in cooperating with business. Relief projects, such as those of the Works Progress Administration, gave jobs to millions of people, and the National Labor Relations Act opened the way for the success of industrial unionization. The Social Security Act established the framework for the modern social-welfare state. FDR's smashing reelection victory in 1936 solidified the Democratic coalition he had forged, including the white South, farmers, urban ethnics, union members, and African-Americans.

How did the New Deal end? (page 595)

The failure of FDR's "court-packing" scheme and the arrival of a recession in 1937 slowed the momentum of the New Deal, and a congressional coalition of Republicans and conservative Democrats made passage of major legislation virtually impossible. The rise of fascism and Nazism in Europe, and Japanese aggression in Asia, took center stage. By 1938, facing rising conservative opposition and menaces abroad, the New Deal's reformist energies faded.

How did the depression and the New Deal affect specific social groups in the United States? (page 597)

Families struggled economically and psychologically during the depression. Industrial workers, with the backing of the administration, organized unions in previously unassailable sectors, such as automobiles. Women and African-Americans continued to face discrimination, while migrant workers were also hard hit. For Native Americans, New Deal legislation restored tribes' legal status, laying the groundwork for future enterprises and treaty claims.

What key developments shaped American culture in the 1930s? (page 603)

American culture in the 1930s reflected the decade's economic and social realities. While the movies and radio offered diversion, writers, painters, and other cultural creators initially expressed despair and cynicism over capitalism's failure. But as New Deal programs assisted writers and artists, and as foreign threats loomed in the later 1930s, the cultural climate grew more patriotic and affirmative.

KEY TERMS continued

Works Progress Administration (WPA) *(p. 589)*

National Labor Relations Act *(p. 590)*

Social Security Act *(p. 591)*

Farm Security Administration (FSA) *(p. 596)*

Fair Labor Standards Act *(p. 597)*

Congress of Industrial Organizations *(p. 599)*

Indian Reorganization Act *(p. 602)*

Popular Front *(p. 604)*

Go to the CourseMate website at **www.cengagebrain.com** for additional study tools and review materials—including audio and video clips—for this chapter.

CHAPTER 25

Americans and a World in Crisis

1933–1945

W. Eugene Smith/Time Life Pictures/Getty Images

Okinawa, 1945

CHAPTER PREVIEW

To most Americans, World War II was "the good war." Unlike the nations of Asia and Europe, the United States suffered no invasion of its homeland, no bombing of its cities, and no mass killing of its civilians. The war lifted the United States out of the Great Depression and propelled many into the middle class, and it gave unprecedented opportunities to millions of minorities and women. That "Good War," however, had little to do with E. B. Sledge's experience fighting in the South Pacific.

E. B. Sledge's harrowing wartime experiences drove him to write a memoir of unrelenting horror, *With the Old Breed.* Describing the battles of Peleliu and Okinawa, Sledge depicts a brutal landscape of war without mercy. He once saw a fellow marine use a knife to try to extract the gold teeth of a wounded Japanese soldier, even as the man thrashed in pain. On Peleliu, unable to reclaim the bodies of his comrades from the battlefield, he watched helplessly as buddies oozed into a wasteland of mud and excreta, land crabs feeding on them. On Okinawa's Half Moon Hill, he dreamed that the decomposed bodies of marines sprawled about him slowly rose, unblinkingly stared at him, and said, "It is over for us who are dead, but you must struggle, and will carry the memories all your life."

The wartime experiences of few Americans matched those of Sledge. Yet World War II fundamentally changed national institutions and transformed individual behavior. The war was a watershed, separating what had come before from what would become the dominant patterns of postwar life. It created a new world order that left the United States at the pinnacle of its power and sowed the seeds of a postwar crisis. It was indeed, in Eleanor Roosevelt's words, "no ordinary time."

THE UNITED STATES IN A MENACING WORLD, 1933–1939

How did the American people and government respond to the international crises of the 1930s?

Apart from improving relations with Latin America, the early administration of President Franklin D. Roosevelt (FDR) remained largely aloof from the crises in the world. Americans reacted ambivalently as Italy, Germany, and Japan grew more aggressive. Millions of Americans, determined not to stumble into war again, supported neutrality. Only a minority wanted the United States to help embattled democracies abroad. All the while, the world slid toward the precipice.

Nationalism and the Good Neighbor

President Roosevelt at first put American economic interests above all else and showed little interest in free trade or international economic cooperation. He did, however, commit himself to an internationalist approach in Latin America, where bitterness over decades of "Yankee imperialism" ran high. FDR announced a **"Good Neighbor" policy,** renouncing any nation's right to intervene in the affairs of another. To that end, Roosevelt withdrew the last U.S. troops from Haiti and the Dominican Republic, and terminated the Platt Amendment, which had given the United States its right to intervene in Cuba since 1901.

"Good Neighbor" policy FDR's less interventionist policy toward Latin America

Cuba and Mexico provided major tests of the Good Neighbor policy. In Cuba, an economic crisis in 1933 brought to power a leftist regime that the United States opposed. Instead of sending in the marines, the United States provided indirect aid to a conservative revolt led by Fulgencio Batista in 1934 that overthrew the radical government. American economic assistance would then allow Batista to retain power until his overthrow by Fidel Castro in 1959. In Mexico, a reform government came to power in 1936 and promptly nationalized several oil companies owned by U.S. and British corporations. While insisting on fair compensation, the United States refrained from military intervention.

Chronology

1931–1932	Japan invades Manchuria
1933	Adolf Hitler becomes chancellor of Germany and assumes dictatorial powers
1934–1936	Nye Committee investigations
1935–1937	Neutrality Acts
1937	Japan invades China
1938	Germany annexes Austria; Munich Pact gives Sudetenland to Germany; *Kristallnacht,* night of Nazi terror against German and Austrian Jews
1939	Nazi-Soviet Pact; Germany invades Poland; World War II begins
1940	Germany conquers most of western Europe; Germany, Italy, and Japan sign the Tripartite Pact; Selective Service Act; Franklin Roosevelt elected to an unprecedented third term
1941	Lend-Lease Act; Roosevelt establishes the Fair Employment Practices Commission (FEPC); Germany invades the Soviet Union; Japan attacks Pearl Harbor; the United States enters World War II; War Powers Act
1942	Battles of Coral Sea and Midway halt Japanese offensive; internment of Japanese-Americans; Revenue Act expands graduated income-tax system; Allies invade North Africa (Operation TORCH); first successful atomic chain reaction; CORE founded
1943	Soviet victory in Battle of Stalingrad; coal miners strike; Smith-Connally War Labor Disputes Act; Detroit and Los Angeles race riots; Allied invasion of Italy; Roosevelt, Churchill, and Stalin meet in Tehran
1944	Allied invasion of France (Operation Overlord); U.S. forces invade the Philippines; Roosevelt wins fourth term; Battle of the Bulge
1945	Yalta Conference; Battles of Iwo Jima and Okinawa; Roosevelt dies; Harry S Truman becomes president; Germany surrenders; Truman, Churchill, and Stalin meet in Potsdam; United States drops atomic bombs on Hiroshima and Nagasaki; Japan surrenders

Although the Good Neighbor policy did not end U.S. interference in Latin American affairs, it did substitute economic leverage for heavy-handed intervention. The better relations fostered by FDR would help the United States pursue hemispheric solidarity in World War II, and later in the Cold War.

The Rise of Aggressive States in Europe and Asia

Benito Mussolini Leader of Italy; founder of fascism

Adolf Hitler Dictatorial leader of resurgent, expansionist Germany

Nazi party Hitler's political party; stressed fascism and anti-Semitism

Meanwhile, powerful forces raged across much of the world. As early as 1922, Italy's economic problems and social unrest had opened the way for **Benito Mussolini** and his Fascist party to seize power in Rome. The regime swiftly suppressed dissent and imposed one-party rule.

The rise of **Adolf Hitler** in Germany proved more menacing. Hitler's National Socialist party, or **Nazi party,** had gained broad support as a result of the depression and German resentment of the harsh Versailles treaty, and Hitler became Germany's chancellor in January 1933. Crushing opponents and rivals, Hitler imposed a brutal dictatorship on Germany and began a program to purify it of Jews—whom he considered an "inferior race" responsible for Germany's defeat in World War I.

Violating the Versailles treaty, Hitler began rearming Germany in 1935. A year later, German troops reoccupied the Rhineland, a region between the

Rhine River and France specifically demilitarized by the Versailles treaty. In 1938, Hitler proclaimed an *Anschluss* (ON-shlooss) (union) between Austria and Germany. Meanwhile, Mussolini, intent on building an empire in Africa, invaded Ethiopia in 1935. London, Paris, and Washington murmured their disapproval but took no action. An emboldened Hitler then claimed Germany's right to the Sudetenland (soo-DATE-un-land), a part of neighboring Czechoslovakia (check-oh-sloh-VAH-kee-uh) containing 3 million ethnic Germans. British prime minister Neville Chamberlain and his French counterpart, insisting that their countries could not endure another war like that of 1914–1918, yielded to Hitler's demands in return for his assurance that Germany had no further territorial ambitions—a policy dubbed **appeasement**—at a conference in Munich in September 1938.

appeasement British policy to avoid war by giving in to German territorial demands for control of Czechoslovakia

In Tokyo, meanwhile, nationalistic militarists gained control of the government and launched a fateful course of expansion, sending troops into the northern Chinese province of Manchuria in 1931. Japan then initiated a full-scale war against China in 1937 and soon controlled key parts of that nation.

The American Mood: No More War

Neutrality Acts Laws passed in the mid-1930s to keep the United States out of any European wars

The feeble American response reflected the people's belief that the decision to go to war in 1917 had been a ghastly mistake. This conviction was rooted in the nation's isolationist tradition as well as in its desire to have the government focus on the problems of the depression, not foreign affairs. A 1934–1936 Senate investigation headed by Republican Gerald P. Nye of North Dakota concluded that war profiteers, whom it called "merchants of death," had tricked the United States into World War I for financial gain. A January 1937 poll showed that 70 percent of the people believed that the United States should have stayed out of World War I.

By the mid-1930s an overwhelming majority of Americans thought that the "mistake" of intervention should not be repeated. In 1935–1937, a series of **Neutrality Acts** echoed the longing for peace. To prevent a repetition of 1917, these measures outlawed arms sales and loans to nations at war and forbade Americans to travel on the ships of belligerent powers.

With the public firmly isolationist and American companies like IBM heavily invested in German industry, confrontation with fascism came solely in sports. At the 1936 Olympics in Berlin, African-American track star Jesse Owens

Thomas D. Mcavoy/Time Life Pictures/Getty Images

Isolationism vs. Interventionism

In front of the White House in 1941, an American soldier grabs a sign from an isolationist picketing against the United States entering the war in Europe. Isolationists ran the gamut from pacifists who opposed all wars, to progressives who feared the growth of business and centralized power, to ultrarightists who sympathized with fascism or shared Hitler's anti-Semitism.

made a mockery of Nazi theories of racial superiority by winning four gold medals. When the black American Joe Louis knocked out German Max Schmeling in the first round of their world heavyweight championship bout in 1938, Americans cheered—but still opposed any policy that might involve them in war.

The Gathering Storm: 1938–1939

The interlude of reduced tension that followed the Munich Pact proved tragically brief. "Peace in our time" lasted a mere 5½ months. At 6:00 A.M. on March 15, 1939, Nazi troops thundered across the border into Czechoslovakia. By evening the Nazi flag flew over the Czech capital of Prague (prahg). Five months later, the signing of the Nazi-Soviet Pact gave Hitler a green light to invade Poland. When Hitler's troops attacked Poland in September, Britain and France declared war on Germany. World War II had begun.

Although isolationist sentiment remained strong in the United States, opinion began to shift. After the fall of Czechoslovakia, Roosevelt called for actions "short of war" to demonstrate America's will to check fascism, and he asked Hitler and Mussolini to pledge no further aggression. A jeering Hitler ridiculed FDR's message, while in Rome Mussolini mocked Roosevelt's physical disability, joking that the president's paralysis must have reached his brain.

Roosevelt, however, did more than send messages. In October 1938, he asked Congress for a $300 million military appropriation; in November, he instructed the Army Air Corps to plan for an annual production of twenty thousand planes; in January 1939, he submitted a $1.3 billion defense budget. Hitler and Mussolini, he said, were "two madmen" who "respect force and force alone."

America and the Jewish Refugees

Hitler and the Nazis translated their hatred of Jews into official policy. The Nuremberg Laws of 1935 stripped Jews of the rights of German citizenship, and increased restrictions on Jews in all spheres of German educational, social, and economic life. This campaign of hatred reached a violent crescendo on November 9–10, 1938, when the Nazis unleashed *Kristallnacht* (cris-TAHL-nocked) (Night of the Broken Glass), a frenzy of arson, destruction, and looting against Jews throughout Germany.

At this point, no one could mistake Hitler's malignant intent. Jews, who had been leaving Germany since 1933, streamed out by the tens of thousands, seeking haven. Between 1933 and 1938, sixty thousand fled to the United States. Most Americans condemned the Jews' persecution, but only a minority favored admitting more refugees. Congress rejected all efforts to liberalize the immigration law, with its discriminatory quotas, and FDR did little to translate his sympathy for the Jews into effective policies.

The consequences of such attitudes became clear in June 1939, when the *St. Louis,* a German liner jammed with 950 Jewish refugees, asked permission to put its passengers ashore at Fort Lauderdale, Florida. Immigration officials refused this request and, according to the *New York Times,* a Coast Guard cutter stood by "to prevent possible attempts by refugees to jump

CHECKING IN

- FDR adopted the Good Neighbor policy toward Latin America.
- Mussolini established a fascist state in Italy in 1922; Hitler and the Nazis took over Germany in 1933 and pursued an expansionist course in Europe; Japan became increasingly militaristic and aggressive in Asia.
- Americans generally remained isolationist; the Neutrality Acts reflected this sentiment.
- When war erupted in Europe, FDR sought increased military funding and ways to evade the Neutrality Acts.
- The American people and government basically ignored the plight of Jews attempting to flee Hitler.

off and swim ashore." The *St. Louis* turned slowly away from the lights of America and sailed back to Germany, where most of its passengers would die from Nazi brutality.

Into the Storm, 1939–1941

What drew the United States into World War II?

Following the lightning German victories in western Europe in the spring of 1940, President Roosevelt's policy of neutrality gave way to a policy of economic intervention. He knew that extending aid to those resisting aggression by the so-called Rome-Berlin-Tokyo Axis, as well as his toughening conduct toward Germany and Japan, could, as he said, "push" the United States into the crisis of worldwide war. Japan's attack on the U.S. fleet at Pearl Harbor provided the final push.

The European War

The war in Europe began on September 1, 1939, as Nazi armies poured into Poland and the *Luftwaffe* (LOOFT-vah-feh) (German air force) devastated Polish cities. Two days later, Britain and France, honoring commitments to Poland, declared war on Germany. Although FDR invoked the Neutrality Acts, he would not ask Americans to be impartial in thought and deed.

Tailoring his actions to the public mood, which favored both preventing a Nazi victory and staying out of war, FDR persuaded Congress in November to amend the Neutrality Acts to allow the belligerents to purchase weapons from the United States if they paid cash and carried the arms away in their own ships. But "cash-and carry" did not stop the Nazis. In spring 1940 Hitler unleashed blitzkrieg (BLITS-kreeg) (lightning war) against western Europe; the Nazi Wehrmacht (VAIR-mokt) (war machine) swept all the way to the English Channel in a scant two months. In early June the British evacuated most of their army, but none of its equipment, from France. On June 22 France surrendered.

Hitler then turned his fury against Great Britain, terror-bombing British cities in hopes of forcing a surrender or, failing that, preparing the ground for a cross-channel invasion. With thousands of civilians killed or wounded and much of London in smoking ruins, Prime Minister **Winston Churchill** pleaded for American aid.

Winston Churchill British wartime Prime Minister; close friend of FDR; staunch ally of the United States

From Isolation to Intervention

In the United States in 1940, news of the "Battle of Britain" competed with speculation about whether FDR would break with tradition and run for an unprecedented third term. Not until the eve of the Democrats' July convention did he reveal that, given the world crisis, he would consent to a "draft" from his party. The Axis threat clinched his renomination and similarly led the Republicans to nominate Wendell Willkie of Indiana, an all-out internationalist who championed greater aid to Britain.

Roosevelt adroitly played the role of a national leader too busy with defense and diplomacy to engage in partisan politics. He appointed Republicans

Henry Stimson and Frank Knox as secretaries of war and the navy. Roosevelt approved a peacetime draft and a dramatic increase in defense funding. In September, he engineered a "destroyers-for-bases" swap with England, sending fifty vintage American ships to Britain in exchange for leases on British air and naval bases in the Western Hemisphere.

These moves infuriated isolationists, particularly the America First Committee. Largely financed by Henry Ford, and featuring Charles Lindbergh as its most popular speaker, the AFC insisted "Fortress America" could stand alone. But a majority of Americans, reassured by the president's promise never to "send an American boy to fight in a foreign war," chose Roosevelt for a third term.

"lend-lease" Program to "loan" war materiel to allies to avoid Neutrality Acts

Roosevelt now called on the United States to become "the arsenal of democracy." He proposed a **"lend-lease"** program to supply war materiel to the cash-strapped British. Despite bitter opposition by the isolationists, Congress approved the lend-lease program in March 1941, and supplies began to flow across the Atlantic. When Hitler's armies invaded the Soviet Union in June 1941, FDR dispatched supplies to the Soviets, despite American hostility toward communism. To defeat Hitler, FDR said, "I would hold hands with the Devil."

Atlantic Charter World War II equivalent of Wilson's Fourteen Points; signed by FDR and Churchill

To counter the menace of German submarines that threatened to choke the transatlantic supply line, Roosevelt in mid-1941 authorized the U.S. Navy to convoy British ships, with orders to destroy enemy ships if necessary. In August, he met with Churchill aboard a warship off Newfoundland. They issued a statement, known as the **Atlantic Charter,** that condemned aggression, affirmed national self-determination, and endorsed the principles of collective security, free trade, and disarmament. After a German submarine fired at an American destroyer in September, Roosevelt authorized naval patrols to shoot on sight all Axis vessels operating in the western Atlantic.

Now on a collision course with Germany, Roosevelt persuaded Congress in November to permit the arming of merchant ships and to allow the transport of lend-lease supplies to belligerent ports in war zones. Unprepared for a major war, America was nevertheless fighting a limited one, and full-scale hostilities seemed imminent.

Pearl Harbor and the Coming of War

Hitler's triumphs in western Europe encouraged Japan to expand farther into Asia. However, the United States opposed Japanese expansion virtually alone. Seeing Germany as America's primary threat, the Roosevelt administration tried to apply enough pressure to deter the Japanese without provoking Tokyo to war before the United States had built the "two-ocean navy" authorized by Congress in 1940.

The Japanese, too, hoped to avoid war, but they would not compromise their desire to create the Greater East Asia Co-Prosperity Sphere (an empire embracing much of China, Southeast Asia, and the western Pacific). Japan saw America's stand as a ploy to block its rise to power, and Americans viewed Japan's talk of legitimate national aspirations as a smoke screen to cloak aggression. Decades of "yellow-peril" propaganda had hardened U.S. attitudes toward Japan, and even those who were isolationist toward Europe tended to be interventionist toward Asia.

The two nations became locked in a deadly dance. In 1940, believing that economic coercion would force the Japanese out of China, the United States ended a long-standing trade treaty with Japan and banned the sale of aviation fuel and scrap metal to it. Tokyo responded by occupying northern Indochina, a French colony, and signing the Tripartite Pact with Germany and Italy in September, creating a military alliance, the Berlin-Rome-Tokyo Axis, that required each government to help the others in the event of a U.S. attack.

When the Japanese then overran the rest of Indochina in July 1941, Roosevelt froze all Japanese assets in the United States and clamped a total embargo on trade with Japan. Tokyo had two choices: submit to the United States to gain a resumption of trade or conquer new lands to obtain vital resources. In October, expansionist war minister General Hideki Tojo (hih-DEH-kee TOH-joh) became Japan's prime minister. Tojo set the first week in December as the deadline for a preemptive strike if the United States did not yield. By late November, U.S. intelligence—after deciphering Japan's top diplomatic code—alerted the Roosevelt administration that war was imminent. Eleventh-hour negotiations under way in Washington made no headway, and warnings went out to all commanders in the Pacific advising them of the threat of an imminent Japanese attack. U.S. officials believed that the Japanese would strike British or Dutch possessions or even the Philippines—but the Japanese gambled on a knockout punch, hoping to destroy the U.S. Pacific Fleet at Pearl Harbor and compel Roosevelt, preoccupied with Germany, to seek accommodation with Japan.

Waves of Japanese dive-bombers and torpedo planes thundered across Hawaii's island of Oahu Sunday morning, December 7, 1941, bombing ships at anchor in Pearl Harbor and strafing planes parked wingtip to wingtip at nearby air bases. In less than three hours, eight battleships, three light cruisers, and two destroyers had been sunk or crippled, and 360 aircraft were destroyed or damaged. The attack killed more than twenty-four hundred Americans and opened the way for Japan's advance toward Australia. Americans had underestimated the resourcefulness, skill, and daring of the Japanese. At the same time, Japanese leaders erred in counting on a paralyzing blow at Pearl Harbor. That miscalculation assured the United States would become an aroused and united nation determined to avenge the attack.

pearl harbor

Roosevelt called December 7 a "date which will live in infamy." On December 8, Congress declared war on Japan. (The sole dissenter was Montana's Jeannette Rankin, who had also cast a nay vote against U.S. entry into WWI.) Three days later, Hitler declared war on the "half Judaized and the other half Negrified" Americans, and Mussolini followed suit. Congress immediately reciprocated without a dissenting vote. America faced a global war that it was not ready to fight.

After Pearl Harbor, U-boats wreaked havoc in the North Atlantic and prowled the Caribbean and the East Coast of the United States. Every twenty-four hours, five more Allied vessels went to the bottom. By the end of 1942, U-boat "wolf packs" destroyed more than a thousand Allied ships, offsetting the pace of American ship production. The United States was losing the battle of the Atlantic.

The war news from Europe and Africa was, as Roosevelt admitted, "all bad." Hitler's rule covered an enormous swath of territory, from the outskirts of Moscow, deep in Russia, to the Pyrenees (PEER-eh-nees) on the French-Spanish border, and from northern Norway to the Libyan (LIB-ee-un) desert. In spring 1942, Nazi armies inflicted more than

CHECKING IN

- The war in Europe went badly for a defeated France and a battered Britain.
- FDR stepped up the American response to the war with cash-and-carry, lend-lease, and naval action programs against German U-boats.
- Isolationism remained strong.
- The Atlantic Charter summed up the Anglo-American vision of a harmonious postwar world.
- Japanese aggression in Asia increased; it became clear war was imminent.
- The Japanese attack on Pearl Harbor shocked Americans and drew the United States into the war.

250,000 casualties on the Soviet army in Crimea (cry-MEE-uh), and Hitler launched a powerful offensive to seize the Caucasian oil fields. German forces moved relentlessly eastward in North Africa, threatening the Suez (soo-EZ) Canal, Britain's oil lifeline.

The Japanese inflicted defeat after defeat on Allied Pacific forces. Tojo followed Pearl Harbor with a rampage across the Pacific that put Guam, Wake Island, Hong Kong, Singapore, Burma, and the Netherlands East Indies under Japan's control by the end of April 1942. American forces in the Philippines, besieged for months on the island of Bataan, surrendered in May. Japan's rising sun flag blazed over hundreds of islands in the central and western Pacific, and over the entire eastern perimeter of the Asian mainland from the border of Siberia to the border of India.

America Mobilizes for War

How did war mobilization transform the American economy and government?

In December 1941, American armed forces numbered only 1.6 million, and war production accounted for just 15 percent of U.S. industrial output. Pearl Harbor changed everything. Within a week of the attack, Congress passed the War Powers Act, granting the president unprecedented authority. Volunteers and draftees swelled the army and navy. By war's end, 15 million men and nearly 350,000 women had served. The far-reaching domestic changes under way would outlast the war and significantly alter the nation's attitudes, behavior, and institutions.

Organizing for Victory

To direct the military engine, Roosevelt formed the Joint Chiefs of Staff, made up of representatives of the army, navy, and army air force. The changing nature of modern warfare also led to the creation of the Office of Strategic Services (OSS), forerunner of the Central Intelligence Agency, to conduct the espionage required for strategic planning.

War Production Board (WPB) Government agency that oversaw the transition from a peacetime to wartime economy

Office of Price Administration (OPA) Government agency that kept inflation down through rationing and strict price controls

Roosevelt established the **War Production Board (WPB)** to allocate materials, to limit the production of civilian goods, and to distribute contracts. The newly created War Manpower Commission (WMC) supervised the mobilization of men and women for the military, war industry, and agriculture; the National War Labor Board (NWLB) mediated disputes between management and labor; and the **Office of Price Administration (OPA)** imposed strict price controls to check inflation.

Although a Nazi commander had jeered, "The Americans can't build planes, only electric iceboxes and razor blades," the United States achieved a miracle of war production in 1942. Car makers retooled to produce planes and tanks; a pinball-machine maker converted to armor-piercing shells. By late 1942, 33 percent of the economy was committed to war production. Whole new industries appeared virtually overnight. With almost all of the nation's crude-rubber supply now in Japanese-controlled territory, the government built some fifty new synthetic-rubber plants. By the end of the war, the United States had become the world's largest exporter of synthetic rubber.

America also became the world's greatest weapons manufacturer, producing more war materiel by 1945 than its Axis enemies combined—three hundred thousand military aircraft, eighty-six thousand tanks, 2.6 million machine guns, and 6 million tons of bombs. The United States built more than five thousand cargo ships and eighty-six thousand warships. Henry J. Kaiser (KYE-zer), who had supervised the construction of the Boulder Dam, introduced prefabrication to cut the time needed to build ships. In 1941, the construction of a Liberty-class merchant ship took six months; in 1943, construction was completed in less than two weeks. By 1945, Kaiser, dubbed "Sir Launchalot," was completing a cargo ship every day.

Such breakneck production had costs. The size and powers of the government expanded as defense spending zoomed from 9 percent of gross national product (GNP) in 1940 to 46 percent in 1945; the federal budget soared from $9 billion to $98 billion. Federal civilian employees mushroomed from 1.1 million to 3.8 million. The executive branch, directing the war effort, grew the most, and an alliance formed between the defense industry and the military. (A generation later, Americans would call these concentrations of power the "imperial presidency" and the "military-industrial complex.")

"Dr. New Deal," in FDR's words, gave way to "Dr. Win the War." To encourage business to convert to war production, the government guaranteed profits, provided generous tax write-offs, and suspended antitrust prosecutions. "If you are going to try to go to war in a capitalist country," said Secretary of War Stimson, "you have to let business make money out of the process or business won't work." Two-thirds of all war-production spending went to the country's hundred largest firms, greatly accelerating trends toward economic concentration.

The War Economy

The United States spent more than $360 billion ($250 million a day) to defeat the Axis, ten times the cost of World War I. Wartime spending and the draft not only vanquished unemployment, but also stimulated an industrial boom that made most Americans prosper. It doubled U.S. industrial output and the per capita GNP, created 17 million new jobs, increased corporate after-tax profits by 70 percent, and raised the real wages or purchasing power of industrial workers by 50 percent.

The federal government poured $40 billion into the West, making it an economic powerhouse as the center of massive aircraft and shipbuilding industries. California alone secured more than 10 percent of all federal funds; by 1945 nearly half the personal income in the state came from the federal government.

A dynamic Sun Belt, stretching from the coastal Southeast to the coastal Southwest, was the recipient of billions spent on military bases and the needs of the armed forces. The South's industrial capacity increased by 40 percent and per capita income tripled.

Full employment, a longer workweek, larger paychecks, and the increased hiring of minorities, women, and the elderly brought a middle-class standard of living to millions of families. The war years produced the only significant shift toward greater equality in the distribution of income in the twentieth century. The earnings of the bottom fifth of all workers rose 68 percent, and those of the middle class doubled. The richest 5 percent, conversely, saw their share of total disposable income drop from 23 to 17 percent.

Large-scale commercial farmers prospered, benefiting from higher consumer prices and increased productivity thanks to improved fertilizers and more mechanization. As sharecroppers, tenants, and small farmers left the land for better-paying industrial jobs, the overall agricultural population fell by 17 percent. Farming became "agribusiness," and organized agriculture wielded power equal to organized labor, big government, and big business.

Organized labor grew mightier as union membership rose from 9 million to 14.8 million workers, in part because of the expansion of the labor force. Although the National War Labor Board attempted to limit wage increases to restrain inflation, unions negotiated unprecedented fringe benefits for workers, including paid vacation time and health and pension plans. As most workers honored the "no-strike" pledge that they had given immediately after Pearl Harbor, less than one-tenth of 1 percent of wartime working time was lost to strikes.

Far more than strikes, inflation threatened the wartime economy. The OPA constantly battled inflation, which was fueled by greater spending power combined with a scarcity of goods. Throughout 1942, prices climbed at a 2-percent-per-month clip; however, at the year's end, Congress gave the president authority to freeze wages, prices, and rents. As the OPA clamped down, inflation slowed dramatically: Consumer prices went up only 8 percent in the war's last two years.

The OPA also instituted rationing to combat inflation and to conserve scarce materials. Under the slogan "Use it up, wear it out, make it do, or do without," the OPA rationed such products as gasoline, sugar, cheese, and meat. Most Americans cheerfully formed carpools, planted victory gardens, and recycled paper and fats, while their children, known as "Uncle Sam's Scrappers" and "Tin-Can Colonels," scoured their neighborhoods for scrap metal.

Buying war bonds further curtailed inflation by decreasing consumer purchasing power, while giving civilians a sense of involvement in the distant war. Small investors bought $40 billion in "E" bonds, and wealthy individuals and corporations invested nearly twice that amount. Bond sales raised almost half the money needed to finance the war. Roosevelt sought to raise the rest by drastically increasing taxes, even though Congress refused the president much of what he sought. Still, the Revenue Act of 1942 raised the top income-tax rate from 60 percent to 94 percent and imposed income taxes on middle- and lower-income Americans for the first time. Beginning in 1943, the payroll-deduction system automatically withheld income taxes from wages and salaries.

"A Wizard War"

Recognizing wartime scientific and technological developments, Winston Churchill dubbed World War II "a wizard war." Mathematicians went to work deciphering enemy codes, psychologists devised propaganda, and, as never before, the major combatants mobilized scientists into virtual armies of invention. In 1941, FDR created the Office of Scientific Research and Development (OSRD) for the development of new weapons and medicines. The OSRD spent more than $1 billion to produce improved radar and sonar, rocket weapons, and proximity fuses for mines and artillery shells. It also funded the development of jet aircraft and high-altitude bombsights. Other OSRD research hastened the widespread use of insecticides, contributed to improved blood transfusions, and produced "miracle drugs," such as penicillin.

The demand for greater accuracy in artillery required the kind of rapid, detailed calculations that only computing machines could supply. By 1944, navy personnel in the basement of Harvard's physics laboratory were operating IBM's Mark I, a cumbersome device fifty-one feet long and eight feet high that weighed five tons. A second-generation computer, ENIAC, soon reduced the time to multiply two tenth-place numbers from Mark I's three seconds to less than three-thousandths of a second.

Nothing saved the lives of more wounded servicemen than improvements in battlefield medical care. Military needs led to advances in heart and lung surgery, and to the use of synthetic antimalarial drugs to substitute for scarce quinine. So-called miracle drugs, antibiotics to combat infections, a rarity on the eve of war, would be copiously produced. The use of DDT cleared many islands of malaria-carrying mosquitoes. Along with innovations like the Mobile Auxiliary Surgical Hospital (MASH), science helped save tens of thousands of soldiers' lives and improved the health of the nation as well. Life expectancy rose by three years during the war.

The atomic bomb project began in August 1939 when Albert Einstein, a Jewish refugee and Nobel Prize–winning physicist, warned Roosevelt that Nazi scientists were seeking to use atomic physics to construct an extraordinarily destructive weapon. In 1941 FDR launched a massive Anglo-American secret program—the Soviets were excluded—to construct an atomic bomb. The next year, the participating physicists, both Americans and Europeans, achieved a controlled chain reaction and acquired the basic knowledge necessary to develop the bomb. By July 1945 this program, code-named the **Manhattan Project,** had employed more than 120,000 people and spent nearly $2 billion.

Manhattan Project Code name for program to develop the atomic bomb

Just before dawn on July 16, 1945, a blinding fireball with "the brightness of several suns at midday" rose over the desert at Alamogordo, New Mexico, followed by a billowing mushroom cloud. Equivalent to twenty thousand tons of TNT, the blast from this first atomic explosion was felt a hundred miles away. The atomic age had dawned.

Propaganda and Politics

People as well as science and machinery had to be mobilized. To sustain a spirit of unity, the Roosevelt administration carefully managed public opinion. The Office of Censorship, established in December 1941, examined all letters going overseas and worked with publishers and broadcasters to suppress information that might damage the war effort, such as details of troop movements.

To shape public opinion, FDR created the Office of War Information (OWI) in June 1942. The OWI employed more than four thousand writers, artists, and advertising specialists to explain the war and to counter enemy propaganda. The OWI depicted the war as a moral struggle between good and evil—the enemy had to be destroyed, not merely defeated. Hollywood films highlighted the heroism and unity of the American forces, while inciting hatred of the enemy. Films about the war portrayed the Japanese, in particular, as treacherous and cruel, as beasts in the jungle, as "slant-eyed rats."

CHECKING IN

- Industrial mobilization was the key to Allied victory, and the United States achieved a miracle of war production.
- Wartime spending lifted the United States out of the Great Depression.
- Government intervened in the economy to direct production and control inflation.
- Science and technology played a major role in the war effort, with the development of radar, sonar, the first computers, and the atomic bomb.
- The war greatly increased government power in shaping public opinion.

While the Roosevelt administration concentrated on the war, Republican critics seized the initiative in domestic politics. Full employment and high wages undermined the Democrats' class appeal, and many of the urban and working-class voters essential to the Roosevelt coalition were serving in the armed forces and did not vote in the 1942 elections. As Republicans gained nine seats in the Senate and forty-six in the House, conservative Republicans and southern Democrats held the power to make or break legislation. Resentful of the wartime expansion of executive authority and determined to curb labor unions and welfare spending, the conservatives abolished the CCC and the WPA, and rebuffed attempts to extend the New Deal.

Despite the strength of the conservative coalition, the war expanded governmental and executive power enormously. As never before, Washington managed the economy, molded public opinion, funded scientific research, and influenced people's daily lives.

THE BATTLEFRONT, 1942–1944

What were the major aspects of Allied military strategy in Europe and Asia?

America's industrial might and Soviet manpower turned the tide of war, and diplomacy followed in its wake. Allied unity diminished as the Axis weakened; increasingly, the United States, Britain, and the Soviet Union each sought wartime strategies and postwar arrangements best suited to its own interests.

Liberating Europe

Joseph Stalin Dictator of the Soviet Union

After Pearl Harbor, British and American officials agreed to concentrate on defeating Germany first and then Japan. However, they differed on where to mount an attack. **Joseph Stalin** demanded a second front, an invasion of western Europe to force Hitler to transfer troops west and thus relieve pressure on the Russians, who faced the full fury of the Nazi armies. Churchill insisted on clearing the Mediterranean before invading France, and he wanted American aid in North Africa to protect the Suez Canal. Roosevelt gave in to Churchill, and so American troops under General Dwight D. Eisenhower landed in Morocco and Algeria. Pushing eastward, they trapped the German and Italian armies being driven westward by the British, and in May 1943 some 260,000 German-Italian troops surrendered, despite Hitler's orders to fight to the death. All of Africa now lay in Allied hands.

Left alone to face two-thirds of the Nazi force, the Soviet Union hung on and, in the turning point of the European war, defeated Germany in the protracted Battle of Stalingrad (STALL-in-grahd) (August 1942–January 1943). As the Russian snow turned red with blood (costing each side more battle deaths in half a year than the United States suffered in the entire war), Soviet forces saved Stalingrad, defended Moscow, and relieved besieged Leningrad. The Red Army then went on the offensive along a thousand-mile front (see Map 25.1).

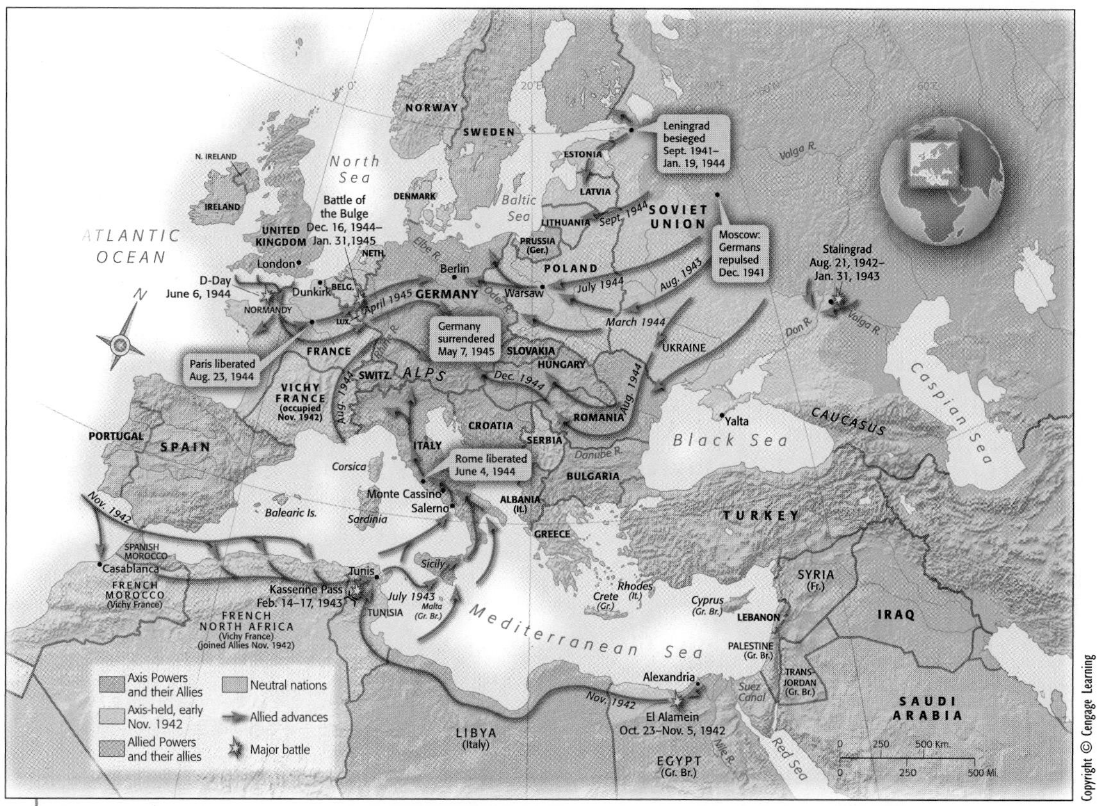

Map 25.1 World War II in Europe and Africa

The momentous German defeats at Stalingrad and in Tunisia early in 1943 marked the turning point in the war against the Axis. By 1945 the Allied conquest of Hitler's "thousand year" Reich was imminent.

 Interactive Map

Although Stalin renewed his plea for a second front, Churchill again objected, and Roosevelt again agreed to a British plan: the invasion of Sicily. In summer 1943 Anglo-American forces gained control of Sicily in less than a month. Italian military leaders deposed and executed Mussolini and surrendered to the Allies on September 8. As Allied forces moved up the Italian peninsula, German troops poured into Italy. Facing elite Nazi divisions in strong defensive positions, the Allies spent eight months inching their way 150 miles to Rome and were still battling through northern Italy when the war in Europe ended in May 1945.

In 1943 and 1944, the United States and Britain turned the tide in the Atlantic and sent thousands of bombers over Germany. At the start of 1943, British and American air forces began round-the-clock bombardment, raining thousands of tons of bombs on German cities. In raids on Hamburg (HAHM-boorg) in July 1943, Allied planes dropping incendiary bombs created terrible firestorms, killing at least thirty-five thousand people and leveling the city, much as they had done earlier at Cologne (koh-LOHN) and would do to Dresden in February 1945, where an estimated sixty thousand people died.

Meanwhile, in July 1943, as the Soviet offensive reclaimed Russian cities and towns from the Nazis, the German armies fell into perpetual retreat. Advancing swiftly, the Red Army drove the Germans out of Soviet territory by mid-1944 and plunged into Poland, where the Soviets set up a puppet government. Late summer and early fall saw Soviet troops seize Romania and Bulgaria and aid communist guerillas under Josip Broz Tito (TEE-toh) in liberating Yugoslavia.

As the Soviets swept across eastern Europe, Allied forces opened the long-promised second front. On June 6, 1944—D-Day—nearly two hundred thousand Allied troops landed in Normandy in northwestern France, gaining a toehold on French soil. Within six weeks, another million Allied troops had waded ashore. Under General Eisenhower, the Allies liberated Paris in August and reached the German border by the end of summer.

Battle of the Bulge Desperate German counteroffensive; launched December 1944; failed to stop the Allied advance into Germany

In mid-December, as the Allies prepared for a full-scale assault on the German heartland, Hitler in a desperate gamble threw his last reserves against American positions. The **Battle of the Bulge**—named for the "bulge" eighty miles long and fifty miles wide that Hitler's troops drove into the Allies' line—raged for nearly a month, and when it ended American troops stood on the banks of the Rhine. The cost was staggering to the United States: fifty-five thousand soldiers dead or wounded and eighteen thousand taken prisoner. But the way to Germany lay open, and the end of the European war was in sight.

War in the Pacific

The day after the Philippines fell to Japan in mid-May 1942, U.S. and Japanese fleets confronted each other in the Coral Sea off northeastern Australia, the first naval battle in history fought entirely from aircraft carriers. Both sides took heavy losses, but the Battle of the Coral Sea stopped the Japanese advance on Australia. Less than a month later, a Japanese armada turned toward Midway Island, the crucial American outpost between Hawaii and Japan. Because the U.S. Signal Corps had broken the Japanese naval code, Japan's plans and the locations of her ships were known. American carriers and their planes consequently won a decisive victory, sinking four Japanese carriers and destroying several hundred enemy planes. Suddenly on the defensive, the stunned Japanese could now only try to hold what they had already won.

On the offensive, U.S. marines waded ashore at Guadalcanal in the Solomon Islands in August 1942. Facing fierce resistance as well as tropical diseases like malaria, the Americans needed six months to take the island, a bitter preview of the battles to come. As the British moved from India to retake Burma, the United States began a two-pronged advance toward Japan in 1943. The army, under General Douglas MacArthur, advanced north on the islands between Australia and the Philippines, and the navy and marines, under Admiral Chester Nimitz, "island-hopped" across the central Pacific to seize strategic bases and put Tokyo in range of American bombers. In fall 1944 the navy annihilated what remained of the Japanese fleet at the battles of the Philippine Sea and Leyte Gulf, giving the United States control of Japan's air and shipping lanes and leaving the Japanese home islands open to invasion (see Map 25.2).

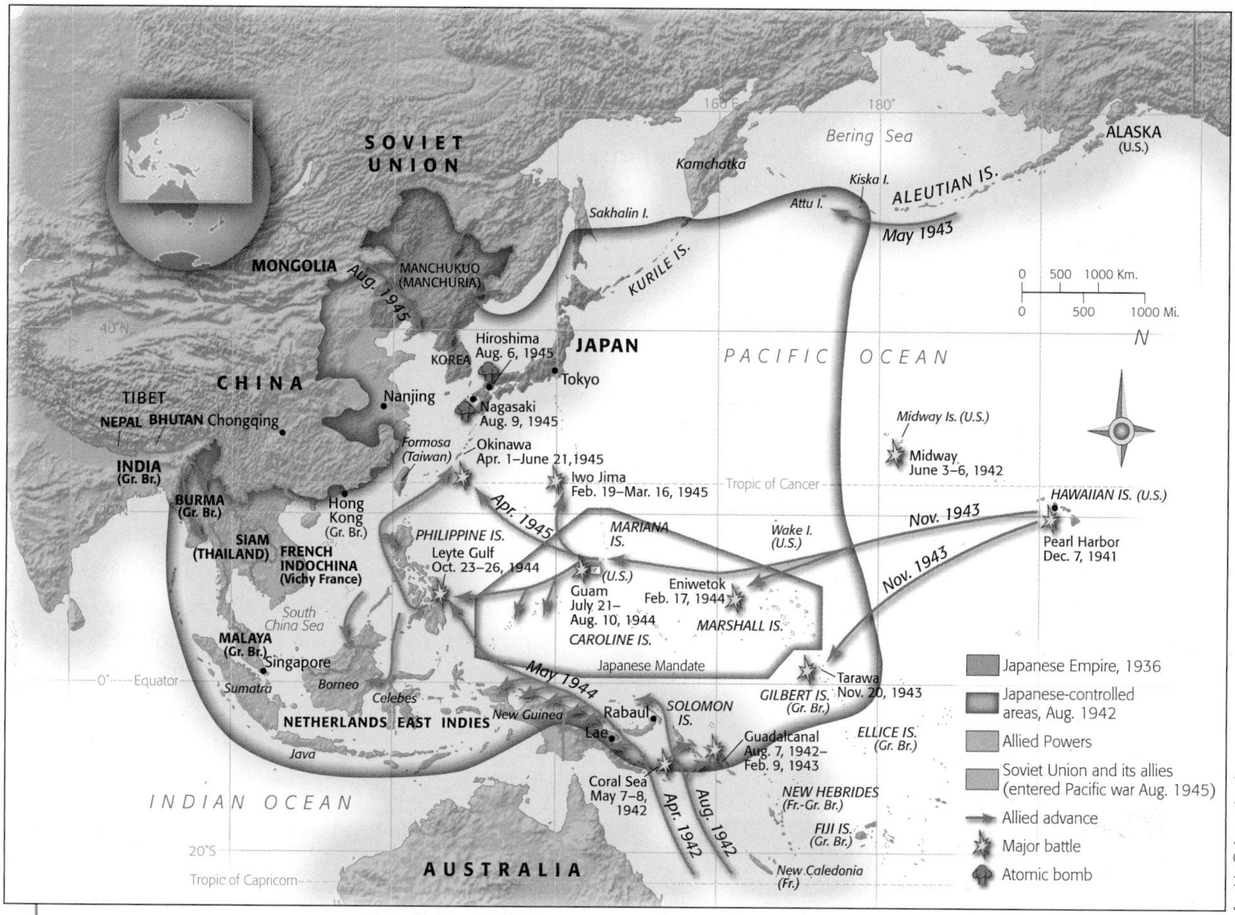

Map 25.2 World War II in the Pacific

American ships and planes stemmed the Japanese offensive at the Battles of the Coral Sea and Midway Island. Thereafter, the Japanese were on the defensive against American amphibious assaults and air strikes.

The Grand Alliance

President Roosevelt had two main goals for the war: the total defeat of the Axis at the least possible cost in American lives, and the establishment of a world order strong enough to ensure peace, open trade, and national self-determination in the postwar era.

Churchill and Stalin had other goals. Britain sought to retain its imperial possessions and a balance of power against the Soviet Union in Europe. The Soviet Union wanted a permanently weakened Germany and a sphere of influence in eastern Europe to protect itself against future attacks from the West. To hold together this uneasy alliance, FDR used personal diplomacy to mediate conflicts.

In January 1943, Roosevelt and Churchill met at Casablanca, Morocco's main port, where they resolved to attack Italy before invading France and proclaimed that the war would continue until the Axis accepted "unconditional surrender." In this

CHECKING IN

- The Anglo-American decision to invade North Africa meant that Russia would remain the only battlefront in Europe, where the Soviet victory at Stalingrad was the turning point in the war.
- On D-Day, June 6, 1944, the Allies launched a cross-channel invasion into France; their offensive stalled until American victory in the Battle of the Bulge in late 1944 opened the path to victory.
- Americans went on the offensive in the Pacific in August 1942, relying primarily on island-hopping and carriers; by late 1944, American forces were poised at the fringe of the Japanese home islands.
- Despite their alliance, the United States, Great Britain, and the Soviet Union had very different war goals.

proclamation they sought to reduce Soviet mistrust of the West, which had deepened because of the postponement of the second front.

In 1943, FDR and Churchill traveled to Tehran, Iran's capital, to confer with Stalin. Here they set the invasion of France for June 1944 and agreed to divide Germany into zones of occupation and to impose reparations on the Reich. Most important to Roosevelt, at Tehran Stalin also pledged to enter the Pacific war after Hitler's defeat.

Roosevelt then turned his attention to domestic politics. Conservative gains in both the Republican Party and the Democratic Party drove FDR to dump the liberal Henry A. Wallace from the ticket and accept Harry S Truman as his vice-presidential candidate. A moderate senator from Missouri, now dubbed "the new Missouri Compromise," Truman restored a semblance of unity to the party for the 1944 campaign. To compete, the Republicans nominated moderate and noncontroversial New York governor Thomas E. Dewey. The campaign focused more on personalities than on issues, and the still-popular FDR defeated his dull GOP opponent, but with the narrowest margin since 1916—winning only 53 percent of the popular vote. A weary Roosevelt, secretly suffering from hypertension and heart disease, now directed his waning energies toward defeating the Axis and constructing an international peacekeeping system.

WAR AND AMERICAN SOCIETY

What were the major effects of World War II on American society, including minorities and women?

The crisis of war altered the most basic patterns of American life. Few families went untouched. More than 15 million Americans served in the armed forces, an equal number moved to find jobs, and millions of women went to work outside the home. As well, the war opened some doors of opportunity for African-Americans and other minorities, although many remained closed. It heightened minority aspirations and widened cracks in the wall of white racist attitudes and policy, while maintaining much of America's racial caste system, thereby tilling the ground for future crises.

The GIs' War

Most Americans in the armed forces griped about regimentation and were more interested in dry socks than in ideology. They knew little of the big strategies and cared less. They wanted to defeat Hitler, avenge Pearl Harbor, and return to a secure, familiar United States.

But the GIs' war dragged on for almost four years, transforming its participants. Millions who had never been far from home traveled to unfamiliar cities and remote lands. Sharing tents and foxholes with fellow Americans of different religions, nationalities, and social backgrounds helped to erase deep-seated prejudices. Besides serving with people they had never previously encountered, over a million GIs married overseas, sowing the seeds of a more tolerant and diverse national culture.

Physical misery, chronic exhaustion, and intense combat left psychological as well as physical wounds. In the Pacific, both American and Japanese troops saw the others in racist terms, as animals to be exterminated. Both sides sometimes behaved brutally, machine-gunning pilots parachuting from damaged planes, torturing and killing prisoners, and mutilating enemy dead. Atrocities also occurred in the war against Germany, although on a lesser scale. A battalion of the Second Armored Division calling itself "Roosevelt's Butchers" boasted that it shot all the German soldiers it captured.

The Home Front

Nothing transformed the social topography more than the vast internal migration of an already-mobile people. Americans swarmed to the centers of war production, especially the Pacific coast states, which manufactured half of the nation's wartime ships and airplanes. Six million people left farms to work in cities, and several million southern whites and blacks migrated northward and westward. They doubled Albuquerque's population and increased San Diego's some 90 percent.

"Rosie the Riveter" Symbol of women who assumed what had been "men's work" in war industries

Lifestyles became freewheeling as Americans moved far from their hometowns, leaving behind their traditional values. Housing shortages left millions living in converted garages, tent cities, or cars. Overcrowding as well as wartime separations strained family and community life. High rates of divorce, family violence, and juvenile delinquency reflected the disruptions.

Millions of American women donned pants, put their hair in bandannas, and went to work in defense plants. Reversing a decade of efforts to exclude women from the labor force, the federal government in 1942 urged women into war production. More than 6 million women entered the labor force during the war, bringing the number of employed women to 19 million. Less than a quarter of the labor force in 1940, women constituted well over a third of all workers in 1945.

National Archives

Rosie the Riveter

Memorialized in song and story, "Rosie the Riveter" symbolized the women war workers who assumed jobs in heavy industry to take up the slack for the absent 15 million men in the armed services. Here a very real Rosie the Riveter is doing her job in April 1943 at the Baltimore manufacturing plant for Martin PMB Mariners.

Before the war most female wage earners had been young and single. By contrast, 75 percent of the new women workers were married, 60 percent were over thirty-five, and more than 33 percent had children under the age of fourteen. Women tended blast furnaces, operated cranes, drove taxis, and worked in shipyards. **"Rosie the Riveter,"** her muscular arms cradling a gun, symbolized the woman war worker; she was, as a popular song put it, "making history working for victory."

Yet traditional attitudes and gender discrimination existed throughout the war. Women earned only about 65 percent of what men earned for the same work, and labor unions often stipulated that women had to give up their jobs to men returning from military service.

The stigma attached to working mothers also shaped government resistance to establishing child-care centers for women employed in defense. "A mother's primary duty is to her home and children," the Labor Department's Children's Bureau stated. "This duty is one she cannot lay aside, no matter what the emergency." Funds for federal child-care centers covered fewer than 10 percent of defense workers' children, and the young suffered. Terms like "eight-hour orphans" and "latch-key children" described children forced to fend for themselves. Fueling fears that the employment of women outside the home would cause the family to disintegrate, juvenile delinquency increased fivefold and the divorce rate nearly doubled.

The impact of war on women and the family proved multifaceted and even contradictory. As the divorce rate soared, so did marriage rates and birthrates. Although some women remained content to roll bandages for the Red Cross, more than three hundred thousand joined the armed forces and, for the first time in American history, were given regular military status and served in positions other than that of nurse—for instance, as mechanics, radio operators, mapmakers, and ferry pilots. Overall, women gained a new sense of their potential. The war proved their capabilities and widened their world.

The loss of students to the armed services and war production forced colleges to admit large numbers of women and to contract themselves out to the military. Military training programs sent nearly a million servicemen and women to college campuses to acquire skills in engineering, foreign languages, economics, and the sciences. Higher education became more dependent on the federal government, and universities competed for federal contracts and subsidies.

The war profoundly affected American culture. Spending on books and theater entertainment more than doubled. More than 60 million people (in a population of 135 million) attended movies weekly. Hollywood turned out a spate of war films that reinforced the image of Nazis and Japanese as fiends. But as the war dragged on, people tired of propaganda, and Hollywood reemphasized romance and adventure with such stars as Katharine Hepburn and Judy Garland.

Similarly, popular music went from "Goodbye, Mama, I'm Off to Yokohama," the first hit of 1942, to songs of lost love and loneliness, like "They're Either Too Young or Too Old." By 1945, bitterness pervaded lyrics, and songs like "Saturday Night Is the Loneliest Night of the Week" revealed impatience for the war's end.

In bookstores, nonfiction crowded the shelves, and every newsmagazine increased its circulation. Wendell Willkie's *One World* (1943) became the fastest-selling title in publishing history to that time, with 2 million copies snapped up in two years. A vision of a world without military alliances and spheres of influence, this brief volume expressed hope that an international organization would extend peace and democracy through the postwar world.

Americans also stayed glued to their radios during the war. The quest for up-to-date information kept radio audiences at record levels. Networks increased their news programs from 4 percent to nearly 30 percent of their daily schedule. Daytime serials, like those featuring Dick Tracy tracking down Axis spies, reached the height of their popularity; a platoon of new comic book superheroes, including Captain America and Captain Marvel, saw action on the battlefield. Even Bugs Bunny put on a uniform to combat America's foes.

Racism and New Opportunities

Realizing that the government needed the loyalty and work of a united people to win the war, African-American leaders saw new pathways to securing equal rights. In 1942 civil-rights spokesmen insisted that African-American support of the war hinged on the United States' commitment to racial justice. They demanded a "Double V" campaign to gain victory over racial discrimination at home as well as over the Axis abroad.

Membership in the National Association for the Advancement of Colored People multiplied nearly ten times, reaching five hundred thousand in 1945. The association pressed for anti-poll tax and anti-lynching legislation, decried discrimination in defense industries and the armed services, and sought to end African-American disfranchisement. The campaign for black voting rights gained momentum when the Supreme Court, in *Smith v. Allwright* (1944), ruled Texas's all-white primary unconstitutional. This decision eliminated a barrier that had existed in eight states, although these states promptly resorted to other devices to minimize African-American voting.

A new civil-rights organization, the Congress of Racial Equality (CORE), was founded in 1942. Employing the strategy of nonviolent resistance to challenge Jim Crow laws, CORE sought to desegregate public facilities in northern cities. Also proposing nonviolent direct action was **A. Philip Randolph,** president of the Brotherhood of Sleeping Car Porters. In 1941 Randolph called for a "thundering march" of one hundred thousand blacks on Washington if the president did not end discrimination in the armed services and the defense industry. FDR agreed to compromise.

A. Philip Randolph Labor leader whose threatened march on Washington led to the creation of the Fair Employment Practices Commission (FEPC)

In June 1941, Roosevelt issued Executive Order 8802, the first presidential directive on race since Reconstruction. It prohibited discriminatory employment practices by federal agencies and all unions and companies engaged in war-related work and established the Fair Employment Practices Commission (FEPC) to enforce this policy. Although the FEPC did not apply to the armed forces and lacked effective enforcement powers, soaring war production and a shrinking labor pool resulted in the employment of 2 million African-Americans in industry and two hundred thousand in the federal civil service. African-American membership in labor unions doubled, and the number of skilled and semiskilled African-American workers tripled. Average earnings for blacks increased from \$457 to \$1,976 a year, compared to \$2,600 for whites.

About 1 million African-Americans served in the armed forces. Due to wartime needs, the military ended its policies of excluding blacks from the marines and coast guard and confining them to mess duty in the navy as well as noncombatant units in the army. In 1944, both the army and navy began token integration in some training facilities, ships, and battlefield platoons. The great majority of blacks, however, served throughout the war in segregated service units commanded by white officers. This indignity, made worse by the failure of military authorities to protect black servicemen off the post and by the use of white military police to keep blacks "in their place," sparked rioting on army bases. At least fifty black soldiers died in racial conflicts during the war.

Violence within the military mirrored growing racial tensions at home. As blacks protested against discrimination, many whites resisted all efforts by blacks to improve their economic and social status. Race riots erupted in 1943 in Harlem, Mobile, and Beaumont, Texas. The bloodiest melee exploded in Detroit that June. By its end, twenty-five blacks and nine whites lay dead, more than seven hundred had been injured, and more than $2 million in property had been destroyed.

Yet the war brought significant changes that would eventually result in a successful drive for black civil rights. The migration of over seven hundred thousand blacks from the South turned a southern problem into a national concern. It created a new attitude of independence in African-Americans freed from the constraints of caste. As the growing numbers of blacks in northern cities began to vote, moreover, African-Americans could hold a balance of power in close elections. This prompted politicians in both major parties to extend greater recognition to blacks and to pay more attention to civil-rights issues.

In addition, the horrors of Nazi racism discredited America's own white supremacist attitudes. A former governor of Alabama complained that Nazism has "wrecked the theories of the master race with which we were so contented so long." A pluralist vision of American society now became part of official rhetoric, as well as the liberal-left agenda. In a massive study of race problems entitled *An American Dilemma* (1944), Swedish economist Gunnar Myrdal concluded that "not since Reconstruction had there been more reason to anticipate fundamental changes in American race relations." Returning black veterans, and African-Americans who had served the nation on the home front, soon expected to gain all the rights enjoyed by whites.

War and Diversity

Wartime winds of change brought new opportunities, and problems, to other American minorities. Twenty-five thousand Native Americans served in the armed forces, including Navajo "code-talkers" who confounded the Japanese by relaying secret messages in an unbreakable code based on their native tongue. Another fifty thousand Indians left reservations to work in defense. For most, it was the first experience of living in a non-Indian world, and after the war some would remain in the cities. Continued discrimination, however, would force a majority back to their reservations, which suffered severely from budget cuts during the war and the immediate postwar years.

To relieve agricultural labor shortages, the federal government negotiated an agreement with Mexico to import temporary workers called *braceros* (brah-SARE-ohs). Classified as foreign workers, not immigrants, an estimated two hundred thousand ***braceros*** received short-term contracts. Farm owners frequently violated these contracts and also encouraged an influx of illegal immigrants.

braceros "Guest workers"; Mexican laborers legally brought into United States

Unable to complain about their working conditions without risking arrest and deportation, hundreds of thousands of Mexicans were exploited by agribusinesses in Arizona, California, and Texas. At the same time, tens of thousands of Chicanos left agricultural work for jobs in factories, shipbuilding yards, and steel mills. By 1943, about half a million Chicanos were living in Los Angeles County, making up 10 percent of the total population.

Much of the hostility toward Mexican-Americans focused on young gang members who wore "zoot suits"—a fashion that originated in Harlem and emphasized broad-shouldered jackets and pleated trousers. Known as *pachucos,* zoot-suited Mexican-Americans aroused the ire of servicemen stationed or on leave in Los Angeles who saw them as delinquents and draft dodgers. After newspaper headlines of a Chicano "crime wave," bands of sailors and soldiers rampaged through Los Angeles in early June 1943, stripping *pachucos,* cutting their long hair, and beating them. Military authorities looked the other way. City police intervened only to arrest Mexican-Americans, and the city council made the wearing of a zoot suit a misdemeanor.

Unlike African-Americans, however, more than 350,000 Mexican-Americans served in the armed forces without segregation, and in all combat units. They volunteered in higher numbers than warranted by their percentage of the population and earned a disproportionate number of citations for distinguished service. And much like black and Indian veterans, Mexican-American veterans organized new groups to press for equal rights.

internment of Japanese-Americans Wartime policy to evacuate from the West Coast and incarcerate all those with Japanese heritage, U.S. citizens included

Thousands of gay men and lesbians who served in the armed forces also found new wartime opportunities. Like other minorities, many gays saw the war as a chance to prove their worth under fire. Yet some suspected of being gay were dishonorably discharged, sent to psychiatric hospitals, or imprisoned in so-called queer stockades. In 1945, gay veterans established the Veteran's Benevolent Association, the first organization in the United States to combat discrimination against homosexuals.

National Archives

Young Nisei Evacuates at the Turlock Assembly Center

While awaiting their turn for baggage inspection on May 2, 1942, these children were interned in remote "relocation centers" along with thirty-seven thousand first-generation Japanese immigrants (Issei) and some seventy-five thousand native-born Japanese-American (Nisei) citizens of the United States. Hastily uprooted from their homes, farms, and stores, most lost all their property and personal possessions, and spent the war under armed guard.

The Internment of Japanese-Americans

Far more than any other minority in the United States, Japanese suffered grievously during the war. The internment of 112,000 Japanese-Americans, two-thirds of them native-born U.S. citizens, in relocation centers guarded by military police was a tragic reminder of the fragility of civil liberties in wartime.

The **internment of Japanese-Americans** policy reflected forty years of anti-Japanese sentiment on the West Coast, rooted in racial prejudice and economic rivalry. Self-serving politicians and farmers who wanted Japanese-American land had long decried the "yellow peril," and after the attack on Pearl Harbor they whipped up the rage and fears of many white Californians. In February 1942, Roosevelt gave in to the pressure and issued Executive Order 9066, authorizing the removal from military areas of anyone deemed a threat. Although not a single Japanese-American was apprehended for espionage or sedition and neither the FBI nor military intelligence uncovered any evidence of disloyal behavior by Japanese-Americans, the military ordered the eviction of all Nisei and Issei from the West Coast. Only Hawaii was excepted. Despite the far larger number of Hawaiians of Japanese ancestry, as well as of Japanese living in Hawaii, no internment policy was implemented there, and no sabotage occurred.

But on the mainland, Japanese-Americans, forced to sell their lands and homes at whatever prices they could obtain, were herded into barbed-wire-encircled detention camps in desolate areas of the West. The Supreme Court, in *Korematsu v. United States* (1944), upheld the constitutionality of the evacuation, stating that it would not question government claims of military necessity during the war. By then, however, the hysteria had subsided, and the government had begun a program of gradual release. In 1982, a special government commission would formally blame the Roosevelt administration's action on "race prejudice, war hysteria, and a failure of political leadership" and would apologize to Japanese-Americans for "a grave injustice." In 1988, Congress voted to pay $20,000 as compensation to each of the nearly sixty thousand Japanese-American internees still alive.

CHECKING IN

- War triggered internal migration, as people sought war industry jobs which, like the military, tossed together Americans of widely different backgrounds.
- Women entered the work force in large numbers but were seen as "temporary workers."
- African-Americans made significant gains and set the stage for the civil-rights drive after the war.
- To take advantage of wartime work, Indians left reservations, and Mexicans entered the United States under the *bracero* program.
- Japanese-Americans, interned in camps, were victims of prejudice and war hysteria.

TRIUMPH AND TRAGEDY, 1945

What new issues did the U.S. government confront in defeating Germany and Japan in 1945?

Spring and summer 1945 brought stunning changes. In Europe, the collapse of the Nazi Third Reich saw a new balance of power emerge. In Asia, continued Japanese resistance and reluctance to surrender led to the use of the atomic bomb. And in the United States, a new president, Harry Truman, presided over the end of World War II and the beginning of a new, "cold" war.

The Yalta Conference

By the time Roosevelt, Churchill, and Stalin met at the Soviet city of Yalta in February 1945, the military situation favored the Soviet Union. The Red Army had overrun Poland, Romania, and Bulgaria; helped drive the Nazis out of Yugoslavia; penetrated Austria, Hungary, and Czechoslovakia; and was massed only fifty miles from Berlin. American forces, in contrast, were still recovering from the Battle of the Bulge and faced stiff resistance en route to Japan. The Joint Chiefs of Staff insisted that obtaining Stalin's help in Asia was worth almost any price. Knowing that the United States did not want to fight a prolonged war against Japan, Stalin had the luxury of deciding whether and when to enter the Pacific war.

Yalta accords 1945 agreements in which FDR made concessions to Stalin to induce him to join the Pacific war

The **Yalta accords** mirrored these realities. Stalin again promised to declare war on Japan "two or three months" after Germany's surrender, and in return Roosevelt and Churchill promised the Soviet Union concessions in Manchuria and the territories that Russia had lost in the Russo-Japanese War forty years before. Stalin accepted the temporary partitioning of Germany and the postponement of discussions about reparations. On the matter dearest to FDR's heart, Stalin approved plans for a United Nations conference to establish a permanent international organization for collective security.

Stalin, however, proved adamant about Soviet domination in eastern Europe, particularly Poland. Twice in the twentieth century German troops had used Poland as a springboard for invading Russia. Stalin would not expose his land again, and after the Red Army captured Warsaw in January 1945, he brutally subdued the noncommunist majority. Roosevelt and Churchill refused to recognize the communist Lublin regime, but they accepted Stalin's pledge to include noncommunist Poles in the new government and to allow free elections. They could do little else. Short of going to war against the Soviet Union while battling Germany and Japan, FDR could only hope that Stalin would keep his word.

Victory in Europe

Meanwhile, Allied armies closed the vise on Germany. In early March 1945, American troops captured Cologne and encircled Germany's industrial heartland. To counter the threat of Soviet power in postwar Europe, Churchill proposed a rapid thrust to Berlin, but Eisenhower, with Roosevelt's backing, overruled the British. Instead, to minimize their casualties and to reassure Stalin, the Americans advanced methodically on a broad front until they met the Russians at the Elbe River at the end of April. By then the Red Army had overrun Vienna and reached the suburbs of Berlin. On April 30 Hitler committed suicide in a bunker under the ruins of Berlin; the city fell to the Soviets on May 2. A hastily assembled German government surrendered unconditionally on May 8.

Jubilant Americans celebrated Victory in Europe (V-E) Day less than a month after they had mourned the death of FDR. On April 12 the exhausted president died of a cerebral hemorrhage. His unprepared successor inherited leadership of the most powerful nation in history—as well as troubles with the Soviet Union that seemed more intractable every day.

Harry S Truman had little familiarity with world affairs. Perhaps sensing his own inadequacies, he adopted a tough pose and counted on American military power to maintain the peace. In office less than two weeks, he lashed out at Soviet ambassador V. M. Molotov that the United States was tired of waiting for Moscow to allow free elections in Poland, and he threatened to cut off lend-lease aid if the Soviet Union did not cooperate. The Truman administration then reduced U.S. economic assistance to the Soviets and stalled on their request for a $1 billion reconstruction loan. Simultaneously, Stalin strengthened his grip on eastern Europe, ignoring the promises he had made at Yalta.

The Truman administration neither conceded the Soviet sphere of influence in eastern Europe nor tried to end it. Truman still sought Stalin's cooperation in establishing the United Nations and in defeating Japan, but Soviet-American relations deteriorated. By June 1945, when the Allied countries framed the United Nations Charter in San Francisco, hopes for a peaceful new international order had dimmed, and the United Nations emerged as a diplomatic battleground. Truman, Churchill, and Stalin met at Potsdam, Germany, from July 16 to August 2 to complete the postwar arrangements begun at Yalta. But the Allied leaders could barely agree to demilitarize Germany and to punish Nazi war criminals. Given the diplomatic impasse, only military power remained to determine the contours of the postwar world.

Holocaust Extermination of 6 million Jews, as well as 6 million others, by Nazis in the name of racial purity

The Holocaust

When news of the **Holocaust** (HAWL-oh-cost)—the term later given to the Nazis' extermination of European Jewry—first leaked out in early 1942, many Americans discounted the reports. Not until November did the State Department admit knowledge of the massacres. A month later, the American broadcaster Edward R. Murrow, who was listened to nationwide, reported on the systematic killing of millions of Jews, "It is a picture of mass murder and moral depravity unequalled in the history of the world. It is a horror beyond what imagination can grasp. . . . There are no longer 'concentration camps'—we must speak now only of 'extermination camps.'"

Most Americans considered the annihilation of Europe's 6 million Jews beyond belief. There were no photographs to prove it, and, some argued, the atrocities attributed to the Germans in World War I had turned out to be false. Therefore, few people took issue with the military's view that the way to liberate those enslaved by Hitler was by speedily winning the war. Pleas by American Jews for the Allies to bomb the death camps and the railroad tracks leading to them fell on deaf ears. In fall 1944, U.S. planes flying over Auschwitz in southern Poland bombed nearby factories but left the gas chambers and crematoria intact, in order, American officials explained, not to divert air power from more vital raids elsewhere.

How much could have been done remains uncertain. Still, the U.S. government never seriously considered rescue schemes or searched for a way to curtail the Nazis' "final solution" to the "Jewish question." Its feeble response was due to its overwhelming focus on winning the war as quickly as possible, congressional and public fears of an influx of destitute Jews into the United States, Britain's wish to placate the Arabs by keeping Jewish settlers out of Palestine, and the fear of some Jewish-American leaders that pressing the issue would increase anti-Semitism at home. The War Refugee Board managed to save the lives of just two hundred thousand Jews and twenty thousand non-Jews, but 6 million other Jews, about 75 percent of the European Jewish population, were gassed, shot, or incinerated, as were several million gypsies, communists, homosexuals, Polish Catholics, and others deemed unfit to live in the Third Reich.

"The things I saw beggar description," wrote General Eisenhower after visiting the first death camp liberated by the U.S. Army. He sent immediately for a delegation of congressional leaders and newspaper editors to make sure Americans would never forget the gas chambers and human ovens. Only after viewing the photographs and newsreels of corpses stacked like cordwood and living skeletons with their vacant, sunken eyes staring through barbed wire did most Americans see that the Holocaust was no myth.

The Atomic Bombs

In the Pacific, the war with Japan ground on. Early in 1945, marines secured the tiny island of Iwo Jima (EE-who jEE muh), seven hundred miles from Japan, at the

AP Photo

Atomic Bombs Bring Relief and Joy to Some

These U.S. servicemen, like many others hearing the news of the atomic bombs and the Japanese surrender, expressed their relief and joy that they would soon be safely coming home rather than having to participate in an invasion of Japan.

cost of twenty-five thousand marine casualties. A month later, Americans landed on Okinawa (oh-kee-NAH-wah), a key staging area for the planned invasion of the Japanese home islands, only 350 miles distant. After eighty-three days of fighting on land and sea, twelve thousand Americans lay dead and three times as many were wounded, a 35 percent casualty rate, which was higher than the losses the United States suffered at Normandy.

The appalling rate of loss on Iwo Jima and Okinawa weighed on the minds of American strategists as they thought about an invasion of the Japanese home islands. The Japanese Cabinet showed no willingness to give up the war despite Japan's being blockaded and bombed daily (in March a fleet of B-29s dropped incendiary bombs on Tokyo, burning most of the city to the ground and killing some eighty-four thousand). Japanese military leaders insisted on fighting to the bitter end. Japan possessed an army of over 2 million, plus up to 4 million reservists. The U.S. Joint Chiefs estimated that American casualties in an invasion of mainland Japan might exceed 1 million.

But the successful test of an atomic weapon at Alamogordo in mid-July presented an alternative. While at Potsdam, Truman, on July 25, ordered that an atomic bomb be used if Japan did not surrender before August 3. He publicly warned Japan to surrender unconditionally or face "prompt and utter destruction." When Japan rejected this **Potsdam Declaration,** Truman gave the military the go-ahead. On August 6, a B-29 named *Enola Gay* dropped a uranium bomb on Hiroshima (hee-roh-SHEE-muh), creating "a hell of unspeakable torments." A searing flash of heat, from a fireball estimated at three hundred thousand degrees centigrade, incinerated buildings and vaporized people. More than sixty thousand died from the blast and another seventy-five thousand later died of burns and radiation poisoning. On August 8, as promised, Stalin declared war on Japan. The next day, much of Nagasaki (nah-gah-SAH-kee) disappeared under the mushroom cloud of a plutonium bomb. On August 14, Japan accepted the American terms of surrender, which implicitly permitted the emperor to retain his throne but subordinated him to the U.S. commander of the occupation forces. General MacArthur received Japan's surrender on the battleship *Missouri* on September 2, 1945. The war was over.

Potsdam Declaration
President Truman's warning to the Japanese, before dropping an atomic bomb on Hiroshima, to surrender or face "utter destruction"

Although Americans at the time overwhelmingly backed the atomic bombings of Japan as the necessary way to end the war quickly and with the least cost in lives, many critics later contended that Japan would have soon surrendered without the horrendous bombing. Some believed that racist American attitudes toward the Japanese motivated the decision. While racial hatred undoubtedly stirred exterminationist sentiment, those involved in the Manhattan Project regarded Germany as the target. Furthermore, considering the ferocity of the Allied bombings of Hamburg and Dresden, there is little reason to assume that the Allies would not have dropped atomic bombs on Germany had they been available. By 1945, the Allies as well as the Axis had abandoned restraints on attacking civilians.

Other critics maintain that demonstrating the bomb's terrible destructiveness on an uninhabited island would have moved Japan to surrender. We will never know for sure. American scientists rejected a demonstration bombing because the United States had an atomic arsenal of only two bombs and they did not know whether the mechanism for detonating them in the air would work. Another line of criticism holds that Truman ordered the atomic attack primarily to end the Pacific war before Stalin could enter it and share in the postwar occupation of Japan. However, the foremost reason for Truman's decision was to shorten the war and save American lives.

The atomic bombs ended the deadliest war in history. A truly global conflict, involving over half the world's peoples, the war affected women, men, and children as victims of civilian bombing campaigns, as war workers, as slave laborers, and as comfort women. Some fifty million died—more than half of them noncombatants. The Soviet Union lost roughly twenty million people, China fifteen million, Poland six million, Germany four million, and Japan two million. Much of Asia and Europe was rubble. Some four hundred thousand American servicemen also perished, and, although physically unscathed, the United States had changed profoundly—for better and worse.

CHECKING IN

- Concessions to the Soviets at Yalta and accepting Soviet dominance of eastern Europe reflected military realities of the time.
- Victory over the Nazis in Europe transitioned quickly into a U.S.-Soviet confrontation.
- The end of the war revealed the horrors of the Holocaust.
- After atomic bombs were dropped on Hiroshima and Nagasaki, and the Soviet Union declared war, Japan surrendered.
- The debate continues about whether use of the atomic bombs was necessary.

Chapter Summary

How did the American people and government respond to the international crises of the 1930s? (page 609)

As war loomed in Europe, most Americans were determined to avoid becoming involved; the Neutrality Acts were one such attempt to prevent involvement. Isolationists formed America First, but FDR sought increased military funding. Americans and the U.S. government turned their backs on Jewish refugees trying to flee Hitler.

What drew the United States into World War II? (page 613)

France had surrendered, and Britain was barely clinging to life by the fall of 1940; despite strong isolationist sentiment, FDR circumvented the Neutrality Acts with cash-and-carry and lend-lease programs for Britain. In Asia, the Japanese became increasingly aggressive but saw the United States as a major obstacle to expansion; their decision to gamble on an all-out attack on American possessions, including Pearl Harbor, precipitated American entry into the war.

How did war mobilization transform the American economy and government? (page 616)

Full mobilization of the industrial economy was the key to Allied victory. U.S. war production boomed as government spending ended the depression. The government established tight control over the economy, the press, and industry. Research and development brought technology to bear on the war, including radar, sonar, the computer, and the atomic bomb.

What were the major aspects of Allied military strategy in Europe and Asia? (page 620)

In Europe, the Soviet Union bore the brunt of the fighting; the battle of Stalingrad was the turning point of the war. The invasion of France on D-Day began the final push to Allied victory. In the Pacific, the United States relied largely on its carrier fleets and island-hopping campaigns. By war's end, however, the U.S.–Great Britain–Soviet Union alliance had seriously eroded because each nation had different war goals.

KEY TERMS

"Good Neighbor" policy *(p. 609)*
Benito Mussolini *(p. 610)*
Adolf Hitler *(p. 610)*
Nazi party *(p. 610)*
appeasement *(p. 611)*
Neutrality Acts *(p. 611)*
Winston Churchill *(p. 613)*
"lend-lease" *(p. 614)*
Atlantic Charter *(p. 614)*
War Production Board (WPB) *(p. 616)*
Office of Price Administration (OPA) *(p. 616)*
Manhattan Project *(p. 619)*
Joseph Stalin *(p. 620)*
Battle of the Bulge *(p. 622)*
"Rosie the Riveter" *(p. 625)*
A. Philip Randolph *(p. 627)*
braceros (p. 628)
internment of Japanese-Americans *(p. 629)*
Yalta accords *(p. 630)*
Holocaust *(p. 632)*
Potsdam Declaration *(p. 634)*

What were the major effects of World War II on American society, including minorities and women? (page 624)

The Sun Belt prospered as government spending there soared; millions of Americans were caught up in a vast internal migration. People of widely diverse backgrounds came together in war jobs and the military. Large numbers of women entered the industrial work force, as did substantial numbers of African-Americans, Indians, and Mexicans. However, wartime propaganda and long-standing prejudice led to the internment of more than one hundred thousand Japanese-Americans solely because of their race.

What new issues did the U.S. government confront in defeating Germany and Japan in 1945? (page 630)

The Yalta conference revealed deep divisions among the Allies; however, FDR made substantial concessions to the Soviet Union because its help was needed to fight Japan. Victory over Germany quickly turned into a U.S.-Soviet confrontation. After viewing evidence, the full horrors of the Holocaust became apparent to Americans who had doubted earlier reports. The use of atomic bombs against Japanese cities was a major factor in convincing Japan to surrender, but the necessity of their use is still being debated.

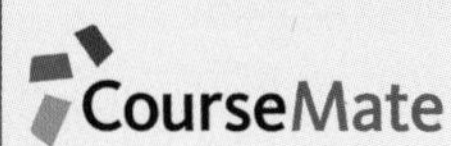

Go to the CourseMate website at **www.cengagebrain.com** for additional study tools and review materials—including audio and video clips—for this chapter.

Chapter 26

The Cold War Abroad and at Home

1945–1960

The Michael Barson Collection/Past Perfect/Picture Research Consultants & Archives

The Day the Communists Took Over America, by Isabel Moore

Chapter Preview

Anticommunism and Containment, 1946–1953
How did the policies of the United States and Soviet Union lead to the beginnings of the Cold War?

The Truman Administration at Home, 1945–1952
What effect did the Cold War have on Truman's domestic program?

The Politics of Anticommunism
How did anticommunist sentiment affect American society and shape Eisenhower's presidency?

The Cold War Continues
In what ways did Eisenhower continue Truman's foreign policy, and in what ways did he change it?

Testifying before the House Un-American Activities Committee in 1948, Whittaker Chambers, a repentant ex-communist, identified Alger Hiss as an underground member of a secret "communist cell" operating in the 1930s. The sad-faced, rumpled Chambers appeared a tortured Christian soul. The handsome Hiss, in contrast, seemed the very symbol of the liberal establishment: Harvard Law graduate, former New Dealer, and now president of the Carnegie Endowment for International Peace. Hiss denied any communist affiliation and claimed not to know Chambers.

Most liberals saw Hiss as the victim of conservatives bent on tarnishing New Deal liberalism. To conservatives, he symbolized every wrong turn the nation had taken since the start of the

New Deal. Under rigorous questioning by freshman Republican congressman Richard Nixon, Hiss eventually admitted he knew Chambers but continued to deny having ever been a communist. Chambers then produced microfilms he had hidden inside a hollowed-out pumpkin. The so-called "pumpkin papers" appeared to be State Department documents from a typewriter once owned by Hiss. Chambers claimed Hiss had stolen the documents in the late 1930s and passed them on to the Soviets.

The Justice Department indicted Hiss for perjury. In January 1950, he was sentenced to five years in federal prison. Although the documents in question seemed insignificant, the conviction of Hiss fueled paranoia of a communist conspiracy. What other "fifth columnists" might be part of a diabolical Red underground in the United States? The Hiss case inspired many Republicans, particularly Nixon and Senator Joseph McCarthy, to press the communists-in-government issue hard. Once-reasonable concerns about American security now mushroomed into witch-hunts and suppression of dissent.

Such was the chilling domestic legacy of what came to be called the Cold War: a new form of international rivalry in which the United States and the Soviet Union avoided direct military conflict while using all their resources to thwart each other's objectives. The conflict transformed the United States' role in the world. The country in 1940 had no military alliances, a small defense budget, and limited troops; by 1960, it had built a massive military establishment, signed mutual-defense pacts with forty countries, erected military bases on every continent, and engaged the USSR in a seemingly unending nuclear-arms race.

Containing communism abroad changed America at home as well. It shifted national priorities, expanded the powers of the presidency, and spawned a second Red Scare that stifled liberalism and empowered Republicans. But Republicans failed to turn back the clock and repeal the New Deal. The politics of deadlock, inherited from the late 1930s, continued into the 1960s. Obsessed with communist spies, Americans increasingly looked to their own prosperity and family life for the joy and blessings denied them by the Cold War.

ANTICOMMUNISM AND CONTAINMENT, 1946–1953

How did the policies of the United States and Soviet Union lead to the beginnings of the Cold War?

The smoldering antagonisms between Moscow and Washington at war's end continued to flare. The "shotgun wedding" that joined the United States and the USSR in an alliance to defeat Hitler dissolved into a struggle to fill the power vacuums left by the defeat of the Axis, the exhaustion and bankruptcy of Western Europe, and the crumbling of colonial empires in Asia and Africa. Misperception and misunderstanding mounted as the two powers sought greater security, each feeding the other's fears, causing a cycle of distrust and animosity. The Cold War resulted.

Polarization and Cold War

The destiny of Eastern Europe, especially Poland, remained at the heart of U.S.-Soviet contention. Wanting to end the Soviet Union's vulnerability to invasions from the west, Stalin insisted on a demilitarized Germany and a buffer of nations friendly to the Soviet Union along its western flank. He considered a Soviet sphere of influence in Eastern Europe essential to national security, a just reward for the Soviet Union's bearing the brunt of the war against Germany, and no different from the American spheres of influence in Western Europe, Japan, and Latin America. Stalin also believed that, at Yalta, Roosevelt and Churchill had implicitly accepted a Soviet zone in Eastern Europe.

With the Red Army occupying half of Europe at the war's end, Stalin installed pro-Soviet governments in Bulgaria, Hungary, and Romania, while communist governments independent of Moscow came to power in Albania (al-BAY-nee-uh) and Yugoslavia. Ignoring the Yalta Declaration of Liberated Europe, the Soviet Union barred free elections in Poland and brutally suppressed Polish democratic parties.

Stalin's insistence on dominance in Eastern Europe collided with Truman's unwillingness to concede Soviet supremacy beyond Russia's borders. What Stalin saw as critical to Russian security Truman viewed as a violation of the right of national self-determination, a betrayal of democratic principles, and a cover for communist aggression. Truman and his advisers believed that the appeasement of dictators only fed their appetite for expansion. Only a new world order based on the self-determination of all nations working in good faith within the United Nations could guarantee peace. Truman also thought that accepting the "enforced sovietization" of Eastern Europe would betray American war aims and condemn nations rescued from Hitler's tyranny to another totalitarian dictatorship.

Domestic political considerations also shaped Truman's response to Stalin. Truman feared that the Democratic Party would invite political disaster if he reneged on the Yalta agreements. The Democrats counted on winning most of the votes of the 6 million Polish-Americans and millions of other Americans of Eastern European origin, who remained keenly interested in the fates of their homelands. He resolved not to appear "soft on communism."

Combativeness fit the temperament of the feisty Truman. Eager to demonstrate that he was in command, the president matched Stalin's intransigence on Polish elections with his own demands for Polish democracy. Emboldened by America's monopoly of atomic bombs and its position as the world's economic superpower, the president hoped that the United States could control the terms of postwar settlement.

The Iron Curtain Descends

Truman's assertiveness deepened Stalin's mistrust of the West. Stalin stepped up his confiscation of materials and factories from occupied territories and forced his satellite nations to close their doors to American trade and influence. In a February 1946 speech that the White House considered a "declaration of World War III," Stalin asserted that there could be no lasting peace with capitalism.

Two weeks later, a sixteen-page telegram from **George F. Kennan,** the American chargé d'affaires in Moscow, reached Washington. A leading student of Soviet

George F. Kennan American diplomat in Moscow, architect of the Cold War policy of containment, or continuous confrontation to stop Soviet expansion

Chronology

1946	George Kennan's "long telegram"; Winston Churchill's "iron curtain" speech; Republicans win control of Congress
1947	Truman Doctrine; Federal Employee Loyalty Program; Taft-Hartley Act; National Security Act; HUAC holds hearings on Hollywood
1948	State of Israel founded; Berlin airlift; Congress approves Marshall Plan to aid Europe; communist leaders put on trial under the Smith Act; Truman elected president
1949	North Atlantic Treaty Organization (NATO) established; East and West Germany founded as separate nations; communist victory in China; People's Republic of China established; Soviet Union detonates an atomic bomb
1950	Soviet spy ring at Los Alamos uncovered; Joseph McCarthy launches anticommunist crusade; Korean War begins; McCarran Internal Security Act; Truman accepts NSC-68
1951	Julius and Ethel Rosenberg convicted of espionage
1952	First hydrogen bomb exploded; Dwight D. Eisenhower elected president
1953	Korean War truce signed
1954	Army-McCarthy hearings
1956	Suez crisis; Eisenhower reelected
1957	Eisenhower Doctrine announced
1959	Fidel Castro comes to power in Cuba
1960	U-2 incident

politics, Kennan warned that the only way to deal with Soviet intransigence was "a long-term, patient but firm and vigilant containment of Russian expansive tendencies." Truman, who had already insisted that it was time "to get tough with Russia," accepted the idea of containment, as did many others in Washington who wanted "no compromise" with the communists. Containment soon became gospel.

In early March 1946, Truman accompanied Winston Churchill to Westminster College in Missouri, where the former British prime minister warned of a new threat to democracy. Stalin, he said, had drawn an "iron curtain" across the eastern half of Europe. Churchill called for an alliance of the English-speaking peoples against the Soviet Union and the maintenance of an Anglo-American monopoly on atomic weapons.

As mutual hostility escalated, the Soviets and Americans rushed to develop doomsday weapons. In 1946, Congress established the Atomic Energy Commission (AEC) to spur both nuclear energy and nuclear weaponry. The AEC, however, devoted more than 90 percent of its effort to atomic bombs. By 1950, one AEC adviser reckoned, the United States "had a stockpile capable of somewhat more than reproducing World War II in a single day."

Thus, less than a year after American and Soviet soldiers had jubilantly met at the Elbe River to celebrate Hitler's defeat, the Cold War had begun. It would involve economic pressure, nuclear intimidation, propaganda, subversion, and proxy wars (fought by governments and peoples allied to the principals rather than directly by the principals themselves). It would affect American life as decisively as any military engagement the nation had ever fought.

Containing Communism

On February 21, 1947, Britain informed the United States that it could no longer afford to assist Greece and Turkey in their struggles against communist insurgents in the eastern Mediterranean. The harsh European winter, the most severe in memory, heightened the sense of urgency in Washington. The economies of Western Europe had ground to a halt, famine and tuberculosis plagued the continent, and colonies in Africa and Asia had risen in rebellion. Communist parties in France and Italy appeared ready to topple democratic coalition governments. Truman resolved to meet the Soviet challenge. But congressional leaders balked, agreeing to support the president only if he could "scare hell out of the country" to gain popular backing for meeting the Soviet threat.

Truman could and did. On March 12, 1947, while addressing a joint session of Congress, he asked for $400 million in military assistance to Greece and Turkey while announcing the **Truman Doctrine.** Truman pictured the matter as a global struggle, pitting "freedom" and "liberty" against "oppression" and "terror," in which the U.S. policy would be to support free peoples everywhere. The Truman Doctrine and the funds appropriated by Congress helped the Greek monarchy to defeat the rebel movement and Turkey to stay out of the Soviet orbit. Moreover, it proclaimed the nation's intention to be a global policeman—everywhere on guard against advances by the Soviet Union and its allies—and it laid the foundation for American foreign policy for much of the next four decades.

Truman Doctrine Implementation of containment: the United States would support any government facing communist challenge

To back up the new international initiative, Congress passed the National Security Act of 1947, unifying the armed forces under a single Department of Defense, creating the National Security Council (NSC) to advise the president on strategic matters, and establishing the Central Intelligence Agency (CIA) to gather information abroad and engage in covert activities in support of the nation's security. In June the administration proposed massive U.S. assistance for European recovery. First proposed by the secretary of state and thus called the **Marshall Plan,** such aid would become another weapon in the arsenal against the spread of communism. Truman wanted to end the economic devastation believed to spawn communism. He correctly guessed that the Soviet Union and its satellites would refuse to take part in the plan, because of the controls linked to it, and accurately foresaw that Western European economic recovery would expand sales of American goods abroad and promote prosperity in the United States.

Marshall Plan Aid to rebuild Western Europe, including Germany

The Marshall Plan fulfilled its sponsors' hopes. By 1952, industrial production had risen 200 percent in Western Europe, and the economic and social chaos that communists had exploited had been overcome in the sixteen nations that shared the $17 billion in aid. Western Europe revived, prospered, and achieved an unprecedented unity. U.S. business, not coincidentally, boomed.

Confrontation in Germany

The Soviet Union reacted to the Truman Doctrine and the Marshall Plan by tightening its grip on Eastern Europe. Then in 1947–1948, communist coups added Hungary and Czechoslovakia to the Soviet bloc, and Stalin turned his sights on Germany.

The 1945 Potsdam Agreement divided Germany into four separate zones (administered by France, Great Britain, the Soviet Union, and the United States) and created a joint four-power administration for Germany's capital, Berlin, which lay 110 miles inside the Soviet-occupied eastern zone. As the Cold War intensified,

Bettmann/Corbis

The Berlin Airlift, 1948

These German children watch an American plane in "Operation Vittles" bring food and supplies to their beleaguered city. The airlift kept a city of 2 million people alive for nearly a year and made West Berlin a symbol of the West's resolve to contain the spread of Soviet communism.

the Western nations began to see a revived Germany as a buffer against Soviet expansion, and they gradually united their zones. In June 1948 Stalin responded by blocking all rail and highway routes through the Soviet zone into Berlin.

Truman resolved neither to abandon Berlin nor to shoot his way into the city and possibly trigger World War III. Instead, he ordered a massive airlift of supplies to the city (the **Berlin airlift**). American cargo planes landed in West Berlin every three minutes around the clock, bringing the mountain of food and fuel necessary to provide the blockaded city with a precarious lifeline. In May 1949, the Soviets ended the blockade. Stalin's gambit had failed. The airlift highlighted American determination and technological prowess, revealed Stalin's readiness to use innocent people as pawns, and dramatically heightened anti-Soviet feeling in the West. Continuing fears of a Soviet attack on Western Europe and public support for "firmness and increased 'toughness' in relations with Russia" then led Truman to push for a rearmed West German state and an Atlantic collective security alliance.

Berlin airlift Use of cargo planes to supply Berlin, blockaded by Stalin, with supplies in 1948

In May 1949, the United States, Britain, and France ended their occupation of Germany and approved the creation of the Federal Republic of Germany (West Germany). A month earlier, ten Western Europe nations had signed the North Atlantic Treaty, establishing a military alliance with the United States and Canada in which "an armed attack against one or more of them . . . shall be considered an attack against them all." After overwhelming Senate approval, the United States officially joined the **North Atlantic Treaty Organization (NATO),** marking the formal end of America's long tradition of avoiding entangling alliances abroad.

North Atlantic Treaty Organization (NATO) U.S.-led political and military alliance against the Soviet Union

Truman was convinced that if NATO had been in existence in 1914 and 1939, the world would have been spared two disastrous wars. Accordingly, he spurred Congress to authorize $1.3 billion for military assistance to NATO nations and authorized the stationing of four American army divisions in Europe as the nucleus of the NATO armed force. The Soviet Union responded by creating the German Democratic Republic (East Germany) in 1949, by exploding its own atomic bomb that same year, and by forming an Eastern bloc military alliance, the Warsaw Pact, in 1955. The United States and Soviet Union had divided Europe into two armed camps (see Map 26.1).

Map 26.1 The Postwar Division of Europe

The wartime dispute between the Soviet Union and the Western Allies over Poland's future hardened after World War II into a Cold War that split Europe into competing American and Soviet spheres of influence. Across an "iron curtain," NATO countries faced the Warsaw Pact nations.

Interactive Map

The Cold War in Asia

Moscow-Washington hostility also carved Asia into contending camps. The Russians created a sphere of influence in Manchuria, the United States denied Moscow a role in postwar Japan, and the two superpowers partitioned a helpless Korea.

As the head of the U.S. occupation forces in Japan, General Douglas MacArthur oversaw the country's transformation from an empire in ruins into a prosperous democracy. In 1952 the occupation ended, but a military security treaty allowed the United States to retain its Japanese bases and brought Japan under the American "nuclear umbrella." In further pursuit of containment, the United States helped crush a procommunist insurgency in the Philippines and aided French efforts to reestablish colonial rule in Indochina (Vietnam, Laos [LAH-oss], and Cambodia [kam-BOH-dee-uh]), despite American declarations in favor of national self-determination and against imperialism.

Mao Zedong Chinese revolutionary whose forces took control of China in 1949

In China, however, U.S. efforts to block communism failed. The Truman administration first tried to mediate the civil war between the nationalist government of Jiang Jieshi (jyang je-SHIRRS) and the communist forces of **Mao Zedong** (MA-oh zay-DONGS), hoping to arrange a coalition government that would end the bloody conflict raging since the 1930s. It also sent nearly $3 billion in aid to the nationalists between 1945 and 1949. But American dollars could not prevent the surrender of Jiang's armies to Mao's forces or the collapse of the nationalists' corrupt regime, whose remnants fled to the island of Taiwan.

Mao's establishment of the communist People's Republic of China shocked Americans. The most populous nation in the world, seen as a counterforce to Asian communism and a market for American trade, had become "Red China." Although Truman blamed Jiang's defeat on his failure to reform China, most Americans were unconvinced. China's "fall" particularly embittered conservatives who believed that America's future lay in Asia, not Europe.

In September 1949, as the "Who lost China" debate raged, the president announced that the Soviet Union had exploded an atomic bomb. The loss of their nuclear monopoly shattered Americans' illusions of invincibility and increased their fear of communism.

Ordinary Americans sought safety in civil defense. Public schools held air-raid drills, teaching students to "duck and cover"—dive under their desks and shield their eyes against atomic blasts. Four million Americans volunteered to be Sky Watchers, looking for Soviet planes. More than a million purchased or constructed their own family bomb shelters. Those who could not afford a bomb shelter were advised by the Federal Civil Defense Administration to "jump in any handy ditch or gutter . . . bury your face in your arms . . . never lose your head."

In January 1950, stung by charges that he was soft on communism, Truman ordered the development of a fusion-based hydrogen bomb (H-bomb), hundreds of times more powerful than an atomic bomb. In November 1952, the United States exploded its first H-bomb in the Marshall Islands, projecting a radioactive cloud 25 miles into the atmosphere and blasting a canyon a mile long and 175 feet deep in the ocean floor. Nine months later, the Soviets detonated their own hydrogen bomb. The balance of terror escalated.

National Security Paper 68 (NSC-68) Blueprint for Cold War; called for military buildup, H-bomb, and worldwide containment

So, too, did nuclear-generated environmental and health problems. Nuclear tests left minimally protected U.S. soldiers and South Pacific islanders exposed to radiation, and radioactive debris from atomic tests contaminated vast areas of Colorado, Utah, Nevada, and Washington.

In April 1950, a presidentially appointed committee issued a top-secret review of defense policy. The report, **National Security Paper 68 (NSC-68),** emphasized the Soviet Union's aggressive intentions and military strength. To counter the Soviets' "design for world domination," NSC-68 called for a vast American military buildup, a large standing army, and a quadrupling of the defense budget to wage a global struggle against communism. By the end of 1950, Truman would order the implementation of NSC-68 and triple the defense budget.

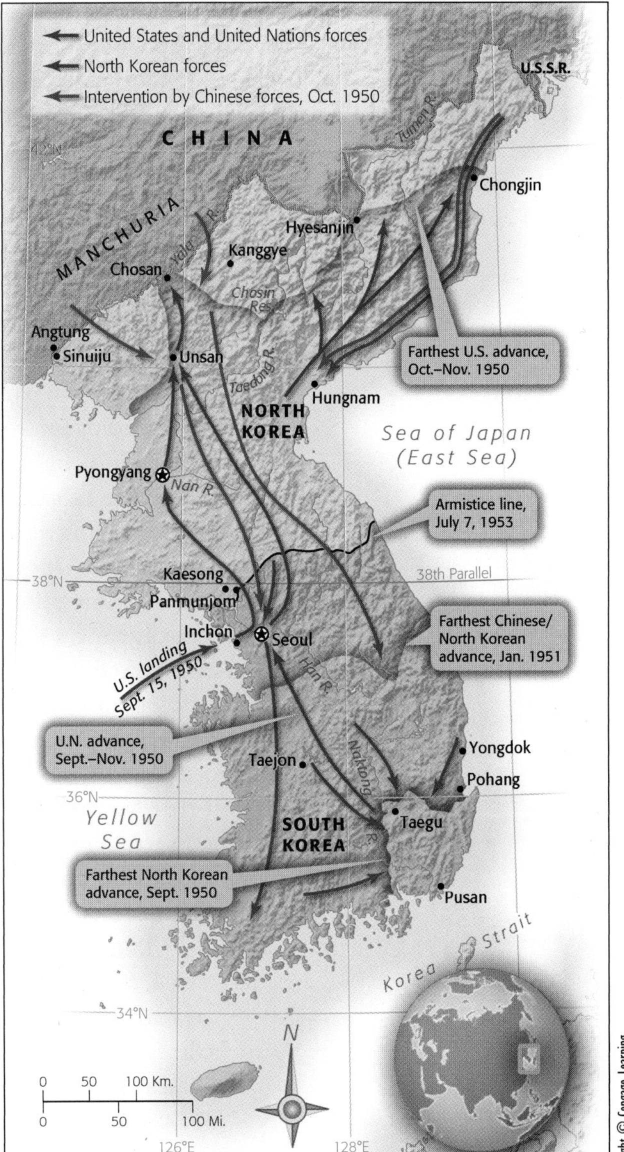

Map 26.2 The Korean War, 1950–1953

The experience of fighting an undeclared and limited war for the limited objective of containing communism confused the generation of Americans who had just fought an all-out war for the total defeat of the Axis.

Interactive Map

The Korean War, 1950–1953

After World War II, the Soviet Union and United States temporarily divided Korea at the thirty-eighth parallel for purposes of military occupation. The dividing line solidified into a political frontier between the Soviet-backed People's Democratic Republic in North Korea and the American-supported Republic of Korea, each claiming the sole right to rule Korea.

On June 24, 1950, North Korean troops swept across the thirty-eighth parallel to attack South Korea. Truman saw the invasion as Soviet-directed aggression. He never doubted that Stalin was testing American will. Mindful of the failure of appeasement at Munich in 1938, Truman said that failure to act would lead to a bloody "third world war." Having been accused of "selling out" Eastern Europe and "losing" China, Truman needed to prove he could stand up to "the Reds."

Without consulting Congress, Truman ordered air and naval forces to Korea from their bases in Japan on June 27. That same day he asked the United Nations to authorize action to repel the invasion. The Soviet delegate was boycotting the Security Council to protest the UN's unwillingness to seat a representative from Mao's China, and Truman gained approval for a UN "police action" to restore South Korea's border. He appointed General Douglas MacArthur to command the UN effort and ordered American ground troops into what became the **Korean War.** The Cold War had turned hot.

Korean War War with communist North Korea to contain the spread of communism in Asia

North Korean forces initially routed the disorganized American and South Korean troops. Then, in mid-September, with UN forces cornered on the southeastern tip of the Korean peninsula, struggling to avoid being pushed into the sea, MacArthur's troops landed at Inchon (in-CHAHN) in a brilliant amphibious maneuver. Within two weeks, U.S. and South Korean forces drove the North Koreans back across the thirty-eighth parallel. Basking in victory, MacArthur persuaded Truman to let him go beyond the UN mandate to repel aggression and to cross the border to liberate all of Korea from communism.

As UN troops approached the Yalu River—the boundary between Korea and China—the Chinese warned that they would not "sit back with folded hands and let the Americans come to the border." Dismissing the threat as "hot air," MacArthur deployed his forces in a thin line below the river. On November 25 thirty-three Chinese divisions (about three hundred thousand men) counterattacked, driving stunned UN forces back below the thirty-eighth parallel. By March 1951, the fighting was stabilized at roughly the original dividing line between the two Koreas (see Map 26.2 on previous page).

Stalemated, Truman reversed course and sought a negotiated peace based on the original objective of restoring the integrity of South Korea. MacArthur rocked the boat, however, urging that he be allowed to seek total victory even at the risk of an all-out war with China. Truman refused. He sought a limited war for a limited objective: to hold the line in Korea. But MacArthur would not accept a stalemate. When he bluntly and repeatedly criticized Truman's limited war—the "appeasement of Communism"—the president fired the general to protect civilian control of the military.

Public opinion, however, backed the general. To Americans accustomed to unconditional victory, the very idea of limited war was baffling. Mounting casualties added anger to the mix. Despite warnings from the chairman of the Joint Chiefs of Staff that MacArthur's proposals would result in "the wrong war at the wrong place in the wrong time and with the wrong enemy," a growing number of Americans listened sympathetically to Republican charges that communist agents controlled American policy.

CHECKING IN

- The Soviet Union moved quickly to establish control over Eastern Europe, as Truman and Stalin's mutual distrust grew.
- The Truman administration adopted containment as the keystone of its foreign policy; the Truman Doctrine in effect made the United States a global policeman.
- The Marshall Plan helped rebuild Western Europe, including Germany but not the Soviet Union.
- The Berlin crisis brought the Cold War very close to the boiling point.
- NSC-68, a top-secret plan, proposed putting the United States on a permanent war footing.
- The Korean War propelled the United States into Asian politics and intensified charges of Soviet influence on American foreign policy.

Truman, meanwhile, found himself bogged down in Korea, unable to win a victory or craft a peace. After two more years of fighting, the two sides reached an armistice in July 1953 that left Korea divided. The "limited" conflict cost the United States 54,246 lives (about 33,700 of them battlefield deaths) with another 103,284 wounded, as well as financial losses of some $54 billion. The Chinese lost nine hundred thousand men, and the two Korean armies lost eight hundred thousand. As in World War II, massive U.S. "carpet bombing" killed at least a million civilians and left North Korea looking like a moonscape.

The Korean War had major consequences. It accelerated implementation of NSC-68 and the expansion of the containment doctrine into a global commitment. From 1950 to 1953, defense spending zoomed from $13 billion to $60 billion—from one-third to two-thirds of the entire federal budget—and the American atomic stockpile mushroomed from 150 to 750 nuclear warheads. The United States acquired new bases around the world, committed itself to rearm West Germany, and joined a mutual-defense pact with Australia and New Zealand. Increased military aid flowed to Jiang Jieshi on Taiwan and to France's fight against communist insurgents in Indochina.

Truman's intervention in Korea preserved a precarious balance of power in Asia and underscored the administration's commitment to the anticommunist struggle. Containment, originally advanced to justify U.S. aid to Greece and Turkey, had become the ideological foundation for a major war in Korea and, ominously, for a deepening U.S. involvement in Vietnam. Truman's actions enhanced the powers of an already powerful presidency and set the precedent for later undeclared wars. They also helped spark an economic boom, added fuel to a second Red Scare, and fostered Cold War attitudes that lasted long after the war ended.

THE TRUMAN ADMINISTRATION AT HOME, 1945–1952

What effect did the Cold War have on Truman's domestic program?

The Cold War profoundly changed the United States for better and for worse. It weakened the nation's commitment to civil liberties while propelling research in medicine and science that, for the most part, made lives longer and better. It spurred more than a quarter of a century of economic growth and prosperity, the longest such period in American history. That, along with a vast expansion of higher education, enabled many Americans to become middle class, diminishing support for federal regulation of business and the expansion of the welfare state. The Cold War context largely determined the domestic record of Truman as well as of Presidents Dwight Eisenhower and John Kennedy.

Truman's Domestic Program

Americans' hunger for the fruits of affluence left them little appetite for extension of the New Deal. Truman's only major domestic accomplishment in the Seventy-ninth Congress was the Employment Act of 1946. It committed the federal government to ensuring economic growth and established the Council of Economic Advisers to confer with the president and formulate policies for maintaining employment, production, and purchasing power. Congress, however, gutted both the goal of full employment and the enhanced executive powers to achieve that objective.

Congressional eagerness to dismantle wartime controls worsened the nation's chief economic problem: inflation. Consumer demand outran the supply of goods, putting intense pressure on prices. The Office of Price Administration (OPA) continued to set price controls after the war, but food producers, manufacturers, and retailers opposed controls strenuously. Many consumers favored preserving the OPA, but others saw the agency as a symbol of irksome wartime regulation. In June 1946, when Congress passed a bill that extended the OPA's life but removed its powers, Truman vetoed the bill. Within a week, food costs rose 16 percent, and the price of beef doubled.

Congress passed, and Truman signed, a second bill extending price controls in weakened form. Protesting any price controls, however, farmers and meat producers threatened to withhold food from the market. Observing that "meatless voters are opposition voters," Truman lifted controls on food prices just before the November 1946 midterm elections. When Democrats fared poorly anyway, Truman ended all price controls. By then, the consumer price index had jumped nearly 25 percent since the end of the war.

Sharp price increases and shrinking paychecks goaded organized labor to demand higher wages. In 1946 alone, more than 4.5 million men and women went on strike. After a United Mine Workers walkout paralyzed the economy for forty days, President Truman ordered government seizure of the mines. A week later the miners returned to work, after Truman pressured owners to grant most of the demands. Six months later the drama repeated itself. In spring 1946 railway engineers and trainmen struck, shutting down the railway system. Truman exploded. "If you think I'm going to sit here and let you tie up this whole country," the president shouted at the heads of the two unions, "you're crazy as hell!" In May, Truman asked Congress for authority to draft workers who struck in vital industries. Before he could finish his speech, the unions gave in. Still, Truman's threat alienated labor leaders.

By fall 1946, Truman had angered most major interest groups; polls showed that less than one-third of Americans approved of his performance. "To err is Truman," some gibed. Summing up public discontent, Republicans asked, "Had enough?" In the 1946 elections they captured twenty-five governorships and, for the first time since 1928, won control of Congress.

The public mood reflected more than just economic discontent; it also revealed a deep current of fear. An NBC Radio program depicted a nuclear attack on Chicago in which most people died instantly. There was much talk of urban dispersal—resettling people in small communities in the country's vast open spaces—and of how to protect oneself in a nuclear attack. The end of World War II had brought an uneasy peace.

The Eightieth Congress, 1947–1948

Many Republicans in the Eightieth Congress interpreted the 1946 elections as a mandate to reverse the New Deal. The Republican-controlled Congress defeated Democratic bills to raise the minimum wage and to provide federal funds for education and housing.

Truman and the conservatives waged their major battle over the pro-union Wagner Act of 1935 (see Chapter 24). Postwar strikes had whipped up a national consensus for curbing union power. In 1947, Congress passed the **Taft-Hartley Act** (the Labor-Management Relations Act), which barred the closed shop—a workplace where only union members could be hired—and permitted the president to call a sixty-day cooling-off period to delay any strike that might endanger national safety or health. Unions termed the law a "slave labor bill" and demanded a presidential veto. Truman did veto the measure, but Congress easily overrode the veto.

Taft-Hartley Act Measure that limited the power of labor unions

Truman, however, had taken a major step toward regaining organized labor's support and reforging FDR's New Deal coalition. Now an unabashed liberal, Truman urged Congress to repeal the Taft-Hartley Act and to provide federal aid to education and housing, national health insurance, and high farm-price supports. To woo ethnic voters of Eastern European descent, Truman railed against Soviet communism; and to court Jewish-American voters, he expressed his deep sympathy toward Holocaust survivors and extended diplomatic recognition to the new state of Israel within hours of its establishment in May 1948.

Still, Truman's chances for victory dimmed as southern segregationists, alarmed by the president's support for civil rights, bolted the Democrats and nominated Governor Strom Thurmond of South Carolina as the candidate of the States' Rights ("Dixiecrat") party. Further diminishing Truman's chances, left-wing Democrats joined with communists to launch a new Progressive Party headed by former vice president Henry A. Wallace. To capitalize on Democratic divisions, Republicans played it safe, nominating the moderate governor of New York, Thomas E. Dewey, for president. Confident of victory, Dewey ran a complacent campaign designed to offend the fewest people. Truman, in contrast, campaigned aggressively, blasting the "no-good, do-nothing" Republicans as "gluttons of privilege." Pollsters applauded Truman's spunk but predicted a Dewey victory.

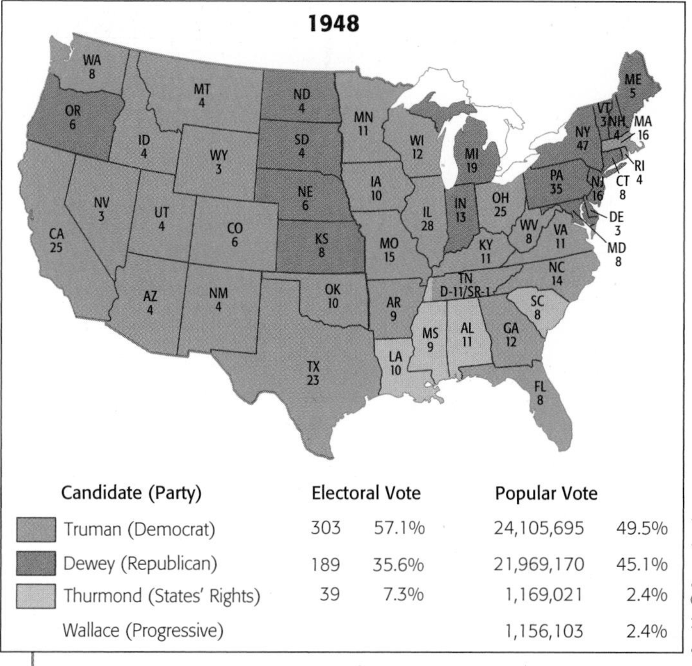

Candidate (Party)	Electoral Vote		Popular Vote	
Truman (Democrat)	303	57.1%	24,105,695	49.5%
Dewey (Republican)	189	35.6%	21,969,170	45.1%
Thurmond (States' Rights)	39	7.3%	1,169,021	2.4%
Wallace (Progressive)			1,156,103	2.4%

Map 26.3 The Election of 1948

Interactive Map

Instead, the president won the biggest Electoral College upset in U.S. history (see Map 26.3). The Progressives and Dixiecrats, ironically, helped Truman. Their radicalism kept most moderates safely in the Democratic fold. Most importantly, Truman succeeded as the defender of the New Deal against the party of Herbert Hoover and the depression. Accordingly, the Roosevelt coalition—organized labor, farmers, urban ethnics, blacks, and most white southerners—held together one more time.

Fair Deal Truman's unsuccessful proposed extension of the New Deal

The Fair Deal

Despite his slim victory, Truman proposed a vast liberal agenda—the **Fair Deal**—that included civil rights, national health-care legislation, and federal aid to education. Unlike New Deal liberalism, the Fair Deal counted on continual economic growth. An expanding economic pie would mean a bigger piece for most Americans and more tax revenue for the government.

Despite prosperity, the bipartisan conservative coalition of northern Republicans and southern Democrats, which had largely controlled Congress since 1938, rejected the Fair Deal. While extending some existing programs, such as the minimum wage and Social Security, and authorizing the construction of eight hundred thousand units of low-income housing, Congress would go no further. Special interest groups, such as the American Medical Association and the National Association of Manufacturers, lobbied extensively against what they called "creeping socialism," and prosperity sapped public enthusiasm for liberal initiatives. By 1950, Truman was once again subordinating domestic issues to foreign policy.

CHECKING IN

- Economic woes, bruising labor battles, and Cold-War anxieties led to widespread disapproval of Truman's presidency.
- The Republican-controlled Eightieth Congress blocked Truman's proposals and reduced organized labor's power by passing the Taft-Hartley Act.
- Controversy split the Democratic Party in 1948 as segregationist southerners walked out to form the Dixiecrats.
- In a stunning upset, Truman defeated Thomas Dewey to win reelection in 1948.
- The Fair Deal was Truman's attempt to continue and enlarge the New Deal; however, Congress rejected virtually all of its measures.

THE POLITICS OF ANTICOMMUNISM

How did anticommunist sentiment affect American society and shape Eisenhower's presidency?

As the Cold War worsened, some Americans concluded that the roots of the nation's foreign difficulties lay in domestic treason and subversion. How else could the communists have taken China and built an atomic bomb? Millions of fearful Americans would eventually enlist in a crusade that would find scapegoats for the nation's problems and equate dissent with disloyalty.

Similar intolerance had prevailed in the Red Scare of 1919–1920 (see Chapter 22), but the Second Red Scare lasted longer, affected more people, and had greater consequences. It took root in the creation of the House Committee on Un-American Activities—later called the **House Un-American Activities Committee (HUAC)** (HYOO-ack)—in 1938 to ferret out fascists, but it quickly became a platform for right-wing denunciations of the New Deal as a communist plot. After World War II, mounting numbers of mainstream Democrats and Republicans climbed aboard the anti-Red bandwagon.

House Un-American Activities Committee (HUAC) "Red-hunting" House committee

The **Second Red Scare** influenced both governmental and personal actions. Millions of Americans were subjected to loyalty oaths and security investigations after the war. Anticommunist extremism destroyed the Left, undermined labor militancy, and discredited liberalism. It spawned a "silent generation" of college students and ensured anticommunist foreign-policy rigidity.

Second Red Scare Postwar anticommunist hysteria that cast a cloud of suspicion over government, academia, and even Hollywood

Loyalty and Security

The U.S. Communist Party claimed eighty thousand members during World War II, and no one knew how many occupied sensitive government positions. In mid-1945, a raid of the offices of a procommunist magazine revealed that classified documents had been stolen from government offices. Ten months later, the Canadian government exposed a major spy network that had passed American atomic secrets to the Soviets during the war. Republicans accused the administration of being "soft on communism."

In March 1947, Truman issued Executive Order 9835 establishing the Federal Employee Loyalty Program to root out subversives in the government. It authorized the attorney general to prepare a list of "subversive" organizations and made association with such groups grounds for dismissal. Those suspected could neither face their accusers nor require investigators to reveal sources.

Mere criticism of American foreign policy could result in an accusation of disloyalty. People lost their jobs because they liked foreign films, associated with radical friends, or favored the unionization of federal workers. Of the 4.7 million jobholders and applicants who underwent loyalty checks by 1952, 560 were fired or denied jobs, and several thousand resigned or withdrew their applications. The probe uncovered no evidence of subversion or espionage, but it did spread fear among government employees.

The Anticommunist Crusade

The very existence of a federal loyalty probe fed mounting anticommunist hysteria and legitimized a witch-hunt for subversives. Universities banned controversial speakers,

The Michael Barson Collection/Past Perfect

The Red Menace, 1949

Although Hollywood generally avoided overtly political films, it released a few dozen explicitly anticommunist films in the postwar era. Depicting American communists as vicious hypocrites, if not hardened criminals, Cold War movies were an effort to protect Hollywood's imperiled public image after HUAC's widely publicized investigation of the movie industry.

and popular magazines ran articles like "Reds Are After Your Child." By the end of Truman's term, thirty-nine states had created loyalty programs. Few had any procedural safeguards. Schoolteachers, college professors, and state and city employees throughout the nation signed loyalty oaths or lost their jobs.

In 1947, HUAC began hearings to expose communist influence in American life. HUAC's probes blurred distinctions between dissent and disloyalty, between radicalism and subversion. People who refused to answer HUAC questions often lost their livelihood. Labor unions expelled communist members and avoided progressive causes, concentrating on securing better pay and benefits and becoming bureaucratic special-interest groups. HUAC also left its mark on the entertainment industry. When several prominent film directors and screenwriters refused to cooperate in 1947, HUAC had them cited for contempt and sent to federal prison. Blacklists in Hollywood and in radio broadcasting barred the employment of anyone with a slightly questionable past, thereby silencing many talented people.

The 1948 presidential campaign fed national anxieties. Truman lambasted Henry Wallace as a Stalinist dupe and the GOP dubbed the Democrats "the party of treason." To blunt such accusations, the Justice Department prosecuted eleven top leaders of the American Communist Party under the Smith Act of 1940, which outlawed any conspiracy advocating the overthrow of the government. In 1951, the Supreme Court upheld the Smith Act's constitutionality, declaring that Congress could curtail freedom of speech if national security demanded such restrictions. Ironically, the Communist Party was fading into obscurity at the very time that politicians were magnifying the threat it posed. By 1950, its membership had shrunk to less than thirty thousand.

McCarthyism

Nothing set off more alarms about the diabolical Red conspiracy in the federal government than the matter of Alger (AL-jurr) Hiss and Whittaker Chambers, discussed at the beginning of this chapter. That an eminent official such as Hiss had been disloyal intensified the widespread fears of a communist underground in the government. Then, a month after Hiss's perjury conviction, another spy case shocked Americans. In February 1950, the British arrested Klaus Fuchs (fooks), a German-born scientist involved in the Manhattan Project, for passing atomic secrets to the Soviets. Fuchs's confession led to the arrest of two Americans, **Ethel and Julius Rosenberg,** as co-conspirators. The Rosenbergs insisted that they were victims of anti-Semitism and were being prosecuted for their leftist beliefs. But in March 1951, a jury found them guilty of conspiring to commit espionage, and in June 1953 they each died in the electric chair—the first American civilians to lose their lives for espionage. The release of classified documents in the 1990s, from the archives of the former Soviet Union, confirmed that Hiss did pass secret information to the Soviets and that Julius Rosenberg, who described himself as a "soldier of Stalin," was part of a spy ring that gave the USSR data on America's atomic bomb project.

Ethel and Julius Rosenberg Julius Rosenberg spied for the Soviets and was executed, along with his wife, in 1953

At this point, some Americans could not separate fact from fantasy. For them, only conspiracy could explain U.S. setbacks. Frustrated by unexpected failure in the 1948 election, Republicans eagerly exploited the fearful mood and accused the "Commiecrats" of selling out America.

Joseph R. McCarthy Redbaiting senator from Wisconsin

Then, in February 1950, Republican senator **Joseph R. McCarthy** of Wisconsin, desperate for an issue on which to run for reelection in 1952, boldly told a West Virginia audience that communists in the State Department had betrayed America. "I have here in my hand a list of 205," McCarthy reported as he waved a laundry list, "who would appear to be either card carrying members or certainly loyal to the Communist Party." McCarthy subsequently lowered his number to 57, then to 10, and then to one "policy risk." McCarthy never released any names or proof. A Senate committee found McCarthy's accusations "a fraud and a hoax," but he persisted, making so many accusations that the facts could never catch up. "McCarthyism" became a synonym for personal attacks on individuals by means of indiscriminate allegations and unsubstantiated charges.

As the Korean War dragged on, McCarthy's efforts to "root out the skunks" escalated. He ridiculed Secretary of State Dean Acheson as the "Red Dean" and charged George Marshall with having "aided and abetted a communist conspiracy so immense as to dwarf any previous such venture in the history of man."

McCarthyism especially appealed to midwestern Republicans opposed to the welfare state and restrictions on business. For them, anticommunism was a weapon of revenge against liberals. McCarthy also won a devoted following among blue-collar workers and among Catholic ethnics, who sought acceptance as "100 percent Americans" through a show of anticommunist zeal. Countless Americans also shared McCarthy's scorn for State Department liberals as the "bright young men who are born with silver spoons in their mouths." And his conspiracy theory offered a simple answer to the perplexing questions of the Cold War: The fault is in Washington.

McCarthy's political power rested on both the Republican establishment and Democrats fearful of antagonizing him. In the 1950 elections, when he helped Republicans defeat Democrats who had denounced him, McCarthy appeared invincible. Few dared incur his wrath.

Over Truman's veto, Congress in 1950 adopted the **McCarran Internal Security Act,** which required organizations deemed communist by the attorney general to register with the Department of Justice. The McCarran Act authorized the arrest and detention during a national emergency of "any person as to whom there is reason to believe might engage in acts of espionage or sabotage." The McCarran-Walter Immigration and Nationality Act of 1952, also adopted over a presidential veto, maintained the quota system that gave immigrants from northern and western Europe 85 percent of available slots, although it did end Asian exclusion. The new law also strengthened the attorney general's authority to exclude or deport aliens suspected of supporting communism.

McCarran Internal Security Act Required all alleged communist organizations to register with the government

Dwight D. Eisenhower Thirty-fourth president; two-term presidency marked by moderation and stability

The Election of 1952

In 1952, public apprehension about the loyalty of government employees combined with frustration over the Korean stalemate to sink Democratic hopes to their lowest level since the 1920s. Truman's approval rating plummeted to 23 percent, the lowest ever recorded by a president. Popular resentment of Truman's handling of the Korean War and revelations of bribery by his political associates gave the GOP ammunition for charging the Democrats with "plunder at home, and blunder abroad."

With Truman too unpopular to seek reelection, dispirited Democrats drafted Governor Adlai E. Stevenson of Illinois. But Stevenson could not dissociate himself from Truman, and his lofty speeches did not stir the average voter. Above all, Stevenson could not overcome the sentiment that twenty years of Democratic rule was enough.

The GOP nominated the hugely popular war hero **Dwight D. Eisenhower.**

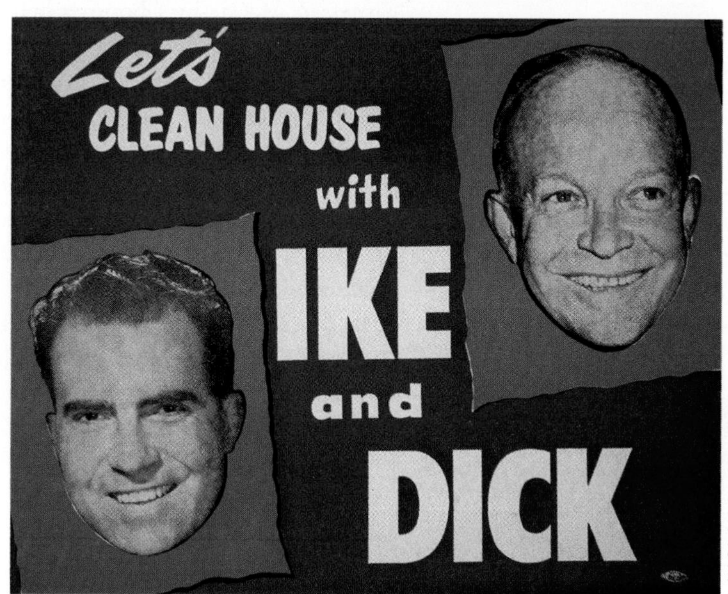

David J. & Janice L. Frent Collection/CORBIS

Ike and Dick

The Republican ticket of Dwight D. Eisenhower and Richard M. Nixon won the 1952 election by capitalizing on frustration over the stalemated Korean War, the fear of communist subversion, and revelations of favoritism and kickbacks on government contracts by the Truman administration.

Although essentially apolitical, Eisenhower answered the call of the moderate wing of the Republican Party and accepted the nomination. "Ike" chose as his running mate Richard M. Nixon, who had won a seat in the Senate in 1950 by redbaiting his opponent, Helen Gahagan Douglas, as "pink right down to her underwear."

Eisenhower and Nixon proved unbeatable. With a captivating grin and an unimpeachable record of public service, Eisenhower projected both personal warmth and the vigorous authority associated with military command. At the same time, Nixon kept public apprehensions at the boiling point. Accusing the Democrats of treason, he charged that a Democratic victory would bring "more Alger Hisses, more atomic spies."

Less than two weeks before the election, Eisenhower dramatically pledged to "go to Korea" to end the stalemated war. It worked: The Republican ticket took 55 percent of the ballots. Ike cracked the Solid South, carrying thirty-nine states. In addition, enough Republicans rode his coattails to give the GOP narrow control of both houses of Congress.

The Downfall of Joseph McCarthy

Although he despised Joseph McCarthy, Eisenhower feared battling the senator. Instead, he allowed McCarthy to grab plenty of rope in hopes that the demagogue would hang himself. He did.

In 1954, McCarthy accused the army of harboring communist spies, and the army charged McCarthy with using his influence to gain preferential treatment for a staff member who had been drafted. The resulting nationally televised Senate investigation, begun in April 1954, brought McCarthy down. A national audience witnessed McCarthy's boorish behavior firsthand on television. His dark scowl, endless interruptions, and disregard for the rights of others repelled many viewers. In June, when McCarthy smeared the reputation of a young lawyer assisting Joseph Welch, the army counsel, Welch struck back: "Until this moment, Senator, I think I really never gauged your cruelty or your recklessness. . . . Have you no sense of decency?" The gallery burst into applause.

The spell of the inquisitor broken, the Senate in December 1954 censured the Wisconsin senator for contemptuous behavior. This powerful rebuke demolished McCarthy as a political force. In 1957, he died from an alcohol-related illness. Still, the paranoia he exploited lingered. Congress annually funded the House Un-American Activities Committee. In addition, state and local governments continued to require loyalty oaths from teachers.

McCarthyism also remained a rallying call of conservatives disenchanted with the postwar consensus. Young conservatives like William F. Buckley, Jr., and the Christian Anti-Communist Crusade continued to claim that domestic communism was a major subversive threat. The John Birch Society denounced Eisenhower as a conscious agent of the communist conspiracy and equated liberalism with treason. Although few saw all the lurking dangers that the John Birch Society did, Barry Goldwater, George Wallace, and Ronald Reagan, among others, used its anticommunist, antigovernment rhetoric to advantage. Stressing victory over communism, rather than its containment, the self-proclaimed "new conservatives" (or radical Right, as their opponents called them) criticized the "creeping socialism" of Eisenhower, advocated a return to traditional moral standards, and condemned the liberal rulings of the Supreme Court.

"Modern Republicanism"

Most Americans in the 1950s did not venture that far Right. They voted for a president who would steer a moderate course and got what they wanted. Rarely in history has a president better fit the national mood than "Ike." Exhausted by a quarter-century of upheaval, Americans craved stability and peace. And Eisenhower, projecting the image of a plain but good man, delivered.

Born on October 14, 1890, in Denison, Texas, Eisenhower grew up in Abilene, Kansas, in a poor, religious family. More athletic than studious, he graduated from the U.S. Military Academy at West Point in 1915. In directing the Allied invasion of North Africa in 1942 and of western Europe in 1944, he revealed himself to be a brilliant war planner, respected for his managerial ability and talent for conciliation. Eisenhower's approach to the presidency reflected his wartime leadership style. He concentrated on major matters, delegated authority, and worked to reconcile contending factions. His restrained view of presidential authority and his low-key style, combined with frequent fishing and golfing vacations, led Democrats to scoff at Eisenhower as a leader who "reigned but did not rule."

The image of passivity, however, masked a "hidden-hand" presidency that enabled Eisenhower to work successfully behind the scenes. More pragmatic than ideological, the president wished to reduce taxes, contain inflation, and, when necessary, check downturns by stimulating the economy. After the Democrats retook Congress in 1954, Eisenhower supported extending social-security benefits, raising the minimum wage, adding 4 million workers to those eligible for unemployment benefits, and providing federally financed public housing for low-income families. He also approved construction of the St. Lawrence Seaway, linking the Great Lakes and the Atlantic Ocean, and creation of the Department of Health, Education, and Welfare. In 1956, Eisenhower backed the largest and most expensive public-works program in American history: the Interstate Highway Act, authorizing construction of a 41,000-mile system of expressways that would soon snake across America, accelerating suburban growth, heightening dependence on imported oil, and contributing to urban decay and air pollution.

Republicans re-nominated Ike by acclamation in 1956, and voters gave him a landslide victory over Democrat Adlai Stevenson. With the GOP crowing, "Everything's booming but the guns," the president won by the greatest popular majority since FDR's victory in 1936.

CHECKING IN

- Truman established the Federal Employee Loyalty Program while HUAC held a series of spectacular hearings to "root out" communism in American life.
- The cases of Alger Hiss and the Rosenbergs, who were accused of spying for the Soviets, increased the public's fear of communism at home.
- Senator Joseph R. McCarthy's reckless anticommunism made him the most feared man in America; he self-destructed in 1954 in the televised Army-McCarthy hearings.
- In the 1952 presidential election, war hero Dwight D. Eisenhower was the easy victor; his laid-back style soothed frayed nerves.
- Pursuing a moderate course, "Ike" won reelection resoundingly in 1956.

THE COLD WAR CONTINUES

In what ways did Eisenhower continue Truman's foreign policy, and in what ways did he change it?

Eisenhower essentially maintained Truman's containment policy. Stalin's death in 1953 and Eisenhower's veiled threat to use nuclear weapons broke the Korean stalemate. The armistice signed in July 1953 set the boundary between North and South Korea once again at the thirty-eighth parallel. Some Americans claimed that communist aggression had been thwarted and containment vindicated; others condemned the truce as peace without honor.

Ike and Dulles

Eager to ease Cold War hostilities, Eisenhower first had to quiet the GOP right wing's clamor to roll back the Red tide. To do so, he chose as his secretary of state **John Foster Dulles** (DULL-us), a rigid, humorless Presbyterian who advocated a holy war against "atheistic communism," backed by the threat of "instant, massive retaliation" with nuclear weapons. Dulles called for "liberation" of the captive peoples of Eastern Europe and for unleashing Jiang Jieshi against communist China. Believing that the Soviet Union understood only force, Dulles insisted on the necessity of "brinksmanship," the art of never backing down in a crisis, even at the risk of war.

John Foster Dulles Eisenhower's secretary of state and anticommunist hard-liner

Such saber rattling pleased the Right, but Eisenhower preferred conciliation, partly because he feared a nuclear war—the Soviet Union had tested its own hydrogen bomb in 1953. Eisenhower refused to translate Dulles's rhetoric into action. Aware of the limits of American power, the United States did nothing to check the Soviet interventions that crushed uprisings in East Germany (1953) and Hungary (1956).

As multimegaton thermonuclear weapons replaced atomic bombs in U.S. and Soviet arsenals, Eisenhower worked to reduce the probability of mutual annihilation. He proposed "atoms for peace," whereby both superpowers would contribute fissionable materials to a new UN agency for use in industrial projects. In the absence of a positive Soviet response, the government began construction of an electronic air defense system to provide early warning of a missile attack.

Work also began on commercial nuclear plants in the mid-1950s, promising electricity "too cheap to meter." However, most money continued to go for nuclear research that was military in nature. Radioactive fallout from atomic tests, especially the 1954 U.S. tests that spread strontium 90 over a wide area, heightened world concern about the nuclear-arms race.

In 1955, Eisenhower and Soviet leaders met in Geneva for the first East-West conference since World War II. Discussions produced no concrete plan for arms control, but mutual talk of "peaceful coexistence" led reporters to hail the "spirit of Geneva." In March 1958, Moscow suspended atmospheric tests of nuclear weapons, and the United States followed suit.

But the Cold War continued. Dulles negotiated mutual-defense pacts with forty-three nations. The United States' "New Look" defense program guaranteed "more bang for the buck" by emphasizing nuclear weapons and reducing conventional forces. It also spurred the Soviets to seek "more rubble for the ruble" by enlarging their nuclear stockpile.

Meanwhile, the focus of the Cold War shifted from Europe to the Third World, the largely nonwhite developing nations. There, the two superpowers waged war by proxy, using local guerrillas and military juntas. There, too, the Central Intelligence Agency (CIA) fought covert wars against those thought to imperil American interests.

CIA Covert Actions

Established in 1947 to conduct foreign intelligence gathering, the CIA soon began to carry out undercover operations to topple regimes friendly to communism.

By 1957, half its personnel and 80 percent of its budget were devoted to "covert action." To woo influential foreign thinkers away from communism, the CIA also sponsored intellectual conferences and jazz concerts. It bankrolled anticommunist cultural events, subsidized magazines to publish articles supporting the United States, and recruited college students and businessmen traveling abroad as "fronts" in clandestine CIA activities.

In 1953, the CIA orchestrated a coup to overthrow the government of Iran. Fearing that the prime minister, who had nationalized oil fields, might open oil-rich Iran to the Soviets, the CIA replaced him with pro-American Shah Reza Pahlavi (REH-zah PAH-lah-vee). The United States thus gained a loyal ally on the Soviet border, and American oil companies prospered when the Shah made low-priced oil available to them. But Iranian hatred of America took root—a hostility that would haunt the United States a quarter-century later.

The CIA also intervened in Philippine elections in 1953 to ensure a pro-American government. The following year, a CIA-supported band of mercenaries in Guatemala overthrew the elected communist-influenced regime, which had seized land from the American-owned United Fruit Company. The new pro-American government restored United Fruit's properties and trampled political opposition.

Troubles in the Third World

Eisenhower first followed Truman's course of aiding France in its battle with Indochinese insurgents. When that failed, he pinned his hopes on the CIA-installed President Ngo Dinh Diem to keep South Vietnam an independent anticommunist nation tied to the United States. That policy, too, appeared to be faltering as he left office (to be further discussed in Chapter 28).

Eisenhower faced his greatest crisis in the Middle East. In 1954, Gamal Abdel Nasser (gu-MAWL AB-dul NASS-er) came to power in Egypt, determined to modernize his nation. To woo him, the United States offered financing for a dam at Aswan (AS-wahn) to harness the Nile River. But when Nasser purchased arms from Czechoslovakia, John Foster Dulles canceled the loan, and Nasser nationalized the British-owned Suez Canal.

Viewing the canal as the lifeline of its empire, Britain planned to take it back by force. Supporting the British were France, which feared Arab nationalism in their Algerian colony, and Israel, which feared the Egyptian arms buildup. The three countries, America's closest allies, coordinated an attack on Egypt in October 1956 without consulting Eisenhower. Ike fumed that the military action would drive the Arab world and its precious oil to the Russians. When Moscow threatened to intervene, Eisenhower forced his allies to withdraw their troops.

The **Suez crisis** had major consequences. It swelled Third World antiwestern sentiment, and the United States replaced Britain and France as the protector of Western interests in the Middle East. Determined to guarantee the flow of oil to the West, in 1957 the president announced the **Eisenhower Doctrine,** a proclamation that the United States would send military aid and, if necessary, troops to any Middle Eastern nation threatened by "communist aggression."

Suez crisis Situation in which Egypt nationalized the Suez Canal, prompting Britain, France, and Israel to take military action

Eisenhower Doctrine Committed the United States to a policy of intervention in the Middle East

Such interventions intensified anti-American feelings in Third World nations. Angry crowds in Peru and Venezuela spat at Vice President Nixon and stoned his car in 1958. In 1959, Fidel Castro overturned a dictatorial regime in Cuba and confiscated American properties without compensation. A tougher blow struck on May 1, 1960, two weeks before a scheduled summit conference with Soviet premier Nikita Khrushchev (KROOSH-chef), when the Soviets shot down a U.S. spy plane far inside their border. Khrushchev displayed the captured CIA U-2 pilot and photos taken of Soviet missile sites. Eisenhower refused to apologize, and the summit collapsed.

military-industrial complex The U.S. arms industry, whose growing influence worried Eisenhower

The Eisenhower Legacy

Just before leaving office, Eisenhower offered Americans a farewell and a warning. The demands of national security, he stated, had produced the "conjunction of an immense military establishment and a large arms industry." Swollen defense budgets had yoked American economic health to military expenditures, and military contracts had become the staff of life for research scholars, politicians, and America's largest corporations. This combination of interests, Eisenhower believed, exerted enormous leverage and threatened the traditional subordination of the military in American life. "We must guard against the acquisition of unwarranted influence . . . by the **military-industrial complex.** The potential for the disastrous rise of misplaced power exists and will persist."

The president concluded that he had avoided war but that lasting peace was not in sight. Most scholars agreed. Eisenhower ended the Korean War, avoided direct intervention in Vietnam, initiated relaxing tensions with the Soviet Union, and suspended atmospheric nuclear testing. At the same time, he presided over an accelerating nuclear-arms race and a Cold War that encircled the globe. So, too, would his successor.

CHECKING IN

- Despite hard-line Dulles rhetoric, Eisenhower pursued a moderate Cold War course and avoided direct confrontation with the Soviet Union.
- The CIA conducted covert operations in Iran and Guatemala to overthrow elected governments not friendly enough to the United States.
- The Middle East remained a hot spot after the Suez crisis, and the Eisenhower Doctrine committed the United States to intervene there against "communist aggression."
- In his farewell address, Eisenhower advised Americans to "guard against the acquisition of unwarranted influence . . . by the military-industrial complex."

Chapter Summary

How did the policies of the United States and Soviet Union lead to the beginnings of the Cold War? (page 638)

The Soviet Union moved quickly to consolidate its hold over Eastern Europe. To Stalin, this policy was primarily defensive; to Truman, it was aggression. What was left of the World War II coalition vanished amid clouds of distrust. Containment became the bedrock of American foreign policy. The Truman Doctrine proclaimed the United States to be a global policeman, while the Marshall Plan helped rebuild Western Europe. NSC-68 placed the country on a permanent war footing and radically increased defense spending. The Korean War thrust the United States squarely into Asian politics.

KEY TERMS

George F. Kennan *(p. 639)*
Truman Doctrine *(p. 641)*
Marshall Plan *(p. 641)*
Berlin airlift *(p. 642)*
North Atlantic Treaty Organization (NATO) *(p. 643)*
Mao Zedong *(p. 644)*
National Security Paper 68 (NSC-68) *(p. 645)*
Korean War *(p. 645)*

What effect did the Cold War have on Truman's domestic program? (page 647)

The Republican-controlled Eightieth Congress blocked most of Truman's proposals; it clipped labor's wings with the Taft-Hartley Act. In 1948, some segregationist southerners left the Democrats and formed their own "Dixiecrat" party. Truman overcame these obstacles and won a surprising reelection victory in 1948. Truman announced the Fair Deal, his attempt to continue and enlarge the New Deal, but virtually none of his new proposals became law.

How did anticommunist sentiment affect American society and shape Eisenhower's presidency? (page 650)

Fear of communism permeated American life. Highly publicized HUAC hearings seemed to reveal communists under every bed. Truman's Federal Employee Loyalty Program and the Hiss and Rosenberg cases intensified the public's jitteriness, thus setting the stage for the emergence of Senator Joseph R. McCarthy. Republicans rode "McCarthyism" back to the seat of power in Washington; Dwight D. Eisenhower easily won the presidency in 1952. While tilting to the Right in favoring private corporations, the Eisenhower administration left New Deal reforms in place, expanded existing social-welfare benefits, and proposed construction of a vast interstate highway system.

In what ways did Eisenhower continue Truman's foreign policy, and in what ways did he change it? (page 655)

Despite the hard-line rhetoric of John Foster Dulles, Eisenhower followed a moderate, nonconfrontational policy in dealing with the Soviet Union. The domino theory led the United States to deeper involvement in Asia; meanwhile, the CIA secretly orchestrated coups in Iran and Guatemala. The Suez crisis underlined the volatile and dangerous nature of Middle Eastern politics, and the resulting Eisenhower Doctrine committed the United States to resisting Soviet influence in the region.

KEY TERMS continued

Taft-Hartley Act *(p. 648)*
Fair Deal *(p. 649)*
House Un-American Activities Committee (HUAC) *(p. 650)*
Second Red Scare *(p. 650)*
Ethel and Julius Rosenberg *(p. 652)*
Joseph R. McCarthy *(p. 652)*
McCarran Internal Security Act *(p. 653)*
Dwight D. Eisenhower *(p. 653)*
John Foster Dulles *(p. 656)*
Suez crisis *(p. 657)*
Eisenhower Doctrine *(p. 657)*
military-industrial complex *(p. 658)*

Go to the CourseMate website at **www.cengagebrain.com** for additional study tools and review materials—including audio and video clips—for this chapter.

CHAPTER 27

America at Midcentury

1945–1961

State Library and Archives of Florida

The Postwar Domestic Ideal

CHAPTER PREVIEW

Postwar Jitters
What were the main sources of the postwar economic expansion and affluence?

The Affluent Society
What, if any, were the negative consequences associated with economic growth and prosperity?

Prosperity and the Suburbs
How accurate is the image of 1950s suburban life as one of contentment, conservatism, and conformity?

Seeds of Disquiet
What actions by minorities and youth foretold the movements for social change to come in the 1960s?

The Other America
In what sense were there two Americas?

The Civil Rights Movement
What innovative strategies were developed by the civil rights movement in this era?

Like no one else, Jackie Robinson personified the accelerating momentum of the struggle against racial discrimination that emerged from World War II. While serving in the war, Robinson was acquitted of insubordination in a court-martial for refusing to accept segregation on army buses. In 1947, he accepted an offer to play baseball for the Brooklyn Dodgers. The grandson of a slave had become the first African-American to play Major League Baseball in the twentieth century. He endured racist insults and bean balls, flying spikes and hate mail, even death threats from fans and other players. But his dazzling play and dignified courage helped the Dodgers win the pennant, and Robinson was named Rookie of the Year.

Robinson became a symbol of progress in race relations and a spur to changes in the United States. In the wake of Robinson's success, professional football and other baseball teams also integrated. The popular press increasingly attacked prejudice, various cities and states passed laws against discrimination, the Supreme Court chipped away at the judicial foundations of segregation, the Truman administration proposed civil-rights legislation, and antiracism took its place in the agenda of liberalism. A new phase in the struggle to end racism in America had begun.

For most white Americans, however, economic growth and prosperity, and the Cold War, defined the postwar era. A new way of life, centered on family "togetherness" and consumption, became the American Dream. Yet Americans also worried about the arms race, and the atmospheric nuclear testing that pumped strontium 90, a cancer-causing chemical, into the world's environment. Fewer middle-class whites paid much attention to critics who railed against mainstream values in the postwar years.

A time of fundamental changes and of portents of yet greater change, the period from 1945 to 1961 brought the advent of an automated postindustrial society, the influence of television, the baby boom, the growth of suburbs and the Sun Belt, high-speed interstate highways, and an enormous internal migration. Midcentury America encompassed booming prosperity and persistent poverty, civil-rights triumphs and rampant racism, consensus and alienation. Much like Jackie Robinson breaking the color line in Major League Baseball, it showcased what we were, and what we would become.

Postwar Jitters

What were the main sources of the postwar economic expansion and affluence?

Americans hailed V-J Day and looked forward to "bringing the boys home." However, the steep decline in defense spending and factory jobs caused many to fear demobilization. Strife between labor and management, as well as inflation and shortages, intensified the anxiety. But by 1947, consumer spending and the Cold War had begun to spur a quarter-century of economic growth and prosperity, the longest such period in American history.

Demobilization and Reconversion

When the war ended, GIs and civilians alike wanted all those who had served overseas "home alive in '45." Troops demanding transport ships barraged Congress with threats of "no boats, no votes." On a single day in December 1945, sixty thousand postcards arrived at the White House with the message "Bring the Boys Home by Christmas." Truman bowed to popular demand, and by 1948 American military strength had dropped from 12 million at war's end to just 1.5 million.

Chronology

1944	Servicemen's Readjustment Act (GI Bill)
1946	ENIAC, the first electronic computer, begins operation
1947	Levittown, New York, development started; Jackie Robinson breaks Major League Baseball's color line; President's Committee on Civil Rights issues *To Secure These Rights*
1948	Bell Labs develops the transistor
1950	David Riesman, *The Lonely Crowd*
1953	Earl Warren appointed chief justice; Operation Wetback begins
1954	*Brown* v. *Board of Education of Topeka; Father Knows Best* begins on TV
1955	Salk polio vaccine developed; AFL-CIO merger; Elvis Presley ignites rock and roll; James Dean stars in *Rebel Without a Cause;* Montgomery bus boycott begins
1956	Interstate Highway Act
1957	Little Rock school-desegregation crisis; Soviet Union launches *Sputnik;* peak of baby boom (4.3 million births); Southern Christian Leadership Conference founded
1958	National Defense Education Act; National Aeronautics and Space Administration (NASA) founded
1960	Sit-ins begin; suburban population almost equals that of central city
1961	Freedom Rides begin

Returning veterans faced readjustment problems intensified by a soaring divorce rate and a drastic housing shortage. As war plants closed, moreover, veterans and civilians feared the return of mass unemployment and economic depression. Defense spending plummeted from $76 billion in 1945 to under $20 billion in 1946, and more than a million defense jobs vanished.

By the end of the decade more women were working outside the home than during World War II. They took jobs in traditional women's fields, especially office work and sales, to pay for family needs. Although the postwar economy created new openings for women in the labor market, many public figures urged women to seek fulfillment at home. Popular culture romanticized married bliss and demonized career women as a threat to social stability.

The GI Bill of Rights

GI Bill Act that allowed education and home ownership for veterans

The Servicemen's Readjustment Act of 1944, commonly called the GI Bill of Rights or **GI Bill,** was designed to forestall the expected recession by easing veterans back into the work force, as well as to reward the "soldier boys" and reduce their fears of female competition. The GI Bill gave veterans priority for many jobs, occupational guidance, and, if need be, fifty-two weeks of unemployment benefits. It also provided low-interest loans to returning GIs who were starting businesses or buying homes, helping to fuel a baby boom, suburbanization, and a record demand for new goods and services.

Most vitally in the long run, the government promised to pay for up to four years of further education or job training for veterans. In 1946, flush with generous stipends, 1.5 million veterans were attending college, spurring a huge increase in higher education and the creation of many new state and community colleges. Veterans made up over half of all college students in 1947.

To make room for the millions of GIs pursuing higher education after the war, many colleges limited the percentage of women admitted or barred students from out of state. As a result, the percentage of female college graduates dropped from 40 percent in 1949 to 25 percent in 1950. By then, most potential women students were the working wives of the veterans who took advantage of the GI Bill to go to college.

The GI Bill democratized higher education. By 1956, nearly 10 million veterans had used the GI Bill to enroll in vocational training programs and colleges. No longer a citadel of privilege, universities awarded twice as many degrees in 1950 as in 1940, propelling millions of veterans into the middle class. Two decades later, these more affluent and educated veterans expected their children to follow suit. Higher education became an accepted part of the American Dream.

The Economic Boom Begins

In addition to the assistance given returning servicemen, a 1945 tax cut of $6 billion spurred corporate investment in new factories and equipment and helped produce an economic boom. Further kindling postwar prosperity, Americans spent much of the $135 billion they had saved from wartime work and service pay to satisfy their desire to consume, causing sales of homes, cars, and appliances to skyrocket. Scores of new products—televisions, high-fidelity phonographs, filter cigarettes, automatic transmissions, freezers, and air conditioners—became hallmarks of the middle-class lifestyle.

Bretton Woods agreement Created the IMF, GATT, and World Bank; secured U.S. dominance in world finance

The **Bretton Woods agreement** (1944) among the Allies set the stage for the United States to become the economic leader of the noncommunist world. In addition to valuing ("pegging") other currencies in relation to the dollar, the Bretton Woods agreement created several institutions to oversee international trade and finance: the International Monetary Fund (IMF), the General Agreement on Tariffs and Trade (GATT), and the World Bank. Since the United States largely controlled and funded these powerful economic institutions, they gave the United States an especially favorable position in international trade and finance.

With many nations in ruins, American firms could import raw materials cheaply; with little competition from other industrial countries, they could increase exports to record levels. U.S. economic dominance also resulted from wartime advances in science and technology, which significantly increased the productivity of American workers, and led to revolutionary developments in such industries as electronics and plastics.

CHECKING IN

- More than a million defense jobs vanished after the war, sparking fears that rapid demobilization would lead to recession.
- The GI Bill helped veterans buy homes and start businesses; it sent millions to college and helped propel even more into the middle class.
- The influx of veterans democratized higher education.
- Pent-up demand triggered a consumer boom, while the Bretton Woods agreement established the United States's leadership in international trade and finance.

THE AFFLUENT SOCIETY

What, if any, were the negative consequences associated with economic growth and prosperity?

In 1958, the economist John Kenneth Galbraith published *The Affluent Society,* a study of postwar America whose title reflected the broad-based prosperity that made the 1950s seem the fulfillment of the American Dream. By the end of the decade, about 60 percent of American families owned homes; 75 percent, cars; and 87 percent, at least one TV. Government spending, a huge upsurge in productivity, and steadily increasing consumer demand pushed the gross national product (GNP) up 50 percent. The United States achieved the world's highest living standard ever. By 1960, the average worker's income, adjusted for inflation, was 35 percent higher than in 1945. With just 6 percent of the world's population, the United States produced and consumed nearly half of everything made and sold on Earth.

The New Industrial Society

Federal spending constituted a major source of economic growth, nearly doubling in the 1950s to $180 billion. Federal expenditures, just 1 percent of the GNP in 1929, reached 17 percent by the mid-1950s. These funds built roads and airports, financed home mortgages, supported farm prices, and provided stipends for education. More than half the federal budget—10 percent of the GNP—went to defense spending. The federal government remained the nation's chief sponsor of scientific and technological research and development (R&D).

Particularly for the West, it was as if World War II had never ended. Politicians from both parties labored to keep defense spending flowing westward. By the late 1950s, California alone received half the space budget and a quarter of all major military contracts. Denver had the largest number of federal employees outside Washington, DC. Government spending transformed the West of rugged individualists into a new West of bureaucrats, defense contractors, and scientists dependent on federal funds.

Government funding and control transformed both the U.S. military and the industrial economy. Financed by the Atomic Energy Commission and using navy scientists, the nation's first nuclear power plant came online in 1957. The chemical industry continued its wartime surge. As pesticides contaminated groundwater supplies and plastics reduced landfill space, Americans—unaware of the hidden perils—marveled at fruits and vegetables covered with Saran Wrap and delighted in their Dacron suits, Acrilan socks, and Teflon-coated pans.

Electricity consumption tripled in the 1950s, and electronics became the fifth-largest American industry, as consumers purchased electric washers and dryers, freezers, blenders, television sets, and stereos. Cheap oil fueled expansion. Domestic oil production and foreign imports rose steeply, and by 1960 oil had replaced coal as the nation's main energy source. Hardly anyone paid attention when a physicist warned in 1953 that "adding 6 billion tons of carbon dioxide to the atmosphere each year is warming up the Earth."

Plentiful cheap gasoline fed the growth of the automobile and aircraft industries. Aerospace, the nation's third-largest industry in the 1950s, depended on defense spending and federally funded research. The automobile industry, still the nation's industrial titan, also applied technological R&D. Between 1945 and 1960, automation halved the number of hours and workers needed to produce a car.

Bettmann/CORBIS

Production Line at Douglas Aircraft Company

The Cold War stimulated an enormous economic boom in defense spending. By midcentury, more than half the federal budget, about 10 percent of the GNP, went to defense contractors like Douglas Aircraft, which helped the economies of the South and the West to flourish.

The Age of Computers

The computer was a key to technological revolution. In late 1946, the military devised ENIAC, the first electronic computer, to improve artillery accuracy. The unwieldy machine, with eighteen thousand vacuum tubes, could perform five thousand calculations per second. Next came the development of operating instructions, or programs, and the replacement of wires by printed circuits. Then, in 1948, Bell Labs invented tiny, solid-state transistors that ended reliance on radio tubes and initiated the age of computers.

Sales of electronic computers to industry rose from twenty in 1954 to more than two thousand in 1960. Major manufacturers used them to monitor production lines, track inventory, and ensure quality control. In government, computers were as indispensable to Pentagon strategists playing war games as to the Census Bureau and the Internal Revenue Service. By the mid-1960s more than thirty thousand mainframe computers would be used by banks, hospitals, and universities.

The development of the high-technology complex known as Silicon Valley began in 1951. Stanford University utilized its science and engineering faculties to design products for the Fairchild Semiconductor and Hewlett-Packard companies. This relationship between universities and corporations became a model followed by other high-tech firms throughout the Santa Clara valley. Similar developments would follow along Massachusetts' Route 128; near Austin, Texas; and in North Carolina's Research Triangle.

The Costs of Bigness

Rapid technological advances accelerated the growth and power of big business. In 1950, twenty-two firms had assets of more than $1 billion; by 1960, fifty did. By then, one-half of 1 percent of corporations earned more than half the total corporate income in the United States. Wealthy firms swallowed weak competitors and became oligopolies. Three television networks monopolized the nation's airwaves; three automobile and three aluminum companies produced 90 percent of America's cars and aluminum; and large corporations controlled the lion's share of assets and sales in steel, petroleum, chemicals, and electrical machinery. Corporations acquired overseas facilities to become "multinational" enterprises. Growth and consolidation meant greater bureaucratization. "Executives" replaced "capitalists." Success required conformity not creativity, teamwork not individuality. According to sociologist David Riesman's *The Lonely Crowd* (1950), the new "company people" were "other-directed," eager to follow the cues from their peers.

Changes in agriculture paralleled those in industry. Farming grew increasingly scientific and mechanized. Between 1945 and 1960, technology halved the work hours necessary to grow crops. Many farm families migrated to cities. Meanwhile, heavily capitalized farm businesses prospered by using more and more machines and chemicals.

Silent Spring Rachel Carson's 1962 book exposing the ecological damage wrought by pesticides

Until the publication of Rachel Carson's ***Silent Spring*** in 1962, few Americans understood the extent to which fertilizers, herbicides, and pesticides poisoned the environment. Carson, a former researcher for the Fish and Wildlife Service, dramatized the problems caused by the use of the insecticide DDT and its spread through the food chain. Her depiction of a "silent spring" caused by the death of songbirds from DDT toxicity led many states to ban its use. The federal government followed suit.

CHECKING IN

- Federal spending, especially in defense industries and military research and development, helped fuel a decade of economic growth.
- The computer industry began a growth spurt as government and business took advantage of the new technology.
- Consolidation and bigness characterized agriculture as well as industry; environmental damage was one result.
- Unions sagged because of prosperity, automation, and an increasingly white-collar work force.

Blue-Collar Blues

Consolidation also transformed the labor movement. In 1955, the AFL and CIO merged, bringing 85 percent of union members into a single unit. Although leaders promised aggressive unionism, organized labor fell victim to its success at the bargaining table. Higher wages, a shorter workweek, paid vacations, health-care coverage, and automatic wage hikes tied to the cost of living led most workers to view themselves as middle class rather than the proletariat.

A decrease in the number of blue-collar workers further sapped labor militancy. Most of the new jobs in the 1950s were in the service sector and in public employment, which banned collective bargaining by labor unions, and automation cut membership in the coal, auto, and steelworkers' unions by more than half. In 1956, for the first time in U.S. history, white-collar workers outnumbered blue-collar workers. Although most service jobs were as routinized as any factory job, few unions sought to woo white-collar workers. The percentage of the unionized labor force dropped from a high of 36 percent in 1953 to 31 percent in 1960, and kept falling.

PROSPERITY AND THE SUBURBS

How accurate is the image of 1950s suburban life as one of contentment, conservatism, and conformity?

As real income (adjusted for inflation) rose, Americans spent less of their income on necessities and more on powered lawn mowers and air conditioners. They heaped their shopping carts with frozen, dehydrated, and fortified foods. When they lacked cash, they borrowed. In 1950, Diners' Club issued the first credit card, and American Express followed in 1958. Installment buying, home mortgages, and auto loans tripled Americans' private indebtedness in the 1950s. In its effort to convince people to buy what they did not need, business spent more on advertising than the nation did on public schools. Thrift and savings were no longer depicted as virtues.

Suburban America

Urged to "Buy Now, Pay Later," Americans purchased 58 million new cars during the 1950s. Manufacturers enticed people to trade in and up by offering flashier models, two-tone color, tail fins, and more powerful engines, such as Pontiac's 1955 "Sensational Strato-Streak V-8," which could go more than twice as fast as any speed limit. The results were increases in highway deaths, air pollution, oil consumption, and "autosclerosis"—clogged urban arteries.

Government policy as well as "auto-mania" spurred white Americans' exodus to the suburbs. Federal spending on highways skyrocketed from $79 million in 1946 to $2.6 billion in 1960. Once-remote areas came within "commuting distance" for urban workers. The income-tax code stimulated home sales by allowing deductions for home-mortgage interest payments and for property taxes. The Federal Housing Administration (FHA) and the Veterans Administration (VA) offered low-interest loans, although both continued to deny loans to blacks who sought to buy homes in white neighborhoods. In 1960, suburbia was 98 percent white.

In 1947 in Long Island, some thirty miles from Manhattan, Alfred and William Levitt used mass-production techniques to construct thousands of look-alike 720-square-foot houses as quickly as possible. With "Levittown" as the ground-breaker, 85 percent of the 13 million new homes built in the 1950s were in the suburbs. In the greatest internal migration in its history, some 20 million Americans moved to the suburbs in the decade—making the suburban population nearly equal to that of the central cities. Although social critics lampooned the

Projected Interstate Highway System, 1957

Touted as the largest public works project in the history of the world, the Highway Act (1956) provided for the nation's first centrally planned transportation system and the construction of a national system of high-speed expressways. The expressways lured more residents and businesses to suburbia and boosted the interstate trucking business. But they also made Americans more dependent on cheap and plentiful gasoline, while hastening the decline of the nation's railroad lines and urban mass-transportation systems. The construction of highways—"white men's roads through black men's bedrooms," as the National Urban League described them—decimated many minority neighborhoods.

"ticky-tacky" houses in "disturbia," suburban life embodied the American Dream for many families who longed for their own home, good schools, and neighbors like themselves.

Americans also moved South and West, into the Sun Belt, lured by job opportunities, the climate, and the pace of life. California, where the population went from 9 to 19 million between 1945 and 1964, supplanted New York as the most populous state. Los Angeles boasted the highest per capita ownership of private homes and cars of any city. Initially designed to lure shoppers downtown, the highway system instead became the road to a home in the suburbs.

Industry, too, also headed South and West, drawn by low taxes, low energy costs, and anti-union right-to-work laws. Senior citizens headed to the easier climate. Both groups brought a conservative outlook. By 1980, the population of the **Sun Belt,** which stretched from the Old Confederacy across Texas to southern California, exceeded that of the North and East. The political power of the Republican Party rose accordingly.

Sun Belt States of the southwestern United States; increasingly populous and conservative in the 1950s

Consensus and Conservatism

Not everyone embraced the conformity of 1950s' consumer culture, however. Intellectuals found a wide audience for their attack on "organization men" bent on getting ahead by going along and on "status seekers" pursuing external rewards to compensate for inner insecurities. Others took aim at the consumerist middle class: "all items in a national supermarket—categorized, processed, labeled, priced, and readied for merchandising."

This criticism oversimplified reality. It ignored ethnic and class diversity, the acquisitiveness and conformity of earlier generations, and the currents of dissent swirling beneath the surface. But it rightly spotlighted the elevation of comfort over challenge, and of private pleasures over public affairs. It was, in the main, a time of political passivity and preoccupation with personal gain.

Togetherness and the Baby Boom

In 1954, *McCall's* magazine coined the term "togetherness" to celebrate the ideal couple: the man and woman who centered their lives on home and children. Americans in the 1950s tended to marry young, have babies quickly, and have more of them. The fertility rate (the number of births per one thousand women) peaked at 123 in 1957, when an American baby was born every seven seconds.

New antibiotics subdued diphtheria and whooping cough, and the Salk and Sabin vaccines eliminated polio. The plunge in childhood mortality helped to raise American life expectancy from 65.9 years in 1945 to 70.9 years in 1970. Coupled with the **baby boom,** this led to a 19 percent population spurt during the 1950s. By 1960, children under fourteen constituted one-third of the population.

baby boom Enormous population spurt from 1946 to 1964

The sheer size of the baby-boom generation (76 million Americans were born between 1946 and 1964) ensured its impact. In the 1950s school construction boomed, as did college enrollments in the 1960s. The 1970s through the 1990s would see peaks in home construction, as the boomers had families, and in retirement investments. In the 1950s the baby boom made child rearing a foremost concern and reinforced the idea that women's place was in the home.

No one did more to emphasize the link between full-time mothers and healthy children than **Dr. Benjamin Spock;** only the Bible outsold his *Baby and Child Care* (1946) in the 1950s. Spock urged mothers not to work outside the home, in order to create an atmosphere of warmth and intimacy for their children. Crying babies were to be comforted; breast-feeding came back into vogue.

Dr. Benjamin Spock Physician and author who urged mothers to devote themselves full time to the welfare of their children

Domesticity

Popular culture throughout the 1950s glorified marriage and parenthood, painting a woman's devotion to life in the home with her children as the most cherished goal. Television mostly pictured women as at-home mothers. Hollywood perpetuated the stereotype of career women as neurotic. As Debbie Reynolds declared in *The Tender Trap* (1955), "A woman isn't a woman until she's been married and had children."

Education reinforced these ideas. Alongside academic subjects, girls studied typing, etiquette, and cooking. Guidance counselors cautioned young women not to miss out on marriage by pursuing higher education. More men than women went to college, and only one-third of college women completed their degrees.

Women both embraced and repudiated the domestic ideal as profound changes accelerated. By 1960, twice as many worked outside the home as in 1940. In 1960, one-third of the labor force was female, and one out of three married women worked outside the home. Most held so-called "pink collar" jobs in the service industry—secretary or clerk, waitress or hairdresser. Their median wage was less than half that for men.

Most women worked to augment family income, not to challenge stereotypes, and took low-paying, low-prestige jobs. Yet many working women developed a heightened sense of expectations and empowerment. Transmitted to their daughters, that experience would fuel a feminist resurgence in the late 1960s.

Religion and Education

Billy Graham Protestant evangelical preacher and outspoken opponent of homosexuality, communism, and working wives

"Today in the U.S.," *Time* claimed in 1954, "the Christian faith is back in the center of things." Evangelist **Billy Graham,** Roman Catholic Bishop Fulton J. Sheen, and Protestant minister Norman Vincent Peale all had syndicated newspaper columns, best-selling books, and radio and television programs. Each promoted a potent mixture of religious salvation and aggressive anticommunism. Hollywood religious extravaganzas, such as *Ben Hur* and *The Ten Commandments,* were the biggest box-office hits of the 1950s, while television promoted the slogan that "the family that prays together stays together."

Congress added "under God" to the Pledge of Allegiance and required "IN GOD WE TRUST" to be put on all U.S. currency. While church membership doubled to 114 million between 1945 and 1960, the intensity of faith diminished for many people, as mainstream churches downplayed sin and evil, and preached Americanism and fellowship.

Similarly, education swelled in the 1950s yet seemed less rigorous than in earlier decades. The baby boom inflated primary-school enrollment by 10 million. California opened a new school every week throughout the decade and still faced a classroom shortage. The proportion of college-age Americans in higher education climbed from 15 percent in 1940 to more than 40 percent by the 1960s. "Progressive" educators promoted sociability and self-expression—"well-roundedness"—over science, math, and history. Surveys of college students found them conservative, conformist, and careerist, a "silent generation" seeking primarily security and comfort.

Few university faculty challenged the reigning thought of the day. Historians downplayed class conflicts and highlighted the pragmatism of most Americans. Consensus—the widely shared agreement on most matters of importance—was frequently depicted as central to America's history and greatness.

Postwar Culture

American culture reflected the spirit of a prosperous era as well as Cold War anxiety. Enjoying more leisure time and bigger paychecks, Americans spent one-seventh of the GNP on entertainment. Spectator sports boomed, new symphony halls opened, and book sales doubled.

New York replaced Paris as the capital of the art world. Like the abstract canvases of Jackson Pollock and the cool jazz trumpet of Miles Davis, the major novels of the 1950s displayed introspection and improvisation. John Cheever's *The Wapshot Chronicles* and John Updike's *Rabbit Run* (1960) presented characters vaguely dissatisfied with jobs and home, longing for a more vital and authentic existence but incapable of decisive action.

Southern, African-American, and Jewish-American writers turned out the decade's most vital fiction. William Faulkner continued his dense saga of a family in Yoknapatawpha County, Mississippi, while Eudora Welty evoked small-town Mississippi life in *The Ponder Heart* (1954). The black experience found memorable expression in James Baldwin's *Go Tell It on the Mountain* (1953) and Ralph Ellison's *Invisible Man* (1951). Philip Roth's *Goodbye, Columbus* (1959) dissected the very different world of upwardly mobile Jews.

Hollywood reflected the diminished concern with political issues, churning out westerns, musicals, and costume spectacles. Most films about contemporary life portrayed Americans as one happy, white, middle-class family. Minorities and the poor remained invisible, and women appeared largely as "dumb blondes" or cute helpmates. But as TV viewing soared, movie attendance dropped by 50 percent, and a fifth of the nation's theaters became bowling alleys or supermarkets.

The Television Culture

No cultural medium ever grew so huge so quickly as television. In 1946, one in every eighteen thousand households had a TV set; by 1960, 90 percent of all households owned at least one TV, and more Americans had televisions than had bathrooms.

Business capitalized on the phenomenon. The three main radio networks—ABC, CBS, and NBC—gobbled up virtually every TV station in the country. *TV Guide* soon outsold all other periodicals. First marketed in 1954, the "TV dinner" changed the nation's eating habits. When Walt Disney produced a show on Davy Crockett in 1955, stores could not keep up with the massive demand for "King of the Wild Frontier" coonskin caps. It seemed that TV could sell anything.

Initially, TV showcased talent and creativity. Opera performances appeared in prime time, as did sophisticated comedies, dramas, and documentaries like Edward R. Murrow's *See It Now*. Early situation comedies such as *The Life of Riley* featured ethnic working-class families. As the price of TV sets fell and the chill of McCarthyism spread, the networks' appetite for a mass audience transformed TV into a cautious celebration of conformity and consumerism. Controversy went off the air. Only a few situation comedies, like Jackie Gleason's *The Honeymooners,* set in Brooklyn, did not feature suburban, consumer-oriented, upper-middle-class families. Most portrayed perfectly coiffed moms who loved to vacuum in high heels, frisky yet ultimately obedient kids, and all-knowing dads. Even Lucille Ball and Desi Arnaz, stars of *I Love Lucy*—a show which no network initially wanted because an all-American redhead was married to a Cuban—had a baby and left New York for suburbia.

Decrying television's mediocrity, in 1961 the head of the Federal Communications Commission called it "a vast wasteland." A steady parade of soaps, unsophisticated comedies, and violent westerns led others to call TV "the idiot box."

Courtesy of Motorola Museum © 1955 Motorola, Inc/Picture Research Consultants & Archives

Motorola TV Family Ad

The television set itself, so grandly advertised and displayed, was a symbol of postwar affluence. Overall, TV powerfully reinforced the conservative, celebratory values of everyday American life in the 1950s.

Measuring television's impact is difficult. Different people read the "texts" of TV (or of movies or books) in their own way and so receive their own messages from the medium. In the main, television reflected American society and stimulated the desire to be included in that society. It spawned mass fads for Barbie dolls and hula hoops and spread the message of consumerism. It reinforced gender and racial stereotypes, rarely showing African-Americans and Latinos—except in servile roles or prison scenes—and extolling male violence in fighting evil; it portrayed women as zany madcaps or self-effacing moms.

Television also changed political life. Politicians could effectively appeal to the voters over the heads of party leaders, and appearance mattered more than content. For example, at least 20 million watched Senator Joseph McCarthy bully and slander witnesses. Richard Nixon reached 58 million and saved his political career with his appeal in the "Checkers" speech, answering charges that he had received gifts and money from California businessmen. In addition, Eisenhower's pioneering use of brief "spot advertisements," combined with Stevenson's avoidance of televised appearances, clinched Ike's smashing presidential victories. In 1960, John F. Kennedy's "telegenic" image would play a significant role in his successful campaign.

Overall, television helped produce a more national culture, diminishing provincialism and regional differences. Its overwhelming portrayal of a contented citizenry reinforced complacency and hid the reality of "the other America."

CHECKING IN

- The baby boom renewed emphasis on the family and "togetherness."
- Motherhood was exalted, although women continued to pursue work outside the home.
- Organized religion and evangelicalism flourished; Billy Graham became a major American figure.
- Americans spent more time and money than ever on entertainment.
- Television became the dominant medium, changing politics as well as enforcing conformity, consumerism, and stereotypes.

SEEDS OF DISQUIET

What actions by minorities and youth foretold the movements for social change to come in the 1960s?

Late in the 1950s, apprehension ruffled the calm surface of American life. Questions about the nation's values and goals, periodic recessions, rising unemployment, and the growing national debt made Khrushchev's boast that "your grandchildren will live under communism" ring in American ears. The growing alienation of American youth and a technological breakthrough by the Soviet Union further diminished national pride.

Sputnik

On October 4, 1957, the Soviet Union launched the first artificial satellite, ***Sputnik*** ("Little Traveler"). Weighing 184 pounds and measuring only twenty-two inches in diameter, it circled Earth at eighteen thousand miles per hour. When *Sputnik II,* carrying a dog, went into a more distant orbit on November 3, critics said that Eisenhower had allowed a "technological Pearl Harbor."

Sputnik First man-made satellite to orbit Earth; launched by the Soviet Union

Although the Eisenhower administration publicly disparaged the Soviet achievement, behind the scenes they pushed to have the American Vanguard missile readied to launch a satellite. On December 6, with millions watching on TV, Vanguard rose six feet into the air and exploded. Newspapers ridiculed America's "Flopnik."

Eisenhower did not laugh, however. Instead, he more than doubled the funds for missile development to $5.3 billion in 1959. He also established the Science Advisory Committee, whose recommendations led to the creation of the National Aeronautics and Space Administration (NASA) in July 1958. By decade's end, the United States had launched several space probes and successfully tested the Atlas intercontinental ballistic missile (ICBM).

Spurred by *Sputnik,* Americans embarked on a crash program to improve American education. The National Defense Education Act (1958) for the first time provided direct federal funding to higher education, especially to improve the teaching of the sciences, mathematics, and foreign languages. Far more funds went to university research to ensure national security. By 1960, the U.S. government was funneling $1.5 billion to universities, a hundred-fold increase over 1940, and nearly a third of scientists and engineers on university faculties worked full-time on government research, primarily defense projects. Some observers dubbed it the "military-industrial-educational complex."

A Different Beat

Few adults considered the implications of affluence for the young, or the consequences of having a teenage generation stay in school instead of working. Few pondered how the young would respond to growing up in an age when traditional values like thrift and self-denial had declining relevance. Despite talk of family togetherness, busy fathers paid little attention to their children, and mothers sometimes spent more time chauffeuring their young than listening to them. Much of what adults knew about teenagers they learned from the mass media, which focused on the sensational and the superficial.

Accounts of juvenile delinquency abounded, portraying high schools as war zones, city streets as jungles, and teenagers as zip-gun-armed hoodlums. In truth, teenage crime barely increased. However, male teenagers sporting black-leather motorcycle jackets, their hair slicked into "ducktails," aroused adult alarm.

Elvis Presley Mississippi-born rock-and-roll singer beloved among younger Americans in the 1950s

Just as dismaying to parents, young Americans embraced rock and roll. In 1952, Cleveland radio host Alan Freed, having observed white teenagers dancing to rhythm-and-blues records by black performers, started a new radio program, "Moondog's Rock and Roll Party," to play "race music." In 1954, Freed took the popular program to New York, creating a national craze for rock and roll.

AP Photo/RCA Victor

"Elvis the Pelvis" in 1956

In 1956 Elvis Presley skyrocketed to rock-and-roll stardom. His rebellious sensuality, which caused girls to scream and faint and boys to imitate his gyrating hips, reflected a hunger for more immediate and vital experiences than was considered "proper" in the 1950s.

White performers transformed black rhythm and blues, with its heavy beat and suggestive lyrics, into "Top Ten" rock and roll. In 1954, Bill Haley and the Comets dropped some of the sexual allusions from Joe Turner's "Shake, Rattle, and Roll," added country-and-western guitar riffs, and produced the first major white rock-and-roll hit. When Haley performed "Rock Around the Clock" in *The Blackboard Jungle,* a 1955 film about juvenile delinquency, many parents linked rock and roll with disobedience and crime. Red-hunters saw it as a communist plot to corrupt youth. Segregationists claimed it was a ploy "to mix the races." Psychiatrists feared it was "a communicable disease." Some churches condemned it as "the devil's music."

"If I could find a white man who had the Negro sound and the Negro feel," said Sam Phillips, the owner of Sun Records in Memphis, "I could make a million dollars." He made it by finding **Elvis Presley.** Born in Tupelo, Mississippi, Elvis melded the Pentecostal music of his boyhood with the powerful beat and sexual energy of rhythm and blues. In songs like "Hound Dog" and "All Shook Up" he seemed to proclaim teenage "separateness." Presley's smirking lips and bucking hips shocked white middle-class adults. However, the more adults condemned rock and roll, the more teenagers loved it. Record sales tripled between 1954 and 1960, and Dick Clark's *American Bandstand* became the decade's biggest TV hit.

Portents of Change

Teens cherished rock and roll for defying adult propriety. They elevated characters like James Dean in *Rebel Without a Cause* (1955) to cult status for rejecting society's mores. They delighted in *Mad* magazine's ridiculing of the phony and pretentious in middle-class America. They customized their cars to reject Detroit's standards. All were signs of their distinctiveness from the adult world.

Beats 1950s poets and writers who criticized American materialism

Nonconformist writers known as the **Beats** expressed a more fundamental revolt against middle-class society. In works like Allen Ginsberg's *Howl* (1956) and Jack Kerouac's *On the Road* (1957), the Beats scorned the conformity and materialism of "square" America. They romanticized society's outcasts and glorified uninhibited sexuality and spontaneity in the search for "It," the ultimate authentic experience.

The mass media scorned the Beats, as they did all dissenters. But some admiring college youth took up the Beat message. They read poetry and listened to jazz, and some students even protested capital punishment and demonstrated against the continuing investigations of the House Un-American Activities Committee. Others decried the nuclear-arms race. In 1958 and 1959, thousands participated in Youth Marches for Integrated Schools in Washington. Together with the Beats and rock music, this vocal minority of the "silent generation" heralded a youth movement that would explode in the 1960s.

CHECKING IN

- The launch of Russia's *Sputnik* satellite spurred crash programs in space research and education to catch up with the Soviets.
- Vast sums of money were channeled into education; government-funded research threatened to dominate universities.
- Rock-and-roll stars like Elvis Presley took center stage in teen music, widening a growing rift between teenagers and their parents.
- Nonconformist writers called "Beats" began to question American culture and society.

THE OTHER AMERICA

In what sense were there two Americas?

"I am an invisible man," declared the African-American narrator of Ralph Ellison's *Invisible Man;* "I am invisible . . . because people refuse to see me." Indeed, few white middle-class Americans of the 1950s perceived the extent of social injustice in the United States. "White flight" from cities to suburbs physically separated races and classes. Popular culture focused on affluent white Americans enjoying the "good life." But poverty and racial discrimination were rife and dire, and the struggles for social justice intensified.

Poverty and Urban Blight

Although the percentage of poor families declined from 1947 to 1960, in 1960 some 35 million Americans, one-fifth of the nation, lived below the poverty line. Some 8 million elderly had yearly incomes of less than a thousand dollars.

One-third of the poor lived in depressed rural areas, and 2 million migrant farm workers lived in the most abject poverty. Observing a Texas migratory-labor camp in 1955, a journalist reported that 96 percent of the children had had no milk in the previous six months, eight out of ten adults had eaten no meat, and most slept "on the ground, in a cave, under a tree, or in a chicken house."

The bulk of the poor huddled in decaying inner-city slums. Displaced southern blacks and Appalachian whites, Native Americans forced off reservations, and newly arrived Hispanics strained cities' inadequate facilities. Nearly two hundred thousand Mexican-Americans herded into San Antonio's Westside barrio; a local newspaper described them as living like cattle in a stockyard. As described by Michael Harrington in *The Other America: Poverty in the United States* (1962), the poor lived trapped in a cycle of want and deprivation. Unable to afford a nutritious diet or doctors, the poor got sick more often and for longer than affluent Americans. Children of the poor started school at a disadvantage and rapidly fell behind; many dropped out. Living with neither hope nor skills, the poor bequeathed a similar legacy to their children.

The pressing need for low-cost housing went unanswered. Slum-clearance and urban-renewal projects shunted the poor from one ghetto to another to make room for parking garages and cultural centers. Bulldozers razed the Los Angeles barrio of Chavez Ravine to make way for Dodger Stadium. Landlords, realtors, and bankers deliberately excluded nonwhites from decent housing. Half of the housing in New York's Harlem predated 1900. There, a dozen people might share a tiny apartment with broken windows, faulty plumbing, and gaping holes in the walls. Harlem's rates of illegitimacy, infant deaths, narcotics use, and crime towered above city and national averages.

Latinos and Latinas

Hispanic-Americans initially made little headway in ending discrimination. High unemployment on the Caribbean island and the advent of direct air service to New York in 1945 brought a steady stream of Puerto Ricans to the city, where they could earn four times the average wage available on the island. By 1960, nearly a million lived in El Barrio in New York City's East Harlem.

In New York Hispanic-Americans suffered from inadequate housing and schools, as well as police harassment; they were denied decent jobs and political recognition. Family frictions flared in the transition to unaccustomed ways. For example, parents felt upstaged by children who learned English and obtained jobs that were closed to them. The relationship between husbands and wives changed as women found readier access to jobs than did men.

Mexican-Americans suffered the same indignities. Most were underpaid and segregated from mainstream American life. After World War II, new irrigation systems added 7.5 million acres to the agricultural lands of the Southwest, stimulating demand for cheap Mexican labor. In 1951, to stem the resulting tide of illegal Mexican immigrants, Congress reintroduced the wartime "temporary worker" program that brought in seasonal farm laborers called *braceros*. Many stayed without authorization, joining a growing number of Latinos who entered the country illegally.

During the 1953–1955 recession, the Eisenhower administration's "Operation Wetback" (a term of derision for illegal Mexican immigrants) deported some 3 million allegedly undocumented entrants. Periodic roundups, however, did not stop the millions of Mexicans who continued to cross the poorly guarded border. The *bracero* program itself peaked in 1959, admitting 450,000 workers.

The swelling Mexican-American population became more urban. In Los Angeles County it doubled to more than six hundred thousand, and the *colonias* (ko-lo-NEE-as) of Denver, El Paso, Phoenix, and San Antonio grew proportionately as large. By 1970, 85 percent of Mexican-Americans lived in urban areas. As service in World War II gave Hispanics an increased sense of their own American identity and a claim on their rights as American citizens, urbanization gave them better educational and employment opportunities. Unions like the United Cannery, Agricultural, Packing, and Allied Workers of America (UCAPAWA) sought higher wages and better working conditions for their Mexican-American members, and such middle-class organizations as the League of United Latin American Citizens (LULAC) campaigned to desegregate schools and public facilities.

In 1954, the Supreme Court banned the exclusion of Mexican-Americans from Texas jury lists, and in 1958 El Paso elected the first Mexican-American mayor. Latinos also took pride in baseball star Roberto Clemente and their growing numbers in the major leagues, in Nobel Prize winners like biologist Severo Ochoa, and in such Hollywood stars as Anthony Quinn. But the existence of millions of undocumented aliens and the continuation of the *bracero* program stigmatized all people of Spanish descent and depressed their wages. The median income of Hispanics was less than two-thirds that of Anglos. At least a third lived in poverty.

Native Americans

Native Americans remained the poorest, most ignored minority. Their death rate was three times the national average, and unemployment on reservations ran a staggering 70 to 86 percent for some tribes. Congress again changed course, moving away from efforts to reassert Indian sovereignty and cultural autonomy and back toward the goal of assimilation. Between 1954 and 1962, Congress terminated treaties and withdrew financial support from sixty-one reservations. First applied to the Menominees (meh-NAH-mih-nees) of Wisconsin and the Klamaths (CLAY-muths) of Oregon, who owned valuable timberlands, the policy was disastrous. Further impoverishing the tribes, it transferred more than five hundred thousand acres of Native American lands to non-Indians.

By 1960, about sixty thousand Indians had been relocated to cities. Some became middle class, some ended up in run-down urban shantytowns, and nearly a third eventually returned to their reservations. The National Congress of American Indians vigorously opposed termination, and most tribal politicians advocated Indian sovereignty, treaty rights, and federal trusteeship.

CHECKING IN

- Michael Harrington's *The Other America* called attention to the poverty and deprivation that existed beneath the complacent surface of the 1950s.
- Many of the poor remained trapped in decaying cities.
- Poverty and discrimination, often sharpened by illegal immigrant status, continued to dog Mexican-Americans; as their population became more urban, Spanish-speakers began to assert their rights.
- Native Americans' welfare slipped even further as government policy veered toward assimilation and termination of treaties.

THE CIVIL RIGHTS MOVEMENT

What innovative strategies were developed by the civil rights movement in this era?

The integration of baseball in 1947, spearheaded by the brilliant Jackie Robinson, symbolized a new robustness in the fight against racial discrimination and segregation in the postwar era. The war had heightened African-American expectations for racial equality, and demands included a permanent Fair Employment Practices Commission (FEPC), the outlawing of lynching, and the right to vote.

The Politics of Race

Fearful of black assertiveness in seeking the vote and in mobilizing grass-roots forces, white racists accelerated their repression and violence. In 1946, whites killed several black veterans in Georgia for daring to vote and blinded a black soldier for failing to sit in the rear of a bus in South Carolina. In Columbia, Tennessee, also in 1946, a white riot against blacks who were insisting on their rights led to the arrest of seventy African-Americans and the jailhouse lynching of two of the prisoners.

President's Committee on Civil Rights Empanelled by Truman; recommended a legal assault on segregation

These events horrified President Truman. Genuinely believing that every American should enjoy the full rights of citizenship, Truman in late 1946 established the **President's Committee on Civil Rights** to investigate race relations. The committee's report, *To Secure These Rights*, published in 1947, called for the eradication of racial discrimination and segregation and proposed anti-lynching and anti-poll tax legislation. Boldly, Truman in February 1948 sent a special message to Congress urging lawmakers to enact most of the committee's proposals. Truman's subsequent actions would fall short of his rhetoric. However, the president issued executive orders barring discrimination in federal employment and creating a committee to ensure "equality of treatment and opportunity" in the armed services.

Jim Crow in Court

During the Truman presidency, moreover, the Supreme Court declared segregation in interstate bus transportation unconstitutional (*Morgan* v. *Virginia*, 1946) and outlawed restrictive housing covenants that forbade the sale or rental of property to minorities (*Shelley* v. *Kraemer*, 1948). Soon thereafter, the NAACP's chief attorney, Thurgood Marshall, undertook a direct attack on segregation itself. He pursued a strategy built on an earlier federal court ruling that had prohibited the segregation of Mexican-American children in California schools.

Earl Warren Chief justice of the Supreme Court who broadened constitutional protections for individual rights

Brown* v. *Board of Education of Topeka 1954 Supreme Court decision that declared "separate but equal" doctrine unconstitutional; paved the way for the end of segregation

In May 1954, the new Chief Justice appointed by Eisenhower, **Earl Warren** (1953), speaking for a unanimous Court, reversed the "separate but equal" doctrine of *Plessy* v. *Ferguson* (see Chapter 20) in the landmark case of ***Brown* v. *Board of Education of Topeka.*** Overturning more than sixty years of legal segregation, the Supreme Court ruled that separate educational facilities for blacks and whites were "inherently unequal," denying black children the "equal protection of the laws" guaranteed by the Fourteenth Amendment. A year later, the Court decreed that school desegregation should proceed "with all deliberate speed."

In the border states, some African-American and white students sat side-by-side for the first time in history. But in the South, where segregation was deeply entrenched in law and custom, politicians vowed resistance. Although not personally racist, Ike never publicly endorsed the *Brown* decision and privately called his appointment of Earl Warren "the biggest damn fool mistake I ever made."

Encouraged by the president's indecisiveness, White Citizens' Councils organized to defend segregation and the Ku Klux Klan revived. Declaring *Brown* "null, void, and of no effect," southern legislatures adopted a strategy of "massive resistance." They closed down or denied state aid to school systems that desegregated and enacted pupil-placement laws that permitted school boards to assign black and white children to different schools. In 1956, more than a hundred members of Congress signed the **Southern Manifesto,** denouncing *Brown*. That year, not a single African-American attended school with whites in the Deep South, and few did so in the Upper South.

Southern Manifesto
1956 statement of southern congressmen opposing the *Brown* decision and defending racial segregation

The Laws of the Land

Southern resistance reached a climax in September 1957. Although the Little Rock school board had accepted a federal court order to desegregate Central High School, Arkansas governor Orval E. Faubus mobilized the state's National Guard to block enforcement and bar nine African-American students from entering the school. After another court order forced Faubus to withdraw the guardsmen, an angry mob of whites blocked the black students' entry.

The Arkansas Democrat-Gazette, Inc.

Little Rock, 1957

Elizabeth Eckford, age fifteen, one of the nine black students to desegregate Central High School, endures abuse on her way to school, September 4, 1957. Forty years later, the young white woman shouting insults asked for forgiveness.

Eisenhower, believing he had to uphold federal authority, nationalized the Arkansas National Guard, augmented by a thousand federal troops, to protect the African-American students for the rest of the academic year. He thus became, albeit reluctantly, the first president since Reconstruction to use federal troops to enforce the rights of blacks. Local authorities, however, shut down Little Rock's public schools the next year, and by decade's end, fewer than 1 percent of African-American students in the Deep South attended desegregated schools.

Clearly, court victories alone would not end Jim Crow laws. Nor would weak legislation. The Civil Rights Act of 1957, the first since Reconstruction, established a permanent commission on civil rights with broad investigatory powers, but did little to guarantee the ballot to blacks; likewise, the Civil Rights Act of 1960 only slightly strengthened the first measure's enforcement provisions. At best, these bills implied a changing view of race relations by the federal government, which further encouraged blacks to fight for their rights.

Mass Protest in Montgomery

To sweep away the separate but rarely equal Jim Crow facilities in the South, African-Americans turned to new tactics, organizations, and leaders. They utilized nonviolent direct-action protest to engage large numbers of blacks in their own freedom struggle and to arouse white America's conscience.

In the 1950s, racism still touched even the smallest details of daily life. In Montgomery, Alabama, black bus riders had to surrender their seats so that no white rider would stand. Although they were more than three-quarters of all passengers, African-Americans had to pay their fares at the front of the bus, leave, and reenter through the back door; sit only in the rear; and then give up their seats to any standing white passengers.

Rosa Parks Civil-rights leader whose refusal to give a white man her bus seat triggered the Montgomery bus boycott

On December 1, 1955, **Rosa Parks,** for many years an officer of the Montgomery NAACP and a veteran of civil-rights protests in the 1930s and 1940s, refused to get up so that a white man could sit. "I was not tired physically," she later wrote. "No, the only tired I was, was tired of giving in." Her arrest sparked a boycott of the buses—the beginning of the mass phase of the civil rights movement. Boycotters founded the Montgomery Improvement Association (MIA) to organize the protest, and elected **Martin Luther King, Jr.,** a twenty-seven-year-old African-American minister, to lead the boycott. Montgomery African-Americans trudged the streets, organized carpools, and raised thousands of dollars to carry on the fight. They persisted for more than a year until the Supreme Court ordered the buses desegregated.

Martin Luther King, Jr. African-American minister whose emphasis on nonviolence catapulted him to leadership of the civil rights movement

The Montgomery bus boycott demonstrated African-American strength and determination. It vaulted Dr. King, whose oratory simultaneously inspired black activism and touched white consciences, into the national spotlight. As no one before, King presented the case for black rights in a vocabulary that echoed both the Bible and the freedom values of the Founding Fathers.

King's philosophy of civil disobedience fused the spirit of Christianity with the strategy of achieving racial justice by nonviolent resistance. His insistence on nonviolence also diminished the likelihood of bloodshed. Preaching that blacks must lay their bodies on the line to provoke crises that would force whites to confront their racism, King urged his followers to love their enemies. By so doing, he believed, blacks would convert their oppressors and bring "redemption and reconciliation." In 1957, King and a group of black ministers formed the Southern Christian Leadership Conference (SCLC). Yet more than on leaders, the movement's triumphs in the decade ahead would depend on the thousands of ordinary people who marched, rallied, and demonstrated extraordinarily in grass-roots protest movements.

New Tactics for a New Decade

Foreshadowing the massive grass-roots activism to come, four black college students in Greensboro, North Carolina, entered the local Woolworth's on February 1, 1960, and sat down at the whites-only lunch counter, defying segregation. "We don't serve colored here," the waitress replied when the freshmen ordered coffee and doughnuts. The blacks remained seated. They would not be moved.

Impatient yet hopeful, the students would not accept the inequality their parents had endured. Inspired by the earlier black struggles for justice, they vowed to sit-in until they were served. Six months later, after prolonged sit-ins, boycotts, and demonstrations by hundreds of students, and violent white resistance, Greensboro's civic leaders grudgingly allowed blacks to sit down at hitherto segregated restaurants and be served.

Meanwhile, the courageous example of the Greensboro "coffee party" catalyzed similar sit-ins throughout the border states and Upper South. Black students confronted humiliations and violence: They endured beatings, cigarette-burnings, tear-gassing, and jailing. Yet they stayed true to nonviolent principles and refused to retaliate.

The determination of the students transformed the struggle for racial equality. Their activism and commitment emboldened black adults and other youths to act. "I myself desegregated a lunch counter, not somebody else, not some big man, some powerful man, but little me," claimed a student. By year's end, nearly fifty thousand people had participated in demonstrations, desegregating lunch counters and other public facilities in 126 southern cities.

Newly encouraged and emboldened, the Congress of Racial Equality (CORE), which had been founded in WWII, organized a "Freedom Ride" through the Deep South in spring 1961 to dramatize the flouting of federal court decisions banning segregation in interstate transportation facilities. It aroused white wrath. Mobs beat the Freedom Riders in Anniston, Alabama, burning their bus, and mauled the protestors in Birmingham. A week later, scores of racist southerners in Montgomery beat Freedom Riders with bats and iron chains, generating international publicity and indignation, which ultimately forced the Interstate Commerce Commission to require the desegregation of all interstate carriers and terminals.

Many of the Freedom Riders were members of the **Student Nonviolent Coordinating Committee (SNCC).** Formed in April 1960 by participants in the sit-ins, SNCC (known as "Snick") stressed both the nonviolent civil disobedience strategy of Martin Luther King, Jr., and the need to stimulate local activism and leadership. In fall 1961, it chose Albany (all-BENNY), Georgia, as the site of a campaign to desegregate public facilities and secure the vote. Wily local authorities avoided the overt violence that had

Student Nonviolent Coordinating Committee (SNCC) Youth auxiliary of the NAACP; involved in sit-ins and rallies

CHECKING IN

- Truman established the President's Committee on Civil Rights; its report, *To Secure These Rights*, pointed the way toward racial equality.
- The *Brown* decision declared the practice of racial segregation in the schools to be unconstitutional.
- White opposition in Little Rock, Arkansas, and throughout the South slowed the process of school integration to a crawl.
- A successful boycott of segregated buses in Montgomery, Alabama, vaulted Martin Luther King, Jr., to the forefront of the civil rights movement.
- CORE, SNCC, and other groups used nonviolent civil disobedience to expose the inherent violence of segregation.

won the Freedom Riders national sympathy. The Albany movement collapsed, but the lesson of Albany, and of the Freedom Rides, had been learned: Only the provocation of vicious white racist violence generated national publicity and forced the federal government to intervene. The young activists who learned that lesson and how to use the media skillfully would chart the course of the 1960s.

Chapter Summary

What were the main sources of the postwar economic expansion and affluence? (page 661)

Although the shift to peacetime production after V-J Day did not always progress smoothly, in general, the postwar era was one of unparalleled affluence for most Americans. Building on the accumulated savings and pent-up demand for consumer goods after World War II, high levels of government spending, the GI Bill, and new technologies that increased productivity spurred an economic boom.

What, if any, were the negative consequences associated with economic growth and prosperity? (page 663)

A decade of sustained prosperity grew in part from massive federal spending, much of it linked to defense. The computer industry began to develop. A new corporate culture emerged, emphasizing conformity over initiative. Meanwhile, the use of chemicals in an increasingly automated agricultural industry caused environmental damage. In addition, union membership sagged, owing to prosperity, automation, and the increasing proportion of Americans working in white-collar positions.

How accurate is the image of 1950s suburban life as one of contentment, conservatism, and conformity? (page 667)

The suburbs boomed, as did the Sun Belt. The baby boom put renewed emphasis on the family and led to the exaltation of motherhood as a woman's principal role; "togetherness" blossomed. Organized religion flourished, as did evangelicalism. Television became the dominant medium, emphasizing conformity and consumerism while changing politics and reinforcing stereotypes.

KEY TERMS

GI Bill *(p. 662)*
Bretton Woods agreement *(p. 663)*
Silent Spring (p. 666)
Sun Belt *(p. 668)*
baby boom *(p. 669)*
Dr. Benjamin Spock *(p. 669)*
Billy Graham *(p. 670)*
Sputnik (p. 673)
Elvis Presley *(p. 674)*
Beats *(p. 675)*
President's Committee on Civil Rights *(p. 678)*
Earl Warren *(p. 678)*
Brown v. *Board of Education of Topeka (p. 678)*
Southern Manifesto *(p. 679)*
Rosa Parks *(p. 680)*
Martin Luther King, Jr. *(p. 680)*
Student Nonviolent Coordinating Committee (SNCC) *(p. 681)*

What actions by minorities and youth foretold the movements for social change to come in the 1960s? (page 673)

The Soviet Union's successful launch of the *Sputnik* satellite shattered American complacency. In response, the government funneled vast sums into education and university research. A new kind of music, rock and roll, emerged to identify a teenage subculture; "Elvis the Pelvis" became the symbol of teen rebellion and parental despair. In their nonconformist writings, the Beats openly questioned American materialism and joined rock and roll in laying the foundation for the youth rebellion of the 1960s.

In what sense were there two Americas? (page 675)

Suburban prosperity left the poor isolated on a remote island of deprivation and powerlessness in "the other America." Poor Americans, rural and urban, lived in a cycle of want and deprivation. Hispanic Americans began to assert their rights, while Native Americans slipped further behind.

What innovative strategies were developed by the civil rights movement in this era? (page 677)

In the courts, the NAACP ceased requesting that separate facilities be equal and instead insisted that true equality required desegregation; this change in strategy resulted in the landmark *Brown* school desegregation decision. And in the streets, Martin Luther King, Jr., SNCC, and CORE employed the techniques of nonviolent civil disobedience to attack Jim Crow laws, bringing some gains and stimulating an insurgency that spurred further challenges to make the nation live up to its ideals.

Go to the CourseMate website at **www.cengagebrain.com** for additional study tools and review materials—including audio and video clips—for this chapter.

CHAPTER 28

Liberalism, Civil Rights, and War in Vietnam

1960–1975

Francis Miller/Time & Life Pictures/Getty Images

Martin Luther King, Jr.

CHAPTER PREVIEW

The Kennedy Presidency, 1960–1963
To what extent did the Kennedy administration's domestic record reflect its liberal rhetoric?

The Continuing Struggle for Black Equality, 1961–1968
What were the major successes and failures of the civil-rights movement from 1961 to 1968?

The Expanding Movement for Equality
How and why did the protest movements of minorities shift from the goals and tactics associated with Martin Luther King, Jr., to those of Black Power?

Liberalism Ascendant, 1963–1968
How did Lyndon Johnson's Great Society program exemplify the new liberalism of the 1960s?

The Vietnam Crusade, 1961–1975
How and why did Kennedy, Johnson, and Nixon each deepen America's involvement in the war in Indochina?

Facing the nearly quarter of a million Americans who had come to Washington, DC, on August 28, 1963, to petition for civil rights, Martin Luther King, Jr., issued an urgent call for change. A century had passed since the Emancipation Proclamation, and yet, "the Negro is still not free." Blacks, King insisted, would brook no further delay:

> We can never be satisfied as long as our children are stripped of their selfhood and robbed of their dignity by signs stating: "For Whites Only." We cannot be satisfied as long as the Negro in Mississippi cannot vote and the Negro in New York believes he has nothing for which to vote. No, no, we are not satisfied and we will not be satisfied until justice rolls down like the waters and righteousness like a mighty stream.

King's speech represented the high-water mark of the black freedom struggle. Along with inspiring the enactment of the Civil Rights Act of 1964 and the Voting Rights Act of 1965, which together sounded the death knell for Jim Crow laws, King would help redefine liberalism to embrace civil rights. Two years earlier, President John Kennedy launched the era with a promise to "pay any price, bear any burden" to win the Cold War and fulfill America's destiny as the last best hope of mankind. JFK's rhetoric, like King's, generated fervent hopes and lofty expectations.

But JFK's assassination, at a time of peace and prosperity, would begin a long descent toward national disillusionment. His successor, Lyndon Baines Johnson (LBJ), brought forth the Great Society—the apex of liberalism. The Great Society promised health care for the aged and indigent, federal aid to education, urban development, environmental safeguards, immigration reform, and an end to racial discrimination and poverty. Nevertheless, the liberal hope to enhance liberty and equality crashed against defeat in Vietnam. The racial strife of the "long hot summers" splintered the civil-rights movement and provoked a growing conservative reaction.

JFK, LBJ, and Richard Nixon all saw the need to thwart the spread of communism in Southeast Asia. The war there would cost America dearly in lives and dollars. It damaged the economy, fomented internal dissent, eroded public faith in elected officials, and transformed the brief era of triumphant liberalism into a time of discord and despair.

THE KENNEDY PRESIDENCY, 1960–1963

To what extent did the Kennedy administration's domestic record reflect its liberal rhetoric?

Projecting an image of youth and vigor, **John F. Kennedy** personified the self-confident liberal who believed that an activist state could improve life at home and confront the communist challenge abroad. His wealthy father, Joseph P. Kennedy, seethed with ambition and instilled in his sons a passion to excel and to attain political power. Despite a severe back injury, John Kennedy served in the navy in World War II and became a war hero. He then used his charm and his father's connections to win election in 1946 to the House of Representatives from a Boston district where he had never lived. Although Kennedy earned little distinction in Congress, Massachusetts voters sent him to the Senate in 1952 and overwhelmingly reelected him in 1958.

John F. Kennedy Thirty-fifth president of the United States; Cold Warrior who projected youthful dynamism

By then he had a beautiful wife, Jacqueline, and a Pulitzer Prize for *Profiles in Courage* (1956), written largely by a staff member. Despite the political liability of his Roman Catholic faith, he won a first-ballot victory at the 1960 Democratic convention. Just forty-three years old, he sounded the theme of a "New Frontier," exhorting Americans to "get this country moving again."

A New Beginning

"All at once you had something exciting," recalled a University of Nebraska student. "You had a guy who had little kids and who liked to play football on his front lawn.

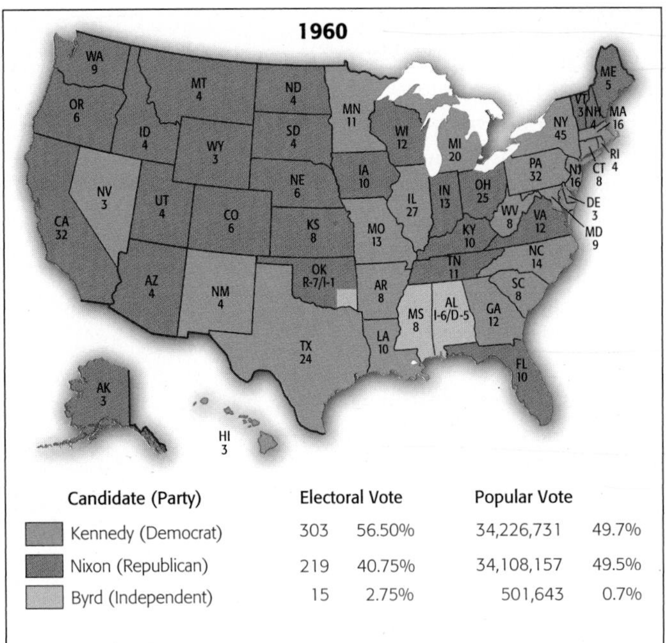

Candidate (Party)	Electoral Vote		Popular Vote	
Kennedy (Democrat)	303	56.50%	34,226,731	49.7%
Nixon (Republican)	219	40.75%	34,108,157	49.5%
Byrd (Independent)	15	2.75%	501,643	0.7%

Map 28.1 The Election of 1960

Interactive Map

Kennedy was talking about pumping new life into the nation and steering it in new directions." But most voters wanted the stability, security, and continuation of Eisenhower's "middle way" promised by the Republican candidate, Vice President Richard M. Nixon. Although scorned by liberals for his McCarthyism, Nixon was better known and more experienced than Kennedy, identified with the still-popular Ike, and a Protestant.

However, Nixon fumbled his opportunity, agreeing to meet Kennedy in a series of televised debates. More than 70 million tuned in to the first televised debate between presidential candidates—a broadcast that secured the dominance of television in American politics. Nixon, sweating visibly, appeared haggard and insecure; in striking contrast, the tanned, telegenic Kennedy radiated confidence. Radio listeners judged the debate a draw, but the far more numerous television viewers declared Kennedy the victor. He shot up in the polls, and Nixon never recovered.

Kennedy also benefited from an economic recession in 1960, and from his choice of a southern Protestant, Senate Majority Leader Lyndon B. Johnson, as his running mate. Still, the election was the closest since 1884. Only 120,000 votes separated the two candidates. Kennedy's religion cost him millions of popular votes, but the Catholic vote in the closely contested midwestern and northeastern states delivered crucial Electoral College votes, enabling him to squeak to victory (see Map 28.1).

Kennedy's inauguration set the tone of a new era: "The torch has been passed to a new generation of Americans." In sharp contrast to the Eisenhower administration's reliance on businessmen, Kennedy surrounded himself with liberal intellectuals.

Kennedy seemed more a celebrity than a politician. Aided by his wife, he adorned his presidency with the trappings of culture and excellence, inviting distinguished artists to perform at the White House and studding his speeches with quotations from Emerson. Awed by his grace and wit, the media extolled him as a vibrant leader and adoring husband. The public knew nothing of his fragile health, frequent use of mood-altering drugs to relieve pain, and extramarital affairs.

Kennedy's Domestic Record

Media images obscured Kennedy's lackluster domestic record. The conservative coalition of Republicans and southern Democrats that had stifled Truman's Fair Deal doomed the New Frontier. Lacking the votes, Kennedy rarely pressed Congress for social legislation.

JFK made stimulating economic growth his domestic priority. To that end, he combined higher defense expenditures with investment incentives for

Chronology

1960	Sit-ins to protest segregation begin; John F. Kennedy elected president
1961	Peace Corps and Alliance for Progress created; Bay of Pigs invasion; Freedom Rides; Berlin Wall erected
1962	Cuban missile crisis
1963	Civil-rights demonstrations in Birmingham; March on Washington; Test-Ban Treaty between the Soviet Union and the United States; Kennedy assassinated; Lyndon B. Johnson becomes president
1964	Freedom Summer in Mississippi; Civil Rights Act; Gulf of Tonkin incident and resolution; Economic Opportunity Act initiates "war on poverty"; Johnson elected president; Bombing of North Vietnam and Americanization of the war begin
1965	Assassination of Malcolm X; civil-rights march from Selma to Montgomery; César Chávez's United Farm Workers strike in California; teach-ins to question U.S. involvement in Vietnam begin; Voting Rights Act; Watts riot in Los Angeles
1966	Black Panthers formed
1967	Massive antiwar demonstrations; race riots in Newark, Detroit, and other cities
1968	Vietnam peace talks open in Paris; Richard Nixon elected president
1970	United States invades Cambodia
1971	United States and South Vietnam invade Laos
1973	Vietnamese cease-fire agreement signed
1974	Indian Self-Determination Act
1975	South Vietnam surrenders following North Vietnam's capture of Saigon

private enterprise. In 1961, he persuaded Congress to boost the defense budget by 20 percent. He vastly increased America's nuclear stockpile and strengthened the military's conventional forces. Kennedy also convinced Congress to finance a "race to the moon," which Americans would win in 1969 at a cost of more than $25 billion. Most importantly, Kennedy took his liberal advisers' Keynesian advice to call for a huge cut in corporate taxes that would greatly increase the deficit but would presumably provide capital for businesses to invest, stimulating the economy and thus increasing tax revenues.

When the Kennedy presidency ended tragically in November 1963, the proposed tax cut was bottled up in Congress. But JFK's economic program had already doubled the rate of economic growth and decreased unemployment, triggering the United States' longest uninterrupted economic expansion.

The boom would both cause further ecological damage and provide the affluence that enabled Americans to care about the environment. The fallout scare of the 1950s raised questions about the planet's well-being. The publication in 1962 of Rachel Carson's *Silent Spring* (see Chapter 27) intensified concern. Additionally, with postwar prosperity, many Americans were concerned less with increased production and more with the quality of life. In 1963, Congress passed a Clean Air Act, regulating automotive and industrial emissions. After decades of heedless pollution, Washington hesitantly began to address environmental problems.

Cold War Activism

Proclaiming in his inaugural address that "we shall pay any price, bear any burden, meet any hardship," to assure the "success of liberty," Kennedy launched a major military buildup and surrounded himself with Cold Warriors who shared his belief that American security depended on superior force and the willingness to use it. He also increased economic assistance to Third World countries to counter the appeal of communism. The Peace Corps, created in 1961, exemplified the New Frontier's liberal anticommunism. By 1963, five thousand Peace Corps volunteers were serving two-year stints as teachers, sanitation engineers, crop specialists, and health workers in more than forty Third World nations.

In early 1961, a crisis flared in Laos, a tiny nation in Southeast Asia, where a civil war between American-supported forces and Pathet Lao rebels seemed headed toward a communist triumph. In July 1962, Kennedy agreed to a face-saving compromise that restored a neutralist government but left communist forces dominant in the countryside.

Spring 1961 brought Kennedy's first major foreign-policy crisis. Despite his military advisers thinking it had little chance of success, he approved a CIA plan, drawn up in the Eisenhower administration, to invade Cuba. In April, fifteen hundred anti-Castro exiles landed at Cuba's Bay of Pigs, assuming that their arrival would trigger a general uprising to overthrow Fidel Castro. It was a fiasco. Deprived of air cover because Kennedy wanted to conceal U.S. involvement, the invaders had no chance against Castro's superior forces.

In July 1961, on the heels of the Bay of Pigs failure, Kennedy met with Soviet premier Nikita Khrushchev, who threatened war unless the West retreated from Berlin. A shaken Kennedy declared the defense of West Berlin essential to the Free World. He doubled draft calls, mobilized reservists, and called for vastly increased defense spending. The threat of nuclear war escalated until mid-August, when Moscow constructed a wall to seal off Soviet-held East Berlin and end the exodus of brains and talent to the West. The Berlin Wall became a concrete symbol of communism's denial of personal freedom until it fell in 1989.

To the Brink of Nuclear War

In mid-October 1962, aerial photographs revealed that the Soviet Union had built bases for intermediate-range nuclear missiles in Cuba, which were capable of striking most U.S. soil. Smarting from the Bay of Pigs disaster and believing his credibility to be at stake, Kennedy responded forcefully. In a somber televised address he announced that the United States would "quarantine" Cuba—impose a naval blockade—to prevent delivery of more missiles and would dismantle by force the missiles already in Cuba if the Soviet Union did not do so.

The world held its breath. The two superpowers appeared to be on a collision course toward nuclear war. Soviet technicians worked feverishly to complete the missile launch pads, and Soviet missile-carrying ships steamed toward the blockade; B-52s armed with nuclear weapons took to the air; and nearly 250,000 troops assembled in Florida to invade Cuba. Secretary of State Dean Rusk reported, "We're eyeball to eyeball."

On October 25, a relieved Rusk announced, "I think the other fellow just blinked." Kennedy received a message from Khrushchev promising to remove the missiles if the United States pledged never to invade Cuba. As Kennedy prepared to respond positively, a second, more belligerent message arrived from the Soviet leader insisting that American missiles be withdrawn from Turkey as part of the deal. Hours later, an American U-2 reconnaissance plane was shot down over Cuba. Robert Kennedy persuaded his brother to accept the first message and simply ignore the second one. In the early morning hours of October 28, Khrushchev pledged to remove the missiles in return for Kennedy's noninvasion promise. Less publicly, Kennedy later removed U.S. missiles from Turkey.

Only after the end of the Cold War did the Russians disclose that Soviet forces in Cuba had possessed thirty-six nuclear warheads as well as nine tactical nuclear weapons for battlefield use, and that Soviet field commanders had independent authority to use these weapons. Worst of all, Kennedy did not know that the Soviets already had the ability to launch a nuclear strike from Cuba.

Chastened by coming so close to the brink of nuclear war, Kennedy and Khrushchev installed a telephone "hot line" so that the two sides could communicate instantly in future crises and then agreed to a treaty outlawing atmospheric and undersea nuclear testing. These efforts signaled a new phase of the Cold War, later called détente (day-TAHNT), in which the superpowers moved from confrontation to negotiation. Concurrently, the **Cuban missile crisis** escalated the arms race by convincing both sides of the need for nuclear superiority.

Cuban missile crisis Brinkmanship between the United States and Soviet Union over nuclear missiles in Cuba in 1962 that nearly led to nuclear war

The Thousand-Day Presidency

On November 22, 1963, during a trip to Texas to shore up his reelection chances, a smiling JFK rode in an open car along Dallas streets lined with cheering crowds. Shots rang out. The president slumped, dying, his skull and throat shattered. Soon after, aboard Air Force One, Lyndon B. Johnson was sworn in as president.

Grief and disbelief numbed the nation as most Americans spent the next four days in front of their television sets staring at replays of the murder of accused assassin Lee Harvey Oswald; at the somber state funeral, with the small boy saluting his father's casket; and at the grieving family lighting an eternal flame at Arlington National Cemetery. Few who watched would forget. Kennedy had helped make TV central to politics; now, in death, it made him the fallen hero-king of Camelot.

More admired in death than in life, JFK ranked as one of the very few "great" presidents in the view of a public that associated him with a spirit of energy and innovation. While Kennedy loyalists continue to stress his intelligence and his ability to change and grow, his detractors point to his lack of achievements, the discrepancy between his public image and his private philandering, his aggressive Cold War tactics, and his vast expansion of presidential powers. Partly because his own personal behavior made him beholden to FBI director J. Edgar Hoover, JFK allowed the agency to infringe on civil liberties.

Internationally, Kennedy left a mixed record. He signed the world's first nuclear-test-ban treaty yet undertook a massive arms buildup. He compromised on Laos but deepened U.S. involvement in Vietnam. He came to question the need for U.S.-Soviet confrontation yet insisted on U.S. global superiority and aggressively prosecuted the Cold War.

CHECKING IN

- Kennedy became the first TV president.
- JFK had relatively few successes in domestic legislation, but he promoted tax cuts that stimulated economic growth.
- The Peace Corps symbolized the optimism and idealism of youth who were confident in the New Frontier.
- Kennedy took a hard line in the Cold War and launched a major military buildup; the Cuban missile crisis took the two superpowers to the brink of war.
- After Kennedy's assassination, the Camelot myth stimulated liberal hopes.

Still, JFK inspired Americans to expect greatness, aroused the poor and the powerless, and stimulated the young to activism. Dying during the calm before the storm, he left his successor soaring expectations at home and a deteriorating entanglement in Vietnam.

THE CONTINUING STRUGGLE FOR BLACK EQUALITY, 1961–1968

What were the major successes and failures of the civil-rights movement from 1961 to 1968?

Following the lunch-counter sit-ins, civil-rights activists tried to convince Kennedy to act on their behalf. He would not do so, however, fearing it would split the Democratic Party and jeopardize his reelection. Yet the movement persisted until it had achieved *de jure,* or legal, equality; made protest respectable; and become an inspiration and model of activism for aggrieved others.

The African-American Revolution

As television coverage brought mounting numbers of African-Americans into the struggle for racial equality, civil-rights leaders pressured Kennedy to intervene. Dismantling segregation piecemeal would take generations, they realized; only comprehensive national legislation, backed by the power of the federal government, could guarantee full citizenship for African-Americans. To get this they needed a crisis that would outrage the conscience of the white majority and force the president's hand.

Library of Congress

Birmingham, 1963
President Kennedy said this photograph of an African-American being attacked by a police dog during the protest demonstrations in Birmingham made him "sick." It helped galvanize the nation's conscience, leading Kennedy to submit a comprehensive civil-rights bill to Congress.

Determined to expose the violent extremism of southern racism, Martin Luther King, Jr., launched nonviolent marches, sit-ins, and pray-ins in Birmingham, Alabama, the most rigidly segregated big city in America. Birmingham's officials had even removed a book from the library that featured white and black rabbits. As such, few doubted Police Commissioner Eugene "Bull" Connor's pledge that "blood would run in the streets of Birmingham before it would be integrated."

In May, thousands of schoolchildren joined King's crusade. The bigoted Connor lost his temper. He unleashed his men—armed with electric cattle prods, high-pressure water hoses, and snarling attack dogs—on the nonviolent demonstrators. The ferocity of Connor's attacks, caught on camera and television, horrified the world. When jailed for instigating the march, King penned the "Letter from Birmingham Jail." It detailed the humiliations of segregation and justified civil disobedience to protest unjust laws.

"The civil-rights movement should thank God for Bull Connor," JFK remarked. "He's helped it as much as Abraham Lincoln." Kennedy arranged a behind-the-scenes compromise ending the Birmingham demonstrations in return for desegregating stores and hiring black workers. By mid-1963, the rallying cry "Freedom Now!" reverberated across the nation as the protests grew. Increasingly concerned about America's image abroad, Kennedy feared that if the government did not act, blacks would turn to violence. When Alabama governor George Wallace in June 1963 refused to allow two black students to enter the University of Alabama, Kennedy forced Wallace to capitulate to a court desegregation order.

On June 11, the president went on television to define civil rights as "a moral issue" and to assert that "race has no place in American life or law." A week later, Kennedy proposed a bill outlawing segregation in public facilities and authorizing the federal government to withhold funds from programs that discriminated. As the bill bogged down in Congress, civil-rights adherents planned to march on Washington to muster support for the legislation.

The March on Washington, 1963

To compel Congress to act, nearly 250,000 Americans converged on the Capitol on August 28, 1963. There they heard the ringing words of **Martin Luther King, Jr.,** proclaiming that he had a dream of brotherhood, of freedom and justice, a dream that "all of God's children, black men and white men, Jews and Gentiles, Protestants and Catholics, will be able to join hands and sing in the words of the old Negro spiritual, 'Free at last! Free at last! Thank God Almighty, we are free at last!'" King had turned a political rally into a historic event with one of the great speeches of history.

Martin Luther King, Jr. Baptist minister whose leadership galvanized the modern, grass-roots civil-rights movement in the 1960s

However, neither Kennedy's nor King's eloquence could quell the anger of white racists. On the night of the president's address, civil-rights leader Medgar Evers was murdered by a sniper in Jackson, Mississippi. In September, the bombing of a black church in Birmingham killed four girls. And still, southern obstructionism kept the civil-rights bill stymied in Congress.

The Civil Rights at High Tide

Kennedy's assassination brought to the White House a southerner, Lyndon Johnson, who knew he had to prove himself on the race issue or the liberals "would get me . . . I had to produce a civil rights bill that was even stronger than the one they'd have gotten if Kennedy had lived."

The resulting **Civil Rights Act,** the most significant civil-rights law in U.S. history, banned racial discrimination and segregation in public accommodations. It outlawed bias in federally funded programs, granted the federal government new powers to fight school segregation, and created the Equal Employment Opportunity Commission (EEOC) to enforce a ban on job discrimination on the basis of race, religion, national origin, or gender.

Civil Rights Act Major legislation that created the Equal Employment Opportunity Commission

The Civil Rights Act of 1964 did not address the right to vote. Therefore, Congress of Racial Equality (CORE) and Student Nonviolent Coordinating Committee (SNCC) activists, believing that the ballot box held the key to power for southern blacks, mounted a major campaign to register black voters. They organized the Mississippi Freedom Summer Project of 1964 to focus on the state most hostile to black rights. One thousand college-student volunteers assisted blacks in registering to vote and in organizing "Freedom Schools" that taught black history and emphasized African-American self-worth. Harassed by Mississippi law enforcement officials and Ku Klux Klansmen, the volunteers endured the firebombing of black churches and civil-rights headquarters as well as arrests and even murders.

The civil-rights workers enrolled nearly sixty thousand disfranchised blacks in the Mississippi Freedom Democratic Party (MFDP). In August 1964, they took their case to the national Democratic convention. But despite stirring testimony from activists like Fannie Lou Hamer, the MFDP was not seated. Rejecting Johnson's offer of two open delegate seats as a "token" gesture, the disillusioned members of the MFDP walked out of the convention.

Determined to win a strong voting-rights law, the Southern Christian Leadership Conference (SCLC) organized mass protests in Selma, Alabama, in March 1965. Blacks were half the population of Dallas County, where Selma was located, but only 1 percent were registered to vote. Alabama state police stormed into defenseless protesters, who were clubbed, shocked with cattle prods, and tear-gassed. Showcased on TV, the spectacle provoked national outrage and support for a voting-rights bill.

Voting Rights Act Law that allowed the federal government to protect the right of blacks to vote; transformed southern politics

Signed by the president in August, the **Voting Rights Act** invalidated the use of any test or device to deny the vote and authorized federal examiners to register voters in states that had disfranchised blacks. The Voting Rights Act of 1965 dramatically expanded black suffrage, boosting the number of registered black voters in the South from 1 million in 1964 to 3.1 million in 1968, and in the process transformed southern politics (see Map 28.2).

The number of blacks holding office in the South swelled from fewer than two dozen to nearly twelve hundred by 1972. That meant jobs for African-Americans, contracts for black businesses, and improvements in facilities and services in black neighborhoods. Most importantly, as Fannie Lou Hamer recalled, when African-Americans could not vote, "white folks would drive past your house in a pickup truck with guns hanging up in the back and give you hate stares. . . . Those same people now call me Mrs. Hamer."

Fire in the Streets

The civil-rights movement changed, but did not revolutionize, race relations. It ended legal segregation and broke the monopoly on political power in the South held by whites. Although the movement raised hopes for the possibility of greater change, its inability to transform equality of opportunity into equality of results underscored the limitations of liberal change, especially in the urban ghetto. The movement did not bring African-Americans economic equality or material well-being, and the anger bubbling below the surface soon boiled over.

On August 11, 1965, five days after the Voting Rights Act had been signed, a confrontation between white police and young blacks in Watts, the largest

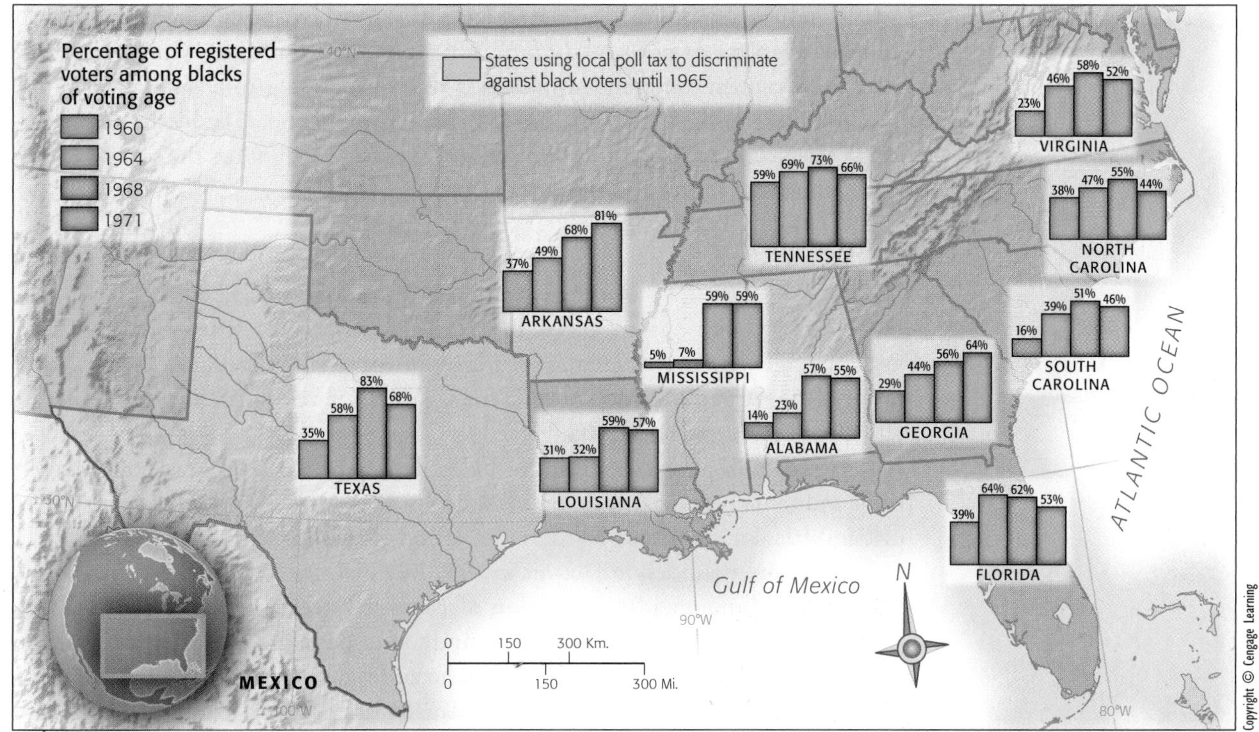

Map 28.2 Voter Registration of African-Americans in the South, 1960–1971

As blacks overwhelmingly registered as Democrats, some former segregationist politicians, among them George Wallace, started to court the African-American vote, and many southern whites began to cast their ballots for Republicans, inaugurating an era of real two-party competition in the South.

African-American district in Los Angeles, ignited the most destructive race riot in decades. For six days, blacks looted shops, firebombed white-owned businesses, and sniped at police officers and firefighters. When the riot ended, thirty-four people were dead, nine hundred injured, and four thousand arrested.

Watts proved to be just a prelude to a succession of "long hot summers." In summer 1966, rioting erupted in more than a score of northern ghettos, forcing whites to heed the squalor of the slums and the savage behavior of police in the ghetto—problems that the civil-rights movement had ignored. The following summer brought nearly 150 racial outbreaks and forty riots—the worst in Detroit, where forty-three people died—the most intense and destructive period of racial violence that the United States had ever witnessed. In 1968, riots would flare again in more than one hundred cities after the assassination of Martin Luther King, Jr. The 1964–1968 riot toll would include two hundred dead, seven thousand injured, forty thousand arrested, and at least $500 million worth of property wrecked.

A frightened, bewildered nation asked why such rioting occurred just when blacks were achieving many of their goals. Militant blacks saw the uprisings as revolutionary violence directed at a racist society. Conservatives described them as senseless outbursts by troublemakers. The National Advisory Commission on

Civil Disorders (the Kerner Commission) indicted white racism for fostering "an explosive mixture" of poverty, slum housing, poor education, and police brutality. The commission recommended increased federal spending to create new jobs for urban blacks, construct additional public housing, and end *de facto* school segregation in the North. Aware of a swelling white backlash, LBJ ignored the commission's advice, and most whites approved of his inaction.

Black Power

Black Power Militant movement for black autonomy and self-respect; rejected the goal of integration

For many young African-Americans, liberalism's response to racial inequality proved "too little, too late." The demand for **Black Power** that sounded in 1966 paralleled the fury of the urban riots; it expressed the eagerness of militant activists for militant self-defense and rapid social change.

Derived from a long tradition of black nationalism, Black Power owed much to the militant rhetoric and vision of Malcolm X. A former drug addict and street hustler, Malcolm X had converted to the Nation of Islam, or the Black Muslim faith, while in prison. Founded in Detroit in 1931 by Elijah Poole (who took the Islamic name Elijah Muhammad), the Nation of Islam insisted that blacks practice self-discipline and self-respect, and it rejected integration. Malcolm X accordingly urged African-Americans to separate themselves from the "white devil" and to take pride in their African roots and their blackness. Blacks, he claimed, had to rely on armed self-defense and had to seize their freedom "by any means necessary." Malcolm X's assassination by members of the Nation of Islam in February 1965, after he had broken with Elijah Muhammad, did not still his voice. *The Autobiography of Malcolm X* (1965) became the main text for the rising Black Power movement.

AP Photo

Bobby Seale and Huey Newton

Founded by Bobby Seale and Huey Newton in Oakland, California, in response to police brutality against African-Americans, the Black Panther Party was organized along semi-military lines and advocated fighting for black justice, in Newton's words, "through the barrel of a gun."

Inspired by Malcolm X, many young, urban blacks abandoned reformist strategies and became more militant. In 1966, CORE and SNCC changed from interracial organizations committed to achieving integration to all-black groups advocating racial separatism and Black Power. Even more militant was the Black Panther Party for Self-Defense, organized that year, which urged black men to overthrow their oppressors by becoming "panthers—smiling, cunning, scientific, striking by night and sparing no one." Violent confrontations with police left some Black Panthers dead and many more in prison—further splintering the black-white civil-rights alliance and contributing to the rightward turn in politics.

Black Power advocates had a real impact on African-American life. They helped to organize self-help groups, establish black studies programs, and encourage African-Americans to see that "black is beautiful."

This message, and Black Power's critique of American society, resonated with other marginalized groups and helped shape their protests.

The Struggle Goes On

As a result of civil-rights activism, millions of blacks experienced significant upward mobility. In 1965, black students accounted for under 5 percent of total college enrollment; by 1990 the figure had risen to 12 percent, close to their proportion in the general population. TV's *The Cosby Show,* a late-1980s comedy in which Bill Cosby played a doctor married to a lawyer, portrayed this upwardly mobile world.

Outside this world lay the inner-city slums, inhabited by perhaps a third of the black population. Here, up to half the young people never finished high school, and the jobless rate soared as high as 60 percent. Cocaine and other drugs pervaded the inner cities. Some black children recruited as lookouts for drug dealers eventually became dealers themselves. With drugs also came violence. In the 1980s, a young black male was six times as likely to be murdered as a young white male. Drug abuse affected all social levels, including yuppies and show-business celebrities. But drug use and trafficking particularly devastated the inner cities.

To compensate for past racial discrimination, some cities set aside a percentage of building contracts for minority businesses. Some educational institutions reserved slots for minority applicants. These so-called **affirmative action** programs faced court challenges, however. In *Bakke* v. *University of California* (1978), the Supreme Court declared strict racial quotas unconstitutional. The Court did, however, uphold programs to encourage minority businesses or minority-student enrollment in higher education, so long as they did not involve specific quotas.

affirmative action Programs that promote opportunities for minorities

CHECKING IN

- The civil-rights movement gained momentum with the violent reactions to nonviolent protests, as well as Martin Luther King, Jr.'s "I Have a Dream" speech.
- The Civil Rights Act of 1964 established the Equal Employment Opportunity Commission, and the Voting Rights Act of 1965 transformed southern politics.
- Race riots stunned the nation from 1965 to 1968.
- Radical leaders like Malcolm X and groups like the Black Panthers emerged to proclaim Black Power and challenge the nonviolent wing of the movement.
- Some African Americans made great gains in education and the professions, but many remained trapped in poverty.

THE EXPANDING MOVEMENT FOR EQUALITY

How and why did the protest movements of minorities shift from the goals and tactics associated with Martin Luther King, Jr., to those of Black Power?

Native Americans, Hispanic-Americans, and Asian-Americans were similarly affected by liberalism. They, too, were inspired by Kennedy's rhetoric, by Johnson's actions, and by the assertive outlook of Black Power. Each followed the black lead in challenging the status quo, demanding full and equal citizenship rights, and emphasizing group identity and pride. And like blacks, each group saw its younger members push for ever more radical action.

Native American Activism

In 1961, representatives of sixty-seven tribes drew up a Declaration of Purposes, and in 1964 hundreds of Indians assembled in Washington to lobby for recognition in the war on poverty. Indians suffered the worst poverty, the highest disease and death rates, and the poorest education and housing of any American group. President Johnson established the National Council on Indian Opportunity in 1965. It funneled more federal funds onto reservations than any previous program.

Militant Native Americans, meanwhile, began to organize. By 1968, younger Indian activists, calling themselves "Native Americans," demanded "Red Power." They protested the lack of protection for Indian land and water rights, and the desecration of Indian sacred sites. They established reservation cultural programs to reawaken spiritual beliefs and teach native languages. The Puyallup (pyoo-AL-up) asserted old treaty rights to fish in the Columbia River and Puget Sound. The Navajo and Hopi protested strip-mining in the Southwest.

American Indian Movement (AIM) Group that attracted attention to problems facing Native Americans by occupying Alcatraz

The most militant group, the **American Indian Movement (AIM),** was founded in 1968 by Chippewas, Sioux, and Ojibwa living in and around Minneapolis. Among its goals was preventing police harassment of Indians in urban "red ghettos." To dramatize the Indian cause, in late 1969 an armed AIM contingent occupied Alcatraz Island in San Francisco Bay, citing a treaty right, and held the island for nineteen months. AIM's militancy aroused other Native Americans to be proud of their heritage. Building on their occupation of Alcatraz Island, members of the militant American Indian Movement briefly occupied the Bureau of Indian Affairs in Washington in 1972. In response to spreading protests, the Indian Self-Determination Act of 1974 granted tribes control of federal aid programs on the reservations and oversight of their own schools.

Many of the eight hundred thousand who identified themselves as Indians in the 1970 census did so for the first time, and by 1990 their number had soared to 1.7 million. This upsurge reflected ethnic pride, as well as the economic advantages associated with tribal membership. Under a 1961 law, tribes launched ventures ranging from gambling resorts to mining and logging operations. Many also reasserted long-ignored treaty rights, resulting in a gain of 40 million acres for Alaskan Indians in 1971. Although high rates of joblessness, alcoholism, and disease persisted among Indians, renewed pride and progress in asserting treaty rights offered hope. In the popular culture, movies such as *Little Big Man* (1970) and *Dances with Wolves* (1990), while idealizing Indians, represented an improvement over the negative stereotypes of earlier films.

Hispanic-Americans Organize

Immigration Act of 1965 Did away with national-origins quotas and increased legal immigration

As occurred earlier in American history, immigration swelled the ranks of minority groups in the second half of the twentieth century. Of enormous significance, Congress enacted the **Immigration Act of 1965,** abolishing the national-origins quotas of the 1920s. Annual legal immigration would increase from about 250,000 before the act to well over 1 million, and the vast majority of new immigrants would come from Asia and Latin America. The Latino, or Hispanic-American, population increased from 4.5 percent in 1970 to nearly 12 percent in 2000. Although less than 1 percent of the U.S. population in 1960, Asian-Americans (discussed in the next section) comprised more than 4 percent in 2000. During the 1960s, these groups contributed to the general spirit of activism.

Like Native Americans, Latinos—the fastest-growing minority—became impatient with their establishment organizations, which had been unable to better their dismal conditions. As they turned to the more militant tactics of the civil-rights movement, Latinos found a charismatic leader in **César Estrada Chávez** (SAY-zar SHAH-vez).

Born on an Arizona farm first cultivated in the 1880s by his grandfather, Chávez grew up a migrant farm worker, joined the U.S. navy in World War II, and then devoted himself to improved working conditions for the mostly Mexican-American farm laborers in California. A magnetic leader, Chávez led a strike against vineyards in the San Joaquin valley in 1965. With United Farm Workers (UFW) cofounder Dolores Huerta, he organized consumer boycotts of table grapes to dramatize the farm workers' struggle, often referred to as *La Causa.* For the first time, farm workers gained the right to unionize to secure better wages; by mid-1970, two-thirds of California grapes were grown under UFW contracts.

Arthur Schatz/Time Life Pictures/Getty Images

Chávez and His Heroes Robert Kennedy and Mohandas Gandhi
César Chávez, from a farm worker family, founded the United Farm Workers to help migrant Mexican farm hands, who worked long hours for meager pay. Chávez and his followers won the enactment in 1975 of a California law requiring growers to bargain collectively with the elected representatives of the farm workers.

César Estrada Chávez Leader of United Farm Workers

Also in the mid-1960s, young Hispanic activists began using the formerly pejorative terms "Chicano" and "Chicana" to express a militant collective identity. Rejecting assimilation, Chicano student organizations came together in 1967 in *El Movimiento Estudiantil Chicano de Aztlan* (MEChA). MEChA demanded bilingual education and more Latino teachers in high schools as well as Chicano studies programs and organizations at colleges. Similar zeal led Jose Angel Gutierrez and others in Texas to create an alternative political party in 1967, *La Raza Unida,* to elect Latinos and instill cultural pride. Across the West, Hispanic-American activists created the "brown is beautiful" vogue and the paramilitary Brown Berets, with conceptual roots in the Black Panthers.

Similarly inspired, Puerto Ricans in New York City founded the Young Lords. Modeled on the Black Panthers, the Young Lords published a newspaper, started drug treatment programs, and even hijacked ambulances and occupied a hospital to demand better medical services in the South Bronx.

Meanwhile, a steady influx of immigrants, both legal and illegal, continued to arrive in the United States. Where most had once come from Europe, some 45 percent now came from the Western Hemisphere and 30 percent from Asia. As in the past, economic need drew these newcomers. Mexico's chronic poverty forced many to seek jobs in the north. But life in the United States was often harsh. Millions of Hispanic immigrants lacked official documentation. Many sweated in the garment trades, cleaned houses, held low-paying service-sector jobs, and labored in agricultural fields. The Immigration Reform and Control Act of 1986, an update of the 1965 Immigration Act, outlawed the hiring of undocumented immigrants, but offered legal status to aliens who had lived in the United States for five years.

Asian-American Activism

Among the rapidly climbing number of immigrants from Asia some, like the Hmong (mong), the indigenous people of Indochina who had supported the United States in the Vietnam War, came mainly for political reasons; others, like those from South Korea and the Philippines, came primarily for economic betterment. Valuing education, many Asian immigrants advanced academically and economically.

Like their counterparts, young activists with roots in the Far East rejected the term "Oriental" and adopted "Asian-American" to signify a new ethnic consciousness. Formed at the University of California in 1968, the Asian American Political Alliance encouraged Asian-American students to claim their own cultural identity. As did other ethnic groups, Asian-American students marched, sat in, and went on strike to gain courses on Asian-American studies. Others agitated to force the United States to make restitution for the internment of Japanese-Americans during World War II.

None of these movements for ethnic pride and power, in later decades, would sustain the fervent activism and media attention they attracted in the late 1960s. But by elevating the consciousness and nurturing the confidence of the younger generation, each contributed to the empowerment of its respective group and to the politics of identity that would continue to grow in importance.

CHECKING IN

- The American Indian Movement occupied Alcatraz, while Indian self-identification increased and long-ignored treaty rights were reasserted.
- César Chávez's successful effort to unionize Latino farm workers was part of a trend toward a more militant collective Chicano identity.
- The activism of Hispanic-American groups like *La Raza Unida* and the Young Lords reflected the influence of Black Power.
- Like Hispanic groups, Asian-Americans molded racial solidarity and created organizations to serve their communities.

LIBERALISM ASCENDANT, 1963–1968

How did Lyndon Johnson's Great Society program exemplify the new liberalism of the 1960s?

Distrusted by liberals as "a Machiavelli in a Stetson," and regarded as a usurper by Kennedy loyalists, **Lyndon Baines Johnson** achieved his highest ambition through the assassination of a popular president in Johnson's home state of Texas. Although just nine years older than Kennedy, he seemed a relic of the past, a back-room wheeler-dealer as crude as his predecessor was smooth.

Lyndon Baines Johnson Thirty-sixth president of the United States; champion of civil-rights legislation and the "war on poverty"

Yet Johnson had substantial political assets. He had served in Washington almost continuously since 1932, accruing enormous experience and a close association with the Capitol Hill power brokers who helped pass bills. He excelled at wooing allies, neutralizing opponents, forging coalitions, and achieving results.

Johnson's first three years in office demonstrated his determination to prove himself to liberals. He deftly handled the transition of power, won a landslide victory in 1964, and guided through Congress the greatest array of liberal legislation in U.S. history, surpassing the New Deal agenda. Nevertheless, LBJ's swollen yet fragile ego could not abide the sniping of Kennedy loyalists and the press. Wondering aloud, "Why don't people like me?" Johnson pressed to vanquish all foes at home and abroad. Ironically, in seeking consensus and affection, Johnson would divide the nation and leave office repudiated.

Johnson Takes Over

Calling for early passage of the tax-cut and civil-rights bills as a memorial to Kennedy, Johnson used his legislative skills to good effect, winning passage of the

Civil Rights Act of 1964 (discussed earlier) and a $10 billion tax-reduction bill, which produced a surge in capital investment and personal consumption that spurred economic growth and shrank the budget deficit. More boldly, Johnson declared "unconditional **war on poverty** in America."

war on poverty Centerpiece of LBJ's Great Society

Largely invisible in an affluent country, according to Michael Harrington's *The Other America* (1962), some 40 million people lived in a "culture of poverty," lacking the education, medical care, and employment opportunities that most Americans took for granted. LBJ championed a campaign to bring these "internal exiles" into the mainstream. Designed to offer a "hand up, not a handout," the Economic Opportunity Act established the Office of Economic Opportunity to fund and coordinate a job corps to train young people in marketable skills; VISTA (Volunteers in Service to America), a domestic peace corps; Project Head Start, to provide compensatory education for preschoolers from disadvantaged families; and an assortment of public-works and training programs.

Great Society LBJ's dream of an American society of equality and opportunity

Barry Goldwater Arizona senator and Republican whose loss in the 1964 presidential election unified conservatives

Summing up his goals in 1964, Johnson offered his vision of the **Great Society.** First, he stated, must come "an end to poverty and racial injustice." In addition, the Great Society would be a place where all children could enrich their minds, where people could renew their contact with nature, and where all would be "more concerned with the quality of their goals than the quantity of their goods."

The 1964 Election

Johnson's Great Society horrified the "new conservatives," such as William F. Buckley, Jr., and the college students of Young Americans for Freedom. The most persuasive critic was Arizona senator **Barry Goldwater,** a western outsider fighting the Washington establishment, a fervent anticommunist, and an advocate of individual freedom. His opposition to big government, deficit spending, racial liberalism, and social-welfare programs found receptive audiences on Sun Belt golf courses and in working-class neighborhoods.

Johnson's advocacy of civil rights frightened southern segregationists and blue-collar workers in northern cities who dreaded the integration of their neighborhoods, schools, and workplaces. Their support of Alabama's segregationist governor George Wallace in early 1964 presidential primaries heralded a "white backlash" against the civil-rights movement.

Buoyed by this backlash, conservatives in 1964 gained control of the GOP. They nominated Barry Goldwater for the presidency and adopted a platform totally opposed to liberalism. Goldwater extolled his opposition to civil-rights legislation, denounced the

Lyndon Baines Johnson LBJ Library and Museum

The LBJ Treatment

Not content unless he could wholly dominate friend as well as foe, Lyndon Johnson used his body as well as his voice to bend others to his will and gain his objectives.

war on poverty, and hinted that he might use nuclear weapons against Cuba and North Vietnam. Goldwater's stance appealed to those angered by the Cold War stalemate, by the erosion of traditional moral values, and by the increasing militancy of African-Americans. But Goldwater's more extreme views made Johnson look like the apostle of restraint. Goldwater's campaign slogan, "In your heart you know he's right," allowed his liberal opponents to quip, "In your guts, you know he's nuts."

LBJ won a landslide victory, capturing 43 million votes to Goldwater's 27 million. The GOP lost thirty-eight congressional and two Senate seats. Many proclaimed the death of conservatism. But Goldwater's coalition of antigovernment westerners, economic and religious conservatives, and anti-integrationist whites presaged conservatism's future triumph. His candidacy transformed the Republicans from a moderate, eastern-dominated party to one decidedly conservative, southern, and western. It built a national base of financial support for conservative candidates and mobilized future leaders of the party, such as Ronald Reagan. But in the short run, the liberals controlled all three branches of government.

The Great Society

"Hurry, boys, hurry," LBJ urged his aides. "Get that legislation up to the hill and out. Eighteen months from now ol' Landslide Lyndon will be Lame Duck Lyndon." Johnson flooded Congress with liberal proposals, and he got most of what he requested.

Medicare Government health insurance for the elderly

The Eighty-ninth Congress enlarged the war on poverty and passed another milestone civil-rights act. It enacted **Medicare** to provide health insurance for the aged under social security and a Medicaid health plan for the poor. By 1975, the two would serve 47 million people and account for a quarter of the nation's health-care expenditures. The legislators appropriated funds for public education and housing and for urban revitalization, and they created new Departments of Transportation and of Housing and Urban Development, as well as the National Endowments for the Arts and the Humanities.

The Great Society also sought to protect the environment. Johnson won the enactment of measures to control air and water pollution, protect endangered species, set aside millions of acres of wilderness, and preserve the natural beauty of the American landscape. As noted, Congress enacted the Immigration Act of 1965, abandoning the quota system enacted in the 1920s that had discriminated against Asians and southern and eastern Europeans, thereby transforming America's racial and ethnic kaleidoscope.

The Great Society improved the lives of millions. The poor, 22 percent of the population in 1960, shrank to 13 percent in 1969. African-American family income rose from 54 percent to 61 percent of white family income, and the segment of blacks living below the poverty line plummeted from 40 percent to 20 percent. But because Johnson oversold the Great Society and Congress underfunded it, rising expectations outdistanced results.

For many in need, the Great Society remained more a dream than a reality. The war against poverty was, in the words of Martin Luther King, Jr., "shot down on the battle-fields of Vietnam." In 1966, Johnson spent twenty times more to wage war in Vietnam than to fight poverty in the United States. Yet the perceived liberality of federal spending and the "ungratefulness" of rioting blacks, as well as the intrusive rulings of the Supreme Court, alienated many middle- and working-class whites. The Democrats' loss of forty-seven House seats in 1966 ended the sway of congressional liberalism.

Miranda* v. *Arizona Supreme Court ruling protecting the rights of the accused

The Liberalism of the Warren Court

The Supreme Court—led by Chief Justice Earl Warren, who was far more liberal than public opinion or Congress—supported an activist government to protect the disadvantaged and accused criminals and expanded individual rights to a greater extent than ever before in American history.

In landmark cases, the Court prohibited Bible reading and prayer in public schools, limited local power to censor books and films, and overturned state bans on contraceptives. It ordered states to apportion legislatures on the principle of "one person, one vote," increasing the representation of urban minorities.

The Court's upholding of the rights of the accused in criminal cases, at a time of soaring crime rates, particularly incensed many Americans. Criticism of the Supreme Court reached a climax in 1966 when it ruled in ***Miranda* v. *Arizona*** that police must advise suspects of their right to remain silent and to have counsel during questioning. In 1968, both Richard Nixon and George Wallace would win favor by promising to appoint judges who emphasized "law and order" over individual liberties.

CHECKING IN

- LBJ declared war on poverty and enlarged New Frontier social goals; his landslide victory in 1964 augmented the Democrats' ruling majority.
- The Great Society marked enormous expansion of federal programs for the poor, elderly, and disadvantaged.
- Rules to protect the environment were established.
- In cases that banned prayer in public schools and protected the rights of the accused, the Warren Court continued to pursue a liberal, activist course.
- Increasing involvement in Vietnam doomed the Great Society.

THE VIETNAM CRUSADE, 1961–1975

How and why did Kennedy, Johnson, and Nixon each deepen America's involvement in the war in Indochina?

The activist liberals who boldly tried to uplift the downtrodden also went to war to contain communism in Vietnam. The nation's longest war, and most controversial, would shatter the liberal consensus and divide the United States as nothing had since the Civil War.

Origins and Causes

American involvement in Vietnam grew out of the containment policy to stop the spread of communism. First as a means of strengthening America's anti-Soviet ally France, President Truman authorized U.S. aid for French efforts to reestablish its colonial rule in Indochina. After the outbreak of war in Korea, Truman ordered vastly increased assistance for the French army fighting the Vietminh, a broad-based Vietnamese nationalist coalition led by the communist Ho Chi Minh. By 1954, the United States was paying three-quarters of the French war costs in Vietnam.

But the French were losing. In early 1954, the Vietminh besieged twelve thousand French troops in the valley of Dien Bien Phu. France appealed for U.S. intervention, and some American officials toyed with the idea of a nuclear strike, which President Eisenhower flatly rejected. In May, the French surrendered at Dien Bien Phu.

An international conference in Geneva arranged a cease-fire and divided Vietnam at the seventeenth parallel, pending elections in 1956 to choose the government of a unified nation.

domino theory The belief that if Vietnam fell to the communists, all of Asia would follow

Although unwilling to go to war, Eisenhower would not accept a communist takeover of Vietnam. In what became known as the **domino theory,** Eisenhower warned that, if Vietnam fell to the communists, then Thailand, Burma, Indonesia, and ultimately all of Asia would follow. The United States refused to sign the Geneva Peace Accords and in late 1954 created the Southeast Asia Treaty Organization (SEATO), a military alliance patterned on NATO.

In June 1954, the CIA installed Ngo Dinh Diem (woh din dee-EM), a fiercely anticommunist Catholic, as premier and then president of an independent South Vietnam. CIA agents helped him eliminate political opposition and block the election to reunify Vietnam specified by the Geneva agreements. As Eisenhower later admitted, "possibly 80 percent of the population would have voted for the communist Ho Chi Minh as their leader." Washington pinned its hopes on Diem to maintain a noncommunist South Vietnam with American dollars rather than American lives.

National Liberation Front (NLF) Insurgent political organization in South Vietnam devoted to overthrowing the government

But the autocratic Diem's Catholicism alienated the predominantly Buddhist population, and his refusal to institute land reform and end corruption spurred opposition. In December 1960, opposition to Diem coalesced in the **National Liberation Front (NLF).** Backed by North Vietnam, the insurgency attracted broad support and soon controlled half of South Vietnam.

Kennedy and Vietnam

Following the 1962 compromise settlement in Laos, President Kennedy resolved, as had President Eisenhower, not to give further ground in Southeast Asia. He ordered massive shipments of weapons to South Vietnam and increased the number of clandestine American forces there from less than seven hundred in early 1961 to more than sixteen thousand by late 1963. He accepted Eisenhower's "domino theory" and viewed international communism as a monolithic force, a single global entity controlled by Moscow and Beijing. He wanted to prove that the United States was not the "paper tiger" mocked by Mao Zedong.

To counter communist gains in the countryside, the United States used both chemical defoliants and napalm to destroy vegetation and expose the enemy. It also uprooted Vietnamese peasants and moved them into fortified villages. But South Vietnamese president Diem rejected American pressure to gain popular support through reform measures, instead crushing demonstrations by students and Buddhists. By mid-1963, Buddhist monks were setting themselves on fire to protest Diem's repression, and Diem's own generals were plotting a coup (coo).

Vietcong Military wing of the National Liberation Front; guerilla army amassed against South Vietnamese and American forces

Frustrated American policy makers concluded that only a new government could stave off a **Vietcong** victory and secretly backed the coup efforts. On November 1, military leaders staged their coup, captured Diem and his brother, and shot them. Although the United States promptly recognized the new government, it made little headway against the Vietcong. JFK now faced two unpalatable alternatives: to use American combat forces or to withdraw and seek a negotiated settlement.

What Kennedy would have done remains unknown. Less than a month after Diem's death, John F. Kennedy himself fell to an assassin's bullet. His admirers contend that by late 1963 he was favoring the withdrawal of American forces after the 1964 election. "It is their war . . . it is their people and their government who have to win or lose the struggle," he proclaimed. Yet the president then restated the domino theory and promised that the United States would not withdraw from the conflict. Virtually all his closest advisers held that an American victory was essential to check communism in Asia. They would counsel Kennedy's successor accordingly.

Lyndon Johnson's Endless War

While privately describing Vietnam as "a raggedy-ass fourth-rate country," LBJ feared that an all-out American military effort might lead to World War III. He foresaw that full-scale U.S. engagement in "that bitch of a war" would destroy "the woman I really loved—the Great Society." Yet Johnson saw his own credibility on the line. He worried that a pullout would make him appear cowardly, threaten his liberal agenda, and leave him vulnerable to conservative accusations that he was "soft" on communism.

Trapped between unacceptable alternatives, Johnson expanded the war, hoping that U.S. firepower would force Ho Chi Minh to the bargaining table. But the North Vietnamese calculated that they could gain more by outlasting the United States than by negotiating.

In 1964, LBJ took bold steps to impress the North Vietnamese with American resolve and to block his opponent, Barry Goldwater, from capitalizing on Vietnam in the presidential campaign. In May his advisers drafted a congressional resolution authorizing an escalation of American military action, and in July LBJ appointed General Maxwell Taylor, an advocate of greater American involvement, as ambassador to Saigon.

In early August, North Vietnamese patrol boats reportedly clashed with two U.S. destroyers patrolling the Gulf of Tonkin (TAWN-kin). Evidence of the attack was unclear. Never admitting that the U.S. destroyers had been aiding the South Vietnamese in clandestine raids against North Vietnam, the president condemned the attacks as unprovoked and called on Congress to pass the previously prepared resolution giving him the authority to "take all necessary measures to repel any armed attack against the forces of the United States and to prevent further aggression." Assured that this power would lead to no "extension of the present conflict," the Senate passed the **Gulf of Tonkin Resolution** by a vote of 98 to 2, and the House by 416 to 0. Privately, Johnson called the resolution "grandma's nightshirt—it covered every thing." He considered it a blank check to commit U.S. forces as he saw fit.

Gulf of Tonkin Resolution
"Blank check" for LBJ to wage war in Vietnam

Early in 1965, Johnson ordered "Operation Rolling Thunder," the sustained bombing of North Vietnam. The United States dropped eight hundred tons of bombs daily on North Vietnam from 1965 to 1968, three times the tonnage used by all combatants in World War II. However, it neither convinced Hanoi to negotiate nor stopped the flow of soldiers and supplies southward from North Vietnam.

Unable to turn the tide by bombing, Johnson committed U.S. combat troops. Adopting a "meat-grinder" or attrition strategy, Johnson sought to inflict unacceptable casualties on the communists to force them to the peace table. Johnson sent 485,000 troops to Vietnam by the end of 1967. But North Vietnam matched each American troop increase with its own, and there was no end in sight.

Paul Szep/Library of Congress

LBJ Haunted by Vietnam

As each step up the escalation ladder led to the next, and then the next, President Johnson increasingly felt trapped—caught in a war that he could not win and that was destroying his dream of a Great Society.

First on college campuses and then in the wider society, a growing number of Americans began to oppose the Vietnam War. In March 1965, students and faculty at the University of Michigan staged the first teach-in to raise questions about U.S. involvement. Later that spring, twenty-five thousand people, mainly students, rallied in Washington to protest the escalation. In 1966, large-scale campus antiwar protests erupted. Students demonstrated against the draft and university research for the Pentagon.

Intellectuals and clergy joined the chorus of opposition to the war. Some decried the massive bombing of an undeveloped nation, some doubted that the United States could win at any reasonable cost, and some feared the demise of liberalism. In 1967, prominent critics, including Robert Kennedy and Martin Luther King, Jr., spurred hundreds of thousands to participate in antiwar protests.

Critics noted that the war fell especially hard on the poor. Owing to college deferments, the use of influence, and a military-assignment system that shunted the better educated to desk jobs, lower-class youths were twice as likely to be drafted and, when drafted, twice as likely to see combat duty as middle-class youths.

TV coverage of the war further eroded support. Scenes of children maimed by U.S. bombs and of dying Americans, replayed in living rooms night after night, undercut the optimistic reports of government officials. Americans shuddered as they watched U.S. troops, supposedly winning the hearts and minds of the Vietnamese, burn villages and leave thousands of civilians mutilated or dead.

Yet for every protestor shouting "Hell No, We Won't Go!" many more war supporters affixed bumper stickers reading "America, Love It or Leave It!" Until 1968, most Americans either supported the war or remained undecided.

"hawks" Term for those who supported American goals in the Vietnam War

"doves" Term for opponents of American military involvement in Vietnam

Equally disturbing was how polarized the nation had grown. **"Hawks"** would accept little short of total victory, whereas **"doves"** insisted on negotiating, not fighting. Civility vanished. Demonstrators paraded past the White House chanting, "Hey, hey, LBJ, how many kids did you kill today?" By 1968, the president had become a prisoner in the White House, unable to speak in public without being shouted down. So ended an era of hope and liberalism.

Eugene McCarthy Minnesota senator opposed to the Vietnam War; challenged LBJ in the 1968 Democratic primaries

The Tet Offensive and a Shaken President

In January 1968, liberal Democratic senator **Eugene McCarthy** of Minnesota, a Vietnam War critic, announced that he would challenge LBJ for the presidential nomination. Pundits scoffed that McCarthy had no chance of unseating Johnson, who had won the presidency in 1964 by the largest margin in U.S. history. But McCarthy persisted, determined that at least one Democrat enter the primaries on an antiwar platform.

Suddenly, America's hopes for victory in Vietnam sank, and with them LBJ's political fortunes. On January 31—the Vietnamese New Year—National Liberation Front (NLF) and North Vietnamese forces mounted a huge offensive, attacking more than a hundred South Vietnamese cities and towns, and even the U.S. embassy in Saigon. U.S. and South Vietnamese troops repulsed the **Tet Offensive** after a month of ferocious fighting, inflicting a major military defeat on the communists (see Map 28.3).

Tet Offensive Coordinated attack by North Vietnam that convinced many Americans that the war could not be won

Victory, however, came at an enormous psychological cost. The dramatic initial reports of the media, highlighting the number of American casualties, undercut Johnson's and General Westmoreland's claims of imminent victory. The Tet Offensive deepened the growing mood of gloom about the war and intensified doubts that the United States could win at an acceptable cost. Public approval of the president's conduct of the war fell to just 26 percent in the immediate aftermath of the Tet Offensive.

After the Tet Offensive, McCarthy's criticism of the war won many new sympathizers. *Time*, *Newsweek*, and the *Wall Street Journal* published editorials urging a negotiated settlement. The nation's most respected newscaster, Walter Cronkite of CBS, observed that "it seems now more certain than ever that the bloody experience of Vietnam is to end in a stalemate." "If I've lost Walter," LBJ sighed, "then it's over. I've lost Mr. Average Citizen." The number of Americans who described themselves as prowar "hawks" slipped from 62 percent in January to 41 percent in March, whereas the antiwar "doves" jumped from 22 percent to 42 percent.

Beleaguered, Johnson pondered a change in American policy. When the Joint Chiefs of Staff sought an additional 206,000 men for Vietnam, he turned to old friends for advice. Dean Acheson, the former secretary of state and a venerable Cold Warrior, told him, "The Joint Chiefs of Staff don't know what they're talking about."

Meanwhile, nearly five thousand college students swarmed to New Hampshire to stuff envelopes and ring doorbells for Eugene McCarthy in the nation's first primary contest. McCarthy astonished the experts by winning nearly half the popular vote in the primary contest of a state usually regarded as conservative.

After this upset, twice as many students converged on Wisconsin to canvass its more liberal voters. Expecting Johnson to lose, Senator **Robert Kennedy,** also promising to end the war, entered the Democratic contest. Projecting the familiar Kennedy glamour and magnetism, Kennedy was the one candidate whom Johnson feared could deny him re-nomination. Indeed, millions viewed Kennedy as the rightful heir to the White House. Appealing to minorities, the poor, and working-class ethnic whites, Kennedy became, according to one columnist, "our first politician for the pariahs, our great national outsider."

Robert Kennedy Brother of John F. Kennedy and former attorney general

On March 31, Johnson surprised a television audience by announcing a halt to the bombing in North Vietnam. Saying that he wanted to devote all of his efforts to the search for peace, Johnson then startlingly announced, "I shall not seek, and I will not accept, the nomination of my party for another term as your president." Embittered by the personal abuse that he had endured, and reluctant to polarize the nation further, the president called it quits. Two days later, McCarthy trounced the president in the Wisconsin primary.

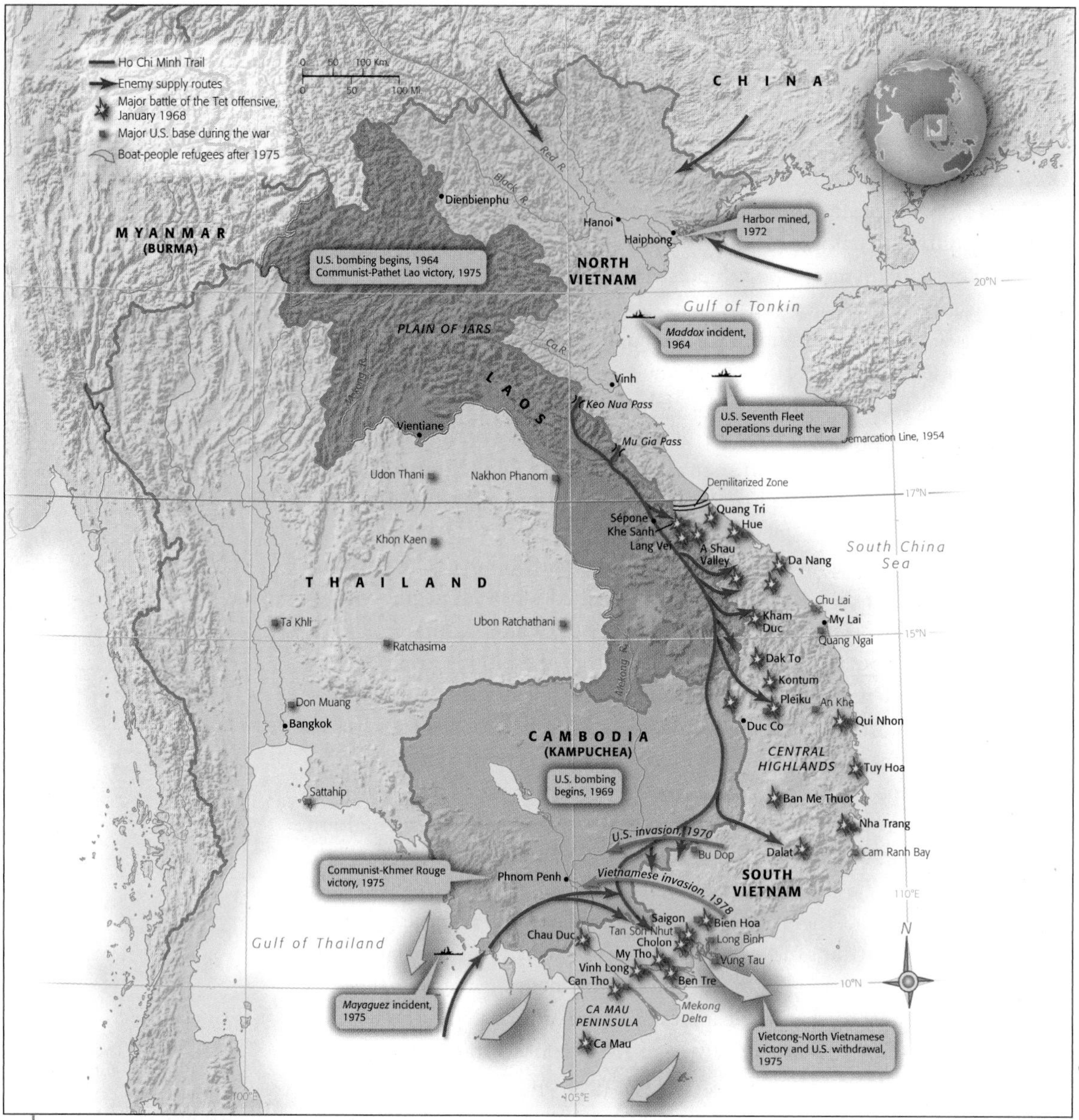

Map 28.3 The Vietnam War

Wishing to guarantee an independent, noncommunist government in South Vietnam, Lyndon Johnson remarked in 1965, "We fight because we must fight if we are to live in a world where every country can shape its own destiny. To withdraw from one battlefield means only to prepare for the next."

Interactive Map

All but forgotten in retirement, Johnson died of a heart attack in January 1973. In many ways a tragic figure, he had carried out Vietnam policies shaped by his predecessors and received little acclaim for his domestic achievements, especially in civil rights. Although he often displayed high idealism and generosity of spirit, the enduring image of LBJ is that of a crude, overbearing politician with an outsized ego that masked deep insecurities.

Nixon's War

Following his election in 1968, President Richard Nixon plotted a strategy of détente—reduced tensions—with the USSR and China that hinged on ending the Vietnam War. He understood that the war had sapped American military strength, hurt the economy, hindered U.S. relations abroad, and devastated Lyndon Johnson.

Announcing the Nixon Doctrine in August 1969, the president redefined America's role in the Third World as that of a helpful partner rather than a military protector. It reflected the president's recognition of war weariness by both the electorate and troops in Vietnam. Johnson's decision to negotiate rather than to escalate had left American troops with the sense that little mattered except survival. Morale plummeted. Discipline collapsed. Army desertions rocketed from twenty-seven thousand in 1967 to seventy-six thousand in 1970. Racial conflict became commonplace, and drug use soared. The army reported hundreds of cases of "fragging"—the practice of enlisted men killing officers.

The toll of atrocities against the Vietnamese mounted. In March 1968, an army unit led by an inexperienced lieutenant, William Calley, massacred several hundred

Ronald S. Haeberle/Time Life Pictures/Getty Images

The My Lai Massacre

Under the command of First Lieutenant William Calley, the men of Charlie Company entered the small village of My Lai in March 1968 to attack the Vietcong believed to be there. Instead, they found unarmed civilians, mostly women and children, and massacred them. When news of the incident surfaced late in 1969, it became symbolic of the war's brutality and the futility of the U.S. effort in the Vietnam War.

My Lai Vietnamese village where American troops massacred more than four hundred civilians

defenseless civilians in **My Lai** (mee lie). Soldiers gang-raped girls, lined up women and children in ditches and shot them, and then burned the village. Revelations of such incidents, and the rising number of returned soldiers who joined Vietnam Veterans Against the War, undercut the already-diminished support for the war.

Despite pressure to end the war, Nixon proved no more willing than his predecessors to accept defeat. Seeking "peace with honor," he acted on three fronts. First was "Vietnamization," replacing American troops with South Vietnamese. By 1972 U.S. forces in Vietnam had dropped from half a million to thirty thousand. Second, Nixon bypassed South Vietnamese leaders by sending Kissinger to negotiate secretly with North Vietnam's foreign minister, Le Duc Tho (lay duck tow). Third, to force the communists to compromise despite the U.S. troop withdrawal, Nixon escalated the bombing of North Vietnam and secretly ordered air strikes on North Vietnamese supply routes in Cambodia and Laos.

The secret B-52 raids against Cambodia neither made Hanoi beg for peace nor disrupted communist supply bases. They did, however, undermine the stability of Cambodia, and increase North Vietnam's infiltration of troops into that tiny republic. Nixon ordered a joint U.S.–South Vietnamese incursion into Cambodia at the end of April 1970. The invaders seized large caches of arms and bought time for Vietnamization. However, the costs were high. The invasion ended Cambodia's neutrality, widened the war throughout Indochina, and provoked massive American protests, culminating in the student deaths at Kent State and Jackson State.

In February 1971, Nixon had South Vietnamese troops invade Laos to destroy communist bases there. The South Vietnamese were routed. Emboldened, North Vietnam mounted a major campaign in April 1972—the Easter Offensive—their largest since 1968. Nixon retaliated by mining North Vietnam's harbors and unleashing B-52s on its major cities. He vowed: "The bastards have never been bombed like they are going to be bombed this time."

America's Longest War Ends

On October 26, just days before the 1972 presidential election, Kissinger announced that "peace is at hand." The cease-fire agreement that he had secretly negotiated required the withdrawal of all American troops, provided for the return of U.S. prisoners of war, and allowed North Vietnamese troops to remain in South Vietnam.

Kissinger's negotiations had sealed Nixon's reelection, but South Vietnam's President Thieu (tyoo) refused to sign a cease-fire agreement permitting North Vietnamese troops to remain in the South. An angry Le Duc Tho then pressed Kissinger for additional concessions. President Nixon again resorted to B-52 raids. The 1972 Christmas bombings of Hanoi and Haiphong, the most destructive of the war, roused fierce opposition domestically and globally but broke the deadlock.

The Paris Accords signed in late January 1973 essentially restated the terms of the October truce. The agreement ended hostilities between the United States and North Vietnam but left unresolved the differences between North and South Vietnam, guaranteeing that Vietnam's future would yet be settled on the battlefield. North Vietnamese troops in the spring of 1975 overran South Vietnam, took control of Saigon, and forced American helicopters to airlift the last remaining officials out of the besieged U.S. embassy.

America's longest war had ended in defeat. It left fifty-eight thousand American dead and three hundred thousand wounded. The expenditure of at least $150 billion (more than $700 billion in 2009 dollars) had diverted resources from reform and triggered huge budget deficits and inflation. It shattered the liberal consensus and inflamed dissent, indelibly scarring a generation. The war also distanced the United States from its allies. "No more Vietnams" decided many in the military: The United States should not fight abroad unless its national security was clearly at stake, there was demonstrable public support, and it had the necessary means to accomplish the goal.

Virtually all who survived, wrote one marine veteran, returned "as immigrants to a new world. For the culture we had known dissolved while we were in Vietnam, and the culture of combat we lived in so intensely . . . made us aliens when we returned." Beyond media attention on the psychological difficulties of readjusting to civilian life, the nation paid little heed to its Vietnam veterans—reminders of a war that Americans wished to forget.

Eager "to put Vietnam behind us," few gave much thought to the 2 million Vietnamese casualties, or to the suffering in Laos, or the price paid by Cambodia. In 1975, the fanatical Khmer Rouge (kmair rooj) (Cambodian communists), led by Pol Pot, took power and turned Cambodia into a genocidal "killing field," murdering some 2 million, an estimated third of the population. "Too many of us have lost touch with the horror of war," complained Tim O'Brien, a veteran and novelist of the war. "But time and distance erode memory. We adjust, we lose the intensity. I fear that we are back where we started. I wish we were more troubled."

CHECKING IN

- The domino theory led the United States to deeper involvement in South Vietnam.
- JFK increased the American military presence in Vietnam and then authorized a military coup against the unpopular Diem regime.
- Pursuant to the Gulf of Tonkin Resolution, LBJ escalated ground combat forces until 485,000 troops were in Vietnam by 1968.
- The United States became increasingly polarized between "hawks" and "doves," with college campuses often the site of massive protests.
- The Tet Offensive resulted in tremendous casualties, undermined public support for the war, and essentially ended LBJ's political career.
- The Nixon Doctrine called for a decreased American role in Vietnam, but Nixon stepped up bombing and expanded the war into Cambodia and Laos.
- The Paris Accords ended American military involvement in Vietnam in January 1973.

Chapter Summary

To what extent did the Kennedy administration's domestic record reflect its liberal rhetoric? (page 685)

Stymied by the conservative coalition in Congress, Kennedy did more to stimulate hope than to achieve change. He got few domestic programs through Congress, although the Peace Corps captured American youth's idealism. JFK took a hard line in the Cold War. The Cuban missile crisis proved a sobering moment and opened the way to détente, as well as to an accelerating arms race.

KEY TERMS

John F. Kennedy *(p. 685)*
Cuban missile crisis *(p. 689)*
Martin Luther King, Jr. *(p. 691)*
Civil Rights Act *(p. 691)*
Voting Rights Act *(p. 692)*
Black Power *(p. 694)*
affirmative action *(p. 695)*
American Indian Movement (AIM) *(p. 696)*

What were the major successes and failures of the civil-rights movement from 1961 to 1968? (page 690)

JFK tried to avoid dealing with civil rights but was drawn into quelling violence against black protesters. Martin Luther King, Jr.'s "I Have a Dream" speech provided inspiration for millions. The Civil Rights Act of 1964 and the Voting Rights Act of 1965 revolutionized southern politics. In the second half of the decade, race riots swept the nation, and radicals like Malcolm X and the Black Panthers emerged to challenge King. After 1965, blacks experienced upward mobility, but the overall poverty rate in the black community remained much higher than among other groups.

How and why did the protest movements of minorities shift from the goals and tactics associated with Martin Luther King, Jr., to those of Black Power? (page 695)

Black Power, which emphasized group identity and pride, inspired other marginalized groups to take action. Native Americans established the American Indian Movement, which dramatized their problems by seizing and occupying Alcatraz. César Chávez organized Latino farm workers, and they gained the right to unionize. Hispanic and Asian students organized and demanded college courses and departments dedicated to their own history.

How did Lyndon Johnson's Great Society program exemplify the new liberalism of the 1960s? (page 698)

Lyndon Johnson's presidency brought the most sweeping reforms since the New Deal. His Great Society legislation promoted health, education, voting rights, urban renewal, immigration reform, federal support for the arts and humanities, protection of the environment, and a war against poverty. The Warren Court continued its activist, liberal course. But race riots at home and increased involvement in Vietnam would spell doom for many Great Society programs.

How and why did Kennedy, Johnson, and Nixon each deepen America's involvement in the war in Indochina? (page 701)

Kennedy significantly increased the number of American advisers in Vietnam and authorized a coup to overthrow the unpopular Diem regime. Inheriting a deteriorating limited war from Kennedy, LBJ also chose to escalate America's involvement. Three years later, after an unprecedented bombing campaign and with a half-million American troops in Vietnam, the United States was no closer to achieving its objective, and Richard Nixon would fare no better. Under Nixon, the war dragged on for four more years, until he finally accepted the limitations of U.S. power and withdrew American forces in 1973.

KEY TERMS continued

Immigration Act of 1965 *(p. 696)*
César Estrada Chávez *(p. 697)*
Lyndon Baines Johnson *(p. 698)*
war on poverty *(p. 699)*
Great Society *(p. 699)*
Barry Goldwater *(p. 699)*
Medicare *(p. 700)*
Miranda v. *Arizona* *(p. 701)*
domino theory *(p. 702)*
National Liberation Front (NLF) *(p. 702)*
Vietcong *(p. 702)*
Gulf of Tonkin Resolution *(p. 703)*
"hawks" *(p. 704)*
"doves" *(p. 704)*
Eugene McCarthy *(p. 704)*
Tet Offensive *(p. 705)*
Robert Kennedy *(p. 705)*
My Lai *(p. 708)*

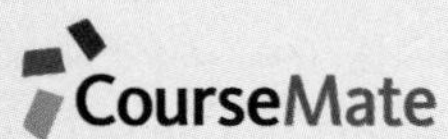

Go to the CourseMate website at **www.cengagebrain.com** for additional study tools and review materials—including audio and video clips—for this chapter.

CHAPTER 29

A Time of Upheaval 1961–1980

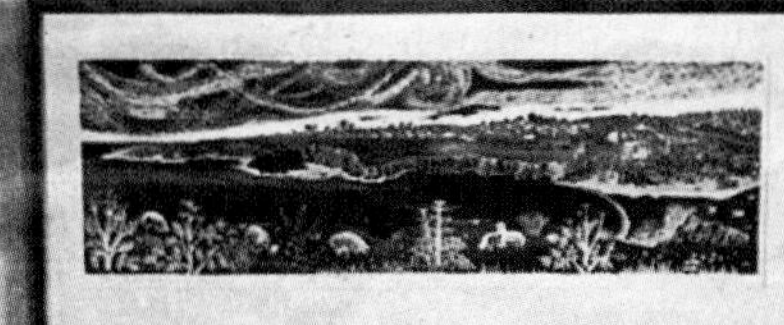

The Joan Baez Sisters and Draft Resistance

National Museum of Natural History, Smithsonian Institution, Washington, D.C. Gift of William Mears

CHAPTER PREVIEW

Coming Apart
What were the major landmarks of the youth movement?

The Countercultural Revolution
In what ways did the counterculture shape the 1960s and 1970s?

Feminism and a Values Revolution
What were the major successes and failures of the Women's Liberation Movement?

A Divided Nation
How did Richard Nixon's political strategy reflect the racial upheavals and radicalism of this era?

Successes Abroad, Crises at Home
What were the main causes of the Watergate scandal?

A Troubled Nation and Presidency
What were the major failures of the Ford and Carter presidencies?

Dorothy Burlage grew up in southeast Texas, a proper southern belle as well as a self-reliant "frontier woman." Her Southern Baptist parents taught her to conform to the conservative values of her old slaveholding community.

During her college years, Burlage's worldview underwent a dramatic transformation. At the University of Texas she watched with awe as black students her age engaged in a civil-rights struggle she likened to a holy crusade. She left her sorority and joined the Christian Faith-and-Life Community, a group committed to nonviolent radical change. The young activists of the civil-rights movement became her political model, their ethos her moral beacon. Burlage attended the founding conference of Students for a Democratic Society (SDS) in 1962. It exhilarated her to be with like-minded idealists, all eager to create a better world. Burlage remained involved in SDS for the rest of the decade until, disillusioned by both the constant need to be "more radical" and the powerful conservative backlash, she ceased her activism and went back to school.

Commitment and then disengagement would be characteristic of many of Dorothy's peers. The baby boomers in college spawned a tumultuous student movement and convulsive counterculture that gave the 1960s its distinctive aura of upheaval. They exploded the well-kept world of the 1950s, when "nice" girls did not have sex or pursue careers, and when African-Americans feared to vote or assert themselves.

But then came 1968. Like an earthquake, the events of that year brought commitments and optimism crashing down. The decade that had begun with high hopes ended in deep disillusionment. One consequence was a widespread turning inward. Many in Dorothy's generation became preoccupied with themselves—which again transformed the nation.

Both agent in and beneficiary of the era's realignment, Republican Richard Nixon would win the presidency in 1968 and then gain an overwhelming reelection victory in 1972. Nixon ended U.S. involvement in Vietnam and inaugurated a period of détente, or reduced tensions, with China and the Soviet Union. In 1974, however, having flouted the very laws he had pledged to uphold, Nixon resigned in disgrace to avoid impeachment. His legacy would be a public disrespect for politics seldom matched in U.S. history.

COMING APART

What were the major landmarks of the youth movement?

By the 1960s, the number of American students pursuing higher education had risen from 1 million in 1940 to 8 million. By then, more than half the U.S. population was under age thirty. Their sheer numbers gave the baby boomers a collective identity and guaranteed that their actions would have an impact.

Most baby boomers followed conventional paths. If they went to college—and fewer than half did—they typically took business and other career-oriented degrees. Whether or not they went to college, the vast majority had their eyes fixed on a good salary, a new car, and a traditional family. Many disdained longhaired protesters and displayed "My Country—Right or Wrong" bumper stickers. Tens of thousands of baby boomers mobilized on the Right, idolizing Barry Goldwater, supporting the war in Vietnam, embracing traditional values, and joining organizations like Young Americans for Freedom (YAF). YAF would be the seedbed of a new generation of conservatives who later gained control of the GOP, yet it was overshadowed in the 1960s by young activists in the New Left.

Toward a New Left

Although a tiny minority of youth, an insurgent band of leftist students got the lion's share of attention. Initially hopeful, they welcomed the idealism of the civil-rights

Chronology

1962	Students for a Democratic Society (SDS) founded
1964	Berkeley Free Speech Movement; the Beatles arrive in the United States
1966	Abolition of automatic student deferments from the draft
1967	March on the Pentagon; Israeli-Arab Six-Day War
1968	Martin Luther King, Jr., assassinated; race riots sweep nation; students take over buildings at Columbia University; Robert F. Kennedy assassinated; violence mars Democratic convention in Chicago; Vietnam peace talks open in Paris; Richard Nixon elected president
1969	*Apollo 11* lands first Americans on the moon; Nixon begins withdrawal of U.S. troops from Vietnam; Woodstock festival
1970	United States invades Cambodia; students killed at Kent State and Jackson State Universities; Beatles disband; Earth Day first celebrated
1971	United States invades Laos; *New York Times* publishes Pentagon Papers; Nixon institutes wage-and-price freeze; South Vietnam invades Laos with the help of U.S. air support
1972	Nixon visits China and the Soviet Union; SALT I agreement approved; break-in at Democratic National Committee headquarters in Watergate complex; Nixon reelected president
1973	Vietnam cease-fire agreement signed; Senate establishes special committee to investigate Watergate; President Salvador Allende ousted and murdered in Chile; Vice President Spiro Agnew resigns; Gerald Ford appointed vice president; *Roe v. Wade;* Yom Kippur War; OPEC begins embargo of oil to the West; Saturday Night Massacre
1974	House Judiciary Committee votes to impeach Nixon; Nixon resigns; Ford becomes president
1975	South Vietnamese government falls; *Mayagüez* incident
1976	Jimmy Carter elected president
1977	Panama Canal treaties ratified; Gay Pride parades in New York and San Francisco
1978	Carter authorizes federal funds to relocate Love Canal residents
1979	Menachem Begin and Anwar el-Sadat sign peace treaty at White House; second round of OPEC price increases; accident at Three Mile Island nuclear plant; Carter establishes full diplomatic relations with the People's Republic of China; Iran hostage crisis begins

movement, supported the campaign against nuclear testing, answered the rousing call of President Kennedy for service to the nation, and admired the mavericks and outsiders of the 1950s.

In June 1962, some sixty students adopted the Port Huron Statement, a broad critique of American society and a call for more genuine human relationships. Proclaiming themselves "a new left," they organized the **Students for a Democratic Society (SDS),** which envisioned a nonviolent youth movement transforming the United States into a "participatory democracy" in which individuals would control the decisions that affected their lives. SDS assumed this could lead to the end of consumerism, militarism, and racism.

Students for a Democratic Society (SDS) Student group opposed to militarism and racism; called for "participatory democracy"

Many idealistic students never joined SDS and instead associated themselves with what they vaguely called "the movement." No matter what the label, a generation of activists found its agenda in the Port Huron Statement. Many became radicalized by the rigidity of campus administrators and mainstream liberalism's inability to achieve swift, fundamental change. Only a radical rejection of the liberal consensus, they presumed, could restructure society and create a genuinely democratic nation.

Berkeley Free Speech Movement (FSM) First major campus protest, which occurred at the University of California, Berkeley

From Protest to Resistance

The first wave of student protest washed across the campus of the University of California, Berkeley. Returning from the Mississippi Freedom Summer in fall 1964, Berkeley graduate student Mario Savio and other student activists tried to solicit funds and recruit volunteers near the campus gate, a spot traditionally open to political activities. Prodded by local conservatives, university administrators suddenly banned such practices; however, when police arrested one of the activists, students surrounded the police car and kept it from moving. Savio then founded the **Berkeley Free Speech Movement (FSM),** a coalition of student groups insisting on the right to campus political activity. Savio likened the university to an impersonal machine, and its students to interchangeable machine parts. More than a thousand students then sat-in on the administrative "gears." Their arrests led to more demonstrations and a strike by nearly 70 percent of the student body.

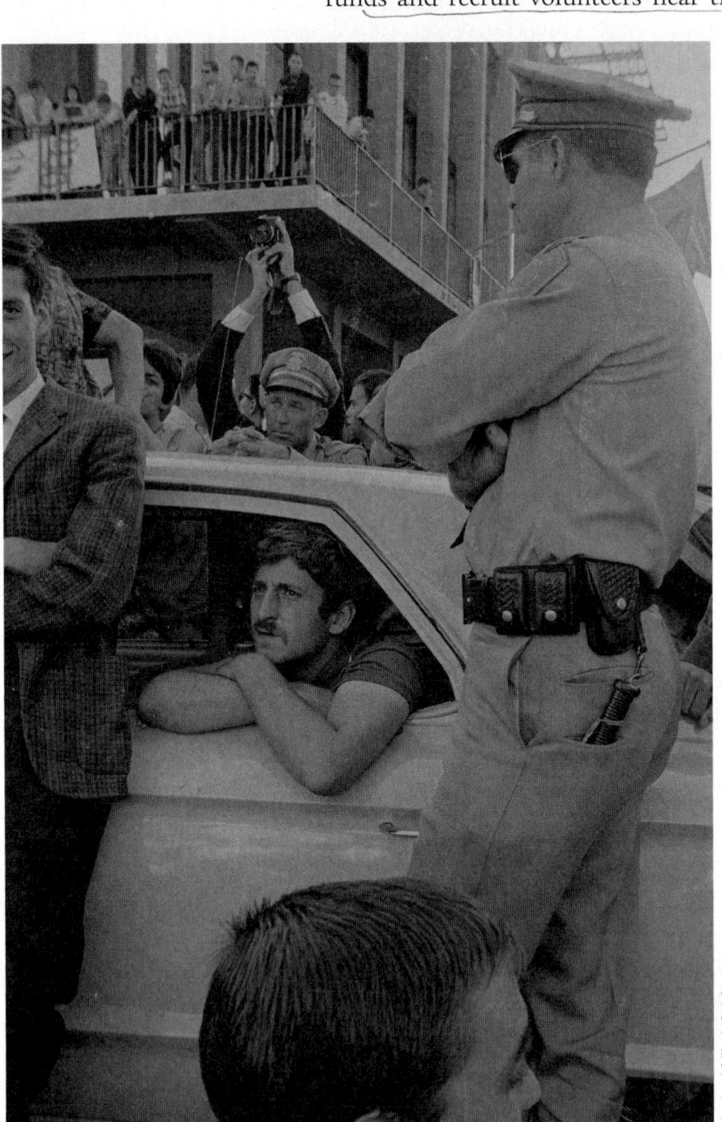

University of California Berkeley

Jack Weinberg in Surrounded Berkeley Police Car

When the police tried to arrest Weinberg for setting up a table in an area that the Berkeley administration had recently banned from all political activity, several hundred students "sat-in" for thirty-two hours, sparking the Free Speech Movement.

The demands and tactics of the FSM reverberated on campuses nationwide. Students disenchanted with filing into impersonal buildings to endure lectures from remote professors initiated a wave of protests seeking greater involvement in university affairs. Their objectives changed the character of American higher education, leading to curricular reform, the end of rules regulating dormitory life, and the admission of more minority students. The escalation of the Vietnam War in 1965 gave the New Left an opportunity to kindle a mass social movement. When the Johnson administration abolished automatic student deferments for the draft in January 1966, more than two hundred new campus chapters of SDS appeared.

In 1966, SDS disrupted ROTC classes, organized draft-card burnings, and harassed campus recruiters for the military and for Dow Chemical Company, the chief producer of napalm and the defoliant Agent Orange, which was used on Vietnam forests. By 1968, it claimed one hundred thousand members and attracted a half-million antiwar protesters to its spring Mobilization to End the War in Vietnam, remembered for the chants of "Burn cards, not people" (meaning draft cards) and "Hell no, we won't go!"

Spring 1968 saw at least forty thousand students on one hundred campuses demonstrate against war and racism. Most, but not all, stayed peaceful. In April, militant Columbia University students took over the administration building and held a dean captive. As the protest expanded, a thousand students barricaded themselves inside five campus buildings, declaring them "revolutionary communes." Galvanized by the brutality of the police who retook the buildings by force, the moderate majority of Columbia students joined a general boycott of classes that shut down the university. Elsewhere, students in Czechoslovakia, France, Germany, Italy, Japan, and Mexico expressed their own revolutionary bombast. Their protests far exceeded in size and ferocity anything that occurred in the United States.

The year 1969 saw the high point of the movement with the New Mobilization, a series of huge antiwar demonstrations culminating in mid-November with the March Against Death. Three hundred thousand protestors descended on Washington to march in a candle-lit parade, carrying signs with the names of soldiers killed or villages destroyed in Vietnam. By 1972, antiwar sentiment would be felt nationwide.

Kent State and Jackson State

Although revulsion against the war continued to grow after Richard Nixon assumed office in 1969, his periodic announcements of troop withdrawals from Vietnam brought a lull in campus demonstrations. On April 30, 1970, however, the U.S. invasion of Cambodia jolted a war-weary nation and reawakened student protests.

At Kent State University in Ohio, as elsewhere, antiwar students broke windows and torched the ROTC building. Nixon branded them "bums," his vice president compared them to Nazi stormtroopers, and the Ohio governor slapped martial law on the university. Three thousand National Guardsmen in full battle gear rolled onto the campus in armored personnel carriers. The next day, as six hundred Kent State students demonstrated, Guardsmen in Troop G, poorly trained in crowd control, fired on students retreating from tear gas, leaving four dead and eleven wounded. None was a campus radical.

Ten days later, Mississippi state patrolmen responding to a campus protest fired into a women's dormitory at historically black **Jackson State College,** killing two students and wounding a dozen. Nationwide, students exploded in anger against the violence, the war, and the president. More than four hundred colleges and universities, many of which had seen no previous unrest, shut down as students boycotted classes. The war had come home.

Jackson State College
Campus where two students were shot to death by highway patrolmen

The nation was polarized. Most students blamed Nixon for widening the war, yet more Americans blamed the victims for the campus violence and criticized students for undermining U.S. foreign policy. Patriotism, class resentment against privileged college students, and a fear of social chaos underlay the condemnation of protesters. Many Kent townspeople shared the view of a local merchant that the guard had "made only one mistake—they should have fired sooner and longer." A local ditty promised, "The score is four, and next time more."

John Filo

"My God, They're Killing Us"

Following President Nixon's announcement of the military incursion into Cambodia, a formally neutral nation, many colleges exploded in anger. To quell the protests at Kent State University, where hundreds of students clashed with local police, Ohio National Guardsmen fired on students, killing four. News of the shootings touched off yet another round of campus protests, which led hundreds of colleges to cancel final exams and shut down for the semester.

Legacy of Student Frenzy

The campus disorders after the invasion of Cambodia were the final spasm of a tumultuous, now fragmenting, movement. When a bomb planted by antiwar radicals destroyed a science building at the University of Wisconsin in summer 1970, killing a graduate student, most deplored the tactic. With the resumption of classes in the fall, the fad of "streaking"—racing across campus in the nude, an act more reminiscent of the 1920s than the 1960s—heralded a change in the student mood.

By then, Nixon had significantly reduced the draft calls, decreasing student opposition to the war. Some antiwar activists turned to other causes, or to communes, careers, and parenthood. A handful of radicals went underground, committing terrorist acts that justified the government's repression of the remnants of the antiwar movement. The New Left fell victim to government harassment, to its own internal contradictions, and to Nixon's winding down of the Vietnam War.

The consequences of campus upheavals outlived the New Left. Student radicalism spurred the resentment of millions of Americans, helping shatter the liberal consensus. It gave religious evangelicals, southern segregationists, and blue-collar workers yet another reason to vote conservative, and propelled Republicans like Ronald Reagan to prominence. "If it takes a bloodbath, let's get it over with," he declared of militants in 1966. "No more appeasement!" In 1966, Reagan won California's governorship, in part because of his opposition to Berkeley demonstrators.

At the same time, the New Left mobilized campuses and made continued American involvement in Vietnam difficult. The Free Speech Movement also liberalized many facets of campus life and made university governance less authoritarian, virtually ending dress codes and curfews, making ROTC an elective rather than a requirement, and forcing the increased recruitment of minority students and the proliferation of Black Studies programs. Such changes, however, fell short of the New Left vision of remaking society and politics. The generation that the New Left had hoped would be the vanguard of radical change preferred pot to politics, and rock to revolution.

CHECKING IN

- SDS produced a manifesto for change.
- Universities became a major site for protests against social ills and the Vietnam War; the Free Speech Movement, sit-ins, and anti-ROTC demonstrations were some of these protests.
- Polarized reactions to the shooting deaths of students at Kent State University and Jackson State College showed how deeply divided the nation had become.
- The New Left movement dissolved in the early 1970s.
- The youth movement left a mixed legacy, including a conservative backlash that would dominate American politics for the rest of the century.

THE COUNTERCULTURAL REVOLUTION

In what ways did the counterculture shape the 1960s and 1970s?

The alienation and hunger for change that drew some youth to politics led others to cultural rebellion, to personal rather than political change, to discarding middle-class conformity, careerism, and sexual repression. In communes and tribes, these "hippies" denounced individualism and private property; in urban areas like Chicago's Old Town or Atlanta's Fourteenth Street, "places where you could take a trip without a ticket," they experimented with drugs. Calling them a **counterculture,** historian Theodore Roszack defined them as "a culture so radically disaffiliated from the mainstream assumptions of our society that it scarcely looks to many as a culture at all, but takes on the alarming appearance of a barbarian intrusion."

counterculture Youth movement led by hippies; promoted drugs and a lack of social restrictions

Hippies and Drugs

Illustrative of the gap between the two cultures, one saw marijuana as "killer weed," a menace to health and life, and the other thought it a harmless social relaxant. At least half the college students in the late 1960s tried marijuana, and a minority used mind-altering drugs, especially LSD. The high priest of LSD was Timothy Leary, a former Harvard psychologist fired in 1963 for encouraging students to experiment with drugs—to "tune in, turn on, drop out." Many youths, distancing themselves from middle-class respectability, flaunted outrageous personal styles. They showed disdain for consumerism by wearing surplus military clothing, torn jeans, and tie-dyed T-shirts. Especially galling to adults, young men sported shaggy beards and long hair, the badge of the counterculture.

Musical Revolution

Popular music both echoed and developed a separate generational identity, a distinct youth culture. In the early 1960s, the revived popularity of folk music mirrored youth's search for an "authentic" alternative to what they considered an artificial consumer culture. Bob Dylan sang hopefully of changes "blowin' in the wind"

Michael Ochs Archives/Corbis

The Beatles in England, 1964

Many Americans, disenchanted with conformity and convention, embraced the Fab Four as much for their mod style and frisky personalities as for their music.

that would transform society. Then in 1964, Beatlemania swept the United States. Moving beyond their early romantic songs, the Beatles gloried in the youth culture's drugs ("I'd love to turn you on"), sex ("Why don't we do it in the road?"), and radicalism ("You say you want a revolution"). They would soon be joined by the Rolling Stones, the Motown rhythm-and-blues black performers, and eardrum-shattering acid rockers—each extolling "sex, drugs, and rock and roll" for a generation at war.

In August 1969, four hundred thousand young people gathered for the **Woodstock festival** in New York's Catskill Mountains to celebrate their vision of freedom and harmony. For one long weekend, they reveled in rock music and openly shared drugs and sexual partners. The counterculture heralded Woodstock as the dawning of an era of love and peace—the Age of Aquarius.

Woodstock festival Outdoor concert in upstate New York that attracted half a million or more young people to celebrate "sex, drugs, and rock and roll"

In fact, the counterculture was disintegrating. The pilgrimage of "flower children" to San Francisco's Haight-Ashbury district and to New York's East Village in the mid-1960s had brought in their wake a train of rapists and organized-crime dope peddlers. A week before the Woodstock festival, hippie Charles Manson and his "family" of runaways ritually murdered a pregnant movie actress and four of her friends in Los Angeles. In December 1969, a Rolling Stones concert at the Altamont Raceway near San Francisco deteriorated into a violent melee in which four concert-goers died. In 1970, the Beatles disbanded. John Lennon sang, "The dream is over."

Nevertheless, the counterculture continued to influence American society long after the 1960s. Advertisers awoke to the economic potential of the youth culture, using "revolution" to sell cars and jeans. Rock groups, commanding huge fees, became big business. Self-fulfillment remained a popular goal, the questioning of conventional values and authority became commonplace, and the repressive sexual standards of the 1950s did not return.

The Sexual Revolution

The counterculture's "if it feels good, do it" approach fit the permissive ethic of the 1960s, leading to a revolution in sexual norms. Although the AIDS epidemic and the graying of the baby boomers in the late 1980s chilled the ardor of promiscuity, liberalized sexual mores were more publicly accepted than ever before, making full gender equality and gay liberation realizable goals.

Many commentators linked the sexual revolution to waning fears of unwanted pregnancy. In 1960, oral contraceptives reached the market, and by 1970, 12 million women were taking "the Pill." Still other women used the intrauterine device (IUD, later banned as unsafe) or the diaphragm. Some states legalized abortion. In New York, one fetus was legally aborted for every two babies born in 1970. The Supreme Court's ***Roe* v. *Wade*** (1973) struck down all remaining state laws infringing on a woman's right to abortion during the first three months of pregnancy.

Roe* v. *Wade Supreme Court decision that a woman's right to abortion is constitutionally protected

The Court also threw out most laws restricting "sexually explicit" art with "redeeming social importance." Mass culture quickly exploited the new permissiveness. *Playboy* magazine featured ever-more-explicit erotica, and women's periodicals encouraged their readers to enjoy recreational sex. Hollywood filled movie screens with scenes of explicit sex, Broadway presented plays featuring frontal nudity and mock orgies, and even television presented frank discussions of once-forbidden subjects.

Attitudinal changes brought behavioral changes, and vice versa. Cohabitation—living together without marriage—became thinkable to average middle-class Americans. Some marital counselors even touted "open marriage" (in which spouses are free to have sex with other partners) and "swinging" (sexual sharing with other couples) as cures for stale relationships. Some Americans' tolerance for unconventional, unrestrained sexuality had changed dramatically by the mid-1970s.

Overall, the baby boomers transformed sexual relations as much as gender and racial relations. The institutions of marriage and family were fundamentally altered. But what some hailed as liberation others bemoaned as moral decay. Offended by open sexuality and its preferences, as well as "topless" bars and X-rated theaters, many Americans applauded politicians who promised a war on immorality. The public association of the counterculture and the sexual revolution with student radicalism and ghetto riots swelled the tide of conservatism in the 1970s.

CHECKING IN

- Hippies denounced materialism and selfishness and created a counterculture on communes and in urban centers like Haight-Ashbury in San Francisco.
- Alienated young people openly experimented with drugs like marijuana and LSD.
- Folk music, the Beatles, and acid rock symbolized the counterculture, culminating in the 1969 festival at Woodstock.
- By 1969, the countercultural movement was deteriorating, although its influence in American culture proved long-lasting.
- The Pill and the legalization of abortion helped launch the sexual revolution that swept from the counterculture into the mainstream.

FEMINISM AND A VALUES REVOLUTION

What were the major successes and failures of the Women's Liberation Movement?

The rising tempo of social activism also stirred a new spirit of self-awareness and dissatisfaction among educated women. Although one of the last of the major social movements to emerge in the 1960s, the second wave of feminism outlasted the others and profoundly altered the economic and legal status of women.

A Second Feminist Wave

Several events fanned the embers of discontent into a flame. The 1963 report of the Presidential Commission on the Status of Women, established by Kennedy, documented occupational inequities that were comparable to those endured by minorities. Women received less pay than men for comparable work. In addition, they made up only 7 percent of the nation's doctors and less than 4 percent of its lawyers. The women who served on the presidential commission successfully urged that the Civil Rights Act of 1964 prohibit gender-based as well as racial discrimination in employment.

Dismayed by the Equal Employment Opportunity Commission's reluctance to enforce the ban on sex discrimination in employment, these women formed the **National Organization for Women (NOW)** in 1966. A civil-rights group for women, NOW labored "to bring women into full participation in the mainstream of American society." It lobbied for equal opportunity, filed lawsuits against gender discrimination, and mobilized public opinion against sexism.

National Organization for Women (NOW) Leading feminist group

NOW's prominence owed much to the publication of journalist Betty Friedan's (free-DANS) critique of domesticity, *The Feminine Mystique* (1963), which posed what Friedan called "the problem that has no name"—the frustration of educated, middle-class wives and mothers who had subordinated their own aspirations to the needs of men. Friedan urged women to pursue careers that would "fulfill their potentialities as human beings."

Still another catalyst for feminism came from the involvement of younger women in the civil-rights and anti–Vietnam War movements. These activists gained confidence in their own potential, an ideology to understand oppression, and experience in the strategy and tactics of organized protest. They also became conscious of their own second-class status, as they were sexually exploited and relegated to menial jobs by male activists. Although small in number, young women who shared such thoughts would soon create a women's liberation movement more critical of sexual inequality than NOW.

Women's Liberation

In 1968, militant feminists adopted "consciousness-raising" as a recruitment device and a means of transforming women's perceptions of themselves and society. Tens of thousands of women assembled in small groups to share their experiences and air grievances. Women learned from such meetings that their individual, personal problems were in fact shared problems with social causes and political solutions—"the personal is political." This new consciousness begot a sense that "sisterhood is powerful." Radical feminists set up "freedom trash cans" into which women could discard high-heeled shoes, bras, girdles, and other symbols of subjugation. They established health collectives and day-care centers and fought negative portrayals of women in the media, in advertising, and in language. Terms like "male chauvinist pig" entered the vocabulary and those like "chicks" exited.

In August 1970, feminists joined the largest women's rights demonstration ever. Commemorating the fiftieth anniversary of woman suffrage, the Women's Strike for Equality brought out tens of thousands of women across the nation to parade for the right to equal employment and to safe, legal abortions. By then the women's movement had already ended newspapers' practice of listing employment opportunities under separate "Male" and "Female" headings, and pressured banks to issue credit to women in their own name.

In the 1970s, feminists focused especially on three issues: equal treatment in education and employment, access to abortion, and passage of the **Equal Rights Amendment (ERA)** barring discrimination on the basis of sex. In 1972, Title IX of the Education Amendments Act prohibited educational institutions that received federal funds from discriminating on the basis of sex. Women won stronger laws on rape and domestic violence. Many single-sex colleges and even military academies became coeducational. The percentage of female students in law schools rose from 5 percent to 40 percent in the 1970s. By century's end, women would constitute about 20 percent of all state and federal legislators.

Equal Rights Amendment (ERA) A proposed amendment to the U.S. Constitution barring discrimination on the basis of sex

The right to control their own sexuality became a feminist rallying cry. In addition to using "the Pill," some women challenged demeaning obstetrical practices. And many, aware of the dangers of illegal abortions, pushed for their legalization, achieved in *Roe* v. *Wade* (1973). *Roe* v. *Wade* and the subsequent doubling of abortions, to 1.5 million by 1980, triggered an enormous backlash from social conservatives, many of whom felt abortion was the moral equivalent of murder. Abortion opponents sought a "right to life" amendment to the Constitution and simultaneously energized Phyllis Schlafly's "STOP ERA" campaign.

In 1972, both houses of Congress passed the ERA with little opposition and, within a year, twenty-eight of the necessary thirty-eight states approved the proposed amendment. Its ultimate adoption seemed self-evident. Then Phyllis Schlafly, a Republican organizer and working-woman herself, took up the fight. Her accusation that feminism was just self-centeredness, and her affirmation of traditional gender roles, struck a responsive chord with many men as well as with working-class women who felt estranged from the largely upper-middle-class feminist movement. Schlafly charged that the ERA would force women into combat roles in the military, necessitate "unisex toilets," and promote lesbianism. Her relentless assault eroded support and helped kill the amendment.

While the number of women working outside the home leaped from under 20 million in 1960 to nearly 60 million by 1990, women's wages still lagged behind those of men, the workplace remained gender-segregated, and the "glass ceiling" that limited their ability to rise beyond a certain corporate level remained in place. As divorce and out-of-wedlock births became more common, the number of women heading families increased; by 1980, only 15 percent of American families with children had a father who worked and a mother who stayed at home. Sociologists began writing about the "feminization of poverty."

Women who worked still bore primary responsibility for their homes and family. Yet day-care centers for working women became commonplace, gender-neutral terms (for example, "firefighter" in place of "fireman") came into vogue, and the ideal male changed from swashbuckler to one more "in touch with his feelings." Few pined for the era when child care, housework, and volunteerism defined "women's sphere."

Gay Liberation

Stimulated by the other protest movements in the 1960s, gay liberation emerged publicly in late June 1969. During a routine raid by New York City police, the homosexual patrons of the Stonewall Inn, a gay bar in Greenwich Village, unexpectedly fought back. The furor triggered a surge of "gay pride," a new sense of identity and self-acceptance, and widespread activism. The **gay liberation** movement that emerged asserted, "We are going to be who we are."

gay liberation Organized attempt to end discrimination against homosexuals

By 1973, eight hundred openly gay groups campaigned for equal rights, for incorporating lesbianism into the women's movement, and for removing the stigma of immorality and depravity attached to being gay. That year the American Psychiatric Association officially ended its classification of homosexuality as a mental disorder. More and more gay men and women, including some elected officials, "came out of the closet," proudly acknowledging their sexual orientation. Organizations like the National Gay Task Force, founded in 1973 (and later renamed the National Gay and Lesbian Task Force), demanded the repeal of anti-gay laws and passage of legislation protecting homosexuals' civil rights. Responding to the pressure, many states and cities repealed laws against same-sex relations between consenting adults.

Like feminism, the gay liberation movement came under attack from conservatives, who feared that protecting gay rights encouraged immoral behavior. In 1977, singer Anita Bryant led a successful campaign to repeal a Miami law banning discrimination against homosexuals, prompting similar antigay campaigns in other cities.

Environmental Activism

Building on the concerns raised in the early 1960s, environmentalists also carried the tide of reform into the 1970s. Following the first Earth Day in April 1970, which attracted some 20 million participants, the media began to highlight acid rain, global warming, nuclear waste disposal, and other human-caused environmental hazards. Well-publicized disasters greatly furthered concern. Cleveland's Cuyahoga River burst into flames, and Lake Erie "died," both contaminated by decades of toxic chemical dumping.

Environmental advocacy groups gained many fresh recruits. Older organizations such as the Sierra Club and the Audubon Society continued their preservation efforts, while newer groups such as Greenpeace and Friends of the Earth rallied against threats to ecological balance. Founded in 1971, Greenpeace worked to preserve old-growth forests and protect the world's oceans. By 2000, it had 250,000 U.S. members. The Save the Whales campaign, launched by the Animal Welfare Institute in 1971, opposed the slaughter of the world's largest mammals.

President Nixon responded to popular pressures by signing bills for cleaner air and water, for reducing toxic wastes, and for the further protection of endangered species and wilderness. Nixon also signed bills creating the Occupational Safety and Health Administration (OSHA), to enforce health and safety standards in the workplace, and the Environmental Protection Agency (EPA), requiring federal agencies to prepare an environmental-impact analysis of all proposed projects.

Environmentalists also targeted the nuclear-power industry. Adopting techniques from the civil-rights and antiwar campaigns, activists protested at planned nuclear-power plants. The movement crested in 1979 when a partial meltdown crippled the **Three Mile Island** nuclear-power plant in Pennsylvania. A Jane Fonda movie released at the same time, *The China Syndrome,* portrayed a fictional but plausible nuclear-power disaster caused by a California earthquake. The Three Mile Island accident deepened public concerns about nuclear power.

Three Mile Island Nuclear-power plant in Pennsylvania where disaster nearly struck in 1979

However, at a time of concern over an energy crisis, and of rising unemployment, Americans divided over environmental issues like construction of the Trans-Alaska Pipeline in 1973 and whether or not to abandon offshore oil drilling and restrictions on logging. A popular bumper sticker read: "If You're Hungry and Out of Work, Eat an Environmentalist." Yet other Americans sought a healthy lifestyle that promoted less consumption. Cigarette smoking declined. Organic food consumption increased. A jogging craze swept the middle class.

The "Me Decade"

Whatever political views Americans held, personal pursuits and self-fulfillment largely shaped 1970s American society. Many citizens—reacting to defeat in Vietnam, an economic downturn, and the corruption of public officials—retreated inward, following the advice of Robert Ringer's best-seller *Looking Out for Number One.*

Highly individualistic pet causes flourished, as did new faiths. Some young people practiced Transcendental Meditation or joined the Reverend Sun Myung Moon's Unification Church. Others embraced the International Society for Krishna Consciousness. Several thousand rural communes arose as some counterculture veterans sought to escape the urban-corporate world and live in harmony with nature. However, most communes proved short-lived.

By the early 1980s, journalists discovered the "yuppie" (young urban professional), preoccupied with physical fitness and consumer goods. Yuppies jogged and bicycled, ate pesticide-free natural foods, and, in a process known as gentrification, purchased and restored run-down inner-city apartments, often displacing poor and elderly residents in the process. Self-indulgence appeared to be their hallmark, and many identified with conservatism's priority on, above all, individual rights.

The 1970s also saw the rise of punk rock, an aggressively anti-establishment genre promoted by groups like the Sex Pistols. Tejano music spread from Texas to win national popularity, the improvised recitations of rap or hip-hop emerged from poor black New York City neighborhoods, and disco music spotlighted the desire to dance on one's own and to pursue individual rather than societal goals.

In the cultural arena, much but not all reflected the era's malaise. Along with films featuring the madness of the war in Vietnam and corruption in high places, blockbuster movies like *Jaws* (1975), *Rocky* (1976), and *Star Wars* (1977) offered escapist fare. *Happy Days,* the top TV show of 1976–1977, evoked nostalgia for the 1950s. The TV series *Dallas,* chronicling the steamy affairs of a Texas oil family, captivated millions. And beginning in 1971 and gaining popularity throughout the decade, *All in the Family* featured a blue-collar working stiff, Archie Bunker, raging against "men with hair down to there" as well as just about everything else associated with the 1960s. The character his creator meant to be a cultural and political dinosaur actually forecast a shift to the Right, a backlash against "the sixties."

CHECKING IN

- *The Feminine Mystique* energized the women's movement; with the formation of NOW, women's liberation became an important force.
- Feminism advanced, but women still bumped up against the "glass ceiling."
- Gay liberation efforts achieved results in the repeal of anti-gay laws; like feminism, the gay rights movement sparked a conservative backlash.
- Environmentalism, particularly concerns about nuclear power, expanded.
- After 1970, personal goals trumped political commitments; the "yuppie," a symbol of the obsession with self-fulfillment, attracted increased attention from the media.

A DIVIDED NATION

How did Richard Nixon's political strategy reflect the racial upheavals and radicalism of this era?

By 1968, the combined stresses and strains in American society had produced the most tumultuous era in the United States since the Civil War. The tensions that year resulted in riots, fiery demonstrations, two stunning assassinations, Lyndon Johnson's retreat in Vietnam and from politics, and an election that marked the demise of liberalism.

Assassinations and Turmoil

On April 4, three days after the Wisconsin primary, Martin Luther King, Jr., was killed in Memphis, Tennessee, where he had gone to support striking sanitation workers.

The assassin was James Earl Ray, a white escaped convict. As the news spread, black ghettos burst into violence in more than a hundred cities. Twenty blocks of Chicago's West Side went up in flames, and Mayor Richard Daley ordered police to shoot to kill arsonists. In Washington, DC, under night skies illuminated by seven hundred fires, army units set up machine-gun emplacements outside the Capitol and White House. The rioting left forty-six dead, three thousand injured, and nearly twenty-seven thousand in jail.

Entering the race as the favorite of the party bosses and labor chieftains, LBJ's vice president, **Hubert Humphrey,** turned the contest for the nomination into a three-cornered scramble. Eugene McCarthy remained the candidate of the "new politics"—a moral crusade against war and injustice directed to affluent, educated liberals. Robert Kennedy campaigned as the tribune of the less privileged, the only candidate who appealed to both white ethnics and the minority poor. But in early June, after his victory in the California primary, the brother of the murdered president was himself assassinated by a troubled Palestinian, Sirhan Sirhan.

Hubert Humphrey LBJ's vice president who ran for president against Nixon in 1968

The deaths of King and Kennedy frustrated untold Americans. The murders denied them a fundamental democratic right, the right to choose their own leaders.

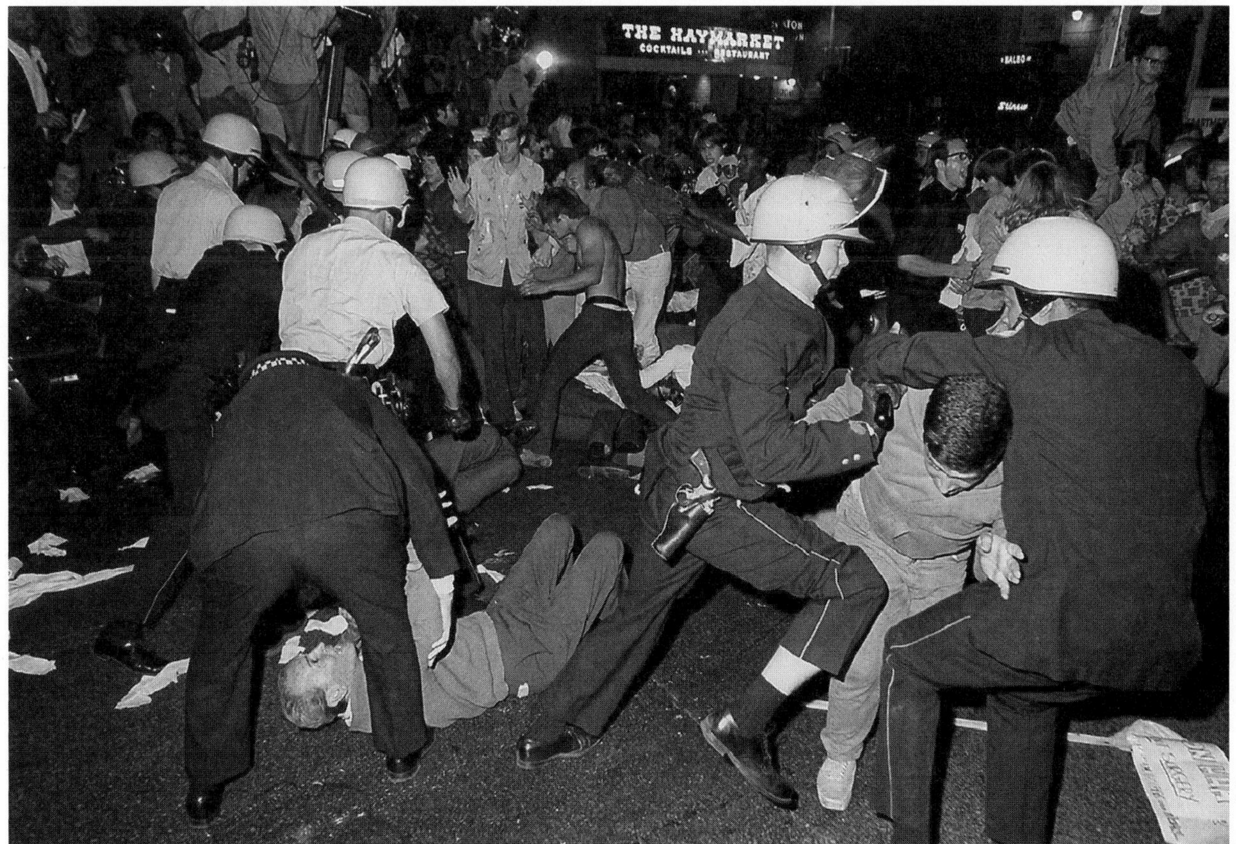

Bettmann/Corbis

"The Whole World Is Watching"

Photographs and televised pictures of Chicago police beating and gassing antiwar protesters and innocent bystanders at the Democratic convention in 1968 linked Democrats in the public mind with violence and mayhem. The scenes made Republican Richard Nixon a reassuring presence to those he would term "the silent majority."

The dream of peace and racial justice turned to despair. "I won't vote," one youth said. "Every good man we get, they kill."

While Kennedy's death cleared the way for Humphrey's nomination, increasing numbers of Democrats turned to third-party candidate George Wallace's thinly veiled appeal for white supremacy or to the GOP nominee Richard M. Nixon. Nixon promised to end the war in Vietnam with honor, to restore "law and order," and to heed "the voice of the great majority of Americans, the forgotten Americans, the nonshouters, the non-demonstrators, those who do not break the law, people who pay their taxes and go to work, who send their children to school, who go to their churches, . . . who love this country." George Wallace tapped into the same wellspring of angry reaction as Nixon. Wallace pitched his message to blue-collar workers and southern whites fed up with antiwar protesters, black militants, hippies, and liberal intellectuals.

In August 1968, violence outside the Democratic National Convention in Chicago reinforced the appeal of both Wallace and Nixon. Determined to avoid the rioting that had wracked Chicago after the assassination of Martin Luther King, Jr., Mayor Richard Daley gave police a green light to attack "the hippies, the **Yippies,** and the flippies." The result was a police riot, televised live to a huge national audience. As protesters chanted, "The whole world is watching," Chicago police clubbed demonstrators and bystanders alike. The brutality on the streets overshadowed Humphrey's nomination, tore the Democrats further apart, and created an enduring image of them as the party of dissent and disorder. The real victor in Chicago was conservatism.

Yippies The Youth International Party, a protest group led by counterculture guru Abbie Hoffman

Conservative Resurgence

Nixon capitalized on the televised turmoil to attract the support of voters desperate for "law and order." He criticized the Supreme Court for safeguarding criminals and radicals, vowed to get people off welfare rolls, promised to crack down on "pot, pornography, protest, and permissiveness," and asserted that "our schools are for education—not integration."

Reaching out even more bluntly to working-class whites, George Wallace stoked the fury of the working class against "bearded anarchists, smart-aleck editorial writers, and pointy-headed professors looking down their noses at us." Promising to keep peace, he vowed that "if any demonstrator ever lays down in front of my car, it'll be the last car he'll ever lie down in front of." Nearly 14 percent of the electorate voted for Wallace in November.

In a narrow outcome with large consequences, Nixon and Humphrey split the rest of the vote almost evenly (see Map 29.1). But with Humphrey receiving just 38 percent of the white vote, the long-dominant New Deal coalition was shattered. The electorate clearly sought stability, not further social change.

The 57 percent of the electorate who chose Nixon or Wallace would dominate American politics for the rest of the century. While the national Democratic Party fractured into a welter of contending groups, the Republicans attracted a new majority who lived in the suburbs and the Sun Belt, regarded the federal government as wasteful, blamed student protestors and hippies for a perceived decline in morality, and objected to special efforts to assist minorities and those on welfare. Wooing these voters became the centerpiece of Nixon's political strategy.

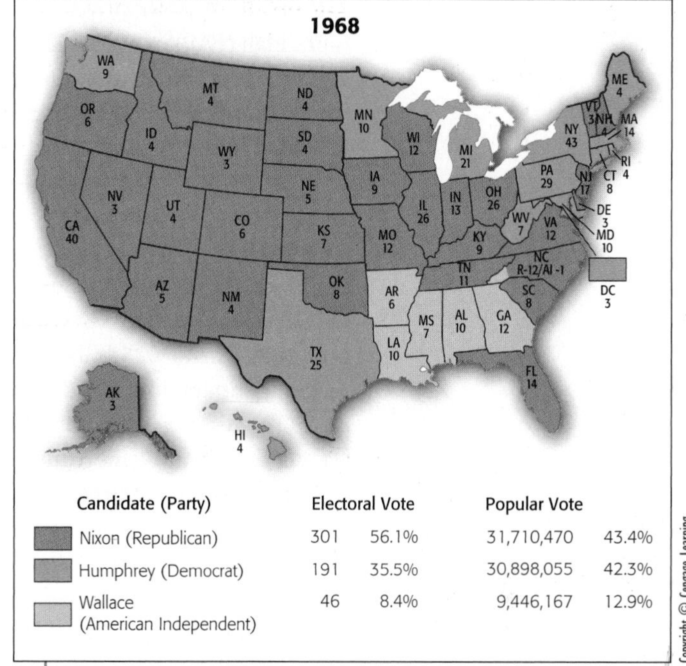

Candidate (Party)	Electoral Vote		Popular Vote	
Nixon (Republican)	301	56.1%	31,710,470	43.4%
Humphrey (Democrat)	191	35.5%	30,898,055	42.3%
Wallace (American Independent)	46	8.4%	9,446,167	12.9%

Map 29.1 The Election of 1968

Interactive Map

A Matter of Character

A Californian of Quaker roots, Richard Milhous Nixon was elected to Congress as a navy veteran in 1946. He won prominence for his role in the HUAC investigation of Alger Hiss (see Chapter 26) and advanced to the Senate in 1950 by accusing his Democratic opponent of disloyalty. He served two terms as Eisenhower's vice president, but lost the presidency to Kennedy in 1960 and a run for the California governorship in 1962. Ignoring what seemed a political death sentence, Nixon campaigned vigorously for GOP candidates in 1966 and won his party's nomination and the presidency in 1968.

Nixon yearned to be remembered as an international statesman, but domestic affairs kept intruding. He tried to reform the welfare system and solve complex economic problems, but the underside of Nixon's personality appealed to the darker recesses of national character and intensified the fears and divisions among Americans.

Although highly intelligent, he displayed the rigid self-control of a man monitoring his own every move. When the private Nixon emerged, he was suspicious, insecure, and vengeful. His conviction that enemies lurked everywhere, waiting to destroy him, verged on paranoia. He sought to annihilate his partisan enemies, especially the "eastern liberal establishment" that had long opposed him.

The classic outsider, reared in pinched surroundings, physically awkward, and unable to relate easily to others, Nixon remained fearful, even at the height of his power, that he would never be accepted. At the beginning of his administration, however, his strengths stood out. He spoke of national reconciliation, took bold initiatives internationally, and dealt with domestic problems responsibly.

Symbolic of this positive start, the nation joined the new president in celebrating the first successful manned mission to the moon. On July 21, 1969, astronaut Neil Armstrong descended from the lunar lander *Eagle* to the surface of the Sea of Tranquility, and announced to enthralled television audiences back on Earth, "That's one small step for man, one giant leap for mankind." Five more lunar expeditions followed, but in 1975 the space race essentially ended as the United States and Soviet Union engaged in cooperative efforts to explore the rest of the universe.

The first newly elected president since 1849 whose party controlled neither house of Congress, Nixon cooperated with the Democrats to increase social-security benefits, build subsidized housing, expand the Job Corps, and grant the vote to eighteen-year-olds. As noted earlier, the president also approved new laws to protect the environment and worker safety.

Conservatives grumbled as government grew larger and more intrusive and as race-conscious employment policies, including quotas, were mandated for all federal contractors. Conservatives grew still angrier when Nixon unveiled the Family Assistance Plan (FAP) in 1969. A bold effort to overhaul the welfare system, FAP proposed a guaranteed minimum annual income for all Americans. Caught between liberals who thought the income inadequate and conservatives who disliked it on principle, FAP died in the Senate.

A Troubled Economy

Nixon inherited the fiscal consequences of Lyndon B. Johnson's effort to wage the Vietnam War and finance the Great Society by deficit financing. Facing a "whopping" budget deficit of $25 billion in 1969 and an inflation rate of 5 percent, Nixon cut government spending and encouraged the Federal Reserve Board to raise interest rates. The result was a combination of inflation and recession that economists called "stagflation" and Democrats termed "Nixonomics" (Figure 29.1).

Accelerating inflation lowered the standard of living for many families and sparked a wave of strikes as workers sought wage hikes to keep up with the cost of living. It also encouraged the wealthy to invest in art and real estate instead of technology and factories. More plants shut down, industrial jobs dwindled, and millions

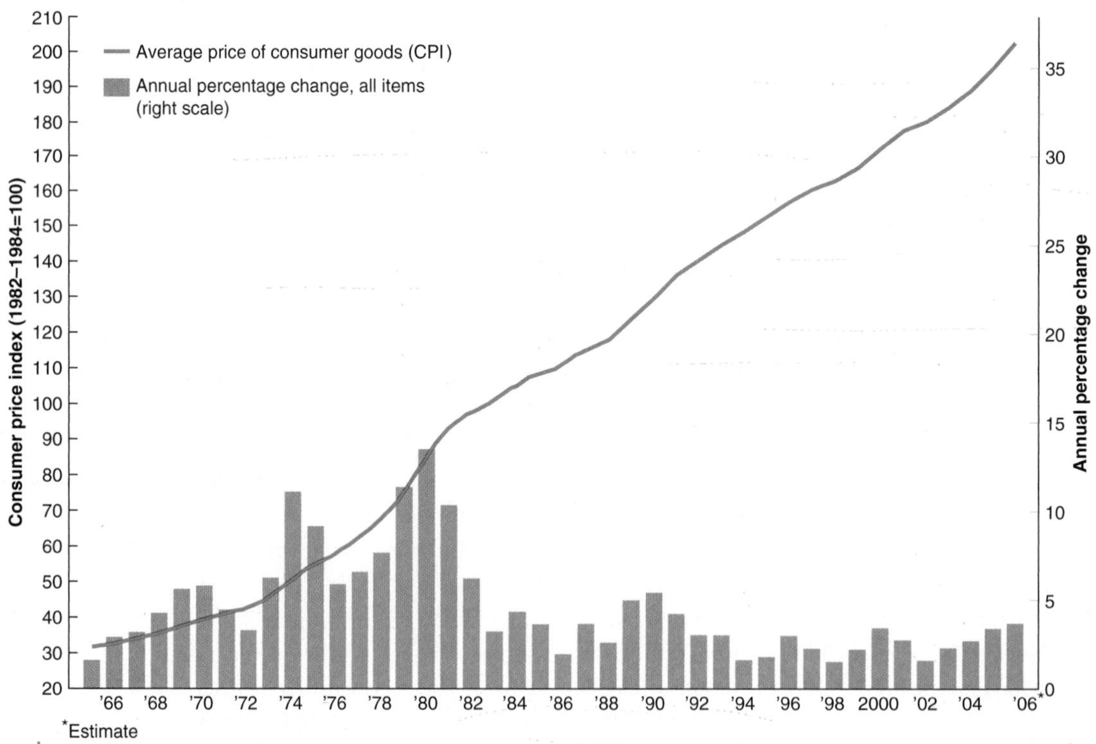

Figure 29.1 Inflation, 1965–2006

Inflation, which had been moderate during the two decades following World War II, began to soar with the escalation of the war in Vietnam in the mid-1960s. In 1979 and 1980, the nation experienced double-digit inflation in two consecutive years for the first time since World War I.

of displaced workers lost their savings, their health and pension benefits, and their homes.

Throughout 1971, Nixon lurched from policy to policy. Declaring, "I am now a Keynesian," he increased deficit spending to stimulate the private sector. It resulted in the largest budget deficit since World War II. Then, Nixon devalued the dollar to correct the balance-of-payment deficit. Finally, he froze wages, prices, and rents for ninety days, a Band-Aid that worked until after the 1972 election. Then Nixon again reversed course, replacing controls with voluntary—and ineffective—guidelines. Inflation and sluggish growth would dog the U.S. economy throughout the decade.

Law and Order

Despite his public appeals for unity, Nixon hoped to divide the American people in ways that would bring about a realignment in politics and create a new Republican majority coalition. His "southern strategy" sought to attract Dixie's white Democrats into the GOP fold, while his stands on crime, drugs, antiwar protestors, and black militants wooed blue-collar laborers and suburbanites—voters whom political strategist Kevin Phillips vividly described as "in motion between a Democratic past and a Republican future."

To combat the militants he despised, Nixon had the IRS audit their tax returns, the Small Business Administration deny them loans, and the National Security Agency illegally wiretap them. The FBI worked with local officials to disrupt and immobilize Black Panthers. The CIA illegally investigated and compiled dossiers on thousands of American citizens. The Department of Justice prosecuted antiwar activists and militant blacks. Nixon himself drew up an "enemies list" of adversaries to be harassed by the government.

In 1970, Nixon widened his offensive against the antiwar movement by approving the Huston Plan, which would use the CIA and FBI in various illegal activities, such as wiretapping and break-ins, to gather or plant evidence. But FBI chief J. Edgar Hoover opposed the Huston Plan as a threat to the bureau's independence. Blocked, Nixon secretly created his own White House unit to discredit his opposition and to ensure executive security. Nicknamed "the **plumbers**" because of their assignment to plug government leaks, the team was headed by former FBI agent G. Gordon Liddy and former CIA operative E. Howard Hunt.

plumbers Group set up by Nixon White House to carry out dirty tricks and undermine opposition to the president

The plumbers first targeted Daniel Ellsberg, a former Defense Department analyst who had turned over to the press the **Pentagon Papers,** a secret chronicle of U.S. involvement in Vietnam. On June 13, 1971, the *New York Times* began publishing the Pentagon Papers, which revealed a long history of White House lies to foreign leaders, Congress, and the American people. Although the papers contained nothing damaging about his administration, Nixon feared that they would undermine public trust in government and establish a precedent for publishing classified material. The Supreme Court, however, ruled that the publication of the Pentagon Papers was protected under the First Amendment. Livid, Nixon directed the Justice Department to indict Ellsberg for theft and ordered the plumbers to break into the office of Ellsberg's psychiatrist in search of information against the man who had become an instant hero to the antiwar movement.

Pentagon Papers Secret chronicle of presidential lies regarding U.S. involvement in Vietnam published by the *New York Times*

CHECKING IN

- The presence of antiwar demonstrators at the Democratic National Convention, and the assassinations of Martin Luther King, Jr., and Robert Kennedy, led to riots.
- Richard Nixon and George Wallace stoked and rode the conservative backlash.
- Despite his enormous political skills, Nixon was a deeply flawed man.
- Early in his presidency, Nixon accepted some moderate social and environmental-protection measures; economic "stagflation" led Nixon to attempt a variety of unsuccessful cures.
- Nixon ordered a secret and frequently illegal campaign against his opponents.
- Nixon's "southern strategy" courted white conservatives by opposing busing and other desegregation measures and promoting law and order.

The Southern Strategy

Nixon especially courted whites upset by the drive for racial equality. The administration opposed extension of the Voting Rights Act of 1965, sought to cripple enforcement of the Fair Housing Act of 1968, pleaded for the postponement of desegregation in Mississippi schools, and filed suits to prohibit busing children to desegregated schools.

The strategy of wooing white southerners dictated Nixon's Supreme Court nominations. To reverse the Warren Court's liberalism, he sought strict constructionists, judges who would not "meddle" in social issues or be "soft" on criminals. In 1969, he appointed Warren Burger as chief justice. Although the Senate then twice rejected southern conservatives nominated by Nixon, the president succeeded in appointing Harry Blackmun of Minnesota, Lewis Powell of Virginia, and William Rehnquist of Arizona. Along with Burger, they steered the Court in a centrist direction, ruling liberally in most cases involving abortion, desegregation, and the death penalty, while shifting to the Right on civil liberties, community censorship, and police power.

As the 1970 congressional elections neared, Nixon's vice president, Spiro T. Agnew, assailed the Democrats as "sniveling hand-wringers" and the news media as "nattering nabobs of negativism." Liberals deplored Agnew's alarming alliterative allegations, but many others found them on target. The 1970 elections were a draw, with the GOP losing nine House seats and winning two Senate seats.

SUCCESSES ABROAD, CRISES AT HOME

What were the main causes of the Watergate scandal?

Above all else, Nixon focused on foreign affairs. Considering himself a master of *realpolitik* (ray-ALL-pol-i-teek)—a pragmatic approach stressing national interest rather than ethical goals—he sought to check Soviet expansionism and limit the nuclear-arms race. He planned to move the United States out of Vietnam and into an era of détente—reduced tensions—with the communist world. To manage diplomacy, Nixon chose **Henry Kissinger,** a refugee from Hitler's Germany and a professor of international relations, who shared Nixon's penchant for secrecy and for the concentration of decision-making power in the White House.

Henry Kissinger Harvard professor chosen to be Nixon's top foreign-policy adviser

In his second inaugural, Nixon pledged to make the next four years "the best four years in American history." Ironically, they would rank among its sorriest. His vice president would resign in disgrace, his closest confidants would go to jail, and he would serve barely a year and a half of his second term before resigning to avoid impeachment.

Détente

détente Effort to reduce tensions between the United States and the communist nations

Disengagement from Vietnam helped Nixon to achieve a turnabout in Chinese-American relations and **détente** with the communist superpowers. These developments, the most significant shift in U.S. foreign policy since the start of the Cold War, created a new relationship among the United States, China, and the Soviet Union.

Presidents from Truman to Johnson had refused to recognize the People's Republic of China, to allow its admission to the United Nations, and to permit American allies to trade with it. But by 1969, a widening Sino-Soviet split made the prospect of improved relations with both nations attractive to Nixon, who hoped to have "closer relations with each side than they did with each other."

In June 1971, Kissinger began secret negotiations with Beijing, laying the groundwork for Nixon's historic February 1972 trip to China "to seek the normalization of relations." The first visit ever by a sitting American president to the largest nation in the world, it ended more than twenty years of Chinese-American hostility. Full diplomatic recognition followed in 1979.

Equally significant, Nixon went to Moscow in May 1972 to sign agreements with the Soviets on trade and technological cooperation. The Strategic Arms Limitation Talks (SALT I) froze each side's offensive nuclear missiles for five years and committed both superpowers to strategic equality rather than nuclear superiority. Although it did not end the arms race, SALT I moved both countries toward "peaceful coexistence" and, in an election year, enhanced Nixon's stature.

Shuttle Diplomacy

However, not even better relations with China and the Soviet Union ensured global stability. In the Middle East, Israel, fearing that a massive Arab attack was imminent, launched a preemptive strike on its Arab neighbors in 1967, routing them in six days. Israel occupied the Egyptian-controlled Sinai (SIE-nie) and Gaza (GAH-zuh) Strip, the Jordanian-ruled West Bank and East Jerusalem, and Syria's Golan (go-LAHN) Heights. Israel promised to give up most of the occupied lands in exchange for a negotiated peace, but the Arab states refused to negotiate with Israel or to recognize its right to exist. Palestinians, many of them refugees, turned to the Palestine Liberation Organization (PLO), which called for Israel's destruction.

War exploded again in 1973 when Egypt and Syria attacked Israel on the Jewish high holy day of Yom Kippur (yawm kip-POOR). Only massive shipments of military supplies from the United States enabled a reeling Israel to stop the assault. In retaliation, the Arab states embargoed shipments of crude oil to the United States and its allies. As the five-month embargo and following spike in oil prices sharply intensified inflation, it dramatized U.S. dependence on foreign energy sources.

The dual shocks of the energy crisis at home and renewed Soviet influence among Arab hardliners spurred Nixon and Kissinger to pursue "shuttle diplomacy." Flying from one Middle East capital to another for two years, Kissinger negotiated a cease-fire, pressed Israel to cede additional captured Arab territory, and persuaded the Arabs to end the oil embargo. Although shuttle diplomacy left the Palestinian issue still festering, it successfully excluded the Soviets from a major role in Middle Eastern affairs.

Nixon-Kissinger *realpolitik* based American aid on a nation's willingness to oppose the Soviet Union, not on the nature of its government. Thus, the Nixon administration liberally supplied arms to the shah of Iran, to President Ferdinand Marcos in the Philippines, and to the white supremacist regime of South Africa, as well as to antidemocratic regimes in Brazil and South Korea and to Portuguese colonial authorities in Angola.

When Chileans elected a Marxist, Salvador Allende (ah-YEN-day), president in 1970, the CIA secretly funded opponents of the leftist regime. The United States also cut off economic aid to Chile. In 1973, a military junta overthrew the Chilean government and killed Allende. Nixon quickly recognized the dictatorship, and economic aid and investment again flowed to Chile.

The Election of 1972

Nixon's reelection appeared certain. He counted on his diplomatic successes and his winding down of the Vietnam War to win over moderate voters. He also expected his southern strategy and law-and-order posture to attract Wallace voters. Continuing Democratic divisions boosted Nixon's optimism. His only major worry, another third-party candidacy by George Wallace, vanished on May 15, 1972, when Wallace was shot during a campaign stop and paralyzed from the waist down. He withdrew from the race, leaving Nixon a monopoly on the white backlash.

George McGovern Liberal senator from South Dakota and Democratic candidate for president in 1972

The Senate's most outspoken dove, **George McGovern** of South Dakota, capitalizing on the antiwar sentiment, blitzed the Democratic primaries and won the nomination on the first ballot. Perceptions of McGovern as inept and radical drove away all but the most committed supporters. McGovern dropped his vice-presidential running mate, Thomas Eagleton, when it became known that Eagleton had received electric-shock therapy for depression. Subsequently, several prominent Democrats publicly declined to run with him. McGovern's endorsement of decriminalization of marijuana, immediate withdrawal from Vietnam, and pardons for those who had fled the United States to avoid the draft exposed him to GOP ridicule as the candidate of the radical fringe.

Remembering his narrow loss to Kennedy in 1960 and too-slim victory in 1968, however, Nixon left no stone unturned. To do whatever was necessary to win, he appointed his attorney general, John Mitchell, to head the Committee to Re-Elect the President (CREEP). Millions in contributions financed a series of "dirty tricks" against Democrats and paid for a special espionage unit, led by Liddy and Hunt, to spy on the opposition. In June 1972, it received Mitchell's approval to wiretap telephones at the Democratic National Committee headquarters in Washington's Watergate complex. A security guard foiled the break-in. Arrested were James McCord, the security coordinator of CREEP, and several other Liddy and Hunt associates.

A White House cover-up began immediately. Nixon announced that "no one in this administration, presently employed, was involved in this bizarre incident." Nixon coached associates on what they should tell investigators, authorized the payment of hush money and hints of a presidential pardon to buy the silence of those arrested, and directed the CIA to halt the FBI's investigation on the pretext that it would damage national security.

With the McGovern campaign a shambles and Watergate seemingly contained, Nixon won the election overwhelmingly, amassing nearly 61 percent of the popular vote and 520 electoral votes. Strongly supported only by minorities and low-income voters, McGovern carried just Massachusetts and the District of Columbia. The election solidified the 1968 realignment.

The Watergate Upheaval

The scheme to conceal links between the White House and the accused Watergate burglars had succeeded during the 1972 campaign. But after the election, federal judge John Sirica (sir-RICK-uh) refused to accept the defendants' claim that they had acted on their own. Threatening severe prison sentences, Sirica coerced James McCord of CREEP into confessing that highly placed White House aides knew in advance of the break-in and that the defendants had committed perjury during the trial. Two *Washington Post* reporters, Carl Bernstein and Bob Woodward, following clues furnished by "Deep Throat," an unnamed informant, wrote a succession of front-page stories tying the break-in to illegal contributions and "dirty tricks" by CREEP.

In February 1973, the Senate established the Special Committee on Presidential Campaign Activities to investigate, and one stunning revelation after another poured forth. The hearings revealed the existence of a White House "enemies list," the president's use of government agencies to harass opponents, and administration favoritism in return for illegal campaign donations. Both the president's special counsel and the acting head of the FBI testified to the White House's involvement in the Watergate break-in, forcing Nixon to announce the resignation of his principal aides and the appointment of a special Watergate prosecutor with broad powers of investigation and subpoena. Then the most dramatic bombshell, the disclosure that Nixon taped every conversation in the Oval Office, meant there was an incontrovertible record of "what the president knew and when he knew it."

When the special prosecutor insisted on access to the tapes, Nixon ordered the attorney general to fire him. The attorney general and the number two man in the Justice Department refused and were dismissed in what became known as the "Saturday night massacre." More than 150,000 telegrams poured into the White House, and eighty-four members of Congress sponsored sixteen different bills of impeachment. The House Judiciary Committee began impeachment proceedings, and Congress went to the Supreme Court to demand access to the original tapes.

Adding to Nixon's woes, Vice President Agnew pleaded no contest to charges of income tax evasion and solicitation of bribes, both as governor of Maryland and as vice president. Agnew left office in October 1973 with a fine and suspended sentence, and was replaced, under provisions of the Twenty-fifth Amendment, by House Minority Leader Gerald R. Ford of Michigan.

A President Disgraced

In late July 1974, the Supreme Court ruled unanimously in *United States* v. *Nixon* that the unedited tapes must be turned over to Congress, and the House Judiciary Committee adopted three articles of impeachment. They charged Nixon with obstruction of justice, abusing the powers of the presidency, and contempt of Congress. Checkmated, Nixon surrendered the subpoenaed tapes.

The tapes produced the "smoking gun" proving that Nixon had ordered the cover-up, obstructed justice by hindering the criminal

Checking In

- Nixon and Kissinger considered themselves masters of *realpolitik,* stressing national interest rather than ethical goals.
- Nixon pursued détente and normalized relations with China.
- Kissinger's shuttle diplomacy guaranteed the United States a preeminent role in the Middle East and helped ease some Israeli-Arab tensions.
- Nixon's reelection strategy involved many "dirty tricks," including breaking into Democratic Party headquarters at the Watergate building to bug telephones.
- A series of House and Senate hearings revealed the extent of illegal activities and the involvement of the president and his chief aides.
- The Supreme Court ruled that Nixon must release taped conversations that incriminated him in the cover-up; rather than be impeached, Nixon resigned the presidency in August 1974.

investigation of the break-in, and lied about his role for more than two years. The revelations confirmed many Americans' distrust of government and cynicism about politics, hastening their disengagement from public affairs.

In trying to explain Watergate, some historians point to the increasing expansion of presidential power, "the imperial presidency," stretching back several decades. Others argue that Nixon simply got caught and that his liberal foes forced him to pay a higher price for his misdeeds than had other presidents. Most focus on Nixon's obsession to destroy his hated adversaries. Whatever the cause, Nixon became the first president to resign—and Gerald Ford took office as the nation's first chief executive who had not been elected either president or vice president.

A Troubled Nation and Presidency

What were the major failures of the Ford and Carter presidencies?

In the aftermath of the Vietnam failure and Richard Nixon's disgrace, Presidents Gerald Ford and Jimmy Carter grappled with inflation, recession, and industrial stagnation as well as humiliations abroad and, for Carter, a maddening hostage crisis. The confident 1950s and early 1960s, when prosperous America had savored its role as the Free World's leader, now seemed remote, even foolhardy. The nation now confronted sobering new realities—particularly significant foreign competition and an energy crisis—beyond its control.

Panic at the Pump

In 1973–1974, Americans sat in their cars and waited in long lines to buy gasoline at skyrocketing prices. Angry and frustrated, motorists fought each other and battled with police. At one service station with no gas to sell, a driver threatened the attendant, "You are going to give me gas or I will kill you."

The nation had long taken cheap, abundant energy for granted, yet remained heavily dependent on the third of its oil it imported. This vulnerability became apparent when Arab nations, angered by Nixon's support of Israel during the 1973 war, cut off the supply of oil to the West. Then the seven Arab members of the **Organization of Petroleum Exporting Countries (OPEC),** a consortium of oil-producing states formed in 1960, quadrupled the cost of a barrel of oil from $3 to $12 in 1976. OPEC would almost triple it again, to $34 in 1979, pushing the price of a gallon of gas over $1 for the first time. Overall inflation soared to 14 percent, turning hard-pressed taxpayers against the welfare programs adopted during past Democratic administrations.

Organization of Petroleum Exporting Countries (OPEC) Oil-exporting nations whose embargo caused fuel prices to spike in 1973 and 1979

Millions of Americans in the 1970s were forced—as one magazine phrased it—to "Learn to Live with Less." Unemployment ranged between 6 and 10 percent, nearly twice the usual postwar level, and the federal deficit soared from $8.7 billion in 1970 to $72.7 billion in 1980. Moreover, the U.S. posted its first trade deficit—importing more than it exported—in almost a century.

Most acutely, higher costs and greater foreign competition ravaged the manufacturing regions of the Midwest and Northeast, soon to be called the "Rust Belt."

AP Photo

The Energy Crisis

The Arab embargo on oil shipments to the United States, begun in 1973, revealed America's dependence on Middle Eastern oil reserves and the end of its unchallenged economic dominance in the world. Dramatic increases in heating oil and gas prices underlined the extent to which Americans no longer could shape their economic future alone.

The automobile industry was especially hard hit by soaring gasoline prices that boosted sales of more fuel-efficient foreign imports, mainly from Japan. Chrysler nearly declared bankruptcy. The Big Three carmakers eliminated the jobs of one in three autoworkers between 1978 and 1982.

Several factors contributed to industrial decline in the United States: aging machinery, inefficient production methods, complacent management, and fierce competition from foreign companies paying lower wages, especially in the countries of the Pacific Rim. American-based manufacturers moved their high-wage jobs overseas. In one five-year period (1979–1983), 11.5 million U.S. workers lost jobs because of plant closings and cutbacks.

With the loss of industrial jobs, the union movement weakened. In 1960, 31 percent of U.S. workers belonged to unions; thirty years later, that figure had been virtually halved to 16 percent, with further declines ahead. However, some workers did join unions in these years, mainly teachers, public employees, and service workers, many of whom were female. A union official lamented "a nation of hamburger stands . . . a country stripped of industrial capacity and meaningful work . . . a service economy."

Gerald Ford, Caretaker

Gerald Ford Thirty-eighth president of the United States; his one term in office was overshadowed by his pardon of Nixon and an economic recession

Former Michigan congressman **Gerald Ford** became vice president after Agnew resigned in disgrace, and then president after Nixon resigned to avoid impeachment. Conveying a likable decency and acknowledging he was "a Ford not a Lincoln," he urged Americans to move beyond the "long national nightmare" of Watergate. But the honeymoon quickly ended as many Americans reacted with outrage when Ford pardoned Nixon for "any and all crimes" committed while in office.

Economic problems, particularly inflation, dogged Ford's presidency. In October 1974, Ford unveiled a program of voluntary price restraint dubbed "Whip Inflation Now" (WIN), but prices continued upward. When the Federal Reserve Board tried to cool the economy by raising interest rates, a severe recession resulted. Unemployment approached 11 percent by 1975, more than twice the postwar average. Americans for the first time since World War II struggled to curb energy consumption. Congress set fuel-efficiency standards for automobiles in 1975 and imposed a national speed limit of fifty-five miles per hour.

National morale sank further in April 1975 when the South Vietnamese government fell, ending two decades of U.S. effort in Vietnam. The TV networks chronicled desperate helicopter evacuations from the U.S. embassy in Saigon (soon renamed Ho Chi Minh City). A few weeks later, Cambodia seized a U.S. merchant ship, the *Mayagüez*. A military rescue ordered by Ford freed the thirty-nine *Mayagüez* crew members but cost the lives of forty-one U.S. servicemen. As the nation entered the election year 1976—also the bicentennial of the Declaration of Independence—Americans found little reason for optimism.

Jimmy Carter, Outsider

Jimmy Carter Thirty-ninth president of the United States; his one-term presidency identified key issues but was plagued by multiple problems

Gerald Ford won the 1976 Republican nomination. **Jimmy Carter,** a Georgia peanut grower and former governor, swept the Democratic primaries by stressing themes that appealed to post-Watergate America: his honesty, his status as a Washington outsider, and his Christian faith.

Carter won by a narrow margin. The vote broke along class lines: the well-to-do went for Ford; the poor, overwhelmingly for Carter. Despite the rising conservative tide, popular revulsion against Nixon and Watergate temporarily interrupted the Republican advance. In office, Carter rejected the trappings of Nixon's "imperial presidency." On inauguration day, he walked from the Capitol to the White House. In an echo of Roosevelt's fireside radio chats, he delivered some TV speeches wearing a sweater and seated by a fireplace.

Despite the populist symbolism, Carter never shaped a clearly liberal agenda. At heart a fiscal conservative, he favored cutting federal spending. "Government cannot solve our problems," he asserted in his second State of the Union address. Carter further disappointed liberals by beginning deregulation—the removal of government controls on the airline, railroad, and trucking industries, as well as on oil and natural gas prices—and by failing to adopt an effective energy policy.

Carter confronted an environmental crisis in Niagara Falls, New York. In a district called Love Canal, schools, homes, and apartments had been built on the site of a former chemical dump. In the 1970s, when residents complained of odors and strange substances oozing from the soil, tests confirmed that toxic chemicals were seeping into basements and polluting the air and water. Medical researchers found elevated levels of cancer, miscarriages, and birth defects among Love Canal residents.

In 1978, President Carter authorized federal funds to relocate Love Canal families. In late 1980, as his term ended, Carter signed legislation creating a federal "Superfund" to clean up the nation's most polluted industrial sites. Carter also signed the Alaska Lands Act, which set aside more than 100 million acres of public land for parks, wildlife refuges, and national forests. These two bills proved to be Carter's rare successes. As a consequence of his own ineptness and the sharp conservative turn in the political climate, Carter, groused one legislator, "couldn't get the Pledge of Allegiance through Congress."

Carter's foreign-policy record proved only somewhat better. As a candidate, he had urged more emphasis on protecting human rights worldwide, in contrast to Henry Kissinger's dominant focus on U.S. national interests. His secretary of state, Cyrus Vance, worked to combat human rights abuses by some, but not all, American allies who committed them, and Carter did raise public awareness of human rights issues. In Latin America, the president completed negotiations on treaties transferring the Canal Zone to Panama by 2000. In a rare success for Carter, the Senate ratified the treaties.

Toward the Soviet Union, Carter first showed conciliation, but toughness ultimately won out. In 1979, Carter and the Soviet leader Leonid Brezhnev signed a new Strategic Arms Limitation Treaty (SALT II), limiting each side's nuclear arsenals. But the treaty failed in the Senate when, in late December 1979, the Soviets invaded Afghanistan. Many Americans saw the invasion as proof of Moscow's expansionist designs. Carter revived registration for the military draft, boycotted the 1980 Summer Olympics in Moscow, and embargoed grain shipments to Russia.

The Middle East and Iran

Carter's proudest achievement and his most bitter setback both came in the Middle East. In September 1978, he hosted Egyptian leader Anwar el-Sadat (AN-wahr el-sah-DAHT) and Israeli leader Menachem Begin (meh-NAKH-em BAY-gin) at Camp David, the presidential retreat in Maryland, where they agreed on a peace framework. The resulting **Camp David Accords** led to Israel's withdrawal from the Sinai Peninsula, captured in the 1967 war; for its part, Egypt recognized Israel as a nation, the first Arab country to do so.

Camp David Accords
Agreement brokered by Jimmy Carter that started a peace process in the Middle East

Carter's efforts for a broader Middle Eastern peace ultimately failed, however. The other Arab states rejected the Camp David Accords and Islamic fundamentalists assassinated Sadat in 1981. Peace remained elusive as ever.

More immediately unsuccessful was Carter's policy toward Iran. Protests against the repressive regime headed by the shah of Iran, a longtime American client and ally, swelled throughout 1978. Iran's Shiite Muslims, inspired by their exiled spiritual head, Ayatollah Ruhollah Khomeini (eye-uh-TOLL-uh roo-HOLL-ah ho-MAY-nee), overthrew the shah's government early in 1979. The shah fled Iran and Khomeini returned in triumph, imposing strict Islamic rule.

On November 4, 1979, after Carter admitted the shah to the United States for cancer treatment, Khomeini supporters stormed the U.S. embassy in Tehran and seized sixty-six American hostages. Thus began a 444-day ordeal that virtually paralyzed the Carter administration. Night after night, TV images of blindfolded hostages, anti-American mobs, and U.S. flags being burned rubbed American nerves raw. A botched rescue attempt in April 1980, in which several U.S. helicopters malfunctioned and eight GIs died, added to the nation's humiliation. Not until January 20, 1981, the day Ronald Reagan took office as the new president, did the Iranian authorities release the hostages.

Americans turned against the remote figure in the White House. When Carter's approval rating sagged to 26 percent in mid-1979 (lower than Nixon's when he resigned as a result of Watergate), he retreated to Camp David and emerged to deliver a televised address that blamed the American people's "crisis of confidence" for leading them to doubt the meaning of their own lives, the future, and the nation's purpose and abilities. But most Americans thought the helpless Carter was the problem. The 1980 Democratic convention glumly re-nominated Carter, but defeat in November loomed. A successful post-presidential career of public service would do much to restore Carter's reputation and bring him the Nobel Peace Prize in 2002. But in 1980, most Americans hungered for a new president and changed policies.

CHECKING IN

- The Ford administration struggled with continued inflation, an oil crisis, and the collapse of South Vietnam.
- Carter was elected as an outsider but found it impossible to govern that way.
- The Carter administration enjoyed few domestic successes but several foreign-policy achievements.
- Carter's greatest achievement came with the Camp David Accords between Egypt and Israel, although subsequent problems overshadowed this accomplishment.
- The Iran hostage crisis undermined and ultimately destroyed Carter's presidency.

Chapter Summary

What were the major landmarks of the youth movement? (page 712)

Campus-based activist groups like SDS and the Free Speech Movement sought a more humane democracy, a less racist and materialistic society, and an end to the war in Vietnam. The New Left movement culminated in a series of mass rallies in 1969. It dissipated after Nixon began to wind down the Vietnam War, and also after the shooting deaths of students at Kent State and Jackson State in 1970. The movement sparked a conservative backlash.

In what ways did the counterculture shape the 1960s and 1970s? (page 717)

The dissatisfaction with the status quo that engendered protest pushed some young people into cultural rebellion. Denouncing materialism and middle-class conventions, hippies "turned on and dropped out," seeking fulfillment in sex, drugs, and rock and roll. Woodstock represented the high point of the counterculture, which declined thereafter, victim to its own excesses and commercial exploitation. The counterculture left behind freer social and sexual norms.

KEY TERMS

Students for a Democratic Society (SDS) *(p. 713)*

Berkeley Free Speech Movement (FSM) *(p. 714)*

Jackson State College *(p. 715)*

counterculture *(p. 717)*

Woodstock festival *(p. 719)*

Roe v. *Wade* *(p. 719)*

National Organization for Women (NOW) *(p. 720)*

Equal Rights Amendment (ERA) *(p. 721)*

gay liberation *(p. 722)*

Three Mile Island *(p. 723)*

What were the major successes and failures of the Women's Liberation Movement? (page 720)

Betty Friedan's *The Feminine Mystique* reinvigorated the feminist movement. Feminists ended some discriminatory hiring practices and made gains in education; the *Roe* v. *Wade* decision protected access to abortion. However, conservatives defeated the Equal Rights Amendment. Gay liberation advocates organized and won passage of some laws protecting homosexuals' civil rights. Environmental advocacy groups won key victories protecting endangered species and for clean air and water. Despite these reforms, most Americans turned away from politics and instead pursued highly individualistic means of self-fulfillment.

How did Richard Nixon's political strategy reflect the racial upheavals and radicalism of this era? (page 724)

The assassinations of Martin Luther King, Jr., and Robert Kennedy in 1968 led to more riots. Richard Nixon and George Wallace capitalized on the resulting conservative backlash, positioning themselves as defenders of law and order and courting white southern conservatives by opposing school busing and other desegregation measures. Nixon was politically skilled, deeply flawed, and convinced that he was surrounded by enemies. He endorsed secret campaigns against his opposition, using the FBI, IRS, CIA, and a shadowy group called "the plumbers."

What were the main causes of the Watergate scandal? (page 730)

During his first term, President Nixon pursued moderate domestic policies while beginning the pullout from Vietnam, normalizing relations with China, enlarging détente with the Soviet Union, and attempting to mediate Middle Eastern politics. Nixon's administration used a variety of "dirty tricks" to attack enemies and win reelection in 1972, resulting most notoriously in the Watergate scandal. Investigative reporters uncovered the extent of illegality, and House and Senate committees revealed how deeply the president and his closest aides were involved. Ultimately, Nixon resigned the presidency rather than be impeached.

What were the major failures of the Ford and Carter presidencies? (page 734)

Neither administration was able to contain inflation, made worse by the OPEC-created oil crisis in 1973. High unemployment and the loss of industrial jobs undermined the unions. The Carter administration did enjoy some foreign-policy successes, notably the Camp David Accords that the president brokered between Egypt and Israel. However, a continuing recession, legislative ineptitude, and, finally, the Iran hostage crisis gravely weakened the Carter administration.

CourseMate

Go to the CourseMate website at **www.cengagebrain.com** for additional study tools and review materials—including audio and video clips—for this chapter.

KEY TERMS continued

Hubert Humphrey *(p. 725)*
Yippies *(p. 726)*
plumbers *(p. 729)*
Pentagon Papers *(p. 729)*
Henry Kissinger *(p. 730)*
détente *(p. 730)*
George McGovern *(p. 732)*
Organization of Petroleum Exporting Countries (OPEC) *(p. 734)*
Gerald Ford *(p. 736)*
Jimmy Carter *(p. 736)*
Camp David Accords *(p. 737)*

Chapter 30

A Conservative Revival and the End of the Cold War

1980–2000

AP Photo/Ira Schwartz

President Ronald Reagan and Soviet Premier Mikhail Gorbachev in Moscow, 1988

Chapter Preview

A Conservative Shift in American Culture and Politics
What core beliefs guided Ronald Reagan's presidency?

Domestic Drift and a New World Order
What were George H. W. Bush's principal achievements and failures as president?

Domestic and Global Issues at Century's End
What policy issues, political events, and economic trends most influenced Bill Clinton's presidency?

Moderation, White House Scandal, and a Disputed Election, 1996–2000
Why did political differences become sharper from 1996 to 2000?

Economic and Cultural Trends at Century's End
What economic trends, technological innovations, and cultural trends shaped American life in the 1990s?

Of all the physical reminders of the Cold War, the most notorious was the Berlin Wall, built by the Russians in 1961. Snaking around the city, this concrete and barbed-wire barrier with its watchtowers and armed guards stood as a stark emblem of Cold War divisions. Over the years, nearly two hundred people had been shot trying to escape across the Wall.

On October 18, 1989, East Germany's communist regime collapsed. When East Berliners rushed to the Wall, guards opened the gates. As people joyously poured through, West Berliners greeted them with flowers, tears, and shouts of welcome. Giddy young people danced on the Wall itself. By November, the wall had practically disappeared. A hated Cold War symbol had faded into history.

The Cold War's end looms large in this chapter. We begin, however, by continuing the story of the post-1960s conservative shift in American politics, which culminated in Ronald Reagan's election as president in 1980. We then examine U.S. politics and foreign affairs during Reagan's presidency, as free-market ideology and a fierce anticommunism shaped policies at home and abroad.

Soon after Reagan left office, Americans welcomed the Soviet Union's collapse. But dangers remained. While U.S. leaders struggled with post–Cold War disorders, an immediate crisis arose in the Middle East as Saddam Hussein's Iraq invaded oil-rich Kuwait, forcing Reagan's successor, President George Bush, to respond.

When Bill Clinton replaced George Bush in the White House in 1993, domestic issues took center stage, although events in the Balkans (BALL-kuns), the Middle East, and elsewhere demanded attention as well. As his term ended in scandal and impeachment, the Supreme Court intervened to resolve the disputed 2000 presidential election. Ostentatious consumption, undercurrents of violence, and deep cultural conflicts shaped American life as the century ended.

A Conservative Shift in American Culture and Politics

What core beliefs guided Ronald Reagan's presidency?

Ronald Reagan won the presidency in 1980 riding the conservative tide that had been building for years. Domestically, Reagan and his congressional allies enacted tax cuts and deregulatory measures reflecting their free-market, small-government ideology. The Reagan era began with a recession and ended with a stock-market crash. In between, though, inflation eased and the overall economy improved. Reagan's economic policies produced mounting federal deficits, however, while economic inequities, inner-city problems, and stubborn unemployment persisted.

An avid Cold Warrior, Reagan boosted military spending and adopted a tough stance toward Russia. He also faced crises in the Middle East. The administration's secretive efforts to overthrow a leftist regime in Latin America triggered a constitutional crisis in Reagan's second term. However, a dramatic easing of Cold War tensions ended his presidency on a high note.

Conservative Cultural Trends in the 1970s

The 1960s was a polarizing decade. Many Americans deplored what they viewed as the decade's radical excesses. As we saw in Chapter 29, Richard Nixon exploited this disaffection to win the White House in 1968.

Even earlier, **William F. Buckley** had launched the conservative *National Review* magazine (1955) and founded Young Americans for Freedom (1960). Barry Goldwater's 1964 presidential campaign, though unsuccessful, gave evidence of conservatism's latent strength. In local communities, especially in the fast-growing

William F. Buckley Author, editor, and commentator who helped shape the modern conservative movement

Chronology

1980	Ronald Reagan elected president
1981	Major cuts in taxes and domestic spending; large increases in military budget
1982	Equal Rights Amendment dies; CIA funds contra war against Nicaragua's Sandinistas; Central Park rally for nuclear weapons freeze
1983	239 U.S. marines die in Beirut terrorist attack; Reagan proposes Strategic Defense Initiative (Star Wars); U.S. invasion of Grenada
1984	Reagan defeats Walter Mondale to win second presidential term
1984–1986	Congress bars military aid to contras
1985	Rash of airline hijackings and other terrorist acts
1986	Congress passes South African sanctions; Immigration Reform and Control Act
1987	Congressional hearings on Iran-contra scandal; Stock-market crash
1988	Reagan trip to Moscow; George H. W. Bush elected president
1989	Massive Alaskan oil spill by *Exxon Valdez;* China's rulers crush prodemocracy movement; Berlin Wall is torn down
1990	Federal Clean Air Act strengthened; Americans with Disabilities Act passed; Iraq invades Kuwait; Recession (1990–1993); Germany reunified; Soviet troops start withdrawal from Eastern Europe
1991	Persian Gulf War; hearings on Clarence Thomas's Supreme Court nomination; collapse of Soviet Union
1992	*Planned Parenthood* v. *Casey* decision approves abortion restrictions; President Bush commits U.S. troops in Somalia; Bill Clinton elected president
1993	Congress approves NAFTA treaty; Clinton health-care reform plan fails (1993–1994); deaths of Branch Davidians in Waco, Texas; World Trade Center bombing kills six
1994	Christian Coalition makes gains; Yasir Arafat and Yitzhak Rabin sign Oslo Accords; Clinton withdraws U.S. forces from Somalia; United States joins the World Trade Organization (WTO); Republicans proclaim "Contract with America" and win control of the House and Senate; Newt Gingrich becomes Speaker of the House
1995	Oklahoma City federal building bombed; Dayton Accords achieve cease-fire in Bosnia; Clinton commits U.S. troops to enforce agreement
1996	Welfare Reform Act; Clinton wins second presidential term
1997	Congressional battle over tobacco industry regulation
1998	Clinton impeached by House of Representatives in sex scandal
1999	Senate dismisses impeachment charges; Columbine High School shootings; U.S. and NATO forces intervene in Kosovo
2000	George W. Bush wins presidency when Supreme Court ends Florida election dispute

South and West, conservatives came together and mobilized politically. Think tanks like the Heritage Foundation helped conservatives solidify their ideology.

Southern California's Orange County vividly illustrates this process. Orange County conservatives—mostly upwardly mobile white evangelical Protestants—were intensely anticommunist, dismayed by 1960s' radicals, and suspicious of the "liberal elites" dominating the media and national politics. Foreshadowing changes ahead nationally, Orange County helped elect Ronald Reagan governor of California in

1966 and in 1978 rallied behind Proposition 13, a state referendum mandating deep cuts in property taxes.

Conservatives mobilized around specific issues, especially abortion. As noted in Chapter 29, in the wake of *Roe* v. *Wade,* "right to life" activists pressed for a constitutional amendment outlawing abortion. Led by Roman Catholic and conservative Protestant activists, "pro-life" advocates rallied, signed petitions, and picketed abortion clinics and pregnancy-counseling centers.

Responding to the pressure, Congress in 1976 ended Medicaid funding for most abortions. Handing conservatives another victory, President Nixon in 1972 vetoed a bill setting up a national network of day-care centers, criticizing its "communal approach to child-rearing." The Equal Rights Amendment, denounced by Phyllis Schlafly and other conservatives, died in 1982—three states short of ratification.

To conservatives, gay and lesbian activism foretold society's moral collapse. "God . . . destroyed the cities of Sodom and Gomorrah because of this terrible sin," thundered TV evangelist Jerry Falwell. In 1977, singer Anita Bryant led a successful campaign against a Miami ordinance protecting homosexuals' civil rights. Soon after, *Good Housekeeping* magazine readers voted Bryant "the most admired woman in America." Other cities, too, reversed earlier measures protecting gay rights.

In 1978, as the backlash intensified, a member of the San Francisco board of supervisors fatally shot gay activist and board-member Harvey Milk and Milk's political ally, Mayor George Moscone. When the killer received a light sentence, riots erupted in the city.

The conservative movement also gained strength from the rapid growth of evangelical Protestantism, with its emphasis on strict morality, biblical authority, and a "born again" conversion experience. Evangelical denominations such as the Assemblies of God and the Southern Baptist Convention grew explosively in the 1970s and 1980s, as did independent suburban megachurches. Meanwhile, liberal denominations lost members.

Modern-day evangelicals preached reform, but of a conservative variety. Jerry Falwell's Moral Majority, founded in 1979 as a "pro-life, pro-family, pro-moral, and pro-America" crusade, supported conservative candidates. So did Pat Robertson, founder of the Christian Broadcasting Network. Tim LaHaye of San Diego, another leading evangelical preacher, was also active in mobilizing grass-roots support for conservative causes.

While battling abortion, homosexuality, and pornography, often in alliance with conservative Catholics, evangelicals also attacked the Supreme Court's 1962 ***Engel* v. *Vitale*** decision banning organized prayer in public schools as a violation of the First Amendment. Evangelicals also advocated home schooling and private Christian schools to shield children from what they saw as the public schools' permissiveness and secularist (nonreligious) values.

Engel* v. *Vitale Supreme Court's 1962 decision prohibiting organized prayer in public schools

Christian bookstores, radio stations, and TV evangelists fueled the revival. Falwell's *Old Time Gospel Hour,* Robertson's *700 Club,* and Jim and Tammy Bakker's *PTL* (Praise the Lord) program attracted a loyal following. The so-called electronic church suffered after 1987 amid sexual and financial scandals, but the evangelical resurgence continued. Evangelicals found certitude in their shared faith and profoundly influenced late-twentieth-century American life.

Ronald Reagan Fortieth president of the United States; his two terms were marked by patriotic rhetoric, tax cuts, and militant anticommunism

Not all evangelicals were political conservatives, however. Most African-American evangelicals retained their Democratic Party loyalties. In general, however, resurgent evangelicalism strengthened the larger conservative movement of the 1970s. **Ronald Reagan** rode this powerful conservative tide to the White House.

Conservatism Triumphant: The 1980 Election

Reagan grew up in Dixon, Illinois, the son of an alcoholic father and a devout mother. In 1937, after a stint as a radio sports announcer, he went to Hollywood for a screen test. His fifty-four films proved forgettable, but he gained political experience as president of the Screen Actors' Guild. A New Dealer in the 1930s, Reagan moved rightward in the 1950s, and in 1954 became the General Electric Company's corporate spokesperson. As governor of California (1967–1975), he espoused conservative ideas and denounced campus demonstrators, but also proved open to compromise.

In the 1980 Republican primaries, Reagan bested his principal opponent, George H. W. Bush (father of the later President George W. Bush), whom he then chose as his running mate. Belying his sixty-nine years, he campaigned vigorously against President Jimmy Carter. In the election, Reagan garnered 51 percent of the vote (see Map 30.1), while Republicans gained eleven Senate seats and trimmed thirty-five seats from the Democrats' majority in the House of Representatives.

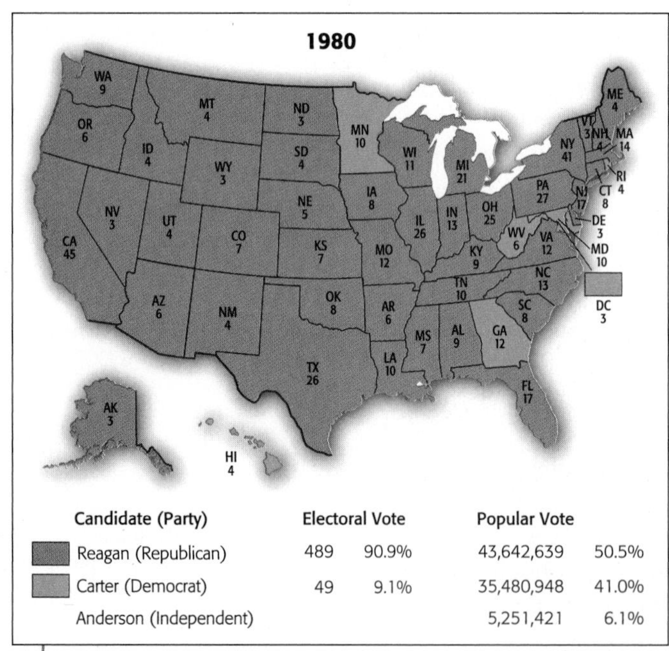

Map 30.1 The Election of 1980
Jimmy Carter's unpopularity and Ronald Reagan's telegenic appeal combined to give Reagan a crushing Electoral College victory.

Interactive Map

Benefiting from the erosion of Democratic strength in the South fostered by George Wallace and Richard Nixon, Reagan carried every southern state except Carter's own Georgia. Over half of white blue-collar workers, once solidly Democratic, voted Republican. Of FDR's New Deal coalition, only black voters remained solidly Democratic.

Jerry Falwell's pro-Reagan Moral Majority registered an estimated 2 million new voters in 1980 and 1984. The organization disbanded after 1984, but Pat Robertson's Christian Coalition took its place, mobilizing evangelicals to elect candidates to town councils and school boards as a stepping stone to expanded national influence.

Reagan embraced the conservative movement's cultural agenda, evoking a somewhat mythic era when American life had seemed simpler and traditional values had prevailed. But other factors also underlay Reagan's appeal. Voters frightened by stagflation welcomed his promise that tax cuts would stimulate the economy. Reagan's anti-government rhetoric resonated with white middle-class and blue-collar Americans. Like his one-time political hero Franklin Roosevelt, Reagan promised a new deal.

But unlike FDR's, Reagan's new deal meant individualism, smaller government, lower taxes, and untrammeled free enterprise.

Reagan, a seasoned actor, wrapped these themes into an appealing message of moral affirmation and support for "traditional values." At a time of national malaise, he seemed confident and assured. His unabashed patriotism and praise of America's greatness soothed the battered psyche of a nation traumatized by Vietnam, Watergate, and the frustrations of the Ford and Carter years. Population changes contributed to Reagan's success. While New York City, Chicago, Detroit, and other Democratic strongholds in the Northeast and Midwest lost population in the 1970s, Texas, California, Florida, and other more conservative Sun Belt states grew.

Enacting the Conservative Domestic Agenda

Reagan's economic plan, dubbed "Reaganomics" by the media, boiled down to the belief that the free-enterprise system, if freed from heavy taxes and regulations, would achieve wonders of productivity. Reagan proposed a 30 percent cut in federal income taxes over three years. Trimming this proposal slightly, Congress voted a 25 percent cut: 5 percent in 1981, 10 percent in both 1982 and 1983.

To partially counterbalance the lost revenues, Congress slashed more than $40 billion from domestic spending. Economists warned that the tax cut would produce huge federal deficits, but Reagan insisted that lower tax rates would stimulate business growth, pushing up tax revenues. In the Republican primaries, George Bush had ridiculed Reagan's rosy predictions as "voodoo economics," but as vice president he tactfully remained silent.

Business deregulation had begun under Carter, but Reagan extended it into new areas such as banking, the savings-and-loan industry, and communications. Interior Secretary James Watt of Wyoming opened federal wilderness areas, forest lands, and coastal waters to oil, gas, and timber companies and cut back on environmental and endangered species protections. Watt earlier spearheaded the so-called Sagebrush Rebellion, a campaign by ranchers, farmers, and mine owners to shift federal lands in the West to state and county control. The Sierra Club and other environmental organizations protested Watt's policies. After various public-relations gaffes, Watt resigned in 1983.

Reagan had little sympathy for organized labor. In 1981, when the Professional Air Traffic Controllers Organization (PATCO) went on strike, Reagan invoked the 1948 Taft-Hartley law against strikes by federal employees and ordered them back to work. When more than eleven thousand PATCO members defied the order, Reagan fired them and barred them permanently from federal employment.

To combat continuing inflation (see Chapter 29), the Federal Reserve Board pushed up interest rates. This harsh medicine, coupled with falling oil prices, pushed the inflation rate down from double digits to around 4 percent by 1983. But high interest rates also brought on a recession. By late 1982, unemployment stood at 10 percent. Reagan's cuts in social programs worsened the plight of the poor, including inner-city blacks and Hispanics. The Fed's policy also drove up the value of the dollar, hurting U.S. exports. With exports declining and U.S. consumers buying cars, TVs, and stereo systems made in Japan and elsewhere, the trade deficit soared to $111 billion in 1984.

Facing a recession and rising federal budget deficits, Reagan in 1982–1983 slowed military spending, approved emergency job programs, restored some spending on social programs, and authorized tax increases disguised as "revenue-enhancement measures." Nevertheless, the recession hurt Reagan's popularity, and in the 1982 midterm elections, the Democrats regained twenty-six House seats.

By 1983, an economic rebound was under way. Encouraged by tax cuts and lower inflation, consumer spending increased and the stock market surged. Brokerage firms lured new investors. Corporate mergers proliferated. Savings-and-loan (S&L) companies, newly deregulated, ladled out billions to developers planning shopping malls, condominiums, and retirement villages.

However, the Wall Street frenzy had an unsavory underside. Famous money manager Ivan Boesky went to prison after a 1986 conviction for insider trading (profiting through advance knowledge of corporate actions). The high-flying S&L industry would collapse in 1988 (as detailed later in this chapter). The 1987 film *Wall Street* captured the spirit of the decade. As protagonist Gordon Gekko, a hard-driving speculator, puts it: "Greed, for lack of a better word, is good. Greed is right, greed works. Greed . . . captures the essence of the evolutionary spirit."

On October 19, 1987, the stock market crashed, reducing the paper value of the nation's stocks by 20 percent overnight. The market soon recovered, but the collapse had a sobering effect on giddy investors. Even during the boom, systemic economic problems persisted. Federal budget deficits surpassed $200 billion in 1985 and 1986. Budget deficits, the trade deficit, and a savings-and-loan crisis related to deregulation rank among the negatives of Reagan's economic legacy.

Reagan also shaped the Supreme Court. His 1981 selection of Sandra Day O'Connor as the first woman Supreme Court justice won praise. He nudged the high court in a conservative direction in 1986 by elevating William Rehnquist, a Nixon appointee, to the chief justiceship upon the retirement of Warren Burger and nominating Antonin Scalia to replace him. Scalia would prove one of the Court's most outspokenly conservative members. When another vacancy opened in 1987, Reagan appointed Anthony Kennedy, a conservative California jurist.

The Cold War Heats Up

The late 1970s' deterioration in U.S.-Soviet relations worsened during Reagan's first term. Addressing a convention of evangelicals, the president demonized the Soviet Union as an "evil empire." Anti-Soviet fury exploded in September 1983 when the Russians shot down a Korean passenger plane that strayed into their airspace, killing all 269 aboard.

Insisting that post-Vietnam America had grown dangerously weak, Reagan launched a major military expansion. The Pentagon's budget nearly doubled. Secretary of State Alexander Haig spoke of using "nuclear warning shots" in a conventional war; other officials mused about the "winnability" of nuclear war. Despite protests across Europe, the administration deployed 572 nuclear missiles in Western Europe in 1983. A Defense Department official proposed backyard

Bill Gentile/Historical/Corbis

Anti-Sandinista Contras on Patrol in Nicaragua, 1987
Under Reagan, the CIA recruited, financed, and equipped an army to overthrow Nicaragua's leftist Sandinista regime. This support continued clandestinely despite congressional prohibitions, leading to the so-called Iran-contra scandal.

shelters as adequate protection in a nuclear war. "With enough shovels," he asserted, "everybody's going to make it."

Such talk, coupled with the military buildup and Reagan's anti-Soviet rhetoric, sparked a grass-roots campaign for a multinational freeze on the manufacture and deployment of nuclear weapons. Antinuclear protesters packed New York's Central Park in June 1982. That November, voters in nine states, including California and Wisconsin, approved nuclear-freeze referenda.

To counter the freeze campaign, Reagan in March 1983 proposed the **Strategic Defense Initiative (SDI),** a computerized antimissile system involving space-based lasers and other high-tech components. Critics quickly dubbed the scheme "Star Wars" and warned of monumental technical hurdles. Nevertheless, Reagan prevailed, and Congress authorized a costly SDI research program.

Strategic Defense Initiative (SDI) Costly "Star Wars" program to build a missile defense system

Fearing communist gains in Latin America, the administration backed El Salvador's ruling military junta in its brutal suppression of a leftist insurgency supported by Fidel Castro's Cuba. In Nicaragua, Reagan vigorously opposed the Sandinista insurgents who overthrew dictator Anastasio Somoza in 1979. In 1982, the CIA organized and financed an anti-Sandinista guerrilla army, called the contras,

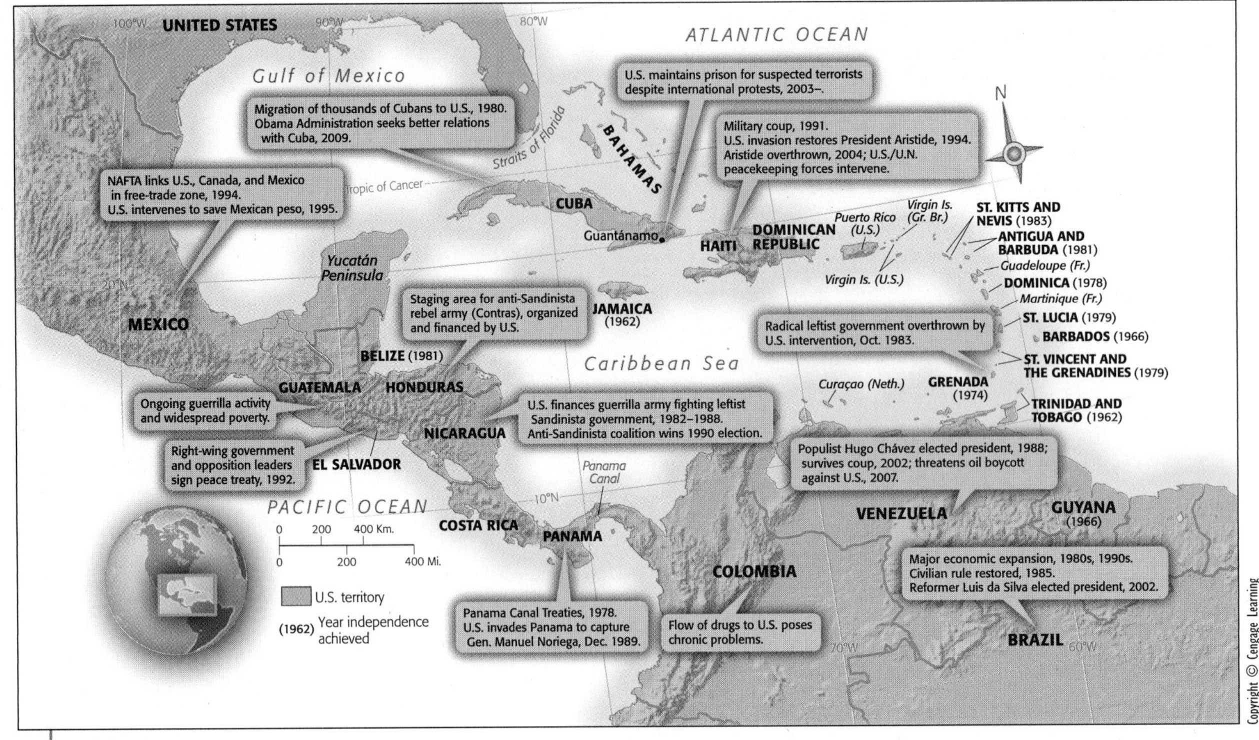

Map 30.2 The United States in Central America and the Caribbean, 1978–2006

Plagued by poverty, population pressures, repressive regimes, and drug trafficking, this region experienced turmoil and conflict—but also hopeful developments—in recent decades.

Interactive Map

based in neighboring Honduras and Costa Rica. The contras conducted raids, planted mines, and carried out sabotage inside Nicaragua that killed many civilians (see Map 30.2).

Fearing another Vietnam, Congress late in 1982 voted a yearlong halt in U.S. military aid to the contras, and in 1984 imposed a two-year ban. Ignoring these prohibitions, the White House secretly continued to funnel money contributed by right-wing groups and foreign governments to the contras. When this subterfuge became known, a major scandal resulted. Reagan's one unqualified success in Latin America involved the tiny island of Grenada, where a 1983 coup had installed a pro-Castro government. In October 1983, two thousand U.S. troops invaded Grenada and substituted a pro-U.S. government.

In Afghanistan, the Reagan administration (extending a policy started by President Carter) secretly funneled funds and equipment to Islamic fighters, called mujahadeen, battling to expel Russian troops that had invaded Afghanistan in 1979. Ironically, young **Osama bin Laden,** a wealthy Saudi Arabian who would later become a deadly foe of America, was also helping to finance the mujahadeen, putting him and the United States briefly on the same side.

Osama bin Laden Radical Islamic terrorist who masterminded murderous attacks against the U.S. military and civilians

Reagan's anticommunist fervor and determination to make America "stand tall" again in the world had broad appeal. So did his tax cuts and celebration of the nation's free-enterprise system. Americans also liked Reagan's upbeat style, typified by his jaunty response in March 1981 when a ricocheting bullet fired by a deranged young man struck him in the chest. Rushed to the hospital, Reagan insisted on walking in. "Please tell me you're all Republicans," he quipped to physicians.

With Reagan's approval ratings rising as the recession faded, he and Vice President Bush were enthusiastically re-nominated at the 1984 Republican convention. Staged for TV, the convention accented themes of patriotism, prosperity, and Reagan's personal charm.

The Democratic hopefuls included civil-rights leader **Jesse Jackson.** In the Democratic primaries, Jackson garnered 3.5 million votes and won five southern states. But former vice president Walter Mondale captured the nomination with backing from traditional Democratic constituencies. His vice-presidential choice, New York congresswoman Geraldine Ferraro, became the first woman to run on a major-party presidential ticket.

Jesse Jackson Civil-rights leader whose "rainbow coalition" campaign for president in 1984 garnered 3.5 million votes

Reagan's ideological and personal appeal, combined with prosperity, proved decisive. Reagan and Bush won 59 percent of the popular vote and carried every state but Mondale's Minnesota plus the District of Columbia. The Republicans' post-1968 dominance of the White House—interrupted only by Jimmy Carter's single term—continued.

In 1985, frustrated by the Democrats' image as a "big government" and "tax-and-spend" party, Arkansas governor Bill Clinton, Tennessee senator Al Gore, and others formed the more centrist Democratic Leadership Council (DLC). Clinton would later use the DLC as a springboard for a presidential bid.

Reagan's second-term achievements included the 1986 Immigration Reform and Control Act and a tax-reform law making the system less complicated. These were overshadowed, however, by a White House scandal involving the abuse of executive power and by a dramatic easing of Cold War hostilities.

The Iran-Contra Scandal and a Thaw in U.S.-Soviet Relations

The worst crisis of Reagan's presidency, the so-called **Iran-contra scandal,** began obscurely in 1986 when a Beirut newspaper reported that in 1985 the United States had shipped, via Israel, 508 antitank missiles to Iran, America's avowed enemy. Admitting the sale, Reagan claimed the goal had been to encourage "moderate elements" in Tehran and to gain the release of U.S. hostages held in Lebanon by pro-Iranian groups. In February 1987, a presidentially appointed investigative panel blamed Reagan's chief of staff, Donald Regan, who resigned.

Iran-contra scandal Scandal in which the Reagan administration sold weapons to Iran to illegally finance contras

Next came the revelation that **Oliver North,** a National Security Council aide in the White House, had secretly diverted profits from the Iran arms sales to the Nicaraguan contras despite Congress's ban on such aid. To hide this crime, North and his secretary had altered and destroyed incriminating documents. A congressional investigative committee convened in May 1987 found no proof that Reagan knew of illegalities, but criticized the lax management and contempt for the law that pervaded the White House. In 1989, North was convicted of obstructing a congressional inquiry and destroying and falsifying official documents. (The conviction was later reversed on a technicality.)

Oliver North Marine colonel at the heart of supplying illegal aid to the contras

Other scandals plagued Reagan's second term. Attorney General Edwin Meese resigned in 1988 amid influence-peddling charges. In 1989 came revelations that former interior secretary James Watt and other prominent Republicans had collected hundreds of thousands of dollars for using their influence to help housing developers seeking federal subsidies. However, Reagan's popularity seemed unaffected; some dubbed him the Teflon president—nothing stuck to him.

Reagan's second term also brought a dramatic warming in Soviet-American relations. At meetings in Europe in 1985 and 1986, Reagan and Soviet premier Mikhail Gorbachev revived the stalled arms-control process. Beset by economic problems at home and by spreading unrest in Eastern Europe, Gorbachev worked to reduce superpower tensions while pursuing his ambitious goals: restructuring the economy, loosening Moscow's grip in Eastern Europe, and bringing more openness to Russia's government. In December 1987, Reagan and Gorbachev signed the **Intermediate-range Nuclear Forces (INF) Treaty,** eliminating twenty-five hundred U.S. and Soviet missiles from Europe. This, in turn, led to Reagan's historic visit to Moscow in May 1988, where the two leaders strolled in Red Square.

Intermediate-range Nuclear Forces (INF) Treaty Title of the first treaty to ban an entire class of nuclear weapons; major U.S.-Soviet agreement

The INF treaty and Reagan's trip to Moscow marked a significant thaw in the Cold War. Historians still debate the relative importance of Reagan's military buildup versus the Soviet Union's internal weaknesses in producing this outcome. Whatever the final judgment on that point, the fact that one of America's most dedicated Cold Warriors presided over the early stages of the Cold War's demise remains a striking irony of recent U.S. history.

Conflict and Terrorism in the Middle East and Beyond

For U.S. diplomats, the Middle East remained a major challenge. Events in this region directly affected U.S. security, economic interests, and international relations. In 1980, Iraq under strongman Saddam Hussein invaded its neighbor Iran. The incoming Reagan administration, hoping to slow the spread of Islamic fundamentalism, backed Iraq in what would prove to be an eight-year war. (Two decades later, the United States would invade Iraq to overthrow Saddam Hussein, covered in Chapter 31.)

As the administration confronted the ongoing conflict among Israel, the Palestinians, and Israel's Arab foes, it faced conflicting interests. The United States gave its ally Israel large annual grants in military aid and other assistance, while also providing aid to Egypt and the Palestinians and importing oil from Saudi Arabia and other Arab states.

In June 1982, when extremists linked to the Palestinian Liberation Organization (PLO) shot and critically wounded Israel's ambassador to Great Britain, Israeli troops under Defense Minister Ariel Sharon attacked PLO bases in southern Lebanon and forced its leaders, including chairman Yasir Arafat (YAH-seer AHR-uh-faht), to evacuate the country.

In September 1982, Reagan ordered two thousand marines to Lebanon as part of a multinational force to keep peace among the country's religious and political factions. On October 23, 1983, a Shiite Muslim crashed an explosives-filled truck into a U.S. barracks, killing 239 marines. Early in 1984, Reagan withdrew the surviving marines.

In 1987, Palestinians launched an intifada, or uprising, against Israeli occupation of Gaza and the West Bank, Palestinian territories occupied by Israel since the 1967 war. In response, Secretary of State George Shultz (who had replaced Alexander Haig in 1982) proposed negotiations leading to an independent Palestinian state. Israel refused to negotiate until the intifada ended, however, and the Palestinians rejected Shultz's proposals for not assuring Palestinian interests. Over U.S. objections, Jewish settlement continued in the occupied territories.

A deadly byproduct of the Middle East conflict was a series of bombings, assassinations, hijackings, and hostage-takings by anti-Israel and anti-American terrorists. At the 1972 Summer Olympics in Munich, Palestinian gunmen killed eleven Israeli athletes. In 1985, terrorists set off bombs in the Vienna and Rome airports and hijacked a TWA flight en route from Athens to Rome, killing one passenger, a U.S. sailor. That same year, armed men demanding the release of Palestinians held by Israel hijacked an Italian cruise ship, dumping a wheelchair-bound Jewish-American passenger into the sea.

A 1986 bombing of a Berlin club popular with Americans killed two GIs and injured others. Accusing Libyan strongman Muammar al-Qaddafi of masterminding this and other attacks, Reagan ordered the bombing of Libyan military sites. But the attacks continued. In December 1988, a bomb detonated aboard Pan Am flight 103, which crashed near Lockerbie, Scotland, killing all 259 aboard, including many Americans.

This terrorism reflected bitter religious and political divisions. Hatred of Israel gripped parts of the Muslim world. Radical Islamic clerics called for jihad (holy war in defense of Islam) against a secular West that seemed increasingly dominant militarily, economically, and culturally. The stationing of U.S. troops in Saudi Arabia, as well as expanding Jewish settlements in the Palestinian territories, also fed the anger that fueled terrorist attacks.

Despite terrorist attacks and festering problems in the Middle East, many Americans felt confident about the nation and its stature in the world as Reagan's term ended. After Nixon's disgrace, Ford's caretaker presidency, and Carter's rocky tenure, Reagan's two terms restored a sense of stability to U.S. politics. Domestically, Reagan compiled a mixed record. Inflation eased, and the economy improved after 1982. But the federal deficit soared, and the reduction of the government's regulatory role planted the seeds of future problems.

Building on Richard Nixon's strategy, Reagan exploited the anxieties of middle-class white voters. He dismissed the social activism of the 1960s, criticized affirmative-action programs, and ridiculed the welfare system by recounting urban legends about Cadillac-driving "welfare queens."

To Reagan's critics, at best his presidency seemed an interlude of nostalgia and drift. Reagan's celebration of individual freedom, they charged, could readily morph into self-centered materialism. Apart from individualism, anticommunism, and flag-waving patriotism, they contended, Reagan offered few common goals around which all Americans could rally. In 1988, former chief of staff Donald Regan published a memoir that portrayed Reagan as little more than an automaton: "Every moment of every public appearance was scheduled, every word was scripted, every place where Reagan was expected to stand was chalked with toe marks."

Reagan's admirers praised him for reasserting the values of self-reliance and free enterprise, criticizing governmental excesses, and

CHECKING IN

- Reagan entered office stressing optimism, patriotism, tax cuts, and cultural conservatism.
- "Reaganomics" led to sharp tax cuts, an even sharper rise in the federal deficit, and reduced federal regulation of business and industry.
- The administration nearly doubled military spending and promoted the controversial "Star Wars" missile defense system.
- Illegal aid to the Nicaraguan contras was the most spectacular of several scandals that beset Reagan's second term.
- Reagan eventually met with the Soviets and reached arms-control agreements that began to wind down the Cold War.
- Major problems flared in the Middle East as the intifada (uprising) erupted among Palestinians; terrorism surfaced as a major threat.

restoring national pride. The mood at the 1984 Summer Olympics in Los Angeles, they suggested, when exuberant American fans waved flags and chanted "USA, USA," captured the nation's newly discovered confidence. Reagan's militant anticommunism and military buildup, they contended, hastened the Soviet collapse and America's Cold War victory. Alzheimer's disease darkened Reagan's post-presidential years, but "the Reagan revolution" still influences American politics.

DOMESTIC DRIFT AND A NEW WORLD ORDER

What were George H. W. Bush's principal achievements and failures as president?

George H. W. Bush Forty-first president; his successes abroad were overshadowed by a mixed record at home

George H. W. Bush, elected president in 1988, was a patrician in politics. Son of a Connecticut senator, a Yale graduate, and a World War II bomber pilot, he entered the Texas oil business, served in Congress, and was a UN ambassador and CIA director before becoming Reagan's running mate in 1980. As president, Bush reacted decisively when Iraq invaded Kuwait, but he proved less impressive on domestic issues.

1988: The Conservative Momentum Continues

Easily winning the 1988 Republican presidential nomination, Bush in his acceptance speech called for a "kinder, gentler America" and pledged, "Read my lips: no new taxes." On the Democratic side, Jesse Jackson again did well in the primaries, but Massachusetts governor Michael Dukakis, winning in New York and California, captured the nomination.

In the campaign, Bush emphasized prosperity and improved Soviet relations, while distancing himself from the Iran-contra scandal. Dukakis emphasized his managerial skills and urged "Reagan Democrats" to return to the fold. But Dukakis seemed wooden, and his focus on competence rather than ideology made it difficult for him to define his political vision. Both candidates relied on sound bites and TV-oriented "photo opportunities." Bush visited flag factories and military plants. Dukakis proved his toughness on defense by posing in a tank. Bush won, carrying forty states and garnering 54 percent of the vote. The Democrats, however, retained control of Congress.

The Cold War Ends; Global Challenges Persist

As Bush took office, the Soviet Union's collapse, heralded by the opening of the Berlin Wall, proceeded with breathtaking rapidity. East Germany's communist regime imploded. The Baltic republics annexed by Moscow in 1940—Estonia, Latvia, and Lithuania—declared independence. The other Soviet republics moved toward autonomy as well. In July 1991, President Bush and Mikhail Gorbachev signed a treaty reducing their nuclear arsenals by 25 percent and NATO announced major troop reductions.

AP Photo/Michael E. Samojeden, FILE

Michael Dukakis Campaigns for President in 1984
To demonstrate his firmness on military preparedness, the Democratic candidate Michael Dukakis posed in a tank, but seemed dwarfed by the helmet and heavy machinery.

In August 1991, die-hard communists tried to overthrow Gorbachev. But thousands of Muscovites, rallied by Boris Yeltsin, president of the Russian Republic, protectively surrounded Moscow's parliament building, and the coup failed. Gorbachev, overwhelmed by forces he himself had unleashed, soon resigned, and Boris Yeltsin filled the power vacuum. The Cold War was over. President Bush proclaimed: "[N]ow we stand triumphant—for a third time this century—this time in the wake of the Cold War. As in 1919 and 1945, we face no enemy menacing our security."

But even as Americans savored the moment, a host of new problems arose. As the Soviet Union fragmented into a loose federation of independent nations, Secretary of State James Baker worked to ensure the security of nuclear missiles based in Russia and in newly independent Ukraine (you-CRANE), Belarus (bell-ah-ROOS), and Kazakhstan (ka-ZAHK-stan), and to prevent rogue states or terrorists from acquiring nuclear materials.

For decades, the superpowers had backed client states and rebel insurgencies around the world. As the Cold War faded, prospects brightened for resolving some local disputes. In Nicaragua, Bush abandoned the U.S.-funded contra war against the leftist Sandinista government. In the Philippines, the United States closed two U.S. naval bases under pressure from the Philippines legislature.

Meanwhile, South Africa's policy of racial segregation—apartheid—provoked worldwide protests. In 1986, over Reagan's veto, Congress joined other nations in imposing economic sanctions against white-ruled South Africa. Yielding to these pressures and to an anti-apartheid campaign in South Africa itself, the South African government in 1990 released black leader Nelson Mandela (man-DELL-uh) after years in prison. When South Africa scrapped its apartheid policy in 1991, President Bush lifted the sanctions. In 1994, Mandela was elected president and his party, the African National Congress, assumed power.

In 1989, Chinese troops brutally crushed a pro-democracy demonstration in Beijing's Tiananmen (tee-yehn-ahn-men) Square, killing several hundred students and workers. The Bush administration curtailed diplomatic contacts, but Bush, committed to expanding U.S. trade, did not break diplomatic relations or cancel trade agreements with Beijing.

The Persian Gulf War, 1991

On August 2, 1990, Iraq invaded neighboring Kuwait (koo-WAIT). Iraq's dictator, Saddam Hussein, viewed Kuwait's ruling sheiks as Western puppets and asserted Iraq's historic claims to Kuwait's vast oil fields.

During the Iran-Iraq War, the United States had backed Iraq. But now, confronted by Iraq's invasion of Kuwait, an important oil-producing nation, Bush responded decisively. In addition to assembling a force of more than five hundred thousand U.S. troops, Bush also built a multi-nation coalition that contributed additional troops. When Saddam ignored UN economic sanctions and a resolution demanding Iraq's withdrawal by January 15, 1991, both houses of Congress endorsed military action. Most Democrats voted against war, however, favoring continued economic sanctions. Memories of Vietnam stirred as Americans debated another war.

Beginning on January 16, U.S. bombers pounded Iraqi troops, supply depots, and command centers in Iraq's capital, Baghdad. In retaliation, Saddam fired Soviet-made Scud missiles against cities in Israel and Saudi Arabia, which supported the U.S.-led war. As TV viewers watched distant explosions filmed through greenish aircraft bombsights, the war seemed hardly real, almost resembling a video game.

On February 23, two hundred thousand U.S. troops moved across the desert toward Kuwait (see Map 30.3). Thousands of Iraqi soldiers fled or surrendered. With Iraqi resistance crushed, President Bush declared a cease-fire, and Kuwait's ruling family returned to power. U.S. casualties numbered 148 dead and 467 wounded. Iraqi military casualties were estimated at twenty-five thousand to sixty-five thousand. The Iraqi government claimed that U.S. bombs also killed twenty-three hundred civilians. For President Bush, the **Persian Gulf War** proved that Americans were prepared to use force to pursue national interests. "By God, we've kicked the Vietnam syndrome once and for all," he declared.

Persian Gulf War Conflict in which a U.S.-led coalition army ousted Saddam Hussein's Iraq army from Kuwait in 1991

Americans with Disabilities Act Law that bars discrimination against handicapped in jobs and education

Bush and his national-security advisers rejected the urging of some who favored invading Iraq itself and overthrowing Saddam Hussein. The UN did impose "no-fly zones" on Iraqi aircraft, and a somewhat chastened Saddam granted UN inspectors access to his weapons-production facilities. Nevertheless, Saddam's army brutally suppressed antigovernment uprisings by Iraq's Shiite Muslims and ethnic Kurds.

Troubles at Home: Economic Woes, Racial Tensions, Environmental Threats

As for Bush's domestic record, a rare accomplishment was the **Americans with Disabilities Act** of 1990. Supported by Bush, this law barred discrimination against disabled persons in hiring or education. Thanks to this law, job opportunities for handicapped persons increased and public schools enrolled more physically or developmentally impaired children. Otherwise, the Bush years saw more problems than achievements on the home front.

By the early 1990s, the impact of Reagan-era tax cuts and deregulation began to hit home. First came the collapse of the savings-and-loan (S&L) industry. In the late 1970s, as inflation pushed up interest rates, the S&Ls offered higher interest to retain investors, even though the S&L's assets were mostly in fixed-rate mortgages. Following the Reagan tax cuts, money flowed into S&Ls. Meanwhile, in the deregulatory fervor, Congress eased the rules governing S&Ls, enabling them to make loans on risky real-estate ventures. As recession hit, many of these investments went bad. In 1988–1990, nearly six hundred S&Ls failed, wiping out depositors' savings.

Because the government insures S&L deposits, the Bush administration in 1989 set up a program to repay depositors and sell hundreds of foreclosed office towers and apartment buildings in a depressed market. Estimates of the bailout's cost topped $400 billion.

Meanwhile, the federal deficit continued to mount, thanks in part to Reagan's tax cuts and military spending. In 1990, Congress and the administration agreed on a deficit-reduction plan involving spending cuts and tax increases.

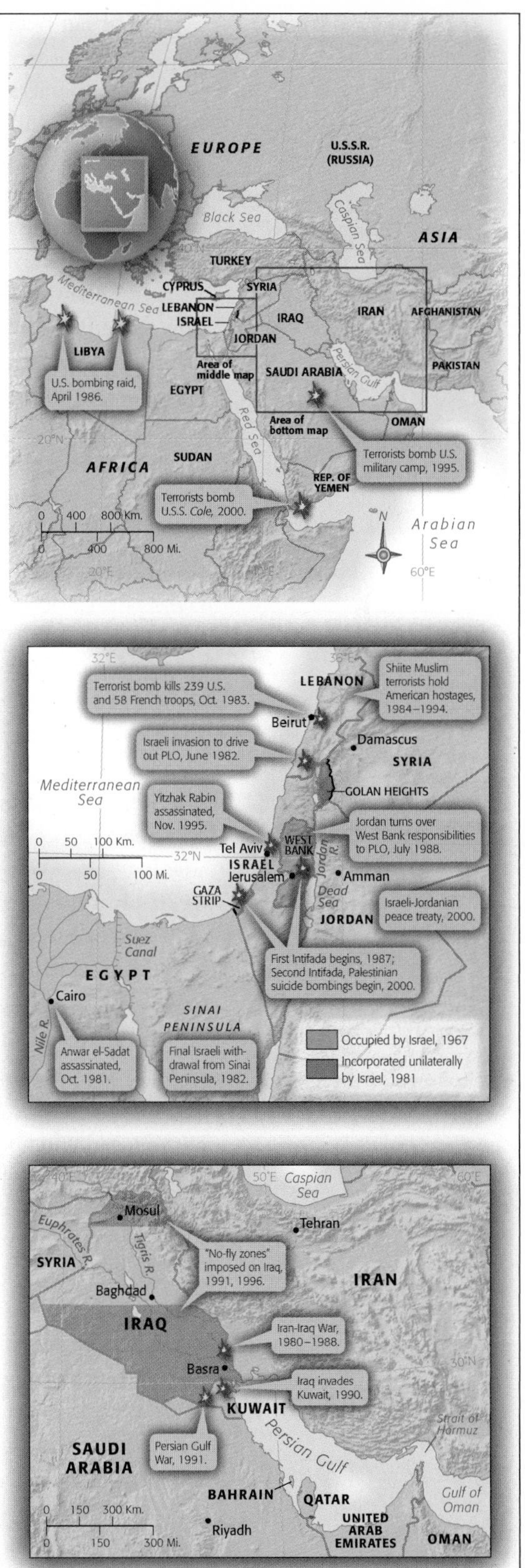

Map 30.3 The Mideast Crisis, 1980–2000

With terrorist attacks, the Iran-Iraq War, the Persian Gulf War, and the ongoing struggle between Israel and the Palestinians, the Middle East saw almost unending violence and conflict in these years.

Interactive Map

Bush's retreat from his "no new taxes" pledge angered voters. Despite this plan, the 1992 deficit neared $300 billion.

Making matters worse, another recession struck in 1990. Retail sales slumped; housing starts fell. General Motors, battered by Japanese imports, laid off more than seventy thousand workers. By 1992, the jobless rate exceeded 7 percent. If 1984 was "morning in America," wrote a columnist, quoting a Reagan campaign slogan, this was "the morning after."

The recession worsened inner-city poverty and despair. In April 1992, an outbreak of arson and looting in Watts, the predominantly black district of Los Angeles and scene of rioting in 1965 (see Chapter 28), left forty persons dead and millions in property damage. The immediate cause was outrage over a jury's acquittal of four white police officers whose brutal beating of a black motorist had been captured on videotape.

America's environmental worries increased during Bush's presidency. In March 1989, a giant oil tanker, the *Exxon Valdez,* ran aground in Alaska's Prince William Sound, spilling more than 10 million gallons of oil. The accident fouled coastal habitats, killed thousands of sea otters and shore birds, and jeopardized Alaska's fisheries. Bush deplored the spill, but insisted that America's energy-hungry economy required ever more quantities of oil, coal, and natural gas.

That summer, air pollution in many U.S. cities exceeded federal standards. A 1991 Environmental Protection Agency study found that pollutants were eroding the atmosphere's ozone layer, which reduces cancer-causing solar radiation. Growing numbers of scientists also warned of global warming related to increasing levels of carbon dioxide in the atmosphere and the role of human activity in causing it. Squeezed between growing environmental concern and his party's free-market ideology, Bush signed a stricter Clean Air Act passed by the Democratic Congress in 1990, but otherwise backed oil exploration in Alaskan wilderness preserves and left other environmental concerns unaddressed.

Clarence Thomas
Ultraconservative Bush appointee to the Supreme Court, who was challenged on grounds of alleged sexual harassment

Of President Bush's two Supreme Court nominations, David Souter, a moderate, won easy confirmation. With **Clarence Thomas,** however, Bush continued Reagan's effort to push the court to the Right. Bush nominated Thomas in 1991 to replace Thurgood Marshall, the black jurist who had played a role in the historic Brown school desegregation case (see Chapter 27). Thomas, also African-American, supported right-wing causes and, as head of the Equal Employment Opportunity Commission (EEOC) under Reagan, had opposed affirmative-action programs. Noting his weak judicial qualifications, critics charged Bush with playing racial politics.

In the Senate confirmation hearings, a former staff member at EEOC, Anita Hill, accused Thomas of sexual harassment. Thomas narrowly won confirmation, but Republican efforts to discredit Hill's testimony alienated many women, and their resentment appeared to play a role when women candidates did well in the 1992 elections.

On the Court, Thomas allied with Antonin Scalia, Chief Justice Rehnquist, and other Republican-appointed justices who supported expanded executive power and a strict interpretation of the Constitution. The conservative bloc narrowed the rights of arrested persons; curbed death-penalty appeals; cut back affirmative-action

Bob Daemmrich Photography

Bill and Hillary Clinton Campaigning in Texas, August 1992

Holding a future voter as microphones record the moment, Bill Clinton demonstrates the popular appeal that helped him win the presidency. Hillary Clinton would soon emerge as a powerful political figure in her own right.

programs; and, in *Planned Parenthood* v. *Casey* (1992), upheld a Pennsylvania law imposing restrictions on abortion providers.

1992: America's Voters Choose a New Course

Given President Bush's popularity after the Persian Gulf War, many top Democrats opted out of the 1992 presidential race. But Arkansas governor **William (Bill) Jefferson Clinton** took the plunge. Fending off reports of marital infidelity, Clinton won the nomination. As his running mate, he chose Tennessee senator **Albert (Al) Gore, Jr.**

President Bush quashed a primary challenge by conservative columnist Pat Buchanan. A third-party candidate, **H. Ross Perot** (pair-OH), founder of a Texas data-processing firm, insisted he could easily solve the nation's economic problems.

William (Bill) Jefferson Clinton Forty-second president; his controversial two-term presidency was marked by a surging economy at home

Albert (Al) Gore, Jr. Tennessee senator and noted expert on environmental issues who served as Clinton's vice president

H. Ross Perot Texas billionaire who ran for president as a third-party candidate in 1992 and 1996

At his peak of popularity, nearly 40 percent of the voters backed Perot, but his eccentricities and thin-skinned response to criticism cost him support.

Bush attacked Clinton for evading the Vietnam-era draft and promised more attention to domestic issues in a second term. Clinton hammered on the recession and the problems of the middle class. He pledged to work for a national health-care system, welfare reform, environmental protection, and economic growth.

Clinton won 43 percent of the vote to Bush's 38 percent. Perot's 19 percent was the best for a third-party candidate since Teddy Roosevelt in 1912. Clinton lured back many blue-collar and suburban "Reagan Democrats." The recession, Bush's lackluster domestic record, and the divisive Perot campaign all helped Clinton. With Democrats now in control of Congress and the White House, an end to the much-deplored "Washington gridlock" seemed possible.

Thirty-eight African-Americans and seventeen Hispanics won congressional seats. The new Senate included six women and the House had forty-seven. Illinois elected the first African-American woman senator, Carol Moseley Braun.

Apart from the Persian Gulf War, President Bush's single term proved unmemorable. A *New York Times* editorial, judging him "shrewd and energetic in foreign policy . . . , clumsy and irresolute at home," went on: "The domestic Bush flops like a fish, leaving the impression that he doesn't know what he thinks or doesn't much care, apart from the political gains to be extracted from an issue."

CHECKING IN

- The Cold War ended suddenly with the collapse of the Soviet Union in late 1991.
- When Saddam Hussein invaded Kuwait, Bush forged a coalition to drive him out; although driven from Kuwait, Saddam retained power in Iraq.
- Despite foreign-policy successes, the Bush administration accomplished little domestically; recession struck, environmental concerns accelerated, and racial tensions exploded into riots.
- Bush attempted to move the Supreme Court to the right with the appointment of the controversial, conservative Clarence Thomas.
- Arkansas governor Bill Clinton defeated Republican George H. W. Bush and third-party candidate Ross Perot to win the presidency in 1992.

DOMESTIC AND GLOBAL ISSUES AT CENTURY'S END

What policy issues, political events, and economic trends most influenced Bill Clinton's presidency?

Clinton's presidency soon encountered setbacks, notably the failure of an ambitious national health-care plan. The 1994 midterm election then produced a Republican landslide. The newly energized congressional Republicans pursued their conservative agenda, including sweeping welfare reform.

Clinton preferred domestic issues, but world events dictated attention to foreign policy. Abroad, four key challenges loomed: promoting stability in the former Soviet Union, improving relations between Israel and the Palestinians, addressing security threats posed by nuclear proliferation and Islamic terrorism, and protecting U.S. trade and investment interests.

Trade, Gay Rights, Health Care: Clinton's Mixed Record

Born in Arkansas in 1946, Bill Clinton was part of the baby-boom generation that admired Elvis and came of age in the era of JFK, Vietnam, and the Beatles. After finishing Yale Law School, he returned to Arkansas, where he was elected governor at age thirty-two. At age forty-six, he was president.

As a founder of the New Democratic Coalition—moderates eager to shed the party's "ultraliberal," "tax and spend" reputation—Clinton in his campaign stressed middle-class concerns and muted the party's traditional attention to the poor and social-justice issues. Seeking middle ground on abortion, he said it should be "safe, legal, and rare." He strongly endorsed environmental protection; indeed, his running mate, Al Gore, in 1992 published an environmental manifesto, *Earth in the Balance*.

Committed to the woman's movement, Clinton named women to head several cabinet departments and advisory panels. To fill a Supreme Court vacancy in 1993, he nominated Judge Ruth Bader Ginsberg. In 1996, he named **Madeleine K. Albright** as secretary of state—the highest U.S. government office ever held by a woman.

Madeleine K. Albright
Clinton's secretary of state; at the time, she had the highest government office ever held by a woman

To reduce the budget deficit and combat the recession, Clinton proposed military spending cuts, tax increases, and programs to stimulate job creation and economic growth. With Clinton's support, Congress in 1993 ratified the **North American Free Trade Agreement (NAFTA),** negotiated by the Bush administration. This pact admitted Mexico to the U.S.-Canadian free-trade zone created earlier. While Ross Perot and others warned that U.S. jobs would flee to Mexico, NAFTA backers predicted a net job gain as Mexican markets opened to U.S. products.

North American Free Trade Agreement (NAFTA)
Agreement to create a free trade community involving the United States, Canada, and Mexico

Other early Clinton initiatives failed, however. Fulfilling a campaign pledge to gay-rights organizations, Clinton proposed to end the ban on gays in the military. When religious conservatives and some military leaders protested, he backed off. A study commission crafted a compromise, summed up in the phrase "Don't ask, don't tell." It continued the ban, but also barred officers from querying service members about their sexual orientation. (This policy remained the law of the land until President Barack Obama signed a repeal act into law in December 2010.)

Health-care reform proved an even greater minefield. With Medicare costs exploding, and millions of citizens lacking health insurance, this issue stood high on Clinton's "to do" list, and he appointed his wife Hillary Rodham Clinton to head a health-care task force. Working in secret, this group devised a sweeping plan for cost containment and universal health insurance. Lobbyists for physicians, insurance and tobacco companies, and other special interests rallied the opposition. By fall 1994, the ambitious plan was dead. Clinton had misread public complaints about the existing system as support for radical change.

Jolted by these setbacks, Clinton in 1994 turned to issues with broad voter appeal: crime and welfare reform. His anticrime bill included a ban on assault weapons and funds for more prisons and police officers. Clinton's welfare-reform bill put a two-year limit on payments from the federal welfare program, Aid to Families with Dependent Children (AFDC). After that, able-bodied recipients would have to find work, in a public-service job if necessary. In 1995, having regained control of Congress, Republicans shaped their own, even tougher bill (discussed shortly).

The approaching midterm election found the administration mired in problems. Republican critics publicized the Clintons' earlier involvement in a murky Arkansas real-estate speculation, the Whitewater Development Company. The 1993 suicide of assistant White House counsel Vincent Foster, the Clintons' close friend, attracted conspiracy theorists. In 1994, Paula Jones, an Arkansas state employee, sued Clinton for alleged sexual harassment during his governorship.

Favorable economic news helped Clinton somewhat. By 1994, the unemployment rate had fallen, inflation remained low, and the federal deficit was dropping.

Christian Coalition Conservative evangelical lobbying group with growing influence over the Republican Party in the 1990s

But radio commentator Rush Limbaugh won fans for his jeering attacks on the Clintons and liberals in general. The religious Right remained a potent political force. In addition, Pat Robertson's **Christian Coalition,** with hundreds of chapters nationwide, controlled several state Republican Parties.

Conservative Resurgence and Welfare Reform: 1994–1996

Bill Clinton had run as a "new Democrat," but by 1994 Republicans tarred him as an old "tax-and-spend" Democrat, beholden to gays, feminists, and other "special interests." The failed health-care plan, they charged, simply perpetuated the New Deal/Great Society style of top-down reform.

A network of conservative organizations, from the Christian Coalition to the National Rifle Association, helped re-energize the rightward swing in U.S. politics. Direct-mail campaigns and conservative radio commentators tirelessly hammered such hot-button issues as abortion, gun control, gay rights, school prayer, "radical feminism," and an alleged erosion of "family values."

Newt Gingrich Republican congressman from Georgia who helped bring his party to power; elected Speaker of the House in 1994

Republican congressman **Newt Gingrich** (GING-rich) of Georgia mobilized the discontent. In September 1994, about three hundred Republican congressional candidates signed Gingrich's "Contract with America" pledging to support tax cuts, tougher crime laws, antipornography measures, a balanced-budget amendment, and other reforms. The Contract nationalized the midterm election, which was normally fought on local issues.

In November, voters gave the GOP control of both houses of Congress for the first time since 1954 and increased the number of Republican governors. Evangelicals turned out in large numbers, mostly to vote Republican. In the Senate, North Carolina's reactionary Jesse Helms became chairman of the Foreign Relations Committee. In the House of Representatives, a jubilant horde of 230 Republicans, seventy-three of them newly elected, chose Newt Gingrich as Speaker, made Rush Limbaugh an "honorary member," and set about enacting the Contract with America. A constitutional amendment requiring a balanced federal budget passed the House but narrowly failed in the Senate. Fulfilling the antipornography pledge, Congress passed a Communications Decency Act strengthening the government's censorship powers. (In 1997, the Supreme Court ruled it unconstitutional.)

The torrent of bills, hearings, and press releases recalled the heady days of the early New Deal and Lyndon Johnson's Great Society. At this time, however, the activist energy came from the conservative side of the political spectrum. The architect of this revolution, Newt Gingrich, stumbled in 1995 when he accepted, then returned, a $4.5 million advance from a publishing house owned by Rupert Murdoch, a media tycoon with interests in federal legislation. Gingrich's network of political action groups also drew critical scrutiny.

Turning to welfare reform, congressional Republicans criticized the existing system on both economic and public-policy grounds. AFDC, with 14.2 million women and children on its rolls, cost about $125 billion in 1994. Though dwarfed by the benefits enjoyed by the middle class through social security, Medicare, farm subsidies, and various tax loopholes, this still represented a budgetary drain. On public-policy grounds, the critics contended that the welfare system encouraged

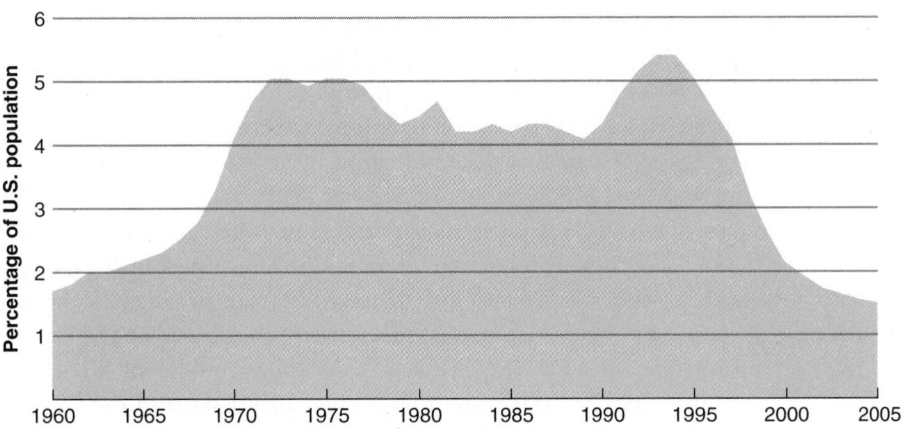

Figure 30.1 Percentage of U.S. Population on Welfare, 1960–2005

From just 1.7 percent in 1960, the percentage of Americans on welfare crept steadily upward until 1994. The post-1994 decline reflected both improved economic conditions and the impact of the Welfare Reform Act of 1996.

Sources: Administration for Children and Families, Department of Health and Human Services; House Committee on Ways and Means, Subcommittee on Human Resources Report, Feb. 26, 2006.

irresponsible social behavior and trapped recipients in a multigenerational cycle of dependence.

As a consensus emerged on the existing system's flaws, debate focused on how to change it. While Clinton favored federally funded child-care and job-training programs to ease the transition from welfare to work, Republicans argued that businesses, the states, and private agencies could best provide these services. After vetoes of two other bills, Clinton eventually signed the **Welfare Reform Act of 1996.** The law replaced AFDC with block grants to states to develop their own programs within funding limits and guidelines restricting recipients to two years of continuous coverage, with a five-year lifetime total.

Welfare Reform Act of 1996 Legislation in which Clinton joined Republicans to end AFDC and move thousands off welfare rolls

Advocates for the poor warned of the effects on inner-city children whose mothers lacked education or job skills, but many observers rated welfare reform at least a qualified success (see Figure 30.1). From 1996 to 2005, the number of families on welfare fell by 57 percent. The percentage of unmarried mothers in the work force rose from around 48 percent in 1996 to around 65 percent in 2000, although many held low-paying, unskilled jobs, and changed jobs frequently.

A Pandora's Box of Dangers in a Post–Cold War World

The aftershocks of the Soviet collapse unsettled the region of southeastern Europe known as the Balkans (BALL-kuns). In Yugoslavia, an unstable nation comprised of Serbia, Bosnia, Croatia, and other enclaves, the ruling Communist Party collapsed in 1990. As Yugoslavia broke apart, Serbian forces launched a campaign of "ethnic cleansing" in neighboring Bosnia, where they killed or drove out Muslims and Croats. In August 1995, after UN peacekeepers failed to stop the killing, a joint U.S. and NATO operation launched air strikes against Bosnian Serb targets.

Kosovo Province of former Yugoslavia victimized by a Serbian ethnic-cleansing campaign

Later in 1995, the Clinton administration flew the leaders of Bosnia's warring factions to Dayton, Ohio, for talks. The resulting Dayton Accords imposed a cease-fire and created a governing framework for Bosnia. Clinton committed twenty thousand U.S. troops to a NATO operation to enforce the cease-fire.

In 1998, when Serbian forces attacked Muslims in Serbia's southern province, **Kosovo,** Clinton approved U.S. bombing of Serbian facilities, including Belgrade, the capital, as part of a NATO response. As Serb forces withdrew from Kosovo, U.S. troops joined a NATO occupying force, and refugees slowly returned. In 2001, a new Serbian government, eager for Western aid, delivered Serbian president Slobodan Milosevic (sluh-BOW-den muh-LOW-sevich) to a war-crimes tribunal at The Hague.

Russia, meanwhile, invaded the breakaway Islamic republic of Chechnya (CHECH-nee-uh) in 1995. This war proved unpopular in Russia, and the Clinton administration watched anxiously as President Boris Yeltsin's position weakened. Hard times and corruption linked to Russia's hasty conversion to a free-market economy further undermined Yeltsin.

Despite Yeltsin's erratic behavior, compounded by alcoholism, the Clinton administration continued to support him. In 1999, the administration backed Russia's admission to the Group of Seven (G-7), a collection of the world's leading industrialized nations. In the same year, however, over Russia's protests, the United States supported NATO's decision to admit three new members from the former Soviet bloc—Hungary, Poland, and the Czech Republic. With Yeltsin's resignation in December 1999, Prime Minister Vladimir Putin (VLAH-dee-meer POO-tun), a former agent of the KGB, the Soviet secret police, succeeded him as president, opening a new chapter in the tortured history of U.S.-Russian relations.

In the Israeli-Palestinian conflict, which was of vital concern to America, prospects brightened in 1993 when Israeli and Palestinian negotiators meeting in Norway agreed on a timetable for peace. The so-called Oslo Accords provided for a Palestinian state, land concessions by Israel, and further talks on Palestinian refugees' claims and the final status of Jerusalem. In 1994, President Clinton presided as Israeli Prime Minister Yitzhak Rabin (YEET-shahk rah-BEEN) and Yasir Arafat of the PLO signed the agreement at the White House.

After hopeful beginnings, however, this initiative failed. In 1995, a young Israeli opposed to the Oslo Accords assassinated Rabin. Israel's next election brought to power Benjamin Netanyahu (net-ahn-YA-hoo) of the hard-line Likud (li-KOOD) Party. Suicide bombings in Israel by Palestinian extremists in 1996–1997 triggered retaliatory attacks. By 2000, the West Bank and Gaza had an estimated two hundred thousand Jewish settlers, with accompanying checkpoints, security forces, and limited-access highways making existence difficult for Palestinians.

In July 2000, Clinton invited Arafat and Israel's new prime minister, Ehud Barak (EH-hood buh-RAHK), of the more moderate Labour Party, for talks at Camp David. Barak made major concessions. Arafat rejected Barak's offer, however, and the summit failed. In September, hundreds of Israeli soldiers and police briefly occupied Jerusalem's Temple Mount, which was sacred to both Muslims and Jews. This action symbolically asserted Israel's control of the site. The Palestinians launched a new intifada, and in 2001 Israelis elected the hard-liner Ariel Sharon prime minister. As Clinton left office, the conflict raged on.

Iraq also claimed Clinton's attention. In 1997, when Saddam Hussein barred UN inspectors from facilities suspected of conducting research on chemical and nuclear weapons, Clinton dispatched ships, bombers, and troops to the Persian Gulf and sought support for a multinational military strike. But France, Russia, and various Arab states resisted, and the stand-off continued.

Other nations, too, posed threats of nuclear proliferation. Neither India nor Pakistan, at odds over the disputed region of Kashmir (KAHSH-meer), had signed the 1968 Nuclear Nonproliferation Treaty. In 1988, India tested a "nuclear device" and Pakistan soon followed. North Korea, despite having signed the Nonproliferation Treaty, also pursued nuclear-weapons development and missile testing. In 1999, confronting famine and economic crisis, North Korea suspended missile testing in return for an easing of U.S. trade and travel restrictions. The country's nuclear intentions remained worrisome, however.

Terrorism: "The War of the Future"

Attacks by anti-American Islamic extremists continued. A February 1993 bomb blast in a parking garage beneath one of the towers of New York's World Trade Center killed six persons, injured hundreds, and forced fifty thousand workers to evacuate. Five Islamic militants were arrested, and three were convicted of murder and given life sentences.

The terrorist threat extended to Africa. In 1992, President Bush committed twenty-six thousand U.S. troops to a UN humanitarian mission in Somalia (soh-MAH-lee-uh), a predominantly Muslim East African nation beset by civil war and famine. As the warring factions battled, forty-four Americans were killed. President Clinton withdrew the U.S. force in 1994, and the UN mission ended a year later. Later evidence implicated Islamic extremists directed by Osama bin Laden (oh-SAHM-uh bin LAH-dun) in the killings. Son of a wealthy Saudi contractor, bin Laden had been expelled from Saudi Arabia in 1991 and settled in Sudan, where he plotted anti-Western terrorist activities.

On August 7, 1998, simultaneous bomb blasts at the U.S. embassies in Nairobi, Kenya, and Dar es Salaam, Tanzania (tan-zuh-NEE-uh), killed 220—including twelve Americans. U.S. intelligence again pinpointed bin Laden, by now organizing terrorist training camps in Afghanistan. Clinton ordered cruise missile strikes on one of these Afghan camps as well as on a suspected chemical-weapons factory in Sudan allegedly financed by bin Laden. On October 12, 2000, a bomb aboard a small boat in the harbor of Aden (AH-den), Yemen (YEH-mun), ripped a gaping hole in the U.S. destroyer *Cole,* killing seventeen sailors.

Defining America's Role amid Global Changes

As Americans confronted these myriad international dangers, the peaceful post–Cold War era that many had anticipated seemed a cruel mirage. The Soviet adversary had collapsed, but crises still flared around the world. Like firefighters battling many small blazes rather than a single conflagration, policy makers now wrestled with a baffling tangle of issues.

globalization The removal of barriers to the flow of capital, goods, and ideas across national borders

Amid the complexities, some larger trends could be discerned. Economic and even cultural **globalization** played an ever greater role. International trade and finance increasingly shaped America's foreign-policy interests. American movies, popular music, and television programs reached a worldwide audience in an age of instant telecommunications.

Along with globalization, however, came a widening chasm that divided the prosperous, comparatively stable industrialized world from societies marked by poverty, disease, illiteracy, and explosive population growth. This vast gulf helped spawn resentment, hatred, and terrorism.

Ancient ethnic hatreds burst into violence as the bipolar Cold War world fragmented. The lethal conflict in the former Yugoslavia was far from unique. Similar clashes erupted in many regions. In the African nation of Rwanda (ruh-WAN-duh), as many as a million people perished in genocidal violence in 1994, as militias of the ruling Hutu ethnic group massacred members of the once-dominant Tutsi group. Thousands more fled in panic, creating a refugee crisis. Traumatized by the Somalia fiasco, President Clinton did not intervene.

Resurgent religious fundamentalism intensified the global unrest. As Muslim fundamentalists denounced Western liberalism and secularism, a small but lethal minority embraced violence as a religious duty. Confronting such complexities, some U.S. citizens simply gave up. In a 1997 poll, only 20 percent of Americans said they followed foreign news, down sharply from the 1980s, with the biggest drop among young people. TV coverage of events abroad fell by more than 50 percent from 1989 to 1995.

Newt Gingrich's 1994 Contract with America largely ignored foreign policy, and key Republican legislators pushed isolationist views. Jesse Helms, as chair of the Senate Foreign Relations Committee, denounced the United Nations, criticized environmental treaties, and belittled UN peacekeeping efforts and America's foreign-aid program. Congressional Republicans refused to pay $1 billion in past UN dues. Bending to such pressures, Clinton in 1998 declined to sign a multinational treaty banning land mines.

Despite isolationist currents, however, opinion polls indicated that most Americans supported internationalist approaches to global problems. The U.S. part in negotiating the Dayton Accords that brought a fragile peace to Bosnia offered a noteworthy instance of this role. Another came in 1995 when President Clinton appointed former Democratic senator George Mitchell as a special envoy to Northern Ireland to promote negotiations between Catholics favoring independence and Protestants advocating continued ties to Great Britain. Mitchell's efforts were rewarded in 1998 when the two sides signed a peace agreement.

With the Cold War's end, the United Nations seemed better positioned to fulfill the role its supporters had envisioned in 1945. Indeed, by 2000, more than forty thousand UN peacekeepers and civilian personnel were deployed in fifteen world trouble spots. A complex network of UN agencies addressed global environmental, nutritional, public-health, and human-rights issues. The UN-sponsored International Court of Justice at The Hague adjudicated disputes between nations and tried perpetrators of mass violence.

CHECKING IN

- Clinton was a fiscally moderate "New Democrat" determined to focus on domestic issues, although his health-care reform initiative failed.
- The 1994 elections brought conservative Republicans to control of Congress; Clinton worked with them for a far-reaching overhaul of welfare.
- Clinton committed U.S. troops to a NATO peacekeeping effort in the Balkans; chastened in Somalia, Clinton did not intervene in the Rwanda genocide.
- The United States helped negotiate the Oslo Accords, providing for a Palestinian state, but progress stalled.
- Nuclear proliferation remained a concern; as terrorism directed at Americans and the West increased, the outlines of a "new world order" became clear.

Moderation, White House Scandal, and a Disputed Election, 1996–2000

Why did political differences become sharper from 1996 to 2000?

Straddling the political center, Bill Clinton won reelection in 1996. Along with sending U.S. forces to Kosovo and the final stab at resolving the Israeli-Palestinian dispute, his second term saw a battle over tobacco-industry regulation and a sex scandal that led to his impeachment. A disputed presidential election in 2000 deepened the nation's divisions.

Clinton Battles Big Tobacco and Woos Political Moderates

Bill Clinton won the nickname "the Comeback Kid" following a long-shot victory in the 1992 New Hampshire primary, and after the 1994 Republican landslide he again hit the comeback trail. In a 1995 budget battle, Clinton outmaneuvered House Speaker Newt Gingrich, who annoyed voters by twice allowing a partial government shutdown.

As the 1996 electoral campaign began, Kansas senator Bob Dole, a partially disabled World War II veteran, won the Republican nomination. Although fundraising scandals marred Clinton's reelection campaign, the seventy-three-year-old Dole ran a lackluster campaign, and Clinton won with 49 percent of the vote to Dole's 41 percent. (Ross Perot garnered 8 percent.) The Republicans retained control of Congress, but proved more subdued than after their 1994 triumph.

Tobacco regulation loomed large as Clinton's second term began. In 1997, facing lawsuits by former smokers and by states saddled with medical costs linked to smoking-related diseases, the tobacco industry agreed to pay some $368 billion in settlement. The agreement limited tobacco advertising, especially when directed at young people.

Since the agreement required government approval, the debate shifted to Washington. The Clinton administration backed a bill imposing tough penalties, higher cigarette taxes, and stronger antismoking measures. The industry struck back with a $40 million lobbying campaign and heavy contributions to key politicians, killing the bill. The Republican Party, commented Arizona Republican senator John McCain, appeared to be "in the pocket of the tobacco companies." In 1998, the tobacco industry and most states reached a new settlement, which was scaled back to $206 billion.

Pursuing his middle-of-the-road strategy, Clinton in his January 1998 State of the Union address offered some initiatives to help the poor, but mostly highlighted proposals attractive to the middle class and fiscal conservatives. Some liberals dismissed the speech as "Progressivism Lite," but it had broad appeal. Further, Clinton's economic policies contributed to the decade's prosperity and in 1998 produced the first federal budget surplus in nearly thirty years. Under normal circumstances, Clinton's record would have assured that his presidency, despite early missteps, would end in a glow of success. But Clinton's situation was far from normal.

A Media Field Day as Scandal Grips the White House

Even as Clinton went about his duties, scandal swirled around his presidency. Adultery charges had long clung to Clinton, and now he faced Paula Jones's sexual-harassment suit, dating from his days as Arkansas governor.

Monica Lewinsky White House intern whose brief liaison with Bill Clinton was discovered by Whitewater investigators

Seeking to document a pattern of sexual harassment, Jones's lawyers quizzed Clinton about rumors linking him to a young White House intern, **Monica Lewinsky.** Under oath, Clinton and Lewinsky denied everything. As the rumors became public, Clinton denounced them as false. Clinton settled Paula Jones's suit, but problems remained. In taped phone conversations, Lewinsky had described a White House affair with Clinton. The tapes were acquired by Kenneth Starr, an independent counsel investigating the Clintons' Arkansas real-estate dealings.

Starr's inquiry now shifted to whether Clinton had committed perjury in his Paula Jones testimony and persuaded Lewinsky to lie. In August, after a promise of immunity, Lewinsky admitted the affair to a grand jury. As the scandal unfolded in tabloid headlines and late-night television jokes, Clinton in a brief TV address conceded "inappropriate" behavior but attacked Starr as politically motivated.

In a September 1998 report to the House Judiciary Committee, Starr recommended Clinton's impeachment for perjury and obstructing justice by coaching his secretary on his version of events. In a party-line vote, the House approved and sent to the Senate two articles of impeachment: perjury and obstruction of justice.

The public, however, sent the Republicans an ominous message: Clinton's approval ratings rose, and the Democrats gained five House seats in the 1998 midterm elections. Few believed the president's actions met the Constitution's "high crimes and misdemeanors" standard for removal from office. With the economy booming and Clinton's political program generally popular, voters appeared willing to tolerate his personal flaws. After a trial presided by Chief Justice William Rehnquist, the Senate rejected both charges in February 1999, and the trial ended. In November, Newt Gingrich, a leader of the impeachment effort but now embroiled in his own ethical controversies, resigned as Speaker and left Congress.

While the impeachment failed, the scandal tarnished Clinton's reputation. Still facing legal liability as he left office in January 2001, the president admitted to perjury, paid a $25,000 fine, and lost his law license for five years.

2000: Divided Nation, Disputed Election

As the 2000 campaign approached, the Democrats nominated Vice President Al Gore for the top job. Distancing himself from the Lewinsky scandal, Gore chose as his running mate Connecticut senator Joseph Lieberman, who had denounced Clinton's behavior.

George W. Bush Forty-third president; son of the former president Bush, he promised to restore dignity to the White House

In the Republican contest, Arizona's somewhat maverick senator John McCain, a Vietnam-era prisoner of war, made a strong bid. But Texas governor **George W. Bush,** with powerful backers, a familiar name, and a folksy manner, won the nomination. The environmentally minded Green Party nominated consumer advocate Ralph Nader.

Both Gore and Bush courted the center while trying to hold their bases. For Bush, this base included corporate interests, energy companies, religious conservatives, and so-called Reagan Democrats in the middle class and blue-collar ranks. Gore's base included liberals, academics and professionals, union members, environmentalists, feminists, and African-Americans. The Hispanic vote remained divided.

Gore boasted of the nation's prosperity and pledged to extend health-care coverage and protect social security. In TV debates, Gore was more articulate and knowledgeable, but some found him rather pompous. Bush, with little experience outside Texas, was widely seen as a lightweight, dependent on family influence. Calling himself a "compassionate conservative," Bush subtly reminded voters of Clinton's misdeeds by promising to restore dignity to the White House. Polls showed that most voters agreed with Gore on the issues, but preferred Bush as a person.

On election day, Gore won the popular vote by more than five hundred thousand. But the all-important Electoral College outcome came down to Florida, where a handful of votes separated the two candidates. Flaws in Florida's voting process quickly emerged. In counties with many black voters, antiquated voting machines rejected thousands of ballots in which the paper tabs, called "chads," were not fully punched out. When election officials began a hand count of rejected ballots, Bush's lawyers sued to prevent it.

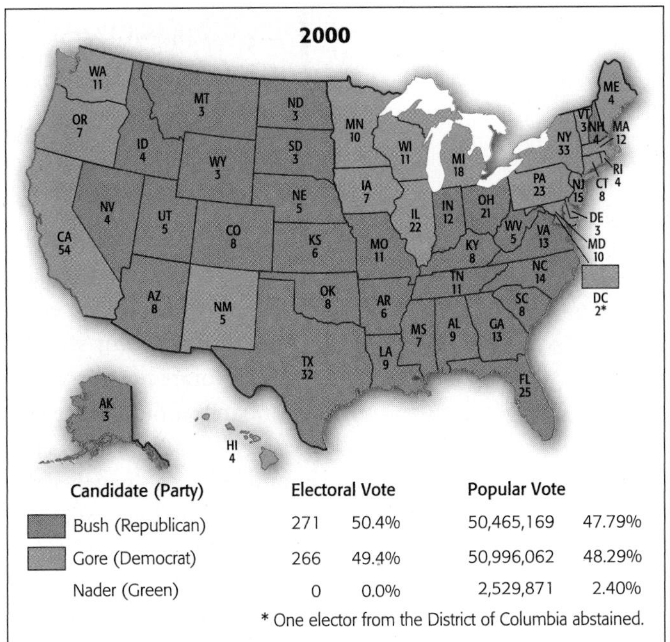

Map 30.4 The Election of 2000

For the first time since 1888, the winner of the popular vote, Al Gore, failed to win the presidency. The Supreme Court's intervention in the disputed Florida outcome put George W. Bush in the White House.

Interactive Map

On November 21, the Florida Supreme Court, with a preponderance of Democrats, unanimously ruled that the ongoing recount should constitute the official result. Bush's legal team appealed to the U.S. Supreme Court (see Map 30.4). Despite a long-established precedent that state courts should decide electoral disputes, the justices accepted the case. On November 26, ignoring the unresolved legal dispute, Florida's secretary of state, Katherine Harris, certified the original, contested Florida vote, awarding Bush the state. (Harris was co-chair of Bush's Florida campaign.)

The Supreme Court on December 12, by a 5-to-4 vote, halted the recount and let Harris's ruling stand. Gore conceded the next day. Five Supreme Court justices (all Republican appointees) had made George W. Bush president. Third-party candidate Ralph Nader also helped Bush win. Had the nearly one hundred thousand Floridians who voted for Nader not had that option, Gore would almost certainly have won the state and the presidency. The election produced an evenly divided Senate, giving Vice President Cheney the deciding vote. The Republicans narrowly held the House of Representatives.

CHECKING IN

- Clinton continued to move to the center, achieving tax cuts and a balanced budget (with surpluses by the end of his term).
- The Monica Lewinsky scandal erupted; Kenneth Starr broadened the Whitewater investigation to include the Lewinsky affair and other accusations of sexual misconduct.
- The Republican-controlled House impeached Clinton, but the Senate did not convict; despite impeachment, Clinton's popularity remained high.
- In the 2000 election, Gore won the popular vote, but the electoral vote remained undecided because of disputed ballots in Florida.
- The Supreme Court intervened, in effect awarding the election to Bush.

ECONOMIC AND CULTURAL TRENDS AT CENTURY'S END

What economic trends, technological innovations, and cultural trends shaped American life in the 1990s?

The 1990s saw sustained economic growth, increased productivity, falling unemployment, low inflation, and the first federal budget surplus in years. Economic globalization fueled U.S. economic growth, but when foreign economies faltered, the American economy stumbled as well.

As corporate profits surged and the stock market soared, America exuded a glow of abundance amid leisure-time diversions and get-rich-quick enthusiasm. But real wages lagged, many workers lacked the skills valued by the emerging knowledge-based economy, and the gap between the super wealthy and most Americans widened. A continuing AIDS epidemic, outbursts of violence, and bitter cultural disagreements also characterized American society as the twentieth century ended.

An Uneven Prosperity

From 1992 to 2000, the unemployment rate fell from 7.5 percent to 4 percent. The gross domestic product, a key economic indicator, rose nearly 40 percent in the decade.

The boom had varied sources, but the revolution in information technology was crucial. Bulky typewriters, calculators, and adding machines—the information technologies of earlier eras—gathered dust as people shifted to computer-based word processing and data management. The computer-based Internet, developed for the Defense Department, initially linked only military installations. By the 1990s, thanks to new software and a system called the World Wide Web, the Internet and e-mail were revolutionizing communications and information-sharing.

Wall Street stock prices far outran many companies' actual earnings prospects. From under 3,000 in 1991, the Dow Jones Industrial Average approached 12,000 by early 2001. Leisure pursuits and consumer spending burgeoned. In 2000, Americans spent $105 billion on new cars and $107 billion on video, audio, and computer equipment. However, a few economists raised cautionary flags. In 1996, Federal Reserve Board chairman Alan Greenspan warned of "irrational exuberance" in the stock market, but with little effect.

Surging information technology (IT) stocks fed the boom. The NASDAQ composite index, loaded with technology stocks, shot up from under 500 in 1991 to over 5,000 by early 2000. Some stock offerings by unknown IT start-up companies hit fantastic levels, turning young entrepreneurs into paper millionaires. As the stock market roared on, companies sought to improve their profitability through mergers and acquisitions. In 2000, communications giant Viacom swallowed CBS for $41 billion.

The prosperity was spotty, however. From 1979 to 1996, the share of the total national income going to the wealthiest 20 percent of Americans increased by 13 percent, while the share going to the poorest 20 percent dropped by 22 percent. Adjusted for inflation, the buying power of the average worker's paycheck fell or remained flat from 1986 to 2000. As corporations maintained profits by downsizing,

Dick Reed/Corbis

The Hummer, Macho Vehicle of the 1990s

The Hummer was a civilian version of the Humvee, a military vehicle used in the Persian Gulf War. These gas-guzzling behemoths became status symbols during the economic boom of the 1990s. General Motors stopped production of the largest model in 2006 and shuttered the brand completely in 2010.

cost cutting, and exporting jobs overseas, workers faced uncertain times. The growing service sector included not only white-collar positions, but also low-paying jobs in fast-food outlets, custodial work, car washes, telemarketing, and so forth. Only 13.5 percent of the labor force was unionized in 2000, eroding this means by which workers had historically bettered their wages and job conditions.

Overall employment statistics also obscured racial and ethnic variables. In 2000, the jobless rate for blacks and Hispanics remained significantly higher than the rate for whites. Some newcomers with training in special skills found well-paying positions, but many took low-paying, unskilled jobs with few benefits or long-term prospects. In short, while many Americans prospered during these boom years, millions more experienced minimal gains or none at all.

As the economy boomed and banks passed out credit cards like candy, consumer debt soared alarmingly. Unscrupulous finance companies offered would-be homeowners mortgages they could ill afford. The deregulation of business and banking that began in the late 1970s and continued through the Clinton years (and beyond) encouraged these dangerous trends. Credit buying and the deregulation mania gave the economy a glow of prosperity, but also laid the groundwork for a harsh recession (see Chapter 31).

America and the World Economy

Multinational economic considerations increasingly shaped U.S. foreign policy. Despite China's human rights abuses and one-party rule, Clinton welcomed Chinese president Jiang Zemin in 1997 and visited China in 1998. This reflected economic realities. In 2000, U.S. imports from China surpassed $100 billion, making it America's fourth largest trading partner, after Canada, Mexico, and Japan.

In 1997–1998, a banking and credit crisis threatened the booming export economies of Thailand, South Korea, Indonesia, and other Asian nations, and indirectly jeopardized the U.S. economy. The International Monetary Fund, a Washington-based agency to which the United States is the largest contributor, put together a $40 billion bailout package to stabilize the situation. As the crisis spread to Japan, Brazil, and Argentina, U.S. prosperity looked increasingly vulnerable. All this underscored how deeply the United States had become enmeshed in a complex global economy.

Affluence and a Search for Heroes

The economic boom produced vast wealth for some and an orgy of consumption that set the decade's tone. Wall Street and Silicon Valley spawned thousands of youthful millionaires. Surveying the lifestyles of the newly rich in 1997, *Vanity Fair* magazine described New York as "the champagne city, making the brash consumption of the 1980s look like the depression." Elegant restaurants offered absurdly expensive cigars and wines; exclusive shops sold $13,000 handbags. Attendance at the Disney

The McMansion: Domestic Architecture as Conspicuous Consumption

As some Americans grew rich in the boom years of the 1980s and 1990s, ostentatious and pretentious houses, nicknamed McMansions, sprang up across the country.

Cal Warlick

theme parks in Florida and California neared 30 million in 2000. The sales of gas-guzzling sport-utility vehicles (SUVs) soared.

The boom encouraged a hard-edged "winner take all" mentality like that of the Gilded Age, when the rich turned their backs on the rest of society. In *Bowling Alone: The Collapse and Revival of American Community* (2000), political scientist Robert Putnam found diminished civic engagement; weakened interest in public affairs; and a more self-absorbed, individualistic society. Meanwhile, the mass culture offered escapist fare. The 1997 film *Titanic* grossed $600 million. The top-rated TV show of 1999–2000, *Who Wants to Be a Millionaire?,* celebrated raw greed. So-called reality shows like *Survivor* offered viewers a risk-free taste of challenges that contemporary American life itself conspicuously lacked.

The Clinton sex scandals often seemed like little more than another media diversion in a sensation-hungry decade. But the popular culture also offered evidence of more complex social crosscurrents. Some critics interpreted *Titanic,* which sided with its working-class hero in steerage against the rich snobs in first class, as a comment on America's widening class differences. One even called the movie "an exercise in class hatred." Dissatisfaction with a materialistic culture and money-driven politics, some suggested, found expression in bestselling books about past heroes and more heroic times, such as David McCullough's *Truman* (1993) and Tom Brokaw's *The Greatest Generation* (1998), about the GIs who fought in World War II.

The 2001 film *Pearl Harbor,* argued critic Frank Rich, reflected a longing "for what is missing in our national life: some cause larger than ourselves." Concluded Rich: "Even those Americans who are . . . foggy about World War II . . . know intuitively that it was fought over something more blessed than the right to guzzle gas."

The AIDS Epidemic Rages On; Outbursts of Violence Stir Concern

Beneath the glow of prosperity, darker currents stirred. The **AIDS** crisis continued its deadly course. By 2000, U.S. deaths from the disease surpassed 458,000. As knowledge about preventive measures spread and medications were developed to treat HIV, an infection that often precedes full-blown AIDS, the crisis abated somewhat by the early twenty-first century—but it was far from over. Tony Kushner's two-part play *Angels in America* (1991–1992), as well as the long-running rock musical *Rent* (1996), explored the human and cultural impact of AIDS.

AIDS Acquired immune deficiency syndrome; first diagnosed in 1981

A popular 1999 film, *American Beauty,* and TV's *The Sopranos,* an HBO series about a mobster and his family, explored dark impulses and a violent substratum in American life. However, the violence was not limited to pop-culture fantasy. True, overall crime rates fell nearly 20 percent between 1992 and 2000. But violent outbursts punctuated the decade. Gun deaths exceeded twenty-eight thousand in 2000. In April 1999, two students at Columbine High School near Denver fatally shot twelve students and a teacher before committing suicide. After this massacre, President Clinton called for stricter gun-control laws, but the National Rifle Association fought such efforts.

The violence sometimes arose from the culture wars. In 1998, two youths tortured and murdered a gay student, Matthew Shepard, at the University of Wyoming because of his sexual orientation. As the abortion controversy raged, some "pro-life" advocates turned violent. In the 1990s, at least five physicians who performed abortions or staff members at clinics providing this service were murdered, and other clinics were bombed.

On April 19, 1995, in the decade's worst incident of mass violence, explosives concealed in a rental truck demolished a federal office building in Oklahoma City, killing 168. Police soon arrested Timothy McVeigh, a Gulf War veteran obsessed with conspiracy theories. McVeigh, convicted of murder, was executed in 2001.

The Oklahoma City bombing came precisely two years after an April 1993 government raid on the Waco, Texas, compound of the Branch Davidians, an apocalyptic religious sect led by David Koresh, who was charged with firearms violations. An earlier confrontation at Waco had left four government agents and six Davidians dead. The April raid ended tragically when fires inside the compound, probably set by Koresh and others, killed some eighty Davidians as federal tanks moved in. Timothy McVeigh boasted that his Oklahoma City attack represented retaliation for Waco.

Culture Wars: A Broader View

While the 1990s' culture wars typically did not descend into violence, they did involve fierce contests that some viewed as a struggle for the nation's soul. The struggle unfolded on many fronts, from televangelists' programs, bookstore shelves, and radio talk shows to school-board protests and demonstrations at family-planning clinics. Some endorsed a constitutional amendment permitting prayer in public-school classrooms; others criticized history textbooks as insufficiently patriotic or excessively multicultural. In 1995, the Smithsonian Institution radically scaled back a planned exhibit marking the fiftieth anniversary of the atomic bombing of Hiroshima and Nagasaki when politicians and veterans' organizations criticized it for graphically documenting the bombs' human toll and for presenting differing contemporary views of the bombings.

As gays and lesbians grew more vocal politically, conservatives resisted their demands for equality. The Southern Baptist Convention, America's largest Protestant denomination, urged a boycott of Disney World for unofficially sponsoring "Gay Pride" days. The fast-growing evangelical movement denounced the nation's alleged moral decline. Bill Clinton's misdeeds underscored for conservatives the moral rot they saw eating away at America. Activists even complained about Republican politicians who courted their votes but ignored their agenda once in power.

Pat Robertson's *The New World Order* (1991) interpreted world history as a vast conspiracy that will soon end in the rule of the Antichrist. The best-selling *Left Behind* series of novels (1995–2004), coauthored by the conservative activist Tim LaHaye, described an approaching end time when satanic forces will take over America and the world, until Jesus Christ returns to destroy all evildoers and establish a righteous kingdom.

But for whom did the culture warriors speak? In *One Nation After All* (1998), sociologist Alan Wolfe found most contemporary Americans surprisingly tolerant of diverse views and lifestyles. "[T]here is little truth to the charge that middle-class Americans, divided by a culture war, have split into two hostile camps," Wolfe concluded. "Middle-class Americans, in their heart of hearts, are desperate that we once again become one nation."

CHECKING IN

- Mass culture in the 1990s was marked by gaudy commercialism, a fixation with scandal, and a decline in civic participation.
- Although crime declined, outbursts of violence such as the Columbine massacre and the Oklahoma City bombing prompted anxieties about public safety.
- In 1993, a government raid on the Waco, Texas, compound of the Branch Davidians, an apocalyptic religious sect, resulted in some eighty deaths.
- Conservatives gained ground in the "culture wars" in the 1990s and built a mass cultural and political movement.
- Evangelical groups espoused an interpretation of current events based in biblical prophecy and called for the nation to restore "traditional values."

Chapter Summary

What core beliefs guided Ronald Reagan's presidency? (page 741)

Under Reagan's economic policies, dubbed "Reaganomics," sharp tax cuts led to steep deficits, and deregulation reduced government oversight of business, with mixed results. Reagan supplied arms and other aid to the contras in Nicaragua, despite a congressional ban. Military spending soared, including funding for the Strategic Defense Initiative ("Star Wars"). Despite second-term scandals, including Iran-contra, Reagan remained popular. He met with Mikhail Gorbachev as the Cold War wound down. Conditions in the Middle East deteriorated, however, as violence between Palestinians and Israel increased, and a surge in terrorist attacks threatened America and other Western nations.

What were George H. W. Bush's principal achievements and failures as president? (page 752)

The collapse of the Soviet Union ended the Cold War, but new problems quickly replaced old ones. Saddam Hussein's invasion of Kuwait provoked a coordinated response by the United States and its allies, driving him out of Kuwait but allowing him to remain in power in Iraq. Recession struck hard, environmental concerns accelerated, and racial tensions exploded into riots. Bush paid the penalty for his neglect of domestic issues when Americans elected Bill Clinton president in 1992.

What policy issues, political events, and economic trends most influenced Bill Clinton's presidency? (page 758)

Clinton preferred to focus on domestic issues; he pushed a major economic reform package through Congress but failed to achieve health-care reform. Conservative Republicans gained control of Congress in 1994; led by Newt Gingrich, they promised radical change but achieved little. Clinton worked with the Republicans to achieve welfare reform. Clinton committed American forces to the Balkans as peacekeepers. He expressed concern about conflicts in Africa but did not intervene. His attempts at forging an Israeli-Palestinian peace faltered. However, Clinton continued to pursue the dismantling of Cold War nuclear arsenals and nonproliferation of nuclear weapons.

KEY TERMS

William F. Buckley *(p. 741)*
Engel v. *Vitale (p. 743)*
Ronald Reagan *(p. 744)*
Strategic Defense Initiative (SDI) *(p. 747)*
Osama bin Laden *(p. 748)*
Jesse Jackson *(p. 749)*
Iran-contra scandal *(p. 749)*
Oliver North *(p. 749)*
Intermediate-range Nuclear Forces (INF) Treaty *(p. 750)*
George H. W. Bush *(p. 752)*
Persian Gulf War *(p. 754)*
Americans with Disabilities Act *(p. 754)*
Clarence Thomas *(p. 756)*
William (Bill) Jefferson Clinton *(p. 757)*
Albert (Al) Gore, Jr. *(p. 757)*
H. Ross Perot *(p. 757)*
Madeleine K. Albright *(p. 759)*
North American Free Trade Agreement (NAFTA) *(p. 759)*
Christian Coalition *(p. 760)*
Newt Gingrich *(p. 760)*
Welfare Reform Act of 1996 *(p. 761)*
Kosovo *(p. 762)*
globalization *(p. 764)*
Monica Lewinsky *(p. 766)*
George W. Bush *(p. 766)*
AIDS *(p. 771)*

Why did political differences become sharper from 1996 to 2000? (page 765)

Once reelected, Clinton moved to the center, supporting tax cuts and a balanced budget, and actually achieved a budget surplus. However, the Monica Lewinsky scandal undermined these successes and nearly undid his presidency. Based on a lurid report by independent counsel Kenneth Starr, a partisan House impeached Clinton, but Republicans could not muster enough votes in the Senate to convict him. In the disputed 2000 presidential election, finally resolved by the Supreme Court, George W. Bush, son of the former president Bush, defeated Vice President Al Gore.

What economic trends, technological innovations, and cultural trends shaped American life in the 1990s? (page 768)

The stock market soared, partially on the wings of technology stocks, and unemployment fell. Nonetheless, income inequality actually increased. Labor unions, their membership numbers depleted, were powerless to stop the exportation of manufacturing jobs and the passage of NAFTA. The proliferation of 24-hour news television and the rise of the Internet provided the context for a fragmented cultural scene in the 1990s. Scandal and violence filled the airwaves while Americans filled their garages with expensive SUVs and their homes with other consumer goods. Against this seeming debauchery arose an opposition movement, rooted in evangelical Christianity and committed to spreading "family values."

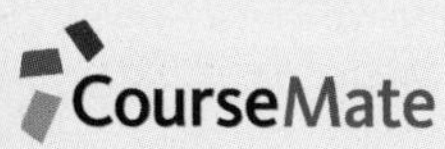

Go to the CourseMate website at **www.cengagebrain.com** for additional study tools and review materials—including audio and video clips—for this chapter.

Chapter 31

Global Dangers, Global Challenges

2001 to the Present

Tannen Maury/epa/Corbis Wire/Corbis

Barack Obama Campaigns in Springfield, Illinois, August 2008

Chapter Preview

America Under Attack: September 11, 2001, and Its Aftermath
How did the Bush administration respond to the September 11, 2001, attacks, internationally and domestically?

Politics and the Economy as a New Century Begins
Beyond security concerns, what economic and social issues did Bush address in his first term?

Debating Iraq and Confronting Other Global Challenges
What challenges faced the United States in the Middle East and elsewhere in the world after 2000?

Social and Economic Trends in Contemporary America
What demographic and economic trends have most shaped contemporary America?

A Floundering Administration Yields to a Renewed Vision
What were the most pressing domestic issues after 2004?

Bao Xiong (bough shong), a Hmong-American born in 1977, spent her first two years in a refugee camp in Thailand. The Hmong (mong) are an Asian ethnic group that originated in northern China and later migrated to the mountainous regions of Laos and Vietnam. During the Vietnam War, the U.S. Central Intelligence Agency recruited many Laotian Hmong to fight the communists. Facing deadly reprisals after the U.S. withdrawal from Vietnam, more than two hundred thousand Hmong, including Bao Xiong's family, fled to refugee camps in Thailand. Here they endured terrible conditions.

In 1979, two-year-old Bao came with her family to America. They settled first in East Moline, Illinois, where her father learned English, enrolled in college, and tried—without success—to resume his teaching career. In 1991, the family moved to Milwaukee, where Bao's mother and father started a laundry while also working in factories. Despite their hard life, Bao Xiong's parents inspired her with their love of learning.

After high school, Bao enrolled in college and majored in elementary education. While pursuing her college degree, she also raised three daughters and taught thirty hours a week in a local ESL (English as a Second Language) program. Bao graduated in 2004 and continued her career as a teacher in the Milwaukee school system. "I want to be a role model for my Hmong students," she said. "I very much want to be an influence in their education and their lives."

The Hmong experience is only one chapter in the larger story of immigration in the contemporary United States. American history from the beginning has been shaped by immigration, voluntary and involuntary, from the British Isles, Africa, Europe, Asia, and Latin America, and this remains true in the early twenty-first century.

This final chapter of *The Enduring Vision* looks at the events and trends shaping U.S. history today. While Americans adapted to new immigration patterns, population movements, and unsettling economic changes, differences over cultural issues persisted and a conservative administration in Washington pursued its vision of the nation's future. Looming over the period were the shocking terrorist attacks of September 11, 2001, and the administration's response, including controversial homeland security measures and a bitterly divisive conflict in Iraq. Despite these troubling times, a historic election in 2008 rekindled hope in the nation's enduring capacity for renewal, even in the face of adversity.

America Under Attack: September 11, 2001, and Its Aftermath

How did the Bush administration respond to the September 11, 2001, attacks, internationally and domestically?

September 11, 2001 Date, emblazoned in national memory, of the terrorist attacks on New York City and Washington, DC

On **September 11, 2001,** a devastating attack horrified the nation. President George W. Bush mobilized a multinational coalition to invade Afghanistan, stronghold of al Qaeda, the organization responsible. Bush also secured new laws and reorganized federal agencies to tighten homeland security. Accusing Iraq's dictator, Saddam Hussein, of complicity in the 9/11 attacks, Bush launched an invasion of Iraq as well.

Colin Powell Commander of U.S. forces in the Persian Gulf War; served as Bush's secretary of state

A New Administration, a Day of Horror

Bush named **Colin Powell,** former head of the Joint Chiefs of Staff, as secretary of state, making him the highest-ranking African-American to serve in a presidential administration. Condoleezza Rice of Stanford University, also African-American, became national security adviser. Other members of the

Chronology

2001	Bush administration repudiates Kyoto protocol; Congress passes $1.35 trillion tax cut bill; stock market falls; wave of corporate bankruptcies and scandals; Congress passes No Child Left Behind Act; terrorist attacks on World Trade Center, Pentagon (September 11); U.S. and allied forces overthrow Taliban regime in Afghanistan; captured Taliban fighters and others imprisoned at Guantánamo Bay, Cuba; USA-Patriot Act passed
2002	Bipartisan Campaign Reform Act (McCain-Feingold law); Department of Homeland Security created; Bush secretly authorizes National Security Administration to spy without warrants; Republicans gain in midterm elections
2003	U.S. and coalition forces invade Iraq (March 21); North Korea withdraws from Nuclear Non-Proliferation Treaty; prescription-drug benefits added to Medicare
2004	Revelation of abuses at Baghdad's Abu Ghraib prison; George W. Bush wins second term
2005	Congress passes Energy Act; trade deficit and budget deficit hit record levels; Bush names John Roberts and Samuel Alito to Supreme Court; Hurricane Katrina devastates New Orleans
2006	Tom Delay resigns House seat; Iran resumes nuclear enrichment program; GM and Ford announce major layoffs; Congress debates immigration-law changes; Democrats gain control of both houses in midterm elections
2007	Bush sends more troops to Iraq; violence declines; real estate market falls; recession begins
2008	United States and Iraq set timetable for U.S. troop withdrawals; recession deepens; major banks fail; job losses increase; Congress passes bank bailout legislation; Barack Obama is elected president; Democrats make gains; Gaza rockets hit Israel; Israel responds with major military attack causing heavy civilian casualties
2009	Obama reverses Bush administration on vehicle emissions, stem-cell research; Congress enacts broad economic stimulus package as recession worsens; unemployment spikes above 10 percent
2010	BP oil spill fouls Gulf of Mexico; Dodd-Frank Wall Street Reform and Consumer Protection Act passed; Tea Party movement builds; Patient Protection and Affordable Care Act passed; "Don't ask, don't tell" policy reversed; Republicans retake House of Representatives
2011	Democratic revolutions overturn dictatorships in Tunisia and Egypt; battle over collective bargaining rights of public sector unions erupts in Wisconsin; unemployment falls below 9 percent; Osama bin Laden killed by U.S. special forces in Pakistan

Bush administration, like Vice President **Richard (Dick) Cheney,** were veterans of earlier Republican administrations with corporate ties. Secretary of Defense **Donald Rumsfeld** had held the same post under President Ford and later headed a pharmaceutical company.

Richard (Dick) Cheney George W. Bush's neoconservative vice president; shaped energy policy and advocated for expanded executive powers

Donald Rumsfeld Secretary of Defense under Bush until 2006

Launching his administration, Bush proposed education reforms, tax cuts favoring the wealthy, an energy bill shaped by the energy industries, and initiatives welcomed by his conservative Christian base (as discussed later in this chapter). Apart from this, however, Bush seemed unfocused and attentive mainly to his core supporters. As the year wore on, his approval ratings fell. This situation changed dramatically on September 11, 2001, a day of horror that energized the administration and dominated Bush's remaining years in office. On that morning, three commercial airplanes hijacked by terrorists slammed into the Pentagon outside Washington, DC, and the twin towers of New York's World Trade Center. As Americans watched in horror, the blazing towers collapsed, carrying more than 2,800 men and women to their deaths.

Hubert Boesl/dpa/Corbis Wire/Corbis

A Day of Horror: September 11, 2001
Smoke billows from the World Trade Center's north tower moments after a commercial aircraft hijacked by terrorists crashed into it.

The Pentagon attack left 245 dead on the ground. A fourth plane crashed in Pennsylvania when heroic passengers overpowered the hijackers. Nearly 250 passengers and crew in the four planes also perished. When investigators identified the nineteen hijackers as Muslims from the Middle East, President Bush urged Americans to distinguish between a few terrorists and the world's 1.2 billion Muslims, including some 6 million in the United States.

As the nation mourned, political divisions faded. The World War II anthem "God Bless America" enjoyed renewed popularity. "United We Stand" proclaimed billboards and bumper stickers. The damaged New York Stock Exchange reopened after six days, but consumer confidence remained fragile. The airline and hospitality industries reeled as jittery travelers canceled trips. Anxiety increased in October, when letters containing deadly anthrax spores appeared in the offices of NBC News, two senators, and a tabloid newspaper. Five persons, including two postal workers, died from anthrax-tainted mail. In 2008, Dr. Bruce Ivins—a researcher at a U.S. Army biological defense research laboratory at Fort Detrick in Frederick, Maryland—committed suicide after the FBI identified him as the likely perpetrator.

Confronting al Qaeda in Afghanistan

President Bush declared the attacks an "act of war," and on September 14 the Senate unanimously authorized Bush to use "all necessary and appropriate force" to retaliate and to prevent future terrorist attacks. The president's approval ratings neared 90 percent. On September 20, before a joint session of Congress, Bush blamed

al Qaeda ("the base"), an organization headed by Osama bin Laden in Afghanistan. Bin Laden, already under indictment for the 1998 attack on U.S. embassies in Africa, had long denounced America for supporting Israel and for stationing "infidel" troops on Saudi soil.

al Qaeda Terrorist organization directed by Osama bin Laden

Bush also targeted the Taliban, a Pakistan-based Muslim fundamentalist movement that had controlled Afghanistan since 1996. This U.S. effort enjoyed NATO backing and broad international support, led by British prime minister Tony Blair. Pakistan's military government also endorsed Bush's decision to invade despite Taliban enclaves in Pakistan's border regions. On October 7, a U.S.-led coalition of forces launched the attack.

The Taliban soon surrendered Kabul, the Afghan capital; by mid-December, the U.S.-led coalition claimed victory. Hundreds of captured prisoners were sent to the U.S. base in **Guantánamo Bay,** Cuba. In June 2002, with U.S. support, Afghan tribal leaders selected Hamid Karzai as leader of an interim government. (Karzai would be elected president in 2004 and reelected in 2009.) However, Osama bin Laden, Taliban leader Mullah Omar, and many al Qaeda loyalists retreated to Afghanistan's mountainous border with Pakistan—prepared to fight on.

Guantánamo Bay Naval base in Cuba; site of a controversial prison holding hundreds of alleged terrorists

Tightening Home-Front Security

In late 2001, Congress created the Transportation Security Administration to oversee an expanded force of twenty-eight thousand airport security personnel. Over the protests of civil liberties advocates and some local officials, the Justice Department rounded up hundreds of Middle Easterners in the United States, some for minor visa violations, and held them without filing charges or even revealing their names.

The **USA-Patriot Act,** the administration's sweeping antiterrorist bill passed by Congress in October 2001, granted the government authority to monitor telephone and e-mail communications. Civil libertarians and others protested this expansion of federal power. (Congress renewed the Patriot Act in 2005, with some added civil liberties safeguards.)

USA-Patriot Act Antiterrorism bill passed after the 9/11 attacks expanding government's powers of investigation and surveillance

Further questions arose as the media reported missed clues before the 9/11 attack. Through the summer of 2001, President Bush's daily security briefings included warnings of an al Qaeda plot to hijack a U.S. airliner. In August 2001, the FBI bungled a Minnesota flight school's warning that a suspicious person named Zacarias Moussaoui wanted to enroll. (Later linked to the 9/11 plot, Moussaoui was arrested, tried, and sentenced to life imprisonment.)

In November 2002, Congress created a new cabinet-level agency, the **Department of Homeland Security,** which absorbed the Federal Emergency Management Agency (FEMA), the Immigration and Naturalization Service, and other agencies. The FBI and the CIA remained independent. However, skeptics questioned whether such a bureaucratic reshuffling actually increased security.

Department of Homeland Security New cabinet-level agency created after 9/11 that was charged with domestic security responsibilities

In 2003, Bush named a bipartisan commission to examine pre-9/11 intelligence failures. Its report pinpointed communication lapses between the FBI and the CIA and urged a restructuring of U.S. intelligence operations. In 2005, Bush appointed a director of national intelligence to coordinate the government's fifteen different intelligence agencies. Nevertheless, when the commission's cochair was asked about homeland security in 2006, he replied: "A lot of the things we need to do . . . to prevent another 9/11 just simply aren't being done." Critics noted, for example, that most incoming shipping containers went unchecked.

War in Iraq, 2003–2004

Although Afghanistan remained unstable and Osama bin Laden uncaptured, the administration's attention shifted elsewhere. In his January 2002 State of the Union address, President Bush identified Iran, Iraq, and North Korea as an "axis of evil." He especially targeted Iraq's ruler, Saddam Hussein, weakened but still in power following the 1991 Persian Gulf War. In a barrage of coordinated speeches and interviews, Cheney, Rumsfeld, Rice, and other officials accused Saddam of complicity in the 9/11 attacks and of developing nuclear, chemical, and biological weapons. The Bush administration clearly believed an invasion of Iraq was necessary and justified.

neoconservatives Political school of thought, ascendant in the Bush administration, espousing enlarged executive powers and a unilateral approach to foreign policy

This focus on Iraq was orchestrated by a close-knit group of Republican **neoconservatives,** including Cheney, Rumsfeld, and their key aides. Throughout the Cold War, some hardliners rejected George Kennan's containment doctrine, advocating instead a policy of overwhelming U.S. military superiority and aggressive challenges to Soviet power. With the Soviet Union's collapse, neoconservatives shifted focus but continued to advocate the aggressive projection of U.S. power worldwide. Any actual or potential threat to America's global interests, they insisted,

Map 31.1 Iraq
With Saddam Hussein's overthrow by U.S.-led forces in 2003, violence erupted among Iraq's ethnic and religious groups, including the majority of Shia Muslims concentrated in the southeast and the minority Sunni Muslims, who ruled the country under Saddam.

Interactive Map

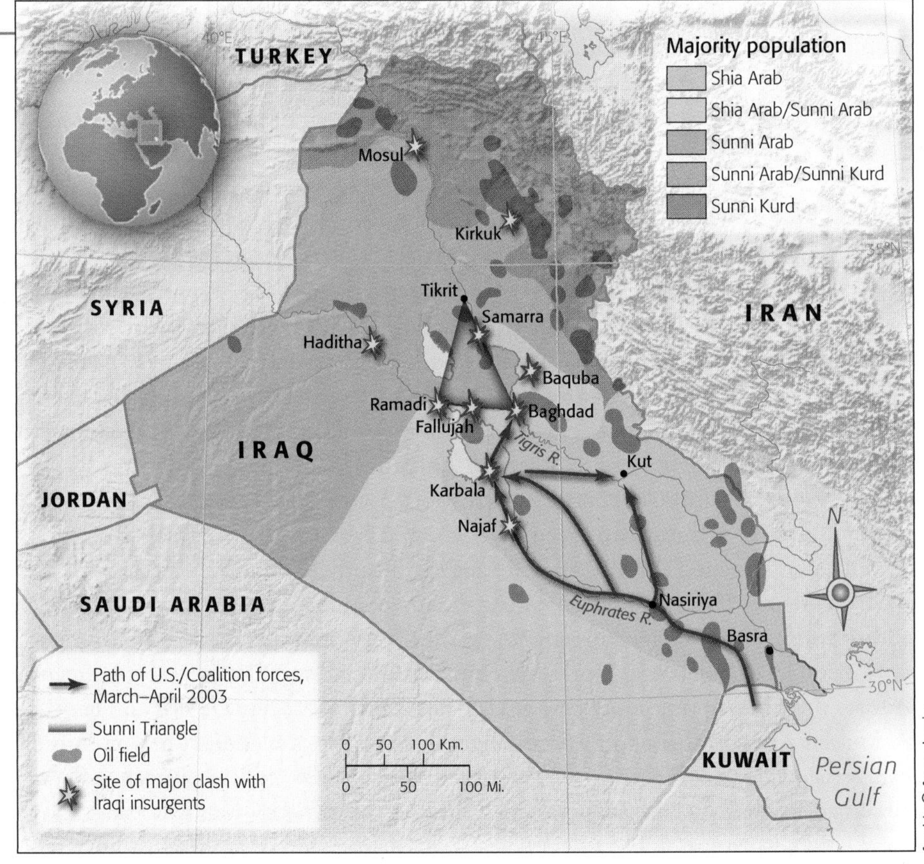

must be resisted by all available means, including preemptive military action. They felt America must primarily act alone in defense of its interests.

These neoconservatives had little patience with the "soft diplomacy" of winning hearts and minds, courting world opinion, or spreading U.S. values of democracy and freedom by example rather than by force. The point was not to negotiate with adversaries, but to defeat them. Neoconservatives attacked President Carter and President Clinton as overly preoccupied with world opinion and too reluctant to use U.S. military power. But they also criticized Republicans like the first President Bush for failing to overthrow Saddam Hussein in the Persian Gulf War. In the Middle East, neoconservatives focused on defending Israel, assuring the flow of oil to meet U.S. energy needs, and promoting democracy. Ending Saddam Hussein's dictatorship, they believed, was crucial to advancing U.S. interests in the region.

George W. Bush's election gave neoconservatives the opportunity to put their ideology into practice. The administration's foreign policy approach came to be called the "Bush Doctrine," which clothed neoconservatism in an aura of religious certitude. "The liberty we prize," Bush said in his 2003 State of the Union address, "is not America's gift to the world, it is God's gift to humanity." Defense Secretary Rumsfeld adorned Iraq combat reports he prepared for Bush with biblical passages proclaiming the triumph of righteousness.

Although a majority of Americans initially supported military intervention in Iraq, the action proved controversial from the outset. Critics challenged the administration to prove its claims. A preemptive war would violate U.S. principles, they charged, and could drag on for years and outrage the Muslim world. Great Britain's Tony Blair backed the administration, but other NATO allies, along with most Arab leaders, objected.

Nevertheless, in October 2002 Congress authorized President Bush to "defend the national security . . . against the continuing threat posed by Iraq." While Republicans supported the resolution, Democrats were divided, with some fearful of opposing a resolution Bush called vital to American security. President Bush would later use this resolution as the legal basis for invading Iraq.

Bolstered by the 2002 midterm elections, in which Republicans regained control of the Senate and increased their House majority, the administration pushed its Iraq invasion plans. On March 19, 2003, U.S. cruise missiles hit Baghdad. Two days later, U.S. and British troops invaded southern Iraq, securing the region's oil fields and moving north (see Map 31.1). Despite unexpected guerrilla resistance, in early April U.S. troops occupied Baghdad and toppled a large statue of Saddam. As the regime fell and Saddam fled, basic municipal services collapsed and widespread looting erupted.

On May 1, aboard the aircraft carrier *Abraham Lincoln* off San Diego, a banner behind President Bush proclaimed "Mission Accomplished." Bush named Paul Bremer, a Foreign Service officer, to administer affairs in Iraq. In December, Saddam was captured; after two trials before Iraqi judges, Saddam was convicted of human-rights abuses in genocidal attacks on Iraq's Kurdish and Shi'ite populations. He was hanged in December 2006.

Checking In

- The September 11, 2001, terrorist attacks were comparable to Pearl Harbor in their effect on Americans; a wave of patriotism swept the country.
- Bush proclaimed war on terrorism; a U.S.-led coalition invaded Afghanistan, routing the pro–al Qaeda Taliban government.
- The administration created a new, cabinet-level Department of Homeland Security, and Congress passed the USA-Patriot Act despite serious concerns about civil liberties.
- In 2002, reflecting the influence of neoconservatives, Bush and his advisers made the case for preemptive war against Iraq; Congress passed a resolution authorizing the use of force.
- The U.S. military operation that toppled Saddam's regime began in March 2003 and was over by April; however, administrative missteps and other factors sparked a violent insurgency that by 2004 threatened all U.S. goals in Iraq.

But conditions in Iraq deteriorated. Iraq's Sunni Muslims, though a minority, had long dominated Iraqi politics and resented Bremer's decision to disband the Iraqi army and dismiss all government officials who had served under Saddam. The resulting power vacuum sparked sectarian violence. Conditions worsened through 2004 as bombings, kidnappings, and deadly highway blasts caused by improvised explosive devices (IEDs) occurred daily. In June, Bremer transferred power to a provisional Iraqi government, but little changed. In September, the toll of U.S. dead in Iraq passed one thousand. Vice President Cheney had predicted that the Iraqis would welcome the Americans as liberators. Now reality blasted such wishful thinking.

Politics and the Economy as a New Century Begins

Beyond security concerns, what economic and social issues did Bush address in his first term?

While pursuing the post–9/11 "war on terror," the early Bush administration also proposed tax cuts and other domestic legislation reflecting its conservative ideology. However, debate over these measures unfolded amid a recession and a cascade of bankruptcies and corporate scandals.

Economic Reverses and Corporate Scandals

George W. Bush's presidency began with a short but sharp recession, led by the high-flying Silicon Valley information technology (IT) companies. An estimated 250 such businesses collapsed in a few months. As the market value of the surviving companies plummeted, instant millionaires watched their portfolios shrivel.

The recession soon spread. The stock market fell by 24 percent. Industrial production dropped; unemployment rose. By mid-2003, 2.6 million workers had lost their jobs. The Bush administration, having inherited a budget surplus, now projected years of deficits. A wave of corporate bankruptcies and scandals in the energy and telecommunications fields further eroded investor confidence. Houston's Enron Corporation, an energy company with close ties to the Bush administration, was an early casualty. In 2000, Enron ranked seventh among America's corporations. The end came with brutal swiftness in 2001 when Enron filed for bankruptcy and admitted to falsifying profit reports. More than five thousand jobless Enron workers also lost their retirement funds, consisting mostly of Enron stock. In 2006, a Houston jury convicted Enron founder Kenneth Lay and the company's CEO Jeffrey Skilling on multiple counts of fraud and conspiracy. The company's logo—a crooked "E"—seemed appropriate.

The parade continued. In 2002 WorldCom, America's second-largest telecommunications company, filed for bankruptcy after admitting that it had overstated profits by billions. CEO Bernard Ebbers, convicted of securities fraud in 2005, received a twenty-five-year prison sentence. Dennis Kozlowski, the CEO of Tyco, an industrial products and service company, was indicted for looting the company of

$600 million, including $2 million for his wife's birthday party on a Mediterranean island. Along with a prison sentence, Kozlowski was fined $70 million and ordered to repay Tyco $134 million. Declared a Wall Street investment banker: "I cannot think of a time when business . . . has been held in less repute." Responding to public anger, Congress in July 2002 imposed stricter financial reporting rules on corporations and toughened criminal penalties for business fraud.

Recovery began in 2003, stimulated by heavy consumer spending (much of it on credit) and a booming housing market. But prosperity was spotty. While the average real income of the nation's richest 1 percent increased by more than 12 percent in 2004, that of the remaining 99 percent grew by only 1.5 percent. Real wages remained flat and job creation weak. Observed economist Paul Krugman: "It's a great economy if you're a high-level corporate executive or someone who owns a lot of stock. For most other Americans, economic growth is a spectator sport." By mid-2006, even this uneven recovery faltered, and the jittery stock market again sank. The worst recession since the 1930s lay ahead.

The Republican Domestic Agenda

In February 2001, President Bush proposed $1.6 trillion in income-tax cuts over a ten-year period. Though the measure reduced all rates, wealthy taxpayers received the highest percentage reduction. Bush argued that the cuts would stimulate investment. However, Democrats attacked the bill for favoring the rich, and warned that such deep cuts would produce even larger federal deficits. In May, Congress passed a $1.35 trillion tax cut that was somewhat less slanted toward the rich. Mounting budget deficits predictably followed, erasing the surplus Clinton had achieved. Nevertheless, the Republican-led Congress cut taxes further in 2003 and 2005.

The administration's 2001 energy bill proposed incentives to expand coal, oil, and natural-gas production and called for drilling in Alaska's **Arctic National Wildlife Refuge (ANWR).** President Bush defended the bill as a way to reduce U.S. dependence on foreign oil. The energy bill finally passed by Congress in August 2005 rejected the provision for drilling in ANWR. It did, however, exempt energy companies from some environmental regulations and grant $14.5 billion in tax breaks to oil, natural gas, coal, and nuclear-power companies. It did not tighten vehicle fuel-efficiency requirements. Overall, the law pleased the energy companies that helped draft it.

Arctic National Wildlife Refuge (ANWR) Vast wildlife area in Alaska in which President Bush called for oil exploration

Bush's education program, labeled **"No Child Left Behind,"** was passed by Congress in 2001 with bipartisan support. It required states to administer standardized reading and math tests in grades four and eight. If test scores still failed to improve, schools faced the loss of federal funds as well as other penalties. Critics worried that teachers would focus too exclusively on the tested subjects. Others warned of federal intrusion in public education, which was traditionally a local matter. As test data accumulated, results proved mixed.

"No Child Left Behind" Label for Bush law mandating standardized testing in reading and math in grades four and eight

Reflecting Republicans' preference for private-sector solutions to social problems, the administration also supported school vouchers, by which children in poorly performing public schools could receive grants to enroll in private, mostly church-sponsored schools. However, teachers' unions criticized vouchers for draining tax dollars from the public schools. Congressional Democrats rejected Bush's call for a federally funded voucher program. Education reformers also supported charter schools, which gain exemption from many regulations governing traditional public schools in exchange for agreeing to contracts mandating specific student achievement goals. By 2009, charter schools across the nation enrolled more than a million students.

Rewarding his conservative religious supporters, Bush created an Office of Faith-Based and Community Initiatives to funnel tax dollars to church-run social programs. Grants went to anti-abortion groups, organizations promoting teenage sexual abstinence, and evangelical prison ministries. A charity operated by televangelist Pat Robertson received $22 million.

President Bush also pleased abortion opponents by restricting stem-cell research. Stem cells are produced during an early stage of human embryo development, and fertility clinics often have "surplus" fertilized embryos. Although stem cells are valuable for medical research, some anti-abortion groups oppose research using fertilized embryos. In 2001, Bush barred federal funding for future research involving stem cells harvested from human embryos.

Committed to a free-market ideology, Bush's appointees throughout the federal bureaucracy reduced regulatory oversight of business and finance and weakened environmental and consumer protection laws.

Campaign Finance Reform and the Election of 2004

Reformers who deplored the role of money in politics targeted so-called soft-money contributions to political parties that then flowed on to specific candidates. In the 2000 election, soft-money contributions reached $400 million. Big contributors ranged from (mostly Republican) business lobbies, anti-abortion groups, and the National Rifle Association to (mostly Democratic) labor unions, trial lawyers, and teachers' unions.

In 2002, President Bush signed a reform bill co-sponsored by Arizona Republican John McCain and Wisconsin Democrat Russell Feingold. It banned soft-money contributions, barred fake TV "issue ads" designed to influence elections, and included other provisions to reduce the power of money in politics. As big contributors sought ways around the law, its impact remained uncertain. In 2007, the Supreme Court, on First Amendment free speech grounds, restricted the law's ban on pre-election "issue ads." Three years later, in *Citizens United v. Federal Election Commission,* the Supreme Court struck down yet another component of the McCain-Feingold law when it ruled that corporate funding of political broadcasts cannot be limited.

As the 2004 election approached, Howard Dean, a former Vermont governor, emerged as the early frontrunner for the Democratic presidential nomination. But while Dean's candor and antiwar position energized the Democratic base, it also alienated many voters. In the campaign's first test, the Iowa primary, he came in a disappointing third. His candidacy quickly faded. Nevertheless, Dean tapped into growing opposition to the Iraq War and demonstrated the Internet's political fundraising potential.

John Kerry Senator from Massachusetts and Vietnam War veteran; Democratic nominee for president in 2004

Senator **John Kerry** of Massachusetts, a decorated Vietnam War veteran, won the nomination. Democratic strategists hoped Kerry's distinguished Vietnam War record would neutralize charges of Democratic weakness on defense. Bush and

Cheney, raising some $150 million from corporations and wealthy individual donors, again headed the Republican ticket. Although Kerry had voted for the Patriot Act and initially supported the Iraq War, he now accused Bush of misleading the nation and criticized parts of the Patriot Act as threats to civil liberties. President Bush defended both the Iraq War and the Patriot Act. Citing Kerry's changing positions, Republicans accused him of "flip-flopping" and indecisiveness. Anti-Kerry TV commercials, funded by a shadowy group called Swift Boat Veterans for Truth, questioned his Vietnam record.

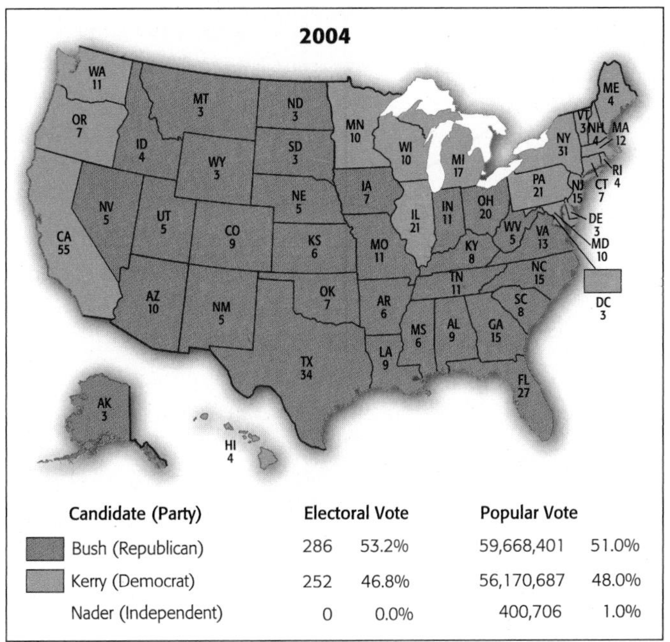

Candidate (Party)	Electoral Vote		Popular Vote	
Bush (Republican)	286	53.2%	59,668,401	51.0%
Kerry (Democrat)	252	46.8%	56,170,687	48.0%
Nader (Independent)	0	0.0%	400,706	1.0%

Map 31.2 The Election of 2004

Interactive Map

The candidates' differences on abortion, the death penalty, gun control, and other issues reflected national divisions. Notably, the issue of same-sex marriage loomed large. In 2004, San Francisco's mayor challenged California law by marrying same-sex couples, and the Massachusetts Supreme Court ruled that banning same-sex marriage violated the state constitution's equal rights clause. The issue energized religious conservatives, who applauded Bush's call for a constitutional amendment banning gay marriage. Antigay marriage referenda passed in all eleven states where the issue was on the ballot. Bush carried nine of the eleven, including Ohio, a key swing state that determined the election's outcome.

Bush won a second term, garnering 50.7 percent of the popular vote (see Map 31.2). Republicans gained a net of four Senate seats and four House seats. Bush, a tax-cutting president seen as a leader in the "war on terror" and a defender of embattled conservative cultural values, had eked out a razor-thin victory. Democrats, however, took heart from the fact that Kerry won 55 percent of voters under thirty, a growing cohort. In Illinois, a charismatic young African-American Democratic state legislator, Barack Obama, won election to the U.S. Senate.

The election highlighted the Internet's political role. During the campaign and after, MoveOn.org raised funds and mobilized e-mails and telephone calls on behalf of liberal candidates and causes. While conservative organizations had long built support through magazines, direct mail, and talk radio, liberals appeared to have the edge in Internet-based activism, especially among young people.

Conservative political groups and those on the religious right, some dating to the 1970s, remained active. But so did progressive organizations such as People for the American Way, Planned Parenthood, the Sierra Club, and Emily's List (which supported women candidates who endorsed liberal and feminist goals). Even among evangelical Christians, support for Bush was not unanimous. Jim Wallis of the evangelical Sojourners movement espoused social justice and the search for peace in his books and *Sojourners* magazine.

Checking In

- The September 11 attacks and the bursting of the technology-stock bubble brought the free-wheeling prosperity of the 1990s to an end.
- A spate of corporate scandals, some involving jail terms for disgraced CEOs of major companies, undermined confidence in corporate America.
- Bush and congressional Republicans passed huge tax cuts, an education bill mandating standardized testing, and an energy bill that favored oil companies.
- Cultural and religious concerns drove Republican opposition to stem-cell research and same-sex marriage.
- Stressing national security and moral issues, Bush defeated Kerry in the 2004 elections.

Debating Iraq and Confronting Other Global Challenges

What challenges faced the United States in the Middle East and elsewhere in the world after 2000?

As the Iraq conflict dragged on, home-front support eroded. Revelations of prisoner abuse, illegal spying on U.S. citizens, and serious distortions in the administration's case for invading Iraq sapped Bush's standing at home and abroad. The Israeli-Palestinian struggle, nuclear proliferation threats, and concern about global warming posed further challenges.

The Continuing Struggle in Iraq

In his second inaugural address in January 2005, Bush described the Iraq War as part of a noble campaign to "[end] tyranny in our world." In Iraq, however, conditions worsened. Sunni insurgents in Baghdad and in Sunni strongholds north of the capital battled to prevent a Shi'ite-dominated government. A November 2004 anti-insurgent operation in Fallujah involved approximately ten thousand U.S. and Iraqi forces. Typically, however, the insurgents returned after the troops withdrew. Followers of the radical Shi'ite cleric Moqtada al-Sadr attacked Sunnis, GIs,

AP Photo/David Guttenfelder

Chaos in Iraq: Aftermath of the Destruction of the Imam Ali Mosque in Najaf, August 29, 2003
As Shi'ite Muslims crowded the mosque for Friday prayers, a car bomb killed at least 125 people, including a top Shi'ite religious leader, and destroyed one of Shia Islam's holiest shrines.

journalists, and foreign contractors alike. Muslim militants from elsewhere, attracted by the U.S. presence and calling themselves al Qaeda in Mesopotamia (the region's ancient name), added to the unrest.

Despite billions in U.S. funds, reconstruction lagged, and basic municipal services remained unpredictable. A subsidiary of the Halliburton Company, once headed by Vice President Cheney, with $3.6 billion in no-bid reconstruction contracts, faced accusations of fraud. Oil exports, vital to Iraq's economy, remained below prewar levels.

Political progress proved equally difficult. Sunnis boycotted a January 2005 election, resulting in a Shi'ite-dominated National Assembly. The prime minister came from a religious party with links to Moqtada al-Sadr. Sunnis accused Shi'ite militias and Interior Ministry "death squads" of kidnapping and killing Sunni leaders and detonating car bombs in Sunni neighborhoods. In February 2006, suicide bombers destroyed the revered Golden Dome Shi'ite mosque in Samarrah, dating to 944 C.E., triggering anti-Sunni reprisal attacks. (The Kurds in northern Iraq, hoping for an independent Kurdish state, remained aloof from the Sunni-Shi'ite sectarian violence.)

As thousands of refugees fled Iraq or sheltered in makeshift camps, an Iraqi leader lamented: "If this is not civil war, then God knows what civil war is." In April 2006, a new Shi'ite prime minister, Nouri al-Maliki, urged "national reconciliation," but the chaos continued. As other coalition forces withdrew, the United States bore the brunt of anti-insurgency fighting.

Sagging Support at Home

Under these circumstances, American public opinion turned decisively against the war. In November 2005, Pennsylvania Democratic congressman Jack Murtha urged immediate withdrawal from Iraq. A decorated Vietnam War veteran, Murtha initially supported the war but now labeled it "a flawed policy, wrapped in an illusion." Even conservative writer William Buckley bluntly declared: "[T]he American objective in Iraq has failed."

The popular culture mirrored the nation's divisions. Michael Moore's anti-Bush satirical documentary *Fahrenheit 9/11* packed movie theaters in 2004. Singers including Bruce Springsteen, Neil Young, Ani DiFranco, and the Dixie Chicks expressed opposition to the administration's policies. Despite these protests, conservative media voices such as radio personality Rush Limbaugh, as well as Bill O'Reilly and other commentators on Rupert Murdoch's Fox News TV channel, supported the president. Bush supporters also posted Internet lists urging boycotts of scores of Hollywood stars who vocally opposed Bush and the Iraq War. In an already polarized climate, Bush's foreign and domestic policies further divided America.

Under critical scrutiny, the administration's arguments for invading Iraq—Saddam Hussein's alleged WMD program and his connections to the 9/11 attacks—crumbled. After the invasion, investigators found no WMDs. A Senate inquiry found that Vice President Cheney and other administration officials pressured the CIA to focus on intelligence supporting their case while ignoring contradictory data. Furthermore, Defense Secretary Rumsfeld's prewar assurances that a small U.S. force equipped with high-tech weaponry would achieve quick victory proved tragically wrong.

Shocking evidence of prisoner mistreatment deepened home-front uneasiness. In 2004, photographs surfaced showing the abuse and sexual humiliation of Iraqis held by U.S. forces at Baghdad's Abu Ghraib prison. Further evidence soon revealed a broader pattern of prisoner abuse, including at Guantánamo, where more than five hundred prisoners from Afghanistan were held without trial. Critics denounced as torture the interrogation techniques used at Guantánamo, including "water boarding," in which the victim is nearly drowned. Evidence also surfaced that the CIA had secretly flown some detainees to an uncertain fate in Egyptian and Eastern European prisons. In a secret 2002 memo, Justice Department lawyer John Yoo argued that the Geneva Conventions protecting prisoners of war did not apply to persons the president designated as "enemy combatants."

In 2005, Congress passed legislation proposed by Senator John McCain forbidding "cruel, inhuman, and degrading" treatment of prisoners. McCain himself had been tortured as a POW in Vietnam. Bush signed the bill, but issued a "signing statement" asserting, in effect, that he was not bound to obey it. This was one of many such pronouncements by which the president "interpreted" bills he was signing, even though the Constitution gave the president no authority to interpret laws as he chose.

Americans also learned in 2005 that President Bush in 2002 had secretly authorized the National Security Agency (NSA), a government body created in 1952, to tap U.S. citizens' overseas phone calls and e-mails without securing a warrant as required by law. Evidence also surfaced that the NSA, in addition to tapping foreign phone calls and e-mails, had tapped domestic ones as well and that the FBI had targeted peace groups and journalists for surveillance. These invasions of privacy disturbed not only the American Civil Liberties Union, but many ordinary citizens as well. For example, the American Library Association protested legislation permitting investigators to access library patrons' records of book borrowing and Internet use.

In *Hamdi* v. *Rumsfeld* (2004), the Supreme Court addressed the Bush administration's claim that "enemy combatants" could be held indefinitely. Eight of the justices agreed that such practices violated a prisoner's Fifth Amendment right to due process. In response to criticism, the Bush administration set up special military tribunals, not bound by the customary rules of courtroom procedure, to try the Guantánamo prisoners. In 2006, the Supreme Court rejected this approach, however, ruling that such tribunals violated both the Constitution and the Geneva Conventions.

In March 2006, *Time* magazine reported that, in November 2005, U.S. marines killed twenty-four unarmed Iraqi men, women, and children after a roadside IED killed one of their unit. As this and other atrocities came to light, memories of the Vietnam-era massacre at My Lai stirred uneasily. Amid a cascade of disturbing news, the reputation not only of the Bush administration but of America itself suffered.

The Bush Administration and the Israeli-Palestinian Conflict

Central to U.S.-Muslim relations was America's support for Israel and Washington's response to Jewish settlements in the West Bank and Gaza. This issue also complicated America's relations with its European allies, many of which supported the Palestinian cause. On this issue, the Bush administration accomplished little. As the Palestinian intifada (uprising) continued, Israeli prime minister Ariel Sharon demanded an end to the violence before resuming talks, while Palestinian leader Yasir Arafat insisted that protests would continue so long as Israel fostered Jewish settlements in Palestinian territory. In 2002, Israel began a security barrier, partially extending into the West Bank, to control access and prevent suicide attacks.

The Bush administration proposed a so-called "road map to peace" in 2003, but it did not push the initiative, and little changed. In 2005, Israel withdrew Jewish settlements from Gaza, but in January 2006 Palestinian elections gave victory to the radical Hamas organization, which condoned attacks on Israel and even denied Israel's right to exist.

Meanwhile, Hezbollah, a militant Lebanon-based Shi'ite organization supported by Iran and Syria, killed or kidnapped several Israeli soldiers and lobbed rockets into northern Israel. In retaliation, Israel invaded Lebanon in July 2006 and bombed not only Hezbollah bases but also bridges, highways, and Beirut's airport, causing heavy casualties and property damage. The Israelis soon withdrew, however, leaving Hezbollah intact and claiming victory. As Hamas militants in Gaza fired rockets into border towns, Israel in December 2008 launched a full-scale air and ground assault on Gaza. Over thirteen hundred Gazans died. The Israelis withdrew after three weeks, leaving Hamas in power and the underlying conflict no nearer to solution.

In eight years, the Bush administration did little to push the negotiations that offered the only prospect of resolving a contentious struggle that jeopardized Israel's security, damaged U.S. interests in the region and beyond, and left the Palestinians demoralized and impoverished.

America Confronts Growing Nuclear Threats

The danger of nuclear proliferation, a grave world threat, worsened in these years. Impoverished and isolated North Korea, ruled by an eccentric dictator, Kim Jong Il, withdrew from the Nuclear Non-Proliferation Treaty and in 2006 tested both a long-range missile and a nuclear weapon. Stop-and-start negotiations appeared to make some progress, but North Korea exploded an even more powerful bomb in May 2009 and fired more missiles, stirring alarmed protests from many nations, including the United States.

Iran, meanwhile, pursued a uranium-enrichment program, allegedly for nuclear-power development. Under UN pressure, Iran suspended this program in 2004 but resumed it in 2006 after the election of Mahmoud Ahmadinejad (AH-mu-din-a-JOD) as president. An Islamic fundamentalist, Ahmadinejad taunted America, called the Holocaust a myth, and denied Israel's right to exist. An Iranian long-range missile test in May 2009 deepened uneasiness about its intentions.

Citing these threats, the Bush administration spent billions on a ground-based version of President Reagan's missile-defense system (see Chapter 30). Although this program violated the 1972 Anti-Ballistic Missile (ABM) Treaty, in 2002 the United States and Russia allowed the ABM treaty to lapse. However, Russian president Vladimir Putin vigorously opposed the administration's plans to build radar facilities in Poland and the Czech Republic as part of its missile-defense program.

In 2006, President Bush agreed to provide fuel and parts for India's nuclear-power reactors even though India refused to sign the Nuclear Non-Proliferation Treaty and barred UN inspectors from its nuclear weapons facilities. Critics warned that this would encourage other nations to pursue nuclear weapons programs. Meanwhile, political instability in Pakistan, a nuclear power, intensified fears of deepening nuclear dangers stalking the world.

A Widening Trade Gap and China's Rising Economic Power

The 2007 U.S. trade deficit approached $800 billion. This massive imbalance mainly reflected imports of oil, automobiles (mostly Japanese), and consumer goods from China. The 2007 trade deficit with China alone surged to $256 billion.

U.S. manufacturers complained that China artificially manipulated its currency, the yuan, to make Chinese exports cheaper. However, big-box discounters welcomed low-priced Chinese imports. When U.S. textile manufacturers pressured President Bush to impose quotas on clothing imported from China, Wal-Mart and other discount chains fought the effort.

China's 2007 gross domestic product (GDP) of $7 trillion ranked second in the world, after the United States. Some economists predicted that China's GDP would surpass America's in twenty years. For China to sustain its growth and provide a higher living standard for its people, the U.S. market was crucial. Critics targeted China's repressive regime, poor quality control on export goods, and massive greenhouse gas emissions. (As host of the 2008 Olympic Games, China did reduce Beijing's notorious air pollution, at least temporarily.)

Environmental Hazards Become a Global Concern

Three Mile Island, Love Canal, and the Exxon Valdez disaster (see Chapters 29 and 30) underscored modern technology's environmental risks. Acid rain carrying pollutants from U.S. factories and vehicle emissions damaged Appalachian forests and Canadian lakes. As fluorocarbons from aerosol cans, air conditioners, and other sources depleted the atmosphere's protective ozone layer, increased solar radiation posed skin cancer risks. A 1986 nuclear-power plant explosion at Chernobyl in the Ukraine and the near-meltdown of the Fukushima nuclear-power facility in Japan (caused by a devastating tsunami) in 2011 highlighted the global scope of these risks.

Environmental hazards included the problem of radioactive waste disposal. In 2002, President Bush designated Nevada's Yucca Mountain as the storage site for nuclear wastes that will remain deadly for thousands of years. But as Nevada politicians protested and scientists warned of seismic activity and water seepage in the area, the project stalled. Meanwhile, dangerous byproducts of aging nuclear-power plants accumulated in temporary sites across the nation.

global warming Worldwide surge in average temperatures most scientists attributed to greenhouse-gas emissions

Above all, **global warming** loomed as a grave threat. The United States, with less than 5 percent of the world's population, accounted for 25 percent of global energy consumption, primarily from fossil fuels widely viewed as contributing to global warming. A 2005 EPA study found significant increases in average U.S. motor vehicles' emissions since 1980. Despite mounting evidence, however, the Bush administration downplayed the environmental impact of fossil fuel consumption. The administration rejected calls for stricter emissions standards, weakened enforcement of existing regulations, and marginalized government scientists who questioned its policies.

A 1997 UN conference on global warming held in Kyoto, Japan, set strict emission targets for industrialized nations. President Clinton signed the **Kyoto Accords** but did not submit the document for Senate ratification, fearing defeat. President Bush repudiated the agreement entirely, on the grounds that it would hurt the U.S. economy. Another conference in Copenhagen in 2009, under the administration of President Barack Obama, also failed to produce a binding worldwide agreement. A 2009 House bill to cap carbon emissions and set up a system to let private industry buy and sell carbon credits ("cap and trade") failed in the Senate. In April 2010, the Deepwater Horizon, a huge oil rig leased to BP, exploded and burned, killing eleven workers and fouling the Gulf of Mexico with over 200 million gallons of oil. It was the most devastating oil spill in American history. But even this disaster had no apparent effect on U.S. energy policy or usage, which continued to depend heavily on fossil fuels.

Hollywood filmmakers both reflected and contributed to global-warming fears. In *The Day After Tomorrow* (2004), a scientist (Dennis Quaid) tries desperately to warn the world of impending disaster and to save his son as the Atlantic engulfs New York City. Al Gore's Academy-Award-winning film *An Inconvenient Truth* (2006) further documented the dangers of global warning. (In 2007, Gore, along with a panel of UN climate scientists, received the Nobel Peace Prize for promoting awareness of global warming.) While such popular culture productions heightened public awareness of global warming, critics charged that they exploited the issue while wildly distorting the actual risks.

Kyoto Accords Agreement reached by most industrial nations, with the exception of the United States and several others, to reduce carbon emissions

CHECKING IN

- Violence in Iraq increased between 2004 and 2006 into a melee of violence, slowing political and economic progress.
- The "surge" of troops in 2007 improved security conditions somewhat, but American opinion had turned against the war, and Bush's approval ratings plummeted.
- The abuse of prisoners and denial of basic rights to "enemy combatants" prompted mounting criticism, as did revelations about a warrantless domestic spying program.
- Israel-Palestinian relations remained tense; in 2006, Israel invaded Lebanon in an effort to root out Hezbollah.
- Nuclear proliferation became a focus of the administration's attention, while the trade deficit with China widened and global warming concerns intensified.

SOCIAL AND ECONOMIC TRENDS IN CONTEMPORARY AMERICA

What demographic and economic trends have most shaped contemporary America?

As a new century began, long-term population shifts to the South and West as well as continued immigration from Asia and Latin America, in addition to other developments, brought significant changes to U.S. society. Profound economic changes benefited some but disadvantaged others, including inner-city residents and displaced industrial workers, widening the economic gap between those at the top and the rest of society.

An Increasingly Diverse People

Americans have long been a people on the move, and this mobility continues. Between 1990 and 2010, the West's population increased by 19.1 million. The South expanded

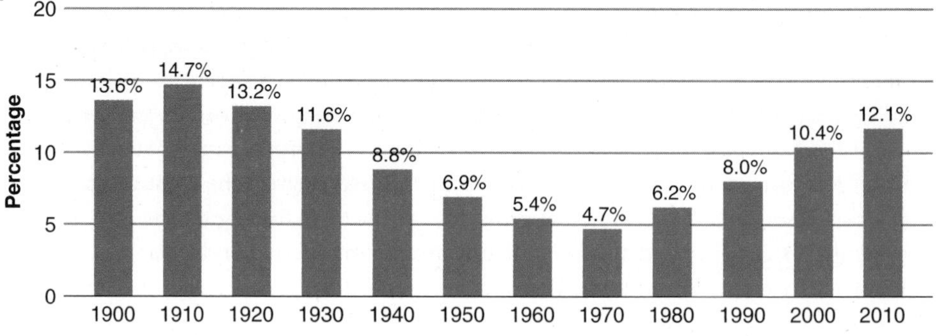

Figure 31.1 Foreign-Born as a Percentage of U.S. Population, 1900–2010

After gradually declining from a peak of nearly 15 percent in 1910 to under 5 percent in 1970, the proportion of the U.S. population that is foreign-born again began to rise.

Source: Bureau of Census, U.S. Dept. of Commerce.

by more than 29 million in the same period. Across the Midwest and Great Plains, by contrast, populations remained stable. In contrast, the population of Michigan actually declined between 2000 and 2010.

Household arrangements changed as well. The proportion of "traditional" families headed by a married heterosexual couple fell from 74 percent in 1960 to under 50 percent by 2007.

Heavy immigration from Asia and Latin America reversed a long decline in the proportion of foreign-born persons in the population. From a low of about 5 percent in 1970, this figure was about 12 percent in 2010 (see Figure 31.1). The 2010 U.S. population of more than 308 million was about 16 percent Hispanic, 12 percent black, 5 percent Asian, and 1 percent American Indian. The nation's Hispanics—nearly 60 percent of Mexican origin, with Puerto Ricans, Cubans, and Salvadorans comprising most of the balance—are predicted to make up 25 percent of the population by 2050. Some 6 million Muslims, mainly from the Middle East and North Africa, add to the ethno-religious mix.

These demographic changes offer more than an interesting snapshot of contemporary American society. They have far-reaching political, economic, and cultural implications and offer a preview of a dynamic future nation very different from that of yesterday or today.

Upward Mobility and Social Problems in a Multiethnic Society

African-American median household income in 2007 approached $35,000. Although below the national median of around $50,700, this represented a substantial gain, in constant dollars, since 1990. College-educated blacks enjoyed significantly higher earnings, and 57 percent of black high school graduates in 2005 went on to college. TV's long-running *The Cosby Show* (1984–1992), starring Bill Cosby as an obstetrician and his wife (Phylicia Rashad) as an attorney, offered a fictional version of this upwardly mobile group of African-Americans.

But many inner-city blacks confronted a different reality, including bleak job prospects, poor schools, and drug-related crime. The black unemployment rate of nearly 15 percent in early 2011 (already well above the national rate) was far higher among high school dropouts and youths lacking a college education. Prison statistics for ill-educated young black males, often involving drug-related offenses, were similarly bleak.

Inner-city black women faced the risks of drug use, HIV/AIDS infection, and out-of-wedlock pregnancy. In 2006, more than 70 percent of black births were to unmarried women, almost twice the percentage in 1970. Many of these unmarried mothers were teenagers, reducing their prospects for education and employment. (Out-of-wedlock births to white women also rose, but at a far lower rate.)

Among Native Americans, renewed tribal pride and activism continued, including federal lawsuits to enforce long-ignored Indian treaties. Tribal gambling casinos, approved by Congress in 1988, proliferated. By 2008, about four hundred casinos generated more than $18 billion in annual income. Some tribal leaders lamented the social problems casinos sometimes brought in their wake, but casino income did help fund tribal schools, museums, job training, and substance-abuse programs.

The Hispanic population resisted sweeping generalizations. While Mexican-Americans concentrated in the Southwest, many lived elsewhere. Cubans, Puerto Ricans, and Haitians (mostly of African origin) resided mainly in Florida, New York, New Jersey, and Illinois.

Hispanic households' median income neared $40,000 by 2008, and unemployment among Hispanics dropped from 9 percent in 1995 to 5.6 percent in 2007. However, in 2007, 21.5 percent lived in poverty, many in troubled inner-city neighborhoods. Religion and family loomed large in Hispanic culture, but stressful social conditions took their toll.

In 2007, more than five thousand Hispanics held elective public office, including Los Angeles mayor Antonio Villaraigosa. Ten million Hispanics streamed to the polls in 2008, making them an increasingly important constituency. In 2009, while filling a Supreme Court vacancy, President Barack Obama nominated Sonia Sotomayor, a U.S. district court judge of Puerto Rican descent. Born in New York City, Sotomayor was reared by her mother after her father's death and went on to

Monica Almeida/The New York Times/Redux Pictures

Americanization, Twenty-First-Century Style

Recent immigrants from Afghanistan join a fitness class in Fremont, California, in 2001.

compile a brilliant college and law school record. Despite some controversy, she won Senate confirmation by a 68–31 vote.

Of the nation's 14.6 million Asian-Americans in 2010, more than 75 percent had arrived since 1980. Prizing education and supported by family networks, many followed a trajectory of academic achievement and upward mobility. Nearly 50 percent of adult Asian-Americans held college degrees; among high school graduates, the college enrollment rate neared 90 percent.

Demographers predict, based on baby-boom mortality and comparative fertility rates, that by 2050 non-Hispanic whites will constitute only about half the U.S. population. Non-Hispanic whites, while still a plurality, will simply be another minority. Many Americans of mixed origins, like the golfer Tiger Woods, of Thai, Chinese, African-American, and American Indian ancestry, resist being pigeonholed. From 1970 to 2005, the number of black-white married couples in the United States rose from 65,000 to 422,000. Recognizing these realities, the Census Bureau now permits citizens to check more than one racial category, or none at all.

With the graying of the baby-boom generation, America is also aging. In 2007, the highest-circulation U.S. magazine was *AARP,* read by 24 million members of the American Association of Retired Persons. The proportion of Americans over sixty-five, about 13 percent in 2009, is projected to reach 20 percent by 2050—a statistic with profound implications for health care, social security and Medicare funding, and other economic and social issues.

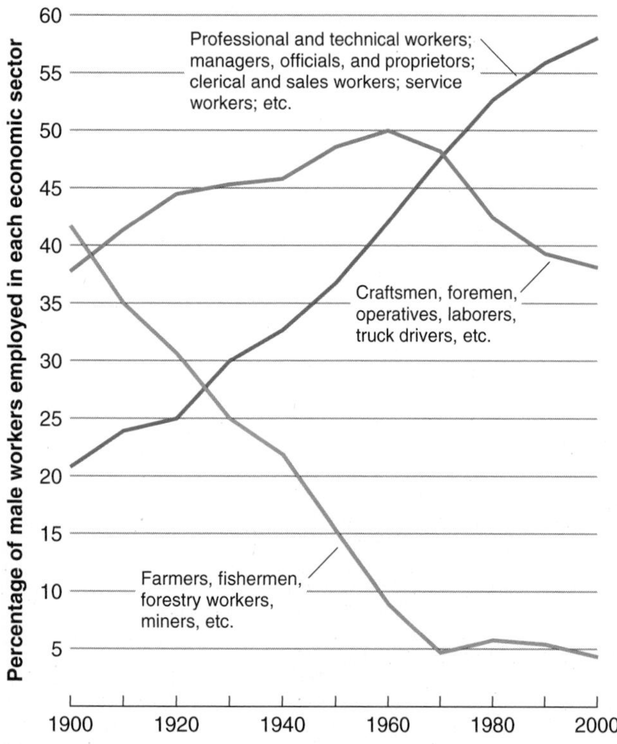

Figure 31.2 Changing Patterns of Work, 1900–2000

This chart illustrates the sweeping changes in the U.S. labor force in the twentieth century. The proportion of male workers in farming, fishing, forestry, and mining fell dramatically. The percentage of workers in industry and related occupations climbed until about 1960, and then began to decline. The service, technical, and professional categories rose steadily throughout the century.

Sources: Historical Statistics of the United States, Colonial Times to 1970 (1975); *Statistical Abstract of the United States, 2002;* Caplow, Hicks, and Wattenberg, *The First Measured Century: An Illustrated Guide to Trends in America* (Washington, DC: The AEI Press, 2001).

The "New Economy" and the Old Economy

In the early twentieth century, industrial production replaced agriculture as America's economic engine. The century's end saw an equally profound transformation: the rise of a professional and service-based economy (see Figure 31.2). Farming and manufacturing continued, of course, but with far fewer workers.

In the U.S. work force of 146 million in 2007, about 60 percent held white-collar jobs, ranging from sales clerks, office workers, and teachers to physicians, lawyers, engineers, computer programmers, and business executives. Service-sector employees in health care, custodial work, restaurants, and so forth accounted for another 16 percent. Only 23 percent worked in manual-labor fields such as manufacturing, farming, construction, trucking, and so on.

This transformation had mixed effects. Young people with education, skills, and contacts did well in the new electronics, programming, and telecommunications fields and in the burgeoning corporate and financial services sectors. For others, supermarkets, car washes, fast-food outlets, and discount superstores provided entry-level jobs, but few long-term prospects.

The computer-based information revolution has had economic ramifications as well. Newspaper circulation fell about 35 percent between 1985 and 2010. Even venerable papers such as the *New York Times* and newsmagazines like *Newsweek* faced problems as Americans turned to TV or online news sources—which for some meant Jon Stewart's satirical TV program, *The Daily Show.* (In 2010, *Newsweek* was obliged to merge with an online news service, *The Daily Beast.*) The new technologies impacted the music industry as well. CD sales peaked in 2000, but then dropped precipitously as fans downloaded albums and songs electronically far more cheaply to their laptops or iPods.

The economic transformation summed up by the term "globalization" complicated all these changes. America's economy has long been enmeshed in transnational patterns of trade and investment, of course, but this involvement has vastly accelerated in recent decades. Today's large corporations and financial institutions are all global in scope. Thanks to regional trading blocs such as NAFTA and multinational agreements administered by the **World Trade Organization (WTO),** the production and marketing of goods now largely ignores national boundaries. The flow of capital among financial institutions is similarly global in scope.

World Trade Organization (WTO) World body governing international trade

The economic well-being of all Americans increasingly depends on developments beyond the nation's borders. As imports replace American-made products and U.S. manufacturers shift operations overseas to cut labor costs, displaced workers face unemployment or lower-wage service-sector jobs. Union membership by 2007 sank to only 12 percent of the labor force, leaving workers even more vulnerable. The recession that hit in 2008 worsened the impact of these longer-term trends.

The decline of the U.S. auto industry typifies the pattern. After losing sales because of rising gasoline prices in the 1970s (see Chapter 29), American carmakers returned to profitability with gas-guzzling SUVs and light trucks. But as gas prices again spiked upward after 2000, car buyers turned to more fuel-efficient imports, particularly Japan's Toyota, Honda, and Nissan brands. By mid-2007, foreign carmakers had captured over half the U.S. market—a historic first.

At GM, a century-old icon of America's industrial might, annual losses spurted to nearly $39 billion in 2008. GM's stock price tumbled, and the company shed tens of thousands of jobs. From 2005 through mid-2008, GM, Chrysler, and Ford eliminated nearly 150,000 jobs and closed thirty-five plants, causing pain across America. Between 2008 and 2010, facing plunging sales and a yawning deficit, GM closed more factories, shuttered several of its oldest brands, and accepted billions of dollars in a government bailout. Chrysler was saved from destruction when it was purchased by Italian carmaker Fiat.

Economists continued to defend globalization as beneficial for America overall, as it lowered consumer prices and opened world markets for U.S. exports. But for displaced workers, this was cold comfort. In addition to the impact on U.S. industrial workers, human rights activists charged that corporations in a "race to the bottom" open factories in poor

Checking In

- The Sun Belt continued to grow, and immigration led to growing diversity.
- Racial problems continued, especially in urban ghettos; Native Americans asserted their treaty rights and built casinos; Hispanic and Asian communities grew dramatically.
- Acceptance of mixed-race celebrities and increasing incidence of interracial marriage hinted at a movement away from fixed notions of race.
- As the population grew increasingly diverse ethnically, the "melting pot" metaphor suggesting sameness and uniformity faded.
- The service economy expanded rapidly, pushing many into low-paying jobs but creating lucrative jobs for the educated; labor unions shrank.

countries where workers live in prison-like barracks and work long hours for low wages. Such factories often are environmental polluters as well.

Amid economic worries and a "war on terror," post-9/11 popular culture reflected crosscurrents of anxiety and escapism. Rupert Murdoch's Fox TV networks, while rallying support for Bush on the Fox News Channel, also offered the top-rated *American Idol* program, in which amateur vocalists competed for audience votes. Such shows, along with the contrived scenarios of so-called "reality" programs and elaborately plotted video games, provided distraction from the stress of contemporary life. A longing to obliterate shadowy enemies perhaps contributed to the success of fantasy movies such as *Iron Man* (2008) and *Avatar* (2009), in which technologically enhanced superheroes battled menacing foes.

A Floundering Administration Yields to a Renewed Vision

What were the most pressing domestic issues after 2004?

President Bush's second term brought multiple setbacks, including the administration's ineffectual response to a devastating hurricane. Two Supreme Court appointments extended Bush's conservative legacy, but lobbying scandals, soaring federal deficits, and discontent with his domestic and foreign policies, capped by a severe recession, all eroded Bush's standing. The watershed 2008 election suggested a renewed national resolve to fulfill the enduring vision of what America might yet become.

Mixed Record, Mounting Deficits, and Disaster in New Orleans

In 2003, Congress enacted Bush's proposal to pay part of seniors' prescription drug expenses under the federal Medicare program. Though older citizens welcomed the help in paying for their medications, many grumbled as they battled the red tape. Democrats charged that the plan mainly benefited drug firms and insurance companies.

The prescription drug benefit helped push the government's share of Medicare costs to $179 billion in 2007, more than five times the 1990 figure. Medicare and social security costs, plus Bush's tax cuts, the Iraq and Afghan wars, and interest payments on the national debt, produced yawning federal deficits from 2002 on. Worsening the problem, Congress members of both parties continued the time-honored practice of quietly inserting into spending bills pet projects known as "earmarks" that benefited their districts.

Launching his second term, Bush proposed a partial privatization of social security, called the New Deal pension program. The social security system faced severe budgetary strains as the baby-boom generation grew older. Under Bush's plan, people could shift some of their social security funds to private investment accounts. However, the proposal failed to win acceptance. Most citizens preferred a government program to the uncertainties of the market.

The administration stumbled over immigration policy. Of the estimated 11 million illegal immigrants in the United States, many worked in a low-wage

Michael Ainsworth/Dallas Morning News/Corbis News/Corbis

New Orleans in the Aftermath of Hurricane Katrina, September 1, 2005
Four days after the city's levees burst and flood waters devastated their homes, New Orleans residents awaited evacuation to the Superdome, which quickly became a scene of nightmarish conditions as thousands of desperate people crowded in.

"shadow economy" as farm laborers, motel cleaners, nursing-home attendants, or employees in food-processing plants. In 2005, the administration proposed a bill by which these workers could eventually gain legal status. The debate that erupted revealed deep divisions in U.S. public opinion and within Bush's own party. Businesses employing immigrants supported the bill, but opponents denounced the plan as "amnesty" for lawbreakers. Deport them, they argued, and the law of supply-and-demand would push up wages for the jobs they held, increasing opportunities for U.S.-born workers.

Late in 2005, the House of Representatives, with strong Republican support, defied the administration by passing a tough immigration bill criminalizing illegal aliens and requiring their deportation; strengthening the U.S.-Mexican border; and making it a felony for anyone, including ministers and health-care providers, to help undocumented immigrants.

The reaction was swift. Protesters, supported by Spanish-language radio and TV, marched in Los Angeles and other cities. The bill's supporters mobilized as well.

Radio personality Rush Limbaugh angrily denounced the marches. In the Southwest, volunteers organized a vigilante-like "Minuteman Project" to patrol the border. With the Hispanic vote in play, politicians proceeded cautiously. Defying the White House, a bloc of Senate Republicans defeated the compromise bill.

Shelving hopes for reform, the Bush administration cracked down on illegal immigration. In 2006, Bush signed a bill to build a 700-mile reinforced fence along the U.S.-Mexican border. In addition, federal agents raided plants employing undocumented Hispanics. While some applauded the administration's harsh policies, humanitarian and civil-rights groups protested, noting the impact on children and disrupted families. A 2008 film, *The Visitor,* portrayed the human consequences of rigidly enforced deportation policies.

Hurricane Katrina Worst natural disaster in U.S. history; destroyed much of New Orleans and the Gulf Coast in August 2005

The administration took another hit in August 2005, when **Hurricane Katrina** struck the Gulf Coast, taking as many as fourteen hundred lives, inflicting heavy property damage, disrupting shipping on the Mississippi River, and smashing oil refineries and offshore oil rigs. New Orleans suffered most. As New Orleans' levees burst under Katrina's storm surge, rampaging water flooded the lower wards, populated mainly by poor blacks. Many residents drowned or died awaiting rescue. Others lost homes and possessions. Thousands poured into New Orleans's Superdome, which soon became a squalid disaster zone.

Washington's response was appallingly inadequate. FEMA head Michael Brown, a political appointee with no disaster experience, proved hopelessly inept. Though praised by Bush, he soon resigned. The distribution of emergency relief funds involved massive fraud and ineptitude. FEMA spent $900 million on twenty-six thousand mobile homes, many of which sat unused. Despite the reorganization of the national security bureaucracy after 9/11, Hurricane Katrina revealed the same pattern of missed warnings, failed communication, and bumbling response. Many blamed Washington as New Orleans neighborhoods stood silent, their streets lined with empty, mud-caked houses, their residents scattered.

Extending Republican Influence: From the Supreme Court to K Street

In July 2005, Supreme Court justice Sandra Day O'Connor, a key swing vote in close decisions, announced her retirement. To replace her, Bush nominated federal judge John Roberts, who had held posts in the Reagan administration. When Chief Justice Rehnquist died in September, Bush nominated Roberts as chief justice. He won easy Senate confirmation while revealing little about his judicial philosophy.

To fill the second vacancy, Bush nominated Samuel Alito, Jr. As a Justice Department lawyer in the Reagan administration, and later as a federal judge, Alito had espoused the broad view of executive powers that the Bush administration used to justify its post-9/11 actions at home and abroad. Alito won confirmation, 58–42.

With Roberts and Alito joining Scalia and Thomas as a bloc of four reliably conservative justices, Justice Anthony Kennedy emerged as the swing vote in close decisions. Pro-choice advocates feared (and abortion opponents hoped) that the high court's growing conservative strength would threaten *Roe* v. *Wade,* the 1973 ruling upholding abortion rights. Although it remained highly contentious, opinion polls showed broad support for *Roe* v. *Wade.* In *Gonzales* v. *Carhart* (2007), the Supreme Court, on a 5–4 vote, upheld a 2003 congressional ban on late-term abortions. In the decision, however, the majority cited *Roe* v. *Wade* as a guiding precedent, thus implicitly reaffirming that ruling.

As Supreme Court politics attracted notice, so did the influence of Washington lobbyists. Long a part of American politics, lobbyists' influence increased during the ascendancy of Texas Republican congressman Tom DeLay, who became House majority leader in 2003. From 2000 to 2005, the ranks of registered Washington lobbyists expanded from around fifteen thousand to nearly thirty-three thousand, with many more unregistered ones. DeLay extracted campaign contributions from lobbyists and pressured them to hire Republican staffers—often members of legislators' families.

An eruption of scandals in 2005 focused attention on lobbyists and money's role in politics. In September, DeLay resigned as majority leader, and soon left Congress altogether, after a grand jury indicted him for violating Texas election laws by engineering a redistricting scheme that benefited Republicans. In December, a federal grand jury indicted Jack Abramoff, a Washington lobbyist with ties to DeLay. Abramoff had collected millions from corporations trying to influence legislation, including $82 million from Indian tribes seeking casino licenses or to prevent rival tribes from getting licenses. Pleading guilty, Abramoff went to prison. As public disgust mounted, politicians scrambled to return tainted contributions and regulate lobbyists more strictly.

A Shifting Political Landscape: The 2006 Election and Beyond

In the 2006 midterm election, voters rendered a stinging judgment on the Bush administration and the Republican-led Congress. Even President Bush admitted that his party had taken a "thumping." Democrats gained thirty-two House seats, retaking control for the first time in twelve years. Democrats also narrowly won control of the Senate, 51 to 49. The number of women senators rose to sixteen, a record high. The Democratic victories brought new congressional leadership, including Nancy Pelosi of San Francisco as Speaker of the House, the first woman to hold that post. The election results signaled discontent with the nation's direction, and especially over the Iraq War. Consequently, President Bush fired Defense Secretary Rumsfeld. Vice President Cheney's influence diminished as well.

By the end of 2007, more than four thousand GIs had been killed in Iraq. After five years, the war's costs had soared to around $600 billion, with billions more projected. Advised by General David Petraeus, the new commander in Iraq, Bush ordered more troops to Iraq in 2007. With additional GIs patrolling Baghdad and other trouble spots, violence declined. An uneasy cease-fire by Shi'ite militias helped as well. Assassinations, suicide bombings, and IED attacks continued, but U.S. military deaths in Iraq for 2008 fell to 314, down sharply from previous years. In November 2008, the Iraqi parliament ratified an agreement with Washington for the withdrawal of U.S. combat forces from urban centers by mid-2009. The conflict, already longer than World War II, was winding down at last.

Despite Bush's claim that Saddam Hussein's overthrow justified the war, most Americans continued to view it as a mistake. A Taliban resurgence in Afghanistan strengthened this view. Reports of poor care in veterans' hospitals, delays in processing wounded veterans' claims, and massive fraud in the Iraq reconstruction program deepened public anger over the war.

Other controversies plagued Bush's final years in office. In March 2007, Vice President Cheney's chief of staff went to prison after his conviction for perjury and obstruction of justice. In August 2007, Attorney General Alberto Gonzales resigned amid an uproar over the hiring and firing of U.S. attorneys and Justice Department lawyers for blatantly political reasons. Gonzales' approval of the Justice Department's "torture memo" and of illegal FBI spying during his tenure as White House counsel added to the firestorm of criticism.

As Bush's presidency wound down, his approval ratings sank to around 25 percent—close to the lowest ever recorded for any president. What caused this reversal? Beyond the unpopular Iraq War and related issues of torture, unlimited detention, and violations of citizens' rights, many saw an arrogant, go-it-alone approach that damaged America's standing worldwide. Critics also targeted the administration's dismissal of scientific evidence on global warming, the politicization of the Justice Department and other federal agencies, and the secretive power exercised by Vice President Cheney and a small circle of like-minded advisers. To his opponents, Bush's black-and-white worldview and preference for snap decisions based on gut instincts further limited his effectiveness.

The Economist, a respected London-based magazine that endorsed Bush in 2000, reached a harsh judgment as his term ended: "He leaves the White House as one of the least popular and most divisive presidents in American history, . . . [and] the most partisan . . . in living memory. . . . Both the country and, ultimately, the Republican Party are left the worse for it."

Millions of Americans continued to support Bush, of course. The Iraq invasion, tax cuts, educational reforms, promotion of international trade, and free-market suspicion of government regulation all had their admirers. Bush himself defended his record, insisting that even his most controversial post–9/11 actions aimed to protect the country from terrorists. The Republican Party retained a large core of loyal supporters. For the moment, however, the party's fortunes stood at a low ebb.

Recession Strikes the U.S. and World Economies

Deepening the national malaise, a recession began in 2007 and quickly worsened. The downturn started in the real estate market. Beginning in the late 1990s, housing prices spiked upward, especially in California, Florida, the Southwest, and the Northeast. The bubble burst in 2007. As real estate prices tumbled, homebuilding and commercial developments stalled.

The crisis soon spread, worsened by lax governmental regulation. In 1999, Congress repealed the Glass-Steagall Act, a 1933 law designed to regulate bank practices and protect depositors. Freed of regulatory constraints, investment banks could now acquire unregulated financial services companies and indulge in other forms of financial wheeling and dealing. During the real estate boom, using slogans like "No credit? No problem," banks and lending companies extended mortgages to homebuyers who could barely afford them. By 2008, nearly 30 percent of all mortgages were rated as "subprime." These risky mortgages were then sold to Wall Street investment banks or other financial institutions that bundled or "securitized" them into stock offerings purchased by investors.

In 2007, it was revealed that billions of dollars of these securities were practically worthless. The resulting credit crisis spooked the financial markets and popped the housing bubble. Rising housing prices had subsidized the American consumer's spending habits since 2001. Now, reports of flat or falling home prices stoked fears of a recession. Worse still, a combination of geopolitical fears and oil speculation drove gas prices above $4 per gallon, the highest ever and more than double the price when George Bush and Dick Cheney—two former oil company executives—took office.

Frustration with the status quo boiled over in the early stages of the 2008 presidential election. Out of a crowded field of contenders, voters in the Republican primaries and caucuses selected Senator John McCain of Arizona to run in the November general election. McCain's plainspoken directness and reputation as a maverick were well suited to a restless electorate. McCain had also criticized Bush's handling of the war in Iraq and advocated sending more U.S. troops into the conflict.

The antiestablishment sentiment was even stronger on the Democratic side. In a hotly contested race, Democratic primary voters rejected two well-known names—Senator John Edwards, who ran for vice president in 2004, and Senator Hillary Clinton, wife of former president Bill Clinton—in favor of a relatively unknown, forty-six-year-old, African-American senator from Illinois, **Barack Obama.** Although little separated the three candidates on the issues, Obama's opposition to the Iraq War, spellbinding oratory, and calls for change jibed well with the mood of Democratic voters.

Barack Obama Forty-fourth U.S. president; first African-American to occupy the Oval Office

The nominees for president formed a study in contrasts. On one side was the energetic and patriotic McCain, seventy-two years of age, a Navy veteran with twenty-six years of experience in Congress. Against him stood the cool and unflappable Obama, a former community organizer and law professor. McCain took a risk in selecting the folksy Sarah Palin, then governor of Alaska, as his vice-presidential running mate. Obama made a comparatively safe choice and partnered with the seasoned Joe Biden, a senator from Delaware. On the campaign trail, Palin hammered away at Obama's past contact with a 1960s-era radical named Bill Ayers (they were once on a charitable foundation together). McCain painted Obama as dangerously untested and even naïve. Unfazed, Obama repeatedly tied McCain's voting record and policies to the deeply unpopular President George W. Bush. Obama's soaring speeches were laced with calls for common purpose and hope for a better day. Chants of "Yes we can!" resounded at his huge rallies.

Pollsters initially predicted a tight race. But then, an economic calamity transformed the election and paved the way for a decisive and historic result. Ever since the collapse of brokerage house Bear Stearns in March 2008, a worried Wall Street struggled to contain the damage from the subprime loan crisis. In early September, anxiety gave way to panic. Saddled with billions in worthless mortgage-backed securities, or **"toxic assets,"** Fannie Mae and Freddie Mac—holding about half of the nation's mortgage debt—were placed under government control. Later that month came the bankruptcies of brokerage giant Lehman Brothers and the huge savings bank Washington Mutual; the fire-sale acquisition of investment bank Merrill Lynch; and the government bailout of the country's largest insurance company, AIG. After a decade when both Washington and American consumers had plunged deeply into

toxic assets Investments comprised of bundled mortgages, which were revealed to be nearly worthless when the real estate market collapsed in 2008

Joe Raedle/Getty Images news/Getty Images

Homeowners Face a Crisis as Recession Hits

As unemployment rose and retirement savings shrunk in value, many homeowners could not meet their mortgage payments. An enterprising real-estate agent in Coral Gables, Florida, organized a "Foreclosure Boat Tour" for potential buyers of foreclosed homes.

debt, the chickens now came home to roost. In 2008, U.S. banks wrote off $41 billion in unpaid credit-card debt.

The news on Main Street was just as dire. The Dow Jones Industrial Average, a bellwether for retirement accounts, fell 35 percent; consumer confidence plunged; and millions of homeowners faced foreclosure. The already weakened U.S. auto companies teetered toward bankruptcy. In 2008, 2.6 million workers lost their jobs, the highest rate of loss in sixty years. (Meanwhile, as late as December 2008, after fourth-quarter losses of $15 billion, Merrill Lynch's CEO doled out millions in bonuses to company executives and spent $2.2 million redecorating his office.) Some economists warned darkly of a "second Great Depression."

President Bush tried to ease the global credit crisis with a $700 billion financial rescue package, called the Troubled Asset Relief Program (TARP). But conservative Republicans in Congress opposed it and many voters saw it as a boondoggle for corporate malefactors. In a moment of high political drama, John McCain abruptly left the campaign trail and went to Washington to save the imperiled rescue package. In the end, both McCain and Obama voted for the bill, which passed. But the incident exposed McCain to attacks that he was "erratic" and linked him more closely to the unpopular George W. Bush. Obama's poll numbers shot up.

On Election Day, Obama took 53 percent of the popular vote and made deep inroads into Republican strongholds, winning North Carolina, Virginia, Florida, and Indiana. Democrats gained eighteen seats in the House and six in the Senate, padding their lead in both chambers. While Republicans lamented their bad luck, Democrats hailed the outcome as a repudiation of Republican policies and a final verdict on the Bush years. Among eighteen- to twenty-four-year-olds, only 32 percent voted for McCain—an ill omen for Republicans' future hopes.

Beyond partisan politics lay deeper meanings. Significantly, the topic of race rarely appeared on the campaign trail. Fears that white Americans would refuse to vote for a black president proved largely unfounded. A majority of whites under the age of thirty and about two-thirds of all Hispanics voted for Obama. It was no doubt too early to conclude that America had entered a "post-racial" age. But it was also clear that something remarkable had happened. Barack Obama—a minority citizen—had been chosen to lead the world's most powerful nation. Facing looming problems at home and abroad, and with hope intermixed with fear, America prepared to inaugurate its first black president on January 20, 2009—almost exactly one hundred years after the founding of the NAACP.

A New Beginning and an Enduring Spirit

Barack Obama was born in Hawaii in 1961, the son of a Kenyan university student and his white wife, an anthropologist from Kansas. After college and Harvard Law School, he worked as a community organizer in Chicago rather than joining a law firm, and in 1996 he won election to the Illinois legislature.

In his inaugural address, President Obama marveled that sixty years earlier, his father could have been denied service in Washington restaurants. He rejected what he called the "worn out dogmas" that blocked bold responses to urgent problems at home and abroad. "[S]turdy alliances and enduring convictions," he said, were as important as military might in achieving security. America's "patchwork heritage" of differing ethnicities and national origins was no liability, he declared, but a great asset as the nation sought to restore its battered reputation in an equally diverse world.

Obama named Hillary Clinton secretary of state. She quickly appointed two seasoned diplomats as special envoys to address the volatile Afghanistan and Pakistan region and the Israeli-Palestinian conflict. Obama's choice as attorney general, Eric Holder, forthrightly declared in his Senate confirmation hearing that water boarding, the interrogation technique used on some Guantánamo prisoners, constituted torture and would not be allowed. In January 2009, Obama signed an executive order stating that Guantánamo would be closed within a year. However, Congress resisted. By 2011, much to the dismay of civil-liberties advocates, Obama had failed to close Guantánamo and had resumed the practice of trying terrorist suspects in military, as opposed to civil, courts—essentially continuing two Bush-era policies that candidate Obama had opposed on the campaign trail.

Obama lifted Bush's ban on stem-cell research and named Steven Chu, a Nobel laureate in physics and advocate of alternative energy sources, to lead the Department of Energy. Reversing Bush-administration policy, Obama announced that by

2016 all new vehicles would be required to meet the tougher fuel-efficiency standards already adopted by California and other states. The new Treasury Secretary Timothy Geithner, formerly president of the Federal Reserve Bank of New York, led Obama's recession-fighting team. (Ironically, he had supported the deregulatory legislation that helped lay the groundwork for the crisis.)

In February 2009, Obama signed a $787 billion economic-stimulus bill. It channeled $120 billion to states for highways, school construction, and other infrastructure projects and cut taxes for middle- and lower-income Americans. Ominously, despite Obama's pleas for bipartisanship, only three Senate Republicans voted for the bill. In July 2010, Obama signed into law the Dodd-Frank Wall Street Reform and Consumer Protection Act, which had narrowly passed through Congress via a party-line vote. The new law significantly reorganized the country's existing financial regulatory agencies while creating a new one, the Bureau of Consumer Financial Protection, to enforce fair lending standards.

While the administration threw a lifeline to the ailing auto industry in the form of a multibillion-dollar emergency bailout, Obama created a White House task force to oversee the industry's long-term restructuring. Chrysler filed for bankruptcy, though a takeover by the Italian automaker Fiat brightened its long-term prospects. As once-mighty General Motors filed for bankruptcy as well, Americans realized the depth of the crisis facing this core domestic industry. Remarkably, after enduring two painful years of steep losses and layoffs, by 2011 General Motors had repaid money loaned to it by the government (plus interest) and had even returned to profitability.

Despite the economic crisis, Obama pursued his top domestic goal, health-care reform, to control runaway costs while extending coverage to the uninsured. Securing cost-cutting pledges from the drug industry, health insurers, hospital associations, and other key players, Obama called on Congress to enact comprehensive health-care legislation.

Orjan F. Ellingvag/Dagens Naringsliv/Corbis News/Corbis

Debating Health Care

With his eye on the cameras, an angry citizen berates Pennsylvania senator Arlen Specter in an August 2009 "town hall" meeting in Lebanon, Pennsylvania, discussing health-care reform.

Reform momentum soon slowed, however. As Congress members returned to their districts, they confronted agitated voters fearful of change. Some critics resorted to scare tactics, conjuring visions of government "death panels" that would deny care to the elderly or terminally ill. As they had since President Truman's day, opponents warned of "socialized medicine" and "a government-run health-care system," even though Medicare, the federal health-insurance program for the elderly, enjoyed broad popularity. The pharmaceutical and health-insurance industries, profiting handsomely under the present system, opposed any cost-control regulations beyond what they had already voluntarily pledged.

Reform proponents, by contrast, pointed to the millions of uninsured Americans, the loss of coverage that often came with unemployment, insurance companies' denial of coverage to high-risk applicants, and the spiraling overall costs of U.S. health care in contrast to other nations with comparable or better medical outcomes.

The loudest opposition to health-care reform came from the so-called **Tea Party,** a loose coalition of citizen groups opposed to big government and activist judges. The Tea Party's name, large outdoor rallies, populist rhetoric, and use of patriotic symbols (notably, the "Don't Tread On Me" Gadsden Flag, which emerged as the movement's standard) tapped into the historical legacy of the Antifederalist movement of the 1780s (see Chapter 6). Like the Antifederalists, they bore a deep suspicion of centralized power and defended personal liberty against government tyranny. Critics, however, pointed out that society had changed greatly since the 1780s and questioned the claim that Tea Party members were oppressed. Surveys showed that they were older, whiter, wealthier, and more educated than average Americans.

Tea Party Conservative or libertarian movement opposed to big government and the Obama administration

Millions identified themselves as "teabaggers." Former Alaska governor Sarah Palin, now a media star and a favorite of the Tea Party, put a face on the movement. But the Tea Party lacked central leadership. In addition, it resisted the temptation to form a separate political party, making it an unpredictable force. In 2010, the movement's political influence was felt most dramatically within the Republican Party. In the primary elections, Tea Party–backed upstarts in New York, Nevada, and Florida defeated prominent moderate Republicans, pushing the party to the Right. In April 2011, the new Tea Party congressional caucus flexed its muscles in the budget debate and pressured the Republican leadership to insist on large spending cuts—nearly forcing a legislative showdown that would have shut down the federal government for the first time in fifteen years.

The emergence of the Tea Party hardened the politics of health-care reform. Even Democrats were divided. Congressional Democrats from conservative districts favored a cautious, incremental approach. Democratic liberals, by contrast, supported a "public option," a government health insurance program supplementing the private system, that would provide a yardstick for efficient, lower-cost coverage. When Massachusetts Democratic senator Edward Kennedy died in August 2009 and voters elected Republican Scott Brown to replace him, the Democratic supermajority in the Senate, and all hope for a public option, vanished.

The end result, the **Patient Protection and Affordable Care Act** of March 2010, represented a major milestone in the history of health care in the United States. The law guaranteed coverage for all patients, even those with pre-existing medical conditions; mandated health insurance for most Americans; and provided subsidies to poor Americans so they could afford health insurance premiums. But while the law's defenders promised that it would reduce the federal budget deficit and expand coverage to millions of uninsured Americans, it was nevertheless a compromise that satisfied few and angered many. Too small to provide the efficiency of public plans, but large enough to be lampooned as a "government takeover of health care," the law faced an uncertain fate in the courts, where it faced constitutional challenges. Politically, health-care reform emerged as a defining issue in the 2010 midterm elections and the early stages of the 2012 presidential election.

Patient Protection and Affordable Care Act Health-care reform mandating and expanding insurance coverage

As the 2010 midterm elections approached, unemployment hovered at around 9.5 percent for the entire year and millions of homes were in foreclosure. Democratic strategists predicted a tough slog. But few predicted such a shockingly lopsided result. Pledging to cut the massive federal budget deficit and repeal "Obamacare," as they called it, Republicans gained six seats in the Senate and sixty-three seats in the House. Republican John Boehner replaced Nancy Pelosi as Speaker of the House. The election also produced a number of new Republican governors, including Scott Walker of Wisconsin, who in early 2011 led an effort to strip away the collective bargaining rights of unions representing public sector employees.

A chastened Obama admitted that his party had taken a "shellacking." His supporters were troubled. The traits that made Obama attractive as a candidate in 2008—a pragmatic, non-ideological approach; a cool, detached demeanor; and an instinct to seek common ground—now seemed ill-suited to an historical moment that demanded pugnacity and bold action. Obama was failing where Ronald Reagan had succeeded: to frame policies as part of clearly articulated values and beliefs.

Nevertheless, Obama's first two years in office produced a record of reform unmatched since the administration of Lyndon Johnson in the 1960s. New laws expanded access to health care and established new financial regulations. In its final months, the lame-duck 111th Congress extended Bush-era tax cuts and ratified the New Strategic Arms Limitation Treaty (New START) with Russia. Fulfilling an Obama campaign pledge, it also ended the military's "Don't ask, don't tell" policy (see Chapter 30), which since 1993 had prevented openly gay citizens from serving in the nation's armed services. Obama also appointed a third woman to the Supreme Court, Elena Kagan, to fill a vacancy created by the retirement of Justice John Paul

David Bathgate/Corbis News/Corbis

U.S. Soldiers in Afghanistan Discuss Tactics for Combating the Taliban

As home-front support for the conflict wavered, American diplomats and military leaders faced major challenges in defining and achieving U.S. objectives in this region of the world.

Stevens. By early 2011, a modest economic recovery had begun to take root and unemployment fell below 9 percent.

Meanwhile, the ten-year war in Afghanistan ground on, with uncertain prospects. With some ninety thousand GIs deployed in that country (plus about forty-two thousand NATO troops), U.S. fatalities by April 2011 exceeded 1,400, with thousands more wounded. As the Islamic fundamentalists known as the Taliban regained control in southern Afghanistan, they weakened the U.S.-backed government of President Hamid Karzai and destabilized neighboring Pakistan as well. Rampant government corruption, accusations of fraud in the elections of August 2009 and September 2010, and Afghanistan's leading role in the cultivation of opium poppies from which heroin is manufactured further complicated the picture. In December 2009, Obama announced that another thirty thousand troops would be sent to Afghanistan, while also setting 2014 as the withdrawal date for American forces there.

A stunning development in May 2011 seemed to increase the likelihood of U.S. troop withdrawals from Afghanistan. In the early morning hours of May 2, 2011, U.S. Navy SEALs launched a daring raid on a compound in Abbottabad, Pakistan, where they found, and killed, Osama bin Laden and several others. This ended a nearly decade-long manhunt for the mastermind of the 9/11 attacks. In the weeks after the raid, al Qaeda named a new chief and vowed revenge, while President Obama's approval ratings soared and commentators speculated about the future. Some congressmen, noting that bin Laden was hiding in plain sight just a mile from a major Pakistan army base, questioned Pakistan's reliability as an ally in the war against the Taliban. Moreover, the killing of Osama bin Laden prompted new questions about the war itself, since the central justification of the Afghanistan war was to prevent the Taliban from giving safe haven to al Qaeda and other terrorist groups.

When President Obama was unexpectedly awarded the Nobel Peace Prize in October 2009, after only nine months in office, it was widely viewed as a gesture of support for his good intentions and an expression of hope for the future—a hope widely shared in a war-weary nation and world. The democratic uprisings that ousted the despots who ruled Tunisia and Egypt in early 2011 elevated hopes that the frontiers of democracy and freedom could be expanded through peaceful means, as opposed to military invasion. Still, Obama continued to cast the Afghan struggle as a "war of necessity." As casualties mounted, home-front support eroded. Ironically, antiwar sentiment was strongest in Obama's own party, while conservative Republicans provided a core of support. Obama's well wishers recalled nervously how the Vietnam War had undermined Lyndon Johnson's domestic program, and how the Iraq War had eroded George W. Bush's effectiveness.

The nation faced uncertain times, but also possessed a history of overcoming challenges and discovering sources of renewal. As President Obama declared in his inaugural address: "The time has come to reaffirm our enduring spirit, to choose our better history, to carry forward that precious gift . . . passed on from generation to generation: the God-given promise that all are equal, all are free, and all deserve a chance to pursue their full measure of happiness."

Checking In

- Bush's plan to privatize social security faltered; a new Medicare drug benefit program, added to the costs of the military operation in Iraq, resulted in ballooning budget deficits.
- Hurricane Katrina obliterated much of New Orleans and the Gulf Coast; the federal response was widely viewed as inadequate.
- Bush appointed two conservatives, John Roberts and Samuel Alito, Jr., to the U.S. Supreme Court; a series of high-profile political scandals disgusted voters.
- Various proposals to reform immigration policy failed, leaving the issue unresolved; Democrats reclaimed the House and Senate in the 2006 midterm elections.
- Falling housing values and rising gas prices deepened the electorate's petulant mood; a yearning for change manifested in the 2008 presidential primaries, when voters showed a preference for antiestablishment candidates.
- Barack Obama, in the face of a conservative movement called the Tea Party, oversaw historic reforms to the health-care and financial industries and also expanded U.S. military involvement in Afghanistan.

Conclusion

In 2001, while accepting the Nobel Peace Prize a few weeks after 9/11, UN Secretary General Kofi Annan said: "We have entered the third millennium through a gate of fire." But Annan went on to evoke the vision that had inspired the UN's founders in 1945. Despite the hatred and inequalities dividing nations and peoples, he insisted, the fate of all Earth's inhabitants is interconnected. The task of the twenty-first century, he said, is to achieve "a new, more profound awareness of the sanctity and dignity of every human life, regardless of race or religion. . . . Humanity is indivisible."

As we conclude this history of America and its people, what is the "enduring vision" of our title? There is, of course, no single vision, but many. That is part of America's meaning. Nor is this a vision of a preordained national destiny unfolding effortlessly, but rather of successive generations' laborious, often frustrating struggle to define what their common life as a people should be. For all the failures, setbacks, and wrong turns, the shared visions, at their best, are rooted in hope, not fear. In 1980, Jesse de la Cruz, a Mexican-American woman who fought for years to improve conditions for California's migrant workers, summed up the philosophy that kept her going: "Is America progressing toward the better? . . . We're the ones that are gonna do it. We have to keep on struggling. . . . With us, there's a saying: *La esperanza muere al ultimo.* Hope dies last. You can't lose hope. If you lose hope, that's losing every thing."

Chapter Summary

How did the Bush administration respond to the September 11, 2011, attacks, internationally and domestically? (page 776)

The 9/11 attacks catapulted the United States into a shadowy war on terrorism. An American-led coalition invaded Afghanistan to drive out al Qaeda and overthrow the Islamic Taliban government. At home, a new cabinet-level agency, the Department of Homeland Security, was created; in addition, Congress enacted the controversial Patriot Act. Bush identified Iraq as part of an "axis of evil" that also included North Korea and Iran. The administration claimed that Saddam Hussein was linked to al Qaeda and that he was building weapons of mass destruction (neither claim turned out to be accurate). With little global support, Bush invaded Iraq and routed Saddam Hussein; a major insurgency followed, fueled largely by sectarian conflicts among the Iraqi people.

Beyond security concerns, what economic and social issues did Bush address in his first term? (page 782)

The collapse of the technology sector of the stock market triggered a recession. The spectacular bankruptcy of the Enron Corporation was only the first of a succession of corporate scandals involving misconduct by top management. On the domestic front, Bush pursued a conservative agenda, including massive tax cuts, education reform called "No Child Left Behind," an energy bill that provided tax breaks to energy companies, and opposition to stem-cell research. Bush won reelection in 2004 by stressing national security and moral issues. Republicans increased their control in Congress.

KEY TERMS

September 11, 2001 *(p. 776)*
Colin Powell *(p. 776)*
Richard (Dick) Cheney *(p. 777)*
Donald Rumsfeld *(p. 777)*
al Qaeda *(p. 779)*
Guantánamo Bay *(p. 779)*
USA-Patriot Act *(p. 779)*
Department of Homeland Security *(p. 779)*
neoconservatives *(p. 780)*
Arctic National Wildlife Refuge (ANWR) *(p. 783)*
"No Child Left Behind" *(p. 783)*
John Kerry *(p. 784)*
global warming *(p. 790)*
Kyoto Accords *(p. 791)*
World Trade Organization (WTO) *(p. 795)*
Hurricane Katrina *(p. 798)*

What challenges faced the United States in the Middle East and elsewhere in the world after 2000? (page 786)

Domestic support for the war eroded amid worsening sectarian violence in Iraq, revelations of abuses by the U.S. military and domestic spying in the name of security, and skepticism about the administration's case for invading Iraq. Other troubling world developments included worsening Israeli-Palestinian relations, nuclear programs in North Korea and Iran, and China's growing economic and military power. As global warming and other environmental hazards roused concern, the Bush administration downplayed the threat and rejected international efforts to address the problem.

KEY TERMS continued

Barack Obama *(p. 801)*

toxic assets *(p. 801)*

Tea Party *(p. 805)*

Patient Protection and Affordable Care Act *(p. 805)*

What demographic and economic trends have most shaped contemporary America? (page 791)

Major social trends in these years included continuing migration to the South and West, chronic inner-city problems, and increasing ethnic diversity as the Hispanic and Asian populations grew. Increased immigration, especially from Latin America and Asia, ignited a debate about whether such an influx could be assimilated and whether American diversity would be a melting pot or a salad bowl in which ethnic identities remained strong. On the economic front, the long-term shift from industrial production to an information-based and service economy proceeded, and a massive tide of foreign imports stirred uneasiness, especially in the troubled domestic auto industry.

What were the most pressing domestic issues after 2004? (page 796)

In his troubled second term, Bush persuaded Congress to pass a costly prescription-drug benefit for Medicare recipients. The administration's inadequate response to Hurricane Katrina prompted questions about its competence. Riding a wave of voter discontent, Democrats reclaimed control of Congress in the 2006 midterm elections. As the Iraq War dragged on, the housing market collapsed, and gas prices spiked, the dominant theme in the early stages of the 2008 presidential campaign was "change." Republicans chose Arizona senator John McCain whereas Democrats opted for Illinois senator Barack Obama. Obama won a decisive victory in the general election and became the nation's first African-American president. In his first two years in office, Barack Obama oversaw landmark reforms to the health-care and financial industries. His early presidency was also marked by the emergence of the libertarian-themed Tea Party and the expansion of U.S. military engagement in Afghanistan.

Go to the CourseMate website at **www.cengagebrain.com** for additional study tools and review materials—including audio and video clips—for this chapter.

Appendix

DECLARATION OF INDEPENDENCE

IN CONGRESS, JULY 4, 1776

The Unanimous Declaration of the Thirteen United States of America

When, in the course of human events, it becomes necessary for one people to dissolve the political bands which have connected them with another, and to assume, among the powers of the earth, the separate and equal station to which the laws of nature and of nature's God entitle them, a decent respect to the opinions of mankind requires that they should declare the causes which impel them to the separation.

We hold these truths to be self-evident: That all men are created equal; that they are endowed by their Creator with certain unalienable rights; that among these are life, liberty, and the pursuit of happiness; that, to secure these rights, governments are instituted among men, deriving their just powers from the consent of the governed; that whenever any form of government becomes destructive of these ends, it is the right of the people to alter or to abolish it, and to institute new government, laying its foundation on such principles, and organizing its powers in such form, as to them shall seem most likely to effect their safety and happiness. Prudence, indeed, will dictate that governments long established should not be changed for light and transient causes; and accordingly all experience hath shown that mankind are more disposed to suffer, while evils are sufferable, than to right themselves by abolishing the forms to which they are accustomed. But when a long train of abuses and usurpations, pursuing invariably the same object, evinces a design to reduce them under absolute despotism, it is their right, it is their duty, to throw off such government, and to provide new guards for their future security. Such has been the patient sufferance of these colonies; and such is now the necessity which constrains them to alter their former systems of government. The history of the present King of Great Britain is a history of repeated injuries and usurpations, all having in direct object the establishment of an absolute tyranny over these states. To prove this, let facts be submitted to a candid world.

He has refused his assent to laws, the most wholesome and necessary for the public good.

He has forbidden his governors to pass laws of immediate and pressing importance, unless suspended in their operation till his assent should be obtained; and, when so suspended, he has utterly neglected to attend to them.

He has refused to pass other laws for the accommodation of large districts of people, unless those people would relinquish the right of representation in the legislature, a right inestimable to them, and formidable to tyrants only.

He has called together legislative bodies at places unusual, uncomfortable, and distant from the depository of their public records, for the sole purpose of fatiguing them into compliance with his measures.

He has dissolved representative houses repeatedly, for opposing, with manly firmness, his invasions on the rights of the people.

He has refused for a long time, after such dissolutions, to cause others to be elected; whereby the legislative powers, incapable of annihilation, have returned to the people at large for their exercise; the state remaining, in the mean time, exposed to all the dangers of invasions from without and convulsions within.

He has endeavored to prevent the population of these states; for that purpose obstructing the laws of naturalization of foreigners; refusing to pass others to encourage their migration hither, and raising the conditions of new appropriation of lands.

He has obstructed the administration of justice, by refusing his assent to laws for establishing judiciary powers.

He has made judges dependent on his will alone, for the tenure of their offices, and the amount and payment of their salaries.

He has erected a multitude of new offices, and sent hither swarms of officers to harass our people and eat out their substance.

He has kept among us, in times of peace, standing armies, without the consent of our legislatures.

He has affected to render the military independent of, and superior to, the civil power.

He has combined with others to subject us to a jurisdiction foreign to our constitution, and unacknowledged by our laws, giving his assent to their acts of pretended legislation:

For quartering large bodies of armed troops among us;

For protecting them, by a mock trial, from punishment for any murders which they should commit on the inhabitants of these states;

For cutting off our trade with all parts of the world;

For imposing taxes on us without our consent;

For depriving us, in many cases, of the benefits of trial by jury;

For transporting us beyond seas, to be tried for pretended offenses;

For abolishing the free system of English laws in a neighboring province, establishing therein an arbitrary government, and enlarging its boundaries, so as to render it at once an example and fit instrument for introducing the same absolute rule into these colonies;

For taking away our charters, abolishing our most valuable laws, and altering fundamentally the forms of our governments;

For suspending our own legislatures, and declaring themselves invested with power to legislate for us in all cases whatsoever.

He has abdicated government here, by declaring us out of his protection and waging war against us.

He has plundered our seas, ravaged our coasts, burned our towns, and destroyed the lives of our people.

He is at this time transporting large armies of foreign mercenaries to complete the works of death, desolation, and tyranny already begun with circumstances of cruelty and perfidy scarcely paralleled in the most barbarous ages, and totally unworthy of the head of a civilized nation.

He has constrained our fellow-citizens, taken captive on the high seas, to bear arms against their country, to become the executioners of their friends and brethren, or to fall themselves by their hands.

He has excited domestic insurrection among us, and has endeavored to bring on the inhabitants of our frontiers the merciless Indian savages, whose known rule of warfare is an undistinguished destruction of all ages, sexes, and conditions.

In every stage of these oppressions we have petitioned for redress in the most humble terms; our repeated petitions have been answered only by repeated injury. A prince, whose character is thus marked by every act which may define a tyrant, is unfit to be the ruler of a free people.

Nor have we been wanting in our attentions to our British brethren. We have warned them, from time to time, of attempts by their legislature to extend an unwarrantable jurisdiction over us. We have reminded them of the circumstances of our emigration and settlement here. We have appealed to their native justice and magnanimity; and we have conjured them by the ties of our common kindred, to disavow these usurpations, which would inevitably interrupt our connections and correspondence. They, too, have been deaf to the voice of justice and of consanguinity. We must, therefore, acquiesce in the necessity which denounces our separation, and hold them, as we hold the rest of mankind, enemies in war, in peace friends.

We, therefore, the representatives of the United States of America, in General Congress assembled, appealing to the Supreme Judge of the world for the rectitude of our intentions, do, in the name and by the authority of the good people of these colonies, solemnly publish and declare, that these United Colonies are, and of right ought to be, FREE AND INDEPENDENT STATES; that they are absolved from all allegiance to the British crown, and that all political connection between them and the state of Great Britain is, and ought to be, totally dissolved; and that, as free and independent states, they have full power to levy war, conclude peace, contract alliances, establish commerce, and do all other acts and things which independent states may of right do. And for the support of this declaration, with a firm reliance on the protection of Divine Providence, we mutually pledge to each other our lives, our fortunes, and our sacred honor.

JOHN HANCOCK *[President]*
[and fifty-five others]

CONSTITUTION OF THE UNITED STATES OF AMERICA

PREAMBLE

We the people of the United States, in order to form a more perfect union, establish justice, insure domestic tranquility, provide for the common defense, promote the general welfare, and secure the blessings of liberty to ourselves and our posterity, do ordain and establish this CONSTITUTION for the United States of America.

ARTICLE I

Section 1. All legislative powers herein granted shall be vested in a Congress of the United States, which shall consist of a Senate and a House of Representatives.

Section 2. The House of Representatives shall be composed of members chosen every second year by the people of the several States, and the electors in each State shall have the qualifications requisite for electors of the most numerous branch of the State Legislature.

No person shall be a Representative who shall not have attained to the age of twenty-five years, and been seven years a citizen of the United States, and who shall not, when elected, be an inhabitant of that State in which he shall be chosen.

Representatives and direct taxes shall be apportioned among the several States which may be included within this Union, according to their respective numbers, *which shall be determined by adding to the whole number of free persons, including those bound to service for a term of years and excluding Indians not taxed, three-fifths of all other persons.* The actual enumeration shall be made within three years after the first meeting of the Congress of the United States, and within every subsequent term of ten years, in such manner as they shall by law direct. The number of Representatives shall not exceed one for every thirty thousand, but each State shall have at least one Representative; *and until such enumeration shall be made, the State of New Hampshire shall be entitled to choose three, Massachusetts eight, Rhode Island and Providence Plantations one, Connecticut five, New York six, New Jersey four, Pennsylvania eight, Delaware one, Maryland six, Virginia ten, North Carolina five, South Carolina five, and Georgia three.*

When vacancies happen in the representation from any State, the Executive authority thereof shall issue writs of election to fill such vacancies.

Note: Passages no longer in effect are printed in italic type.

The House of Representatives shall choose their Speaker and other officers; and shall have the sole power of impeachment.

Section 3. The Senate of the United States shall be composed of two Senators from each State, *chosen by the legislature thereof,* for six years; and each Senator shall have one vote.

Immediately after they shall be assembled in consequence of the first election, they shall be divided as equally as may be into three classes. The seats of the Senators of the first class shall be vacated at the expiration of the second year, of the second class at the expiration of the fourth year, and of the third class at the expiration of the sixth year, so that one-third may be chosen every second year; and if vacancies happen by resignation or otherwise, during the recess of the legislature of any State, the Executive thereof may make temporary appointments until the next meeting of the legislature, which shall then fill such vacancies.

No person shall be a Senator who shall not have attained to the age of thirty years, and been nine years a citizen of the United States, and who shall not, when elected, be an inhabitant of that State for which he shall be chosen.

The Vice President of the United States shall be President of the Senate, but shall have no vote, unless they be equally divided.

The Senate shall choose their other officers, and also a President *pro tempore,* in the absence of the Vice President, or when he shall exercise the office of the President of the United States.

The Senate shall have the sole power to try all impeachments. When sitting for that purpose, they shall be on oath or affirmation. When the President of the United States is tried, the Chief Justice shall preside: and no person shall be convicted without the concurrence of two-thirds of the members present.

Judgment in cases of impeachment shall not extend further than to removal from the office, and disqualification to hold and enjoy any office of honor, trust or profit under the United States; but the party convicted shall nevertheless be liable and subject to indictment, trial, judgment and punishment, according to law.

Section 4. The times, places and manner of holding elections for Senators and Representatives shall be prescribed in each State by the legislature thereof; but the Congress may at any time by law make or alter such regulations, except as to the places of choosing Senators.

The Congress shall assemble at least once in every year, and such meeting *shall be on the first Monday in December, unless they shall by law appoint a different day.*

Section 5. Each house shall be the judge of the elections, returns and qualifications of its own members, and a majority of each shall constitute a quorum to do business; but a smaller number may adjourn from day to day, and may be authorized to compel the attendance of absent members, in such manner, and under such penalties, as each house may provide.

Each house may determine the rules of its proceedings, punish its members for disorderly behavior, and with the concurrence of two-thirds, expel a member.

Each house shall keep a journal of its proceedings, and from time to time publish the same, excepting such parts as may in their judgment require secrecy; and the yeas and nays of the members of either house on any question shall, at the desire of one-fifth of those present, be entered on the journal.

Neither house, during the session of Congress, shall, without the consent of the other, adjourn for more than three days, nor to any other place than that in which the two houses shall be sitting.

Section 6. The Senators and Representatives shall receive a compensation for their services, to be ascertained by law and paid out of the treasury of the United States. They shall in all cases except treason, felony and breach of the peace, be privileged from arrest during their attendance at the session of their respective houses, and in going to and returning from the same; and for any speech or debate in either house, they shall not be questioned in any other place.

No Senator or Representative shall, during the time for which he was elected, be appointed to any civil office under the authority of the United States, which shall have been created, or the emoluments whereof shall have been increased, during such time; and no person holding any office under the United States shall be a member of either house during his continuance in office.

Section 7. All bills for raising revenue shall originate in the House of Representatives; but the Senate may propose or concur with amendments as on other bills.

Every bill which shall have passed the House of Representatives and the Senate, shall, before it become a law, be presented to the President of the United States; if he approve he shall sign it, but if not he shall return it with objections to that house in which it originated, who shall enter the objections at large on their journal, and proceed to reconsider it. If after such reconsideration two-thirds of that house shall agree to pass the bill, it shall be sent, together with the objections, to the other house, by which it shall likewise be reconsidered, and, if approved by two-thirds of that house, it shall become a law. But in all such cases the votes of both houses shall be determined by yeas and nays, and the names of the persons voting for and against the bill shall be entered on the journal of each house respectively. If any bill shall not be returned by the President within ten days (Sundays excepted) after it shall have been presented to him, the same shall be a law, in like manner as if he had signed it, unless the Congress by their adjournment prevent its return, in which case it shall not be a law.

Every order, resolution, or vote to which the concurrence of the Senate and House of Representatives may be necessary (except on a question of adjournment) shall be presented to the President of the United States; and before the same shall take effect, shall be approved by him, or being disapproved by him, shall be repassed by two-thirds of the Senate and House of Representatives, according to the rules and limitations prescribed in the case of a bill.

Section 8. The Congress shall have power

To lay and collect taxes, duties, imposts, and excises, to pay the debts and provide for the common defense and general welfare of the United States; but all duties, imposts and excises shall be uniform throughout the United States;

To borrow money on the credit of the United States;

To regulate commerce with foreign nations, and among the several States, and with the Indian tribes;

To establish an uniform rule of naturalization, and uniform laws on the subject of bankruptcies throughout the United States;

To coin money, regulate the value thereof, and of foreign coin, and fix the standard of weights and measures;

To provide for the punishment of counterfeiting the securities and current coin of the United States;

To establish post offices and post roads;

To promote the progress of science and useful arts by securing for limited times to authors and inventors the exclusive right to their respective writings and discoveries;

To constitute tribunals inferior to the Supreme Court;

To define and punish piracies and felonies committed on the high seas and offenses against the law of nations;

To declare war, grant letters of marque and reprisal, and make rules concerning captures on land and water;

To raise and support armies, but no appropriation of money to that use shall be for a longer term than two years;

To provide and maintain a navy;

To make rules for the government and regulation of the land and naval forces;

To provide for calling forth the militia to execute the laws of the Union, suppress insurrections, and repel invasions;

To provide for organizing, arming, and disciplining the militia, and for governing such part of them as may be employed in the service of the United States, reserving to the States respectively the appointment of the officers, and the authority of training the militia according to the discipline prescribed by Congress;

To exercise exclusive legislation in all cases whatsoever, over such district (not exceeding ten miles square) as may, by cession of particular States, and the acceptance of Congress, become the seat of government of the United States, and to exercise like authority over all places purchased by the consent of the legislature of the State, in which the same shall be, for erection of forts, magazines, arsenals, dock-yards, and other needful buildings;—and

To make all laws which shall be necessary and proper for carrying into execution the foregoing powers, and all other powers vested by this Constitution in the government of the United States, or in any department or officer thereof.

Section 9. *The migration or importation of such persons as any of the States now existing shall think proper to admit shall not be prohibited by the Congress prior to the year 1808; but a tax or duty may be imposed on such importation, not exceeding $10 for each person.*

The privilege of the writ of habeas corpus shall not be suspended, unless when in cases of rebellion or invasion the public safety may require it.

No bill of attainder or ex post facto law shall be passed.

No capitation, or other direct, tax shall be laid, unless in proportion to the census or enumeration herein before directed to be taken.

No tax or duty shall be laid on articles exported from any State.

No preference shall be given by any regulation of commerce or revenue to the ports of one State over those of another; nor shall vessels bound to, or from, one State, be obliged to enter, clear, or pay duties in another.

No money shall be drawn from the treasury, but in consequence of appropriations made by law; and a regular statement and account of the receipts and expenditures of all public money shall be published from time to time.

No title of nobility shall be granted by the United States: and no person holding any office of profit or trust under them, shall, without the consent of the Congress, accept of any present, emolument, office, or title, of any kind whatever, from any king, prince, or foreign state.

Section 10. No State shall enter into any treaty, alliance, or confederation; grant letters of marque and reprisal; coin money; emit bills of credit; make anything but gold and silver coin a tender in payment of debts; pass any bill of attainder, ex post facto law, or law impairing the obligation of contracts, or grant any title of nobility.

No State shall, without the consent of Congress, lay any imposts or duties on imports or exports, except what may be absolutely necessary for executing its inspection laws: and the net produce of all duties and imposts, laid by any State on imports or exports, shall be for the use of the treasury of the United States; and all such laws shall be subject to the revision and control of the Congress.

No State shall, without the consent of Congress, lay any duty of tonnage, keep troops or ships of war in time of peace, enter into any agreement or compact with another State, or with a foreign power, or engage in war, unless actually invaded, or in such imminent danger as will not admit of delay.

ARTICLE II

Section 1. The executive power shall be vested in a President of the United States of America. He shall hold his office during the term of four years, and, together with the Vice President, chosen for the same term, be elected as follows:

Each state shall appoint, in such manner as the legislature thereof may direct, a number of electors, equal to the whole number of Senators and Representatives to which the State may be entitled in the Congress; but no Senator or Representative, or person holding an office of trust or profit under the United States, shall be appointed an elector.

The electors shall meet in their respective States, and vote by ballot for two persons, of whom one at least shall not be an inhabitant of the same State with themselves. And they shall make a list of all the persons voted for, and of the number of votes for each; which list they shall sign and certify, and transmit sealed to the seat of government of the United States, directed to the President of the Senate. The President of the Senate shall, in the presence of the Senate and the House of Representatives, open all the certificates, and the votes shall then be counted. The person having the greatest number of votes shall be the President, if such number be a majority of the whole number of electors appointed; and if there be more than one who have such majority, and have an equal number of votes, then the House of Representatives shall immediately choose by ballot one of them for President; and if no person have a majority, then from the five highest on the list said house shall in like manner choose the President. But in choosing the President the votes shall be taken by States, the representation from each State having one vote; a quorum for this purpose shall consist of a member or members from two-thirds of the States, and a majority of all the States shall be necessary to a choice. In every case, after the choice of the President, the person having the greatest number of votes of the electors shall be the Vice President. But if there should remain two or more who have equal votes, the Senate shall choose from them by ballot the Vice President.

The Congress may determine the time of choosing the electors and the day on which they shall give their votes; which day shall be the same throughout the United States.

No person except a natural-born citizen, *or a citizen of the United States at the time of the adoption of this Constitution,* shall be eligible to the office of President; neither shall any person be eligible to that office who shall not have attained to the age of thirty-five years, and been fourteen years a resident within the United States.

In case of the removal of the President from office or of his death, resignation, or inability to discharge the powers and duties of the said office, the same shall devolve on the Vice President, and the Congress may by law provide for the case of removal, death, resignation, or inability, both of the President and Vice President, declaring what officer shall then act as President, and such officer shall act accordingly, until the disability be removed, or a President shall be elected.

The President shall, at stated times, receive for his services a compensation, which shall neither be increased nor diminished during the period for which he shall have been elected, and he shall not receive within that period any other emolument from the United States, or any of them.

Before he enter on the execution of his office, he shall take the following oath or affirmation:—"I do solemnly swear (or affirm) that I will faithfully execute the office of the President of the United States, and will to the best of my ability preserve, protect and defend the Constitution of the United States."

Section 2. The President shall be commander in chief of the army and navy of the United States, and of the militia of the several States, when called into the actual service of the United States; he may require the opinion, in writing, of the principal officer in each of the executive departments, upon any subject relating to the duties of their respective offices, and he shall have power to grant reprieves and pardons for offenses against the United States, except in cases of impeachment.

He shall have power, by and with the advice and consent of the Senate, to make treaties, provided two-thirds of the Senators present concur; and he shall nominate, and by and with the advice and consent of the Senate, shall appoint ambassadors, other public ministers and consuls, judges of the Supreme Court, and all other officers of the United States, whose appointments are not herein otherwise provided for, and which shall be established by law: but Congress may by law vest the appointment of such inferior officers, as they think proper, in the President alone, in the courts of law, or in the heads of departments.

The President shall have power to fill up all vacancies that may happen during the recess of the Senate, by granting commissions which shall expire at the end of their next session.

Section 3. He shall from time to time give to the Congress information of the state of the Union, and recommend to their consideration such measures as he shall judge necessary and expedient; he may, on extraordinary occasions, convene both houses, or either of them, and in case of disagreement between them, with respect to the time of adjournment, he may adjourn them to such time as he shall think proper; he shall receive ambassadors and other public ministers; he shall take care that the laws be faithfully executed, and shall commission all the officers of the United States.

Section 4. The President, Vice President and all civil officers of the United States shall be removed from office on impeachment for, and on conviction of, treason, bribery, or other high crimes and misdemeanors.

ARTICLE III

Section 1. The judicial power of the United States shall be vested in one Supreme Court, and in such inferior courts as the Congress may from time to time ordain and establish. The judges, both of the Supreme and inferior courts, shall hold their offices during good behavior, and shall, at stated times, receive for their services a compensation which shall not be diminished during their continuance in office.

Section 2. The judicial power shall extend to all cases, in law and equity, arising under this Constitution, the laws of the United States, and treaties made, or which shall be made, under their authority;—to all cases affecting ambassadors, other public ministers and consuls;—to all cases of admiralty and maritime jurisdiction;—to controversies to which the United States shall be a party;—to controversies between two or more States;—*between a State and citizens of another State;*—between citizens of different States;—between citizens of the same State claiming lands under grants of different States, and between a State, or the citizens thereof, and foreign states, citizens or subjects.

In all cases affecting ambassadors, other public ministers and consuls, and those in which a State shall be party, the Supreme Court shall have original jurisdiction. In all the other cases before mentioned, the Supreme Court shall have appellate jurisdiction, both as to law and fact, with such exceptions, and under such regulations, as the Congress shall make.

The trial of all crimes, except in cases of impeachment, shall be by jury; and such trial shall be held in the State where said crimes shall have been committed; but when not committed within any State, the trial shall be at such place or places as the Congress may by law have directed.

Section 3. Treason against the United States shall consist only in levying war against them, or in adhering to their enemies, giving them aid and comfort. No person shall be convicted of treason unless on the testimony of two witnesses to the same overt act, or on confession in open court.

The Congress shall have power to declare the punishment of treason, but no attainder of treason shall work corruption of blood, or forfeiture except during the life of the person attainted.

ARTICLE IV

Section 1. Full faith and credit shall be given in each State to the public acts, records, and judicial proceedings of every other State. And the Congress may by general laws prescribe the manner in which such acts, records, and proceedings shall be proved, and the effect thereof.

Section 2. The citizens of each State shall be entitled to all privileges and immunities of citizens in the several States.

A person charged in any State with treason, felony, or other crime, who shall flee from justice, and be found in another State, shall on demand of the executive authority of the State from which he fled, be delivered up, to be removed to the State having jurisdiction of the crime.

No person held to service or labor in one State, under the laws thereof, escaping into another, shall, in consequence of any law or regulation therein, be discharged from such service or labor, but shall be delivered up on claim of the party to whom such service or labor may be due.

Section 3. New States may be admitted by the Congress into this Union; but no new State shall be formed or erected within the jurisdiction of any other State; nor any State be formed by the junction of two or more States, or parts of States, without the consent of the legislatures of the States concerned as well as of the Congress.

The Congress shall have power to dispose of and make all needful rules and regulations respecting the territory or other property belonging to the United States; and nothing in this Constitution shall be so construed as to prejudice any claims of the United States, or of any particular State.

Section 4. The United States shall guarantee to every State in this Union a republican form of government, and shall protect each of them against invasion; and on application of the legislature, or of the executive (when the legislature cannot be convened); against domestic violence.

ARTICLE V

The Congress, whenever two-thirds of both houses shall deem it necessary, shall propose amendments to this Constitution, or, on the application of the legislatures of two-thirds of the several States, shall call a convention for proposing amendments, which, in either case, shall be valid to all intents and purposes, as part of this Constitution, when ratified by the legislatures of three-fourths of the several States, or by conventions in three-fourths thereof, as the one or the other mode of ratification may be proposed by the Congress; provided *that no amendments which may be made prior to the year one thousand eight hundred and eight shall in any manner affect the first and fourth clauses in the ninth section of the first article;* and that no State, without its consent, shall be deprived of its equal suffrage in the Senate.

ARTICLE VI

All debts contracted and engagements entered into, before the adoption of this Constitution, shall be as valid against the United States under this Constitution, as under the Confederation.

This Constitution, and the laws of the United States which shall be made in pursuance thereof; and all treaties made, or which shall be made, under the authority of the United States, shall be the supreme law of the land; and the judges in every State shall be bound thereby, anything in the Constitution or laws of any State to the contrary notwithstanding.

The Senators and Representatives before mentioned, and the members of the several State legislatures, and all executive and judicial officers, both of the United States and of the several States, shall be bound by oath or affirmation to support this Constitution; but no religious test shall ever be required as a qualification to any office or public trust under the United States.

ARTICLE VII

The ratification of the conventions of nine States shall be sufficient for the establishment of this Constitution between the States so ratifying the same.

Done in Convention by the unanimous consent of the States present, the seventeenth day of September in the year of our Lord one thousand seven hundred and eighty-seven and of the Independence of the United States of America the twelfth. In witness whereof we have hereunto subscribed our names.

[Signed by]
G° WASHINGTON
Presidt and Deputy from Virginia
[and thirty-eight others]

AMENDMENTS TO THE CONSTITUTION

AMENDMENT I*

Congress shall make no law respecting an establishment of religion, or prohibiting the free exercise thereof; or abridging the freedom of speech, or of the press; or the right of the people peaceably to assemble, and to petition the government for a redress of grievances.

AMENDMENT II

A well-regulated militia being necessary to the security of a free State, the right of the people to keep and bear arms shall not be infringed.

AMENDMENT III

No soldier shall, in time of peace, be quartered in any house without the consent of the owner, nor in time of war, but in a manner to be prescribed by law.

AMENDMENT IV

The right of the people to be secure in their persons, houses, papers, and effects, against unreasonable searches and seizures, shall not be violated, and no warrants shall issue but upon probable cause, supported by oath or affirmation, and particularly describing the place to be searched, and the persons or things to be seized.

AMENDMENT V

No person shall be held to answer for a capital, or otherwise infamous crime, unless on a presentment or indictment of a grand jury, except in cases arising in the land or naval forces, or in the militia, when in actual service in time of war or public danger; nor shall any person be subject for the same offense to be twice put in jeopardy of life or limb; nor shall be compelled in any criminal case to be a witness against himself, nor be deprived of life, liberty, or property, without due process of law; nor shall private property be taken for public use without just compensation.

* The first ten Amendments (Bill of Rights) were adopted in 1791.

AMENDMENT VI

In all criminal prosecutions, the accused shall enjoy the right to a speedy and public trial, by an impartial jury of the State and district wherein the crime shall have been committed, which district shall have been previously ascertained by law, and to be informed of the nature and cause of the accusation; to be confronted with the witnesses against him; to have compulsory process for obtaining witnesses in his favor, and to have the assistance of counsel for his defense.

AMENDMENT VII

In suits at common law, where the value in controversy shall exceed twenty dollars, the right of trial by jury shall be preserved, and no fact tried by a jury shall be otherwise reexamined in any court of the United States, than according to the rules of the common law.

AMENDMENT VIII

Excessive bail shall not be required, nor excessive fines imposed, nor cruel and unusual punishments inflicted.

AMENDMENT IX

The enumeration in the Constitution, of certain rights, shall not be construed to deny or disparage others retained by the people.

AMENDMENT X

The powers not delegated to the United States by the Constitution, not prohibited by it to the States, are reserved to the States respectively, or to the people.

AMENDMENT XI [*Adopted 1798*]

The judicial power of the United States shall not be construed to extend to any suit in law or equity, commenced or prosecuted against one of the United States by citizens of another State, or by citizens or subjects of any foreign state.

AMENDMENT XII [*Adopted 1804*]

The electors shall meet in their respective States, and vote by ballot for President and Vice President, one of whom, at least, shall not be an inhabitant of the same State with themselves; they shall name in their ballots the person voted for as President, and in distinct ballots the person voted for as Vice President, and they shall make distinct lists of all persons voted for as President, and of all persons voted for as Vice President, and of the number of votes for each, which lists they shall sign and certify, and transmit sealed to the seat of government of the United States, directed to the President of the Senate;—the President of the Senate shall, in the presence of the Senate and House of Representatives, open all the certificates and the votes shall then be counted;—the person having the greatest number of votes for President shall be the President, if such number be a majority of the whole number of electors appointed; and if no person have such majority, then from the persons having the highest numbers not exceeding three on the list of those voted for as President, the House of Representatives shall choose immediately, by ballot, the President. But in choosing the President, the votes shall be taken by States, the representation from each State having one vote; a quorum for this purpose shall consist of a member or members from two-thirds of the States, and a majority of all the States shall be necessary to a choice. And if the House of Representatives shall not choose a President whenever the right of choice shall devolve upon them, before *the fourth day of March* next following, then the Vice President shall act as President, as in the case of the death or other constitutional disability of the President.

The person having the greatest number of votes as Vice President shall be the Vice President, if such a number be a majority of the whole number of electors appointed; and if no person have a majority, then from the two highest numbers on the list the Senate shall choose the Vice President; a quorum for the purpose shall consist of two-thirds of the whole number of Senators, and a majority of the whole number shall be necessary to a choice. But no person constitutionally ineligible to the office of President shall be eligible to that of Vice President of the United States.

AMENDMENT XIII [*Adopted 1865*]

Section 1. Neither slavery nor involuntary servitude, except as a punishment for crime whereof the party shall have been duly convicted, shall exist within the United States, or any place subject to their jurisdiction.

Section 2. Congress shall have power to enforce this article by appropriate legislation.

AMENDMENT XIV [*Adopted 1868*]

Section 1. All persons born or naturalized in the United States, and subject to the jurisdiction thereof, are citizens of the United States and of the State wherein they reside. No State shall make or enforce any law which shall abridge the privileges or immunities of citizens of the United States; nor shall any State deprive any person of life, liberty, or property, without due process of law; nor deny to any person within its jurisdiction the equal protection of the laws.

Section 2. Representatives shall be apportioned among the several States according to their respective numbers, counting the whole number of persons in each State, excluding Indians not taxed. But when the right to vote at any election for the choice of Electors for President and Vice President of the United States, Representatives in Congress, the executive and judicial officers of a State, or the members of the legislature thereof, is denied to any of the male inhabitants of such State, being twenty-one years of age and citizens of the United States, or in any way abridged, except for participation in rebellion, or other crime, the basis of representation therein shall be reduced in the proportion which the number of such male citizens shall bear to the whole number of male citizens twenty-one years of age in such State.

Section 3. No person shall be a Senator or Representative in Congress or Elector of President and Vice President, or hold any office, civil or military, under the United States, or under any State, who, having previously taken an oath, as a member of Congress, or as an officer of the United States, or as a member of any State legislature, or as an executive or judicial officer of any State, to support the Constitution of the

United States, shall have engaged in insurrection or rebellion against the same, or given aid and comfort to the enemies thereof. Congress may, by a vote of two-thirds of each house, remove such disability.

Section 4. The validity of the public debt of the United States, authorized by law, including debts incurred for payment of pensions and bounties for services in suppressing insurrection or rebellion, shall not be questioned. But neither the United States nor any State shall assume or pay any debt or obligation incurred in aid of insurrection or rebellion against the United States, or any claim for the loss or emancipation of any slave; but all such debts, obligations, and claims shall be held illegal and void.

Section 5. The Congress shall have the power to enforce, by appropriate legislation, the provisions of this article.

AMENDMENT XV [*Adopted 1870*]

Section 1. The right of citizens of the United States to vote shall not be denied or abridged by the United States or by any State on account of race, color, or previous condition of servitude.

Section 2. The Congress shall have power to enforce this article by appropriate legislation.

AMENDMENT XVI [*Adopted 1913*]

The Congress shall have power to lay and collect taxes on incomes, from whatever source derived, without apportionment among the several States, and without regard to any census or enumeration.

AMENDMENT XVII [*Adopted 1913*]

Section 1. The Senate of the United States shall be composed of two Senators from each State, elected by the people thereof, for six years; and each Senator shall have one vote. The electors in each State shall have the qualifications requisite for electors of [voters for] the most numerous branch of the State legislatures.

Section 2. When vacancies happen in the representation of any State in the Senate, the executive authority of such State shall issue writs of election to fill such vacancies: Provided, that the Legislature of any State may empower the executive thereof to make temporary appointments until the people fill the vacancies by election as the Legislature may direct.

Section 3. This amendment shall not be so construed as to affect the election or term of any Senator chosen before it becomes valid as part of the Constitution.

AMENDMENT XVIII [*Adopted 1919; repealed 1933*]

Section 1. *After one year from the ratification of this article the manufacture, sale, or transportation of intoxicating liquors within, the importation thereof into, or the exportation thereof from the United States and all territory subject to the jurisdiction thereof, for beverage purposes, is hereby prohibited.*

Section 2. *The Congress and the several States shall have concurrent power to enforce this article by appropriate legislation.*

Section 3. *This article shall be inoperative unless it shall have been ratified as an amendment to the Constitution by the legislatures of the several States, as provided by the Constitution, within seven years from the date of the submission thereof to the States by the Congress.*

AMENDMENT XIX [*Adopted 1920*]

Section 1. The right of citizens of the United States to vote shall not be denied or abridged by the United States or by any State on account of sex.

Section 2. The Congress shall have the power to enforce this article by appropriate legislation.

AMENDMENT XX [*Adopted 1933*]

Section 1. The terms of the President and Vice President shall end at noon on the 20th day of January, and the terms of Senators and Representatives at noon on the 3d day of January, of the years in which such terms would have ended if this article had not been ratified; and the terms of their successors shall then begin.

Section 2. The Congress shall assemble at least once in every year, and such meeting shall begin at noon on the 3d day of January, unless they shall by law appoint a different day.

Section 3. If, at the time fixed for the beginning of the term of the President, the President-elect shall have died, the Vice President-elect shall become President. If a President shall not have been chosen before the time fixed for the beginning of his term, or if the President-elect shall have failed to qualify, then the Vice President-elect shall act as President until a President shall have qualified; and the Congress may by law provide for the case wherein neither a President-elect nor a Vice President-elect shall have qualified, declaring who shall then act as President, or the manner in which one who is to act shall be selected, and such persons shall act accordingly until a President or Vice President shall have qualified.

Section 4. The Congress may by law provide for the case of the death of any of the persons from whom the House of Representatives may choose a President whenever the right of choice shall have devolved upon them, and for the case of the death of any of the persons from whom the Senate may choose a Vice President whenever the right of choice shall have devolved upon them.

Section 5. Sections 1 and 2 shall take effect on the 15th day of October following the ratification of this article.

Section 6. This article shall be inoperative unless it shall have been ratified as an amendment to the Constitution by the Legislatures of three-fourths of the several States within seven years from the date of its submission.

AMENDMENT XXI [*Adopted 1933*]

Section 1. The eighteenth article of amendment to the Constitution of the United States is hereby repealed.

Section 2. The transportation or importation into any State, Territory, or Possession of the United States for delivery or use therein of intoxicating liquors, in violation of the laws thereof, is hereby prohibited.

Section 3. This article shall be inoperative unless it shall have been ratified as an amendment to the Constitution by conventions in the several States, as provided in the Constitution, within seven years from the date of submission thereof to the States by the Congress.

AMENDMENT XXII [*Adopted 1951*]

Section 1. No person shall be elected to the office of President more than twice, and no person who has held the office of President, or acted as President, for more than two years of a term to which some other person was elected President shall be elected to the office of President more than once. But this article shall not apply to any person holding the office of President when this article was proposed by the Congress, and shall not prevent any person who may be holding the office of President, or acting as President, during the term within which this article becomes operative from holding the office of President or acting as President during the remainder of such term.

Section 2. This article shall be inoperative unless it shall have been ratified as an amendment to the Constitution by the legislatures of three-fourths of the several States within seven years from the date of its submission to the States by the Congress.

AMENDMENT XXIII [*Adopted 1961*]

Section 1. The District constituting the seat of Government of the United States shall appoint in such manner as the Congress may direct:

A number of electors of President and Vice President equal to the whole number of Senators and Representatives in Congress to which the District would be entitled if it were a State, but in no event more than the least populous State; they shall be in addition to those appointed by the States, but they shall be considered for the purposes of the election of President and Vice President, to be electors appointed by a State; and they shall meet in the District and perform such duties as provided by the twelfth article of amendment.

Section 2. The Congress shall have the power to enforce this article by appropriate legislation.

AMENDMENT XXIV [*Adopted 1964*]

Section 1. The right of citizens of the United States to vote in any primary or other election for President or Vice President, for electors for President or Vice President, or for Senator or Representative in Congress, shall not be denied or abridged by the United States or any State by reason of failure to pay any poll tax or other tax.

Section 2. The Congress shall have the power to enforce this article by appropriate legislation.

AMENDMENT XXV [*Adopted 1967*]

Section 1. In case of the removal of the President from office or of his death or resignation, the Vice President shall become President.

Section 2. Whenever there is a vacancy in the office of the Vice President, the President shall nominate a Vice President who shall take office upon confirmation by a majority vote of both Houses of Congress.

Section 3. Whenever the President transmits to the President pro tempore of the Senate and the Speaker of the House of Representatives his written declaration that he is unable to discharge the powers and duties of his office, and until he transmits to them a written declaration to the contrary, such powers and duties shall be discharged by the Vice President as Acting President.

Section 4. Whenever the Vice President and a majority of either the principal officers of the executive departments or of such other body as Congress may by law provide, transmit to the President pro tempore of the Senate and the Speaker of the House of Representatives their written declaration that the President is unable to discharge the powers and duties of his office, the Vice President shall immediately assume the powers and duties of the office as Acting President.

Thereafter, when the President transmits to the President pro tempore of the Senate and the Speaker of the House of Representatives his written declaration that no inability exists, he shall resume the powers and duties of his office unless the Vice President and a majority of either the principal officers of the executive department[s] or of such other body as Congress may by law provide, transmit within four days to the President pro tempore of the Senate and the Speaker of the House of Representatives their written declaration that the President is unable to discharge the powers and duties of his office. Thereupon Congress shall decide the issue, assembling within forty-eight hours for that purpose if not in session. If the Congress, within twenty-one days after receipt of the latter written declaration, or, if Congress is not in session, within twenty-one days after Congress is required to assemble, determines by two-thirds vote of both Houses that the President is unable to discharge the powers and duties of his office, the Vice President shall continue to discharge the same as Acting President; otherwise, the President shall resume the powers and duties of his office.

AMENDMENT XXVI [*Adopted 1971*]

Section 1. The right of citizens of the United States, who are eighteen years of age or older, to vote shall not be denied or abridged by the United States or by any State on account of age.

Section 2. The Congress shall have power to enforce this article by appropriate legislation.

AMENDMENT XXVII* [*Adopted 1992*]

No law, varying the compensation for services of the Senators and Representatives, shall take effect, until an election of Representatives shall have intervened.

* Originally proposed in 1789 by James Madison, this amendment failed to win ratification along with the other parts of what became the Bill of Rights. However, the proposed amendment contained no deadline for ratification, and over the years other state legislatures voted to add it to the Constitution; many such ratifications occurred during the 1980s and early 1990s as public frustration with Congress's performance mounted. In May 1992 the Archivist of the United States certified that, with the Michigan legislature's ratification, the article had been approved by three-fourths of the states and thus automatically became part of the Constitution. But congressional leaders and constitutional specialists questioned whether an amendment that took 202 years to win ratification was valid, and the issue had not been resolved by the time this book went to press.

PRESIDENTIAL ELECTIONS, 1789–2008

Year	States in the Union	Candidates	Parties	Electoral Vote	Popular Vote	Percentage of Popular Vote
1789	11	GEORGE WASHINGTON	No party designations	69		
		John Adams		34		
		Minor candidates		35		
1792	15	GEORGE WASHINGTON	No party designations	132		
		John Adams		77		
		George Clinton		50		
		Minor candidates		5		
1796	16	JOHN ADAMS	Federalist	71		
		Thomas Jefferson	Democratic-Republican	68		
		Thomas Pinckney	Federalist	59		
		Aaron Burr	Democratic-Republican	30		
		Minor candidates		48		
1800	16	THOMAS JEFFERSON	Democratic-Republican	73		
		Aaron Burr	Democratic-Republican	73		
		John Adams	Federalist	65		
		Charles C. Pinckney	Federalist	64		
		John Jay	Federalist	1		
1804	17	THOMAS JEFFERSON	Democratic-Republican	162		
		Charles C. Pinckney	Federalist	14		
1808	17	JAMES MADISON	Democratic-Republican	122		
		Charles C. Pinckney	Federalist	47		
		George Clinton	Democratic-Republican	6		
1812	18	JAMES MADISON	Democratic-Republican	128		
		DeWitt Clinton	Federalist	89		
1816	19	JAMES MONROE	Democratic-Republican	183		
		Rufus King	Federalist	34		
1820	24	JAMES MONROE	Democratic-Republican	231		
		John Quincy Adams	Independent Republican	1		
1824	24	JOHN QUINCY ADAMS	Democratic-Republican	84	108,740	30.5
		Andrew Jackson	Democratic-Republican	99	153,544	43.1
		William H. Crawford	Democratic-Republican	41	46,618	13.1
		Henry Clay	Democratic-Republican	37	47,136	13.2
1828	24	ANDREW JACKSON	Democratic	178	642,553	56.0
		John Quincy Adams	National Republican	83	500,897	44.0
1832	24	ANDREW JACKSON	Democratic	219	687,502	55.0
		Henry Clay	National Republican	49	530,189	42.4
		William Wirt	Anti-Masonic	7	33,108	2.6
		John Floyd	National Republican	11		

Because candidates receiving less than 1 percent of the popular vote are omitted, the percentage of popular vote may not total 100 percent.

Before the Twelfth Amendment was passed in 1804, the Electoral College voted for two presidential candidates; the runner-up became vice president.

PRESIDENTIAL ELECTIONS, 1789–2008 (*continued*)

Year	States in the Union	Candidates	Parties	Electoral Vote	Popular Vote	Percentage of Popular Vote
1836	26	MARTIN VAN BUREN	Democratic	170	765,483	50.9
		William H. Harrison	Whig	73		
		Hugh L. White	Whig	26	739,795	49.1
		Daniel Webster	Whig	14		
		W. P. Mangum	Whig	11		
1840	26	WILLIAM H. HARRISON	Whig	234	1,274,624	53.1
		Martin Van Buren	Democratic	60	1,127,781	46.9
1844	26	JAMES K. POLK	Democratic	170	1,338,464	49.6
		Henry Clay	Whig	105	1,300,097	48.1
		James G. Birney	Liberty		62,300	2.3
1848	30	ZACHARY TAYLOR	Whig	163	1,360,967	47.4
		Lewis Cass	Democratic	127	1,222,342	42.5
		Martin Van Buren	Free Soil		291,263	10.1
1852	31	FRANKLIN PIERCE	Democratic	254	1,601,117	50.9
		Winfield Scott	Whig	42	1,385,453	44.1
		John P. Hale	Free Soil		155,825	5.0
1856	31	JAMES BUCHANAN	Democratic	174	1,832,955	45.3
		John C. Frémont	Republican	114	1,339,932	33.1
		Millard Fillmore	American	8	871,731	21.6
1860	33	ABRAHAM LINCOLN	Republican	180	1,865,593	39.8
		Stephen A. Douglas	Democratic	12	1,382,713	29.5
		John C. Breckinridge	Democratic	72	848,356	18.1
		John Bell	Constitutional Union	39	592,906	12.6
1864	36	ABRAHAM LINCOLN	Republican	212	2,206,938	55.0
		George B. McClellan	Democratic	21	1,803,787	45.0
1868	37	ULYSSES S. GRANT	Republican	214	3,013,421	52.7
		Horatio Seymour	Democratic	80	2,706,829	47.3
1872	37	ULYSSES S. GRANT	Republican	286	3,596,745	55.6
		Horace Greeley	Democratic	*	2,843,446	43.9
1876	38	RUTHERFORD B. HAYES	Republican	185	4,034,311	48.0
		Samuel J. Tilden	Democratic	184	4,288,546	51.0
		Peter Cooper	Greenback		75,973	1.0
1880	38	JAMES A. GARFIELD	Republican	214	4,453,295	48.5
		Winfield S. Hancock	Democratic	155	4,414,082	48.1
		James B. Weaver	Greenback-Labor		308,578	3.4
1884	38	GROVER CLEVELAND	Democratic	219	4,879,507	48.5
		James G. Blaine	Republican	182	4,850,293	48.2
		Benjamin F. Butler	Greenback-Labor		175,370	1.8
		John P. St. John	Prohibition		150,369	1.5

*When Greeley died shortly after the election, his supporters divided their votes among the minor candidates.

Because candidates receiving less than 1 percent of the popular vote are omitted, the percentage of popular vote may not total 100 percent.

Presidential Elections, 1789–2008 (*continued*)

Year	States in the Union	Candidates	Parties	Electoral Vote	Popular Vote	Percentage of Popular Vote
1888	38	BENJAMIN HARRISON	Republican	233	5,477,129	47.9
		Grover Cleveland	Democratic	168	5,537,857	48.6
		Clinton B. Fisk	Prohibition		249,506	2.2
		Anson J. Streeter	Union Labor		146,935	1.3
1892	44	GROVER CLEVELAND	Democratic	277	5,555,426	46.1
		Benjamin Harrison	Republican	145	5,182,690	43.0
		James B. Weaver	People's	22	1,029,846	8.5
		John Bidwell	Prohibition		264,133	2.2
1896	45	WILLIAM McKINLEY	Republican	271	7,102,246	51.1
		William J. Bryan	Democratic	176	6,492,559	47.7
1900	45	WILLIAM McKINLEY	Republican	292	7,218,491	51.7
		William J. Bryan	Democratic; Populist	155	6,356,734	45.5
		John C. Wooley	Prohibition		208,914	1.5
1904	45	THEODORE ROOSEVELT	Republican	336	7,628,461	57.4
		Alton B. Parker	Democratic	140	5,084,223	37.6
		Eugene V. Debs	Socialist		402,283	3.0
		Silas C. Swallow	Prohibition		258,536	1.9
1908	46	WILLIAM H. TAFT	Republican	321	7,675,320	51.6
		William J. Bryan	Democratic	162	6,412,294	43.1
		Eugene V. Debs	Socialist		420,793	2.8
		Eugene W. Chafin	Prohibition		253,840	1.7
1912	48	WOODROW WILSON	Democratic	435	6,296,547	41.9
		Theodore Roosevelt	Progressive	88	4,118,571	27.4
		William H. Taft	Republican	8	3,486,720	23.2
		Eugene V. Debs	Socialist		900,672	6.0
		Eugene W. Chafin	Prohibition		206,275	1.4
1916	48	WOODROW WILSON	Democratic	277	9,127,695	49.4
		Charles E. Hughes	Republican	254	8,533,507	46.2
		A. L. Benson	Socialist		585,113	3.2
		J. Frank Hanly	Prohibition		220,506	1.2
1920	48	WARREN G. HARDING	Republican	404	16,143,407	60.4
		James N. Cox	Democratic	127	9,130,328	34.2
		Eugene V. Debs	Socialist		919,799	3.4
		P. P. Christensen	Farmer-Labor		265,411	1.0
1924	48	CALVIN COOLIDGE	Republican	382	15,718,211	54.0
		John W. Davis	Democratic	136	8,385,283	28.8
		Robert M. La Follette	Progressive	13	4,831,289	16.6
1928	48	HERBERT C. HOOVER	Republican	444	21,391,993	58.2
		Alfred E. Smith	Democratic	87	15,016,169	40.9
1932	48	FRANKLIN D. ROOSEVELT	Democratic	472	22,809,638	57.4
		Herbert C. Hoover	Republican	59	15,758,901	39.7
		Norman Thomas	Socialist		881,951	2.2

Because candidates receiving less than 1 percent of the popular vote are omitted, the percentage of popular vote may not total 100 percent.

PRESIDENTIAL ELECTIONS, 1789–2008 (*continued*)

YEAR	STATES IN THE UNION	CANDIDATES	PARTIES	ELECTORAL VOTE	POPULAR VOTE	PERCENTAGE OF POPULAR VOTE
1936	48	FRANKLIN D. ROOSEVELT	Democratic	523	27,752,869	60.8
		Alfred M. Landon	Republican	8	16,674,665	36.5
		William Lemke	Union		882,479	1.9
1940	48	FRANKLIN D. ROOSEVELT	Democratic	449	27,307,819	54.8
		Wendell L. Willkie	Republican	82	22,321,018	44.8
1944	48	FRANKLIN D. ROOSEVELT	Democratic	432	25,606,585	53.5
		Thomas E. Dewey	Republican	99	22,014,745	46.0
1948	48	HARRY S TRUMAN	Democratic	303	24,105,812	49.5
		Thomas E. Dewey	Republican	189	21,970,065	45.1
		Strom Thurmond	States' Rights	39	1,169,063	2.4
		Henry A. Wallace	Progressive		1,157,172	2.4
1952	48	DWIGHT D. EISENHOWER	Republican	442	33,936,234	55.1
		Adlai E. Stevenson	Democratic	89	27,314,992	44.4
1956	48	DWIGHT D. EISENHOWER	Republican	457	35,590,472	57.6
		Adlai E. Stevenson	Democratic	73	26,022,752	42.1
1960	50	JOHN F. KENNEDY	Democratic	303	34,227,096	49.7
		Richard M. Nixon	Republican	219	34,108,546	49.5
		Harry F. Byrd	Independent	15	502,363	.7
1964	50	LYNDON B. JOHNSON	Democratic	486	43,126,506	61.1
		Barry M. Goldwater	Republican	52	27,176,799	38.5
1968	50	RICHARD M. NIXON	Republican	301	31,770,237	43.4
		Hubert H. Humphrey	Democratic	191	31,270,533	42.7
		George C. Wallace	American Independent	46	9,906,141	13.5
1972	50	RICHARD M. NIXON	Republican	520	47,169,911	60.7
		George S. McGovern	Democratic	17	29,170,383	37.5
1976	50	JIMMY CARTER	Democratic	297	40,827,394	49.9
		Gerald R. Ford	Republican	240	39,145,977	47.9
1980	50	RONALD W. REAGAN	Republican	489	43,899,248	50.8
		Jimmy Carter	Democratic	49	35,481,435	41.0
		John B. Anderson	Independent		5,719,437	6.6
		Ed Clark	Libertarian		920,859	1.0
1984	50	RONALD W. REAGAN	Republican	525	54,451,521	58.8
		Walter F. Mondale	Democratic	13	37,565,334	40.5
1988	50	GEORGE H. W. BUSH	Republican	426	47,946,422	54.0
		Michael S. Dukakis	Democratic	112	41,016,429	46.0
1992	50	WILLIAM J. CLINTON	Democratic	370	43,728,275	43.2
		George H. W. Bush	Republican	168	38,167,416	37.7
		H. Ross Perot	Independent		19,237,247	19.0

Because candidates receiving less than 1 percent of the popular vote are omitted, the percentage of popular vote may not total 100 percent.

PRESIDENTIAL ELECTIONS, 1789–2008 (*continued*)

YEAR	STATES IN THE UNION	CANDIDATES	PARTIES	ELECTORAL VOTE	POPULAR VOTE	PERCENTAGE OF POPULAR VOTE
1996	50	WILLIAM J. CLINTON	Democratic	379	47,401,185	49.2
		Robert Dole	Republican	159	39,197,469	40.7
		H. Ross Perot	Reform		8,085,294	8.4
2000	50	GEORGE W. BUSH	Republican	271	50,456,141	47.9
		Albert Gore Jr.	Democratic	266	50,996,039	48.4
		Ralph Nader	Green		2,882,807	2.7
2004	50	GEORGE W. BUSH	Republican	286	60,608,582	51.0
		John Kerry	Democratic	252	57,288,974	48.0
		Ralph Nader	Independent		406,924	1.0
2008	50	BARACK OBAMA	Democratic	365	69,456,897	52.9
		John McCain	Republican	173	59,934,814	45.7

Because candidates receiving less than 1 percent of the popular vote are omitted, the percentage of popular vote may not total 100 percent.

Index

Fundamentals of Nursing Test Success

Ruth A. Wittmann-Price, PhD, CNS, RN, CNE, is Chairperson and Professor at Francis Marion University Department of Nursing in South Carolina. Dr. Wittmann-Price has been an obstetrical/women's health nurse for 32 years. She received her AAS and BSN degrees from Felician College in Lodi, New Jersey (1978 and 1981, respectively) and her MS as a perinatal CNS from Columbia University, New York City (1983). Ruth completed her PhD at Widener University, Chester, Pennsylvania (2006) and was awarded the Dean's Award for Excellence. She developed a midrange nursing theory "Emancipated Decision Making in Women's Health Care." Besides continuing her research about decisional science, she studies developmental outcomes of preterm infants. She has also been the Director of Nursing Research for Hahnemann University Hospital (2007–2010) to oversee all evidence-based practice projects for nursing. Hahnemann University Hospital was awarded initial Magnet status (AACN) in December 2009. Ruth has taught all levels of nursing students over the past 15 years (AAS, BSN, MSN, and DNP) and completed an international service-learning trip (2007) to rural Mexico with undergraduate nursing and physician assistant students. She was the coordinator for the Nurse Educator track in the DrNP program at Drexel University in Philadelphia (2007–2010) and sits on four dissertation committees.

Dr. Wittmann-Price is coeditor and chapter contributor of three books, *Nursing Education: Foundations for Practice Excellence* (with B. A. Moyer, ed.; AJN Book of the Year Award Winner, 2008), *The Certified Nurse Examination (CNE) Review Manual*, and *NCLEX-RN® EXCEL Test Success Through Unfolding Case Study Review* (with B. R. Thompson, ed.). She has published "The Newborn at Risk" in *Maternal-Child Nursing Care: Optimizing Outcomes for Mothers, Children, and Families*, a section in *Giving Through Teaching: How Nurse Educators Are Changing the World* (with M. Godshall and A. Pasco), and "The Role of the Educator" in *Role Development for Doctoral Advanced Nursing Practice* (with R. Waite and D. L. Woda).

Frances H. Cornelius, PhD, MSN, RN-BC, CNE, is Associate Clinical Professor, Chair of the MSN Advanced Practice Role Department and Coordinator of Informatics Projects at Drexel University, College of Nursing and Health Professions. Dr. Cornelius has taught nursing since 1991, at several schools of nursing. She taught community health at Madonna University (Livonia, MI), Oakland (MI) University, University of Pittsburgh, and Holy Family College (Philadelphia). Fran taught Adult Health and Gerontology at Widener University School of Nursing until 1997, when she began teaching at Drexel. In 2003, she was a Fellow at the Biomedical Library of Medicine. She is a certified nurse informaticist and has been the recipient of several grants. She has collaborated on the development of mobile applications as Coordinator of Informatics Projects including Patient Assessment and Care Plan Development (PACPD) tool, which is a PDA tool with a web-based companion, and Gerontology Reasoning Informatics Programs (the GRIP project). She is the coeditor of Cornelius/Gallagher-Gordon, PDA Connections (LLW), an innovative textbook designed to teach health care professionals how to use mobile devices for "point-of-care" access of information. She has written six book chapters and has published 19 journal articles on her work. She has delivered 26 presentations and more than 50 peer-reviewed presentations mostly in the United States, but also in Spain, Canada, and Korea. She is a member of STTI, the American Informatics Association, the American Nursing Informatics Association, the International Institute of Informatics and Systemics (IIIS), NANDA, ANA, and the PSNA.

Fundamentals of Nursing Test Success: Unfolding Case Study Review

Ruth A. Wittmann-Price, PhD, CNS, RN, CNE
Frances H. Cornelius, PhD, MSN, RN-BC, CNE,

Springer Publishing Company, LLC
11 West 42nd Street
New York, NY 10036
www.springerpub.com

Acquisitions Editor: Margaret Zuccarini
Composition: S4Carlisle Publishing Services

ISBN: 978-0-8261-9393-3
E-book ISBN: 978-0-8261-9394-0

12 13 14 15/ 5 4 3 2 1

Library of Congress Cataloging-in-Publication Data
Wittmann-Price, Ruth A.
Fundamentals of nursing test success : an unfolding case study review/Ruth A. Wittmann-Price, Frances H. Cornelius.
p. ; cm.
Includes bibliographical references and index.
ISBN 13: 978-0-8261-9393-3
ISBN 10: 0-8261-9393-5
I. Cornelius, Frances H. II. Title.
[DNLM: 1. Nursing Care—methods—Problems and Exercises. 2. Nursing Process—Problems and Exercises.
WY 18.2]
610.73—dc23

2012029826

Printed in the United States of America by Bang Printing

This effort, like all efforts of nurse educators,
is dedicated to our students!

Contents

Preface

This book is unique! Unlike the other review books published that require students to answer question after question, this book uses unfolding case studies to simulate real-life learning. This book has technological links that encourage learners to use the most up-to-date resources available and to apply them to achieve quality patient care. This is one of the rare review books for nursing fundamentals learners, and we know if the foundational concepts are not conquered well at the outset, it becomes more difficult, at best, to comprehend, internalize, and effectively apply more advanced concepts in nursing.

Through short, interesting, real-to-life case studies that you can work through at your own pace, we have devised an interesting method for you to understand and apply foundational nursing concepts. If you work through this book, you will be able to move onto the more advanced concepts presented in our other unfolding case study books, which include the following:

- *NCLEX-RN® EXCEL: Test Success Through Unfolding Case Study Review*
- *Maternal-Child Nursing Test Success: Unfolding Case Study Content and NCLEX-RN Review*

Unfolding case studies is a great method for learning and retaining concepts because it provides the learner with memorable situations that promote reflection and clinical decision making. This series of books also holds the learner's attention by using many alternative question formats interposed in the cases. We are sure you will enjoy this type of learning and it will be a welcome relief from the NCLEX-RN question-after-question review!

Thank you for delving into a different learning format; it will be nurses, like yourself, who are open to new ideas and situations that will make positive changes for patients, families, and in the health care system of the United States.

We wish you the best of luck in your nursing career.

Ruth A. Wittmann-Price
Frances H. Cornelius

Acknowledgments

Thank you to Margaret Zuccarini for her endless publishing support.

1

Understanding Your Nursing Education and the Need for NCLEX-RN® Success!

Beginning Nursing Education

Nursing education is intense and very differently designed compared with other disciplines, for several reasons. First, the obvious reason: As a nurse you will serve people at very vulnerable moments in their lives. Your care must be safe and accurate. Second, nursing education is different because there is such a large amount of information to learn, which is updated on almost a daily basis. Technology and health care science expand exponentially. A third and very real difference in nursing education is that it is laden with standardized and high-stakes testing. In order to obtain a license, you must pass a national exam and because of this you will most likely be tested all the way through your educational program.

The good news is that there are ways to assist you in these high-stakes testing situations, and by learning those methods now, at the level of your fundamental course, you will prepare yourself for a successful journey. Many fundamental courses do not discuss test-taking strategies; it is done later in your educational program. But just as we learn in fundamentals of nursing that to prepare a patient for discharge, discharge teaching begins on admission, we need to consider that same principle valid for ourselves: Test-taking preparation begins in fundamentals. This chapter will give you an overview of what to expect with testing and how to prepare yourself for tests.

What to Expect in Testing Situations

Test-taking situations are anxiety provoking and you need to be aware of how you currently cope with stressful situations. Reflect on your coping mechanisms and how you manage them and decide if they are within "normal range." Table 1.1 provides a self-reflective format to help you.

If you are unsure about your coping skills or if they are ineffective in test-taking situations, go to your student counseling center. There you will find professionals who can help you with relaxation techniques or obtain the documentation you need to make alternative testing accommodations. Many

Table 1.1

During test-taking situations, do you find that you experience . . .	Yes	No	How do you cope with this symptom?
Sleeplessness the night before the test?			
Muscle tension that produces muscle pain?			
Headaches?			
Gastrointestinal (GI) upset?			
Nervousness with an inability to focus on the material any longer?			
Anxiety with sweating and trembling?			
Tendency to overeat before the test?			
Mood changes before the test including irritability or depression?			

Source: Adapted from MedicineNet.com (2011, p. 3).

learners say to me, "How can I have accommodations for testing when I am going to be a nurse that has to be on the top of her/his game all the time?" Here is what I tell them:

> Pretend you are a pediatric nurse and you are taking care of two 10-year-olds in a double-bedded room and they are being prepped for tonsillectomies. You need to teach both children what to expect. The child in bed A is an auditory learner that needs a room with no background noise in order to concentrate on what you are saying, so ... you turn off the TV. The other child in bed B is a visual learner so you draw a sketch of what the OR (operating room) will look like. Who is the better learner? Neither; they are just different types of learners so you alter your approach.

So why would you not alter your approach in the classroom in order to facilitate your learning?

So if you have a "different" learning need, address it immediately because you will be in test-taking situations throughout your nursing educational program, sometimes for progression in the program. This is done to make sure that you are prepared for the NCLEX-RN® exam or the final high-stakes test. Each test is a milestone that needs to be passed, so that the accumulation of knowledge is appropriate for the NCLEX-RN. If testing is viewed in this way rather than in a negative, "Why are they putting us through all these hoops?" way you will fare better, learn more, and feel more accomplished.

Normally high-stakes tests in a nursing educational program are static, even if they are computerized. This means that you answer one question after another and the final score determines a pass or fail. Some tests are teacher-made, whereas other schools buy tests from companies that specialize in test making. These companies sell their tests to many schools and then compare grades. Most companies that make tests have an end-of-the-program test, sometimes called a "predictor test." The predictor tests tell how likely you are to "pass" the NCLEX-RN. Most of these companies have tests that are similar to teacher-made tests and score it by the number of questions a learner gets correct, but some companies are now making computer adaptive tests (CATs) similar to the NCLEX-RN.

The NCLEX-RN®

The NCLEX-RN is a CAT-style exam, which means the learner is scored on each question in a different way. It works like this: The first question is easy. If the learner answers the question correctly, the next question offered is more difficult. If the learner answers that one correctly, the third question offered is more difficult, and so on. If the learner gets a question wrong, the computer drops back to a less difficult level for the next question. This pattern continues until the learner correctly answers a total of 60 progressively higher-level questions. The minimum number of questions it takes to pass the NCLEX-RN is 75. This is because 15 questions on every exam are "test" questions that the National Council of the State Board of Nursing (NCSBN) is evaluating for inclusion on future tests. The maximum number of questions that a candidate or learner can take is 265 questions; therefore, the easy-to-challenging test question cycle can go up and down quite a few times.

The maximum time a candidate is allowed to complete the NCLEX-RN is 6 hours. So if you divide 6 hours by 265 questions, you have an average of 1.36 minutes per question, but remember some questions take longer than others to answer, so consider the 1.36 minutes per question as an average. This may be why some instructors in your nursing education program give you 1.36 minutes per question on tests; it is to "tune you in" to NCLEX-RN test-taking time. Every test you take in your nursing educational program is preparing you to pass your NCLEX-RN, which is your licensure test! Once you pass the NCLEX-RN, the public is ensured that you meet the minimal competencies in knowledge and skill that it takes to be a successful RN.

The NCLEX-RN is a test that follows a well thought-out test plan and includes a certain percentage of questions that are given to each part of the plan. The plan is updated and changed every 3 years depending on patients' needs at that time in history in the clinical setting. Figure 1.1 shows the test plan.

Understanding what each NCLEX category labels means will help you to understand what will be expected of you when you get to the NCLEX-RN and it will also help you to frame content that you learn throughout your nursing education. The first category is Safe and Effective Care Environment and is divided into two subcategories: Management of Care and Safety and Infection Control. Questions from this category can make up 24% to 36% of the NCLEX-RN exam, so think of it

Figure 1-1 NCLEX-RN© test plan. (Portions copyrighted by the National Council of State Boards of Nursing, Inc. All Rights Reserved, 2009.)

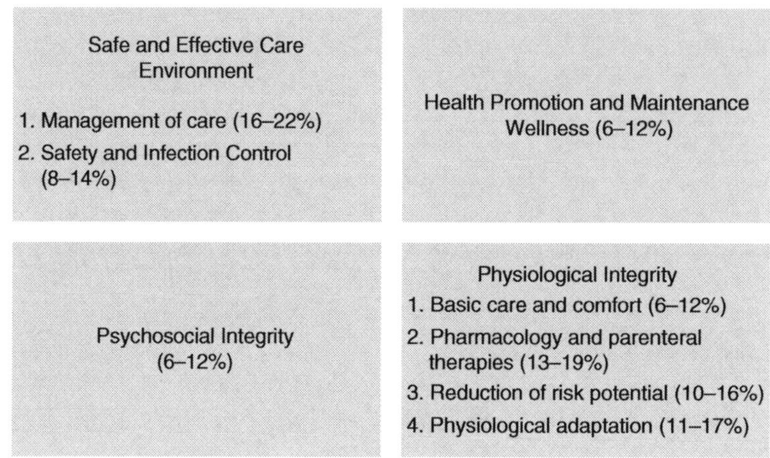

as a quarter or more of the content. Management of Care is understanding the issues that go into caring for people in the health care environment, such as legal rights, privacy issues, ethical issues, and referring patients and families to other health care professionals, if needed; communicating your patient's needs to other authorized health care professionals; establishing priorities in caring for patients; and delegating nursing tasks safely to other members of the health care team.

The second subcategory is Safety and Infection Control and addresses issues such as disasters, triaging, environmental hazards, infection control in hospitals, violence, reporting mistakes, and understanding proper use of equipment, technology, and restraints. Think of this entire category as a snapshot of a hospital unit or a community center that has people, equipment, and a system that are trying to safely and respectfully take care of patients in the most humanistic way possible (National Council of State Boards of Nursing [NCSBN], 2009).

The next major category is Health Promotion and Wellness; let us estimate about 10% of your questions will come from this category. This category contains issues such as growth and development, which you will learn in pediatrics. It also has things that promote wellness such as breast self-exams and testicular-self exams. Other issues that support wellness may also be included such as proper nutrition and exercise as well as the effects of smoking, alcohol, and drugs (NCSBN, 2009).

Psychosocial Integrity is the next category, and you can estimate about 10% of questions will come from this category. This has to do with mental and cognitive abilities of patients. It is not only about how to help them if they have a mental illness, but it also includes people's ability to cope with illness, learn about care, and understand the social structure that patients live in such as healthy or unhealthy families. Another important topic in this category is therapeutic communication, which is needed for ***all*** patient interactions (NCSBN, 2009).

The next large category of questions will come from Physiological Integrity and this is how we usually think about nursing—taking care of people's bodies so they can regain their health or die peacefully. This large category is broken up into four sections. The first is Basic Care and Comfort, and again you can think of this as about 10% of the questions. Basic Care and Comfort includes many of the concepts we learned from Florence Nightingale: rest, elimination, food, hygiene, comfort measures, and mobility.

The next topic is a big one—Pharmacology and Parenteral Therapies—so drugs and IVs are about 15% of the test. Know your drug categories, how to administer them safely, how to calculate the right amount to give, and how the drugs and IV fluids will work on a person's body. The next category is Reduction of Risk Potential; this means being able to tell when things are not within normal limits (WNL) such as vital signs (VS) or lab results. It also includes what testing does and what complications can happen from the diagnostic test. This section is approximately 15% of the exam.

The final section of content in this large category is Physiological Adaptation and is about 15% of the total test. It deals with actual disease processes in the body and how to manage them. It includes pathophysiology as well as emergencies such as hemorrhage. This is the nitty-gritty stuff you will hear in medical–surgical nursing (NCSBN, 2009).

Test Question Levels

The actual questions on the NCLEX-RN are developed for different levels of difficulty; remember, we mentioned before it goes from easy to more difficult. Those levels are derived from Bloom's taxonomy (Bloom, 1956), which is the way in which people learn, from simple to complex. The first or simplest level of learning is ***remembering***. Your instructor tells you that infants get intramuscular (IM) shots in their vastus lateralis (leg muscle) and on a test you see a question that states:

The nurse is giving vitamin K IM to a day-old infant. It should be administered in the:

A. Rectus gluteus

B. Vastus lateralis

C. Vastus rectus

D. Deltoid muscle

If you remember what your instructor said in class or clinical, you will know the answer. The next level is ***understanding*** or knowing ideas or concepts.

The nurse understands that vitamin K is administered IM to infants because:

A. It is difficult to start IVs on infants

B. Subcutaneous (SC) injections are absorbed too fast

C. Vitamin K PO does not taste good

D. IM injections are absorbed slowly

To answer this question, the student would have to understand the concept of IM injections. The next level of questions is ***applying***. In this level, you need to use the information for patient care. Many questions are written on this level. Here is an example:

> An infant is born whose mother is positive for hepatitis B. The one-time dose of immunoglobulin should be given within 12 hours, so it can be absorbed readily. The best method would be:
>
> A. IV
>
> B. IM
>
> C. Sub q
>
> D. Dermal

The answer would be IM because you know it is faster and it is for a one-time dose instead of starting an IV. The next level is even more tricky—it is ***analyzing*** and many of these questions wind up to be exhibit questions or questions that provide you with a bunch of information and you have to decide what fits best. Here is an example:

> The nurse reviews the following lab data on a day-old, small-for-gestational-age (SGA) infant:
>
> Hct 62%
>
> Glucose 35 mg/dL
>
> Blood type B+
>
> Coombs test +
>
> What intervention would be a priority?
>
> A. Check the mother's blood type
>
> B. Feed the infant
>
> C. Draw a bilirubin level
>
> D. Notify the primary care practitioner

Yes, you would feed the infant first because a low glucose could lead to seizures. There may also be a blood incompatibility (problem) going on, but it is not as urgent.

One of the highest levels of questions is ***evaluating***. These are few and far between but sometimes they have to do with nurses evaluating their care such as:

> The nurse teaches a postoperative mastectomy patient about home care and evaluates that the teaching is effective when the patient states:
>
> A. It is okay for me to lift as long as it is not too heavy or too big
>
> B. I can take a shower with the drain if I tape it on my shoulder
>
> C. I will have to lie in bed for at least another day so it can drain
>
> D. I should tell health care providers to take my blood pressure on my other arm

Yes, you have evaluated right if "D" was your answer.

So these are just a couple of short examples showing how Bloom's taxonomy is used to formulate questions to help instructors understand if students have the knowledge they need to move on in the program.

Summary

Now that you have the knowledge you need about tests and are starting to analyze the way you react to tests, you are well on your way to successful test taking. Every test is an evaluation of your accumulated knowledge and is important, so treat each one with respect and be ready. As you successfully master the content, you will gain insight and confidence but always keep in mind the end goal—to become an RN. In order to accomplish that you need to begin here with a solid understanding of nursing education testing and fundamentals of care! Enjoy the journey!

References

Bloom, B. S. (1956). *Taxonomy of educational objectives, handbook I: The cognitive domain.* New York, NY: David McKay.

MedicineNet.com. (2011). Retrieved from http://www.medicinenet.com/stress/page3.htm

National Council of State Boards of Nursing. (2009). *NCLEX-RN test plan.* Chicago, IL: Author.

2

Nursing History, Theory, and Importance of Evidence-Based Practice

Unfolding Case Study 1 Aubree

Aubree is a first-semester nursing student. She is very happy that she was accepted into the program since nursing education has become so competitive. All national indicators predict a shortage of nurses in the near future.

Exercise 2-1: *Select All That Apply*

The shortage of nurses is due to a number of variables, which include the following:

- ❑ Lack of space in schools of nursing
- ❑ Increase in the birthrate of the nation
- ❑ Increase in teenage pregnancy
- ❑ Increase in the geriatric population
- ❑ Increase in acute illnesses
- ❑ Decrease in the number of insured

Aubree learns about the history of nursing, which is accented by many famous nurses who paved the way for all nurses today. Although initially Aubree thought it was useless information, she began to realize that the past paved the way for her current career goal: to be a professional nurse!

Exercise 2-2: *Matching*

Match the name in column A to the description in column B.

Column A		Column B
A. Florence Nightingale	______	One of the first to receive a doctorate
B. Clara Barton	______	Mother of psychiatric nursing
C. Isabel Hampton Robb	______	Henry Street Settlement
D. Dorothea Dix	______	Frontier midwifery school

The Answers section can be found on page 17.

Column A		Column B
E. Susie King Taylor	______	First nursing philosopher
F. Mary Breckinridge	______	Founded *American Journal of Nursing (AJN)*
G. Lillian Wald	______	Started documentation in nursing
H. Linda Richards	______	Most influential nurse in 20th century
I. Sister Mary B. Beck	______	Superintendent of nurses in Union Army
J. Hildegard Peplau	______	Civil War nurse—worked in South Carolina battlefields
K. Virginia A. Henderson	______	Founded the American Red Cross

e **eResource 2-1:** The students visit several web resources that highlight the history of nursing:

- A selection of letters written by Florence Nightingale: http://clendening.kumc.edu/dc/fn/
- University of Pennsylvania's Nursing History and Health Care website: www.nursing.upenn.edu/nhhc/Pages/Welcome.aspx
- Dianne Brownson's nursing history links: http://diannebrownson.tripod.com/history.html

Nursing has grown as a profession over the past few decades and meets the criteria of a profession.

Exercise 2-3: ***Select All That Apply***

The following characteristics define a profession:

- ❑ Requires extended education based on a strong liberal arts foundation
- ❑ Has a body of knowledge
- ❑ Has leaders
- ❑ Has an honor society
- ❑ Has a specific service
- ❑ Members have autonomy
- ❑ There is a code of ethics

The American Nurses Association (ANA) publishes two sets of standards:

- Standards of Professional Performance for Nurses
- Standards of Professional Practice

Exercise 2-4: ***True/False***

The American Nurses Association (ANA) Standards of Professional Performance for Nurses calls primarily for nurse managers to be involved in quality improvement (QI) activities.

- ❑ True
- ❑ False

The Answers section can be found on page 17.

The ANA Standards of Professional Practice distinguish between a Registered Nurse and other health care practitioners.

eResource 2-2: To learn more about ANA Standards of Professional Performance for Nurses and Standards of Professional Practice, visit the following websites:

- *Current Nursing* (open access journal): www.currentnursing.com/nursing_management/nursing_standards.html
- Ferris State University's overview of Standards of Professional Nursing Practice: www.ferris.edu/HTMLS/colleges/alliedhe/Nursing/Standards-of-Professional-Nursing-Practice.htm

Exerci.se 2-5: *True/False*

One of the similarities in roles between an RN and an LPN (licensed practical nurse) is that they can both provide health teaching to patients and families.

- ❑ True
- ❑ False

Aubree knows that one of the great things about becoming a nurse is that it is a profession that has many career paths. She hopes someday to be able to continue her education and become a nurse practitioner.

Exercise 2-6: *Select All That Apply*

The following nursing specialties are included in advanced practice nursing and require a master's degree:

- ❑ Certified Nurse Midwife (CNM)
- ❑ Certified Emergency Department RN
- ❑ Clinical Nurse Leader
- ❑ Pediatric Nurse Practitioner
- ❑ Clinical Nurse Specialist
- ❑ Lactation Consultant
- ❑ Nurse Anesthetist
- ❑ Nurse Administrator

eResource 2-3: To learn more about available career paths and available specialties in nursing, Aubree visits the American Nurses Credentialing Association (ANCC; www.nursecredentialing.org).

In addition, she views a brief video providing an overview of the benefits of certification (www.nursecredentialing.org/CertificationVideo.aspx).

Aubree knows that the terminal degree for a nurse is a doctorate.

The Answers section can be found on page 17.

Exercise 2-7: *Multiple Choice Question*

Aubree's instructor knows that more teaching is indicated when Aubree states:

A. "I think the best degree to get for an NP will eventually be the doctorate of nursing practice (DNP)."
B. "If I want to be a researcher I should get a DNP."
C. "I know that some states grant nurse practitioners prescription privileges."
D. "I want to get a PhD in nursing with an emphasis on curriculum to teach."

Regardless of which degree Aubree pursues, she realizes that being a nurse is a lifelong learning adventure because most states require continuing education (CE) units to renew your license every 2 years.

Aubree thinks about all the current issues that will influence what she does as a nurse. She knows from the television and newspaper that the health care reform movement will increase the number of Americans who will have health care insurance. Although it is good that more people will have access to health care, Aubree knows it will put a strain on the system. Demographic changes of the country are also increasing the need for nurses.

Exercise 2-8: *Select All That Apply*

The following are current demographic facts in the United States:

- ❑ Decreasing life span
- ❑ Increase in short-term illnesses
- ❑ Increasing medically underserved
- ❑ Increase in obesity
- ❑ Increase in urban populations
- ❑ Increase in psychiatric illness

Exercise 2-9: *Multiple Choice Question*

Women's health care has become an issue because many of women's symptomologies has been undetected due to:

A. Pharmaceutical companies concentrating on male-focused drugs.
B. Many traditional research studies included only men.
C. Men seek health care more often.
D. Women are less likely to get ill.

Exercise 2-10: *Multiple Choice Question*

The patient who is least likely to be medically underserved would be the person who:

A. Lives in the country
B. Lives in the city
C. Is employed
D. Is on Medicaid

The Answers section can be found on page 17.

eResource 2-4: To learn more about the medically underserved and resources available to this population, visit the U.S. Department of Health and Human Services, Health Resources and Services Administration (HRSA) website:

- Medically Underserved Areas and Populations (MUA/Ps): http://bhpr.hrsa.gov/shortage/muaps/index.html
- HRSA Mobile, a smartphone application, which can help locate federally funded health centers that provide healthcare to the uninsured, regardless of ability to pay: www.hrsa.gov/about/mobile

Aubree knows that another topic that is well-discussed in nursing is evidence-based practice, so she is trying to understand how to look at health care research with an eye for appraisal.

Exercise 2-11: *Multiple Choice Question*

One of the reasons for encouraging evidence-based practice in nursing is to:

A. Decrease health care utilization
B. Increase individualistic health care
C. Provide every option to all
D. Maintain costs

eResource 2-5: To learn more about evidence-based practice in nursing, view the University of Minnesota Libraries' Evidence-Based Practice Interprofessional Tutorial: www.hsl.lib.umn.edu/learn/ebp

Aubree is very interested in evidence-based practice and is looking forward to her research course next semester so she can do a group project on a clinical issue.

There are also many nursing concepts that are abstract, and Aubree hears about them often from senior nursing students. They are often confusing because Aubree does not have the clinical experience to understand them.

Exercise 2-12: *Matching*

Match the concept in column A to the definition in column B

Column A	Column B
A. Autonomy	______ Addresses the person as a whole to assist
B. Care giving	______ Asserts rights for people
C. Accountability	______ Uses critical thinking skills
D. Advocate	______ Responsible
E. Clinical decision maker	______ Self-governing

Aubree is also taking a class about nursing theory. She is interested in its relationship to research. It is explained to her that one supports the other and both support the practice of nursing. It is described as a triangle of knowledge development (Figure 2.1).

The Answers section can be found on page 17.

Figure 2-1

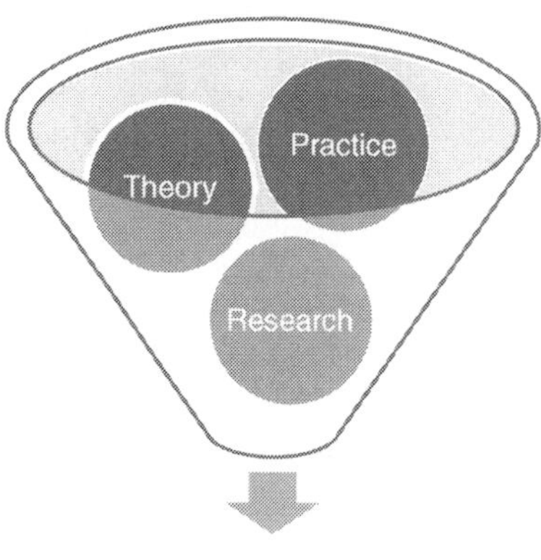

Nursing Knowledge

Aubree is glad that Benner's theory, *From Novice to Expert*, is explained to her because she better understands how she will have to grow professionally (Benner, 1984).

Exercise 2-13: *Matching*

Match the label of Benner's stage in column A to its characteristics in Column B.

Column A		Column B
A. Novice	______	Greater than 2–3 years of experience, sees situation as a whole and can transfer knowledge.
B. Advanced beginners	______	No previous level of experience.
C. Competent	______	Intuitive grasp of actual or impending situations.
D. Proficient	______	Some level of experience that allows nurse to identify priorities.
E. Expert	______	Has 2–3 years of experience and understands the organization and what each patient needs.

eResource 2-6: To review Benner's theory, visit *Current Nursing's* site: www.currentnursing.com/nursing_theory/Patricia_Benner_From_Novice_to_Expert.html

Other nursing theories that Aubree learned about had to do with the four metaparadigms of nursing. She understands that all nursing theories have these four elements.

The Answers section can be found on page 17.

Exercise 2-14: *Select All That Apply*

- ❑ Nurse
- ❑ Skills
- ❑ Person
- ❑ Environment
- ❑ Caring
- ❑ Health

Exercise 2-15: *Fill-in*

The basic building blocks of a theory are ________________________.

Aubree understands that nurses write theories because they experience a phenomenon in clinical practice working with patients, and the theory helps to describe it. There are three levels of theories:

- Grand theories are those that are broad in scope and usually have many concepts and can fit to most populations;
- Middle-range theories are those that deal with more specific phenomena but one that can cross several populations; and
- Practice theories are the most specific and are useful in a specific clinical situation or with a specific population.

eResource 2-7: To review the basics of Nursing Theory, visit *Current Nursing's "Introduction to Nursing Theories"*: www.currentnursing.com/nursing_theory/introduction.html

Aubree is excited to get her career started and cannot wait to get into the clinical area so she can "feel" more like a nurse than she does in the classroom and lab. Clinical starts next week and Aubree is nervous but anxious!

Reference

Benner, P. (1984). *From novice to expert.* Menlo Park, CA: Addison-Wesley.

The Answers section can be found on page 17.

Answers

Exercise 2-1: *Select All That Apply*

The shortage of nurses is due to a number of variables, which include the following:

☒ **Lack of space in schools of nursing—YES, nursing schools are having difficulty accommodating all the students.**

☐ Increase in the birthrate of the nation—NO, the birthrate is decreasing.

☐ Increase in teenage pregnancy—NO, teenage pregnancy rate is decreasing.

☒ **Increase in the geriatric population—YES, this is putting a tremendous burden on our health care system.**

☐ Increase in acute illnesses—NO, there is actually an increase in chronic illness.

☐ Decrease in the number of insured—NO, more people will be insured with the new health care plan.

Exercise 2-2: *Matching*

Match the name in column A to the description in column B.

Column A	Column B
A. Florence Nightingale	**I** One of first to receive a doctorate
B. Clara Barton	**J** Mother of psychiatric nursing
C. Isabel Hampton Robb	**G** Henry Street Settlement
D. Dorothea Dix	**F** Frontier midwifery school
E. Susie King Taylor	**A** First nursing philosopher
F. Mary Breckinridge	**C** Founded *American Journal of Nursing* (AJN)
G. Lillian Wald	**H** Started documentation in nursing
H. Linda Richards	**K** Most influential nurse in 20th century
I. Sister Mary B. Beck	**D** Superintendent of nurses in Union Army
J. Hildegard Peplau	**E** Civil War nurse—worked in South Caroliana battlefields
K. Virginia A. Henderson	**B** Founded the American Red Cross

Exercise 2-3: *Select All That Apply*

The following characteristics define a profession:

☒ **Requires extended education based on a strong liberal arts foundation.**

☒ **Has a body of knowledge—YES, every profession has its own body of knowledge.**

❑ Has leaders—NO, this is not a criterion but often is true.

❑ Has an honor society—NO, this is not a criterion but nursing has one.

☒ **Has a specific service—YES, every profession provides a service to mankind.**

☒ **Members have autonomy—YES, members of a profession can autonomously provide the service of the profession.**

☒ **There is a code of ethics—YES, all professions have a code of ethics.**

Exercise 2-4: *True/False*

The ANA Standards of Professional Performance for Nurses call primarily for nurse managers to be involved in quality improvement (QI) activities.

❑ True

☒ **False—All nurses must be involved in QI.**

Exercise 2-5: *True/False*

One of the similarities in roles between an RN and an LPN (licensed practical nurse) is that they can both provide health teaching to patients and families.

❑ True

☒ **False—NO, only RNs can provide teaching; LPNs can reinforce the education.**

Exercise 2-6: *Select All That Apply*

The following nursing specialties are included in advanced practice nursing and require a Master's degree:

☒ **Certified Nurse Midwife (CNM)—YES, in the past not all CNM had an MSN but now it is required.**

❑ Certified Emergency Department RN.

☒ **Clinical Nurse Leader—YES, this nurse is a specialist in generalist practice.**

☒ **Pediatric Nurse Practitioner—YES, all nurse practitioners (NPs) are an advanced practice registered nurse (APRN), and many have a doctorate of nursing practice (DNP) degree.**

☒ **Clinical Nurse Specialist—YES, this is one of the original APRN roles.**

❑ Lactation Consultant.

☒ **Nurse Anesthetist—YES, this is an APRN role.**

❑ Nurse Administrator.

Exercise 2-7: *Multiple Choice Question*

Aubree's instructor knows that more teaching is indicated when Aubree states:

A. "I think the best degree to get for an NP will eventually be the doctorate of nursing practice (DNP)."—NO, this is true and advocated by some of the accrediting agencies in nursing.

B. **"If I want to be a researcher I should get a DNP."—YES, a PhD is more suited for research than a DNP, which is a practice doctorate.**

C. "I know that some states grant nurse practitioners prescription privileges."—NO, this is true.

D. "I want to get a PhD in nursing with an emphasis on curriculum to teach."—NO, there are degrees with this emphasis.

Exercise 2-8: *Select All That Apply*

The following are current demographic facts in the United States:

☐ Decreasing life span—NO, the life span is increasing.

☐ Increase in short-term illnesses—NO, short-term illnesses still exist.

☒ **Increasing medically underserved—YES, we are becoming a more diverse population.**

☒ **Increase in obesity—YES, this is a major health problem.**

☒ **Increase in urban populations—YES, people are moving to the cities for work.**

☒ **Increase in psychiatric illness—YES, there is a rise in mental health issues.**

Exercise 2-9: *Multiple Choice Question*

Women's health care has become an issue because many of women's symptomologies has been undetected due to:

A. Pharmaceutical companies concentrating on male-focused drugs—NO, they produce drugs for both men and women.

B. **Many traditional research studies included only men—YES, traditionally women have not been included as research participants.**

C. Men seek health care more often—NO, this is not true.

D. Women are less likely to get ill—NO, this is not true.

Exercise 2-10: *Multiple Choice Question*

The patient who is least likely to be medically underserved would be the person who:

A. **Lives in the country—YES, rural residents are underserved by primary care practitioners.**

B. Lives in the city—NO, there is more access to health care providers in urban areas.

C. Is employed—NO, employed individuals are more likely to have health insurance.

D. Is on Medicaid—NO, Medicare recipients are more likely to seek health care.

Exercise 2-11: *Multiple Choice Question*

One of the reasons for encouraging evidence-based practice in nursing is to:

A. Decrease health care utilization—NO, we want people to have access to care.
B. Increase individualistic health care—NO, evidence uses the best knowledge for everyone.
C. Provide every option to all—NO, this is costing too much money; the options that work the best should be presented.
D. **Maintain costs—YES, using the correct interventions will decrease the cost of repetitive care or using many interventions for one situation.**

Exercise 2-12: *Matching*

Match the concept in column A to the definition in column B

Column A	Column B
A. Autonomy	**B** Addresses the person as a whole to assist
B. Care giving	**D** Asserts rights for people
C. Accountability	**E** Uses critical thinking skills
D. Advocate	**C** Responsible
E. Clinical decision maker	**A** Self-governing

Exercise 2-13: *Matching*

Match the label of Benner's stage in column A to its characteristics in column B.

Column A	Column B
A. Novice	**C** Greater than 2–3 years of experience, sees situation as a whole and can transfer knowledge.
B. Advanced beginners	**A** No previous level of experience.
C. Competent	**E** Intuitive grasp of actual or impending situations.
D. Proficient	**D** Some level of experience that allows nurse to identify priorities.
E. Expert	**B** Has 2–3 years of experience and understands the organization and what each patient needs.

Exercise 2-14: ***Select All That Apply***

☒ **Nurse**

☐ Skills

☒ **Person**

☒ **Environment**

☐ Caring

☒ **Health**

Exercise 2-15: ***Fill-in***

The basic building blocks of a theory are **Concepts**.

3

Health Care Delivery Today

Unfolding Case Study 2 Connor

Connor is a second degree student who has returned to school to be a nurse due to life-altering family circumstances. Connor's older brother died from ALS (amyotrophic lateral sclerosis, sometimes called Lou Gehrig's disease). Connor was in awe of the nurses who helped him and his family care for his brother and vowed that after his brother's death he too would become a nurse to help people. Connor finally met all the prerequisite courses and is now in the Fundamentals of Nursing course. He realizes that there are many skills that he needs to learn in order to be a nurse, but he did not realize that understanding the health care environment in which he will function is so complex. Connor listens attentively in class because he has been hearing much about "health care reform" on the news and is curious about how it will affect his role as a nurse.

Exercise 3-1: ***Multiple Choice Question***

The major force driving health care reform in the United States is:

A. Patient advocacy
B. Primary care provider billing
C. Immigrant populations
D. Health care costs

eResource 3-1: To learn more about the history of Health Care Reform in the United States, visit the Kaiser Family Foundation website: www.healthreform.kff.org/flash/health-reform-new.html

Connor recognizes that there are many terms to describe the method in which health care is paid for by insurance companies.

The Answers section can be found on page 31.

Exercise 3-2: *Matching*

Match the term in column A to the definition in column B.

Column A		Column B
A. Managed care	______	Hospitals are reimbursed a set amount of money for each diagnosis
B. Medicare	______	People can only pick from a list of certain providers
C. Medicaid	______	Provides care to a specific group of people who voluntarily enroll
D. Capitation	______	People pay a yearly premium to be part of a limited number of patients for a provider
E. PPO (provider preferred organization)	______	Federally funded program to assist people with a low income
F. VIP care	______	Federally funded health care for people older than 65 years of age
G. DRG (diagnostic related groups)	______	Providers get a fixed amount per person in the health plan

While listening to the news, Connor begins to understand that the country is in need of health care attention.

eResource 3-2: To better understand Health Care Reform and the issues surrounding it, Connor watches:

1. *"Illustrating Health Reform: How Health Insurance Coverage Will Work."* http://www.youtube.com/watch?v=3-Ilc5xK2_E
2. The Kaiser Foundation's:
   - *Medicare: The Basics* www.kaiseredu.org/tutorials/Medicare101/player.html
   - *Medicaid: The Basics* www.kaiseredu.org/tutorials/medicaidbasics2009/player.html

Exercise 3-3: *Select All That Apply*

The current health care reform is actually two bills (Patient Protection and Affordable Care Act and the Health Care and Education Reconciliation Act of 2010) and increases health care coverage to:

- ❑ Small business employees
- ❑ Large business employees
- ❑ High school students
- ❑ Young adults
- ❑ Elderly
- ❑ City workers

The Answers section can be found on page 31.

Another health care issue for Americans is the "cost of dying." Our culture is a "cure" not "care" one, so many patients spend their last days in the ICUs (intensive care units) instead of in palliative care (comfort care).

eResource 3-3: To better understand palliative care, Connor:

1. Watches the PBS's The Open Mind Video: *Palliative Medicine: Care vs. Cure?* http://video.pbs.org/video/1824648879/
2. Consults MedlinePlus on his mobile device: [Pathway: m.medlineplus.gov enter "palliative care" in the search field].

Exercise 3-4: *Fill-in*

Do not resuscitate (DNR) is a term that is being replaced by an AND or ________.

There are many other levels of care that patients can interact with in the health care system and nursing. There are now six levels of care defined.

Exercise 3-5: *Ordering*

Place the levels of care in order from preventative care to continuing care.

_______ Preventive care
_______ Restorative care
_______ Primary care
_______ Tertiary care
_______ Secondary care
_______ Continuing care

Connor knows that, in the scheme of things, people seek health care at different places. Some places are inpatient and some are out patient.

Exercise 3-6: *Multiple Choice Question*

The nurse understands that the patient needs further teaching during discharge planning, the patient states:

A. "I need restorative care in my rural hospital"
B. "I know that I can get primary care at my doctor's office"
C. "I have home health for restorative care"
D. "Respite care will provide some care my family needs"

Other services that a patient may receive after discharge are rehabilitative services.

Exercise 3-7: *Select All That Apply*

Rehabilitative services include:

- ❑ Occupational therapy
- ❑ Physical therapy
- ❑ Social service
- ❑ Speech therapy
- ❑ Spiritual counseling

The Answers section can be found on page 31.

Exercise 3-8: *Multiple Choice Question*

A patient care facility that is considered an intermediate facility may include skilled care such as IVs, wound care, ventilator care, etc., is called:

A. Primary care
B. Block nursing center
C. Home care extender
D. Skilled nursing facility

Exercise 3-9: *Matching*

Match the name of the facility or service in column A to the definition in column B.

Column A		Column B
A. Respite care	______	Family centered and allows patient to die with dignity
B. Assisted living	______	Services are offered during the day, so family can work
C. Hospice	______	Long-term care in a home environment
D. Adult day care center	______	Short-term time off as care provider

Connor is excited to start clinical because he is anxious to start doing "real patient care." Before his clinical group can start patient care they are told that they need to pass "competencies." Competencies are usually demonstrations that show a learner knows how to do something, such as take and accurate finger-stick reading for a patient's glucose. Competencies help ensure a safe work place because people practice according to policies and procedures. Another safeguard that is in place to promote best practice is evidence-based practice (EBP).

eResource 3-4: Connor is interested in learning more about:

- Patient safety, visit Quality and Safety in Education for Nurses (QSEN) for prelicensure nurses: www.qsen.org/ksas_prelicensure.php
- Evidence-based competencies for prelicensure nurses, visit QSEN: www.qsen.org/ksas_prelicensure.php#evidence-based_practice

Exercise 3-10: *Multiple Choice Question*

Evidence-based practice was instituted to:

A. Simplify the research process
B. Develop policies and procedures
C. Get hospitals to get special accreditation status
D. Bridge the research–practice gap

eResource 3-5: To learn more about evidence-based practice, Connor visits CurrentNursing.com: www.nursingplanet.com/research/evidence_based_nursing.html

Another concept that was reviewed with the incoming Fundamentals of Nursing ("fundies") clinical group was delegation. Many health care organizations use assistive

The Answers section can be found on page 31.

personnel (AP), sometimes referred to as unlicensed assistive personnel (UAP). Also licensed practical nurses (LPNs) are used in many institutions, and in some areas, they are called LVNs (licensed vocational nurses).

Exercise 3-11: ***Select All That Apply***

The five rights of delegation include:

- ❑ Task to be delegated
- ❑ Circumstance under which the task is being delegated
- ❑ Person to whom the task is being delegated
- ❑ Correct patient or family for personality mix
- ❑ Directions and communication to clarify delegated task and expectations of health care provider
- ❑ Follow-up

eResource 3-6: As a review, Connor also reads the National Coalition of State Boards of Nursing overview of the five rights of delegation: www.ncsbn.org/fiverights.pdf

The clinical instructor provides Connor and his classmates with a case study about delegation. Connor reads the case:

A RN is working on a medical surgical unit and is assigned six patients along with an LPN and an AP. The nurse needs to divide up the work so that all the patient care is completed in 8 hours. The patients are as follows:

1. A 58-year-old women who is post hysterectomy (removal of the uterus) and is being discharged today
2. A 64-year-old man who is diabetic with IV insulin and is hypertensive
3. An 80-year-old man who is confused and a fall risk with a stage 3 decubiti (open wound)
4. A 24-year-old athlete who was being watched for a head trauma
5. A 27-year-old postoperative bariatric surgery patient on TPN (total parenteral nutrition)
6. A 75-year-old on a cardiac monitor for dysrhythmias (abnormal heart beats)

The case then provides a list of tasks to be performed:

A. Divide up patients
B. Hang IV insulin
C. Wound care for the decubiti
D. VS (vital signs) on all patients
E. Baths on four patients who are remaining
F. Hourly checks on the fall risk patient
G. Blood glucose monitoring 4×/day on the diabetic
H. STAT (immediate) nitroglycerin to be given for the patient with dysrhythmias if there is a report of chest pain

The Answers section can be found on page 31.

eResource 3-7: Fall prevention programs centered on awareness of conditions that predispose a person to fall: www.youtu.be/hXcaoh2IFzI

Exercise 3-12: ***Exhibit Question***

Using the information in the case above helps Connor delegate the patients and functions to the correct health care provider:

1. RN
   Patients: __________, ______________, ______________.
   Functions: __________, ______________, ____________.
2. LPN
   Patients: __________, ______________, ______________.
   Functions: __________.
3. APN
   Functions: __________, ______________, ____________, __________.

Exercise 3-13: ***Multiple Choice Question***

The RN understands that to complete delegation, it requires:

A. Supervision and evaluation
B. Evaluation and written critique
C. Supervision and checkups
D. Huddles and checkups

eResource 3-8: To learn more about delegation, Connor also reads the American Nurses Association (ANA)'s and National Coalition of State Boards of Nursing (NCSBN)'s joint statement: www.ncsbn.org/Joint_statement.pdf

Connor's first clinical day was interesting, and the RN he was assigned was an expert nurse who was good at precepting (or guiding) novice student nurses.

Exercise 3-14: ***Matching***

A. A short-term relationship between an expert and a novice	_______	Mentoring
B. A long-term relationship between an expert and a novice	_______	Precepting

Connor's preceptor explained the importance of quality patient care to reduce health care error, save finances, and improve patient satisfaction. Connor asked how the organization monitored patient satisfaction. Connor's preceptor told him about standardized surveys that patients receive after discharge. Patient satisfaction is shared with the staff each month, and the trends are followed. Patient satisfaction is also information that the public has access to and is benchmarked (or one facility is compared to another with good results). Connor explains what he has learned about patient

The Answers section can be found on page 31.

satisfaction to his clinical group in postconference, and a related concept arises that his instructor expands on "knowing" patients. Some of the steps that help nurses know their patients better include the following:

- Reviewing the patient's health history
- Apply principles of therapeutic communication
- Use your observational skills
- Interact with family
- Use your time with the patient effectively
- Talk to other nurses who have had the patient for additional information
- Make rounds on the patient regularly

Exercise 3-15: *Multiple Choice Question*

Knowing patients is a concept that is thought to be critical for:

A. Completing work
B. Handing-off report
C. Teaching
D. Decision making

Connor is exhausted by the end of his first clinical day but has reaffirmed in his head that this is indeed what he wants to do!

The Answers section can be found on page 31.

Answers

Exercise 3-1: *Multiple Choice Question*

The major force driving health care reform in the United States is:

A. Patient advocacy—NO, patient advocacy is important, but it is not the primary thrust of the reform

B. Primary care provider billing—NO, primary care billing is a problem, but alone is not the only concern

C. Immigrant populations—NO, immigrant population care is a concern for health care providers, but it is not the major initiative for reform

D. **Health care costs—YES, this is the major concern for the nation.**

Exercise 3-2: *Matching*

Match the term in column A to the definition in column B.

Column A		Column B
A. Managed care	**G**	Hospitals are reimbursed a set amount of money for each diagnosis
B. Medicare	**E**	People can only pick from a list of certain providers
C. Medicaid	**A**	Provides care to a specific group of people who voluntarily enroll
D. Capitation	**F**	People pay a yearly premium to be part of a limited number of patients for a provider
E. PPO (provider preferred organization)	**C**	Federally funded program to assist people with a low income
F. VIP care	**B**	Federally funded health care for people older than 65 years of age
G. DRG (diagnostic related groups)	**D**	Providers get a fixed amount per person in the health plan

Exercise 3-3: *Select All That Apply*

The current health care reform is actually two bills (Patient Protection and Affordable Care Act and the Health Care and Education Reconciliation Act of 2010) and increases health care coverage to:

☒ **Small business employees**

☐ Large business employees

☐ High school students

☒ **Young adults**

☒ **Elderly**

☐ City workers

Exercise 3-4: *Fill-in*

Do not resuscitate (DNR) is a term that is being replaced by AND or **Allow Natural Death.**

Exercise 3-5: *Ordering*

Place the levels of care in order from preventative care to continuing care.

1 Preventive care
5 Restorative care
2 Primary care
4 Tertiary care
3 Secondary care
6 Continuing care

Exercise 3-6: *Multiple Choice Question*

The nurse understands that the patient needs further teaching during discharge planning, the patient states:

A. **"I need restorative care in my rural hospital."—YES, restorative care is rarely done in the hospitals anymore**
B. "I know that I can get primary care at my doctor's office."—NO, this is true that many patients get primary care at a physician's office
C. "I have home health for restorative care."—NO, home health is usually for restorative care
D. "Respite care will provide some care my family needs."—NO, this is correct. Respite care provides temporary relief from care-taking duties

Exercise 3-7: *Select All That Apply*

Rehabilitative services include:

☒ **Occupational therapy—YES**

☒ **Physical therapy—YES**

☒ **Social service—YES**

☒ **Speech therapy—YES**

☐ Spiritual counseling—NO, this is usually done by requested referral

Exercise 3-8: *Multiple Choice Question*

A patient care facility that is considered as an intermediate facility may include skilled care such as IVs, wound care, ventilator care, etc. is called:

A. Primary care—NO, this is usually an outpatient facility

B. Block nursing center—NO, this is usually where nurses live, similar to a parish nurse concept

C. Home care extender—NO, this is usually an APN or UAP who goes into the home

D. **Skilled nursing facility—YES, this is the facility type now used for subacute in patient care**

Exercise 3-9: *Matching*

Matching the name of the facility or service in column A to the definition in column B.

Column A		Column B
A. Respite care	**C**	Family centered and allows patient to die with dignity
B. Assisted living	**D**	Services are offered during the day, so family can work
C. Hospice	**B**	Long-term care in a home environment
D. Adult day care center	**A**	Short-term time off as care provider

Exercise 3-10: *Multiple Choice Question*

Evidence-based practice was instituted to:

A. Simplify the research process—NO, this was not the primary reason

B. Develop policies and procedures—NO, EBP informs policies and procedures

C. Get hospitals to get special accreditation status—NO, it assists with hospital accreditation but is not the sole criteria

D. **Bridge the research—practice gap—YES, EBP puts best practice into use sooner than traditional research, which can take up to 17 years**

Exercise 3-11: *Select All That Apply*

The five rights of delegation include:

☒ **Task to be delegated**

☒ **Circumstance under which the task is being delegated**

☒ **Person to whom the task is being delegated**

☐ Correct patient or family for personality mix

☒ **Directions and communication to clarify delegated task and expectations of health care provider**

☒ **Follow-up**

Exercise 3-12: *Exhibit Question*

Using the information in the case above helps Connor delegate the patients and functions to the correct health care provider:

1. **RN**

   Patients: __2__, __5__, __6__.

   Functions: __A__, __B__, __H__.

2. **LPN**

   Patients: __1__, __3__, __4__.

   Functions: __C__

3. **AP**

   Functions: __D__, __E__, __F__, __G__.

Exercise 3-13: *Multiple Choice Question*

The RN understands that to complete delegation, it requires:

A. **Supervision and evaluation—YES, these are the follow-up components needed**

B. Evaluation and written critique—NO, it does not have to be written, just communicated

C. Supervision and checkups—NO, checkup should not always be necessary

D. Huddles and checkups—NO, huddles are used for team information

Exercise 3-14: *Matching*

A. A short-term relationship between an expert and a novice	**B**	Mentoring
B. A long-term relationship between an expert and a novice	**A**	Precepting

Exercise 3-15: *Multiple Choice Question*

Knowing patients is a concept that is thought to be critical for:

A. Completing work—NO, this is important but not the priority

B. Handing-off report—NO, this is important but not the priority

C. Teaching—NO, this is important but not the priority

D. **Decision making—YES, it increases safe decision making**

4

Health and Wellness Concepts of Patients and Families

Unfolding Case Study 3 Alita

Alita is in her Nursing Fundamentals class and is anxious to understand what she needs to know for clinical, but currently they are reviewing many abstract concepts. She understands this is necessary, but thinks she will prefer the skills portion of the class.

Exercise 4-1: ***True/False***

Health is the absence of disease.

- ❑ True
- ❑ False

eResource 4-1: To better understand the concept of health, Alita's instructor directs her to look at the World Health Organization's (WHO) definition of health: http://www.who.int/about/definition/en/print.html

How people handle their lives in relation to their health is called their health beliefs. It includes attitudes, convictions, and values about health and illness. What people believe about health can be true or false, and what they do about their health is mostly based on their beliefs. An example is if a person believes that he or she is getting all the vitamins that are recommended in a day (recommended daily amount [RDA]), that person will not be likely to take a multivitamin. There are many things that influence a person's health beliefs, and they are all a concern of nursing since they all play a part in holistic care.

Exercise 4-2: ***Multiple Choice Question***

Holistic nursing care can best be described as:

A. Using complementary medicine methods to heal
B. Focused health care on the problem
C. Using resources to help patients get well
D. Accepting patients as health care decision makers

The Answers section can be found on page 45.

Exercise 4-3: *Matching*

Place the letter in front of the variables that affect health beliefs onto the internal or external factor category.

A. Developmental stage of the patient	___________ Internal factors
B. Socioeconomic status	___________ External factors
C. Emotional factors	
D. Perception of functioning	
E. Cultural background	
F. Family practices	
G. Intellectual background and education	

eResource 4-2: To learn more about Health Beliefs and Culture, Alita

- Reads CurrentNursing.Com's overview of the Health Belief Model: www.currentnursing.com/nursing_theory/psychosocial_models_nursing_hbm.html
- Watches "Infusing Cultural and Linguistic Competence into Health Promotion Training—Part 1" from the National Center for Cultural Competence (NCCC) at Georgetown University: www.youtu.be/PPq_Rg9OmVI

Alita is from a family that has a strong history of heart disease (HD) and so she is aware of risk factors for health care problems.

Exercise 4-4: *Select All That Apply*

What other risk factors are involved in health-related consequences:

- ☐ Genetic factors
- ☐ Age
- ☐ Marital status
- ☐ Socioeconomic status
- ☐ Lifestyle
- ☐ Environment

eResource 4-3: To learn more about determinants of health, Alita

- Reads Healthy People 2020 description of the determinants of health: www.healthypeople.gov/2020/about/DOHAbout.aspx
- Views the video entitled Determinants of Health: A Framework for Reaching Healthy People 2020 Goals: www.youtu.be/5Lul6KNIw_8

Alita understands that there are three types of disease prevention: primary, secondary, and tertiary. Primary prevention occurs before any disease is detected; secondary prevention helps patients who are sick to avoid complications; and tertiary prevention aims to keep patients with permanent disabilities or disease functioning at the highest possible level.

The Answers section can be found on page 45.

Exercise 4-5: *Fill-in*

Fill in the blank: 1 = primary prevention; 2 = secondary prevention, and 3 = tertiary prevention

_______ Physical therapy for a paraplegic

_______ Antibiotics for an ear infection

_______ Daily jogging

_______ HPV (human papillomavirus) vaccine

_______ Hospice care for a terminally ill patient

_______ Casting a broken leg

_______ Diabetic teaching

_______ High school course about STIs (sexually transmitted infections)

_______ Universal hearing screens done on infants for hearing loss

e **eResource 4-4:** To reinforce her understanding of this concept, Alita plays a levels of prevention game on Wisc-Online: www.wisc-online.com/objects/ViewObject.aspx?ID=NUR3403

Alita also understands that the concept of illness can be subdivided into categories and when a patient is ill it has an effect on the person's body image, self-concept, family roles, and dynamics. Many times it also causes an economic strain.

Exercise 4-6: *Matching*

Match the definition to the concept.

A. Short-term illness, often severe	_______ Chronic
B. Illness lasting longer than 6 months	_______ Acute

Alita's father had heart surgery while she was in high school. She remembers the nurses being very ***caring*** to her father and her family. She wants to be a caring nurse and knows a caring person when she meets one, but she is interested in the behavior that makes a nurse caring. Caring is also referred to as the ***art*** of nursing. One theory about caring is that it has five dimensions: knowing, being with, doing for, enabling, and maintaining belief (Swanson, 1991). This makes sense to Alita because the behavior of getting to ***know*** your patients shows caring, as does ***presence*** or being with them when they need you. Enabling is a misunderstood word sometimes but really means helping a patient get through by supporting them with either actions or words. Maintaining belief is providing hope in a realistic manner when patients and families are in crises; they appreciate a nurse who is appropriately optimistic about the future without focusing on all the negative consequences.

Alita now understands that a person cannot be separated from his or her ***family*** when sick or in need of nursing care. Although Alita is from a traditional family, she understands that not every patient will be from a traditional family, and that she will need to understand what ***family-centered nursing care*** encompasses.

The Answers section can be found on page 45.

Exercise 4-7: ***Select All That Apply***

Characteristics of a family include:

- ❑ At least two adults
- ❑ Legally married
- ❑ Biologically connected
- ❑ Live together
- ❑ Have a relationship

Exercise 4-8: ***Multiple Choice Question***

Current family trends include all the following except:

A. More and more people are creating households with more than one person
B. Divorce rates are increasing to over 50% of marriages
C. The majority of women work outside the home
D. Homosexual couples can marry in some states

Alita and her classmates in Fundamentals identify other societal influences that have affected family composition and functioning.

- Teenage pregnancy rates are decreasing but is still a concern
- Increase in single-parent families
- Changing economic status
- Caregiver strain

Exercise 4-9: ***Multiple Choice Question***

The fastest growing number of citizens in the United States are:

A. Immigrants
B. Infants of teenage mothers
C. Jobless young adults
D. Geriatric

eResource 4-5: To learn more about changing demographics in the United States, Alita uses her smartphone to search the U.S. Census database: www.census.gov/main/www/srchtool.html

Economics plays a direct relationship to health care. As more and more people lose jobs, less have health insurance and are likely not to seek care unless it is an emergency. Another great concern for the nurse is the increasing number of ***vulnerable populations*** in the United States.

Exercise 4-10: ***Multiple Choice Question***

The fastest growing number of the "homeless" population are:

A. Geriatric families
B. Drug/alcohol-addicted individuals
C. Families with children
D. Mentally incompetent individuals

The Answers section can be found on page 45.

eResource 4-6: To understand more about vulnerable populations and which populations are most vulnerable in the United States, Alita explores the Office of Minority Health and Health Disparities: http://www.cdc.gov/omhd/Populations/definitions.htm

Alita and three of her classmates have to do a group project on a vulnerable population. They choose patients with ***HIV***. Each of them develops a part of a PowerPoint® presentation about ***AIDS*** to show to the class during presentation day. Alita researches the history of the disease.

Exercise 4-11: ***Multiple Choice Question***

Currently the fastest method by which HIV is being transmitted is:

A. Heterosexually
B. Piercing/tattooing
C. Homosexually
D. Mother to infant

The presentation goes well, and Alita's group gets an "A." The following group presents on another vulnerable population, ***victims of family violence***. Alita and her classmates learn that family violence is a multifaceted phenomenon that has long-term physical and emotional effects on a person.

Exercise 4-12: ***Select All That Apply***

Factors associated with family violence include:

- ❑ Stress
- ❑ Single-parent family
- ❑ Poverty
- ❑ Parents who themselves were abused as children
- ❑ Homosexual families
- ❑ Mental illness
- ❑ Drug/alcohol abuse

The increase in family violence is disheartening, and Alita sometimes feels that there are so many problems in society that she does not know how she will make a difference as a nurse. She writes about these feelings in her reflective journal, which she gives to her clinical instructor to review. Her clinical instructor sets up a meeting with her to talk about feelings of ***helplessness***. One concept that is discussed is "reciprocity." The clinical instructor tells Alita that when a patient/family/population appreciates the care a nurse gives, it increases ***self-worth*** and rebuilds meaning to the role. Alita understands that it is helping one person/family/population at a time that is rewarding. They also discuss how healthy families function, and list characteristics of healthy families:

- Can adapt to change of parenting
- Communicate openly and express concern for each other

The Answers section can be found on page 45.

- Can flex role assignments
- Volunteer help to one another
- Have specific roles—financier, problem solver, decision maker, nurturer, manager, gatekeeper for information

In contrast, unhealthy families have characteristics, such as:

- Blaming others
- Keeping secrets
- Hiding feelings

Exercise 4-13: *Select All That Apply*

Select the following tasks that families are responsible for:

- ❑ Physical maintenance of members
- ❑ Socialization of members
- ❑ Allocation of resources
- ❑ College educating
- ❑ Maintenance of order
- ❑ Division of labor
- ❑ Reproduction, recruitment, and release of members
- ❑ Placement of members in larger society
- ❑ Maintaining motivation and morale

Alita and her classmates learn that ***healthy families*** have ***hardiness*** and ***resiliency*** and can deal with the stress of illness better than families who are ***dysfunctional***.

Exercise 4-14: *Ordering*

Correctly order following classic lifecycles with numbers 1 through 8:

_______ Launching family
_______ Marriage or establish a relationship and family plan
_______ Older age/retirement
_______ Family with school-age children—keeping up with demands of education
_______ Family with adolescent children teaching responsible freedom
_______ Family of middle years or two-partner nuclear family
_______ Early childbearing period—starts with incorporating first child into family
_______ Family with preschool children dealing with growth and development

A third presentation about families is presented by Alita's classmates the following week, and their topic is ***culturally marginalized populations***. Culture plays an important role in health care, and the diverse population of the United States calls for nurses not only to be diverse themselves but also to be culturally competent. Cultural, ethnic, and racial disparities exist in the United States. For example, an

The Answers section can be found on page 45.

infant of a mother from Black or African American descent has an increased chance of dying compared with an infant of a mother from an Eastern European White descent. These types of statistics are unacceptable and health care must better understand cultural diversity.

Exercise 4-15: *Matching*

Match the word in column A to the definition in column B.

Column A		Column B
A. Cultural backlash	_______	Shared values related to cultural and racial identity
B. Enculturation	_______	Identification with two or more cultures
C. Assimilation	_______	Distinct identities from the dominant culture
D. Acculturation	_______	Socialization into a person's primary culture
E. Ethnicity	_______	Rejecting a culture due to a bad experience
F. Subcultures	_______	Thinking that your own culture is superior
G. Ethnocentrism	_______	Adapting to the new culture
H. Biculturalism	_______	Giving up identity to fit into dominant culture

eResource 4-7: To learn more about health disparities and culture, the students visit the following resources:

- Healthy People 2020: www.healthypeople.gov/2020/about/DisparitiesAbout.aspx
- The Provider's Guide to Quality and Culture: http://erc.msh.org/mainpage.cfm?file=1.0.htm&module=provider&language=English
- U.S. DHHS, Office of Minority Health's information on Cultural Competency: www.minorityhealth.hhs.gov/templates/browse.aspx?lvl=2&lvlid=11

Alita learned from the presentation that ***transcultural nursing*** is the study of cultures related to nursing care and that nurses need to provide ***culturally congruent care***. Culturally competent care does not mean that Alita needs to know every value and custom about every culture, but nurses do need to bridge cultural gaps. Culturally competent care consists of five components (Campinha-Bacote, 2002).

eResource 4-8: The students learn more about Transcultural Nursing: Basic Concepts and Case Studies by reviewing: www.culturediversity.org/index.html

The Answers section can be found on page 45.

Exercise 4-16: *Matching*

Match the concept in column A to the example in column B.

Column A	Column B
A. Cultural awareness	_______ Having an understanding of a diverse group
B. Cultural knowledge	_______ Motivation and commitment to care for diverse groups
C. Cultural skill	_______ Engaging in cultural interactions
D. Cultural encounters	_______ Examining one's own background and biases
E. Desire	_______ Assessing cultural issues that affect nursing care

eResource 4-9: To better understand cultural competency from a patient and provider perspective, view these videos:

- Cultural Competence for Health Care Providers: www.youtu.be/dNLtAj0wy6I
- Cultural Awareness for Health Care Professionals: www.youtu.be/Gxp_7aRA_tQ
- Cultural Competence: Becoming Culturally Competent: www.youtu.be/gdhpWhXv4YQ

Exercise 4-17: *Hot Spot*

If the center ring in the diagram below represents a specific culture, label the other two rings as emic or etic worldviews (Figure 4.1):

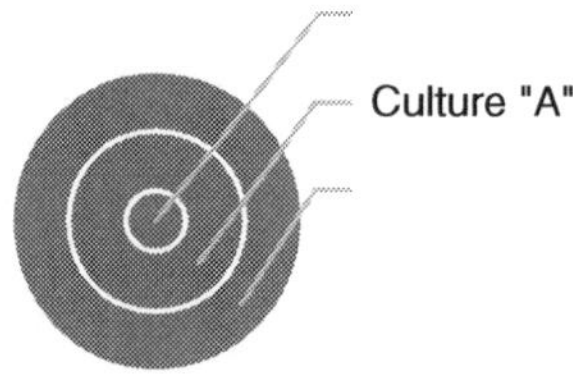

eResource 4-10: Alita finds some tip sheets, Culture Clues™, from the University of Washington Medical Center: www.depts.washington.edu/pfes/CultureClues.htm

Alita is overwhelmed by the amount of information that needs to be acquired to become culturally competent. She journals her feelings, and her instructor discusses that making a good cultural assessment is the key. Some of those main features are to understand the following:

- The history of the group
- What health care needs the group has

The Answers section can be found on page 45.

- How they are socially organized
- What their spiritual beliefs are
- Communication pattern
- Time orientation
- Caring beliefs
- Their past experiences with health care

eResource 4-11:

- To learn more about the concept of cultural health care delivery, Alita watches U.S. DHSS, Office of Minority Health's two-part video series, *Think, Speak and Act Cultural Health:*
  - Part I: www.thinkculturalhealth.hhs.gov/FlashPlayer/play508.asp?Video=QHpart1
  - Part 2: www.thinkculturalhealth.hhs.gov/FlashPlayer/play508.asp?Video=QHpart2
- To build her cultural competency, Alita registers for the U.S. DHHS, Office of Minority Health's free self-directed training module, Culturally Competent Nursing Care: A Cornerstone of Caring: https://ccnm.thinkculturalhealth.hhs.gov/

The instructor provides Alita with some case scenarios and asks her to assess feature that was missed in the cultural assessment.

Exercise 4-18: *Exhibit Question*

A nurse is educating a Muslim patient about nutrition and is frustrated because he only eats 10% of his lunch during the month of Ramadan. What cultural feature was not assessed?

A. The history of the group
B. What health care needs the group has
C. How they are socially organized
D. What their spiritual beliefs are
E. Communication patterns
F. Time orientation
G. Caring belief
H. Their past experiences with health care

Exercise 4-19: *Exhibit Question*

The nurse is taking care of Hindu patient in labor who is obviously uncomfortable. Her husband is not in the labor room at the time, and the patient is asked to make a decision about pain medication but tells the nurse that she cannot tell her until her husband returns. What cultural feature was not assessed?

A. The history of the group
B. What health care needs the group has

The Answers section can be found on page 45.

C. How they are socially organized
D. What their spiritual beliefs are
E. Communication patterns
F. Time orientation
G. Caring belief
H. Their past experiences with health care

Exercise 4-20: *Exhibit Question*
A nurse is caring for an older American-born patient who was a young woman during the Great Depression. The woman keeps large amounts of leftover food at her bedside, which the nurse keeps throwing away. What cultural feature was not assessed?

A. The history of the group
B. What health care needs the group has
C. How they are socially organized
D. What their spiritual beliefs are
E. Communication patterns
F. Time orientation
G. Caring belief
H. Their past experiences with health care

Alita better understands the implications of caring for patients, families, or groups of different cultures and has begun to journal her reflections about her own cultural beliefs and values so she can become more aware of any biases that may stand in the way of her cultural competence.

References

Campinha-Bacote, J. (2002). The process of cultural competence in the delivery of healthcare services: A model of care. *Journal of Transcultural Nursing, 13*(3), 181–184.

Swanson, K. (1991). Empirical development of a middle-range theory of caring. *Nursing Research, 40*(3), 161–166.

The Answers section can be found on page 45.

Answers

Exercise 4-1: ***True/False***

Health is the absence of disease.

❑ True

☒ **False—Health care is more than just the absence of disease; it includes health promotion and maintenance**

Exercise 4-2: ***Multiple Choice Question***

Holistic nursing care can best be described as:

A. Using complementary medicine methods to heal—NO, this is just a part of holistic health

B. Focused health care on the problem—NO, it is focused on the whole person

C. Using resources to help patients get well—NO, this is just one aspect

D. **Accepts patients as health care decision makers—YES, this is the main concept; the patient is the expert about his or her health**

Exercise 4-3: ***Matching***

Place the letter in front of the variables that affect health beliefs onto the internal or external factor category.

A. Developmental stage of the patient	**A, C, D**	Internal factors
B. Socioeconomic status	**B, E, F, H**	External factors
C. Emotional factors		
D. Perception of functioning		
E. Cultural background		
F. Family practices		
H. Intellectual background and education		

Exercise 4-4: ***Select All That Apply***

What other risk factors are involved in health-related consequences:

☒ **Genetic factors—YES**

☒ **Age—YES**

❑ Marital status—NO, although there are some long-term longitudinal studies that suggest married people live longer, it is not related to a specific illness

☒ **Socioeconomic status—YES**

☒ **Lifestyle—YES**

☒ **Environment—YES**

Exercise 4-5: *Fill-in*

Fill in the blank: 1 = primary prevention; 2 = secondary prevention, and 3 = tertiary prevention

___**3**___ Physical therapy for a paraplegic
___**2**___ Antibiotics for an ear infection
___**1**___ Daily jogging
___**1**___ HPV (human papillomavirus) vaccine
___**3**___ Hospice care for a terminally ill patient
___**2**___ Casting a broken leg
___**2**___ Diabetic teaching
___**1**___ High school course about STIs (sexually transmitted infections)
___**2**___ Universal hearing screens done on infants for hearing loss

Exercise 4-6: *Matching*

Match the definition to the concept.

A. Short-term illness often severe	**B**	Chronic
B. Illness lasting longer than 6 months	**A**	Acute

Exercise 4-7: *Select All That Apply*

Characteristics of a family include:

☐ At least two adults—NO, it can be an adult and a child

☐ Legally married—NO, they do not have to be legally married

☐ Biologically connected—NO, they can just have a relationship

☐ Live together—NO, some families are separated

☒ **Have a relationship—YES, this is the only criterion needed**

Exercise 4-8: *Multiple Choice Question*

Current family trends include all the following except:

A. **More people are creating households with more than one person—YES, this is not true—more and more people live alone**
B. Divorce rates are increasing to over 50% of marriages—NO, this is true
C. The majority of women work outside the home—NO, this is true
D. Homosexual couples can marry in some states—NO, this is true

Exercise 4-9: *Multiple Choice Question*

The fastest growing number of citizens in the United States are:

A. Immigrants—NO
B. Infants of teenage mothers—NO

C. Jobless young adults—NO

D. **Geriatric—YES, the aging of the baby boomers (born 1946–1960; post-World War II)**

Exercise 4-10: *Multiple Choice Question*

The fastest growing number of the "homeless" population are:

A. Geriatric families—NO

B. Drug/alcohol-addicted individuals—NO

C. **Families with children—YES**

D. Mentally incompetent individuals—NO

Exercise 4-11: *Multiple Choice Question*

Currently the fastest method by which HIV is being transmitted is:

A. **Heterosexually—YES, this is now the population most affected along with IV drug users**

B. Piercing/ tattooing—NO

C Homosexually—NO

D. Mother to infant—NO

Exercise 4-12: *Select All That Apply*

Factors associated with family violence include:

☒ **Stress**

☐ Single-parent family

☒ **Poverty (Note: Poverty increases stress, but abuse crosses all socioeconomic boundaries)**

☒ **Parents who themselves were abused as children**

☒ **Homosexual families**

☒ **Mental illness**

☒ **Drug/alcohol abuse**

Exercise 4-13: *Select All That Apply*

Select the following tasks that families are responsible for:

☒ **Physical maintenance of members**

☒ **Socialization of members**

☒ **Allocation of resources**

☐ College educating—NO, college is not a requirement for all families

☒ **Maintenance of order**

☒ **Division of labor**

☒ **Reproduction, recruitment, and release of members**

☒ **Placement of members in larger society**

☒ **Maintaining motivation and morale**

Exercise 4-14: *Ordering*

Correctly order following classic lifecycles with numbers 1 through 8:

__6__ Launching family
__1__ Marriage or establish a relationship and family plan
__8__ Older age/retirement
__4__ Family with school-age children—keeping up with demands of education
__5__ Family with adolescent children teaching responsible freedom
__7__ Family of middle years or two-partner nuclear family
__2__ Early childbearing period—starts with incorporating first child into family
__3__ Family with preschool children dealing with growth and development

Exercise 4-15: *Matching*

Match the word in column A to the definition in column B.

Column A		Column B
A. Cultural backlash	E	Shared values related to cultural and racial identity
B. Enculturation	H	Identification with two or more cultures
C. Assimilation	F	Distinct identities from the dominant culture
D. Acculturation	B	Socialization into a person's primary culture
E. Ethnicity	A	Rejecting a culture due to a bad experience
F. Subcultures	G	Thinking that your own culture is superior
G. Ethnocentrism	D	Adapting to the new culture
H. Biculturalism	C	Giving up identify to fit into dominant culture

Exercise 4-16: *Matching*

Match the concept in column A to the example in column B.

Column A		Column B
A. Cultural awareness	C	Having an understanding of a diverse group
B. Cultural knowledge	E	Motivation and commitment to care for diverse groups
C. Cultural skill	D	Engaging in cultural interactions
D. Cultural encounters	A	Examining one's own background and biases
E. Desire	B	Assessing cultural issues that affect nursing care

Exercise 4-17: ***Hot Spot***

If the center ring in the diagram below represents a specific culture, label the other two rings as emic or etic worldviews (Figure 4.2):

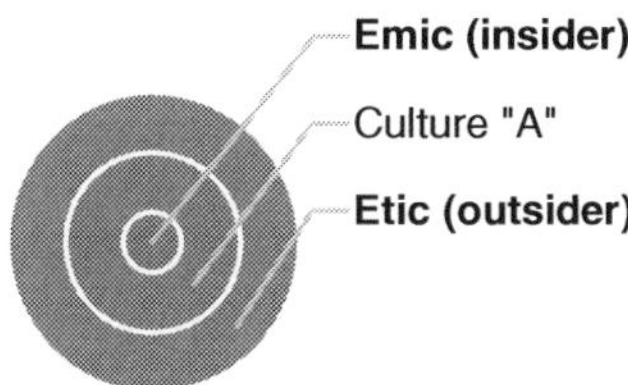

Exercise 4-18: ***Exhibit Question***

A nurse is educating a Muslim patient about nutrition and is frustrated because he only eats 10% of his lunch during the month of Ramadan. What cultural feature was not assessed?

A. The history of the group
B. What health care needs the group has
C. How they are socially organized
D. **What their spiritual beliefs are**
E. Communication patterns
F. Time orientation
G. Caring belief
H. Their past experiences with health care

Exercise 4-19: ***Exhibit Question***

The nurse is taking care of Hindu patient in labor who is obviously uncomfortable. Her husband is not in the labor room at the time, and the patient is asked to make a decision about pain medication but tells the nurse that she cannot tell her until her husband returns. What cultural feature was not assessed?

A. The history of the group
B. What health care needs the group has
C. **How they are socially organized**
D. What their spiritual beliefs are
E. Communication patterns
F. Time orientation
G. Caring belief
H. Their past experiences with health care

Exercise 4-20: *Exhibit Question*

A nurse is caring for an older American-born patient who was a young woman during the Great depression. The woman keeps large amounts of leftover food at her bedside, which the nurse keeps throwing away. What cultural feature was not assessed?

A. **The history of the group**
B. What health care needs the group has
C. How they are socially organized
D. What their spiritual beliefs are
E. Communication patterns
F. Time orientation
G. Caring belief
H. Their past experiences with health care

5

Understanding Human Growth and Development Theory

Unfolding Case Study 4 ▒ Connor

The fundamentals class is being tested on human growth and development, and Connor is studying for the test because it is 20% of the total class grade. Ten percent of the test will be evaluating the learner's understanding of growth and development theories, and the other 10% will be applying the theories to health promotion concepts. Connor inquired of the professor why growth and development is such a large portion of the course but now understands the reason.

Exercise 5-1: *Multiple Choice Question*

Understanding of human growth and development is needed in order for the nurse to:

A. Pick appropriate games
B. Know medication dosages
C. Understand age-appropriate nursing interventions
D. Understand body proportions

eResource 5-1: To learn more about normal growth and development, Conner uses his computer to visit MedlinePlus: [Pathway: www.nlm.nih.gov → select "MedlinePlus" → enter "Normal Growth and Development" into the search field].

Connor understands that human growth is fairly predictable and can be assessed to establishe norms (such as height compared with a growth chart). Physical growth and development are different concepts. ***Physical growth*** can be measured in things such as height, weight, and number of teeth erupted. ***Development*** is the capacity of a human to function, and it follows a few simple rules.

Exercise 5-2: *Multiple Choice Question*

Which statement does not apply to human growth and development?

A. Complex to simple
B. Head to toe (***cephalocaudal***)

The Answers section can be found on page 59.

C. General to specific
D. Trunk to extremities (***proximodistal***)

Connor understands the concept of maturation, which is the development of increasing integration of complex behavior into a person's life, and he knows that it takes time for an individual to grow. Part of that growth has to do with ***differentiation*** of cell function. Before birth, fetal cells develop into different organs. Human bodies grow and develop in four areas:

- Physical
- Cognitive
- Moral
- Psychological

There are many different developmental theories, and Connor finds them confusing, so he reviews the main theories for the test.

Exercise 5-3: *Matching*
Match the name of the theory or theorist in column A to the overall concept of the theory in column B.

Column A		Column B
A. Gesell	_______	Essential tasks must be attained and come from internal and external sources
B. Freud	_______	Adults shed childhood beliefs in order to mature
C. Erikson	_______	Change is driven by libido and aggression
D. Havighurst	_______	Eight stages, each with a task and an opposing conflict
E. Gould	_______	Growth is directed by the genetic makeup of the person
F. Piaget	_______	Theory of cognitive development with four stages

Connor gets the major developmental theories and theorists straight in his mind and then concentrates on the important subdivisions in each theory. Gesell's theory (1948) is easy to remember because he uses G-G or Gesell-Genetics. This theory basically describes development as being predetermined by genetic makeup.

Sigmund Freud's theory is an older but well-known one and contains five stages of human development that are grounded around psychosexual behavior. Connor remembers Freud-Five, for five stages.

The Answers section can be found on page 59.

Exercise 5-4: *Ordering*

Place the numbers 1 to 5 to designate the correct order of Freud's stages from birth to death.

_______ Phallic
_______ Oral
_______ Genital
_______ Anal
_______ Latency

eResource 5-2: To review Freud's theory, Connor reads an overview of the stages outlined by Freud: www.allpsych.com/psychology101/sexual_development.html

Connor knows that Freud's theory is important because it was a theory that drove the development of many other significant developmental theories like the one developed by Erikson (1963). Erikson's theory of development is widely used and is based on eight stages of life. Conner remembers Erikson-Eight!

Exercise 5-5: *Matching*

Match the name of the stage in column A to the description in column B.

Column A	Column B
A. Trust vs. mistrust	_______ This is developed with consistent care giving in the first year
B. Autonomy vs. shame	_______ Toddler finds newfound independence (1–3 years) and doubt
C. Initiative vs. guilt	_______ Child likes to pretend and explore environment (3–6 years)
D. Industry vs. inferiority	_______ Children thrive on accomplishments and praise (6–11 years)
E. Identity vs. role	_______ Preoccupied with body image and appearance (puberty) confusion
F. Intimacy vs. isolation	_______ Capacity to love others (young adulthood)
G. Generativity vs. self-absorption and stagnation	_______ Focus on supporting next generations (middle adulthood)
H. Integrity vs. despair	_______ Dealing with physical and social losses (old age)

The Answers section can be found on page 59.

eResource 5-3: To learn more about Erikson's theory, Conner

- Reads CurrentNursing.com's overview of the theory: www.currentnursing.com/nursing_theory/theory_of_psychosocial_development.html
- Watches a video that summarizes the eight stages of development: www.youtu.be/577GqQDMX08

Once Connor has an understanding of Erikson's theory, he looks at Havighurst's developmental theory. Havighurst's theory is based on accomplishing a series of essential tasks that come from three internal and external pressures but are predictable. (Connor remembers Havighurst has pressure!)

Exercise 5-6: ***Multiple Choice Question***

Select the concept that is not considered an internal or external pressure in Havighurst's theory:

A. Sexual awareness
B. Physical maturity
C. Cultural
D. Personal goals

Another theory is Gould's theory. Gould's theory makes sense to Connor because it is all about adult maturation and he likes having the understanding of some of the things he is going through living away from home at his college dorm. Connor remembers Gould-Grown, since the theory is about adults.

Exercise 5-7: ***Select all that apply***

Select Gould's five stages of adult development out of the seven listed below:

- ❑ 20s—developing independence from parents
- ❑ 30s—taking control of life
- ❑ Late 30s—reexamining if this is the way I want to be
- ❑ 40s—possibilities become more limited
- ❑ Late 40s—midlife crises—finding self-attractive
- ❑ 50s—realization of mortality and less regret
- ❑ 60s—despair related to life regrets

Connor has also heard of Piaget from his developmental psychology course (Polan & Taylor, 2011). Just like Gould deals with (Grown) adults, Piaget deals with four stages of children and cognitive development.

Connor remembers Piaget-Pre-grown.

The Answers section can be found on page 59.

Exercise 5-8: *Matching*

Match the Piaget stage in column A to the descriptor in column B.

Column A	Column B
A. Sensorimotor	_______ Develops object permanence (birth to 2 years)
B. Preoperational	_______ Thinking can be abstract (11 to adulthood)
C. Concrete operations	_______ Can perform mental operations (7–11 years)
D. Formal operations	_______ Develops parallel play and use of symbols (2–7 years)

eResource 5-4: To review Piaget's stages of development, Conner

- Reads CurrentNursing.com's overview: www.nursingplanet.com/theory/Piaget's_cognitive_development_theory.html
- Watches the following video on his iPhone: www.youtu.be/TRF27F2bn-A

Once Connor breaks the theories down into simple subconcepts, they are not that difficult to remember. He reads about one more theory that is interesting to him because his mom always described him as an "easy child" as opposed to his older sister who was always described as a "difficult child." Theorists Chess and Thomas (1986) studied children's temperament and actually did find that they could categorize children into one of the three categories: easy, difficult, or slow to warm-up. These different child temperaments are described as follows:

- Easy—predictable, adaptable, positive, and mild-to-moderate moods
- Difficult—active, irritable, negative, and intense moods
- Slow-to-warm-up—adapts slowly to change, mildly negative

eResource 5-5: Conner views a video in which theorists Chess and Thomas discuss temperament qualities in children: www.youtu.be/mgXwCqzh9B8

Also on the exam will be questions about moral development, which differs from physical growth and development, because besides actual human physical and cognitive growth and functioning, it takes into account another dimension that needs to be developed in humans: the reasoning about what is right and wrong. Two moral developmental theories are well known and used to guide nursing care; they are Piaget and Kohlberg. Connor studies each one to prepare for the test.

The Answers section can be found on page 59.

Exercise 5-9: *Matching*

Match Piaget's moral developmental stage in column A with its description in column B.

Column A	Column B
A. Premoral	_______ Can decide on internalized principles
B. Conventional	_______ Follows rules without understanding them
C. Autonomous	_______ Understands the reason for the rules

Kohlberg's moral developmental theory (1983) has six stages, so Connor studies the major issues of each stage in order in an attempt to assimilate the learning into his long-term memory for the test and for practice.

eResource 5-6: To supplement his study materials, Conner reviews two web-based overviews of Kohlberg's model.

- AllPsych.com: www.allpsych.com/psychology101/moral_development.html
- CurrentNursing.com: www.currentnursing.com/nursing_theory/Theory_of_Moral_Development.html

Exercise 5-10: *Select All That Apply*

Select Kohlberg's six stages of moral development out of the following eight:

- ❑ Punishment and obedience orientation—obedience to authority unquestioned
- ❑ Family awareness orientation—wants to please parents
- ❑ Instrumental relativist orientation—recognizes that there is more than one view
- ❑ Good boy–nice girl orientation—good behavior wins approval of others
- ❑ Society-maintenance orientation—expands to being concerned for social order
- ❑ Social disregard orientation—believes authority is personally oppressive
- ❑ Social contract orientation—understands that laws can be changed to help society
- ❑ Universal ethical principle orientation—self chooses ethical principles

After reviewing the material, Connor feels better prepared for the fundamentals test on the theoretical portion about growth and development. Just to be sure he is ready for the test this week; he does the following five questions that he finds on the CD that came with his textbook.

The Answers section can be found on page 59.

Exercise 5-11: *Multiple Choice Question*

Parents of a child on a pediatric unit described their child's behavior as standoffish and independent. The nurse can best help them understand this behavior by educating them about which developmental theory:

A. Piaget
B. Freud
C. Gould
D. Chess and Thomas

Exercise 5-12: *Multiple Choice Question*

The nurse is caring for an older adult who is depressed because the patient lost her spouse and has very few friends. The nurse recognizes this as Erikson's stage of:

A. Identity vs. role
B. Intimacy vs. isolation
C. Generatively vs. self-absorption and stagnation
D. Integrity vs. despair

Exercise 5-13: *Multiple Choice Question*

The nurse is caring for a psychiatric patient who is detained for multiple counts of shoplifting. Which one of Kohlberg's stages has not likely been achieved?

A. Instrumental relativist orientation
B. Good boy–nice girl orientation
C. Society-maintenance orientation
D. Social contract orientation

Exercise 5-14: *Multiple Choice Question*

The nurse applies which stage of Gould's themes to a patient who is 36 and deciding on moving to a better climate to improve her health?

A. Developing independence from parents
B. Taking control of life
C. Reexamining if this is the way she wants to be
D. Possibilities become more limited

Exercise 5-15: *Multiple Choice Question*

An 8-month-old child is brought into the ED (emergency department) and is septic and placed in isolation. The parents want the child to have the stuffed animal that has been in the crib at home. The nurse explains to them that the child will not miss it because the child is in what developmental stage according to Piaget:

A. Sensorimotor
B. Preoperational
C. Concrete operations
D. Formal operations

The Answers section can be found on page 59.

eResource 5-7: As a final step in preparing for the test, Connor watches a video that provides an overview of nursing considerations when assessing an infant's growth and development during a well-baby visit: www.youtu.be/tcqXsdU7Lm0

Connor is successful on the practice questions and now has the confidence to move on to studying the application portion for the growth and development test. For now, he is going to relax, watch a little TV, and get a good night's sleep!

References

Chess, S., & Thomas, A. (1986). *Temperament in clinical practice.* New York, NY: Guilford Press.

Erikson, E. H. (1963). *Childhood and society.* New York, NY: Norton Publishing.

Gesell, A. (1948). *Studies in child development.* New York, NY: Harper Publishing.

Kohlberg, L. (1981). *The philosophy of moral development: Moral stages and idea of justice.* San Francisco, CA: Harper and Row Publishers.

Polan, E. U., & Taylor, D. R. (2011). *Journey across the life span: Human development and health promotion* (4th ed.). Philadelphia, PA: F.A. Davis.

The Answers section can be found on page 59.

Answers

Exercise 5-1: *Multiple Choice Question*

Understanding of human growth and development is needed in order for the nurse to:

A. Pick appropriate games—NO, this is important but does not include all interventions

B. Know medication dosages—NO, this is important but does not include all interventions

C. **Understand age-appropriate nursing interventions—YES, this is the most important reason**

D. Understand body proportions—NO, this is important but does not include all interventions

Exercise 5-2: *Multiple Choice Question*

Which statement does not apply to human growth and development?

A. **Complex to simple—YES, this does not apply; it is simple to complex**

B. Head to toe (***cephalocaudal***)—NO, this is true

C. General to specific—NO, this is true

D. Trunk to extremities (***proximodistal***)—NO, this is true

Exercise 5-3: *Matching*

Match the name of the theory or theorist in column A to the overall concept of the theory in column B.

Column A		Column B
A. Gesell	**D**	Essential tasks must be attained and come from internal and external sources
B. Freud	**E**	Adults shed childhood beliefs in order to mature
C. Erikson	**B**	Change is driven by libido and aggression
D. Havighurst	**C**	Eight stages, each with a task and an opposing conflict
E. Gould	**A**	Growth is directed by the genetic makeup of the person
F. Piaget	**F**	Theory of cognitive development with four stages

Exercise 5-4: *Ordering*

Place the numbers 1 to 5 to designate the correct order of Freud's stages from birth to death.

__3__ Phallic

__1__ Oral

__5__ Genital

__2__ Anal

__4__ Latency

Exercise 5-5: *Matching*

Match the name of the stage in column A to the description in column B.

Column A		Column B
A. Trust vs. mistrust	A	This is developed with consistent care giving in the first year
B. Autonomy vs. shame	B	Toddler finds newfound independence (1–3 years) and doubt
C. Initiative vs. guilt	C	Child likes to pretend and explore environment (3–6 years)
D. Industry vs. inferiority	D	Children thrive on accomplishments and praise (6–11 years)
E. Identity vs. role	E	Preoccupied with body image and appearance (puberty) confusion
F. Intimacy vs. isolation	F	Capacity to love others (young adulthood)
G. Generativity vs. self-absorption and stagnation	G	Focus on supporting next generations (middle adulthood)
I. Integrity vs. despair	H	Dealing with physical and social losses (old age)

Exercise 5-6: *Multiple Choice Question*

Select the concept that is not considered an internal or external pressure in Havighurst's theory:

A. **Sexual awareness—YES, this is not a concept in Havighurst's theory**
B. Physical maturity—NO, this is a concept in Havighurst's theory
C. Cultural—NO, this is a concept in Havighurst's theory
D. Personal goals—NO, this is a concept in Havighurst's theory

Exercise 5-7: ***Select all that apply***

Select Gould's five stages of adult development out of the seven listed below:

☒ **20s—developing independence from parents**

☒ **30s—taking control of life**

☒ **Late 30s– reexamining if this is the way I want to be**

☒ **40s—possibilities become more limited**

❑ Late 40s—midlife crises – finding self-attractive

☒ **50s—realization of mortality and life regret**

❑ 60s—despair related to life regrets

Exercise 5-8: ***Matching***

Match the Piaget stage in column A to the descriptor in column B.

Column A	Column B
A. Sensorimotor	__**A**__ Develops object permanence (birth to 2 years)
B. Preoperational	__**D**__ Thinking can be abstract (11 to adulthood)
C. Concrete operations	__**C**__ Can perform mental operations (7–11 years)
D. Formal operations	__**B**__ Develops parallel play and use of symbols (2–7 years).

Exercise 5-9: ***Matching***

Match Piaget's moral developmental stage in column A with its description in column B.

Column A	Column B
A. Premoral	__**C**__ Can decide on internalized principles
B. Conventional	__**A**__ Follows rules without understanding them
C. Autonomous	__**B**__ Understands the reason for the rules

Exercise 5-10: ***Select all that apply***

Select Kohlberg's six stages of moral development out of the following eight:

☒ **Punishment and obedience orientation—obedience to authority unquestioned**

❑ Family awareness orientation—wants to please parents

☒ **Instrumental relativist orientation—recognizes that there is more than one view**

☒ **Good boy–nice girl orientation—good behavior wins approval of others**

☒ **Society-maintenance orientation—expands to being concerned for social order**

❑ Social disregard orientation—believes authority is personally oppressive

☒ **Social contract orientation—understands that laws can be changed to help society**

☒ **Universal ethical principle orientation—self chooses ethical principles**

Exercise 5-11: *Multiple Choice Question*

Parents of a child on a pediatric unit described their child's behavior as standoffish and independent. The nurse can best help them understand this behavior by educating them about which developmental theory:

A. Piaget—NO, Piaget describes cognitive and moral development
B. Freud—NO, Freud describes personality development using a psychoanalytical model
C. Gould—NO, Gould describes adult development
D. **Chess and Thomas—YES, this theory describes temperament**

Exercise 5-12: *Multiple Choice Question*

The nurse is caring for an older adult who is depressed because they lost their spouse and has very few friends. The nurse recognizes this as Erikson stage of:

A. Identity vs. role—NO, this describes young adult's sexual maturation
B. Intimacy vs. isolation—NO, this describes young adult's capacity to love
C. Generatively vs. self-absorption and Stagnation—NO, this describes middle-aged patients' focus on next generations
D. **Integrity vs. despair—YES, this describes older adults who have difficulty finding meaning in their lives**

Exercise 5-13: *Multiple Choice Question*

The nurse is caring for a psychiatric patient who is detained for multiple counts of shoplifting. Which one of the Kohlberg's stages has not likely been achieved?

A. Instrumental relativist orientation—NO, this is when a child recognizes that there can be more than one view and the world is not black and white
B. Good boy–nice girl orientation—NO, this is children's behavior when they are pleasing their friends to be accepted
C. **Society-maintenance orientation—YES, this person may not have developed the morality of social order**
D. Social contract orientation—NO, this is when it is recognized that laws can be changed to improve society

Exercise 5-14: ***Multiple Choice Question***

The nurse applies which stage of Gould's themes to a patient who is 36 and deciding on moving to a better climate to improve her health:

A. Developing independence from parents—NO, this is a task of college-aged adults

B. Taking control of life—NO, this is an early 30s task

C. **Reexamining if this is the way I want to be—YES, late 30s patients will ask if their lives are going in the right direction**

D. Possibilities become more limited—NO, this happens in the 40s, with increasing responsibility and less time in life to do things

Exercise 5-15: ***Multiple Choice Question***

An 8-month-old child is brought into the ED (emergency department) and is septic and placed in isolation. The parents want the child to have the stuffed animal that has been in the crib at home. The nurse explains to them that the child will not miss it because the child is in what developmental stage according to Piaget:

A. **Sensorimotor—YES, the child does not have object permanence yet**

B. Preoperational—NO, this is 2 to 7 years, and the child would have object permanence

C. Concrete operations—NO, this is 7 to 11 years

D. Formal operations—NO, this is 11 years to adulthood

6

Applying Growth and Development Concepts to Health Promotion

Unfolding Case Study 5 Connor

Connor now starts to take a serious look at how growth and development principles are applied for safe nursing care in order to assist patients in health promotion. Connor is going to study this information broken down into life stages, so he can best organize it in his mind. Even though he has not studied specific health conditions yet, he gets a basic understanding of developmentally appropriate care. He starts by reviewing nursing interventions that are done for the newborn infant in order to prevent complications and ensure health promotion.

Exercise 6-1: *Multiple Choice Question*

The primary defense in the newborn nursery for prevention of infection is:

A. Erythromycin ointment 0.5% to each eye

B. Vitamin K IM

C. Cleaning the umbilical stump at each diaper change

D. Adult hand washing

e **eResource 6-1:** Connor visits the CDC website to learn more about hand hygiene in health care settings (www.cdc.gov/handhygiene/Basics.html). There he finds several handy reference guides and learns that unless his hands are visibly soiled, it is recommended that a hand hygiene solution be utilized:

- How to hand wash: www.who.int/gpsc/5may/How_To_HandWash_Poster.pdf
- How to hand rub: www.who.int/gpsc/5may/How_To_HandRub_Poster.pdf

The Answers section can be found on page 73.

Exercise 6-2: *Matching*

Match the health-promoting intervention in column A with the rationales in column B.

Column A	Column B
A. Erythromycin ointment 0.5% to each eye	______ Protect airway
B. Vitamin K (*Aqua-Mephyton*) 1 mg IM	______ Prevent cold stress
C. Clean umbilical stump each diaper change	______ Prevent ophthal mic conjunctivitis
D. Keep a bulb syringe within reach	______ Prevent ascending bacteria into blood stream
E. Maintain a head covering	______ Prevent hemorrhagic disease of the newborn

Connor learns that monitoring an infant's weight gain and growth is also a part of health promotion. Parental teaching is extremely important, especially to prevent sudden infant death syndrome (SIDS). This health promotion piece has made an impact, and since nurses have been teaching parents' methods to prevent SIDS, the incidence or the number of infants who have died from it has decreased by almost 50%!

Exercise 6-3: *Select All That Apply*

Select all the proper things to teach parents in order to decrease the risk of SIDS for their baby:

- ❑ Using a pacifier may be beneficial
- ❑ Wrap the infant tightly in a blanket
- ❑ Keep the infant on a firm mattress
- ❑ Place the infant on their back to sleep
- ❑ Keep the infant in a warm room
- ❑ Sleep with the infant in your bed

eResource 6-2: Connor is eager to learn more, so he looks for more information about SIDS and finds several helpful resources:

- A brief tutorial developed by South Carolina's Healthy Start Program: www.youtu.be/t-Q9qfOKUNE
- A brief audio clip about "Back to Sleep" initiative from the American Academy of Pediatrics: www.aap.org/audio/mfk/011408.mp3
- Additional patient teaching material regarding a safe sleeping environment for the infant at: www.cdc.gov/SIDS

Screening is another aspect of health promotion that is done for infants. Infants are screened for a number of potential health care issues that, if caught early, can be overcome or minimized.

The Answers section can be found on page 73.

Exercise 6-4: *Multiple Choice Question*

Screening infants for inborn errors of metabolism (IEM) is done in order to:

A. Decrease failure to thrive

B. Limit intake to highly efficient proteins

C. Establish a diet until adulthood

D. Prevent permanent intellectual disability

eResource 6-3:

- To ensure that he has reference material readily available on his mobile device, Connor downloads and installs Mobile Merck Medicus, a free mobile resource for health care professionals from Merck & Co., Inc. (available in multiple mobile device platforms). Connor uses the Merck Manual to learn more about screening of neonates. [Pathway: Merck Manual → Topics → Neonate → Evaluation and Care ... (scroll down to) "screening."]
- To find more information regarding screening guidelines, Connor goes to the National Guideline Clearinghouse (NGC) to view Practice Guidelines: www.guideline.gov [Pathway: NGC → enter "newborn screening guidelines" into the search field to find relevant practice guidelines.]
- Connor finds additional information regarding screening guidelines at the CDC www.cdc.gov [Pathway: CDC.gov → enter "newborn screening" into the search field → select "Newborn Screening" → scroll down to view selected screening guidelines.]

Another screening that is completed on all infants is a hearing screen called Universal Newborn Hearing Screen (UNHS). This is done to detect any congenital hearing deficit but cannot detect a progressive hearing loss that occurs after birth.

Exercise 6-5: *Multiple Choice Question*

The nurse should explain to parents that they should be aware of progressive types of hearing loss, which may be detected by the infant:

A. Not smiling back

B. Having delayed speech

C. Pulling on their ears

D. Moving their heads side to side

eResource 6-4: To better understand strategies to educate new parents regarding newborn screening, Connor views the following tutorial from MedlinePlus: www.nlm.nih.gov/medlineplus/tutorials/newbornscreening/htm/_yes_50_no_0.htm

Connor also reads the accompanying reading materials: www.nlm.nih.gov/medlineplus/tutorials/newbornscreening/pd089103.pdf

Other health promotion concerns for infants are safe cribs and car seats.

The Answers section can be found on page 73.

Exercise 6-6: *Multiple Choice Question*

The nurse explains to parents that a child should be in a rear-facing car seat in the back seat until they are:

A. 6 months
B. 1 year old
C. 2 years old
D. 3 years old

Another health promotion issue is shaken baby syndrome and child abuse. It is illegal for a nurse not to report suspected child abuse. Parents must be educated that they can never shake a baby.

Knowing that there are some difficult children, the nurse must equip parents with interventions when they become frustrated.

eResource 6-5: To learn more about shaken baby syndrome, Connor visits the CDC website and reads about the CDC's public health campaign:

- *Heads Up: Prevent Shaken Baby Syndrome*: www.cdc.gov/concussion/HeadsUp/sbs.html and
- Listens to a CDC Expert Commentary: *Shaken Baby Syndrome: Making the Diagnosis, which provides* an overview of signs and symptoms as well as preventative measures: www.medscape.com/viewarticle/725823

Exercise 6-7: *Select All That Apply*

When a child is frustrating a caregiver, some positive interventions are:

- ❑ Gently rock the baby
- ❑ Call a family member or friend for help
- ❑ Jog with the baby in a back pack
- ❑ Place in a room and let the baby cry it out
- ❑ Use a pacifier

Connor also understands that toddlers have great health promotion needs due to their increasing independence and mobility. Some of the dangers for toddlers are car accidents, falls, and poisonings.

Exercise 6-8: *Multiple Choice Question*

The nurse asks the parents what year their house was built in order to ascertain if there is a danger of:

A. Banister accidents
B. Faulty windows
C. Gas leaks
D. Lead paint

The Answers section can be found on page 73.

eResource 6-6: To learn more about these health risks and prevention measures, Connor finds information online at two reputable governmental websites:

- The EPA: www.epa.gov/pesticides/factsheets/child-ten-tips.htm
- The CDC:
  - Lead poisoning prevention tips: www.cdc.gov/nceh/lead/tips.htm
  - Podcast: http://www2c.cdc.gov/podcasts/player.asp?f=10543

Preschoolers are also at risk for poisoning, and health promotion efforts are needed for parents to keep them safe.

Exercise 6-9: *Multiple Choice Question*

The nurse understands that the leading cause of death for children in the United States is:

A. Cancer
B. Unintentional injury
C. SIDS
D. Poisoning

eResource 6-7:

- Connor learns more about the leading causes of death and injury for children at the CDC website: /www.cdc.gov/safechild/Child_Injury_Data.html
- To supplement his understanding of the issue, he also listens to the CDC's Keeping Kids Safe podcast in which Dr. Julie Gilchrist discusses how to prevent these injuries among children: www2c.cdc.gov/podcasts/player.asp?f=10620

Preschoolers should also be checked for vision problems.

Exercise 6-10: *Multiple Choice Question*

Preschoolers who are at high risk for vision problems would be those who:

A. Have a history of prolonged oxygen use as an infant
B. Do not eat vegetables
C. Play out in the sun often
D. Have sleep disturbances

Accidents continue to be a threat to school-age children, and at this stage health promotion gets more complicated. School-age children should be educated, age-appropriately, about HIV and nutrition to prevent obesity. Connor sees the link between the education and the preadolescent stage that will bring with it a very fast period of development. Sexually transmitted infection (STI) prevention is paramount since the majority of STIs are in the young adult group. Although accidents continue to be the leading cause of death in adolescents, the second and third causes are homicide and suicide.

The Answers section can be found on page 73.

eResource 6-8:

- Connor reads more about youth risk behaviors on the CDC website (www.cdc.gov/healthyyouth/yrbs/index.htm) and learns that many young people engage in sexual risk behaviors that can result in unintended health outcomes (www.cdc.gov/healthyyouth/sexualbehaviors/index.htm).
- Connor also uses the Merck manual on his mobile device to learn more about adolescent health risks and health care provider considerations. [Pathway: Merck Manual → Topics → Adolescents → select "Care of....," "Suicide in...," and "Violence and...."]
- Connor also uses the Merck manual on his mobile device to learn more general preventive measures for suicide and to learn more about suicidal behavior. [Pathway: Merck Manual → select "Topics" → enter "suicide" into the search field → select "prevention of..." and also select "Suicidal Behavior."]

Exercise 6-11: *Select All That Apply*

The nurse should teach parents and adolescents that the warning signs of suicide are:

- ❑ Declining grades
- ❑ Sadness
- ❑ Withdrawing from friends
- ❑ Verbalization that "I am okay"
- ❑ Sleep disturbances
- ❑ Loss of energy
- ❑ Crying

Young adulthood brings another set of health teaching as students begin going to college or living independently. College-age children should continue to receive immunization for meningitis and HPV before going off to college. Other college health promotion is education about alcohol and drugs.

Exercise 6-12: *Multiple Choice Question*

Off-campus housing is a concern for:

A. Transportation to and from campus
B. Infestation of bed bugs
C. Poor Internet access for school work
D. Fire safety

Connor considers the implications of young adults in relation to preconceptual health. Preconceptual health is so very important since the critical time in fetal development is the first 8 weeks. Health risks include STIs, alcohol, smoking, and drugs. Habits of good nutrition and exercise should also be established by this time.

The Answers section can be found on page 73.

Exercise 6-13: ***Multiple Choice Question***

The nurse understands that the patient needs more teaching about fetal alcohol syndrome (FAS) and fetal alcohol effects (FAEs) when she states:

A. "Drinking alcohol is a teratogen"
B. "I can drink alcohol up until the time of conception"
C. "I just need to avoid alcohol the first 8 weeks"
D. "I know that binge drinking may cause FAS"

eResource 6-9:

- Connor visits the CDC to view a video that provides a good overview of the long-term impact of FAS. [Pathway: www.cdc.gov/fasd → scroll down to locate and select the **"View 'Story of Iyal' Video link." Note: There is considerable information on this website that can contribute to your understanding and support patient education.]**
- To learn more about FAS and the clinical presentation, Connor uses his mobile device and opens the Merck manual [Merck manual → Topics → enter "neonate" into the search field → scroll down and select "drug withdrawal in." → select "Prenatal Drug Exposure" → tap on the menu icon on the upper right corner of the screen and select "Alcohol."]
- In addition, Connor opens Medscape from WebMD on his mobile device. [Pathway: Medscape → enter "fetal" into the search field at the top of the screen → select "fetal alcohol syndrome."]

Young adulthood is a stressful developmental stage and includes childbearing and rearing. Many marriages unfortunately end in divorce, and families struggle economically. Another increasing societal health concern is partner abuse.

Exercise 6-14: ***Multiple Choice Question***

The nurse understands that partner abuse is related to:

A. Sex
B. Money
C. Power
D. Obedience

Connor's parents are in the middle adult years and are sandwiched between launching him and his sister and taking care of Connor's grandparents. With all their responsibilities, they verbalize that it is difficult to keep up a healthy lifestyle. For many middle-aged adults, this is the period in which there is an onset of chronic health issues such as diabetes, hypertension, and obesity. It is important to encourage patients in this developmental phase to engage in an exercise program.

Connor's grandparents are elderly but are living in their own home.

The Answers section can be found on page 73.

eResource 6-10: To better understand the stressors experienced by his parents, Connor does a bit of research.

- Connor also views this short video about the "lived experience" of the sandwich generation: www.youtube.com/watch?v=t7tDSI-Ncsk
- He also goes to MedlinePlus to learn more about healthy aging: www.nlm.nih.gov/medlineplus/healthyaging.html

Exercise 6-15: ***Select All That Apply***

The reason that the older adult population is increasing is:

- ❑ Financial stability
- ❑ Improved health care
- ❑ Genetic changes
- ❑ Amount of people older than 65

Connor notices that he needs to speak louder to his grandparents.

Exercise 6-16: ***Multiple Choice Question***

Elderly patients often suffer from:

A. Presbycusis
B. Presbyopia
C. Hyposmia
D. Retinopathy

Connor feels like he is in good shape for both parts of the test: the theory and the application piece. It is true you need to know what affects patients at different ages in order to develop appropriate nursing care interventions!

The Answers section can be found on page 73.

Answers

Exercise 6-1: *Multiple Choice Question*

The primary defense in the newborn nursery for prevention of infection is:

A. Erythromycin ointment 0.5% to each eye—NO, this just prevents eye infections

B. Vitamin K HIM—NO, this prevents bleeding

C. Cleaning the umbilical stump at each diaper change—NO, this prevents an infected cord

D. **Adult hand washing—YES, this is primary prevention for all infections**

Exercise 6-2: *Matching*

Match the health-promoting intervention in column A with the rationale in column B

Column A		Column B
A. Erythromycin ointment 0.5% to each eye	**D**	Protect airway
B. Vitamin K (*Aqua-Mephyton*) 1 mg IM	**E**	Prevent cold stress
C. Clean umbilical stump each diaper change	**A**	Prevent ophthalmic conjunctivitis
D. Keeping a bulb syringe within reach	**C**	Prevent ascending bacteria into blood stream
E. Maintaining a head covering	**B**	Prevent hemorrhagic disease of the newborn

Exercise 6-3: *Select all that apply*

Select all the proper things to teach parents in order to decrease the risk of SIDS for their baby:

☒ **Using a pacifier may be beneficial—YES**

❑ Wrap the infant tightly in a blanket—NO, one loose blanket should be over the infant below the armpits

☒ **Keep the infant on a firm mattress—YES**

☒ **Place the infant on their back to sleep—YES**

❑ Keep the infant in a warm room—NO, the room should not be exceptionally warm

❑ Sleep with the infant in your bed—NO, there have been reports of infants suffocating in parents' bed

Exercise 6-4: *Multiple Choice Question*

Screening infants for inborn errors of metabolism (IEM) is done in order to:

A. Decrease failure to thrive—NO, this may be a consequence but not the main manifestation

B. Limit intake to highly efficient proteins—NO, each IEM may need a different dietary restriction or medication

C. Establish a diet until adulthood—NO, most are diet for life

D. **Prevent permanent intellectual disability—YES, this is what is normally prevented**

Exercise 6-5: *Multiple Choice Question*

The nurse should explain to parents that they should be aware of progressive types of hearing loss, which may be detected by the infant:

A. Not smiling back—NO, this is done from visual stimuli also

B. **Having delayed speech—YES, this is usually an indication of hearing loss**

C. Pulling on their ears—NO, this may indicate an ear infection

D. Moving their heads side to side—NO, this is usually not an indicator

Exercise 6-6: *Multiple Choice Question*

The nurse explains to parents that a child should be in a rear-facing car seat in the back seat until they are:

A. 6 months—NO

B. 1 year old—NO

C. **2 years old—YES or until the weight limit is reached**

D. 3 years old—NO

Exercise 6-7: *Select All That Apply*

When a child is frustrating a caregiver, some positive interventions are:

☒ **Gently rock the baby**

☒ **Call a family member or friend for help**

☐ Jog with the baby in a back pack—NO, in rare instances vigorous jogging can produce shaken baby syndrome

☒ **Place in a room and let the baby cry it out**

☒ **Use a pacifier**

Exercise 6-8: *Multiple Choice Question*

The nurse asks the parents what year their house was built in order to ascertain if there is a danger of:

A. Banister accidents—NO, although this may be a concern if they are weak or not updated to specify the correct distance between each one

B. Faulty windows—NO, although this too is a concern if they are not secure

C. Gas leaks—NO, the house may not be fueled by gas but if it is, there should be a carbon monoxide monitor

D. **Lead paint—YES, most have some lead-based paint**

Exercise 6-9: *Multiple Choice Question*

The nurse understands that the leading cause of death for children in the United States is:

A. Cancer—NO

B. **Unintentional injury—YES**

C. SIDS—NO

D. Poisoning—NO

Exercise 6-10: *Multiple Choice Question*

Preschoolers who are at high risk for vision problems would be those with a:

A. **History of prolonged oxygen use as an infant—YES, this can cause retinopathy**

B. Do not eat vegetables—NO, there is no direct correlation

C. Play out in the sun often—NO, there is no direct correlation

D. Have sleep disturbances—NO, there is no direct correlation

Exercise 6-11: *Select all that apply*

The nurse should teach parents and adolescents the warning signs of suicide are:

☒ **Declining grades**

☒ **Sadness**

☒ **Withdrawing from friends**

☐ Verbalization that "I am okay"—NO, many times they verbalize about dying

☒ **Sleep disturbances**

☒ **Loss of energy**

☒ **Crying**

Exercise 6-12: *Multiple Choice Question*

Off-campus housing is a concern for:

A. Transportation to and from campus—NO, this is a concern if the student does not have transportation

B. Infestation of bed bugs— NO, this is only a concern if there is infestations

C. Poor Internet access for school work—NO, this may be a concern, but they can access it at school

D. Fire safety—YES, many college-age students die in off-campus fires

Exercise 6-13: *Multiple Choice Question*

The nurse understands that the patient needs more teaching about fetal alcohol syndrome (FAS) and fetal alcohol effects (FAEs) when she states:

A. "Drinking alcohol is a teratogen."—NO, this is true

B. "I can drink alcohol up until the time of conception."—NO, this is true

C. **"I just need to avoid alcohol the first 8 weeks."—YES, this is a concern because they are not sure at what developmental stage alcohol affects the fetus**

D. "I know that binge drinking may cause FAS."—NO, this is true

Exercise 6-14: *Multiple Choice Question*

The nurse understands that partner abuse is related to:

A. Sex—NO

B. Money—NO

C. **Power—YES, it is control and power**

D. Obedience—NO

Exercise 6-15: *Select all that apply*

The reason that the older adult population is increasing is:

❑ Financial stability—NO, many older Americans are below poverty level

☒ **Improved health care—YES**

❑ Genetic changes—NO, this has not been supported

☒ **Amount of people older than 65—YES, because of the baby boomers**

Exercise 6-16: *Multiple Choice Question*

Elderly patients often suffer from:

A. **Presbycusis**—YES, this is an age-related hearing loss

B. Presbyopia—NO, this is a visual problem or inability to focus

C. Hyposmia—NO, this is poor sense of smell

D. Retinopathy—NO, this is related to preterm infant vision loss

7

The Nursing Process: Assessment

Unfolding Case Study 6 Alita

Connor did well on the developmental test and has been studying with one of his classmates, Alita. The next few classes they are going to be learning about the nursing process.

Exercise 7-1: *Ordering*

Place the steps of the nursing process in order from 1 to 5.

_______ Diagnose

_______ Implement

_______ Assess

_______ Evaluate

_______ Plan

Alita is not sure why they have to spend so much time on the nursing process.

e **eResource 7-1:** To learn more about the nursing process, Alita visits the American Nurses Association website: www.nursingworld.org/EspeciallyForYou/What-is-Nursing/Tools-You-Need/Thenursingprocess.html

Exercise 7-2: *Multiple Choice Question*

The main goal of the nursing process is to:

A. Diagnose conditions that nurses are licensed to treat

B. Formulate a care plan for the patient

C. Determine if nursing can affect the patient's health

D. Organize and deliver nursing care

Exercise 7-3: *Select All That Apply*

By using the nursing process, the nurse will be able to:

❑ Make sound clinical decisions

❑ Use critical thinking

❑ Develop individualized care

The Answers section can be found on page 83.

- ❑ Use her intuition to make decisions
- ❑ Ask the patient to participate
- ❑ Modify care on common practice

Alita is anxious to learn how to use the nursing process to the best of her ability. The first step is assessing or collecting data that will influence your nursing decisions.

eResource 7-2: In order to better understand the steps in the nursing process and utilization of the nursing process, she watches a brief video that highlights the steps within the nursing process: www.youtu.be/kph8xm2CVnI

Exercise 7-4: *True/False*

Asking the patient is a method of collecting secondary data.

- ❑ True
- ❑ False

Alita learns that there are several approaches to collecting data about a patient and to establishing a ***database***. Some of the methods include Gordon's 11 Functional Health Patterns, Pender's Health Promotion Model, or Agency for Health Care Research and Quality (AHRQ)'s standards for pain assessment.

eResource 7-3: To better understand these methods, Anita reads the following materials:

- CurrentNursing.com's overview of
  - Gordon's Functional Health Patterns: www.nursingplanet.com/theory/functional_health_patterns.html
  - Pender's Health Promotion Model: www.nursingplanet.com/health_promotion_model.html
- AHRQ's guidelines for pain assessment: www.guideline.gov [Pathway: AHRQ Home → Pain → Assessment and management of pain → Scroll down and select "recommendation."]

Most often the approach that is most practical is the problem-oriented approach, which answers the question, "Why is the patient here for nursing care?" Once that is established and dealt with, the other approaches are easy to incorporate. Alita asks her instructor to give her an example to help her better understand.

Exercise 7-5: *Multiple Choice Question*

A 25-year-old woman presents in the ED (emergency department) with acute abdominal pain in her right lower quadrant. This is the woman's first time in a hospital; the nurse should first assess her:

A. Abdomen
B. Respiratory status
C. Circulation
D. Pain

The Answers section can be found on page 83.

Alita understands that once the initial assessment is completed for the presenting problem, the other models of assessment can be used to provide information in the database. Gordon's Functional Health Patterns are popular because they ***holistically*** assess the patient.

eResource 7-4: The instructor reviews the process of a *Head To Toe Nursing Assessment:* www.youtu.be/9Fxb8icOTOA

Exercise 7-6: *Matching*

Match Gordon's Functional Health Pattern in column A with the example in column B.

Column A	Column B
A. Health perception and health management	_______ Assess if patient is in a relationship
B. Nutrition and metabolism	_______ Assess what patient does for relaxation
C. Elimination	_______ Assess occupation
D. Activity and exercise	_______ Assess daily routine
E. Cognition and perception	_______ Assess smoking and alcohol use
F. Sleep and rest	_______ Assess if sedentary lifestyle exists
G. Self-perception and self-concept	_______ Assess frequency of urination
H. Roles and relationships	_______ Assess if patient would like spiritual referral
I. Sexuality and reproduction	_______ Assess how many glasses of water/day
J. Coping and stress tolerance	_______ Assess if patient has social contacts
K. Values and belief	_______ Assess how patient describes herself

Assessment is a complex process that yields a lot of data. Data are often organized into ***objective*** and ***subjective*** data.

Exercise 7-7: *Multiple Choice Question*

The nurse is eliciting objective data when asking the patient to:

A. State her name, the time, and where she is
B. State if her pain is a 6 or a scale of 0 to 10
C. State when the pain started
D. State if she could be pregnant

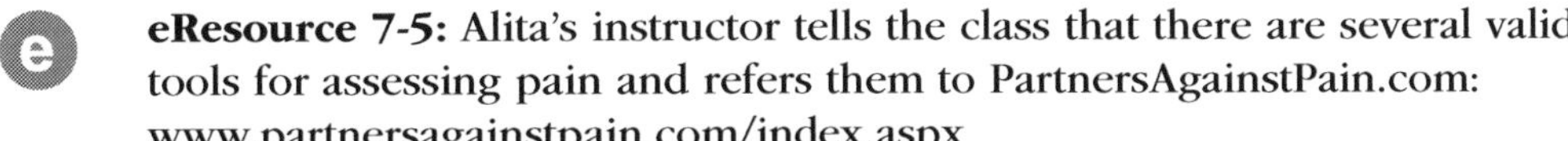

eResource 7-5: Alita's instructor tells the class that there are several valid tools for assessing pain and refers them to PartnersAgainstPain.com: www.partnersagainstpain.com/index.aspx

Alita understands that objective data are based on standards or norms.

The Answers section can be found on page 83.

Exercise 7-8: *Fill-in*

The standard norm for an adult blood pressure would be ________________.

Exercise 7-9: *Select All That Apply*

A nurse may gather assessment data from which of the following sources:

- ❑ Nursing experience
- ❑ Other health care team members
- ❑ Patient's roommate
- ❑ Family
- ❑ Medical records
- ❑ Patient

Alita role-plays in the lab with her peers. She is the nurse doing the assessment on the patient who presents in the ED with acute abdominal pain. She interviews the patient in order to find out more about the patient's current condition.

Exercise 7-10: *Multiple Choice Question*

The three phases of a nurse–patient interview are:

A. Introduction, working, termination
B. Introduction, ongoing, termination
C. Orientation, working, ongoing
D. Orientation, working, termination

In the first phase, during the role-playing, Alita focuses on introducing herself and assuring the patient that she will keep everything confidential.

Exercise 7-11: *Fill-in*

The law that provides for patient confidentiality is called: ________________.

The initial interview phase is important because it is at this phase that the nurse gains the patient's trust and confidence. Alita is performing well during her role-playing, and by closing the door, facing the patient, and listening attentively, she is establishing a positive nurse–patient relationship. Alita also uses conducive, nonverbal clues, such as:

- ❑ Maintaining eye contact
- ❑ Nodding her head affirmatively as she listens
- ❑ Smiling
- ❑ Leaning forward to show interest
- ❑ Using touch appropriately

During the second phase of the interview, Alita moves into collecting data about the patient's health status. Some of the techniques Alita demonstrates to her peers are open-ended sentences to elicit more data about a subject.

The Answers section can be found on page 83.

Exercise 7-12: *Multiple Choice Question*

Which is an open-ended question?

A. Does it hurt when you urinate?
B. How often have you taken pain medication?
C. Do you think you may have eaten something bad?
D. Tell me about your pain.

At some points during the interview, Alita needed to use close-ended questions. This was done to get more specific information about an issue being discussed. Most patient health histories are done electronically, so the computer prompts the nurse about what to ask the patient. Many include a ROS (review of systems), which asks specifically about each body system in order to get a comprehensive "look" at the patient. The ROS includes:

- Skin, hair, and nails
- Musculoskeletal system
- Head and neck
- Endocrine
- Reproductive
- Chest and lungs
- Heat and circulation
- Gastrointestinal
- Nutrition
- Genitourinary
- Neurologic
- Psychiatric

Exercise 7-13: *Multiple Choice Question*

After the review of systems is documented, the nurse's next assessment step is to:

A. Perform a physical examination
B. Look at the laboratory data
C. Medicate
D. Make a nursing diagnosis

Exams are usually started with vital signs as well as height and weight. Then they proceed from head to toe. Currently Alita is in her physical assessment class where she learns to perform a physical assessment from head toe. She now understands why these classes are taken together. Next Alita checks the computer for any laboratory data or diagnostic tests that will help her understand the patient's problem. After her patient–nurse role-playing interaction, Alita describes it as obtaining "a mountain of information" and now asks—how do I organize this in order to deliver the most important nursing care first? Her instructor explains that the next step in the nursing process is formulating a nursing diagnosis.

The Answers section can be found on page 83.

eResource 7-6: To review the process of taking a patient history, Alita's instructor shows the class the following video, *Taking a Patient's History (Nurse/Patient):* www.youtu.be/NW-ZRo6GJnA

Reference

Gordon, M. (1994). *Nursing diagnosis: Process and application* (3rd ed.). St. Louis, MO: Mosby.

The Answers section can be found on page 83.

Answers

Exercise 7-1: *Ordering*

Place the steps of the nursing process in order from 1 to 5.

__2__ Diagnose

__4__ Implement

__1__ Assess

__5__ Evaluate

__3__ Plan

Exercise 7-2: *Multiple Choice Question*

The main goal of the nursing process is to:

A. Diagnose conditions that nurses are licensed to treat—NO, this is just one part of the nursing process

B. Formulate a care plan for the patient—NO, this is just one part of the nursing process

C. Determine if nursing can affect the patient's health—NO, we know that nurses can affect individual's health

D. **Organize and deliver nursing care—YES, this is why it is done**

Exercise 7-3: *Select All That Apply*

By using the nursing process, the nurse will be able to:

☒ **Make sound clinical decisions—YES**

☒ **Use critical thinking—YES**

☒ **Develop individualized care—YES**

☐ Use her intuition to make decisions—NO, decisions should be made of systematic collection of valid data

☒ **Ask the patient to participate—YES**

☐ Modify care on common practice—NO, care is provided on the basis of evidence

Exercise 7-4: *True/False*

Asking the patient is a method of collecting secondary data.

☐ True

☒ **False—NO, it is primary**

Exercise 7-5: *Multiple Choice Question*

A 25-year-old women presents in the ED (emergency department) with acute abdominal pain in her right lower quadrant. This is the woman's first time in a hospital; the nurse should first assess her:

A. Abdomen—NO, this is important but not the first assessment
B. Respiratory status—NO, this is important but not the first assessment
C. Circulation—NO, this is important but not the first assessment
D. **Pain—YES, this is why the patient presents to the nurse**

Exercise 7-6: *Matching*

Match Gordon's Functional Health Pattern in column A with the example in column B.

Column A		Column B
A. Health perception and health management	**I**	Assess if patient is in a relationship
B. Nutrition and metabolism	**J**	Assess what patient does for relaxation
C. Elimination	**E**	Assess occupation
D. Activity and exercise	**F**	Assess daily routine
E. Cognition and perception	**A**	Assess smoking and alcohol use
F. Sleep and rest	**D**	Assess if sedentary lifestyle exists
G. Self-perception and self-concept	**C**	Assess frequency of urination
H. Roles and relationships	**K**	Assess if patient would like spiritual referral
I. Sexuality and reproduction	**B**	Assess how many glasses of water/ day
J. Coping and stress tolerance	**H**	Assess if patient has social contacts
K. Values and belief	**G**	Assess how patient describes herself

Exercise 7-7: *Multiple Choice Question*

The nurse is eliciting objective data when asking the patient to:

A. **State her name, the time, and where she is—YES, this is a neurological assessment**
B. State if her pain is a 6 or a scale of 0 to 10—NO, this is subjective to how the patient feels
C. State when the pain started—NO, this is subjective to the patient and not witnessed by the nurse
D. State if she could be pregnant—NO, this is subjective until supported by a diagnostic test

Exercise 7-8: *Fill-in*

The standard norm for an adult blood pressure would be 120/80.

Exercise 7-9: *Select All That Apply*

A nurse may gather assessment data from which of the following sources:

- ☒ **Nursing experience—YES**
- ☒ **Other health care team members—YES**
- ☐ Patient's roommate—NO, this violates HIPAA (Health Insurance Portability and Accountability Act)
- ☒ **Family—YES**
- ☒ **Medical records—YES**
- ☒ **Patient—YES**

Exercise 7-10: *Multiple Choice Questions*

The three phases of a nurse–patient interview are:

A. Introduction, working, termination—NO

B. Introduction, ongoing, termination—NO

C. Orientation, working, ongoing—NO

D. **Orientation, working, termination—YES, these are the three phases of a nurse–patient interview**

Exercise 7-11: *Fill-in*

The law that provides for patient confidentiality is called: HIPAA (Health Insurance Portability and Accountability Act).

Exercise 7-12: *Multiple Choice Question*

Which is an open-ended question?

A. Does it hurt when you urinate?—NO, the patient can answer yes or no

B. How often have you taken pain medication?—NO, this is asking for an amount and time specifically

C. Do you think you may have eaten something bad?—NO, the patient can answer yes or no

D. **Tell me about your pain—YES, this elicits a description**

Exercise 7-13: *Multiple Choice Question*

After the review of systems is documented, the nurse's next assessment step is to:

A. **Perform a physical examination—YES, this is the next logical step**

B. Look at the laboratory data—NO, finish with the patient first

C. Medicate—NO, finish collecting data

D. Make a nursing diagnosis—NO, you do not have all the information yet

8

The Nursing Process: Nursing Diagnosis

Unfolding Case Study 7 Alita and Connor

Alita and Connor return to class the following week and are taught about nursing diagnosis. They are instructed that there is a distinct difference between nursing diagnosis and medical diagnosis.

Exercise 8-1: ***Matching***

Match the type of diagnosis in column A to the definition in column B.

Column A		Column B
A. Nursing diagnosis	_______	Identification of a disease condition on the basis of assessment information
B. Medical diagnosis	_______	Clinical judgment about responses to actual or potential health problems

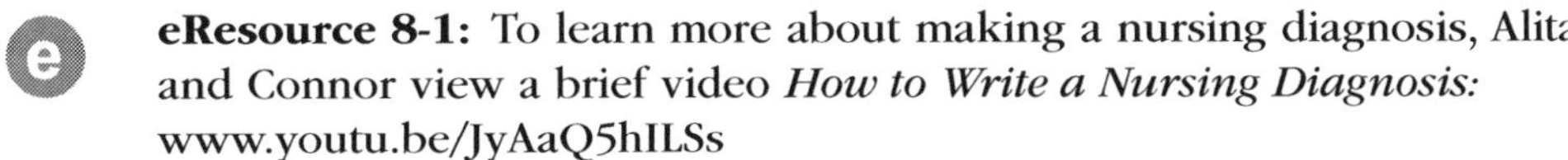

eResource 8-1: To learn more about making a nursing diagnosis, Alita and Connor view a brief video *How to Write a Nursing Diagnosis:* www.youtu.be/JyAaQ5hILSs

The fundamentals class is taught that nursing diagnosis is developed by ***NANDA-I*** (North American Nursing Diagnosis Association-International) in order to standardize the language or ***taxonomy*** of nursing. The Center for Nursing Classification and Clinical Effectiveness at the University of Iowa College of Nursing is another organization that works to standardize the language of ***nursing interventions classification (NIC)*** and ***nursing outcomes classification (NOC).***

eResource 8-2: Alita reviews additional materials to build her understanding of standardized language:

- Rutherford's (2008) article explaining the benefits of standardized language for nursing: www.nursingworld.org/MainMenuCategories/ThePracticeofProfessionalNursing/Health-IT/StandardizedNursingLanguage.html

The Answers section can be found on page 95.

- NANDA-I: *The Structure of Nanda Diagnosis,* describing the four categories of nursing diagnosis: www.nursing-diagnosis-nanda.blogspot.com/2011/05/structure-of-nanda-diagnosis.html
- NIC list of interventions: http://www.nursing.uiowa.edu/sites/default/files/documents/cncce/LabelDefinitionsNIC5.pdf
- NOC overview: http://www.nursing.uiowa.edu/cncce/nursing-outcomes-classification-overview

Alita raises her hand in class and asks the instructor, "I understand NANDA-I, NIC, and NOC (NNN), but how does it relate to the assessment pieces we learned last week?"

The instructor answers Alita, "That is a great question. The bridge from the assessment data you collect to the nursing diagnosis that you make is built on ***critical thinking***!" Critical thinking is a way of thinking about things meaningfully. In order to do this, a nurse must find relationships among concepts or think about how things go together.

Exercise 8-2: *Matching*

Match the attribute or characteristic of critical thinking in column A to the description in column B.

Column A		Column B
A. Interpretation	_______	Looking for patterns in your assessment data and classifying trends
B. Analysis	_______	Closely examining the assessment data and comparing them against criteria or standards
C. Evaluation	_______	Assessing the results of care critically by looking at outcomes
D. Explanation	_______	Supporting and justifying your findings, telling why
E. Inference	_______	Speculating on the meaning of the assessment data
F. Self-regulation	_______	Self-correcting or preventing yourself from jumping to conclusions without looking at all the possibilities

The class begins to discuss other ways of thinking that all lead to understanding ***clinical decision making*** for nurses. ***Reflection*** is another term used to describe thinking and involves thinking about what happened, how you handled it or behaved, and if you would change your actions or reactions if that situation arose again.

Exercise 8-3: *Multiple Choice Question*

The following statement by a nurse demonstrates reflection:

A. "I do not know why that happened; it is not supposed to be a side effect of the medication"
B. "I just use my sixth sense, and it worked for that patient"
C. "I do not think we will know the outcome for a while"
D. "I think next time I may do the intervention a little differently"

The Answers section can be found on page 95.

Alita wants to become a reflective practitioner because it makes sense to her. With reflection, a nurse can grow in her role and learn how to critically think. ***Intuition*** is another type of knowledge Alita learns, but it is a knowledge that comes with nursing experience so that you can describe a situation without reflecting on it because you have experienced it so many times before.

Exercise 8-4: *Multiple Choice Question*

Patient's assessment data are organized and analyzed by the nurse, and then the next step is for the nurse to develop:

A. A nursing diagnosis
B. Critical thinking
C. Intuition
D. Reflection

To arrive at an appropriate nursing diagnosis, Alita is told that assessment data must be interpreted into categories or patterns.

Exercise 8-5: *Exhibit Question*

Below are assessment data from an adult patient (25-year-old female) assessment:

- Major complaint: chronic fatigue (tiredness)
- Health history: no major surgeries, no pregnancies, no chronic or acute illnesses
  - Sleeping: 7 hours a night
  - Nutrition: eats three vegetarian meals a day
- Social history: last month broke up with long-term partner
- Physical examination: skin pale, BMI (body mass index), WNL (within normal limits)
  - VS (vital signs) 98.6 – 76–20, 120/78
- Diagnostic exams: CBC (complete blood count)
  - RBCs (red blood cells) 4.8×10^{12} cells per liter
  - WBCs (white blood cells) $.9 \times 10^{9}$ cells per liter
  - Hct (hematocrit) 35%

Is the patient's VS WNL? __________

Exercise 8-6: *Multiple Choice Question*

According to the data above, what pattern can the nurse detect?

A. The patient may be grieving a loss
B. The patient has a lack of iron (Fe)
C. The patient needs a lifestyle change
D. The patient is a suicide risk

eResource 8-3: Alita turns to her mobile device and consults several resources:

- Pocket Guide to Diagnostic Tests in Mobile MerckMedicus. [Pathway: Pocket Guide to Diagnostic Tests → Laboratory Tests → enter

The Answers section can be found on page 95.

"CBC" into the search field → select "RBC count," "WBC count," and "Hematocrit" to check for normal values.]

- McGraw-Hill's *Diagnosaurus* (www.books.mcgraw-hill.com/medical/diagnosaurus). [Pathway → Diagnosaurus → select "Symptoms" → enter "fatigue" into the search field → review list of potential diagnosis.]

Now that Alita understands how to detect a pattern, she is ready to make a nursing diagnosis.

Exercise 8-7: *Multiple Choice Question*

Which would be an appropriate diagnosis for the patient information described in Exercise 8-5?

A. Risk for spiritual distress
B. Post-trauma syndrome
C. Sleep deprivation
D. Imbalanced nutrition: less than body requirements

Alita understands the example and the steps to arrive at a diagnosis:

- First, she reviewed the assessment database (patient history, medical records, physical examination, and diagnostic tests)
- Then, she looked for trends in the data (low Hct, fatigue, dietary restrictions of meat)
- Next, she clusters these pieces of information together and they become defining characteristics and validate her choice of nursing diagnosis

eResource 8-4: To review the process leading to a nursing diagnosis, Alita watches a series of videos regarding *Constructing a Care Plan*:

- Introduction: www.youtu.be/ClY21HJbOTw
- Data clustering: www.youtu.be/p1fS4QaOnQE

Alita is taught that there are three types of nursing diagnosis:

- ❑ Actual
- ❑ Risk
- ❑ Wellness

Exercise 8-8: *Matching*

Match the type of nursing diagnosis in column A to the description in column B.

Column A		Column B
A. Risk	______	Describes a human response to a health condition
B. Wellness	______	Describes a response to health conditions that may develop in a vulnerable population
C. Actual	______	Describes a human response that is ready for enhancement

The Answers section can be found on page 95.

In order to formulate a diagnosis, Alita is taught the P-E-S (Problem-Etiology-Signs and Symptoms) format. The problem is actually the diagnostic label that is defined by NANDA-I. Alita has a list of nursing diagnosis on her iPad that she can access readily. Alita and Connor make up short patient scenarios to practice developing five nursing diagnostic statements.

eResource 8-5: Before proceeding, they watch the third video of videos regarding *Constructing a Care Plan: Formatting a Nursing Diagnosis*: www.youtu.be/lCA1C1Z1F40

Exercise 8-9: ***Fill-in***

Finish the nursing diagnosis:

A 27-year-old woman delivered her first baby 6 hours ago and is unable to void (urinate). Her perineum is swollen from the delivery. Fill in the *actual* diagnosis part that is missing.

P—Urinary retention

E—Related to perineal trauma

S—As evidenced by ______________________

Exercise 8-10: ***Fill-in***

An 80-year-old man with COPD (chronic obstructive pulmonary disease) is being seen for SOB (shortness of breath) and inability to walk short distances related to SOB. Fill in the *actual* diagnosis part that is missing.

P—Impaired gas exchange

E—Related to COPD (the etiology can be a medical diagnosis)

S—As evidenced by ______________________

Exercise 8-11: ***Fill-in***

A nursing student makes an appointment with the student services counselor in order to find a resource for her test anxiety. Fill in the *wellness* diagnosis part that is missing.

P—Readiness for enhanced coping

E—Related to ____________________

S—As evidenced by making an appointment with a counselor

Exercise 8-12: ***Fill-in***

A visiting nurse observes a poorly secured window in a second floor apartment in which there is a 3-year-old. Fill in the *risk* diagnosis part that is missing.

P—Risk for injury

E—Related to ____________________

S—There is no "S" in risk diagnosis because it has not happened yet, so there are no manifestations

The Answers section can be found on page 95.

Exercise 8-13: *Fill-in*

An adolescent boy is being bullied in school and has become depressed and withdrawn. Fill in the *risk* diagnosis part that is missing.

P—Risk for suicide

E—Related to ____________________

S—There is no "S" in risk diagnosis because it has not happened yet, so there are no manifestations

Alita learns that nursing diagnoses are a part of the ***nursing care plan,*** and that there are many different formats that can be used to record a care plan. One of the common formats is a ***care map,*** sometimes called a ***concept map.*** A care map is a visual display of the nursing care needed for a patient.

eResource 8-6: To make sure she understands how to use a concept map in care planning, Alita conducts an Internet search and locates:

- *Concept Map Care*, an overview of the process: www.snjourney.com/ClinicalInfo/CarePlans/conceptmapguide.pdf
- Additional resources from Student Nurse Journey: [Pathway: www.snjourney.com → select "Care Plans" from the Resource menu].

Here is an example:

Let us use that adult patient in Exercise 8-10 with COPD and make a care map (Figure 8.1). An 80-year-old man with COPD is being seen for SOB and inability to walk short distances related to SOB.

Figure 8.1

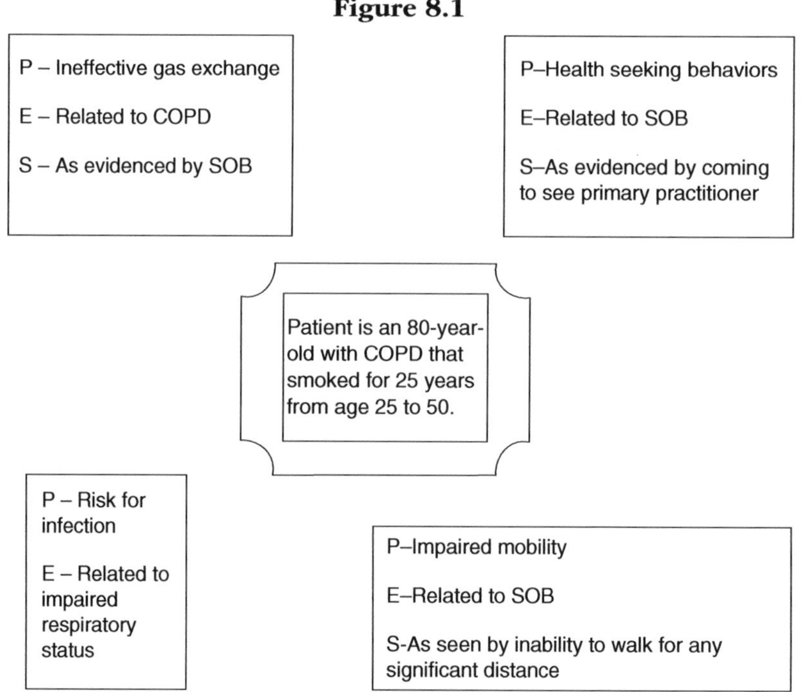

The Answers section can be found on page 95.

In the figure above, draw lines that connect the patient to the diagnosis and some of the diagnoses to each other. Alita explains that holistically one thing affects another in the lives of humans. COPD manifestations prompt the patient to initiate health-seeking behaviors because the impaired mobility can place people at risk for respiratory infections. Others like to prioritize nursing diagnoses. The first priority would be the diagnosis that is most threatening to life or safety.

Exercise 8-14: *Fill-in*

On the following care map (Figure 8.2) in the small boxes in the upper right of the diagnostic box, place the numbers 1 to 4 to designate the first to fourth priority in the care for the patient with COPD.

Figure 8.2

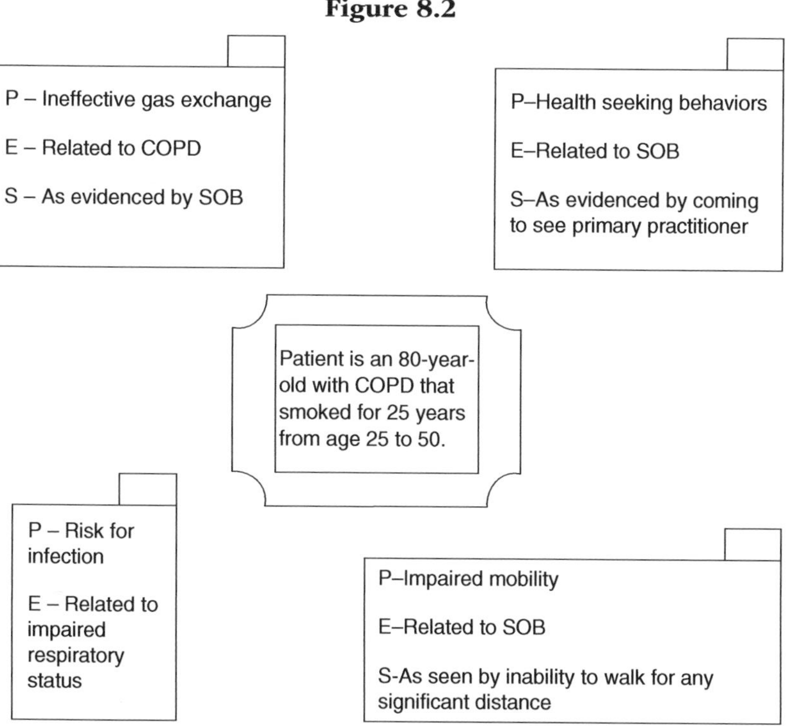

eResource 8-7: Alita wants to get started using concept mapping to link patient assessment data together. She downloads a free concept mapping tool Knowledge Notebook (www.knowledgenotebook.com). To get started, she watches a brief tutorial on how to use (www.youtu.be/FUkteJDFpHI).

Alita also learns that there may be errors in diagnostic statements if any of the major components are missed.

The Answers section can be found on page 95.

Exercise 8-15: *Multiple Choice Question*

The primary reason for diagnostic statements that do not depict the problems of the patient is:

A. Poor assessment
B. Using the wrong type of diagnosis
C. Clustering too many patterns
D. Overanalyzing the data collected

Alita and Connor feel as if they have a good understanding of steps 1 and 2 of the nursing process and are now anxious to learn how to plan their patients' care!

Reference

Rutherford, M. (2008). Standardized nursing language: What does it mean for nursing practice? *OJIN: The Online Journal of Issues in Nursing, 13*(1).

The Answers section can be found on page 95.

Answers

Exercise 8-1: *Matching*

Match the type of diagnosis in column A to the definition in column B.

Column A		Column B
A. Nursing diagnosis	B	Identification of a disease condition on the basis of assessment information
B. Medical diagnosis	A	Clinical judgment about responses to actual or potential health problems

Exercise 8-2: *Matching*

Match the attribute or characteristic of critical thinking in column A to the description in column B.

Column A		Column B
A. Interpretation	A	Looking for patterns in your assessment data and classifying trends
B. Analysis	B	Closely examining the assessment data and comparing them against criteria or standards
C. Evaluation	C	Assessing the results of care critically by looking at outcomes
D. Explanation	D	Supporting and justifying your findings, telling why
E. Inference	E	Speculating on the meaning of the assessment data
F. Self-regulation	F	Self-correcting or preventing yourself from jumping to conclusions without looking at all the possibilities

Exercise 8-3: *Multiple Choice Question*

The following statement by a nurse demonstrates reflection:

A. "I do not know why that happened; it is not supposed to be a side effect of the medication."—NO, the nurse is not showing the spirit of inquiry to find out why it happened

B. "I just use my sixth sense, and it worked for that patient."—NO, this is just guessing

C. "I do not think we will know the outcome for a while."—NO, this is passing off any type of evaluation
D. **"I think next time I may do the intervention a little different."—YES, this is an example of reflective thinking. You are thinking about what you did, how it turned out, and how you can do it better next time**

Exercise 8-4: *Multiple Choice Question*

Patient's assessment data are organized and analyzed by the nurse, and then the next step is for the nurse to develop:

A. **A nursing diagnosis—YES, this is step 2**
B. Critical thinking—NO, this is needed but not defined as an actual step
C. Intuition—NO, this is sometimes used by expert nurses
D. Reflection—NO, this is needed but not an actual step

Exercise 8-5: *Exhibit Question*

Below are assessment data from an adult patient (25-year-old female) assessment:

- Major complaint: chronic fatigue (tiredness)
- Health history: no major surgeries, no pregnancies, no chronic or acute illnesses
  - Sleeping: 7 hours a night
  - Nutrition: eats three vegetarian meals a day
- Social history: last month broke up with long-term partner
- Physical examination: skin pale, BMI (body mass index), WNL (within normal limits)
  - VS (vital signs) 98.6 – 76–20, 120/78
- Diagnostic exams: CBC (complete blood count)
  - RBCs (red blood cells) 4.8×10^{12} cells per liter
  - WBCs (white blood cells) 7.9×10^{9} cells per liter
  - Hct (hematocrit) 35%

Is the patient's VS WNL? **YES**

Exercise 8-6: *Multiple Choice Question*

According to the data above, what pattern can the nurse detect?

A. The patient may be grieving a loss—NO, there is one incident that lends itself to grieving
B. **The patient has a lack of iron (Fe)—YES, the patient has no meat in her diet, is tired, and has a low Hct**
C. The patient needs a lifestyle change—NO, this is not indicated in the information provided
D. The patient is a suicide risk—NO, this is also not indicated in the information provided

Exercise 8-7: *Multiple Choice Question*

Which would be an appropriate diagnosis for the patient information described in Exercise 8-7?

A. Risk for spiritual distress—NO, this may be but is not indicated
B. Post-trauma syndrome—NO, there is no indication of this

C. Sleep deprivation—NO, this is not stated

D. **Imbalanced nutrition: less than body requirements—YES, the low Hct and dietary restrictions indicate this**

Exercise 8-8: *Matching*

Match the label of the diagnosis in column A to the description in column B.

A. Risk	**C**	Describes a human response to a health condition
B. Wellness	**A**	Describes a response to health conditions that may develop in a vulnerable population
C. Actual	**B**	Describes a human response that is ready for enhancement

Exercise 8-9: *Fill-in*

Finish the nursing diagnosis:

A 27-year-old woman delivered her first baby 6 hours ago and is unable to void (urinate). Her perineum is swollen from the delivery. Fill in the *actual* diagnosis part that is missing.

P—Urinary retention

E—Related to perineal trauma

S—As evidenced by **inability to void**

Exercise 8-10: *Fill-in*

An 80-year-old man with COPD (chronic obstructive pulmonary disease) is being seen for SOB (shortness of breath) and inability to walk short distances related to SOB. Fill in the *actual* diagnosis part that is missing.

P—Impaired gas exchange

E—Related to COPD (the etiology can be a medical diagnosis)

S—As evidenced by **SOB**

Exercise 8-11: *Fill-in*

A nursing student makes an appointment with the student services counselor in order to find a resource for her test anxiety. Fill in the *wellness* diagnosis part that is missing.

P—Readiness for enhanced coping

E—Related to **awareness of test anxiety**

S—As evidenced by making an appointment with a counselor

Exercise 8-12: *Fill-in*

A visiting nurse observes a poorly secured window in a second floor apartment in which there is a 3-year-old. Fill in the *risk* diagnosis part that is missing.

P—Risk for injury

E—Related to **unsecured second floor windows**

S—There is no "S" in risk diagnosis because it has not happened yet, so there are no manifestations

Exercise 8-13: *Fill-in*

An adolescent boy is being bullied in school and has become depressed and withdrawn. Fill in the *risk* diagnosis part that is missing.

P—Risk for suicide

E—Related to **depression**

S—There is no "S" in risk diagnosis because it has not happened yet, so there are no manifestations

Exercise 8-14: *Fill-in*

On the following care map in the small boxes in the upper right of the diagnostic box, place the numbers 1 to 4 to designate the first to fourth priority in the care for the patient with COPD (Figure 8.3).

Figure 8.3

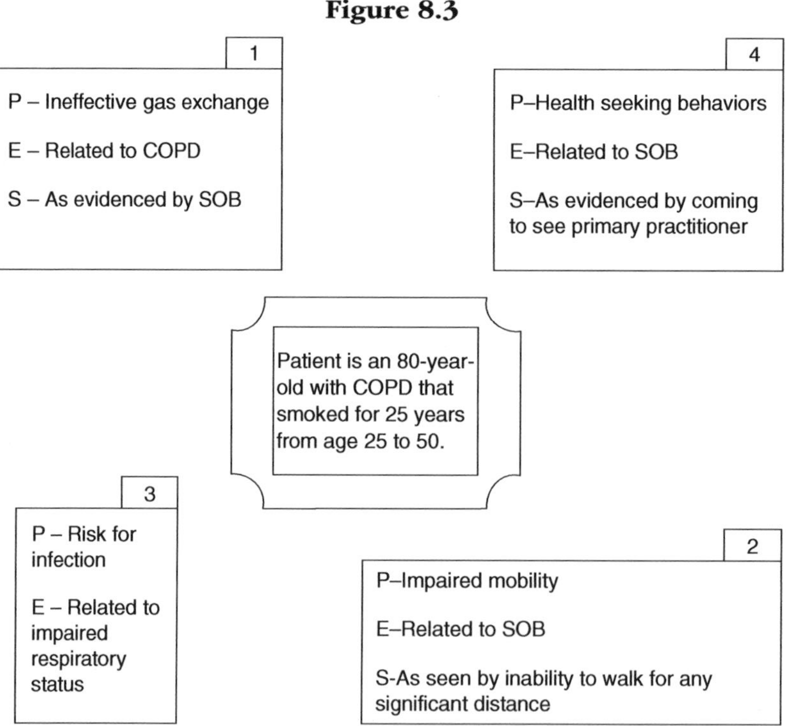

The first priority for this patient would be the gas exchange (nurses have been taught care priorities for years as A-B-C (Airway-Breathing-Circulation). Now nurses are being challenged to think of S-A-B-C (Safety first!). The second priority is the impaired mobility because this will lead to infection and infection is the third priority. Lastly, although important and something nurses want to promote, is health seeking.

Exercise 8-15: *Multiple Choice Question*

The primary reason for diagnostic statements that do not depict the problems of the patient is:

A. **Poor assessment—YES, this is usually the primary reason**
B. Using the wrong type of diagnosis—NO, this happens but is not the usual cause
C. Clustering too many patterns—NO, this happens but is not the usual cause
D. Overanalyzing the data collected—NO, this happens but is not the usual cause

9

Planning, Intervention, and Evaluation of Nursing Care

Unfolding Case Study 8 Alita and Connor

Connor and Alita are studying the next chapter for developing patient care plans. Alita realizes that she has already done a part of this by prioritizing nursing diagnoses after she developed them. Prioritizing is how to start your plan of care.

Exercise 9-1: ***Multiple Choice Question***

In order to prioritize nursing care, the nurse should start with the diagnosis that:

A. Affects circulation
B. Affects airway
C. Affects safety
D. Affects breathing

Exercise 9-2: ***Multiple Choice Question***

The nurse realizes those nursing diagnoses that are not a priority may:

A. Be incorrect for that patient
B. Affect lifestyle
C. Reduce focus on priorities
D. Emerge as urgent

eResource 9-1: Connor and Alita feel that the best way to understand planning nursing care is to practice. To get started on this, they view a brief video that provides an overview of nursing care plans (NCPs): *Nursing Student Guide for Nursing Care Plans*: www.youtu.be/XOpT_SMLuGw

Exercise 9-3: ***Ordering***

Order the following nursing diagnoses from highest priority 1 to least priority 5 for an infant who has a congenital heart disease:

_______ Alternation in nutrition
_______ Ineffective breastfeeding
_______ Decreased cardiac output

The Answers section can be found on page 107.

_______ Ineffective breathing pattern
_______ Impaired family coping

Exercise 9-4: *Ordering*

Order the following nursing diagnoses from highest priority 1 to least priority 5 for an adult with a fractured leg:

_______ Activity intolerance
_______ Risk for infection
_______ Acute pain
_______ Self-care deficit: bathing
_______ Impaired family coping

Now Connor and Alita understand that you have to deal with ***first things first!*** The next step is to develop ***goals and outcomes*** for your care or what you believe your care will help the patient, family, or community achieve.

eResource 9-2: To better understand the process of planning nursing care and how to develop goals, they view an additional video from the series Constructing a Care Plan: *Developing Patient Goals*: www.youtu .be/yKt2zhZL9qM

Goals are often divided into short term and long term, and in order for the patient to reach the goal, there should be measurable outcomes along the way.

Here is an example for the patient with the leg fracture (Figure 9.1):

Figure 9.1 Goals for a Patient With a Leg Fracture

Assessement	• Fractured leg falling from roof • Leg is in a cast
Diagnoses	• Acute pain related to break as evidenced by rating pain as an 8 on a scale of 0 to 10
Long term goal	• Report that pain management regimen achieves comfort-function goal without adverse effects.
Short term goal	• Use a self-report pain tool to identify current pain level and establish a comfort-function goal
Outcomes	• Describe non-pharmacological methods that will help • Notify member of the health care team promptly for pain level greater that the comfort-function goal

The Answers section can be found on page 107.

Connor and Alita realize that sometimes nurses speak about goals and outcomes in the same statement. Goals and outcomes can be written by the ***NOC (Nursing Outcomes Classification)*** terminology.

Exercise 9-5: *Select All That Apply*

Goals and outcomes of patient care should be:

- ❑ Patient centered
- ❑ Evidence based
- ❑ Measurable
- ❑ Realistic
- ❑ Nursing based

Connor and Alita now move onto understanding how to meet those goals and outcomes.

Exercise 9-6: *Multiple Choice Question*

In order to meet the goals and outcomes developed, the nurse must choose:

A. New goals
B. Supporting diagnosis
C. Evaluation mechanisms
D. Interventions

There are three types of interventions that have to be distinguished: nurse initiated, physician initiated, and collaborative. The nurse-initiated responses are the interventions that students learn about throughout the nursing program because they are independent responses a nurse can make.

The ***NIC (Nursing Interventions Classification)*** system provides nursing interventions that nurses can use in their plan of care. Not all schools use the exact NIC terminology, but all nursing schools do teach interventions that are nurse initiated. Alita reads Connor NIC examples for the nursing diagnosis of acute pain:

1. Assess pain level in the patient using a valid and reliable self-report pain tool
2. Assess the patient for pain presence routinely at frequent intervals
3. Prevent pain during procedures if possible (cast adjustments)
4. Determine the patient's current medication use (Ackley & Ladwig, 2011)

Connor and Alita enter the interventions on their care plan (which, of course, they now know can be a care map).

Exercise 9-7: *Multiple Choice Question*

The most appropriate intervention for a family that is grieving would be to:

A. Request a psychiatric consult
B. Administer a pain medication
C. Teach coughing and deep breathing
D. Develop a trusting relationship

Connor and Alita have it—the interventions need to move the patient toward the goals and outcomes set and need to be logical. Now they need to just learn how to do the interventions!

The Answers section can be found on page 107.

eResource 9-3: To reinforce their understanding, Alita and Connor view two short videos on the topic:

- An additional video from the series Constructing a Care Plan: *Formulating Nursing Interventions*: www.youtu.be/il_JWCzkFfY
- From Kent State University depicting an overview of *Nursing Interventions:* www.youtu.be/xRFIDg9BPnQ

Interventions can be done by protocol, standing or newly provided physician orders, or independent nursing care. A ***protocol*** contains nursing interventions that are done in a specific circumstance. The instructor gives Connor and Alita an example: An infant is delivered with no complications, and the protocol is to give 1 mg (0.5 ml) of vitamin K IM (intramuscularly) after the initial bath. The protocol is written down, and although a nurse cannot prescribe medications, there is an order sheet prestamped with the vitamin K order, which is called a **standing order**. The infant is now in the nursery and is having respiratory distress. You call the pediatrician and receive an order to place the baby under oxygen. This order is a newly issued order, not a standing order.

eResource 9-4: The instructor tells Connor and Alita that protocols are developed using best practice evidence and directs them to explore the National Guideline Clearinghouse (NGC; www.guideline.gov) to learn more about available protocols for nursing care. [Pathway: NGC → enter "nursing protocols" into the search field → scroll down to view list of protocols.]

Connor and Alita are told that before they provide direct care, they must organize their resources.

Exercise 9-8: *Select All That Apply*

Choose the resources below that are needed by nurses to deliver patient care:

- ❑ Equipment
- ❑ Skilled personal
- ❑ Condition of the patient
- ❑ Identifying areas of assistance
- ❑ Physician assistance in the hospital

When providing interventions, many of them are ***direct care***. Direct care can be anything from ***ADLs (activities of daily living)*** to lifesaving measures such as starting ***CPR (cardiopulmonary resuscitation).***

Exercise 9-9: *Select All That Apply*

Select some of the direct care interventions done by nurses:

- ❑ Teaching
- ❑ Checking emergency cart
- ❑ Bathing
- ❑ Health promotion measures

The Answers section can be found on page 107.

❑ Delegation

❑ Counseling

Exercise 9-10: *Multiple Choice Question*

Outcomes are directly a result of the:

A. Assessment
B. Diagnosis
C. Planning
D. Implementation

Connor and Alita realize they will learn many skills that are considered direct care in fundamentals and are looking forward to it. There are also nursing interventions that are considered indirect care that nurses perform and include skills in communication and delegation. Once the interventions are done for a patient, the instructor tells the fundies students they need to evaluate their care. ***Evaluation*** is the final step of the nursing process.

Exercise 9-11: *True/False*

Evaluation is done by comparing the patient's condition with the diagnosis.

❑ True

❑ False

The process of evaluation takes judgment, and the nurse has to summarize and look at findings before he or she can say that the problem is solved or the problem needs to be reassessed and the care plan revised. Alita draws the process out for Connor (Figure 9.2).

Figure 9.2 Nursing Care Process Diagram Starting With Assessment

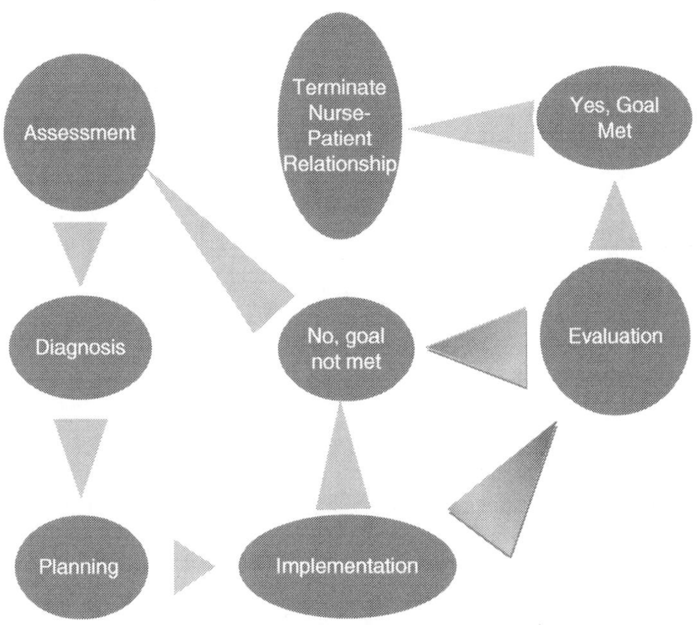

The Answers section can be found on page 107.

Both Alita and Connor feel ready for the next test about care planning. They understand the five steps and the pieces that go into each step. For the next fundamental unit, they will learn about how care is delivered or how the nurses organize themselves to make sure that each patient is cared for on a patient care hospital unit.

Reference

Ackley, B. J., & Ladwig, G. B. (2011). *Nursing diagnosis handbook: An evidence-based guide to planning care* (9 th ed.). St. Louis, MO: Mosby Elsevier.

The Answers section can be found on page 107.

Answers

Exercise 9-1: *Multiple Choice Question*

In order to prioritize nursing care, the nurse should start with the diagnosis that:

A. Affects circulation—NO, this is important but not a first priority if the patient is not safe

B. Affects airway—NO, this is important but not a first priority if the patient is not safe

C. **Affects safety—YES, if the patient is not safe, you will not be able to do anything else**

D. Affects breathing– NO, this is important but not a first priority if the patient is not safe

Exercise 9-2: *Multiple Choice Question*

The nurse realizes those nursing diagnoses that are not a priority may:

A. Be incorrect for that patient—NO, they are needed

B. **Affect lifestyle—YES, they may have to do with social or emotional issues**

C. Reduce focus on priorities—NO, nurses know how to prioritize

D. Emerge as urgent—NO, although this is possible, it is not likely in the current patient situation

Exercise 9-3: *Ordering*

Order the following nursing diagnoses from highest priority 1 to least priority 5 for an infant who has a congenital heart disease:

__3__ Alternation in nutrition—NO, this can be used interchangeably with diagnosis 2 in this case

__2__ Ineffective breastfeeding—NO, if the infant is not perfusing, he or she cannot expend energy to eat, so this is the next concern

__1__ **Decreased cardiac output—YES, this is the main concern or problem**

__5__ Ineffective breathing pattern—NO, because it is a cardiac issue and there is no mention of respiratory distress

__4__ Impaired family coping—NO, there is no assessment of this, but it is probably a diagnosis with a lesser priority

Exercise 9-4: *Ordering*

Order the following nursing diagnoses from highest priority 1 to least priority 5 for an adult with a fractured leg:

__3__ **Activity intolerance—NO, but activity intolerance and mobility will be a concern after the pain is under control**

__2__ Risk for infection—NO, but a definite concern when a procedure is done

__1__ **Acute pain—YES, until the pain is under control, the other diagnosis will be difficult to address**

__4__ Self-care deficit: Bathing—NO, not a high-priority diagnosis

__5__ Impaired family coping—NO, not a high-priority diagnosis

Exercise 9-5: *Select All That Apply*

Goals and outcomes of patient care should be:

☒ **Patient centered—YES**

☒ **Evidence based—YES**

☒ **Measurable—YES**

☒ **Realistic—YES**

❑ Nursing based—NO, they should be patient based

Exercise 9-6: *Multiple Choice Question*

In order to meet the goals and outcomes developed, the nurse must choose:

A. New goals—NO, the first goals need evaluation
B. Supporting diagnosis—No, the diagnosis is already completed
C. **Evaluation mechanisms—YES, the nurse must evaluate systematically if the goals were met**
D. Interventions—NO, these should have been completed

Exercise 9-7: *Multiple Choice Question*

The most appropriate intervention for a family that is grieving would be to:

A. Request a psychiatric consult—NO, although this may be needed, there is no indication for it yet
B. Administer a pain medication—NO, this may mask the grieving process
C. Teach coughing and deep breathing—NO, this is unrelated
D. **Develop a trusting relationship—YES, this is essential at such a vulnerable time**

Exercise 9-8: *Select All That Apply*

Choose the resources below that are needed by nurses to deliver patient care:

☒ **Equipment—YES, properly checked and functioning equipment is essential**

☒ **Skilled personnel—YES, assistive personnel are needed**

❑ Condition of the patient—NO, all patient conditions will need resources

☒ **Identifying areas of assistance—YES, the nurse should be able to identify the interventions that will require assistance**

☐ Physician assistance in the hospital—NO, some places do not have MDs in house at all times

Exercise 9-9: ***Select All That Apply***

Select some of the direct care interventions done by nurses:

☒ **Teaching—YES, the nurse directly teaches the patient and family**

☐ Checking emergency cart—NO, this is indirect

☒ **Bathing—YES, this is direct care**

☒ Health promotion measures**—YES, this is direct care, such as immunizing**

☐ Delegation—NO, this is indirect

☒ **Counseling—YES, this is direct care**

Exercise 9-10: ***Multiple Choice Question***

Outcomes are directly a result of the:

A. Assessment—NO, even though proper assessment ensures outcomes, they occur after the nursing care is provided
B. Diagnosis—NO, even though proper diagnosis ensures outcomes, they occur after the nursing care is provided
C. Planning—NO, even though proper planning ensures outcomes, they occur after the nursing care is provided
D. **Implementation—YES, outcomes are met after the interventions are completed**

Exercise 9-11: ***True/False***

Evaluation is done by comparing the patient's condition with the diagnosis.

☐ True

☒ **False—Evaluation is done by comparing the patient's condition to the goals**

10

Care Delivery Models

Unfolding Case Study 9 ■ Aubree, Alita, and Connor

Aubree is a classmate of Alita and Connor and asks them if she can join their study group. Aubree did not do as well as she would have liked on the nursing process test. The abstract things in nursing are more difficult for some than the actual learned skills. All three classmates meet to start studying for the next test, which is about how to deliver the care patients need.

Exercise 10-1: *Matching*

Match the following classic models used to deliver patient care in column A with their description in column B.

Column A		Column B
A. Functional nursing	______	RN is responsible for all aspects of care
B. Team nursing	______	Supports the development of a nurse–patient relationship by making the nurse accountable for care
C. Total patient care	______	Leads a group of RNs, LPNs, and UAP to deliver care
D. Primary nursing	______	Focuses on the tasks to be completed

e **eResource 10-1:** Connor, Aubree, and Alita seek out additional resources to help them understand the different models of care. Connor finds two resources for the group to use for studying:

- CurrentNursing.com's overview of *Models of Nursing Care Delivery:* www.currentnursing.com/nursing_theory/models_of_nursing_care_delivery.html

The Answers section can be found on page 115.

- University of Carolina at Chapel Hill's learning activity, *Nursing Care Delivery Systems: Models of Care*: **www.unc.edu/courses/2005fall/nurs/079/960/delivery_systems/activity2.html**

Exercise 10-2: *Multiple Choice Question*

A nurse in a case management role is best described as:

A. A liaison between inpatient and outpatient care
B. A nurse who assists the family members also
C. A nurse who provides total patient care
D. A communicator to other nurses about patient needs

Aubree also learns that most nursing units run as ***decentralized*** or the people who work there have a say in the management of the unit. This is called ***self-governance.***

Exercise 10-3: *Multiple Choice Question*

Which nursing care activity exemplifies self-governance in nursing?

A. The manager makes the schedule
B. The staff nurses punch a clock
C. The manager does the yearly evaluations
D. The staff nurses run the policy and procedure committee

In a decentralized system, the staff nurses have a lot of responsibility for the way the unit runs and functions. Along with this freedom comes accountability and responsibility.

Exercise 10-4: *Matching*

Match the concept in column A to the definition in column B.

Column A	Column B
A. Authority	______ The independence to make a decision about patient care
B. Accountability	______ The completion of the work a nurse is hired to perform
C. Responsibility	______ Having the right to manage patient care activities
D. Autonomy	______ The nurse is answerable for actions taken

eResource 10-2: To further her understanding, Aubree reviews the American Nurses Association (ANA)'s Code of Ethics for Nurses with interpretive statements: www.nursingworld.org/MainMenuCategories/EthicsStandards/CodeofEthicsforNurses/Code-of-Ethics.pdf

Aubree is taught that all nurses are leaders of patient care, that this is a skill she and the others will learn and includes:

- Making clinical decisions
- Setting priorities

The Answers section can be found on page 115.

- Managing time
- Using resources appropriately
- Organizing skills
- *Collaborating* or talking with other health care team members

One of the important ways that nurses accomplish their patient care is through delegation. Delegation is assigning the right task to the right person.

Exercise 10-5: *Select All That Apply*

Select the five rights of delegation from the list:

- ❑ Right person
- ❑ Right patient
- ❑ Right method
- ❑ Right circumstance
- ❑ Right task
- ❑ Right direction
- ❑ Right communication or direction

e **eResource 10-3:** To support her understanding of the five rights of delegation, Aubree refers to the National Council of State Boards of Nursing's publication: www.ncsbn.org/fiverights.pdf

Aubree raises her hand and asks the instructor just what the other members of the health care team can do. The instructor provides Aubree with an example.

Exercise 10-6: *Fill-in*

Write RN, LPN, or UAP in front of the tasks listed below (can be more than one):

_______ Bathe patient A with a possible neck injury
_______ Redress a surgical incision on patient B
_______ Teach patient C when to call the primary care provider for complications of GI surgery
_______ Administer medication in pill form to patient D for pain
_______ Assess patient C for bowel sounds
_______ Take patient A's vital signs
_______ Ambulate patient B in the hallway
_______ Reinforce with patient D when to call for pain medication
_______ Hang IV antibiotics on patient B

Aubree, Alita, and Connor are starting to understand how complex nursing care on the nursing care unit can be. Before they can wrap their heads around what leadership skills are needed for delegation, the instructor starts to talk about ***quality improvement (QI).*** QI is the process of continuously studying what we do as nurses to see if the process can be improved. Often there are standards to base the QI on and try to fix the process to meet the standard. QI is a team effort. Aubree asks for an example,

The Answers section can be found on page 115.

and the instructor provides one. The local standard for waiting in an ED (emergency department) for being seen by a primary care practitioner is 1 hour.

Exercise 10-7: *Select All That Apply*

The nurse is evaluating wait times in the ED, where wait times are longer than the benchmark. What issues should be investigated?

- ❑ The type of patients serviced
- ❑ Availability of staff at heavy volume times
- ❑ The mix of staff
- ❑ The personal preferences of staff
- ❑ The equipment and beds available
- ❑ The documentation system
- ❑ The throughput or the time it takes ED patients to be admitted

Once an improvement plan is put into place, it then needs to be tracked and evaluated to make sure it does resolve the issues.

eResource 10-4: To learn more about quality improvement in health care, Aubree consults several resources recommended by her instructor:

- Quality and Safety Education for Nurses (QSEN): www.qsen.org/ksas_prelicensure.php
- Agency for Research and Health Care Quality's *Improving Health Care Quality Fact Sheet:* www.ahrq.gov/news/qualfact.htm
- The National State Board of Nurses response to *The Future of Nursing: Leading Change, Advancing Health* report: www.ncsbn.org/NCSBN_BOD_Response_TheFutureofNursing_June2011.pdf

The Answers section can be found on page 115.

Answers

Exercise 10-1: *Matching*

Match the following classic models used to deliver patient care in column A with their description in column B.

Column A		Column B
A. Functional nursing	C	RN is responsible for all aspects of care
B. Team nursing	D	Supports the development of a nurse–patient relationship by making the nurse accountable for care
C. Total patient care	B	Leads a group of RNs, LPNs, and UAP to deliver care
D. Primary nursing	A	Focuses on the tasks to be completed

Exercise 10-2: *Multiple Choice Question*

A nurse in a case management role is best described as:

A. **A liaison between inpatient and outpatient care—YES, a case manager often makes sure that the patient has the resources at home available to continue the plan of care**

B. A nurse who assists the family members also—NO, they do assist the family members, but this does not describe the primary responsibility of their jobs

C. A nurse who provides total patient care—NO, this is a hospital-based concept and one that does not prepare the patient for home care

D. A communicator to other nurses about patient needs—NO, they do communicate with other professional members, but this does not describe the primary responsibility of their jobs

Exercise 10-3: *Multiple Choice Question*

Which nursing care activity exemplifies self-governance in nursing?

A. The manager makes the schedule—NO, this is authoritarian-type governance

B. The staff nurses punch a clock—NO, this is authoritarian-type governance

C. The manager does the yearly evaluations—NO, this is authoritarian-type governance

D. **The staff nurses run the policy and procedure committee—YES, the staff participates in the unit's management**

Exercise 10-4: *Matching*

Match the concept in column A to the definition in column B.

Column A	Column B
A. Authority	B. **D** The independence to make a decision about patient care
C. Accountability	D. **C** The completion of the work a nurse is hired to perform
E. Responsibility	F. **A** Having the right to manage patient care activities
G. Autonomy	H. **B** The nurse is answerable for actions taken

Exercise 10-5: *Select All That Apply*

Select the five rights of delegation from the list:

☒ **Right person**

❑ Right patient—NO, delegation has to do with other staff members

❑ Right method—NO, the right method of delegation is clear communication

☒ **Right circumstance**

☒ **Right task**

☒ **Right direction**

☒ **Right communication or direction**

Exercise 10-6: *Fill-in*

Write RN, LPN, or UAP in front of the tasks listed below (can be more than one):

RN, LPN, UAP Bathe patient A with a possible neck injury

RN, LPN Redress a surgical incision on patient B

RN Teach patient C when to call the primary care provider for complications of GI surgery

RN, LPN Administer medication in pill form to patient D for pain

RN Assess patient C for bowel sounds

RN, LPN, UAP Take patient A's vital signs

RN, LPN, UAP Ambulate patient B in the hallway

RN, LPN Reinforce with patient D when to call for pain medication

RN, LPN Hang IV antibiotics on patient B

Exercise 10-7: *Select All That Apply*

The nurse is evaluating wait times in the ED, where wait times are longer than the benchmark. What issues should be investigated?

☒ **The type of patients serviced**

☒ **Availability of staff at heavy volume times**

☒ **The mix of staff**

❑ The personal preferences of staff

☒ **The equipment and beds available**

☒ **The documentation system**

☒ **The throughput or the time it takes ED patients to be admitted**

11

Legal and Ethical Issues in Nursing

Unfolding Case Study 10 Aubree, Alita, and Connor

Aubree, Alita, and Connor read the chapters on ethical and legal issues in nursing before the next class. They discover that there are a lot of ethical definitions they need to know, and many of them are abstract concepts. They are told in class that ethics and bioethics (the study of ethical principles in health care) are derived from ethical philosophies:

- ***Deontology*** is the theory of deciding if something is right or wrong. Is it fair, just, and truthful? The consequence is not the issue
- ***Utilitarianism*** is ***consequentialism*** or deciding on the usefulness of the outcome
- ***Teleology*** is the greatest good for most of the people involved

eResource 11-1: To reinforce their understanding of ethical philosophies and the responsibility of nurses, Aubree, Alita, and Connor view several videos:

- *Ethical Issues In Nursing—Respect: Dignity, Autonomy, and Relationships:* www.youtu.be/-GxuvKRL7ks
- *Ethical Issues In Nursing—Commitment: Patients, Professionalism, and Boundaries*: www.youtu.be/XtuanLybaZs

Exercise 11-1: *Fill-in*

Fill in the following nursing situations with a D—deontology, U—utilitarianism, or T—teleology to denote how the nurse decided in the situation:

________ The nurse votes for national health care

________ The nurse tells parents of a dying child about organ donation

________ The nurse honors a patient's right not to take chemotherapy for aggressive CA (cancer)

________ The nurse educator gives back a test question to the class because several people did not understand the wording

The Answers section can be found on page 133.

_______ The nurse educator gives points for the right answer regardless of the calculation method the student uses

_______ The nurse tells the student the proper step-by-step procedure for NG (nasogastric) tube insertion

Once the class understands the philosophies of ethical principles, they are introduced to some of the important definitions.

Exercise 11-2: *Matching*

Match the concept in column A with the definition in column B.

Column A	Column B
A. Autonomy	_______ The patient has the ability to answer for his or her own actions
B. Beneficence	_______ Following through on promises made
C. Nonmaleficence	_______ The person is reliable and can be depended upon
D. Justice	_______ Person's right to be independent
E. Fidelity	_______ Involves federal regulations known as HIPAA
F. Accountability	_______ Being truthful
G. Responsibility	_______ Doing the most good
H. Confidentially	_______ Being fair
I. Veracity	_______ Avoiding harm

To Aubree, Alita, and Connor, this is overwhelming, because they never really thought they would have so many things to consider. Aubree asks how a nurse would start to understand an ethical situation in health care. The answer is to start by clarifying your own values. A ***value*** is the worth a person places on something. The process of looking at one's own values and how they affect their nursing care is ***value clarification***. Values are formed during a person's development and even changes as a person matures and gains experiences. Many values are derived from a nurse's culture and upbringing.

e **eResource 11-2:** Their instructor gives the class a values clarification worksheet (www.itp.edu/resources/crc/pdf/values.pdf) and asks them to complete it and save it. She points out that values change over time and instructs the class to do the exercise again when they finish their nursing education.

Exercise 11-3: *True/False*

Ethnocentrism is the consideration of other people's cultural values in health care.

- ❑ True
- ❑ False

The Answers section can be found on page 133.

Alita asks the instructor how they would go about making an ethical decision if they needed to. The instructor tells them that there is a process, and that there are also resources to assist the nurse.

eResource 11-3: To clarify this point, the instructor shows the class several videos:

- *Ethical Issues In Nursing Introduction: Concepts, Values, and Decision Making*: www.youtu.be/9VRPMJUyE7Y
- *Patient Privacy Rights:* www.youtu.be/X65QlPO4VI0

Every health care organization has an ethics committee to help when an ethical dilemma occurs, and nurses collaborate with other health care professions in order to solve dilemmas. There are seven steps to solving an ethical dilemma (Figure 11.1).

Figure 11.1

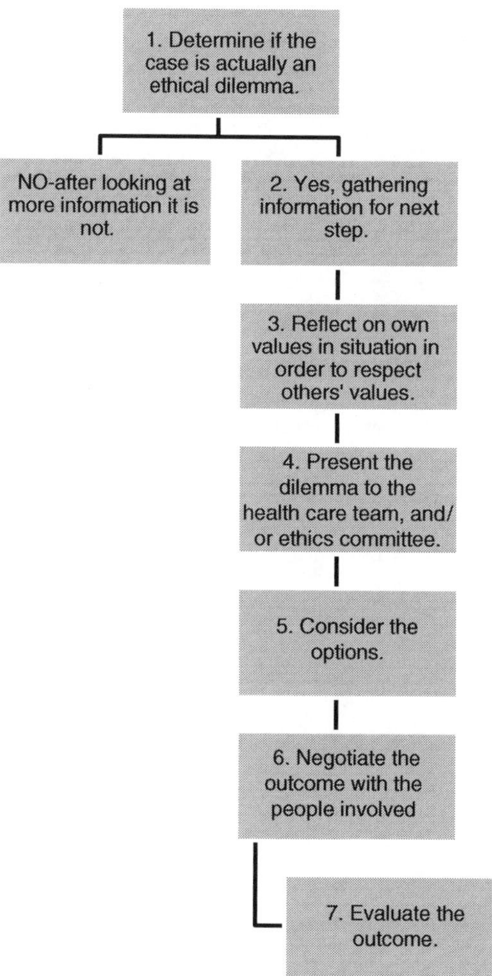

The Answers section can be found on page 133.

The instructor provides the following as an ethical dilemma that a nurse may experience.

Exercise 11-4: *Fill-in*

A nurse has a living will from a patient who states that if he is unresponsive he does not want a feeding tube. He does become unresponsive, and the family is called in and his daughter wants a feeding tube placed, stating, "I am not going to watch my father starve to death." The nurse determines that this is an ethical dilemma and is a matter of which principle from Exercise 11-2. ______________________________

Why? ______________________________

Exercise 11-5: *Fill-in*

A nurse is caring for an adult patient who does not want to take antibiotics for a leg wound that is contaminated because it makes her stomach very upset and she is going to use herbal medicine. The nurse determines that this is NOT an ethical dilemma and is a matter of which principle from Exercise 11-2. ______________________________

Why? ______________________________

Exercise 11-6: *Fill-in*

A nurse is caring for a child who is a Jehovah Witness and needs life-saving transfusions. The parents refuse to have the child given blood. This is an ethical dilemma that is quickly brought to the ethics committee and is a matter of which principle from Exercise 11-2. ______________________________

Why? ______________________________

Aubree, Alita, and Connor really like the examples; it makes things clearer.

eResource 11-4: As a way to build understanding of the decision process utilized when dealing with ethical dilemmas, they also view *The ABCDE of Medical Ethics for Medical Students*: www.youtu.be/dGLcYVQeUAE

The instructor tells them that some of the most common ethical dilemmas that a nurse will face have to do with:

- Quality of life
- Genetic screening
- Futile care
- Allocation of resources

The instructor tells the class that quality of life is defined by the individual. Connor asks for an example, and the instructor provides one:

A child is born with severe brain damage and a TE fistula (***tracheoesophageal fistula*** is a congenital communication between the trachea and the esophagus), so if the baby is fed it would choke to death. TE fistulas are repairable. One mother may choose to have it repaired, but another may decide not to, because of the quality of life.

The instructor further discusses genetic screening. It may become more and more important over the next few decades since there is research in the fields of genetic

The Answers section can be found on page 133.

manipulation. It will undoubtedly raise questions about what is acceptable to manipulate and what is not. Futile care and allocation of resources are often discussed together. A large problem in this county is the amount of health care dollars spent on end-of-life care. Futile care is performing interventions even though the person is not going to recover. The reason this is done is that our society has been so "cure" oriented. New initiatives such as hospice and "allow natural death" are trying to find ways to assist people to a peaceful passing.

One of Aubree's classmates asks about a fairly recently publicized case of a nurse who used medication to kill end-of-life victims, and how that was dealt with being completely on the other end of the spectrum. The instructor advised the class about ***Nurse Practice Acts*** that explain the nurses' scope of practice in each state. The Nurse Practice Acts defines the ***Standards of Care***.

eResource 11-5: The class refers to the ANA (2010) Nursing: Scope and Standards of Practice, by revisiting the following websites:

- Current Nursing (open access journal): www.currentnursing.com/nursing_management/nursing_standards.html
- Ferris State University's overview of Standards of Professional Nursing Practice: http://www.ferris.edu/HTMLS/colleges/alliedhe/Nursing/Standards-of-Professional-Nursing-Practice.htm

Exercise 11-7: *True/False*

The *ANA (2010) Nursing: Scope and Standards of Practice* obligate a nurse to report another nurse they suspect of misusing drugs on patients.

❑ True

❑ False

Exercise 11-8: *Multiple Choice Question*

The Standards of Nursing Care are defined by each state in the state:

A. Constitution

B. Nursing amendments

C. Nurse education documents

D. Practice act

Exercise 11-9: *True/False*

The Standards of Care cannot be used in a nursing malpractice suit.

❑ True

❑ False

Aubree asks her fundamentals instructor if there are any other regulations that she needs to know. The instructor describes the process of regulations. Besides the state Nurse Practice Act, there are organizations that have published standards that must be followed. Those, of course, cannot supersede the state practice act. The ANA (American Nurses Association) has practice guidelines that define scope of practice for nurses.

The Answers section can be found on page 133.

Nursing specialties also have ANA (2010) Nursing: Scope and Standards of Practice. Health care institutions also have policies that guide nursing practice.

Exercise 11-10: *Fill-in*
The regulating bodies in order from overriding policies to specific policies for nursing practice use the following governing bodies: state, hospital, critical care nurse (CCN) organization, and ANA (Figure 11.2). Please place in order from 1 to 4.

Figure 11.2 Regulating Bodies for Nursing

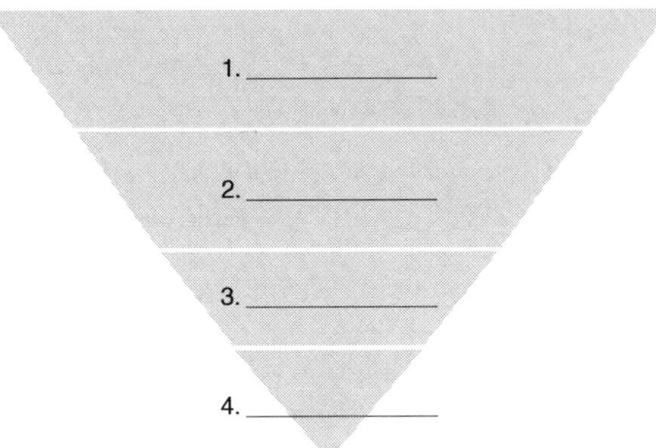

The fundamental instructor provides the students with a real case in order to clarify malpractice for nursing negligence.

Exercise 11-11: *Exhibit*
An infant who has ROP (retinopathy of prematurity), a progressive degenerative eye disease, is discharged from the NICU (neonatal intensive care unit), and the primary nurse tells the parents it is very important to take the baby back to the eye doctor. The parents indicate they understand and make an appointment but do not tell the eye doctor's scheduler it is for an infant with ROP. The appointment is made for a couple of weeks later, and the infant suffers from blindness. The hospital policy of that NICU says, "the discharge nurse should make an outpatient appointment with the ophthalmologist." Under what Standard of Care was the nurse found negligent?

A. State
B. Hospital
C. Neonatal Intensive Care Nursing Standards
D. ANA

This lawsuit demonstrates that nurses, by virtue of their license, can be sued for negligence.

The Answers section can be found on page 133.

Exercise 11-12: ***Select All That Apply***

In order for negligence to be proven, the following nursing actions are demonstrated:

- ❑ The nurse performed her duty to the patient
- ❑ There was an injury involved that included loss of money, pain, suffering, or death
- ❑ If the nurse functioned within her duty, the injury would not have occurred
- ❑ The patient did not follow the nurse's instructions
- ❑ The Standard of Care was unreasonable in that situation

One of the classmates of Aubree, Alita, and Connor has a hearing disability and has an amplifier for her stethoscope. Some of the students are questioning how she can perform as a nurse. The instructor discusses with them the ADA (Americans with Disabilities Act) and its history. The ADA gives people with physical and cognitive disabilities access to places and education. It was put into law in 1990 and made stronger in 2008. It started in Tennessee, when a man in a wheelchair, George Lane, could not appear in a second-floor courtroom without crawling up the steps. There were no elevators in the building. He crawled up the steps once, and it was humiliating, so he refused to do it again and was in contempt of court.

eResource 11-6: To learn more about the Americans with Disabilities Act, the class visits the ADA website (www.ada.gov) and about the extensive resources available as well as established guidelines for accessible design (http://www.ada.gov/stdspdf.htm)

Exercise 11-13: ***Multiple Choice Question***

Under the ADA law, accommodations need to be made for physically disabled persons that:

A. Are reasonable
B. Provide them with anything they need to succeed
C. Make them equal to the others
D. Decrease standards, so they can succeed

After the ADA discussion, Alita says that in high school, she was given a longer time to take her tests in a quiet room. She wonders if that can happen in nursing school. Alita asks the instructor if she can have a longer time in a quiet environment to take the test.

Exercise 11-14: ***True/False***

The instructor tells her it is not allowed because when she takes the NCLEX-RN exam, it is not done.

- ❑ True
- ❑ False

The Answers section can be found on page 133.

Exercise 11-15: *Ordering*

Place the following steps in order from 1 to 5 that a student needs to take in order to receive accommodations in nursing school:

_______ Have a licensed practitioner diagnose a cognitive or physical disability

_______ Provide the instructor with the documentation

_______ Receive documentation of the disability

_______ Provide the student service center or counseling center on campus with the documentation

_______ Arrange with the instructor how the accommodation will be carried out

Exercise 11-16: *Multiple Choice Question*

In order for the nursing instructor to make an accommodation, he or she needs:

A. To know what the disability is
B. To know what the student would like
C. The documentation from student services
D. A copy of the college policy

Aubree asks the instructor about hospitals, "Do they all have to be handicap accessible or can a handicapped person be sent to a hospital that is accessible?" A discussion ensued in the classroom about emergency medical treatment.

Exercise 11-17: *True/False*

A person can be turned away from an ED (emergency department) if the facility cannot treat their specific health care need.

❑ True
❑ False

Alita asks, "What if you cannot get the patient to consent for treatment?" The instructor tells her that in an emergency, it may need to be obtained later but as soon as possible.

Exercise 11-18: *Select All That Apply*

An informed consent is needed for:

❑ All routine treatment
❑ Special procedures
❑ Research participation
❑ All medication
❑ Chemotherapy

Exercise 11-19: *Multiple Choice Question*

An informed consent should include:

❑ Complete explanation of what is to be done
❑ Who will do the procedure
❑ The time of the procedure

The Answers section can be found on page 133.

- ❑ A list of possible complications including death if it is a possibility
- ❑ Alternative therapies
- ❑ Right to refuse beforehand
- ❑ The loss of right to refuse once the procedure is started

e

eResource 11-7: Alita views two short video presentations:

- Informed Consent—Introduction: www.youtu.be/0XIlx533Pd4
- What is "Informed Consent?": www.youtu.be/-aDHQnsEcQs

Exercise 11-20: *Select All That Apply*

The proper procedure for a nurse to witness an informed consent for a foreign language-speaking patient is to:

A. Find a person on staff who can speak the language
B. Ask a family member to interpret
C. Use a certified language line
D. Use a free web translation program to convert the consent to their language

Connor then asks, "What if a person comes to the ED with a mental health problem? They are threatening to commit suicide, and the hospital does not have a psychiatric ward?" The instructor explains that psychiatric patients who present can be admitted voluntarily or involuntarily, and the hospital would have to find an appropriate place for them.

Exercise 11-21: *Multiple Choice Question*

In order for a hospital to keep a psychiatric patient involuntarily, they must believe that the patient is:

A. Hallucinating
B. A threat to himself or herself and others
C. Combative
D. Unlawful in public

Alita then asks the instructor if psychiatric patients can be kept involuntarily as long as the psychiatric staff sees fit. The instructor tells her there needs to be a court order granted within 96 hours of the detainment. Connor asks if patients who refuse treatment can also be detained in the hospital this way.

Exercise 11-22: *True/False*

Hospitals cannot detain patients for refusing treatment if they are not an immediate harm to themselves or others.

- ❑ True
- ❑ False

Aubree asks if the person can be restrained in the ED if they are violent.

The Answers section can be found on page 133.

Exercise 11-23: *Multiple Choice Question*

A restraint can be placed on a patient in the ED without a doctor's order only if:

A. There is no doctor available
B. There is no medication that can calm the patient
C. There is no other way to provide treatment
D. There is an immediate risk to self or others

Exercise 11-24: *Multiple Choice Question*

A restraint can be ordered by a physician but is usually renewed every:

A. 12 hours
B. 24 hours
C. 48 hours
D. 72 hours

The instructor tells the class that this is a good time to talk about Civil and Common Law issues that can affect nursing practice.

Exercise 11-25: *Matching*

Match the terminology in column A to the definition in column B.

Column A		Column B
A. Tort	_______	Touching a person without consent
B. Intentional tort	_______	Civil wrong against property or person
C. Malpractice	_______	Threatening a person
D. Assault	_______	Negligence by a nurse
E. Battery	_______	Willfully violating a patient's rights
F. Negligence	_______	Publically damaging a patient's reputation
G. Slander	_______	Publishing false information
H. Malice	_______	Verbal mistruth
I. Libel	_______	Practice that is below standard
J. Defamation of character	_______	Written mistruth

Patients who do not have an immediate psychiatric problem have choices all the time in hospitals, the instructor explains.

Exercise 11-26: *Multiple Choice Question*

Two advanced directives provided to patients admitted to the hospital are:

A. Against medical advice (AMA) documents if needed and power of attorney
B. Power of attorney and consent to treat
C. Patients' bill of rights and living will
D. Living will and power of attorney

The Answers section can be found on page 133.

eResource 11-8: Aubree views a video to learn more about *Advance Medical Directives:* www.youtu.be/Hh8M-gx8Kt0

Exercise 11-27: *Multiple Choice Question*

The hospital is responsible under the Patient Self-determination Act of 1991 to:

A. Provide verbal information about patients' rights
B. Provide written information about patients' rights
C. Assist the patient to designate a power of attorney
D. Assist the patient to create a living will

Exercise 11-28: *Multiple Choice Question*

A document that designates another person to make health care decisions for a patient if the patient cannot do it for themselves is:

A. Living will
B. Proxy permission
C. Durable power of attorney
D. Next of kin statement

eResource 11-9: Aubree wants to have a mobile resource readily available to access while in clinical and finds the University of California School of Medicine's *Ethics Fast Facts:* [Pathway: www.missinglink.ucsf.edu/lm/ethics/index.htm → select "Review Fast Facts" → starting with "Basic Principles Overview" select topic of choice].

The instructor provides the class with a case study to better understand these concepts of patient rights.

Exercise 11-29: *Exhibit Question*

The nurse on a long-term hospital unit is not starting an IV or tube feeding on an 88-year-old who has terminal cancer that has ***metastasized*** (spread throughout his body). His wife of 55 years is upset and asking why he is "starving to death." The nurses have the right not to start these interventions because the following witnessed document is present in the patient's chart:

A. Durable power of attorney who is not the wife
B. Against medical advice document
C. Self-determination papers
D. Living will

eResource 11-10: To highlight the issues surrounding end-of-life, the class watches a short video segment from PBS Frontline: "Facing Death": www.youtu.be/N4objV7cLYg

Also on the same patient's chart is an order by the primary care provider to Allow Natural Death.

The Answers section can be found on page 133.

Exercise 11-30: *Fill-in*

Allow Natural Death (AND) is another term that is more user friendly than ________ ________________________.

The instructor tells the class that another consideration in care of adults who are terminally ill and are 18 years or older is the National Organ Transplant Act of 1984.

Exercise 11-31: *Multiple Choice Question*

In many states, a person's intent to donate organs in the event of death as outlined by the Uniform Anatomical Gift Act of 1987 is documented on their:

A. Medical record
B. Marriage certificate
C. Will
D. Driver's license

Aubree asks, "If the next of kin needs to be told about a patient's condition who should do it?"

The instructor tells the class that it is usually a hospital administrator and that it is regulated by privacy acts or HIPAA (Health Insurance Portability and Accountability Act). Alita then reminds the class that is why they see the signs in the hospital elevators reminding people not to discuss patient information. The instructor provides them with a recent real example of a HIPAA violation involving nursing students.

Exercise 11-32: *Exhibit Question*

A nursing student used a personal mobile electronic device (MED) in the clinical area to take a picture of a delivered, detached placenta before it was discarded for educational purposes and then posted the picture on Facebook. This was deemed a violation of HIPAA because:

A. A placenta is the personal property of a patient
B. A placenta is identifiable to the patient
C. The student did not have permission to take the picture
D. The student did not have permission to post the picture on Facebook

eResource 11-11: To better understand HIPAA and the responsibilities of the health care provider, the class views *Privacy and Security: The New HIPAA Rule:* www.youtu.be/fTjZ7GokQw4

The instructor reminds them that all work involving materials should be excluded from social networking. Even inferences about being tired at work, being busy, or specific unit characteristics are not professional. Connor asks why.

Exercise 11-33: *Exhibit Question*

The instructor gives them a real-life example. A nurse posts on Facebook (after work) that she should get paid extra because her unit was "busy and smelly." A person reading the entry knows the nurse works on a unit where his or her family member is a

The Answers section can be found on page 133.

patient! This makes the person upset that their family member is in a place with these conditions and complains to nursing administration. The nurse who posted the statement is most likely in conflict with:

A. HIPAA
B. Hospital policy
C. Unit policy
D. Professional standards

The instructor tells the class that HIPAA is based on laws of invasion of privacy. Patients have the right to privacy. Aubree is overwhelmed; there is "so much to worry about." The instructor assures her that sound clinical decision making, critical thinking, and common sense are the tools that will prevent any charges of wrongdoing. Connor then asks a related but different question, "What will be my obligation as a bystander in a public situation like witnessing a car accident?"

Exercise 11-34: *Multiple Choice Question*
Nurses are protected by which law if they act within their licensure in an emergency situation:

A. Self-determination act
B. Good Samaritan Law
C. HIPAA
D. Standards of Professional Practice

Exercise 11-35: *True/False*
A nurse stops at a car accident, and the parent is unconscious; she can still render care to the child without permission.

❑ True
❑ False

Aubree asks the instructor, "Can student nurses be sued?"

Exercise 11-36: *Multiple Choice Question*
An inappropriate answer to the question "Can student nurses be sued?" by a nurse educator is:

A. "No, they are working under the license of their instructor"
B. "Yes, if they do something that they have not been taught"
C. "Yes, if they do not act prudently"
D. "No, if they are prudent and under the Good Samaritan Law"

Exercise 11-37: *True/False*
Nurses should always have their own malpractice insurance.

❑ True
❑ False

Aubree raises her hand in class and states, "I have one more question: What is the correct procedure if I do make a mistake in the hospital?"

The Answers section can be found on page 133.

Exercise 11-38: ***Ordering***

Place the steps that should be taken in the correct order if an error is made by a nurse:

_______ Call the physician
_______ Notify the nursing supervisor
_______ Assess the patient
_______ Render any needed interventions
_______ Fill out an incident report for risk management
_______ Document the care given

Exercise 11-39: ***Multiple Choice Question***

Incident reports should be documents that are:

A. Kept in the patient's medical record
B. Discussed at unit meetings
C. Copied and retained by the nurse
D. Kept separate from the patient's medical record

Aubree, Alita, and Connor decide that there is a lot of information about ethical and legal issues in nursing. They have made a study schedule to work together to study for the next fundamentals test.

The Answers section can be found on page 133.

Answers

Exercise 11-1: *Fill-in*

Fill in the following nursing situations with a D—deontology, U—utilitarianism, or T—teleology to denote how the nurse decided in the situation:

__**U**__ The nurse votes for national health care

__**T**__ The nurse tells parents of a dying child about organ donation

__**D**__ The nurse honors a patient's right not to take chemotherapy for aggressive CA (cancer)

__**T**__ The nurse educator gives back a test question to the class because several people did not understand the wording

__**U**__ The nurse educator gives points for the right calculation answer regardless of the calculation method the student uses

__**D**__ The nurse tells the student the proper step-by-step procedure for NG (nasogastric) tube insertion

Exercise 11-2: *Matching*

Match the concept in column A with the definition in column B.

Column A		Column B
A. Autonomy	**F**	The patient has the ability to answer for his or her own actions
B. Beneficence	**E**	Following through on promises made
C. Nonmaleficence	**G**	The person is reliable and can be depended upon
D. Justice	**A**	Person's right to be independent
E. Fidelity	**H**	Involves federal regulations known as HIPAA
F. Accountability	**I**	Being truthful
G. Responsibility	**B**	Doing the most good
H. Confidentially	**D**	Being fair
I. Veracity	**C**	Avoiding harm

Exercise 11-3: *True/False*

Ethnocentrism is the consideration of other people's cultural values in health care.

❑ True

☒ **False—It considers one's own values superior**

Exercise 11-4: *Fill-in*

A nurse has a living will from a patient who states that if he is unresponsive he does not want a feeding tube. He does become unresponsive, and the family is called in and his daughter wants a feeding tube placed, stating, "I am not going to watch my father starve to death." The nurse determines that this is an ethical dilemma and is a matter of which principle from Exercise 11-2. **Teleology**

Why? **The outcome of starving is what is being judged.**

Exercise 11-5: *Fill-in*

A nurse is caring for an adult patient who does not want to take antibiotics for a leg wound that is contaminated, because it makes her stomach very upset and she is going to use herbal medicine. The nurse determines that this is NOT an ethical dilemma and is a matter of which principle from Exercise 11-2. **Deontology**

Why? **Because it is right for that patient.**

Exercise 11-6: *Fill-in*

A nurse is caring for a child who is a Jehovah Witness and needs life-saving transfusions. The parents refuse to have the child given blood. This is an ethical dilemma that is quickly brought to the ethics committee and is a matter of which principle from Exercise 11-2. **Deontology**

Why? **Because it is *right* for that family.**

Exercise 11-7: *True/False*

The *Standards of Care* obligate a nurse to report another nurse they suspect of misusing drugs on patients.

☒ **True—YES, because they endanger others**

❑ False

Exercise 11-8: *Multiple Choice Question*

The Standards of Nursing Care are defined by each state in the state:

A. Constitution—NO

B. Nursing amendments—NO, this is part of the Nurse Practice Act

C. Nurse education documents—NO, this is part of the Nurse Practice Act

D. **Practice act—YES**

Exercise 11-9: *True/False*

The Standards of Care cannot be used in a nursing malpractice suit.

❑ True

☒ **False—This is normally what the suit is based on**

Exercise 11-10: *Fill-in*

The regulating bodies in order from overriding policies to specific policies for nursing practice use the following governing bodies: state, hospital, critical care nurse (CCN) organization, and ANA (Figure 11.3).

Figure 11.3

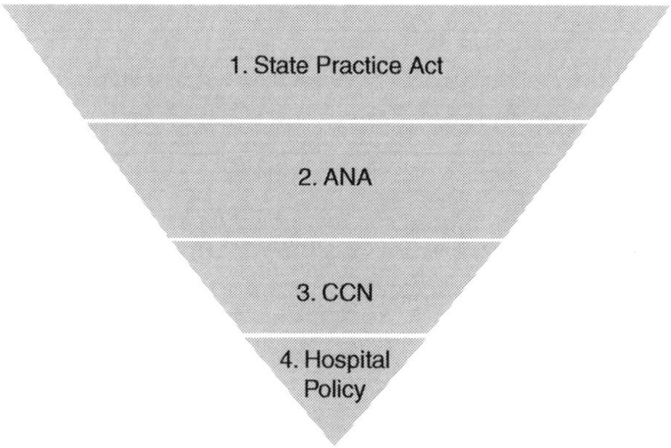

1. State Practice Act
2. ANA
3. CCN
4. Hospital Policy

Exercise 11-11: *Exhibit*

An infant who has ROP (retinopathy of prematurity), a progressive degenerative eye disease, is discharged from the NICU (neonatal intensive care unit), and the primary nurse tells the parents it is very important to take the baby back to the eye doctor. The parents indicate they understand and make an appointment but do not tell the eye doctor's scheduler it is for an infant with ROP. The appointment is made for a couple of weeks later, and the infant suffers blindness. The hospital policy of that NICU says, "the discharge nurse should make an outpatient appointment with the ophthalmologist." Under what Standard of Care was the nurse found negligent?

A. State—NO, the state practice act does not mandate how referrals are done
B. **Hospital—YES, it was a hospital policy**
C. Neonatal Intensive Care Nursing Standards—NO, organizations do not mandate how referrals are done
D. ANA—NO, organizations do not mandate how referrals are done

Exercise 11-12: *Select All That Apply*

In order for negligence to be proven, the following nursing actions are demonstrated:

- ❑ The nurse performed her duty to the patient—NO, then he or she is not liable
- ☒ **There was an injury involved that included loss of money, pain, suffering, or death—YES, there is permanent injury from the act**
- ☒ **If the nurse functioned within her duty, the injury would not have occurred—YES, the injury would have been prevented if the nurse did the right thing**

❑ The patient did not follow the nurse's instructions—NO, this is the patient's responsibility

❑ The Standard of Care was unreasonable in that situation—NO, the Standards of Care are for all situations

Exercise 11-13: *Multiple Choice Question*

Under the ADA law, accommodations need to be made for physically disabled persons who:

A. **Are reasonable—YES, they must be reasonable for the institution to do**

B. Provide them with anything they need to succeed—NO, not if it is a burden to the institution

C. Make them equal to the others—NO, not if it is a burden to the institution

D. Decrease standards, so they can succeed—NO, they should be held to the same standards

Exercise 11-14: *True/False*

The instructor tells her it is not allowed because when she takes the NCLEX-RN© exam, it is not done.

❑ True

☒ **False—NCLEX-RN© does make provisions**

Exercise 11-15: *Ordering*

Place the following steps in order from 1 to 5 that a student needs to take in order to receive accommodations in nursing school:

__1__ Have a licensed practitioner diagnose a cognitive or physical disability

__4__ Provide the instructor with the documentation

__2__ Receive documentation of the disability

__3__ Provide the student service center or counseling center on campus with the documentation

__5__ Arrange with the instructor how the accommodation will be carried out

Exercise 11-16: *Multiple Choice Question*

In order for the nursing instructor to make an accommodation, he or she needs:

A. To know what the disability is—NO, they do not need to know

B. To know what the student would like—NO, the student does not decide

C. **The documentation from student services—YES, the documentation is needed**

D. A copy of the college policy—NO, this should be accessible to all in the catalog

Exercise 11-17: ***True/False***

A person can be turned away from an ED (emergency department) if the facility cannot treat their specific health care need.

❑ True

☒ **False—The Emergency Medical Treatment and Active Labor Act (EMTALA) of 1986 states that an appropriate medical evaluation must be done**

Exercise 11-18: ***Select All That Apply***

An informed consent is needed for:

☒ **All routine treatment—YES, a general consent that covers routine procedures is signed by all admitted patients**

☒ **Special procedures—YES**

☒ **Research participation—YES**

❑ All medication—NO, some are considered routine

☒ **Chemotherapy—YES, this is not routine**

Exercise 11-19: ***Multiple Choice Question***

An informed consent should include:

☒ **Complete explanation of what is to be done—YES**

☒ **Who will do the procedure—YES**

❑ The time of the procedure—NO, this is not included since procedure times change

☒ **A list of possible complications including death if it is a possibility—YES**

☒ **Alternative therapies—YES**

☒ **Right to refuse beforehand—YES**

❑ The loss of right to refuse once the procedure is started—NO, a patient can stop and refuse at any time

Exercise 11-20: ***Select All That Apply***

The proper procedure for a nurse to witness an informed consent for a foreign language-speaking patient is:

A. Find a person on staff who can speak the language—NO, this is a breach of privacy and may be an inaccurate translation

B. Ask a family member to interpret—NO, this is a breach of privacy and may be an inaccurate translation

C. **Use a certified language line—YES, this is a source of people who are educated about confidentiality and health care terminology**

D. Use a free web translation program to convert the consent to their language—NO, this may not accurately translate health care terminology

Exercise 11-21: *Multiple Choice Question*

In order for a hospital to keep a psychiatric patient involuntarily, they must believe that the patient is:

A. Hallucinating—NO, this alone is not a reason

B. **A threat to himself or herself and others—YES, this is the only reason**

C. Combative—NO, this may be dealt with by communication

D. Unlawful in public—NO, this may not be a threat

Exercise 11-22: *True/False*

Hospitals cannot detain patients for refusing treatment if they are not an immediate harm to themselves or others.

☒ **True—Patients can refuse treatment and leave if there is no immediate danger**

☐ False

Exercise 11-23: *Multiple Choice Question*

A restraint can be placed on a patient in the ED without a doctor's order only if:

A. There is no doctor available—NO, this is not a choice for an ED

B. There is not a medication that can calm the patient—NO, medication is also considered a restraint, a chemical restraint

C. There is no other way to provide treatment—NO, they can refuse treatment

D. **There is an immediate risk to self or others—YES, this is the key indicator for restraints**

Exercise 11-24: *Multiple Choice Question*

A restraint can be ordered by a physician but is usually renewed every:

A. 12 hours—NO, although this may be policy at some health care organizations

B. **24 hours—YES, at least every 24 hours is the standard**

C. 48 hours—NO, too long

D. 72 hours—NO, too long

Exercise 11-25: *Matching*

Match the terminology in column A to the definition in column B.

Column A	Column B
A. Tort	**E** Touching a person without consent
B. Intentional tort	**A** Civil wrong against property or person
C. Malpractice	**D** Threatening a person
D. Assault	**C** Negligence by a nurse
E. Battery	**B** Willfully violating a patient's rights
F. Negligence	**J** Publically damaging a patient's reputation
G. Slander	**H** Publishing false information
H. Malice	**G** Verbal mistruth
I. Libel	**F** Practice that is below standard
J. Defamation of character	**I** Written mistruth

Exercise 11-26: *Multiple Choice Question*

Two advanced directives provided to patients admitted to the hospital are:

A. Against medical advice (AMA) documents if needed and power of attorney—NO
B. Power of attorney and consent to treat—NO
C. Patients' bill of rights and living will—NO
D. **Living will and power of attorney—YES, these are provided by law**

Exercise 11-27: *Multiple Choice Question*

The hospital is responsible under the Patient Self-determination Act of 1991 to:

A. Provide verbal information about patients' rights—NO
B. **Provide written information about patients' rights—YES, this must be done**
C. Assist the patient to designate a power of attorney—NO
D. Assist the patient to create a living will—NO

Exercise 11-28: *Multiple Choice Question*

A document that designates another person to make health care decisions for a patient if the patient cannot do it for themselves is:

A. Living will—NO, this is a set of preferences that the patient writes
B. Proxy permission—NO, the durable power of attorney person is the proxy
C. **Durable power of attorney—YES, the person has power of attorney for health care**
D. Next of kin statement—NO, this does not necessarily have to be the person

Exercise 11-29: *Exhibit Question*

The nurse on a long-term hospital unit is not starting an IV or tube feeding on an 88-year-old who has terminal cancer that has ***metastasized*** (spread throughout his body). His wife of 55 years is upset and asking why he is "starving to death." The nurses have the right not to start these interventions because the following witnessed document is present in the patient's chart:

A. Durable power of attorney who is not the wife—NO, this is not the case
B. Against medical advice document—NO, this is done by a conscious patient
C. Self-determination papers—NO, this the general term for durable power of attorney and living wills
D. **Living will—YES, the patient put preferences in a living will and it is respected**

Exercise 11-30: *Fill-in*

Allow Natural Death (AND) is another term that is more user friendly than **Do Not Resuscitate.**

Exercise 11-31: *Multiple Choice Question*

In many states, a person's intent to donate organs in the event of death as outlined by the Uniform Anatomical Gift Act of 1987 is documented on their:

A. Medical record—NO, this may be a place but not always
B. Marriage certificate—NO

C. Will—NO, this may be the place but not always
D. **Driver's license—YES, many states place it on the driver's license**

Exercise 11-32: *Exhibit Question*

A nursing student used a personal mobile electronic device (MED) in the clinical area to take a picture of a delivered, detached placenta before it was discarded for educational purposes and then posted the picture on Facebook. This was deemed a violation of HIPAA because:

A. **A placenta is personal property of a patient—YES, this is a violation of confidentiality because it is a part of a person's body**
B. A placenta is identifiable to the patient—NO, this is not the best reason because it may not be identifiable, but in a rare case it may be identifiable by circumstance of time and day
C. The student did not have permission to take the picture—NO, even though they did not have permission to do this, it is not the best answer. To take a picture in the hospital, you must have a written consent
D. The student did not have permission to post the picture on Facebook—NO, pictures of any patient area, patient part, or hospital unit should never be posted on a social network

Exercise 11-33: *Exhibit Question*

The instructor gives them a real-life example. A nurse posts on Facebook (after work) that she should get paid extra because her unit was "busy and smelly." A person reading the entry knows the nurse works on a unit where his or her family member is a patient! This makes the person upset that their family member is in a place with these conditions and complains to nursing administration. The nurse who posted the statement is most likely in conflict with:

A. HIPAA—NO, specific patient information is not revealed
B. Hospital policy—NO, the hospital policy may not cover this
C. Unit policy—NO, the unit's policy may not cover this
D. **Professional standards—YES, this is not professional talking negatively about your work on a social network**

Exercise 11-34: *Multiple Choice Question*

Nurses are protected by which law if they act within their licensure in an emergency situation:

A. Self-determination act—NO, this is a patient responsibility
B. **Good Samaritan Law—YES**
C. HIPAA—NO, this is confidentiality
D. Standards of Professional Practice—NO, this is not the best answer

Exercise 11-35: *True/False*

A nurse stops at a car accident, and the parent is unconscious; she can still render care to the child without permission.

☒ **True—YES, in an emergency situation care can be rendered**

☐ False

Exercise 11-36: *Multiple Choice Question*

An inappropriate answer to the question "Can student nurses be sued?" by a nurse educator is:

A. **"No, they are working under the license of their instructor."—YES, this is not true; students are responsible for their actions**
B. "Yes, if they do something that they have not been taught."—NO, this is true
C. "Yes, if they do not act prudently."—NO, this is true
D. "No, if they are prudent and under the Good Samaritan Law."—NO, this is true

Exercise 11-37: *True/False*

Nurses should always have their own malpractice insurance.

☒ **True—Hospitals and nurses are sued as well as primary care providers**

☐ False

Exercise 11-38: *Ordering*

Place the steps that should be taken in the correct order if an error is made by a nurse:

__4__ Call the physician
__3__ Notify the nursing supervisor
__1__ Assess the patient
__2__ Render any needed interventions
__6__ Fill out an incident report for risk management
__5__ Document the care given

Exercise 11-39: *Multiple Choice Question*

Incident reports should be documents that are:

A. Kept in the patient's medical record—NO, they are internal records to help prevent errors in the future
B. Discussed at unit meetings—NO, they are not usually public knowledge
C. Copied and retained by the nurse—NO, they should not be removed from the hospital
D. **Kept separate from the patient's medical record—YES, they are for preventing errors in the future**

12

Communication

Unfolding Case Study 11 ▒ Aubree, Alita, and Connor

The fundamentals class has a laboratory component, and this week, the students are learning communication in the lab. Alita read her chapter on communication, so she feels prepared to role-play and practice in the lab. The instructor tells the students that ***therapeutic communication*** is a critical skill for any nurse. Without the use of therapeutic communication, the other aspects of nursing would not be able to be completed; an example is that a nurse would never elicit an accurate patient history if he or she did not communicate effectively and therapeutically. Developing communication skills takes time and practice. How a person interprets communication through sight, hearing, touch, taste, and smell has to do with his or her perceptions.

Exercise 12-1: *Multiple Choice Question*

When a person's culture, background, values, and education overshadow their perceptions, it is called perceptual:

A. Acculturation
B. Assimilation
C. Overcasting
D. Bias

The instructor has the students in the lab break up into small groups to practice communication skills. Alita, Aubree, and Connor are in one group. The instructor tells them about three types of communication.

Exercise 12-2: *Matching*

Match the name of the communication type in column A to the definition in column B.

Column A	Column B
A. Intrapersonal	_______ Communication with the spiritual domain
B. Interpersonal	_______ Communication with your inner thoughts
C. Transpersonal	_______ Person-to-person communication

The Answers section can be found on page 153.

Other types of communication that nurses are called to do are small group, such as teaching a group of patients about a procedure and public speaking to an audience. The instructor tells the class that there are basic elements of the communication process, all of which are important.

Exercise 12-3: *Fill-in*

Use the following words to fill in the blanks.

Referent, Sender, Receiver, Message, Channels, Feedback, Interpersonal variables, Environment

A. This motivates people to speak to one another ____________________

B. This is the content of the communication process____________________

C. This is the setting for the communication interaction ____________________

D. This is the means through which the communication is conveyed, such as auditory ____________

E. This is the person who encodes the message ________________________

F. This is the return of the message, and lets the person know if it was understood ____________________

G. This is the person who decodes the message that was sent ______________

e **eResource 12-1:** To learn more about the communication process, Alita reads:

- *Communication*: www.nursingplanet.com/pn/communication.html
- *Therapeutic Communication in Psychiatric Nursing*: www.nursingplanet.com/pn/therapeutic_communication.html

Alita realizes that besides the communication process itself, there are different forms of communication. They are verbal and nonverbal, but what she did not realize is how many elements each one of those had!

Exercise 12-4: *Fill-in*

In front of each variable, place a "V" for verbal and an "N" for nonverbal:

_______ Vocabulary
_______ Connotative meaning (a word with several meanings)
_______ Facial expression
_______ Personal space
_______ Eye contact
_______ Pacing or speed of message
_______ Sounds that are not words
_______ Intonation (tone)
_______ Posture and gait
_______ Clarity
_______ Brevity
_______ Personal appearance

The Answers section can be found on page 153.

_______ Relevance

_______ Timing

eResource 12-2: To supplement her understanding of the communication process, Alita reads *Interpersonal Communication*: www.uc.edu/armyrotc/ms2text/MSL_201_L08b_Interpersonal_Communication.pdf

Aubree raises her hand and asks about personal space. She says that she is from an English background and they are not a physically close family. She is worried that this will be interpreted as standoffish. The instructor tells her about how personal space is rated, and that helps students to understand boundaries and appropriateness.

Exercise 12-5: *Matching*

Match the zone in column A to the descriptors in column B.

Column A	Column B
A. Intimate zone	_______ 4 to 12 ft
B. Personal zone	_______ 0 to 18 in.
C. Social zone	_______ 12 ft or more
D. Public zone	_______ 18 in. to 4 ft

The instructor tells the class that a concept closely related to personal space in communication is touch, and that there are different zones for that also that the nurse must be aware of to use it therapeutically.

Exercise 12-6: *Multiple Choice Question*

The nurse touching the hands of a mother in encouragement who is stroking her sick child's head is classified as touch in the:

A. Social zone
B. Consent zone
C. Vulnerable zone
D. Intimate zone

Exercise 12-7: *Multiple Choice Question*

The nurse helping the patient do a Sitz bath is considered the:

A. Social zone
B. Consent zone
C. Vulnerable zone
D. Intimate zone

The Answers section can be found on page 153.

Exercise 12-8: *Multiple Choice Question*

The nurse touches an elderly man's mouth to give mouth care; this touch is classified as being in the:

A. Social zone
B. Consent zone
C. Vulnerable zone
D. Intimate zone

Exercise 12-9: *Multiple Choice Question*

The nurse holds the patient around the neck in order to help her keep steady for an epidural; this type of touch is in the:

A. Social zone
B. Consent zone
C. Vulnerable zone
D. Intimate zone

Alita asks the instructor about using drawings or music to help patients, if that is a form of communication.

Exercise 12-10: *Multiple Choice Question*

Using art forms in nursing to communicate and relate to patients is called:

A. Nonverbal communication
B. Metacommunication
C. Territorial communication
D. Symbolic communication

Connor admits to the class that he is glad to know all this because nurse–patient relationships make him nervous, and many times there are numerous families around to deal with also. The instructor tells them that the nurse–patient or nurse–family relationship should be thought of in phases, as illustrated in Figure 12.1:

Figure 12.1 Phases of a nurse-patient relationship

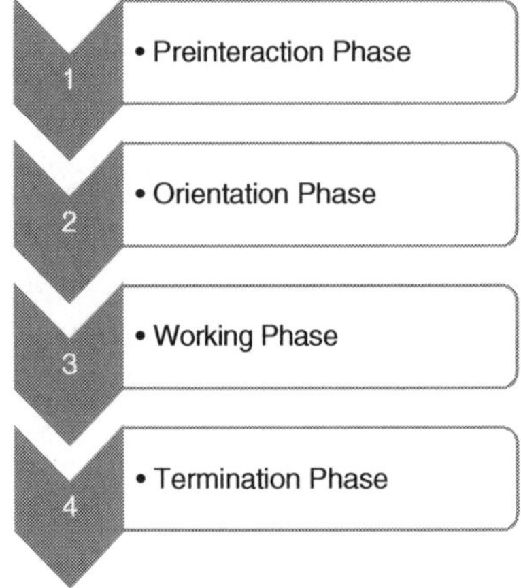

The Answers section can be found on page 153.

Exercise 12-11: *Matching*

Match the phase in column A to the characteristics of the phase in column B.

Column A		Column B
A. Preinteraction phase	______	Develops the initial tone for the relationship
B. Orientation phase	______	Relinquishes responsibility to the patient
C. Working phase	______	Provides care and information to the patient
D. Termination phase	______	Reviews data about the patient

Exercise 12-12: *Select All That Apply*

Select some of the interactions you would expect to see between a nurse and a patient in the orientation phase of a relationship:

- ❑ Introductions
- ❑ Preparing the patient for a procedure
- ❑ Assessment
- ❑ Goal setting
- ❑ Reading the medical record
- ❑ Role clarification
- ❑ Prioritizing care

Exercise 12-13: *Multiple Choice Question*

The nurse and the patient talk about the patient's hospital stay and look back and discuss the events. The phase that the relationship is in would be the:

A. Preinteraction
B. Orientation
C. Working
D. Termination

Exercise 12-14: *Multiple Choice Question*

The patient is telling the nurse that he is misinterpreting his preference for pain medication. The relationship phase that the nurse and patient are in is the:

A. Preinteraction
B. Orientation
C. Working
D. Termination

Aubree raises her hand and asks the instructor about the "other things" that they have been taught since childhood, and how important are they in a nurse–patient relationship. The instructor asks the class to name important elements of a communication process, and here is the class list:

- Courtesy
- Using correct names
- Privacy and confidentiality

The Answers section can be found on page 153.

- Trust
- Responsibility
- Assertiveness and aggressiveness

The instructor tries to place these terms in context for the beginning students by playing a matching game.

Exercise 12-15: *Matching*

Match the word in column A to the descriptor in column B.

Column A	Column B
A. Courtesy	______ The nurse covers the portable computer screen while in the room with visitors
B. Using correct names	______ The nurse lets the patient know he or she is comfortable doing the procedure
C. Privacy	______ The nurse chooses the option for the patient
D. Trust	______ The nurse knocks on the door before entering the patient's room
E. Responsibility	______ The nurse tells the patient her name and role
F. Assertiveness	______ The nurse takes the initiative to call for stronger medication
G. Aggressiveness	______ The nurse returns at the set time that he or she indicated

The class then discusses contextual factors that influence communication such as gender, culture, emotional, and developmental factors. Because all these factors play into any nurse–patient relationship, there are ***therapeutic communication techniques*** that are used to elicit and exchange information in an open environment that is safe for patients and nurses.

eResource 12-3: Handout: Therapeutic Communication Techniques for health care: http://www.snjourney.com/ClinicalInfo/PracticeAreas/Therapeutic_Communication_Techniques.pdf

Exercise 12-16: *Matching*

Match the therapeutic communication technique in column A to the description in column B.

Column A	Column B
A. Clarifying	______ Allowing time to continue what someone means
B. Paraphrasing	______ Reviewing main issue
C. Reflecting	______ Setting priorities

The Answers section can be found on page 153.

Column A		Column B
D. Silence	______	Restating
E. Structuring	______	Open-ended information gathering
F. Pinpointing	______	Following up to make sure you understand
G. Questioning	______	Letting the patient know you understand his or her feeling
H. Directing	______	Encouraging person to go on
I. Summarizing	______	Pointing out issues or inconsistencies

eResource 12-4: The instructor provides the class with a handout that summarizes therapeutic communication techniques that facilitate communication and those that block communication: www.snjourney.com/ClinicalInfo/PracticeAreas/Therapeutic_Communication_Techniques.pdf The class uses the handout as a reference during role-playing exercises in the lab to practice using therapeutic communication techniques. Aubree, Conner, and Alita videotape themselves and help each other identify ***nontherapeutic communication*** during the simulated interaction. A couple are identified, and then the instructor gives the class some "clicker (audience response) questions" to clarify concepts.

Exercise 12-17: *Multiple Choice Question*

The nurse asks the patient who is a victim of partner abuse if she loves her partner. This form of nontherapeutic communication is:

A. Asking for explanation
B. Approving or disapproving
C. Showing sympathy
D. Asking personal questions

Exercise 12-18: *Multiple Choice Question*

The nurse tells the patient that she would not trust her toddler to a daycare. This form of nontherapeutic communication is:

A. Asking for explanation
B. Providing personal opinion
C. Automatic response
D. Asking personal questions

Exercise 12-19: *Multiple Choice Question*

The patient explains to the nurse the events leading up to the illness, and the nurse responds, "It is what it is." This form of nontherapeutic communication is:

A. Automatic response
B. Approving or disapproving
C. Asking for an explanation
D. Asking personal questions

The Answers section can be found on page 153.

Exercise 12-20: *Multiple Choice Question*

The nurse responds to a patient who just said "I hate my mother" with "that is not right." This form of nontherapeutic communication is:

A. Showing sympathy
B. Approving or disapproving
C. Automatic response
D. Asking personal questions

Alita asks the instructor the difference between empathy and sympathy.

Exercise 12-21: *Fill-in*

Place an E next to the statement that displays empathy and an S next to the statement that uses sympathy.

_______ "I feel so sorry for you, you have had such a hard year"
_______ "I can only imagine how hard it has been"
_______ "I'm sure it is difficult to describe the feeling you had at the time"
_______ "You have been hit with your share more than anyone I know"
_______ "That happened to me once, and I got depressed too"

eResource 12-5: Aubree and her classmates view a video that presents the value of therapeutic communication from a patient's perspective, *Qualities of a nurse-Therapeutic communication for nurses*: www.youtu .be/Nipj7PwCjTc

After viewing it, they have a better understanding of this important aspect of nursing care.

There are also communication issues with special populations of people, the class is told. Aubree asks how to communicate with a person with whom she has difficulty speaking due to illness.

Exercise 12-22: *Select All That Apply*

Some of the communication techniques that can be used for a patient who has suffered speech impairment due to an illness are:

- ❑ Speak louder
- ❑ Use questions that can be answered "yes" or "no"
- ❑ Do not encourage the patient to converse
- ❑ Use a communication board
- ❑ Let the patient know if he or she is understood

The instructor asks them to think of other patients who may have difficulty, and Connor says, "hearing impaired, which is also sometimes the elderly." Hearing impairment is common in the elderly, but some rules of communication hold true for all patients who are hearing impaired.

The Answers section can be found on page 153.

Exercise 12-23: *Multiple Choice Question*

The nurse is caring for an elderly patient with a hearing deficit. During a teaching session, the nurse should encourage:

A. The family to leave, so the patient receives the instructions directly
B. Helping the patient by finishing his or her sentences
C. Trying to anticipate their questions
D. Using short sentences and simple words

eResource 12-6: The instructor provides the class with a handout that serves as an easy reference of tips from Culture Clues™ *Communicating With Your Deaf Patient*: www.depts.washington.edu/pfes/PDFs/DeafCultureClue.pdf

Aubree asks the instructor, "How do I deal with a patient who is unresponsive?" The instructor tells the class some of the best ways to communicate with an unresponsive patient.

Exercise 12-24: *Fill-in*

What is a method that can be used to communicate with an unresponsive patient?

____

Alita asks the instructor about intellectually disabled individuals.

Exercise 12-25: *Select All That Apply*

Select the communication techniques that assist intellectually disabled patients to understand:

❑ Speak loudly
❑ Use short sentences
❑ Have family present
❑ Give short explanations
❑ Do not worry about them doing other things during the communication

The students have a better idea of how to communicate, but now need actual patient practice to use the new techniques they have learned. They are anxious to get into the hospital again and practice!

The Answers section can be found on page 153.

Answers

Exercise 12-1: *Multiple Choice Question*

When a person's culture, background, values, and education overshadow their perceptions, it is called perceptual:

A. Acculturation—NO, this is when you learn a new culture
B. Assimilation—NO, this is when you become part of the new culture
C. Overcasting—NO
D. **Bias—YES, this is biasness against another group**

Exercise 12-2: *Matching*

Match the name of the communication type in column A to the definition in column B.

Column A	Column B	
A. Intrapersonal	**C**	Communication with the spiritual domain
B. Interpersonal	**A**	Communication with your inner thoughts
C. Transpersonal	**B**	Person-to-person communication

Exercise 12-3: *Fill-in*

Use the following words to fill in the blanks.

Referent, Sender, Receiver, Message, Channels, Feedback, Interpersonal variables, Environment.

A. This motivates people to speak to one another **Referent**
B. This is the content of the communication process **Message**
C. This is the setting for the communication interaction **Environment**
D. This is the means through which the communication is conveyed, such as auditory **Channel**
E. This is the person who encodes the message **Sender**
F. This is the return of the message, and lets the person know if it was understood **Feedback**
G. This is the person who decodes the message that was sent **Receiver**

Exercise 12-4: *Matching*

In front of each variable place a "V" for verbal and an "N" for nonverbal:

V Vocabulary
V Connotative meaning (a word with several meanings)
N Facial expression

__**N**__ Personal space
__**N**__ Eye contact
__**V**__ Pacing or speed of message
__**N**__ Sounds that are not words (sounds that are not words are not considered intentional forms of communication)
__**V**__ Intonation (tone)
__**N**__ Posture and gait
__**V**__ Clarity
__**V**__ Brevity
__**N**__ Personal appearance
__**V**__ Relevance
__**V**__ Timing

Exercise 12-5: *Matching*

Match the zone in column A to the descriptors in column B.

Column A	Column B
A. Intimate zone	__**C**__ 4 to 12 ft
B. Personal zone	__**A**__ 0 to 18 in.
C. Social zone	__**D**__ 12 ft or more
D. Public zone	__**B**__ 18 in. to 4 ft

Exercise 12-6: *Multiple Choice Question*

The nurse touching the hands of a mother in encouragement who is stroking her sick child's head is classified as touch in the:

A. **Social zone—YES, hands are considered in the social zone**
B. Consent zone—NO
C. Vulnerable zone—NO
D. Intimate zone—NO

Exercise 12-7: *Multiple Choice Question*

The nurse helping the patient do a Sitz bath is considered the:

A. Social zone—NO
B. Consent zone—NO
C. Vulnerable zone—NO
D. **Intimate zone—YES, rectal and perineal touch is in the intimate zone**

Exercise 12-8: *Multiple Choice Question*

The nurse touches an elderly man's mouth to give mouth care; this touch is classified as being in the:

A. Social zone—NO
B. **Consent zone—YES, the mouth is part of the consent zone**
C. Vulnerable zone—NO
D. Intimate zone—NO

Exercise 12-9: *Multiple Choice Question*

The nurse holds the patient around the neck in order to help her keep steady for an epidural; this type of touch is in the:

A. Social zone—NO

B. Consent zone—NO

C. **Vulnerable zone—YES, this is the vulnerable zone**

D. Intimate zone—NO

Exercise 12-10: *Multiple Choice Question*

Using art forms in nursing to communicate and relate to patients is called:

A. Nonverbal communication—NO

B. Metacommunication—NO, this is communicating about communicating

C. Territorial communication—NO

D. **Symbolic communication—YES, art and music are types of symbolic communication**

Exercise 12-11: *Matching*

Match the phase in column A to the characteristics of the phase in column B.

Column A		Column B
A. Preinteraction phase	**B**	Develops the initial tone for the relationship
B. Orientation phase	**D**	Relinquishes responsibility to the patient
C. Working phase	**C**	Provides care and information to the patient
D. Termination phase	**A**	Reviews data about the patient

Exercise 12-12: *Select All That Apply*

Select some of the interactions you would expect to see between a nurse and a patient in the orientation phase of a relationship:

☒ **Introductions**

☒ **Preparing the patient for a procedure**

☒ **Assessment**

☒ **Goal setting**

❑ Reading the medical record—NO, this is the preinteraction phase

☒ **Role clarification**

☒ **Prioritizing care**

Exercise 12-13: *Multiple Choice Question*

The nurse and the patient talk about the patient's hospital stay and look back and discuss the events. The phase that the relationship is in would be the:

A. Preinteraction—NO

B. Orientation—NO

C. Working—NO

D. **Termination—YES, reminiscing about the relationship is part of termination**

Exercise 12-14: *Multiple Choice Question*

The patient is telling the nurse that he is misinterpreting his preference for pain medication. The relationship phase that the nurse and patient are in is the:

A. Preinteraction—NO
B. Orientation—NO
C. **Working—YES, this is when the nurse and the patient work toward the goals together**
D. Termination—NO

Exercise 12-15: *Matching*

Match the word in column A to the descriptor in column B.

Column A		Column B
A. Courtesy	C	The nurse covers the portable computer screen while in the room with visitors
B. Using correct names	E	The nurse lets the patient know he or she is comfortable doing the procedure
C. Privacy	G	The nurse chooses the option for the patient
D. Trust	A	The nurse knocks on the door before entering the patient's room
E. Responsibility	B	The nurse tells the patient her name and role
F. Assertiveness	F	The nurse takes the initiative to call for stronger medication
G. Aggressiveness	D	The nurse returns at the set time that he or she indicated

Exercise 12-16: *Matching*

Match the therapeutic communication technique in column A to the description in column B.

Column A		Column B
A. Clarifying	D	Allowing time to continue what someone means
B. Paraphrasing	I	Reviewing main issue
C. Reflecting	E	Setting priorities
D. Silence	B	Restating
E. Structuring	G	Open-ended information gathering
F. Pinpointing	A	Following up to make sure you understand
G. Questioning	C	Letting the patient know you understand his or her feeling
H. Directing	H	Encouraging person to go on
I. Summarizing	F	Pointing out issues or inconsistencies

Exercise 12-17: *Multiple Choice Question*

The nurse asks the patient who is a victim of partner abuse if she loves her partner. This form of nontherapeutic communication is:

A. Asking for explanation—NO, this is asking the patient to expand on the same subject
B. Approving or disapproving—NO
C. Showing sympathy—NO
D. **Asking personal questions—YES, this is personal and not the priority when safety is the issue**

Exercise 12-18: *Multiple Choice Question*

The nurse tells the patient that she would not trust her toddler to a daycare. This form of nontherapeutic communication is:

A. Asking for explanation—NO
B. **Providing personal opinion—YES, it is not necessary to tell patients what you did or would do**
C. Automatic response—NO
D. Asking personal questions—NO

Exercise 12-19: *Multiple Choice Question*

The patient explains to the nurse the events leading up to the illness, and the nurse responds, "It is what it is." This form of nontherapeutic communication is:

A. **Automatic response—YES, this is an unnecessary automatic response and does not help**
B. Approving or disapproving—NO
C. Asking for an explanation—NO
D. Asking personal questions—NO

Exercise 12-20: *Multiple Choice Question*

The nurse responds to a patient who just said "I hate my mother" with "that is not right." This form of nontherapeutic communication is:

A. Showing sympathy—NO
B. Approving or disapproving—YES, this is disapproving of her feelings
C. Automatic response—NO
D. Asking personal questions—NO

Exercise 12-21: *Fill-in*

Place an E next to the statement that displays empathy and an S next to the statement that uses sympathy.

__**S**__ "I feel so sorry for you, you have had such a hard year"
__**E**__ "I can only imagine how hard it has been"
__**E**__ "I'm sure it is difficult to describe the feeling you had at the time"

S "You have been hit with your share more than anyone I know"

S "That happened to me once, and I got depressed too"

Exercise 12-22: *Select All That Apply*

Some of the communication techniques that can be used for a patient who has suffered speech impairment due to an illness are:

- ❑ Speak louder—NO, this is for hearing impaired
- ☒ **Use questions that can be answered "yes" or "no"—YES, this makes it easier for them**
- ❑ Do not encourage the patient to converse—NO, encourage them
- ☒ **Use a communication board—YES, this helps**
- ☒ **Let the patient know if he or she is understood—YES, this encourages them**

Exercise 12-23: *Multiple Choice Question*

The nurse is caring for an elderly patient with a hearing deficit. During a teaching session, the nurse should encourage:

A. The family to leave, so the patient receives the instructions directly—NO, the family can assist
B. Helping the patient by finishing his or her sentences—NO, give them time
C. Trying to anticipate their questions—NO, encourage them to ask questions
D. **Using short sentences and simple words—YES, this will increase understanding**

Exercise 12-24: *Fill-in*

What is a method that can be used to communicate with an unresponsive patient? **Touch**

Exercise 12-25: *Select All That Apply*

Select the communication techniques that assist intellectually disabled patients to understand:

- ❑ Speak loudly—NO, they are not hearing impaired
- ☒ **Use short sentences—YES, this will increase understanding**
- ☒ **Have family present—YES, this will help everyone to understand**
- ☒ **Give short explanations—YES, this is easier to comprehend**
- ❑ Do not worry about them doing other things during the communication—NO, try to gain their attention

13

Patient Education

Unfolding Case Study 12 ▒ Aubree, Alita, and Connor

Aubree, Alita, and Connor did well on the communication test and the practicum in the lab. They had to be videotaped with a standardized patient (SP) who was a live actor and use therapeutic communication to interact. During the simulation experience, they used their therapeutic communication to record a health history that they can use for the Physical Assessment Course. Now they are back in the classroom learning about patient teaching, and then they will have the opportunity to practice in the lab with each other.

Exercise 13-1: ***Multiple Choice Question***

Patient education is one of the most important nursing roles because the goal of it is to:

A. Establish a therapeutic nurse–patient relationship

B. Understand the needs of the patient

C. Advocate for the patient to other health professionals

D. Promote healthy behaviors

eResource 13-1: To provide the class with an introduction to the concept of patient teaching, the instructor provides the following reading assignments:

- A guide for nurses: Teaching health care effectively to patients by Lara Alspaugh: www.healthcareersjournal.com/a-guide-for-nurses-teaching-healthcare-effectively-to-patients
- The art of patient care: Patient teaching: www.art-of-patient-care.com/patient-teaching.html

The instructor explains to the class that the other functions of patient teaching are to help patients and families understand how to restore health and cope with impaired functioning.

The Answers section can be found on page 167.

Exercise 13-2: *Fill-in*

All the patient education content below is completed by nurses to promote, restore, or cope with health care issues. Place a "P" for those that promote, "R" for restore, and "C" for cope in front of the educational content. The nurse teaches the patient and family about:

- ________ Self-help devices
- ________ Exercise
- ________ Nutrition
- ________ Antibiotics
- ________ Rationale for treatments
- ________ Home care
- ________ Immunizations

The instructor explains that teaching and learning are interactive, and that patients need the ***motivation*** to learn. Motivation to learn can originate within the person ***(internal)*** because they want to stay well, get better, or live better or it can come from ***external*** factors such as "I want to see my daughter graduate college."

eResource 13-2: Connor's roommate tells him about the Center for Health Communications Research, which provides a wealth of information regarding the topic. [Pathway: http://chcr.umich.edu/index.php → select "How We Do It" → select "Health Behavior Theories" and "Tailoring".]

Exercise 13-3: *Multiple Choice Question*

The nurse understands that patient teaching is successful when:

A. It changes behavior
B. It is demonstrated back correctly once
C. It is evaluated by testing
D. The patient asks questions

The instructor tells the students that there are three domains of learning for humans whether they are students or patients.

Exercise 13-4: *Select All That Apply*

The three domains of learning are:

- ❑ Psychomotor
- ❑ Spiritual
- ❑ Cognitive
- ❑ Intellectual
- ❑ Affective

The instructor tells the students that they can verify that learning has taken place when teaching patients by understanding the behaviors that signify that the knowledge has been learned for each of the domains.

The Answers section can be found on page 167.

Exercise 13-5: *Fill-in*

Place a "C" for cognitive learning, an "A" for affective learning, or a "P" for psychomotor learning in front of the patient learning outcomes below:

_______ The patient tells the nurse that mobility is very important.
_______ The patient reorganizes his or her work space to increase safety
_______ The patient re-explains the procedure to the nurse
_______ The patient is content with the health care decision
_______ The patient explains how to apply the child safety rules at camp
_______ The patient demonstrates the dressing change to the nurse

eResource 13-3: To supplement their understanding of learning domains, Connor, Alita, and Aubree read the web resource Bloom's Taxonomy of Learning Domains—*The Three Types of Learning:* www.nwlink.com/~donclark/hrd/bloom.html

Connor asks a great question in class, "What factors need to be present in order for people to keep up their motivation?" The instructor tells them about the concept of ***adherence,*** which used to be termed ***compliance.*** It is theorized that people with ***self-efficacy***, or the people who have the perception of themselves as being able to succeed in a specific situation, will be more adherent than those who lack self-efficacy. Then Connor asks, "How can the nurse affect a person's self-efficacy, so the person succeeds in changing the behavior and sustaining the change?"

Exercise 13-6: *Multiple Choice Question*

Nurses can assist patients to increase their self-efficacy in health-promoting situation by:

A. Telling them they can do it
B. Showing them repeatedly how to do it
C. Telling them the consequences of not following through
D. Assisting them to master the experience

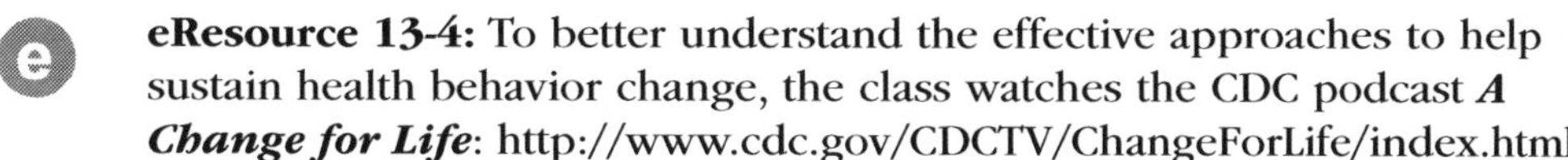

eResource 13-4: To better understand the effective approaches to help sustain health behavior change, the class watches the CDC podcast ***A Change for Life***: http://www.cdc.gov/CDCTV/ChangeForLife/index.html

The instructor tells the students that another consideration when teaching patients is not only their developmental stage, but also how they psychologically react to the illness diagnosis and what stage of diagnosis acceptance or rejection they are in.

Exercise 13-7: *Ordering*

Place the psychological adaptation to illness in order from one to five.

_______ Resolution
_______ Anger
_______ Disbelief

The Answers section can be found on page 167.

_______ Acceptance

_______ Bargaining

At this point in the class, the instructor asks the students to team up and to randomly pick a diagnosis from a hat that also has a psychological adaptation stage on the paper. One of the team members is the patient and acts out the stage, while the other two guess what stage the "patient" is in!

Exercise 13-8: *Fill-in*

The instructor understands that learning is best facilitated by ___________ rather than passive learning.

In the next class exercise the teacher has the student participate in providing a verbal case study to the entire class while music was playing on the computer and the lights were dimmed in the front of the room. The students started to raise their hands, and Alita asked, "Please turn off the music; it is difficult for me to hear."

Exercise 13-9: *Multiple Choice Question*

The class exercise demonstrates that an important variable to consider while educating patients is the:

A. Time of day
B. Subject
C. Environment
D. Nurse

The instructor tells the students that they have a written assignment of developing a teaching plan for a patient who has to learn how to turn a bedridden relative who is a hospice patient in their home.

Exercise 13-10: *Multiple Choice Question*

The first part of developing a teaching plan for a patient is to devise the:

A. Long-term goal
B. Intervention
C. Method
D. Learning outcome

Next the nurse must select the teaching method that will be used to convey the knowledge.

Exercise 13-11: *Multiple Choice Question*

The best method to teach a patient how to position a bedridden relative would be:

A. Simulation
B. One-on-one discussion
C. Using story telling
D. Group discussion

The instructor provides the class with another example.

The Answers section can be found on page 167.

Exercise 13-12: *Multiple Choice Question*

The best method to assist a patient to work through the grieving process from a loss that occurred 6 months ago is:

A. Simulation
B. Demonstration
C. Using story telling
D. Group discussion

A final example that the instructor provides helps the students to understand that their teaching plan is dependent on the subject to be taught and the patient situation.

eResource 13-5: Aubree performs a search on the Internet and locates the U.S. Department of Health and Human Services, Office of Disease Prevention and Health Promotion's: *Quick Guide to Health Literacy*, which offers considerable information, including information about effective teaching strategies: www.health.gov/communication/literacy/quickguide/healthinfo.htm

Exercise 13-13: *Multiple Choice Question*

The best method to teach a dressing change on an ambulatory patient's leg is:

A. Simulation
B. Demonstration
C. Using story telling
D. Group discussion

Exercise 13-14: *Matching*

Match the learning factor in column A with the descriptor in column B.

Column A	Column B
A. Developmental level	_______ Personal space
B. Language	_______ Organization and confidence
C. Culture	_______ Terminology
D. Previous experience	_______ Comfort and privacy
E. Physical environment	_______ Age and ability
F. Skill of instructor	_______ Familiarity

The instructor tells the students that more and more information is on the World Wide Web (WWW) and is therefore available to them and to the patients.

Exercise 13-15: *Select All That Apply*

The nurse understands that in order to use health information from the WWW in the teaching plan for a patient, consideration must be given to the:

❑ Source
❑ Font size
❑ Grade level of the writing
❑ Copyright issues

The Answers section can be found on page 167.

- ❑ Background color
- ❑ Biasness

Exercise 13-16: *Multiple Choice Question*

The nurse understands that when making written patient information, the reading difficulty should be at grade level:

A. 4 to 6
B. 6 to 8
C. 8 to 10
D. 10 to 12

eResource 13-6: The instructor provides additional information to the students so that they better understand the considerations associated with readability of health education material: www.healthcommunications.org

- *Improving Readability by Design*: www.slideboom.com/presentations/85901/Introduction
- *Key Terms and Definitions:* http://www.slideboom.com/presentations/85904/Key-Terms-and-Definitions
- *Design Elements and Scorecard:* www.slideboom.com/presentations/86246/Design-Elements-and-Scorecard
- *Fonts:* http://www.slideboom.com/presentations/165238/The-first-design-element%3A-font
- *Paragraphs:* www.slideboom.com/presentations/165262/The-second-design-element%3A-paragraphs
- *Line Length:* www.slideboom.com/presentations/169492/The-third-design-element%3A-line-length
- *Color:* www.slideboom.com/presentations/164835/The-sixth-design-element%3A-color

In addition, the instructor provides links to free readability calculators that can be used to assess reading level of educational materials: www.readabilityformulas.com/free-readability-calculators.php

Evaluating patient teaching is necessary because just because a nurse has a well-thought-out teaching plan and implements it without difficulty does not mean that learning has occurred. There needs to be a change in behavior and that is what is documented to ensure that the process of teaching–learning is complete.

Exercise 13-17: *Multiple Choice Question*

The nurse understands that further teaching is needed when the patient:

A. Does a return demonstration correctly
B. Asks questions about the information
C. Answers questions correctly
D. Self-reports the change

The Answers section can be found on page 167.

The students feel as if they understand the teaching–learning process between the nurse and the patient fairly well and can develop a teaching plan according to the grading rubric provided. They ask the instructor to also provide them with a few review questions to help validate the knowledge, so the instructor gives them three more examples.

Exercise 13-18: *Multiple Choice Question*

A patient is learning how to use crutches for the first time. This skill will require learning in which domain:

A. Cognitive
B. Affective
C. Global
D. Psychomotor

Exercise 13-19: *Multiple Choice Question*

The nurse is teaching a group of older adolescents the proper method to use a condom, using a banana. This is an example of:

A. Discovery
B. Analogy
C. Demonstration
D. Selling approach

Exercise 13-20: *Multiple Choice Question*

The nurse is teaching a postoperative young man who had weight control surgery about nutrition, and should:

A. Explain to him things to avoid eating
B. Teach him to calorie count
C. Complete a literature search about complications
D. Build on the knowledge that the patient has

The Answers section can be found on page 167.

Answers

Exercise 13-1: ***Multiple Choice Question***

Patient education is one of the most important nursing roles because the goal of it is to:

A. Establish a therapeutic nurse–patient relationship—NO, the relationship should be established before the teaching takes place

B. Understand the needs of the patient—NO, this should be completed in the assessment phase

C. Advocate for the patient to other health professionals—NO, this is a different patient intervention, although important

D. **Promote healthy behaviors—YES, this is the goal of patient education**

Exercise 13-2: ***Fill-in***

All the patient education content below is completed by nurses to promote, restore, or cope with health care issues. Place a "P" for those that promote, an "R" for restore, and a "C" for cope in front of the educational content. The nurse teaches the patient and family about:

__**C**__ Self-help devices

__**P**__ Exercise

__**P**__ Nutrition

__**R**__ Antibiotics

__**R**__ Rationale for treatments

__**C**__ Home care

__**P**__ Immunizations

Exercise 13-3: ***Multiple Choice Question***

The nurse understands that patient teaching is successful when:

A. **It changes behavior—YES, this is the goal to change the patient's health behavior**

B. It is demonstrated back correctly once—NO, the change must be sustained

C. It is evaluated by testing—NO, the test is one way to indicate it but not a long-term method

D. The patient asks questions—NO, this usually means further teaching is needed

Exercise 13-4: ***Select All That Apply***

The three domains of learning are:

☒ **Psychomotor**

❑ Spiritual

☒ **Cognitive**

❑ Intellectual

☒ **Affective**

Exercise 13-5: ***Fill-in***

Place a "C" for cognitive learning, an "A" for affective learning, or a "P" for psychomotor learning in front of the patient learning outcomes below:

A The patient tells the nurse that mobility is very important.

P The patient reorganizes his or her work space to increase safety

C The patient re-explains the procedure to the nurse

A The patient is content with the health care decision

C The patient explains how to apply the child safety rules at camp

P The patient demonstrates the dressing change to the nurse

Exercise 13-6: ***Multiple Choice Question***

Nurses can assist patients to increase their self-efficacy in health-promoting situation by:

A. Telling them they can do it—NO, this is only a temporary encouragement

B. Showing them repeatedly how to do it—NO, this is not helping them to build self-efficacy

C. Telling them the consequences of not following through—NO, this is not helping them to build self-efficacy

D. **Assisting them to master the experience—YES, this is the best way to increase self-efficacy**

Exercise 13-7: ***Ordering***

Place the psychological adaptation to illness in order from one to five.

4 Resolution

2 Anger

1 Disbelief

5 Acceptance

3 Bargaining

Exercise 13-8: ***Fill-in***

The instructor understands that learning is best facilitated by **active** rather than passive learning.

Exercise 13-9: *Multiple Choice Question*

The class exercise demonstrates that an important variable to consider while educating patients is the:

A. Time of day—NO, this is not what is demonstrated in the example although it can have an effect on patient teaching
B. Subject—NO, this is not what is demonstrated in the example although it can have an effect on patient teaching
C. **Environment—YES, the environment as well as privacy is very important**
D. Nurse—NO, this is not what is demonstrated in the example although it can have an effect on patient teaching

Exercise 13-10: *Multiple Choice Question*

The first part of developing a teaching plan for a patient is to devise the:

A. Long-term goal—NO
B. Intervention—NO
C. Method—NO
D. **Learning outcome—YES, what it is you would like the patient to learn**

Exercise 13-11: *Multiple Choice Question*

The best method to teach a patient how to position a bedridden relative would be:

A. **Simulation—YES, showing them on a manikin or simulated patient**
B. One-on-one discussion—NO
C. Using story telling—NO
D. Group discussion—NO

Exercise 13-12: *Multiple Choice Question*

The best method to assist a patient to work through the grieving process from a loss that occurred 6 months ago is:

A. Simulation—NO
B. Demonstration—NO
C. Using story telling—NO
D. **Group discussion—YES, group discussion is effective for affective learning**

Exercise 13-13: *Multiple Choice Question*

The best method to teach a dressing change on an ambulatory patient's leg is:

A. Simulation—NO
B. **Demonstration—YES, this is most effective because the patient can see the psychomotor learning**
C. Using story telling—NO
D. Group discussion—NO

Exercise 13-14: *Matching*

Match the learning factor in column A with the descriptor in column B.

Column A	Column B
A. Developmental level	**C** Personal space
B. Language	**F** Organization and confidence
C. Culture	**B** Terminology
D. Previous experience	**E** Comfort and privacy
E. Physical environment	**A** Age and ability
F. Skill of instructor	**D** Familiarity

Exercise 13-15: *Select All That Apply*

The nurse understands that in order to use health information from the WWW in the teaching plan for a patient consideration must be given to the:

☒ **Source**

☒ **Font size**

☒ **Grade level of the writing**

☒ **Copyright issues**

☒ **Background color**

☒ **Biasness**

Exercise 13-16: *Multiple Choice Question*

The nurse understands that when making written patient information, the reading difficulty should be at grade level:

A. **4 to 6—YES, health literature should not be above a sixth grade level**
B. 6 to 8—NO, too high for many Americans
C. 8 to 10—NO, too high for many Americans
D. 10 to 12—NO, too high for many Americans

Exercise 13-17: *Multiple Choice Question*

The nurse understands that further teaching is needed when the patient:

A. Does a return demonstration correctly—NO, this shows that learning has occurred
B. **Asks questions about the information—YES, this indicates that more information is needed by the receiver**
C. Answers questions correctly—NO, this shows that learning has occurred
D. Self-reports the change—NO, this shows that learning has occurred

Exercise 13-18: *Multiple Choice Question*

A patient is learning how to use crutches for the first time. This skill will require learning in which domain:

A. Cognitive—NO
B. Affective—NO

C. Global—NO
D. **Psychomotor—YES**

Exercise 13-19: *Multiple Choice Question*
The nurse is teaching a group of older adolescents the proper method to use a condom, using a banana. This is an example of:
A. Discovery—NO
B. Analogy—NO
C. **Demonstration—YES**
D. Selling approach—NO

Exercise 13-20: *Multiple Choice Question*
The nurse is teaching a postoperative young man who had weight control surgery about nutrition, and should:
A. Explain to him things to avoid eating—NO, this will not be most effective since he probably knows this from multiple attempts at weight loss
B. Teach him to calorie count—NO, this will not be most effective since he probably knows this from multiple attempts at weight loss
C. Complete a literature search about complications—NO, this is all anticipatory and may not be relevant to him
D. **Build on the knowledge that the patient has—YES, this is the first step, to see what he currently knows**

14

Documentation

Unfolding Case Study 13 Aubree, Alita, and Connor

Now that the fundamental students have some of the theory about nursing behind them, it is time for them to learn how to document what they do for patients.

Exercise 14-1: ***Multiple Choice Question***

All of the following reasons are important for accurate documentation except:

A. Track patient care outcomes
B. Assists the hospital or health care institution with accreditation
C. Serves to justify what nurses do
D. Used for health insurance reimbursement

The instructor explains that the medical record of a patient is a multidisciplinary communication tool. All caregivers use it and protect the confidentiality of it.

Exercise 14-2: ***Select All That Apply***

The following pieces are usually standard parts of a patient's medical record (MR):

- ❑ Demographic page
- ❑ Informed consent
- ❑ Nursing admitting history
- ❑ Incident reports
- ❑ Physician orders
- ❑ Medication record
- ❑ Mediation reconciliation
- ❑ Nurses or interdisciplinary care notes

The Answers section can be found on page 181.

eResource 14-1: To learn more about nursing documentation, Alita reviews:

- South Carolina Department of Health and Human Services' Guidelines: www.ddsn.sc.gov/providers/manualsandguidelines/Documents/HealthCareGuidelines/NursingDocumentation.pdf
- A presentation on nursing considerations related to documentation: www.slideshare.net/cslonern/documentation-4617068

Alita is overwhelmed and asks the instructor, "How will I ever be able to know all the parts of the MR and what is important?" The instructor ensures her that it will happen, and the learning curve starts in fundamentals when the students "look up" their patient information. The other functions of documenting or what many nurses call "charting" have to do with research, legal, and educational functions. Often MRs are used to collect research data for investigational studies. They are also reviewed by lawyers if there happens to be a legal issue. The education that is done for a patient is also documented in the MR. Understanding the basics of documenting makes the process easy. There are some well-established rules.

eResource 14-2: To help the class better understand their responsibilities, the instructor:

- Shows the class a video *Documentation: Avoiding the Pitfalls* in which a lawyer discusses the importance of proper documentation: www.youtu.be/yeFr66flhXg
- Gives the class an article to read: *Nursing Documentation: Let's Get Back to Basics*: http://www.proassurance.com/pdfindex/tmp/KeyCon_2008_Q4.pdf?d=20120325070936
- *Do's and Don'ts of Documentation:* www.nso.com/nursing-resources/article/24.jsp
- *Eight Common Charting Mistakes to Avoid:* http://www.nso.com/nursing-resources/article/16.jsp

Exercise 14-3: *Select All That Apply*

Select the following guidelines that assist if the MR is used for legal purposes:

- ☐ If you make an error in documenting, erase it
- ☐ Do not write retaliatory comments
- ☐ Document facts
- ☐ You can correct errors the next day
- ☐ Leave a space before your name
- ☐ If handwritten, use blue ink
- ☐ If computerized, protect your password
- ☐ Document for your unlicensed assistive personnel (UAP)
- ☐ Start each entry with the time and date

The Answers section can be found on page 181.

Alita tells the instructor that when she went into the hospital she read her patient's chart and saw that some nurses used terms such as "appears asleep." The instructor tells the class they should only chart factual information they can support objectively not subjectively.

Exercise 14-4: *Multiple Choice Question*

The nurse finds the patients wandering in the hall and trying to find his room. The best documentation would be:

A. Patient confused
B. Patient in hall unable to locate room
C. Patient appears disoriented
D. Patient seems out of touch with reality

Alita said she also saw WNL on her patient's chart and did not know what it was. The instructor tells her that WNL means ***Within Normal Limits*** and some charting systems use this term because those normal limits are defined in that system. But for most systems, WNL is not acceptable, and the instructor laughs and tells the class when she was a student she was taught that WNL meant "We Never Looked." Alita groans, "There are different charting systems?" "Yes, but although there are many variations, there are only a few ways to organize documents." The instructor also tells the class that there are other commonly used abbreviations used in clinical documentation, and that each organization typically has a list of approved abbreviations; however, more and more, there is a shift toward a universal list to minimize the risk of error and improve patient safety. The instructor goes on to say that no matter which abbreviations are approved at any organization, there is a list of abbreviations that should *never* be used due to high risk of misinterpretation.

eResource 14-3: The instructor provides the class with two important resources that provide updated lists of Error-Prone Abbreviations to health care professionals:

- Institute for Safe Medication Practice: www.ismp.org/Tools/errorproneabbreviations.pdf
- The Joint Commission: http://www.jointcommission.org/assets/1/18/Do_Not_Use_List.pdf

Exercise 14-5: *Matching*

Match the type of charting system in column A to the description in column B.

Column A		Column B
A. Problem-orientated medical record	_______	It has defined norms in the system
B. Narrative	_______	Organized so each discipline has a separate section
C. Source records	_______	Data in the record is organized by patient needs
D. Charting by exception	_______	Traditional method of recording each event

The Answers section can be found on page 181.

The instructor tells the students that nurses often write ***progress notes.*** Over the years, people have created acronyms for ways to chart the pertinent patient information. One of them is ***SOAP*** or ***SOAPIE,*** and often it is used by nurses who still narrative note or advanced practice RNs (APRNs).

- S = Subjective
- O = Objective
- A = Assessment
- P = Plan
- I = Interventions
- E = Evaluations

Another charting acronym is ***PIE***.

- P = Problem
- I = Intervention
- E = Evaluation

A third is ***DARP***.

- D = Data
- A = Action
- R = Response
- P = Plan

Many of these progress note methods of documenting patient care will no longer be used in the near future in larger health care systems. The move toward electronic medical records (EMRs) will make them obsolete and make checklist type of charting more common.

eResource 14-4: To learn more about nursing documentation, the class views episode no. 182 of "*The Nursing Show*" hosted by Jamie Davis: www.nursingshow.com/?powerpress_pinw=4522-studio_video

Exercise 14-6: *Multiple Choice Question*

The nurse encounters a patient situation that was unusual but not a safety risk, and it is not covered in the EMR checklist. The nurse should:

A. Not document it
B. Document it on an incident report
C. Call the supervisor
D. Write it in the narrative note space in the system

The instructor tells the class that flow sheets either paper or electronic are used for routinely done interventions such as vital signs.

Exercise 14-7: *Multiple Choice Question*

The nurse understands that flow sheets are charts that are used because:

A. All personnel can write or record on them
B. They easily show trends

The Answers section can be found on page 181.

C. Large narrative notes or checklists do not have to be used
D. They are not part of the permanent patient MR

Aubree raises her hand and asks where the nursing care plans go in the MR. The instructor tells her that many places use standardized care plans, and often they are part of the EMR.

Exercise 14-8: *Multiple Choice Question*
Standardized care plans are used because:
A. All patients will receive the same care
B. Nurses will not have to make them
C. Decrease variation in the nursing workload
D. They are a starting point and can be individualized

Aubree also tells the class that she saw nurses using a ***Kardex*** when they were giving report. She asks if the Kardex is kept with the MR, and the instructor tells her that it is not.

Exercise 14-9: *True/False*
The Kardex is a legal document.
❑ True
❑ False

Reporting off from one shift to another is very interesting to the students since they have observed this being done in their clinical rotations. Change of shift reports are done a number of ways and sometimes include room-to-room ***walking rounds***.

Exercise 14-10: *Multiple Choice Question*
The nurse understands that caution is needed for walking rounds because:
A. It is easy to confuse patients
B. It is easy to violate HIPAA
C. Patient rooms are far apart
D. The other end of the unit is unattended

The instructor tells the class there are other instances where patient reports are communicated among nursing staff or interprofessionally. ***Huddles*** are done during a shift to bring all the staff together briefly in order to identify important patient issues on the unit. Huddles usually take no more than 10 minutes out of the work day.

Exercise 14-11: *Multiple Choice Question*
The nurse understands that the priority topic for a huddle would be:
A. Open beds
B. Critical lab reports
C. Procedure or operating room (OR) schedules
D. Safety issues

The Answers section can be found on page 181.

eResource 14-5: To demonstrate the information that is needed for a nursing report, the instructor provides the class with a *Nurse Report Sheet* template: www.northcountryhospital.org/docs/4-Nursing_Report_V1_1.pdf

Another reporting tool is a ***handoff***. A handoff is usually done interdepartmentally. If a patient is being transported to another department for a different type of nursing cares or procedures, a handoff can be used. It is a short report that cuts to the main issue but provides enough information for the receiving person to care for them. Many institutions have handoff forms that have prefilled clues, so the nurse can fill in the important data. In addition, another common reporting method used by nurses is ***SBAR***:

- S = Situation
- B = Background
- A = Assessment
- R = Recommendation

SBAR is usually used for a single event that needs resolution. If a nurse needs to call another department or a primary care provider for orders, SBAR is the method of choice. This provides the other person with a snapshot of the issue and YOUR recommendation. Your recommendation is important because you are the nurse there and have a "bird's eye view" of what is taking place. Often the result of the SBAR will be a telephone order from the physician.

eResource 14-6: For a comprehensive review of SBAR and Huddles and to see additional examples of charting, Aubree reads *A Guide For Collaborative Structured Communication:* www.health.gov.bc.ca/library/publications/year/2010/LPNGuide_collaborative_structured_communication.pdf

Exercise 14-12: *Select All That Apply*

Proper recording of a telephone order from a physician includes:

- ❑ Delegating the call to a licensed practical nurse (LPN)
- ❑ Recording the time and date the order was received, not the time and date of the call
- ❑ Only used in an emergency situation
- ❑ Must be physically signed by the physician within 72 hours
- ❑ When obtained, the nurse cannot write it in the physician order section of the MR
- ❑ The nurse must repeat it back for clarification

Alita raises her hand and asks what if the patient's condition is declining, what communication method should we use? The instructor takes a deep breath and says "actually if the patient's condition is declining use the ***Rapid Response Team (RRT)***!" All the students groan, what is that? The RRT is a method for nurses, and in many

The Answers section can be found on page 181.

institutions, families to "pull the panic button" so to speak to get help to them immediately. Before RRTs, nurses had to telephone the nursing supervisor, the physician, the repertory therapists, or the code team for assistance. RRTs are able to respond before the patient's condition deteriorates, and it is an emergency. RRTs are a safety net that helps to save lives.

eResource 14-7: To help the students better understand the decision-making process involved in initiating the RRT, the instructor provides a Rapid Response Team Algorithm: www.healthynh.com/fhc/quality/qualitydownloads/CMC-RapidResponseTeamAlgorithm.pdf

The students are overwhelmed to do all the different types of documenting and reporting. The instructor tells them to take out their clickers, and she will provide them with some questions for practice!

Exercise 14-13: *Multiple Choice Question*

A patient has discussed signing out AMA (Against Medical Advice) due to family issues that need attention at home. The nurse should document this with the following method:

A. SBAR
B. Kardex
C. DARP
D. RRT

Exercise 14-14: *Multiple Choice Question*

A patient's blood pressure has dropped dangerously low after taking her antihypertensive medication. The nurse should communicate this incident to the rest of the professional team with the following method:

A. SBAR
B. Kardex
C. DARP
D. RRT

Exercise 14-15: *Multiple Choice Question*

A patient's pain is not alleviated by the current medication at 3 a.m.; the nurse needs to call the physician for a stronger pain medication. The nurse should use the following method:

A. SBAR
B. Kardex
C. DARP
D. RRT

The Answers section can be found on page 181.

Exercise 14-16: *Multiple Choice Question*

A patient is going to the radiology department to confirm placement of a nasogastric (NG) tube. The nurse should report to the transfer team with the following method:

A. Walking round
B. Kardex
C. Huddle
D. Handoff

Exercise 14-17: *Multiple Choice Question*

A patient fell while trying to get to the bathroom. The nurse should report this occurrence to administration with the following method:

A. SBAR
B. Incident report
C. Huddle
D. Handoff

The students enjoyed questions using the clickers and feel more prepared for the next unit test.

eResource 14-8: To prepare for the test, the students also review a presentation about documentation: www.slideshare.net/Bates2ndQuarterLPN/nursing-skills-charting

The Answers section can be found on page 181.

Answers

Exercise 14-1: *Multiple Choice Question*

All of the following reasons are important for accurate documentation except:

A. Track patient care outcomes—NO, this is important

B. Assists the hospital or health care institution with accreditation—NO, this too is important for hospitals to maintain accreditation

C. **Serves to justify what nurses do—YES, this is not the reason; nurses' work is not usually quantified in this manner**

D. Used for health insurance reimbursement—NO, this is looked at on the MR

Exercise 14-2: *Select All That Apply*

The following pieces are usually standard parts of a patient's medical record (MR):

☒ **Demographic page**

☒ **Informed consent**

☒ **Nursing admitting history**

❑ Incident reports—NO, incident reports only go to risk management and are never mentioned on the chart. The incident is documented not that a report was made and sent to risk management

☒ **Physician orders**

☒ **Medication record**

☒ **Mediation reconciliation**

☒ **Nurses or interdisciplinary care notes**

Exercise 14-3: *Select All That Apply*

Select the following guidelines that assist if the MR is used for legal purposes:

❑ If you make an error documenting, erase it—NO, never erase

☒ **Do not write retaliatory comments**

☒ **Document facts**

❑ You can correct errors the next day—NO, put a single line through them and correct them that day

❑ Leave a space before your name—NO, never leave any space

❑ If handwritten, use blue ink—NO, use black; it copies better if the documentation needs copying for legal purposes

☒ **If computerized, protect your password**

☐ Document for your unlicensed assistive personnel (UAP)—NO, only document for yourself, never anyone else

☒ **Start each entry with the time and date**

Exercise 14-4: *Multiple Choice Question*

The nurse finds the patients wandering in the hall and trying to find his room. The best documentation would be:

A. Patient confused—NO, making a judgment
B. **Patient in hall unable to locate room—YES, this is exactly what is happening**
C. Patient appears disoriented—NO, making a judgment
D. Patient seems out of touch with reality—NO, making a judgment

Exercise 14-5: *Matching*

Match the type of charting system in column A to the description in column B.

Column A		Column B
A. Problem-orientated medical record	D	It has defined norms in the system
B. Narrative	C	Organized so each discipline has a separate section
C. Source records	A	Data in the record is organized by patient's needs
D. Charting by exception	B	Traditional method of recording each event

Exercise 14-6: *Multiple Choice Question*

The nurse encounters a patient situation that was unusual but not a safety risk, and it is not covered in the EMR checklist. The nurse should:

A. Not document it—NO, everything should be documented
B. Document it on an incident report—NO, it was not a risk so it does not have to go to risk management
C. Call the supervisor—NO, it is not a risk
D. **Write it in the narrative note space in the system—YES, this is the proper place to document something unusual**

Exercise 14-7: *Multiple Choice Question*

The nurse understands that flow sheets are charts that are used because:

A. All personnel can write or record on them—NO, this is true but not the reason for their existence
B. **They easily show trends—YES, it is easy to visually pick up trends on flow sheets**
C. Large narrative notes or checklists do not have to be used—NO, they are necessary
D. They are not part of the permanent patient MR—NO, they are placed in the MR when complete

Exercise 14-8: ***Multiple Choice Question***

Standardized care plans are used because:

A. All patients will receive the same care—NO, care plans should always be individualized

B. Nurses will not have to make them—NO, this is not the main reason

C. Decrease variation in the nursing workload—NO, this is not the reason

D. They are a starting point and can be individualized—YES, this helps nurses' workload

Exercise 14-9: ***True/False***

The Kardex is a legal document.

❑ True

☒ **False—It is just for reporting and keeping track of care; it is not a part of the permanent record**

Exercise 14-10: ***Multiple Choice Question***

The nurse understands that caution is needed for walking rounds because:

A. It is easy to confuse patients—NO, this is important but not the main concern

B. **It is easy to violate HIPAA—YES, reporting in the room or hallway means that extra precautions must be taken so the health information is not overheard by others**

C. Patient rooms are far apart—NO

D. The other end of the unit is unattended—NO

Exercise 14-11: ***Multiple Choice Question***

The nurse understands that the priority topic for a huddle would be:

A. Open beds—NO, this is not the main reason for this activity

B. Critical lab reports—NO, this is not the main reason for this activity

C. Procedure or operating room (OR) schedules—NO, this is not the main reason for this activity

D. **Safety issues—YES, it alerts all staff on a unit to safety issues such as patients who are fall risks**

Exercise 14-12: ***Select All That Apply***

Proper recording of a telephone order from a physician includes:

❑ Delegating the call to a licensed practical nurse (LPN)—NO, LPNs cannot take telephone orders

❑ Recording the time and date the order was received not the time and date of the call—NO, the time the call was made as well as the callback time is important

☒ **Only used in an emergency situation**

☐ Must be physically signed by the physician within 72 hours—NO, 24 hours

☐ When obtained, the nurse cannot write it in the physician order section of the MR—NO, that is where it should go, so it is sequenced with all the other orders

☒ **The nurse must repeat it back for clarification**

Exercise 14-13: *Multiple Choice Question*

A patient has discussed signing out AMA (Against Medical Advice) due to family issues that need attention at home. The nurse should document this with the following method:

A. SBAR—NO, not until you notify the physician
B. Kardex—NO, this is not the official place to document it
C. **DARP—YES, it should be in the progress notes**
D. RRT—NO

Exercise 14-14: *Multiple Choice Question*

A patient's blood pressure has dropped dangerously low after taking her antihypertensive medication. The nurse should communicate this incident to the rest of the professional team with the following method:

A. SBAR—NO, this will take too much time
B. Kardex—NO, this is for shift report
C. DARP—NO, this is for later to document in narrative format
D. **RRT—YES, get help now**

Exercise 14-15: *Multiple Choice Question*

A patient's pain is not alleviated by the current medication at 3 a.m.; The nurse needs to call the physician for a stronger pain emaciation. The nurse should use the following method:

A. **SBAR—YES, this is a great reporting system for telephone orders**
B. Kardex—NO, this is for the end of the shift
C. DARP—NO, this is done after the care in the narrative notes
D. RRT—NO, this is not an emergency

Exercise 14-16: *Multiple Choice Question*

A patient is going to the radiology department to confirm placement of a nasogastric (NG) tube. The nurse should report to the transfer team with the following method:

A. Walking round—NO, this is for end of the shift report
B. Kardex—NO, this is to pass the information on to the next shift
C. Huddle—NO, this involves everyone on the unit
D. **Hand-off—YES, this is used for interdepartmental communication**

Exercise 14-17: *Multiple Choice Question*

A patient fell while trying to get to the bathroom. The nurse should report this occurrence to administration with the following method:

A. SBAR—NO, this is usually to receive orders

B. **Incident report—YES, this is the method to report an incident to administration and risk management**

C. Huddle—NO, this is for all staff on the unit

D. Handoff—NO, this is for patients leaving the unit

15

Patient Psychosocial Concepts

Unfolding Case Study 14 Aubree, Alita, and Connor

Connor is apprehensive about this unit of fundamentals that is about to be presented. He is envisioning abstract concepts that are difficult to understand. The instructor reassures the class that she will break it down into chunks, so they can "wrap their heads around the concepts." The instructor begins by explaining that when individuals seek health care, they present with psychosocial history that affects the way they deal with health and illness. These include many things, but a few of the important ones are:

- Self-concept
- Sexuality
- Spirituality
- Coping
- Grief reaction

Self-concept is closely related to self-esteem, and these are developed from childhood to adulthood.

Exercise 15-1: ***Select All That Apply***

Select all the variables that may contribute to a positive self-concept:

- ❑ Job satisfaction
- ❑ Chronic illness
- ❑ Good appearance
- ❑ Competency
- ❑ Physical changes of aging
- ❑ Being culturally different
- ❑ Unrealistic expectations
- ❑ Spiritual identity

The Answers section can be found on page 199.

Exercise 15-2: *Multiple Choice Question*

The nurse is aware that adolescence's self-identity may be negative when the patient:

A. Talks about going to college
B. Finds a part-time job
C. Volunteers at church
D. Joins a street gang

Many components contribute to a person's identity, such as culture, body image, and role performance. Connor gets it now! Even in nursing school, students have identities within the group, such as smartest and best clinically prepared.

Exercise 15-3: *Fill-in*

An individual's overall sense of self-worth is called their self-________________.

There are many life circumstances that can alter a person's identity, the class is asked to discuss and name a few. Some of the ones that they come up with are:

- Role confusion
- Body image stress
- Overload
- Role performance

Then the fundamental students in the class realize that all these stressors can be produced by illness, and they understand the nurse's role in maintaining the patient's self-identity.

Exercise 15-4: *Multiple Choice Question*

The nurse understands that the initial step in preserving a patient's self-esteem is:

A. Introducing her- or himself properly
B. Understanding the patient's health care concerns
C. Self-reflecting on his or her feelings about health and illness
D. Being aware of his or her nonverbal communication

eResource 15-1: The instructor shows the class a short video, which depicts a *Medical Interview—Social History*: www.youtu.be/luNHxkuaYGc

One of the components of self-identity in humans is sexuality, and the class needs to understand how this element affects patients who are sick. Sexual identity occurs in infancy and in today's environment, it actually happens often in utero because people find out if they are having a boy or girl. Children are treated differently according to their gender and therefore grow up with a sexual identity.

The Answers section can be found on page 199.

Exercise 15-5: *Multiple Choice Question*

The nurse caring for a school-age child is asked by the child about sex and love. The nurse answers the child:

A. By providing written material
B. With factual information
C. By telling the child to ask a parent
D. By trying to find out why the child is asking

Exercise 15-6: *Multiple Choice Question*

The nurse is caring for an adolescent child who asks about sex and love; one of the most prominent needs of adolescents is for:

A. Prenatal care information
B. Sexually transmitted diseases and birth control
C. All about different sexual orientations
D. Embryology and organogenesis

Exercise 15-7: *Multiple Choice Question*

The nurse understands that female geriatric patients have a decline in sexual activity related to:

A. Lack of interest and time
B. Poor physical and psychological health
C. Fear of disease and injury
D. Increased widowhood and divorce

The class talks about the health of lesbian, gay, bisexual, and transgender (LGBT) people. They are marginalized groups and do not always have access to appropriate health care.

Exercise 15-8: *Select All That Apply*

LGBT youth have higher incidence of the following:

- ❑ Homelessness
- ❑ Abuse
- ❑ HIV and AIDS
- ❑ Anorexia
- ❑ Suicide

e **eResource 15-2:** To expand upon the health needs of LGBT people, the instructor shows the class a video describing the health care challenges and concerns that gay and bisexual men experience: www.youtu.be/x024AUwrCCo

The instructor points out to students that a subpopulation of concern is LGBT youth because they are vulnerable due to their age as well as their sexual orientation. Societal attitudes toward LGBT people put youth who are LGBT at increased risk for experiences with violence than their heterosexual counterparts.

The Answers section can be found on page 199.

eResource 15-3: The class explores several U.S. Government websites devoted to assisting this vulnerable population:

- Facts about LGBT: www.hhs.gov/ash/oah/resources-and-publications/info/parents/just-facts/lgbtq-youth.html
- Strategies to prevent and address bullying of LGBT youth: www.stopbullying.gov/at-risk/groups/lgbt/index.html
- Resources for LGBT youth: www.cdc.gov/lgbthealth/youth-resources.htm

STD (sexually transmitted disease) is a large concern for both LGBT and straight couples.

Exercise 15-9: *Multiple Choice Question*

The most common STD is:

A. Chlamydia
B. Gonorrhea
C. Syphilis
D. Herpes

eResource 15-4: Connor does a quick search on the Internet for information about STDs and finds the Centers for Disease Control and Prevention (CDC) website, which offers current information about STDs, incidence, and treatment guidelines: www.cdc.gov/std/

Connor and his classmates decide to make this link a favorite on their smartphones.

Exercise 15-10: *Multiple Choice Question*

The age group with the highest STDs is:

A. 13- to 14-year-olds
B. 15- to 24-year-olds
C. 25- to 29-year-olds
D. 30- to 35-year-olds

Connor and his classmates know they will learn more about STDs in the women's health course but for now they are interested in learning the basics, so they care for people in the clinical area and answer questions if they come up. Another topic comes up, contraception. The instructor briefly reviews contraception.

Exercise 15-11: *Matching*

Match the type of contraception in column A to its description in column B.

Column A		Column B
A. Male condom	______	Implanted under the skin and lasts 3 years
B. Depo-provera®	______	Refrain from sex during fertile period
C. Implanon	______	Polyurethane sheath placed into vagina to block sperm
D. ParaGard IUD	______	Injectable progesterone given every 12 weeks

The Answers section can be found on page 199.

Column A		Column B
E. Mirena IUD	______	T-shaped device that is inserted into the uterus that lasts 10 years and releases copper
F. Fertility awareness	______	Fallopian tubes are blocked
G. Female surgical sterilization	______	Vas deferens are cut surgically
H. Ortho Erva patch	______	Monthly injections of progesterone and estrogen
I. Female condom	______	Transdermal patch that releases estrogen and progesterone into the circulation
J. Sponge	______	Pills that suppress ovulation; can be progesterone only or estrogen and progesterone
K. Postcoital emergency	______	Disk-shaped contraceptive device that covers the cervix, was temporarily taken off the market but is now available OTC (over the counter)
L. Oral contraceptives	______	A plastic ring with estrogen and progesterone that is inserted into the vagina for 3 weeks each month
M. NuvaRing®	______	Progestin-only pills taken within 72 hours of unprotected intercourse
N. Cervical cap	______	A sheath placed over the penis to block sperm
O. Diaphragm	______	Shallow latex cup that has to be fitted to each woman, so the rim fits well into the vagina
P. Lunelle injectable	______	T-shaped device inserted into the uterus; lasts 5 years and releases synthetic progesterone
Q. Male sterilization	______	Latex device that just covers the cervix

Exercise 15-12: *Multiple Choice Question*

The best contraceptive protection against HIV is:

A. Diaphragm
B. Cervical cap
C. Condom
D. IUD

eResource 15-5: To supplement the information provided about contraception, the students read information provided by the CDC on *Unintended Pregnancy Prevention: Contraception:* www.cdc.gov/reproductivehealth/UnintendedPregnancy/Contraception.htm

Other issues that Connor and his classmates discuss revolve around the endless commercial that is now out for medication for sexual dysfunction. The instructor explains that both men and women can experience sexual dysfunction, and it is actually very

The Answers section can be found on page 199.

common. Establishing a trusting relationship with the patient will allow you to elicit information that you will need to assess sexual function. Assessing sexual function is difficult because it is such a sensitive issue for many patients. Another sensitive issue is spirituality, and one that is important to many patients when their health is threatened. There is a relationship between health and spirituality. ***Spiritual well-being*** exists when there is harmony between a person's state of being and a unifying purpose or belief. It is important to note that there does not always exist a supreme being for all people.

Exercise 15-13: *Multiple Choice Question*

The nurse is assessing a patient who has just arrived and understands that when the patient states, "I believe that is up to me and each of us to live correctly because we do not know what happens after we die," that the patient is probably:

A. Atheist
B. Agnostic
C. Jewish
D. Christian

Conner, Aubree, and Alita listen intently to the instructor because they understand that this realm of nursing care is filled with abstract concepts, but they want to know how to care for people not only physically and psychologically, but also spiritually.

Exercise 15-14: *Matching*

Match the concept in column A to the definition in column B.

Column A		Column B
A. Faith	_______	A concept that provides comfort in threatening situations
B. Transcendence	_______	A person trying to connect with something for meaning in life
C. Hope	_______	A relationship that involves a higher power without proof
D. Religion	_______	Using activities to connect the mind and body
E. Coherence	_______	Understanding that there is more in life than what can be seen
F. Individuation	_______	A system of practices associated with worshiping

Alita understands that ***spiritual distress*** occurs when people's faith is disrupted. The class names things that commonly place people in spiritual distress, such as:

- Acute illness
- Near death experiences
- Terminal illness
- Chronic illness

The Answers section can be found on page 199.

Exercise 15-15: ***Select All That Apply***

Nursing interventions that assist patients with spiritual distress include:

- ❑ Presence
- ❑ Therapeutic communication
- ❑ Tell patient about your own experiences
- ❑ Encourage the patient to journal
- ❑ Encourage the patient to describe support systems

Aubree, Alita, and Connor understand that they will be dealing with people who are experiencing a loss and are grieving. There are many types of losses patients may experience, all of which are significant to the patient.

Exercise 15-16: ***Matching***

Match the type of loss in column A to the description in column B.

	Column A	Column B
A.	Necessary losses	_______ A loss due to natural development in life
B.	Actual losses	_______ A loss that is expected and cannot be prevented
C.	Perceived losses	_______ An unexpected loss due to an event
D.	Maturational losses	_______ A loss that is internal to the patient
E.	Situational losses	_______ A loss of person or object that cannot be recovered

e **eResource 15-6:** To highlight the importance of the nursing role for people who are experiencing loss and grieving, the instructor shows the class a video depicting one patient's positive experience with health care professionals: www.youtu.be/K7PO8a-N0zU

The human reaction to loss is a significant health care concern for nurses. The reaction is labeled ***grief,*** and the internal process of the person feeling the grief that includes mourning is called ***bereavement***. Theorists have described stages and phases of the grief process that humans go through, and these assist nurses to recognize the reactions and provide the appropriate care to patients.

Exercise 15-17: ***Ordering***

Order (1 to 5) the stages of grief described by Dr. Kübler-Ross (1969).

_______ Depression
_______ Anger
_______ Denial
_______ Acceptance
_______ Bargaining

Patients work through these stages at different rates and in different intensities.

The Answers section can be found on page 199.

eResource 15-7: To help clarify this, the instructor shows a video describing the Köbler-Ross' stages of grief: www.youtu.be/x39p3x0chYU

Once the acute grief is over, many people face the long task of mourning. Another theorist, Worden (1982), helps nurses to understand the tasks that relate to mourning:

- Accept the reality of the loss
- Work through the grief and pain
- Adjust to the environment from which the deceased person is missing
- Emotionally relocate the deceased and move on with life

Aubree asks the instructor if everyone goes through these stages progressively. The instructor tells Aubree that grief expression can be different for different people, and sometimes can be considered "out of the norm" and then describes the types of grief that nurses may encounter patients experiencing.

Exercise 15-18: ***Matching***

Match the type of grief pattern in column A to its description in column B.

Column A	Column B
A. Anticipatory grief	_______ Displacing the grief to another area in life
B. Complicated grief	_______ Mourning over a long period
C. Chronic grief	_______ Cannot openly acknowledge or show grief
D. Delayed grief	_______ Not progressing through the normal stages of grief
E. Exaggerated grief	_______ Process of letting go before the death
F. Masked grief	_______ Active grieving is held back and resurfaces later
G. Disenfranchised grief	_______ Overwhelmed by the grief and nonfunctional

The way individual patients react to loss and display the grieving process is dependent on many factors including their:

- Developmental phase
- Spiritual beliefs
- Socioeconomic status
- Nature of the loss to them
- Psychological perspectives
- Relationships with others
- Culture and ethnicity

Exercise 15-19: ***True/False***

Nurses themselves also experience grief related to patient care.

- ❑ True
- ❑ False

Connor asks, "What can nurses do if their patient is grieving?"

The Answers section can be found on page 199.

Exercise 15-20: *Select All That Apply*

The nursing interventions appropriate to a grieving patient are:

- ❑ Using therapeutic communication
- ❑ Facilitating mourning
- ❑ Determining patient's perception of loss
- ❑ Concentrating on patient and not family
- ❑ Discussing healthy ways of dealing with grief
- ❑ Telling patient how long each phase should last

Alita makes a comment in class that talking about grief and imagining caring for patients who are experiencing a loss sounds ***stressful***. The instructor acknowledges that it is and says that stress is both a physiological and a psychological response that is normal but can be detrimental if uncontrolled. At that point in class, the building's fire alarm sounds!

Exercise 15-21: *Multiple Choice Question*

The first physiological reaction to an emergency situation in a fight-or-flight mode diverts blood to:

A. Musculoskeletal system
B. Gastrointestinal tract
C. Genital urinary system
D. Immunological system

Exercise 15-22: *Multiple Choice Question*

The fight-or-flight response in humans is regulated by the following mechanisms:

A. Hypothalamus, cortex, spinal cord
B. Medulla oblongata, reticular system, hypothalamus
C. Reticular system, cortex, spinal cord
D. Medulla oblongata, pituitary gland, reticular system

Exercise 15-23: *Ordering*

Place the stages of the general adaptation syndrome reaction to stress in order from 1 to 3:

_______ Resistance stage
_______ Exhaustion stage
_______ Alarm stage

Exercise 15-24: *Fill-in*

During a fight-or-flight reaction, the hypothalamus excretes ___________________.

The students filter out of the classroom to the outside of the building for the fire drill, and the instructor asks them to take their pulse. They all agree that their hearts are beating faster.

The Answers section can be found on page 199.

Exercise 15-25: *Fill-in*

The word for healthy motivating stress is called ________________.

After the building is checked by maintenance, the students are let back to their classroom. The instructor finishes the lesson on stress and describes a case study to exemplify ***post-traumatic stress disorder (PTSD).***

Classroom case study:

A young woman is an army nurse and is called to duty in a war zone. She witnesses a car bomb explosion in which several service man and women are killed or severely injured. After she is discharged, she returns home and displays at least three dissociative symptoms that consistent with the diagnosis for PTSD.

Exercise 15-26: *Select All That Apply*

Using the above case, select the dissociated symptoms that are correlated with PTSD; the discharged veteran:

- ❑ Avoids looking at her army gear
- ❑ Shows symptoms immediately after the trauma only
- ❑ Has decreased arousal to life stimuli
- ❑ Experiences flashbacks

eResource 15-8: To better understand PTSD, Alita, Aubree, and Connor do some additional research on the topic. They find several very informative materials:

- Overview of PTSD by Dr. Ram Randhawa, Director of the Anxiety Clinic at the University of British Columbia: www.youtu.be/lpZk4woJ8g0
- Patient education presentation regarding PTSD: www.youtu.be/ZGWSSUNXn4A
- Post-Traumatic Stress Disorder (PTSD) Fact Sheet: www.report.nih.gov/NIHfactsheets/ViewFactSheet.aspx?csid=58&key=P#P

The instructor explains that for situations of PTSD, intensive therapy is needed. Alita asks the million dollar question, "What can nurses do for patients who are experiencing a more normal stress reaction to a situational or developmental health care crisis?"

Exercise 15-27: *Multiple Choice Question*

A patient has just told the nurse that he or she is experiencing chronic stress. The nurse understands that the patient needs further teaching when they state:

A. "I should talk to my sister about this because she is my best support system"
B. "I should not exercise because this will increase the stress"
C. "I should reflect in a journal to better understand my feelings"
D. "I should make a calendar to get my schedule under control"

The Answers section can be found on page 199.

Aubree asks the instructor if there are specific places for patients to go when experiencing acute stress. The instructor describes the functions of ***crisis intervention*** care.

Exercise 15-28: *Multiple Choice Question*

The nurse understands that by working in a crisis intervention center that the nurse will provide intervention that will:

A. Use spontaneous psychotherapy
B. Only refer the patient to long-term therapy
C. Provide shelter and food
D. Use prescribed brief psychotherapy

Aubree states, "How do nurses continually deal with patients and families who are in crises; do they not ***burn out***?" The instructor tells the class that there are things they can do to prevent burn out, such as exercise, understanding your scope at work, and making a clear separation between work and home.

eResource 15-9: To reinforce the concept of self-care to prevent burnout, the instructor provides the class with a few additional resources:

- Burnout Self-Test from MindTools.com: www.mindtools.com/stress/Brn/BurnoutSelfTest.htm
- Suggested approaches to avoid burnout: http://www.starcityblog.typepad.com/files/strategies-to-avoid-burnout.pdf

Exercise 15-29: *Multiple Choice Question*

The nurse understands that the following symptom is not associated with burnout:

A. Depersonalization of others
B. Emotional exhaustion
C. Increased perception of personal accomplishments
D. Intense involvement with patients

The students feel well prepared for the next unit test, which is on abstract concepts. They are starting to relate the concepts to people and situations they have known in their lives and are anxious to have the opportunity to recognize them in patients.

Reference

Kübler-Ross, E. (1969). *On death and dying*. New York, NY: Macmillan.

Worden, J. W. (1982). *Grief counseling and grief therapy: A handbook for the mental health practitioner.* New York, NY: Springer Publishing.

The Answers section can be found on page 199.

Answers

Exercise 15-1: *Select All That Apply*

Select all the variables that may contribute to a positive self-concept:

☒ **Job satisfaction**

❑ Chronic illness

☒ **Good appearance**

☒ **Competency**

❑ Physical changes of aging

❑ Being culturally different

❑ Unrealistic expectations

☒ **Spiritual identity**

Exercise 15-2: *Multiple Choice Question*

The nurse is aware that adolescence's self-identity may be negative when the patient:

A. Talks about going to college—NO, this is positive and future oriented
B. Finds a part-time job—NO, this is positive
C. Volunteers at church—NO, this is positive
D. **Joins a street gang—YES, this usually means they are looking to identify with something**

Exercise 15-3: *Fill-in*

An individual's overall sense of self-worth is called their __**self-esteem**__.

Exercise 15-4: *Multiple Choice Question*

The nurse understands that the initial step in preserving a patient's self-esteem is:

A. Introducing her- or himself properly—NO, this is important but not the initial step
B. Understanding the patient's health care concerns—NO, this is important but not the initial step
C. **Self-reflecting on his or her feelings about health and illness—YES, you need to do this first**
D. Be aware of his or her nonverbal communication—NO, this is important but not the initial step

Exercise 15-5: *Multiple Choice Question*

The nurse caring for a school-age child is asked by the child about sex and love. The nurse answers the child:

A. By providing written material—NO, this is not effective and is impersonal
B. **With factual information—YES, this is the best way to answer a school-age child**
C. By telling the child to ask a parent—NO, this is not effective and is impersonal
D. By trying to find out why the child is asking—NO, this is not effective and is impersonal

Exercise 15-6: *Multiple Choice Question*

The nurse is caring for an adolescent child who asks about sex and love; one of the most prominent needs of adolescents is for:

A. Prenatal care information—NO, this should not occur yet
B. **Sexually transmitted diseases and birth control—YES, this is very important**
C. All about different sexual orientations—NO, this is important but not the priority
D. Embryology and organogenesis—NO, this is not the priority

Exercise 15-7: *Multiple Choice Question*

The nurse understands that female geriatric patients have a decline in sexual activity related to:

A. Lack of interest and time—NO, this is not the reason
B. Poor physical and psychological health—NO, this is not the reason
C. Fear of disease and injury—NO, this is not the reason
D. **Increased widowhood and divorce—YES, this is often the reason**

Exercise 15-8: *Select All That Apply*

LGBT youth have higher incidence of the following:

☒ **Homelessness**

☒ **Abuse**

☒ **HIV and AIDS**

☐ Anorexia—NO, actually there is a higher incidence of obesity

☒ **Suicide**

Exercise 15-9: *Multiple Choice Question*

The most common STD is:

A. **Chlamydia—YES, this is the most common STD**
B. Gonorrhea—NO, but this is often a diagnosis with Chlamydia
C. Syphilis—NO, but this is on the rise
D. Herpes—NO, but this too is on the rise

Exercise 15-10: *Multiple Choice Question*

The age group with the highest STDs is:

A. 13- to 14-year-olds—NO, but STDs are on the rise in this age group

B. **15- to 24-year-olds—YES, this age group accounts for 50% of STDs**
C. 25- to 29-year-olds—NO
D. 30- to 35-year-olds—NO

Exercise 15-11: *Matching*

Match the type of contraception in column A to its description in column B.

Column A		Column B
A. Male condom	**C**	Implanted under the skin and lasts 3 years
B. Depo-provera®	**F**	Refrain from sex during fertile period
C. Implanon	**I**	Polyurethane sheath placed into vagina to block sperm
D. ParaGard IUD	**U**	Injectable progesterone given every 12 weeks
E. Mirena IUD	**D**	T-shaped device that is inserted into the uterus that lasts 10 years and releases copper
F. Fertility awareness	**G**	Fallopian tubes are blocked
G. Female surgical sterilization	**V**	Vas deferens are cut surgically
H. Ortho Erva patch	**B**	Monthly injections of progesterone and estrogen
I. Female condom	**H**	Transdermal patch that releases estrogen and progesterone into the circulation
J. Sponge	**L**	Pills that suppress ovulation; can be progesterone only or estrogen and progesterone
K. Postcoital emergency	**J**	Disk-shaped contraceptive device that covers the cervix, was temporarily taken off the market but is now available OTC (over the counter)
L. Oral contraceptives	**R**	A plastic ring with estrogen and progesterone that is inserted into the vagina for 3 weeks each month
R. NuvaRing®	**K**	Progestin-only pills taken within 72 hours of unprotected intercourse.
S. Cervical cap	**A**	A sheath placed over the penis to block sperm
T. Diaphragm	**T**	Shallow latex cup that has to be fitted to each women, so the rim fits well into the vagina
U. Lunelle injectable	**E**	T-shaped device inserted into the uterus lasts 5 years and releases synthetic progesterone
V. Male sterilization	**S**	Latex device that just covers the cervix

Exercise 15-12: *Multiple Choice Question*

The best contraceptive protection against HIV is:

A. Diaphragm—NO, vaginal mucous membranes are still exposed

B. Cervical cap—NO, vaginal mucous membranes are still exposed

C. Condom—YES, this is the best protective device to date

D. IUD—NO, vaginal and cervical tissue are still exposed

Exercise 15-13: *Multiple Choice Question*

The nurse is assessing a patient who has just arrived and understands that when the patient states, "I believe that is up to me and each of us to live correctly because we do not know what happens after we die," that the patient is probably:

A. Atheist—NO, they believe there is no afterlife

B. **Agnostic—YES, they believe you cannot prove that there is a higher being**

C. Jewish—NO, they believe there is an afterlife

D. Christian—NO, they believe there is an afterlife

Exercise 15-14: *Matching*

Match the concept in column A to the definition in column B.

Column A		Column B
A. Faith	**C**	A concept that provides comfort in threatening situations
B. Transcendence	**F**	A person trying to connect with something for meaning in life
C. Hope	**A**	A relationship that involves a higher power without proof
D. Religion	**E**	Using activities to connect the mind and body
E. Coherence	**B**	Understanding that there is more in life than what can be seen
F. Individuation	**D**	A system of practices associated with worshiping

Exercise 15-15: *Select All That Apply*

Nursing interventions that assist patients with spiritual distress include:

☒ **Presence**

☒ **Therapeutic communication**

☐ Tell patient about your own experiences—NO, this is usually not therapeutic and not respecting professional boundaries

☒ **Encourage the patient to journal**

☒ **Encourage patient to describe support systems**

Exercise 15-16: *Matching*

Match the type of loss in column A to the description in column B.

Column A		Column B
A. Necessary loses	D	A loss due to natural development in life
B. Actual losses	A	A loss that is expected and cannot be prevented
C. Perceived losses	E	An unexpected loss due to an event
D. Maturational losses	C	A loss that is internal to the patient
E. Situational losses	B	A loss of person or object that cannot be recovered

Exercise 15-17: *Ordering*

Order (1 to 5) the stages of grief described by Dr. Kübler-Ross (1969):

__4__ Depression
__3__ Anger
__1__ Denial
__5__ Acceptance
__2__ Bargaining

Exercise 15-18: *Matching*

Match the type of grief pattern in column A to its description in column B.

Column A		Column B
A. Anticipatory grief	G	Displacing the grief to another area in life
B. Complicated grief	C	Mourning over a long period
C. .Chronic grief	F	Cannot openly acknowledge or show grief
D. Delayed grief	B	Not progressing through the normal stages of grief
E. Exaggerated grief	A	Process of letting go before the death
F. Masked grief	D	Active grieving is held back and resurfaces later
G. Disenfranchised grief	E	Overwhelmed by the grief and nonfunctional

Exercise 15-19: *True/False*

Nurses themselves also experience grief related to patient care.

☒ **True**

❑ False

Exercise 15-20: *Select All That Apply*

The nursing interventions appropriate to a grieving patient are:

☒ **Using therapeutic communication**

☒ **Facilitating mourning**

☒ **Determining patient's perception of loss**

❑ Concentrating on patient and not family—NO, it is important to include the family

☒ **Discussing healthy ways of dealing with grief**

❑ Telling patient how long each phase should last—NO, because each patient will progress at their own rate

Exercise 15-21: ***Multiple Choice Question***

The first physiological reaction to an emergency situation in a fight-or-flight mode diverts blood to:

A. **Musculoskeletal system—YES, to increase flight**
B. Gastrointestinal tract—NO, blood is diverted away to heart, brain, and muscles
C. Genital urinary system—NO, blood is diverted away to heart, brain, and muscles
D. Immunological system—NO, blood is diverted away to heart, brain, and muscles

Exercise 15-22: ***Multiple Choice Question***

The fight-or-flight response in humans is regulated by the following mechanisms:

A. Hypothalamus, cortex, spinal cord—NO, the spinal cord reacts not regulates
B. Medulla oblongata, reticular system, hypothalamus—NO, the hypothalamus reacts
C. Reticular system, cortex, spinal cord—NO
D. **Medulla oblongata, pituitary gland, reticular system—YES**

Exercise 15-23: ***Ordering***

Place the stages of the general adaptation syndrome reaction to stress in order from 1 to 3:

__**2**__ Resistance stage
__**3**__ Exhaustion stage
__**1**__ Alarm stage

Exercise 15-24: ***Fill-in***

During a fight-or-flight reaction, the hypothalamus excretes __**endorphins**__.

Exercise 15-25: ***Fill-in***

The word for healthy motivating stress is called __**eustress**__.

Exercise 15-26: ***Select All That Apply***

Using the above case, select the dissociated symptoms that are correlated with PTSD; the discharged veteran:

☒ **Avoids looking at her army gear—YES, avoiding triggers of the memory**

❑ Shows symptoms immediately after the trauma only—NO, it is usually delayed weeks

❑ Has decreased arousal to life stimuli—NO, experiences hyperarousal

☒ **Experiences flashbacks—YES**

Exercise 15-27: *Multiple Choice Question*

A patient has just told the nurse that he or she is experiencing chronic stress. The nurse understands that the patient needs further teaching when they state:

A. "I should talk to my sister about this because she is my best support system."—NO, support system identification is important
B. **"I should not exercise because this will increase the stress."—YES, this is wrong, exercise decreases stress**
C. "I should reflect in a journal to better understand my feelings."—NO, this is a good intervention to decrease stress
D. "I should make a calendar to get my schedule under control."—NO, time management decreases stress

Exercise 15-28: *Multiple Choice Question*

The nurse understands that by working in a crisis intervention center that the nurse will provide intervention that will:

A. Use spontaneous psychotherapy—NO, this is a preplanned intervention
B. Only refer the patient to long-term therapy—NO, there needs to be an immediate intervention
C. Provide shelter and food—NO, these are just physiological interventions
D. **Use prescribed brief psychotherapy—YES, this is an immediate, proven interventions**

Exercise 15-29: *Multiple Choice Question*

The nurse understands that the following symptom is not associated with burnout:

A. Depersonalization of others—NO, this is associated
B. Emotional exhaustion—NO, this is associated
C. **Increased perception of personal accomplishments—YES, there is a decreased perception of personal accomplishments**
D. Intense involvement with patients—NO, this is associated

16

Vital Signs

Unfolding Case Study 15 Aubree, Alita, and Connor

Aubree, Alita, and Connor are going to the clinical area again. They are assigned to an extended care facility. They drive over to the facility the night before in their uniforms and introduce themselves to the staff and look up their patient information. They are responsible to resource the patient's diagnosis and provide comfort care and the collection of accurate vital signs (VS).

Exercise 16-1: ***Select All That Apply***

Accurate vital signs are needed in order for the nurse to:

- ❑ Assess physiological functioning
- ❑ Monitor the patient's condition
- ❑ Determine the safety of medication administration
- ❑ Assess spiritual health
- ❑ Determine appropriate nursing interventions

Exercise 16-2: ***Select All That Apply***

The techniques used to assess vital signs include:

- ❑ Observation
- ❑ Inspection
- ❑ Auscultation
- ❑ Light palpation
- ❑ Deep palpation

e **eResource 16-1:** The instructor provides supplemental materials to reinforce the students' understanding of vital signs: www.prohealthsys.com/physical/vital_signs.php

The Answers section can be found on page 217.

The class is provided additional videos to support their understanding of how to take patient vital signs:

- General video providing an overview on how to take vital signs: www.youtu.be/ZRhDMxWZ1Hc
- For a more detailed training video on how to take a blood pressure, the students view the following: www.youtu.be/t0IngUYN2OA

Aubree's patient is an 89-year-old man who has moderate dementia and a history of heart disease. Convner's patient is a 32-year-old woman who is a motorcycle accident victim and has paralysis from the waist down, and Alita's patient is a 79-year-old woman who is recovering from a broken hip. They write down all the patient information they need to get started the next morning.

Exercise 16-3: ***Multiple Choice Question***

The nurse understands that for HIPAA regulations, they should use the following patient identifier when collecting data and writing it down:

A. The patient's bar code
B. The patient's initials
C. A room number
D. An assigned letter such an A, B, or C

The next morning all three fundamental students are anxious and at clinical on time. They tell their instructor and group about their patients in preconference and outline what they are going to do for the day. They all go to their patients' rooms and introduce themselves and ask their patients if they have any immediate needs. Next they take their vital signs.

Exercise 16-4: ***Select All That Apply***

The nurse understands that the following parameters are included in routine vital sign (VS) assessment:

- ❑ Temperature
- ❑ Pain
- ❑ Pulse pressure
- ❑ Blood pressure
- ❑ Respirations
- ❑ Pulse
- ❑ Orientation to time, place, person

Exercise 16-5: ***Multiple Choice Question***

The nurse understands that when assessing the vital signs (VS) of an 89-year-old man who has moderate dementia and a history of heart disease, the following findings should be reported:

A. Temperature of 99°F
B. Pulse of 92 BPM

The Answers section can be found on page 217.

C. Respirations of 18 breaths per minute
D. Blood pressure of 106/52

eResource 16-2: The students use the *Vital Signs Table*, a web resource to refresh their understanding of normal vital sign ranges: www .prohealthsys.com/physical/vital_signs_table.php

Exercise 16-6: ***Multiple Choice Question***

The nurse understands that the next action after assessing the VS of a 32-year-old woman who is a motorcycle accident victim and has paralysis from the waist down as 98.2–82–16–128/88 pain level 1 is to:

A. Notify the primary health care provider
B. Reassess the routine VS in 30 minutes
C. Document the findings
D. Reposition and reassess

Exercise 16-7: ***Multiple Choice Question***

The nurse understands when assessing the VS of a 79-year-old woman who is recovering from a broken hip, an important priority is noted when the patient:

A. Is found trying to get over the side rails
B. Has a 99.2°F
C. Complains of a pain level of 5
D. Tells the nurse she is depressed

The instructor asks Alita if she is describing a surface or core temperature on her patient.

Exercise 16-8: ***Select All That Apply***

The nurse understands that the following methods are methods of assessing core temperature:

❑ Rectal
❑ Axillary
❑ Oral
❑ Tympanic
❑ Skin

Exercise 16-9: ***True/False***

When the body is overheated, the hypothalamus causes vasoconstriction.

❑ True
❑ False

Exercise 16-10: ***Multiple Choice Question***

The nurse understands that basal metabolic rate (BMR) of humans is calculated on the basis of body surface and heat production:

A. During rapid eye movement sleep
B. After 30 minutes of low-level exercise

The Answers section can be found on page 217.

C. After 30 minutes of vigorous exercise
D. At complete rest

The instructor asks the students during their morning break if they remember the modes of heat loss that patients can experience.

Exercise 16-11: *Matching*

Match the mode of heat loss in column A to the situation in column B.

Column A		Column B
A. Convection	______	The nurse does not dry a patient well after a bath
B. Evaporation	______	The nurse places the patient on a cold metal shower chair
C. Radiation	______	The nurse examines the patient's lung sounds next to a swinging door
D. Conduction	______	The nurse dresses the patient next to an outside window in the winter

Exercise 16-12: *Fill-in*

Connor reads an abbreviation in his patient's chart that says FUO and asks the instructor what it means. The instructor tells him it means ______________________.

eResource 16-3: To learn more about FUO, Connor opens MerckMedicus on his mobile device and goes to the Merck Manual: [Pathway: Merck Manual → Topics → enter "Fever" into the search field → select "of unknown origin"].

The instructor reviews some other terms related to body temperature to familiarize the students with them.

Exercise 16-13: *Matching*

Match the term in column A to the definition in column B.

Column A		Column B
A. Hyperthermia	______	Core temperature of 95°F or below
B. Hypothermia	______	Anesthetic drugs cause uncontrolled heat production
C. Malignant hyperthermia	______	Excessive fluid loss
D. Heatstroke	______	Describes heat loss by infants and young children
E. Heat exhaustion	______	Causes permanent circulatory damage
F. Frost bite	______	Elevated temperature
G. Cold stress	______	Produces confusion and delirium, and extreme body temperatures up to 113°F

Alita notes that most of the residents have axillary temperatures taken. She asks why different places use different types of thermometers.

The Answers section can be found on page 217.

Exercise 16-14: *Multiple Choice Question*

The nurse understands that choosing a type of thermometer is best done when considering:

A. Availability
B. Institutional policy
C. Nurse comfort level with equipment
D. Patient condition

eResource 16-4: Alita watches two videos reviewing the different ways to take a temperature:

- www.youtu.be/dDHDCyyhyGg
- www.youtu.be/lpbQqk3hX-M

Exercise 16-15: *Ordering*

Place the following steps regarding obtaining a rectal temperature in order from 1 to 12.

_______ Attach the red probe tip to the thermometer
_______ Lubricate
_______ Slide plastic cover on thermometer tip
_______ Dispose soiled probe
_______ Wipe patient anal area clean
_______ Explain to the patient what you are going to do
_______ Put on gloves
_______ Dispose gloves and clean equipment
_______ Provide privacy
_______ Position patient
_______ Separate the buttock cheeks with nondominant hand
_______ Insert the thermometer 1 in. to 1.5 in.

Exercise 16-16: *Multiple Choice Question*

Medications that reduce body temperature are called:

A. Anitpyretics
B. Antibiotics
C. Antiviral
D. Analgesics

Alita asks what she can do for a fever if there is no medication order.

Exercise 16-17: *Multiple Choice Question*

The nurse understands that the following nursing intervention is acceptable to reduce fever in a patient:

A. Tepid alcohol baths
B. Ice packs to the groin area
C. Place a cooling fan in the room
D. Use a hypothermia blanket

The Answers section can be found on page 217.

Conner approaches the clinical instructor about his patient. He asks if he should feel "normal" pedal pulses on her since she is paralyzed. The instructor tells him that the pumping action of the heart should definitely be reaching all areas of her body even if the nerve innovation is absent.

Exercise 16-18: *Matching*

Match the pulse that can be assessed in column A with the body area in which it is found in column B.

Column A	Column B
A. Temporal	______ Thumb side of the wrist
B. Carotid	______ In the inguinal area
C. Apical	______ Top of the foot
D. Brachial	______ Lateral to the eye
E. Radial	______ In the neck
F. Ulnar	______ Inner side of the ankle
G. Femoral	______ Fourth or fifth intercostal space
H. Popliteal	______ Between biceps and triceps
I. Posterior tibial	______ Behind knee
J. Dorsalis pedis	______ Little finger side of wrist

e **eResource 16-5:** The instructor provides Connor with a diagram of the circulatory system with pulse landmarks depicted: www.prohealthsys .com/physical/images/veins.jpg

Conner asks how to describe a pulse, and the instructor reviews the important points about rate, rhythm, and quality.

Exercise 16-19: *Fill-in*

An apical pulse should be counted for ______________ (how long).

Exercise 16-20: *Matching*

Matching the descriptor in column A to the definition in column B.

Column A	Column B
A. Tachycardia	______ Slow heart rate
B. Bradycardia	______ Abnormal heart rhythm
C. Dysrhythmia	______ Fast heart rate

Exercise 16-21: *Select All That Apply*

The nurse understands the following issues may affect a patient's pulse rate, quality, or rhythm:

- ❑ Activity intolerance
- ❑ Anxiety or fear

The Answers section can be found on page 217.

- ❑ Pain
- ❑ Content state of being
- ❑ Impaired gas exchange

Exercise 16-22: *Multiple Choice Question*

The nurse understands that the normal pulse quality is described as:

A. 1+
B. 2+
C. 3+
D. 4+

Connor states that he now understands and describes his patient's radial pulse as regular and 2+ at 82 beats per minute. But now Aubree asks questions about her patient's respirations. He is 89 years old and confused, so Aubree is having difficult listening to lung sounds because the patient keeps trying to get up and walk around his room.

Exercise 16-23: *Multiple Choice Question*

The nurse understands that when dealing with distracted patients, the best intervention is to:

A. Speak loudly
B. Turn on soft music
C. Turn on the television
D. Turn off the television

The instructor explains that respirations can vary on people from 12 to 20 breaths per minute, and that many mechanisms regulate breathing, including CO_2, O_2, and blood pH.

Exercise 16-24: *Multiple Choice Questions*

The nurse understands that the chemoreceptors in the carotid artery increase respiratory rate by responding to:

A. Hyperglycemia
B. Hypoglycemia
C. Hyperoxemia
D. Hypoxemia

The students know that they have to assess the respirations for three parameters.

Exercise 16-25: *Fill-in*

The three respiratory parameters to assess for are:

A. R__________
B. D__________
C. R__________

The Answers section can be found on page 217.

Exercise 16-26: *Multiple Choice Question*

Which patient should the nurse obtain a pulse oximeter reading for:

A. An 89-year-old man who has moderate dementia and a history of heart disease
B. A 32-year-old woman who is a motorcycle accident victim and has paralysis from the waist down
C. A 79-year-old woman who is recovering from a broken hip
D. An 80-year-old woman with abdominal ascites (edema)

Conner assists in obtaining the pulse oximetry. The patient with a chronic disease can have a lower reading, but it should never be too low or the organs will not be receiving enough oxygen.

Exercise 16-27: *Fill-in*

The lower limit of an acceptable pulse oximetry reading for a patient with a chronic respiratory disease is _________%.

Exercise 16-28: *Matching*

Match the respiratory rate in column A with the population it is WNL for in column B.

Column A (breaths per minute)	Column B
A. 30 to 60	_______ Child
B. 30 to 50	_______ Adult
C. 25 to 32	_______ Infant
D. 20 to 30	_______ Adolescent
E. 16 to 19	_______ Toddler
F. 12 to 20	_______ Newborn

Aubree asks Connor to double check the blood pressure she heard for her patient. She heard the systolic at 150 mmHg and she is unsure of the diastolic. Aubree knows that the diastolic is important because it is the minimal exertion of pressure on the walls of the arteries from the heart's pumping action. Conner hears the diastolic at 90 mmHg.

Exercise 16-29: *Calculation*

The pulse pressure for Aubree's patient is _________________.
Formula systolic − diastolic = _________________.

Exercise 16-30: *Select All That Apply*

An increase in pulse pressure is expected due to:

- ❑ The normal aging process
- ❑ Lower heart stroke volume
- ❑ Stiffening of the arteries
- ❑ Dehydration

The Answers section can be found on page 217.

Exercise 16-31: *Fill-in*

The nurse understands that hypertension is considered if the reading is over _______________ mmHg.

eResource 16-6: To reinforce his understanding of blood pressure, Connor views a brief presentation by cardiologist Dr. Eric Fisher who answers the question: *What Is the Normal Blood Pressure Range?* www.youtu.be/ZN0ToPpr36E

Exercise 16-32: *Multiple Choice Question*

The priority nursing action for a patient with known orthostatic hypotension is:

A. Increase PO fluids
B. Maintain bed rest
C. Ambulate q.i.d
D. Dangle before rising

Exercise 16-33: *Multiple Choice Question*

The nurse understands that which Korotkoff sound is the diastolic sound for adult patients:

A. First
B. Third
C. Fourth
D. Fifth

eResource 16-7: Alita, Connor, and Aubree view a brief video in which the difference between systolic and diastolic blood pressure is explained: www.youtu.be/AKdZ1dPMXIY

Once Alita, Connor, and Aubree finish vital signs, they immediately record them in the electronic medical records (EMRs) and on the paper flow sheet. It is important to record them as soon as possible to keep all interdisciplinary health care professionals up to date on the patients' statuses.

The Answers section can be found on page 217.

Answers

Exercise 16-1: ***Select All That Apply***

Accurate vital signs are needed in order for the nurse to:

☒ **Assess physiological functioning—YES**

☒ **Monitor the patient's condition—YES**

☒ **Determine the safety of medication administration—YES**

❑ Assess spiritual health—NO, this is a subjective assessment parameter

☒ **Determine appropriate nursing interventions—YES**

Exercise 16-2: ***Select All That Apply***

The techniques used to assess vital signs include:

☒ **Observation—YES**

☒ **Inspection—YES**

☒ **Auscultation—YES**

☒ **Light palpation—YES**

❑ Deep palpation—NO, deep palpation is not needed to assess VS

Exercise 16-3: ***Multiple Choice Question***

The nurse understands that for HIPAA regulations, they should use the following patient identifier when collecting data and writing it down:

A. The patient's bar code—NO, this is a HIPAA violation

B. The patient's initials—NO, this may be traceable back to the patient

C. A room number—NO, this may be traceable back to the patient

D. **An assigned letter such as A, B, or C—YES, this is not traceable back to the patient**

Exercise 16-4: ***Select All That Apply***

The nurse understands that the following parameters are included in routine vital sign (VS) assessment:

☒ **Temperature—YES**

☒ **Pain—YES, this is the fifth VS**

❑ Pulse pressure—NO, this is not a routine VS

☒ **Blood pressure—YES**

☒ **Respirations—YES**

☒ **Pulse—YES**

❑ Orientation to time, place, person—NO, this is not considered a VS

Exercise 16-5: *Multiple Choice Question*

The nurse understands that when assessing the vital signs (VS) of an 89-year-old man who has moderate dementia and a history of heart disease, the following findings should be reported:

A. Temperature of 99°F—NO, this is just a slight elevation

B. Pulse of 92 BPM—NO, this is just a slight elevation

C. Respirations of 18 breaths per minute—NO, this is WNL

D. **Blood pressure of 106/52—YES, this is low for his age and condition**

Exercise 16-6: *Multiple Choice Question*

The nurse understands that the next action after assessing the VS of a 32-year-old woman who is a motorcycle accident victim and has paralysis from the waist down as 98.2–82–16–128/88 pain level 1 is to:

A. Notify the primary health care provider—NO, they are WNL

B. Reassess the routine VS in 30 minutes—NO, they are WNL

C. **Document the findings—YES**

D. Reposition and reassess—NO, they are WNL

Exercise 16-7: *Multiple Choice Question*

The nurse understands when assessing the VS of a 79-year-old woman who is recovering from a broken hip, an important priority is noted when the patient:

A. Is found trying to get over the side rails—YES, this is a safety risk

B. Has a 99.2°F—NO, this is only slightly elevated but needs to be watched

C. Complains of a pain level of five—NO, this is important but not the priority

D. Tells the nurse she is depressed—NO, this is important but not the priority

Exercise 16-8: *Select All That Apply*

The nurse understands that the following methods are methods of assessing core temperature:

☒ **Rectal—YES**

❑ Axillary—NO

☒ **Oral—YES**

☒ **Tympanic—YES**

❑ Skin—NO

Exercise 16-9: *True/False*

When the body is overheated, the hypothalamus causes vasoconstriction.

❑ True

☒ **False—It vasodilates**

Exercise 16-10: *Multiple Choice Question*

The nurse understands that basal metabolic rate (BMR) of humans is calculated on the basis of body surface and heat production:

A. During rapid eye movement sleep—NO
B. After 30 minutes of low-level exercise—NO
C. After 30 minutes of vigorous exercise—NO
D. **At complete rest—YES**

Exercise 16-11: *Matching*

Match the mode of heat loss in column A to the situation in column B.

Column A		Column B
A. Convection	**B**	The nurse does not dry a patient well after a bath
B. Evaporation	**D**	The nurse places the patient on a cold metal shower chair
C. Radiation	**A**	The nurse examines the patient's lung sounds next to a swinging door
D. Conduction	**C**	The nurse dresses the patient next to an outside window in the winter

Exercise 16-12: *Fill-in*

Conner reads an abbreviation in his patient's chart that says FUO and asks the instructor what it means. The instructor tells him that it means **Fever of Unknown Origin**.

Exercise 16-13: *Matching*

Match the term in column A to the definition in column B.

Column A		Column B
A. Hyperthermia	**B**	Core temperature of 95°F or below
B. Hypothermia	**C**	Anesthetic drugs cause uncontrolled heat production
C. Malignant hyperthermia	**E**	Excessive fluid loss
D. Heatstroke	**H**	Describes heat loss by infants and young children
E. Heat exhaustion	**F**	Causes permanent circulatory damage
F. Frost bite	**A**	Elevated temperature
G. Cold stress	**D**	Produces confusion and delirium, and extreme body temperatures up to 113°F

Exercise 16-14: *Multiple Choice Question*

The nurse understands that choosing a type of thermometer is best done when considering:

A. Availability—NO
B. Institutional policy—NO, this is important, but not the first consideration
C. Nurse comfort level with equipment—NO
D. **Patient condition—YES, the patient's condition is the important deciding factor, and this is most likely supported by institutional policy**

Exercise 16-15: *Ordering*

Place the following steps regarding obtaining a rectal temperature in order from 1 to 12.

5 Attach the red probe tip to the thermometer
7 Lubricate
6 Slide plastic cover on thermometer tip
10 Dispose soiled probe
11 Wipe patient anal area clean
1 Explain to the patient what you are going to do
3 Put on gloves
12 Dispose gloves and clean equipment
2 Provide privacy
4 Position patient
8 Separate the buttock cheeks with nondominant hand
9 Insert the thermometer 1 in. to 1.5 in.

Exercise 16-16: *Multiple Choice Question*

Medications that reduce body temperature are called:

A. **Anitpyretics—YES**
B. Antibiotics—NO, these are for bacterial infections
C. Antiviral—NO, these are for viral infections
D. Analgesics—NO, this is for pain

Exercise 16-17: *Multiple Choice Question*

The nurse understands that the following nursing intervention is acceptable to reduce fever in a patient.

A. Tepid alcohol baths—NO, this is no longer used because it can chill patients too fast
B. Ice packs to the groin area—NO, this is no longer used because it can chill patients too fast
C. Place a cooling fan in the room—NO, this is no longer used because it can chill patients too fast
D. **Use a hypothermia blanket—YES, this is the only recommended method because it can be regulated best**

Exercise 16-18: *Matching*

Match the pulse that can be assessed in column A with the body area in which it is found in column B.

Column A		Column B
A. Temporal	E	Thumb side of the wrist
B. Carotid	G	In the inguinal area
C. Apical	J	Top of the foot
D. Brachial	A	Lateral to the eye
E. Radial	B	In the neck
F. Ulnar	I	Inner side of the ankle
G. Femoral	C	Fourth or fifth intercostal space
H. Popliteal	D	Between biceps and triceps
I. Posterior tibial	H	Behind knee
J. Dorsalis pedis	F	Little finger side of wrist

Exercise 16-19: *Fill-in*

An apical pulse should be counted for **1 minute** (how long).

Exercise 16-20: *Matching*

Matching the descriptor in column A to the definition in column B.

Column A		Column B
A. Tachycardia	B	Slow heart rate
B. Bradycardia	C	Abnormal heart rhythm
C. Dysrhythmia	A	Fast heart rate

Exercise 16-21: *Select All That Apply*

The nurse understands the following issues may affect a patient's pulse rate, quality, or rhythm:

☒ **Activity intolerance—YES**

☒ **Anxiety or fear—YES**

☒ **Pain—YES**

☐ Content state of being—NO, this usually keeps the pulse rate stable

☒ **Impaired gas exchange—YES**

Exercise 16-22: *Multiple Choice Question*

The nurse understands that the normal pulse quality is described as:

A. 1+—NO

B. **2+—YES, this is normal**

C. 3+—NO

D. 4+—NO, this is bounding

Exercise 16-23: *Multiple Choice Question*

The nurse understands that when dealing with distracted patients, the best intervention is to:

A. Speak loudly—NO, this will add to the overstimulation

B. Turn on soft music—NO, this will add to the overstimulation

C. Turn on the television—NO, this will add to the overstimulation

D. **Turn off the television—YES, decrease environmental stimulation**

Exercise 16-24: *Multiple Choice Question*

The nurse understands that the chemoreceptors in the carotid artery increase respiratory rate by responding to:

A. Hyperglycemia—NO, glucose is not involved

B. Hypoglycemia—NO, glucose is not involved

C. Hyperoxemia—NO, this is not the usual trigger to increase breathing rate

D. **Hypoxemia—YES, decrease in O_2 is the trigger**

Exercise 16-25: *Fill-in*

The three respiratory parameters to assess for are:

A. **Rate**

B. **Depth**

C. **Rhythm**

Exercise 16-26: *Multiple Choice Question*

Which patient should the nurse obtain a pulse oximeter reading for:

A. An 89-year-old man who has moderate dementia and a history of heart disease—NO, although this may be a good idea, this is not the priority patient

B. A 32-year-old woman who is a motorcycle accident victim and has paralysis from the waist down—NO, there is no lung involvement

C. A 79-year-old woman who is recovering from a broken hip—NO, there is no lung involvement

D. **An 80-year-old woman with abdominal ascites (edema)—YES, the ascites may be severe enough to be pressing on the diaphragm and impeding respirations**

Exercise 16-27: *Fill-in*

The lower limit of an acceptable pulse oximetry reading for a patient with a chronic respiratory disease is **85%**.

Exercise 16-28: ***Matching***

Match the respiratory rate in column A with the population it is WNL for in column B.

Column A	Column B
A. 30 to 60	__D__ Child
B. 30 to 50	__F__ Adult
C. 25 to 32	__B__ Infant
D. 20 to 30	__E__ Adolescent
E. 16 to 19	__C__ Toddler
F. 12 to 20	__A__ Newborn

Exercise 16-29: ***Calculation***

The pulse pressure for Aubree's patient is **60 mmHg**.
Formula systolic – diastolic = **60 mmHg**.

Exercise 16-30: ***Select All That Apply***

❑ An increase in pulse pressure is expected due to:
☒ **The normal aging process—YES**
❑ Lower heart stroke volume—NO, this will decrease pulse pressure
☒ **Stiffening of the arteries—YES**
❑ Dehydration—NO, this will decrease pulse pressure

Exercise 16-31: ***Fill-in***

The nurse understands that hypertension is considered if the reading is over **120/80** mmHg.

Exercise 16-32: ***Multiple Choice Question***

The priority nursing action for a patient with known orthostatic hypotension is:

A. Increase PO fluids—NO, this is important but not the priority
B. Maintain bed rest—NO
C. Ambulate q.i.d.—NO
D. **Dangle before rising—YES, ambulate slowly**

Exercise 16-33: ***Multiple Choice Question***

The nurse understands that which Korotkoff sound is the diastolic sound for adult patients:

A. First—NO, this is systolic
B. Third—NO
C. Fourth—NO, this is for a child
D. **Fifth—YES, this is the diastolic for an adult**

17

Infection Control

Unfolding Case Study 16 ▪ Alita

Alita is assigned in the clinical area a patient who is HIV positive. In preconference, the nurse educator goes over the principles of infection control and communicable diseases.

Exercise 17-1: ***Ordering***

Place the chain of infection in the correct order from 1 to 6.

_______ Mode of transmission

_______ Portal of entry

_______ Infectious agent (pathogen)

_______ Susceptible host

_______ Source for pathogen to grow (reservoir)

_______ Way to exit the reservoir

Exercise 17-2: ***Select All That Apply***

Infection agents include:

- ☐ Protozoa
- ☐ Bacteria
- ☐ Insects
- ☐ Fungi
- ☐ Viruses
- ☐ Nonvertebrates

The nurse educator explains that **resident** organisms live on a person and usually do not cause harm. **Transient** organisms are not the ones that usually live on a person's skin or body but make contact during ADLs (activities of daily living). Alita says, "Oh that is why hand washing is so important!" Correct.

The Answers section can be found on page 231.

eResource 17-1: To reinforce the importance of infection control, the instructor shows the class several videos:

- *Infection Control: Basic Infection Prevention Techniques:* www.youtu.be/JHRu8eSUHU8
- *Infection Control: Precautions and Sterile Dressing Changes:* www.youtu.be/w7bJ4rMhfXE
- *Infection Control: Core Measures:* www.youtu.be/EdHFqEzch2k

Exercise 17-3: *Multiple Choice Question*

The nurse understands that there is an increased chance of an organism in causing a disease if:

A. The organism is not virulent
B. The organism has insufficient number of infection cells
C. The patient is hydrated
D. The patient is immunocompromised

Alita asks the instructor, "What is the most common reservoir for pathogens?"

Exercise 17-4: *Multiple Choice Question*

The most common place for pathogens to grow on or in the human body is:

A. Skin
B. Bowel
C. Genitourinary tract
D. Respiratory tract

The nurse educator goes on and explains that pathogens need specific things such as oxygen and water in order to grow.

Exercise 17-5: *Fill-in*

Aerobic bacteria require oxygen to grow, but ________________ bacteria such as *Staphylococcus aureus* do not.

The students name other factors that may influence or deter specific pathogenic growth, such as:

- Light
- Temperature
- pH
- Food

The students also identify the portals of entry in humans for an infection:

- Respiratory tract
- Skin and mucous membranes
- Urinary tract
- Gastrointestinal tract

The Answers section can be found on page 231.

- Reproductive tract
- Blood

The way a pathogen is transmitted from one person to another is called the ***mode of transmission***.

Exercise 17-6: *Matching*

Match the mode of transmission in column A with an example in column B.

Column A	Column B
A. Direct contact	_______ Contaminated food
B. Air	_______ Tick
C. Vehicle	_______ Sneezing
D. Vector	_______ Contaminated needle
E. Indirect contact	_______ Contaminated hands

The nurse educator keeps the students in preconference in order to fully review the principles of an infectious process to safe guard them and the patients. The nurse educator tells them the infection can be localized or systemic, and that systemic infections can be fatal. Fortunately, the human body has defenses against infection. One of the first responses to an invading pathogen is ***inflammation.***

Exercise 17-7: *Select All That Apply*

Signs of an inflammatory response are:

- ☐ Redness
- ☐ Swelling (***edema***)
- ☐ Coolness of site
- ☐ Pain
- ☐ Numbness
- ☐ Loss of function

The nurse educator tells the clinical group that by surrounding the pathogen and producing ***exudate*** the body is trying to get rid of the infection. In order for the body to do this, it generates WBCs (white blood cells) to the site for ***phagocytosis*** with ***neutrophils*** and ***monocytes*** to ingest the pathogens.

Exercise 17-8: *Matching*

Match the type of exudates in column A with the descriptor in column B.

Column A	Column B
A. Serous	_______ Contains RBCs (red blood cells)
B. Sanguineous	_______ Contains WBCs
C. Purulent	_______ Clear

The Answers section can be found on page 231.

Exercise 17-9: *Multiple Choice Question*

The nurse understands that for systemic infections, leukocytosis occurs producing a WBC count:

A. 2,500/mm^3
B. 5,000/mm^3
C. 10,000/mm^3
D. 15,000/mm^3

Before the preconference ends, the nurse educator speaks to the group about how "dangerous" it is for patients in the hospital because of the high likelihood of getting an infection in a hospital.

Exercise 17-10: *Multiple Choice Question*

An infection acquired in the hospital is called:

A. Nosocomial
B. Iatrogenic
C. Exogenous
D. Endogenous

The students leave preconference and introduce themselves to their patients. Alita's patient is immunocompromised due to HIV, and she uses strict ***aseptic technique.***

Exercise 17-11: *Multiple Choice Question*

Aseptic technique includes all the following actions except:

A. Vigilant hand washing (10–15 seconds)
B. Sterile gloves
C. Cleaning an object that fell to the floor
D. Considering used objects contaminated

Exercise 17-12: *Multiple Choice Question*

The student nurses know that it is safe to use alcohol-based antiseptic solution:

A. After contact with blood
B. Hands are visibly dirty
C. After removing gloves
D. After contacting body fluid

eResource 17-2: Alita and her classmates review proper hand washing procedures by viewing the video *A Complete Guide to Hand Washing:* www.youtu.be/mWe51EKbewk

Alita's patient is on isolation precautions. The patient is suspected to have TB (tuberculosis) and is having tests to confirm it.

The Answers section can be found on page 231.

Exercise 17-13: *Multiple Choice Question*

The nurse understands that TB is a droplet nuclei of less than 5 mcm and therefore requires:

A. Standard precautions
B. Airborne precautions
C. Droplet precautions
D. Contact precautions

Alita knows that a respiratory protective device that is fitted specifically to her must be worn because of the suspected TB. Alita also has an order to collect a stool specimen from her patient. The principles of ***specimen collection*** include clean gloves and sterile equipment. The collection equipment is then put in an ***impervious bag*** or one in which fluids cannot seep through.

Exercise 17-14: *Multiple Choice Question*

The nurse understands that if it is impossible not to contaminate the outside of an impervious bag, the next step is to:

A. Change it to an uncontaminated bag
B. Leave it in the room until housekeeping can come with a bin
C. Clean the outside of the bag
D. Double bag

eResource 17-3: Alita reviews the basic principles of universal precautions by viewing a short video *Universal Precautions-Infection Control Procedures in Health Care:* www.youtu.be/nmyTbQPNpLM

A new order is written for Alita's patient to collect a sterile urine specimen. This will require sterile technique or ***surgical asepsis.***

Exercise 17-15: *Ordering*

Place the steps in order from 1 to 13 collect a sterile urine specimen:

_______ Obtain equipment
_______ Open package away from body first
_______ Make a sterile field
_______ Position the patient
_______ Identify the patient
_______ Explain the procedure
_______ Clean the area
_______ Put on sterile gloves
_______ Insert catheter
_______ Place sterile urine in collection cup and secure lid
_______ Wipe off patient
_______ Dispose all contaminated equipment in an impervious bag
_______ Remove catheter

The Answers section can be found on page 231.

eResource 17-4: Before completing the procedure, Alita reviews

- An overview of catheterization from Assisted Learning for All (ALFA): http://alfa.saddleback.edu/N170/urinarycatheterization.aspx
- A video demonstration of a straight catheterization: www.youtu.be/sZHlY0WI9as

Alita reports her day in postconference. She was successful in getting the sterile urine specimen and maintaining airborne isolation. Her patient thanked her for her careful and thoughtful care, which is the best reward a student nurse can get!

The Answers section can be found on page 231.

Answers

Exercise 17-1: ***Ordering***

Place the chain of infection in the correct order from 1 to 6.

__**4**__ Mode of transmission

__**6**__ Portal of entry

__**1**__ Infectious agent (pathogen)

__**5**__ Susceptible host

__**2**__ Source for pathogen to grow (reservoir)

__**3**__ Way to exit the reservoir

Exercise 17-2: ***Select All That Apply***

Infection agents include:

☒ **Protozoa—YES**

☒ **Bacteria—YES**

❑ Insects—NO, they are sometimes the vector but not the agent

☒ **Fungi—YES**

☒ **Viruses—YES**

❑ Nonvertebrates—NO, they are sometimes the vector but not the agent

Exercise 17-3: ***Multiple Choice Question***

The nurse understands that there is an increased chance of an organism in causing a disease if:

A. The organism is not virulent—NO, virulence causes disease
B. The organism has insufficient number of infection cells—NO, there needs to be an adequate amount of cells
C. The patient is hydrated—NO, this is a mechanism that detracts from infection
D. **The patient is immunocompromised—YES, these patients are more susceptible**

Exercise 17-4: ***Multiple Choice Question***

The most common place for pathogens to grow on or in the human body is:

A. Skin—NO, they can grow here, but it is not the most common
B. Bowel—NO, they can grow here, but it is not the most common
C. Genitourinary tract—NO, they can grow here, but it is not the most common
D. **Respiratory tract—YES, this is the most common place—think of how many times you have gotten URIs (upper respiratory infections) in your life**

Exercise 17-5: *Fill-in*

Aerobic bacteria require oxygen to grow, but __**anaerobic**__ bacteria such as *Staphylococcus aureus* do not.

Exercise 17-6: *Matching*

Match the mode of transmission in column A with an example in column B.

Column A	Column B
A. Direct contact	__**C**__ Contaminated food
B. Air	__**D**__ Tick
C. Vehicle	__**B**__ Sneezing
D. Vector	__**E**__ Contaminated needle
E. Indirect contact	__**A**__ Contaminated hands

Exercise 17-7: *Select All That Apply*

Signs of an inflammatory response are:

☒ **Redness—YES, this is a sign of inflammation**

☒ **Swelling (*edema*)—YES, this is a sign of inflammation**

❑ Coolness of site—NO, the area is usually warm

☒ **Pain—YES, this is a sign of inflammation**

❑ Numbness—NO, the area is usually tender

☒ **Loss of function—YES, this is a sign of inflammation**

Exercise 17-8: *Matching*

Match the type of exudates in column A with the descriptor in column B.

Column A	Column B
A. Serous	__**B**__ Contains RBCs (red blood cells)
B. Sanguineous	__**C**__ Contains WBCs
C. Purulent	__**A**__ Clear

Exercise 17-9: *Multiple Choice Question*

The nurse understands that for systemic infections, leukocytosis occurs producing a WBC count:

A. 2,500/mm^3—NO, this is too low

B. 5,000/mm^3—NO, this is WNL (within normal limits)

C. 10,000/mm^3—NO, this is WNL

D. **15,000/mm^3—YES, this is elevated**

Exercise 17-10: *Multiple Choice Question*

An infection acquired in the hospital is called:

A. **Nosocomial—YES**
B. Iatrogenic—NO, this is an infection from a procedure
C. Exogenous—NO, this is an infection from an outside source
D. Endogenous—NO, this is overgrowth of normal floras

Exercise 17-11: *Multiple Choice Question*

Aseptic technique includes all the following actions except:

A. Vigilant hand washing (10–15 seconds)—NO, this is part of aseptic technique
B. **Sterile gloves—YES, this is surgical asepsis or sterile technique**
C. Cleaning an object that fell to the floor—NO, this is part of aseptic technique
D. Considering used objects contaminated—NO, this is part of aseptic technique

Exercise 17-12: *Multiple Choice Question*

The student nurses know that it is safe to use alcohol-based antiseptic solution when:

A. After contact with blood—NO, this should be washed off with soap and water
B. Hands are visibly dirty—NO, this should be washed off with soap and water
C. **After removing gloves—YES**
D. After contacting body fluid—NO, this should be washed off with soap and water

Exercise 17-13: *Multiple Choice Question*

The nurse understands that TB is a droplet nuclei of less than 5 mcm and therefore requires:

A. Standard precautions—NO, protective gear is not needed
B. **Airborne precautions—YES, this is airborne and needs a respirator mask**
C. Droplet precautions—NO, just a regular mask is needed
D. Contact precautions—NO, gown and gloves but no mask is needed

Exercise 17-14: *Multiple Choice Question*

The nurse understands that if it is impossible not to contaminate the outside of an impervious bag, the next step is to:

A. Change it to an uncontaminated bag—NO, this will contaminate you
B. Leave it in the room until housekeeping can come with a bin—NO, you cannot leave the contamination unattended
C. Clean the outside of the bag—NO, this will contaminate you
D. **Double bag—YES**

Exercise 17-15: *Ordering*

Place the steps in order from 1 to 13 collect a sterile urine specimen:

__1__ Obtain equipment
__5__ Open package away from body first
__6__ Make a sterile field
__4__ Position the patient
__2__ Identify the patient
__3__ Explain the procedure
__8__ Clean the area
__7__ Put on sterile gloves
__9__ Insert catheter
__10__ Place sterile urine in collection cup and secure lid
__13__ Wipe off patient
__12__ Dispose all contaminated equipment in an impervious bag
__11__ Remove catheter

18

Medication Administration—Part I

Unfolding Case Study 17 Aubree, Alita, and Connor

Aubree, Alita, and Connor are back in the lab to learn administration of medication. They are anxious because they realize that it is a big responsibility.

Exercise 18-1: *Multiple Choice Question*

The U.S. legal agency that regulates medications is the:

A. Pure Food and Drug Act
B. Health Science Regulatory Agency
C. Center for Disease Control
D. Food and Drug Administration

Alita, Aubree, and Connor are very much amazed at all the ways drugs can be administered, and all the different forms they come in!

Exercise 18-2: *Select All That Apply*

Select the forms of medications that are used for patients:

- ❑ Caplet
- ❑ Tablet
- ❑ Intraocular disk
- ❑ Transdermal patch
- ❑ Intraaural disk
- ❑ Vaginal suppository
- ❑ Rectal suppository

Besides there being many forms of medications, there are many routes of medication.

Exercise 18-3: *Fill-in*

The quickest route of administration for drug absorption is ____________.

Aubree asks the instructor what some of the reasons that absorption rate is affected.

The Answers section can be found on page 249.

Showing her a web-based reference sheet, the instructor tells her that factors can be related to the drug itself or related to the body.

eResource 18-1: *Factors Affecting Absorption of Drugs:* www.howmed.net/pharmacology/factors-affecting-absorption-of-drugs/

Exercise 18-4: *Select All That Apply*

The following are factors in drug absorption:

- ❑ Route
- ❑ Dissolvability
- ❑ Blood flow
- ❑ Age of patient
- ❑ Gender of patient

eResource 18-2: To better understand this, the class watches:

- *How Medicines Work: Drug Actions 2—Drug Absorption, Elimination, Distribution*: www.youtu.be/bosxbO-hw9c
- *Pharmacology: Oral Meds Absorption:* www.youtu.be/xiuWdJYyIKs

Once drugs are in a human body, they need to be metabolized to be used and then eventually excreted.

Exercise 18-5: *Multiple Choice Question*

The organ that plays the largest role in detoxifying medication is the:

A. Lungs
B. Liver
C. Kidneys
D. Intestines

Exercise 18-6: *Multiple Choice Question*

The organ that plays the largest role in medication excretion is:

A. Lungs
B. Liver
C. Kidneys
D. Intestines

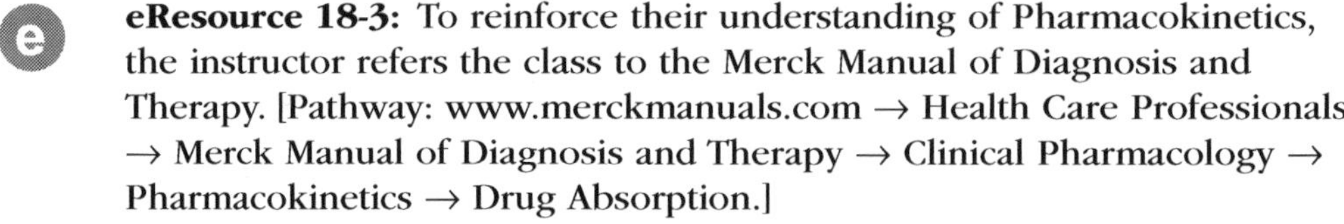

eResource 18-3: To reinforce their understanding of Pharmacokinetics, the instructor refers the class to the Merck Manual of Diagnosis and Therapy. [Pathway: www.merckmanuals.com → Health Care Professionals → Merck Manual of Diagnosis and Therapy → Clinical Pharmacology → Pharmacokinetics → Drug Absorption.]

The instructor tells the class that humans react differently to medications, and that nurses must be able to recognize a reaction.

The Answers section can be found on page 249.

Exercise 18-7: *Matching*

Match the reaction in column A to the description in column B.

Column A		Column B
A. Therapeutic effect	_______	A reaction to a medication that is different from the norm
B. Side effect	_______	Caused by an accumulation of the drug
C. Allergic reaction	_______	Unintended effects of a drug
D. Adverse effect	_______	Immunologically sensitized to the drug
E. Toxic effect	_______	Severe response to a drug
F. Idiosyncratic ration	_______	Predicted response to the drug

eResource 18-4:

- The class is instructed to open MerckMedicus on their mobile device and go to the Merck Manual. [Pathway: Merck Manual → Topics → enter "Drugs" into the search field → select "hypersensitivity" → select "hypersensitivity reactions to" and read about Adverse Drug Reactions, Anaphylaxis and Drug Hypersensitivity.]
- To better understand drug reactions, Aubree uses the browser on her mobile device to read more in the Merck Manual of Diagnosis and Therapy. [Pathway: www.merckmanuals.com → Health Care Professionals → Merck Manual of Diagnosis and Therapy → Clinical Pharmacology → Adverse Drug Reactions.]

Exercise 18-8: *Multiple Choice Question*

Common side effects of medication include:

A. Shortness of breath, rash, pruritus
B. Pruritus, rhinitis, diarrhea
C. Diarrhea, stomach upset, constipation
D. Constipation, urticaria, stomach upset

Exercise 18-9: *Exhibit Question*

A 24-year-old college student is brought to the student health center, wheezing with strider (Table 18.1).

Table 18.1

Vital signs (VS)	Medications	Laboratory tests
Temperature = 99.0°F	Doxycycline 3 3 days for acne	Finger-stick glucose 5 78
Respirations 5 36	Birth control pills	
Pulse 5 98		
Blood pressure 5 128/88		

The Answers section can be found on page 249.

The nurse would recognize this as a(n):

A. Anaphylactic reaction
B. Side effect
C. Idiosyncratic reaction
D. Therapeutic effect

The instructor tells the students to use Epocrates, a drug reference, to see if there are any side effects associated with doxycycline. Some of the students use their laptops to go online, while others consult the Epocrates mobile version on their smartphones:

eResource 18-5:

- Epocrates online. [Pathway: http://online.epocrates.com/ → tap on the "Drugs" tab → enter "Doxycycline" in the search field to view content → select "Adverse Reactions" to view severe and common drug reactions.]
- Mobile Epocrates. [Pathway: Epocrates → tap on the "Drugs" icon → enter "doxycycline" in the search field to view content → select "Adverse Reactions" to view severe and common drug reactions.]

The instructor then goes on to explain to the learners in the fundamental class that when a patient takes more than one medication or uses complementary and alternative medicine (CAM), they can affect each other.

Exercise 18-10: ***Multiple Choice Question***

When medications taken together potentiate each other, this reaction is called:

A. Antagonistic
B. Idiosyncratic
C. Detrimental
D. Synergistic

The instructor gives the students another example of how medications are monitored.

Exercise 18-11: ***Exhibit Question***

An infant is receiving gentamicin IV for sepsis (blood infection), and the neonatal nurse practitioner orders a peak and trough with the next dose. The nurse checks the trough half an hour before and it is WNL and administers the dose. One hour later, the peak is drawn and should be between 4 and 8 mcg/ml (Table 18.2).

Table 18.2

Vital signs (VS)	Medications	Laboratory tests
Temperature 98.4°F axillary	Gentamicin 1.5 mg/kg/q 12 hr	Gentamicin trough , 1 mcg/mL (WNL)
Respirations 5 56/min		
Apical 5 134 BPM		Gentamycin peak 6 mcg/mL

The Answers section can be found on page 249.

After the results are received, the priority nursing intervention would be:

A. Call the neonatal nurse practitioner
B. Administer a second dose
C. Increase the plain IV to dilute the medication in the blood stream
D. Continue to monitor the patient

eResource 18-6: To check the therapeutic levels for Gentamycin, Alita opens Mobile MerckMedicus on her smartphone. [Pathway: MerckMedicus → select "Pocket Guide to Diagnostic Tests" → select "All Tests" → enter "Gentamicin" in the search field → select "Gentamicin" to read about effective concentrations]

Alita raises her hand and asks the instructor a question about a drug's ***half-life.***

Exercise 18-12: *Multiple Choice Question*

The half-life of a drug is the amount of time it takes for:

A. To be totally excreted by the kidneys
B. The blood concentration is at half-strength
C. The drug to reach its therapeutic effect
D. The body to respond to the therapeutic effect

In order to keep a drug at the desired level in a person's body, it usually has to be given at specific times during the day. Nurses use abbreviations for those times, and it is very important for proper drug administration to know them.

Exercise 18-13: *Matching*

Match the abbreviation in column A to the descriptor in column B.

Column A	Column B
A. ac	_______ hour
B. Ad lib	_______ every 8 hours
C. bid	_______ immediately
D. H	_______ before meals
E. pc	_______ every hour
F. prn	_______ twice a day
G. Q h	_______ every 6 hours
H. q 2 h	_______ as desired or at liberty
I. q 6 h	_______ every 2 hours
J. q 8 h	_______ after meals
K. tid	_______ as needed
L. stat	_______ three times a day

eResource 18-7: Connor finds an online abbreviations dictionary to look up definitions of abbreviations with which he is unsure: www.medilexicon.com

The Answers section can be found on page 249.

The instructor tells the students they will go to the lab for the rest of the class and look at the different type of medications. First, they look at orally administered medications because this is the easiest method to administer drugs. Besides swallowing pills, tablets, caplets, capsules, or elixirs, medications can be given sublingual and buccal.

Exercise 18-14: ***Multiple Choice Question***

The nurse understands that the patient needs further teaching when he states:

A. "I should put my buccal medication in the same cheek each time"
B. "I should not swallow the medication"
C. "I should not drink water while taking the medication"
D. "I should not chew the medication"

eResource 18-8: The instructor shows the students an image depicting sublingual and buccal medication administration, which can be used for patient education: http://alfa.saddleback.edu/N170/oralmedications.aspx

The students practice opening pill packages, reading labels, and checking doses. The instructor calls them back to the classroom to go over medications that are given ***parenterally***.

Exercise 18-15: ***Matching***

Match the parenteral administration method in column A with the description in column B.

Column A	Column B
A. Intradermal	_______ Injection into a muscle
B. Subcutaneous	_______ Injection just under the skin
C. Intramuscular	_______ Injection into a vein
D. Intravenous	_______ Injection into tissue under the skin

The instructor tells the students that there are other ways drugs are given, such as inhalers for asthma, transdermal disks like those used for birth control sometimes, eye drops are intraocular, and instillations can be given in the ear, nose, rectum, or bladder.

The next most important thing about drug administration is knowing conversions, so the right dose can be calculated.

Exercise 18-16: ***Fill-in***

A. 1 gram (g or GM) = _______________ milligrams (mg)
B. 1 liter (L) = _______________ milliliters (mL)
C. 1 tablespoon (tbsp) = _______________ teaspoons (tsp)
D. 1 teaspoon (tsp) = _______________ mL

eResource 18-9: The instructor tells the students about a free resources that provide calculation support *MedCalc* (www.medcalc.com/wtmeas.html) for an online weight conversion calculator offered by MedCalc.com.

The Answers section can be found on page 249.

[Pathway: Tap on "General" → "Weights and Measures" to access the conversion calculator.] Use this resource to check your answers for Exercise 18-17 through 18-19.

Now that Aubree, Alita, and Connor understand these basic conversions, they can attempt some calculations.

Exercise 18-17: *Calculation*

The order is written for 5 mL q 6 hours of an antibiotic, amoxicillin. The nurse tells the patient to take how many tsp? ________________

Exercise 18-18: *Calculation*

The nurse instructs a patient to take an ounce of cough syrup that is 30 mL. How many tbsp should the patient take? ________________

Exercise 18-19: *Calculation*

The nurse is to give an IV of 250 mL. The solution comes in a 1-L bag. The nurse understands that she is given _____ of a bag.

Exercise 18-20: *Calculation*

The order is written for 500 mg of an antihypertensive medication. The nurse understands that this is ______________ g.

eResource 18-10: *Archimedes*, a free mobile calculator from Skyscape, Inc. available in PC and multiple mobile device platforms can also be used on your PDA or smartphone to perform weight conversions. [Download: www.skyscape.com and enter "Archimedes" into search field. [Once installed, the pathway on device: Skyscape → Archimedes → Weight Conversion → enter 500 into input field and select units.]

The instructor then tells the class about medicating children. Medications for children are calculated on the weight of the child since children can be such different sizes at all ages.

Exercise 18-21: *Fill-in*

A. 1 pound (lb) = __________ kg

B. 1 kg = __________ g

Alita, Aubree, and Connor will feel more comfortable with these conversions if they practice.

Exercise 18-22: *Calculation*

The nurse is medicating a child who is 15 pounds. The order for the medication is written in mg per kg. How many kg is the child? ________________

The Answers section can be found on page 249.

Exercise 18-23: *Calculation*

A child is 4,200 g; how many kg is the child? _____________ How many lbs is the child? ________

eResource 18-11: Use *Archimedes* or MedCalc mobile, a free mobile calculator for iPhone/iPod/iPad (www.apple.com/itunes/) to check weight conversions.

Pediatric medications are often written in upper and lower limits. For example, the Gentamicin is 1.2 to 1.5 mg/kg/q 12 hours. So the nurse has to calculate if the dose written is in between those parameters. In order to know this, you have to do the calculation twice, one with the lower limit number and one with the higher limit number.

Exercise 18-24: *Calculation*

A dose of Gentamicin is ordered for an 11-lb child who is 12 mg/kg/day in two divided doses.

A. Change 11 lbs to kg ____________________

B. 12 mg/day would be how many mg per 12 hours? _________mg

C. How much should you give? ____________________

Connor asks how will he know what medication to give, when, and how much? The instructor tells him that medication administration is an ***interdisciplinary*** function because it involves a provider (physician or nurse practitioner) who orders the patient medication, a pharmacist (who dispenses the medication), and a nurse (who administers the medication). When physicians or nurse practitioners order medication, they can do it by several methods, including:

- Electronic orders by putting it into the patients electronic health record (EHR),
- Verbally telling the nurse that the patient should receive a medication,
- Calling the medication in to the nurse (telephone order), and
- Hand writing the medication in the patient record.

Exercise 18-25: *Multiple Choice Question*

The nurse understands that the safest way to receive a medication order is by:

A. EHR

B. Verbally

C. Telephone

D. Written

eResource 18-12: To help the class better understand how the EHR can improve safety, the instructor tells the students about computerized physician order entry in the EHR and about Leapfrog, a voluntary organization that works to improve hospital systems to minimize risk of harm to patients. To highlight important points, the instructor provides the class with a fact sheet: http://www.leapfroggroup.org/media/file/FactSheet_CPOE.pdf

The Answers section can be found on page 249.

Exercise 18-26: *Select All That Apply*

The components of a medication order include:

- ❑ Patient's name
- ❑ Date
- ❑ Times to give
- ❑ Expiration of the order
- ❑ What type of nurse should give the medication (RN, LPN)
- ❑ Amount

The Joint Commission (TJC), a hospital accrediting agency, has banned some abbreviations from being used when prescriptions are written because they are dangerous. It is important not to use them because they are associated with patient medication errors in the past.

Exercise 18-27: *Matching*

Match the different types of orders in column A with the description in column B.

Column A	Column B
A. Standing orders	_______ Give once
B. PRN orders	_______ Give until it is cancelled or expires
C. Single-time orders	_______ Give immediately
D. STAT orders	_______ Give if needed

e **eResource 18-13:** The instructor reminds the class that there are some abbreviations that are not to be used due to risk of error and asks them to review the two important resources that provide updated lists of error-prone abbreviations to health care professionals:

- Institute for Safe Medication Practice: www.ismp.org/Tools/errorproneabbreviations.pdf
- The Joint Commission: http://www.jointcommission.org/assets/1/18/Do_Not_Use_List.pdf

Most hospitals have automated medication dispensing systems in which the nurse needs an ID number or to be fingerprinted in order to gain access. Aubree asks if this helps safe medication administration, and the instructor answers that it does but they still need to know (and follow) the "six rights" each time they administer medications.

e **eResource 18-14:** Aubree reviews her notes to reinforce her knowledge: www.dhhs.nh.gov/dcbcs/bds/nurses/documents/sectionIV.pdf

Exercise 18-28: *Select All That Apply*

The nurse understands that each and every time he or she administers medication, they must check:

- ❑ Right medication
- ❑ Right patient

The Answers section can be found on page 249.

- ❑ Right situation
- ❑ Right route
- ❑ Right time
- ❑ Right documentation
- ❑ Right dose

Alita groans, "That is so much to remember." The instructor agrees but tells them that it is necessary to reduce medication errors and that some even cause ***sentinel events*** or very serious injury or death. Conner asks, "What if the patient does not want a medication?"

Exercise 18-29: *True/False*

The nurse understands that the patient has the right to refuse a medication.

- ❑ True
- ❑ False

eResource 18-15: Additional information regarding the patient's rights to refuse can be found in the University of California Medical School's Ethics Resource: [Pathway: www.missinglink.ucsf.edu/lm/ethics → select "Refusal for Treatment" to read overview of this topic].

The instructor also tells the students that patients have the right to be informed about their medication and cannot be given an experimental drug unless they are aware and agree. This is to safeguard the patient.

eResource 18-16: Additional information regarding the informed consent can be also found in the University of California Medical School's Ethics Resource: [Pathway: www.missinglink.ucsf.edu/lm/ethics → select "Informed Consent" to read overview of this topic].

Exercise 18-30: *Fill-in*

The nurse understands that the term used to describe patients who are taking many medications that may interact with one another is ____________________________.

The instructor takes the class into the lab in order to practice medication administration in a safe environment. They start with oral medications. This is usually the easiest method to administer a medication.

Exercise 18-31: *Multiple Choice Question*

The nurse understands that PO (oral) medications are contraindicated in patients who:

A. Are elderly
B. Are infants
C. Have gastrointestinal (GI) disorders
D. Can only sit at a 30° angle

Oral medication can be dispensed in liquid form, capsule, pill, or tablet form.

The Answers section can be found on page 249.

Exercise 18-32: *Multiple Choice Question*

The nurse understands that most tablets and capsules should be swallowed with ____ of fluid.

A. 10 to 20 mL
B. 20 to 50 mL
C. 60 to 100 mL
D. 100 to 150 mL

After Conner, Alita, and Aubree practice dispensing oral medications they move on to topical. Topical medication can be administered through the skin or mucous membranes.

Exercise 18-33: *Multiple Choice Question*

The nurse understands that when administering a topical skin medication, he or she should wear gloves because:

A. They will contaminate the skin
B. The patient will be infectious
C. The gloves will assist it to go on smoothly
D. The gloves will prevent the nurse from getting the drug's effect

eResource 18-17: AFLA's topical medication administration tip sheet can be found at: http://alfa.saddleback.edu/N170/topicalmedications.aspx

Exercise 18-34: *Ordering*

Place the steps to administer ophthalmic (eye) medication in order from 1 to 7:

_______ Drop prescribed number of drops into the conjunctival sac
_______ With nondominant hand, hold the upper and lower lids open
_______ ID the patient
_______ Ask the patient to close his or her eye
_______ Slightly hyperextend head
_______ Don gloves
_______ Wipe away any excess medication that is dripping

Exercise 18-35: *Fill-in*

When instilling eye ointment, it is placed in the eye from the ______ to the _______ canthus.

eResource 18-18: Aubree, Alita, and Conner review proper administration of eye medication by consulting the ALFA website: http://alfa.saddleback.edu/N170/eyemedications.aspx

Next Aubree moves on to ear medication and reviews the different positioning for adults and children.

The Answers section can be found on page 249.

Exercise 18-36: *Matching*

Match child or adult in column A to the proper method to position the ear in column B.

Column A	Column B
A. Child	_______ Down and backward
B. Adult	_______ Up and outward

Aubree, Alita, and Connor also learn about vaginal and rectal instillation of medication.

Exercise 18-37: *Multiple Choice Question*

Rectal suppositories should be positioned:

A. Above the internal anal sphincter
B. Above the external anal sphincter
C. Below the internal anal sphincter
D. Just inside the external anal sphincter

Exercise 18-38: *Multiple Choice Question*

Rectal suppositories should be instilled:

A. Lubricated with petroleum jelly (Vaseline)
B. Without additional lubrication
C. Moistened with water
D. Lubricated with water-soluble jelly

eResource 18-19: Aubree, Alita, and Connor review proper medication administration references on the ALFA website.

- Vaginal medication administration: http://alfa.saddleback.edu/N170/vaginalmedications.aspx
- Rectal medication administration: http://alfa.saddleback.edu/N170/rectalmedications.aspx

The next subject that is addressed in the lab session and the final subject for today is inhalation medication. Many individuals in the United States have asthma and use inhalers, but there are many other diseases of the lung that benefit from inhalation medications. Medications are delivered by spray, mist, or powder and they are easily absorbed in the lungs, producing local and systemic effects.

Many handheld inhalers are now equipped with spacers or an attachment that separates the inhaler from the patient in order to further break down the medication and enhance its absorption. The students manipulate ***placebo*** (fake) inhalers in order to learn the proper administration of inhaled medication.

Exercise 18-39: *Multiple Choice Question*

After inhaling medication, the patient should:

A. Exhale immediately
B. Hold the breath for 10 seconds

The Answers section can be found on page 249.

C. Expectorate

D. Tilt his or her head back

eResource 18-20: Aubree, Alita, and Connor also review the proper inhalation medication administration technique: http://alfa.saddleback.edu/N170/inhaledmedications.aspx

Aubree, Alita, and Connor's class is over for the day. They have learned a tremendous amount of information about medication administration, which is a large portion of nurses' jobs and a big responsibility. Next class medication administration will continue with parenteral medication or those given by injection or intravenous.

The Answers section can be found on page 249.

Exercise 18-1: ***Multiple Choice Question***

The U.S. legal agency that regulates medications is the:

A. Pure Food and Drug Act—NO, this regulates medication labeling

B. Health Science Regulatory Agency—NO, this is not a regulatory agency

C. Center for Disease Control—NO, this regulates immunizations

D. **Food and Drug Administration—YES, the FDA regulates medications that can be safely used**

Exercise 18-2: ***Select All That Apply***

Select the forms of medications that are used for patients:

☒ **Caplet**

☒ **Tablet**

☒ **Intraocular disk**

☒ **Transdermal patch**

❑ Intraaural disk—NO, ear medication comes in drops (gtts)

☒ **Vaginal suppository**

☒ **Rectal suppository**

Exercise 18-3: ***Fill-in***

The quickest route of administration for drug absorption is ***intravenous.***

Exercise 18-4: ***Select All That Apply***

The following are factors in drug absorption:

☒ **Route**

☒ **Dissolvability**

☒ **Blood flow**

☒ **Age of patient**

☒ **Gender of patient**

Exercise 18-5: ***Multiple Choice Question***

The organ that plays the largest role in detoxifying medication is the:

A. Lungs—NO, only if the medication is inhaled

B. **Liver—YES, the liver detoxifies most medications**

C. Kidneys—NO, the kidneys excrete what the liver detoxifies
D. Intestines—NO, this is where medication is usually absorbed

Exercise 18-6: *Multiple Choice Question*

The organ that plays the largest role in medication excretion is:

A. Lungs—NO, minimal amounts are excreting through breathing
B. Liver—NO, the liver detoxifies
C. **Kidneys—YES, kidney function is important for excreting drugs**
D. Intestines—NO, most are excreting through the kidneys

Exercise 18-7: *Matching*

Match the reaction in column A to the description in column B.

Column A		Column B
A. Therapeutic effect	**D**	A reaction to a medication that is different from the norm
B. Side effect	**E**	Caused by an accumulation of the drug
C. Allergic reaction	**B**	Unintended effects of a drug
D. Adverse effect	**F**	Immunologically sensitized to the drug
E. Toxic effect	**C**	Severe response to a drug
F. Idiosyncratic reaction	**A**	Predicted response to the drug

Exercise 18-8: *Multiple Choice Question*

Common side effects of medication include:

A. Shortness of breath, rash, pruritus—NO, shortness of breath (SOB) is severe
B. Pruritus, rhinitis, diarrhea—NO, rhinitis is severe
C. **Diarrhea, stomach upset, constipation—YES, these are common**
D. Constipation, urticaria, stomach upset—NO, urticaria is severe

Exercise 18-9: *Exhibit Question*

A 24-year-old college student is brought to the student health center, wheezing with strider (Table 18.3).

Table 18.3

Vital signs (VS)	Medications	Laboratory tests
Temperature 5 99.0°F	Doxycycline 3 3 days for acne	Finger-stick glucose 5 78
Respirations 5 36	Birth control pills	
Pulse 5 98		
Blood pressure 5 128/88		

The nurse would recognize this as a(n):

A. **Anaphylactic reaction—YES, this is anaphylaxis**
B. Side effect—NO, this is not as severe
C. Idiosyncratic reaction—NO, this is an immune reaction
D. Therapeutic effect—NO, this is what is supposed to happen

Exercise 18-10: *Multiple Choice Question*

When medications taken together potentiate each other, this reaction is called:

A. **Antagonistic—YES**
B. Idiosyncratic—NO
C. Detrimental—NO
D. Synergistic—NO

Exercise 18-11: *Exhibit Question*

An infant is receiving Gentamycin IV for sepsis (blood infection) and the neonatal nurse practitioner orders a peak and trough with the next dose. The nurse checks the trough half an hour before and it is WNL and administers the dose. One hour later, the peak is drawn and should be between 4 and 8 mcg/mL (Table 18.4).

Table 18.4

Vital signs (VS)	Medications	Laboratory tests
Temperature 98.4°F axillary	Gentamycin 1.5 mg/kg/q 12 hr	Gentamycin trough , 1 mcg/ mL (WNL)
Respirations 5 56/min		
Apical 5 134 BPM		Gentamycin peak 6 mcg/mL

After the results are received, the priority nursing intervention would be:

A. Call the neonatal nurse practitioner—NO
B. Administer a second dose—NO
C. Increase the plain IV to dilute the medication in the blood stream—NO
D. **Continue to monitor the patient—YES, the peak should be between 5 and 8 mcg/mL and the trough <2 mcg/mL**

Exercise 18-12: *Multiple Choice Question*

The half-life of a drug is the amount of time it takes for:

A. It to be totally excreted by the kidneys—NO
B. **The blood concentration is at half-strength—YES**
C. The drug to reach its therapeutic effect—NO
D. The body to respond to the therapeutic effect—NO

Exercise 18-13: *Matching*

Match the abbreviation in column A to the descriptor in column B.

Column A	Column B
A. ac	**D** hour
B. Ad lib	**J** every 8 hours
C. bid	**L** immediately
D. H	**A** before meals
E. pc	**G** every hour
F. prn	**C** twice a day
G. Q h	**I** every 6 hours
H. q 2 h	**B** as desired or at liberty
I. q 6 h	**H** every 2 hours
J. q 8 h	**E** after meals
K. tid	**F** as needed
L. stat	**K** three times a day

Exercise 18-14: *Multiple Choice Question*

The nurse understands that the patient needs further teaching when he states:

A. **"I should put my buccal medication in the same cheek each time."—YES, it should be alternated**
B. "I should not swallow the medication."—NO, this is true
C. "I should not drink water while taking the medication."—NO, this is true
D. "I should not chew the medication."—NO, this is true

Exercise 18-15: *Matching*

Match the parenteral administration method in column A with the description in column B.

Column A	Column B
A. Intradermal	**C** Injection into a muscle
B. Subcutaneous	**A** Injection just under the skin
C. Intramuscular	**D** Injection into a vein
D. Intravenous	**B** Injection into tissue under the skin

Exercise 18-16: *Fill-in*

A. 1 gram (g or GM) = **1000** milligrams (mg)
B. 1 liter (L) = **1000** milliliters (mL)
C. 1 tablespoon (tbsp) = **3** teaspoons (tsp)
D. 1 teaspoon (tsp) = **5** mL

Exercise 18-17: *Calculation*

The order is written for 5 mL q 6 hours of an antibiotic, Amoxicillin. The nurse tells the patient to take how many tsp? **one**

Exercise 18-18: *Calculation*

The nurse instructs a patient to take an ounce of cough syrup that is 30 mL. How many tbsp should the patient take? **2**

Exercise 18-19: *Calculation*

The nurse is to give an IV of 250 ml. The solution comes in a 1-L bag. The nurse understands that she is given **1/4 or 0.25** of a bag.

Exercise 18-20: *Calculation*

The order is written for 500 mg of an antihypertensive medication. The nurse understands that this is **1/2 or 0.50** g.

Exercise 18-21: *Fill-in*

A. 1 pound (lb) = **0.45** kg
B. 1 kg = **1000** g

Exercise 18-22: *Calculation*

The nurse is medicating a child who is 15 pounds. The order for the medication is written in mg per kg. How many kg is the child? **15 × 0.45 = 6.75 kg**

Exercise 18-23: *Calculation*

A child is 4,200 g; how many kg is the child? **4.2 kg** How many lbs is the child? **4.2 × 2.2 = 9.25 lbs.**

Exercise 18-24: *Calculation*

A dose of Gentamycin is ordered for an 11-lb child who is 12 mg/kg/day in two divided doses.

A. Change 11 lbs to kg **11 × 0.45 = 4.95 kg**
B. 12 mg/day would be how many mg per 12 hours? **12 mg divided by 2 = 6 mg**
C. How much should you give? **29.7 mg**

Exercise 18-25: *Multiple Choice Question*

The nurse understands that the safest way to receive a medication order is by:

A. **EHR—YES, this is the safest way**
B. Verbally—NO, this is often miscommunicated
C. Telephone—NO, this is often miscommunicated
D. Written—NO, handwriting can be difficult to read

Exercise 18-26: *Select All That Apply*

The components of a medication order include:

☒ **Patient's name**

☒ **Date**

☒ **Times to give**

❑ Expiration of the order—NO, this is usually known by hospital policy

❑ What type of nurse should give the medication (RN, LPN)—NO, the order does not note this—this is part of the nurse practice act

☒ **Amount**

Exercise 18-27: *Matching*

Match the different types of orders in column A with the description in column B.

Column A	Column B
A. Standing orders	**C** Give once
B. PRN orders	**A** Give until it is cancelled or expires
C. Single-time orders	**D** Give immediately
D. STAT orders	**B** Give if needed

Exercise 18-28: *Select All That Apply*

The nurse understands that each and every time he or she administers medication, they must check:

☒ **Right medication**

☒ **Right patient**

❑ Right situation—NO, this is not one of the rights for medication it is for delegation

☒ **Right route**

☒ **Right time**

☒ **Right documentation**

☒ **Right dose**

Exercise 18-29: *True/False*

The nurse understands that the patient has the right to refuse a medication.

☒ **True**

❑ False

Exercise 18-30: *Fill-in*

The nurse understands that the term used to describe patients who are taking many medications that may interact with one another is **polypharmacy**.

Exercise 18-31: ***Multiple Choice Question***

The nurse understands that po (oral) medications are contraindicated in patients who:

A. Are elderly—NO, this is not necessarily true
B. Are infants—NO, this is not necessarily true
C. **Have gastrointestinal (GI) disorders—YES, this may be a problem for absorption**
D. Can only sit at a 30° angle—NO, they should sit up to take po medications to prevent aspiration

Exercise 18-32: ***Multiple Choice Question***

The nurse understands that most tablets and capsules should be swallowed with ____ of fluid.

A. 10 to 20 mL—NO, too little
B. 20 to 50 mL—NO, too little
C. **60 to 100 mL—YES**
D. 100 to 150 mL—NO, may be too much

Exercise 18-33: ***Multiple Choice Question***

The nurse understands that when administering a topical skin medication, he or she should wear gloves because:

A. They will contaminate the skin—NO, cross contamination may be an issue, but it is not the primary reason
B. The patient will be infectious—NO, contamination may be an issue, but it is not the primary reason
C. The gloves will assist it to go on smoothly—NO
D. **The gloves will prevent the nurse from getting the drug's effect—YES, the nurse will absorb it through her skin**

Exercise 18-34: ***Ordering***

Place the steps to administer ophthalmic (eye) medication in order:

__5__ Drop prescribed number of drops into the conjunctival sac
__4__ With nondominant hand hold the upper and lower lids open
__1__ ID the patient
__6__ Ask the patient to close his or her eye
__3__ Slightly hyperextend head
__2__ Don gloves
__7__ Wipe away any excess medication that is dripping

Exercise 18-35: ***Fill-in***

When instilling eye ointment, it is placed in the eye from the **inner** to the **outer** canthus.

Exercise 18-36: *Matching*

Match child or adult in column A to the proper method to position the ear in column B.

Column A		Column B
A. Child	**A**	Down and backward (remember children are "down" closer to the floor)
B. Adult	**B**	Up and outward

Exercise 18-37: *Multiple Choice Question*

Rectal suppositories should be positioned:

A. **Above the internal anal sphincter—YES, or else it will be pushed out involuntarily**
B. Above the external anal sphincter—NO
C. Below the internal anal sphincter—NO
D. Just inside the external anal sphincter—NO

Exercise 18-38: *Multiple Choice Question*

Rectal suppositories should be instilled:

A. Lubricated with petroleum jelly (Vaseline)—NO, this is not water soluble
B. Without additional lubrication—NO, they should be lubricated
C. Moistened with water—NO, water will melt the suppository
D. **Lubricated with water-soluble jelly—YES**

Exercise 18-39: *Multiple Choice Question*

After inhaling medication, the patient should:

A. Exhale immediately—NO, this does not give the medication time to absorb
B. **Hold the breath for 10 seconds—YES**
C. Expectorate—NO, this will lose some of the medication
D. Tilt his or her head back—NO, this should be done before administration of the medication

19

Medications—Part II

Unfolding Case Study 18 Aubree, Alita, and Connor

Back in lab the following week, Aubree, Alita, and Connor continue to learn about medication administration. The content for this week will focus on parenteral medications that are given by injection.

Exercise 19-1: ***Fill-in***

Since administering medication parenterally is an invasive procedure, it is done under _______________ technique.

The instructor provides the students with various types and size of syringes. The syringes range from 1 to 60 mL, and some have a tip that the needle can screw into and others do not. All syringes are packaged sterilely. Different-sized syringes are used for different medications.

Exercise 19-2: ***Matching***

Match the medication or route in column A to the size of the syringe in column B.

Column A	Column B
A. Insulin syringe	_______ 1-mL syringe
B. Tuberculin syringe	_______ 3-mL syringe
C. Intramuscular (IM) syringe	_______ 0.3- to 1-mL syringe

Next the instructor reviews the differences between needles. Today, all needles are disposable and are considered contaminated waste and need to be disposed of in a nonpermeable sharp container in order to protect workers when removing the trash.

The Answers section can be found on page 265.

Exercise 19-3: ***Label the Diagram***

Draw a line from the label to the part of the picture it represents.

A. Bevel

B. Shaft

C. Hub

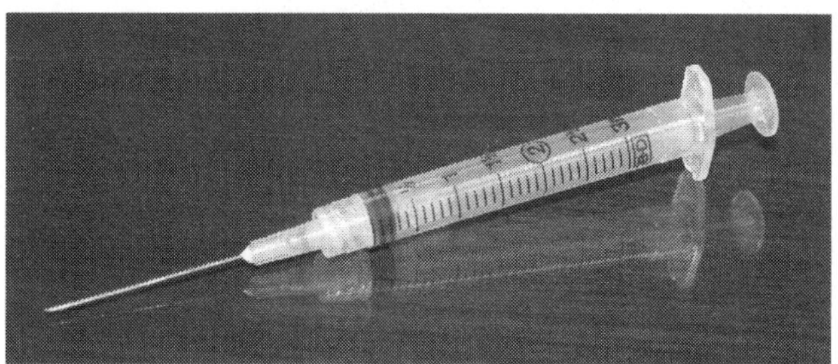

Needles come in sizes, different lengths, and different thickness or gauge. As the gauge number becomes smaller, the circumference of the needle becomes larger. So an 18 gauge needle is larger than a 23 gauge needle. An 18 gauge needle would be used for blood since it is more viscous and needs a larger lumen or needle to go through. The length of needles varies depending on the size of the patient and the medication. IM needles need to be longer than subcutaneous or sc needles in order to reach the muscle.

eResource 19-1: IV basics provide an overview of IV administration as well as information regarding needle sizes. [Pathway: www.employees.csbsju.edu/mbyrne/IVSite/basics_page_abciv.htm → select "Basics" → select "Needles".]

There are also prefilled syringes that insert into a device that holds them while you give the injection. The most popular of these devices are called Tubex or Carpuject and are the brand names of the device.

Most medication comes in ampules or vials that have to be withdrawn. An ampule is a small glass bottle that has to be snapped off at the neck. Once this is done, the fluid can be withdrawn with a filter needle attached to the syringe, so glass shards are not injected into the patient. Then the filter needle is changed for a regular needle.

Exercise 19-4: ***Ordering***

Place the steps of withdrawing medication from an ampule in order from 1 to 8:

_______ Snap at the neck away from the hands

_______ ID the patient

_______ Check the MAR (Medication Administration Record)

_______ Cover the top of the ampule with a gauze or unopened alcohol swab

_______ Don gloves

_______ Change the filter needle to a regular injection needle

_______ Withdraw with a filter needle

_______ Give the medication as ordered

The Answers section can be found on page 265.

Withdrawing medication from a vial is different because there is a rubber top on a vial. The rubber top keeps the vial air tight, so air has to be injected to displace the fluid. Many vials are multidose, so the vial top has to be cleaned well with alcohol each time it is used. Some vials contain powder that needs to be reconstituted in order to inject. Solution is injected into the powder than with drawn with a clean needle. Drawing up insulin is also important. There are many kinds of insulin, and often patients are on a short and long acting insulin.

Exercise 19-5: *Multiple Choice Question*

The nurse understands that the patient needs more teaching when he says:

A. "I will draw up the clear insulin first"
B. "I will draw up the insulin with a sterile needle"
C. "I will inject air without touching the needle to the liquid"
D. "I will draw up the insulin and place it on the side until after I eat breakfast"

The students practice reconstituting and drawing up solutions. The use of manikins and injection pillows allow students to practice techniques.

Exercise 19-6: *Matching*

Match the type of injection in column A with the angle it is given in column B.

Column A	Column B
A. Intradermal (ID)	_______ 90° angle
B. Subcutaneous (SC)	_______ 5° to 15° angle
C. Intramuscular (IM)	_______ 45° to 90° angle

Exercise 19-7: *Hot Spot*

Place an X on three approximate spots for a subcutaneous injection.

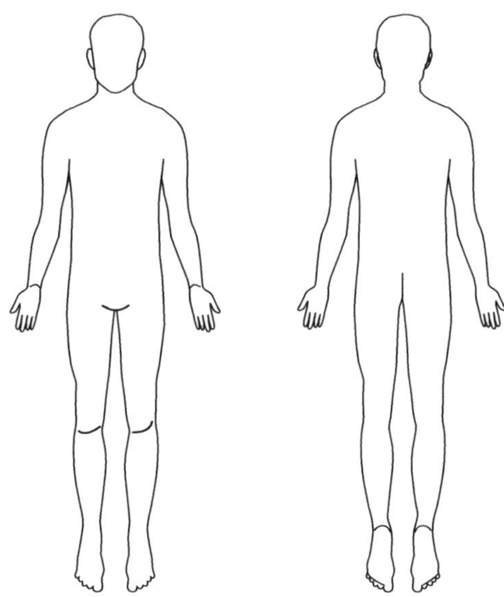

The Answers section can be found on page 265.

eResource 19-2: Tip sheet and video demonstration for SQ injections (scroll down to bottom of page to view videos:

- Insulin: http://alfa.saddleback.edu/N170/insulin.aspx
- Heparin: http://alfa.saddleback.edu/N170/heparin.aspx

Exercise 19-8: *Multiple Choice Question*

The nurse understands that he or she should administer the IM injection to the 6-month-old infant in the following muscle:

A. Ventrogluteal

B. Deltoid

C. Dorsogluteal

D. Vastus lateralis

Alita, Connor, and Aubree practice marking the spots where IM injections are given to patients.

Exercise 19-9: *Hot Spot*

Mark the spot for a ventrogluteal injection.

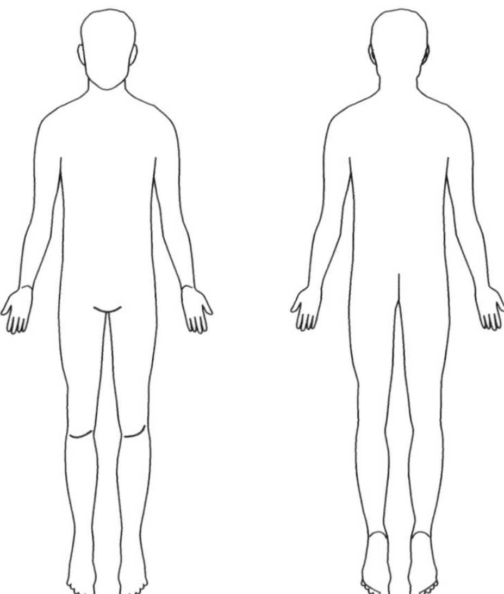

Exercise 19-10: *Multiple Choice Question*

The risk identified in giving an IM injection in the dorsogluteal muscle is:

A. Soreness when the patient sits

B. High incidence of skin reaction

C. Damage to the sciatic nerve

D. High incidence of bruising

eResource 19-3: IM injections:

- Overview of intramuscular injections: http://alfa.saddleback.edu/N170/intramuscularOverview.aspx

The Answers section can be found on page 265.

- Administering IM injections: www.saddleback.edu/alfa/N170/adminintramuscular.aspx Scroll down to bottom of page to view two videos demonstrating:
  - Ventrogluteal IM injection
  - Deltoid IM injection

Exercise 19-11: *Multiple Choice Question*

The nurse understands that a reason to use a Z-track method of IM injection is:

A. To prevent skin irritation

B. To increase muscle penetration on obese patients

C. To decrease hematoma formation

D. To increase medication absorption

eResource 19-4: The students watch another video demonstration depicting the proper technique for administering an Z-track IM injection: www.youtu.be/IPp28ZGgobw

Exercise 19-12: *Select All That Apply*

The nurse understands that the needle should be changed before giving IM injection that involves:

- ❑ Z-track technique
- ❑ Dorsogluteal injections
- ❑ Two types of insulin
- ❑ Medication extraction from an ampule
- ❑ Medication extraction from a vial

The class also talks about safety. Needle sticks are a serious health care issue, and prevention should be practiced. Occupational Safety and Health Association (OSHA) has clear preventative guidelines in order to decrease needle-stick injuries.

eResource 19-5: The instructor provides several important handouts designed to heighten awareness of health care workers on steps to prevent injuries:

- CDC sharp safety for health care settings: www.cdc.gov/sharpssafety/
- Sharps safety training program: www.absa50.org/pdf/204Brack.pdf
- The CDC's one and only campaign: www.oneandonlycampaign.org/content/audio-video

Exercise 19-13: *Multiple Choice Question*

The nurse is finished performing an IM injection, and the sharps container in the patient's room is full. The nurse should:

A. Recap the needle and take it to the nurses' station

B. Leave the needle in the room and go get a new sharps box

C. Carefully try to squeeze in the needle

D. Do not recap the needle, and take it to the nearest sharps box that is not full

The Answers section can be found on page 265.

Exercise 19-14: *Multiple Choice Question*

In an emergency, a needle may need to be recapped, in order to perform this technique properly, the nurse should:

A. Hold the cap in your nondominant hand and the needle in your dominant hand
B. Use sterile gloves
C. Ask a colleague to hold the cap
D. Use one hand

Alita, Aubree, and Connor are now ready to move onto intravenous (IV) basics. This seems like the most confusing of all medication administration. The instructor tells them that once they understand the principles of IV medication administration, they will feel more comfortable.

There are three ways that medication is given by the IV route:

- In bolus form or IV push, which is small amounts given directly into the vein through the IV line or a port called a heparin lock or saline lock;
- IV piggy bag (IVPB) in which a small volume IV bag (50–100 ml) is attached to shorter IV tubing that is attached to the main IV line; and
- IV mixtures or medications mixed in a large IV bag (1,000 ml or 1-L bag) such as magnesium sulfate (MgSO4), which comes in the IV bag from the company or the hospital pharmacy.

eResource 19-6: Alita, Aubree, and Connor review what they have learned about administering medications by the IV route by reading supplemental materials and viewing videos:

- IV push medications: http://alfa.saddleback.edu/N172/IVP.aspx
- IV piggy bag (IVPB) via infusing IV: http://alfa.saddleback.edu/N172/IVPB.aspx

Exercise 19-15: *Multiple Choice Question*

The nurse understands that IV medication administration poses additional risks because:

A. Larger amounts are given
B. More potent drugs are always given
C. Medications are immediately available to the blood stream
D. Vein's absorption is unpredictable

Medication in IV bags is premixed in the pharmacy. Very rarely do nurses inject medication into IV bags. This regulates medication administration and decreases mistakes. IV medications are always given by a dose-regulated pump. They are never hung "free flow" because if it should "run in" fast there could be grave consequences for the patient. IV flow rate is dependent on the type of tubing that is delivering the solution. Giving IV medications and calculating IV flow rate are done in the adult health courses, but it is necessary for fundamental students to know the principles of IV medication administration.

The Answers section can be found on page 265.

Exercise 19-16: *Fill-in*

On the following chart, put an X in the box that denotes the appropriate task for the skill level.

Task	RN	LPN (licensed practical nurse)	UAP (unlicensed assistive personnel or certified nursing assistant [CAN])
IV push medication			
Check IV site			
Administer IVPB medication			
Administer large volume IV medication			

Alita, Aubree, and Connor are through with medication class and feel that they can handle administering PO, IV, sub q., and IM medications in their clinical learning experience. They also start to study for the medication administration test!

The Answers section can be found on page 265.

Exercise 19-1: *Fill-in*

Since administering medication parenterally is an invasive procedure, it is done under **aseptic** technique.

Exercise 19-2: *Matching*

Match the medication or route in column A to the size of the syringe in column B.

Column A	Column B
A. Insulin syringe	**B** 1-mL syringe
B. Tuberculin syringe	**C** 3-mL syringe
C. Intramuscular (IM) syringe	**A** 0.3- to 1-mL syringe

Exercise 19-3: *Label the Diagram*

Draw a line from the label to the picture it represents.

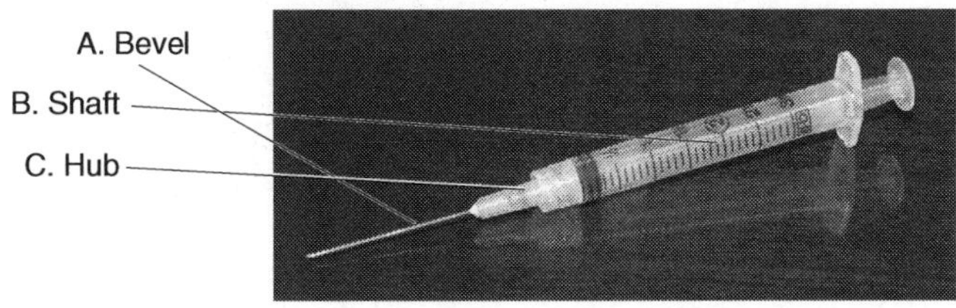

Exercise 19-4: *Ordering*

Place the steps of withdrawing medication from an ampule in order.

5 Snap at the neck away from the hands
2 ID the patient
1 Check the MAR (Medication Administration Record)
4 Cover the top of the ampule with a gauze or unopened alcohol swab
3 Don gloves
7 Change the filter needle to a regular injection needle
6 Withdraw with a filter needle
8 Give the medication as ordered

Exercise 19-5: ***Multiple Choice Question***

The nurse understands that the patient needs more teaching when he says:

A. **"I will draw up the clear insulin first."—YES, the cloudy is drawn up first**

B. "I will draw up the insulin with a sterile needle."—NO, it should be a sterile needle

C. "I will inject air without touching the needle to the liquid."—NO, this is the right method

D. "I will draw up the insulin and place it on the side until after I eat breakfast."—NO, it needs to be administered right away or it could decompensate and not be as effective

Exercise 19-6: ***Matching***

Match the type of injection in column A with the angle it is given in column B.

Column A	Column B
A. Intradermal (ID)	__C__ 90° angle
B. Subcutaneous (Sub q.)	__B__ 5° to 15° angle
C. Intramuscular (IM)	__A__ 45° to 90° angle

Exercise 19-7: ***Hot Spot***

Place an X on three approximate spots for a subcutaneous injection.

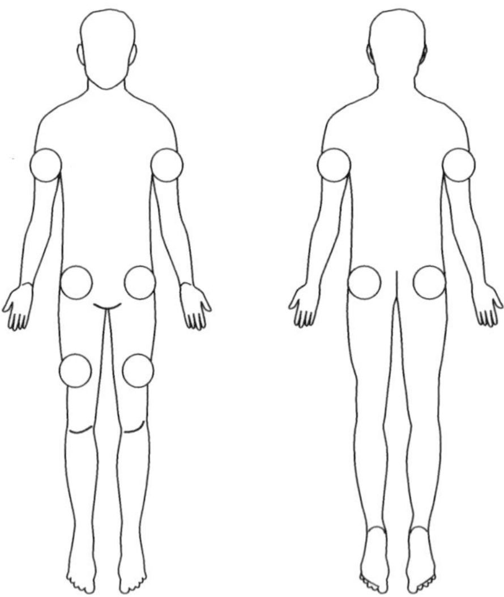

Exercise 19-8: ***Multiple Choice Question***

The nurse understands that he or she should administer the IM injection to the 6-month-old infant in the following muscle:

A. Ventrogluteal—NO, this muscle is not developed until the child is walking for a while

B. Deltoid—NO, this muscle is too small on a child

C. Dorsogluteal—NO, this muscle is not developed until the child is walking for a while

D. **Vastus lateralis—YES, this is the best muscle until they are walking for about a year**

Exercise 19-9: ***Hot Spot***

Mark the spot for a ventrogluteal injection.

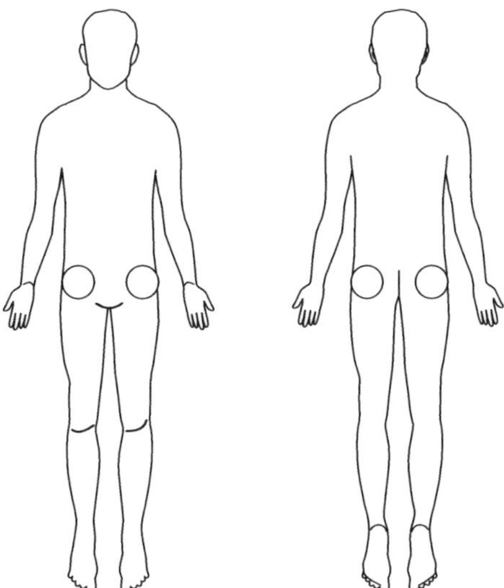

Exercise 19-10: ***Multiple Choice Question***

The risk identified in giving an IM injection in the dorsogluteal muscle is:

A. Soreness when the patient sits—NO, this could happen but is not the most important reason

B. High incidence of skin reaction—NO, this not specific to the spot

C. **Damage to the sciatic nerve—YES, this is the main concern**

D. High incidence of bruising—NO, this could happen but is not the most important reason

Exercise 19-11: ***Multiple Choice Question***

The nurse understands that a reason to use a Z-track method of IM injection is:

A. **To prevent skin irritation—YES, this is done when administering irritating solutions**

B. To increase muscle penetration on obese patients—NO, this can be done with needle length

C. To decrease hematoma formation—NO, this is not the main concern

D. To increase medication absorption—NO, this is not affected

Exercise 19-12: ***Select All That Apply***

The nurse understands that the needle should be changed before giving IM injection that involves:

☒ **Z-track technique—YES, because the solution is irritating and could be on the needle that was used to withdraw it from the medication container**

❑ Dorsogluteal injections—NO

❑ Two types of insulin—NO

☒ **Medication extraction from an ampule—YES, the filter needle needs to be changed before it is given**

☐ Medication extraction from a vial—NO

Exercise 19-13: *Multiple Choice Question*

The nurse is finished performing an IM injection, and the sharps container in the patient's room is full. The nurse should:

A. Recap the needle and take it to the nurses' station—NO, try not to recap
B. Leave the needle in the room and go get a new sharps box—NO, this is a patient safety issue
C. Carefully try to squeeze in the needle—NO, this will cause you injury
D. **Do not recap the needle and take it to the nearest sharps box that is not full—YES, this is your best option for safety**

Exercise 19-14: *Multiple Choice Question*

In an emergency, a needle may need to be recapped, in order to perform this technique properly, the nurse should:

A. Hold the cap in your nondominant hand and the needle in your dominant hand—NO, this is not the recommended method
B. Use sterile gloves—NO, clean gloves are all that are needed
C. Ask a colleague to hold the cap—NO, you may stab the other person
D. **Use one hand—YES, use the one-handed method**

Exercise 19-15: *Multiple Choice Question*

The nurse understands that IV medication administration poses additional risks because:

A. Larger amounts are given—NO, this is a concern but not the most important concept
B. More potent drugs are always given—NO, this is not always true
C. **Medications are immediately available to the blood stream—YES, the absorption is fast**
D. Vein's absorption is unpredictable—NO, this is not true

Exercise 19-16: *Fill-in*

On the following chart, put an X in the box that denotes the appropriate task for the skill level.

Task	RN	LPN (licensed practical nurse)	UAP (unlicensed assistive personal or certified nursing assistant [CAN])
IV push medication	X		
Check IV site	X	X	X
Administer IVPB medication	X	X (in some states, this is covered by the LPN practice act but not all states)	
Administer large volume IV medication	X	X (in some states, this is covered by the LPN practice act but not all states)	

20

Complementary or Alternative Medications and Therapies

Unfolding Case Study 19 Aubree, Alita, and Connor

Aubree, Alita, and Connor are confused why they would need to read a chapter on CAM (Complementary or alternative medicine). In class, the instructor tells them that it is an important part of holistic care, and that it is estimated that a large percent of patients use CAM along with traditional therapies. Nurses need to know about the patient's use of CAM, in case there are any contraindications or adverse effects as well as positive outcomes.

Exercise 20-1: ***Matching***

Match the terms in column A to the description in column B.

Column A	Column B
A. Allopathic medicine	_______ Used instead of traditional medical therapy
B. Complementary therapies	_______ Combination of traditional and alternative therapies
C. Alternative therapies	_______ Traditional therapies
D. Integrative therapies	_______ Used to augment traditional therapies

eResource 20-1: The instructor tells the students that CAM and associated therapies have been gaining acceptance among Western health care providers and refers them to the National Institute of Health (NIH)'s Complementary and Alternative Medicine Online Continuing Education Series: www.nccam.nih.gov/training/videolectures

There are many CAM, but they all come under five categories, which include:

- ❑ Alternative medical systems
- ❑ Biologically based therapies
- ❑ Mind–body therapies
- ❑ Manipulative therapies
- ❑ Energy field therapies

The Answers section can be found on page 275.

Exercise 20-2: *Hot Spot*

Place an X that represents the concepts of CAM:

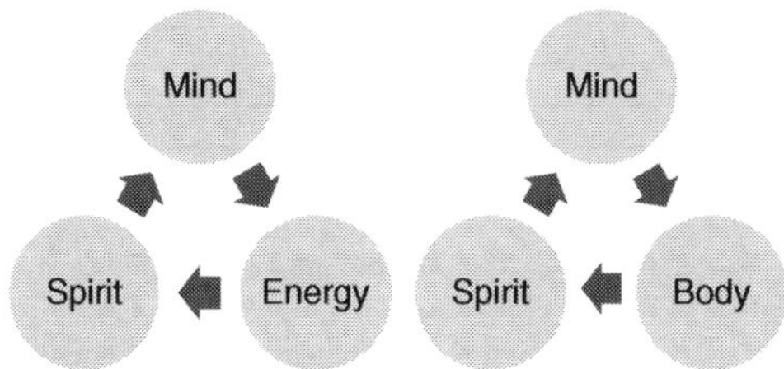

Exercise 20-3: *Fill-in*

On the following chart, place an X on the classification in which the type of therapy represents:

	Alternative medical	Biologically based	Manipulative	Mind–body	Energy
Acupuncture					
Reiki					
Biofeedback					
Herb					
Massage					

Nurses have actually been using types of CAM and therapies for years such as breathing exercises, visualization, and relaxation techniques.

Exercise 20-4: *Multiple Choice Question*

A patient who is being prepared for a diagnostic test is extremely stressed and anxious. The nurse teaches him to isolate one muscle group at a time and concentrate on relating that muscle group. This type of CAM and therapy is:

A. Therapeutic touch
B. Passive relaxation
C. Progressive relaxation
D. Mind–body response

Exercise 20-5: *Select All That Apply*

The nurse is assisting the patient to meditate and therefore should provide the following:

❑ Quiet space
❑ Relaxing picture
❑ Receptive attitude
❑ A mantra

The Answers section can be found on page 275.

Exercise 20-6: *Multiple Choice Question*

The nurse is caring for a patient in labor who is becoming uncomfortable. She provides a moving picture of a waterfall for the patient to look at and hear. This type of therapy is called:

A. Biofeedback
B. Meditation
C. Therapeutic touch
D. Visualization

eResource 20-2: The class views a short video on the use of meditation as a means to reduce stress by relaxing the body and calming the mind. The students learn that there is evidence that there are health benefits and more research is currently underway: www.nihseniorhealth.gov/cam/faq/video/cam3_na.html?intro=yes

Exercise 20-7: *Multiple Choice Question*

The nurse understands that biofeedback therapy involves:

A. Laying on of hands
B. Manipulation of the spine
C. Word association
D. Electronic impulses

Exercise 20-8: *True/False*

Therapeutic touch (TT) always involves the direct contact.

❑ True
❑ False

The class discusses chiropractic medicine, and many of the students have been to see a chiropractor for spinal manipulation for different reasons such as pain or headaches.

eResource 20-3: To learn more about Chiropractic Therapy as a supplement to traditional health care, the students visit NIH Complementary and Alternative Medicine website: www.nccam.nih.gov/health/chiropractic/introduction.htm

One student raised her hand and said she has had acupuncture for headaches also and that it worked. Acupuncture is a traditional Chinese medicine (TCM). Other TCMs include acupressure, exercise, and herbs. Patients' herbal intake is very important for nurses to know since herbs can enhance or deter the therapeutic effects of traditional medicine.

eResource 20-4: To understand more about acupuncture, Connor views two brief videos:

- *How does acupuncture work?* Dr. Zhen Zheng from RMIT University: www.youtu.be/dhhdmahBQU8
- *How does acupuncture work?* Perspective from Dr. Craig Schadow: www.youtu.be/4PgjZ2rj63U

The Answers section can be found on page 275.

Exercise 20-9: *Matching*

Match the commonly used herb in column A with its therapeutic effect and usage in column B.

Column A	Column B
A. Aloe	_______ Increased physical endurance: fatigue
B. Chamomile	_______ Inhibits serotonin uptake: depression
C. Garlic	_______ Antiemetic: morning sickness
D. Ginger	_______ Anti-inflammatory: used for burns
E. Gingko biloba	_______ Anti-inflammatory used for respiratory system
F. Ginseng	_______ Lowers lipids: high cholesterol
G. St. John's wort	_______ Helps memory: dementia

The students are told that there are very many herbs used, and that the most important thing is to maintain a therapeutic nurse–patient relationship in order for patients to feel comfortable enough during the assessment process to tell which herbs are being used.

eResource 20-5: Aubree finds several websites that provide information about herbs and their medicinal value:

- Memorial Sloan-Kettering Cancer Center: [Pathway: www.mskcc.org/ → enter "Integrative Medicine" into the search field → select "About Herbs, Botanicals & Other Products"].
- American Botanical Council: www.herbmed.org/

Exercise 20-10: *Multiple Choice Question*

The nurse is interviewing a patient, and the patient says that she takes garlic along with her medication to lower her cholesterol. The best response for the nurse is:

A. "You should stop taking that because the medication is doing the same thing."
B. "Taking garlic along with your medication may drop your cholesterol too low."
C. "I understand that herbs are good but they should only be prescribed by your health care provider."
D. "How much garlic do you take in 1 day and in what form?"

The students understand the role of CAM and therapies and will now include it into their patient history taking during the assessment phase of the nursing process.

The Answers section can be found on page 275.

Answers

Exercise 20-1: *Matching*

Match the terms in column A to the description in column B.

Column A	Column B
A. Allopathic medicine	__**C**__ Used instead of traditional medical therapy
B. Complementary therapies	__**D**__ Combination of traditional and alternative therapies
C. Alternative therapies	__**A**__ Traditional therapies
D. Integrative therapies	__**B**__ Used to augment traditional therapies

Exercise 20-2: *Hot Spot*

Place an X on the figure that represents the concepts of CAM.

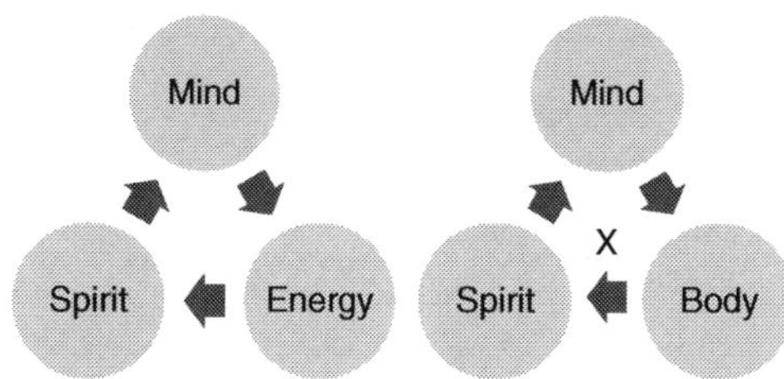

Exercise 20-3: *Fill-in*

On the following chart, place an X on the classification in which the type of therapy represents:

	Alternative medical	Biologically based	Manipulative	Mind–body	Energy
Acupuncture	**X**				
Reiki					**X**
Biofeedback				**X**	
Herb		**X**			
Massage			**X**		

Exercise 20-4: *Multiple Choice Question*

A patient who is being prepared for a diagnostic test is extremely stressed and anxious. The nurse teaches him to isolate one muscle group at a time and concentrate on relating that muscle group. This type of CAM and therapy is:

A. Therapeutic touch—NO, this is using the energy of the provider
B. Passive relaxation—NO, this is self-directed by the patient
C. **Progressive relaxation—YES**
D. Mind–body response—NO, this is usually done using thought processes

Exercise 20-5: *Select All That Apply*

The nurse is assisting the patient to meditate and therefore should provide the following:

☒ **Quiet space**
☐ Relaxing picture—NO, usually the visualization is internal
☒ **Receptive attitude**
☐ A mantra—NO, each person chooses their own mantra

Exercise 20-6: *Multiple Choice Question*

The nurse is caring for a patient in labor who is becoming uncomfortable. She provides amoving picture of a water fall for the patient to look at and hear. This type of therapy is called:

A. Biofeedback—NO, this is electric impulse driven
B. Meditation—NO, this is concentration
C. Therapeutic touch—NO, this is energy driven
D. **Visualization—YES, this is looking at a focal point**

Exercise 20-7: *Multiple Choice Question*

The nurse understands that biofeedback therapy involves:

A. Laying on of hands—NO, this is therapeutic touch (TT)
B. Manipulation of the spine—NO, this is chiropractic medicine
C. Word association—NO, this is cognitive therapy
D. **Electronic impulses—YES**

Exercise 20-8: *True/False*

Therapeutic touch (TT) always involves the direct contact.

☐ True
☒ **False—Hands can be over the patient for it to be effective**

Exercise 20-9: ***Matching***

Match the commonly used herb in column A with its therapeutic effect and usage in column B.

Column A		Column B
A. Aloe	**F**	Increased physical endurance: fatigue
B. Chamomile	**G**	Inhibits serotonin uptake: depression
C. Garlic	**D**	Antiemetic: morning sickness
D. Ginger	**A**	Anti-inflammatory: used for burns
E. Gingko biloba	**B**	Anti-inflammatory used for respiratory system
F. Ginseng	**C**	Lowers lipids: high cholesterol
G. St. John's wort	**E**	Helps memory: dementia

Exercise 20-10: ***Multiple Choice Question***

The nurse is interviewing a patient, and the patient says that she takes garlic along with her medication to lower her cholesterol. The best response for the nurse is:

A. "You should stop taking that because the medication is doing the same thing."—NO, this is not therapeutic and will close off any open discussion and you may not receive any more information from the patient

B. "Taking garlic along with your medication may drop your cholesterol too low."—NO, this is not therapeutic and will close off any open discussion and you may not receive any more information from the patient

C. "I understand that herbs are good, but they should only be prescribed by your health care provider."—NO, this is not therapeutic and will close off any open discussion, and you may not receive any more information from the patient

D. **"How much garlic do you take in 1 day and in what form?"—YES, this will help you know if it is a problem. Think assessment first**

21

Patient Mobility and Safety

Unfolding Case Study 20 Aubree, Alita, and Connor

Aubree, Alita, and Connor have read the chapter in the book about rest and exercise, but because they are young they are having difficulty grasping the importance on health promotion in patients. The instructor tells them that illness and inactivity can take a serious toll on muscle tone, balance, and posture. Also, as nurses they must learn body mechanics in order to protect themselves from back injuries. Nurses are often injured when moving patients.

eResource 21-1: The students review supplemental learning materials to support their understanding of these concepts:

- Body Mechanics and Patient Transfers Handout: http://moon.ouhsc.edu/belledge/ptcare/bodmech.pdf
- Body Mechanics Skills Demonstration Video: www.youtu.be/NYzMmYA-dJY

Exercise 21-1: *Multiple Choice Question*

The nurse understands that the immobile patient is exerting opposing friction when being moved, and therefore the nurse should:

A. Increase body surface by uncrossing the patient's arms
B. Instruct the patient to remain still and let the nurse do the work
C. Lift the patient's body and not the sheet
D. Lift instead of pushing the patient in bed

The instructor explains that activity helps to keep the skeletal system in good shape in order to maintain posture and the person's center of gravity.

Exercise 21-2: *Select All That Apply*

The skeletal system is responsible for the following human functions:

- ❑ Support
- ❑ Protection
- ❑ Movement

The Answers section can be found on page 285.

❑ Vitamin storage
❑ Mineral storage
❑ Hematopoiesis

The instructor explains that many patients are at risk for ***activity intolerance*** due to congenital anomalies such as spinal bifida, bone and joint disorders such as osteoporosis, central nervous system damage such as hemiplegic, and musculoskeletal traumas such as cervical injuries from falls.

Exercise 21-3: *Multiple Choice Question*

The nurse understands that the most important body mechanics consideration for a patient who is bedridden is:

A. Keeping the body aligned
B. Using a footboard
C. Referring the patient to physical therapy (PT)
D. Keeping the call bell within reach

Exercise 21-4: *Multiple Choice Question*

The nurse is teaching a patient with a back injury how to lift properly. The nurse understands that the patient needs more teaching when the patient states:

A. "I will tighten my stomach muscles before I lift"
B. "I will bend at the knees"
C. "I will keep the object at arm's length"
D. I will avoid twisting while I lift"

The next day is clinical in a geriatric setting and Aubree has a patient who needs help ambulating due to left-sided weakness. Aubree ambulates the patient safely in the hall.

Exercise 21-5: *Multiple Choice Question*

The instructor assists the nursing student to document the ambulation of a patient in the following manner:

A. Ambulated to nurses' station and back
B. Ambulated for 20 minutes
C. Ambulated with minimal assistance
D. Ambulated 20 ft and back

Connor's patient has a walker, which is one of many assistive devices. Walkers help patients to ambulate safely as do canes, either straight canes or quad canes. Alita's patient is elderly and has crutches due to a motor vehicle (MV) accident that left his leg broken in several spots.

Exercise 21-6: *Multiple Choice Question*

The nurse understands that if a patient cannot weight bear at all on one foot, the following crutch-walking technique cannot be used:

A. Four-point alternating gait
B. Three-point alternating gait

The Answers section can be found on page 285.

C. Three-point gait
D. Swing through gait

Alita's patient is being taught to go up and down the stairs in order to get ready for discharge.

Exercise 21-7: ***Multiple Choice Question***
The nurse understands that the patient is using the crutches safely when ascending the stairs when the patient:
A. Leads with the affected leg
B. Leads with the unaffected leg
C. Uses the railings
D. Uses the crutches on one side to balance

Exercise 21-8: ***Multiple Choice Question***
The nurse understands that the patient is using the crutches safely when descending the stairs when the patient:
A. Leads with the affected leg
B. Leads with the unaffected leg
C. Uses the railings
D. Uses the crutches on one side to balance

Alita is doing a discharge assessment on her patient in order to determine if the home environment is safe for an elderly patient with crutches. The patient lives in a ranch house that is all on one floor, so access is not a problem.

Exercise 21-9: ***Multiple Choice Question***
A safety concern when a patient is living in a house with an attached garage is:
A. Fire
B. Hypothermia
C. Hyperthermia
D. Carbon dioxide

Alita is able to accompany the home health nurse after the patient is discharged. The home health nurse is assessing the environment for fall risks. Things that are assessed are lighting, flooring, obstacles, and bathroom hazards. The patient's house is uncluttered, but the fire alarm battery was not functioning, so they made sure that it was changed. The home health nurse is scheduled to check on Alita's patient twice a week. The home health nurse uses a fall assessment scale in order to record the patient's risk factors.

eResource 21-2: The home health nurse shows Alita several different tools to assess risk for falling:

- Morse Fall Scale: www.sandiego.networkofcare.org/library/Morse%20Fall%20Scale.pdf
- Hendrich II Fall Risk Model: Overview: *Fall Risk Assessment for Older Adults: The Hendrich II Fall Risk Model*: www.nursingcenter.com/pdf.asp?AID=751195 (Gray-Miceli, 2007)

The Answers section can be found on page 285.

Connor is just as concerned about his patient who is in the hospital because he knows the majority of incident reports are reporting falls.

eResource 21-3:

- Connor is excited to find out that the hospital has initiated a project to reduce patient falls using the Hendrich II Fall Risk Model to improve patient safety. The head nurse shows him a video that highlights the benefits of implementing this fall reduction program: www.downloads.lww.com/wolterskluwer_vitalstream_com/AJN/TRYTHIS_EP4_CH4_FINAL.wmv
- Connor also learns that the U.S. Department of Veterans Affairs has also implemented a very broad fall reduction education program and is excited to share this resource with his classmates: www.patientsafety.gov/CogAids/FallPrevention/index.html#page=page-1

Other types of hospital incidence have to do with client-inherent incidents such as a seizure, a procedure-related incident such has wrong medication, and equipment-related incidents such as malfunctioning IV pumps. All are a concern to the nurse and must be guarded against.

Exercise 21-10: ***Ordering***

If the nurse witnesses a patient seizure, the following steps should be taken:

_______ Answer the patient's questions
_______ Time the seizure
_______ Have seizure precaution equipment (airway, suction, gloves) in room
_______ Position patient
_______ Protect the patient's head
_______ Loosen clothing

Exercise 21-11: ***Select All That Apply***

The nurse understands that after making a medication error, he or she should:

- ❑ Document it in an incident report
- ❑ Document it on the patient's EMR
- ❑ Call the nursing supervisor
- ❑ Call the primary care provider
- ❑ Tell the patient and family
- ❑ Monitor the patient
- ❑ Wait and see if there are any adverse effects, then report it

eResource 21-4: To learn more about medication errors, the class visits the U.S. Food and Drug Administration (FDA) website: [Pathway: www.fda.gov/ → select the 'Drugs' tab → 'Drug Safety and Availability' → 'Medication Errors'].

The Answers section can be found on page 285.

Exercise 21-12: *Multiple Choice Question*

The nurse understands that the root cause of most patient accidents that occur in the hospital are:

A. Lack of communication
B. Carelessness
C. Inexperience
D. Knowledge deficit

eResource 21-5: The instructor gives the students additional patient teaching materials to empower patients/family members to become partners in efforts to reduce medication errors:

- *Where medical errors occur and how to avoid them*: www.youtu.be/WkmfYZg4bnk
- 20 tips to help prevent medical errors: www.ahrq.gov/consumer/20tips.pdf

Connor's elderly patient becomes disoriented as the day wears on and starts to wander in the hall and go into other patient's rooms. Connor persuades him to get back to bed four separate times.

Exercise 21-13: *Select All That Apply*

The nurse understands that to avoid using patient restraints, they should:

- ❑ Orient patient to the environment
- ❑ Get a sitter
- ❑ Do not encourage family to stay
- ❑ Use consistent scheduling of patient activities
- ❑ Place the patient away from the nurses' station, so they are not disturbed
- ❑ Ask for medication from the primary care provider

eResource 21-6: To learn more about strategies to avoid using restraints, Connor watches some additional videos:

- *Healthcare and nursing training: avoiding use of restraints*: www.youtu.be/BIZZuTa9lyM
- *Avoiding restraints in older adults with dementia:* www.consultgerirn.org/resources/media/?vid_id=4475795#player_container
- *Communication difficulties: assessment and interventions in hospitalized older adults with dementia*: www.consultgerirn.org/resources/media/?vid_id=4610524#player_container

The instructor tells Connor that restraints are used as infrequently as possible to prevent injury but at times cannot be avoided. There are several different types of restraints including vest (Posey), belt, ankle, wrist, mitten, elbow, and mummy.

The Answers section can be found on page 285.

Exercise 21-14: *Multiple Choice Question*

Many institutions have banned this type of restraint because of incidents of accidental strangulation:

A. Belt
B. Elbow
C. Wrist
D. Posey

Exercise 21-15: *Multiple Choice Question*

The nurse understands that if a restraint is needed, it should be:

A. Released once a day
B. Tied to itself so the patient cannot get out
C. Be the least restrictive as possible
D. Unpadded so it does not become loose

eResource 21-7: Connor locates the National Council for Community Behavioral Health's *Restraints and Seclusion Rules*: www.thenationalcouncil.org/cs/public_policy/restraints_seclusion_rules_chart

Exercise 21-16: *Fill-in*

Patients who are restrained should be checked every ______ hour(s).

The instructor explains to Connor that sometimes the primary care provider is not in the hospital when the restraint is needed and a phone order must be obtained in order to apply them.

Exercise 21-17: *Fill-in*

The nurse understands that if he or she receives a verbal order for restraints that the primary care provider must sign them within ______ hour(s).

The instructor tells Connor about other devices that help keep patients safe such as beds enclosed by netting and alarms that are placed either on the bed or on the patient and signal if they try to ambulate.

Connor admits that he had an interesting clinical day and that safety is a large issue to think about at many levels when you are a nurse. Aubree agrees and they cannot wait to hear about Alita's day in home care. Tomorrow they will return to the facility and help bathe patients. In long-term care facilities, baths are given on a schedule, and the students will be able to practice that skill tomorrow.

References

Gray-Miceli, D. (2007). Fall risk assessment for older adults: The Hendrich II Fall Risk Model. *Try This: Best Practices in Nursing Care to Older Adults*, (8). The Hartford Institute for Geriatric Nursing, New York University, College of Nursing. Retrieved from http://consultgerirn.org/uploads/File/trythis/try_this_8.pdf

The Answers section can be found on page 285.

Answers

Exercise 21-1: *Multiple Choice Question*

The nurse understands that the immobile patient is exerting opposing friction when being moved, and therefore the nurse should:

A. Increase body surface by uncrossing the patient's arms—NO, this will increase body surface and friction
B. Instruct the patient to remain still and let the nurse do the work—NO, this will increase friction, you should ask the patient to help if they can
C. Lift the patient's body and not the sheet—NO, you should use the sheet
D. **Lift instead of pushing the patient in bed—YES, this will overcome friction**

Exercise 21-2: *Select All That Apply*

The skeletal system is responsible for the following human functions:

☒ **Support**

☒ **Protection**

☒ **Movement**

❑ Vitamin storage—NO, it does not store vitamins

☒ **Mineral storage**

☒ **Hematopoiesis**

Exercise 21-3: *Multiple Choice Question*

The nurse understands that the most important body mechanics consideration for a patient who is bedridden is:

A. **Keeping the body aligned—YES, this is the most important thing and must be done at all times**
B. Using a footboard—NO, although this is important it is not as important as keeping the entire body aligned
C. Referring the patient to physical therapy (PT)—NO, although this is important, it is not as important as keeping the entire body aligned
D. Keeping the call bell within reach—NO, although this is important always, it is not specific to body mechanics

Exercise 21-4: *Multiple Choice Question*

The nurse is teaching a patient with a back injury how to lift properly. The nurse understands that the patient needs more teaching when the patient states:

A. "I will tighten my stomach muscles before I lift."—NO, this is correct
B. "I will bend at the knees."—NO, this is correct
C. **"I will keep the object at arm's length."—YES, this needs correcting, the lifted object should be close to the body**
D. I will avoid twisting while I lift."—NO, this is correct

Exercise 21-5: *Multiple Choice Question*

The instructor assists the nursing student to document the ambulation of a patient in the following manner:

A. Ambulated to nurses' station and back—NO, this is not specific enough
B. Ambulated for 20 minutes—NO, this does not tell distance
C. Ambulated with minimal assistance—NO, this does not tell distance or specifically what minimal assistance was
D. **Ambulated 20 ft and back—YES, this is specific**

Exercise 21-6: *Multiple Choice Question*

The nurse understands that if a patient cannot weight bear at all on one foot, the following crutch-walking technique cannot be used:

A. Four-point alternating gait—NO, this uses both feet
B. Three-point alternating gait—NO, this uses both feet
C. Three-point gait—NO, this uses both feet
D. **Swing through gait—YES, this uses one foot**

Exercise 21-7: *Multiple Choice Question*

The nurse understands that the patient is using the crutches safely when ascending the stairs when the patient:

A. Leads with the affected leg—NO
B. **Leads with the unaffected leg—YES, weight is transferred to crutches, then unaffected leg, after which crutches are moved to that stir and the unaffected leg is moved up**
C. Uses the railings—NO
D. Uses the crutches on one side to balance—NO

Exercise 21-8: *Multiple Choice Question*

The nurse understands that the patient is using the crutches safely when descending the stairs when the patient:

A. Leads with the affected leg—NO
B. **Leads with the unaffected leg—YES, the unaffected leg leads, then crutches and affected leg**

C. Uses the railings—NO
D. Uses the crutches on one side to balance—NO

Exercise 21-9: *Multiple Choice Question*

A safety concern when a patient is living in a house with an attached garage is:
A. Fire—NO, this is always a concern
B. Hypothermia—NO, heat should not be affected
C. Hyperthermia—NO, heat should not be affected
D. **Carbon dioxide—YES, this can be produced by a car if it is not turned off**

Exercise 21-10: *Ordering*

If the nurse witnesses a patient seizure, the following steps should be taken:
__6__ Answer the patient's questions
__5__ Time the seizure
__1__ Have seizure precaution equipment (airway, suction, gloves) in room
__2__ Position patient
__3__ Protect the patient's head
__4__ Loosen clothing

Exercise 21-11: *select all that apply*

The nurse understands that after making a medication error, he or she should:

☒ **Document it in an incident report—YES**

☐ Document it on the patient's EMR—NO, the incident should not be recorded, only the actions taken

☒ **Call the nursing supervisor—YES**

☒ **Call the primary care provider—YES**

☐ Tell the patient and family—NO, this is done by the primary care provider

☒ **Monitor the patient—YES**

☐ Wait and see if there are any adverse effects, then report it—NO, do not wait

Exercise 21-12: *Multiple Choice Question*

The nurse understands that the root cause of most patient accidents that occur in the hospital are:
A. **Lack of communication—YES, this is the main cause**
B. Carelessness—NO, this is a contributing factor but not the overriding cause
C. Inexperience—NO, this is a contributing factor but not the overriding cause
D. Knowledge deficit—NO, this is a contributing factor but not the overriding cause

Exercise 21-13: *Select All That Apply*

The nurse understands that to avoid using patient restraints, they should:

☒ **Orient patient to the environment—YES**

☒ **Get a sitter—YES**

- ❑ Do not encourage family to stay—NO, it is safer if they stay
- ☒ **Use consistent scheduling of patient activities—YES**
- ❑ Place the patient away from the nurses' station, so they are not disturbed—NO, place the patient by the nurses' station
- ❑ Ask for medication from the primary care provider—NO, often increasing medications makes patients more confused

Exercise 21-14: *Multiple Choice Question*

Many institutions have banned this type of restraint because of incidents of accidental strangulation:

A. Belt—NO, this is a safety concern but has not been banned
B. Elbow—NO, this is a safety concern but has not been banned
C. Wrist—NO, this is a safety concern but has not been banned
D. **Posey—YES**

Exercise 21-15: *Multiple Choice Question*

The nurse understands that if a restraint is needed, it should be:

A. Released once a day—NO, they should be released every 2 hours
B. Tied to itself, so the patient cannot get out—NO, they should be slipped knotted to the bed
C. **Be the least restrictive as possible—YES**
D. Unpadded, so it does not become loose—NO, padding should be used

Exercise 21-16: *Fill-in*

Patients who are restrained should be checked every __**1**__ hour(s).

Exercise 21-17: *Fill-in*

The nurse understands that if he or she receives a verbal order for restraints that the primary care provider must sign them within __**24**__ hour(s).

22

Hygiene and Oxygen Therapy

Unfolding Case Study 21 ▪ Aubree, Alita, and Connor

Alita, Aubree, and Connor are at the clinical site at 7 a.m. with their instructor and peers for report. They are aware that today is "bath day," and each resident in the east wing of the facility will be bathed. Connor asks in preconference, "Why do the residents not get bathed every day?"

The instructor asks them to list some of the variables that affect hygiene.

Exercise 22-1: *Select All That Apply*

Variables that affect the frequency of hygiene practices include:

- ❑ Lifestyle
- ❑ Economics
- ❑ Physical condition
- ❑ Culture
- ❑ Peer pressure
- ❑ Health beliefs

The instructor reminds the students of two concepts before they participate in morning baths:

- Allow patients to do as much as they can for themselves
- Provide privacy

Aubree receives report on her patient, and her patient needs a complete bath. Alita is going to help Aubree with the bath and in return Aubree can assist her with the shower ordered for her patient.

eResource 22-1: Before going into the patient's room, Aubree quickly reviews the video, www.youtu.be/hYXYcOHT6aE

Connor has a patient who needs a partial bath.

The Answers section can be found on page 299.

Exercise 22-2: ***Ordering***

Place the bathing steps in order for complete and partial bath preparation:

_______ Adjust room temperature
_______ Fill wash basin
_______ Wash feet
_______ Remove soiled linen
_______ Perineal care
_______ Wash face
_______ Wash legs
_______ Redress
_______ Wash chest
_______ Wash arms
_______ Wash abdomen
_______ Turn and wash back

Aubree also provides her patient with a backrub.

Exercise 22-3: ***Multiple Choice Question***

The nurse understands that backrubs have all the following therapeutic effects except:

A. Decrease muscle tension
B. Decrease blood pressure
C. Stimulation
D. Increased skin circulation

Exercise 22-4: ***Multiple Choice Question***

The nurse should question the UAP (unlicensed assistive personal) when he or she is about to perform foot care on a patient if:

A. The patient is elderly
B. The patient is unconscious
C. The patient is a diabetic
D. The patient has chronic obstructive pulmonary disease (COPD)

Alita transfers her patient onto the shower chair and washes her patient. She folds the wash cloth in order to make a mitt. Alita is careful not to get the surrounding floor wet and create a safety hazard.

Exercise 22-5: ***Multiple Choice Question***

The nurse understands that besides hygiene, the bath process provides assessment of:

A. Mobility
B. Functioning
C. Cultural values
D. Skin

After Alita provides her patient with a shower, she makes her bed. She is very glad that they have fitted sheets, so she does not have to struggle with mitered corners. She does

The Answers section can be found on page 299.

make sure that she uses a draw sheet in order to move the patient easier if needed. Connor does fine with his partial bath, but his patient has chronic obstructive pulmonary disease (COPD) and was getting short of breath (**dyspnea**) just from the bath.

Exercise 22-6: *Matching*

Match the respiratory term in column A with the description in column B.

Column A		Column B
A. Hyperventilation	_______	Inadequate tissue oxygenation at the cellular level
B. Hypoventilation	_______	Collapse of the alveoli
C. Hypoxia	_______	Blue discoloration of the mucus membranes from decreased oxygen
D. Atelectasis	_______	Excessive respirations
E. Cyanosis	_______	Bloody sputum
F. Wheezing	_______	High-pitched cough
G. Hemoptysis	_______	Respirations that do not meet the body's oxygen demand

Connor reports this assessment finding to the instructor.

Exercise 22-7: *Multiple Choice Question*

The nurse understands that the next assessment step for a patient who is having dyspnea would be:

A. Ambulate to expand lungs
B. Send for a chest x-ray
C. Check oxygen saturation
D. Place on 100% oxygen

The instructor notifies the primary care provider who orders blood gases for Connor's patient.

Exercise 22-8: *Multiple Choice Question*

The nurse understands that normal blood gas findings are:

A. PaO_2 95 to 100 mmHg; $PaCO_2$ 35 to 45 mmHg
B. PaO_2 92 to 98 mmHg; $PaCO_2$ 22 to 25 mmHg
C. PaO_2 95 to 100 mmHg; $PaCO_2$ 25 to 35 mmHg
D. PaO_2 100 mmHg; $PaCO_2$ 35 to 45 mmHg

Exercise 22-9: *Multiple Choice Question*

The nurse understands that the following blood pH should be reported to the primary care practitioner:

A. 7.35
B. 7.40

The Answers section can be found on page 299.

C. 7.45
D. 7.50

Connor also raises the head of the bed (HOB) to assist the patient to breathe easier.

Exercise 22-10: *Fill-in*

The condition in which a patient must sit up to breathe is called ______.

Exercise 22-11: *Matching*

Match the bed position in column A to the picture on the bed placement in column B.

Column A	Column B
A. Fowler's	
B. Semi-Fowler's	
C. Trendelenburg	
D. Reverse Trendelenburg	

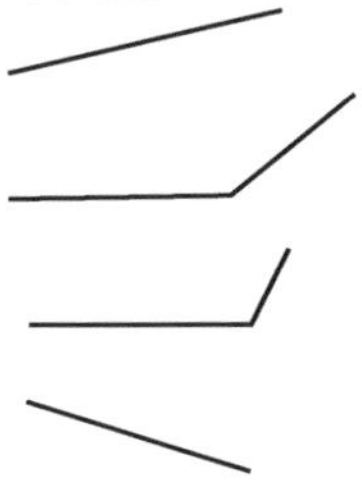

Connor also noted that his patient was coughing and was expectorating sputum, which is common in COPD. The instructor encourages Connor to listen to his patient's breathing pattern.

Exercise 22-12: *Matching*

Match the name for the breathing pattern in column A with its description in column B.

Column A	Column B
A. Eupnea	______ Absence of breathing
B. Tachypnea	______ Normal breathing
C. Bradypnea	______ Breathing below 10 breaths per minute
D. Apnea	______ Fast breathing seen with metabolic acidosis
E. Kussmaul	______ Breathing above 35 breaths per minute

The primary care practitioner calls the instructor back and orders a pulmonary function test. The respiratory therapist (RT) comes to the patient's room to perform it.

Exercise 22-13: *Matching*

Match the pulmonary function measurement in column A with its normal value in column B.

Column A	Column B
A. Tidal volume (V)	______ 4,500–4,800 mL
B. Residual volume (RV)	______ 5–10 mL/kg
C. Functional residual capacity (FRC)	______ 1,000–1,200 mL
D. Vital capacity (VC)	______ 5,000–6,000 mL
E. Total lung capacity (TLC)	______ 2,000–24,000 mL

The Answers section can be found on page 299.

Connor's patient had decreased lung function, so the primary care practitioner ordered a nebulizer treatment (a process that mixes medication with air), which eased his dyspnea. They also humidified low-level oxygen by cannula, which also helped and the added water to the oxygen is gentler on the lungs than dry oxygen. The RT came and also gave the patient chest physiotherapy (CPT) to help loosen up the secretions.

Exercise 22-14: *Multiple Choice Question*

The nurse understands that before the patient receives CPT, they should make sure that the following equipment is in the room for patient safety:

A. Call bell
B. Suctioning
C. IV
D. Restraint

Exercise 22-15: *Matching*

Match the lung segment affected by postural drainage in column A to the position in column B.

Column A		Column B
A. Left anterior upper lobe	_______	Prone, elevate thorax, and abdomen
B. Right anterior upper lobe	_______	Side lying, left side elevated on pillow
C. Left posterior upper lobe	_______	Trendelenburg, left lateral
D. Right posterior upper lobe	_______	Trendelenburg, ¾ supine
E. Right middle lobe anterior	_______	Prone, Trendelenburg
F. Right middle lobe posterior	_______	Supine, HOB elevated 15° to 30°
G. Bilateral anterior lower lobes	_______	Side lying, right side elevated on pillow
H. Left lower lobe lateral segment	_______	Trendelenburg, right lateral
I. Right lower lobe lateral segment	_______	Supine, HOB elevated
J. Left lower lobe anterior	_______	Supine, Trendelenburg

The nurse comes into Connor's patient's room to suction him.

eResource 22-2: Nasopharyngeal suctioning: http://www.youtube.com/watch?v=TwNSNodYfEw

Exercise 22-16: *Multiple Choice Question*

The nurse understands that suctioning a patient's nasopharynx is an intervention done under:

A. Sterile technique
B. Clean technique

The Answers section can be found on page 299.

C. Negative air conditions
D. Droplet precautions

Connor's patient is hypoxic even after nasopharyngeal suctioning, so the primary nurse that is his preceptor does orotracheal suctioning and then provides the patient with oxygen via a mask and his pulse oximeter reading returns to 97%. The nurse asks Connor if he would like to observe her suctioning a patient with a tracheotomy.

eResource 22-3: Tracheostomy suction—Registered nurse training: www.youtu.be/jcO9dE8CDhU

Exercise 22-17: *Ordering*

Place the steps in order from 1 to 10 for suctioning a tracheotomy tube:

_______ Identify patient
_______ Clean patient, patient area, and equipment
_______ Apply sterile gloves
_______ Document
_______ Insert catheter
_______ Gather equipment and check suction
_______ Apply intermittent suction
_______ Hyperoxygenate patient
_______ Slowly withdraw catheter
_______ Apply face mask

Connor sees an oral airway taped in a clean bag above the bed of the patient and asks the nurse about it. She tells him that it is a simple device to keep a patient's tongue from obstructing the airway should a patient become unconscious. She role-played for Connor how it works on a pretend patient.

Exercise 22-18: *Multiple Choice Question*

The nurse places an airway in a patient's mouth by:

A. Inserting the curved end directly back
B. Inserting the curved end laterally and then turning it up
C. Inserting the curved end up and back
D. Inserting the curved end laterally and then turning it down

Aubree accompanies a nurse to teach a patient incentive spirometry.

eResource 22-4: The nurse shows the patient a short video *How to Use an Incentive Spirometer*: www.youtu.be/L17uEjiPAZ4

Exercise 22-19: *Fill-in*

Incentive spirometry is used while the patient is breathing _______.

Aubree also accompanies her nurse to a room with a patient with chest tubes for a pneumothorax, which is a collection of air in the pleural space that causes the lung to collapse. The collection system of the chest tubes is a sealed plastic system with a

The Answers section can be found on page 299.

water seal that creates negative pressure and re-expands the lungs. The tubes leading room the patient's chest to the system should not be closed off. The nurse checks that the tubes are not kinked and that the system is standing upright lower than the chest. She also checks that the dressing is in place.

eResource 22-5: *Maintaining Chest Tubes:* http://alfa.saddleback.edu/N172/maintainChestTube.aspx

Exercise 22-20: ***Multiple Choice Question***

Emergency equipment needed in a patient's room who is receiving chest tube therapy is:

A. Petroleum jelly
B. CPR board
C. Disposable scalpel
D. Two kelly clamps

Alita calls her primary nurse to report that her patient's pulse oximeter reading is only 90%. The instructor and the primary nurse are aware that the patient often requires oxygen to increase perfusion, so they check that they have a prn oxygen order.

Exercise 22-21: ***Multiple Choice Question***

The nurse understands that oxygen should be treated as a(n):

A. Drug
B. Intervention
C. Assessment
D. Therapy

Exercise 22-22: ***Select All That Apply***

Safety measures that should be taken when patients are receiving oxygen include:

❑ No smoking signs are posted
❑ All electrical equipment is out of the room
❑ Know the location of the fire extinguisher
❑ Keep visitors to a minimum
❑ Keep room door closed
❑ Know fire evacuation route

The nurse in charge of Alita's patient chooses a nasal cannula to deliver the oxygen that the patient needs. She sets the flow rate at 3 liters per minute and places the cannula on the patient. She explains to Alita that the cannula is placed in the patient's nose and then the tubing is looped around the patient's ears and secured under the chin with a built-in tubing clip. After 30 minutes, Alita checks her patient's oximetry again and it is now up to 96%.

eResource 22-6: Overview of oxygen therapy:

- *Oxygen therapy skills demonstration (1 of 2):* http://www.youtube.com/watch?v=wP1_CqcEV5Y
- *Oxygen therapy skills demonstration (2 of 2):* http://www.youtube.com/watch?v=4BnPy9ppSHw

The Answers section can be found on page 299.

Exercise 22-23: *Multiple Choice Question*

Another method nurses can apply for delivering oxygen to a patient who can accommodate up to 10 L of oxygen per minute is:

A. Tightly applied cannula
B. Ventilator
C. Continuous positive airway pressure (CPAP)
D. Mask

Alita confides in the nurse that is precepting her that she is fearful of someone needing cardiopulmonary resuscitation (CPR). The nurse explains to her the value of keeping her CPR certification for health care providers up to date because the procedure changes often. The nurse also tells Alita that as her experience grows she will understand how to better assess patients who are in cardiac or respiratory failure. One of the things that helps is to remember the A-B-Cs of resuscitation.

Exercise 22-24: *Multiple Choice Question*

A-B-C of resuscitation stands for:

A. Alarm, breathing, cardiac
B. Airway, back position, circulation
C. Alarm, breathing, circulation
D. Airway, breathing, circulation

The nurse explains to Alita that once a patient has had CPR and is stable, the next step is cardiopulmonary rehabilitation.

Exercise 22-25: *Select All That Apply*

The nurse understands that the following interventions are included in cardiopulmonary rehabilitation:

- ❑ Exercise
- ❑ Nutrition
- ❑ Scheduled rest periods
- ❑ Stress management
- ❑ Compliance with medication

Exercise 22-26: *Multiple Choice Question*

Two concepts that are important to teach patients experiencing cardiopulmonary conditions are:

A. Hydration and coughing techniques
B. Hydration and sodium consumption
C. Coughing techniques and sneezing
D. Sneezing and allergy prevention

The Answers section can be found on page 299.

The nurse also tells Alita that many patients with respiratory conditions such as COPD used pursed lip breathing in order to create an end pressure to keep the alveoli open. Diaphragmatic breathing is also taught in order for the patient to practice better lung expansion.

eResource 22-7: To learn more about the two different breathing techniques, Alita watches two brief videos:

- *Living with COPD part 2 pursed lip breathing:* www.youtu.be/jFqrWVeskR0
- *Living with COPD part 3 diaphragmatic breathing:* www.youtu.be/if2yyaFp1dI

Alita, Conner, and Aubree are thankful for all they have learned today at clinical, and the staff has been exceptional role models and preceptors for them. For postconference, they talk about bathing and oxygenation techniques and discuss expectations for the next clinical day!

The Answers section can be found on page 299.

Answers

Exercise 22-1: *Select All That Apply*

Variables that affect the frequency of hygiene practices include:

☒ **Lifestyle—YES**

☒ **Economics—YES**

☒ **Physical condition—YES**

☒ **Culture—YES**

❑ Peer pressure—NO, peer pressure is usually not a concern

☒ **Health beliefs—YES**

Exercise 22-2: *Ordering*

Place the bathing steps in order for complete and partial bath preparation:

1 Adjust room temperature
2 Fill wash basin
10 Wash feet
12 Remove soiled linen
9 Perineal care
3 Wash face
8 Wash legs
11 Redress
4 Wash chest
5 Wash arms
6 Wash abdomen
7 Turn and wash back

Exercise 22-3: *Multiple Choice Question*

The nurse understands that backrubs have all the following therapeutic effects except:

A. Decrease *muscle* tension—NO, this is a therapeutic effect
B. *Decrease* blood pressure—NO, this is a therapeutic effect
C. **Stimulation—YES, they relax not stimulate**
D. Increased skin circulation—NO, this is a therapeutic effect

Exercise 22-4: *Multiple Choice Question*

The nurse should question the UAP (unlicensed assistive personal) when he or she is about to perform foot care on a patient if:

A. The patient is elderly—NO, they can perform routine foot care for elderly
B. The patient is unconscious—NO, they can perform routine foot care
C. **The patient is a diabetic—YES, diabetics should have foot care done by a podiatrist due to vascular occlusion that decreases circulation to the feet, and any nick or cut can turn into a wound that heals poorly and easily gets infected**
D. The patient has chronic obstructive pulmonary disease (COPD)—NO, they can perform routine foot care

Exercise 22-5: *Multiple Choice Question*

The nurse understands that besides hygiene, the bath process provides assessment of:

A. Mobility—NO, the patient does not stand
B. Functioning—NO, the fine and gross motor is not completely assessed
C. Cultural values—NO, cultural values have to do with other ADLs also such as nutrition
D. **Skin—YES, an accurate and complete assessment of the skin can be completed**

Exercise 22-6: *Matching*

Match the respiratory term in column A with the description in column B.

Column A		Column B
A. Hyperventilation	C	Inadequate tissue oxygenation at the cellular level
B. Hypoventilation	D	Collapse of the alveoli
C. Hypoxia	E	Blue discoloration of the mucus membranes from decreased oxygen
D. Atelectasis	A	Excessive respirations
E. Cyanosis	G	Bloody sputum
F. Wheezing	F	High-pitched cough
G. Hemoptysis	B	Respirations that do not meet the body's oxygen demand

Exercise 22-7: *Multiple Choice Question*

The nurse understands that the next assessment step for a patient who is having dyspnea would be:

A. Ambulate to expand lungs—NO, this may increase the stress on the respiratory system
B. Send for a chest x-ray—NO, this is not necessary

C. **Check oxygen saturation—YES, this is the next assessment step**
D. Place on 100% oxygen—NO, you need to know the pulse oximetry reading first

Exercise 22-8: *Multiple Choice Question*
The nurse understands that normal blood gas findings are:
A. PaO_2 95 to 100 mmHg; $PaCO_2$ 35 to 45 mmHg—NO
B. PaO_2 92 to 98 mmHg; $PaCO_2$ 22 to 25 mmHg—NO
C. PaO_2 95 to 100 mmHg; $PaCO_2$ 25 to 35 mmHg—NO
D. **PaO_2 100 mmHg; $PaCO_2$ 35 to 45 mmHg—YES**

Exercise 22-9: *Multiple Choice Question*
The nurse understands that the following blood pH should be reported to the primary care practitioner:
A. 7.35—NO
B. 7.40—NO
C. 7.45—NO
D. **7.50—YES, this is outside normal range**

Exercise 22-10: *Fill-in*
The condition in which a patient must sit up to breathe is called **orthopnea**.

Exercise 22-11: *Matching*
Match the bed position in column A to the picture on the bed placement in column B.

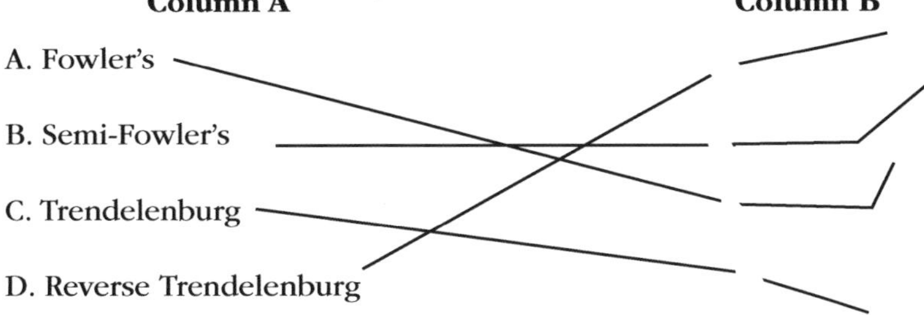

Exercise 22-12: *Matching*
Match the name for the breathing pattern in column A with its description in column B.

Column A	Column B
A. Eupnea	**D** Absence of breathing
B. Tachypnea	**A** Normal breathing
C. Bradypnea	**C** Breathing below 10 breaths per minute
D. Apnea	**E** Fast breathing seen with metabolic acidosis
E. Kussmaul	**B** Breathing above 35 breaths per minute

Exercise 22-13: *Matching*

Match the pulmonary function measurement in column A with its normal value in column B.

Column A		Column B
A. Tidal volume (V)	**D**	4,500–4,800 mL
B. Residual volume (V)	**A**	5–10 mL/kg
C. Functional residual capacity (FRC)	**B**	1,000–1,200 mL
D. Vital capacity (VC)	**E**	5,000–6,000 mL
E. Total lung capacity (TLC)	**C**	2,000–24,000 mL

Exercise 22-14: *Multiple Choice Question*

The nurse understands that before the patient receives CPT, they should make sure that the following equipment is in the room for patient safety:

A. Call bell—NO, although this is always important
B. **Suctioning—YES, you run the risk of dislodging excessive secretions**
C. IV—NO
D. Restraint—NO

Exercise 22-15: *Matching*

Match the lung segment affected by postural drainage in column A to the position in column B.

Column A		Column B
A. Left anterior upper lobe	**F**	Prone, elevate thorax, and abdomen
B. Right anterior upper lobe	**C**	Side lying, left side elevated on pillow
C. Left posterior upper lobe	**H**	Trendelenburg, left lateral
D. Right posterior upper lobe	**E**	Trendelenburg, ¾ supine
E. Right middle lobe anterior	**J**	Prone, Trendelenburg
F. Right middle lobe posterior	**A**	Supine, HOB elevated 15° to 30°
G. Bilateral anterior lower lobes	**D**	Side lying, right side elevated on pillow
H. Left lower lobe lateral segment	**I**	Trendelenburg, right lateral
I. Right lower lobe lateral segment	**B**	Supine, HOB elevated
J. Left lower lobe anterior	**G**	Supine, Trendelenburg

Exercise 22-16: *Multiple Choice Question*

The nurse understands that suctioning a patient's nasopharynx is an intervention done under:

A. Sterile technique—NO, only if suctioning is needed in the trachea
B. **Clean technique—YES, the oropharynx is not sterile**
C. Negative air conditions—NO
D. Droplet precautions—NO, only if secretions are infectious

Exercise 22-17: *Ordering*

Place the steps in order from 1 to 10 for suctioning a tracheotomy tube:

__3__ Identify patient
__9__ Clean patient, patient area, and equipment
__4__ Apply sterile gloves
__10__ Document
__6__ Insert catheter
__2__ Gather equipment and check suction
__7__ Apply intermittent suction
__5__ Hyperoxygenate patient
__8__ Slowly withdraw catheter
__1__ Apply face mask

Exercise 22-18: *Multiple Choice Question*

The nurse places an airway in a patient's mouth by:

A. Inserting the curved end directly back—NO, this will push the tongue back
B. Inserting the curved end laterally and then turning it up—NO, this will put pressure on the palate
C. Inserting the curved end up and back—NO, this will put pressure on the palate
D. **Inserting the curved end laterally and then turning it down—YES, this will hold the tongue in place**

Exercise 22-19: *Fill-in*

Incentive spirometry is used while the patient is breathing __**in (inspiration)**__.

Exercise 22-20: *Multiple Choice Question*

Emergency equipment needed in a patient's room who is receiving chest tube therapy is:

A. Petroleum jelly—NO, this is used for dressing sometimes, but not put on in an emergency
B. CPR board—NO, we do not expect the person to code unless there are other complications
C. Disposable scalpel—NO, there is no incision to be made
D. **Two kelly clamps—YES, the tubing may have to be clamped off**

Exercise 22-21: *Multiple Choice Question*

The nurse understands that oxygen should be treated as a(n):

A. **Drug—YES, it is prescribed as is any medication**
B. Intervention—NO, it is not an automatic nursing intervention
C. Assessment—NO, although there are some conditions, it is used for assessment purposes; this is not the norm
D. Therapy—NO, it is a therapy but is considered a potentially toxic drug

Exercise 22-22: *Select All That Apply*

Safety measures that should be taken when patients are receiving oxygen include:

☒ **No smoking signs are posted—YES**
☐ All electrical equipment is out of the room—NO, they need to be functioning properly but not out of the room
☒ **Know the location of the fire extinguisher—YES**
☐ Keep visitors to a minimum—NO, this does not support patient-centered care
☐ Keep room door closed—NO, this is not necessary
☒ **Know fire evacuation route—YES**

Exercise 22-23: *Multiple Choice Question*

Another method nurses can apply for delivering oxygen to a patient who can accommodate up to 10 L of oxygen per minute is:

A. Tightly applied cannula—NO, this would cause nasal breakdown
B. Ventilator—NO, this is not done by liters
C. Continuous positive airway pressure (CPAP)—NO, this is applied by primary care practitioners
D. **Mask—YES, mask can deliver a higher concentration of oxygen**

Exercise 22-24: *Multiple Choice Question*

A-B-C of resuscitation stands for:

A. Alarm, breathing, cardiac—NO
B. Airway, back position, circulation—NO
C. Alarm, breathing, circulation—NO
D. **Airway, breathing, circulation—YES**

Exercise 22-25: *Select All That Apply*

The nurse understands that the following interventions are included in cardiopulmonary rehabilitation:

☒ **Exercise—YES**
☒ **Nutrition—YES**
☐ Scheduled rest periods—NO, this is not usually necessary
☒ **Stress management—YES**
☒ **Compliance with medication—YES**

Exercise 22-26: *Multiple Choice Question*

Two concepts that are important to teach patients experiencing cardiopulmonary conditions are:

A. **Hydration and coughing techniques—YES, these are needed to keep mucus loose and expectorate it by teaching coughing techniques**
B. Hydration and sodium consumption—NO, although important, this has to do with fluid retention
C. Coughing techniques and sneezing—NO, sneezing does not clear the lower respiratory tract
D. Sneezing and allergy prevention—NO, sneezing and allergies do not clear the lower respiratory tract

23

Fluid and Electrolytes

Unfolding Case Study 22 ■ Aubree, Alita, and Connor

Aubree, Connor, and Alita review fluid and electrolytes before the next fundamentals class. This is a subject that seems as if some extra studying may be needed.

Exercise 23-1: *Fill-in*

Write an "I" for intracellular fluid and an "E" for extracellular fluid, which is contained in the following anatomical areas:

_______ Inside the body cells
_______ Interstitial
_______ Intravascular
_______ Lymph
_______ Blood vessels
_______ Cerebral spinal fluid
_______ Pleural fluid

The nursing instructor describes electrolytes that are in the body fluids and the importance of them being in balance. Electrolytes are minerals and salts that are in the liquids of the body, and once in the liquid they break up and produce ***anions*** (−) and ***cations*** (+). ***Milliequivalents*** (mEq) is how the amount of anions or cations is measured in the solution or liquid. The fluid moves by ***osmosis*** to the lesser concentration of solutes or ions (anions and cations).

eResource 23-1: The instructor shows the students some additional material to help them better understand the concept of body fluids:

- An overview of *Body Fluids* by Dr. Joe Patlak, Department of Physiology, University of Vermont: http://physioweb.uvm.edu/bodyfluids/ (Patlak, 2000).
- *Osmotic Pressure* learning activity from Wisc-Online: [Pathway: www.wisc-online.com/ → select "Learning Objects" → "Health" → "Nursing" → scroll down and select "Osmotic Pressure"].

The Answers section can be found on page 321.

Exercise 23-2: *Matching*

Match the osmolarity descriptor in column A to what it does in the body in column B.

Column A		Column B
A. Isotonic	______	Pulls fluid from cells
B. Hypertonic	______	Pushes fluid into cells
C. Hypotonic	______	Expands the blood volume without movement of fluid in or out of the cells

Exercise 23-3: *Matching*

Match the electrolyte in column A to its correct normal values in column B.

Column A		Column B (mEq/L)
A. Sodium (Na^+)	______	22 to 26
B. Potassium (K^+)	______	1.5 to 2.5
C. Calcium (Ca^+)	______	135 to 145
D. Bicarbonate (HCO_3^-)	______	1.7 to 4.6
E. Chloride (Cl^-)	______	3.5 to 5.0
F. Magnesium (Mg^{2-})	______	90 to 110
G. Phosphate (PO_4^{3-})	______	4.5 to 5.5

eResource 23-2: *Electrolyte Panel Game*, another learning activity from Wisc-Online: [Pathway: www.wisc-online.com/ → select "Learning Objects" → "Health" → "Clinical Lab Technician" → scroll down and select "Electrolyte Panel Game"].

Exercise 23-4: *Multiple Choice Question*

An excess of fluid being pushed into the intravascular space results in:

A. Sore joints
B. Flushing
C. Itching
D. Edema

eResource 23-3: Alterations in fluid balance learning activity from Wisc-Online: [Pathway: www.wisc-online.com/ → select "Learning Objects" → "Health" → "Nursing" → scroll down and select "Alterations in Fluid Balance"].

Exercise 23-5: *Fill-in*

The balance of body fluids is called ***homeostasis.***

The Answers section can be found on page 321.

Exercise 23-6: *Multiple Choice Question*

The nurse understands that patients may be suffering from hypovolemia when they experience:

A. Thirst
B. Water intoxication
C. Nausea
D. Constipation

The instructor tells the students that humans ingest approximately 2,200 to 2,700 mL per day between fluids and food.

Exercise 23-7: *Select All That Apply*

The following patients are at highest risk for dehydration:

- ☐ Elderly
- ☐ Adults
- ☐ Adolescents
- ☐ Children
- ☐ Infants
- ☐ Patients with neurological issues
- ☐ Patients with psychological issues

The instructor refreshes the students' memory about hormonal regulation of fluid. ***Antidiuretic hormone (ADH)*** from the posterior pituitary responds if the ***osmolarity*** of the blood is unbalanced and it responds on the kidneys to retain fluid. Aldosterone secreted by the adrenal cortex responds to an imbalance in K^+ and increases the absorption of Na^+. Renin from the kidneys responds to decreased kidney perfusion by producing angiotensin 1, which converts to angiotensin II and vasoconstricts selectively to increase perfusion to the kidneys. In addition, the blood pH or acid–base balance is maintained by hydrogen, carbon dioxide excreted by the lungs, and bicarbonate excreted by the kidneys.

eResource 23-4: To reinforce the discussion, the instructor shows the class a ADH Tutorial: www.youtu.be/qqrUEjQXRak

Exercise 23-8: *Multiple Choice Question*

The nurse understands that normal blood acid–base balance is a pH from:

A. 7.15 to 7.25
B. 7.25 to 7.35
C. 7.35 to 7.45
D. 7.45 to 7.55

The Answers section can be found on page 321.

Exercise 23-9: *Matching*

Match the condition in column A to the description in column B.

Column A	Column B
A. Hyponatremia	______ Low serum potassium
B. Hypernatremia	______ Low serum calcium
C. Hypokalemia	______ High serum chloride
D. Hyperkalemia	______ High serum potassium
E. Hypocalcemia	______ High serum magnesium
F. Hypercalcemia	______ Low serum magnesium
G. Hypomagnesemia	______ Low serum sodium
H. Hypermagnesemia	______ High serum calcium
I. Hypochloremia	______ High serum sodium
J. Hyperchloremia	______ Low serum chloride

Exercise 23-10: *Multiple Choice Question*

A patient is admitted to the hospital with kidney disease resulting in a salt-wasting syndrome; the nurse would expect to see the following serum laboratory finding for this patient:

A. Hypernatremia
B. Hyponatremia
C. Hyperkalemia
D. Hypocalcemia

eResource 23-5: The class views several video lectures by D. J. Hennager from Kirkwood Community College that further explain these important concepts of *Sodium Homeostasis*:

- *Video Lecture Part 1*: www.youtu.be/W3t8gtN-Wfk
- *Video Lecture Part 2*: www.youtu.be/yiZrbulz3xI
- *Accompanying Handout:* www.kirkwood.edu/pdf/uploaded/695/sodium_homeostasisyt.pdf

Exercise 23-11: *Multiple Choice Question*

A patient is admitted to the hospital with severe dehydration; the nurse would expect to see the following serum laboratory finding for this patient:

A. Hypernatremia
B. Hyponatremia
C. Hyperkalemia
D. Hypocalcemia

The Answers section can be found on page 321.

Exercise 23-12: *Multiple Choice Question*

A patient uses potassium-wasting diuretics; the nurse would expect to see the following serum laboratory finding for this patient:

A. Hypernatremia
B. Hypokalemia
C. Hyperkalemia
D. Hypocalcemia

eResource 23-6: The class views several more video lectures by D. J. Hennager from Kirkwood Community College that further explain these important concepts of *Potassium Homeostasis*:

- *Video Lecture Part 1*: www.youtu.be/TjlZpCPXrhs
- *Video Lecture Part 2*: www.youtu.be/gghbd53nH0A
- *Accompanying Handout:* www.kirkwood.edu/pdf/uploaded/695/potassium_homeostasisyt.pdf

Exercise 23-13: *Multiple Choice Question*

A patient is admitted with massive cellular damage due to a burn; the nurse would expect to see the following serum laboratory finding for this patient:

A. Hypernatremia
B. Hypokalemia
C. Hyperkalemia
D. Hypocalcemia

Exercise 23-14: *Multiple Choice Question*

A patient has vitamin D deficiencies; the nurse would expect to see the following serum laboratory finding for this patient:

A. Hypercalcemia
B. Hypokalemia
C. Hyperkalemia
D. Hypocalcemia

Exercise 23-15: *Multiple Choice Question*

A patient has taken an excessive amount of TUMS® (calcium carbonate); the nurse would expect to see the following serum laboratory finding for this patient:

A. Hypercalcemia
B. Hypokalemia
C. Hyperkalemia
D. Hypocalcemia

Electrolyte evaluation is done along with fluid intake and output assessment. They are very interdependent concepts. If a patient is putting out too much fluid, they can lose electrolytes or concentrate the electrolytes that are left in their bodies. If a patient is not

The Answers section can be found on page 321.

putting out enough fluid, they can be holding onto excessive electrolytes or diluting them in their bodies. The fluid and electrolyte risk depend on the disease and what organ it affects. A patient's total body water depends on a number of factors including size and age.

Exercise 23-16: *Multiple Choice Question*

The nurse understands that the patient with the highest risk for fluid loss is the:

A. Infant
B. Toddler
C. Child
D. Adolescent

The instructor explains that other patients who are at risk or those with chronic and acute illnesses, the elderly, and those patients whose lifestyle and nutrition do not consider proper fluid intake. Nurses record intake and output for patients during their shift and for 24 hours. Sometimes a urine specimen is collected to look at the ***specific gravity***. Specific gravity is the concentration of molecules in the urine and is an indicator of kidney function.

Exercise 23-17: *Multiple Choice Question*

The normal range for adult specific gravity of urine is:

A. 1.010 to 1.020
B. 1.020 to 1.030
C. 1.030 to 1.040
D. 1.040 to 1.050

eResource 23-7: To learn more about urine specific gravity and the disorders associated with abnormal values, the students view *Nursing Review (urine specific gravity):* www.youtu.be/QghgEOPbQR4

Alita asks how urine is collected for a specific gravity from an infant. The instructor tells her that a cotton ball is placed in the diaper and that when the infant urinates, the cotton ball is placed in a barrel of a 5 mL syringe, and the plunger is then replaced. A few drops are squeezed out onto a specific gravity meter, which either digitally reads out the specific gravity or it shows up on a chart that can be visualized.

Connor asks how to measure the output of an infant. The instructor tells them that 1 g is equivalent to 1 mL. So if an infant's diaper weighs 50 g wet and a dry diaper weighs 20 g, then the infant ***voided*** 30 mL.

Exercise 23-18: *Calculation*

The nurse is calculating a 24-hour urine output on an infant. The diapers weigh 24 g dry. The infant was changed every 4 hours during the day and the weight of six diapers is 28, 54, 37, 42, 79, and 63 g. The infant's output in 24 hours is ________ mL.

Alita asks about balancing patient's intake and output (I & O). The instructor gives the students case studies to practice.

The Answers section can be found on page 321.

Exercise 23-19: *Calculation*

A patient takes in three 8-ounce glasses of water, 1,000 mL IV, 4 ounces of orange juice, a 16-ounce soda, and two 4-ounce cups of coffee. The patient voids seven times during the 24 hours. The voided amounts are 550, 700, 430, 300, 200, 200, and 200 mL. What is her ***fluid volume deficit (FVD)*** for the day? ________________ mL.

	Intake	Output
TOTAL	______	______

Exercise 23-20: *Calculation*

The nurse is caring for a pediatric patient. The child consumed one bowl of cereal with 4 ounces of milk, one 3-ounce glass of apple juice, one 2-ounce drink of water, two teaspoons of medication, 4 ounces of apple juice for lunch, a 6-ounce juice for snack, and 8 ounces of juice for supper. The child also had 200 mL of IV fluid in each 8-hour shift. The child voided 150, 275, 100, 480, 215, and 350 mL. The child's fluid volume deficit is _________ mL.

	Intake	Output
TOTAL	______	______

Besides having fluid volume deficit (FVD), a patient can actually be overhydrated or suffer from a fluid volume excess (FVE). The following case studies help the students to calculate FVE.

The Answers section can be found on page 321.

Exercise 23-21: *Calculation*

A patient takes in three 8-ounce glasses of water, 1,000 mL IV, 4 ounces of orange juice, a 16-ounce soda, and two 4-ounce cups of coffee. The patient voids five times during the 24 hours. The voided amounts are 350, 500, 330, 250, and 200 mL. What is her ***fluid volume excess (FVE)*** for the day? _________ mL.

	Intake	Output
TOTAL	______	______

Exercise 23-22: *Calculation*

The nurse is caring for a pediatric patient. The child consumed one bowl of cereal with 4 ounces of milk, one 3-ounce glass of apple juice, one 2-ounce drink of water, 2 teaspoons of medication, 4 ounces of apple juice for lunch, a 6-ounce juice for snack, and 8 ounces of juice for supper. The child also had 100 mL of IV fluid in each 8-hour shift. The child voided 50, 175, 100, 380, 215, and 350 mL. The child's fluid volume excess is _________ mL.

	Intake	Output
TOTAL	______	______

Another nursing intervention that monitors fluid balance is daily patient weights. A sudden increase in weight means fluid retention, and this can happen with patients who are in congestive heart failure. A sudden loss in weight may indicate dehydration.

The Answers section can be found on page 321.

Exercise 23-23: *Fill-in*

To monitor a patient's weight accurately, the nurse must weigh the patient on the same ______, at the same ________________, with the same ______________________.

Fluid and electrolyte replacement is necessary for patients with imbalances. If patients have fluid restrictions, strict I&O is adhered to, and all fluids are counted even ice chips and gelatin. If a patient had a FVD often, parenteral fluids are given to replace losses. Parenteral or IV replacement is of three types:

- Total parenteral nutrition (TPN), which includes fluids with electrolytes, glucose, fats, and nutrients usually in cases of severe nutritional deficit such as someone who cannot eat at all;
- Crystalloids are infusions of solutions with electrolytes; and
- Colloids are blood and its by-products.

In order to receive parenteral fluid, a patient needs a venous access that can be done by a peripheral catheter. For longer-term access, a patient may have a threaded cannular (peripherally inserted central catheter or PICC line), or an infusion port placed under the skin. Most often crystalloids are used for short-term therapy.

Exercise 23-24: *Matching*

Match the type of IV crystalloid fluid in column A with its osmolarity effect in column B.

Column A	Column B
A. Hypotonic	_______ Equal to the osmolarity of body fluids
B. Isotonic	_______ Greater than the osmolarity of body fluids
C. Hypertonic	_______ Less than the osmolarity of body fluids

Exercise 23-25: *Matching*

Match the solution in column A to the type of osmolarity in column B (use the descriptors in column B more than once).

Column A	Column B
A. Dextrose 5% in water (D5W)	_______ Hypotonic
B. Dextrose 10% in water (D10W)	_______ Isotonic
C. 0.45% sodium chloride (normal saline solution [NSS])	_______ Hypertonic
D. 0.9% sodium chloride (0.9% NSS)	
E. D5 in 0.9 NSS (D5/NSS)	
F. D5 in 0.45 NSS (D5 ½NSS)	
G. Lactated Ringer's or Ringer's Lactate (RL)	
H. D5RL	

The Answers section can be found on page 321.

To deliver fluids, the patient has to have an access line. Most times, the veins in the hand or arms are used.

Exercise 23-26: *Ordering*

Place the following steps to starting an IV in order:

_______ Insert catheter
_______ Collect equipment
_______ Place the tourniquet on above the site
_______ Dress the site per policy, usually using a transparent dressing to be able to visualize site
_______ Release tourniquet
_______ Wash hands
_______ Attach IV
_______ Put on gloves
_______ Regulate IV flow on pump
_______ Cleanse patient skin per protocol

Exercise 23-27: *Hot Spot*

Please identify the median cubital, cephalic, basilic, and antebrachial veins on the diagram.

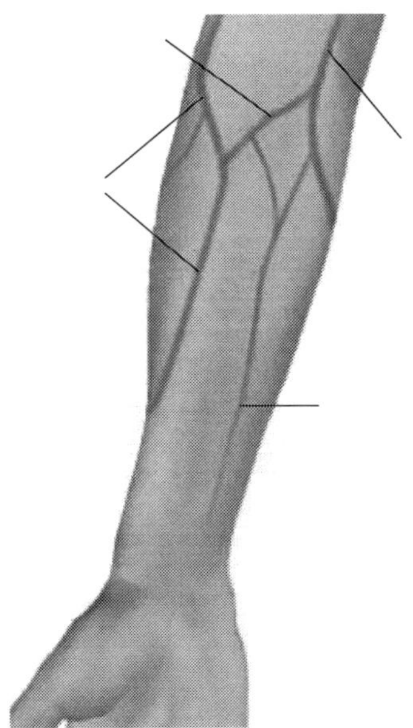

The instructor explains that IV tubing comes in different delivery sizes. Macro tubing will give 1 mL in 10 or 15 drops (gtts) depending on the company that made the tubing. A micro drip tubing breaks each 1 mL down to 60 gtts. This is used for smaller amounts of fluid. All IV fluids should be hung using an IV pump to regulate flow. IV Piggy Backs (IVBP) are medications that are in a smaller amount of fluid such as 50 to 100 mL that are attached to the main IV and infused in 30 to 60 minutes. Although IVs

The Answers section can be found on page 321.

are hung using a pump, the flow rate should still be calculated by the nurse to make sure that they are not infusing too slow or too fast.

Exercise 23-28: *Calculation*

The IV order is RL 1,000 mL infused in 8 hours. How many mL should be delivered to the patient each hour? _____

Exercise 23-29: *Calculation*

The IV order is NSS 200 mL per hour, and the tubing delivers 10 gtts/mL. How many gtts per minute should the nurse set the pump? _____

Exercise 23-30: *Calculation*

The IV order reads 1,000 mL of D5W over 12 hours. The IV pump delivers 60 gtts/mL. How many gtts/min should the nurse set the pump at? ______

The instructor goes on to tell Aubree, Alita, and Connor about complications of IV sites. IV sites should be checked often, usually every few hours depending on policy.

Exercise 23-31: *Matching*

Match the IV complication term in column A to the descriptor in column B.

Column A	Column B
A. Infiltration	___ Inflammation of the vein
B. Erythema	___ IV fluids infusing into surrounding spaces
C. Phlebitis	___ Redness of the skin around IV site

After talking about IVs in class, Alita asks if they always use veins for drawing blood and inserting IVs. The instructor tells her that arteries are often used for specific tests. Aubree, Alita, and Connor ask more questions about the electrolytes and how they can be affected by different conditions as they move onto a more in-depth discussion of acid–base balance.

Exercise 23-32: *Multiple Choice Question*

The nurse understands that the best method to assess acid–base balance in a patient is to obtain:

A. A pulse oximetry reading
B. Blood pressure
C. Hemoglobin and Hematocrit
D. Arterial blood gas

The instructor explains that six values are assessed to understand a patient's acid–base value.

The Answers section can be found on page 321.

Exercise 23-33: *Select All That Apply*

The following six values are assessed for acid–base value:

- ❑ Hematocrit
- ❑ pH
- ❑ $PaCO_2$
- ❑ PaO_2
- ❑ HCO_3^-
- ❑ Base excess
- ❑ Potassium
- ❑ Oxygen saturation

Exercise 23-34: *Matching*

Match the acid–base value obtained when getting an arterial blood gas (ABG) in column A with the normal value expected in column B.

Column A	Column B
A. $PaCO_2$	______ ± 2
B. PaO_2	______ 95% to 99%
C. O_2 saturation	______ 35 to 45 mmHg
D. Standard base excess (SBE)	______ 22 to 26 mEq/L
E. Bicarbonate	______ 80 to 100 mmHg

eResource 23-8: To better understand ABGs, the class participates in two ABG Interpretation learning activities from Wisc-Online: [Pathway: www.wisc-online.com/ → select "Learning Objects" → "Health" → "Nursing" → select and view the following: *ABG Interpretation: Partially and Fully Compensated Conditions* and *ABG Interpretation: Uncompensated Conditions*].

The instructor explains that there are four imbalances that patients can experience:

- Respiratory acidosis—an increase in $PaCO_2$ and a decrease in pH
- Respiratory alkalosis—a decrease in $PaCO_2$ and an increase in pH
- Metabolic acidosis—decreases bicarbonate
- Metabolic alkalosis—increases bicarbonate in the serum

eResource 23-9: The class views several video lectures by D. J. Hennager from Kirkwood Community College that further explain these important concepts:

- *pH (Acid) Homeostasis*:
  - *Part 1:* www.youtu.be/HrUvft2d8Zo
  - *Part 2:* www.youtu.be/-8tcJ8uBn-Q and
  - *Accompanying Handout:* www.kirkwood.edu/pdf/uploaded/695/acid_homeostasisyt.pdf

The Answers section can be found on page 321.

- *Acidosis and Alkalosis: Metabolic or Respiratory*:
  - *Part 1:* Video Lecture: www.youtu.be/eK2dBdBRvCU
  - *Part 2:* Video Lecture: www.youtu.be/K0UMXxjoAaw with an
  - *Accompanying Handout:* www.kirkwood.edu/pdf/uploaded/695/acidosisd.pdf

Exercise 23-35: *Multiple Choice Question*

The nurse interprets the following ABGs, pH = 7.2, $PaCO_2$ = 60 mmHg, SBE = 0 mEq/L as:

A. Respiratory acidosis

B. Respiratory alkalosis

C. Metabolic acidosis

D. Metabolic alkalosis

Exercise 23-36: *Multiple Choice Question*

The nurse interprets the following ABGs, pH = 7.30, $PaCO_2$ = 30 mmHg, SBE = −10 mEq/L as:

A. Respiratory acidosis.

B. Respiratory alkalosis

C. Metabolic acidosis

D. Metabolic alkalosis

Aubree, Alita, and Connor are overwhelmed; the instructor tells them not to be because acid–base balance as well as blood transfusions will not be on a fundamental's test and it will be gone over many times in their adult health class. Aubree, Alita, and Connor feel like they have covered a lot of material with fluid and electrolytes and make a study schedule to start studying for the next test.

Reference

Patlak, J. (2000). *Body fluids.* Department of Physiology, University of Vermont. Retrieved from http://physioweb.uvm.edu/bodyfluids/

The Answers section can be found on page 321.

Answers

Exercise 23-1: *Fill-in*

Write an "I" for intracellular fluid and an "E" for extracellular fluid, which is contained in the following anatomical areas:

__I__ Inside the body cells
__E__ Interstitial
__E__ Intravascular
__E__ Lymph
__E__ Blood vessels
__E__ Cerebral spinal fluid
__E__ Pleural fluid

Exercise 23-2: *Matching*

Match the osmolarity descriptor in column A to what it does in the body in column B.

Column A		Column B
A. Isotonic	B	Pulls fluid from cells
B. Hypertonic	C	Pushes fluid into cells
C. Hypotonic	A	Expands the blood volume without movement of fluid in or out of the cells

Exercise 23-3: *Matching*

Match the electrolyte in column A to its correct normal values in column B.

Column A		Column B (mEq/L)
A. Sodium (Na^+)	D	22 to 26
B. Potassium (K^+)	F	1.5 to 2.5
C. Calcium (Ca^+)	A	135 to 145
D. Bicarbonate (HCO_3^-)	G	1.7 to 4.6
E. Chloride (Cl^-)	B	3.5 to 5.0
F. Magnesium (Mg^{2-})	E	90 to 110
G. Phosphate (PO_4^{3-})	C	4.5 to 5.5

Exercise 23-4: *Multiple Choice Question*

An excess of fluid being pushed into the intravascular space results in:

A. Sore joints—NO, this is not a typical complaint

B. Flushing—NO, this is a vasoconstriction issue

C. Itching—NO, this occurs from irritants

D. **Edema—YES, this is misplaced fluid in the spaces outside the cells**

Exercise 23-5: *Fill-in*

The balance of body fluids is called **homeostasis**.

Exercise 23-6: *Multiple Choice Question*

The nurse understands that patients may be suffering from hypovolemia when they experience:

A. **Thirst—YES, this may be an indicator of hypovolemia**

B. Water intoxication—NO

C. Nausea—NO

D. Constipation—NO

Exercise 23-7: *Select All That Apply*

The following patients are at highest risk for dehydration:

☒ **Elderly—YES, due to increased insensible water loss**

☐ Adults—NO, healthy adults should not normally be at risk

☐ Adolescents—NO, healthy adolescents should not normally be at risk

☒ **Children—YES, due to inability for self-care if they are very young**

☒ **Infants—YES, due to large body surface**

☒ **Patients with neurological issues—YES, may lack sensation of thirst**

☒ **Patients with psychological issues—YES, may lack cognitive ability to hydrate**

Exercise 23-8: *Multiple Choice Question*

The nurse understands that normal blood acid–base balance is a pH from:

A. 7.15 to 7.25—NO

B. 7.25 to 7.35—NO

C. **7.35 to 7.45—YES, this is the normal values**

D. 7.45 to 7.55—NO

Exercise 23-9: *Matching*

Match the condition in column A to the description in column B.

Column A	Column B
A. Hyponatremia	__C__ Low serum potassium
B. Hypernatremia	__E__ Low serum calcium
C. Hypokalemia	__J__ High serum chloride
D. Hyperkalemia	__D__ High serum potassium
E. Hypocalcemia	__H__ High serum magnesium
F. Hypercalcemia	__G__ Low serum magnesium
G. Hypomagnesemia	__A__ Low serum sodium
H. Hypermagnesemia	__F__ High serum calcium
I. Hypochloremia	__B__ High serum sodium
J. Hyperchloremia	__I__ Low serum chloride

Exercise 23-10: *Multiple Choice Question*

A patient is admitted to the hospital with kidney disease resulting in a salt-wasting syndrome; the nurse would expect to see the following serum laboratory finding for this patient:

A. Hypernatremia—NO, this would happen if the body were holding onto sodium
B. **Hyponatremia—YES, this is low sodium**
C. Hyperkalemia—NO, this is high potassium
D. Hypocalcemia—NO, this is low calcium

Exercise 23-11: *Multiple Choice Question*

A patient is admitted to the hospital with severe dehydration; the nurse would expect to see the following serum laboratory finding for this patient:

A. **Hypernatremia—YES, because there has been a loss of water**
B. Hyponatremia—NO, this would happen if it were diluted
C. Hyperkalemia—NO, this would be a late sign
D. Hypocalcemia—NO, this would not be affected

Exercise 23-12: *Multiple Choice Question*

A patient uses potassium-wasting diuretics; the nurse would expect to see the following serum laboratory finding for this patient:

A. Hypernatremia—NO
B. **Hypokalemia—YES**
C. Hyperkalemia—NO
D. Hypocalcemia—NO

Exercise 23-13: *Multiple Choice Question*

A patient is admitted with massive cellular damage due to a burn; the nurse would expect to see the following serum laboratory finding for this patient:

A. Hypernatremia—NO
B. Hypokalemia—NO
C. **Hyperkalemia—YES, due to massive cell damage**
D. Hypocalcemia—NO

Exercise 23-14: *Multiple Choice Question*

A patient has vitamin D deficiencies; the nurse would expect to see the following serum laboratory finding for this patient:

A. Hypercalcemia—NO
B. Hypokalemia—NO
C. Hyperkalemia—NO
D. **Hypocalcemia—YES, vitamin D helps absorb calcium**

Exercise 23-15: *Multiple Choice Question*

A patient has taken an excessive amount of TUMS® (calcium carbonate); the nurse would expect to see the following serum laboratory finding for this patient:

A. **Hypercalcemia—YES, this is a calcium-based medication and should not be taken in excess**
B. Hypokalemia—NO
C. Hyperkalemia—NO
D. Hypocalcemia—NO

Exercise 23-16: *Multiple Choice Question*

The nurse understands that the patient with the highest risk for fluid loss is the:

A. **Infant—YES, due to their large body surface**
B. Toddler—NO
C. Child—NO
D. Adolescent—NO

Exercise 23-17: *Multiple Choice Question*

The normal range for adult specific gravity of urine is:

A. 1.010 to 1.020—NO
B. **1.020 to 1.030—YES, this is the normal value**
C. 1.030 to 1.040—NO
D. 1.040 to 1.050—NO

Exercise 23-18: *Calculation*

The nurse is calculating a 24-hour urine output on an infant. The diapers weigh 24 g dry. The infant was changed every 4 hours during the day and the weight of six diapers is 28, 54, 37, 42, 79, and 63 g. The infant's output in 24 hours is __**159**__ mL.

Exercise 23-19: *Calculation*

A patient takes in three 8-ounce glasses of water, 1,000 mL IV, 4 ounces of orange juice, a 16-ounce soda, and two 4-ounce cups of coffee. The patient voids seven times during the 24 hours. The voided amounts are 550, 700, 430, 300, 200, 200, and 200 mL. What is her ***fluid volume deficit (FVD)*** for the day? __**20 mL**__

	Intake	**Output**
Water = 720 mL		
IV 1,000 mL		
120 mL OJ		
Soda = 480 mL		
Coffee = 240 mL		
TOTAL	**2,560 mL**	**2,580 mL**

Exercise 23-20: *Calculation*

The nurse is caring for a pediatric patient. The child consumed one bowl of cereal with 4 ounces of milk, one 3-ounce glass of apple juice, one 2-ounce drink of water, two teaspoons of medication, 4 ounces of apple juice for lunch, a 6-ounce juice for snack, and 8 ounces of juice for supper. The child also had 200 mL of IV fluid in each 8-hour shift. The child voided 150, 275, 100, 480, 215, and 350 mL. The child's fluid volume deficit is __**150**__ mL.

	Intake	**Output**
Milk = 120 mL		
Juice = 90 mL		
Water = 60 mL		
Medication = 10 mL		
Juice for lunch = 120 mL		
Snack juice = 180 mL		
Supper juice = 240 mL		
IV = 600 mL		
TOTAL	**1,420 mL**	**1,570 mL**

Exercise 23-21: *Calculation*

A patient takes in three 8-ounce glasses of water, 1,000 mL IV, 4 ounces of orange juice, a 16-ounce soda, and two 4-ounce cups of coffee. The patient voids five times during the 24 hours. The voided amounts are 350, 500, 330, 250, and 200 mL. What is her ***fluid volume excess (FVE)*** for the day? **450** mL

	Intake	Output
Water = 240 mL		
IV = 1,000 mL		
OJ = 120 mL		
Soda = 480 mL		
Coffee 240 mL		
TOTAL	**2,080 mL**	**1,630 mL**

Exercise 23-22: *Calculation*

The nurse is caring for a pediatric patient. The child consumed one bowl of cereal with 4 ounces of milk, one 3-ounce glass of apple juice, one 2-ounce drink of water, 2 teaspoons of medication, 4 ounces of apple juice for lunch, a 6-ounce juice for snack, and 8 ounces of juice for supper. The child also had 100 mL of IV fluid in each 8-hour shift. The child voided 50, 175, 100, 380, 115, and 150 mL. The child's fluid volume excess is **150** mL.

	Intake	Output
Milk = 120 mL		
Juice = 90 mL		
Water = 60 mL		
Medication = 10 mL		
Juice for lunch = 120 mL		
Snack juice = 180 mL		
Supper juice = 240 mL		
IV =300 mL		
TOTAL	**1,120 mL**	**970 mL**

Exercise 23-23: *Fill-in*

To monitor a patient's weight accurately, the nurse must weigh the patient on the same **scale**, at the same **time** with the same **clothes**.

Exercise 23-24: *Matching*

Match the type of IV crystalloid fluid in column A with its osmolarity effect in column B.

Column A		Column B
A. Hypotonic	**B**	Equal to the osmolarity of body fluids
B. Isotonic	**C**	Greater than the osmolarity of body fluids
C. Hypertonic	**A**	Less than the osmolarity of body fluids

Exercise 23-25: *Matching*

Match the solution in column A to the type of osmolarity in column B (use the descriptors in column B more than once).

Column A		Column B
A. Dextrose 5% in water (D5W)	**C**	Hypotonic
B. Dextrose 10% in water (D10W)	**A,D,G**	Isotonic
C. 0.45% sodium chloride (normal saline solution [NSS])	**B,C,E,F, H**	Hypertonic
D. 0.9% sodium chloride (0.9% NSS)		
E. D5 in 0.9 NSS (D5/NSS)		
F. D5 in 0.45 NSS (D5 ½NSS)		
G. Lactated Ringer's or Ringer's Lactate (RL)		
H. D5RL		

Exercise 23-26: *Ordering*

Place the following steps to starting an IV in order:

__**6**__ Insert catheter
__**1**__ Collect equipment
__**4**__ Place the tourniquet on above the site
__**10**__ Dress the site per policy, usually using a transparent dressing to be able to visualize site
__**8**__ Release tourniquet
__**2**__ Wash hands
__**7**__ Attach IV
__**3**__ Put on gloves
__**9**__ Regulate IV flow on pump
__**5**__ Cleanse patient skin per protocol

Exercise 23-27: *Hot Spot*

Place an X on the cephalic vein in the arm and a zero on the basilica vein.

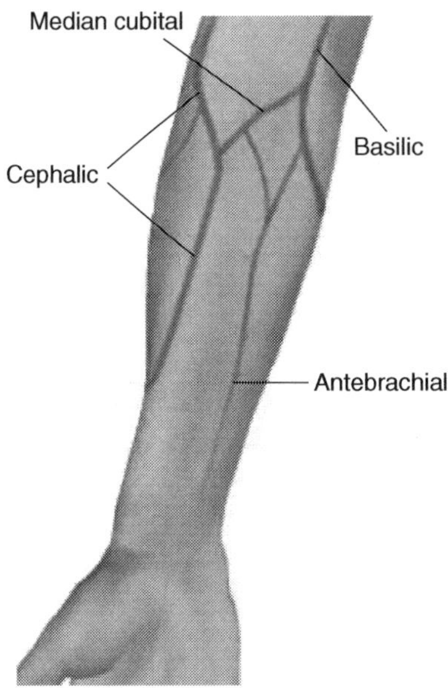

Exercise 23-28: *Calculation*

The IV order is RL 1,000 mL infused in 8 hours. How many mL should be delivered to the patient each hour? **125**

1,000 mL divided by 8 hr = 125 mL/hr

Exercise 23-29: *Calculation*

The IV order is NSS 200 mL per hour, and the tubing delivers 10 gtts/mL. How many gtts per minute should the nurse set the pump? **33 gtts/min**

200 mL divided by 60 min = 3.3 mL/min × 10 gtts/min = 33 gtts/min

Exercise 23-30: *Calculation*

The IV order reads 1,000 mL of D5W over 12 hours. The IV pump delivers 60 gtts/mL. How many gtts/min should the nurse set the pump at? **88 gtts/min**

1,000 mL divided by 12 hr = 83 mL/hr

88 mL divided by 60 min = 1.4 mL/min

1.4 mL/min × 60 gtts/min = 88 gtts/min

Exercise 23-31: *Matching*

Match the IV complication term in column A to the descriptor in column B.

Column A		Column B
A. Infiltration	**C**	Inflammation of the vein
B. Erythema	**A**	IV fluids infusing into surrounding spaces
C. Phlebitis	**B**	Redness of the skin around IV site

Exercise 23-32: *Multiple Choice Question*

The nurse understands that the best method to assess acid–base balance in a patient is to obtain:

A. A pulse oximetry reading—NO, this assesses peripheral oxygenation
B. Blood pressure—NO, this assesses vascular resistance
C. Hemoglobin and Hematocrit—NO, this assesses iron-carrying capacity of the blood
D. **Arterial blood gas—YES, this assesses acid–base balance**

Exercise 23-33: *Select All That Apply*

The following six values are assessed for acid–base value:

❑ Hematocrit
☒ **pH**
☒ **$PaCO_2$**
☒ **PaO_2**
☒ **HCO_3^-**
☒ **Base excess**
❑ Potassium
☒ **Oxygen saturation**

Exercise 23-34: *Matching*

Match the acid–base value obtained when getting an arterial blood gas (ABG) in column A with the normal value expected in column B.

Column A		Column B
A. $PaCO_2$	**D**	± 2
B. PaO_2	**C**	95% to 99%
C. O_2 Saturation	**A**	35 to 45 mmHg
D. Standard base excess (SBE)	**E**	22 to 26 mEq/L
E. Bicarbonate	**B**	80 to 100 mmHg

Exercise 23-35: *Multiple Choice Question*

The nurse interprets the following ABGs, pH = 7.2, $PaCO_2$ = 60 mmHg, SBE = 0 mEq/L as:

A. **Respiratory acidosis—YES, this is probably a patient with respiratory depression: The pH is acidic and the $PaCO_2$ is acidic or low and the SBE is normal, so it is not metabolic**

B. Respiratory alkalosis—NO

C. Metabolic acidosis—NO

D. Metabolic alkalosis—NO

Exercise 23-36: *Multiple Choice Question*

The nurse interprets the following ABGs, pH = 7.30, $PaCO_2$ = 30 mmHg, SBE = –10 mEq/L as:

A. Respiratory acidosis—NO

B. Respiratory alkalosis—NO

C. **Metabolic acidosis—YES, the pH is acid, the $PaCO_2$ is low, and the SBE is high**

D. Metabolic alkalosis—NO

24

Sleep and Comfort

Unfolding Case Study 23 Aubree, Alita, and Connor

Aubree, Alita, and Connor did well on their fluid and electrolyte test, and they are ready for the next lecture, which is about sleep and comfort. During the instructor's presentation, the students are told about the importance of sleep for mental and physiological functioning. Sleep deprivation causes impairment of judgment and is the cause of many accidents. Promoting sleep is difficult in the hospital, and many patients have pre-existing sleep disorders. Sleep disorders are classified into four categories:

- Dyssomnias—these can be from intrinsic, extrinsic, or circadian disorders
- Parasomnias—behaviors such as arousal disorders
- Sleep disorders—due to medical or psychiatric disorders
- Proposed sleep disorders—such as pregnancy associated

Exercise 24-1: *Multiple Choice Question*

The patient describes his sleep patterns to the nurse and states, "I go to bed at 10:30 and then lie awake most of the night no matter what I do." The patient is describing:

A. Narcolepsy
B. Sleep apnea
C. Hypersomnolence
D. Insomnia

The instructor tells the students that many patients suffer from sleep disorders. Sleep tests are often done overnight in a sleep lab, and patients are tested with a polysomnogram, which uses a combination of electroencephalogram (EEG), electrooculogram (EOG), electromyogram (EMG), and an electrocardiogram (ECG or EKG) to monitor sleep.

The Answers section can be found on page 341.

Exercise 24-2: *Select All That Apply*

Patients who are high risk for obstructive sleep apnea are:

- ❑ Middle-aged men
- ❑ Thin patients
- ❑ Patients who snore
- ❑ Patients with nasal polyps
- ❑ Patients who have had a tonsillectomy

Exercise 24-3: *Multiple Choice Question*

The nurse understands that a condition patients may have is a dysfunction in alternating wake and sleep patterns that may cause them to fall asleep at any time. This condition is called:

A. Narcolepsy
B. Sleep apnea
C. Hypersomnolence
D. Insomnia

Aubree, Alita, and Connor ask about working nights and how that affects nurses. The instructor tells them that there have been many sleep studies on shift workers, and sleep deprivation negatively affects the physical, mental, social, and spiritual health of people.

Exercise 24-4: *Multiple Choice Question*

Patients mostly at risk for sleep deprivation are those:

A. On a medical surgical hospital unit
B. In a hospice unit
C. On the maternity unit
D. In the intensive care unit (ICU)

The instructor explains that ***parasomnias*** are sleep issues that often occur in children.

Exercise 24-5: *Matching*

Match the disorder in column A to the description in column B.

Column A	Column B
A. Sudden infant death syndrome (SIDS)	______ Night bed wetting
B. Somnambulism	______ Teeth grinding
C. Nocturnal enuresis	______ Prolonged apnea
D. Bruxism	______ Sleep walking

Exercise 24-6: *Fill-in*

Infants should sleep ______ hours each 24 hours, and adults should sleep ______ hours each night.

Hypnotics and sedatives are often ordered for patients in the hospital to promote sleep.

The instructor explains to the students the importance of promoting sleep hygiene for patients in the hospital including a bedtime routine.

The Answers section can be found on page 341.

Exercise 24-7: *Select All That Apply*

The following medications are to decrease anxiety:

- ❑ Alprazolam (Xanax)
- ❑ Diazapam (Valium)
- ❑ Florazepam (Dalmane)
- ❑ Oxazepam (Serax)

Exercise 24-8: *Select All That Apply*

Medications used as antiinsomnia are:

- ❑ Alprazolam (Xanax)
- ❑ Diazapam (Valium)
- ❑ Florazepam (Dalmane)
- ❑ Oxazepam (Serax)
- ❑ Lorazepam (Ativan)
- ❑ Temazepam (Restoril)

Exercise 24-9: *Calculation*

The order is to administer oxazepam (Serax) 15 mg three times a day. The oxazepam (Serax) is dispensed in 30-mg tablets. How many tables should the nurse administer for one dose ________?

Exercise 24-10: *Calculation*

The order reads triazxolam (Halcion) 0.25 mg 1 hour before bedtime. The triazxolam (Halcion) is dispensed in tablets of 0.125 mg. How many tablets should the nurse administer for one dose________?

Medication may be avoided if routine comfort measures are provided and improve the patient's relaxation. Another reason that patients may be unable to sleep in the hospital is pain!

Exercise 24-11: *Multiple Choice Question*

The patient tells the nurse that she is feeling a sharp pain in her abdomen that has just started an hour ago. The nurse understands that the patient is describing a pain that is:

A. Chronic
B. Dull
C. Idiopathic
D. Acute

Exercise 24-12: *Multiple Choice Question*

The primary care provider runs tests on a patient complaining of pain and cannot find the cause. This type of pain is called:

A. Chronic
B. Dull
C. Idiopathic
D. Acute

The Answers section can be found on page 341.

eResource 24-1: The instructor provides additional resources to the class to help better understand pain:

- Pain: [Pathway: → www.anaesthetist.com/ → select "Pain Anatomy" to review materials: lecture on the Anatomy and Physiology of Pain, Practical Pain Management and a Pain Physiology].
- Pain animation, which demonstrate the physiology of pain: www.bayareapainmedical.com/nervanim.html

The instructor reviews how to assess for pain with Aubree, Alita, and Connor. They understand that some of the important assessment questions are those that describe pain by:

- Intensity
- Onset
- Duration
- Location
- Contributing factors

To assess pain, the nurse should use an age-appropriate pain scale.

Exercise 24-13: ***True/False***

The nurse understands that pain scales are inappropriate for infants.

- ❑ True
- ❑ False

eResource 24-2: The instructor tells Aubree, Alita, and Connor that there are a variety of established, age-appropriate tools that can be used for pain assessment and can even be utilized for patients with limited cognitive capability. She points to two resources as good starting points:

- The NIH Pain Consortium's list of *Pain Intensity Scales*: [Pathway: www.painconsortium.nih.gov → select "Pain Intensity Scales" to view].
- *Geriatric Pain Assessment* Resources: [Pathway: www.geriatricpain.org → Pain Assessment → review the resources listed:
    - Core Principles of Pain Assessment for Providers
    - Choosing and Using Observational Pain Tools
        - Part I
        - Part II
    - Pain Assessment Terminology—Glossary of Terms
    - Cognitively Intact—Tools and Resources
    - Cognitively Impaired—Tools and Resources]

Connor asks about pain relief. The instructor tells Connor that there are nonpharmacological methods and pain medications. Nonpharmacological methods are aimed at relaxation or a mental state free from stress.

The Answers section can be found on page 341.

Exercise 24-14: *Multiple Choice Question*

Voluntarily controlling physiological responses is called:

A. Cutaneous feedback
B. Biofeedback
C. Guided imagery
D. Acupressure

eResource 24-3: The International Association for the Study of Pain (IASP) provides extensive evidence-based resources at no charge. In IASP's free online publication, *Guide to Pain Management in Low-Resource Settings*, there is a discussion of Complementary Therapies for Pain Management by Cassileth and Gubili (2010): [Pathway: → www.iasp-pain.org → select "Publications" → "Free Books" → select "Guide to Pain Management in Low-Resource Settings" book icon → scroll down to Table of Contents and select "9. Complimentary Therapies. . ."].

The instructor tells the students that another strategy called Distraction Therapy has also been found to be effective in reducing the pain experience.

eResource 24-4: She shows Connor a short video demonstrating an approach utilized at Johns Hopkins Medical Institution for Bronchoscopies: www.webmd.com/pain-management/video/distraction-therapy-pain-control

The instructor tells the students that another method of pain control is TENS (transcutaneous electrical nerve stimulation). This stimulates the skin with mild electrical currents that detract from the pain being perceived. Herbals are another method used to help pain.

Exercise 24-15: *Select All That Apply*

The nurse understands that:

- ❑ Herbs may interact with other medications
- ❑ Many clients self-medicate with herbs
- ❑ They are usually harmless
- ❑ They are not addicting
- ❑ Many clients readily tell health care professions that they are using them

Often pain medication is used in order to make patients comfortable.

Exercise 24-16: *Multiple Choice Question*

Pain medication is called:

A. Antiarrythmias
B. Antianxiety
C. Analgesics
D. Antipyretics

The Answers section can be found on page 341.

The instructor explains to the students that pain is a “subjective” experience, and the nurse’s job is to understand all the variables that can affect a patient’s pain level.

Exercise 24-17: *Multiple Choice Question*

The nurse is caring for a patient who is walking in the hall and chatting with another patient. A short while later, the nurse finds the patient in bed reading and asks the patient to tell him his pain level on a scale of 1 to 10. The patient reports his pain level as 6; the nurse should:

A. Administer analgesics if it is time
B. Respond, can you describe your pain?
C. Call the primary care provider to communicate the observation
D. Give the patient a placebo

eResource 24-5: The instructor also shares with the class the *Pain Care Bill of Rights* published by the American Pain Foundation: www.painfoundation.org/learn/publications/pain-care-bill-of-rights.html

The instructor teaches the students that pain is managed in many ways with different types of pharmacological agents.

Exercise 24-18: *Matching*

Match the category of pharmacological agent in column A with its action in column B.

Column A		Column B
A. Opioids	______	Non-narcotic
B. Adjuvants	______	Potentiate narcotics
C. Nonsteroidal anti-inflammatory drugs (NSAIDs)	______	Narcotics

Exercise 24-19: *Select All That Apply*

Medications that fit into the NSAIDs category are:

- ❑ Acetylsalicylic acid (Aspirin)
- ❑ Naproxan
- ❑ Darvocet
- ❑ Ibuprofen

Exercise 24-20: *Multiple Choice Question*

The nurse is caring for a 34-year-old patient on heparin for a deep vein thrombosis (DVT) of the right leg who is requesting a non-narcotic pain relief medication. Which order should the nurse question?

A. Acetylsalicylic acid 650 mg po q 4 h
B. Naproxan 250 mg q 6 h
C. Darvocet 325 mg q 4 h
D. Ibuprofen 400 mg q 6 h

The Answers section can be found on page 341.

Another method of drug delivery explained to the students is a patient-controlled anesthesia (PCA) pump. This is used most often for patients with postoperative pain. A narcotic is attached to a pump, which is attached to the IV line. The pump is set at a specific dosage to be infused, and the patient can press a button to deliver a dose of pain medication as needed within a limit.

eResource 24-6: The class meets with a staff nurse who goes over the use of an IV PCA: www.youtu.be/KqGCOLIglqE

Exercise 24-21: *Calculation*

The order read morphine sulfate (MSO_4) 50 mg in 50 mL of NS via PCA pump. Deliver 1 mg per hour basal dose and 1 mg PRN q 10 minutes. What is the maximum amount of MSO_4 the patient can have in 1 hour _______?

The students ask more questions about operative pain such as, "Is there anything that can be done prior to the operation, other than anesthesia, to control pain postoperatively?"

The instructor tells them about topical and regional anesthesia that can help patients. The instructor gives Aubree, Alita, and Connor an example: When an infant boy is scheduled for a circumcision, the primary care provider uses ***EMLA*** (Eutectic Mixture of Local Anesthesia) cream 15 minutes before the procedure. EMLA comes in a patch or cream and "numbs" the area. After the area is numb, the primary care provider uses a local anesthesia injected intradermally and then subcutaneously. The injections block the nerve conduction. After the injections take effect, the procedure can be done more comfortably.

eResource 24-7: Students review both intradermal and subcutaneous injection techniques by viewing the following videos:

- *Administering Intradermal Injections*: http://alfa.saddleback.edu/N170/intradermal.aspx (scroll down to bottom of page to view video).
- *How to give a Subcutaneous Injection*: www.youtu.be/pNl29347FcI

Another way to "numb" large areas of the body is regional anesthesia such as an ***epidural anesthesia***. Epidural anesthesia is administered into the epidural space either by one injection or by continuous catheter into the lumbar area to numb or decrease pain in the back or legs.

eResource 24-8: Students also listen to a presentation by Anesthetist, Dr. Daman Mulhi, in which she explains the epidural procedure: www.youtu.be/uNDcf3Vw1vo

The Answers section can be found on page 341.

Exercise 24-22: *Multiple Choice Question*

Epidural anesthesia is often preferred over spinal anesthesia because a fairly common spinal anesthesia risk is:

A. Permanent numbness
B. Itching
C. Nausea
D. Headache

The instructor sums up the class and tells the students that pain relief for patients is a major nursing responsibility. If a patient had unrelieved pain and no appropriate pain medication order, then the nurse would advocate for the patient by calling the primary care provider and using the SBAR format to report the recommendation.

eResource 24-9: Student Nurses Journey web resource: [Pathway: www.snjourney.com → select "Care Plans and Maps"→ "Writing And Reporting" → "Nursing Notes and SOAP Notes"].

Exercise 24-23: *Multiple Choice Question*

Studies show that nurses tend to under medicate patients because they:

A. Do not want to mask signs of complications
B. Understand when a patient is "faking"
C. Are afraid that patients will become addicted
D. Encourage coping skill development

Aubree, Alita, and Connor ask for some more pharmacology practice questions, and the instructor gives them the following to take home and work on to ready themselves for the next test, which will have calculations.

Exercise 24-24: *Multiple Choice Question*

The order reads Daypro (oxaprozin) 1.8 g PO once a day. The drug is supplied as 600 mg per tablet. How many tablets will you administer to your patient?

A. 1 tablet
B. 2 tablets
C. 3 tablets
D. 4 tablets

eResource 24-10: Connor uses MedCalc on his smartphone to quickly double check his conversion of milligrams to grams: [Pathway: MedCalc → Units Conversion (Physics) → select "weight" icon].

The Answers section can be found on page 341.

Exercise 24-25: *Multiple Choice Question*

The order reads Dilaudid (hydromorphone) 4 milligrams (mg) every 4 hours PRN (as needed). The vial of Dilaudid has 10 mg/mL. How many mL (milliliters) of this drug will you give?

A. 0.4 mL
B. 4.0 mL
C. 0.5 mL
D. 5.0 mL

eResource 24-11: Alita finds a terrific online resource to help master medmath and shares it with the class: www.dosagehelp.com/

Exercise 24-26: *Multiple Choice Question*

The order reads acetylsalicylic acid (aspirin) 80 mg PO 4 times a week for heart health. The OTC (over the counter) tablets come in 40 mg. How many should the patient take at one time?

A. 1 tablet
B. 1.5 tablets
C. 2 tablets
D. 2.5 tablets

Reference

Cassileth, B., & Gubili, J. (2010). Complementary therapies for pain management. In A. Kopf & N. B. Patel (Eds.), *Guide to pain management in low-resource settings* (pp. 59–64). Seattle, WA: The International Association for the Study of Pain. Retrieved from http://www.iasp-pain.org

The Answers section can be found on page 341.

Answers

Exercise 24-1: ***Multiple Choice Question***

The patient describes his sleep patterns to the nurse and states, "I go to bed at 10:30 and then lie awake most of the night no matter what I do." The patient is describing:

A. Narcolepsy—NO, this is falling asleep during the day
B. Sleep apnea—NO, this is waking at night due to airway obstruction
C. Hypersomnolence—NO, this is excessive tiredness
D. **Insomnia—YES, this is the inability to fall asleep**

Exercise 24-2: ***Select All That Apply***

Patients who are high risk for obstructive sleep apnea are:

☒ **Middle-aged men—YES, middle-aged, obese men are mostly at risk**

❑ Thin patients—NO

☒ **Patients who snore—YES, this may indicate an obstruction**

☒ **Patients with nasal polyps—YES, polyps may obstruct the airway**

❑ Patients who have had a tonsillectomy—NO, tonsils may obstruct the airway

Exercise 24-3: ***Multiple Choice Question***

The nurse understands that a condition patients may have is a dysfunction alternating wake and sleep patterns that may cause them to fall asleep at any time. This condition is called:

A. **Narcolepsy—YES, narcoleptics can fall asleep anytime**
B. Sleep apnea—NO, this is airway obstruction
C. Hypersomnolence—NO, this is excessive sleeping
D. Insomnia—NO, this is inability to sleep

Exercise 24-4: ***Multiple Choice Question***

Patients mostly at risk for sleep deprivation are those:

A. On a medical surgical hospital unit—NO, there is a risk but not the most at risk
B. In a hospice unit—NO, there is a risk but not the most at risk
C. On the maternity unit—NO, there is a risk but not the most at risk
D. **In the intensive care unit (ICU)—YES, this is the place where activity and monitors are going all night long**

Exercise 24-5: *Matching*

Match the disorder in column A to the description in column B.

Column A	Column B
A. Sudden infant death syndrome (SIDS)	**C** Night bed wetting
B. Somnambulism	**D** Teeth grinding
C. Nocturnal enuresis	**A** Prolonged apnea
D. Bruxism	**B** Sleep walking

Exercise 24-6: *Fill-in*

Infants should sleep **16 to 20** hours each 24 hours, and adults should sleep **6 to 8** hours each night.

Exercise 24-7: *Select All That Apply*

The following medications are to decrease anxiety:

☒ **Alprazolam (Xanax)—YES, this is an antianxiety medication**

☐ Diazapam (Valium)—NO, this is a relaxant

☐ Florazepam (Dalmane)—NO, this is an antiinsomnia medication

☒ **Oxazepam (Serax)—YES, this is an antianxiety medication**

Exercise 24-8: *Select All That Apply*

Medications used as antiinsomnia are:

☐ Alprazolam (Xanax)—NO, antianxiety

☒ **Diazapam (Valium)—YES**

☒ **Florazepam (Dalmane)—YES**

☐ Oxazepam (Serax)—NO, antianxiety

☐ Lorazepam (Ativan)—NO, antianxiety

☒ **Temazepam (Restoril)—YES**

Exercise 24-9: *Calculation*

The order is to administer oxazepam (Serax) 15 mg three times a day. The oxazepam (Serax) is dispensed in 30-mg tablets. How many tables should the nurse administer for one dose? **0.5 tablet**

Exercise 24-10: *Calculation*

The order reads triazxolam (Halcion) 0.25 mg 1 hour before bedtime. The triazxolam (Halcion) is dispensed in tablets of 0.125 mg. How many tables should the nurse administer for one dose?

0.125 mg × 2 = 0.25 mg **2 tablets**

Exercise 24-11: *Multiple Choice Question*

The patient tells the nurse that she is feeling a sharp pain in her abdomen that has just started an hour ago. The nurse understands that the patient is describing a pain that is:

A. Chronic—NO, this is pain that has a long duration
B. Dull—NO, this is an aching type of pain sensation
C. Idiopathic—NO, this just means that the cause of the pain is unknown even after diagnostic tests
D. **Acute—YES, sudden onset and usually intense**

Exercise 24-12: *Multiple Choice Question*

The primary care provider runs tests on a patient complaining of pain and cannot find the cause. This type of pain is called:

A. Chronic—NO, this is pain that has a long duration
B. Dull—NO, this is an aching type of pain sensation
C. **Idiopathic—YES**
D. Acute—NO, this is a sudden onset pain and usually intense

Exercise 24-13: *True/False*

The nurse understands that pain scales are inappropriate for infants.

☐ True

☒ **False—Infant pain scales rate the behavior of the infant such as crying and muscle tenseness**

Exercise 24-14: *Multiple Choice Question*

Voluntarily controlling physiological responses is called:

A. Cutaneous feedback—NO, this is usually done with adjunct stimulation
B. **Biofeedback—YES**
C. Guided imagery—NO, this is a cognitive therapy, one that uses pictures to take the mind off the pain.
D. Acupressure—NO, this is done by another person.

Exercise 24-15: *Select All That Apply*

The nurse understands that if a patient is using herbs that they may:

☒ **Herbs may interact with other medications—YES**

☒ **Many clients self-medicate with herbs—YES**

☐ They are usually harmless—NO, they are often not harmless

☐ They are not addicting—NO, many are not addicting

☒ **Many clients readily tell health care professions that they are using them—YES, often the patient does not tell health care providers about them for fear of being ridiculed for using them**

Exercise 24-16: *Multiple Choice Question*

Pain medication is called:

A. Antiarrythmias—NO, these are cardiac medications
B. Antianxiety—NO, these decrease anxiety
C. **Analgesics—YES**
D. Antipyretics—NO, these decrease fever

Exercise 24-17: *Multiple Choice Question*

The nurse is caring for a patient who is walking in the hall and chatting with another patient. A short while later, the nurse finds the patient in bed reading and asks the patient to tell him his pain level on a scale of 1 to 10. The patient reports his pain level as 6; the nurse should:

A. **Administer analgesics if it is time—YES, always believe the patient; individual patients manifest pain differently**
B. Respond, can you describe your pain?—NO, this is questioning his perception
C. Call the primary care provider to communicate the observation—NO, this is undermining the patient's right to care
D. Give the patient a placebo—NO, this is ethically inappropriate and goes against the concept of veracity or telling the truth

Exercise 24-18: *Matching*

Match the category of pharmacological agent in column A with its action in column B.

Column A		Column B
A. Opioids	C	Non-narcotic
B. Adjuvants	B	Potentiate narcotics
C. Nonsteroidal anti-inflammatory drugs (NSAIDs)	A	Narcotics

Exercise 24-19: *Select All That Apply*

Medications that fit into the NSAIDs category are:

❑ Acetylsalicylic acid (Aspirin)

☒ **Naproxan—YES**

❑ Darvocet

☒ **Ibuprofen—YES**

Exercise 24-20: *Multiple Choice Question*

The nurse is caring for a 34-year-old patient on heparin for a deep vein thrombosis (DVT) of the right leg who is requesting a non-narcotic pain relief medication. Which order should the nurse question?

A. **Acetylsalicylic acid 650 mg po q 4 h—YES, aspirin decreases clotting time**
B. Naproxan 250 mg q 6 h—NO, this is safe
C. Darvocet 325 mg q 4 h—NO, this is safe
D. Ibuprofen 400 mg q 6 h—NO, this is safe

Exercise 24-21: ***Calculation***

The order read Morphine Sulfate (MSO_4) 50 mg in 50 mL of NS via PCA pump. Deliver 1 mg per hour basal dose and 1 mg PRN q 10 minutes. What is the maximum amount of MSO_4 the patient can have in 1 hour?

7 mg (1 mg basal + 6 mg for every 10 minutes to 60 minutes or 1 hour)

Exercise 24-22: ***Multiple Choice Question***

Epidural anesthesia is often preferred over spinal anesthesia because a fairly common spinal anesthesia risk is:

A. Permanent numbness—NO, this is not a common complication
B. Itching—NO, this is a common side effect of epidurals
C. Nausea—NO, this is not a side effect of spinals or epidurals
D. **Headache—YES, many patients experience spinal headaches**

Exercise 24-23: ***Multiple Choice Question***

Studies show that nurses tend to under medicate patients because they:

A. Do not want to mask signs of complications—NO, this is not the reason
B. Understand when a patient is "faking"—NO, this is not the reason
C. **Are afraid that patients will become addicted—YES, this is a misconception if pain medication is used correctly**
D. Encourage coping skill development—NO, this is not the reason

Exercise 24-24: ***Multiple Choice Question***

The order reads Daypro (oxaprozin) 1.8 g PO once a day. The drug is supplied as 600 mg per tablet. How many tablets will you administer to your patient?

A. 1 tablet—NO, this is only 0.6 g
B. 2 tablets—NO, this is only 1.2 g
C. **3 tablets—YES, 1.8 g = 1800 mg, divide by 600 mg = 3 tablets**
D. 4 tablets—NO, this is 2.4 g

Exercise 24-25: ***Multiple Choice Question***

The order reads Dilaudid (hydromorphone) 4 milligrams (mg) every 4 hours PRN (as needed). The vial of Dilaudid has 10 mg/mL. How many mL (milliliters) of this drug will you give?

A. **0.4 mL—YES, every 0.1 mL is equal to 1 mg, so 0.4 mL = 4 mg**
B. 4.0 mL—NO, this is 40 mg
C. 0.5 mL—NO, this is 5 mg
D. 5.0 mL—NO, this is 50 mg

Exercise 24-26: *Multiple Choice Question*

The order reads acetylsalicylic acid (aspirin) 80 mg po 4 times a week for heart health. The OTC (over the counter) tablets come in 40 mg. How many should the patient take at one time?

A. 1 tablet—NO, this is only 40 mg
B. 1.5 tablets—NO, this is 60 mg
C. **2 tablets—YES, this is 80 mg**
D. 2.5 tablets—NO, this is 100 mg

25

Nutrition

Unfolding Case Study 24 ▪ Aubree, Alita, and Connor

Aubree, Alita, and Connor attend a conference at the clinical site with the rest of their clinical group. It is provided by a nutritionist who works for the hospital and consults about patients every day. The nutritionist goes over basic concepts with the students, and then explains how he applies them to the care of patients. He is an important member of the interdisciplinary team because nutritional needs of patients can be very diverse, and many Americans need nutritional teaching.

Exercise 25-1: *Matching*

Match the nutritional term in column A to the correct description in column B.

Column A	Column B
A. Basal metabolic rate (BMR)	_______ The number of nutrients you are getting for the calories
B. Resting energy expenditure (REE)	_______ Metabolic rate + energy to digest meals
C. Nutrients	_______ Energy to maintain life
D. Nutrient density	_______ Necessary elements needed by the body

The nutritionist tells the students that he is going to talk a little bit more in depth about carbohydrates, fats, and proteins. Carbohydrates are derived from glucose, which is the main energy for the body and produce 4 kcal (kilocalorie) per gram. Most carbohydrates come from plant food or milk (lactose). They are classified according to the type of saccharides; they are simple (monosaccharides and disaccharides) or complex (polysaccharides).

Exercise 25-2: *Multiple Choice Question*

A complex carbohydrate (polysaccharide) that humans cannot digest is called a:

A. Sucrose

B. Starch

C. Maltose

D. Fructose

The Answers section can be found on page 359.

Proteins are also produce 4 kcal/g energy and are needed for DNA and RNA. Most protein comes from animal sources; others come from legumes, which are beans and peas. Animal proteins provide complete proteins or essential amino acids, while beans and peas are usually incomplete proteins but can be mixed together to make complete proteins (complementary proteins). Proteins also ensure nitrogen balance in the body. If the body consumes less protein than needed, it is in negative nitrogen balance.

eResource 25-1: The instructor uses a variety of active learning modules from Wisc-Online to help the students better understand the concepts associated with nutrition: [Pathway: www.wisc-online.com/ → select "Learning Objects" → "Health" → "Dietary" → scroll down and select the following: (a) *Classifying Foods According to Nutrient Density*, (b) *Digestion and Absorption of Carbohydrates*, and (c) *Digestion and Absorption of Protein*].

Exercise 25-3: *Multiple Choice Question*

Risk factors for negative nitrogen balance include:

A. Burns, sepsis, starvation
B. Edema, obesity, colds
C. Hypothermia, diabetes, sepsis
D. Obesity, burns, sutured wounds

Fats are the most dense of the nutrients and are 9 kcal/g. They are made up of triglycerides and fatty acids. Fatty acids are either saturated or unsaturated.

eResource 25-2: Nutrition Glossary: [Pathway: http://nutritiondata.self.com/ → select "help" → scroll down and select "glossary"].

Exercise 25-4: *Multiple Choice Question*

The nurse understands that the patient needs additional teaching about nutrition when the patient states:

A. "Vegetable oils have more unsaturated fatty acids"
B. "Animal fat has more saturated fat"
C. "I should have 50% saturated and unsaturated fats"
D. "I should have linoleic acid, which is an essential fatty acid"

The instructor tells the students that there are other important nutrients needed besides carbohydrates, fats, and proteins. There is a need for vitamins and minerals.

eResource 25-3: The instructor uses a variety of active learning modules from Wisc-Online to help the students better understand the concepts associated with nutrition: [Pathway: www.wisc-online.com/ → select "Learning Objects" → "Health" → "Dietary" → scroll down and select the following: (a) *Classifying Foods According to Nutrient Density*, (b) *Digestion and Absorption of Carbohydrates*, and (c) *Digestion and Absorption of Protein*].

The Answers section can be found on page 359.

Exercise 25-5: *Multiple Choice Question*

Water comprises what percent of the total body weight?

A. 60% to 70 %
B. 50% to 60%
C. 40% to 50%
D. 30% to 40%

Exercise 25-6: *Matching*

Place the vitamin in column A in the correct category in column B.

Column A	Column B
A. Vitamin A	_______ Fat soluble
B. Vitamin B complex	_______ Water soluble
C. Vitamin C	
D. Vitamin D	
E. Vitamin E	
F. Vitamin K	

The instructor tells Aubree, Alita, and Connor that nutrition also depends on an intact gastrointestinal (GI) system. Food is moved along the GI track by peristalsis, where enzymes work on the food to digest it and use the nutrients.

Exercise 25-7: *Multiple Choice Question*

The nurse is delegating tasks to the unlicensed assistive personnel (UAP). Which task should the nurse not delegate?

A. Feeding a patient with a long-term feeding tube
B. Cutting up the meat for a patient with a paralyzed right hand
C. Assisting a wheelchair patient to the dining room
D. Feeding a dysphagic patient

All food that people buy in the United States has daily values called recommended daily allowances (RDA).

Exercise 25-8: *Multiple Choice Question*

The nurse understands that RDA are based on:

A. A 1,500 calorie daily diet
B. A 2,000 calorie daily diet
C. A 2,500 calorie daily diet
D. A 3,000 calorie daily diet

Aubree asks if humans throughout their lives need the RDA of calories each day. The instructor explains that it differs with each developmental stage. Infants grow quickly and double their birth weight by 4 to 5 months and triple it by a year. Their digestive tracks are immature, and they can digest simple carbohydrates, proteins, and some fats.

The Answers section can be found on page 359.

Exercise 25-9: *Multiple Choice Question*

Breast milk and formula for full-term infants provide an infant with how many kcal per ounce?

A. 15 kcal/30 mL
B. 20 kcal/30 mL
C. 25 kcal/30 mL
D. 30 kcal/30 mL

Infants grow rapidly but only need formula for the first 4 to 6 months of life.

Exercise 25-10: *Multiple Choice Question*

Infants should be introduced to solid foods one at a time, 5 to 7 days apart in order to:

A. Introduce them to different textures separately
B. Make sure they acquire a taste for each new food substance
C. Determine their likes and preferences to enhance intake
D. Monitor them for any food allergies

Exercise 25-11: *Multiple Choice Question*

Toddlers are weaned off milk and provided with increased amounts of protein in order to prevent:

A. Anemia
B. Baby bottle teeth
C. Constipation
D. Lactose intolerance

Exercise 25-12: *Multiple Choice Questions*

Schools have initiated a nutritional program to provide breakfast for students because:

A. Most eat at home but the wrong things
B. Protein assists them to learn
C. Carbohydrates keep them awake in class
D. They are complaining about being hungry by lunch

Exercise 25-13: *Multiple Choice Question*

An adolescent female is exercising excessively and has stopped having her menses; the nurse suspects that she may be suffering from:

A. Body dysmorphia
B. Excessive sport competitiveness
C. Anorexia
D. Pregnancy

The instructor tells the students how important nutrition is in adulthood. Growth has stopped and the amount of calories needed is less. The students are done with class for the day and get themselves ready to go to the clinical area to get the information they need to care safely for their patients tomorrow.

The Answers section can be found on page 359.

eResource 25-4: A good starting place for patient education material is the U.S. Department of Agriculture Center for Nutrition and Prevention Policy: www.cnpp.usda.gov/Publications.htm

Aubree's patient is a middle-aged woman who was admitted for a ***cholecystectomy*** (gall bladder removal). She is recovering well according to the chart, but requesting pain medication every 4 to 6 hours and will still have an IV tomorrow. Aubree gets all the information she can off the chart and records it on her care plan without identifying patient data. Her patient is married with three grown children. She works at a computer job full time and cooks at home. She is obese with a BMI of 31. Aubree develops a care plan, and within the plan, she addressed "alteration in nutrition: more than body requirements."

Connor's patient is a young woman who is in for an exploratory lab for infertility. She is 32 years old and of normal weight. He is also going to address preconceptual nutritional needs with her.

Alita's patient is elderly and having issues with mobility due to a fractured hip repair. He also has a hearing deficit and wears glasses. He lives alone and is responsible for his own meals. Alita will address his nutritional needs also.

The next clinical day the instructor starts the students in pre-clinical conference and they share their patient data and describe the interventions they will carry out for the day. Aubree tells about her patient first and asks how she is going to teach her patient about healthy eating.

Exercise 25-14: *Select All That Apply*

The nurse should include the following information in nutritional teaching of an obese patient:

- ❑ Use fats, sweets, and oils sparingly
- ❑ Have four to five servings of milk a day
- ❑ Increase vegetable intake
- ❑ Use whole grain wheat
- ❑ Decrease fiber
- ❑ Increase exercise

Exercise 25-15: *Multiple Choice Question*

In order to decrease neural tube defects (NTDs) in children, preconceptual nutrition should include:

A. Vitamin B12
B. Thiamine
C. Protein
D. Folic acid

The Answers section can be found on page 359.

Exercise 25-16: ***Multiple Choice Question***

A nursing mother should increase her daily intake in order to feed her infant by:

A. 200 kcal

B. 300 kcal

C. 400 kcal

D. 500 kcal

Alita is concerned about her patient going home and being able to cook his own meals. Since her patient has some sensory deficits, home safety is an issue.

Exercise 25-17: ***Multiple Choice Question***

Elderly patients who live alone may benefit most from a referral to:

A. Occupational therapy

B. Recreational therapy

C. Meals on wheels

D. Local YMCA

Alita's patient is discharged, and she is assigned another patient for the remainder of the day. The objectives will be to assess this new patient's nutritional needs. Alita's new patient does not eat meat, so protein must be acquired from other sources.

Exercise 25-18: ***Matching***

Match the type of vegetarian in column A with the food substances that are withheld in column B.

Column A	Column B
A. Ovolactovegitarian	______ Only eat food from plants
B. Lactovegitarian	______ Do not eat meat, fish, or poultry
C. Vegans	______ Only eat fruit, nuts, honey, and olive oil
D. Fruitarian	______ Consume milk but not eggs

Alita's patient has iron-deficiency anemia and is put on iron. Alita discusses with him how to consume combinations of incomplete proteins to make a balanced diet. Her patient is receptive to learn and understands the implications of a protein-poor diet. Alita also initiates the process for her patient to have a dietician come and consult with him.

Exercise 25-19: ***Multiple Choice Question***

The nurse understands that iron absorption is increased when iron tablets are consumed with:

A. Water

B. Meals

C. Vitamin C

D. Vitamin A

In postconference, the clinical group discusses dietary habits of different ethnic and religious groups that they may care for in their professional lives. Understanding

The Answers section can be found on page 359.

different dietary habits plays a large part in promoting cultural sensitivity and respect. Food is a universal need, so all cultures deal with it, but all cultures do not deal with the consumption of food with the same beliefs.

Connor asks the instructor, "What is the best way to assess a person's nutrition?" The instructor tells the students about several common tests that are done. ***Anthropometry*** measures height to body size by measuring the wrist, arm, or skin folds.

Exercise 25-20: *True/False*

All patients admitted to the hospital must be weighed.

- ❑ True
- ❑ False

Another method of determining ideal body weight is ***body mass index (BMI)***, which uses height and weight.

Exercise 25-21: *Multiple Choice Question*

The nurse understands that if the patient has a BMI of 25.5, the patient is considered:

A. Underweight
B. Normal weight
C. Overweight
D. Obese

e **eResource 25-5:** A variety of tools for calculating BMI are available:

- MedCalc.com for an online calculator: [Pathway: www.medcalc.com → Tap on "General" → "Body Mass Index" to access the calculator].
- Skyscape's Archimedes on your mobile device: [Pathway: Archimedes → enter "BMI" into the search field →scroll down to "BMI (Adult)" or "BMI(Child)"].
- MedCalc on your mobile device: [Pathway: MedCalc →tap on "BMI" in the "All Formulas" search field].

Exercise 25-22: *Select All That Apply*

Laboratory tests that are used to assess a patient's nutritional status are:

- ❑ Albumin
- ❑ Prealbumin
- ❑ Bilirubin
- ❑ Retinol-binding protein
- ❑ Erythrocyte sedimentation rate
- ❑ Total iron binding
- ❑ Hemoglobin (Hgb)

The instructor tells the students that for many years, nurses have been accurately assessing patients' nutritional status by taking 24-hour dietary histories. Having intake of a typical day can help nurses and dieticians look for nutritional deficits. Having

The Answers section can be found on page 359.

patients write their intake down also works as a self-reflective mechanism and can be an excellent teaching tool when reviewed with the nurse. So for homework, the students are keeping a dietary history to analyze.

The following day, Aubree, Alita, and Connor are back for more clinical experience with a focus on patient nutrition. They are also writing down their own intakes. Alita has a patient on chemotherapy that is having difficulty eating. She looks for intervention to increase her patient's intake.

Exercise 25-23: *Select All That Apply*

Some nursing interventions to increase a patient's appetite include:

- ❑ Spraying air freshener
- ❑ Brushing the patient's teeth after feeding
- ❑ Cleaning the over-bed table
- ❑ Selecting foods that are fried

Aubree's patient has an order to advance diet PRN. Her patient was postoperative from yesterday and was on clear liquids last evening.

Exercise 25-24: *Multiple Choice Question*

The nurse understands that the patient who is advancing his diet from clear liquids needs further teaching when he makes a breakfast selection of:

A. A sausage sandwich with orange juice
B. Toast and tea
C. Farina and cranberry juice
D. Yogurt and a banana

Connor's patient was diagnosed with an ilius (or bowel section that is not responding normally) and cannot be feed. Connor assesses the patient and he has very hypo bowel sounds and he is gastrically distended. There is an order to place a ***nasogastric (NG)*** tube. The instructor reviews the procedure with Connor, and then they collect the equipment and double check the order.

Exercise 25-25: *Multiple Choice Question*

The nurse understands that the correct anatomical marks used to measure a NG tube are:

A. Bridge of the nose to the earlobe to the xiphoid process
B. Tip of the nose to the top of the pina to the umbilicus
C. Tip of the nose to the earlobe to the xiphoid process
D. Bridge of the nose to the top of the pina to the xiphoid process

eResource 25-6: As part of the review, Connor views a brief video tutorial *Nasogastric Intubation Demonstration NGT*: www.youtu.be/WgfNa7dzSn0

The Answers section can be found on page 359.

Exercise 25-26: *Ordering*

Place the following steps in order from one to nine:

_______ Insert tube through nostril to back of the throat aiming back and down
_______ Wash hands
_______ Place in high Fowler's position
_______ Aspirate gastric content
_______ Measure length of tube
_______ Put on gloves
_______ Fasten tube to patient gown with a pin and rubber band
_______ Apply tape
_______ Advance tube as patient swallows

Exercise 25-27: *Multiple Choice Question*

The preferred method of verifying initial tube placement is:

A. Testing gastric pH
B. Listening for inserted air over stomach
C. Marking the tube at the nostril
D. Obtaining an x-ray

Exercise 25-28: *Multiple Choice Question*

If gastric pH may be used to verify placement of a NG tube, but it would not be affected by:

A. How long ago the patient ate
B. The respiratory status of the patient
C. If the feeds were continuous or intermittent
D. If the tube was placed in the jejunum

eResource 25-7: Connor views an overview of the NG tube insertion process and notes that step 17 of the procedure provides information regarding verification of tube placement: http://alfa.saddleback.edu/N170/nasogastrictube.aspx (Note, there are additional instructional videos to view if you scroll down to view videos.)

Alita's patient is not consuming enough calories and is showing signs of malnutrition. The decision is made to start enteral feeding by a percutaneous endoscopic gastrotomy (PEG) tube in order to assist her to stay well nourished while receiving chemotherapy. The instructor explains to Alita that there are four types of enteral formulas used on patients.

- Polymeric formula—this type of formula delivers whole nutrients at 1.0 to 2.0 kcal/mL
- Modular formula—delivers 3.8 to 4.0 kcal/mL and are single macronutrients incomplete by themselves because they are just protein or glucose or lipids
- Elemental formula—this is 1.0 to 3.0 kcal/mL of predigested formula
- Specialty formula—made for specific patient needs such as for someone with liver failure

The Answers section can be found on page 359.

Exercise 25-29: *Multiple Choice Question*

The nurse is preparing to administer an enteral feed to a patient that has limited gastrointestinal (GI) enzymes functioning. The nurse would expect to administer which type of formula?

A. Polymeric formula
B. Modular formula
C. Elemental formula
D. Specialty formula

eResource 25-8: Enteral Tube Feedings:

- Enteral Nutrition: http://alfa.saddleback.edu/N170/tubefeeding.aspx
- Administration: http://alfa.saddleback.edu/N170/tubefeeding-administration.aspx
- Step-by-Step Procedure: www.youtu.be/wcnGOIX3tuw

Exercise 25-30: *Select All That Apply*

The following manifestations could indicate that a patient is not tolerating enteral feeding:

- ❑ Nausea
- ❑ Headache
- ❑ Muscle twitching
- ❑ Diarrhea
- ❑ Abdominal cramping
- ❑ Leg cramping

Exercise 25-31: *Multiple Choice Question*

The nurse understands that the risk of enteral feedings through an NG tube is:

A. Short gut syndrome
B. Aspiration
C. Stomach acid deficiency
D. Liver overload

eResource 25-9: To learn more about potential complications associated with tube feedings and how to manage these complications, Connor, Aubree, and Alita review additional materials:

- Management of complications: http://alfa.saddleback.edu/N170/tubefeeding-complications.aspx
- An active learning module from Wisc-Online about common problems: [Pathway: www.wisc-online.com/ → select "Learning Objects" → "Health" → "Nursing" → scroll down and select "Correcting Common Problems with Parental Nutrition"].

The Answers section can be found on page 359.

Alita's patient also is ordered medications through the PEG tube, which is a first-time skill for her. The instructor goes over the procedure after verifying with the pharmacy that each medication can be given by the enteral route and can be dispensed in liquid form.

Exercise 25-32: *Multiple Choice Question*

The nurse understands that the most important method of preventing enteral tube occlusion is:

A. Aspirating before administering each medication
B. Crushing each medication if not in liquid form
C. Administering medication mixed with the formula
D. Flushing with 30 ml of water before and after each medication

Alita's patient does well with the PEG tube and she understands that it is temporary and necessary to keep her strength up during chemotherapy treatment.

In postconference, the students discuss their day with their patients, and they indicate they have a deeper understanding of nutritional needs. Also, the students review their 24-hour diet intake charts and are amazed at the how many calories are inadvertently consumed when there is not a conscious effort to monitor intake. They analyze Connor's diet before they go home.

Exercise 25-33: *Exhibit Question*

The 24-hour diet intake history includes:

Last night's supper: Pork chop, baked potatoes, beans, cake
Last night snack: Popcorn and a glass of milk
Breakfast: Bowl of cereal and OJ
Lunch: Ham sandwich on white bread and potato chips
Three glasses of water, two glasses of milk, and three colas during the last 24 hours

According to the above diet, the nurse would include in her teaching:

A. Increase meat servings
B. Increase potatoes servings
C. Increase vegetable and fruit servings
D. Increase dairy servings

The Answers section can be found on page 359.

Answers

Exercise 25-1: *Matching*

Match the nutritional term in column A to the correct description in column B.

Column A		Column B
A. Basal metabolic rate (BMR)	D	The number of nutrients you are getting for the calories
B. Resting energy expenditure (REE)	A	Metabolic rate + energy to digest meals
C. Nutrients	B	Energy to maintain life
D. Nutrient density	C	Necessary elements needed by the body

Exercise 25-2: *Multiple Choice Question*

A complex carbohydrate (polysaccharide) that humans cannot digest is called a:

A. Sucrose—NO, this is a disaccharide
B. **Starch—YES, this is a complex carbohydrate**
C. Maltose—NO, this is a disaccharide
D. Fructose—NO, this is a simple carbohydrate

Exercise 25-3: *Multiple Choice Question*

Risk factors for negative nitrogen balance include:

A. **Burns, sepsis, starvation—YES, these are common causes for negative nitrogen balance**
B. Edema, obesity, colds—NO, an upper respiratory infection (URI) should not cause it
C. Hypothermia, diabetes, sepsis—NO, diabetes should not cause it unless it is very uncontrolled
D. Obesity, burns, sutured wounds—NO, obesity should not cause it

Exercise 25-4: *Multiple Choice Question*

The nurse understands that the patient needs additional teaching about nutrition when the patient states:

A. "Vegetable oils have more unsaturated fatty acids."—NO, this is true
B. "Animal fat has more saturated fat."—NO, this is true
C. **"I should have 50% saturated and unsaturated fats."—YES, they should have less saturated fat**
D. "I should have linoleic acid, which is an essential fatty acid."—NO, this is true

Exercise 25-5: *Multiple Choice Question*

Water comprises what percent of the total body weight?

A. **60% to 70%—YES**
B. 50% to 60%—NO
C. 40% to 50%—NO
D. 30% to 40%—NO

Exercise 25-6: *Matching*

Place the vitamin in column A in the correct category in column B.

Column A	Column B
A. Vitamin A	**A, D, E, K** Fat soluble
B. Vitamin B complex	**C and B complex** Water soluble
C. Vitamin C	
D. Vitamin D	
E. Vitamin E	
F. Vitamin K	

Exercise 25-7: *Multiple Choice Question*

The nurse is delegating tasks to the unlicensed assistive personnel (UAP). Which task should the nurse not delegate?

A. Feeding a patient with a long-term feeding tube—NO, this can be delegated safely
B. Cutting up the meat for a patient with a paralyzed right hand—NO, this can be delegated safely
C. Assisting a wheelchair patient to the dining room—NO, this can be delegated safely
D. **Feeding a dysphagic patient—YES, this patient has an increased risk of choking**

Exercise 25-8: *Multiple Choice Question*

The nurse understands that RDA are based on:

A. A 1,500 calorie daily diet—NO
B. **A 2,000 calorie daily diet—YES**
C. A 2,500 calorie daily diet—NO
D. A 3,000 calorie daily diet—NO

Exercise 25-9: *Multiple Choice Question*

Breast milk and formula for full-term infants provide an infant with how many kcal per ounce?

A. 15 kcal/30 mL—NO
B. **20 kcal/30 mL—YES**
C. 25 kcal/30 mL—NO
D. 30 kcal/30 mL—NO

Exercise 25-10: ***Multiple Choice Question***

Infants should be introduced to solid foods one at a time, 5 to 7 days apart in order to:

A. Introduce them to different textures separately—NO, this is not necessary
B. Make sure they acquire a taste for each new food substance—NO, this is not necessary
C. Determine their likes and preferences to enhance intake—NO, this is not necessary
D. **Monitor them for any food allergies—YES, this is important**

Exercise 25-11: ***Multiple Choice Question***

Toddlers are weaned off milk and provided with increased amounts of protein in order to prevent:

A. **Anemia—YES, meat protein is needed to increase iron content**
B. Baby bottle teeth—NO, although this is a concern
C. Constipation—NO
D. Lactose intolerance—NO

Exercise 25-12: ***Multiple Choice Questions***

Schools have initiated a nutritional program to provide breakfast for students because:

A. Most eat at home but the wrong things—NO, most are not eating at home
B. **Protein assists them to learn—YES, they need nutrition for brain functioning**
C. Carbohydrates keep them awake in class—NO, carbohydrate loads decrease wakefulness
D. They are complaining about being hungry by lunch—NO, although this would be a concern

Exercise 25-13: ***Multiple Choice Question***

An adolescent female is exercising excessively and has stopped having her menses; the nurse suspects that she may be suffering from:

A. Body dysmorphia—NO, this is not the overt diagnosis
B. Excessive sport competitiveness—NO
C. **Anorexia—YES, this is the reason that is most common and likely**
D. Pregnancy—NO, although a pregnancy test should be done

Exercise 25-14: ***Select All That Apply***

The nurse should include the following information in nutritional teaching of an obese patient:

☒ **Use fats, sweets, and oils sparingly**

☐ Have four to five servings of milk a day

☒ **Increase vegetable intake**

☒ **Use whole grain wheat**

☐ Decrease fiber

☒ **Increase exercise**

Exercise 25-15: *Multiple Choice Question*

In order to decrease neural tube defects (NTDs) in children, preconceptual nutrition should include:

A. Vitamin B12—NO, this is important but not directly correlated with NTDs
B. Thiamine—NO, this is important but not directly correlated with NTDs
C. Protein—NO, this is important but not directly correlated with NTDs
D. **Folic acid—YES, this is correlated with NTDs and the intake should be 0.4mg/ day**

Exercise 25-16: *Multiple Choice Question*

A nursing mother should increase her daily intake in order to feed her infant by:

A. 200 kcal—NO
B. 300 kcal—NO
C. 400 kcal—NO
D. **500 kcal—YES**

Exercise 25-17: *Multiple Choice Question*

Elderly patients who live alone may benefit most from a referral to:

A. Occupational therapy—NO, although this may be helpful, it will not directly address the nutritional issue
B. Recreational therapy—NO, although this may be helpful, it will not directly address the nutritional issue
C. **Meals on wheels—YES, this will ensure a hot meal at least a few times each week**
D. Local YMCA—NO, although this may be helpful, it will not directly address the nutritional issue

Exercise 25-18: *Matching*

Match the type of vegetarian in column A with the food substances that are withheld in column B.

Column A	Column B
A. Ovolactovegitarian	__C__ Only eat food from plants
B. Lactovegitarian	__A__ Do not eat meat, fish, or poultry
C. Vegans	__D__ Only eat fruit, nuts, honey, and olive oil
D. Fruitarian	__B__ Consume milk but not eggs

Exercise 25-19: *Multiple Choice Question*

The nurse understands that iron absorption is increased when iron tablets are consumed with:

A. Water—NO
B. Meals—NO, although taking Fe medication with meals decreases nausea

C. **Vitamin C—YES, vitamin C helps absorption**
D. Vitamin A—NO

Exercise 25-20: *True/False*
All patients admitted to the hospital must be weighed.
☒ **True—This is done to decrease weight-based medication errors**
❑ False

Exercise 25-21: *Multiple Choice Question*
The nurse understands that if the patient has a BMI of 25.5, the patient is considered:
A. Underweight—NO, this is a BMI under 18
B. Normal weight—NO, this is a BMI 18 to 25
C. **Overweight—YES**
D. Obese—NO, this is a BMI over 30

Exercise 25-22: *Select All That Apply*
Laboratory tests that are used to assess a patient's nutritional status are:
☒ **Albumin—YES, tests long-term protein content of blood serum**
☒ **Prealbumin—YES, tests short-term protein content of blood serum**
❑ Bilirubin
☒ **Retinol-binding protein—YES, used to determine visceral (organ) protein mass**
❑ Erythrocyte sedimentation rate
☒ **Total iron binding—YES, tests capacity to bind iron with transferring**
☒ **Hemoglobin (Hgb)—YES, tests the amount of iron present**

Exercise 25-23: *Select All That Apply*
Some nursing interventions to increase a patient's appetite include:
❑ Spraying air freshener—NO, odors will not help
❑ Brushing the patient's teeth after feeding—NO, brush before to decrease bad tastes for patients
☒ **Cleaning the over-bed table—YES, cleaning the environment is important**
❑ Selecting foods that are fried—NO, lighter foods are more appetizing

Exercise 25-24: *multiple choice question*
The nurse understands that the patient who is advancing their diet from clear liquids needs further teaching when they make a breakfast selection of:
A. **A sausage sandwich with orange juice—YES, these are difficult to digest solids**
B. Toast and tea—NO, these are easy to digest
C. Farina and cranberry juice—NO, farina is a soft substance
D. Yogurt and a banana—NO, these are considered soft food and are the next step in advancing from a liquid to a solid diet

Exercise 25-25: ***Multiple Choice Question***

The nurse understands that the correct anatomical marks used to measure a NG tube are:

A. Bridge of the nose to the earlobe to the xiphoid process—NO
B. Tip of the nose to the top of the pina to the umbilicus—NO
C. **Tip of the nose to the earlobe to the xiphoid process—YES**
D. Bridge of the nose to the top of the pina to the xiphoid process—NO

Exercise 25-26: ***Ordering***

Place the following steps in order from one to nine:

__**5**__ Insert tube through nostril to back of the throat aiming back and down
__**1**__ Wash hands
__**2**__ Place in high Fowler's position
__**7**__ Aspirate gastric content
__**4**__ Measure length of tube
__**3**__ Put on gloves
__**9**__ Fasten tube to patient gown with a pin and rubber band
__**8**__ Apply tape
__**6**__ Advance tube as patient swallows

Exercise 25-27: ***Multiple Choice Question***

The preferred method of verifying initial tube placement is:

A. Testing gastric pH—NO, although this may be used, it is not the best initial check
B. Listening for inserted air over stomach—NO, although this may be used, it is not the best initial check
C. Marking the tube at the nostril—NO, although this may be used, it is not the best initial check
D. **Obtaining an x-ray—YES, this confirms placement initially**

Exercise 25-28: ***Multiple Choice Question***

If gastric pH may be used to verify placement of a NG tube, but it would not be affected by:

A. How long ago the patient ate—NO, this will affect it
B. **The respiratory status of the patient—YES, unless it was placed wrong this should not affect it**
C. If the feeds were continuous or intermittent—NO, this will affect it
D. If the tube was placed in the jejunum—NO, this will affect it

Exercise 25-29: *Multiple Choice Question*

The nurse is preparing to administer an enteral feed to a patient that has limited gastrointestinal (GI) enzymes functioning. The nurse would expect to administer which type of formula?

A. Polymeric formula—NO, this is whole nutrients
B. Modular formula—NO, this is specific nutrients
C. **Elemental formula—YES, this is predigested**
D. Specialty formula—NO, this is specific nutrients

Exercise 25-30: *Select All That Apply*

The following manifestations could indicate that a patient is not tolerating enteral feeding:

- ☒ **Nausea—YES, this is a GI symptom**
- ☐ Headache—NO, this is not directly correlated with GI disturbances
- ☐ Muscle twitching—NO, this is not directly correlated with GI disturbances
- ☒ **Diarrhea—YES, this is a GI symptom**
- ☒ **Abdominal cramping—YES, this is a GI symptom**
- ☐ Leg cramping—NO, this is not directly correlated with GI disturbances

Exercise 25-31: *Multiple Choice Question*

The nurse understands that the risk of enteral feedings through an NG tube is:

A. Short gut syndrome—NO, this is a condition usually due to surgical resection of the intestines
B. **Aspiration—YES, there is a risk of the tube displacing into the trachea**
C. Stomach acid deficiency—NO
D. Liver overload—NO

Exercise 25-32: Multiple Choice Question

The nurse understands that the most important method of preventing enteral tube occlusion is:

A. Aspirating before administering each medication—NO, this is not necessary
B. Crushing each medication if not in liquid form—NO, this is done if appropriate for that medication but is not the primary mechanism of preventing occlusions
C. Administering medication mixed with the formula—NO
D. **Flushing with 30 mL of water before and after each medication—YES, this is the suggested mechanism to prevent occlusions**

Exercise 25-33: Exhibit Question

The 24-hour diet intake history includes:

Last night's supper: pork chop, baked potatoes, beans, cake

Last night snack: popcorn and a glass of milk

Breakfast: bowl of cereal and OJ

Lunch: ham sandwich on white bread and potato chips

Three glasses of water, two glasses of milk, and three colas during the last 24 hours

According to the above diet, the nurse would include in her teaching:

A. Increase meat servings—NO, he has two (pork and ham)

B. Increase potatoes servings—NO, he has six breads and cereals (potato, cake, popcorn, cereal, bread, and potato chips), although some are very unhealthy and should be substituted

C. **Increase vegetable and fruit servings—YES, he only has OJ and beans and needs at least three more**

D. Increase dairy servings—NO, he has two (milk and yogurt)

26

Urinary Elimination

Unfolding Case Study 25 Aubree, Alita, and Connor

The following week in class, Aubree, Alita, and Connor learn about "output" or urinary elimination. They are anxious to learn about catheters since they have seen them used so much in the clinical area for patients. The instructor reviews the anatomy of the kidneys and urinary tract.

Exercise 26-1: *Matching*

Match the renal structure or substance in column A to its function in column B.

Column A	Column B
A. Renal artery	_______ Kidneys produce this, and it stimulates RBC production
B. Nephron	_______ Hormone that regulates kidney blood flow
C. Erythroprotein	_______ The path by which blood reaches the kidneys from the aorta
D. Renin	_______ Connect renal pelvis to bladder
E. Ureters	_______ Functional unit of the kidney

The instructor also reviews some disorders of the urinary tract in order to familiarize the students with patient manifestations they may come across in the clinical area.

Exercise 26-2: *Multiple Choice Question*

The nurse understands that proteinuria is a sign of:

A. Bladder injury
B. Dehydration
C. Glomerular injury
D. Medication side effect

The Answers section can be found on page 373.

Exercise 26-3: *Multiple Choice Question*

An obstruction of a ureter is most commonly caused by a(n):

A. Hematoma
B. Emboli formation
C. Contracture
D. Renal calculus

Exercise 26-4: *Multiple Choice Question*

A condition that is caused by a spinal cord injury and produces an involuntarily ***micturation:***

A. Reflex bladder
B. Kidney dysfunction
C. Urinary retention
D. Uremic syndrome

Alita asks the instructor, "How much urine can a bladder hold before the feeling to micturate is initiated?" The instructor tells her that in a child this occurs when the bladder has 50 to 100 mL in it.

Exercise 26-5: *Multiple Choice Question*

An adult bladder normally can hold up to ________ mL of urine:

A. 400
B. 500
C. 600
D. 700

The instructor also tells them some terms associated with urine output.

Exercise 26-6: *Matching*

Match the term in column A to the definition in column B.

Column A		Column B
A. Oliguria	______	Excessive urine output
B. Anuria	______	Increased urine production
C. Polyurina	______	Low urine output
D. Dieresis	______	No urine output

When kidneys become damaged to the point that they are permanently altered, patients must be placed on a transplantation list or receive ***dialysis***. Dialysis can be accomplished one of two ways. **Peritoneal dialysis** uses the perineal membrane as a filtering system. Fluid or dialysate is inserted into the peritoneal cavity via a surgically placed tube. The dialysate absorbs the waste products and then is drained off. ***Hemodialysis*** uses a machine to filter the blood. Patients go to hemodialysis several times a week.

The Answers section can be found on page 373.

eResource 26-1: Overview of the Hemodialysis Procedure: www.youtu.be/x_ra9YUX9fk

Exercise 26-7: *Multiple Choice Question*

The patient asks for an explanation of why a urinary diversion is needed; the nurse explains that it is a bypass from:

A. The aorta to the urethra
B. The ureter to the urethra
C. Kidneys to the ureter
D. Kidneys to a stoma

The instructor gives the students a list of common medications used on the renal unit for patient problems associated with urinary dysfunction and how they may affect output.

Exercise 26-8: *Matching*

Match the medication or classification of medications in column A with the urinary tract effect in column B (descriptors can be used for more than one medication and/or classification).

Column A	Column B
A. Diuretics	______ May cause urinary retention
B. Anticholinergics	______ Colors the urine bright orange or rust
C. Antihistamines	______ May be toxic to the kidneys
D. Antihypertensives	______ May color the urine green or blue
E. Phenazopyridine (pyridium)	______ Increases excretion of water
F. Amitriptyline	______ May color the urine brown or black
G. Levdopa	
H. Chemotherapy	

In the afternoon, the students go to clinical for "pickup," so they can look at the data about their patients. Aubree is assigned a patient with ***urinary retention***. Alita is assigned a patient experiencing a ***urinary tract infection (UTI)***. Connor's patient has ***urinary incontinence***.

The following morning in preconference, the students tell their instructor about the information they researched pertaining to their patient. Aubree tells the group that urinary retention in her patient is a result of a urethral obstruction due to an enlarged prostate gland. This causes her patient to become restless as his bladder fills and at times produces overflow or a small bit on incontinence. Surgical relief is needed until the primary cause is determined or a prostectomy is performed. Aubree's patient is scheduled for an ureterostomy today.

The Answers section can be found on page 373.

Exercise 26-9: *Multiple Choice Question*

The nurse understands that the preoperative ureterostomy patient requires further teaching when he states:

A. "I will have a stoma in my abdomen after surgery"
B. "I will be able to control my urination"
C. "I will be taught to take care of the stoma before discharge"
D. "I will have to wear a bag"

Alita's patient is also elderly and was admitted for a UTI. Like many older adults, the UTI and the change in environment have caused her to become slightly confused. Alita is careful to keep the environment safe since her patient is mobile but unsure of where she is.

Exercise 26-10: *Multiple Choice Question*

One of the most common causes of UTIs is:

A. *Streptococcus*
B. Methicillin-resistant *Staphylococcus aureus* (MRSA)
C. Vancomycin-resistant *Enterococcus*
D. *Escherichia coli*

Exercise 26-11: *Matching*

Match the term in column A to the description in column B.

Column A		Column B
A. Bacteriuria	______	Blood in the urine
B. Urosepsis	______	Pain when urinating
C. Pyelonephritis	______	Bacteria in the urine
D. Hematuria	______	Organisms in kidneys and blood
E. Cystitis	______	Infection in the kidneys
F. Dysuria	______	Irritated bladder

Alita makes sure her patient gets her antibiotics on time and drinks plenty of clear fluid. Her patient has a walker, so she places a water bottle in her walker bag in order to encourage her to drink. Alita also accompanies her patient to the bathroom and assists her with perineal care. She uses a peri bottle of warm water to wash her patient from front to back after urinating.

Connor's patient is incontinent and confused. Connor finds it difficult to keep his patient clean but asks the unlicensed assistive personnel (UAP) who is familiar with the patient for assistance with custodial care. His patient's skin is starting to break down due to being wet all the time. The primary care provider orders a urinary catheter, so Connor and the instructor review the procedure to insert a female urinary catheter.

eResource 26-2: Before proceeding, Connor reviews the standard procedure and views a video tutorial on catheterization: http://alfa.saddleback.edu/N170/urinarycatheterization.aspx

The Answers section can be found on page 373.

Exercise 26-12: *Ordering*

Place the following steps of inserting a Foley catheter in order from 1 to 11:

_______ Lubricate the catheter tip 2 in. for women (it would be lubricated at least 7" for men)

_______ Test the catheter balloon before insertion by inflating and deflating

_______ Wash hands

_______ Inflate balloon

_______ Cleanse urinary meatus

_______ Hold open labia with nondominant hand and using forceps with dominant hand

_______ Clean down with three cotton balls with antiseptic solution

_______ Gather supplies

_______ Open sterile package

_______ Position patient and drape

_______ Insert catheter until urine appears and insert slightly more

_______ Tape to inner thigh

Connor also has an order to send a sterile urine specimen to the lab.

Exercise 26-13: *Multiple Choice Question*

The nurse understands that the proper method for obtaining a sterile urine specimen is:

A. Taking it from the collection bag
B. Detaching the catheter tube and letting it drip into the sterile cup
C. Using the port in the tube with a sterile syringe to withdraw the urine
D. Assisting the physician with a suprapubic tap for urine

Alita's patient has an order for a clean catch urine specimen, so Alita assists her client to obtain the specimen.

Exercise 26-14: *Multiple Choice Question*

The nurse understands that the patient needs further teaching regarding obtaining a clean catch or midstream urine specimen when she states:

A. "I will increase my fluids 30 minutes before"
B. "I will release my labia before I remove the specimen cup"
C. "I will clean my perineum from front to back"
D. "I will void 1 to 2 ounces in the cup"

Exercise 26-15: *Select All That Apply*

Methods to assist patients to stimulate micturation are:

❑ Sitting on the toilet
❑ Run the water
❑ Credé the bladder
❑ Have the patient lean forward
❑ Run cold water over the perineum

The Answers section can be found on page 373.

Before going home for the day, Connor provides his patient with catheter care. He washes the insertion site with soap and water to prevent any ascending bacteria. He also makes sure his patient has plenty of fresh water to drink.

eResource 26-3: Foley care procedure handout including video tutorials: http://alfa.saddleback.edu/N170/urinarycatheterization.aspx

Exercise 26-16: ***Multiple Choice Question***

In order to prevent urinary infections in patients with indwelling urinary catheters, the nurse should:

A. Change the bag every 8 hours
B. Keep the bag lower than the bladder
C. Place the bag under the bed on the floor
D. Keep the bag level with the abdomen

In postconference, the group discusses types of urinary catheters, and the instructor tells them about condom catheters for males. These are attached by a sheath to the penis. The end of the sheath has a catheter attached, which is then attached to a drainage bag that often can be worn as a leg bag under pants.

eResource 26-4: The students review a tutorial entitled *Infection Control for Student Nurses*: http://faculty.ccc.edu/tr-infectioncontrol/index.htm

Exercise 26-17: ***Multiple Choice Question***

The primary advantage of a condom catheter for a male would be:

A. More accurate I&O
B. Less leakage
C. Less invasive
D. Less infections

They also talk about patients who have spinal cord injuries and self-catheterize. This is done in the home without risk of ***nosocomial infection*** (hospital-induced infection), so it is done under clean rather than sterile technique. In other cases, bladder training can be done if a patient who has been incontinent does pelvic floor exercises or biofeedback and strengthens their muscles. Sometimes bladder training can be successful during the day, but patients may still need adult diapers at night for ***noctoria***. The students tell the instructor they feel they have a good understanding of the concepts of urinary elimination, and they discuss that next week they will focus on bowel elimination in class and clinical.

eResource 26-5: To learn more about hospital-induced infections, the students view a presentation on Nosocomial Infections: www.youtu.be/shvCWXTvheg

The Answers section can be found on page 373.

Answers

Exercise 26-1: ***Matching***

Match the renal structure or substance in column A to its function in column B.

Column A		Column B
A. Renal artery	C	Kidneys produce this, and it stimulates RBC production
B. Nephron	D	Hormone that regulates kidney blood flow
C. Erythroprotein	A	The path by which blood reaches the kidneys from the aorta
D. Renin	E	Connect renal pelvis to bladder
E. Ureters	B	Functional unit of the kidney

Exercise 26-2: ***Multiple Choice Question***

The nurse understands that proteinuria is a sign of:

A. Bladder injury—NO

B. Dehydration—NO

C. **Glomerular injury—YES, these are usually filtered out**

D. Medication side effect—NO

Exercise 26-3: ***Multiple Choice Question***

An obstruction of a ureter is most commonly caused by a(n):

A. Hematoma—NO

B. Emboli formation—NO

C. Contracture—NO

D. **Renal Calculus—YES**

Exercise 26-4: ***Multiple Choice Question***

A condition that is caused by a spinal cord injury and produces an involuntarily ***micturation***:

A. **Reflex bladder—YES, loss of voluntary control of bladder**

B. Kidney dysfunction—NO

C. Urinary retention—NO

D. Uremic syndrome—NO

Exercise 26-5: *Multiple Choice Question*

An adult bladder normally can hold up to __________ mL of urine:

A. 400—NO

B. 500—NO

C. **600—YES**

D. 700—NO

Exercise 26-6: *Matching*

Match the term in column A to the definition in column B.

Column A		Column B
A. Oliguria	C	Excessive urine output
B. Anuria	D	Increased urine production
C. Polyurina	A	Low urine output
D. Dieresis	B	No urine output

Exercise 26-7: *Multiple Choice Question*

The patient asks for an explanation of why a urinary diversion is needed, the nurse explains that it is a bypass from:

A. The aorta to the urethra—NO

B. The ureter to the urethra—NO

C. Kidneys to the ureter—NO

D. **Kidneys to a stoma—YES, this is to bypass the damaged ureters**

Exercise 26-8: *Matching*

Match the medication or classification of medications in column A with the urinary tract effect in column B (descriptors can be used for more than one medication and/or classification).

Column A		Column B
I. Diuretics	B, C, D	May cause urinary retention
J. Anticholinergics	E	Colors the urine bright orange or rust
K. Antihistamines	H	May be toxic to the kidneys
L. Antihypertensives	F	May color the urine green or blue
M. Phenazopyridine (pyridium)	A	Increases excretion of water
N. Amitriptyline	G	May color the urine brown or black
O. Levdopa		
P. Chemotherapy		

Exercise 26-9: *Multiple Choice Question*

The nurse understands that the preoperative ureterostomy patient requires further teaching when he states:

A. "I will have a stoma in my abdomen after surgery."—NO, this is correct

B. **"I will be able to control my urination."—YES, this is incorrect; patients are not able to control urination**

C. "I will be taught to take care of the stoma before discharge."—NO, this is correct

D. "I will have to wear a bag."—NO, this is correct

Exercise 26-10: *Multiple Choice Question*

One of the most common causes of UTIs is:

A. *Streptococcus*—NO

B. Methicillin-resistant *Staphylococcus aureus* (MRSA)—NO

C. Vancomycin-resistant Enterococcus—NO

D. ***Escherichia coli*—YES, this is the most frequent causative agent**

Exercise 26-11: *Matching*

Match the term in column A to the description in column B.

Column A	Column B
A. Bacteriuria	**D** Blood in the urine
B. Urosepsis	**F** Pain when urinating
C. Pyelonephritis	**A** Bacteria in the urine
D. Hematuria	**B** Organisms in kidneys and blood
E. Cystitis	**C** Infection in the kidneys
F. Dysuria	**E** Irritated bladder

Exercise 26-12: *Ordering*

Place the following steps of inserting a Foley catheter in order from 1 to 11:

8 Lubricate the catheter tip 2 in. for women (it would be lubricated at least 7" for men)

4 Test the catheter balloon before insertion by inflating and deflating

1 Wash hands

10 Inflate balloon

6 Cleanse urinary meatus

5 Hold open labia with nondominant hand and using forceps with dominant hand

7 Clean down with three cotton balls with antiseptic solution

2 Gather supplies

4 Open sterile package

5 Position patient and drape

9 Insert catheter until urine appears and insert slightly more

11 Tape to inner thigh

Exercise 26-13: *Multiple Choice Question*

The nurse understands that the proper method for obtaining a sterile urine specimen is:

A. Taking it from the collection bag—NO, this is not the correct technique

B. Detaching the catheter tube and letting it drip into the sterile cup—NO, this is not the correct technique, and it contaminates the closed system

C. **Using the port in the tube with a sterile syringe to withdraw the urine—YES, this is the right way—wash off the port and use a sterile needle**

D. Assisting the physician with a suprapubic tap for urine—NO, this is not necessary

Exercise 26-14: *Multiple Choice Question*

The nurse understands that the patient needs further teaching regarding obtaining a clean catch or midstream urine specimen when she states:

A. "I will increase my fluids 30 minutes before."—NO, this is correct

B. **"I will release my labia before I remove the specimen cup."—YES, the labia are released after the cup is removed to decrease contamination**

C. "I will clean my perineum from front to back."—NO, this too is correct

D. "I will void 1 to 2 ounces in the cup."—NO, this is correct (30–60 mL in preferred)

Exercise 26-15: *Select All That Apply*

Methods to assist patients to stimulate micturation are:

☒ **Sitting on the toilet—YES, sitting in a natural position helps some patients**

☒ **Run the water—YES**

☐ Credé the bladder—NO, this is only done for a neurogenic bladder

☐ Have the patient lean forward—NO, this may make the patient unsteady

☐ Run cold water over the perineum—NO, warm water may help

Exercise 26-16: *Multiple Choice Question*

In order to prevent urinary infections in patients with indwelling urinary catheters, the nurse should:

A. Change the bag every 8 hours—NO, it should remain a closed system.

B. **Keep the bag lower than the bladder—YES, so there is no back flow.**

C. Place the bag under the bed on the floor—NO, it should be off the floor.

D. Keep the bag level with the abdomen—NO, it should be lower than the bladder.

Exercise 26-17: *Multiple Choice Question*

The primary advantage of a condom catheter for a male would be:

A. More accurate I&O—NO, this is not facilitated and often leakage prevents accurate I&O

B. Less leakage—NO, these types are more prone to leak

C. Less invasive—NO, although this is true, it is not the primary advantage

D. **Less infections—YES, and this is most important**

27

Bowel Elimination

Unfolding Case Study 26 ■ Aubree, Alita, and Connor

The next week in class Aubree, Alita, and Connor learn about bowel elimination and nursing care of patients experiencing gastrointestinal (GI) difficulties. Many patients experience difficulty in bowel elimination due to their illness, medication, or disruption in daily routine or nutrition.

Exercise 27-1: *Select All That Apply*

The following are variables that promote normal bowel function:

- ☐ Fiber
- ☐ Rest
- ☐ Fluid
- ☐ Squatting position
- ☐ Valsalva maneuver

Exercise 27-2: *Multiple Choice Question*

Patients who have difficulty digesting milk and its by-products are considered to have:

A. Colitis
B. Crohn's disease
C. Lactose intolerance
D. Paralytic ileus

The students are amazed as they listen to all the diseases that affect the bowel and know that they are going to spend 2 days in the clinical area taking care of patients on a GI unit of an acute care hospital. In class, they practice nursing histories and include:

- Determining the patient's bowel pattern
- Stool characteristics
- Routines

The Answers section can be found on page 387.

- Use of laxatives or enemas
- Changes in appetite and diet history
- Fluid intake
- Medication
- Exercise
- Social history

The students also review bowel sound assessment and look at diagnostic tests that may be ordered for their patients.

Exercise 27-3: *Multiple Choice Question*

The nurse understands that the following laboratory test will be ordered if a bile duct obstruction is suspected:

A. Hemoglobin
B. White blood cell count
C. Bilirubin
D. Blood urea nitrogen

Exercise 27-4: *Matching*

Match the diagnostic laboratory test specific to the GI tract in column A with its purpose in column B.

Column A		Column B
A. Alkaline phosphate	_______	Increased in hepatobiliary diseases; normal range is 30 to 85 ImU/mL
B. Amylase	_______	Increase with GI cancer or inflammation; normal range is <5 ng/mL
C. Carcinoembryonic antigen (CEA)	_______	Increased in disease of the pancreas; normal range is 56 to 190 IU/L

The instructor tells the student about other diagnostic tests that are used to collect assessment data on patient with GI disturbances. One test that can be completed at the bedside is fecal occult blood testing (FOBT).

eResource 27-1: To learn more about fecal occult blood testing, Connor opens Mobile MerckMedicus on his smartphone: [Pathway: MerckMedicus → Pocket Guide to Diagnostic Tests → enter "fecal occult blood test" into the search field].

Exercise 27-5: *Ordering*

Place the steps needed to obtain a FOBT in order from one to six:

_______ Use the wooden tip to smear fecal matter on ***guaiac*** paper in both spots that are indicated

_______ Obtain fecal specimen

The Answers section can be found on page 387.

_______ Wash hands

_______ Close cover, turn card over open second cover and apply developer

_______ Put on gloves

_______ Assess color of spots in 30 to 60 seconds (blue indicates blood in stool)

eResource 27-2: The Atlas of Gastrointestinal Endoscopy: www .endoatlas.com/atlas_1.html

Other tests that are done include visualization of the GI tract. Often patients need sedation to undergo a colonoscopy. The patient's symptoms may be upper or lower GI manifestations, and this will determine the type of test that is to be completed.

Exercise 27-6: *Multiple Choice Question*

The patient undergoing this GI test will be given an opaque contrast medium to drink:

A. Colonoscopy
B. Barium enema
C. Barium swallow
D. Upper endoscopy

Exercise 27-7: *Multiple Choice Question*

The nurse understands that the patient needs further teaching about the barium enema procedure when the patient states:

A. "A contrast medium will be used"
B. "I will not eat anything after midnight"
C. "I will have to have enemas to clean me out"
D. "I will not be exposed to any radiation"

The instructor tells the students that an important concept is knowing that a colonoscopy is not only a diagnostic test, but also a generalized screening test and can reduce the incidence of death from GI cancer through early detection.

eResource 27-3: Colonoscopy and Sigmoidoscopy:

- *About the Colonoscopy Procedure*: www.youtu.be/wA9QtgVQWOw
- *Flexible Sigmoidoscopy*: www.youtu.be/VBpj0eUs9JA
- Center for Excellence Medical Media's (CEMM) Guide to Colonoscopy and Sigmoidoscopy: www.colonscope.org/
- An interactive web-based animation *Look at Your Colon* from Aetna visually demonstrates scope placement for colonoscopy and sigmoidoscopy: www.intelihealth.com/IH/ihtIH/WSIHW000/23722/29680.html

Exercise 27-8: *Select All That Apply*

A colonoscopy should be done for the following risk factors:

❑ Patients over 40 years of age

❑ Family history of colon cancer

The Answers section can be found on page 387.

- ❑ High-fiber diet
- ❑ History of GI polyps
- ❑ BMI over 30

After class, the students go to the hospital to copy the information about their patients for the following day. Aubree's patient is fecal impacted and immobile. Alita's patient has a fresh ostomy.

eResource 27-4: Alita recalls a recent presentation by a classmate demonstration patient teaching regarding Colostomy Surgery: www.youtu.be/ewirBo6rvVA

Connor's patient has high serum potassium and will be treated with a polystyrene sulfonate (Kayexalate) enema.

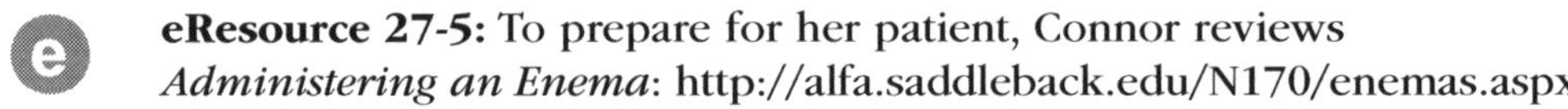

eResource 27-5: To prepare for her patient, Connor reviews *Administering an Enema*: http://alfa.saddleback.edu/N170/enemas.aspx

The students diligently look up everything they can the evening before clinical to prepare themselves for the next day.

eResource 27-6: In addition to her textbook, Alita consults several additional resources:

- National Guideline Clearinghouse to determine best practices related to management of constipation: [Pathway: www.guideline.gov → enter "constipation" into the search field → select "management of constipation" to view guidelines].
- MerckMedicus on her mobile device
  - Merck Manual: [Pathway: Merck Manual → Topics → enter "constipation" into the search field → select "constipation" and listen to podcast, *Constipation in Adults*].
  - Harrison's Practice: [Pathway: Merck Manual → Topics → enter "constipation" into the search field → review content focusing particularly on treatment and ongoing care].

In preconference the next day, students describe to the instructor how they are going to assess and plan their nursing care. The students are a bit nervous but know that their instructor will help them perform skills the first time they do them.

Aubree's patient is confused and in bed due to a hip fracture. After breakfast, she places her on the fracture pan to see if she can stimulate her to have a bowel movement.

Exercise 27-9: ***Select All That Apply***

The nurse understands that the following interventions are therapeutic to a patient trying to move their bowels while on bed rest:

- ❑ Provide privacy
- ❑ Lie the patient flat
- ❑ Powder the bedpan, so it does not stick

The Answers section can be found on page 387.

- ❑ Place a small pillow behind the lumbar curve for support
- ❑ Raise their knees
- ❑ Cover their legs

Aubree's attempts to stimulate her patient to have a bowel movement are unsuccessful, and the patient is uncomfortable. Aubree has an order to digitally remove the fecal impacted stool from her patient. She explains the procedure to the patient and places her in a side lying position. She puts the bed pan close to the patient and lubricates her gloves and gently removes the stool. After she is done and cleans the patient, the patient is less restless.

eResource 27-7: Fecal Impaction videos providing comprehensive overview of this disorder:

- Dr. Carlo Oller discusses aspects of Fecal Impaction and associated treatment: www.youtu.be/WkwFOrVuwlU
- Fecal Impaction Overview: www.youtu.be/eN7Qsf94hJ8

Exercise 27-10: *Multiple Choice Question*

A risk factor associated with digital removal of stool is:

A. Bradycardia
B. Tachycardia
C. Hypertension
D. Tachypnea

Aubree consults with the dietitian to increase fiber in her patient's diet in order to prevent her from becoming fecal impacted in the future.

Alita has been interacting with her patient all morning who has a fresh stoma from an ileostomy due to severe Crohn's disease. The ***enterostomal nurse (ET)*** comes to visit the patient and begin stoma teaching. All ostomies are attached to a pouch that collects the effluent from the bowel. The pouch is connected to the skin by an adhesive skin barrier. The pouch usually detaches from the skin barrier piece, so it can be emptied.

eResource 27-8: Colostomy Care Videos

- Colostomy Care and Pouching (part 1 of 2): www.youtu.be/fOPWxRF6_z8
- Colostomy Care and Pouching (part 2 of 2): www.youtu.be/_51a9JW8Msc
- Some Resources: http://alfa.saddleback.edu/N170/colostomy.aspx

Exercise 27-11: *Multiple Choice Question*

When measuring the stoma, the nurse should use a pouch size no bigger than:

A. 1/16" larger than the stoma
B. 1/8" larger than the stoma
C. 1/4" larger than the stoma
D. 1/2" larger than the stoma

The Answers section can be found on page 387.

Alita's patient is only expected to have the ostomy temporarily. It is anticipated that it will be reversed after the Crohn's disease exacerbation slows. At that point, he will need bowel training. Nevertheless, he will need appropriate discharge planning and teaching about how to care for the ostomy at home. Alita reviews materials for patient education.

eResource 27-9: Discharge Planning Checklist: www.ostomy.org/ostomy_info/wocn/wocn_discharge_planning.pdf

Exercise 27-12: *Multiple Choice Question*

Suppositories used for bowel training are best administered:

A. 15 minutes before toileting
B. 30 minutes before toileting
C. 1 hour before toileting
D. 2 hours before toileting

Connor is preparing to give his patient an enema that will assist with drawing off K+. Connor explains the procedure to the patient. He receives the enema from the pharmacy since it is a drug-containing enema.

Exercise 27-13: *Ordering*

Place the following steps in order from one to nine regarding the proper method to administer an enema to patients:

_______ Position the patient in a Sim's position
_______ Gently and steadily insert the prescribed amount of fluid
_______ Wash hands
_______ Clean patient
_______ Ask patient to hold fluid if possible
_______ Put on gloves
_______ Assist patient to bathroom or on bedpan
_______ Lubricate tip
_______ Insert tip no more than 4 inches "for an adult"

eResource 27-10: Connor reviews what he has learned previously regarding body positions:

- A learning activity from Wisc-Online describing the various body positions for medical exams and procedures: [Pathway: www.wisc-online.com/ → select "Learning Objects" → "Health" → "Medical Assistant" → scroll down and select "Positions Used in Medical Examinations"].
- To make sure he has "it down," he takes a practice quiz regarding body positions: www.funtrivia.com/playquiz/quiz579116a3ed0.html

The Answers section can be found on page 387.

Connor finds the intervention a bit more daunting than he expected because his patient has hemorrhoids. After the procedure, he calls the primary care provider (PCP) for an order to decrease his patient's hemorrhoid discomfort.

Exercise 27-14: *Multiple Choice Question*

The nurse should question the following intervention for hemorrhoid care:

A. Sitz bath

B. Increased fluids

C. Ice

D. Stool softener

The students review their day in postconference and are thankful that their patients were cooperative. They are becoming more aware of the holistic caring aspect of patients and realize how one health care deficit affects so many activities of daily living. Next week, they will be studying immobility and its health care effects.

The Answers section can be found on page 387.

Answers

Exercise 27-1: *Select All That Apply*

The following are variables that promote normal bowel function:

☒ **Fiber—YES, this increases peristalsis**

❑ Rest—NO, activity increases peristalsis

☒ **Fluid—YES**

☒ **Squatting position—YES, this is a natural position**

☒ **Valsalva maneuver—YES, this is contracting abdominal muscles while holding an expiration**

Exercise 27-2: *Multiple Choice Question*

Patients who have difficulty digesting milk and its by-products are considered to have:

A. Colitis—NO, this is an irritable bowel condition

B. Crohn's disease—NO, this is an inflammatory bowel disease

C. **Lactose intolerance—YES, this is a condition in which the patient lacks an enzyme to break down lactose**

D. Paralytic ileus—NO, this is lack of peristalsis

Exercise 27-3: *Multiple Choice Question*

The nurse understands that the following laboratory test will be ordered if a bile duct obstruction is suspected:

A. Hemoglobin—NO, this is for iron content in the blood

B. White blood cell count—NO, this is for diagnosis of an infection

C. **Bilirubin—YES, this will be elevated if the bile duct is obstructed, and bilirubin, which is the breakdown of heme from hemoglobin, cannot travel from the liver to the GI tract**

D. Blood urea nitrogen—NO, this is for kidney function

Exercise 27-4: *Matching*

Match the diagnostic laboratory test specific to the GI tract in column A with its purpose in column B.

Column A		Column B
A. Alkaline phosphate	A	Increased in hepatobiliary diseases; normal range is 30 to 85 ImU/mL
B. Amylase	C	Increase with GI cancer or inflammation; normal range is <5 ng/mL
C. Carcinoembryonic antigen (CEA)	B	Increased in disease of the pancreas; normal range is 56 to 190 IU/L

Exercise 27-5: *Ordering*

Place the steps needed to obtain a FOBT in order from one to six:

__4__ Use the wooden tip to smear fecal matter on guaiac paper in both spots that are indicated
__3__ Obtain fecal specimen
__1__ Wash hands
__5__ Close cover, turn card over open second cover and apply developer
__2__ Put on gloves
__6__ Assess color of spots in 30 to 60 seconds (blue indicates blood in stool)

Exercise 27-6: *Multiple Choice Question*

The patient undergoing this GI test will be given an opaque contrast medium to drink:

A. Colonoscopy—NO, this is a scope that is inserted rectally after a sedative is given
B. Barium enema—NO, this contrast is inserted rectally
C. **Barium swallow—YES, the patient drinks this, and then X-rays are done**
D. Upper endoscopy—NO, this is a scope procedure

Exercise 27-7: *Multiple Choice Question*

The nurse understands that the patient needs further teaching about the barium enema procedure when the patient states:

A. "A contrast medium will be used."—NO, this is true
B. "I will not eat anything after midnight."—NO, this is true
C. "I will have to have enemas to clean me out."—NO, this is true
D. **"I will not be exposed to any radiation."—YES, an x-ray will be done**

Exercise 27-8: *Select All That Apply*

A colonoscopy should be done for the following risk factors:

❑ Patients over 40 years of age—NO, patients over 50 should have it done every 10 years
☒ **Family history of colon cancer—YES**
❑ High-fiber diet—NO, low-fiber diets place a patient at risk
☒ **History of GI polyps—YES**
☒ **BMI over 30—YES, obese patients are at risk**

Exercise 27-9: ***Select All That Apply***

The nurse understands that the following interventions are therapeutic to a patient trying to move their bowels while on bed rest:

☒ **Provide privacy—YES**

☐ Lie the patient flat—NO, sitting the patient up when possible helps

☒ **Powder the bedpan so it does not stick—YES**

☒ **Place a small pillow behind the lumbar curve for support—YES**

☒ **Raise their knees—YES**

☒ **Cover their legs—YES, helps to provide privacy**

Exercise 27-10: ***Multiple Choice Question***

A risk factor associated with digital removal of stool is:

A. **Bradycardia—YES, this is an effect of a Valsalva maneuver.**
B. Tachycardia—NO
C. Hypertension—NO
D. Tachypnea—NO

Exercise 27-11: ***Multiple Choice Question***

When measuring the stoma, the nurse should use a pouch size no bigger than:

A. **1/16" larger than the stoma—YES, it should be very close to the actual size of the stoma**
B. 1/8" larger than the stoma—NO
C. 1/4" larger than the stoma—NO
D. 1/2" larger than the stoma—NO

Exercise 27-12: ***Multiple Choice Question***

Suppositories used for bowel training are best administered:

A. Fifteen minutes before toileting—NO, some more time is needed for them to work if possible
B. **Thirty minutes before toileting—YES**
C. One hour before toileting—NO, too long and difficult for patients to hold
D. Two hours before toileting—NO, too long and difficult for patients to hold

Exercise 27-13: ***Ordering***

Place the following steps in order from one to nine regarding the proper method to administer an enema to patients:

__3__ Position the patient in a Sim's position
__6__ Gently and steadily insert the prescribed amount of fluid
__1__ Wash hands
__9__ Clean patient
__7__ Ask patient to hold fluid if possible
__2__ Put on gloves

__**8**__ Assist patient to bathroom or on bedpan
__**4**__ Lubricate tip
__**5**__ Insert tip no more than 4 inches "for an adult"

Exercise 27-14: *Multiple Choice Question*

The nurse should question the following intervention for hemorrhoid care:

A. Sitz bath—NO, this is often used
B. Increased fluids—NO, this will increase the softness of the stool
C. **Ice—YES, this is not therapeutic**
D. Stool softener—NO, this will increase the softness of the stool

28

Immobility

Unfolding Case Study 27 ▒ Aubree, Alita, and Connor

The following week in class, Aubree, Alita, and Connor learn about mobility, body mechanics, and ergonomics. This subject is important for not only patients but also nurses. Nurses are at high risk for back injuries because of the nature of patient interactions. Many health care facilities have a "no-lift" policy that prevents nurses from moving patients unassisted. These policies are put in place to decrease patients' and nurses' injuries. In order to understand the dynamics of body mechanics, the instructor reviews some terminology.

eResource 28-1: The instructor reminds the students of what they have learned previously to ensure that they are working safely:

- Body Mechanics and Patient Transfers Handout: http://moon.ouhsc.edu/belledge/ptcare/bodmech.pdf
- Body Mechanics Skills Demonstration Video: www.youtu.be/NYzMmYA-dJY

Exercise 28-1: *Matching*

Match the term in column A to the description in column B.

Column A	Column B
A. Body alignment	_______ Controls the speed and direction of movement
B. Friction	_______ Applying force to one end to lift another end
C. Concentric tension	_______ No muscle contraction but increases tone
D. Eccentric tension	_______ Center of gravity is stable
E. Isometric	_______ Active movement of muscles
F. Isotonic	_______ Opposite force from the movement
G. Leverage	_______ Increased muscle contractions

The Answers section can be found on page 395.

Exercise 28-2: ***Multiple Choice Question***

When a patient is immobile or on bed rest for therapeutic reasons, a risk factor is:

A. Muscle tone
B. Muscle atrophy
C. Concentric tension
D. Leverage

The instructor tells the students that bed rest can be therapeutic but that it comes with many risks, particularly for the elderly. That is why patients are kept on bed rest as little as possible.

eResource 28-2: The instructor shows the students:

- An article "Effects of bedrest 3: musculoskeletal and immune systems, skin and self-perception" (Nigam, Knight, and Jones, 2009): www.nursingtimes.net/effects-of-bedrest-3-musculoskeletal-and-immune-systems-skin-and-self-perception/5003298.article
- A table depicting the interaction between aging and hospitalization: www.annals.org/content/118/3/219/T1.large.jpg (Creditor, 1993).
- A diagram depicting the "cascade of dependency" resulting from bed rest: www.annals.org/content/118/3/219/F1.large.jpg (Creditor, 1993).

Exercise 28-3: ***Select All That Apply***

Complications that can occur from prolonged bed rest include:

- ❑ Thrombus formation
- ❑ Hypostatic pneumonia
- ❑ Diarrhea
- ❑ Disuse osteoporosis
- ❑ Contractures
- ❑ Pressure ulcers

The students now realize that the nursing care of patients on bed rest or who are immobile must be carefully planned in order to prevent complications. After class, they go to the long-term care facility and receive information on their patients for the next day. Aubree's patient will be a fresh postoperative patient from abdominal surgery. Alita's patient has quadriplegia, and Connor's patient is in traction. The students go to the hospital and find the patients' medical records and extract the data they need to do their research.

eResource 28-3: The following resources were reviewed by the students as part of their clinical preparation:

- Overview of *Postsurgical Recovery Experiences:* www.youtu.be/s000pUVwyhw
- *Safe Transfer Techniques*: www.youtu.be/H23EZlPIcZU

The Answers section can be found on page 395.

The following day in preconference, the instructor stresses that they are not to move patients alone or without assistive devices. They discuss their plans for the day briefly because they realize that immobile patients need much of their ADLs completed for them.

Aubree introduces herself to her patient who is uncomfortable. His orders are pain medication q 4 h PRN, OOB to chair, progress diet, and continue IV fluids at 100 ml/hr. Aubree medicates him for pain and then sits him up in the bed to eat breakfast, which is now a "soft" diet of grits, juice, and scrambled eggs. Alita's patient is also eating but needs assistance due to limited arm movement. Connor's patient can use the trapeze bar to maneuver the top portion of himself in bed to eat.

Exercise 28-4: *Multiple Choice Question*

The nurse understands that UAP needs guidance when he states:

A. "I took off the patient's compression stockings, so he can eat"
B. "I put the patient's compression stockings on as soon as he got back in bed"
C. "I turned the patient's compression stockings off just before I assisted him to the chair"
D. "I check the patient's skin under his compression boots every 2 hours"

After the patients finish their breakfast, the students provide AM care. Aubree carefully assists her patient to a sitting position in bed and places a ***gait belt*** around his waist.

eResource 28-4: *Using a Gait Belt Safely and Effectively On Any Size Person*: www.youtu.be/SaGHn0JOpkQ

Exercise 28-5: *Multiple Choice Question*

The nurse understands that having a patient dangle for a few minutes before rising may prevent which bed rest complication:

A. Emboli
B. Pneumonia
C. Footdrop
D. Orthostatic hypotension

Aubree places her feet in front of the patient's when he rises in order to prevent him from slipping. She has the chair adjacent to the bed, so the patient can pivot and lower himself into the chair using his arms.

Alita performs range-of-motion (ROM) exercises on her patient. She also inspects her patient for any skin breakdown during his AM care.

eResource 28-5: Passive and assistive range-of-motion exercises:

- ROM Exercises Video Demonstration:
  - http://alfa.saddleback.edu/video_only.aspx?ID=10
  - www.youtu.be/RGCtC3PclFU
- Handout: www.alsworldwide.org/pdfs/rom_exercises.pdf

The Answers section can be found on page 395.

Alita is getting ready to move her patient from the bed to his wheelchair. She removes the footboard used to prevent footdrop and places her patient on the hydraulic lift with the assistance of the UAP. This is the preferred method of moving completely immobilized patients, but nurses must be knowledgeable regarding the equipment.

eResource 28-6: Alita reviews a video on how to use a Hoyer lift to *Transfer Bed to Wheelchair and Wheelchair to Bed*: www.youtu.be/5jequ72bduY

Connor finishes AM care for his patient, but his patient needs to continue with traction.

Exercise 28-6: ***Multiple Choice Question***

The nurse understands that preventing pneumonia on a patient with limited mobility is a primary concern and can be accomplished best by:

A. Turning in bed q 2 h
B. Taking deep breaths q 8 h
C. Limiting visitors with URIs
D. Incentive spirometry use

The students are tired when they get back to postconference, but they review methods that will keep their backs healthy throughout their nursing careers.

Exercise 28-7: ***Select All That Apply***

Positive self-care activities for nurses to prevent back injuries include:

- ❏ Using assistive devices to move patients
- ❏ Exercising regularly
- ❏ Keeping objects away from the body while lifting
- ❏ Placing feet together when lifting
- ❏ Using draw sheets to move patients

References

Creditor, M. C. (1993). Hazards of hospitalization of the elderly. *Annals of Internal Medicine, 118*, 219–223.

Nigam, Y., Knight, J., & Jones, A. (2009). Effects of bedrest 3: Musculoskeletal and immune systems, skin and self-perception. *Nursing Times, 16(105)*, 18–22. Retrieved from http://www.nursingtimes.net/effects-of-bedrest-3-musculoskeletal-and-immune-systems-skin-and-self-perception/5003298.article

The Answers section can be found on page 395.

Answers

Exercise 28-1: *Matching*

Match the term in column A to the description in column B.

Column A		Column B
A. Body alignment	D	Controls the speed and direction of movement
B. Friction	G	Applying force to one end to lift another end
C. Concentric tension	E	No muscle contraction but increases tone
D. Eccentric tension	A	Center of gravity is stable
E. Isometric	F	Active movement of muscles
F. Isotonic	B	Opposite force from the movement
G. Leverage	C	Increased muscle contractions

Exercise 28-2: *Multiple Choice Question*

When a patient is immobile or on bed rest for therapeutic reasons, a risk factor is:

A. Muscle tone—NO, this just describes the shape of the muscles

B. **Muscle atrophy—YES, this is muscle wasting due to bed rest**

C. Concentric tension—NO, this is increased muscle contraction

D. Leverage—NO, this is using opposing ends to lift

Exercise 28-3: *Select All That Apply*

Complications that can occur from prolonged bed rest include:

☒ **Thrombus formation—YES**

☒ **Hypostatic pneumonia—YES**

❑ Diarrhea—NO, normally patients get constipated from bed rest

☒ **Disuse osteoporosis—YES**

☒ **Contractures—YES**

☒ **Pressure ulcers—YES**

Exercise 28-4: *Multiple Choice Question*

The nurse understands that UAP needs guidance when he states:

A. **"I took off the patient's compression stockings, so he can eat."—YES, the stocking should be left on while the patient is in bed**
B. "I put the patient's compression stockings on as soon as he got back in bed."—NO
C. "I turned the patient's compression stockings off just before I assisted him to the chair."—NO
D. "I check the patient's skin under his compression boots every 2 hours."—NO

Exercise 28-5: *Multiple Choice Question*

The nurse understands that having a patient dangle for a few minutes before rising may prevent which bed rest complication:

A. Emboli—NO
B. Pneumonia—NO
C. Footdrop—NO
D. **Orthostatic hypotension—YES, this is a drop in blood pressure**

Exercise 28-6: *Multiple Choice Question*

The nurse understands that preventing pneumonia on a patient with limited mobility is a primary concern and can be accomplished best by:

A. Turning in bed q 2 h—NO, although this is a good thing, it is not the best intervention; it is most effective in preventing skin break down
B. Taking deep breaths q 8 h—NO, although this is a good intervention to maintain healthy respiratory function, it should be done q 2 h
C. Limiting visitors with URIs—NO, limiting visitors does not decrease nosocomial infections
D. **Incentive spirometry use—YES, this is used to increase lung function**

Exercise 28-7: *Select All That Apply*

Positive self-care activities for nurses to prevent back injuries include:

☒ **Using assistive devices to move patients—YES**
☒ **Exercising regularly—YES**
☐ Keeping objects away from the body while lifting—NO, objects should be lifted close to the body
☐ Placing feet together when lifting—NO, a wide gait increases balance
☒ **Using draw sheets to move patients—YES**

29

Wounds and Sensory Considerations

Unfolding Case Study 28 Aubree, Alita, and Connor

The next class, the students learn about wound care. The specific topic is pressure ulcers. Pressure ulcers are a "nurse-sensitive" issue. Nurse sensitive means that nurses are accountable to keep patients from developing or having existing pressure ulcers become worse. Insurance companies now have reimbursement guidelines that can exclude payment for nurse-sensitive issues.

Exercise 29-1: ***Select All That Apply***

The following factors increase the risk of patients developing pressure ulcers:

- ❑ Hypersensitive skin perception
- ❑ Malnutrition
- ❑ Impaired mobility
- ❑ Being turned regularly
- ❑ Friction and shearing
- ❑ Level of consciousness

The instructor teaches Aubree, Alita, and Connor how pressure ulcers are classified. They are classified in to four stages.

Exercise 29-2: ***Matching***

Match the pressure ulcer stage in column A with the description in column B.

Column A	Column B
A. Stage I	_______ Full-thickness skin loss
B. Stage II	_______ Reddened area
C. Stage III	_______ Damage to muscle
D. Stage IV	_______ Partial-thickness skin loss

The Answers section can be found on page 403.

The instructor reviews other descriptive words regarding pressure ulcers that the students may hear in the clinical area.

eResource 29-1: Pressure Ulcers:

- Pressure Ulcer Treatment Guidelines: www.pressureulcerguidelines.org/therapy/
- Braden Scale for Predicting Pressure Sore Risk: www.bradenscale.com/images/bradenscale.pdf

Exercise 29-3: *Multiple Choice Question*

Old skin that must be removed from a wound before it can heal is called:

A. Granulation tissue

B. Eschar

C. Exudates

D. Edema

The students go to the acute care facility to collect their patient care data. Aubree's patient has a stage III pressure ulcer or decubiti that she was admitted with from home. Alita's patient is a fresh postoperative patient with a Jackson Pratt drain, and Connor's patient needs a wet-to-dry dressing change. Aubree assesses her patient's pressure ulcer. It is healing by ***secondary intention*** because the skin is not approximated. The wound is draining.

eResource 29-2: The students review materials related to wounds and wound healing:

- Animation depicting healing by secondary intention: http://www.argosymedical.com/Cellular/samples/animations/Tissue%20Repair/index.html
- *Wound Healing*: http://alfa.saddleback.edu/N170/woundhealing.aspx
- *Wound Classification Systems*: http://alfa.saddleback.edu/N170/woundclassification.aspx
- *Caring for a Jackson-Pratt Drain and Hemovac Drain*: www.youtu.be/L2hsNE-hn-8

Exercise 29-4: *Matching*

Match the name of the wound drainage in column A to the description in column B.

Column A	Column B
A. Serous	_______ A mixture of clear and red fluid
B. Purulent	_______ Bright red drainage
C. Serosanguinous	_______ Clear watery drainage
D. Sanguinous	_______ Thick yellow drainage

The Answers section can be found on page 403.

Aubree's patient's pressure ulcer is on her left buttock and requires a ***wound vacuum-assisted closure (Wound V.A.C.)***. This is an occlusive negative pressure dressing that is attached to a catheter, which is attached to a vacuum. The negative pressure removes bacteria and fluid and increases circulation to the site. The wound care nurse demonstrates its use to Aubree and then dresses the wound with ***hydrogel ointment*** and covers it with a clear covering.

eResource 29-3: To help Aubree understand VAC, the wound care nurse gives Aubree some information:

- *Science Behind Wound Therapy: Understanding the Science of V.A.C. Therapy* [Pathway: *www.kci1.com/KCI1/vactherapy* → select "Science Behind Wound Therapy"].
- *VAC Therapy Demonstration Video*: www.youtu.be/J3eD18GZKV8

Aubree provides her patient with a pain medication because all the moving was uncomfortable.

Alita assesses her patient's incision. It is a staple closure with a ***Jackson-Pratt drain***.

Exercise 29-5: *Multiple Choice Question*

The nurse is caring for a patient with a Jackson-Pratt drain that will no longer hold suction. The priority intervention would be to:

A. Remove it
B. Clamp the tubing for the patient to the drain
C. Leave it open
D. Notify the primary care provider

Aubree teaches her patient that the staple and drain will come out in approximately 2 to 3 days. Aubree empties 20 ml of serosanguinous drainage for the drain. The patient asks if they should have a dressing on, and Aubree tells him that exposure to air increases healing.

eResource 29-4: Aubree shows her patient a brief video about normal *Wound Healing*: www.youtu.be/zZpMQ_7qiRg

Connor's patient needs a wet-to-dry dressing change and he assists the wound care nurse.

Exercise 29-6: *Ordering*

Place the steps in order for 1 to 6 to complete a wet-to-dry wound dressing:

_______ Wash hands
_______ Apply moist gauze into wound
_______ Explain procedure to the patient
_______ Put on sterile gloves
_______ Cover with a sterile dry dressing
_______ Clean wound with sterile saline

The Answers section can be found on page 403.

Exercise 29-7: *Multiple Choice Question*

The nurse understands that when packing a wet-to-dry dressing, the moist gauze:

A. Should not touch the skin area
B. Should not be packed
C. Should not be placed in a wound that is tunneling
D. Should be packed with clean gloves

Alita's patient is complaining about abdominal pain when rising. The patient rates the pain as a 6 on a scale of 1 to 10 and has had pain medication 2 hours ago. Alita gets an order for an abdominal binder to help the patient with support of abdominal muscles. This seems to help the patient's ability to move around his room. He is able to ambulate to the chair for lunch. Aubree notices that her patient feels his way to the chair. She investigates his past medical history and finds out that he has a history of cataracts. Visual deficits are an added safety concern.

Exercise 29-8: *Matching*

Match the visual deficit in column A to the description in column B.

Column A		Column B
A. Presbyopia	_______	Changes in blood vessels of the retina
B. Dry eye	_______	Increased intraocular pressure due to an obstruction in the canal of Schlemm
C. Open-angle glaucoma	_______	Inability to focus on close objects
D. Diabetic retinopathy	_______	Macular loses ability to function
E. Macular degeneration	_______	Tear gland deficit

Aubree explains to her patient what is on his plate and she makes sure he can feel the call bell and instructs him not to get out of the chair without help. During postconference, they discuss Aubree's patient and the complications that sensory deficits produce for patients. Alita says her grandmother has difficulty hearing and that it is often frustrating to try to speak with her on the phone.

Exercise 29-9: *Multiple Choice Question*

Progressive age-related hearing loss is called:

A. Conductive hearing loss
B. Sensorineuro hearing loss
C. Presbycusis
D. Auditory neuropathy spectrum disorder

eResource 29-5: To better understand the changes that occur with aging, Aubree reviews a handout *Understanding Sensory Deficits in the Elderly*: www.loyolaems.com/ce/ce_nov07.pdf

The instructor tells the students that deficits in ***olfactory*** (smell) and ***gustatory*** (taste) senses interfere with a patient's ability to eat.

The Answers section can be found on page 403.

Exercise 29-10: *Multiple Choice Question*

A safety priority for a nurse when providing discharge teaching for a patient with an olfactory deficit would be:

A. Food preparation
B. Cleanliness of the home
C. Air fresheners
D. Fire alarms

The instructor also reminds the students that specific drugs can affect the senses.

Exercise 29-11: *Fill-in*

Medications that can damage the auditory nerve are said to be ____________________.

The students have learned a tremendous amount during their clinical rotation for wound care, and in order to care for the patients holistically, the students needed to better understand sensory deficits.

The Answers section can be found on page 403.

Answers

Exercise 29-1: ***Select All That Apply***

The following factors increase the risk of patients developing pressure ulcers:

- ☐ Hypersensitive skin perception—NO, patients with decreased sensitivity have increased pressure ulcers
- ☒ **Malnutrition—YES, this is one of the main causes**
- ☒ **Impaired mobility—YES, static body parts have pressure on them from the mattress**
- ☐ Being turned regularly—NO, patients should be turned at least every 2 hours
- ☒ **Friction and shearing—YES, these injure the skin and make it more likely to break down**
- ☒ **Level of consciousness—YES, reduced level of consciousness makes it difficult for the patient to verbalize pain or pressure**

Exercise 29-2: ***Matching***

Match the pressure ulcer stage in column A with the description in column B.

Column A	Column B
A. Stage I	**C** Full-thickness skin loss
B. Stage II	**A** Reddened area
C. Stage III	**D** Damage to muscle
D. Stage IV	**B** Partial-thickness skin loss

Exercise 29-3: ***Multiple Choice Question***

Old skin that must be removed from a wound before it can heal is called:

A. Granulation tissue—NO, this is healing skin
B. **Eschar—YES, this is ischemic or dead skin that must be removed for new growth to take place**
C. Exudates—NO, this is discharge
D. Edema—NO, this is swelling

Exercise 29-4: *Matching*

Match the name of the wound drainage in column A to the description in column B.

Column A	Column B
A. Serous	__C__ A mixture of clear and red fluid
B. Purulent	__D__ Bright red drainage
C. Serosanguinous	__A__ Clear watery drainage
D. Sanguinous	__A__ Thick yellow drainage

Exercise 29-5: *Multiple Choice Question*

The nurse is caring for a patient with a Jackson-Pratt drain that will no longer hold suction. The priority intervention would be to:

A. Remove it—NO, drains are removed by the primary care provider (PCP)
B. Clamp the tubing for the patient to the drain—NO, this will obstruct suction
C. Leave it open—NO, this will not create suction
D. **Notify the primary care provider—YES, the drain is not functioning correctly or is no longer needed and either has to be replaced or discontinued**

Exercise 29-6: *Ordering*

Place the steps in order for 1 to 6 to complete a wet-to-dry wound dressing:

__1__ Wash hands
__5__ Apply moist gauze into wound
__2__ Explain procedure to the patient
__3__ Put on sterile gloves
__6__ Cover with a sterile dry dressing
__4__ Clean wound with sterile saline

Exercise 29-7: *Multiple Choice Question*

The nurse understands that when packing a wet-to-dry dressing, the moist gauze:

A. **Should not touch the skin area—YES, the wet gauze should not be contaminated by the skin**
B. Should not be packed—NO, it should be gently packed
C. Should not be placed in a wound that is tunneling—NO, wet gauze should be in the tunneling area
D. Should be packed with clean gloves—NO, this is sterile

Exercise 29-8: *Matching*

Match the visual deficit in column A to the description in column B.

Column A		Column B
A. Presbyopia	**D**	Changes in blood vessels of the retina
B. Dry eye	**C**	Increased intraocular pressure due to an obstruction in the canal of Schlemm
C. Open-angle glaucoma	**A**	Inability to focus on close objects
D. Diabetic retinopathy	**E**	Macular loses ability to function
E. Macular degeneration	**B**	Tear gland deficit

Exercise 29-9: *Multiple Choice Question*

Progressive age-related hearing loss is called:

A. Conductive hearing loss—NO, sound is stopped at the middle or inner ear
B. Sensorineuro hearing loss—NO, sound is stopped in the inner ear or at the nerve level
C. **Presbycusis—YES, this is common progressive hearing loss**
D. Auditory neuropathy spectrum disorder—Sound enters ear but is not organized in a way that it can be cognitively understood

Exercise 29-10: *Multiple Choice Question*

A safety priority for a nurse when providing discharge teaching for a patient with an olfactory deficit would be:

A. Food preparation—NO, this is a concern but not the priority; a diminished olfactory sense may not allow a patient to detect spoiled food
B. Cleanliness of the home—NO, this is not a related concern
C. Air fresheners—NO, this will not be necessary
D. **Fire alarms—YES, they may not be able to smell something burning**

Exercise 29-11: *Fill-in*

Medications that can damage the auditory nerve are said to be **ototoxic**.

30

Perioperative Nursing

Unfolding Case Study 29 Aubree, Alita, and Connor

The next class covers perioperative topics for the class. Surgical interventions have progressed, and many of the surgical interventions are now done as an outpatient procedure. This is called ***ambulatory surgery***, and it is more cost effective and many times more comfortable for the patient to be at home. ***Laparoscopic*** surgery is often done as an outpatient procedure because large incisions do not have to be made. The instructor explains that there are many different types of surgeries.

Exercise 30-1: *Matching*

Match the surgical term in column A to the description in column B.

Column A		Column B
A. Major surgery	_______	Restores function
B. Minor surgery	_______	Needs to be done immediately to save a life
C. Elective surgery	_______	Minimally alters the body
D. Urgent surgery	_______	Done to improve personal appearance
E. Emergency surgery	_______	Done by choice
F. Diagnostic surgery	_______	Just decreases symptoms or pain
G. Reconstructive surgery	_______	Allows practitioner to confirm diagnosis
H. Procurement surgery	_______	Extensive surgery
I. Cosmetic surgery	_______	Needs to be done within a reasonable timeframe
J. Palliative surgery	_______	Done to harvest organs

The next day the students are scheduled to have experiences in the operative suite of the acute care hospital. The clinical area is set up with a preoperative room and a postoperative suite. The next day Aubree is in the postoperative recover unit or post-anesthesia care unit (PACU). Alita and Connor are in the preoperative unit.

The first patient to go into the OR is a patient for bariatric surgery who is above a BMI of 30.

The Answers section can be found on page 413.

eResource 30-1: Bariatric Surgery: www.youtu.be/lTlVIcWg4gw

Exercise 30-2: ***Select All That Apply***

An obese patient undergoing anesthesia for surgery has an increased risk of:

- ❑ Diabetes
- ❑ Dehiscence
- ❑ Atalectasis
- ❑ Wound infection
- ❑ Pneumonia

In the preoperative area, Alita and Connor watch the nurses do preoperative teaching. The nurses also check that all the preoperative information needed is present. Preoperative checklists usually include pertinent laboratory data, diagnostic tests, and informed consent, and patient identification is verified. The patient's medical record follows the patient to the OR.

Patients going for surgery also need to remove makeup and prosthesis.

Exercise 30-3: ***True/False***

Patients with dentures do not have to remove them.

- ❑ True
- ❑ False

Exercise 30-4: ***Multiple Choice Question***

The patient tells the nurse that she does not understand what was on the consent for surgery. The nurse should:

A. Re-explain the surgical procedure
B. Read the consent to the patient
C. Call the surgeon to explain
D. Ask a family member to witness the explanation

eResource 30-2: The nurse can consult the University of California School of Medicine's *Ethics Fast Facts*: [Pathway: www.missinglink.ucsf.edu/lm/ethics/index.htm → select "Review Fast Facts" → starting with "Informed Consent"].

Another important aspect of preoperative nursing is marking the surgical site on the patient. This allows for clear communication if surgery is on a left or right body part. Alita and Connor assisted with making sure that the patient's ID be intact, placing OR caps on them, and helping with inserting Foley catheters. Patients also need an IV to go to surgery.

eResource 30-3: World Health Organization's Surgical Safety Checklist:

- Handout of the 19-point checklist: http://whqlibdoc.who.int/publications/2009/9789241598590_eng_Checklist.pdf
- Video: www.youtu.be/SMfYv84j_ME

The Answers section can be found on page 413.

Exercise 30-5: *Multiple Choice Question*

The most important purpose of an IV access site for surgery is:

A. To keep hydrated
B. Keep NPO
C. Have a line to give emergency medication
D. Have a line to give postop antibiotics if needed

Exercise 30-6: *Multiple Choice Question*

Many patients have Foley catheters put in for surgery. The reason for this intervention is to:

A. Prevent accidental nicking of the full bladder
B. Calculate I&O accurately
C. Prevent patients from stopping surgery to urinate
D. Keep the sterile field clean

eResource 30-4: Urinary Catheterization: www.youtu.be/YpzGfxyG69s

Exercise 30-7: *Multiple Choice Question*

Patients are often asked to remove nail polish from at least one fingernail in order to:

A. Identify the patient
B. Have a spot for the finger pulse oximeter
C. Assess if the blood pressure cuff is on too tight on the OR
D. Assess capillary refill

Also during the preoperative preparation, patients are taught about what they can expect postoperatively after the anesthesia starts to wear off. Some of the routine postoperative care will be deep breathing, coughing, and turning.

eResource 30-5: Frequently patients will be shown educational videos prior to 1:1 instruction on the use of the incentive spirometry device: http://www.youtube.com/watch?v=VHN5zPaw96w

Exercise 30-8: *Multiple Choice Question*

The nurse understands that the disease prevention reason for postoperative coughing and deep breathing is to:

A. Prevent emboli
B. Increase airflow to alveoli
C. Prevent pneumonia
D. Increase circulation

Exercise 30-9: *Multiple Choice Question*

The nurse understands that turning is important for circulation and to decrease pressure on boy prominences. The patient is reluctant to turn due to operative pain; therefore the nurse should:

A. Explain the rationale for turning
B. Ask a family member to assist

The Answers section can be found on page 413.

C. Report it to the primary care provider
D. Medicate the patient 30 minutes before turning

The nurses also tell the preoperative patient that they will be doing leg exercises while they are on bed rest postoperatively. They demonstrate the exercises expected and then ask the patients to practice.

eResource 30-6: Review Passive and Assistive Range-of-Motion Exercises presented previously in Chapter 28:

- ROM Exercises Video Demonstration:
  - http://alfa.saddleback.edu/video_only.aspx?ID=10
  - www.youtu.be/RGCtC3PclFU
- Handout: www.alsworldwide.org/pdfs/rom_exercises.pdf

Exercise 30-10: *Multiple Choice Question*
The nurse understands that the patient needs further teaching when the patient states:

A. "Leg exercise will increase my ability to voluntarily urinate after anesthesia"
B. "If I do leg exercises, I can go home earlier"
C. "Leg exercises may prevent thromboses from forming"
D. "Leg exercises will prevent postoperative gas buildup"

Another question that the nurse asked every preoperative patient was about allergies.

Exercise 30-11: *Multiple Choice Question*
A major operative concern regarding allergies is:

A. Peanuts
B. Environmental
C. Smoke
D. Latex

Alita goes into the OR with the patient who is undergoing bariatric surgery. The patient is slide onto the operative table using a slide board. Three people help pull the draw sheet over the slide board, so no one hurts their back. There are several nurses in the OR to assist getting things setup.

Exercise 30-12: *Multiple Choice Question*
The charge nurse in the OR is making assignments; what is the best assignment to delegate to the UAP?

A. Circulating nurse
B. Admitting nurse
C. Postanesthesia
D. Scrub nurse

The anesthesiologist explains to Alita about the different types of anesthesia. General is used to produce amnesia and a totally relaxed patient; regional is used when there is a need to lose sensation in a specific body part. Local is used if the OR team would like a specific site numb. Many outpatient procedures are now completed under conscious sedation.

The Answers section can be found on page 413.

Exercise 30-13: ***Multiple Choice Question***

When a patient is under conscious sedation, they:

A. Need an assistive device to maintain their airway
B. Can feel pain
C. Can follow verbal commands
D. Have reduced fear

After Alita watches the surgery, she accompanies the patient to the PACU, and Aubree is there helping the staff care for patients. Normally patients stay in the PACU for 1 to 2 hours depending on their reaction to the anesthesia and the stability.

eResource 30-7: Surgical Recovery in the PACU: www.youtu.be/s000pUVwyhw

Exercise 30-14: ***Multiple Choice Question***

The PACU nurse expects the patient to come to the unit with:

A. A ventilator
B. Liquid diet ordered
C. Anti-emboli hose (AE hose)
D. Discharge order

After the nurses recover the patient, they assess their ability to be transferred to a surgical hospital unit. If the patient is recovering in an acute care facility, a Postanesthesia Recovery Score (PARS) and if they are being recovered in an ambulatory care facility, they may use an assessment tool called Postanesthesia Recovery Score for Ambulatory Patients (PARSAP).

Exercise 30-15: ***Multiple Choice Question***

The patient after 3 hours in the PACU has not reached a PARS level of 8 to 10, which is needed before transport to the surgical unit is done. The PACU nurse should expect that:

A. The patient will stay longer
B. The patient will be transferred to an ICU
C. The patient will be put on a one-to-one observation overnight
D. Have a family stay with the patient on the surgical unit

The PACU nurse also tells Aubree and Connor that they are always on the lookout for postanesthesia complications. One of the complications that they learn about is malignant hyperthermia. This can be a life-threatening complication.

eResource 30-8: To learn more about the causes of malignant hyperthermia (MH), the students:

- Review a video: www.youtu.be/LVSIFoVYr24
- Read a brief overview of MH: www.ncbi.nlm.nih.gov/pubmedhealth/PMH0002292/

The Answers section can be found on page 413.

Exercise 30-16: *Multiple Choice Question*

In order to assess the development of malignant hyperthermia, the nurse would frequently assess:

A. Orientation to person, place, and time
B. Pulse
C. Respirations
D. Temperature

In postconference, the instructor and the students discuss other operative complications such as paralytic ileus, pain, and constipation. The students discuss nursing interventions that decrease the risk of patients developing these complications.

eResource 30-9: Postoperative Complications:

- Postop algorithm: paralytic ileus: www.youtu.be/aRLG8IJ9J2U
- MerckMedicus on their mobile device
  - Merck Manual: [Pathway: Merck Manual→Topics→ enter "constipation" into the search field → select "constipation" and listen to podcast, *Constipation in Adults*].
  - Harrison's Practice: [Pathway: Merck Manual → Topics→ enter "constipation" into the search field → review content focusing particularly on treatment and ongoing care].
- Postoperative Pain
  - Postop Algorithm: pain: www.youtu.be/MOE4WpUjoU4
  - World Health Organization Pain Ladder: www.who.int/cancer/palliative/painladder/en/

Exercise 30-17: *Multiple Choice Question*

The nurse understands that the most effective method of preventing ***paralytic ileus*** postoperatively is:

A. Enemas
B. Rectal tubes
C. Early ambulation
D. Liquid diet

The students cannot believe that class and clinical are over for the semester. They are anxious about the final exam, which is cumulative, but they are comfortable with the material. Their clinical instructor evaluates their performance in clinical and all three of them pass with competency levels that are above average. Next semester, they are registered for mental health nursing and adult health. They are looking to enjoying the semester break!

The Answers section can be found on page 413.

Answers

Exercise 30-1: *Matching*

Match the surgical term in column A to the description in column B.

Column A		Column B
A. Major surgery	G	Restores function
B. Minor surgery	E	Needs to be done immediately to save a life
C. Elective surgery	B	Minimally alters the body
D. Urgent surgery	I	Done to improve personal appearance
E. Emergency surgery	C	Done by choice
F. Diagnostic surgery	J	Just decreases symptoms or pain
G. Reconstructive surgery	F	Allows practitioner to confirm diagnosis
H. Procurement surgery	A	Extensive surgery
I. Cosmetic surgery	D	Needs to be done within a reasonable timeframe
J. Palliative surgery	H	Done to harvest organs

Exercise 30-2: *Select All That Apply*

An obese patient undergoing anesthesia for surgery has an increased risk of:

❑ Diabetes—NO, this is a risk but not specific to surgery

☒ **Dehiscence—YES, there is an increased chance due to adipose mass**

☒ **Atalectasis—YES, there is an increased chance due to adipose mass**

☒ **Wound infection—YES, there is an increased chance due to adipose mass**

☒ **Pneumonia—YES, there is an increased chance due to adipose mass**

Exercise 30-3: *True/False*

Patients with dentures do not have to remove them.

❑ True

☒ **False—They are considered a prosthesis**

Exercise 30-4: *Multiple Choice Question*

The patient tells the nurse that she does not understand what was on the consent for surgery. The nurse should:

A. Re-explain the surgical procedure—NO, if the patient does not understand the major premise of the intervention, it needs to be the responsibility of the primary care provider

B. Read the consent to the patient—NO, this is the responsibility of the primary care provider

C. **Call the surgeon to explain—YES, it is the surgeon's responsibility for patients to understand what is going to be done to them**

D. Ask a family member to witness the explanation—NO, this is a HIPAA violation

Exercise 30-5: *Multiple Choice Question*

The most important purpose of an IV access site for surgery is:

A. To keep hydrated—NO, this is important but not the most important

B. Keep NPO—NO, this is important but not the most important

C. **Have a line to give emergency medication—YES, anesthesia places patients in high-risk positions, and emergency medication if needed is most effective by IV**

D. Have a line to give postop antibiotics if needed—NO, this is important but not the most important

Exercise 30-6: *Multiple Choice Question*

Many patients have Foley catheters put in for surgery. The reason for this intervention is to:

A. **Prevent accidental nicking of the full bladder—YES**

B. Calculate I&O accurately—NO, but this is also done

C. Prevent patients from stopping surgery to urinate—NO

D. Keep the sterile field clean—NO

Exercise 30-7: *Multiple Choice Question*

Patients are often asked to remove nail polish from at least one fingernail in order to:

A. Identify the patient—NO, this is done by the arm bands

B. Have a spot for the finger pulse oximeter—NO, this will not interfere with the pulse oximeter

C. Assess if the blood pressure cuff is on too tight on the OR—NO, this should be assessed at the cuff site

D. **Assess capillary refill—YES, this is the safety reason**

Exercise 30-8: *Multiple Choice Question*

The nurse understands that the disease prevention reason for postoperative coughing and deep breathing is to:

A. Prevent emboli—NO, this is done by compression stockings or anti-emboli stockings
B. Increase airflow to alveoli—NO, this is an effect but not the primary reason
C. **Prevent pneumonia—YES, this is disease prevention**
D. Increase circulation—NO, this may be a secondary affect, but not the primary reason

Exercise 30-9: *Multiple Choice Question*

The nurse understands that turning is important for circulation and to decrease pressure on boy prominences. The patient is reluctant to turn due to operative pain; therefore the nurse should:

A. Explain the rational for turning—NO, this is a good intervention but not the priority
B. Ask a family member to assist—NO, this could cause a visitor injury
C. Report it to the primary care provider—NO
D. **Medicate the patient 30 minutes before turning—YES, Maslow's needs—comfort is needed**

Exercise 30-10: *Multiple Choice Question*

The nurse understands that the patient needs further teaching when the patient states:

A. "Leg exercise will increase my ability to voluntarily urinate after anesthesia."—NO
B. "If I do leg exercises, I can go home earlier."—NO
C. **"Leg exercises may prevent thromboses from forming."—YES, this is the important reason**
D. "Leg exercises will prevent postoperative gas buildup."—NO

Exercise 30-11: *Multiple Choice Question*

A major operative concern regarding allergies is:

A. Peanuts—NO, this is a common allergy but not an operative concern
B. Environmental—NO, this is a common allergy but not an operative concern
C. Smoke—NO, this is not an operative concern
D. **Latex—YES, many health care products contain latex**

Exercise 30-12: *Multiple Choice Question*

The charge nurse in the OR is making assignments; what is the best assignment to delegate to the UAP?

A. Circulating nurse—NO, this must be an RN
B. Admitting nurse—NO, only an RN can do an assessment
C. Postanesthesia—NO, RNs need to assess patients in PACU
D. **Scrub nurse—YES, a scrub tech or LPN can scrub**

Exercise 30-13: ***Multiple Choice Question***

When a patient is under conscious sedation, they:

A. Need an assistive device to maintain their airway—NO, this is usually not necessary
B. Can feel pain—NO, they should not be in pain
C. Can follow verbal commands—NO, they are in another level of consciousness
D. **Have reduced fear—YES, they are not afraid during the procedure**

Exercise 30-14: ***Multiple Choice Question***

The PACU nurse expects the patient to come to the unit with:

A. A ventilator—NO, they should be weaned in the OR
B. Liquid diet ordered—NO, they should be NPO
C. **Anti-emboli hose (AE hose)—YES, these should be put on preoperative if possible**
D. Discharge order—NO, this is not usual practice

Exercise 30-15: ***Multiple Choice Question***

The patient after 3 hours in the PACU has not reached a PARS level of 8 to 10, which is needed before transport to the surgical unit is done. The PACU nurse should expect that:

A. The patient will stay longer—NO, this is usually not a solution if the patient is not responding as expected
B. **The patient will be transferred to an ICU—YES, they will need more supportive interventions**
C. The patient will be put on a one-to-one observation overnight—NO, this may be dangerous if they need supportive interventions
D. Have a family stay with the patient on the surgical unit—NO, this may be dangerous if they need supportive interventions

Exercise 30-16: ***Multiple Choice Question***

In order to assess the development of malignant hyperthermia, the nurse would frequently assess:

A. Orientation to person, place, and time—NO, this is not the most astute assessment
B. Pulse—NO, this is not the most astute assessment
C. Respirations—NO, this is not the most astute assessment
D. **Temperature—YES, this is the distinguishing factor of this complication**

Exercise 30-17: ***Multiple Choice Question***

The nurse understands that the most effective method of preventing paralytic ileus postoperatively is:

A. Enemas—NO, this is a late intervention
B. Rectal tubes—NO, this is a late intervention
C. **Early ambulation—YES, this is the most effective**
D. Liquid diet—NO, this is not preventative

Index